W9-CDW-185

Identification	Education and the Preschool Child	Education and the Schoolchild	Collaboration for Inclusion
Differing concepts of disability, prevalence rates	IDEA services	Special education defined, problems of special education, using proven practices	Advocacy groups
Referrals, types of assessments, identification process	Individualized Family Service Plan (IFSP)	Individualized Education Program (IEP)	LRE, continuum and array of services, in general education, in statewide assessments
Under- and overrepresentation, special testing concerns	Head Start, cultural awareness	Cultural diversity, language and instruction, building self-esteem	Partnerships with community groups
Curriculum based measurement, discrepancy formulas	Early intervention preschool programs, screening	Reading, learning strategies	Conditions for successful inclusion, teachers working together
Speech impairments, language impairments	Strategies that promote preschoolers' communication	Instructional enhancements, language instruction	Adjusting teachers' language, phonological awareness, SLPs in general education
Adaptive behavior, mental age, diversity	The power of early intervention	Functional curriculum, community based instruction, making choices	Multidisciplinary teams, teacher training, good inclusion practices
Underrepresentation of culturally and linguistically diverse students, alternative methods	Enriched experiences, differentiated programs	Gifted approaches, service delivery options	Acceleration, enrichment triad, "cultural brokers," community partners
Ecological assessments, screening instruments	Early identification and intervention, relationship to delinquency and later aggression	Curriculum based measurement, effective discipline, corporal punishment, self-determination	Placement rates, programs with community agencies
Multidisciplinary teams	Motor development and positioning, developing communication skills	Instructional and physical accommodations, designing learning environments	Multidisciplinary teams, instructional accommodations
Methods to test hearing, behavioral supports	Language development, modes of communication	Instructional considerations, instructional methods, teaming with educational interpreters	Teaming with interpreters, determining LRE
Methods to test vision	Play, learning independence, quality indicators of preschool programs	Classroom organization and instructional management, literacy, orientation, and mobility	Multidisciplinary teams and families, alternative programs
Checklists, functional assessment	Systematic instruction; Early signs of autism, delayed language; Deaf–blindness: Inhibited mobility, problems with incidental learning	Teaching functionally equivalent behaviors, incidental teaching	Multidisciplinary teams and families, placement and curricular issues

Introduction to
Special Education

Introduction to Special Education

Teaching in an Age of Opportunity

FOURTH EDITION

Deborah Deutsch Smith

Peabody College

Vanderbilt University

Allyn and Bacon

Boston • London • Toronto • Sydney • Tokyo • Singapore

Vice President, Editor-in-Chief, Education: Paul A. Smith
Series Editor: Virginia Lanigan
Developmental Editor: Alicia Reilly
Series Editorial Assistant: Jennifer Connors
Senior Marketing Manager: Brad Parkins
Production Manager: Elaine M. Ober
Composition and Prepress Buyer: Linda Cox
Manufacturing Buyer: Megan Cochran
Cover Administrator: Linda Knowles
Photo and Fine Art Researcher: Helane M. Prottas/Posh Pictures
Editorial-Production Service: Barbara Gracia
Interior Designer: Melinda Grosser for *silk*
Electronic Composition: Schneck-DePippo Graphics

Copyright © 2001, 1998, 1995, 1992 by Allyn and Bacon
A Pearson Education Company
160 Gould Street
Needham Heights, MA 02494-2310

Internet: www.abacon.com

All rights reserved. No part of the material protected by this copyright notice may be reproduced or utilized in any form or by any means, electronic or mechanical, including photocopying, recording, or by any information storage and retrieval system, without written permission from the copyright owner.

Library of Congress Cataloging-in-Publication Data

Smith, Deborah Deutsch.
     Introduction to special education: teaching in an age of
  challenge/Deborah Deutsch Smith.—4th ed.
        p.   cm.
     Includes bibliographical references and indexes.
     ISBN 0-205-29222-4
     1. Special education—United States. I. Title.
LC3981.S56 2000   00—036215
371.9′0973—dc21   CIP

Printed in the United States of America

10 9 8 7 6 5 4 3   —VHP—04 03 02

Copyright © 2000 by Maya Angelou. Reprinted by permission of The Helen Brann Agency, Inc.

Photo Credits
P. 11: © Kate Brooks/SABA; p. 12: Lyrl Ahern (left), Evans Picture Library (right); p. 17: Courtesy of the National Easter Seal Society; pp. 18, 19: AP/Wide World Photos; p. 22: Simon R. Fulford; p. 23: Noel Saltzman/PBS; p. 45: Will Hart; p. 53: Tony Freeman/PhotoEdit; p. 58: Michael Newman/PhotoEdit; p. 61: Jim Pickerell; p. 64: Larry Wilson/Vanderbilt University 1999; p. 70: James Shaffer/PhotoEdit; p. 82: Tony Freeman/PhotoEdit; p. 84: Luc Novovitch/Gamm Liaison; pp. 90, 96: Will Hart; p. 100: Paul Gish/Monkmeyer; p. 103: Brian Smith; p. 112: Will Hart; p. 130: Stephen Marks; p. 133: Courtesy of the Council for Exceptional Children; p. 140: Brian Smith; p. 145: Bernard Wolf/Monkmeyer; p. 150: Will Faller; p. 164: Will Hart; p. 169: © Lernout & Hauspie Speech Products, Burlington, MA; p. 182: Will Hart; p. 185: Will Faller; p. 194: Courtesy of the American Speech, Language, and Hearing Association; p. 204: Will Faller; p. 208: Will Faller; p. 217: Photographs of Liberator II system users courtesy of the Prentke Romich Company, Wooster, Ohio; p. 218: © Kevin Thomas; p. 231: Will Hart; p. 236: David Young-Wolf/PhotoEdit; p. 242: Paul Kennedy/Liaison International; p. 249: Paul Conklin/PhotoEdit; p. 252: Vic Bider/PhotoEdit; p. 256: Michael Newman/PhotoEdit; p. 258: AP/Wide World Photo; p. 276: Will Hart; p. 285: Special Collections, Milbank Memorial Library, Teachers College, Columbia University; p. 292: David Young-Wolf/PhotoEdit; p. 299: Jim Pickerall; p. 302: Will Hart; p. 312: David Young-Wolf/PhotoEdit; p. 323: Will Hart; p. 330: Stephen Marks;

Photo credits are continued on page 629 and are considered an extension of the copyright page.

To Jim who achieved his goals,
Steve who will,
and Victor who will never get it quite right

PAEAN

The bells are a clamor
Chimes have been loosed
There is a banquet of hosannas in the air.

We have endured endless peaks of pain and valleys of loneliness
We have lost beloved's we could not live without
Yet we have lived.

We have encountered unforgivable cruelties
Yet we have forgiven
Yet we have been forgiven.

We have survived, flourished, and thrived
With passion, compassion, humor and style
We have been fortunate and worthy.

Now we stand, heavy laden, before a great gate
Which leads to the rest of all time.
It swings ajar, and we know at this critical moment
That not all we carry need enter when we enter.

We can evict hate and scorn from our souls
We can open clenched fists and let bigotry
Malice and enmity fall back down the slope to yesterday.

We can lay down our burden of violence
And step lightly over the lintel into a vernal and newly-minted tomorrow

We, who never saw a new century
We, who never saw a new one thousand years,
Can join the hallelujah, the hymns, the paeans, the voices all over the world.

We can shout or whisper, scream or mumble
Happy New Millennium!
 Happy New Century !
  Happy New Year !

Maya Angelou
Performed at the Washington, D.C. Millenium Celebration

[blank page vi]

Contents

CHAPTER **4**

Learning Disabilities 122

CHAPTER **5**

Speech or Language Impairments 176

CHAPTER **6**

Mental Retardation   224

CHAPTER 7

Giftedness and Talent Development 270

CHAPTER 8

Emotional or Behavioral Disorders 318

CHAPTER 9

Physical Impairments and Special Health Care Needs 362

CHAPTER 10

Deafness and Hard of Hearing 410

CHAPTER *11*

Low Vision and Blindness 458

CHAPTER 12

Autism, Deaf-Blindness, and Traumatic Brain Injury: Low Incidence Disabilities 502

Preface

TO THE STUDENT AND PROFESSOR

At the start of a new century, it seems to me that people are more optimistic about life's potential than they were several decades ago. Rather than focusing on problems, I think we are looking for opportunities that might nourish change. For this reason, what used to be *Introduction to Special Education: Teaching in an Age of Challenge* has been retitled *Introduction to Special Education: Teaching in an Age of Opportunity.* Some new features were created for this fourth edition that stress the importance of learning from the past, pondering the present, and thinking about how things can be better. I want to help you think about individuals with disabilities and the special response to their education we as a society should provide. In Chapter 1, you are asked questions which are meant to broaden your considerations about people with disabilities and think about societies' responses to them across time. Starting with Chapter 2 and continuing throughout the text, two features present timely and critical examinations the field of special education at the dawn of the twenty-first century. At the beginning of each chapter, a section called *Opportunities for the New Millennium* helps to explain the legacy of the twentieth century and the dilemmas that need to be addressed if special education is to better meet the needs of students with exceptionalities. Likewise, in the margins you will find notations entitled *New Directions for the Millennium: Legacies and Opportunities*; these summarize a specific topic about the "state of the field" in special education, and prompt you to think critically about ideas for the future. In these sections, and also through the *Concepts and Controversy* features, you are asked to consider important issues and wrestle with problems still left to resolve as we enter a new century.

ORIENTATION

As with previous editions, I have attempted to write a thorough, comprehensible introduction to the field of special education and the schooling of students with special needs. My intention is that the content and examples provided give a basic understanding of exceptionalities (disabilities and giftedness) and how these students' unique characteristics create special needs that must be addressed if they are to fulfill their potential. My aim is for the text to be practical and applied; therefore, it is filled with real-life examples, mostly in school settings. Verified instructional procedures are explained to show how the education system and the instructional practices of special educators make real differences in the outcomes of their students. Special education is important work, and my hope is that you will also choose to devote your career to students with special needs and their families.

The following are some of the major themes you will find as you study this text. These themes run throughout the entire book, and, I believe, are critical dimensions to the nature of the work we have come to call special education.

Theme 1: Think of People First. Facts, figures, research findings, and the special education and disability knowledge base are important to all professionals and to the public so that the needs of people with disabilities, as well as those with unique gifts and talents, are met at school and in the community. Such information is important, but it is not the entire essence of this field. To approach what is really important about special education we must listen to individuals with disabilities, those who are gifted, and their family members. We as a society must hear their voices; see their accomplishments; and become caring, sensitive, and respectful in all of our interactions with them. For these reasons, some very special features are included in this text.

First, each chapter opens with a work of art created by a master who had or has a disability or unique challenge. All of the artists included here were or are exceptional in ways beyond their creative and artistic abilities. The inclusion of this artwork is intended to make an important point: People, irrespective of disabilities, are capable of creating great beauty.

Second, near the beginning of every chapter you will find a vignette called *A Personal Perspective,* written by a person with a disability, a family member, or a professional. I tried to create a personal experience for you, wherein the stories of real people—their hopes, challenges, and achievements—come to life. Through these stories, I hope you will come to a better understanding and acceptance of differences. Listen carefully and hear their messages about persistence, dealing positively with crisis and conflict, and solving problems so that quality of life is always improving, always just that much better.

And, in every chapter, real-life examples are provided to make a point or illustrate a concept. What is so important to remember in your studies, is that special education is about the lives of people, and what we do in the classroom, on the playground, and after school makes a difference.

Theme 2: Special education is individually determined and requires continual evaluation. For special education to be truly special, it must be individualized. The services it provides must be responsive to the age of the learner as well as his or her abilities and needs. In other words, there can be no single answer to the question about what comprises an appropriate education for an individual child. And what might be the correct educational response at one point in time may not be the right response at another. Decisions about the appropriateness of services and educational programs should always be made from information gathered directly from student performance. The application of these principles are feasible only when a full array of services is available and they are flexibly applied. Therefore, you will find examples of many different service delivery options described in the *Educational Interventions* sections in every categorical chapter in this text. These descriptions range across all ages where special education is delivered: from birth to age 21.

Theme 3: Integration and inclusion does not happen by accident. As you will learn, placement alone does not guarantee full participation in the general education curriculum or in activities with peers. Many accommodations and special efforts are often required to provide students with special needs access to instruction and to their nondisabled classmates. In most cases, integration requires continual application of problem solving skills, collaboration, and partnerships from teams of people that include family members, all educators, and community resources. Pay attention to the sections called *Collaboration for Inclusion* and the boxes entitled

Accommodating for Inclusive Environments, where you will learn about the complexity of issues relating to achieving full participation in school and in the community.

Theme 4: Good special education is based on proven practices. Special education has a knowledge base that was developed through systematic research. Unfortunately, the field does not always use proven practices, and instead reaches out for what seem to be good ideas or appear to be quick solutions. Typically, students and their families do not benefit from easy answers to complex problems. To me, it is vital that special educators become critical consumers of research who consistently evaluate their own actions. This value is woven throughout the text. For this edition, I asked some researchers to share the findings of their studies. I asked them to write about their investigations in a format that allows you to understand the methods and procedures they developed, apply them to classroom settings, and get similar results. My motivation for this new feature is simple. Gifted students and students with disabilities and their families deserve to receive assistance that has been proven effective through carefully conducted research. The implementation of fads and unproven interventions is common practice in special education, and, I believe, should not continue. Educators need to become sophisticated consumers of research, and I hope that the *Research to Practice* boxes will help focus the attention of those concerned about the best interests of individuals with disabilities, and make us insist on knowing the efficacy of what we apply in classrooms.

You also find boxes that indicate how to create good classroom environments where disruption is held to a minimum. In the *Achieving Discipline* boxes, proven techniques that match infractions with levels of intervention are explained so they can be implemented easily at school.

Theme 5: Cultural and linguistic diversity is part of the fabric of American schools. The diversity of America's schoolchildren is reflected in almost every school in this country. In some school districts, children come to school speaking over a hundred different languages and many students do not understand the culture of the classroom or the teacher providing instruction. Cultural and language differences present challenges to the educational system, challenges that are often inappropriately answered with special education placements. Culturally and linguistically diverse students are overrepresented in programs for students with cognitive disabilities and underrepresented in gifted education. These problems must be corrected, for misidentification, improper labeling, and inappropriate placement in special education can have tragic results for these individuals and their families. And failure to provide unique programs that develop talents can result in missed opportunities for a richer society. Therefore, an entire chapter is devoted to cultural and linguistically diverse learners, and in most chapters particular attention is paid to unbiased identification procedures and instructional methods that are culturally sensitive.

Theme 6: Legislation is one foundation of special education. Unlike other areas of education, special education—the rights of students with disabilities to a free appropriate education in the least restrictive environment—is outlined in legislation. The Individuals with Disabilities Education Act (IDEA) and the U.S. Department of Education's regulations for this federal law drive much of what we do in special education. These provisions provide many guarantees to students with disabilities and their families. For example, they outline individualized education programs and the plans that guarantee the delivery of a free appropriate public education in least restrictive environments. They provide guidelines about the implementation of disciplinary actions with students with disabilities, their access to the general education curriculum, their participation in national assessments, and the array of related services (including assistive technology) which provide them supports in school. All educators must understand these fundamentals of special education, and I have attempted to explain them simply and concisely.

ORGANIZATION OF THIS TEXT

In the first three chapters, the fundamentals of special education are presented. The context of special education, the services it provides, the laws and court cases that guarantee fundamental education rights to students with disabilities are discussed in Chapters 1 and 2. The third chapter focuses on the diversity of American schoolchildren and the very special educational needs that culturally and linguistically diverse students can present to the educational system. The subsequent categorical chapters are ordered by prevalence of the disability: the chapter covering the largest category, learning disabilities, comes first, followed by the other high incidence disability categories. Low incidence disabilities, as defined by the federal government, come next. And a chapter about three very low incidence disabilities—autism, traumatic brain injury, and deaf–blindness—brings the text to a close.

TOOLS FOR LEARNING

In this book you will find many features to facilitate your study. At the beginning of every chapter is a set of Advance Organizers. The chapter overview, the five self-test questions, and one challenge question should help focus your attention on important concepts presented in that chapter. These questions are repeated and answered in the Summary found at the end of the chapter. This feature should allow you to check your understanding of some of the most important concepts presented in the text.

The advance organizer/summary feature is only one of many elements of this text that should help you master the content. Chapters 3 through 12 are written using a *consistent organizational format*, so you will know where to find topical information on a specific disability. These chapters have the following structure:

- Definition, identification, and significance
- History of the field
- Prevalence
- Causes and prevention
- Students with this disability
- Educational considerations, such as early intervention, placement and inclusion, interventions, collaborating with partners, and making accommodations that facilitate integration, transition through adulthood
- Technology
- Families
- Concepts and controversy
- Supplemental resources, including selected scholarly readings, popular books and videos portraying individuals with disabilities, contact information for consumer and professional organizations and agencies

Key terms and brief definitions are found in the margin on the page where an important concept is first introduced and discussed. The *Glossary* at the end of the text provides you with an alphabetically organized set of these terms and their definitions. Reviewing the glossary at the end of the term should give you a good overview and review of the content. Another feature should help you bridge information across chapters: The *Making Connections* statements found in the margins are intended to help you find supporting and complementary information across the text, as is the *content matrix* found on the inside front and back covers. The sources cited in each chapter are organized in the *References* section by chapter, under headings that correspond to the standard outline. If you want to learn more about a topic or write a paper, the arrangement of these references should be helpful.

At the end of each chapter, there is a brief list of resources to enrich your study. Although certainly not exhaustive, some scholarly references are listed so you can seek out additional information, more than can be offered in an introductory text. Over the years, exceptional individuals have been included in fictional and nonfictional roles in both books and films. (Only videos and DVDs that can be rented at many large video stores are included. Unfortunately, copies of many excellent television shows and movies are not readily available, so they were not included.)

I would also like to call your attention to the *Student's Resource Manual and Study Guide* that accompanies this text. There you will find many tips on how to study more efficiently and effectively for this and other courses you are taking. The manual also includes many practice activities to help you learn the content of the course and practically apply your knowledge to classroom settings. In addition, the resource book includes practice test items to help you self-test and assess your mastery of the content presented in each chapter. To augment the brief listing of resources (organizations and agencies, scholarly references) and creative works (popular books and videos) at the end of each chapter in the main text, more complete lists are found in the *Student's Resource Manual*.

TO THE PROFESSOR

Unlike previous editions, the fourth edition does not provide you with a separate annotated instructor's edition of the text. The supporting information you found before in the Instructor's Section at the front of the text is now found in the *Instructor's Resource Manual and Test Bank (IRM)*. Your feedback about the previous editions was used to improve and update the text and its accompanying instructional package. Thank you for your suggestions, and please continue to let me know about what works and what still needs to be improved. I hope you will agree that the fourth edition has retained those elements that made this text both useful and unique, while the new features further improve it and its supporting materials.

ELEMENTS AND FEATURES OF THE FOURTH EDITION

You will find this to be a very current, and hopefully provocative, edition. Not only does this edition cite 664 new references, but it also has a modern orientation. It explains *and* interprets the 1999 U.S. Department of Education's regulations for IDEA throughout the text and highlights those changes in a new box feature, *What IDEA Says About. . . .* This is the first introduction to special education text of the new millennium, and so should be a text that challenges college students to wrestle with dilemmas facing the field. The "millennium approach" and the Concepts and Controversy sections, described earlier in this preface, provided me with the opportunity to encourage the reader to think critically about important issues facing students with disabilities and their families.

You will find many changes and new features in this edition, but the basic order of the twelve chapters is unchanged. I was encouraged to write a thirteenth chapter, focusing on attention deficit/hyperactivity disorder, but I decided not to. Instead, increased coverage of ADHD is found across the text. For example, issues about whether it is or is not a disability are discussed in Chapter 1, its identification in Chapter 2, its characteristics which overlap with learning disabilities in Chapter 4, those that overlap with behavioral disorders in Chapter 8, and how it can now be considered as a health impairment in Chapter 9. Putting all of the information about this condition, which Congress specifically called out in IDEA '97 in the health impairment category, in a separate chapter would have been easier than the approach I elected. But I felt it would have left students with the wrong impression: that ADHD is a disability category. Remember, most special education students with ADHD receive services under the learning disabilities and emotional and behavioral disorders categories. Now, another identification option is available, but as the officials of the federal government made clear in the 1999 regulations of IDEA '97, more students are *not* expected to join the special education rolls because of the inclusion of ADHD in the health impairments category.

The first chapter is new, and hopefully provides an exciting launch to the academic term. In this chapter I call out some of the major concerns about special education (e.g., its efficacy and costs) that are often the focus of newspaper articles and television news shows. My experience is that students know about these issues but think it is "politically incorrect" to raise them in class, leaving them with incomplete understandings of important problems that need to be resolved. Issues are presented in a question–answer format. You should be able to use these questions as platforms for provocative class discussions. Within this format, however, I still provide foundation information about the context of special education—what special education is, its history, and the laws and court cases that support it. Chapter 2 continues to include fundamental information about individualized education programs and plans, and, once again, the chapter displays a sample IEP. A sample IFSP and ITP are included as IRM handouts to complete your class discussion about these requirements of IDEA.

At the heart of much of the controversy over the reauthorization of IDEA were issues related to students' behavior and discipline. These issues contributed to the delay in the passage of IDEA this time in Congress and continued through the drafting of its regulations by the Department of Education. In fact, final agreement and resolution about how students should be disciplined for violations of rules of conduct at school has not yet been achieved; it seems that at almost every opportunity the issue resurfaces in Congressional hearings and debates. Because discipline is such an important topic, a new box, *Achieving Discipline*, describes a school situation in need of intervention and lists the steps to take to solve the problem.

Here are just a few of the features you will find in this edition:

- Enhanced emphasis on trends, issues, and dilemmas to solve in this new century
- Expanded coverage of ADHD
- Stressed importance of translating research to practice
- Increased attention to developing literacy, reading, and pre-reading milestones (phonemic awareness)
- Discussions about the positive influence of collaboration and partnerships among teachers, schools, families, and community agencies

- Explanations of specific accommodations needed to foster integration and inclusion
- The latest information about IDEA '97, its 1999 regulations, and current implementations
- An applied, practical, and methods orientation
- Stress on the importance of educators being sensitive to students' diversity of culture and language

COMPONENTS OF THE INSTRUCTIONAL PACKAGE*

I view this edition, and the previous ones, as a complete instructional package designed to make your teaching of this course easier, more interesting, and complete. The supplements are an important part of the instructional package we offer you. We believe you will find an outstanding array of resources to facilitate your instructional efforts:

- A Companion Website with Online Practice Tests
- An accompanying *Instructor's Resource Manual (IRM)*, which includes a Test Bank, a special instructors' section (including PlanAhead, lecture notes, discussion questions, Web activities), Transparency Masters, Handout Masters (including case studies), and listings of supplemental resources (organizations and agencies, popular books, and popular videos)
- A Computerized Test Bank
- A *Student's Resource Manual and Study Guide*
- The *Allyn and Bacon Transparencies for Special Education*
- The *Allyn and Bacon Digital Media Archive for Special Education*
- The *SNAPSHOTS Inclusion Video*
- *SNAPSHOTS 2: Video for Special Education*
- *Teaching Students with Special Needs* from the Allyn and Bacon *Professionals in Action* video series

THE *INSTRUCTOR'S RESOURCE MANUAL*

The *Instructor's Resource Manual and Test Bank (IRM)* is available to all adopters. Be sure to request your copy from Allyn and Bacon. The materials provided there are designed to enrich your lectures and the course in general. The IRM—created by Naomi Chowdhuri Tyler, Zina Yzquierdo McLean, and myself—provides helpful suggestions and ideas for teaching the content and also includes supplemental materials which should enhance this course about students with disabilities and their lives at school, at home, and in the community. Also included are listings of organizations and associations, updated by Claudia C' de Baca, that include the most current Web sites at the time of development. The lists of popular books and videos in which people with disabilities are depicted was updated by Steven Smith, and Chris Curren prepared the case studies. The test bank section was written by Naomi Chowdhuri Tyler.

First, you will find an opening section intended to help you prepare for the entire semester. This feature, called PlanAhead, includes ideas for panels, guest speakers, and

---

*For more information about the instructor and student supplements that accompany and support the text, ask your local Allyn & Bacon representative, or write to: Allyn & Bacon, Sales Support Department, 160 Gould Street, Needham Heights, Massachusetts 02494.

field trips. To help you achieve balance across these activities, you have been provided with a matrix to check off where you have planned to include which type of activity. You should also note that we shaded in sections of the matrix where we thought the activity might be most appropriately applied (a panel of multidisciplinary team members with Chapter 2). PlanAhead also gives you many suggestions for materials to order; some of these could be used as student handouts and others will provide you with background information to enhance your lectures. Phone numbers and addresses of the groups that produce these materials are included for your convenience. All of these are in checklist formats so you will have a record of the materials you actually requested.

The IRM also includes sections that correlate to each chapter in the text. So that you will know what materials (test bank items, IRM Transparency Masters, IRM Student Handouts, A&B transparencies, Snapshots videos) support each chapter, a listing is provided. Following that you will find a brief Chapter Overview or summary that highlights the content of the chapter found in the student edition. This information should provide you with a quick refresher to review before class. The Advance Organizer Questions are restated. You might find them useful for a general review of the chapter's content. In every chapter in the text, Key Terms are listed and defined in the margins the first time the term is used and explained in the text. For your use in the IRM, we have listed each chapter's terms. These terms are also listed in the *Student's Resource Manual and Study Guide* to ensure students learn them. We suggest that some class time be spent reviewing each of these terms to be certain that your students have a sufficient understanding of them.

To assist with the development of your class presentation for each chapter, we have prepared Lecture Notes for your use. These outlines should help you provide full coverage of each chapter's information in your lectures. In each chapter of the IRM and also in the *Student's Resource Manual*, you will find a historical Time Line. In many of the suggested assignments and activities, we present various ideas about how these time lines could be used so students have a better understanding of how the field evolved and developed across time. At the end of the Lecture Notes sections, you will find Lecture Enhancements that give you more information about a topic discussed in the text or somehow related to the chapter's content. In some cases, in this section you will find an additional Concepts and Controversy to use in class to stimulate further discussion; in other cases, you will find background information to use in your lectures.

Following the Lecture Notes section, you will find Class Discussion Questions. These can be used to encourage class discussion or homework assignments. Also, you will find Activities and Assignments that might give you some ideas about how to more actively involve your students and engage them in their study of students with disabilities. Each IRM chapter includes at least one Web-based activity.

We also created black-and-white IRM Transparency Masters and reproducible IRM Student Handouts to support your lectures and instruction. Some of these transparencies and handouts are popular features not retained in this edition (e.g., Focus on Diversity, Teaching Tactics, and Tips for Teachers boxes). Each IRM chapter includes at least one case study as a student handout. A list of these can be found at the beginning of each IRM chapter.

A directory of Supplemental Resources follows. It includes organizations and agencies which focus their efforts on the disability area discussed in the chapter, as well as professional journals for that field. You and your students will find that many of these organizations are available to provide additional information or answer specific questions that might arise. Popular books and popular videos (and DVDs), in which people with disabilities are central characters, are also listed. We, and many of our colleagues, have found that having students select one of these books or videos to read or watch and then write a critical review is a highly popular assignment. (The directory also appears in the *Student's Resource Manual,* so students can have their own set of this information, making duplication unnecessary for the instructor.)

TEST BANK

The Test Bank contains over 1,200 items with 100 questions for each chapter. Three types of questions are available: true/false, multiple choice, and discussion (essay). The items are grouped together by each major section for each chapter. The test bank can be accessed in several ways. All of the items appear in the IRM. By covering over the answers (which appear in the margin) with a piece of paper and the creative use of a copy machine, tests and quizzes can be easily generated. Also available from Allyn and Bacon is a computerized version of the Test Bank. The Computerized Test Bank is available for both Macintosh and IBM computers.

COMPANION WEBSITE WITH ONLINE PRACTICE TESTS

The Companion Website with Online Study Guide supports the text on a chapter-by-chapter basis. It includes: learning objectives, study questions with text page references, "live" links to relevant Web sites, and additional enrichment material. You can access the Web site by using the Allyn and Bacon internet address: www.abinteractive.com

SUPPORTING ALLYN AND BACON VIDEOS

Allyn and Bacon has developed a number of videotapes that were specially prepared to support your course instruction. Usually it is not possible to schedule actual observations of students with all of the different types of disabilities in one academic term. Therefore, these videos should help to: introduce your college students to persons with disabilities and their families and their teachers, stimulate student discussions and critical thinking, and counter stereotypical views of individuals with disabilities. We recommend that these video programs be used as advanced organizers to introduce your discussion of a particular disability area.

The popular *SNAPSHOTS* videos series—*SNAPSHOTS 2* and the *Inclusion Video*—are available as Allyn and Bacon supplements. The *SNAPSHOTS Inclusion Video* profiles three students in inclusive class settings who are of differing ages and have various disabilities. *SNAPSHOTS 2: Video for Special Education* is a set of six videotaped segments (traumatic brain injury, behavior disorders, learning disabilities, mental retardation, hearing impairments, visual disabilities) profiling three individuals, their families, teachers, and experiences. Each program runs approximately 20 minutes in length, and was designed to introduce your instruction on these topics.

The *Teaching Students with Special Needs* video, from the Allyn and Bacon *Professionals in Action* video series, presents viewpoints and approaches to teaching students with various disabilities across the continuum of classroom settings. The video uses actual classroom footage, and also shows interviews with general and special education teachers, parents, and students. All of these videos were designed specifically for use in college courses.

TRANSPARENCY PACKAGE

The *Allyn and Bacon Transparencies for Special Education* has been revised and expanded since the last edition of this text, and includes approximately 100 acetates, over half of which are full color.

DIGITAL MEDIA ARCHIVE

The *Allyn and Bacon Digital Media Archive for Special Education* provides charts, graphs, tables, figures, weblinks, and audio and video clips on one cross-platform CD-ROM. There's a dynamic lecture presentation, too.

STUDENT'S RESOURCE MANUAL AND STUDY GUIDE

The *Student's Resource Manual and Study Guide* is an applications-based workbook, and can be ordered through your bookstore for students to purchase. The contents of this booklet were provided by Diane Bassett, Claudia C' de Baca, Naomi Tyler, and myself. The manual provides an opening chapter giving college students many helpful hints about how to study more efficiently and effectively. This section provides students with many study strategies they can apply before (e.g., time and organizational management), during (e.g., listening, notetaking, and reading strategies), and after (e.g., test taking skills) to their study. The manual offers students units for each chapter found in the text; each unit begins with the advance organizer Important Points to Remember. The Manual also contains proven learning strategies (e.g., mnemonics, clustering information into main ideas and details, study organizers) and numerous ways of having students apply the information presented in the text. Some of the application features include: define-the-terms activities, alphabet soup (where the special education "language of letters"—IEP, LRE, FAPE, ITP—is practiced), legislation and litigation sections, mini case studies, short sample tests, and "Test Yourself" crossword and other word puzzles on special terms and topics. The manual also includes historical time lines, a directory of resources (organizations, agencies, and journals), and listings of popular books and videos depicting individuals with disabilities.

ACKNOWLEDGEMENTS

Some very special people deserve "first thanks." To the guy who once again lost his playmate and travel companion, was sure the book must be done by now, and insisted on some normalcy during these once-every-eighteen-months periods of craziness: thanks for your endurance. Jim, we survived again! The debt of gratitude to "my team" can never be fully repaid. To Naomi Chowdhuri Tyler, who coordinated the preparation of the supplements that accompany this text, created the Test Bank, developed many of the activities included in the Instructors' and Students' Resource Manuals—our partnership and friendship means so much to me; thanks. Recognition for their excellence, acknowledgement for extraordinary dedication to me and this project, and my very special thanks are owed to some wonderful people: Valerie Easterling, once again, who handled all of the permissions; Zina Yzquierdo McLean, for her outstanding assistance with the *Instructor's Resource Manual*; and Claudia C'de Baca for ensuring that the agency and organization information found at the end of each chapter and in the resource manuals is as up-to-date as possible. Without the wonderful people at the Alliance Project, work at my real job would have suffered and life would have been even nuttier than it was. For all of your help and support, my thanks: Janet Church, Cindy Cantou Clarke, Pam Dismuke, Jeff Easterling, and Debbie Whelan. Thanks also go to Chris Curren of Central Washington State University for helping to conceptualize the advance organizer component and for the case study handouts that were first used in the third edition and carried forth into this edition. And, finally, but certainly not least, a special "hat's off" goes to the dedicated student workers whose attention to details guaranteed that references actually match citations, "lost" articles were only temporarily misplaced, the "very safe place" where important figures and tables surfaced, and resource information was at my fingertips: Tara Stewart, Emily Jordon, and Julia Weller, and Lore Rodriguez.

As in the other editions, voices from the disability community—people with disabilities, their family members, and special education professionals—resonate throughout this text. They are heard most loudly in the Personal Perspective sections found at the beginning of each chapter. To those who so generously shared their individual stories and "spoke" for so many others, a special thanks is extended to: Megan Askim, Karen Canellas-U'Ren, Omar Chavez, Betty Dominguez, Gloria Inlow, Jean Gibson, Tom Hehir, Leslie Palanker, Ann Park, Samantha Reid, and Rebecca Viers.

I believe that the Research to Practice boxes, written specifically for this text by those scholars who conducted the studies presented, add immensely to the applied nature of this book. My thanks are extended to: Cynthia Neese Bailes, Gallaudet University; Jamie Dote-Kwan, California State University–Los Angeles; Doug Fuchs, Vanderbilt University; Lynn Fuchs, Vanderbilt University; Robert H. Horner, University of Oregon; Ann Kaiser, Vanderbilt University; Charles Kinzer, Vanderbilt University; Norma Lopez-Reyna, University of Illinois–Chicago Circle; Herb Rieth, University of Texas–Austin; and George Sugai, University of Oregon.

Many, many people supported my writing effort. Some of them I've never met in person, but they unselfishly assisted in finding the right information or the correct resource. For example, the staff at Gallaudet University and Gallaudet Research Institute was so helpful (again and again and again) while I was preparing the chapter about deaf and hard of hearing students. In particular, my gratitude is extended to: Sue Hotto, Michael Karchmer, Susan King, and Kay Lamb. While revising, I reconnected with an old friend, Judy Yale, and learned of the outstanding work of those associated with the Chicago Youth Centers (CYC). I decided to highlight CYC because the partnerships and collaborative models they use make a real difference in the lives of children living in urban, inner city settings. In that regard, Mary Erangey of CYC made the task so easy. My gratitude is also extended to Jean Lundy of Metropolitan State College of Denver, and Stacey Nordwall of the American Institutes for Research, John C. Flanagan Research Center in Palo Alto, for their help to ensure information contained in this edition is technically accurate.

I am also blessed with many close friends and colleagues, who seem always to be standing ready to lend a hand, help make a connection, remember that reference, or offer needed guidance. To all who went the very extra mile, I owe "ya": Leonard Baca, BUENO Center at the University of Colorado–Boulder; Lilly Cheng, San Diego State University; Phil Chinn, California State University–Los Angeles; Anne Corn, Vanderbilt University; Laura Davis, Vanderbilt University; Elise MacMillian, John F. Kennedy Center of Vanderbilt University; Karl Murray, National Association for State

Directors of Special Education; Dan Reschly, Vanderbilt University; Steve Smith, Destination Films; Judy Smith-Davis, Director of the Metropolitan Washington DC office of the Alliance Project; and Matt Timm, Tennessee Voices for Children.

Many professionals have reviewed the drafts of the four editions of this text. Those who helped with earlier editions were acknowledged previously; however, my thanks for their time and expertise continues. I want to extend a special appreciation to those who assisted specifically with the development of this fourth edition: Sister Carmela Abbruzzese, Regis College; Brian Berry, Holy Family College; Helen Brantley, South Carolina State University; Rachelle Bruno, Northern Kentucky University; Karen Cole, Northern Illinois University; Nancy T. Cupolo, Hudson Valley Community College; Paul A. Haubrick, University of Wisconsin–Milwaukee; Nedra Irvin, South Carolina State University; Melanie Jephson, Stephen F. Austin State University; John W. Keck, Lesley College; Cathy Kea, North Carolina State University; Thomas M. LaGrasta, Lesley College; Jeanette W. Lee, West Virginia State College; Sister Rosemary Lesser, St. Joseph's College; August J. Mauser, University of South Florida; Ellen Marshall, San Antonio College; Christina Ramirez-Smith, Christopher Newport University; Marianne Reynolds, Mercer County Community College; Helene Schaumberger, Adelphi University; Rick Shade, Ball State University; Janet Spector, University of Maine; and Jim Yanok, Ohio University.

And, finally, I want to thank the Allyn and Bacon team. My continued gratitude is extended to Ray Short, my editor for the first three editions, who helped facilitate the project in every way possible and advocated for elements that I wanted included but made his job more difficult. When Ray retired from A&B, the revision of my text landed in the very capable hands of Virginia Lanigan. It has been my pleasure to work with her on her first cycle of productions; she's super! It has been such an honor to once again collaborate with Elaine Ober, Allyn and Bacon's Production Manager, who decided during the development of the last edition to take this book on as one of "her own." She immediately caught my vision and added her creativity and sense of aesthetics to the project; the outcome is wonderful and apparent.

How can you ever thank someone who answers e-mails and telephone calls on evenings, weekends, and holidays; is always cheerful, even when things seem impossible; solves problems and doesn't ever create them; quickly gets questions answered; and is also a heck of a lot of fun? Well, maybe these sentences do so in some small way. If any of you elect to create a personal nightmare and write an intro text, may you have a developmental editor as wonderful as Alicia Reilly.

Toward the end of a big book project like this one, nothing is more important to an author than to work with a production packager who is professional and efficient, attends to details from the beginning, is available and pleasant, and sets the highest quality standard for those in her business. Barbara Gracia and I have worked together three times, and I hope we will be able to do so again. And, to those wonderful people who made this edition interesting to look at and easier for you to use, many thanks as well: Melinda Grosser, text designer; William Heckman, copy editor; Deborah Schneck, text composition and art rendering; and Helane Prottas, photo researcher.

D.D.S.

A Reflection

My career in special education is long, beginning when I was a teenager. What has sustained me over the years is the excitement of watching a child with disabilities achieve an important goal, perform a task that seemed impossible to accomplish only a few weeks before, and share a funny happening with everyone in class. In no way would I intend to minimize disabilities, but I also would not describe them as so complex and difficult that many cannot be compensated for or even reduced. One important message I want to convey is that people with disabilities can assume their places, alongside people without significant disabilities, in modern society when special education is truly special. May a child's laughter and joy over an accomplishment entice you, too, to devote your career to the field of disabilities as it did me.

Another message is that every school, not just isolated examples, are places where all children—those with and without disabilities—are engaged and excited by learning. Schools should be places where students learn with and from each other, helped by excellent teachers and other professionals—places where families are integral to the educational process and their family traditions, culture, and language are respected and reflected in educational programs. I realize that this vision is just that: a vision of what schools should and could be.

Lilly Cheng of San Diego State University often tells the following story. Think of the possibilities if each of us stops to save just one starfish!

An old man was walking on a beach one morning and saw some movements from a distance. He was very curious about the movements and as he walked closer, he saw a young girl picking something from the beach and throwing it into the ocean. When he got very near, he saw that the girl was throwing starfish that had washed up on the beach into the ocean. The old man said to the girl, "The sun is out and there are hundreds of starfish on the beach. You can't save them all. They'll all perish." The young girl picked up one more starfish, and while she was throwing the starfish into the ocean, she said, "This one won't."

The son of a Dutch pastor, **Vincent van Gogh** was drawn to the pulpit early in life. At the same time, he was also influenced by his three uncles who were very active in the art world. His many remaining letters give much insight into his early career indecision and his continuing loneliness, melancholy, and emotional disturbance. Yet the impact and beauty of his most productive artistic life are almost beyond comparison (Stein, 1986; Walther & Metzger, 1993).

Van Gogh left many self-portraits. This painting, *Portrait of the Artist Holding a Palette* (1889), is one made during the last years of his life, and sends a message about his state of well-being. The painting on the cover of this book, also painted by van Gogh, is representative of this period when use of bold color became his trademark.

Vincent van Gogh, *Self-Portrait* (1889). Collection of Mr. and Mrs. John Hay Whitney. Photograph © 1999 Board of Trustees, National Gallery of Art, Washington.

C H A P T E R 1

Toward the beginning of every chapter in this text you will find a section called A Personal Perspective. Each of these stories was written by a person with a special need, a family member of an individual with disabilities, or a professional who has devoted his or her career to special education. I decided, in this edition, to take the opportunity to share my perspective in this opening chapter.

I began working with children with disabilities as a teenage volunteer. IDEA—the law that guarantees children with disabilities a right to a free appropriate education—had not yet been passed, and many children were denied access to schools. I realize that it is hard to believe today that not so long ago parents were turned away from schools, and told that "no children like yours go to school in this district." But it's true! It was commonplace that children who were not toilet trained, or could not walk, or could not talk, or acted very differently were excluded. Many states in the late 1960s and early 1970s had "permissive" education laws. (Permissive education meant that school districts did not have to provide schooling to all of their students with disabilities.) This is when I began in special education, and it was a time of great energy because there were so many "wrongs" to be "righted," and so many possibilities to make a difference. Special education was a movement, and the excitement surrounding it was irresistible.

As a teenager, I volunteered at a private school in Los Angeles, the Marianne Frostig School, specifically for children with learning disabilities. (The school at that time only had classes for elementary students, leaving many of these families without educational options for their children during the high school years.) After earning a bachelor's degree in psychology from Pitzer College, one of the Claremont Colleges

The Context of Special Education:
The Legacy of the Twentieth Century and the Promise of the Millennium

in Southern California, I pursued general and special education teaching certificates at California State University–Northridge. After my "fifth year," I had finished the general education requirements, but only a few of those needed for a special education license. Regardless, job opportunities were everywhere and emergency certificates were easy to arrange. (Sadly, some things have definitely not changed over the years. How can special education be very special when its teachers are unprepared to meet the challenges their students present?) Instead of taking a job, I accepted a fellowship at the University of Missouri–Columbia, and received a masters' degree in special education. And soon after that I enrolled in a doctoral program at the University of Washington in Seattle.

The models we had to learn about special education were very different from today's. My field experience, student teaching, internship, and teaching assignments were in self-contained special education classes, many of which were housed in separate special education schools. Some of these programs were even considered experimental, because they served students who at that time were not typically provided education in the public system. One was even housed in an old rural farmhouse where almost all of the students traveled long distances from the same city to attend school out in the country. The children who participated in that program all were toilet trained and were able to walk; those who did not meet these requirements either stayed home or went to institutions. Another class I worked in was in the basement of an old public school, which gave the children, teachers, and parents plenty of opportunities for seasonal decorations which could be hung from the exposed pipes that ran along the ceiling!

By the end of the 1970s, the battles about children's rights to a public education were won. Although not always completely welcome, arguments about whether children with disabilities could come to school were over. Of course, for many coming to school meant attending separate schools far from home or separate classes in portable buildings set on the back side of playgrounds. Since then, parents and professionals have advocated for more integrated settings and for curriculum and individualized procedures necessary for the delivery of an appropriate education to each child with a disability. While some focused more on placement issues, I concentrated on instruction (though, of course, they go hand in hand). I was interested in helping to shape what should comprise the educational programs for students with disabilities. And I decided that my contribution to effect widespread change was to prepare new university faculty members who would generate knowledge about improved instructional methods, and train special education teachers who would implement quality programs to children with disabilities and their families. I am a committed advocate for culturally and linguistically diverse children with disabilities and their very special educational needs. I also write textbooks to explain how effective procedures should be put into practice. For the last two decades, I have dedicated myself to those goals.

With the passion I felt as a teenager, I remain committed to the concept of special education today. I know that the individualized instruction and the special techniques (proven through systematic research) make a real difference in the outcomes of students with disabilities. Many more adults with disabilities are able to participate fully in American society because of the educational experiences they received. I remain excited about the future and the possibilities it holds. I am also worried because special education cannot be special when a large proportion of its teaching force is unprepared and unable to translate research to practice. Hopefully, the stories you will read this semester, written by people with disabilities, their family members, and friends, will engage you. Possibly, the challenges faced by students with disabilities and those who work with them will excite you—and the fact that you can make a real difference in the lives of people will convince you, as it did me so long ago, that special education is a wonderful career opportunity. Please share my enthusiasm for the field of special education and the education of students with disabilities.

1. What factors might interest you in pursuing a career in special education?

2. What do you think the future holds for people with disabilities?

Advance Organizers

MAKING CONNECTIONS

Use the learning strategy—Advance Organizers—to help focus your study of this chapter's content, and reinforce your learning by reviewing answers to the Focus and Challenge questions at the end of the chapter.

Overview   As the nation begins a new millennium and a time for new beginnings, special education and the related services it provides are poised for new directions, meeting challenges with new approaches. As the 1990s drew to a close, the programs and services provided to students with disabilities and their families became controversial. Special education was developed to allow students with disabilities, when they are adults, to participate fully in mainstream society. And, to a great extent, special education has made a real difference in the lives of children and youth with disabilities and their families. However, it has received some criticism for not meeting its goals, being too expensive, being a major source of discipline problems at schools, discriminating against the very students it intended to help, and being burdensome. The time is right to use opportunities created at the close of the last century to develop responsive and informed solutions to the special education dilemmas yet to be resolved.

Focus Questions

Self-Test Questions

- What does it mean to have a disability?
- Where did special education come from and why did it develop?
- Why did the federal government and the public call for national intervention?
- Why is special education controversial?
- What is the legacy of the evolution of special education as the new millennium begins?

Challenge Question

What are the solutions to problems faced by students with disabilities and the educators charged with meeting their needs?

Beginning in Chapter 2, two features are found in every chapter that will help you think about unresolved dilemmas left from the twentieth century and our opportunities to develop effective solutions:

- Sections called Opportunities for the New Millennium
- Marginal annotations New Directions for the Millennium

*I*n this chapter and as you study throughout this academic term, let's think together about answers to some very important questions. Everyone interested in individuals with disabilities should be prepared to discuss the complex issues that are imbedded in questions called out in this chapter. The questions are important, are being talked about today, and currently have no complete resolution. In other words, no consensus has been reached on most of the dilemmas these questions present. First, let's quickly look at the basis for controversy in the field of special education.

Although the services special education provides were acclaimed during most of the latter part of the century, some aspects of special education were criticized toward the end of the twentieth century. Despite great advances in results experienced by children with disabilities and their families, special education was accused by some of being immoral, ineffective, racist, too costly, and inequitable (Gartner & Lipsky, 1987; Gubernick & Conlin, 1997; Stainback et al., 1994). Attacks came from all fronts and were very public: from politicians, family members of students with disabilities, people with disabilities themselves, members of the press, and the entire education community. Debates about special education's effectiveness—who should receive special education services, how and where they should be delivered, and who should deliver them—raged. Although full agreements have not been reached about actions that should be taken to solve special education's problems, many professionals, members of the press, and the disability community believe its problems can be solved (Audette & Algozzine, 1997; Chaifetz, 1999; Edgar, 1997). To respond intelligently to such charges requires deliberation and informed debate.

Across the academic term, consider the questions raised in this chapter, and try to form your own conclusions about the merits of what we as a society call special education. At first glance, many of these questions seem simple and straightforward, but resist the temptation to be deceived by that illusion. They are complicated and complex. Resist the temptation of thinking in terms of "black and white," "yes and no," and looking to debate issues that can be clearly articulated "on one side or the other." Remember, people and cultures have different perspectives on complex issues. None of us truly lives in a world of black and white; for most issues, we live in "gray-space." As Hungerford wisely pointed out over a half a century ago, "only the brave dare look upon the gray—upon the things which cannot be explained easily" (1950, p. 417). Take the time to ponder all possibilities, as you spend the academic term developing your own understanding of special education and the students and families it serves.

The sets of questions and answers discussed in this chapter are organized around five major topics:

- The essence of disabilities
- Origins of special education
- Necessity for national intervention
- The legacy of the twentieth century
- The development of informed and effective solutions

As we ponder these important issues, let's not lose sight of the fact that we are thinking about people, people who are important members of society.

THE ESSENCE OF DISABILITIES

WHAT IS A DISABILITY?

You would think that a question like "What is a disability?" has a simple and straight-forward answer. It does not. Remember, nothing is absolute when studying the human condition, and not all concepts are consistent across cultures. Many answers have been suggested to resolve this question. Definitions of disability differ because of differences in attitudes, beliefs, orientation, discipline, and culture. For example, different disciplines offer different definitions of disabilities; some definitions include analyses of a group of individuals' common characteristics (e.g., cognitive abilities, stereotypic behaviors). Other concepts take a more sociological view and discuss how differences are socially constructed and are more a function of the social system than the individual (Danforth & Rhodes, 1997).

Explanations of the concept of disability vary, as do opinions on whether its presence has to impair a person's ability to participate in mainstream society. For example, some scholars propose that the concept of disabilities is a political and economic necessity of societies that require a class structure (Erevelles, 1996; Grossman, 1998). The assumption implied by this position is that disability would disappear if society were organized some other way. Other scholars do not accept the position that disability is the result of a stratified society, and reject the idea that everyone should be treated alike (Kauffman, 1997). An extreme need for "sameness" forces people to minimize disability, even deny its existence. It is this logic that downplays the importance of extra educational supports necessary to make maximal achievements. Other experts hold other positions about disability and what it means. Instead of focusing on the concept of "sameness" they focus on the concept of "difference" and the related necessity of making value judgements. To them, it is these relationships that set the stage for mainstream society's concept of "disabilities" (Artiles, 1998). This mind-set drives us to identify more and more deviant groups, more different types of disabilities. (The 1990 reauthorization of IDEA called out two more separate special education categories—traumatic brain injury and autism—and IDEA '97 included attention deficit hyperactivity disorder as part of the health impairments category.)

You can see that there are different ways to understand and answer what appears to be a simple question. As you think about these points, study Figure 1.1, which illustrates adjectives often used to reference differences and disability. Do the words in the right-hand column define for you the concept of disability?

When it comes to schoolchildren, the federal government has elected to define disabilities by using a **categorical** approach and by whether a child needs special services (U.S. Department of Education, 1999). Here are the thirteen special education categories defined as disabilities in Public Law 105–17, the **Individuals with Disabilities Education Act of 1997 (IDEA '97)**:

$\overset{\text{M}_{A_{K_{I}N_G}}}{\underset{\text{C}^{O^{N_{N_{E_{C_{T_{I}O}}}}N^S}}}{}}$

In every chapter about an exceptionality, you will find a section devoted to definitions.

categorical. A system of classification using specific categories such as learning disabilities or mental retardation.

Individuals with Disabilities Education Act (IDEA). New name given in 1990 to the Education for All Handicapped Children Act (EHA).

Autism	Deaf-blindness
Deafness	Emotional disturbance
Hearing impairment	Mental retardation
Multiple disabilities	Orthopedic impairment
Other health impairment	Specific learning disability
Speech or language impairment	Traumatic brain injury
Visual impairment	

same	different
able	disabled
normal	abnormal
competent	impaired
typical	atypical
perfect	defective
functioning	dysfunctional
usual	delayed
standard	deviant
ordinary	exceptional

Figure 1.1 Comparisons of Difference: Defining Disabilities

The government says that if a child is identified as having one of these conditions (or a condition that is subsumed under one of these categories—such as attention deficit hyperactivity disorder, part of the "other health impairment" category), he or she is a student with a disability.

The courts have also wrestled with the problem of defining disabilities, and found the task daunting. Each time the Supreme Court has to fulfill its responsibility to clarify a law passed by Congress, it has to resolve conflicts about differing interpretations. In three recent cases—*Sutton v. United Airlines, Murphy v. United Parcel Service,* and *Albertsons v. Kirkingburg*—the Supreme Court clarified the **Americans with Disabilities Act (ADA),** and had to find a definition that was faithful to the law. The justices had to think about whom Congress wanted to protect when it passed the ADA law in 1990. In other words, what was the "Congressional intent" of the legislation? The ADA law defines disability as an impairment that "substantially limits one or more of the major life activities." What do you think Congress meant by this definition of disability? This is a question that continues to plague the court system.

So, can you define the concept of disabilities for yourself? Not yet? Maybe it would be helpful to consider whether the presence of a disability makes a difference in a person's life. Let's think about another question which might have seemed so simple only a few paragraphs ago: "Is a disability a handicap?"

IS HAVING A DISABILITY NECESSARILY A HANDICAP?

Americans with Disabilities Act (ADA). Federal disability antidiscrimination legislation passed in 1990.

We learned from the civil rights movements of the 1960s that discrimination and bias can "handicap" groups of individuals or keep them from participating fully in society. A discussion about the relationship between disabilities and being handicapped is not only an important concept, but an interesting one too. The way people are treated can limit their independence and opportunities. But we are still left with the question about whether the terms "disability" and "handicap" are synonymous. If they are, disability could then be viewed as a difference, a characteristic that sets an individual apart from everyone else, something that makes the individual less able or inferior. Many professions (medicine, psychology) view disabilities in terms of deviance, a model whereby the majority of the population is considered normal and a disability sets the individual apart. In that view, it is the disability that restricts an individual's ability to reach his or her potential, rather than the individual being handicapped by society's attitudes. And what of gifted individuals with exceptional talents and outstanding intellect? Do people's attitudes about their differences handicap them and limit them from achieving their potential?

Some evidence exists that might sort out this dilemma, or may blur the issue even more. Read the story, in the box about the settlers of Martha's Vineyard, of deaf Americans who were not stigmatized by their immediate society. Absent of bias, their rates of success and failure were similar to everyone else's, showing that how people are treated does influence their lives.

Now, we must consider whether the experience of the early settlers of Martha's Vineyard is an aberration. Is it so peculiar that we should not generalize from this case to other possibilities? Perhaps the story would be different if these early settlers

For other discussions about Deaf Culture and its history, see the History and Deaf Culture sections of Chapter 10.

Disability Does Not Equal Handicap: The Case of Martha's Vineyard

The seventeenth-century settlers of Martha's Vineyard came from Kent, England. Apparently, they carried with them both a recessive gene for deafness and the ability to use sign language. The hearing people living on the island were bilingual, developing their oral and sign language skills simultaneously early in life. Generation after generation, the prevalence of deafness on the island was exceptionally high, being 1:4 in one small community and 1:25 in several others. Probably because deafness occurred at such a high rate and in almost everyone's family, people who were deaf were not treated like deaf people who lived on the mainland. They were integrated into society and were included in all of the community's work and play situations.

So what were the results of such integration and adaptation to the needs of people with this disability, rather than requiring them to adapt to the ways of those without it? These individuals were free to marry whomever they wished. Of those born before 1817, 73% of the Vineyard Deaf* married, whereas only 45% of deaf Americans married. Only 35% of the Vineyard Deaf married other deaf people, compared to 79% of deaf mainlanders. According to tax records, they generally earned average or above-average incomes, with

*A capital D is used here because the Deaf people on Martha's Vineyard represent an important historical group in Deaf culture. See Chapter 10.

some Deaf people actually being quite wealthy. Also, these individuals were active in all aspects of church affairs. Deaf individuals did have some advantages over their hearing neighbors and family members. They were better educated than the general population because they received tuition assistance to attend the school for the deaf in Connecticut. According to the reports of their descendants, these people were able to read and write, and there are numerous accounts about hearing people asking their Deaf neighbors to read something to them or write a letter for them.

The amazing story about the English settlers on Martha's Vineyard shows how deafness, a disability historically considered to be extremely serious, did not affect the way of life or achievement of those who lived on the island. For more than two hundred years, life on this relatively restricted and confined environment was much the same for those who had this disability and those who did not. Groce (1985) provides an explanation for this situation:

> The most striking fact about these deaf men and women is that they were not handicapped, because no one perceived their deafness as a handicap. As one woman said to me, "You know we didn't think anything special about them. They were just like anyone else. When you think about it, the Island was an awfully nice place to live." Indeed it was. (p. 110)

had a genetically caused cognitive disability instead of deafness. Clearly, what happened at Martha's Vineyard was not commonplace. Regardless, it is information you need to consider as you develop your own perspective about disability, its meaning, its impact, and its implications for social response. Thinking about the Martha's Vineyard experience, is it possible that disability and a response to it, special education, are phenomena of the twentieth century?

IS THE NOTION OF DISABILITIES A MODERN-DAY INVENTION?

The answer to this question is quite straightforward: No. Evidence abounds that disabilities are part of the human condition. From the earliest written records, we know that people with disabilities existed. Some, particularly those who were blind, or deaf, or a "bit eccentric," or who acquired their disability while adults, fared well and are part of the written record (Bragg, 1997). An example is Aesop, the blind Greek poet of ancient times whose morality lessons are still read in schools today. Could it be possible that disabilities do not signal a social problem worthy of concern? Could it be that the important issue is not whether disabilities exist, but rather how people react to them? If people are treated fairly and can achieve their potential without considerable supports from others, maybe we are expending considerable energy where it is not necessary. So let's examine how people with disabilities have been treated historically. This analysis might also help us understand the nature of the condition better.

M A K I N G
C O N N E C T I O N S

For these reasons, Chapters 3–12 include sections titled History of the Field.

HOW HAVE PEOPLE WITH DISABILITIES BEEN TREATED OVER THE COURSE OF HISTORY?

The answer to this question is: Inconsistently, but often badly. As you have learned, examples of humane treatment can be documented. Here's another example to consider: People with disabilities who served as court jesters in palaces and royal courts of the Middle Ages and Renaissance were protected. Although we might think they were unfairly treated because they were kept for the amusement of royalty, they lived better than most common people of their times. Typically, however, people with disabilities were victims of discrimination and cruelty. It was common practice to leave defective babies in the woods or to throw them into rivers to die. For most who lived to adulthood, their treatment was harsh. For example, Balbus Balaesus the Stutterer, who lived during ancient Roman times, was caged and placed along the Appian Way to amuse travelers who thought his speech was funny. Some people with disabilities were locked away in asylums or monasteries, while others were thought to be possessed by demons and some were tried as witches (Bragg, 1997).

You might think that such stories are relegated to ancient history. Certainly, many people with disabilities are included in today's mainstream society. They now have access to public buildings, find suitable accommodations when they travel, and assume active roles in society. Unfortunately, positive stories are not always the case. For example, we know that during the middle of the last century Nazi Germany sent millions of Jews, people with disabilities, and members of other targeted groups to their deaths in concentration camps. But that was over fifty years ago; certainly, you might think, such inhumane acts could not occur today. Well, many documented cases of abuse and neglect of children with disabilities do occur today. Exposé after exposé, particularly in Third World and developing countries (including members of

outcomes. The results of decisions and actions.

Without guarantees of civil and human rights around the world, many children with disabilities are forced to live in deplorable conditions. Such treatment is not "a thing-of-the-past."

the former USSR) reveal horrible conditions in orphanages and institutions where imperfect children are kept until they die (Bennett, 1997; Powell & Dlugy, 1998). However, inhumane treatment of people with disabilities is not just a problem of other countries. Think about American adults with mental illness who are left to wander streets and have few supports to assist them.

So, as you construct a concept of disabilities, think about the information you can use to advocate for good solutions and think about what educational programs should comprise. First, definitions of disability vary because people do not share the same attitudes, beliefs, orientation, discipline, and culture. So there is not an absolute nature to disabilities. Second, bias and discrimination influence people's **outcomes** in such a way that what is thought of as a severe disability in one society might not handicap a person from achieving his or her potential in another society. Third, disabilities have existed since the beginning of time, and are not a construct or phenomenon created in the twentieth century. Fourth, the plight of children with disabilities has been terrible, and cruel treatment continues today in some parts of the world.

To further our understanding about disabilities and to be able to suggest a vision for this millennium, it might be helpful to think about one of western civilization's responses to disabilities: special education. To get a better understanding of services that need to be provided to students with disabilities and their families, let's think about when special education emerged, and how it developed.

ORIGINS OF SPECIAL EDUCATION

IS SPECIAL EDUCATION A NEW IDEA?

MAKING
CONNECTIONS

For more on the importance of Itard and Victor, see the History section of Chapter 6.

Although many Americans believe that special education began in the United States in 1975 with the passage of the national law we now call IDEA, special education began over 200 years ago. The legend of its beginnings is not only famous, it's true! A short synopsis of the story of Itard and Victor is presented in the accompanying box. Although Itard did not evaluate his long-term efforts with Victor positively, his work did spawn a new era for children with disabilities. His work saw the beginning of a positive period when education was thought to be one answer to the problems associated with disabilities.

The Origins of Special Education: The Story of Itard and Victor

In 1799 a young child, who had probably been left to die in the woods of southern France because he was "defective," was found by some farmers. These farmers were concerned about the child's welfare, and had heard of a doctor in Paris who was specializing in the treatment of deaf children. They took the child to this physician, Jean-Marc-Gaspard Itard, who is now considered to be the father of special education. Itard named the young boy Victor, but because he was thought to be a "wild child," untouched by civilization, he was often referred to as the Wild Boy of Aveyron. It is likely that he had mental retardation as well as environmental deprivation. Most people thought the case was hopeless. But Itard, believing in the power of education, took on the task of teaching Victor all the things that typical children learn from their families and in school. He used carefully designed techniques to teach Victor to speak a few words, to walk upright, to eat with dishes and utensils, and to interact with other people.

Fortunately, Itard wrote detailed reports of his techniques and his philosophy, as well as of Victor's progress. Many of these techniques are still used in modern special education. Here are Itard's five aims for Victor's "mental and moral education."

> First aim: To interest him in social life …
> Second aim: To awaken his nervous sensibility …
> Third aim: To extend the range of his ideas …
> Fourth aim: To lead him to the use of speech …
> Fifth aim: To make him exercise the simplest mental operations …
> (Itard, 1806/1962, pp. 10–11)

Measures of success are subjective. Today we would credit Itard with the achievement of making great gains with Victor. Victor learned many basic skills of life, but he never became "normal." He was unable to develop oral language beyond a few words, and he did not learn all forms of socially acceptable behavior. Itard thought himself a failure, perhaps because his goals were unrealistic, and Victor lived out his life on Itard's country estate with a housekeeper attending to his needs.

Jean-Marc-Gaspard Itard, considered to be the father of special education, kept a detailed diary on his teaching of Victor.

Victor, the wild boy of Aveyron, contributed to the development of special education theory and techniques as a student of Itard.

For more stories of these and other special education pioneers, see the History sections found in each chapter, beginning with Chapter 3.

The movement was brought to the United States by a student of Itard, Edouard Seguin. In 1846, Seguin published *The Moral Treatment, Hygiene, and Education of Idiots and Other Backward Children*, the first special education treatise addressing the needs of children with disabilities. He believed that sensorimotor exercises could help stimulate learning for children with disabilities (a belief that continually gained and lost popularity during the ensuing 150 years). In 1876, Sequin also helped found the oldest and largest interdisciplinary professional association in the field of mental retardation, which is now called the American Association on Mental Retardation (AAMR). Attitudes gradually changed. Professionals and the public shifted from a belief that people with disabilities should be shunned to the position that they should be protected, cared for, and instructed—even if it took an extraordinary effort.

While the special education effort gained steam in the United States, it also became popular across Europe. In Italy, Montessori worked first with children with cognitive disabilities. She showed that children could learn at young ages through concrete experiences offered in environments rich with manipulative materials. In 1817, Thomas Hopkins Gallaudet went to Europe to bring experts in deaf education back to the United States to implement model education programs. Samuel Gridley Howe, the famous American reformer and abolitionist, founded the New England Asylum for the Blind (later the Perkins Institute) in 1832, and created the Massachusetts School for Idiotic and Feeble-Minded Children in 1848. And so it continued: In state after state, educational programs for students with disabilities were initiated. Many of these programs followed Howe's and Gallaudet's model, and established residential schools; others followed the example of those begun by Elizabeth Farrell (1898) and were offered in public schools. So did the concept of treating disabilities through educational services become commonly accepted? What was the orientation of those programs? Were they successful? Let's explore these questions a bit more, again with the notion of gaining a better understanding of students with disabilities and the education they require.

WERE SPECIAL EDUCATIONAL OPPORTUNITIES CONSISTENTLY AVAILABLE?

As most of us do today, professionals in the late nineteenth century believed in the individual worth of each student, regardless of that student's special learning needs. They were prepared to work hard to make achievement a reality for all students. And it became widely accepted that special education teachers needed special training to do this important work. The first training opportunity for teachers of special classes was offered in 1905 at the New Jersey Training School for Feebleminded Boys and Girls (Kanner, 1964). In 1907, the tuition for a six-week summer course in special education was $25. (See Figure 1.2 on page 14.)

The era of optimism, however, did not last. Public school classes were not widespread, and residential schools took on the nature of repressive institutions. To develop a lasting vision about the education of students with disabilities, it might help to understand the reasons for shifting attitudes. First, there were not enough classes. Second, many children were excluded from public schools because they did not meet entrance criteria—because they were not toilet trained, could not walk, or could not speak. What happened to them? Many functioned to some degree in their home communities, rarely found employment, and lived with their parents. Others were forced to enter isolated, segregated institutions. Certainly, some died from lack of care, and others were hidden by families fearing discrimination and prejudice.

The Training School

Entered March 14, 1904, at Vineland, N.J., as second-class matter, under act of Congress of July 16, 1894.

No. 36.   FEBRUARY 1907.   25c. per Annum.

"I gave a beggar from my little store
Of well-earned gold. He spent the
*   shining ore*
And came again, and yet again, still
*   cold*
*   And hungry as before.*

I gave a thought and through that
*   thought of mine*
He found himself a man, supreme,
*   divine,*
Bold, clothed, and crowned with bless-
*   ings manifold,*
*   And now he begs no more."*

THE SUMMER SCHOOL FOR TEACHERS.

The announcements of our Summer School for 1907 are now ready for distribution. The purpose of the School is to give professional training to those who desire to teach in the special classes in the public schools and to fit teachers and others to better understand peculiar, backward and "special" children. We have unusual facilities for this work, a splendid general equipment and quite a complete laboratory. The plan of work includes observation and teaching, laboratory work, lectures and reading. The tuition fee is $25 and those students who first apply may be boarded at the School at an additional cost of $25. The course extends from July 15th to August 24th.

Information concerning the Summer School may be obtained by addressing E. R. Johnstone, Vineland, N. J.

AS IT APPEARS TO THE PSYCHOLOGIST.

You remember the fable of the lion looking at the picture of a man conquering a lion and saying: "if a lion had painted the picture the man would have gotten the worst of it." It makes a difference who paints the picture.

Men strong of intellect have for long had a monopoly of painting the picture of the feeble-minded. While at times the feeble-minded child has been regarded as a supernatural being possessed of a spirit either good or bad, he has been among the more intellectual races more often treated much as the Spartans treated him—regarded as an outcast and either exposed to die or, where some reverence for human life as such has developed, been preserved from death indeed, but preserved for a life that is possibly worse than death. He has been not only useless, but a drag on society, an incurable disease, a horrible nightmare, one of God's blunders.

But how would the picture look if the lion and not the man painted it?

The feeble-minded child is a human being. He differs from those who call themselves normal, in degree, not in kind. No one of us but might have been of his grade had any one of a score of very possible contingencies taken place. Not one of us but might tomorrow become as "defective" as any of these by the slightest change in our organism. (It is true we should call it insanity, but that is only a matter of terminology.)

What then are we and who is this child? He is somewhere near the

Figure 1.2 Newsletter from the Training School in Vineland, New Jersey.

For more about the twentieth century reaction to people with disabilities and how they were shunned, see the History section of Chapter 6.

While the residential schools first started at the end of the nineteenth century were thought of as educational programs, they became warehouses where people were isolated from society. Possibly, like Itard, professionals and the public became disillusioned about special education, for it was unable to "remove" disabilities, "cure" children, or make them "normal." Children with disabilities apparently were not worthy of investment. Rather, people with disabilities came to be viewed as the source of problems in society: one source of crime, a group that could bring society down (Winzer, 1993). Although not a widely held attitude at the very beginning of the twentieth century, negative beliefs about people with disabilities took hold in the first decades of the century. While children without disabilities were required to attend school under compulsory school attendance laws, children with disabilities were prevented from attending school. The excuses presented for excluding these children from school are shocking by today's standards. One state supreme court justified excluding a young boy with cerebral palsy because he "produces a depressing and nauseating effect upon the teachers and school children" (*State ex rel. Beattie v. Board of Education*, 1919). Bias against people with disabilities lasted through the first half of the century. The purpose of residential special education programs had changed, and no longer was to provide intensive education. From the beginning of the twentieth century until the end of World War II, the primary purpose of institutions was to protect society from those who were different.

Attitudes changed during the last half of the century. The end of World War II saw a time of increased opportunities for people, eventually leading to the Civil Rights Movement of the 1960s and advocacy for people with disabilities during the 1970s. Let's look at these changes in beliefs to see if we can better understand the nature of disabilities and what measures are necessary to guarantee fair treatment to people with disabilities—and to those who are gifted as well.

NECESSITY FOR NATIONAL INTERVENTION

WHY DID CONGRESS PASS A NATIONAL SPECIAL EDUCATION LAW?

In 1975, the stage was clearly set for a national special education law. In the 1970s, the courts and Congress addressed the issue of education for children with disabilities. Table 1.1 on page 16 summarizes early landmark court cases that prepared the way for national special education consistently offered to all children with disabilities.

Years of exclusion, segregation, and denial of basic educational opportunities to students with disabilities and their families set an imperative for a civil rights law guaranteeing these students access to the education system. Why was this so? In 1948, only 12% of all children with disabilities received special education (Ballard et al., 1982). Even as late as 1962, only sixteen states had laws that included students with even mild mental retardation under mandatory school attendance requirements (Roos, 1970). In most states, even those children with the mildest levels of disabilities were not allowed to attend school. Children with more severe disabilities were routinely excluded even until the 1970s.

Clearly, Congress, when first considering passage of a national special education law, recognized the importance of special education for children with disabilities and was concerned about widespread discrimination. It pointed out that many students with disabilities were excluded from education, and that those who did

Table 1.1 Landmark Court Cases Setting the Stage for Special Education

Case	Date	Ruling	Importance
Brown v. Board of Education	1954	Ended white "separate but equal" schools	Basis for future rulings that children with disabilities cannot be excluded from school
Pennsylvania Association for Retarded Children (PARC) v. Commonwealth of Pennsylvania	1972	Guaranteed special education to children with mental retardation	Court case that signaled a new period for special education
Mills v. Board of Education of the District of Columbia	1972	Extended the right for special education to children with all disabilities	Reinforced the right to a free public education to all children with disabilities

For specifics about the last reauthorization of the Individuals with Disabilities Education Act, see the boxes called What IDEA '97 Say About, which are found throughout the text.

attend school frequently failed to benefit because their disabilities went undetected or ignored. Congress realized that special education could make a positive difference in the lives of these children and their families with proper financial assistance and educational support. It found these facts so compelling (see the box on congressional findings) that it declared it was "in the national interest" to stop discrimination against children with disabilities.

Congress has deemed it necessary to continue supporting this education law (first named the **Education for All Handicapped Children Act,** and now called the **Individuals with Disabilities Education Act—IDEA**). **Public Law (PL) 94–142** was

1975 Congressional Findings: The Justification for a National Special Education Law

Here are Congress's 1975 findings that caused it to pass PL 94–142, the special education law now known as IDEA:

1. There are more than 8 million children with disabilities in the United States today;
2. The special educational needs of such children are not being fully met;
3. More than half of the children with disabilities in the United States do not receive appropriate educational services which would enable them to have full equality of opportunity;
4. 1 million of the children with disabilities in the United States are excluded entirely from the public school system and will not go through the educational process with their peers;
5. There are many children with disabilities throughout the United States participating in regular school programs whose handicaps prevent them from having a successful educational experience because their disabilities are undetected;

6. Because of the lack of adequate services within the public school system, families are often forced to find services outside the public school system, often at great distance from their residence and at their own expense;
7. Developments in the training of teachers and in diagnostic and instructional procedures and methods have advanced to the point that, given appropriate funding, State and local educational agencies can and will provide effective special education and related services to meet the needs of children with disabilities;
8. State and local educational agencies have a responsibility to provide education for all children with disabilities, present financial resources are inadequate to meet the special educational needs of children with disabilities; and
9. It is in the national interest that the Federal Government assist State and local efforts to provide programs to meet the educational needs of children with disabilities in order to assure equal protection of the law. (20 U.S.C. section 1400[b])

For *some* kids school segregation DIDN'T END IN THE SIXTIES.

Students with disabilities should be evaluated individually to decide their best situations for learning. Because when students are kept apart just for being different, it teaches all the wrong things.

GIVE ABILITY A CHANCE

Education for All Handicapped Children Act (EHA) or Public Law (PL) 94-142. A federal law, PL 94-142, passed in 1975 with many provisions for assuring free appropriate public education for all students with disabilities; in 1990 renamed the **Individuals with Disabilities Education Act (IDEA).**

reauthorization. The act of amending and renewing a law.

Section 504 of the Rehabilitation Act of 1973. This law set the stage for both the Individuals with Disabilities Education Act, passed in 1975, and the Americans with Disabilities Act, passed in 1990, by outlining basic civil rights of people with disabilities.

initially passed in 1975 and implemented in 1977. It has been reauthorized three times since: PL 99-475, PL 101-476, and PL 105-17. The last **reauthorization** was passed in 1997, so the law is now referred to as IDEA '97. With each enactment, the law has been expanded or strengthened, and it now protects the education rights of children and youth with disabilities from birth to the age of 21.

IDEA was not Congress's first attempt to correct the injustices it saw in the way people with disabilities were treated in America; it also was not its last. IDEA is a children's law, a law that protects their rights to education. To end discrimination and to guarantee basic civil rights to this group, Congress has taken additional measures. Perhaps broadening our discussion to adults, if for only a few paragraphs, might help us understand the nature of disabilities and the supports these individuals require.

WAS A SPECIAL EDUCATION LAW SUFFICIENT TO END DISCRIMINATION AGAINST PEOPLE WITH DISABILITIES?

At last, a question with a straightforward, simple, and resounding answer of *no.* The nation's policymakers, both in Congress and in the courts, saw injustices in society that they believed had to be corrected, and recognized that it would take national action to solve these problems. Congress's first attempt at a national civil rights law for people with disabilities was passed before IDEA was drafted, and it was part of a larger act. In 1973, Congress passed **Section 504 of the Rehabilitation Act.** This law set the stage for IDEA because it included some protection of the rights of students with disabilities to public education and required accommodations for people with disabilities like access to public buildings. After almost twenty years of implementation, Congress felt that Section 504 was not sufficient and did not end discrimination for adults with disabilities. It took stronger measures by passing yet another law.

On July 26, 1990, President Bush signed the Americans with Disabilities Act (ADA), which bars discrimination in employment, transportation, public accommodations, and telecommunications. He said, "Let the shameful walls of exclusion finally come tumbling down." Senator Tom Harkin (D–IA), the chief sponsor of the act, spoke of this law as the "emancipation proclamation" for people with disabilities (West, 1994). ADA guarantees access to all aspects of life—not just those that are federally funded—to people with disabilities and implements the concept of normalization across all of American life.

Both Section 504 of the Rehabilitation Act of 1973 and ADA are considered civil rights and antidiscrimination laws (Roberts & Mather, 1995). ADA supports and extends Section 504, and provides adults with disabilities greater access to employment and participation in everyday activities that adults without disabilities enjoy. ADA requires employers not to discriminate against qualified applicants or employees with disabilities. It requires new public transportation (buses, trains, subways) and new or remodeled public accommodations (hotels, stores, restaurants, banks, theaters) to be accessible to persons with disabilities. It also requires telephone companies to provide relay services so that deaf individuals and people with speech impairments can use ordinary telephones. For students who are making the transition from school to adult life, these improvements in access and nondiscrimination should help them achieve genuine participation in their communities.

Beginning with Chapter 3, every chapter includes a Technology section featuring developments that will benefit students and adults with disabilities.

HAVE THE PROTECTIONS OF NATIONAL LAWS MADE A DIFFERENCE IN THE LIVES OF PEOPLE WITH DISABILITIES?

Here the answer is a resounding *yes!* ADA, and American attitudes that allowed its passage, have brought many personal benefits to people with disabilities. Businesses have made accommodations that allow all employees, including those with disabilities, to perform at levels they might not otherwise achieve. Equipment is now available in the workplace that supports people with disabilities: voice-activated computers, closed circuit TV equipment that magnifies printed material, and physical accommodations like ramps. Of course, the ADA law alone cannot be credited with all these changes and benefits, but it is clearly one part of the civil rights movement for citizens with disabilities that has made a real difference.

For many people with disabilities, access and participation in mainstream society is an expectation today. These adults actively participate in all aspects of daily life, from employment to recreation. Here are some examples that illustrate improved access and participation: wheelchair marathon races, tactile museum exhibits for blind people, accessible trails in national and state parks, captioned television and movies, and audio descriptions of visual images for people with limited visual abilities (DVS, 1999). Even Barbie has a doll-friend, Share a Smile Becky, who uses a wheelchair (even though the first version demonstrated how inaccessible Barbie's doll house and accessories really were!). People with disabilities are included in TV and magazine advertisements, and have taken jobs in the entertainment industry as newscasters, actors, and comedians. All of these examples demonstrates how attitudes have changed, improving the quality of life for many people with disabilities.

Many secondary benefits have resulted from the passage of the ADA law. For example, books like

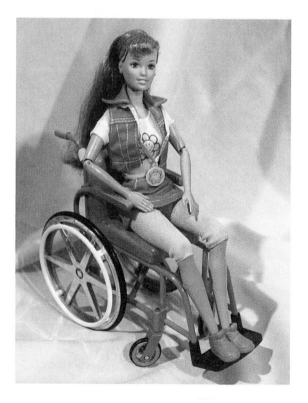

Barbie now has a friend, Share a Smile Becky, who provides a role model for girls with disabilities in a fashion similar to the one Barbie provides for girls without disabilities.

Charles Ruff was headed to the floor of the congressional chamber to defend President Clinton in his impeachment hearings. He reported finding the floor not very accessible!

Fodor's *Great American Vacations for Travelers with Disabilities,* which contains helpful information on accommodations and accessibility of places of interest, are now widely available. And many books aimed at a more general audience, like Fodor's *Complete Guide to America's National Parks,* include accessible features of travel destinations which help people with and without disabilities plan holidays appropriate for their individual abilities. The benefits to the tourist industry are great as well. The Census Bureau reports that the 49 million people with disabilities have a combined disposable income of $188 billion, and these individuals do travel, spending 3.5 times more nights in hotels a year than most other Americans (Vukelich, 1995). People with disabilities are profiting in other ways from the ADA law. Architects are now using a concept called "universal design" to remodel and build homes that are accessible to everyone (Werne, 1995). Lever handles on doors are easier to use for those whose arms are laden with shopping bags, those who have arthritis, and those with restricted mobility. Wheelchairs can roll under sinks. Driveways gradually slope to the level of the front door, which eliminates the need for steps and is also aesthetically pleasing. The principles of universal design can have great benefits to almost everyone, not just those with disabilities.

Section 504 and ADA do affect the education system, but there are some important differences between them and IDEA that you should understand. Section 504 and ADA have a broader definition of disabilities than does IDEA, for they guarantee the right to accommodations even for those who do not need special education services and to those beyond school age. For example, it is under the authority of ADA that college students are entitled to special testing situations (untimed tests, someone to read the questions to the test taker, a special braille version).

ADA does not come without controversy, however. On the first level, many individuals with disabilities do not believe that the law is being implemented or enforced (West, 1994). Disappointment is felt by some members of the disability community who still cannot find jobs to suit their interests, training, or skills. On the second level are the many small-business owners who claim that ADA requires them to make expensive accommodations to their businesses that are never used. Take the case of Blair Taylor, owner of the Barolo Grill in Denver, who bore the expenses for building a ramp (it even took ten months to obtain the necessary variances from the city) and sacrificed four of his twenty-eight dining tables (all twenty-four are now accessible). The ramp has never been used, and Taylor is certain that seventeen wheelchairs will never be in his business at the same time (Mills, 1995). Despite the controversy, and in some cases even hard feelings, the overwhelming opinion of most Americans is that the ADA law guarantees people with disabilities the rights to which they are entitled: participation in and access to the mainstream of American society. In particular, people with disabilities overwhelmingly support continuation of the ADA law despite their continued frustration with specifics about its implementation (Pfeiffer, 1996).

So, while federal legal protections have clearly made a difference in the lives of people with disabilities, sometimes the requirements of these laws have not been entirely clear. As you will see next, the courts had to become involved to clarify and interpret Congress's intent.

WHY DID THE COURTS HAVE TO FURTHER INTERPRET AND DEFINE IDEA?

Although Congress thought it was clear in its intentions about the educational guarantees it believed were necessary for children with disabilities and their families, no legal language is perfect. It is the role of the courts to clarify laws passed by Congress and implemented by the administration (for example, implementation of IDEA is the responsibility of the U.S. Department of Education). Since 1975, when PL 94–142 became law, a very small percentage of all children served have been involved in formal disputes. Those disputes concern the identification of children with disabilities, evaluations, educational placements, and the provision of a free appropriate public education. Many of these disputes are resolved in noncourt proceedings (due process hearings).

Some disputes, however, must be settled in courts of law—a few even in the U.S. Supreme Court. Through such **litigation,** many different questions about special education have been addressed and clarified. A few of the more important cases the Supreme Court has decided are listed in Table 1.2.

THE LEGACY OF THE TWENTIETH CENTURY

IS THE FEDERAL GOVERNMENT THE ONLY VOICE HEARD ABOUT THE RIGHTS OF PEOPLE WITH DISABILITIES?

The answer is definitely *no.* Professionals, along with people with disabilities and their families, have become very effective advocates. The laws and court cases you have just learned about were, in part, stimulated by organized advocacy efforts. In the early twentieth century, the job of raising America's consciousness about problems of people with disabilities rested primarily with professional organizations, but in the latter part of the century people with disabilities began to speak on their own behalf. Let's look at a bit of this history to understand an important aspect of the legacy given to those of us living in the new millennium.

In 1922, the International Council for the Education of Exceptional Children (CEC) was founded (Aiello, 1976) when members of a summer special education class conducted at Teachers' College, Columbia University, decided to meet annually to continue sharing exciting ideas about special education. Their professor, Elizabeth Farrell, became the group's first president. Membership grew, and CEC remains the largest special education professional organization in the United States, with about 61,000 members. CEC was not the only professional organization concerned about people with disabilities. The American Speech-Language-Hearing Association (ASHA) was established in 1935 and has a current membership of about 85,000 professionals. The American Occupational Therapy Association (AOTA), the

C O N N E C T I O N S
M A K I N G

The self-advocacy movement is discussed in the History sections of Chapters 6 and 9.

litigation. A lawsuit or legal proceeding.

Table 1.2 U.S. Supreme Court Cases Interpreting IDEA

Case	Date	Issue	Finding
Rowley v. Hendrick Hudson School District	1984	Free appropriate public education (FAPE)	School districts must provide those services that permit a student with disabilities to benefit from instruction.
Irving Independent School District v. Tatro	1984	Defining *related services*	Clean intermittent catheterization (CIC) is a related service when necessary to allow a student to stay in school.
Smith v. Robinson	1984	Attorneys' fees	IDEA does not provide for attorneys' fees for special education litigation. Congress objected to this interpretation and passed a law authorizing fees to parents who win their case.
Burlington School Committee v. Department of Education	1984	Private school placement	In some cases, public schools may be required to pay for private school placements when an appropriate education is not provided by the district.
Honig v. Doe	1988	Exclusion from school	Students whose misbehavior is related to their disability cannot be denied education.
Timothy W. v. Rochester New Hampshire School District	1989	FAPE	Regardless of the existence or severity of a student's disability, a public education is the right of every child.
Zobrest v. Catalina Foothills School District	1993	Paid interpreter at parochial high school	Paying a sign language interpreter does not violate the constitutional separation of church and state.
Florence County School District 4 v. Carter	1993	Reimbursement for private school	A court may order reimbursement for parents who unilaterally withdraw their children from a public school that provides inappropriate education and place their child in a private school that is proper under IDEA but does not meet all requirements.
Doe v. Withers	1993	FAPE	Teachers are responsible for the implementation of accommodations specified in individual students' IEPs.
Cedar Rapids School District v Garret F.	1999	Related services	Health attendants are a related service if they maintain students in education programs, and are therefore to be provided at the school's expense.

National Association of Social Workers (NASW), and the American Physical Therapy Association (APTA) have all been instrumental in advocating for the availability of related services for all students with disabilities who need them.

Many volunteer and parent organizations began to organize after World War II to fight for the initiation of educational services in the public schools for students with disabilities. The Arc (formerly the Association for Retarded Citizens of the United States), founded in 1950 as the National Association of Parents and Friends of Mentally Retarded Children, worked to have special education services provided to all students with disabilities through the public education system. Other influential groups were United Cerebral Palsy Associations, Inc. (UCP), which began in 1949; the National Society for Autistic Children, formed in 1961; the Learning

People with disabilities participate in a wide range of leisure time and sports activities with just as much enjoyment as people without disabilities.

The story of Ed Roberts is found in Chapter 9.

normalization. Making available ordinary patterns of life and conditions of everyday living.

Disability Association of America (LDA), founded in 1963 as the Association for Children with Learning Disabilities; and the Epilepsy Foundation of America, which grew out of several earlier epilepsy groups in 1968. The power and importance of these parent advocacy groups must be recognized and applauded. It continues to be the strength of the parent movement that improves federal laws. Parents argue successfully for funding at the state and national levels, and serve as a "watchdog" over local education programs to ensure that each student with a disability has access to a free appropriate public education.

People with disabilities formed their own advocacy groups, becoming effectively organized during the late 1980s and 1990s. The first phase was a quest for civil rights; the second phase is focusing on the development of a disability culture (Longmore, 1995; Treanor, 1993). Ed Roberts, founder of the World Institute on Disability and himself a person with disabilities, was a catalyst in organizing people with disabilities to demand access to mainstream U.S. society and the fulfillment of basic civil rights. The Council for Citizens with Disabilities (a coalition of many advocacy groups) was instrumental in shaping the ADA and provided considerable input during the last reauthorization of IDEA. It continues to be active in shaping national laws and policies. Today there are many adult advocacy organizations and many other less formal support groups formed by and for adults with disabilities who seek to change laws, policies, and practices that affect their lives. In many respects, the development and passage of the ADA law in 1990 was due to the advocacy and vigilance of adults who believe they have been handicapped by society's treatment of them. Today, parents and people with disabilities are the two most powerful lobbying groups at work on behalf of people with disabilities. They have created powerful political action organizations that work to improve opportunities available to all individuals with disabilities.

One of the formative principles that guide advocacy efforts is the notion of normalization. **Normalization** is an essential dimension of special education and a guiding concept for adults with disabilities. Although the concept was suggested in 1959 by Bank-Mikkelsen of Denmark (Biklen, 1985), the word itself was coined by Bengt Nirje of Sweden (1969, 1976), who, along with Wolf Wolfensberger, encouraged the United States to incorporate this principle in services to people with disabilities (Wolfensberger, 1972, 1995). According to Nirje (1985), normalization means "making available to all persons with disabilities or other handicaps, patterns of life and conditions of everyday living which are as close as possible to or indeed *the same* as the regular circumstances and ways of life of society" (p. 67; emphasis in original). The principle of normalization applies to every aspect of a student's life. Nirje referred to a set of normal life patterns: the normal rhythm of the day, the normal rhythm of the week, the normal rhythm of the year, and the nor-

MAKING CONNECTIONS

Normalization and its evolution are also discussed in Chapter 6.

mal development of the life cycle. Until the 1970s, much of the day-to-day work in institutions—such as caring for individuals with severe disabilities or performing farm or laundry work—was provided by residents with mild and moderate disabilities. Because of the widely held belief that individuals with disabilities would contaminate the "normal" population, many people spent their entire lives in these institutions, isolated from mainstream society. Institutional living conflicts with the principle of normalization, and advocacy efforts have resulted in most people, even those with severe disabilities, living in community settings and having a voice about issues like how and where they live (Johnson, 1998). As you think about what the American response to children and adults with disabilities should be, remember the normalization principle.

Another signal of a new era has been the approval of disabilities studies as a bona fide major at many colleges and universities. As with women's studies or Black studies, this major represents an interdisciplinary study of the history and culture of a group of people. What is also very interesting is an emerging attitude that one must have disability status (be a person with a disability) to be seen as an expert in the field of disabilities (Cassuto, 1999).

HAS SOCIETY INCREASED ITS SENSITIVITY REGARDING PEOPLE WITH DISABILITIES AND THEIR NEEDS?

MAKING CONNECTIONS

Brief listings of popular books and films available on video or DVD are found in the Resources section at the end of each chapter.

Possibly stimulated by national policies, society now reflects a more sensitive and understanding way of regarding and talking about the minority group that includes children and adults with disabilities. People with disabilities are visible members of communities, very different from some fifty years ago when great lengths were taken to hide President Franklin Roosevelt's use of crutches and a wheelchair from the public (Gallagher, 1994). They have also begun to advocate for themselves in expressing some strong feelings about the words and phrases used to describe them. The Getting It Right box explains how this has influenced the language we use, and how most people with disabilities prefer to be referred to when spoken or written about.

One way to measure and evaluate how any group of people is perceived by a society is to analyze how that group is portrayed in film. Film not only reflects public attitudes, it has the potential to influence the way people think and interact with others (Safran, 1998, 2000). It can also perpetuate stereotypes. Films produced at the beginning of the last century rarely depicted people with disabilities in a positive light. They were people who were villainous or evil, being punished through their disabilities by God, or were bitter and self-pitying. Another theme was that through the miracles of modern medicine, people

Filmmaker Walter Brock and Arthur Campbell, Jr. discuss the impact of their film, *If I Can't Do It*, which was part of the PBS series P.O.V. The film portrays both Brock's striving for independence and the history of the disability rights movement before and after the passage of the Americans with Disabilities Act.

Getting It Right: Talking About People with Disabilities

Language evolves to reflect changing concepts and beliefs. What is socially acceptable at one point in history can be viewed as funny or offensive at another. For example, at the beginning of the twentieth century terms like *imbecile, moron,* and *mental retardate* were commonly used. Other references, which we think of today as cruel, came and went. In most cases, they were not originally thought of as harmful, but they took on negative connotations. As a result of grassroots advocacy, people with disabilities and their families have influenced the language we use to talk about members of this minority group. This issue is very important to people with disabilities because words send a message to others about our respect for them. Although most of us try to "get it right" all of the time, we occasionally use language offensive to others. The language preferred by people with disabilities can be confusing because different groups and individuals have very different preferences. Although there are some exceptions (especially for the Deaf), there are two basic rules to follow:

- Put people first
- Do not make the person equal the disability

In light of these rules, therefore, it is proper to use phrases such as the following: students *with* mental retardation, individuals *who have* learning disabilities. Two groups of individuals with disabilities prefer a different descriptive approach: Specifically, the Deaf (who prefer this term as a reflection of their heritage and culture) and those who are blind provide for most of the exceptions found in accepted disability terminology. You might find the "Do Say" and "Don't Say" tables (Tables 1.3 and 1.4) helpful as you explain the language of disabilities and its exceptions. Remember, however, that not all members of any group agree unanimously on every issue; some people with disabilities might not agree with the rules of language described here. And the rules will probably change over time.

Table 1.3 Getting It Right: Do Say

Adjective	People	Qualifier
Culturally and linguistically diverse	students with … students who have … individuals with … individuals who have … children with … youth with … toddlers with … adults with …	• disabilities • mental retardation • learning disabilities • speech impairments • language impairments • emotional disturbance • behavioral disorders • cerebral palsy • physical disabilities • hearing impairments • visual disabilities
Exceptions		
	people toddlers	• who face physical challenges • who use a wheelchair
Blind	students youth	• who are blind • who have low vision
Deaf	individuals	• who are deaf • who are hard of hearing
	the deaf the blind	

Table 1.4 Getting It Right: Don't Say

Article	Adjective or Noun
The	crippled disabled disturbed handicapped hearing impairments learning disabled mentally retarded wheelchair bound

with paralysis or blindness could be cured. Comparisons of some acclaimed and Academy Award winning films make it clear that the message has changed over a century of movies: *Frankenstein* (1931), *The Best Years of Our Lives* (1946), *My Left Foot* (1989), and *Shine* (1996). Not all of the disability themes found in motion pictures across time are negative, and some evidence points to more accurate representations of what life is like for many people with disabilities.

Despite important changes in the ways people with disabilities are portrayed and included in society, stigma and bias are a long way from being eliminated. Many people with disabilities and observers of societies across the world would agree with Kitchin's comments, "Disabled people are marginalized and excluded from 'mainstream' society. . . . Disabled people represent one of the poorest groups in Western society" (1998, p. 343). Most definitely, people with disabilities drop out of school at alarming rates, are unemployed and underemployed far more than people without disabilities, and face discrimination in the workplace and in the community (U.S. Department of Education, 1998). And think again about adults with mental illness in this country who are left homeless on the streets of America because changes in public policy made them vulnerable to neglect.

We should now understand the climate of advocacy, the atmosphere of sensitivity, and the acknowledgement that as a minority group, people with disabilities have had to fight for their places in American society. But to achieve the level of participation they desire requires them to be prepared to assume independence and access to work and life in the community. Preparation for these responsibilities begins at school, with an education. So let's turn our attention back to what actually is the focus of this text: the special educational opportunities available to students with disabilities.

WHAT IS SPECIAL EDUCATION?

To improve any process or program requires an understanding of what needs to be modified. Let's see if we can come to an understanding of the concept of special education, with the goal in mind of determining solutions that will improve the education and outcomes of students with disabilities.

Special education is described, defined, and explained in many ways. These different perceptions about what special education is result from people's diverse orientations and experiences. For example, as you can see from the story in the box on page 26, one way special education is defined is by the teachers who have dedicated themselves to the field. It can also be defined as a service or supportive part of the educational system where professionals either consult with teachers or provide a considerable amount of direct instruction and collaborate with others who also teach and work with students with disabilities. Like so many answers to the questions we've investigated so far, special education means different things to different people. Let's look at a couple of other definitions of special education; maybe we can get closer to a more specific answer.

Congress explained what it meant by special education in the original passage of IDEA in 1975 by using these words:

> It is the purpose of this chapter to assure that all handicapped children have available to them . . . a free appropriate public education which emphasizes special education and related services designed to meet their unique needs, to assure that the rights of handicapped children and their parents or guardians are protected, to assist States and localities to provide for the education of all handicapped children,

MAKING CONNECTIONS

See Figure 2.3 for the proportions of professionals from disciplines supporting the special education enterprise through the delivery of related services.

Special Education in 1891: As Defined by Its Teachers

In 1891, one superintendent of a residential school described the perfect special education teacher. He urged the teachers to be "sweet-tempered":

> The ideal teacher is well educated, refined, intensely interested in her pupils, and has a professional zeal to grow in her work: she is original, striving to introduce new and bright methods, but not passing hastily from subject to subject before the child has grasped the first.

She is patient but energetic, sweet-tempered but persistent, and to the influences of her education and character she adds the charms of personal neatness and attractive manners. She possesses naturally a well grounded religious sense, which finds its best expression in self-sacrifice, conscientious duty, and instinctive kindness. (Isaac N. Kerlin, *Manual of Elwyn,* 1891, quoted in Nazzaro, 1977, p. 11)

More about special education and the individualized education it offers is found in Chapter 2.

special education. Individualized education for children and youth with special needs.

related services. A part of special education that includes services from professionals from a wide range of disciplines typically outside of education, all designed to meet the learning needs of individual children with disabilities.

and to assess and assure the effectiveness of efforts to educate handicapped children. (20 U.S.C. section 1400[c])

The United States Department of Education, in its regulations implementing IDEA '97, says that special education means:

> specially designed instruction, at no cost to the parent, to meet the unique needs of a child with a disability, including instruction conducted in the classroom, in the home, in hospitals and institutions, and in other settings; and instruction in physical education. (1999, p. 12425).

Another way to conceptualize **special education** is by looking at the wide variety of services it provides to children with disabilities and their families. Special education is supposed to be individualized and to provide a tailor-made education for each child with a special need. These programs are also supposed to hold high expectations that lead to reasonable outcomes achieved by students with disabilities. Special educaton includes direct instruction in the classroom, consultation and collaboration with the general education teacher, coordination of the student's educational program, and orchestration of those learning opportunities necessary for each youngster to profit from instruction. It also includes a wide array of the **related services,** which include these professionals:

Adaptive PE teachers	Assistive technologists
Counselors	Audiologists
Interpreters for the deaf	Diagnostic staff
Physical therapists	Paraprofessionals (teacher aides)
Occupational therapists	Psychologists
Rehabilitation counselors	Recreational therapists
Supervisors and administrators	School social workers
Work study coordinators	Vocational education teachers

Special education can also be defined by the eight fundamental provisions outlined in IDEA '97. These provisions are listed here, and the two most often misunderstood are clarified in their respective What IDEA '97 Says boxes.

- Free appropriate public education (FAPE)
- Parental rights to notification of evaluation and placement decisions, including the rights to due process hearings in the case of disagreements

Least Restrictive Environment (LRE)

- To the maximum extent possible, children with disabilities are educated with nondisabled peers
- Ensures a continuum of alternative placements
- Provides for supplementary services (resource room or itinerant instruction) in conjunction with general education
- Is individually determined and is based on evaluations of the student
- Is evaluated at least annually
- Is based on the child's IEP
- Is as close to the child's home as possible, and whenever possible is at that child's neighborhood school

Free Appropriate Public Education (FAPE)

- Must be based on each child's identified special education and related service needs
- Guarantees parents that special education services will be at no cost to them
- Is determined by the child's unique needs, not on what is assumed by the special education category the child's been assigned to
- Ensures that there is no delay in implementing a child's individualized education plan, once it has been developed

- Individualized education and services to all children with disabilities
- Provision of necessary related services
- Individualized assessments
- Individualized education program (IEP) plans
- Education provided to the fullest extent possible in the least restrictive environment (LRE)
- Federal assistance to state and school districts to ease the burden of the excess costs for special education

WHAT DO MANY PEOPLE SEE AS PROBLEMS OF SPECIAL EDUCATION?

It is impossible to ignore the fact that special education became controversial at the end of the twentieth century. Criticisms came from all sectors of American society. This program that had once been acclaimed appears to be falling out of favor. Although schooling is no longer denied to any child and the outcomes of students with disabilities are significantly improved over previous times, complaints about special education, its costs, and its practices continue to be pervasive in the press, in public conversations, and in Congress (Gubernick & Conlin, 1997). Special education is blamed for many problems found in the public schools.

Clearly, the fairly recent but overwhelming negative feelings about special education held by many in American society are one of the significant legacies of the twentieth century. Here are some of the major concerns and issues that must be resolved in this new millennium.

Special education:

- Is ineffective and unnecessary
- Is discriminatory
- Segregates children from their peers
- Serves too many children
- Should include all students with ADHD
- Is too expensive and places too much of a burden on local schools
- Unequally protects children who are violent and present discipline problems

To get a better understanding of concerns about special education, let's briefly look at these issues to gain a perspective that might lead to effective solutions.

Is special education ineffective and unnecessary? The answer to this question would definitely help us sort out whether special education costs are too great. Unfortunately, like most of the other questions we have grappled with, the question cannot be answered at this time (or answered simply). The debates about special education's effectiveness are often emotional, and irrational. There is great confusion about what standards should be applied to measure special education's effectiveness. The goals for special education are implied and not specific. Many policymakers, educators, and parents also seem unclear about their expectations for special education. Many of them believe that special education is only effective if it "cures" or "fixes" disabilities, makes them go away (Lovitt & Cushing, 1999). Using these unreasonable expectations, special education will always be judged ineffective. The related attitude of minimizing the impact of disabilities leads to arguments that "good teaching" and "high expectations" in general education classes ("the mainstream") alone can meet the needs of students with disabilities. Others, however, recognize that special education teachers work with students who are "difficult to teach," who present some of the most serious challenges to the educational system, but the goals for their efforts are not clearly articulated. Regardless, evidence does exist that the long-term benefits of educating students with disabilities are positive (Hehir, 1996). Individuals who have received special education now, as adults, work and live in the community, pay taxes, and need fewer supports than those individuals with disabilities who had no access to the educational system. Balancing the financial costs of life long residential services and an inability to work against the costs of special education show that the cost-effectiveness of special education is great. Also, the personal costs to individuals who are unable to assume a productive place in the community are immeasurable. It is always tempting to make short-term savings without regard to long-term consequences. Considering the relatively short history of special education and the participation of all students with disabilities in the education system, I worry about how vulnerable they and their participation in the educational system are.

Is special education discriminatory? A commonly held belief, particularly among leaders from many culturally and linguistically diverse groups, is that too many students of color are placed in special education programs (Artiles et al., 1998; Artiles & Trent, 1994; Artiles & Zamora-Duran, 1997; Harry, 1994; Oswald et al., 1999). It is a fact that their rates of placement in special education exceed their proportions in the school population. Many different explanations for their disproportionate representation exist, ranging from documentation of these youngsters' low academic achievement and disruptive behaviors, to expected outcomes of poverty and limited access to health care, to institutional racism (MacMillan et al., 1998; Patton,

MAKING CONNECTIONS

- Discussions throughout this text, particularly in Chapter 3, focus are the unique learning needs of culturally and linguistically diverse students.
- In particular, study the sections in Chapter 3 about the over- and underrepresentation of diverse students in special education.

1998; Reschly, 1997). So, to some educators, special education is being provided to students who are not succeeding in the general education curriculum, and it is giving them the extra assistance and supports they require. To others, special education is a way to remove disruptive students from the general education classroom. And to some, it is perceived as a sentence to low achievement and a "watered down" curriculum guaranteeing poor lifetime opportunities.

Does special education unnecessarily segregate students with disabilities from their nondisabled peers? Historically, there is no question that this was a problem; to many, it remains a problem (Danforth & Rhodes, 1997; Gardner & Lipsky, 1987). See if you think it still is. When the field of special education began, the few services that were available were offered primarily in segregated settings. Sometimes these services were provided in special schools within a school district, but more often in residential schools, which in many cases became terrible institutions, geographically isolated in the rural parts of a state. As public school programs became more available and **mainstreaming** was limited, students with disabilities often found themselves in separate schools or separate classes, removed from their neighborhood peers. The concept of least restrictive environment (review again the IDEA '97 box about LRE) is guided by the principle of normalization, and the result is that most students with disabilities attend their neighborhood schools. Today, according to the U.S. Department of Education, all children with disabilities have access to public education. The vast majority (73%) receives their education predominately in the general education setting. To many professionals and parents, this percentage is insufficient, particularly since it includes children who leave the general education classroom for their instruction for large portions of the schoolday. However, positions about placement (where students receive their education) vary wildly, ranging from support for full inclusion in general education classes to full-time placement in center (residential) schools. As debates continue about placement, particularly among professionals and federal policymakers, it is important to listen to the other voices. For example, according to a Gallup/Kappan public opinion poll, two-thirds (66%) of Americans believe that students with learning problems belong in separate classes (Rose & Gallup, 1998). And many (though not all) students themselves prefer to receive their instruction outside of the general education setting (Klingner et al., 1998; Lovitt et al., 1999).

Should the medical diagnosis of attention deficit hyperactivity disorder (ADHD) automatically qualify a student for special education? Since the 1990 reauthorization of IDEA, Congress and the U.S. Department of Education have wrestled with this issue. In IDEA '97 ADHD was included under the special education category of "other health impaired," but both Congress and the Department of Education (in its IDEA regulations) were clear that not all children with ADHD qualify for or need special education. Most of these children's educational accommodations are covered under Section 504 and their needs for more structured general education classroom experiences are protected in that section of the Rehabilitation Act (Deveres, 1999). Estimates indicate that the percentage of the school population included in special education would exceed 20% if all ADHD students were included, but the federal government insists that students with ADHD whose condition adversely affects their educational performance have been consistently included in special education. The symptoms of ADHD are commonly acknowledged symptoms of learning disabilities and emotional or behavioral disorders, and many of these students receive dual diagnoses. It is interesting, at a time when

CONNECTIONS

For more information about inclusion and educational placements, see:
- Collaboration for Inclusion sections in Chapters 3–12
- Discussions about FAPE and LRE in Chapter 2

CONNECTIONS

Information about ADHD is found in these chapters:
- Chapter 4
- Chapter 8
- Chapter 9

mainstreaming. Including students with special needs in general education classrooms for some or all of their school day.

special education is being criticized as ineffective, that many parents are trying desperately to get their children identified as having a disability and qualified for special education services.

Are too many students included in special education? Clearly, the number of students participating in special education has increased since the initial passage of IDEA in 1975. However, the overall student population in America has also increased, so increases in numbers are to be expected. Also, in 1975 many children were still excluded from public schools, so that date should probably not be the benchmark used to evaluate whether the number or percentage of students participating in special education is increasing. So it is important to think about the proportion of students identified as having disabilities, rather than the sheer number of them, to be able to make fair comparisons. **Prevalence** is the term professionals use to refer to the total number of cases at a given time. When Congress passed IDEA in 1975, estimates were that special education would not serve any more than 12% of schoolchildren. According to the *Twentieth Annual Report to Congress on the Implementation of the Individuals with Disabilities Act*, 4,966,776 children and youth from ages 6 through 17 are served in special education programs under the IDEA (U.S. Department of Education, 1998). This total represents 10.78% of all children and youth in this age group. Although the percentage of students served through special education is still below original estimates, many administrators and policymakers think the number served is too high. Could it be that general education is failing to meet the educational needs of a large number of students? Certainly, if the nation decides that this percentage or the number of students receiving services through special education is too great, a lower cap or limit could be developed. And more alternatives to the present general and special education options might be warranted.

Is special education too costly and does it create a financial burden on states and local school districts? It is true: Many state and school district officials believe that the costs for special education services infringe on services available to general education students, and that the federal share of special education costs is insufficient. In 1975 when IDEA was first passed, Congress authorized the federal government to pay up to 40% of the extra funds, referred to as **excess cost**, needed to provide special education services. (Notice that Congress used the phrase "up to" in the original law.) Although federal appropriations have increased considerably over the years, the federal share of costs is only about 10%, and many districts believe that they are left with an unfair burden (Parrish, 1999). Let's look at national averages for an example to help us understand their concerns. Nationally, the average expenditure for a typical general education student is a bit more than $6,060 (Education Commission

For specific prevalence figures for each exceptionality, see the Prevalence sections in Chapters 3–12.

Printed with permission of the Des Moines Register.

With the costs of education rising and the number of special needs students rising, many school districts are searching for ways to save money. One alternative used is to reduce the number of special education programs, particularly resource room programs.

The Stay-Put Provision and Discipline

- Placement decisions may be made without consulting with the student's IEP committee
- Students with disabilities can be removed from school for a total of ten days for minor disciplinary infractions
- Services must resume after the tenth day of explusion
- Students with disabilities can be removed from their school placements for up to forty-five days for major infractions, like involvement with drugs or weapons, and placed in alternative programs or schools
- An IEP meeting does not have to be held each time the child is suspended

Issues related to discipline are included throughout the text, but in particular see:
- The IEP Process section in Chapter 2
- Achieving Discipline boxes in Chapters 3–12

prevalence. The total number of cases at a given time.

excess cost. Expenses for the education of a child with disabilities that exceed the average expenses of education for a child without disabilities.

of the States [ECS], 1999). The additional cost for a student with autism is $13,902; with visual disabilities, $8,982; with mental retardation, $8,393; with learning disabilities, $4,865. In general, the common notion is that the educational costs for a student with disabilities is 2½ times that of a student without special needs. And with increasing legal costs stemming from disputes between parents and school districts about services children with disabilities are entitled to, and with increased costs because the Supreme Court ruled that schools must provide attendant care for students with significant health care needs as a related service (*Cedar Rapids School District v. Garret*) special education costs will certainly rise (Grupé, 1999). Many questions, value judgments, and concerns stem from these data. The nation must evaluate its educational investments in all children. It is impossible to know whether expenditures made on students with disabilities actually reduce the amount available for students without disabilities, or if less were spent on students with disabilities that more would be spent on other students. We do know, however, that improved academic achievement is associated with school expenditures, particularly for low-income and diverse students (Grissmer et al., 1998).

Are special education students a primary source of disruption and violence in school settings? During the last reauthorization of IDEA, and since, many congressional leaders have taken the position that what has been known as the "stay-put provision" of IDEA is unfair and unequal. Up until the passage of IDEA '97, students with disabilities could not be expelled or removed from school, or from the educational program specified in their individualized education plan, because of their disabilities or behaviors relating to them. Many people believe that this provision unfairly protected students with disabilities who are disruptive or violent. School administrators, the public, the press, and many members of Congress thought that the provision contributed to the excessive violence that occurs in the public schools (Trump, 1999). Specifically, Congress was concerned that students with disabilities could bring guns to school and yet could not be expelled as could their nondisabled violent peers (Briand, 1995; Garnett, 1996). This protection led some to joke that IDEA was "The Students with Disabilities Right to Bear Arms at School Act." Of course, the nation is, and should be, especially concerned about school violence. Incidents of students assaulting their teachers, killing their classmates, and causing disruptions to the learning environments are well acknowledged. To what degree students with disabilities are responsible for disruption and violence is not clear, though at times public opinion places much of the blame squarely on special education students. In the last reauthorization of IDEA in 1997, Congress amended the "stay-put provision" and two years later the U.S. Department of Education (1999) interpreted the law in its regulations (see the What IDEA '97 Says box for a summary). Although not enough time has passed to evaluate the effectiveness of the new discipline regulations, Congress remains concerned and continues to propose more **legislation** to tighten standards (Jennings, 1999). Only time will tell whether this amendment makes America's schools less disruptive and safer.

THE DEVELOPMENT OF INFORMED AND EFFECTIVE SOLUTIONS—THE OPPORTUNITY OF THE NEW MILLENNIUM

We have only glimpses of what computer technology will bring to daily life in years to come, but those glimpses show that access to information and accommodations for differing abilities will increase. Medical advances, both in the areas of prevention and treatment, will eliminate some conditions that result in disabilities and reduce the impact of others. Most surely, possibilities will exist of which we cannot even dream. But as we imagine a "new world," we must address the real legacies of the last century. Immediate problems must be studied. Our collective attention to these problems will become opportunities for creative solutions.

One lesson of previous times is that we must conduct the business of special education differently. Although great strides on behalf of people with disabilities have been made, there is great dissatisfaction and confusion surrounding the special education endeavor. Let's think together about a few ways to resolve just a few of the problems that were unsolved at the turn of the century. Here are three ideas:

- Being responsive to constituents
- Developing reasonable goals and expectations for the field
- Using validated methods

As we explore these issues in the rest of this chapter and as you read the entire text, think about other ways special education can come to better meet the needs of students with disabilities.

Any endeavor, if it is to survive, must have support both financially and psychologically. And if that endeavor is part of the public sector, it must derive at least part of its strength from attitudes and opinions regarding its merits. Its consumers must be satisfied and the general public must believe in the effort. If these two events do not occur, then the activity should and will be discontinued. Consumer satisfaction is important, and as with all good businesses, the special education community must find ways to listen to the voices of all its constituents: taxpayers, students with disabilities, families of students with disabilities, as well as its alumni (Kortering & Braziel, 1999; Lovitt & Cushing, 1999). Many responsibilities are associated with satisfying the consumer. The consumer must be informed about services provided, believe they are worthy, and feel confident that they make a difference.

Possibly one place to start is to develop reasonable expectations for the pursuit itself. Quite likely, a major source of problems special education faced at the end of the last century was confusion about its purpose. Without a clear articulation of what it is supposed to accomplish, no standards to judge its effectiveness can be de-

legislation. Laws passed by a legislature or the Congress and signed by a governor or the President.

veloped. Just as it is a tragic error to have low expectations for students with disabilities, it is also a mistake to minimize disabilities. If disabilities were not serious, why would the nation spend so much money toward prevention, treatment, education, and supports? What are its goals? Certainly, the outcomes for special education cannot be to "cure" disabilities, but this expectation may be the unspoken understanding of many parents and a reason for dissatisfaction (Lovitt & Cushing, 1999). Possibly a more reasonable expectation is for special education to result in adults with disabilities being able to compensate for their disabilities by drawing strength from developed abilities. But evaluation of this expectation must be left until a time when it is too late to adjust instruction. So, we will have opportunities to "get it right," but we must first decide what "it" is. And maybe "it" is the wrong referent. Remember the overriding principle of special education: first and foremost it is individualized, where each student's performance guides the selection and application of interventions. This approach demands an array of services offered both flexibly and responsibly.

Another solution to the special education dilemma is to make special education truly special. Whether we are professionals or concerned citizens, we have an obligation to ensure that special education makes a difference. Is this a hopeless pursuit? Clearly it is not; and, collectively, we do have the opportunity to make a positive difference. Obviously, not all procedures or methods associated with the education of students with disabilities are effective. Research findings, however, are available which document the power and effectiveness of selected strategies (Fuchs & Fuchs, 1998). But if special education is to become special, educators (and related service providers) must use them. Policy decisions of the twentieth century were often made from assumptions and were not always guided by findings of research (Cook et al., 1997). It is imperative that special educators, early childhood specialists, speech/language pathologists, and all professionals who work with students with disabilities become sophisticated consumers of research. Tolerance for using unproven or ineffective educational practices should be zero! The growing special education research base allows professionals and parents to make educational decisions with some confidence, and nothing less should be expected (Abbott et al., 1999; Fey & Johnson, 1998; Warby et al., 1999; Wilcox et al., 1998).

MAKING CONNECTIONS

See the Research to Practice boxes in Chapters 3–12.

Professionals working in this new millennium have the opportunity to avoid two bad practices that were common in the last century. First, no longer should one fad after another be adopted and then abandoned because it was ineffective. Second, widespread policy decisions should not be made until research guides practice. Special education, like many other fields, has often changed its directions because parents and professionals believed in an idea or thought a new approach "made sense." Being too anxious to use a new technique, a yet unproven strategy, is an urge that must be resisted. Years of systematic research can and should guide action. Considerable work is left to be done to identify and develop instructional methods that will meet all of the challenges of teaching students with disabilities effectively. However, a vast amount of knowledge is available, and it should be used (Forness et al., 1997; Lloyd et al., 1998). Here are some special education approaches proven effective through research: mnemonic strategies, enhanced reading comprehension, behavior modification, direct instruction, cognitive behavior modification, formative evaluation (curriculum based measurement), early intervention. Here are some practices which are often associated with special education (and used by many teachers) that research has shown not to be effective or improve academic learning:

modality instruction, diet, perceptual training. Researchers who have conducted **meta-analyses** make these general recommendations about how educators should teach students with disabilities:

- Intervene early
- Monitor students' progress and provide positive consequences for improvement
- Teach cognitive-behavioral self-management
- Teach academic and cognitive skills directly and systematically
- Use behavioral techniques to promote acquisition of academic and social behaviors
- Teach mnemonic strategies for understanding and remembering what one learns (Lloyd et al., 1998, p. 198)

meta-analysis. A research method that allows for the synthesis of many individual research studies to determine the power or effectiveness of an educational practice.

Think again about the range of issues presented in this chapter. What should be clear is that we are left with no single "right answer" to any of the questions we considered. To many of us, exceptionality is a difference that demands an extraordinary response (Kauffman, 1997). Special education is a dynamic, changing, exciting, and controversial field. Although great strides have been made in the past fifty years, much work remains to be done as we strive to "get it right" and provide wonderful educational programs that truly meet the needs of each student with a disability. This job requires everyone to work together to arrive at solutions whereby all children have the access and opportunities they deserve.

In Conclusion

MAKING CONNECTIONS

Look again at the Advance Organizers at the beginning of the chapter; to help you study the chapter's content, the answers to the Focus and Challenge questions are found here. Test yourself to see if you have mastered the major points of this chapter.

Summary

After centuries of neglect and exclusion, all children and youth with disabilities today have the right to receive a free appropriate public school education. Thus, many children receive special education services for at least part of their school career. However, special education has come under attack in recent years, and the issues that surround it and the concept of disabilities are complex. The time is now for important questions to be addressed and solutions to the special education dilemma developed.

Focus Questions

Self-Test Questions

- *What does it mean to have a disability?*

  In part, the significance of having a disability is determined by whether the difference experienced by the individual is also a handicap. Disability is a relative concept with differing definitions and connotations depending on culture, attitudes, beliefs, discipline, and orientation. Regardless, disability has been part of the human condition since its beginning; across history, people with disabilities typically have been treated harshly.

- *Where did special education come from and why did it develop?*

  Special education began in the late 1700s when farmers from the southern part of France found a young boy in the woods who had been abandoned. They brought the boy to Jean-Marc-Gaspard Itard, a doctor who worked in Paris. Itard named the boy Victor, and spent years trying to teach him to speak, read, write, and possess the social skills required in French society. Special education in America has its roots in Europe, beginning through the efforts of Seguin, a student of Itard's who emigrated to America. It soon flourished and both residential and public day schools developed throughout the twentieth century. Until 1975 and the passage of the first Individuals with Disabilities Education Act (IDEA; PL 94–142), availability of educational opportunities to students with disabilities was inconsistent. Special education developed as a continuum of services to meet the needs of students with disabilities who had been denied placements in general education or who were not succeeding in those classes.

- *Why did the federal government and the public call for national intervention?*

  In 1975, Congress passed a national law guaranteeing students with disabilities access to education that is free and appropriate, offered in the public system and at no cost to parents. Overwhelming evidence convinced Congress that legislated protections were necessary. Findings included the following:

  - Millions of children with disabilities were Americans,
  - The needs of students with disabilities who were receiving public education were not being fully met,
  - Educational services available were typically inappropriate,
  - A million children were excluded from educational opportunities,
  - Many students with disabilities were not identified and therefore not being adequately served,
  - Families were forced to obtain special services for their children with disabilities at considerable hardship,
  - The delivery of special education and related services could be effective,
  - The states needed federal assistance to pay for special education, and
  - It was in the interests of the nation to assure children with disabilities equal protections of the law.

- *Why is special education controversial?*

  Although applauded throughout most of the twentieth century, during the last decade special education was accused of: being ineffective, being discriminatory, segregating children from their peers, serving too many students, costing too much and placing a financial burden on local schools, and protecting violent and unruly children. Debates about the efficacy of special education rage, and at the center of continuing controversy is where students with disabilities should receive their education. Unfortunately, research findings have not been used to direct the field, making it vulnerable to fads and policy changes that may or may not prove effective.

- *What is the legacy of the evolution of special education as the new millennium begins?*

  Special education must gain support from its constituents: students with disabilities, families of students with disabilities, adults with disabilities, the public, the press, education professionals, and public policymakers. At the end of the last millennium, special education lacked direction, was embroiled in controversy and criticism, was confused about its purpose, and did not set practices from research findings. Possibly, it was trying to do too much for too many, and educators lost sight of its original necessity: to provide an individualized education to a very diverse and heterogeneous population of learners who are difficult to teach.

Challenge Question

- *What are the solutions to problems faced by students with disabilities and the educators charged with meeting their needs?*

  Solutions to complex questions cannot be predicted. They must be developed through responsive, flexible, and creative problem solving techniques. Regardless, a few observations can be made about likely sets of solutions to the dilemmas faced by special educators. Educators must be responsive to students and families, listening to multiple perspectives about how satisfied they are about the services provided. Special education also needs to develop goals for itself by determining and articulating its purpose, expectations for its outcomes, and standards against which it can measure its effectiveness. And special educators must become sophisticated evaluators of research, and apply only those methods, approaches, techniques, and practices that have been verified through stringent research trials. Clearly, the rapid development of technology (both computer based and medical) will influence the lives of people with disabilities, and it is special educators' opportunity to exploit gains made in their own and in related disciplines.

 **Supplementary Resources**

Scholarly Readings

Artiles, A. J. (1998). The dilemma of difference: Enriching the disproportionality discourse with theory and context. *The Journal of Special Education, 32,* 32–36.

Artiles, A. J., & Zamora-Duran, G. (Eds.). (1997). *Reducing disproportionate representation of culturally diverse students in special and gifted education.* Reston, VA: Council for Exceptional Children.

Kauffman, J. M., Hallahan, D. P., & Ford, D.Y. (Eds.). (1998). Special issue. *The Journal of Special Education, 32,* 3–62.

Lloyd, J. W., Forness, S. R., & Kavale, K. A. (1998). Some methods are more effective than others. *Intervention in School and Clinic, 33,* 195–200.

Oswald, D. P., Coutinho, M. J., Best, A. M., & Singh, N. N. (1999). Ethnic representation in special education: The influence of school-related economic and demographic variables. *The Journal of Special Education, 32,* 194–206.

Reschly, D. J. (1997). Utility of individual ability measures and public policy choices for the 21st century. *School Psychology Review, 26,* 234–241.

Safford, P. L., & Safford, E. J. (1996). *A history of childhood and disability.* New York: Teachers College Press.

Popular Books

Bauby, J.-D. (1997). *The diving bell and the butterfly.* New York: Knopf.

Gallagher, H. G. (1994). *FDR's splendid deception* (Rev. ed.). Arlington, VA: Vandamere Press.

Treanor, R. B. (1993). *We overcame: The story of civil rights for disabled people.* Falls Church, VA: Regal Direct Publishing.

Parent, Professional, and Consumer Organizations and Agencies

Council for Exceptional Children (CEC)
1920 Association Drive
Reston, VA 22091
Phone: (703) 620-3660
Web site: http://www.cec.spec.org

ERIC
Clearinghouse on Disabilities and Gifted Education (CEC)
1920 Association Drive
Reston, VA 22091
Phone: (703) 264-9476; (888) CEC-SPED
TTY: (703) 724-9480
Web site: http://www.ericec.org

NICHY
National Information Center for Children and Youth with Disabilities
P.O. Box 1492
Washington, DC 20013
Voice/TTY: (800) 695-0285 and (202) 884-8200
E-mail: nichy@aed.org
Web site: http://www.nichy.org

Office of Special Education Programs
U.S. Office of Special Education and Rehabilitative Services
U.S. Department of Education
Washington, DC 20202-2641
Phone: (202) 205-9675
Web site: www.ed.gov/offices/osers/osep

National Clearinghouse for Professions in Special Education (CEC)
1920 Association Drive
Reston, VA 22091-1589
Phone: (703) 274-9476
E-mail: ncpse@cec.sped.org
Web site: www.specialedcareers.org/

President's Committee on Employment of People with Disabilities
1331 F. Street N.W.
Washington, DC 20002
Phone: (202) 376-6200
Web site: http://www.pcepd.gov

Henri de Toulouse-Lautrec, born into a noble French family, was closely related to the royal families of France and England. His childhood was privileged, but also tragic. Probably due to a hereditary condition, he had a speech impairment and was frail. He was highly intelligent but missed months of school. His bones were weak and he used a wheelchair for many long periods during his childhood. Early on Lautrec retreated to painting and became highly productive and successful. However, because of his disabilities, his adult life was often in turmoil and plagued by alcoholism. (Denvir, 1991; Perruchot, 1962).

At the Moulin Rouge was painted in 1895, and is now on display at the Art Institute of Chicago. This painting follows a typical theme of Lautrec, who was fascinated by the nightlife of Paris. Here, he included himself in the background.

Henri de Toulouse-Lautrec, *At the Moulin Rouge,* oil on canvas, 1893–95, 123 × 141 cm, Helen Birch Bartlett Memorial Collection, 1928.610. Photograph courtesy of The Art Insitute of Chicago.

CHAPTER 2

A Changing Vision of Special Education

Tom Hehir is the former director of the federal office that administers the programs Congress authorizes through the Individuals with Disabilities Education Act. Dr. Hehir, a longtime professional in special education, held this post for most of the Clinton administration. He now works at Harvard University and at Educational Development Center in Boston. Tom's perspective about how life for children and youth with disabilities has improved across the years and yet the tenuous nature of the guarantees that enable this improved quality of life is important for all of us to understand.

I can still recall the smell, a mix of ammonia and human excrement. I still can recall the sight of rows of metal beds in which were entombed living children and adults with cerebral palsy for almost their entire day and night. I can still recall the racket that enveloped the ward, created by the simultaneous crying, moaning, yelling, and pleading of the residents. I was an undergraduate taking my first course in special education, Nature and Needs of the Mentally Retarded. This scene occurred during a field trip to a state school for the mentally retarded. The year was 1971.

It was not only the images that stayed in my mind, but also the attitudes expressed by staff. "This is all you can expect of these people. They're severely brain damaged, vegetables." I kept wondering where the school was. When we returned to the college, we discussed our feelings about what we had seen. Our professor assured us that these children and adults were capable of far more and we would visit other sites that would prove these kids could learn and have full lives. At that time the more positive sites were special schools and classes in which more fortunate kids were learning to read, write, and laugh. However, though some

Individualized Educational Programs: Planning and Delivering Services

children were getting a chance at a better life, children with significant disabilities were not guaranteed a right to an education. They could be denied entrance to school.

My professor also predicted that the time would come when all disabled kids would be entitled to public education. He told us about lawsuits and legislative initiatives that were seeking to extend education to all disabled kids. We also showed us a book, *Christmas in Purgatory,* by Burton Blatt, a professor of special education at Syracuse University, which exposed the inhumane treatment of people with mental retardation in state institutions. As special educators in training, he made it clear to us that our job would be to expand educational opportunity to children with disabilities.

When I finished my undergraduate work, I decided to pursue a master's degree and had the great fortune to study under Burt Blatt. It was a heady time for special education as lawsuits were proceeding through the courts challenging exclusion from school and exposing the miseries of institutionalization. Syracuse University was in the middle of it all with Burt serving as an expert witness in several cases. One course I took, taught by Doug Biklen and Bob Bogdan, was entitled Law and Human Abuse. The course focused on how the law at that time was being used to deny people with disabilities basic human rights. The professors argued that this needed to be turned around; that law should promote, not deny, rights. I left Syracuse energized and pleased that I had chosen a career of such importance, teaching kids with disabilities.

I returned to Massachusetts and began teaching at a vocational high school, Keefe Tech in Framingham. The school was brand new and from its inception included a broad range of kids with disabilities. The state had just passed a comprehensive special education law, Chapter 766, which required that all kids with disabilities receive publicly funded education in the least restrictive environment. A number of my students had started their lives in the state institutions I had visited three years before. Most of the kids with disabilities thrived in this new environment, achieving at levels few would have predicted and going on to real competitive employment jobs. During my experience at Keefe I also served some kids who had needs that had not been addressed and who could not read due to dyslexia. These students too were benefiting from the new special education law.

I eventually left Keefe Tech at the behest of the Massachusetts Department of Education to set up similar programs in the other vocational schools in the state. This ultimately led me to the Boston Public Schools, where I eventually became Director of Special Education. I left Boston in 1987 to pursue a doctorate at Harvard. Though I was very pleased with the education I received there, I was concerned with the lack of attention paid to students with disabilities in the education reform debates. It seemed that in the eyes of many we were still out of sight and mind.

When I graduated from Harvard in 1990, I headed for Chicago as Associate Superintendent of Schools with special education as one of my primary responsibilities. At that time Chicago was undergoing a major reform effort and students with disabilities were very much part of the effort. Indeed, many of the parent activists in the school reform movement were parents of students with disabilities. Though I was pleased with the role of special education activists in the reform movement, I was dismayed by the lack of compliance with IDEA in the district. Too many children were still being inappropriately segregated and many children were waiting months to be assessed and placed.

Through hard work and focused activity, the special educators, general educators, the disability community, and parents of Chicago demonstrated that a large school district could make progress expanding educational opportunity to students with disabilities while improving education for all. Noncompliance with special education law dropped markedly while overall performance of students increased. I witnessed in Chicago what many in special education are seeing throughout the country, that the principles upon which IDEA is based—individualization, innovation, and strong parental involvement—can benefit all children.

In 1993 I had the great honor of being asked by the Clinton Administration to serve as Director of the Office of Special Education Programs (OSEP). The early years of the Clinton Administration were exciting times as we planned our legislative agenda. Assistant Secretary Judy Heumann and Secretary Riley made sure that students with disabilities were included in all the reform legislation, particularly Goals 2000 and the Improving America's Schools Act. I was optimistic that special education had come of age. My optimism was dashed a bit when the Congress changed hands in 1994. Shortly thereafter, powerful interests began to call for a significant scaling back of IDEA. One influential group, the Heritage Foundation, called for the repeal of the law. Another legislative threat included a plan to block grant the Medicaid program, which is the primary health insurer for large numbers of children and adults with disabilities. I had a deep concern about this because the Medicaid program mandates comprehensive health coverage for children, which many children and families need to keep students in their communities and enable them to attend school. I feared that, absent this support, children might be sent back to institutions.

Both the threat to IDEA and to Medicaid were turned back because a coalition of parents of students with disabilities, people with disabilities, and special educators joined together to impress upon the Congress that we needed to move forward, not backward. The message was clear that people with disabilities needed to be full participants in all aspects of our society and that education and health care were necessary for that goal to be achieved. I was heartened to see that we had friends on "both sides of the aisle." I recall discussing my surprise over the threats to IDEA with the parent of a young woman with Down syndrome. As a veteran parent activist, he replied, "We have made progress but we still have far to go. These issues are never finally resolved because we have yet to reach the point where people with disabilities are fully accepted. We must be constantly vigilant and never go back."

When I reflect on my decision to pursue a career in special education almost thirty years ago, I consider myself truly fortunate to have entered a field that has been so rewarding. I think back on that institution I visited as a student and now see similar children attending school in their communities with their brothers and sisters and friends. I also agree with the parent who reminds us we have far to go and must be constantly vigilant. I would encourage those of you who are reading this text to seriously consider a career in special education. All good educators liberate the mind. However, in a very real sense, special educators, through their efforts to enable children with disabilities to access education, liberate people.

1. How has life changed for people with disabilities over the last thirty years?

2. Why does Dr. Hehir believe that national protections still need to be in place to ensure good outcomes for students with disabilities?

dvance Organizers

CONNECTIONS

Use the learning strategy—Advance Organizers—to help focus your study of this chapter's content, and reinforce your learning by reviewing answers to the focus and challenge questions at the end of the chapter.

Overview IDEA '97 mandates that students with disabilities receive a free appropriate education in the least restrictive environment possible. Designing an appropriate education requires the combined efforts of educators, related service providers, and the child's family. Individualized education program plans are required by IDEA '97. These plans include Individualized Family Service Plans (IFSP) and Individualized Education Programs (IEP), and are the blueprints for the special education every student with disabilities receives.

Focus Questions

Self-Test Questions

- What are the six steps to developing an individualized program for each student with disabilities?
- What roles does the IEP Team fill?
- What factors must be considered when determining the least restrictive environment for individual students?
- What are the different educational placement options that comprise the continuum of services for special education?
- What are the different purposes of IDEA '97's various program plans?

Challenge Question

- How should the array of educational services and supports available to students with disabilities be implemented?

While you read this chapter, consider our discussions in Chapter 1. Think about the basic rights that the Individuals with Disabilities Education Act (IDEA '97) guarantees to students with disabilities and their families. In this chapter, we will see how those civil rights are exercised through a balance of two concepts: a free appropriate public education (FAPE) and least restrictive environment (LRE). Here is another way of conceptualizing special education: It is an array of educational services, a consortium of professionals from a variety of disciplines, the availability of specialized expertise, and individualized educational programs that are directed by goals and objectives and evaluated by curriculum based benchmarks. After studying some problems left for us to solve in this new millennium, let's look at the services special education provides.

See the Problems of Special Education section in Chapter 1.

Opportunities for the New Millennium

IDEA was a reaction to the injustices experienced by children with disabilities and their families during most of the twentieth century. When it was first passed in 1975, the law was hailed as the way to guarantee rights and access to appropriate education for all students with disabilities. IDEA is a very important civil rights law, a national law that imposes many requirements on states and local school systems. And, because it includes many safeguards for these children's rights, it is perceived by many at the local level as cumbersome and costly. The IEP process is at the heart of these safeguards, but many of its features are the cause of criticism and complaints. The authors of IDEA '97 attempted to address concerns about special education and its law, but some think it only created more problems.

Legacies from the Twentieth Century

At the close of the century, complaints about special education and the requirements of the IEP process came from all quarters. Special education teachers believed that the development of IEPs contributed to a burden of too much paperwork, reducing the amount of instructional time available to work with students. Some special educators believed that students with disabilities were excluded from large-scale achievement assessments, and therefore were not part of the education reform movement. General education teachers thought that they were ill prepared to teach students with disabilities and did not have enough planning time to collaborate with special educators and related service providers about students with disabilities integrated into their classrooms. Principals and other administrators often stated that relationships between parents and schools had changed because of the "legal atmosphere" created by mediation, due process, and civil actions used to resolve disputes with families about services and placement. Administrators also continue to complain that the regulations are too complicated and confusing. Superintendents and state officials are concerned that the costs of educating students with disabilities are too great, taking away from what would otherwise be available for nondisabled students. And Congress and other policymakers have felt that the IEP results in unequal treatment of students with disabilities because, unlike their nondisabled classmates, they cannot be expelled from school for violent, disruptive, or potentially dangerous behaviors at school.

Thinking About Dilemmas to Solve

As you read this chapter, think about ways to guarantee the education rights of students with disabilities and yet address these issues listed here. Think about how to:

- Reduce the paperwork burden
- Have Congress increase the federal contribution to the education costs of students with disabilities
- Increase planning time for general education teachers to collaborate with special educators and related service providers
- Streamline the legal requirements of IDEA
- Make the IEP process less contentious

SPECIAL EDUCATION SERVICES

CONNECTIONS
MAKING

For background about IDEA and other laws protecting the rights of persons with disabilities, see the Necessity for National Intervention section in Chapter 1.

As discussed in Chapter 1, the law that provides the framework for special education is the Individuals with Disabilities Education Act (IDEA '97). Originally passed as Public Law (PL) 94–142 in 1975, IDEA '97 remains first a civil rights law, guaranteeing a free appropriate public education (FAPE) for all youngsters with disabilities from birth through age 21. The law also provides states and local school districts with some federal funding to support the programs (individualized education in the least restrictive environment possible) that it mandates.

SERVICE DELIVERY OPTIONS

Special education should always be based on the individual needs of the student and his or her family, not on what is available at a neighborhood school. This individualized instruction is delivered by professionals who fulfill a broad array of services that are delivered in a wide range of settings. For example, some special education professionals are itinerant, like **itinerant teachers** or **speech/language pathologists (SLPs),** who travel from school to school. Others might work at one school delivering a very special set of skills, like some **audiologists** who only work with Deaf students at one **center school,** a separate school that only students with disabilities attend. Although IDEA '97 requires placement in the least restrictive environment (LRE), where the educational services are delivered and who delivers those services do not always indicate whether an environment is least restrictive or appropriate.

Special education, as you are learning, is an evolving concept. **Service delivery options** continue to expand and change. Unfortunately, like many wide-scale education reform movements, modifications to special education are usually not the result of carefully conducted research about the efficacy of new practices (Cook et al., 1997; Manset & Semmel, 1997). Toward the end of the last century, a model called **full inclusion** gained momentum. One version of this model became known as **pull-in programming.** In this system, children with disabilities receive all of their education in the **general education** classroom. Under this approach, special education *and* related service therapies (e.g., speech, physical therapy) are brought to the child in the general education classroom (Welch et al., 1995). Recently, other full inclusion models have gained in popularity. For example, team teaching, **co-teaching,** and **consultation/collaborative teaching** are now being tried in the schools (Vaughn, Elbaum, Schumm, & Hughes, 1998). Results from these new approaches are mixed, with some results positive and others not (Fox & Ysseldyke, 1997; Hunt & Goetz, 1997; Klingner et al., 1998; Salend & Duhaney, 1999; Vaughn et al., 1996; Waldron & McLesky, 1998). Why might this be so? One reason is that people have different criteria to judge the merits of special education. Some think that gains in social skills are more important than gains in academic or life skills. Another reason is that what works for some special needs students does not work for others. Regardless, what is clear both from teachers' comments and from research findings is that fully including students with disabilities is hard work and is only successful when teams of professionals commit considerable effort to the endeavor (Kennedy et al., 1997). Full inclusion and other service delivery options are listed and explained in Table 2.1 on page 46.

Let's consider each of these commonly used service delivery options. Figure 2.1 on page 47 compares percentages of students with disabilities who received their

itinerant teachers. Teachers who teach students or consult with others in more than one setting.

speech/language pathologist (SLP). A professional who diagnoses and treats problems in the area of speech and language development.

audiologist. A professional trained to diagnose hearing losses and auditory problems.

center schools. Separate schools (some residential), typically dedicated to serving students with a particular disability.

service delivery options. Different special education services and placements, sometimes described as a continuum and other times as an array.

General and special education teachers work side by side in the pull-in service delivery model.

full inclusion. An interpretation that states that the least restrictive environment for all children with disabilities is the general education classroom.
pull-in programming. Rather than having students with disabilities leave the general education classes for special education or for related services, delivering those services to them in the general education classroom.
general education. A typical classroom and curriculum designed to serve students without disabilities.
co-teaching. General education and special education teachers teaching together in the same classroom for the entire school day.
consultation/ collaborative teaching. General education and special education teachers working together to meet the needs of special needs students.

education in each of the government's official educational categories from the 1991–1992 school year through the 1995–1996 school year. These data reveal a lot of information. First, most students with disabilities receive their education primarily in general education settings, with some support. Some 80% of students with disabilities between the ages of 6 and 17 receive their education in either the general education classroom or in a combination of general education and resource room classes (U.S. Department of Education, 1998). And approximately 95% of students with disabilities receive their education and related services in schools with nondisabled peers. Second, the data in Figure 2.1 show that placement rates are changing, with resource rooms becoming a less common placement option. This fact worries some learning disabilities experts who are concerned that a needed option for many students with disabilities is disappearing, while the use of self-contained classes for students with disabilities is increasing (Roberts & Mather, 1995).

Be careful not to make assumptions about data from large groups. You might think that, because each state has about the same proportion of youngsters with disabilities, and because students with disabilities have similar needs for education no matter where they live, we would see in each state roughly the same percentages of students in each type of educational environment. However, the rates at which states use each type of placement vary tremendously. For example, New York's rate of segregated day and residential placements is more than four times Oregon's rate. Placement rates also vary wildly by state and by disability. For example, in North Dakota 83% of all students with visual disabilities receive their education in general education classrooms, while in Washington, DC only 3% of them do. Clearly, it is not only students' characteristics that determine their LRE. Such variations may well contribute to some of the criticism special education has received. What do you think are some reasons for the differences between states? Do you think that this is a problem the federal and state governments should address?

Special education services should be flexible and responsive to the needs of each student. Children and youth with special needs should have access to a variety of services, according to the support needed to achieve their potential. This support will vary by type, intensity, location, personnel, and duration of special education. One way to think about special education and related services is to think about a support system that contains a rich array of services that consists of components

Table 2.1 Service Delivery Options

Type	Description	Government Category	Government Criterion
Pull-In Programming (Full Inclusion)	All special education and related services are brought to the student in the general education classroom setting.	Regular (general education) class	No separate government category exists. Although all services are delivered in the general education category, placement data are reflected in the "less than 21%" category.
Co-teaching	General education and special education teachers teach together in the same classroom for the entire school day. Students may be "pulled out" for related services.	Regular (general education) class	No separate government category exists. Although all services are delivered in the general education category, placement data are reflected in the "less than 21%" category.
Consultation/ Collaborative Teaching	General education and special education teachers work together to meet the needs of special needs students. Students are seldom removed from the general education class.	Regular (general education) class	Students receive special education and related services outside the general education class for less than 21% of the school day.
Itinerant or Consultative	The teacher and/or student receives assistance from a specialist who may serve many students at many schools.	Regular (general education) class	Students receive special education and related services outside the general education class for less than 21% of the school day.
Resource Room (Pull-Out Programming)	Student attends a regular class most of the day but goes to a special education class several hours per day or for blocks of time each week.	Resource room	Includes students who receive special education and related services for at least 21% and not more than 60% of their school day.
Special Education Class (Partially Self-Contained)	Student attends a special class but is integrated into regular education classes for a considerable amount of time each day.	Separate class	Students receive special education for more than 60% of their day, outside of the general education classroom.
Special Education Class (Self-Contained)	Student attends a special class most of the school day and is included in regular education activities minimally.	Separate class	Students receive special education for more than 60% of their day, outside of the general education classroom.
Special Education Schools (Center Schools)	Center schools—some private, others supported by the state—serve only students with a specific category of disability. Some offer residential services; others do not.	Public separate school facility; private separate school facility; public residential facility; private residential facility.	Includes students who receive their education for more than 50% of the day in: (a) a separate day school, (b) a public or private residential facility at public expense, (c) a hospital setting, or (d) at home.

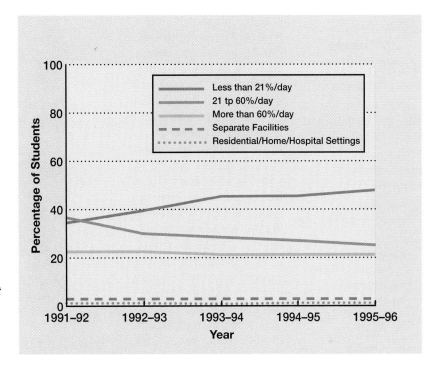

Fiᵍure 2.1 Percentage of Students Served in Different Environments (1991–1992 to 1995–1996)

Source: From *Twentieth Annual Report to Congress on the Implementation of the Individuals with Disabilities Education Act* (p. III–36) by the U.S. Department of Education, 1998, Washington, DC: U.S. Government Printing Office.

that are individually determined and applied. The term **array of services** implies that students do not have to travel step by step up and down a ladder of services but have available many selections. For example, in some cases, the general education classroom can meet the needs of the student with some support from a consulting teacher or specialist (for instance, an SLP). Other cases require more intensive services from many different specialists.

The most common way to describe the educational services and settings available is to use the term **continuum of services**. IDEA '97 reaffirms the belief that a continuum of services be available to children and youth with disabilities and their families, and the law does *not* suggest that a single service delivery option (such as only the general education class) should be the only alternative. The concept of "continuum" implies a full range of alternatives. For example, a continuum of living arrangements for people with disabilities would probably include a large congregate institution, smaller congregate facilities, foster care, structured group homes, independent group homes, apartments with roommates, and independent apartments and homes. For special education, this conceptualization of educational services begins with hospital and homebound, moves to residential center schools, and ends with general education placements.

An older description of the continuum model is **cascade of services** (Deno, 1970). This conceptualization of special education has many pitfalls, but it was most often criticized because it became lockstepped, and students found it difficult, almost impossible, to move to each successively more integrated placement. As a result, many students who were placed in a self-contained classroom for special

array of services.
A constellation of services, personnel, and educational placements.
continuum of services. A graduated range of educational services, each level of service leading directly to the next one.
cascade of services. A linear and sequential model used to describe educational environments from the most to the least restrictive.

NEW DIRECTIONS
FOR THE
MILLENNIUM

Legacy: Determining LRE for each individual student with disabilities is challenging, and judgments are often subjective.

Opportunities:

- Articulate the purpose of every type of education option and curriculum available
- Create flexible approaches but provide guidelines for placement decisions

Review the What IDEA '97 Says About FAPE and LRE boxes in Chapter 1.

education remained in that type of placement throughout their school careers, even though their educational needs changed and an appropriate educational experience for them would have been a resource room or a general education class. Another problem with the cascade model is that professionals may assume that a classroom placement necessarily corresponds to a determination of the severity of the student's disability. They might incorrectly assume, for instance, that youngsters with the most severe disabilities belong automatically in a full-time, self-contained classroom. But that assumption is often erroneous. It may be that one student with a severe disability is most appropriately served in the general education classroom and another with a moderate disability requires temporary placement in a full-day special education classroom. For example, one child with a severe physical disability may require accommodations to the physical organization of a classroom environment but no modification to the instructional program. Another child with a learning disability may not be able to profit from the type of initial reading instruction offered in the general education classroom and until his basic reading skills are mastered would be better served in an intensive special education program.

Figure 2.2 Achieving a Balance Between FAPE and LRE Can Be a Difficult Goal

Unfortunately, the problems associated with the cascade model are likely to follow the concept of "continuum of services." Since some criticisms of special education from the last century focus on special education segregating students with disabilities from their nondisabled peers, professionals and parents will need to work hard to find ways that services needed for an appropriate education do not unnecessarily segregate children. To avoid the problems of the past, a fluid approach is necessary when professionals determine services, supports, and placements for students with disabilities. A key factor in this process is the analysis of the outcomes or goals for each student. For example, careful consideration of the goals of integrated employment, community living, citizenship and involvement, and personal autonomy and life satisfaction should all factor into the decisions about the topics of instruction each individual should receive. When identifying what services an individual requires and where they should be delivered, the student with disabilities and the family should be the focus. The balance between FAPE and LRE can be challenging to achieve, but it is this tension that keep special education fluid and continually responsive to individual needs (see Figure 2.2).

SPECIAL EDUCATION AND RELATED SERVICE PROFESSIONALS

At the heart of special education are the wonderful professionals who provide services to students with disabilities and their families. Together, they provide the multidisciplinary services required by individuals with disabilities. A special educator might be a paraprofessional (teacher's aide), a resource specialist, a consultant, an itinerant teacher, a special education classroom teacher, a job coach, a **home or hospital teacher**, a diagnostician, or an administrator. In addition, a special education professional might work in a related service as a school psychologist, an SLP, an **assistive technology** specialist, an audiologist, an **occupational therapist (OT)**, a **physical therapist (PT)**, a counselor, a nurse or physician, a transportation specialist, a recreational therapist, a supported living worker, a personal care attendant, or a vocational rehabilitation worker. Also contributing to the appropriate education of many students with disabilities are lawyers and **school nurses.** Although not listed in IDEA '97 as related services, the services of these professionals are vital to the educational programs for many students with disabilities. School nurses, for example, are particularly important resources to teachers who work with children with special health care needs, and lawyers can be helpful in ensuring that students' rights under IDEA '97 are protected.

Let's look at some examples of how an array of flexible services might be implemented. Deaf individuals might need the services of an audiologist, an SLP, and possibly an interpreter. Many students with disabilities also require and profit from the services of an assistive technology expert, who can help the individuals learn compensatory skills through the use of technological aids such as communication devices. In some cases, assistive technology is included in a child's special education program, but in other cases (e.g., when a special device needs to be created or adapted specially for the student by an expert) it is a related service (Menlove, 1996). To visualize what a multidisciplinary special education is like, it is helpful to see the proportion that each discipline represents in the total enterprise of special education related services (see Figure 2.3, page 50).

Special education teachers, related services providers, and general education teachers collaborate—work cooperatively—to ensure that each student receives an appropriate education in the least restrictive setting possible. Together they form teams and use a method called **collaboration** to adapt and modify instruction so students with disabilities can participate and be included in the general education curriculum to the maximal extent possible. A key person in the collaborative effort at every school is the school principal (Williams & Katsiyannis, 1998). Principals are likely to be the school district's representative on the IEP Team. Since they often coordinate site-based management efforts, they can be most helpful in developing and ensuring the delivery of accommodations (particularly for large-scale assessments), and can facilitate the coordination of services throughout the school and across the district.

PARTICIPATION IN THE GENERAL EDUCATION CURRICULUM

IDEA '97 stresses the importance of students with disabilities participating in the general education curriculum. One criticism of special education at the end of the last century was that special education was ineffective. Of course, that evaluation is dependent on the goals held for special education: achieving the skills necessary for

home or hospital teacher. A special teacher who teaches in the child's home or hospital when the child must be absent from school due to health problems.

assistive technology. Devices that help students with disabilities in their daily lives; they include hearing aids, wheelchairs, computers that offer augmentative communication, and a wide array of equipment that helps compensate for an individual's disabilities.

occupational therapist (OT). A professional who directs activities that help improve muscular control and develop self-help skills.

physical therapist (PT). A professional who treats physical disabilities through many nonmedical means.

school nurses. Professionals who participate in delivering FAPE to students with disabilities; they are not listed by IDEA as an actual related service.

collaboration. Professionals working cooperatively to provide educational services.

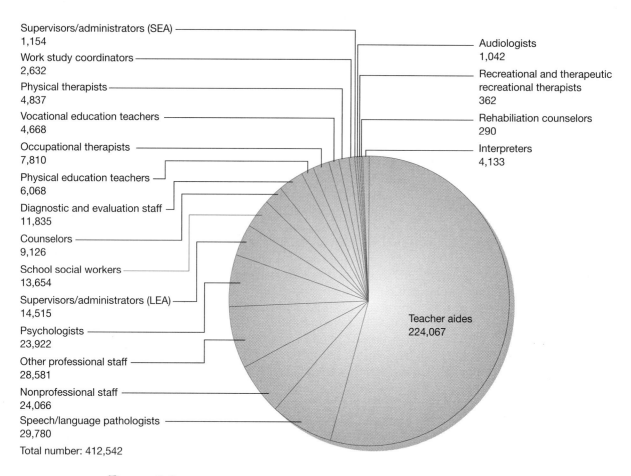

Supervisors/administrators (SEA)
1,154

Work study coordinators
2,632

Physical therapists
4,837

Vocational education teachers
4,668

Occupational therapists
7,810

Physical education teachers
6,068

Diagnostic and evaluation staff
11,835

Counselors
9,126

School social workers
13,654

Supervisors/administrators (LEA)
14,515

Psychologists
23,922

Other professional staff
28,581

Nonprofessional staff
24,066

Speech/language pathologists
29,780

Total number: 412,542

Audiologists
1,042

Recreational and therapeutic
recreational therapists
362

Rehabiliation counselors
290

Interpreters
4,133

Teacher aides
224,067

Figure 2.3 **Number of Related Services and Support Positions**

Source: From *Twentieth Annual Report to Congress on the Implementation of the Individuals with Disabilities Education Act* by the U.S. Department of Education, 1998, Washington, DC: U.S. Government Printing Office.

Note: Data include all positions, including those filled by certified and noncertified personnel, along with those positions unfilled.

independent living or passing state-adopted competency tests required to achieve a standard high school diploma. Regardless, of this there is no doubt: The likelihood of passing statewide competency tests is low for those who do not participate in the curriculum the tests reflect. So, let's look at these new, important requirements of IDEA '97 — participating in the general education curriculum and in statewide or district-wide assessments.

Access to the General Education Curriculum. A new requirement of IDEA '97 is for students with disabilities to have access to the general education curriculum and to reforms that occur in general education at the state, district, and local school level. Each student's IEP must now address participation and access to the general education curriculum (see the What IDEA '97 Says box on page 52), and specifically delineate why a student cannot participate at a particular point in time (Project Forum, 1999). Why did federal lawmakers and advocates for students with disabilities insist

NEW DIRECTIONS
FOR THE
MILLENNIUM

Legacy: Students with disabilities must now be included in large-scale achievement testing, but the ramifications of their participation were not studied before these policies were put into place.

Opportunities:

- Assess the progress of students with different types and levels of disabilities in the general education curriculum
- Carefully monitor risk factors associated with high stakes testing: dropout, placements in more restrictive settings, special education referral rates

that IDEA be changed to include these requirements? Little consensus about the purpose of IEPs existed (Yell & Shriner, 1997). Some teachers felt that IEPs were only supposed to include descriptions about special education and related services provided to the student and the family. Others believed that IEPs were to focus primarily on the child's needs and problems and were not supposed to articulate the student's strengths and areas of participation in the general education curriculum. By not connecting the goals and objectives, along with benchmarks marking achievement, it was felt that those connections would not occur (McLaughlin & Warren, 1995). Many professionals thought that these factors contributed to "fractured programs," programs which lacked continuity.

The disconnect between general and special education can be documented time and time again. Possibly, the best example is the absence of special educators in the conversation about general education reforms. The IEP process now requires professionals who have knowledge about the general education curriculum and resources that can be made available to students. Students with disabilities should participate in the general education curriculum, and only be removed and placed in an alternative curriculum when "supplementary support and services can be demonstrated as benefiting the student" (Yell & Shriner, 1997, p. 7). This change in IDEA may well become a new defining feature of LRE: Rather than access to a place, it is access to a curriculum.

Participation in Statewide or Districtwide Assessments. Although special education students experience frequent—and for many, daily—assessments of their educational progress, they have not consistently participated in the large-scale assessments designed to evaluate the progress of their nondisabled peers. At the end of the last century, general dissatisfaction grew about the educational results of all students

Source: Trevor, Albuquerque Journal. Reprinted by permission.

What IDEA '97 Says About

Access to the General Education Curriculum

The IEP of each student with a disability must

- Indicate how the disability affects involvement and progress in the general education curriculum
- Include annual goals that reflect inclusion in the general education curriculum
- Describe how the educational program will be modified
- Indicate how the student will participate in extracurricular and nonacademic activities
- Discuss plans for integrating the student with his or her nondisabled peers

attending public schools, particularly those students going to schools in the inner cities (Rose & Gallup, 1998). For these reasons, calls for more assessment of students' progress were heard from the public, in the press, in Congress, and in state legislatures. And, in many states, policymakers have added both incentives and disincentives to schools based on students' overall performance. What is often called **high stakes testing** has now become a system of rewarding schools for good student achievement on these standardized tests and sanctioning schools that do not meet the mark.

Although the nation has expressed concern about public education and has spent years discussing ways to improve the achievement of America's students, most remarkably, the results of students with disabilities were not part of those discussions (Vanderwood et al., 1998). In fact, in most **statewide and districtwide assessments,** students with disabilities were not included. Because they were not in the accountability systems, we do not even know to what extent they did participate in such tests nationally (Thurlow, 1998). We do know that participation rates, even within the same school district, varied widely, with all students with disabilities at one school participating and few participating at other schools (VanEtten, 1998). Considering the difficulties that many students with disabilities have with academic subjects, why would their exclusion from these tests be considered a problem? Here's one answer: "Assessments frequently serve as the cornerstone of efforts to improve education. If students with disabilities are excluded from the development and administration of statewide assessments, it is less likely that they will benefit from overall school reform improvements" (Landau et al., 1998, p. 1).

high stakes testing. Placing incentives and disincentives on schools and school districts for their students' academic achievement. **statewide and districtwide assessments.** Part of the national education reform movement that includes annual achievement testing of all schoolchildren for the purpose of increasing the accountability of schools for children's progress in the curriculum.

But some special educators are concerned that general educators will now see a risk to including students with disabilities in their classes. They are afraid that they will be held responsible for these students' insufficient progress in the general education curriculum. These educators are worried that including difficult-to-teach students at their schools and in their classes will result in disincentives, such as reductions in the school's budget, bad reports in the press, or poor public image. Others say that if students with disabilities participate in the development of these tests (are part of the groups used to norm these tests), these concerns will disappear (Thurlow, 1998). Still others believe that if students with disabilities receive proper accommodations while taking these tests, they can and will perform well. And some also believe that the process will become more equitable (Elliott et al., 1998). Here's a listing of the types of accommodations students with disabilities profit from:

- Braille versions of tests
- Tests read to the student
- Directions explained several ways
- Extended time to take tests
- Breaks in the testing sessions

- Aids or adaptive equipment
- Directions signed to the student
- Dictating answers to an assistant
- Taking tests in a quiet space
- Tests given over several days

Participation of most students with disabilities in statewide achievement tests is an expectation outlined in IDEA '97. Although many of these students will need accommodations, the hope is that such participation will contribute to greater access to the general education curriculum for them.

INDIVIDUALIZED SPECIAL EDUCATION PROGRAMS

To safeguard the principles contained in the concept of a free appropriate public education, IDEA '97 requires that an individual program plan be developed and implemented for every child identified as having a disability and in need of special education. Individualized plans are required by other laws as well. For example, federal regulations, such as those for Medicaid and Social Security, require that individualized plans also be developed and implemented for individuals residing in institutions or community-based living arrangements, such as group homes. Individual written rehabilitation plans are also required for people receiving vocational rehabilitation. Individualized plans thus cover a range of educational, social, and vocational goals of people with disabilities. Although the various types of plans respond to different goals, all share some basic principles. For example, such plans typically include a description of the individual's current abilities and disabilities, goals and related objectives, a summary of services to be provided, and the ways these services are to be evaluated. For those concerned with schools and educational systems, it is only IDEA '97 that requires an individual plan for children. So, only students with disabilities have individual programs that detail the services they require for an appropriate education that has been agreed upon by their parents.

CRITICAL FEATURES OF SPECIAL EDUCATION PROGRAMS

Six fundamental principles are integral to the implementation of IDEA '97 and are stressed by the federal government as being critical features of special education programs offered to children and youth with disabilities (Office of Special Education Programs, 1999):

- A free appropriate public education (FAPE)
- An individualized education program

- The least restrictive environment (LRE)
- Appropriate evaluations
- Parent and student participation in decision making
- Procedural safeguards

Let's briefly review these fundamental provisions of IDEA '97, the foundations for individualized educational programs offered through special education. Then, we'll turn attention to the IEP process where all of these provisions are put together.

MAKING CONNECTIONS

Review the What IDEA '97 Says About FAPE box in Chapter 1.

Free Appropriate Public Education (FAPE). IDEA '97 guarantees all children and youth with disabilities and their families a free appropriate public education. This also applies to students in the juvenile justice system (Robinson & Rapport, 1999). The word education here is broadly defined to include all types of supportive services and a curriculum that may differ from that presented in general education (Levine & Edgar, 1994). To be appropriate the program must be highly individualized. Because few special education graduates, particularly those with cognitive disabilities, successfully complete the postsecondary general education curriculum, either because they drop out or cannot pass the final competency tests, possibly the education community should consider more curricular options designed specifically to prepare youngsters to assume the responsibilities of adulthood immediately after high school. The concept of an array of curricular options fits with the concept of FAPE. For some students with disabilities, it may include a functional curriculum where the traditional emphasis on academics is less important than focusing on adult outcomes, such as living and working in the community satisfactorily (Edgar & Polloway, 1994). And for some youngsters it may mean the need for community based instruction that allows students to learn important job and life skills in the natural environment—that is, in the community, not in a general education class.

Each student with disabilities is entitled to a tailor-made educational program complete with supportive services and individually designed to meet the needs of the child. The costs of these services are the responsibility of the state and public school system, not the family. The services delivered are determined by the needs of the child, and not the convenience of the school district. Also, the cost of the services cannot be a factor in whether they are provided to a child who requires them (Parette et al., 1996). For example, if Samantha requires a special communications device to benefit from special education and to participate in a general education placement for part of the day, that device and the training in how to use it must be part of her IEP. The school district must provide the equipment for Samantha. Because of districts' limited resources, many are looking to community leaders to help find private funding to provide the equipment students need. Teachers must understand that when the school district purchases equipment, the district, not Samantha, owns the device. Depending on the district's policy, Jane may or may not be able to take the equipment home with her or practice using the equipment in a variety of settings. If Sam's insurance company purchases the assistive technology equipment, however, then it belongs to Sam.

As a final note about these IDEA '97 requirements, FAPE is a guarantee to all students with disabilities. Therefore, states and schools are obligated to specifically seek out and identify *all* children with disabilities. This obligation in the law is referred to as **child find**, and particularly in the early days of IDEA was a major effort

free appropriate public education (FAPE). One of the provisions of IDEA that ensures that children with disabilities receive necessary education and services without cost to the child and family.
child find. A function or office in each state's department of education that helps refer and identify children with disabilities.

in most states. Child find systems are now well in place and states use public information campaigns, direct contact with social service agencies, and other types of outreach efforts to locate and provide services to every child with a disability.

Individualized Education Program (IEP). As just mentioned, for an educational program to be appropriate for each child with a disability, it must be individualized. Therefore, it seems impossible that there is a single answer to the educational needs of all students with disabilities: no standard program, no single service delivery option, no single place where education is received, and no single curriculum.

MAKING CONNECTIONS

Review the What IDEA '97 Says About LRE box in Chapter 1.

Least Restrictive Environment (LRE). The concept of LRE is controversial, and is at the heart of many of the debates which divided the field of special education during the last century. The debate and serious questioning about LRE began in 1986 when the then director of the federal Office of Special Education Programs, Madeline Will, began the push for more integration of students with disabilities into general education (then called the Regular Education Initiative).

Does LRE always equal placement in the general education classroom? Do "restriction" and feelings of isolation go hand-in-hand with segregated special education settings? Special educators must be constantly aware of how placement decisions can segregate students by removing them from normal role models, social interactions, and curriculum—and can fragment their daily lives. Placement decisions further identify a student as being different. Finally, removing a child from the general education classroom has serious implications for today and the future. IDEA '97 is clear that LRE must be individually determined, and a continuum of services must be available, but it does require that the student be integrated with nondisabled peers as much as possible and included in the mainstream of society. Possibly, gaining a better understanding and sensitivity to the concept of LRE is helpful. Table 2.2 on page 56 might help us think about how to make LRE decisions that are not too restrictive and do not result in lockstepped, rigid programs.

Debate among parents, special educators, general educators, politicians, and the media continually focuses on the concept of LRE and how it should be interpreted. On one side of the issue are those who believe that a full array of options should be available to youngsters with disabilities (Commission on the Deaf, 1988; Hallahan & Kauffman, 1995; Vaughn et al. 1998; Vaughn & Schumm, 1995). They believe in integration in general classrooms and general education activities whenever possible, but they also argue that other services, even separate schooling, may be necessary. On the other side of the issue is the interpretation that LRE is a legal mandate and ethical obligation that ensures the right of those with disabilities to be fully included in general education settings (Turnbull et al., 1995; Sailor, 1991; Snell, 1988; Stainback et al., 1994). No side is arguing for complete segregation, but how to make decisions about LRE and integration has not been resolved. As some professionals have pointed out, the general education classroom teacher referred the child in the first place, indicating that at least this professional believes that the general education classroom, as it is currently structured, is not the most appropriate placement for the child (Keogh, 1988; MacMillan & Forness, 1998; Smith, 1988). In that teacher's view, the child needs additional support in the general education classroom, supplemental services, or possibly a separate curriculum in order to have a successful educational experience. Finally, many parents and

individualized education program (IEP). A requirement of IDEA that guarantees a specifically tailored program to meet the individualized needs of each student with disabilities.

least restrictive environment (LRE). One of the principles outlined in IDEA that must be balanced when considering the best educational placement for an individual student with disabilities.

Table 2.2 Making LRE Decisions

Feature	Application
Maximum freedom	The ability to physically and intellectually explore environments should not be restricted.
Similar to age-peers	Activities should be age appropriate.
Not hindering	Access to appropriate curricula (general education curriculum), life skills (functional), or a combination is determined through the IEP process.
Not harmful	Some restrictions may be necessary to protect the individual or may be extended until specific skills are mastered.
Similar to peers with similar ability	Activities and freedom should consider both the individual's ability and age, being careful not to put the individual in a dangerous situation.
Not controlling	Rather than others controlling the many aspects of the lives of individuals with disabilities, they need to develop those skills necessary to control their own worlds.
Not dangerous	Care must be taken to balance the "dignity of risk" principle and safety.
Not intrusive	Although teaching others is an intrusive activity, respect privacy and dignity of each student.
Most respectful	Teachers must be sensitive, considerate, and respectful of the needs and wishes of students and their families.
Most appropriate	The essence of individualization is to develop students' educational program with their unique needs, abilities, learning styles, family circumstances, age, and all other relevant factors.
Most integrated	Full acceptance by peers and others, being able to be oneself in group situations, and being spontaneously included are measures of integration.
Most normalized	Making available to students with disabilities opportunities for lives similar to others in their society.

evaluation. Assessment or judgment of special characteristics such as intelligence, physical abilities, sensory abilities, learning preferences, and achievement. **authentic assessments.** Performance measures that use work generated by the student or observational data on social behaviors for assessment and evaluation purposes.

professionals, particularly those concerned with blind or deaf students, also feel that the array of placement options must include residential center schools. Clearly, the debate about full inclusion and where students with disabilities should receive their education is one of the hottest and most contentious issues that must be resolved in these new times.

As professionals argue about LRE, what it is, where it can happen, and how it should be determined, the children and youth who are experiencing whatever it is that adults have decided for them are typically left out of the conversation. And evidence is mounting that many of them have some strong feelings about their education and where they receive it. In one study, 60% of high school students reported strong negative experiences in general education classes, often preferring placement in special education (Lovitt et al., 1999). In another study, 76% of elementary students with disabilities indicated that they liked going to special education classes, and 90% believed that the services provided in those classes were beneficial (Padeliadu & Zigmond, 1996). And in yet another study, children with learning disabilities preferred pull-out programs because they thought they received special assistance and could work in a quieter setting (Klingner et al. 1998). Maybe we should listen to the collective voices of students with disabilities to learn about what services

NEW DIRECTIONS
FOR THE
MILLENNIUM

Legacy: The search for a single definition for LRE and for the concept of inclusion (reinforced by phrases such as "all means all") remain illusive.

Opportunities:

- Develop an array of definitions for the concept of inclusion that can be flexibly applied across the school years
- Match desired individual student's outcomes with supports, curriculum, and instructional procedures required to achieve them

curriculum based measurement (CBM). A method of evaluating students' performance by collecting data on their daily progress.
portfolio assessment. An alternative form of individualized assessment that includes many samples of the student's work across all curriculum targets and reports of teachers and parents about that individual's social skills.

they prefer and what practices are effective! At least from the limited studies conducted, it seems that while some students prefer to receive all of their education in general education classes, others do not. This certainly speaks to retaining different options for special education.

Appropriate Evaluations. Assessments of student performance have many different purposes. Three types of **evaluation** are particularly important in special education, and each serves a different function:

1. Identify and qualify students for special education
2. Guide instruction, continually ensuring that practices implemented are effective, so a minimal amount of instructional time is wasted using a tactic that is ineffective or has lost its power for an individual child
3. Determine annual or long-term gains, possibly through statewide or districtwide achievement tests given to entire classes of students, or to show progress on achieving benchmarks listed on IEPs

Remember, evaluation instruments or procedures selected should reflect the purpose or intended outcomes of the evaluation process.

Evaluations of students with disabilities usually include a "battery of tests" (more than one test or type of assessment). They often include standardized tests which were normed on large groups of people (intelligence and achievement tests are examples of standardized instruments). The use of standardized tests concerns many educators because they contribute to the overrepresentation of culturally and linguistically diverse students in special education. In an attempt to resolve or at least monitor this problem, the authors of IDEA '97 now require states to collect data and change practices that may be discriminatory.

Also, states now encourage diagnosticians to use a full array of evaluation instruments and procedures, and rely exclusively on standardized tests. Today, many professionals are advocating the use of **authentic assessments,** which use the work students generate in classroom settings as the assessment measurements (Fuchs & Deno, 1994; Fuchs & Fuchs, 1998). In other words, evaluation is made directly from the curriculum and the students' work. Results on students' class assignments (spelling tests, math tests), anecdotal records, writing samples, and observational data are examples of authentic assessments. Authentic assessments also include ongoing, frequent evaluations of students' performance. One method that many special educators use is a data collection system, **curriculum based measurement (CBM),** which is often thought of as a self-correcting instructional method combined with an evaluation system (Reschly, 1999). Here, teachers collect data about a child's daily progress on each instructional task (Fuchs & Fuchs, 1998). For example, a teacher instructing a youngster in math would keep a daily record of the number or percentage of problems the child correctly solved. This record helps the teacher judge whether the instructional methods selected are both efficient and effective. With CBM, teachers know how well their students are learning and whether the chosen instructional methods help the child meet the goals and objectives of the individualized plan.

Also considered a form of authentic assessment, **portfolio assessment** adds a considerable portion of student involvement in the process. Students can select a variety of samples of their work over a period of time to show growth and development (Bloom & Bacon, 1995; Curran & Harris, 1996; Salend, 1998). The portfolio may also include prizes, certificates of award, pictures, dictated work, photographs, lists of books read, and selections from work done with others. Finally, a portfolio might include narratives written by the teacher or others who work with the child about challenging situations or patterns of behavior that should be a target of concern.

Functional behavioral assessment, another type of authentic assessment, is typically used to understand a student's problem behaviors (Horner, 1994; Fitzsimmons, 1998). This well-researched system was developed with students with severe disabilities, and leads teachers directly to socially validated outcomes, and holds much promise for all students (Larson & Maag, 1998). It helps determine the nature of the behavior of concern, the reason or motivation for the behavior, and under what conditions the behavior does not occur. For example, are a student's temper tantrums a result of frustration by academic work that is too difficult? And does the frequency of the disruptive behaviors diminish when the target student is assigned a peer tutor who can help the student with an assignment? These are the five steps followed when conducting a functional assessment:

1. Verify the seriousness of the problem
2. Define the problem behavior in concrete terms
3. Collect data on possible causes of problem behavior
4. Analyze the data
5. Formulate and test a hypothesis (Fitzsimmons, 1998, pp. 1–2.)

IDEA '97 suggests that functional behavioral assessments be conducted when students with disabilities are faced with disciplinary actions.

Parent and Student Participation in Decision Making. IDEA '97 stresses the importance of involving families and students with disabilities in the IEP process.

See the Research to Practice box in Chapter 12 about functional assessments.

CONNECTIONS

For more information about parent involvement of diverse families, see these sections in Chapter 3:
• Prevalence
• Causes and Prevention
• Families

When parents, teachers, and students share the results from IEP team meetings, everyone understands goals, expectations, and the purpose of instruction.

functional behavioral assessment. A behavioral evaluation technique that determines the exact nature of problem behaviors, the reasons why they occur, and under what conditions the likelihood of their occurrence is reduced.

Procedural Safeguards

Parents of each student with a disability have the right to

- Be notified and invited to all meetings held about their child's educational program
- Give permission for their child to be evaluated and to obtain independent evaluations
- Access to their child's educational records
- Participate in all decisions about their child's educational program, placement, goals and objectives,
- Mediation, due process, and civil action

A major goal of the IEP meeting is to form a partnership between the parents, the schools, and professionals who will provide needed services. Educators need to recognize, however, that many parents feel that the schools control the special education process. They feel disenfranchised or confused about rules, regulations, and the purpose of special education. For families that do not speak English well enough to understand the complicated language we use to talk about special education issues, participation may seem impossible (Winzer & Mazurek, 1998). In such instances, schools must welcome family members or people from the community who are fluent in the family's native language and also knowledgeable about the special education process. Even though the law encourages their maximal participation, it is the obligation of educators to include and inform parents and students about the efforts which will be made on their behalf.

procedural safeguards. IDEA '97 guarantees students with disabilities and their parents the right to a free appropriate public education in the least restrictive environment possible, through a process to resolve disagreements and disputes beginning with mediation and ending with civil action.
mediation. A meeting of parents and school officials to resolve disagreements about the IEP and the student's placement and services.

Procedural Safeguards. IDEA '97 protects the rights of students with disabilities and their families to FAPE and LRE. The law also guarantees their rights to involvement in the educational process, written notifications, and consent. The IDEA laws prior to 1997 included many **procedural safeguards,** and the 1997 reauthorization expanded some of those protections. The What IDEA '97 Says box lists many of these protections, but a few important points that educators should keep in mind are summarized here.

The first point to remember is that it is important to communicate with parents and family members, and that communication must be meaningful. Therefore, to ensure that communication with parents about their children's educational programs has occurred, notification about meetings and other important events (change in the IEP, change in the child's placement, plans for evaluation) need to be in writing. Also, parents need to understand the meaning of communications from school, so these need to be in the native language of the parents, and they need to be clear and free from special education jargon. Second, many parents do not know their rights or have knowledge of the special education process. It is the school's obligation to be sure they know that they have to give permission for their children to be tested or evaluated, have a right to participate in the special education planning process, have the right to examine their child's records, and can obtain an independent educational evaluation of their child.

Parents have a right to challenge any of the school's decisions about the education of their child. IDEA '97 requires that parents notify the state education agency or the school district that they are filing a complaint. The disagreement may then be taken to a **mediation** process, where discussions are confidential and the family's lawyer's fees are the responsibility of the parents. If agreement between the two parties cannot be reached, a **due process hearing** may be called, in which an impartial third party settles the dispute. If either party does not agree to the decision made at the due process hearing, they can appeal to the state education agency. If they still do not agree, they may take the matter to the civil courts, and have a **judicial hearing.** These rights include the right to legal counsel and other rights concerning witnesses, written evidence, verbatim documentation of the hearing, and an appeal. The state or school district is obligated to pay the parents' legal costs (possibly at reduced fees, however) if the parents prevail.

THE IEP PROCESS

The IEP process is required by law, and is systematically applied for every student with disabilities. The process is to include considerable participation by the family, the student (whenever possible), and a team of experts. The IEP process is meant to be deliberate and equitable; and its results, individualized program plans, are the means by which the educational concepts outlined in IDEA '97 are guaranteed to each student and that student's family. The formation of an individualized program involves six steps in a comprehensive process, beginning with pre-referral and ending with evaluation of a youngster's program (Council for Exceptional Children [CEC], 1999):

1. Referral
2. Evaluation
3. Eligibility
4. Development of the IEP
5. Implementation of the IEP
6. Annual review

The IEP process is also sometimes called the IEP cycle (CEC, 1999). It is initiated as a result of a series of pre-referral interventions. The point here is to avoid unnecessary referrals, which are costly in terms of time, money, and resources. Before any special education referral is made, teachers and family members should work together to see if educational or behavioral difficulties can be resolved in the general education classroom by general education teachers. During this pre-referral period, teachers should try different teaching approaches and make basic accommodations to the instructional program. They can also seek assistance and consultation with resources available at the school (principal, resource room teachers, special educators, districtwide methods and materials teachers). If concerns continue, a referral to special education and the initiation of the IEP process should begin. Let's look at the six steps of the IEP process to get a better understanding of what each means and how they add up to a process or cycle.

Step 1: Referral. In this step, a child is actually referred for special education services. The parents must be invited to a meeting where a committee decides whether the student's problems are significant enough to warrant formal assessment. In its consideration, the committee looks at all of the information collected during the pre-referral process, which includes samples of the student's work and descriptions of the effectiveness of changes in teaching style and other accommodations. Parents must give permission for the next step in the IEP process (evaluation), and must be invited to all meetings where their child's **identification,** evaluation, and placement are considered.

due process hearing. A noncourt proceeding before an impartial hearing officer that can be used if parents and school personnel disagree on a special education issue.

judicial hearing. A hearing before a judge in court.

identification. The process of seeking out and designating children with disabilities who require special education and related services.

school psychologist. A psychologist trained to test and evaluate individual students' abilities.

acuity. Sharpness of response to visual, auditory, or tactile stimuli.

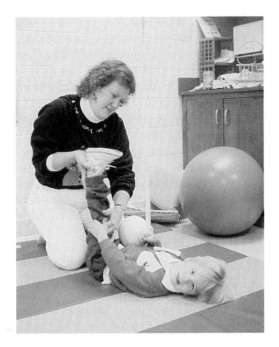

Some children require the services of professionals from different disciplines, such as physical therapy.

Referrals can come from many different sources. For preschoolers, the referral can come from parents, a social service agency, a public health nurse, a day care or preschool teacher, or a doctor. Typically, children with severe disabilities begin the referral process sooner than do other children with disabilities. For example, some infants with severe disabilities may be identified at birth or early in infancy. Children who are at risk because of improper prenatal care, low birth weight, accident, or trauma during infancy are also often referred for special services by public health nurses or day care professionals. Parents might be concerned about a child who is not walking by age 2 or not talking by age 3. Preschool teachers may be troubled by children who have frequent and excessive bursts of violent behavior or inappropriate displays of temper. Pediatricians may be concerned about children whose physical or motor development is slow. Delayed language, difficulties in eating, inability to locate the source of sounds, or excessive crying are other signals that normal child development may be delayed. All of these indicators can signal a referral of an infant or toddler to special education.

For schoolchildren, referral usually begins when the general education teacher becomes concerned about a particular student's behavior or academic achievement. Candidates for referral are students whose academic performance is significantly behind their classmates' or who continually misbehave and disrupt the learning environment. Students who are thought to be gifted and talented because of their accelerated academic performance or high levels of creativity may also experience the IEP process. Although gifted education is not included in IDEA '97, many states follow the requirements of IDEA '97 and develop IEPs for gifted students as they do for students with disabilities.

MAKING CONNECTIONS

For more information about evaluation and student assessment, see these features:

• Step 2 in the IEP process in the next section of this chapter

• The Identification section (Defined) in Chapters 3–12

• The IDEA '97 box about nondiscriminatory testing in the Identification section of Chapter 3

Step 2: Evaluation. The purpose of this step in the IEP process is to determine whether a youngster has a disability, whether special education is required, and what types of special or related services are needed. Evaluations must be conducted by multidisciplinary teams, and assess the student's strengths and needs. If a child is suspected of having a language impairment, an SLP should be a member of the multidisciplinary team. If a hearing problem is possible, an audiologist must be a team member, and so on. And, any information provided by the parents must be considered by the multidisciplinary team. In many states, the team leader is a **school psychologist,** an educational diagnostician, or a psychometrician.

Many different types of data are used to inform the team about the student's abilities. Medical history, information about social interactions at school and at home, adaptive behavior in the community, educational performance, and other relevant factors are considered. Evaluations must include an array of assessment instruments and procedures. Formal tests—tests of intelligence, academic achievement, **acuity** (vision and hearing), and learning style—and less formal assessments, such as classroom observations of social behavior, curriculum based measurements (CBM), samples of academic performance—may be used as well. The information

IEP Team. The multidisciplinary team of education professions that develops and evaluates, along with students with disabilities and their parents, the individualized education program plan for each student with a disability.

benchmarks. Indicators of accomplishments for IEP goals and objectives.

manifestation determination. The result of a process that determines whether or not a student's disciplinary problems are a result of the student's disability.

Behavioral Intervention Plan. The plan developed for any student with disabilities that includes a functional behavioral assessment and describes procedures to use to prevent and intervene if the student is violent, brings weapons to school, or is involved in drugs; the result of disciplinary action.

interim alternative setting. A temporary (no more than 45-day) educational placement for a student with disabilities who is violent, brings a gun to school, or is involved with drugs; not considered a change in educational placement, and a new IEP is not required for this action.

collected should also relate to the individual's major life activities: how the child performs at home, at school, in interpersonal relationships, and during leisure time. So, evaluations may also include interviews of extended family members as well as others who know the child well.

Because of the potentially negative effect on the individual and the family of incorrectly identifying an individual as having a disability, IDEA '97 is quite specific, stressing that tests must be nondiscriminatory and be given in children's native language or other mode of communication (such as sign language). The team must give considerable weight to samples of students' classroom work, CBM summaries, and teachers' descriptions of social behavior. The details of the identification procedure are established by each state. Because the state determines the process used to identify children with disabilities, teams of professionals must be involved to ensure that the procedures adopted represent the points of view of all culturally and linguistically diverse groups.

In all cases, evaluation should contribute to the development of an appropriate education for those students identified as having disabilities. The information gathered about the child during this stage is used throughout the rest of the process. Assessment is the foundation for the planning process. The team's thinking and planning should focus on life goals and outcomes, so instruction is relevant to the individual's long-term needs (living independently, holding a job, participating in the community). And the result should be a baseline of performance that guides the development of the individualized education program and will later be used to judge the effectiveness of the educational program that was implemented.

Step 3: Eligibility. The assessment process, first, identifies whether a student has a disability and, second, classifies the disability (mental retardation, learning disabilities, emotional or behavioral disorders, low vision or blindness, deafness or hard of hearing, speech or language impairment). Although IDEA '97 and its regulations, which were prepared by the U.S. Department of Education, provide definitions of the special education categories, each state has written its own definitions. Typically, children who are younger than 5 are not assigned to a disability category, and a trend not to use disability or special education categories for mild disabilities (high incidence disabilities) is developing (Reschly, 1996). Regardless, once it is determined that a child has a disability—whether labeled as having mental retardation, learning disabilities, or emotional or behavioral disorders—the committee needs to determine if the child also needs special education.

Step 4: Development of the IEP. What happens next? Very few children tested are ineligible for special services because they do not meet the criteria set by individual states (Algozzine et al., 1983; Kroth, 1990). These youngsters continue to be served by general education. Special education is intended only for those students with disabilities. For them, the next step requires decisions about appropriate education, services, and placement. The assessment results are used to help make these decisions. It is at this point that the **IEP Team** begins its work. Representation on the IEP Team is specified by IDEA '97 (see the What IDEA '97 Says box). Collectively, the members should be knowledgeable about the student, resources and services available from the school district, the general education curriculum, implications of evaluation results, and the IEP process. At least one team member should be prepared to explain the process and the student's IEP goals and objectives to the parents. If an interpreter is needed for a family that is not proficient in English, one must be provided.

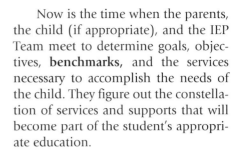

What IDEA '97 Says About

IEP Team Members

The IEP Team for each student with a disability must include

- At least one general education teacher (if the student is participating in general education)
- At least one special educator or related service provider
- A representative of the school district
- The parents
- The student (if appropriate)
- Other people the parents or school invite

NEW DIRECTIONS
FOR THE
MILLENNIUM

Legacy: Disciplining, particularly being able to expel, students with disabilities was one of the hottest issues surrounding IDEA's last reauthorization, and the issue continues to resurface in congressional debates.

Opportunities:

- Determine if students with disabilities are a major source of disciplinary problems
- Develop alternative educational placements for all students so no student is expelled or experiences reduced educational opportunities

Now is the time when the parents, the child (if appropriate), and the IEP Team meet to determine goals, objectives, **benchmarks,** and the services necessary to accomplish the needs of the child. They figure out the constellation of services and supports that will become part of the student's appropriate education.

Step 5: Implementation of the IEP. After the development of the IEP, the student's services and individualized program begin. Of course, minor changes in students' goals and objectives, or the benchmarks that indicate their achievement, do not indicate a need for a new IEP or another IEP meeting. The annual IEP meeting sets the stage for a productive year, and no other meetings are necessary. However, any major change in the student's program or placement does require written notification of the parents and possibly necessitates a meeting. Most actions related to discipline fall into the category of major change.

For students with disabilities who commit serious infractions that would cause a nondisabled peer to be suspended or expelled, the implementation of the IEP can become more challenging and confusing (Katsiyannis & Maag, 1998). For example, the school district has to notify parents on the same day a decision to discipline their child is made. The school district has a number of options available to it when a student with a disability is violent, brings a gun or weapon to school, or is involved with drugs. School officials can, for no more than a total of ten school days in any one academic year, suspend the student or place the student in another school. However, once the ten-day rule is exceeded, the IEP Team must meet. The team has several important jobs to complete (Katsiyannis & Maag, 1998). It must determine whether the behavior that caused the disciplinary action is a result of the student's disability. This process is called **manifestation determination.** It must see that a functional behavioral assessment is conducted in order to develop and implement a **Behavioral Intervention Plan.** The IEP team may also identify an **interim alternative setting** in which the student will continue to receive services, make progress on IEP goals and objectives, and also address the behaviors which were the cause of disciplinary actions (Bear, 1999; Voyles, 1999). IDEA '97 mandates that the interim alternative setting cannot be used for more than 45 school days, after which a formal request to change the student's placement is necessary. If problems continue beyond that time period, then the school can request a change of placement during a new IEP meeting, where the parents participate. If the parents disagree with the placement change, they are entitled to their procedural safeguards (mediation, due process hearings, followed by civil action if disagreements continue).

Step 6: Annual Review. The IEP is reviewed annually by the IEP Team and the parents. The purpose of the annual review meeting is to be sure the student is meeting the goals and objectives specified in the IEP. This is done by evaluating whether the student is making progress toward or has achieved the benchmarks specified for

The preschool at the John F. Kennedy Center at Vanderbilt University—named after Susan Gray, a pioneer in the Head Start movement—remains an active research center. Here, young children with and without disabilities learn together.

each objective. For evaluation purposes, most educators are careful to specify goals, objectives, and benchmarks in terms that can be evaluated. And, of course, the goals need to reflect tasks and skills the student needs to learn to have greater success with the general education curriculum or for independence and a community presence later in life.

Although the IEP process only requires an annual review, the individualized program—whether it is for an infant or toddler (an IFSP) or a schoolchild (an IEP)—must contain frequent evaluations of student performance. A student's individualized program is typically evaluated to guide instruction and to be sure the interventions scheduled are effective, ongoing and frequent assessments in the curriculum are used for these purposes, and to reevaluate the continuing needs of the student. As the student grows and learns, the educational decisions made one year may not be the best for the ensuing years. At the time of the annual review, a new program is developed. Decisions about placement, supportive services, and the goals and objectives for the upcoming year are made. In some cases, a child's progress may have been so great that special services are no longer required. In other cases, the degree of special services may change. For example, a child's progress may indicate that only periodic support from a special educator is necessary to maintain growth and continued progress. In other cases, more intensive special services may be needed. For example, a student with a behavior disorder may have been placed in a resource room under a behavior management program. If the student showed insufficient progress over the year, this student may need to spend at least part of the upcoming year in a self-contained special education class taught by a teacher specially trained to work with children with emotional or behavioral disorders.

MAKING CONNECTIONS

See the Education and the Preschool Child (Educational Interventions) sections in Chapters 3–12.

THE INDIVIDUALIZED EDUCATION PLANS

IDEA '97 specifies that an Individualized Family Service Plan (IFSP) be developed for each infant and toddler with disabilities and an Individualized Education Program (IEP) be developed for all preschool through high school students with disabilities (students from ages 3 to 21). A component of older children's IEPs specifies the services necessary to help them make successful transitions from school to work. The transition component is initiated at age 14 and continues until the student leaves the public schools. Let's first look at the IFSP in a little more detail.

Individualized Family Service Plan (IFSP). A written plan that identifies and organizes services and resources for infants and toddlers with special needs who are under age 3 and their families.

Individualized Family Service Plans (IFSPs). Infants or toddlers (birth through age 2) with disabilities or who are at risk for disabilities were originally guaranteed the right to early intervention programs through PL 99–457, passed in 1986, and that right continues through IDEA '97. Children who are age 3 or older receive an IEP and are served through school districts. The process starts with referral and assessment, and, for those who qualify for services, results in the development of the plan drawn up by the IFSP.

The required contents of the IFSP differ somewhat from those of plans for older children. One key difference is that, like all individualized programs, the plan is evaluated once a year, but the IFSP must also be reviewed with the family every six months. The key components of the IFSP include the following descriptions:

- The child's current functioning levels in all relevant areas (physical development, cognitive development, language and speech development, psychosocial development, and self-help skills)
- The family's strengths and needs, to assist them in enhancing the development of their child
- The major outcomes expected, including criteria, procedures, and a time line, so progress can be evaluated
- The services necessary and a schedule for their delivery
- Projected dates for initiation of services
- The name of the service manager
- A biannual review with the child's family of progress made and the need for modifications in the IFSP
- Indication of methods for transitioning the child to services available for children ages 3 to 5

To many **service managers** and early childhood specialists, the IFSP is a working document for an ongoing process in which parents and specialists work together, continually modifying, expanding, and developing a child's educational program. Children and families who participate in early intervention programs often find these years to be an intense period, with many professionals offering advice, training, guidance, personalized services, and care and concern. The transition to preschool at the age of 3 can be particularly difficult and frightening, so IDEA '97 includes transition efforts for these youngsters and their families (CEC, 1999).

Individualized Education Program (IEP). The IEP is a management tool designed to ensure that schoolchildren with special needs receive the special education and related services appropriate to their needs. First required in 1975 by PL 94–142, the IEP remains a cornerstone of every educational program planned for each student with a disability. Congress delineated the minimal contents of the IEP, and it is important that every educator knows these key components (CEC, 1999; U.S. Department of Education, 1999):

- The student's present levels of educational performance
- Indications about ways in which the student's disability influences participation and progress in the general education curriculum
- Statement of measurable annual goals including benchmarks or short-term instructional objectives that are related to participation in the general education curriculum, as well as meeting other educational needs resulting from the disability
- Specific educational services to be provided, including program modifications or supports which will allow participation in the general education curriculum and extracurricular activities
- Explanation of the extent to which the child will not participate in general education classes and extracurricular activities with nondisabled peers

service manager. The case manager who oversees the implementation and evaluation of an Individualized Family Service Plan. **Individualized Education Program (IEP).** A management tool used to identify and organize individualized education and related services for preschoolers and schoolchildren.

- Description of modifications in statewide or districtwide assessments (if the student will not be participating, a statement of those reasons for nonparticipation and how the student will be assessed must be specified)
- Projected date for initiation of services
- Expected duration of those services
- Beginning at age 14, an annual statement of the transition service needs, and at age 16, a statement of needed transition services
- Statement of how the student's progress will be measured and how parents will be informed about the progress for at least the same grade reporting periods as apply to nondisabled peers, as well as informed about annual progress made on the IEP

A sample IEP form is found in Figure 2.4 on pages 67–69. It shows all the components of what needs to be included in an IEP. Notice that the IEP is not too complicated. Completing one should not be frightening.

Bateman and Linden (1998) remind us of five important principles that should be followed when developing and implementing IEPs. These principles are included in the law and have been verified and supported through hundreds of rulings from a variety of agencies and the courts. First, all of the student's needs must be met, not just a selected few. Academic areas may be reflected, but they might also represent areas not typically part of educational programs of students without disabilities (e.g., fine and gross motor skills, functional life skills). Second, whether services are available does not determine whether they are included on the IEP. If a student needs the services of an assistive technologist, they shall be made available. Third, the IEP indicates services that must be provided. Through this process, they become legally binding. They cannot be denied without another IEP meeting and mutual approval by the family and the school district. Fourth, the IEP should be individually determined. All students who need services of an SLP, for example, should not have identical IEPs.

Another important principle should be followed when implementing IEPs: Communicate their contents to everyone who should have the information. Too often teachers do not know what the student's IEP comprises, and at the secondary level, many general education teachers of specific students with disabilities do not even know that they have an IEP that spells out accommodations and modifications that should be met (Bateman & Linden, 1998; Lovitt et al., 1994; Pautier, 1995). This situation leaves one to ask: How can an appropriate education be delivered when the educators who interact with students with disabilities do not even know what services, goals, and objectives their education should include? The answer is obvious. An appropriate education cannot be delivered under these circumstances. At least some modifications in instruction and accommodations to the learning environment are required for even those with the mildest disabilities. Although IEPs are part of the students' school records, they are not private for those educators who have legitimate educational reasons for having access to them (Bateman & Linden, 1998).

MAKING
CONNECTIONS

See the Transitional (Educational Interventions) sections in Chapters 3–12.

IEP Component for Transitional Services. IDEA '97 included some changes about transitional services and adolescents with disabilities. Guidelines about transition were initiated in PL 101–476, the 1990 amendments of IDEA, and were expanded in this last reauthorization (see the What IDEA '97 Says box on page 71). The law stresses the importance of vocational and life skills for these individuals, and it ensures that transitional services are provided throughout the school years (NICHCY, 1998; Patton & Blalock, 1996).

Name _Estelle Wong_   Grade _11_   Date of Birth _3-3-81_

Parent/Guardian _Lawrence Wong_   School _Henderson High_

Primary language: Student _English_   Home _English_

Disability classification: _Mild mental retardation_   Secondary _Orthopedic impairment_

Present Levels of Performance, Goals and Objectives

Skill Area: *Math calculation*

Estelle is an 11th grade young lady whose math skills limit her success in regular math classes. Estelle can use a calculator to solve whole number addition, subtraction, multiplication, and division problems with decimals. She cannot calculate total cost of groceries, total outlay for utility bills, or expenditures for retail purchases. Estelle cannot calculate correct change, balance a checkbook, or calculate net income.

Annual Goal: Estelle will improve her ability to total different types of bills from present levels of performance.

Short-term Objective: Given $10.00, three items from the grocery store, and a calculator, Estelle will total the cost of the items and state whether the money covers the cost of the items with 100% accuracy for 3 consecutive trials.

Short-term Objective: Given three utility bills and a calculator, Estelle will calculate the cost of utilities with 100% accuracy over 3 consecutive trials.

Short-term Objective: Given receipts from her monthly retail purchases and a calculator, Estelle will calculate the cost of her purchases with 100% accuracy over 3 consecutive trials.

Annual Goal: _____

Short-term Objective: _____

Short-term Objective: _____

Short-term Objective: _____

Skill Area: *Reading*

Estelle is able to read and comprehend written passages at a 3.0 grade level, which limits her independent success in the regular high school curriculum. She can read and follow printed directions on simple recipes and work tasks when given help in reading unfamiliar words. She has difficulty reading the classified ads (e.g., headings, abbreviations) to search for potential jobs.

Annual Goal: Estelle will improve reading skills for task sequences.

Short-term Objective: When given a new simple recipe, Estelle will read the recipe and follow it with no assistance, with at least 80% accuracy over 2 trials.

(continued)

Figure 2.4 **Individualized Education Program**

Source: From *Guide to Writing Quality Individualized Education Programs: What's Best for Students with Disabilities?* by G. Gibb and T. Dyches, 2000, Boston: Allyn and Bacon. Reprinted by permission.

Short-term Objective: When given a written sequence for a work task, Estelle will read the sequence and follow it with no assistance, with at least 80% accuracy over 2 trials.

Annual Goal: _____

Short-term Objective: _____

Short-term Objective: _____

Short-term Objective: _____

Skill Area: *Social Skills*

Estelle is a very friendly young lady who enjoys the company of others. However, her socializing often distracts her from working in general and special education settings and at job sites. When not reminded, Estelle socializes rather than works for periods of up to 50 minutes.

Annual Goal: Estelle will limit her socialization with friends to free time and decrease her socialization during work time.

Short-term Objective: When Estelle has free time at school and work (e.g., before/after work periods, breaks, lunch), she will socialize with her friends with 100% accuracy over 5 consecutive days.

Short-term Objective: _____

Skill Area: *Daily Living Skills*

Estelle has deficits in daily living skills which currently limit her independence. She is able to plan and prepare 6-8 simple meals independently, but she often chooses food from only one or two food groups. She also needs several reminders to clean areas of the house when they are not tidy. She needs verbal cues to complete such tasks as dusting, vacuuming, and doing laundry.

Annual Goal: Estelle will independently plan and prepare at least 15 well-balanced meals.

Short-term Objective: Given a food pyramid chart to guide her selection of foods, Estelle will plan and prepare 1 of 15 meals containing food from each food group, with at least 80% accuracy over 3 meals.

Short-term Objective: When it is mealtime, Estelle will plan and prepare 1 of 15 meals containing food from each food group, with at least 80% accuracy over 3 meals.

Annual Goal: _____

Short-term Objective: _____

Short-term Objective: _____

Skill Area: *Motor Skills*

Estelle is able to walk independently in spite of her orthopedic impairment, but she is unable to use stairs and ramps without physical assistance for balance. She gets nervous when the hallways are crowded because she thinks she might fall down the stairs, so she waits for the other students to leave. This limits her ability to get to her general education classes on time.

(continued)

Figure 2.4 **Individualized Education Program** *(continued)*

Annual Goal: Estelle will increase her independent use of stairs and ramps.

Short-term Objective: When Estelle is let out of class 5 minutes early to avoid the crowd, she will ascend/descend the stairs or ramp independently within 10 minutes with 100% accuracy over 4 days.

Short-term Objective: When Estelle is let out of class 3 minutes early to avoid the crowd, she will ascend/descend the stairs or ramp independently within 7 minutes with 100% accuracy over 4 days.

Short-term Objective: When Estelle is let out of class at the bell, she will ascend/descend the stairs or ramp independently within 5 minutes with 100% accuracy over 4 days.

Special Education and Related Services

Type of Service, Aid or Modification	Location	Time per day/week	Begin Date	Duration
Special Education/General Education Team Teach	Regular class	3 hrs./day	11/3/98	1 year
Special Education	Self-contained class	1 hr./day	11/3/98	1 year
Vocational Training	Work site	2 hrs./day	11/3/98	1 year
Physical Therapy	Hallways	30 min./week	11/3/98	1 year

Non-Participation in the General Curriculum

Estelle will spend 55% of her time not participating in the general curriculum.

Transition Planning (for students 14 and over)

_____ Transition planning will be addressed through the student's Student Advisement Program

__X__ Transition planning is addressed on the IEP addendum (see attached)

_____ Transition planning is not needed due to the age of the student

Participation in Statewide or District Assessments

Estelle is unable to participate in statewide and district assessments due to her inability to read, write and comprehend concepts beyond a 10-year developmental level. Her progress will be assessed using the Brigance Employability Skills Inventory and the Checklist of Adaptive Living Skills.

Scheduled Reports to Parents

Estelle's parents will be informed of her progress toward her annual goals on the same schedule as the rest of the school: parent/teacher conferences and quarterly report cards. These reports will include the number of annual goals Estelle has met and an estimate of her rate of progress toward meeting all of the annual goals.

Signature   Position   Date

_____   _____   _____

_____   _____   _____

Figure 2.4 **Individualized Education Program** *(continued)*

Many businesses are now helping individuals with disabilities find their places in the community and in employment settings.

Beginning at age 14 and every year thereafter, students' IEPs must include a statement of transitional services, and at age 16, the IEP must include a statement of interagency responsibilities and linkages to ensure continuity of services when the student leaves school. This features adds an important dimension to adolescents' educational programs. In the past, there was little dialogue between special educators and the vocational rehabilitation counselors who assume some responsibility for many of these youngsters after their school years. As a result, many young adults with disabilities were ill prepared for community living or the world of work. Collaboration of special and vocational education has great benefits, including the preparation for independent living and employment. Because young adults with disabilities often interact with so many different social service agencies, postsecondary job training opportunities, and potential employers, the transition component of students' IEPs facilitates the process involved in becoming an independent adult (Blalock, 1996).

The transition component supplements and complements the school-based IEP process. While the IEP describes the educational goals and objectives that a student should achieve during a schoolyear, the transitional services part of the IEP addresses the skills and the supportive services required in the future (being able to shop, make leisure time choices, and cooperate with co-workers). It ensures that the IEP reflects goals and objectives relating to skills necessary at work, at home, and in the community. Some goals might relate to desired outcomes (integrated employment, community living, citizenship and involvement, and personal autonomy and life satisfaction), while some might be specific to skill acquisition (money management, independent travel from home to work, time management), and should reflect a life skills curriculum (Clark, 1996; Patton et al., 1997).

By the time some youngsters reach high school, their attitudes and their involvement with school and the educational process have lessened. Unfortunately, many adolescents with disabilities find the process used to develop IEPs and transition plans frustrating and meaningless (Lovitt et al., 1994). These last years of school, however, can be critical to their achievement of special education outcomes and to their smooth and successful transition to adulthood. Recognizing the importance of these last years of schooling, Congress strongly suggests in IDEA '97 that students be involved in the development of their own IEPs. By participating in the IEP meetings, adolescents can become more involved in the process and become motivated to achieve transitional goals (Lehmann et al., 1999). Certainly, the needs and feelings of the students themselves must be considered. At the conclusion of several research projects that focused on high school students with disabilities, the researchers made these suggestions about educational programs and these adolescents (Hasazi et al., 1999; Lovitt et al., 1999; Sands, 1999):

Transition Services

For every student with a disability over the age of 14, the IEP must

- Include a statement about transitional service needs
- At the age of 16, also add information about the coordination of services across agencies (education, social services, vocational rehabilitation)
- Describe how the educational program will be modified
- Indicate how the student will participate in extracurricular and nonacademic activities
- Include a statement that the student has been informed about the rights that obtain upon attainment of the age of majority

---

- Assist them in becoming more independent, self-sufficient, and vocal about their needs
- Include more instruction on social skills
- Make them more aware of their IEP goals, the instructional practices being implement to achieve those goals, and how they are being evaluated
- Identify and focus on students' strengths that are valued by the student and others
- Help develop positive self-identities
- Expand school options to include learning in the community, even for students with mild disabilities
- Give students information about options they might explore after leaving high school
- Continue working on the mastery of basic skills, if necessary

CONCEPTS AND CONTROVERSY: HIGH STAKES TESTING: FOR WHOM ARE THE STAKES THE HIGHEST?

See the Access to the General Education Curriculum section of this chapter.

Partly as a reaction to charges that special education was ineffective, special education students are evaluated more than other students in the education system. They are assessed to determine their eligibility for special education, to monitor their progress in the curriculum, and to judge their annual achievement of individually specified goals and objectives. And IDEA '97 now mandates that most students with disabilities also participate in statewide or districtwide high stakes assessments. Assessments, however, have been criticized for not providing relevant information necessary to implement an effective special education program (Voyles, 1998). So, for a group of students who are assessed considerably, here is yet another evaluation for them to complete. And, although there was no pilot testing of this concept, IDEA '97 mandates that students with disabilities participate.

Besides the time away from instruction that assessments require, other concerns perplex some parents and educators. Schools and teachers are being held accountable for the performance of their students on these statewide or districtwide tests (Consortium on Renewing Education, 1998). High performing schools are being rewarded with more funds to support their efforts, while low performing teachers and schools are experiencing negative consequences (reductions in budget, poor public relations, being held in receivership). The motivation to remove students with disabilities from classes, schools, and these high stakes tests must be high. Tolerance for poorly performing students is low, and the adverse responses to students, particularly those with mild disabilities, is high.

What is the benefit to students with disabilities who cannot perform well on these tests? What safeguards protect their inclusive education? Well, students who cannot perform on large-scale achievement tests (such as those with severe cognitive disabilities) can take alternative assessments, or receive accommodations on these achievement tests (Tindal et al., 1998; Ysseldyke & Olsen, 1999). So why take them? These questions will need to be resolved, but of more importance is that reactions to children with disabilities are at least monitored to ensure that positive attitudes about their participation do not change to hostile and angry ones.

 n Conclusion

Look again at the Advance Organizers found at the beginning of the chapter; to help you study the content of this chapter, the answers to the Self-Test and Challenge questions are found here. Test yourself to see if you have mastered the major points of this chapter.

Summary

A cornerstone of the federal laws assuring a free appropriate education to all children and youth with disabilities is a mandated process of individualized educational programs. They are the Individualized Family Service Plan, the Individualized Education Program, and the supplemental Individualized Transition Plan. Each of these management tools guides the education system as it plans for and delivers an appropriate education to these individuals.

Focus Questions

Self-Test Questions

• *What are the six steps to developing an individualized program for each student with disabilities?*

The six steps to every individualized special education program are: referral, evaluation, eligibility, development of the IEP, implementation of the IEP, and annual review. All of these programs (IFSPs, IEPs, and ITPs) follow a general process in the development of individualized program plans. For youngsters first being considered for placement into special education, three steps are completed before the program plan is written: referral, evaluation, and eligibility. Not all children referred for special education services qualify. Some referred do not have a disability and do not require special assistance; others with disabilities do not require special services to meet their educational needs. A wide range of services is available to children with disabilities, from short-term assistance of a specialist to intensive full-time services. Also, many different professionals are available to children with disabilities: special education teachers, speech/language pathologists, occupational therapists, physical therapists, vocational educators, audiologists, counselors, assistive technology experts, social workers. Special education placement decisions must be made by balancing an appropriate education with the concept of least restrictive environment. Every student receiving special services must have a program individually tailored to meet his or her needs, and this program must be specified in terms of annual goals and objectives, complete with benchmarks and measurable ways to evaluate their attainment. Evaluation and review of these goals and objectives must occur at least once a year. At the time of the annual evaluation, a determination about next year's program must be made. For children requiring continuing special services, a new program plan is developed. For those who no longer require special services, transition to the general education system is made.

- *What roles do the IEP Team fill?*

  The IEP Team is comprised of at least one general education teacher (if the student is participating in general education), at least one special educator or related service provider, a representative of the school district, the parents, the student (if appropriate), and other people the parents or school invite. The IEP Team begins its work when the IEP is being developed to determine services, resources, and the needs of the student now identified as having a disability. The team sets the goals, objectives, and benchmarks which comprise the IEP. The team meets each time the student's placement is to be changed or when the goals and objectives need considerable modification. It is also responsible for evaluation of the student's annual review.

- *What factors must be considered when determining the least restrictive environment for individual students?*

  All children and youth with disabilities, ages birth to 21, are entitled to a free appropriate education in the least restrictive environment possible. These rights are guaranteed by the Individuals with Disabilities Education Act. When balancing FAPE with LRE, parents and professionals should consider the goals and objectives developed for the student. These goals, of course, should reflect the adult outcomes that will need direct intervention to achieve. These outcomes should include integrated employment, community living, citizenship, and life satisfaction. Attaining these outcomes requires substantial effort by many, including the students with disabilities themselves, their families, and the array of educators and related service professionals who have dedicated their careers to these goals. Most important, LRE must be individually determined, with no single service delivery option being able to meet the needs of all students with any single disability or all students with disabilities. It requires an array of educational placements and services to meet the needs of these students and to define LRE for each of them.

- *What are the different educational placement options that comprise the continuum of services for special education?*

New and innovative placement options and service delivery systems are being developed by the creative professionals who work to see special education evolve and improve. For example, pull-in programs have not yet become part of the federal accountability system but are being implemented in many schools today. Under this fully inclusive system, special education and related services are brought to the individual in the general education setting, instead of having the student go to the services. The more traditional options that tend to comprise the continuum of services include itinerant or consultative general education placements, resource rooms, special education classes or self-contained special education classes, special schools or center schools, and homebound services.

- *What are the different purposes of IDEA '97's various program plans?*

For infants and toddlers, IDEA '97 mandates that an Individualized Family Service Plan be developed and implemented. The IFSP must contain information about the child's current functioning levels, the strengths and needs of the family, measurable goals and objectives, the services required and the time of their delivery, and the name of the person responsible for coordination of these services. Developing IFSPs is the responsibility of a multidisciplinary team of professionals who must address the needs of the child and the family. Usually, services are provided by many different professionals, with some or all of these services provided in the child's home. As a culminating activity, the multidisciplinary team assists the child and the family in making a transition to preschool.

Children with disabilities from ages 3 to 21 are served by the public schools. IDEA '97 mandates that Individualized Education Programs be prepared for them. The IEP is the management tool that guides their educational program, including related services. It includes an assessment of the child's present level of educational performance, annual goals and objectives, the extent to which the student will participate in general education, the specific services to be provided, and the date for initiation of those services. For students with disabilities who are 14 years and older, a transitional services plan must be part of the IEP. It helps the student prepare for employment and community-based independent living. When students reach the age of 16, the plan begins the preparation for moving from the schools to other service agencies.

Challenge Question

- *How should the array of educational services and supports available to students with disabilities be implemented?*

The array of educational services should be, first, individually determined, and second, delivered to support the child with disabilities and his or her family at the intensity required and only for the duration needed for the problem to be met. Participation by the student and the family must be integral components of the educational decision-making process. The development of a partnership among school officials, the student's teachers, the student, and the family should be a most important element that is active when determining and implementing educational services. One criticism of the continuum of special education services model, one that has been widely voiced nationwide for over thirty years, is that it is too lockstepped. In other words, students become identified with a level of classroom placement and seem unable to move to a less restrictive placement despite the academic and social progress they make. "Once a self-contained special education classroom student, always a special education classroom student" seems to be the common trap of this model. Therefore the array of services model is being used to describe supports and placements because it tends to be a more fluid and flexible approach. The array provides many options of programs, placements, intensities of services, and duration of support. It is neither rigid nor unidimensional.

 # Supplementary Resources

Scholarly Readings

Bateman, B. D., & Linden, M. A. (1998). *Better IEPs: How to develop legally correct and educationally useful programs* (3rd ed.). Longmont, CO: Sopris West.

Council for Exceptional Children. (1999). *IEP Team Guide*. Reston, VA: Author.

Hallahan, D. P., & Kauffman, J. M. (1995). *The illusion of inclusion*. Austin, TX: Pro-Ed.

NICHCY (1998, June). The IDEA Amendments of 1997 (Special Issue). *News Digest, 26,* 1–39.

Patton, J. R., & Blalock, G. (1996). *Transition and students with learning disabilities: Facilitating the movement from school to adult life.* Austin, TX: Pro-Ed.

Parent, Professional, and Consumer Organizations and Agencies

American Bar Association: Commission on Mental and Physical Disability Law
1800 M Street, NW
Suite 200 South
Washington, DC 20036-5886
Phone: (202) 331-2200
E-mail: cmpdl@abanet.org
Web site: http://www.abanet.org/disability

National Association of State Directors of Special Education (NASDSE)
1800 Diagonal Road, Suite 320
Alexandria, VA 22314
Phone: (703) 519-3800; (888) 438-1938
TTY: (703) 519-7008
Web site: http://www.nasdse.com

National Council on Disability
1331 F Street, NW
Washington, DC 20004
Phone: (202) 272-2004
Web site: http://www.ncd.gov

National Association of School Psychologists
1929 K Street, Suite 250
Washington, DC 20006
Phone: (301) 657-0270
Web site: http://www.naspweb.org

NICHCY
P.O. Box 1492
Washington, DC 20013-1492
Voice/TTY: (800) 695-0285
Voice/TTY: (202) 884-8200
E-mail: nichcy@aed.org
Web site: http://www.nichcy.org

Harry L. Davis is a professional artist who lives in Wilmington, North Carolina. To balance his life as a busy artist, he is an active wheelchair athlete, a dedicated weight lifter, an avid fisherman, a student of the martial arts, and a teacher of African American history at his church. Davis became interested in painting after an accidental shooting while he was in the 82nd Airborne Division. The incident left him using a wheelchair. He developed his painting skills through a trial-and-error process, first beginning with landscapes and eventually honing his expressive talents by painting people of the American South and of rural Africa. Immensely popular, Davis's work is part of many important public and private collections, including those of Nell Carter, Bill Cosby, Home Savings and Loan of Washington, DC, the University of North Carolina at Wilmington, and Denzel Washington. The piece shown here, *Blue Queen,* is representative of Davis's remarkable use of color and attention to detail.

Harry Davis, *Blue Queen.* Reprinted by permission of the artist and by Davis Studio, Wilmington, NC.

C H A P T E R **3**

Bilingual Education Experience Gone Right

Omar Chavez is a 17-year-old college student who recently completed high school. A very intelligent and talented young man, he began school in the United States with no command of the English language. His dream today is to study astrophysics.

School is a little more challenging in Mexico. They teach you harder stuff at a younger age. It was easy up to the eighth grade. During high school I learned new stuff. The teachers are more strict in Mexico. One teacher takes the second grade class all the way to sixth grade. It's just one teacher.

To this day I don't know why they put me into the sixth grade. It might be because of the language. I was in the seventh grade in Mexico, but when I came to the United States they put me in sixth grade. I think it was because of the language. I was a year or two younger than the rest of the students. We came here on vacation and all of a sudden I found myself in school. I didn't bring my transcript.

I've been successful mostly because of my parents' support and understanding and teachers' support and encouragement. When I was 3, my mom taught me to read and write before I went to school. From the beginning they treated me as if I was really smart. Not like, "You're a kid and you don't need to know this or that!" At first my mom taught me the alphabet. She taught me how to write it despite the fact my mother didn't have the opportunity to complete middle school. That was

Multicultural and Bilingual Special Education

the first thing I learned. I skipped through first and second grade. I only went to kindergarten for a month. Actually, I didn't mind. It was fun. When I got to second grade, it was fun learning new things. The students were already learning mathematics. I was almost 6. A lot of parents don't take the time; I'm glad mine did. My parents were very involved in my education. They always kept an eye on me and how I was doing. They kept close to me even when I came to school here in Albuquerque. Up to high school in the tenth grade they told me, "This is your responsibility now. If you fail, it is going to be your fault. We can't keep an eye on you every single day."

My teachers tried not to treat me differently because I didn't speak English. They tried to encourage me to learn it. They saw that I was getting the stuff okay, but still they tried to encourage me to learn more in spite of my language problem at the time. They realized that I was understanding the stuff pretty well. They didn't do anything to give me more work.

When I first came to the United States, the teacher introduced me to another student. He was the first person I met, and he helped me a lot. The teacher knew he spoke Spanish and English. We were friends throughout middle school and part of high school. One day he dropped out of school. He had to uh, I don't know. Some economical problems or something. I lost track of him.

Since the beginning, when I went from the sixth grade to the eighth grade, I took ESL. I had the same teacher for my ESL classes. This teacher was very supportive of the students in the class. When she taught, she was very calm, and very, very patient with her students. There were a couple of Vietnamese students. I got to meet a lot of interesting people from diverse cultures in the high school. Especially in my communications class. There were some students from Vietnam, China, and India. The teacher was very patient with the students who couldn't understand the lessons well. Sometimes we had tutors going in and working with one special group, like the Vietnamese people or the Hispanics. It was pretty fun.

Up to the eighth grade I had all my classes bilingual. In middle school they have lots of tutors and student teachers. They helped us a lot. Almost 80 percent of the teachers weren't bilingual, so they offered us a bilingual class which used the tutors. The teachers who didn't speak Spanish gave a format to the tutor which described what we were going to do and what we were going to talk about. But that was in the eighth grade and I was speaking and understanding English a little better then. I didn't need it too much. By the time I was in high school I didn't have bilingual classes anymore.

In high school, none of my teachers knew I was in ESL. I was in regular English throughout ninth grade and tenth grade, and my tenth grade teacher recommended me for enriched English. So I took enriched English in my junior year, and during my junior year my teacher recommended me for honors English. My junior and senior year I took honors English. They asked, "Do you want to do this," and I said, "I'll give it a try." Honors English was a real challenge for me. I did learn, but it was really a challenge.

1. Does Omar fit your stereotype of students who begin school without knowing how to speak English?

2. What challenges do you think you would face if you had to move to a foreign country and begin school without speaking the host language?

3. What do you think contributed to Omar's successes in school?

Advance Organizers

CONNECTIONS MAKING

Use the learning strategy—Advance Organizers—to help focus your study of this chapter's content, and reinforce your learning by reviewing answers to the focus and challenge questions at the end of the chapter.

Overview

Only about 3% of Americans can consider themselves true natives; the rest of us are immigrants or the descendants of immigrants. The diversity of America's schools is changing more rapidly than ever before. Schoolchildren today come from hundreds of different cultures and speak almost as many languages. These children are at great risk for being overidentified as having disabilities and underidentified as being gifted. Culturally and linguistically diverse students with exceptionalities require special education programs that accommodate both their diversity and their disabilities.

Focus Questions

Self-Test Questions

- What is meant by multicultural special education, and who is served by these programs?
- What is meant by bilingual special education, and who is served by these programs?
- Why are educators so concerned about culturally and linguistically diverse children?
- In what ways can biases occur in the identification and assessment process?
- How can school personnel integrate children's home cultures and languages into the educational environment and curriculum?

Challenge Question

- Why is there such a national debate about the issue of the overrepresentation of culturally and linguistically diverse students in disability categories and their underrepresentation in gifted education?

As it has since its founding, the face of the United States continues to change. As this new century has begun, predictions about the nation's increasing diversity have proven true. The **demographics** of the nation and its schools have changed. America's schoolchildren are diverse in so many different ways. Their racial and ethnic diversity is a fact. The languages and cultures they bring with them to school represent cultures from all over the world, not just from several continents. And *all schools* and teachers face the challenges of creating appropriate educational opportunities where instruction is effective for *all students* who now comprise the school population. Their heterogeneity is marked along multiple dimensions: language, values,

demographics. The racial and ethnic composition of a country or regional area.

See the Prevalence
section found later in
this chapter.

culture, and abilities. It is a fact that the United States is a multicultural country. In and of itself, this is neither bad nor good. It is what we do about and with our diversity, how we treat each other, how we understand each other's similarities and differences, and how we learn from one another that require value judgments.

As you read this chapter, reflect about how mainstream culture treats people who come from diverse groups. Remind yourself about how they are thought of as "different," and the impact that conceptualization has on children from diverse language and cultural backgrounds. Artilles (1998) believes that being seen as different puts people on distinct trajectories before they have an opportunity to display their own strengths, weaknesses, and characters. His point is well worth consideration. Educators must embrace the belief that schools are better places for all children and their parents if educators both understand and capitalize on their students' diversity of race, ethnicity, culture, language, socioeconomic class, religion, regional differences, and gender. By using this diversity to our advantage, the educational environment can be richer, and all children can flourish.

Opportunities for the New Millennium

Throughout the twentieth century, Americans held differing views about themselves, their nation, and people from different countries. Most definitely, the ways in which they welcomed others to their new homeland changed across time. At one point, Americans prided themselves in being seen as part of a cultural "melting pot," where everyone was included into a new American culture. At other times, cultural pluralism was valued as a way for people to retain their traditions and cultures but still feel part of America. And at other times, groups of Americans were segregated and denied opportunities. Attitudes by the larger society affect the educational system. As the nation wrestles with increasing diversity of language and cultures, so will the schools. Undoubtedly, those children who do not fit easily in the general education system are likely to interface with special education.

See the Problems of
Special Education
section in Chapter 1.

Legacies from the Twentieth Century Accusations that special education contributed to racist practices of the last century remain as the new millennium begins. Charges abound that special education placement legitimizes segregation and results in poor outcomes. However, American society and the schools during the twentieth century did not do well with poor children. The associations among poverty, access to health care, having a disability, participation in special education, dropping out of school, and renewing a cycle of poverty became clear. Regardless of race or ethnicity, poor children did not fare well. And culturally and linguistically diverse children remain at the greatest risk not only for being poor, but also for being disproportionately represented in special education programs and underrepresented in gifted education.

Thinking About Dilemmas to Solve As you read this chapter, consider children who are not native English language speakers or who are not from the dominant culture in American society. Think about how:

- We can create opportunities for children from cultural and linguistically diverse backgrounds to have equal chances to succeed
- They and their families can become better connected and involved with schools

- General education can become more responsive to diverse learners
- Issues relating to disproportionate representation in special education can be resolved
- Views about participation in special education can be changed so it is thought to be valuable

MULTICULTURAL AND BILINGUAL SPECIAL EDUCATION DEFINED

For more information about the relationships among disabilities and poverty, see
- Causes and Prevention in this chapter
- Information about access to health care in Chapter 6 (Prevention section)

Culturally and linguistically diverse students are at greater risk for being identified as having a disability, particularly because of factors associated with poverty (e.g., access to health care). Those who do have disabilities deserve and require a very special education. Multicultural and bilingual special education is a combination of the fields of multicultural education, bilingual education, and special education. Table 3.1 on page 82 was designed to help you understand each of these three educational systems. As you study this table and read this chapter, think about how teachers might, using these approaches, stress the acquisition of academic and social skills in culturally and linguistically diverse children with disabilities.

TYPES OF CULTURALLY AND LINGUISTICALLY DIVERSE STUDENTS

Sometimes it is helpful to understand how the federal government classifies its citizenry and how people describe themselves. In national census reports and other official documents, citizens are divided into five general ethnic groups: Native American, Asian/Pacific Islander, White (non-Hispanic), Hispanic, and Black (African American).* The diversity within each of these groups is enormous along a multitude of dimensions: language, home country, years and generations in the United States, ethnicity, and social and economic status (SES).

More about LEP students is found in this chapter in the section called Exceptional Culturally and Linguistically Diverse Children.

In addition to classifying students by ethnic groups, educators often base their research and clinical findings on two dimensions of diversity: linguistic and cultural. Remember, these issues are not mutually exclusive. Many students who do not come from the dominant U.S. culture (Western European) also are not native English speakers. Some families have retained their cultural heritage even though they have been in this country for several generations, and many have not. Clearly, it is important not to make any assumptions.

Linguistically Diverse Students. One of the fastest growing segments of the U.S. student population is **limited English proficient (LEP)**, sometimes called **English Language Learners (ELL)**. These students' native languages are not English. In classrooms where English is the language of instruction, their reading, writing, speaking,

limited English proficient (LEP) or English Language Learners (ELL). Limited ability to read, write, or speak English.

*The terms used in this text reflect national preferences. For example, Hispanic is used rather than the term Latino, which has a more regional popularity. African American and Black are used interchangeably. Native American is used when all native populations are discussed, and American Indian is used when referring to tribal groups who reside in the lower 48 states.

Table 3.1 Multicultural Education, Bilingual Education, and Bilingual Special Education Definitions

Concepts	Definitions	Sources
Multicultural education	The educational strategy which supports and extends the concepts of students' cultural backgrounds. Concepts of culture, differences, equality, and democracy are used to develop effective classroom instruction and school environments.	Gollnick & Chinn (1998)
Bilingual education	The purpose of this educational methodology is to develop greater competence in English, more proficiency in the dominant language, and increased educational opportunity. While affirming the importance of English, bilingual education uses and develops the child's native language for primary instruction until sufficient command of English is attained.	U.S. Office of Education, Office of Bilingual Education (1980)
Bilingual special education	Bilingual special education begins with an individually designed educational program that uses the home language and home culture, along with English, as the foundations for and the means of delivering special instruction that emphasizes the academic and social needs of the child.	Baca and Cervantes (1998)

and understanding skills usually hinder their ability to learn successfully. Their exact number is unknown, but some estimates are available (Baca, 1998). It is thought that 20% come from homes where a language other than English is spoken, and over 10% of the overall student population in the nation are ELL students. Nationally, the vast majority (some 80%) of these students are Spanish-speaking, but great variance exists by locale, and changes in regional demographics are occurring rapidly. For example, estimates indicate that Asian Americans constitute over 10% of the California school population and are one-fourth of the LEP population in that state (Cheng, 1995).

The challenges these students present school district personnel are great. Some of these students come to school speaking no English. Many others are able to communicate in English but are not proficient enough to profit from academic instruction without supports. And being able to determine when they have truly mastered the language can be difficult. The challenges these students present are compounded by the number of languages they speak. In many school districts, including New York City, Chicago, Los Angeles, and Fairfax County, Virginia, children speak over 100 languages. Not enough teachers who speak these children's native

All children's language skills develop when they are engaged, excited, and work together on activities that support academic instruction.

See Over- and Under-
representation in the
Prevalence section of
this chapter.

NEW DIRECTIONS
FOR THE
MILLENNIUM

Legacy: Diverse students
often do not feel in-
cluded or accepted in
classroom settings.

Opportunities:

• Know and respect the
cultural styles of each
student

• Enrich instruction
with multicultural
examples

languages are available. Many of these children do not have a teacher who can speak their language and have to rely on a parent, community member, or paraprofessional for language support.

As you will learn in this chapter, many of these students are at great risk of being incorrectly identified as having a disability. Their language differences do impair their educational opportunities and can mask their potential. Clearly, they do need special programs. For those students without disabilities, however, the answer should not be special education.

Culturally Diverse Students. Only about 3% of us can claim native status (American Indians, Eskimos, Aleutian Islanders, and Hawaiians), and such diversity demands changes in the way teachers teach (Tiedt & Tiedt, 1999). As there are hundreds of languages spoken at schools across the nation, there must be thousands of different cultures represented by its schoolchildren. Being from a culture different from the dominant American culture does not directly cause disabilities or poor academic performance. However, culturally diverse students are more likely to live in poverty, a definite risk factor for having a disability. And culture does influence an individual's learning style and experiences, influences which must be reflected in the assessment process and in the delivery of instruction (Baca & Cervantes, 1998; Gollnick & Chinn, 1998).

Why is culture related to children and their schooling? The values, traditions, and beliefs that children bring to school provide the experiences on which new knowledge is learned and understood. Children from different backgrounds often approach learning in different ways, and if the instructional methods used at school conflict with their home culture, their educational performance can ultimately be affected. For example, some cultures value cooperation and do not value competitiveness. For children from these cultures, cooperative learning activities rather than competitive games might be better instructional strategies to implement. In some cultures it is considered a sign of disrespect for a child to gain eye contact with an adult, but unknowing teachers think students who avoid eye contact are untruthful or rebellious (Holman, 1997). This example of "culture clash" illustrates the importance of teachers understanding their own beliefs and culture, but also knowing those of their students.

Certainly, educators must be sensitive to children's cultural and learning styles when they select their instructional methods, but that is not enough. They must also respect these students and the cultures they come from (Ogbu, 1992). What teachers do and say sends important messages to children about their abilities and their worth. So, too, do the curriculum adopted and the instructional materials used. Children learn best when they can associate new concepts with those they have already learned and understand. Banks (1994) suggests that the curriculum should be modified to reflect "the experiences, cultures, and perspectives of a range of cultural and ethnic groups as well as both genders" (p. 11). The benefits of broadening the curriculum can be many. One benefit is that students' motivational levels are peaked when they learn information they can connect with. Another is that they learn about different approaches to solving problems and understand multiple perspectives about daily situations.

A Very Special Population: Native Americans. Of the almost 86,000 public schools in this country, 149 are recognized as tribal schools and another 1,260 schools have high enrollments (over 25%) of Native American students. However, the majority of the 445,425 American Indian/Alaska Native students attend public

Valuing every student's culture provides a wealth of rich experiences that can enhance instruction about traditional topics.

schools with a low native enrollment (Amos, 1997). Half of the Native American population is concentrated in five states (Alaska, Arizona, California, New Mexico, and Oklahoma). Native Americans represent over 5% of all schoolchildren in seven states: Alabama, Arizona, Montana, New Mexico, North Dakota, Oklahoma, and South Dakata (National Center for Education Statistics [NCES], 1997). This group represents hundreds of different tribes, but together they make up less than 1% of America's population. Navajo Nation claims the largest resident population, with 143,000 people living on the reservation. Native Americans speak as many as 187 languages, and many of these children, particularly those living in rural areas and on reservations, come to school without previous exposure to the English language (Krause, 1992). As a group, Native Americans face many serious challenges. They experience high rates of unemployment, low educational attainment, a 36% dropout rate (25% higher than the national average), and increased health problems (U.S. Department of Education, NCES, 1999). These children experience high rates of otitis media (which interrupts normal language development), fetal alcohol syndrome (the number one cause of mental retardation), and other health problems (Amos, 1997). They are the poorest group in the United States: 88% of students attending tribal schools and 61% of those attending schools with a high enrollment of American Indians receive free lunches (a signal for poverty status).

These students are more likely to attend isolated, rural schools that offer few resources. Unfortunately, many of their teachers do not speak these children's native languages or understand their cultures, which are often in conflict with their own. Conflict between teachers' and students' communication styles, cultural preferences, and values is a common experience for native children. "Caught between two cultures" is a phrase frequently used to describe the situation native students experience: The culture of school and the culture of home are at odds—the dilemma most diverse students confront. As an example, native children's communication at home tends to be symbolic and filled with nonverbal nuances. To these children, adults at school talk too much, are overly direct, and ask questions that are inappropriately personal. Also, values about what is important often differ between home and school. The result is disengagement and eventual dropout (Amos, 1997).

Many questions were raised in the twentieth century about these children and their education. Should individual tribes take over educational responsibilities for their children? Should the federal Bureau of Indian Affairs retain a role in the education of American Indian children? Should states insist that the curriculum offered on reservations match the curriculum taught in that state's local public schools?

MAKING CONNECTIONS

The Transition section in this chapter has more about dropout rates of poor and diverse students.

NEW DIRECTIONS
FOR THE
MILLENNIUM

Legacy: Many diverse students are incorrectly identified as having disabilities.

Opportunities:

- Find ways to increase the academic achievement levels of diverse students attending general education

- Develop flexible assessment procedures which reflect students' abilities to learn and perform in the general education curriculum

nondiscriminatory testing. Assessment that properly takes into account a child's cultural and linguistic diversity.
underrepresentation. The lack of presence of a group or groups of individuals in a special education category; smaller numbers than would be predicted by their proportion in the overall school population.
overrepresentation. Too many students from a cultural or ethnic group participating in a special education category, beyond the level one might expect from their proportion of the overall school population.

Clearly, how to better meet the needs of these children must receive policymakers' attention in this new century.

IDENTIFICATION

In recent years it has become commonly accepted that standardized tests used in schools frequently discriminate against culturally and linguistically diverse students. In the early 1970s it became apparent that standard methods of testing and evaluation were identifying too many of them as having disabilities and too few as being gifted. The question "Are intelligence (IQ) tests discriminating against culturally and linguistically diverse students?" was asked and re-asked over and over during the 1970s by educators, policymakers, court judges, and parents. Two California cases, *Larry P. v. Riles* and *Diana v. State Board of Education*, dramatically illustrated the problem. These cases brought national attention to the overrepresentation of African American children in classes for students with mental retardation, the misidentification of bilingual children as having disabilities, and the possibility of bias and discrimination in intelligence testing. These cases also made educators aware of diverse students' underrepresentation in gifted education (Ochoa et al., 1999).

How can discrimination in the assessment process occur? There are many reasons for bias, but some of the major ones are worthy of attention and thought. The content level of the test's items might give preference toward specific groups' experiences and interests. For example, asking a child who has never been fishing to explain how to bait a fishing line might negatively affect the impression others have of that child's expressive language and cognitive abilities. When minority groups are not represented in the standardization population, or when an individual untrained in multicultural and bilingual techniques conducts the evaluation, opportunities for unfair evaluations are created. To stress the importance of nonbiased evaluations, IDEA '97 requires that **nondiscriminatory testing** be established in each state. Take a look at the What IDEA '97 Says box on page 86 to see what the law and its regulations say about this important issue.

Courts have challenged schools' use of standardized tests of intelligence, saying that they place many students from various ethnic and racial groups at a disadvantage because many of the test items are unfair to students from different cultures. The use of such tests has contributed to some students being misidentified as having a disability; for others, test results present an incorrect and depressed picture of their abilities. Remember, the **underrepresentation** of these students in gifted education is just as unfortunate as their **overrepresentation** in disability categories. Despite all of the negative attention given to IQ and other standardized tests and despite decisions in the courts indicating that bias exists in these testing procedures, educators still rely on what appears to be the simplest and most clear-cut form of student evaluation: the standardized test. Unfortunately, these tests do not guarantee fair or accurate results. For example, some exceptionalities are especially difficult to diagnose when the child has difficulty with English. Another problem with standardized tests is that they take a very narrow view of intelligence, one that only reflects students' abilities to achieve academically. This restricted concept of ability is one reason why students from culturally and linguistically diverse groups continue to be unidentified, misidentified, and underrepresented in gifted education (Tomlinson et al., 1998).

One solution to the problem of both under- and overrepresentation in special education may be to broaden our concept about ability. Although thought of more

What IDEA '97 Says About

Nondiscriminatory Testing

Tests, assessment procedures, and evaluation materials used to determine students' eligibility for special education must

- not be discriminatory on a racial or cultural basis
- be administered in the child's native language (unless it is definitely not possible)
- measure whether a child has a disability and not that child's English proficiency
- include a variety of assessment tools
- be administered by trained and knowledgeable personnel

when considering gifted children, educators of diverse children have had a growing interest in Gardner's (1983) theory of **multiple intelligences.** To Gardner, intelligence centers on problem solving abilities. He identified seven different intelligences: linguistic, logical-mathematical, spatial, musical, bodily-kinesthetic, interpersonal, and intrapersonal. Maker and her colleagues (Maker et al., 1994) applied Gardner's theory to children from diverse backgrounds. They make the point that one's culture may influence how ability is expressed. They give the example that oral storytelling may be a common form of linguistic giftedness in one culture, where writing a novel may be another form in another culture. Maker and her colleagues developed a matrix of problem solving skills requiring a range of divergent and convergent thinking across Gardner's seven intelligences. They claim that students identified as gifted through this process, many of whom are not so recognized through traditional methods, do exceptionally well in special enrichment programs. In fact, culturally and linguistically diverse students identified in this way often make gains equal to or greater than those of students identified through the standard IQ testing process. Applying this innovative concept to all special education assessments also may well reduce the number of these students who are inappropriately identified for participation in disability categories.

What are some other ways that might solve this disproportionality problem? Innovative, performance based diagnostic procedures, such as authentic and portfolio assessments, have particular merit for students at risk for over- or underrepresentation in special education (Rueda & Garcia, 1997). Curriculum based measurement has also been suggested as a means of more fairly evaluating students' abilities because assessment is based on classroom performance (Reschly, 1997; Reschly et al., 1999). New, flexible identification systems need to be developed that change depending on the individual's situation, family, culture, and region. The referral process should change and include input from multiple sources such as parents, extended family members, church and community leaders, and service clubs (Rogers-Dulan, 1998; Patton, 1998; Patton & Baytops, 1995). It also needs to be sensitive to issues like how long the child and family have lived in the United States, their economic status, and the child's prior educational experience (Curraco, 1996). The argument for innovative and flexible identification procedures can be made for all children, but particularly for those who are culturally and linguistically diverse.

Experts agree: Even minor changes in current practice can make a difference (Amos, 1997; Ortiz, 1997; Yates & Ortiz, 1995). Local school districts and state education agencies could alter standard practices when assessing culturally and linguistically diverse students. The goal of these modifications is to reduce the number of these children incorrectly identified as having disabilities. Here are some of their recommendations:

The theory of multiple intelligences is discussed in the Defined section of Chapter 7.

Refer back to the Development of Informed and Effective Solutions section in Chapter 1 for an explanation of the concerns about placement.

**NEW DIRECTIONS
FOR THE
MILLENNIUM**

Legacy: High school
dropout rates of diverse
students, particularly
Hispanics, are
unacceptable.

Opportunities:
- Find ways to make
  education relevant,
  meaningful, and
  interesting
- Create ways that all
  teachers can anchor
  instruction with
  culturally relevant
  examples

multiple intelligences.
A multidimensional
approach to intelli-
gence, providing an
alternative view for the
concept of IQ, allow-
ing those exceptional
in any one of seven
areas to be identified
as gifted.

melting pot. The
concept of a homog-
enized United States
where cultural tradi-
tions and home lan-
guages are abandoned
for the new American
culture.

- Assess students in their dominant language.
- If interpreters are necessary, be sure they are proficient in the child's native language, understand the special education system and the assessment process, and know how to report student responses accurately.
- Evaluation should include a comparison of students' academic achievement and their language skills.
- Assessment should determine the level of students' competence in their own milieu, in their own cultures.
- Both informal and formal diagnostic procedures should be used, and results from both types of assessments should be compared.
- If tests' norms or the standardized testing procedures were altered, the results should be described but actual scores should not be reported.
- Multidisciplinary teams must include professionals with expertise about culturally and linguistically diverse students.
- Include parents and community members from the child's culture in the referral process.

SIGNIFICANCE

Unfortunately, many educators lack positive attitudes about students who do not come from the dominant culture or from middle-class backgrounds (Banks, 1994). When teachers believe students from a language-different background, students of color, and low-income students are unable to achieve at high levels of academic achievement, their expectations for these students are lower (Baca & Cervantes, 1998; Gollnick & Chinn, 1998). Without high expectations for students, many teachers tend to slow the pace of instruction, select instructional materials that are not challenging, and teach "down" to their students. The result of such negative attitudes and low expectations often is low achievement. Students tend to internalize negative expectations and perceptions. Internalizing negative attitudes can lead to reduced motivation to learn difficult skills and concepts. This situation may also be the explanation for high dropout rates these students experience (Winzer & Mazurek, 1998). Leaving school before completion has serious long-term effects, including an inability to break the poverty cycle. Educators must create positive learning climates in which children are stimulated to do their best, supported to take risks, and encouraged to have fun learning.

HISTORY OF THE FIELD

Education in the United States has been faced with issues of bilingualism and multiculturalism throughout its history. In the late nineteenth and early twentieth centuries, total exclusion (or separate language schools) began to give way to a new era of "Americanization." Antiforeign feelings and sentiments were on the rise. The guiding principle during the new period was the **melting pot** model, in which individuals were expected to assimilate and abandon their home languages and cultures as soon as possible for a new, homogenized American experience. But the melting pot model appears to have failed. Instead of creating a harmonious new culture, it led to racism, segregation, poverty, and aggression toward individuals in each new immigrant group. It also led to a loss of the richness that can result when a country welcomes many cultures and languages.

Cultural pluralism, a model that was reproposed in the 1960s, actually emerged in the early years of the twentieth century (between 1915 and 1925) as an alternative to the assimilation argument (Banks, 1994). Cultural pluralism does not require abandoning one's home culture, as did the melting pot model. Rather, it allows people to maintain their various ethnic languages, cultures, and institutions while encouraging their participation in society as a whole. Both early in the century and later, the belief was that diversity would enrich the nation and guide the development of policies for educational and social systems.

The concern about overrepresentation of culturally and linguistically diverse students in disability categories is not new. This issue was brought to national attention in several ways. First, in 1968, Lloyd Dunn published an article in which he estimated that about 60% to 80% of special education students, particularly those with mental retardation, were culturally and linguistically diverse. In 1970, the President's Committee on Mental Retardation (PCMR) published *The Six Hour Retarded Child,* which dramatically exposed the ways in which cultural differences were causing some children to be inappropriately labeled as having mental retardation. In California, also in 1970, the case of *Diana v. State Board of Education* began to bring issues about bias in the assessment process into focus. This case was a class action suit on behalf of Hispanic children placed in classrooms for students with mental retardation on the basis of IQ tests that were argued to be discriminatory. Additionally in California, the case of *Larry P. v. Riles* (1971) brought to the attention of the courts and schools the overrepresentation of African American children in classes for students with mental retardation and the possibility of discrimination in intelligence testing. In 1974, the U.S. Supreme Court ruled in a case brought in San Francisco on behalf of students with limited English proficiency (LEP) who were Chinese-speaking (*Lau v. Nichols,* 1974). Following the favorable decision in *Lau,* Congress enacted legislation that incorporated the Court's rationale:

> Public education is not a "right" granted to individuals by the Constitution. But neither is it merely some governmental "benefit" indistinguishable from other forms of social welfare legislation. Both the importance of education in maintaining our basic institutions, and the lasting impact of its deprivation on the life of the child, mark the distinction. The American people have always regarded education and the acquisition of knowledge as matters of supreme importance. We have recognized the public school as a most vital civic institution for the preservation of a democratic system of government, and as the primary vehicle for transmitting the values on which our society rests.... In sum, education has a fundamental role in maintaining the fabric of our society. We cannot ignore the significant social costs borne by our Nation when select groups are denied the means to absorb the values and skills upon which our social order rests. (Citations omitted; p. 2397)

cultural pluralism.
All cultural groups are valued components of the society, and the language and traditions of each group are maintained.

Nationally normed, standardized tests continue to be at the center of concern about accurate identification of diverse students. Jane Mercer (1973) viewed mental retardation from a sociological perspective (rather than a psychological construct). She extended her work from theory to practice with the development of a test aimed at reducing bias in the identification process. The test, *The System of Multicultural Pluralistic Assessment (SOMPA),* significantly decreased the number of African American and Hispanic children placed in special education classes (Gonzales, 1989).

Attention to the very special learning needs of this unique and heterogeneous group of learners was brought to the professional community in the professional literature. The journal of the Council for Exceptional Children, *Exceptional Children,* published a special issue on cultural diversity in 1974 (Bransford et al., 1974) that brought together many authors to discuss multicultural and bilingual special education issues. Several landmark books called professionals' attention to the unique learning needs of these students. For example, Donna Gollnick and Phil Chinn, in their 1983 landmark book *Multicultural Education in a Pluralistic Society*, helped educators better understand the influence of culture on children's educational performance. Leonard Baca and Hermes Cervantes's textbook *The Bilingual Special Education Interface*, first published in 1984, brought the question of language-different youngsters with disabilities to the attention of people in the fields of multicultural education, bilingual education, and special education.

Children's right to an education even gained the attention of the courts. Some states attempted to limit the right to education and to exclude culturally and linguistically diverse children who are not citizens (children who do not have immigration papers). In 1982, the Supreme Court decided a Texas case that questioned whether undocumented children of Mexican nationals residing in Texas without proper documentation had a right to free public school education (*Phyler v. Doe*, 1982). The Supreme Court ruled that children do have this right. Interestingly, history seems to be repeating itself. In 1994, California voters passed Proposition 187, prohibiting undocumented immigrants from receiving public benefits, including education. This component of Proposition 187 was put on the state ballot despite the *Phyler v. Doe* decision but was later ruled illegal by the federal government. And, in 1998, California voters passed a ban on bilingual education through Proposition 227, thereby implementing an almost "English only" policy for the state's schools, and to some degree limiting these students' access to a meaningful education.

The issue of "English Only" is debated in the Concepts and Controversy section of this chapter.

PREVALENCE

The number of children and youth from different ethnic groups served by special education should generally reflect the prevalence of those groups in the general population. So, are the nation's demographics changing? In 1997, the U.S. Population Reference Bureau estimated that 27% of America's population was comprised of three groups: Blacks, Hispanics, and Asians (Chinn, 1999). And that percentage is increasing because of immigration and birth rates. Whites are experiencing only 2% growth while Blacks are increasing by 14%, Hispanics by 36%, and Asians by 39%. Culturally and linguistically diverse students represent a large segment of the school population (NCES, 1997). Here are a few examples of states with large proportions of diverse students in their overall school populations:

- More than 60%—Hawaii and the District of Columbia
- More than 50%—Mississippi, New Mexico, New York, and Texas
- Almost 40% or more—Arizona, California, Georgia, Louisiana, Maryland, and South Carolina

How do these national data play out in general education classes? In that regard, Baca (1998) helps us visualize what a typical American classroom might look like (see Figure 3.1 on page 91). You might be surprised to learn that 30% of the students are culturally or linguistically diverse, 20% are from homes where languages other than English are spoken, and about half of them are themselves LEP. Of course, it is important to remember that these are national statistics, in some schools almost all of the students are from diverse backgrounds, and in other schools relatively few.

The fact that these children are from diverse backgrounds should not be disturbing. What should be disconcerting is the fact that youngsters from underrepresented groups have a much higher probability of having been born of mothers who did not receive early prenatal care, and of living in poverty, having limited access to health care, and being raised in a single-parent household (Children's Defense Fund [CDF], 1999). All of these factors put children at great risk of having a disability. In addition, for many, their cultural and language differences increase their chances for failure in the educational system and the likelihood of being referred to special education. The sad fact is that so many of these youngsters are misidentified.

OVERREPRESENTATION

Review again the IDEA '97 box about nondiscriminatory testing found in the Identification section of this chapter.

From the early days of special education, professionals called the nation's attention to the disproportionate participation of various racial and ethnic groups in special education programs (Deno, 1970; Dunn, 1968). Over thirty years ago, higher percentages of African American students than should be expected were identified as having mental retardation. Despite the attention that overrepresentation of some of these groups of students in some disability categories received in the press, in the courts (e.g., *Diana v. State Board of Education, Larry P. v. Riles, Lau v. Nichols*), in Congress (e.g., Individuals with Disabilities Act, 1997), and by the federal government (e.g., U.S. Department of Education, 1993, 1998), the situation persists. Although some of the national data should cause concern, the data from some locales are truly alarming.

First, consider the most current national data available. Take a look at Table 3.2 on page 92. You should see that 5.7% of all White students are identified as having learning disabilities, and that the same percentage holds for Black and Hispanic students. The table shows a higher percentage (7.3%) of American Indians served in this special education category, but that figure could be skewed upward because of the smaller number of children from this group overall (which can distort data when using percentages). Now let's compare students from different racial and ethnic groups who are identified as having mental retardation: 1.2% of the White student population, 2.6% of the Black student population, .09% of Hispanic students, and only .5% of Asian students. Although the overall percentages are not great, this is where the concern about overrepresentation of African American students in disability programs arises.

Nationally, Black students are two and a half times more likely to be identified as having mild mental retardation and about one and a half times more likely to have behavioral disorders or emotional disturbance when compared to their peers (Oswald et al.,

Sometimes, assessment and testing situations discriminate against culturally and linguistically diverse students. Every attempt must be made to help all children reach their potential.

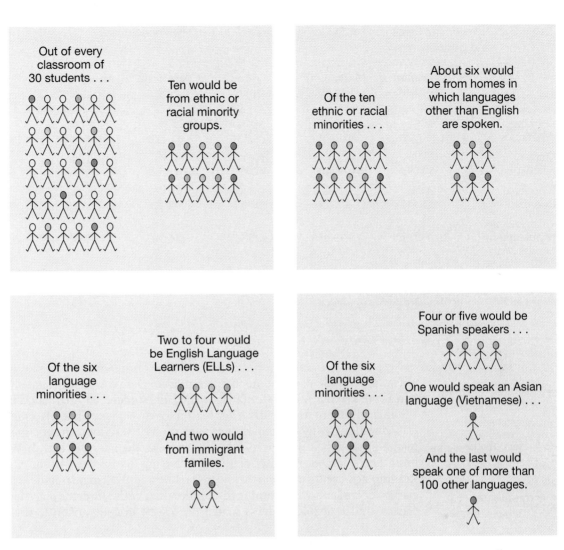

Figure 3.1 Diversity in America's Classrooms

Source: From the Diversity of America's Schoolchildren by L. M. Baca. In R. Thorp (1998) *Teaching Alive* CD ROM. Santa Cruz, CA: The Center for Research on Education, Diversity, and Excellence, University of California–Santa Cruz. Reprinted by permission.

1999). And a connection to poverty is clear: As degree of poverty increases, African American students are more likely to be identified as having mental retardation and less likely to be identified as having emotional disturbance.

At the local level, more disconcerting data are available about the overrepresentation of diverse students in special education programs. Data from Hawaii's Department of Education show why educators are concerned about diverse children's disproportional participation in special education. While Hawaiian and part-Hawaiian children represent about 25% of the overall student population, they represent about 34% of the special education student population. Compare this to their peers from Japanese backgrounds, who represent about 12% of students in the public education system, and only 9% of special education students. The situation

Table 3.2 Number and Percentage of Students in Special Education by Race/Ethnicity and Disability: 1994

	White, non-Hispanic	Black, non-Hispanic	Hispanic	American Indian	Asian/Pacific Islander	Total
Learning disabilities	5.7% 1,587,918	5.7% 407,848	5.7% 308,136	7.3% 32,413	2.0% 31,968	5.5% 2,368,283
Mental retardation	1.2% 350,699	2.6% 190,885	0.9% 50,091	1.6% 7,152	0.5% 8,197	1.4% 607,024
Emotional disturbance	0.8% 214,442	1.1% 80,253	0.5% 25,514	0.9% 4,227	0.2% 2,786	0.8% 327,222
Total students population by race/ethnicity	28,039,068	7,193,038	5,425,976	445,105	1,588,124	42,691,311

Source: U.S. Department of Education, Office for Civil Rights, 1994 Elementary and Secondary School Compliance Reports; as reported in *Twentieth Annual Report to Congress on the Implementation of the Individuals with Disabilities Education Act,* U.S. Department of Education, 1998.

NEW DIRECTIONS
FOR THE
MILLENNIUM

Legacy: Disproportionate representation is one reason some consider special education to be racist and discriminatory.

Opportunities:

- Ensure that all students have basic academic skills—reading and math—mastered
- Create systems that pay careful attention to the academic achievement levels of culturally and linguistically diverse students and are responsive when achievement is insufficient

of Hawaiian students is not much different from Native American students in North and South Dakota and in Montana, or Hispanic students in Arizona (Harry, 1994).

It is important to consider a key reason for diverse students' placements in special education: Many of them do not perform well at school. Despite the varied explanations for their poor academic achievement, the reality is that they are far behind their peers, even those identified as having disabilities (Artiles et al., 1998). Reading achievement is much lower for Black and Hispanic students placed in classes for students with learning disabilities than White students placed in the same classes. And Hispanic students scored the lowest in comparison to the other two groups.

Is overrepresentation in disability categories a problem? This is a complex question. Possibly, the simplest answer would be "no" if special education is truly and universally special. Unfortunately, in many cases it is not very special and does not lead to positive outcomes for children (Gottlieb et al., 1994). For many it leads to lower educational expectations and stigmatization. The problem is compounded because special education is plagued by an excessive number of untrained teachers (those teaching before they are licensed) and a high attrition rate (U.S. Department of Education, 1998). Some experts maintain that the number of diverse students identified for special education is expected and not significantly disproportional (Reschly, 1997; Reschly et al., 1999). Some other experts support this belief, saying that data from individual children indicate that school districts are very careful not to overidentify diverse students as having disabilities, and diverse students who are assigned to special education have extremely poor academic achievement as compared to White peers attending the same special education classes (Macmillian et al., 1998).

Other questions to ask are: How much overrepresentation of culturally and linguistically diverse students exists? And at what point should their participation in special education be considered disproportional? These questions spark heated debates (Daniels, 1998; Ford, 1998; Harry, 1994; Kauffman et al., 1998; Patton, 1998; Reschly et al., 1999). Here are some percentages for you to consider as you make up your own mind about these confusing statistics and issues:

- The overall special education identification rate for high incidence disabilities is 7.7% for African American students, 5.33% for Hispanic students, and 5.73% for White students.
- Three special education categories—LD, SED, and MR—serve 7.7% of all African American pupils in the United States.
- About 2.1% of all African American students in the United States are served in programs for students with mild mental retardation.
- Twenty-four percent of the mild mental retardation special education category is comprised of African American students.

Some experts, like Reschly and Macmillian and their colleagues, take the position that the overall identification of students with disabilities is small. And with the high correlation of poverty to disabilities and the high probability of members of minority groups being in the lower-income categories, the higher rate of special education identification for these groups of students should be expected. It also could be that poor children are less ready for school and that children who are not from the dominant culture and language system are more vulnerable to school failure. What do you think?

UNDERREPRESENTATION

The Concepts and Controversies section in Chapter 7 reinforces these concepts.

While African American, Hispanic, Hawaiian, and Native American students are overrepresented in many special education categories, they are underrepresented in gifted education (Ford, 1998). But, as you have learned, not all diverse students are included in special education at a rate greater than their proportion in the overall school population. For example, students from an Asian background are less than half as likely to be identified as having a disability (U.S. Department of Education, 1998). Remember the statistics about Native American students in Alaska, Montana, South Dakota, and Arizona; these students are overwhelmingly identified as having disabilities. In Alaska, for example, where Native Americans comprise 25% of the population, only 15% of them are receiving educational services in gifted programs (Harry, 1994).

CAUSES AND PREVENTION OF DISABILITIES IN DIVERSE STUDENTS

Diversity does not cause disabilities, of course, although poverty and related life circumstances can result in a variety of disabilities. This is important, but the impact of multiculturalism must be separated from the effects of poverty. Terrible mistakes are made when people assume that all diverse students are poor or all poor students have disabilities. Unfortunately, the economic conditions for many families from historically underrepresented groups did not improve greatly during the last decades of the twentieth century, but many culturally and linguistically diverse students do not live in poverty. In fact, three out of five children of poverty are White (CDF, 1998). The issues of multiculturalism, bilingualism, cultural and linguistic

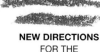
Legacy: Poverty contributes to children's rates of disabilities and low academic achievement.

Opportunities:

- Guarantee all expectant mothers' and young children's access to health care
- Ensure access to high-quality early intervention programs to all culturally and linguistically diverse students and their families

diversity, and poverty are complex and intertwined. It is important not to oversimplify the causes of disabilities in students from diverse backgrounds or how they can be prevented.

CAUSES

Social and economic inequities have a significant impact on our nation's children (CDF, 1998; Kozol, 1991, 1995; Reed & Sautter, 1990). The rate of childhood poverty is a major problem in the United States. The Children's Defense Fund (CDF, 1998, p. xv) gives us some alarming facts to consider when we think about the relationship between the conditions of children and the prevalence of children receiving special education:

- 1 in 2 preschoolers has a mother in the workforce
- 1 in 3 will be poor sometime during childhood
- 1 in 4 is born poor
- 1 in 4 is born to a mother who did not finish high school
- 1 in 5 is poor now
- 1 in 5 is born to a mother who did not receive prenatal care during the first three months of pregnancy
- 1 in 7 has no health insurance
- 1 in 8 is born to a teenage mother
- 1 in 13 is a low birth weight baby
- 1 in 680 is killed by gunfire before the age of 20

These risk factors are important to consider, but other evidence supports the notion that disabilities, poverty, and diversity are related. For example, research findings show that diverse students from low income families are more likely to be identified as having learning disabilities than diverse students from families with higher income levels (Artiles et al., 1998). Also, statewide data are available to illustrate this point. These data come from one state, but remember that such comparisons repeat themselves all across the nation. So, let's look at the case of students living in Hawaii. Study Table 3.3. Notice that in 1997 the proportion of Asian students from three particular groups (Chinese, Japanese, and Korean) who received special education was far less than their proportion in the overall student population. These students also participate less in free lunch programs, a signal for poverty. Now look at the column for Hawaiian students, and you'll find the opposite relationship: a higher proportion of them participate in both free lunch programs and in special education compared to the general school population.

The federal government also concludes that one reason for the increased proportion of diverse students who are identified as having disabilities is poverty (U.S. Department of Education, 1998). Here is the logic it uses to make this conclusion:

- Poor children are more likely than wealthy children to be identified as having disabilities.
- African American children are more likely to be identified for some special education categories (mental retardation and emotional disturbance) than White or Asian children.
- Poverty is the primary contributor to the disproportionality of African American students in special education.
- Addressing the assessment process alone will not eliminate overrepresentation.

MAKING CONNECTIONS

The Defined section in Chapter 4 includes information about the identification of students with learning disabilities.

Table 3.3
The Link Between Poverty and Disabilities

	Chinese, Korean, & Japanese Students	Hawaiian & Part Hawaiian Students
School population	17%	25%
Percentage of those receiving free lunches	6%	37%
Proportion of special education	12%	34%

Source: Hawaii Department of Education. (1999). *Hawaii's state demographics—1997*. Honolulu, HI: Author.

The federal perspective about the relationship between poverty and disabilities has been supported through research (Artiles et al., 1998; Fujiura & Yamaki, 1997; Oswald et al., 1999). Advocacy groups like the Children's Defense Fund are also convinced that poverty and the factors associated with it place diverse students at incredible risk for special education needs (CDF, 1997, 1998). The lifelong impact of poor nutrition, anemia (which stops blood cells from carrying oxygen to the brain), lead poisoning, and low birth weight during childhood is undeniable. During the school years, the effects can be seen in learning and behavior problems. Across a life span, the effects can be seen in employment and life satisfaction outcomes.

Causation of disabilities must also be viewed within a cultural context. Different cultures sometimes think about the causes of disabilities in children differently. Because of various conceptions and definitions of what disability is, cultures do not always agree about the presence of a disability (Holman, 1997). In general, people from the dominant American culture believe in a direct scientific cause-and-effect relationship between a biological problem and the developing baby. Those from other cultures may, in contrast, consider fate, bad luck, sins of a parent, food the mother ate, or evil spirits potential causes of disabilities (Cheng, 1995; Lynch, & Hanson, 1998). These alternative views affect the way a child with a disability is considered within the culture and the types of intervention services a family might be willing to pursue to address the child's disabilities and needs.

PREVENTION

For more information about the importance of access to health care, see the Causes and Prevention section in Chapter 6.

What interventions can make a difference and reduce the number of diverse students with disabilities? Of course, prenatal care, removing the risk variables of poverty, improving health care access, vaccination against disease, and safe living environments can make a real difference (CDF, 1998). Home environments rich with books and family members who provide stimulating experiences for their children, whether they are economically advantaged or not, also make real differences in the lives of children.

Remember, in the twentieth century poverty was a major factor in the high referral rates and eventual placements of diverse students in special education, but it does not explain all of the reasons for overrepresentation. Many experts are working on finding solutions. They are focusing on other variables that could reduce the referral rates of diverse children for special education. Children from diverse backgrounds, across their school careers, are not taught by many teachers who reflect their diversity. For example, only .04% of today's special education elementary teachers and 2.2% of secondary special education teachers are African American males (Voltz, 1998). So, all teachers must be better prepared to work with children from many different backgounds (Obiakor & Utley, 1997; Voltz, 1998; Sileo & Prater, 1998). The thought is that if teachers were prepared to work with diverse

The importance of reading becomes real when parents and children have fun reading together.

MAKING
CONNECTIONS

The evaluation (assessment) sections in Chapter 2 give more detail about alternative assessments, including portfolios.

MAKING
CONNECTIONS

For more information about discipline, see:
- Implementation of the IEP section in Chapter 1
- The Achieving Discipline boxes in Chapters 3 through 12

populations of learners, educational needs would be better met. The results would be less bias, higher expectations for all children, adjusting instruction to meet different learning styles of students from different cultures (more active learning, less competition, more group work), and greater parent involvement.

Another solution may lie in changing the referral and assessment process. Possibly alternative assessments, like portfolios, would give teachers and diagnosticians better indicators of children's potential (Rueda & Garcia, 1997). Or including more individuals from the student's home culture in the referral process would give a better understanding about how well the child can perform outside of the school setting (Amos, 1997).

It is clear, and noted by both educators and researchers for many years, that a student's inappropriate behavior can trigger the special education referral process (Rivera & Smith, 1997). Boys who "act out" and do not comply with expectations at school are more likely to be referred for special education services. Many of these children do not understand that one behavior is acceptable in one setting but not another. For example, having fun with a group of friends, making spontaneous and clever jokes, and kidding around by physically touching a peer might bring positive attention and make the child popular after school. However, during class time or during period changes, such behaviors are troubling to teachers and school administrators. Most children learn to sort out the different behavioral expectations across a variety of settings and situations, but many do not. The Achieving Discipline box provides an illustration of how educators can help students learn these important skills, and another outcome can be a reduction in the special education referral and placement rates.

EXCEPTIONAL CULTURALLY AND LINGUISTICALLY DIVERSE CHILDREN

Culturally and linguistically diverse children with special education needs often have problems in several unique areas. First, language and communication differences can cause challenges for these children and for special education personnel. Second, cultural differences may raise questions about the behavior of these children and their families and about the appropriateness of interventions. In addition, mobility (homelessness, migrant worker transience, or refugee circumstances) can add stress and logistical difficulties to educating some children.

Achieving Discipline

SCHOOLWIDE DISCIPLINARY ACTIONS: CONSISTENCY

Teachers and administrators at John Murray Elementary School, an inner-city school in a large urban area, were becoming very concerned about many aspects of their school. They felt that they were offering a curriculum which held high standards, and that they had high expectations for their pupils. They coordinated units and activities, so students across the grades received motivating instruction supported by excellent and engaging activities. They believed they were anchoring their instruction to experiences of their students, and were sensitive to the many different cultures and backgrounds of their students and families. However, each educator had individual concerns about the educational program they were collectively offering. Concerns stemmed from their own informal observations and from the overall evaluation data about John Murray students' outcomes. John Murray had one of the highest special education referral rates in the city, overall achievement levels were low, many students were being assigned to in-school suspension, and a high number of negative notes were being sent home.

Individually, teachers, support staff, paraprofessionals, and parents voiced their concerns with the school's principal, Ms. Mims. She decided to call for a meeting of the school's community, including elected student representatives, to discuss the problems and see if they could arrive at some solutions. At the first meeting, people discussed both the strengths and weaknesses of the school's programs, and they listed their concerns. At the end of the first meeting, everyone agreed that an outside professional was needed to work with the community and create a professional development plan. Using the resources and expertise available in the district, several problem solving meetings were held where it became clear to everyone that each teacher had a set of rules and expectations, but they differed across teachers and settings. They also came to realize that the consequences for inappropriate behavior were not consistently applied. One teacher would ignore a fight in the hall, while another would assign in-school suspension for such violations. No one wanted a structure that would restrict students' freedom to discover, think creatively, acquire basic knowledge, or develop personally. But they also wanted to create a positive climate where students were free to learn and disruption was held to a minimum. To achieve their goals, they developed a schoolwide code of conduct, where standards for acceptable behavior in all settings were clear and where consequences for levels of infractions were consistently applied.

Steps used to create schoolwide discipline

- All stakeholders contribute to a process in which problems are identified and understood.
- All stakeholders participate in developing solutions.
- A plan is developed that includes clear examples of acceptable and unacceptable behaviors in all different settings and situations.
- Levels of consequences for violations of the code of conduct are clearly listed.
- The community—everyone, including students—comes to understand the code and the consequences for infractions.
- The plan is implemented schoolwide.

LANGUAGE AND COMMUNICATION DIFFERENCES

Linguistically diverse children exhibit language differences—and many culturally diverse children present communication differences—that often raise educational issues which should not always result in special education (Cheng, 1999). Some children may speak forms of a language that vary from its literate or standard form. For

See Chapter 5:
- Language Impairments section (Causes) for more about language differences
- Speech Impairments sections (Defined, Causes, Children with Speech or Language Impairments) for more about articulation.

NEW DIRECTIONS
FOR THE
MILLENNIUM

Legacy: The overidentification of language-different children as children with disabilities contributes to the overrepresentation of culturally and linguistically diverse students in special education.

Opportunities:
- Improve the preparation of teachers
- Develop more effective ways to sort students with language differences from those with language impairments and learning disabilities

example, the spoken Spanish used in South Texas usually varies from the spoken Spanish used in New Mexico, both of which may vary from the standard form of Spanish. These variations are dialects and should not automatically be considered language deficiencies. Some languages do not have certain sounds or grammatical structures found in English. For example, the *f, r, th, v,* and *z* sounds do not exist in Korean. Many English consonant sounds do not exist in Chinese, so a Chinese-speaking child's difficulty with some English sounds may be a result of the child's inexperience with the sounds rather than a speech or language impairment. Although many of these children are referred for speech therapy for an articulation problem, their distinctive speech is simply an accent and therapy is unnecessary.

Detecting the difference between a language impairment or a learning disability and a language difference can be difficult, even for well-trained professionals. Sometimes children are identified who do not have a language impairment or learning disability, only a language difference. Other times, children's disabilities are masked by the language difference and they wait years for special services. Why might this be so? First, the diagnosis of a learning disability is supposed to depend on a significant discrepancy between the IQ and academic achievement scores. Diverse children with genuine learning disabilities may not score well on a standardized test of intelligence, so they do not show the necessary discrepancy between potential and achievement to qualify for services. On the other hand, some children may be wrongly identified as having a learning disability when in fact it is their difficulty with English—their underachievement in a second language—that causes their poor academic achievement (McLean, 1999; Ruiz, 1995). Second, to find a speech or language impairment in a bilingual child, the impairment must occur in both English and the child's dominant language. For example, a Spanish-speaking child who converses perfectly in Spanish with his brothers on the playground but who has limited ability to discuss academic subjects in English in the classroom certainly has a problem; however, it is due to a communication difference, not a language impairment. McLean (1999) helps us visualize these differences (see Figure 3.2).

Language is a major issue for many students, even those who speak English at home. Many African American children, for example, come to school speaking a **dialect** of English. While many Hispanic children come to school speaking Spanish, some come to school speaking combinations of two languages (Sileo et al., 1996). Native Americans speak over 187 different languages (Krause, 1992), and people from Southeast Asia and the Pacific speak hundreds of different languages and dialects (Cheng & Chang, 1995). And remember that some 20% of the current school population does not speak English at home (Baca, 1998). When there is a critical mass of these youngsters (enough who speak the same language), many professionals recommend that a bilingual education approach be implemented (Cheng, 1995). Under this system, children are taught in both their primary language and in English until such time that their English proficiency is good enough to benefit from academic instruction in this language.

Another group of learners and their language differences has come to the attention of educators, Congress, and the public. These children speak a variance of standard English often referred to as **Ebonics**. Interestingly, although this form of American English is often considered substandard, it is used to generate millions of dollars in advertisements, music, television, and film. What is the concern? Should Ebonics be banned from use at school? The language of the schools and the language of mainstream America does not accept this form of English, and many leaders in the Black community believe its use in inappropriate settings has a negative

Possesses accent and/or dialect which may impede communication intent.	Uses and interprets nonverbal cues such as facial expressions, gestures, physical proximity, posture to convey their communication.	Uses spoken language efficiently within own cultural group.	Has same cognitive ability to learn Standard American English (SAE) as other children.	Use of home language skills may oppose school language expectations.

LANGUAGE DIFFERENCE

LANGUAGE DISORDER

Exhibits deficits in receptive and/or expressive language.	Has limited ability to use and interpret nonverbal language.	Has difficulty using language within own cultural group.	Has difficulty understanding and formulating language structures and components.	Presents an inability to meet school language expectations.

Figure 3.2 Distinctions Between Language Differences and Language Disorders
Source: Courtesy of and thanks to Zina Yzquierdo McLean, Department of Special Education, Vanderbilt University, 1999. Reprinted by permission.

impact on those individuals who cannot "switch codes." They believe strongly that schools must "teach standard English to all of our nation's children yet celebrate their diversity and their ability to communicate effectively in a variety of settings" (Taylor, 1997, p. 3), and many professionals support this approach (Seymour et al., 1999). In his testimony to the U.S. Senate, Orlando Taylor made some important points for all educators to consider:

dialect. Words and pronunciation typical of a particular area and different from the forms of the language used by the normative group.
Ebonics. A learned and rule-governed social dialect of nonstandard English, spoken by many African American children.

1. Many African American children come to school using a rule-governed, non-standard language system that is deeply rooted in complex social, political, economic, social, and educational factors.
2. African American children are not the only group of learners coming to school using nonstandard English or social dialects, and attention needs to be paid to all groups of children who have language differences.
3. Slang and dialect are different: one reflects the use of rapidly changing vocabulary and phrases; the other is a rule-based language system.
4. By using and recognizing the language system that children know, educators can bridge instruction to teach a new language system while presenting academic instruction.
5. Being able to use more than one language effectively is a benefit to those proficient in two languages.

Possibly the most important point is implied in Dr. Taylor's remarks: Educators need to continually find effective ways to teach students who come to school without

Allowing children to play at school as they do after school can help them see connections between school and their communities. These experiences can be used to provide opportunities to understand the different language expectations at school and at home as well.

a basic mastery of English. If they do not succeed, the outcomes are serious. Language and communication differences influence students' oral language skills and their overall academic performance. Recognize that these differences also affect the acquisition of reading skills, imperative to academic success. The overall low achievement of diverse children is very troubling, for, at least in American society, academic achievement is a predictor of future success.

CULTURAL DIFFERENCES

Refer back to the Achieving Discipline box found in the Prevention section of this chapter.

Cultural conflicts may well contribute to some diverse children being identified as having disabilities (Cummins, 1984; Sileo et al., 1996). For some, behaviors perceived as problems in the school setting might be related to differences between the standards of behavior in the home and standards of behavior in school. Table 3.4 compares the Hawaiian and dominant White values and clearly illustrates how cultures can differ and how those differences can affect children's learning.

Other issues can arise when behavior appropriate in one environment, such as the home, is inappropriate in another environment, such as the school. A silent child might behave in a desirable way according to standards of his home culture, for example, but be characterized at school as "withdrawn" or "anxious." Look at Table 3.4 again. Contrast the White culture's focus on individual competitiveness and the standard of cooperation preferred in the Hawaiian culture. A similar case can be made for Native Americans and other diverse learners. For these children, intense competitiveness at home might be interpreted as a behavior disorder, and its absence at school could be interpreted as lack of motivation. When home and school cultures clash, children can become terribly confused and poorly educated (Obiakor, 1994). Keep in mind that another way to help children sort out the differences between behavioral expectations at school, at home, and in the community is for educators to help students learn and understand what is appropriate in school settings.

MOBILITY

Some culturally and linguistically diverse children experience great mobility in their lives. Homeless children and children of immigrants and migrant workers often experience disruption and dislocation, circumstances that can adversely affect their

Table 3.4 Hawaiian American Compared with White American Values

Hawaiian	White
Overall Values	
Affiliation/maintenance of interpersonal harmony	Personal achievement
Group goals	Individual goals
Affirmation of relationships as status	Accumulation of material capital as status
Deference to rank and authority	Personal autonomy
Interdependency	Independence
Care and affection	Development of competencies
Learning Styles	
Na'au (sharing of personal information, establishing lineage, relationships)	Separation of public and private life
Ho'olohe (listen)	Questions encouraged
'Ike pono (look)	Adult–child interchanges and feedback
Ho'opili (watch and mimic)	Originality encouraged
Peers as source of information	Adults as source of information
Risk minimization ("ain't no big thing")	Creativity and spontaneity rewarded
Educational Process	
Hawaii Education Process	*Special Education Process*
Group	Individual
Social-interpersonal skills	Individual achievement in math and reading
Ho'oponopono as conflict resolution	Due process
Verbal word important	Written paper trails
Deference to experts	Equal partnerships
Holistic view of child	Fragmented

Source: From Kishi, G., Hanohano, M. (1992, November), Pihana Nā Mamo: The Native Hawaiian Special Education Project. Presentation at Council for Exceptional Children Multicultural Conference, Minneapolis, MN. Reprinted by permission.

physical, mental, and academic abilities. Because many homeless, refugee, or migrant children have little formal experience with school, special education teachers may need to address years of missed educational opportunities in addition to language and cultural issues. Estimates about the number of children who are homeless vary widely because they "fall between the cracks" of different social service agencies, and because they are so mobile. What we do know is that there are many of them, they tend not to attend school, and many of them have disabilities (Walther-Thomas et al., 1996).

The impact of being homeless is great (Zima et al., 1998). In one study, researchers tested children who were living in an urban shelter, and here's what they found: 46% of all the children had a disability. The most common disability was behavioral disorders or emotional disturbance: 30% of the children identified as

Legacy: Migrant children, particularly those with disabilities, receive sporadic and incomplete educational services

Opportunities:

- Speed up the process of transferring school records from one district to another
- Initiate research agenda to develop "best practices" for the instruction of migrant students with disabilities

For proven instructional practices, see the Research to Practice boxes in this and the remaining chapters in the text.

having a disability. Diverse children were the most likely to find themselves in this situation: 44% of the children were Black and 35% Hispanic. Although the Education for Homeless Children's Act of 1994 guarantees children a right to an education and allows them to attend any school the parent requests, many of these youngsters experience a fractured education.

Comparable results would probably be found with children of migrant workers. Over 80% of migrant and seasonal farmworkers are U.S. citizens or legal immigrants (Henning-Stout, 1996). These workers earn less than $7,500 a year, clearly below the federal poverty level. Most migrant families live in Florida, Texas, or California between November and April and move to find agricultural work the rest of the year. Approximately one-half million migrant students live in the United States, and about 75% are Hispanic. These culturally and linguistically diverse children are very likely to be affected by disabilities because of the poverty and health problems that accompany migrant working. This group experiences high rates of tuberculosis, cervical cancer, and hypertension (Henning-Stout, 1996). Although 64% of these students are reported as having learning disabilities, they tend to be underidentified and underserved in special education. These children face other hardships. Their parents must make a difficult choice: keeping their families together but being highly mobile, or separating the family by leaving their children with relatives for a more stable school experience. Many middle and high school students also work long hours in the fields before and after school. Their high mobility only aggravates their educational problems.

Homeless and migrant children with special needs can experience exceptional hardships because they may have to move from a school where these needs were being met (or were in the process of being assessed) to a different school or maybe a series of schools, depending on the shelter(s) to which a homeless child is sent, or the new site(s) of the migrant parents' work. The stress, hunger, disease, and feelings of hopelessness that often accompany homelessness and mobility can create new special education needs in a child or exacerbate existing ones. The ability of the family to implement aspects of an IEP at home are impaired when the family is separated in large dormitories, for example, or when living conditions are so crowded or dangerous that physical survival requires all the family's energy (Kozol, 1988).

EDUCATIONAL INTERVENTIONS

Clearly, teachers are working in an age of challenge. The demands on them and their students, though great, can be met with innovative, individually sensitive, and culturally responsive approaches. As we begin this century, teachers across the nation are dealing with a variety of learning styles, values, customs, and behavioral patterns in the classroom. Predictions are that these challenges will only increase (Chinn, 1999). The hope is that teachers will meet them with an awareness of some important differences among students, and that teachers will celebrate the unique diversity every child brings to school.

The professional educator must assist culturally and linguistically diverse students in their mastery of English, address their academic needs, help them develop self-confidence, and heighten their awareness of and sensitivity to other linguistic and cultural backgrounds. Unfortunately, little actual research is available to guide teachers as they design appropriate instruction for culturally and linguistically diverse students with disabilities (Artiles et al., 1997). Most of the research findings that are available focus on the identification process, and not on solutions to instructional dilemmas these children often present to their teachers. In particular, a striking lack of attention has been paid to Asian or Native American students with disabilities.

EDUCATION AND THE PRESCHOOL CHILD

MAKING CONNECTIONS

More information about the concept of "at risk" is found in Education and the Preschool Child (Educational Interventions) in Chapter 5.

Young children benefit from early educational experiences in many ways. Headstart programs were initiated in 1964, as part of the federal initiative called the "War on Poverty," and are for children from low-income families. Many eligible children, 3- to 5-year-olds, attend Headstart programs, but most do not (Currie & Thomas, 1995). Many Headstart children could be considered **at risk** for being identified as having disabilities during their school careers, and participation in this program reduces these risk factors. Headstart services include a physical examination and full health assessments (immunization status, growth, vision, hearing, speech, anemia, sickle cell anemia, lead poisoning, tuberculosis, and infections). Access to health care is an important factor in preventing disabilities.

Children have an awareness of cultural differences very early. Some believe that by age 3, the first year children typically attend preschool, they already recognize physical differences between groups of people (King et al., 1994). It also appears that they are being taught to be more aware of their own cultural identities early in life. Preschool teachers often report their children introducing themselves on the first day of school: "My name is Diana, and I am a Chicana." "My name is Tega. I am beautiful, and I am Black." What should teachers do about this early cultural

The cultural reality of children's lives is an important component of their experiences. Creative teachers incorporate this reality into school learning experiences.

at risk. Children whose condition or situation makes it probable for them to develop disabilities.

awareness? King and her colleagues (King et al., 1994) believe that cultural knowledge and experiences should be infused into the curriculum. They argue that having a "unit" on each cultural group is insufficient. Rather, the history, customs, art, literature, music, and famous people from all cultures should be woven into every curriculum topic presented across the schoolyear (not just during a designated week). Despite the fact that they have received little or no preparation for multicultural teaching during college or while they are working, most early intervention specialists believe they are doing a good job of weaving culture into instruction (Sexton et al., 1997). Imagine how well they could increase their students' information and also reduce stereotypes and fear of people who may seem different or strange if they were trained in effective methods to accomplish these aims. (Some suggestions for culturally sensitive accommodations are found in the box nearby.)

EDUCATION AND THE SCHOOLCHILD

Indicators, such as the high dropout rates of diverse students, make it clear that America's schools are not meeting the needs of many of these children. As you read the rest of this section which includes information about cultural diversity, and language and instruction, be reminded of Artiles's sage advice: "Indeed, special educators must begin to hear the voices of the students we serve." (1998, p. 34)

Cultural Diversity. Siccone (1995) points out a very important fact, one that we all should think about: Only about 3% of Americans can truly claim to be native. The rest of us are immigrants or descendants of immigrants. Many of our families retained at least a part of their cultural heritage; some replaced the old with newer American traditions. The United States is ever evolving, with one guarantee: Its diversity is increasing. U.S. classrooms are, and will be, comprised of students from different ethnic groups and different cultures. Teachers must provide culturally responsive instruction by "anchoring" their teaching with examples from many American experiences (Kea & Utley, 1998). How can a teacher incorporate multicultural and bilingual aspects in a classroom? Instructional materials should reflect the cultural diversity of students (Artiles & Zamora-Duran, 1997). Some teachers have their students celebrate local holidays, and they incorporate culturally relevant examples in their instruction. Schools can also recognize and value different cultures by supporting their clubs and groups (e.g., ESL clubs, Movimiento Estudiantil Chicano de Aztlan [MEChA] clubs, chapters of African American sororities and fraternities, arts, music, dance, and crafts clubs).

We are cautioned, however, not to become "cultural tourists," celebrating holidays of countries or traditions of places these students have never visited (Thorp, 1997). Instead of decorating classrooms with posters from foreign countries students have never been to, pictures of events from the local community are more meaningful to students. Many teachers have found that using magazines for supplemental reading activities (like *Essence, Ebony, Canales, Latina, Pamir, Indian Country Today*) also retains students' interests and can provide them with excellent role models (Connie Chung, the journalist; Michael Chang, the tennis star; Zubin Mehta, the musician) to emulate (Jairrels et al., 1999; Sileo & Prater, 1998). In attempting to incorporate cultural diversity into the day-to-day activities of a school, teachers must be careful not to use stereotypical images of students' cultures, yet they should select content that reflects central aspects of a culture (Lynch & Hanson, 1998). For example, the assumption that a second-generation, American-born child

Accommodating for Inclusive Environments

HELPING EVERYONE BECOME CULTURALLY SENSITIVE

1. Reflect the various cultural groups at school by providing in the different languages of the community:

   - signs in public areas that welcome people
   - sections in the school newsletters and other official school communications

2. Provide opportunities for students from the same ethnic group to:

   - communicate with one another in their home language
   - work together in extracurricular activities
   - study elective subjects in their primary language
   - read literature written in their native language and work in small groups to discuss what they have read
   - share information about special holidays and events with their classmates

3. Recruit volunteers and/or parents who can:

   - tutor students in their primary language
   - serve as translators in meetings with non–English speaking parents
   - help in the classroom, library, playground, and in clubs
   - act as resources
   - present at awards ceremonies
   - be active partners in classroom instruction
   - connect the curriculum with the students' personal experiences

4. Decorate the school and classrooms with:

   - pictures and objects of the various cultures represented at the school
   - pictures of culturally diverse individuals in the professions and high-status occupations
   - calendars which show special holidays from different countries

of Japanese heritage maintains the same cultural belief system as a recent Japanese immigrant is just as erroneous as the assumption that a child of Cherokee heritage who lives in Denver is completely assimilated into the dominant U.S. culture. In other words, children must not be stereotyped, and neither should their education be stereotyped.

Teachers can help students become more sensitive to other cultures by helping them understand that there are many different ways to accomplish the same tasks and that not all cultures value the same experiences in the same ways. Students also need to understand that each of them enters the classroom with a set of values, beliefs, cognitive and behavioral styles, and verbal and nonverbal communication styles unique to their life situations (Sileo & Prater, 1998). These beliefs can be influenced not only by the cultural background of students, but also by such factors as the length of time their families have been in the United States; the geographic region of the country in which they live; the age, gender, and birthplace of each child; the language spoken at home; the religion practiced by the family; the proximity to other extended family members; and the socioeconomic level of the family (Gollnick & Chinn, 1998). Teachers must become aware of and respect the cultural differences among their students, and their students must gain such acceptance as well. Teachers must come to understand and appreciate different communication styles. For example, American Indian students often find the direct and personal nature of White teachers offensive and confusing (Amos, 1997).

CONNECTIONS

- The "English only" debate and the halting of bilingual education in California is presented in the Concepts and Controversy section of this chapter.
- Review the definition of bilingual education found in Table 3.1.

Language and Instruction. What language does the teacher use to teach culturally and linguistically diverse students? As you learned in the history section, this question was easily answered for most of our nation's history—English. Educators believed that bilingualism caused academic problems and that bilingual children would suffer unless they were transformed into monolingual children. Educators believed that children's learning problems would be aggravated if they were required to deal with two languages of instruction. In recent years, bilingual education has come under attack, and bilingual approaches are even being banned through the recent passage of state laws (California being the most publicized example). However, bilingual approaches can be very effective in teaching students their new language, English, and also their academic subjects (Lemberger, 1996; Lyons, 1998). Bilingual education practices vary greatly, and linguistically diverse students with disabilities can provide unique challenges to schools. Like their LEP peers, they often do not find the typical general education classroom supportive of their developing language skills. However, like their special education peers, LEP students with disabilities often do not find the bilingual education classroom individualized enough to support their academic needs (Fletcher et al., 1999). For example, bilingual education teachers tend to use whole group, undifferentiated instruction rather than an individualized approach. And they do not provide enough accommodations, for they typically only make adjustments to a child's seating arrangement, or adjust the amount of time allowed to complete assignments, or lower their expectations, or provide cooperative learning activities. Linguistically diverse students with disabilities need more assistance and special instruction than the bilingual teacher can offer.

Research indicates a few key elements included in effective bilingual and bilingual special education programs, and one of those important keys is sensitivity to the background of the individual child (Lemberger, 1996; Pyle, 1996). For example, immigrant children who have already received two to three years of schooling in their native language and come from homes in which their parents are highly educated seem to cope in immersion classes with some supports and achieve equally to their English-speaking peers in about five years (Collier, 1995). Other key elements include: expanding vocabularies in both the home language and in English, using both languages during instruction, learning to read in two languages, and supporting and respecting both languages the child is developing. Children who do not possess the prerequisites for academic learning are better served in programs that stress the development of language proficiency in both languages (Collier, 1995). Greater academic gains are achieved when they are instructed in their native language until English is completely mastered. In such bilingual programs, students out-achieve many other groups. They typically score at or above grade level in all subjects when tested in their first language and surpass their native English-speaking peers after four to seven years. Language acquisition and the development of enough proficiency to profit from academic instruction in English is a slow and complex process—and, as Gersten and his colleagues point out, is not an automatic or natural process for many children (Gersten et al., 1994). It often requires that teachers help students make explicit connections between what they read and write in one language and their activities in the other language. Teachers also need to understand that the mere ability to translate from one language to another is not sufficient (Cheng, 1996). Complete understanding also requires understanding of feelings, anecdotes, and culturally based nonverbal messages.

A number of different instructional approaches are used with bilingual children. Table 3.5 provides a summary of the most commonly adopted. Dual language

Table 3.5 Approaches Used with Bilingual Students

Approach	Explanation
English as a second language (ESL)	Children are taught English in their classrooms or in special classes until English proficiency is achieved. This method is used when teachers fluent in the child's native language are not available.
Bilingual transitional approach	Students are taught academic subjects in their native language and English is emphasized with the purpose of being able to participate in an English-only curriculum as soon as possible. Although three years of exposure to English is not always sufficient, that is usually how long students are taught in their native language.
Bilingual maintenance approach	Students are taught partly in English and partly in their home language so that they maintain proficiency in the home language but also gain proficiency in English. This method is not used very much today.
Total immersion*	Frequently used in Canada or with very young children; the student is taught entirely in English, and no English instruction or home language instruction is provided. Usually, the other students are also non–native English speakers, and the teacher speaks the students' home language.

*This approach should not be confused with *submersion*, placement in an all-English classroom with no assistance.

English as a second language (ESL). Instructing children in English in their classrooms or in special classes until English proficiency is achieved.
bilingual transitional approach. Teaching students primarily in English and partly in their home language until they learn enough English to learn academic subjects.
bilingual maintenance approach. Teaching students partly in English using ESL strategies and partly in their home language so that they maintain proficiency.
total immersion. The student is taught entirely in English; all the other students are also non–native English speakers, and the teacher can speak the students' home language.

instruction, bilingual education, is particularly effective for ELL students with disabilities. Unfortunately, it is not always possible to provide bilingual education (or bilingual special education), because teachers are not trained in this methodology or because teachers who themselves are bilingual are not available. For example, over 1.3 ELL students attend California K–12 classes, and when bilingual education was allowed, the annual shortage of trained teachers was over 20,000 (Housman & Simmons, 1998). And when bilingual special education teachers are available at a school, the demands on them are great (Salend et al., 1997). They are expected to meet the needs of all bilingual students at the school, to be the cultural resource for every child's multicultural education, and to provide ESL and language support to general education students.

Experts in the field of bilingual education now tend to agree that the appropriate time to move a child from the bilingual class to the all-English class is when the dominant language is fully developed, which is at about age 12. The proper timing for such a move is crucial. Research conducted by Cummins (1984) highlights the issues. The first stages of language proficiency include conversational fluency, the mastery of pronunciation, vocabulary, and grammar. Only later does the individual develop the more complex, conceptual linguistic ability, the deeper functions of language necessary for competent participation in academic settings. (See Figure 3.3 on page 109, which shows the surface and the deeper levels of language proficiency.) Cummins cautions that children first develop face-to-face conversational skills and are then transferred to all-English instruction because they appear to have English proficiency. But they then fall further and further behind academically because they do not have the more complex linguistic abilities required for academic success. Their **basic interpersonal communicative skills (BICS)** are more developed than their **cognitive/academic linguistic proficiency (CALP)**. Conversational skills in a second language can be acquired within two to three years, but the more complex language abilities required for academic work require about five to seven years of meaningful exposure and practice.

The student's understanding is affected by how many contextual clues accompany the language, such as explanatory pictures, specific people speaking, or particular tone of voice. In addition, understanding is affected by how demanding the activity is; if the task is concrete, it is easier to understand than if it is quite complex. Second-language ability must be greater when fewer contextual clues suggest meaning, or when the communication requires more cognitive ability. The bottom half of the pyramid in Figure 3.3 requires the highest level of language and cognitive skills.

Most Americans are not proficient in two languages, and no teacher speaks all of the over 100 different languages spoken by children attending American schools. Bilingual education is not a possibility for most children who come to school not speaking English. What can teachers do when they do not speak the child's native language? One approach often suggested is to create **cooperative learning** groups, in which children work together on academic tasks (Fletcher et al., 1999). It is thought that this approach is powerful in several different ways. Children who come from cultures that do not value individual competition will be more comfortable, and peers can help each other learn academic tasks. Research indicates, however, that students merely being assigned to small groups and being told to help each other does not guarantee desired academic improvement (Lopez-Reyna, 1997). Students also need structure and guidance from the teacher. They need instructional prompts to help them learn to write coherent and thoughtful stories. They must help children expand their vocabularies and increase the complexities of their language use. The Research to Practice box on page 110 gives some tips on how to make cooperative learning more effective with LEP learners.

COLLABORATION FOR INCLUSION

basic interpersonal communicative skills (BICS). Face-to-face conversational language.
cognitive/academic linguistic proficiency (CALP). The abstract language abilities required for academic work.
cooperative learning. Groups of more than two students collaborating as they learn the same material.

As you will learn throughout this text, the word *inclusion* means many different things to people. You will also learn that issues related to inclusion are extremely complex and vary from individual to individual and group to group. For homeless children, it might mean gaining access to school (Walther-Thomas et al. 1996). To LEP students, who in general are more likely to attend segregated classes, it might mean attending general education classes alongside their English-speaking peers (Hoff, 1995). For all culturally and linguistically diverse children, it means including their families and their communities in the educational system. This last level of inclusion requires partnerships and the development of collaborative relationships with groups that can provide a network of supports.

Building the right partnerships often requires working in difficult situations, for many of these families and communities are fighting for their own survival and are often disenfranchised (Walther-Thomas et al., 1996). Collaboration needs to occur in meaningful ways, often with nontraditional partners. For example, innovative approaches for homeless children might bring educators together with staff from shelters. It might mean finding ways for family members who have no means of transportation to get to meetings at schools. It could be identifying creative ways of communicating with families that have no consistent mailing addresses. For families

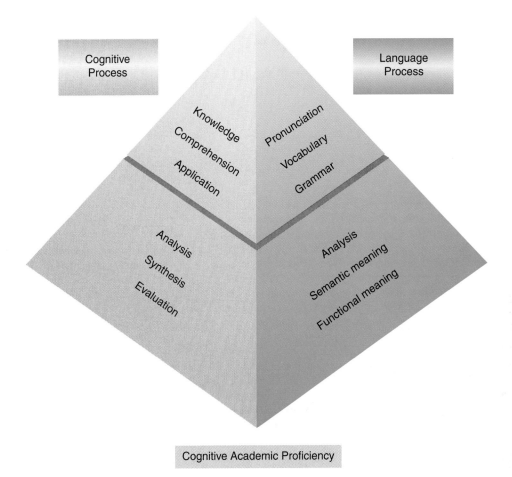

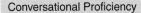

Figure 3.3 Surface and Deeper Levels of Language Proficiency

Source: Bilingualism and Special Education: Issues in Assessment and Pedagogy (p.138) by J. Cummins, 1984, Austin, TX: Pro-Ed. Reprinted by permission.

that do not speak English well, it means finding interpreters very familiar with the special education process who can explain it to people who have no knowledge of the American educational system. It definitely means finding ways to change attitudes of community members who feel alienated from the educational system, as well as professionals from social service agencies.

Why might the community be a good source of partnerships for those working at schools where many students from diverse groups attend? One reason is that they stand ready to help. The Meenendiwin Model gives us an illustration that is quite helpful in this regard (see Figure 3.4 on page 111). *Meenendiwin* is the Ojibwe word for "mutual gifting," and the model compares the traditional American view to a diverse perspective for delivery of services and supports (Vraniak, 1998). The traditional perspective could be characterized as being "top down," while the diverse perspective describes "many serving one." When studying these illustrations, the

Research to Practice: Teaching with Confidence

USING COOPERATIVE LEARNING STRUCTURES TO OPTIMIZE LEARNING FOR ALL STUDENTS

NORMA A, LOPEZ-REYNA
University of Illinois at Chicago

RESEARCH

Cooperative learning methods that divide students into small teams of interdependent members have been found to be consistently more successful than individual learning methods for improving academic achievement, interethnic relations, and prosocial development. For second-language learners, the use of their native language to discuss and explain instructions to one another and to negotiate and construct meaning collaboratively is a well-documented result of cooperative structures. Research suggests that conceptual knowledge developed through the students' native language transfers positively into English. Several of my studies found that when Spanish-speaking students discuss in their native language to clarify meaning when reading English texts, their comprehension is increased. Similarly, cooperative learning groups have been observed to provide a supportive learning environment in which second-language learners are encouraged by their peers who are more proficient in English to participate in activities to learn content knowledge, improve social skills, and develop language skills, As such, cooperative learning is frequently promoted for English as a second language (ESL) learners and ESL students with learning disabilities. While research with students with disabilities is limited, it has been noted that both the skill levels and willingness to collaborate are critical for successful group membership. When they are taught and encouraged to work collaboratively and are closely moni-

tored, students are able to support one another during cognitively demanding instructional tasks, and thus they gain access to alternative or supplemental modes of comprehension beyond what the teacher is able to provide.

PRACTICE

Obviously, cooperative learning involves much more than simply instructing students to work together or placing them in small groups. Students need to be made responsible for their own learning as well as that of others. It is very important to organize children into heterogeneous groups. Dependent on the goals of the lesson, students may be grouped according to their varying levels of content knowledge, English language fluency, social status characteristics, or ability and willingness to work with others. It is best to change groupings several times during the schoolyear to maintain heterogeneity. A critical feature of cooperative learning structures is for the teacher to model high expectations, mutual trust, and respect. With a student who has special learning needs, it is important that the teacher identify cognitive skill areas in which the student is an expert, provide opportunities for teaching others, and point out to the rest of the class the value of the skill. Another means of incorporating students with disabilities is to prepare them prior to the lesson in such a way that significant participation is guaranteed. This serves both to improve the student's involvement and expectations for him/herself and to reinforce perceptions for high expectations on the part of classmates.

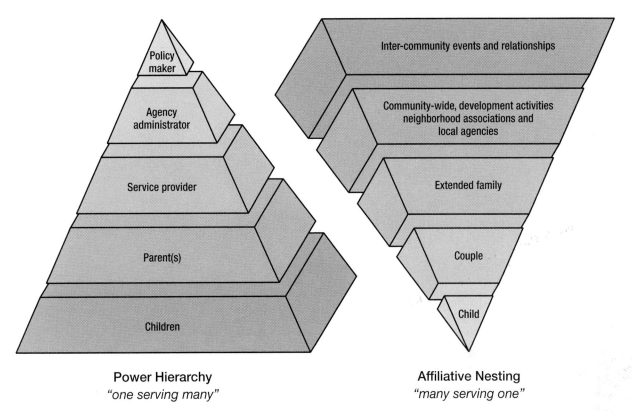

Power Hierarchy	**Affiliative Nesting**
"one serving many"	*"many serving one"*

Fiɡure 3.4 **The Meenendiwan Model: Ojibwe for "Mutual Gifting"**

The Western system of support and services is based on the principle of "one serving many": one physician serving many patients; one therapist serving many clients; ione teacher serving many students; one social worker serving many families. This system is hierarchical, specialized, and control-oriented. A contrasting model, grounded in American Indian cultural beliefs, is "many serving one": many women baby-showering one pregnant woman; many mourners visiting one widower; many celebrants congratulating one graduate; many families celebrating one marriage. This contrasting model is horizontal, affiliative, and ecological. The principle of many-serving-one is at the heart of the Meenendiwin model.

Source: From "Developing systems of support with American Indian Families of Youth with Disabilities" by D. Vraniak, 1998 summer, *Health Issues for Children & Youth & Their Families, 6,* p. 9. Reprinted by permission.

phrase adopted by many African American communities comes to mind: "It takes a whole village to raise a child."

Another reason is that the community is a more permanent part of these individuals' lives than any single school. Also, such supports for these children continue even if they move from school to school, and district to district, frequently. And they also often exist after the school day and during the summer months. An excellent example of a service group that offers a full range of services and supports is the Chicago Youth Centers (CYC). CYC enrolls over 700 children in its early intervention programs, programs which have received accreditation from the National Association for the Education of Young Children (only 5% of child development centers in the United States have been so acknowledged). CYC's After-School Programs

Partnerships between community agencies and schools help children see the value of doing well in school, becoming self-directed, and being responsible for their own actions.

have over 8,000 students. Even more notably, CYC has developed a partnership and collaborative agreement with many Chicago inner-city schools, and provides early intervention and prevention programs that uniquely complement the work of public schools while serving the needs of children. CYC approached principals, guidance counselors. and teachers in Chicago public xchools, offering to set up innovative programs. That initiative has resulted in programs that bring CYC program directors into schools to conduct weekly sessions addressing basic life skills issues. Some of the topics presented focus on: communication skills, conflict resolution, family relationships and responsibilities, gender stereotyping, cultural diversity, assertiveness techniques (especially in resisting sexual and peer pressure), child and sexual abuse, drug use prevention, gang alternatives, goal setting, and sexual relationships and parenthood. Each of these sensitive and volatile issues is addressed through school-approved curricula that incorporate CYC's experience and ability to teach through stories and example, role-playing and videos. CYC also calls upon its own community relationships and sometimes invites guest speakers, such as a recent program that brought in officers from the area Sheriff's Department to speak on dating and violence.

Another innovative program resulting from this partnership is known as "Girl Power," which was begun in 1998. This program, offered by Lowell Elementary School in Chicago's tough Humboldt Park neighborhood, has sixth-, seventh-, and eighth-grade girls meet with CYC staff as part of a voluntary after-school program. The girls are encouraged to write their thoughts and questions in journals, which are collected weekly. The journal writings are then used as the basis for open discussions of teen pregnancy, suicide, peer/gang pressure, and relationship issues. The popularity of these programs, both with students and with school personnel, attests to the power of collaborative partnerships between the community and schools.

Besides social service agencies like CYC, other excellent sources for partnerships and assistance exist in inner-city areas. Educators can seek out community leaders as they seek help from community groups, churches, and volunteer organizations (Rogers-Dulan, 1998). One place to start is with students' parents, who will know of other resources in the local community. Educators must be cautioned, however: Partnerships are built from a sense of equity. Community leaders must feel welcome at school, be allowed to become actively involved at school, and have a voice in the schools' life (Thorp, 1997). Many opportunities for inclusion exist; we just need to be creative and seize them.

The Native American dropout problem is also discussed in the Defined section of this chapter.

NEW DIRECTIONS FOR THE MILLENNIUM

Legacy: Many families of diverse students do not participate in school activities, leaving them with feelings of being disconnected from their children's education.

Opportunities:
- Increase opportunities for community partnerships
- Apply culturally and personally sensitive approaches when working with all families

TRANSITION THROUGH ADULTHOOD

The relationship between education and wages is clear: High school graduates are less likely to be unemployed. Every year of high school completed increases lifetime wages by 8% and improves job satisfaction (Currie & Thomas, 1995). Statistics show that low-income and culturally and linguistically diverse students tend to drop out of school at a higher rate than do others. Although there has been improvement in the past twenty years, the dropout rate remains troubling, particularly for poor children. Native Americans have the worst overall dropout rate of all ethnic groups. As an example, 31% of all Navajo students leave school before completion (Jordon et al., 1997). Data are available to compare some poor children within and across ethnic groups: while 3% of high-income White students drop out of school, 19% of poor White students do; 4% of high-income Blacks drop out compared to 19% of poor Blacks; and 6% of high-income Hispanics drop out compared to 41% of poor Hispanics (CDF, 1995; U.S. Department of Education, NCES, 1999). These issues relate directly to the under- and unemployment rates for these groups. High school graduation is one criterion for entrance into college and, as you have just learned, is important to future employment opportunities and the potential for economic success. Unfortunately, data indicate that African American and Hispanic students are underrepresented in colleges and universities. In many cases, minority students are advised not to take the core required courses for college entrance (e.g., enough science, math, and foreign language courses). Often, they attend high schools with fewer financial resources, which translates to outdated textbooks, old instructional materials, and less experienced teachers.

For most Americans, employment is one important goal of education, but for some the possibilities of economic independence appear bleak. Those living on the White Mountain Apache Indian Reservation are a good example (Ramasamy, 1996). Of those students from both general and special education who graduated from high school across a five-year period, only 33% were employed (27% of special education graduates and 35% of general education graduates). This situation is partly due to the paucity of jobs on the reservation, but other factors need to be considered as well. Only two individuals had requested assistance from rehabilitation services. The vast majority of the entire group were satisfied with their employment situation. Possibly, transition goals for individuals who live on reservations where employment opportunities are limited should be developed with traditional values (participation in cultural and religious activities) considered.

FAMILIES

Families of culturally and linguistically diverse children often have very special needs when interacting with social service agencies, particularly schools. Many come to the school situation with feelings of distrust, alienation, and lack of information (Linan-Thompson & Jean, 1997; Voltz, 1994). For some, their children are the first generation in their family to enter an education system where English is spoken. These families may speak little, if any, English at home. Even those who speak English may not have enough comfort or proficiency in this second language to truly understand and communicate with educators using technical language or jargon (Holman, 1997). To them, "disability" may have a meaning (only a physical or sensory disability, or only a severe disability) different from our view of disability (Thorp, 1997). Teachers must know about and respect the cultural background of their students' families, dissolve barriers, and develop partnerships with all family members who wish to be included. Most important, educators must develop trust and respect between home and school. Let's first think together about some reasons family–school partnerships are sometimes difficult to establish with diverse families, and then look at ways these partnerships can be fostered.

CROSS-CULTURAL DISSONANCE AND OTHER BARRIERS TO PARTNERSHIPS

Many teachers often express disappointment about parents of their students with disabilities. They comment that these parents seem detached, appear uninvolved in their children's lives, and do not participate in school events (Thorp, 1997). Most likely, only the last part of this observation is true: many parents of diverse students are not involved in school life. Probably as a result of the exclusion these families feel, diverse families tend not to access social services available to them (Bailey et al., 1999; Little, 1998). Some barriers which keep diverse families who have children with disabilities from participating in important services may be only perceived, but certainly not all. Regardless, efforts to reduce or remove factors that inhibit the development of meaningful partnerships is everyone's responsibility.

Teachers and service providers may inadvertently set up barriers to the development of effective partnerships by excluding diverse family members in many different ways (Thorp, 1997). The roots of these barriers are many, but a few reasons for us to examine are: conflict between home and school cultures, poor communication, no mutual respect, misunderstanding about ability to fulfill promises, and lack of information.

In many school–home relationships, **cross-cultural dissonance**—a situation of extreme misunderstanding of fundamental issues and values about education, disability, and home–school interaction—may undermine special education for students with disabilities (Harry, 1992). Or parents might not understand how their child could be considered as having a disability by schools when the child's behavior does not fit their concept of "disability." Teachers may use language and special education jargon that parents do not understand. For those who speak a language other than English, the interpreter selected might not understand the special education process.

Teachers often assign parents to an inferior role, in which the parents believe that their beliefs are not valued (Thorp, 1997). They need to be respected and not be given assignments they are unable to complete. For example, many parents who are not proficient in English are embarrassed that they cannot help their children with their homework (Milian, 1999). They might commit to helping their children with schoolwork, but are unable to follow through. Likewise, educators should not make promises they cannot keep. Parents are often limited to roles of "consent giver" and "educational planner" rather than being accepted as full partners in the special education of their sons and daughters (Harry, 1992). Instead of assuming that parents will be loyal supporters and passive recipients of information, educators should seek parents' input about how they would like to be involved in their child's educational program (Prater & Tanner, 1995; Thorp, 1997). They need information. For example, to be full partners, parents need to understand the special education process and their child's progress in the system. They need to know what educational options are available—like phonics versus whole language approaches—and why

cross-cultural dissonance. When the home and school cultures are in conflict.

one method was selected over another or how they are being used in combination. Such openness in communication can foster active dialogues about children's instructional programs.

FAMILY–SCHOOL PARTNERSHIPS

The benefits to children are great when schools develop meaningful, quality partnerships with families (Voltz, 1994). But partnerships require effort and participation. How can teachers help solve problems associated with lack of parent participation? Experts have been pondering this question, studying dynamics of diverse families, and analyzing schools (Bailey et al., 1999; Holman, 1997; Linan-Thompson & Jean, 1997; Thorp, 1997; Milian, 1999). Here's what they suggest educators consider when they seek to foster these special partnerships:

- Develop an atmosphere of trust and respect
- Be sure the family and community feel welcome
- Ensure that teachers and parents understand each other's cultures, beliefs, and values
- Identify families' preferred means of communication and use it effectively
- Communicate on a regular, ongoing basis (not just when there is a problem)
- Use titles (Mr., Mrs., Ms., Dr.) when addressing family members (unless directly told otherwise)
- Incorporate materials that reflect the diversity of the community
- Seek meaningful ways to involve the family and community (as they feel comfortable)
- Treat families with individual respect and avoid stereotyping on any characteristic (race, ethnicity, language, or socioeconomic class).

Parents also need to be asked about which family members they would like to be involved in their children's programs. Children from diverse backgrounds may have a family constellation that differs from that of children from the dominant culture. Often, these **extended family** members play a crucial role in the life of the individual with disabilities. The families of culturally and linguistically diverse children may include many extended family members as well as individuals outside the family. For example, for some African American families church and community leaders often lend support and resources to the student with disabilities (Rogers-Dulan, 1998). For that child, the concept of extended family may well include key members from the community. For Native American children, it may be tribal elders whose exclusion would be considered an offense (Vraniak, 1998). Before making any decisions about treatments or educational strategies, it may be necessary to consult with these tribal elders and allow time for such consultations. Without understanding the cultural demands and expectations of the child's family, educators can inadvertently create unfortunate and unnecessary barriers.

In part, a child's success in school depends on respect between the school and the family. Children must feel confident that their cultural heritage and language are valued by the teacher and school. To encourage confidence and cooperation, a teacher can bring the strengths, contributions, culture, and language of the family directly into the school experience. For example, a grandfather might teach the class a special skill like making silver jewelry. A grandmother who creates pottery following the ancient techniques might demonstrate her art. A mother who programs computers might teach the class how to make drawings or large signs using the computer. A

- For more about Native Americans, review the Very Special Population section (Defined) found earlier in this chapter.
- For more about developing proficiency in English, see Language and Instruction (Educational Interventions) in this chapter.

extended family. Includes immediate family members— mother, father, and siblings—and other relatives—aunts, uncles, grandparents.

parent who is a migrant agricultural worker might sing folk songs in the home language or tell traditional stories. An aunt who has recently immigrated might have photos, musical instruments, examples of clothing, or other items from her home country to help students dramatize a myth and better understand the customs of the country. A church leader could explain a religious holiday or event. Finally, a tribal leader might be asked to officiate at a school awards ceremony. Any such family participation in school events helps foster home–school partnerships and promote children's success at school.

TECHNOLOGY

Technology has changed all of our lives. There is no question that it will continue to impact the lives of those with disabilities and their families. In each section on technology you will come to wonder about the future possibilities. Our hope is to have you dream with us about how even the greatest challenges can be facilitated by advances in technology.

As **computerized language translators** are developed, they may have a significant impact for special education students with a primary language other than English. For instance, the student may be able to use a computer to write an assignment in his or her primary language, check the spelling and punctuation, and then press a button to translate the work into English and give it to the teacher. Students could write their assignments in a dialect, and then have the computer translate it into the standard English. Computers can save time for the bilingual teacher or volunteer by being used for immediate translations of specific words or explanations of phrases and idioms.

CONCEPTS AND CONTROVERSY: CHANGING POLICIES AFFECT CULTURALLY AND LINGUISTICALLY DIVERSE INDIVIDUALS

Probably because of the rising numbers of immigrants coming to the United States seeking a new life free from political injustice and economic hardship, the nation is experiencing a change of attitudes about access to public services, language use, and affirmative action (Smith, 1998). State legislatures and voters across the country, particularly in Texas and California, are changing policies that affect the lives of diverse individuals. These policies are far-reaching, changing their access to school, how they are taught, and employment opportunities. Are such changes in the sociopolitical context of America the right thing to do? Do these changes solve issues of equity? Let's examine a few of these changes.

Twenty-five states have now passed English-only laws; although unsuccessful so far, legislation has been introduced in the U.S. Congress, and the Supreme Court is considering the issue (Lyons, 1998; U.S. English, Inc., 1999). In California, one extension of the English-only attitudes was the passage of Proposition 227, which banned bilingual education. Formal organizations have been created (e.g., U.S. English) to promote official language policies. Most likely, these actions are in response to the recent influx of immigrants from non-European countries and to the increase in the number of foreign languages spoken in this country. Estimates are

computerized language translators. Microcomputers that provide translations of written text from one language to another.

that over six million students in America are English Language Learners, and, proportionally, they are dramatically overrepresented in general education classes which creates a challenge for the teachers who must accommodate instruction for their diversity (NABE, 1998). Proponents of English-only laws argue that for the social fabric of the United States to stay intact, for economic stability, and to guarantee the American lifestyle, this nation must use one language: English. Defenders of this position maintain that English is a unifying force in the United States, and they fear that the country is being divided along language lines (Piatt, 1990; Tatalovich, 1995). They also cite research findings which indicate that children of immigrant families prefer English to their parents' native language (Portes & Rumbaut, 1996). Many look to the recent problems in Canada with conflict over the use of French and English and strengthen their stance that we should adopt a single-language policy. Those wanting to maintain the use of multiple languages in the United States and retain the availability of bilingual education to students not proficient in English are many. For example, two-thirds of Hispanic voters in California voted against the English-only initiative, and 80% of Hispanics who had children in school voted to retain the bilingual education option. Bilingual education was halted because 81% of Republican males voted against its use (Lyons, 1998; Pachon, 1998)

What motivates the development of single-language policies? What would be so wrong with an English-only America? What might be the outcomes of such laws? It is possible that English-only laws could cause discrimination against bilingual individuals. They could create an atmosphere of hostility, repression, and divisiveness in cities and towns with large communities of non-English speakers. As seen with

Source: Albuquerque Tribune

the passage of California Proposition 227, funding and use of bilingual education would be stopped. A climate could emerge in favor of certain other initiatives, such as the recently passed California Proposition 209, which banned affirmative action procedures in the state's college and university admission policies.

So, should speaking more than one language be regarded as a valued skill? Supporters of the alternative position, English Plus, contend that pluralism is an American strength, and that there are great benefits to proficiency of English plus mastery of at least a second language. Four states (New Mexico, Oregon, Washington, and Rhode Island) along with some major cities (Atlanta, Cleveland, Dallas, San Antonio, Tucson, and Washington, DC) have laws or resolutions supporting the concept of English Plus. How will this national debate conclude? What issues should be considered in this national conversation? What will be the impact on bilingual education and bilingual special education?

In Conclusion

MAKING CONNECTIONS

Look again at the Advance Organizers found at the beginning of the chapter; to help you study the content of this chapter, the answers to the Self-Test and Challenge questions are found here. Test yourself to see if you have mastered the major points of this chapter.

Summary

Education should reflect the rich diversity of culture and language found in communities across this country, and special education should capitalize on each student's background as an appropriate individualized education program is created. Many exceptional children are bilingual, and many more come from diverse cultural backgrounds. The combinations of disability, giftedness, cultural diversity, and LEP (ELL) present many challenges to these children, their families, and educators as schools attempt to ensure that special education services are delivered to children who need and are entitled to them.

Focus Questions

Self-Test Questions

• *What is meant by multicultural special education, and who is served by these programs?*

The demographics of the United States and its school population are changing rapidly, creating complex challenges for educators and the educational system. The number of multicultural and bilingual students in the United States is increasing rapidly. Almost one-third of today's public schoolchildren come from diverse backgrounds, and it is predicted that by 2026 White children will represent only one-third of the school population. Today, in twenty-five of the country's largest cities and metropolitan areas, at least half the students are from culturally and linguistically diverse groups. The largest and fastest-growing group is Hispanic, which includes 75% of all LEP students.

• *What is meant by bilingual special education, and who is served by these programs?*

Bilingual special education stresses the development of academic and social skills through an individually designed program that capitalizes on the child's home language and culture, along with English, as a foundation for delivering instruction to culturally and linguistically diverse children with exceptionalities. These programs typically serve children who have limited English proficiency, have not mastered English well enough to receive academic instruction in their nondominant language, and have been identified as having a disability. A central issue in the instruction of LEP students is the type of instructional approach to use. Four basic instructional approaches are often used in bilingual special education classes: English as a second language (ESL), the bilingual transitional approach, the bilingual maintenance approach (not used much today), and the total immersion approach. It is difficult to implement bilingual special education, using any of the four available approaches, because of the unavailability of trained teachers who are also proficient in the child's native language. In such cases, teachers must seek help from family and community volunteers and bilingual paraprofessionals to help children to become proficient in English as quickly as possible.

- *Why are educators so concerned about culturally and linguistically diverse children?*
  Culturally and linguistically diverse children are at great risk for disabilities and for low educational achievement; this risk is far greater for them than for children who come from mainstream society. Many of these families face social and economic inequities that can result in risk factors for their children. For example, poverty reduces a family's access to health care, which can lead to increased school absences and, in some cases, disabilities. Cultural differences in classroom settings require that teachers adjust their instructional techniques to match differences in learning styles. Those children whose home language is not English face additional risks and challenges. The development of second-language acquisition and proficiency concurrent with academic instruction presented in English requires many accommodations. When insufficient numbers of educators who speak the family's primary language are available, the challenges of cultural differences are compounded by language differences. Schools must address the needs of children from different cultures and different languages. If they do not, students from diverse backgrounds will continue to be overrepresented in disability categories and underrepresented in gifted education. They will also continue to drop out of school at alarming rates. Not finishing high school is associated with reduced employability and increased contacts with the juvenile justice system.

- *In what ways can biases occur in the identification and assessment process?*
  One risk in the assessment and identification process is discrimination. When testing culturally and linguistically diverse children, bias can occur for many reasons: the information (content level) being tested is not known by culturally and linguistically diverse students, minority groups are not represented in the standardization population, the administrator of the test is not trained in multicultural or bilingual techniques, or the child does not adequately comprehend the language used in the testing situation. Bias in the testing process is a major factor in the overrepresentation of culturally and linguistically diverse children in special education programs and their underrepresentation in gifted education.

- *How can school personnel integrate children's home cultures and languages into the educational environment and curriculum?*

Educators have the opportunity to demonstrate their cultural awareness and sensitivity to their students' diversity throughout every school day in every instructional unit by the examples and resources they integrate into their lessons. They can show their acceptance of different languages by posting signs, publishing columns in school newsletters, displaying posters from different countries, and learning welcoming phrases in their students' native languages. They can enrich their instruction by encouraging students to read literature from their home cultures, work together in study groups, and join clubs that offer common interests and additional supports. Educators can seek the assistance of parents, family members, and community volunteers to work with students as language and academic tutors, enhance instructional units with culturally relevant illustratives, connect the curriculum with students' personal experiences, and become active partners in classroom instruction.

Challenge Question

- *Why is there such a national debate about the issue of the overrepresentation of culturally and linguistically diverse students in disability categories and their underrepresentation in gifted education?*

Clearly, culturally and linguistically diverse children are overrepresented in disability categories and underrepresented in gifted education. Multiculturalism and bilingualism do not cause disabilities or the likelihood of being gifted, but many correlates of being diverse do. One of the main culprits here is poverty, because in the United States factors associated with poverty (e.g., access to health care) do result in a variety of disabilities. Many culturally and linguistically diverse students do not live in poverty; but for those who do, the effects of poverty are sometimes confused with the effects of diversity. Cultural and linguistic diversity can mask a child's giftedness and inappropriately suggest a cognitive disability or language impairment. Language and communication differences often challenge both the child and special education personnel, and cultural differences may raise questions about the behavior of the child and family and about the appropriateness of interventions. In addition, mobility (e.g., homelessness, migrant worker transience, and immigrant or refugee circumstances) interrupts education, aggravates educational problems, creates great disadvantages in learning and academic experience, adds stress, and causes logistical difficulties in the education of some children.

 **Supplementary Resources**

Scholarly Readings

Baca, L. M., & Cervantes, H. T. (Eds.). (1998). *The bilingual special education interface* (2nd ed). Columbus, OH: Merrill.

Baker, C., & Jones, S. P. (1998). *Encyclopedia of bilingualism and bilingual education.* Philadelphia: Multilingual Matters, Ltd.

Banks, J. A. (1994). *An introduction to multicultural education.* Boston: Allyn and Bacon.

Cheng, L. L. (Ed.). (1995). *Integrating language and learning for inclusion: An Asian-Pacific focus.* San Diego: Singular Publishing Group.

Gollnick, D. M., & Chinn, P. C. (1998). *Multicultural education in a pluralistic society* (5th ed.). Columbus, OH: Merrill.

Lynch, E. W., & Hanson, M. J. (1998). *Developing cross-cultural competence: A guide for working with young children and their families* (2nd ed). Baltimore: Paul H. Brooks.

Tiedt, P. L., & Tiedt, I. M. (1999). *Multicultural teaching: A handbook of activities, information, and resources* (5th ed.). Boston: Allyn and Bacon.

Popular Books

Anaya, R. A. (1979). *Tortuga.* Berkeley, CA: Editorial Justa.

Dorris, M. (1989). *The broken cord.* New York: Harper & Row.

Kenzaburo, O. (1994). *The pinch runner memorandum.* London: M. E. Sharpe.

Kozol, J. (1995). *Amazing grace: The lives of children and the conscience of a nation.* New York: Crown.

Ng, F. M. (1993). *Bone: A novel.* New York: Hyperion.

Rechy, J. (1993). *The miraculous day of Amalia Gomez.* New York: Arcade.

Wilson, A. (1993). *Two trains running.* New York: NAL-Dutton.

Videos and DVDs

To kill a mockingbird. (1960). United Artists.
The Milagro beanfield war. (1988). Universal Films.
Stand and deliver. (1989). Warner Brothers.

Professional, Parent, and Consumer Organizations and Agencies

Division for Culturally and Linguistically Diverse Exceptional Learners (DDEL)
Council for Exceptional Children (CEC)
1920 Association Drive
Reston, VA 22091
Phone: (888) CEC-SPED; (703) 620-3660
Web site: http://www.cec.sped.org

National Association for Bilingual Education (NABE)
1220 L Street NW, Suite 605
Washington, DC 20005
Phone: (202) 898-1829
E-mail: nabe@nabe.org
Web site: http://www.nabe.org

National Clearinghouse for Bilingual Education
1118 22nd Street NW
Washington, DC 20037
Phone: (800) 322-6223
E-mail: askncbe@ncbe.gwu.edu
Web site: http://www.ncbe.gwu.edu

National Association for Multicultural Education (NAME)
1511 K Street NW, #43
Washington, DC 20005
Phone: (202) 628-NAME
E-mail: name@nicom.com

P. Buckley Moss is a highly successful contemporary artist who faced a childhood filled with school failure and challenge. She says of her schooling, "I was totally unprepared for the discipline of school; and the reading that I knew would be so easy turned out to be a frustration I would never overcome" (Moss, 1989, p. 19). She remembers being described as inattentive, a slow learner, and even stupid. She knew she was not stupid; and when the diagnosis of learning disabilities was made, it was almost a relief. Moss is not only a well-recognized American artist, she is also a supporter of many associations concerned with learning disabilities.

Evening Time (1985) represents a common theme for P. Buckley Moss, who enjoys capturing the spirit, honesty, and happiness of her Amish and Mennonite neighbors living in Virginia's Shenandoah Valley. Much of her work presents the strong family values, the fun and enjoyment found in life's simple pleasures which are an integral part of these people's simple lifestyle. *Evening Time* is a good illustration of her typical message— life can be very good without the complications and confusion of overly materialistic attitudes.

Evening Time, copyright P. Buckley Moss, 1985. Reprinted by permission.

C H A P T E R **4**

Personal Perspective:

Educating Erin

Megan and Tim Askim and I met recently. We were on vacation at a cooking school in Italy, coming from different parts of America. Megan and I were attracted to each other almost immediately. It had not occurred to either of us that we would go halfway across the world to meet someone else whose life is immersed in issues related to students with disabilities. After a few days of traveling and cooking together, I asked Megan if she would share her story—the story of her daughter, Erin, who has very serious learning disabilities, the Askim family, and a special mom who exemplifies the modern parent advocate—a writing task Megan found to be more difficult than she expected. Megan has not had to fight for Erin to be able to go to school, though she continually has to monitor her daughter's education. What you will learn, and maybe be surprised about, is that services do not automatically kick into place when a child's disability is suspected, nor are they "seamless" as children move through the educational system.

> We were a young couple when Erin was born. She was a second child, and we had no reason to suspect problems. But she stayed like a baby for a long time. "Well, it's a good thing we like having a baby," we would say. "She is taking her sweet time growing up. Not too fast for us; that's okay." She was a little slow crawling, a little slow walking, and she talked a funny kind of language—we called it *ewock*. What we slowly learned was that how Erin is in the world is just different. Our family calls Erin "inside-out, upside-down, and backwards." I realized that Erin really had difficulties when I sent my son off to kindergarten. I knew that Erin wouldn't be ready for that program in two or three years. Honestly, I knew there was something wrong from the second day she was with us. She was fretful. She

Learning Disabilities

was sleeping and eating, but she would start to cry for no apparent reason. I had a 2-year-old, he didn't do that, and I could comfort him. I looked for help from our pediatrician, but he said, "Erin's fine." I asked family members, but only got a lot of opinions that weren't very helpful. I had a friend who was an educator, and her expertise was early childhood development. So I invited her over for lunch and expressed my concern that there was something "not quite right." I asked her straight out what she thought, and she said, "There is something drastically wrong with Erin." Although I knew that, it was hard to accept. Fortunately, with that profound statement I got a helping hand and a list of phone numbers.

Hours, days, and weeks with countless interviews, needs assessments to fill out, and about a million phone calls later (not really; it just felt like it), we had an appointment with the county office of education for the assessment they felt was necessary. Educators, speech and language pathologist, OT, psychologist—all deemed her to be fine. "No way," I said. "There is something wrong!" Luckily, there was one speech pathologist who said, "Well, let's look more." Finally, Erin, at 3 years and 3 months, was eligible to receive special education services. The help meant a special education preschool that had the specialists needed to teach her. Help meant putting a little 3-year-old girl on a little yellow school bus to go ten miles away to school at 6:50 in the morning. I sent her blanket with her, but that was never enough of a blanket for me. I kept thinking that it wasn't supposed to be like this; Erin's barely out of her crib!

At age 5, Erin's school program changed. She went from that preschool far away to an elementary school in our school district. She attended a special day class for K–2. Here she stayed until 7. In spite of all the intensive teaching, the speech therapy, and OT, she still couldn't count to 10 or learn the ABCs. The school was truly puzzled. We needed more assessments! This would come in the form of an intense four-day stay at our state diagnostic center, which included psychologists, speech and language evaluation, occupational therapy, medical evaluation, and numerous educational tests. More reports, and confirmation of many specific learning disabilities, and a very specific plan with the recommended interventions. In order for her to participate in the amount of therapies and the intense intervention needed, she would have to change schools. This move meant a special school, which is considered one of the most restrictive environments in education, but for Erin (at this time) it was the least restrictive environment. She had the program that was necessary for her to learn. She stayed at this school for four years. She learned to read and write. She made friends. Erin grew into a confident and motivated learner with a lot of help—and I mean a lot of help—and some very intense learning strategies. However, this school was twenty miles away from home. With all the very positive things going on in her education, she was beginning to realize that she didn't go to school with her friend down the street.

Erin, now a middle-school student, told us she was ready for a change, and it was our responsibility to make that happen. The thought of a neighborhood middle school for her was terrifying to us. So the place to start was by reconvening the IEP committee to have discussions from everyone involved about what her program might look like. The details are irrelevant and too numerous, but it is critical for you to know that we ended up being the experts who made decisions about what Erin's program would be. Anyway, Erin did transition to our neighborhood school in seventh grade, into a "full inclusion program." She was now enrolled in all general education classes, like all typical seventh graders, but it seemed like meetings with teachers were endless. For an example, the math teacher was concerned that the curriculum would be too difficult. I recommended he present the math curriculum as it was, and if Erin "hit a wall" we would be open to alternatives. She has not hit the wall yet. Erin received real grades (for the first time ever), and she has thrived. (She still receives special education services with what the district calls a "one-to-one aide," and also continuing speech and language therapy.)

Erin is now a sophomore in high school, and we have different issues to deal with. My challenge now is to have relationships with all the different teachers. I have to, because her general teachers do not understand disabilities in general and how they specifically impact individual students. I can plead Erin's case very effectively, but I keep wondering why do I still have to? And I worry about those parents who are unable to advocate effectively on their own child's behalf. Our family is still dealing with teachers who actively question our decisions about Erin's education. After all these years—with all the professionals, the educational therapists, the medical evaluations, the IEPs, the team meetings, support from family and friends and teachers, making decisions based on past history and high expectations for the future—how can a teacher say, "Well, Mrs. Askim, I really don't think this is the best class for Erin"? It is my responsibility to advocate on Erin's behalf, but should it be my responsibility to convince teachers that my child deserves to be taught? My response in my own mind is that Erin hasn't "hit the wall" in learning but some teachers have "hit the wall" in teaching. My child has been a challenge to teach all along and she has been the teacher to many teachers. They are the teachers who admit they don't have all the answers but are willing to be persistent, supportive, and have high expectations for a little girl, and now a young lady, who sees the world "inside-out, upside-down, and backwards."

1. Why do you think Erin's high school teachers were so concerned about including Erin in the general education curriculum?

2. What's do you think might be next for Megan and Erin?

Advance Organizers

CONNECTIONS
MAKING

Use the learning strategy, Advance Organizers, to help focus your study of this chapter's content, and reinforce your learning by reviewing answers to the Focus and Challenge Questions which are found at the end of the chapter.

Overview

Learning disabilities is the largest special education category, with well over 50% of all students with disabilities identified as having it as their primary disabling condition. Although these individuals comprise a heterogeneous group, they all share several defining characteristics: unexpected underachievement and difficulty mastering academic subjects, particularly reading. Many of these students also display characteristics associated with attention deficit hyperactivity disorder (ADHD). Partly because of the ease of identifying students as belonging to this special education category and the size of this group, much controversy surrounds these children and their educational programs. Although some have questioned whether this disability even exists, considerable evidence indicates not only that it does exist but also that it is a lifelong disability.

Self-Test Questions

- What are the differences and similarities between the two major definitions of learning disabilities?
- Why can students be identified as having learning disabilities in one state or school district but not qualify for special education services elsewhere?
- Why is it correct to consider learning disabilities a lifelong condition?
- What are some learning characteristics that contribute to these students' poor academic performance?
- How might teachers and diagnosticians better identify students with ADHD who qualify for special education services and those who do not?

Challenge Question

- What constitutes an appropriate education for these students, and in what setting should it be provided?

We have all had the experience that no matter how hard we try, we have trouble understanding the information presented. In school we might sit through lectures and not understand the messages the instructor is trying to deliver. We may not understand the reading material for a particular class. We find it impossible to organize our thoughts to write a coherent essay or report. Sometimes we stumble over words and are unable to convey our thoughts, feelings, or knowledge. And occasionally we are uneasy and uncomfortable with other people. For most of us, these situations are infrequent. For people with **learning disabilities (LD)**, however, one or more of these situations is commonplace. People with learning disabilities belong to a group of very diverse individuals, but they do share one common problem: They do not learn in the same way or as efficiently as their nondisabled peers. Although most possess normal intelligence, their academic performance is significantly behind their classmates'. Some have great difficulty learning mathematics, but most find the mastery of reading and writing to be their most difficult challenge (Kavale & Forness, 1996).

In this chapter, you will come to understand learning disabilities. You will learn that because of this group's **heterogeneity**, there is no single answer about why such otherwise normal individuals have problems learning at the same rate and in the same style as their nondisabled classmates. You will learn that learning disabilities is the largest special education category, one that includes students who do not have this disability. You will also learn about students with learning disabilities who also have ADHD. As we begin the new millennium, professionals in this area have not come to agreement about how best to teach these individuals. However, you must recognize that many individuals overcome their learning disabilities through highly specialized, intensive, individualized instructional programs. Unfortunately, for many others, a learning disability will last a lifetime.

learning disabilities (LD). A disability in which the individual possesses average intelligence but is substantially delayed in academic achievement. **heterogeneity.** Variation among members in a group.

Opportunities for the New Millennium

Although learning disabilities is one of the newest special education categories, being initiated in the 1960s, study of history shows that this condition is not a phenomenon that began in the twentieth century. The American educational system is finally responding to a disability that had previously been either ignored or misdiagnosed. However, this burgeoning special education category is now serving over half of the children identified as having special education needs, and the numbers continue to increase year after year. Possibly, by the end of the century this field had lost its direction and was no longer serving its original purpose.

Legacies from the Twentieth Century Mostly in response to its increasing size, concerns about the learning disabilities category of special education were voiced across the last two decades of the twentieth century. Because the operational definition of this disability is so broad, identifying a student who is not succeeding in general education classes as having a learning disability is not difficult. So, some education professionals began to question whether learning disabilities was simply an educational response to students' failure in the general education curriculum rather than an actual disability. Had it become a "dumping ground" for unsuccessful students? Or could the students placed in this disability area possess different types of problems—some may actually have a disability, while others may be either low achieving or not performing well for a variety of reasons?

Thinking About Dilemmas to Solve As you read this chapter, think about children who are unable to achieve to their potential in the general education curriculum and the services and supports they need. Think about whether:

- This disability area should be discontinued and replaced with a more general "high incidence" special education category combining all mild disabilities
- The size of the category should be limited
- The operational definition should become more restrictive
- Research findings are leading to effective practices for a unique set of learners
- As with other disability areas, learning disabilities range from mild to severe cases

LEARNING DISABILITIES DEFINED

Students who qualify for special education services because of a learning disability must meet specific criteria established by the state and the school district in which they live. These criteria are based on the federal definition, but usually include some modifications suggested by professional and parent organizations. However, actual interpretation of the definition and identification of these students vary considerably from state to state (ranging from 5.8% of all schoolchildren to 1.7%), district to district, and even school services committee to school services committee (Lester & Kelman, 1997; MacMillan et al., 1998; Mercer et al., 1996).

Legacy: The heterogeneity of characteristics included in the definitions of learning disabilities contributes to the large size of this special education category.

Opportunities:

- Accept the wide range of abilities and problems associated with this disability
- Redefine the disability to be more restrictive

MAKING
CONNECTIONS

See the History Section of this chapter.

dyslexia. Severely impaired ability to read; presumed to be caused by a central nervous system dysfunction.
central nervous system dysfunction. Some brain or neurological damage that impedes individuals' motor and/or learning abilities.

Nationally, two definitions of learning disabilities are the basis for many states' definitions. One is included in the U.S. Department of Education's regulations for IDEA '97; the other was adopted by a coalition of professional and parent organizations concerned with learning disabilities. Here is the federal government's definition:

> "Specific learning disability" means a disorder in one or more of the basic psychological processes involved in understanding or in using language, spoken or written, that may manifest itself in an imperfect ability to listen, think, speak, read, write, spell, or to do mathematical calculations, including conditions as perceptual disabilities, brain injury, minimal brain dysfunction, dyslexia, and developmental aphasia. The term does not include learning problems that are primarily the result of visual, hearing, motor disabilities, mental retardation, emotional disturbance, or environmental, cultural, or economic disadvantages. (U.S. Department of Education, 1999)

The National Joint Committee on Learning Disabilities (NJCLD) definition is as follows:

> Learning disabilities is a general term that refers to a heterogeneous group of disorders manifested by significant difficulties in the acquisition and use of listening, speaking, reading, writing, reasoning or mathematical skills. These disorders are intrinsic to the individual, presumed to be due to central nervous system dysfunction, and may occur across the life span. Problems in self-regulatory behaviors, social perception, and social interaction may exist with learning disabilities but do not by themselves constitute a learning disability. Although learning disabilities may occur concomitantly with other handicapping conditions (for example, sensory impairment, mental retardation, serious emotional disturbance) or with extrinsic influences (such as cultural differences or insufficient or inappropriate instruction), they are not the result of those conditions or influences. (NJCLD, 1994)

Basically, the difference between these two definitions rests in orientation about the causes of the disability. The federal definition is older and has a medical orientation, reflecting the earliest work done in this field by doctors helping individuals who suffered injuries to the brain. Notice that terms like brain injury and **dyslexia** are included in the federal definition but not in the NJCLD definition. The NJCLD definition states that an individual's learning disability may be due to a **central nervous system dysfunction** but allows for the inclusion of individuals who do not have such a documented dysfunction. There are other differences between these two definitions; see whether you can identify several more.

The NJCLD definition requires that the primary reason for a student's disability be learning disabilities but allows for another disability as well. Therefore we now see educational records indicating that a student is deaf and has a learning disability, or is gifted and has a learning disability. Although many states insist that students be classified and served by their primary disability and will *not* "serve a student twice," professionals are becoming increasingly aware of students who have characteristics of learning disabilities along with other disabilities (Rock et al., 1997; Rosenberg, 1997). Of course, the combinations seem endless, but most commonly professionals see the strong relationships between early identification of language impairments and learning disabilities (Schoenbrodt et al., 1997). Also, gifted students with learning disabilities have received considerable attention from researchers and school district personnel for many years (Maker, 1986; Robinson, 1999).

Table 4.1 Key Features of Definitions of Learning Disabilities

Intelligence scores within the normal range

A significant discrepancy between academic achievement and expected potential

Not caused by other factors, such as cultural differences, educational opportunities, poverty, or other disabilities: the exclusion clause

Often manifested in language-related areas, such as communication, written language, or reading

Problems intrinsic to the individual involving that person's central nervous system, specific deficits in information processing, or the ability to learn

Learning problems specific and confined to one or two cognitive areas

See the section on gifted students with disabilities in Chapter 7.

The NJCLD definition also reflects the now acknowledged problems many of these individuals have in the social domain. For over fifteen years, parents and professionals have recognized a relationship between social skills and learning disabilities, with consensus that some 75% of these students have difficulty achieving social competence (Kavale & Forness, 1996). This characteristic might not be a defining characteristic of learning disabilities, but rather one more related to low achievement (Haager & Vaughn, 1995). Remember, however, the predominant problem these students face is developing academic competence, as reflected in their unexpected underachievement (Fuchs & Fuchs, 1998; MacMillan et al., 1998).

Considerable debate about the definition of learning disabilities, and which students should be identified as having this disability, raged during the twentieth century. Thus some argue that another definition of learning disabilities should be developed, and the search for better ways to operationalize a definition continues (Kauffman et al., 1998; NJCLD, 1998; Swanson, 1998). Why are there different positions about what a definition should include? Some differences are due to philosophical orientations about what causes the disability and how it should be treated. Some hold to a medical orientation; others believe that an educational framework should be used. Some believe that the current definition is not scientific enough, leaving the field open to politics (Kavale & Forness, 1998). Regardless, there appears to be consensus about some key features that define this disability; they are summarized in Table 4.1.

TYPES OF LEARNING DISABILITIES

For more information about ADHD, see:

- Problems of special education question in Chapter 1
- Sections about ADHD in the "Children with" sections of this chapter, Chapter 8, and Chapter 9

Because learning disabilities are manifested in different ways with different individuals, there is no uniform classification system for students with learning disabilities. According to the definitions of the disability, these students are supposed to have normal intelligence, but they do not achieve academically as well as could be expected. The most common problem is in the area of reading. Many of these students have other problems as well, such as poor social skills, different learning styles, and symptoms of ADHD. Such characteristics can interfere with efficient learning.

Practitioners typically do not further divide this large group of diverse learners into specific types. Although for many years researchers have worked to identify groups of individuals with learning disabilities, definitive groups have not yet been identified. Some researchers are focusing on subtypes by academic area (Padget,

Also refer to the section on Reading found in the Interventions section of this chapter.

1998), and others are focusing on psychological processes (Shafrir & Siegel, 1994). Other researchers are working to identify a clear neurological basis for many learning disabilities (Rourke, 1994). Such work is still in its formative stages and so far cannot give teachers useful information about how to work effectively with specific subgroups.

Remember, one defining characteristic of learning disabilities is "unexpected underachievement." In other words, these students perform significantly below their peers and below levels teachers and parents would expect from children of their ability. Often, their academic achievement in reading is significantly below the levels of their nondisabled classmates and is the most common reason for referrals to special education. In fact, reading problems are the basis for referral twice as often as mathematics problems (Kavale & Reese, 1992). Reading and writing, obviously, are important skills; in school, students must be able to read information from a variety of texts (social studies, science, literature) and write in varying formats (essays, reports, creative writing, notes). As the complexity of academic tasks increases, students who are not proficient in reading and writing cannot keep pace with the academic expectations of school settings. A small percentage of students with learning disabilities have difficulties only in mathematics; however, most find all areas of academics challenging. In the past, students with specific academic difficulties were grouped together. For example, those with severe reading problems were called dyslexic. Students with writing disorders were said to have **disgraphia,** and those unable to learn mathematics readily had **discalculia.** These terms imply that the individual has experienced brain injury that resulted in the disorder. Given that very few students with learning disabilities have documented brain damage, such terms should be applied cautiously.

Some youngsters with learning disabilities display behavioral problems along with poor academic performance. These characteristics are often associated with

One way to determine whether a child's academic achievement is equal to his overall intellectual abilities is to use standardized achievement tests. Another method is to collect data on his daily academic performance.

disgraphia. Severely impaired ability to write; presumed to be caused by central nervous system dysfunction.
discalculia. Severely impaired ability to calculate or perform mathematical functions; presumed to be caused by central nervous system dysfunction.

ADHD. For example, many are **hyperactive** or **impulsive,** seem unable to control their behavior, and display excessive movement. These children are unable to sit or concentrate for very long; their parents and teachers comment that they are in constant motion. Both hyperactivity and impulsivity are characteristics frequently associated with other disabilities (traumatic brain injury, emotional disturbance) as well as ADHD.

IDENTIFICATION

Some experts have referred to the category of learning disabilities as a "soft" form of disability, because it has no specific physical markers, like visual or auditory acuity, that can be reliably measured (Reschly, 1996). The key defining feature included in all definitions is a significant difference between intelligence and achievement. However, quantifying this discrepancy has proven difficult, complicated, and unreliable, making the category of learning disabilities in the last two decades of the twentieth century too inclusive and too large to many school district and government officials.

The majority of school districts' and states' identification policies require the use of **discrepancy formulas** to quantify the identification process. However, school services committees often ignore these policies and identify students as having learning disabilities who do not have the required discrepancy between their ability and academic expectations (Lester & Kelman, 1997; MacMillan et al., 1998). Why would they violate state and school district guidelines? The answers are many. In some cases, they are attempting to avoid negative labels such as mental retardation. In other instances, they are desperately trying to get special help to students who might not otherwise qualify for special education. Some of these students might not yet meet the cutoff score. For them, the current difference between achievement and intelligence is not great enough, but because of the growing disparity between these scores it is only a matter of time before their low academic achievement will qualify them for special services. Other students are low achievers, who perform to their expectations, demonstrate no discrepancy, but cannot keep up with their general education classmates. And some other students are linguistically diverse and are struggling to master English. For some of them, well-intentioned teachers refer them to special education in hopes of getting them the additional help they need to succeed in school.

Other criticisms about the use of discrepancy formulas to identify students with learning disabilities center on these assessment procedures (Tomasi & Weinberg, 1999). Discrepancy formulas are complicated, and are difficult to use. Therefore, some states have endorsed the use of special computer programs to compute the discrepancy between a student's achievement and intelligence scores, while others have developed printed tables for diagnosticians to use. This system is also being criticized because the results do not help teachers determine the effectiveness of classroom placements. These cumbersome systems have not met their purpose, for they have not accurately identified students with this disability, have not contained the numbers included in this category, and do not indicate the adequacy of student progress (Fletcher et al., 1998). How might these problems be solved?

Researchers and parent groups, like the Learning Disabilities Association (LDA), are suggesting that the field adopt alternative methods of assessment for identification purposes (Harrison, 1997). Some researchers believe that skills like listening, which are not currently measured, should become key components in the assessment

C O N N E C T I O N S
M A K I N G

In Chapter 3, review the sections about:
- Overrepresentation
- Prevalence

hyperactive. Impaired ability to sit or concentrate for long periods of time.

impulsive. Impaired ability to control one's own behavior.

discrepancy formulas. Formulas developed by state educational agencies or local districts to determine the difference between a child's actual achievement and expected achievement based on the student's IQ scores.

For a review of assessment procedures, see:
- The evaluation sections in Chapter 2
- The Identification sections (Defined) in Chapters 3, and 5–12

In Chapter 5, review the sections about:
- Communicative competence (Types of Language Impairments)
- Prevalence of preschoolers with language impairments

postsecondary. Education that comes after high school (e.g., community college, technical/vocational school, college, university, continuing education).

lateral dominance. A preference for using either the right or the left side of the body for one's motoric responses; some believe that mixed dominance or lateral confusion is associated with poor reading performance.

battery for learning disabilities (Fletcher et al., 1998). New assessment devices are doing just that. The *Learning Disabilities Diagnostic Inventory (LDDI)* has moved away from sole dependence on intelligence and achievement and measures students' abilities in: listening, speaking, reading, writing, mathematics, and reasoning. Other researchers advocate for different measurement systems, like curriculum based measurement (CBM) (Fuchs & Fuchs, 1998). CBM uses direct and frequent measurements of students' performance. Advocates of CBM indicate that this system is sensitive to different students' learning patterns and expectations. It can be used to compare one student's daily achievements and track trends across time with classmates'. And it provides useful feedback to teachers about the effectiveness of their instructional methods for the entire class.

SIGNIFICANCE

As with other groups of individuals with disabilities, those with learning disabilities range in abilities. Some children have a mild learning disability. With assistance, they profit from the standard curriculum offered in general education and are college bound. Children with severe disabilities, however, require intensive remediation and support throughout their schoolyears and into adulthood. Students with learning disabilities are different from their nondisabled classmates. These students are the lowest of low achievers (MacMillan et al., 1998).

Most children with learning disabilities are not identified as having a learning disability until they have attended school for several years. And what happens in those early schoolyears can set the stage for future success or failure. Parents and researchers are concerned about the growing trend, and governmental support, for grade retention (Cannon, 1998). While the call for the end of social promotion practices is being made by government officials and education policymakers alike, research results do support this practice. Retention actually increases the probability that a student will eventually drop out of school (New Mexico Learning Disabilities Association, 1994). Those who are retained once are 30% to 40% more likely to drop out, and those who have been retained twice have a 100% chance of leaving school before graduation. Despite the fact that retaining students does not improve either academic or social adjustment, 58% of students with learning disabilities had repeated a grade before being referred and identified as having a learning disability (McLeskey, 1992). Grade retention does not reduce costs either, and parents argue that school districts spend $13,000 for each grade repeated, money that should be spent on extra services, like summer school, smaller class size, and earlier identification for special education (Cannon, 1998; King, 1998). Because the outcomes for those who are retained are not good and because more and more of these students are being included in general education classes with fewer supports, it is important for educators and parents to change their beliefs about the effectiveness of retention.

As the demands of school increase, many of these students fall further and further behind their classmates in academic achievement. Most (60%) are identified by third grade (Kavale & Reese, 1992) when reading and writing take on greater importance. At this time, students begin to read textbooks to gain information and are required to write reports and themes. It is a time when curriculum materials require use and comprehension of figurative and symbolic language, communication skills that are difficult for many individuals with learning disabilities (Abrahamsen & Sprouse, 1995). Also, teachers expect students at this age to work at their desks independently for longer periods of time. Some develop behavioral problems, and many develop poor self-esteem (Kavale & Forness, 1996).

Most individuals with learning disabilities have a lifelong disability. Table 4.2 on page 134 shows that students' learning difficulties can be present from the pre-school years through adulthood. Some remedial procedures are effective, however, and Table 4.2 also describes a few treatment plans.

HISTORY OF THE FIELD

The field of learning disabilities began in the twentieth century. The term *learning disabilities* was coined on April 6, 1963, by Professor Sam Kirk and others at a meeting of parents and professionals in Chicago. From this date, the field of education has experienced an explosion in the number of pupils identified, teachers trained, and classroom programs offered. Services began in elementary schools, later extended to high schools, and continue to expand, as programs for **postsecondary** students and adults with disabilities proceed to develop.

Investigation of learning disabilities, however, put down roots long before 1963 (Wiederholt, 1974). In 1919, Kurt Goldstein began working with young men with brain injuries who had returned to the United States after World War I. He found many of them distractible, unable to attend to relevant cues, confused, and hyperactive. They also could no longer read or write well. Some years later, Alfred Strauss and Heinz Werner expanded on Goldstein's work. Strauss and Werner worked at the Wayne County Training Center in Michigan with pupils who were thought to be brain injured. They found many similarities to the group of World War I veterans that Goldstein had studied earlier. However, there was one important difference between these two groups: Goldstein's group lost their abilities to read, write, and speak well; Strauss and Werner's group had never developed these abilities. Study of learning disabilities thus originated in the work of these pioneers, and their concentration on brain injury continues to affect the field today.

During the 1920s and 1930s, Samuel Orton, a specialist in neurology, developed theories and remedial reading techniques for children with severe reading problems, whom he called "dyslexic" and believed to be brain damaged. He emphasized the importance of **lateral dominance.** In the late 1930s, Newell Kephart worked with Strauss at the Wayne County School and further studied a group of children who were considered to have mental retardation but behaved like Goldstein's brain-injured subjects. Both Kephart and Laura Lehtinen developed teaching methods for what they thought were a distinct subgroup of children with disabilities. Kephart's approach was motoric; he sought to remediate these children's difficulties through physical

NEW DIRECTIONS
FOR THE
MILLENNIUM

Legacy: In desperate searches for techniques and approaches that would solve learning disabilities, parents and teachers have submitted children to one ineffective strategy after another only to be disappointed time and time again.

Opportunities:

- Insist that research be carefully and systematically conducted before approaches are adopted
- Special educators become sophisticated "consumers of research" and evaluate the effectiveness of the procedures they select with each individual student

Sam Kirk is considered by many to be the "father" of the field of learning disabilities, in part because he helped coin the term at a meeting in 1963 of what was to become the Learning Disabilities Association of America.

Table 4.2 Life Span View of Learning Disabilities

	Preschool	Grades K–1	Grades 2–6	Grades 7–12	Adult
Problem areas	Delay in developmental milestones (e.g., walking) Receptive language Expressive language Visual perception Auditory perception Short attention span Hyperactivity	Academic readiness skills (e.g., alphabet knowledge, quantitative concepts, directional concepts, etc.) Receptive language Expressive language Visual perception Auditory perception Gross and fine motor Attention Hyperactivity Social skills	Reading skills Arithmetic skills Written expression Verbal expression Receptive language Attention span Hyperactivity Social-emotional	Reading skills Arithmetic skills Written expression Verbal expression Listening skills Study skills (metacognition) Social-emotional-delinquency	Reading skills Arithmetic skills Written expression Verbal expression Listening skills Study skills Social-emotional
Assessment	Prediction of high risk for later learning problems	Prediction of high risk for later learning problems	Identification of learning disabilities	Identification of learning disabilities	Identification of learning disabilities
Treatment types	Preventive	Preventive	Remedial Corrective	Remedial Corrective Compensatory Learning strategies	Remedial Corrective Compensatory Learning strategies
Treatments with most research and/or expert support	Direct instruction in language skills Behavior management Parent training	Direct instruction in academic and language areas Behavior management Parent training	Direct instruction in academic areas Behavior management Self-control training Parent training	Direct instruction in academic areas Tutoring in subject areas Direct instruction in learning strategies (study skill) Self-control training Curriculum alternatives	Direct instruction in academic areas Tutoring in subject (college) or job area Compensatory instruction (e.g., using aids such as tape recorder, calculator, computer, dictionary) Direct instruction in learning strategies

Source: Students with Learning Disabilities (4th ed., p. 50) by C. Mercer, 1991. Reprinted by permission of Prentice-Hall, Inc., Upper Saddle River, NJ.

Evaluate the effectiveness of these approaches by reading again the Development of Informed and Effective Solutions section in Chapter 1.

Review the Problems of Special Education question (Legacies of the 20th Century) in Chapter 1.

process/product debate. Argument that either perceptual training or direct instruction was more effective for instruction.

direct instruction. Specifically focusing instruction on the desired, targeted behavior.

Attribute Treatment Interaction Approach. Selecting instructional methods that match a student's modality strength; visual learners receive visually-based procedures, and so on.

exercises. Lehtinen developed a set of instructional procedures similar to those used by some classroom teachers today. At about the same time, Sam Kirk, who also worked at the Wayne County School, helped to develop a set of word drills and other teaching procedures he referred to throughout his career. In 1961, he and his colleagues published the *Illinois Test of Psycholinguistic Abilities (ITPA)*. Although developed to identify individuals' strengths and weaknesses and their learning styles and preferences (whether they learned better by seeing or by hearing information presented), it was used for many years to identify students with learning disabilities.

During the early years of learning disabilities programs, professionals supported perceptual approaches. In the 1960s, Marianne Frostig, for example, developed materials that were used to improve students' visual perceptual performance. The thought was that many students with learning disabilities were unable to process information accurately through the visual channel. So the logic was that if their visual perceptual skills were enhanced, their reading abilities would also show improvement. The 1970s saw the field of learning disabilities embroiled in heated debate about perceptual training, or process, approaches and their use in the remediation of students' academic deficits. This debate, which raged for years, seriously divided the field and was known as the **process/product debate.** The dispute was resolved when research data showed that perceptual approaches were seldom effective in teaching academic skills, and **direct instruction** techniques do make a difference (Hammill & Larsen, 1974). Remnants of this debate continue today, as educators argue about the effectiveness of the **Attribute Treatment Interaction Approach.** This approach supports the belief that the best way to teach these students is to match teaching method with each student's modality strength. Visual learners should be taught using procedures that use the visual channels, auditory learners should profit most from oral instructions, and so on. The concept has considerable allure, or what some have called "irresistable appeal," and many teachers today believe that this approach must be effective. Unfortunately, this has not proven to be the case (Kavale et al., 1998).

Periodically across the twentieth century, various fads that were supposed to remediate learning disabilities became popular with the press and the public. One fad suggested teaching students with learning disabilities to crawl again, regardless of their age. Others claimed that various diets improved students' academic and behavioral performances. Fluorescent lighting was blamed as the cause of learning disabilities. Plants placed on students' desks were given credit for improving academic skills. In most of these instances, people made claims about students' improvement, but offered little if any research data to support the method being advocated. Parents spent considerable money, time, and resources chasing one cure after another, but the problems did not disappear. The best tool we have for evaluating recommended programs is research. To be better consumers, parents, and advocates, we must consistently and persistently ask for data that prove the benefits of such treatments.

PREVALENCE

Great concern about this category of disabilities is felt by many professionals and parents. With charges that special education is too expensive and expenditures being some 2.3 times that of general education, one major concern is the size of this category (Parrish, 1995). Another concern, as mentioned earlier, is the inclusion of students who do not have a disability or have a different disability, like mental retardation, which is a disability that with the proper application of the definition cannot coexist with learning disabilities (MacMillan et al., 1998). These considerations have caused some researchers to call the category of learning disabilities a "dumping ground" where any student unsuccessful in the general education curriculum can be placed (Reschly, 1996).

Learning disabilities has grown to be the largest category of exceptional learners in the United States, with about two and a half million children (5% of the nation's schoolchildren and over half of all special education students) identified as having learning disabilities. The number and percentage of students served in the learning disabilities category has grown since the original passage of IDEA. In 1976–1977, almost 25% of schoolchildren with disabilities had a learning disability, while today it is well over 50%. The rate at which learning disabilities has increased far surpasses that for students with speech or language impairments or behavioral disorders, while the prevalence of students with mental retardation and has decreased slightly over the years. These relationships are shown in Figure 4.1.

How much might ADHD contribute to the prevalence of learning disabilities? As you will learn in the remaining sections of this chapter, many of the behaviors associated with learning disabilities are also associated with ADHD. IDEA '97 includes ADHD under the category of "Other Health Impaired" and stresses that to qualify for special education services the condition must adversely affect educational performance. The What IDEA '97 Says box about ADHD gives more information. One very carefully conducted study gives us a hint about the ratio of students with learning

Figure 4.1 The Relationship Among the Number of Children with Learning Disabilities, Mental Retardation, Emotional Disturbance, and Speech or Language Impairments Served under IDEA, Ages 6 to 21: School Years 1987–88 through 1996–97.

Source: From the *Twentieth Annual Report to Congress on the Implementation of the Individuals with Disabilities Education Act,* U.S. Department of Education, 1999. Washington, DC: Government Printing Office.

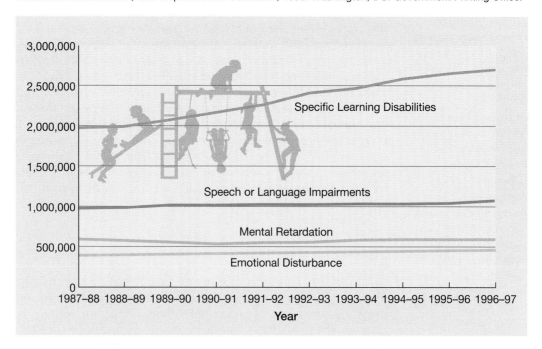

What IDEA '97 Says About

Attention Deficit Hyperactivity Disorder (ADHD)

- Children with ADHD are not automatically protected by IDEA '97
- All children with ADHD, even those with medical diagnoses and medication, clearly are *not* eligible for special education or related services
- Some children with ADHD are eligible for special education under categories, like learning disabilities, health impairments, and emotional disturbance
- To receive special education the condition must adversely affect educational performance
- The only category where ADHD is specifically called out is health impairments. Not all disabilities or conditions are named in IDEA '97 (e.g., Tourette's syndrome)

disabilities who also have ADHD (Mac-Millan et al., 1998). When strictly adhering to state guidelines, of the twenty-nine students the researchers identified as having learning disabilities, nine (or 31%) also met the criteria for identification as having ADHD. Might ADHD, then, be the reason for the increased number of students identified with learning disabilities? Probably not: 48% of the students the school district identified as having learning disabilities did not when state definitions and guidelines were followed. In these researchers' analyses of the sixty-one students identified as having learning disabilities, ten did not meet the criterion for any special education category and nineteen had IQ scores below 76, which should have qualified them for services in the mental retardation category.

So is the overidentification of students in the learning disabilities category a problem? Does it matter, if a child qualifies for special education, what label he or she receives? If a student is performing poorly at school, is it more important to follow state guidelines for identification as having a disability or to get the student special services? These are serious questions that professionals, parents, state legislators, educators, and the federal government need to answer early in this new millennium. The answers are far reaching: They will affect the lives of students and their families. They will affect entire school systems because they influence how many students are served without special education supports by general educators and could alter the depth of content covered and the instructional methods used.

CAUSES AND PREVENTION

People with learning disabilities comprise a heterogeneous group of individuals. Their learning disabilities are manifested in different ways and at different levels of severity. Unfortunately, researchers do not have much concrete information about the causes of learning disabilities (Bender, 1998; Hallahan et al., 1996).

CAUSES

As the field has wrestled with definitions of learning disabilities, so too has it argued over the causes of the problem. Little is actually known about the causes of learning disabilities, but we can presume that students who have them are as diverse as are the types. Some students may have a central nervous system dysfunction that inhibits their learning. Some may have proven brain damage—caused by an accident or by a lack of oxygen before, during, or after birth—resulting in neurological difficulties that affect their ability to learn. Some may have inherited their disability, and as we learn more about genes, this association will become clearer (Decker & Defries, 1980, 1981; New Mexico Learning Disabilities Association, 1994; Oliver et al., 1991). Diet and various environmental factors have also been suggested as causes of learning disabilities.

Teachers need to recognize the uncertainty about what causes learning disabilities and not make assumptions about the students they teach. In the majority of cases of learning disabilities, there is no physical evidence or actual medical diagnosis of brain injury or damage to the central nervous system. Using terms like *assumed brain injury* or *presumed central nervous system dysfunction* may lead to a conclusion that cannot be proven and may be misleading. The use of the term *brain injury* can give the impression that nothing can be done about the condition. This impression can lead parents, educators, and the individuals concerned to give up or not try to remediate identified educational difficulties. They might also set expectations too low. We know from research on education that when expectations and goals are set low, they are usually met but not exceeded. For a child with a learning disability, if goals are set too low, the child may never reach his or her potential. For these reasons, many special educators oppose the use of medical terms associated with brain injury.

PREVENTION

In Chapter 5, review all of the sections about language impairments, particularly in these sections:

• Identification
• Causes
• Children with

In Chapter 3, see Education and the Preschool Child.

Providing guidelines about preventing learning disabilities is difficult because we cannot pinpoint causes. Methods of preventing or reducing the effects of this disability do exist, however. For instance, developing adequate language and sound awareness skills, particularly during the preschool years, may be beneficial, as shown by apparently strong relationships between poor language development and learning disabilities (Schoenbrodt et al., 1997; Wallach & Butler, 1995). Young children who do not develop good language skills during their early childhood years tend to be at risk for academic problems during their later schoolyears. Children who develop language very late tend to have poor cognition; they do not reason or solve problems well. And children who do not learn to recognize and discriminate sounds in the words they hear are at risk for reading problems. There is strong evidence that early intervention programs, such as Headstart and other well-structured preschool programs, positively influence children's language and thinking skills and their later success in school (Currie & Thomas, 1995). Children who are at risk or show developmental lags in these areas should be referred to an early intervention program, even if they have not yet been identified as having a disability.

Special instruction programs during the schoolyears, as you will learn later in this chapter, can make a real difference. Instruction sensitive to individual differences in learning rates and styles includes different amounts of drill, practice, and review. Many experts believe that these youngsters may not process information properly or may need to learn how to learn (Bos & Vaughn, 1994; Deshler & Schumaker, 1986; Lerner, 1993). Those who do not receive enough repetition to master the skills being taught are left behind. Because the concept currently taught often builds on one that was just presented, lack of mastery of basic concepts could result in children falling further and further behind their peers' academic achievement. To prevent the compounding effects of learning disabilities, these children need special assistance, either from a special educator or their general education teacher, as soon as possible.

CHILDREN WITH LEARNING DISABILITIES

Providing a profile for children with learning disabilities is difficult because the most cited characteristic of this group is their individual differences. Time after time, reference is made to the group's heterogeneity (Haager & Vaughn, 1995). Despite the diversity in this group of learners, many of these youngsters share some common characteristics and patterns of behavior that have been noted by their teachers, peers, and parents (see Table 4.3 for a listing of these). In this section, you will find information about these students' typical learning and social characteristics, and you will also learn about a condition—attention deficit hyperactivity disorder—that is often a secondary diagnosis for children with learning disabilities.

LEARNING CHARACTERISTICS

Let's be clear. The predominant problem of all students with learning disabilities is learning and mastering academic tasks (Fuchs & Fuchs, 1998; Kavale & Forness, 1996). These students' low achievement is often described as unexpected, because it is far below what their intellectual abilities would predict, and it is below that of almost all of their classmates (Gresham et al., 1996). Although individuals might differ in their strengths and weaknesses, learning styles, and personalities, all have learning difficulties that result in poor academic performance. For most, the learning impairment is so severe that by the time they are in high school, they are many years behind their classmates in achievement. Many researchers feel that the following learning characteristics impede these students' abilities to learn efficiently:

Table 4.3 Signs or Characteristics of Learning Disabilities

Academic	Social	Behavioral Style
Exhibits a significant discrepancy between potential and achievement	Possesses immature social skills	Does not pay attention during lectures or class discussions; distractible
Demonstrates an inability to solve problems	Chooses less socially acceptable behavior patterns	Exhibits excessive movement; hyperactive
Experiences substantial delays in academic achievement	Misinterprets social and nonverbal cues	Is impulsive
Has uneven academic abilities	Makes poor decisions	Has poor motor coordination and spatial relation skills
Is not actively involved in learning tasks	Is victimized more often	Is disorganized
Evidences poor language and/or cognitive development	Cannot predict behavioral consequences	Seems poorly motivated
Has not acquired basic reading and decoding skills	Uses social conventions (manners) improperly	Tends to be overreliant on teacher and peers for class assignments
	Experiences rejection from peers	
	Is too trusting of others' motivations and sincerity; naive	
	Is shy, withdrawn, and distractible	

Motivation and attribution are directly related to success in school. Many students with learning disabilities become poorly motivated to accomplish educational tasks and may attribute their difficulties to external factors.

lack of motivation, inattention, inability to generalize, and insufficient problem solving, information processing, and thinking skills (Rivera & Smith, 1997). Depending on a student's learning style, altering these characteristics can lead to substantial improvement in achievement.

Motivation and Attribution. **Motivation** is usually defined as the inner stimulus that causes individuals to be energized and directed in their behavior. Motivation can be explained as a person's trait (a need to succeed, a need not to fail, a great interest in a topic) or as a temporary state of mind (a test or class presentation tomorrow, a passing interest in the topic). **Attributions** are the self-explanations about the reasons for one's success or failure. Differences in motivation and attributions may account for differences in the way people approach tasks and for differences in their success with those tasks. Clearly, year after year of frustration and failure at school can affect students' motivation and their approach to the task of learning.

By the time most students are identified as having a learning disability, they have experienced many years of failure. Research findings show that many students with learning disabilities, probably because of their excessive number of failure experiences, have a greater incidence of overall negative attitudes (Yasutake & Bryan, 1995). School failure can result in both academic and motivational deficits and, in turn, poor motivation can contribute to poor academic performance (Hock, 1997). Students can develop a negative attitude and come to believe that their failure is a result of lack of ability, rather than a signal to work harder or ask for help. They lower their expectations and believe that success is an unattainable goal. They do not believe in themselves and do not try to learn. When people expect to fail, they can also become too dependent on others—a situation referred to as **learned helplessness**—and increase the likelihood of poor performance. They come to believe that they are not responsible for their achievements and that luck is the reason for their successes and failures, not effort (Pearl, 1982; Switzky & Schultz, 1988). Also, a student who has a fear of failure or low self-esteem is less likely to have a positive motivation to learn. Teachers can help students overcome these problems by involving the student in the learning process, responding positively, praising students, promoting mastery, and creating a challenging and stimulating instructional environment (Dev, 1997). Further, students benefit by being shown the relationship between effort and accomplishment, and teaching them learning strategies they know are effective (Hock, 1997; Sexton et al., 1998).

Students who expect academic failure tend to be passive. This trait is seen in many students with learning disabilities, who are said to be **inactive learners** (Torgesen & Licht, 1983). They do not approach the learning task purposefully and are not actively involved in their learning. They do not ask questions, seek help, or read other related material to learn more. They often attribute their success to luck rather than to their abilities or effort (Dohrn & Bryan, 1994), and 70% attribute poor performance to lack of ability (Kavale & Forness, 1996). These characteristics are just the opposite of those of **high achievers,** who tend to expect success and view it as an

motivation. Internal incentives that are influenced by previous success or failure.
attributions. The explanations individuals give themselves for their successes or failures.
learned helplessness. A phenomenon in which individuals gradually, usually as a result of repeated failure or control by others, become less willing to attempt tasks.

A fuller section about ADHD is found later in this section of this chapter.

inactive learners. Students who do not become involved in learning situations, do not approach the learning task purposefully, do not ask questions, do not seek help, or do not initiate learning.

high achievers. Students who expect success and view it as an incentive to work harder.

low achievers. Students who expect failure and see little use in expending effort to learn.

attention deficits. A characteristic often associated with learning disabilities in which students do not pay attention to the task or the correct features of a task to learn how to perform it well.

advance organizers. Previews to lectures that acquaint students with the content, its organization, and importance.

generalization. The transfer of learning from particular instances to other environments, people, times, and events.

incentive to work harder. Thus students with learning disabilities tend to be **low achievers;** they expect failure and see no use in expending more effort.

By comparing low-achieving students' motivation and attributions with those of high-achieving students, we can better understand the concepts of attribution and learned helplessness. Let's look at a classroom situation, such as writing a social studies term paper, to see how students' motivation affects the way they approach the task. High achievers, when given the assignment of writing a term paper on, say, the Revolutionary War, approach the task with confidence, knowing that they are capable of producing a thorough and well-written paper. They realize that if they read their textbook and other materials available at the library, they will know enough about the topic to prepare the paper. Because of past successes, they know that making an effort results in success. Therefore these students will proofread their term papers and even add extras (such as maps and diagrams) to their final products. The low-achieving students, in contrast, do not approach this assignment with much vigor. They seem overwhelmed by the assignment and complain that it is too difficult. These children believe that it is useless to ask for assistance, spend time in the library, or read extra materials. Instead, they write a short and incomplete term paper that is probably not developed with care or proofread.

Attributions and motivation can be altered (Fulk, 1996). With intensive efforts from teachers and parents, youngsters can learn that their efforts can lead to success. Students and adults need to discuss actual performance and how it can be improved. Students also need to be helped to approach learning strategically; they need to be taught strategies for approaching the learning task. For example, by breaking tasks into smaller units, students realize that many tasks are easily mastered and are not as difficult as originally perceived and that with more effort and greater persistence success can be achieved.

Attention Deficits. Another learning characteristic commonly observed by teachers and researchers is inattention, or **attention deficits** (Mercer, 1997). Children who do not focus on the task to be learned or who pay attention to the wrong features of the task are said to be distractible. One characteristic of students with learning disabilities and also ADHD is impulsivity. This factor may be why these children are unable to focus on the relevant components of problems that need to be solved or tasks that need to be learned, and why they may disrupt the learning environment for an entire class. (See the Achieving Discipline box for a suggestion about how to solve this problem.)

A related problem is developing good organizational skills (Stormont-Spurgin, 1997). Becoming better organized can be taught though a variety of means: classmates helping each other, better communication between home and school, rewards, and structured routines and lists. Clearly, creating structure helps students become better organized and also contributes to focusing attention so learning is more probable. Several researchers (Lenz et al., 1987) have found that **advance organizers,** like those found at the beginning of every chapter in this text, help to focus students' attention by providing an introductory overview of the material to be presented. These introductory statements explain why the information is important and provide a key to the crucial elements of the presentation.

Generalization. Most students with learning disabilities also have difficulty transferring or generalizing their learning to different skills or situations (Rivera & Smith, 1997). They might apply a newly learned study skill in history class but not in English class. Or a child might master borrowing in subtraction with a zero in the

Achieving Discipline

CREATE A COMMUNITY OF HELPERS: PEER MANAGEMENT

Marc, a student with both learning disabilities and ADHD, was a fourth-grader at Pearson Elementary School. He had a terrible time concentrating on his school work, seemed always to be restless, and had poor basic reading and writing skills. Ms. Reilly's general education class was a bit larger than she wanted, particularly with the number of special education students she had included in her class. Marc kept disturbing everyone by interrupting class discussions, Ms. Reilly's presentations, and small group work. It seemed that Marc was getting all of the attention, and instructional time was being reduced. Ms. Reilly feared that the entire class was suffering, not only from Marc's disruptions but also from her being distracted, and he was not the only child who needed special attention!

She decided that she could not accomplish her goals alone. She needed a new plan, one that would first address small group work, a time when chaos seemed to be the greatest. Ms. Reilly held several class discussions about the situation. Students talked about their frustrations with not being able to get their work done, and the difficulties they had when their attention was disrupted. The class agreed that intervention was needed, that they could work together, and evaluate the intervention's effectiveness. The students agreed to help each other with their group assignments and also with staying on task. The students wanted their teacher to move from group to group, helping them with the assignments. So Ms. Reilly divided her thirty students into six groups of five, and was careful to create groups which were equally represented by academically strong students, students

with special needs, and youngsters who understood the classroom rules and were well behaved. She also carefully considered individual students she assigned to each group, not mixing children who did not get along. Each time the class worked in small groups, she reminded them of their individual commitments to help each other and work together cooperatively. She also had students create records about their progress. The class learned a lot. First, they learned that classmates can help each other in many ways. They can help each other behave more appropriately, learn, and complete their academic assignments. Most important, students are a key part of the environment that fosters a climate of support for each other. Whether students serve as peer tutors, where they help each other with academic assignments, or behavioral managers, where they model expected behavior or dispense praise and rewards, students themselves are powerful assets in the instructional setting.

Steps used to create a community of helpers

- The teacher included her students in describing the problem.
- The teacher and students worked together to identify some solutions.
- Everyone made a commitment to help each other.
- Ability groups were mixed.
- The intervention was phased in, and not scheduled for all types of activities across the entire day.
- They included an evaluation component to the intervention process.

MAKING CONNECTIONS

For other useful strategies see the Achieving Discipline boxes found in each chapter.

units column but not apply that rule when borrowing with two zeros. Again, research has shown that some teaching methods can actually interfere with students learning the concept of generalization (Ellis, 1986). The overuse of feedback on performance (knowledge of results) reinforces dependency, learned helplessness, and learning inactivity.

Teachers help students learn to generalize by having students take more responsibility for managing their own instructional programs. For example, a special education teacher who is concerned about a student who is not applying a recently learned study skill to a general education science class might remind the student to use the

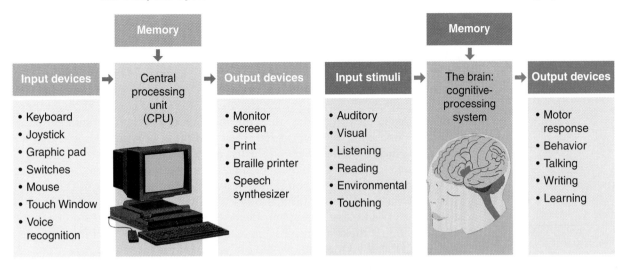

The Computer System

Input devices	Memory ↓ Central processing unit (CPU)	Output devices
• Keyboard • Joystick • Graphic pad • Switches • Mouse • Touch Window • Voice recognition		• Monitor screen • Print • Braille printer • Speech synthesizer

The Human Information-Processing System

Input stimuli	Memory ↓ The brain: cognitive-processing system	Output devices
• Auditory • Visual • Listening • Reading • Environmental • Touching		• Motor response • Behavior • Talking • Writing • Learning

Figure 4.2 Information Processing Theory and Its Similarities to the Computer System
Source: Lerner, Janet, *Learning Disabilities: Theories, Diagnosis, and Teaching Strategies*, Sixth Edition. Copyright © 1993 by Houghton Mifflin Company. Adapted with permission.

study skill when preparing for the next science test. Next, the teacher might collaborate with the science teacher, explaining the strategy and asking that teacher to remind the student to apply the strategy while studying. Then the special education teacher might ask the student to keep a record of the times the strategy was used. Finally, the teacher might reward the student for improved performance in science class.

Processing Information. Many people with learning disabilities have difficulty learning to read and write, understanding things they are told, and even expressing themselves through oral communication. To explain why, researchers are studying theories of learning and then applying them to the way students with learning disabilities actually learn. One theory, **information processing**, follows the flow of information while people learn new skills; the theory begins with the input of information, shows how information is processed, and ends with its output. Lerner (1993) helps us to understand this theory by comparing the way computers work and the way people learn (see Figure 4.2). Like the computer, the human brain takes in information, processes that information (makes associations, stores information, calls it up, acts upon it), and generates responses from it. This model is currently guiding researchers in their study of students with learning disabilities and how they learn (Swanson, 1987, 1990).

> **information-processing theory.** Suggests that learning disabilities are caused by an inability to organize thinking and approach learning tasks systematically.

Even though research on information processing is preliminary, it provides educators with some guidelines for the instructional process. To benefit from the information they receive in class, students must pay attention and must remember the information. Educators can help by repeating important information, presenting material that is organized and grouped in a systematic fashion, and providing students with information that is meaningful to them and associated with other information they are already familiar with. In addition, educators can help students manipulate information—that is, use the information in their writings and discussions.

Problem Solving and Thinking Skills. Many researchers feel that students with learning disabilities have poor **problem solving** and thinking skills (Rivera & Smith, 1997). They are not strategic learners. To study efficiently and remember content, students must be proficient in the following thinking skills: classifying, associating, and sequencing. **Classifying** allows the learner to categorize and group items together by common characteristics. Usually, people will remember more items in a list if they approach the task by **chunking,** or clustering, the information presented. For example, if you forget your grocery list and are already at the store, you might try to remember what items you need by thinking about groups of items. You might recall that potatoes and corn were on the list when you think of vegetables and that ice cream, pizza, and TV dinners were on the list when you think of frozen foods.

People are more strategic in their learning and remembering when they relate or associate information by some common denominator (for example, softness or hardness, style of painting). **Association** also helps individuals see the relationships that exist among and between different knowledge bases. By associating facts or ideas, the mind is able to find the relationships and connections that units of information possess. By using this thinking skill, people can relate information on different dimensions. **Sequencing** information also facilitates memory and learning. Items can be sequenced in many ways. For example, physical items can be sorted and sequenced by size, weight, or volume. Facts, events, and ideas can be sequenced by time, importance, or complexity. These thinking skills—classifying, associating, and sequencing—help students approach learning tasks more purposefully. With guided practice, these abstract skills can be learned and developed into useful tools for learning.

SOCIAL SKILLS CHARACTERISTICS

Although deficits in social skills may not be the defining characteristic of learning disabilities, problems in this area are quite common (Bryan, 1997). Overwhelmingly, teachers rate their students with learning disabilities significantly lower in social competence and school adjustment than their other students (Tur-Kaspa & Bryan, 1995). Pervasive problems in the social domain, particularly when they persist into adulthood, can be devastating to both the individuals and their family members (Bryan, 1994). Because of the importance of developing friends, getting along with others, and understanding appropriate social interaction conventions, let's look at two important areas: social competence and social status.

Social competence relates in some way to almost all actions and skills that people perform. It is the ability to perceive and interpret social situations, generate appropriate social responses, and interact with others. Through a comprehensive analysis of 152 independent research studies, Kavale and Forness (1996) found that almost 80% of students with learning disabilities are perceived to have a deficit in social competence. More than any other group of students, including those with other disabilities, boys with learning disabilities feel alienated, which results in their seeking to avoid everything and everyone connected with school (Fulk et al., 1998). They are naive and unable to accurately judge other people's intentions (Donahue, 1997). This trusting nature can get them into trouble.

Social competence and communicative competence are related because many skills associated with understanding and using language are also associated with social abilities. How might language be associated with social competence? Many students with learning disabilities do not understand implied messages, abstractions, or nonliteral language. This point was well illustrated in a study about these students'

problem solving. Finding answers or solutions to situations.
classifying. The ability to categorize items or concepts by their common characteristics.
chunking. Grouping information into smaller pieces so that it can be more easily remembered.
association. In thinking, the ability to see relationships among different concepts or knowledge bases.
sequencing. Mentally categorizing and putting items, facts, or ideas in order according to various dimensions.
social competence. The ability to understand social situations, respond to others appropriately, and interact with other people.

Read the Social
Competence Section
found in the Children
with Speech or
Language Impairment
section of Chapter 5.

abilities to comprehend the moral messages included in fables (brief tales in which animals replace human characters and relate indirect messages that have great social meaning). This study showed that students with learning disabilities do not comprehend the meaning of these stories, cannot understand even rudimentary metaphors, and are unable to create meaning from abstract language (Abrahamsen & Sprouse, 1995). Such inability in pragmatic language skills, once again, demonstrates the relationship between communicative competence and social competence. It is important to realize the broad and negative impact that lack of communicative competence can have on an individual's overall performance: understanding stories read in the general education class, grasping teachers' explanations of concepts, and understanding the implicit rules of social interactions.

Difficulty with social skills, coupled with low achievement and inappropriate classroom behavior, influences the social status of children with learning disabilities. Teachers note that these children often are not accepted by their classmates and have difficulties making friends. These children, regardless of placement, are rejected by their classmates without learning disabilities and are considered by their teachers to be poorly adjusted (Kavale & Forness, 1996). They are less likely to be selected for extracurricular activities, which also reduces the likelihood of their developing leadership skills, friendships, and a sense of competence outside of academic situations (Geisthardt & Munsch, 1996). Parents suggest that their children's social immaturity and social skills deficits are the primary reason for their children's lack of friends (Wiener & Sunohara, 1998). The social status of these children needs to be given greater attention by educators and parents.

Signs of these problems begin early, during the preschool years, as these children experience strong feelings of loneliness and lack of friends (Margalit, 1998; Tur-Kaspa et al., 1998). And rejection and inadequate social skills persist through adolescence (Hartas & Donahue, 1997). During the later schoolyears, they do not seek the support of peers or friends as do their classmates without disabilities, leaving them with feelings of rejection and isolation. Of even more concern is their tendency to be victimized—threatened, physically assaulted, subjected to theft of their belongings—more than their peers (Sabornie, 1994). In particular, children who either act out or are withdrawn are more likely to be rejected by their nondisabled classmates. However, students with learning disabilities who did not display either behavioral excesses or deficits did not experience rejection from their peers (Roberts & Zubrick, 1993). Teachers can play an instrumental role in reducing

Although a learning disability is usually thought of in terms of academic problems, many students with this disability lack friends and are excluded from social interactions with classmates. Teachers can help children become more sensitive to each others' feelings and encourage them to play in group activities during recess.

peer rejection by pairing these students with nondisabled classmates in areas of mutual interest. For example, teachers might plan activities for which students with common interests (sports, music, hobbies) are assigned to work together on an academic task such as a social studies report.

ATTENTION DEFICIT HYPERACTIVITY DISORDER

See the section on ADHD in the Children with EBD section of Chapter 8.

Sometimes called attention deficit disorder (ADD), **attention deficit hyperactivity disorder (ADHD)** has been estimated to affect between 10% and 20% of the school-age population in the United States (Shaywitz & Shaywitz, 1992). This condition can be confusing to parents, professionals, and people in the community. The story of Joey Pigza, taken from a popular book, also shows the confusion these individuals experience themselves (see Joey's story in the accompanying box).

The Story of Joey Pigza

At school they say I'm wired bad, or wired mad, or wired sad, or wired glad, depending on my mood and what teacher has ended up with me. But there is no doubt about it, I'm wired.

This year was no different. When I started out all the days there looked about the same. In the morning I'd be okay and follow along in class. But after lunch, when my meds had worn down, it was nothing but trouble for me.

One day, we were doing math drills in class and every time Mrs. Maxy asked a question, like "What's nine times nine?" I'd raise my hand because I'm really quick at math. But each time she called on me, even though I knew the answer, I'd just blurt out, "Can I get back to you on that?" Then I'd nearly fall out of my chair from laughing. And she'd give me that white-lipped look which meant, "Settle down." But I didn't and kept raising my hand each time she asked a question until finally no other kid would raise their hand because they knew what was coming between me and Mrs. Maxy.

"Okay, Joey," she'd say, calling on me and staring hard at my face as if her eyes were long fingers that could grip me by the chin. I'd stare right back and hesitate a second as if I was planning to answer the question and then I'd holler out really loud, "Can I get back to you on that?" Finally, after a bunch of times of me doing that in a row, she jerked her thumb toward the door. "Out in the hall," she said. And the class cracked up.

So I went and stood in the hall for about a second until I remembered the mini-Superball in my pocket and started to bounce it off the lockers and ceiling and after Mrs. Deebs in the next class stuck her head out her door and yelled, "Hey, cut the racket," like she was yelling at a stray cat, I remembered something I wanted to try. I had seen the Tasmanian Devil on TV whirling around like a top so I unbuckled my belt and pulled on the end really hard, as if I was trying to start a lawn mower. But that didn't get me spinning very fast. So I took out my high-top shoelaces and tied them together and then to the belt and wrapped it all around my waist. Then I grabbed one end and yanked on it and sort of got myself spinning. I kept doing it until I got better and better and before long I was bouncing off the lockers because I was dizzy too.

Then I gave myself one more really good pull on the belt and because I was already dizzy I got going really fast and began to snort and grunt like the Tasmanian Devil until Mrs. Maxy came out and clamped her hands down on my shoulders. She stopped me so fast I spun right out of my shoes and they went shooting up the hall.

"You glue your feet to the floor for five whole minutes or you can just spin yourself down to the principal's office," she said. "Now, what is your choice going to be?"

"Can I get back to you on that?" I asked.

Source: From *Joey Pigza Swallowed the Key*, pp. 3–6, by Jack Gantos, 1998, New York: Farrar, Straus, and Giroux.

Not all students diagnosed as having ADHD qualify for special education services (Lerner et al., 1995). Those who do are covered by various special education categories and are considered to have a coexisting condition. Most have the primary identification of learning disabilities, others are identified as having behavior disorders, and a few have ADHD and another disability. These children's primary problem is neither intellectual, emotional, or the result of defiance, but they do not meet expectations of their families or of school. Hyperactivity and attention problems are common among children with learning disabilities and are characteristics of the ADHD condition. Also, children with ADHD are at significant risk for academic failure, as are children with learning disabilities (Riccio, Gonzalez, & Hynd, 1994). Therefore it is not surprising that some 25% to 50% of children with ADHD are identified as having learning disabilities as well (Shelton & Barkley, 1994).

So, what is ADHD? According to the *DSM-IV* (American Psychiatric Association, 1994), ADHD "is a persistent pattern of inattention and/or hyperactivity-impulsivity that is more frequent and severe than is typically observed in individuals at a comparable level of development" (p. 78). Symptoms of the condition must occur in more than one setting. The *DSM-IV* also establishes criteria for determining whether a child has ADHD; those criteria are listed in Table 4.4 on page 148. As you read this table, think about what ADHD is and what it is not.

Although the *DSM-IV* definition is widely accepted in the United States, it is not the definition used worldwide. In Europe, particularly in Britain, the World Health Organization's definition is more commonly accepted, and results in fewer students being identified with this condition (Reason, 1999). This definition requires that the individual have *both* significant inattention and hyperactivity. When both characteristics are required, the prevalence falls to between 0.5% and 1% of the student population, as compared to the range of 2% to 10% identified in the United States. A key difference between these two definitions is the emphasis on problems associated with impulsivity, and British psychologists believe that their more stringent view of ADHD reduces the risk of including children from different cultural backgrounds who come from homes where behaviors expected in school are not instilled from early childhood.

How does a teacher help the student with ADHD? Like their counterparts who only have learning disabilities, students with ADHD respond well to highly structured learning environments where topics are taught directly. Professionals suggest that carefully planned educational procedures, such as giving rewards, making assignments more interesting, letting students chose their academic assignments from a group of alternatives selected by the teacher, shortening the task, giving clear and precise instructions are effective procedures that can lead to academic improvement (Lerner et al., 1995; Powell & Nelson, 1997). Peer tutoring has proven to be very effective with students with ADHD, as well as those with learning disabilities (Fuchs & Fuchs, 1998; DuPaul et al., 1998). Over 50% improvement in academic tasks has been achieved by involving peers in the instructional program. Although it is important for teachers and parents to pay attention to these students' academic problems, it is also imperative that they help these students develop social skills that are acceptable to their peers.

Students with ADHD, whether also having learning disabilities or not, are often rejected by their peers because of their hyperactivity and poor social skills (Bryan, 1997). Rejection by classmates can leave these children lonely and without friends. They come to judge themselves as social failures and tend to engage in solitary activities (playing computer games, watching television, feeling sorry for themselves).

attention deficit hyperactivity disorder (ADHD). A condition that describes students who display hyperactive behaviors, have difficulty attending to the task at hand, and tend to be impulsive.

Table 4.4 *DSM-IV* Diagnostic Criteria for Attention Deficit/Hyperactivity Disorder

Either inattention or hyperactivity/impulsivity must have persisted for at least six months. Either condition must be at a level that is both maladaptive and inconsistent with development and must include six (or more) of the following symptoms:

Inattention

- Often fails to give close attention to details or makes careless mistakes in schoolwork, work, or other activities
- Often has difficulty sustaining attention in tasks or play activities
- Often does not seem to listen when spoken to directly
- Often does not follow through on instructions and fails to finish schoolwork, chores, or duties in the workplace (not due to oppositional behavior or failure to understand instructions)
- Often has difficulty organizing tasks and activities
- Often avoids, dislikes, or is reluctant to engage in tasks that require sustained mental effort (such as schoolwork or homework)
- Often loses things necessary for tasks or activities (e.g., toys, school assignments, pencils, books, or tools)
- Is often easily distracted by extraneous stimuli
- Is often forgetful in daily activities

Hyperactivity/Impulsivity

- Often fidgets with hands or feet or squirms in seat
- Often leaves seat in classroom or in other situations in which remaining seated is expected
- Often runs about or climbs excessively in situations in which it is inappropriate (in adolescents or adults, may be limited to subjective feelings of restlessness)
- Often has difficulty playing or engaging in leisure activities quietly
- Is often "on the go" or often acts as if "driven by a motor"
- Often talks excessively
- Often blurts out answers before questions have been completed
- Often has difficulty awaiting turn
- Often interrupts or intrudes on others (e.g., butts into conversations or games)

Also, some hyperactive-impulsive or inattentive symptoms were present before age 7 years.

The symptoms must be present in two or more settings (e.g., at school [or work] and at home).

Clear evidence of clinically significant impairment in social, academic, or occupational functioning must be demonstrated.

The symptoms do not occur exclusively during the course of a pervasive developmental disorder, schizophrenia, or other psychotic disorder and are not better accounted for by another mental disorder (e.g., mood disorder, anxiety disorder, disassociative disorder, or a personality disorder).

Source: Reprinted with permission from the *Diagnostic and Statistical Manual of Mental Disorders,* Fourth Edition (*DSM-IV*), pp. 83–85. Washington, DC: American Psychiatric Association, 1994.

This characteristic contributes to more alienation and withdrawal. Classroom behavior that classmates find more desirable can be improved by using direct instruction techniques. For example, self-management strategies that include contingencies for conforming to classroom rules improve behavior (Shapiro et al., 1998). For those who do not qualify for special education services, general educators must accommodate their problems and differences in learning styles by providing them with instruction that meets their individual needs.

Many physicians prescribe drugs, such as Ritalin or Dexedrine, to help children with ADHD focus their attention on assigned tasks (Gulley & Northup, 1997). Controversy surrounds the usefulness of behavior-control drugs for these youngsters, though. Clinical evidence indicates that these drugs are effective in reducing the hyperactivity for some of these children but that the drugs do not seem to positively influence academic performance. For many, the drugs are unnecessary and can even be harmful (Armstrong, 1995). Instead, behavioral techniques, direct and systematic instruction that is evaluated on a frequent basis, and highly motivating instructional materials have proven successful with many children currently identified as having ADHD.

EDUCATIONAL INTERVENTIONS

You have already learned that considerable debate surrounds the issue of properly identifying students with learning disabilities. Professionals also debate the content of educational programs and where students are best educated. In this section, you will learn about educational programs for students with learning disabilities, programs that span preschool through young adulthood. You will learn about the successes, failures, and work that still needs to be done. You will also learn of some alarming data about the dropout rate of students with learning disabilities and why transitional services for these youngsters are so important. The issues presented here have not been resolved and will require the attention of current and future special education professionals.

EDUCATION AND THE PRESCHOOL CHILD

CONNECTIONS
MAKING

- Chapter 3, Prevention section discusses the benefits of early intervention programs, particularly Headstart.
- Also, see the Prevention section of this chapter.

Many professionals are reluctant to identify or label children as having a learning disability in the preschool years or even by first grade. One reason is that young children do not develop at exactly the same rate, and some youngsters are not as ready for school as their classmates. Some children may not have developed as quickly as their peers but do not have a disability and will catch up. Still others are the youngest in their class and are not and should not be developmentally equal to their classmates. Because of the close ties between learning disabilities and language abilities, many children who are later identified as having a reading problem or a learning disability are identified during their preschool years as having a language impairment (Schoenbrodt et al., 1997; Webster et al., 1997). And, for all children who appear to be delayed in developing language and pre-academic skills or show signs of being at risk for school failure, there is a growing trend to not assign a categorical label to them, but rather to serve them in noncategorical programs (McCarthy et al., 1997).

Although educators are reluctant to label preschoolers as having a disability, there are several good reasons for identifying those who are at risk for disabilities or show early signs of having a disability. First, the effects of early intervention are powerful, and children who would benefit from special programs at an early age should receive these services as soon as possible. Who might be likely candidates? Children who are not talking by age 3 and children who were low birth weight and premature babies are at risk for developing learning disabilities, and benefit from good early childhood programs (American Academy of Pediatrics, 1992). And young children who are not developing skills related to later reading abilities benefit from specific instruction (Torgesen & Wagner, 1998). New, exciting research about precursors to

Learning basic reading skills, like sound to symbol relationships, is essential for reading success. Students who do not learn these skills naturally, must receive direct instruction aimed at achieving mastery.

reading have promise of reducing reading difficulties experienced by many students by the third grade. Let's take a look at these new findings. The link between phonological awareness and successful early reading performance is now confirmed (Majsterek & Ellenwood, 1995). Phonological awareness is the ability to identify sound segments in words (the three sounds in *cat*) and the ability to manipulate sound segments (understanding that *fall* and *wall* rhyme). Those preschoolers who cannot identify letters and cannot correctly associate sounds with their symbols should be candidates for direct instruction on such reading skills during first grade. According to Reid Lyon of the National Institutes of Health's Child Health and Human Development Branch, some 20% of young children have difficulty with phonological awareness and about 7% to 10% have major problems. He is convinced that if these children do not receive direct instruction on phonics by age 9, 70% of them will have problems through high school (CEC Today, 1995).

The relationship between long-term reading achievement and early instruction that promotes **phonemic awareness** is clear (Torgesen et al., 1994). This awareness is demonstrated by an ability to divide words into segments even smaller than syllables and is clearly a precursor to later reading abilities. So, is it possible to identify very young children who are likely to experience difficulties in mastering reading during the schoolyears? The answer now is yes. Researchers have identified a number of skills that are related to later success in reading (Badian, 1998; Torgesen & Wagner, 1998). What are the predictors of reading failure? Young children who have problems with the following skills also seem to have problems learning to read:

- Letter naming
- Sentence memory
- Decoding words quickly and accurately
- Naming items they have seen
- Having an awareness of rhymes
- Demonstrating phonological awareness (being able to break words into sound parts)
- Color naming

So why are researchers and teachers excited by these findings? Not only is it important to be able to identify skills related to later reading abilities, but it is now known that these early precursors of reading can be taught and later reading failure avoided or minimized (Chard & Dickson, 1999; Lyon & Moats, 1997; Smith, 1998;

phonemic awareness. An oral language skill that enables children to understand words can be represented in print.

Vandervelden & Siegel, 1997). Being able to not only identify discrete characteristics that contribute to later academic problems, but also to prevent later difficulties with interventions that preschool and elementary school teachers can easily implement, provide great promise that reading failure can be reduced significantly.

Teachers need to remember that classrooms need to support the acquisition of reading skills and comprehension. Children also need to learn that reading is important to them and that it is fun. "Literacy rich environments" can help preschoolers gain these skills and attitudes (Katims, 1994). By retelling and reenacting their favorite stories, the important concept that print has meaning is understood early and becomes a foundation to future instruction.

EDUCATION AND THE SCHOOLCHILD

As we discussed, most students with learning disabilities have not learned how to learn. They are not well organized and do not approach learning situations strategically. Teachers can help them become more efficient and effective by incorporating some simple principles into the classroom setting. So many easy-to-use and proven instructional methods for students with learning disabilities have been verified (Lovitt, 1995) that it was difficult deciding which ones to highlight in this chapter. Two areas have been selected for discussion: reading and learning strategies. Because reading is so central to academic success and it is the most prevalent problem for this population of learners, and since some important new research findings are available in this area, it merits some focus. Also, because "learning how to learn" is often posed as an area on which teachers must concentrate, and the learning strategies approach has proven so effective, a section is devoted to this topic.

Particularly for students with learning disabilities, it is important to underscore two important principles: Select instructional techniques that are verified through rigorous research, and collect information about the effectiveness of the methods selected for each student. The field of learning disabilities, in particular, has a history of advocating one instructional method after another that has not been thoroughly tested first. There are many examples to cite, but let's take sensory integration as a case in point. Sensory integration is based on the importance of sensory (visual, auditory, tactile) stimulation, particularly in the context of motor activity. It is from this theory that perceptual motor training as a prerequisite to reading instruction for students with learning disabilities gets its roots. Years ago, elementary-age children were taught to crawl again, engage in patterning exercises, walk balance beams, make angels in the snow, and draw lines on dittos from one pattern to another. These sensory integration activities were thought to be related to improved reading. Periodically, despite consistent evidence that these procedures are absolutely ineffective, they gain in popularity (Hoehn & Baumeister, 1994). Unfortunately, teachers do not carefully select their instructional procedures from those proven effective through carefully conducted research or do not know how to implement proven methods (Talbott et al., 1994). For example, a National Institutes of Health study found that only 10% of teachers know how to teach reading to students who do not acquire this skill naturally (*New York Times*, 1997). It may not be as exciting to use **best practices** that are "tried and true" as to use those that sound new and innovative, but that may well be our obligation to the students we are responsible to teach. Educators must become good consumers, and "shop" for the instructional tactics they use as they would shop for major, personal purchases. For example, many school district administrators have selected SUCCESS for ALL, an instructional and

MAKING
CONNECTIONS

- For proven instructional practices, see the Research to Practice boxes in this and the remaining chapters in the text.
- Review again the discussion in Chapter 1 about special education interventions proven through research.

best practices. Instructional techniques or methods proven through research to be effective.

curriculum package which addresses all instructional targets, not just reading (Slavin, 1997). It is based on solid research findings and is very effective with students who are at great risk for poor academic performance and for dropping out of school.

Besides using instructional methods that have passed the scrutiny of research, it is very important that teachers be certain the tactics they select are actually working with each student. Remember, students with learning disabilities comprise a heterogeneous group of learners, each possessing different learning needs and styles. Therefore it is necessary to ensure that the "right" instructional method has been selected, and to do that requires that data be collected about how well the student is performing the academic task being taught. Curriculum based measurement (CBM), whereby students' performance on each learning task is evaluated directly to determine whether the intervention is effective, whether the intervention is effective enough, and whether the child's progress is sufficient to move on to other tasks. So, now let's turn our attention to the area of reading.

Reading. Of this there is no doubt: Most students with learning disabilities have difficulty learning to read. Unfortunately, these students are not alone. Reading is a problem area for many Americans, with some estimating that 20% of children and adults have significant difficulties learning to read (Lyon & Moats, 1997). Because this basic skill is used in almost all other curriculum areas, students must receive as much effective instruction as possible in this area. As you have learned, research conducted in the 1990s helps teachers identify preschoolers who are at risk for reading failure and offers ways to prevent these youngsters from having reading problems during the schoolyears. But what about those students who continue to have difficulties mastering reading after third grade?

Fortunately, research findings give teachers guidance. And while some techniques are highly effective, others are not. Let's first turn our attention to one popular method which, for students having difficulties acquiring reading, is not effective. The whole language approach is widely used in general education classes. It emphasizes the "wholeness" of reading and writing and seeks complete infusion into the entire curriculum. All methods that promote "natural learning" are encouraged, but direct instruction on decoding, isolated vocabulary development, or discrete skills that are components of the reading process is considered unacceptable (Mather, 1992). Teaching independent skills, such as sound–symbol associations, is also not endorsed. Reading is integrated into the entire curriculum, across the school day, for the entire class. For children experiencing reading failure, including those with learning disabilities, "substantial contemporary evidence documents the efficacy of explicit systematic instruction of important reading skills—that is, research supports practices explicitly inconsistent with whole language" (Pressley & Rankin, 1994, p. 161). Research has shown that the whole language approach is not effective for students with learning disabilities (Mastropieri & Scruggs, 1997; Mather, 1992).

For students who do not learn to read as most of their classmates do, teachers need to select individualized instructional procedures that systematically and explicitly focus on the basic skills (phonics) and component parts (sound blending) of reading (Lovett & Steinback, 1997; Lyon & Moats, 1997). Direct instruction on these basic skills helps students to decode words, but for many continued specific instruction aimed at the improvement of reading comprehension is necessary. Here research findings are again helpful. The following tactics have proven helpful in improving reading comprehension: teacher-lead questioning, text enhancements (like illustrations and study guides), students restating the content of passages just read,

NEW DIRECTIONS
FOR THE
MILLENNIUM

Legacy: Disagreements between special and general educators about effective methods to teach reading persist, the result being children who lack proficiency in the basic skills necessary to succeed in the later years of school.

Opportunities:

- Make instructional decisions, regardless of placement, based on the educational outcomes of individual students
- Use more than one reading method (e.g., whole language) in general education settings

MAKING CONNECTIONS
Curriculum based measurement (CBM) is also discussed in Chapters 2 and 4.

skill based instruction (vocabulary development, decoding words) and rewards, and increased fluency in oral reading rates (Bakken, Mastropieri, & Scruggs, 1997; Biemiller & Siegel, 1997; Lebzelter & Nowacek, 1999; Markell & Deno, 1997). Others have found that a technique called "cooperative story mapping" also promotes greater reading comprehension (Mathes et al., 1997; Swanson & De La Paz, 1998). Using this procedure, children work together in groups and develop a graphic representation of the elements of the story they have just read. Every story map includes information about: the main character, setting, problem (what the main character must solve), major events, and the outcome of the story.

Many teachers are most excited about PALS, an instructional tactic that consistently improved the reading performance of students often referred to as difficult to teach. PALS, which stands for peer-assisted learning strategies, is implemented for entire classes of students. This highly effective technique is effective with a wide range of students who attend general education classes (Fuchs & Fuchs, 1998; Fuchs et al., 1997). PALS was developed by Lynn and Doug Fuchs and has received national awards; it is described in the nearby Research to Practice box. Teaching students with learning disabilities how to read can be an arduous task, with each component skill requiring teacher-directed instruction (Prater et al., 1998). The teaching tactics that are successful in teaching these skills often vary by student. For this reason, many teachers incorporate CBM into their teaching routines to ensure that their instruction continues to be as powerful as possible.

Learning Strategies. Experts in the field of learning disabilities consistently advocate that these students receive direct instruction in learning how to learn. To accomplish this, specialists recommend a **learning strategies** approach. For those working with middle school and secondary students, researchers at the University of Kansas Center for Research on Learning have diligently worked for years to develop and verify the usefulness of this approach (Deshler et al., 1996; Deshler & Schumaker, 1986). The results are impressive! The learning strategies method helps students learn and remember information more efficiently. For many years, teachers of these students practiced "crisis teaching"—that is, they tutored their students with learning disabilities to prepare for imminent academic crises, so that they might have a better chance of receiving a passing grade on tomorrow's test or term paper. The learning strategies approach goes beyond crisis teaching and helps students meet the demands of the general education secondary curriculum. Another strategy has students group activities by main ideas and details, which helps them remember a great amount of information. Youngsters are also taught how to read difficult passages in high school social studies and science texts and how to write themes and reports in systematic ways. In addition, strategies have been developed that help students study more efficiently and take tests more effectively.

Key features of the University of Kansas approach are that the materials, which are highly structured, all use advance organizers, **mnemonics,** and built-in systems of evaluation. Mnemonics have proven to be effective memory aids (Mastropieri & Scruggs, 1998; Mastropieri, Scruggs, & Whedon, 1997). For example, many people remember the names of the Great Lakes by associating them with the mnemonic HOMES (Huron, Ontario, Michigan, Erie, and Superior).

Other researchers have developed teaching tactics that include many of the elements found in the Kansas learning strategies approach—advance organizers, mnemonics, systematic instruction, CBM measures. They, too, have proven to be powerful interventions with this group of learners. For example, Mastropieri and Scruggs

---

MAKING CONNECTIONS

For other examples of learning strategies, see:
- The Student's Resource Manual that accompanies this text
- The Advance Organizers and accompanying summary section and questions that are found at the beginning and end of each chapter in this text

learning strategies. Instructional methods to help students read, comprehend, and study better by helping them organize and collect information strategically.

mnemonics. A learning strategy that promotes the remembering of names by associating the first letters of items in a list with a word, sentence, or picture.

Research to Practice: Teaching with Confidence

PEER-ASSISTED LEARNING STRATEGIES (PALS): HELPING TEACHERS FACE THE CHALLENGE OF STUDENT DIVERSITY

LYNN FUCHS AND DOUGLAS FUCHS

RESEARCH

PALS was developed for reading in grades K–12, and for math in grades 2–6. Research indicates that, when used within general education classrooms, PALS improves the reading and math achievement of students with disabilities along with their low-, mid-, and high-achieving classmates. Based on this strong research base for PALS, the U.S. Department of Education, Program Effectiveness Panel, has awarded PALS its "Certificate of Validation."

TO PRACTICE

With PALS, a teacher pairs all the students in her class; each dyad includes a stronger- and a weaker-performing student. During classwide peer tutoring sessions, students in each pair take turns helping each other on highly structured activities. Teachers use PALS to supplement their reading and mathematics instructional programs so that students receive additional instruction and practice on skills and strategies with which they need extra help.

In reading at grades 2–6, for example, students practice three structured activities during each PALS session. In *Partner Reading,* one student in the pair reads aloud for five minutes, while the other student monitors and corrects reading errors; then, students take turns retelling the events that occurred in the story. In *Paragraph Shrinking,* students take turns reading paragraphs. After each paragraph, the student identifies the main idea by stating who or what the paragraph was mainly about, identifying the most important thing about the who or what, and shrinking this information to ten or fewer words. In *Prediction Relay,* students take turns making predictions. They predict what will occur next in the story; they read aloud the next page; they confirm or correct their prediction; they generate a main idea statement; they then formulate their next prediction; and so on.

Using this basic structure, teachers differentiate activities according to students' needs by varying the types and difficulty levels of the reading material. Also, as needed, they incorporate PALS decoding activities developed for beginning readers.

(1998) have developed the pictorial mnemonic, a tactic that uses a visual image to help children remember important information. Figure 4.3 shows the illustration used to help them remember which animals are vertebrates. Other researchers have shown that math test scores improve when students are taught to be more strategic (organized and preparatory in the way they approached the problems). For example, they were taught to prepare for the next test by reviewing the problems they had correctly solved on the previous test. While taking the test, they were taught to do the problems they were sure of first, circle the number of each problem they were "kinda sure of" as a marker to come back to those first, and then tackle the ones they did not think they knew how to solve (Winnery & Fuchs, 1993). Another example was applied to difficult spelling words (Greene, 1994). Children are taught to use cues (like making the two *o* letters in the middle of the word *look* into eyes) to help

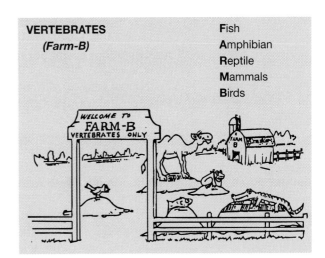

Figure 4.3 A Pictorial Mnemonic Representation of the Vertebrates: Fish, Amphibians, Reptiles, Mammals, and Birds.

Source: From *A Practical Guide for Teaching Science to Students with Special Needs in Inclusive Settings,* p. 158, by M. A. Mastropieri and T. E. Scruggs, 1993, Austin, TX: Pro-Ed. Reprinted by permission.

them remember the correct spelling for words they find difficult. Clearly, this group of tactics, often generally referred to as "learning strategies," have met the test. They have been proved through research to be effective tactics with many students with learning disabilities. Teachers also indicate that students enjoy creating their own mnemonics and strategies.

COLLABORATION FOR INCLUSION

The majority of parents of children with learning disabilities and professionals agree: Most students with learning disabilities should receive a substantial proportion of their education in general education classrooms alongside their nondisabled peers. And their education *must* be accompanied by an array of special services, supports, and curricular options that will meet their individual needs. Although some educators believe that the general education setting should be the "only" placement option for students with learning disabilities, a recent court decision reminds us that there is no single answer to "What is the least restrictive environment for the education of students with learning disabilities?" In fact, in *Zumwalt School District v. Missouri State Board of Education,* the courts ruled that the school district should pay for the cost of a private, segregated school because the student's self-esteem, behavior, and academics were negatively affected by his association with students from whom he felt different (Kahn, 1996).

Many parents and professionals worry about the implementation of a full inclusion policy for students with learning disabilities (Council for Learning Disabilities, 1993; Learning Disabilities Association, 1994; National Joint Committee on Learning Disabilities, 1993). They are concerned that the array of special services now available will disappear and that in the future the general education option, without sufficient supports, will be the only one available. They also worry about the current emphasis on national assessments and high test scores. What is the underlying concern? It is that such efforts will become disincentives to include students with learning disabilities. The outcomes could be higher referrals of non–academically competitive students to special education and ultimately a higher dropout rate for students with learning disabilities. How can their fears be put to rest? The only way is to be certain that students with learning disabilities receive effective instruction that helps them achieve their individual goals and the outcomes of adult independence and fulfillment. First, let's take a closer look at the reasons for concerns about inclusion, and then let's see how those problems can be overcome.

Not all general education instructional procedures or organizational structures foster positive results for these students with disabilities. The accommodations required to attain the desired outcomes for a student can take teacher's time and extra planning (see the Accommodating for Inclusive Environments box for some ideas). Sometimes this is more time that a teacher has available to spend for the benefit of one student. Some special education instructional methods are inconsistent with the philosophy of some general education teachers. For example, general education teachers use group, rather than individualized, instruction. They tend not to make special arrangements for students with special needs, even when only 40% of them are successfully participating in a group activity (O'Connor & Jenkins, 1996a). Possibly because of the importance of getting through an assignment and moving on to the next, little if any time is spent on direct reading instruction (word analysis or reading strategies) (O'Connor & Jenkins, 1996b). Other findings also show that when attending most general education settings, these students do not receive differentiated instruction (tailored to their individual needs), are not engaged in the learning process, participate very little, interact with their teachers and fellow students infrequently, and make few academic gains (McIntosh et al., 1993; Zigmond & Baker, 1994). And some research shows that some special education strategies might not be as effective in general education settings (Scanlon et al., 1996). Also, when compared with students who learned strategies in a special education setting and applied them in a general education setting, these students had much poorer outcomes in strategy mastery and use.

General education placements can be positive for students with learning disabilities, but for this to occur requires special educators and general educators to work closely together. Collaboration is one key to the development of successful educational experiences for students who are difficult to teach (Friend and Bursuck, 1999). "True" collaboration exists under some important conditions:

- Participation is voluntary
- Parity exists in the relationship
- Goals are shared
- Responsibility for outcome-accountability is mutual
- Decision making is done as a team
- Resources are pooled
- Trust and respect are the basis of the partnership

When characteristics of collaborative settings exist, all students profit. General education students can benefit from the unique expertise of the special educator, and students with disabilities find the general education classroom responsive to their learning needs. Collaboration requires communication, planning, and continual evaluation of students' performance. Figure 4.4 on page 158 provides excellent examples of the questions that teachers working together should ask each other. Although designed to address assistive technology needs of students with learning disabilities, the questions listed could be applied to almost every curriculum area.

Years of research findings show that there is no single answer to what comprises an appropriate or effective education for these students (Roberts & Mather, 1995).

MAKING CONNECTIONS

For more suggestions on accommodating students' learning needs in general education settings, see the Accommodating for Inclusive Environments boxes found in Chapters 3 through 12.

Accommodating for Inclusive Environments

STEPS FOR SUCCESS IN THE ACADEMIC CURRICULUM

1. *Provide structure and a standard set of expectations:*
   Help students develop organizational skills,
   Establish sets of rules for academic and social activities and tasks.
   Adhere to a well-planned schedule.
   Match your language to the comprehension level of the student.
   Be consistent.

2. *Adjust instructional materials and activities:*
   Individualize instruction; be sure the reading level is appropriate.
   Break tasks down into smaller pieces (or chunks).
   Begin lessons with advance organizers.
   Supplement oral and written assignments with learning aids (computers).
   Assign a peer tutor.
   Modify tests, allowing the student to take more time or complete it in a different way (listen to a tape of the test).

   Evaluate the effectiveness of your instructional interventions and when they are not effective, change them.

3. *Give students feedback and reinforcement for success:*
   Tell students when they are behaving properly.
   Reward students for improvement.
   Praise students when they have done well or accomplished a goal.
   Inform students when they are not meeting expectations.
   Encourage students to develop partnerships among each other, and reinforce those who do so.

4. *Make tasks interesting:*
   Develop attention by making assignments interesting and novel.
   Vary the format of instruction and activities.
   Use high-interest curriculum materials.
   Encourage students to work together during extracurricular activities.

Even in the best settings, where teachers are well-informed about instructional practices that have been verified through research and where collaboration between special educators and general educators is ongoing, individual students' progress must be carefully monitored (Vaughn et al., 1998). While some students make excellent progress in general education settings, others do not. Teachers must be responsive to students' instructional needs; they need to know when the instructional program needs to be adjusted.

Which students placed in general education classes are particularly at risk for continued poor academic performance? Very poor readers are the most likely candidates. In fact, in one research study these students made no progress over an entire school year (Klingner et al., 1998). Why might this be so? Students with very serious reading problems in grades 3 through 6 tend not to profit from group instruction. They do, however, benefit from one-on-one intensive reading instruction (Torgesen et al., 1997).

There are other differences between the education delivered in special education settings and general education settings. These findings imply the need for a continuum or an array of special education offerings. The question then arises: For students with learning disabilities, is special education a good or bad alternative? When asked, these students seem to support special education classes (Guterman,

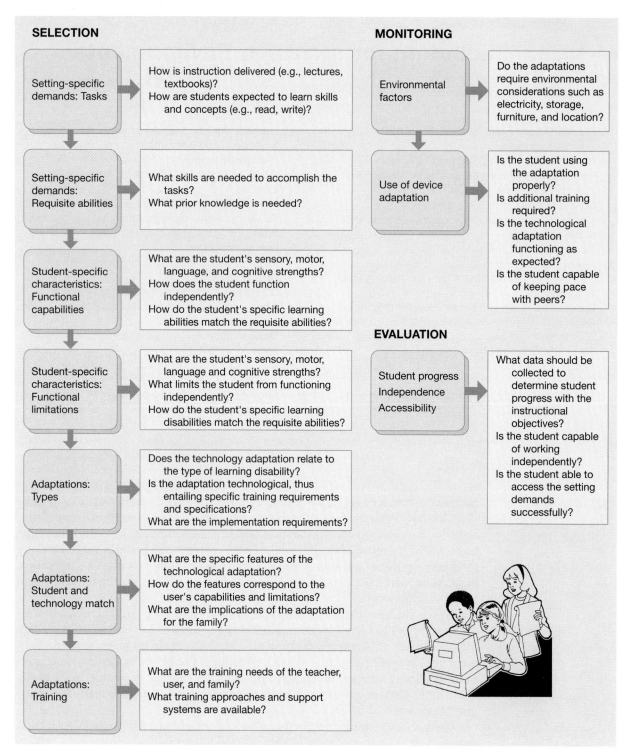

SELECTION

Setting-specific demands: Tasks	How is instruction delivered (e.g., lectures, textbooks)? How are students expected to learn skills and concepts (e.g., read, write)?
Setting-specific demands: Requisite abilities	What skills are needed to accomplish the tasks? What prior knowledge is needed?
Student-specific characteristics: Functional capabilities	What are the student's sensory, motor, language, and cognitive strengths? How does the student function independently? How do the student's specific learning abilities match the requisite abilities?
Student-specific characteristics: Functional limitations	What are the student's sensory, motor, language and cognitive strengths? What limits the student from functioning independently? How do the student's specific learning disabilities match the requisite abilities?
Adaptations: Types	Does the technology adaptation relate to the type of learning disability? Is the adaptation technological, thus entailing specific training requirements and specifications? What are the implementation requirements?
Adaptations: Student and technology match	What are the specific features of the technological adaptation? How do the features correspond to the user's capabilities and limitations? What are the implications of the adaptation for the family?
Adaptations: Training	What are the training needs of the teacher, user, and family? What training approaches and support systems are available?

MONITORING

Environmental factors	Do the adaptations require environmental considerations such as electricity, storage, furniture, and location?
Use of device adaptation	Is the student using the adaptation properly? Is additional training required? Is the technological adaptation functioning as expected? Is the student capable of keeping pace with peers?

EVALUATION

Student progress Independence Accessibility	What data should be collected to determine student progress with the instructional objectives? Is the student capable of working independently? Is the student able to access the setting demands successfully?

Figure 4.4 Assistive Technology Adaptation—Integration Questions.

Source: From "Using assistive technology adaptations to include students with learning disabilities in cooperative learning activities" by D. P. Bryant and B. R. Bryant, 1998, *Journal of Learning Disabilities, 31,* p. 45. Reprinted by permission.

1995; Padeliadu & Zigmond, 1996). They understand that they get more academic assistance in these settings where the environment is more reinforcing and organized. Because of such results, many professionals and parents argue that a full continuum and array of educational options must be retained and be available for these students.

The type of educational and supportive programs a student with learning disabilities receives must be determined by that child's individual needs, wherever the program is delivered. Most students with learning disabilities included in the general education classroom need at least some extra assistance and accommodations. They might require the adaptation and modification of commercially available textbooks and instructional materials. They may require more instructional time for explanations, drill, practice, and feedback. In many cases, these students need to learn how to apply a specific strategy to the learning process; others require some tutoring in mastering academic tasks. Some students with learning disabilities do not profit from the standard curriculum used in general education. For them, an educational experience with a life-skills, functional, or vocational emphasis is more appropriate. Of this there is no doubt: For students with disabilities to achieve their potential requires many partnerships, along with real collaboration between general and special educators.

TRANSITION THROUGH ADULTHOOD

The experiences of adults with learning disabilities are about as varied as the population itself (Patton & Blalock, 1996a). Many drop out of high school, and yet others complete graduate school; some become chronically unemployed, and others become successful professionals. Reports about highly successful adults who had problems in school because of learning disabilities have colored the public's perception about the devastating effects of this disability. Stories about highly successful adults who had or have learning disabilities are often told. For example, Hans Christian Andersen, Leonardo da Vinci, Thomas Edison, Nelson Rockefeller, and Woodrow Wilson are thought to have had a learning disability. Some present-day celebrities—Cher, Magic Johnson, Brook Theiss, Bruce Jenner, and Greg Louganis, among others—have acknowledged having a learning disability. Charles Schwab, the millionaire discount broker, has also revealed his lifelong reading problem (Colvin, 1996). Schwab's significant learning disability created challenges for him, particularly throughout his academic career. These public figures show the gains that an individual with a learning disability can make. Such cases are not typical, however.

Longitudinal or follow-up studies provide valuable information about how adults with learning disabilities fare in society. These studies give us insight into the nature of this disability, and should inform educators about the educational requirements of these individuals while in elementary, middle, and secondary schools, and the types of support they need throughout their lives. Here are a few of the dismal adult outcomes found in these research studies. Many of these adults

- Left high school without a diploma (Aune & Friehe, 1996; Dunn, 1996)
- Are unemployed or underemployed at far greater rates than their special education and general education classmates (Blalock, 1997; Murray et al., 1997; Sitlington & Frank, 1993)

Dropout rates are also discussed in Chapters 3 and 8.

- Do not possess the basic mathematical skills necessary for daily living (Johnson & Blalock, 1987)
- Are extremely dependent upon their families (White, 1992)
- Have difficulties with social relationships and desperately wish to have friends (Learning Disabilities Association of America, 1994)
- Regardless of their abilities, work in fast-food and service-related jobs that do not require them to read or write (Haring et al., 1990; Sitlington & Frank, 1993)
- Are not satisfied with their jobs (Patton & Blalock, 1996a)
- Express great concerns about having low incomes and few opportunities for job and career advancement (Learning Disabilities Association of America, 1994)
- (Over half) are unable to live independently (Schalock et al., 1992; Sitlington & Frank, 1993)
- Are in the majority not self-supporting (White, 1992)

The outcomes for students with learning disabilities, however, is not always bleak. For example, those who graduate from college have very positive outcomes. One study (Greenbaum et al., 1996) followed up adults who had graduated from the University of Maryland between 1980 and 1992. All of them had received support services from the Office of Disabled Student Services while attending college, and graduated at about age 22. Their outcomes are quite different from most young adults with learning disabilities. They were happy with their lives, were employed primarily in white-collar jobs (71% professional/technical, 23% clerical/sales, and 6% service), and participated in recreational and community activities. Why is this group so different from their peers with learning disabilities? They may well comprise a subgroup that has greater abilities and skills. They also possessed important characteristics that enabled them to succeed in school and work: understanding of their disability and their strengths and weaknesses, determination, perseverance, abilities to seek accommodations and self-advocate (Greenbaum et al., 1995). Another common characteristic may well be the most important: This group also came from well-educated, middle- to upper-middle-class families who offered considerable emotional and financial support to them. Parents' **socioeconomic status** and educational status were found to be key variables in the success of adults with learning disabilities in prior research as well (O'Connor & Spreen, 1988).

socioeconomic status. The status an individual or family unit holds in society, usually determined by job, level of education, and the amount of money available to spend.
life skills. Those skills used to manage a home, cook, shop, and organize personal living environments.

When such support from family is unavailable, carefully designed transitional services should compensate, but what actually does the typical adolescent with learning disabilities receive? Patton and Blalock (1996b) help us better understand why adult outcomes are not as universally positive. These students

- Receive inadequate vocational experiences
- Obtain little help from school personnel in finding either a job or work experience
- Tend not to access postsecondary options within five years of leaving high school, only 16% attending vocational schools, 12% attending two-year colleges, and 4% going to four-year colleges
- Are less adept in using community resources

Now, let's see whether the programs available to these students actually meet their needs.

High School Options. Students with learning disabilities tend to follow one of three paths during their high school years: some receive the traditional college preparatory, general education curriculum; some receive a transitional curriculum that focuses on vocational and functional or life skills; and the majority drop out of school, although an increasing number of these individuals complete high school later through a GED option.

Systematic transitional services and alternative curriculum programs are not typically available to students with learning disabilities. The increasing trend is for them to remain in general education classrooms and fulfill general education requirements. More and more states require students to complete all course and exit examination requirements to attain a standard diploma (Thurlow et al., 1997). Traditional high school experiences are difficult for most students with learning disabilities. Even for those who are successful, it can be fraught with frustration and failure. Also, there is a strong relationship between poor school performance, absenteeism, feelings of social isolation, and dropping out of school. For those who do not see the importance of school, who are faced with constant failure, and who do not believe that they will graduate, dropping out may seem like the best option. (See the accompanying box on page 162 for the comments of one dissatisfied midschooler.) Students with disabilities drop out at a rate almost double the rate for students without disabilities; only about one-third of them leave school with a diploma or a certificate (U.S. Department of Education, 1998). And students with learning disabilities represent the group with the largest number of dropouts (the largest percentage is for students with behavior disorders and emotional disturbance). Only about 4% go immediately on to a four-year college (Aune & Friehe, 1996). For those who are definitely college bound, high school experiences should prepare them well for academic success. For them, the curriculum should not be "watered down" and should include those learning strategies which will provide them with the knowledge, study skills, thinking skills, and real-world contexts necessary for advanced study (Ellis, 1997).

What are some solutions to the dropout problem? Students with disabilities have these suggestions (Kortering & Braziel, 1999):

- Change attitudes and get them to work harder
- Have parents take them to school and be sure they go
- Teachers need a better attitude
- Textbooks that are easier to read and understand
- Teachers become more helpful
- More participation in sports

Because of the high dropout rates among students with learning disabilities, more attention has recently been given to developing alternative curricular options for them in high school. Now may well be the time to seize the moment to develop innovative transitional programs for these students (Bassett & Smith, 1996). One option seeks to assist students more consistently with their transition from school to the world of work (Dunn, 1996). These programs should be individually tailored for the needs of each student and should include curriculum topics beyond traditional vocational education or job placements, such as self-determination, understanding of one's disability, psychosocial issues, and problem solving. Another option is to add **life skills** to these students' curriculum. Programs should include instruction about budgeting, banking, caring for a home or apartment, cooking, comparison shopping,

NEW DIRECTIONS
FOR THE
MILLENNIUM

Legacy: The number of students with learning disabilities who drop out of school is extremely high, and the percentage who participate in postsecondary education is very low.

Opportunities:
- Develop strategies to help students prepare for college and other postsecondary educational options
- Create an array of curricular options which stress job and life skills

A Middle School Student Considers Dropping Out

Will's comments help us understand why so many high school students with learning disabilities drop out of school.

When did you start skipping school, or decide that skipping school was a better choice than being in school?

Will: Sixth grade.

Why?

Will: Well, I just wanted to go hunting or something, hang out with friends and it was boring in school.

How was that?

Will: Well, I'd go to class and they'd tell me to do something; I couldn't do it. But I had to do it anyway. So I figured they didn't need me here.

If they gave you things you couldn't do, how did that go?

Will: Well, I'd just mark down some answers. It didn't matter.

Did they give you help?

Will: No.

So you felt it didn't matter if you were in school?

Will: Yeah, 'cause I wasn't learning anything.

Source: From "Persistence of Reading Disabilities: The Voices of Four Middle School Students," by R. Kos, 1991, *American Educational Research Journal, 28,* p. 887. Reprinted by permission.

and independent living skills (Cronin, 1996). A life-skills approach could focus on the mathematics needed in the home and community (Patton et al., 1997). Many such skills could be included in adaptations to general mathematics instruction that would provide interest to many students with disabilities and make the curriculum more real and meaningful. For example, topics related to mathematics use and work could use wages, net pay, time worked, and deductions to teach basic concepts related to time and money. Household repairs and maintenance could be used to teach knowledge and skills related to capacity, volume, length, weight, and temperature. The list goes on. Think about other ways that real-life skills could be taught in instructional units in mathematics, reading, and writing.

Postsecondary Options. Increasingly, more students are identified as having a learning disability after they are enrolled in college programs; an estimated 50% are identified during their college years (Ganschow et al., 1999). The reluctance of many states and school districts to identify and serve students who are highly able, who can cope with the general education curriculum, but also have a substantial discrepancy between their potential and achievement (those who are gifted and have learning disabilities) is one explanation for this situation (MacMillian et al., 1998).

The end of the twentieth century witnessed an increase in the postsecondary educational options available for students with learning disabilities. Many two-year community college and technical/vocational school programs are now designed specifically for these students. Several guides are available to help students and their parents select a college. *Peterson's Colleges with Programs for Students with Learning Disabilities* (Mangrum & Strichart, 1997) lists 800 colleges and universities in the United States and Canada that have special programs to support students with learning disabilities, and the *K&W Guide to Colleges for the Learning Disabled* (Kravets, 1999) provides detailed information about 200 specific programs. Many traditional colleges and universities are now offering students with learning disabilities a variety of academic supports. A rise in support services is also available in professional programs (dental, medical, and law schools) and other graduate programs (Ganschow et al., 1999). Supporting programs or accommodations typically include extra time (up to double the assigned time) to complete tests, student support services, and other special programs (Thomas, 1997). Meanwhile, the NCAA has instituted barriers to college admission for athletes who have identified learning disabilities. Cutoff scores for grade-point averages in "core" high school courses and college-bound tests where they do not permit accommodations impede access to postsecondary educational opportunities with the financial support that would be available to those who could otherwise earn scholarships for participation in sports (Hishinuma & Fremstad, 1997). With the increased supportive services available on college campuses for students with learning disabilities, the NCAA's rulings seem somewhat out-of-date.

FAMILIES

For more about families of students with disabilities see the Families sections in Chapters 3 through 12.

As discussed earlier in this chapter, most children with learning disabilities are not identified until they are of school age, and some are not identified until they are in college. In contrast, most deaf children, blind children, or those with severe disabilities are diagnosed when they are very young by medical professionals. The parents are aware of their children's disabilities during their early years of life. Most have prepared themselves to cope with the day-to-day challenges a disability can present, and many have become active participants in their children's educational programs during the preschool years. Many parents of children with learning disabilities, however, do not suspect that their children have a disability until difficulties at school become apparent, and it is often school personnel who have to deliver the bad news to them. This is a crucial time for parents and for the children who are diagnosed as having a learning disability. It is a time of confusion and concern—and often a time of anger, frustration, and stress. If the identification process were speedier and even earlier, some think, the emotional turmoil families often experience would be lessened (Dyson, 1996). Besides finances, think of some reasons that the identification process might not seem efficient to family members.

The challenges that family members of individuals with disabilities face can be great. A disability can affect every aspect of a person's life. Many family members have found that gaining support from others can be helpful. Often, educators offer considerable assistance. Because learning disabilities are academically related disabilities, many parents find that connections with teachers, school administrators, special education teachers, and whoever else can help their children accomplish realistic goals in school is crucial. And it may be for some of these reasons that the role of teachers is expanding (O'Shea et al., 1994). Let's examine two means of home–school communication: parent conferencing and homework.

PARENT CONFERENCING

Educators can develop good relationships with parents if they use good conferencing skills when meeting with them. At least four factors contribute to successful meetings (Kroth, 1978; Kroth & Edge, 1997). First, the area selected should be comfortable

Teachers view homework as an important part of school. Parents who actively participate in their children's efforts typically also build partnerships with teachers.

and free from interruptions. A desk or table between the parents and the educator can act as a barrier to discussion; a round table might get better results. Second, the professional must be a good listener. By listening carefully, the professional can help parents solve problems, and parents can come to a better understanding of how the family and the school can develop a partnership. Third, teachers should write down significant information shared by the parents. This note helps the teacher remember and stresses to the parent the importance of the meeting. Finally, parents should know how many meetings are planned and how long the meetings will last. Time periods should be adhered to; limiting the number and the length of the meetings seems to enhance their effectiveness. Even under the best of circumstances, where meetings are skillfully conducted, many parents report that they are overwhelmed with the amount and sophistication of the information presented (Simpson, 1996). Because of the emotionally charged nature of parent–teacher meetings, particularly the initial one, parents often indicate that they remember nothing after terms like *brain damaged* were used. To solve this problem, educators may need to schedule extra meetings to ensure the following results:

- The purpose of the meeting is specified
- The information given is clear and precise
- Information is restated using different words and examples
- Jargon is not used
- A professional attitude is maintained
- Feedback on the child's social and academic performance is provided
- The results of the meeting are recorded

Home–school communications can also be improved if educators are flexible in their scheduling to better accommodate parents' other obligations (Jayanthi et al., 1995). For example, meetings can be scheduled during the day if teachers have release time. Or, if teachers can receive extra pay, meetings can be scheduled early in the morning or in the evenings.

HOMEWORK

The word *homework* can bring horror to the minds of parents of students with learning disabilities, and probably to the children as well.

> The mere mention of the word may bring to mind memories of many long, unpleasant nights spent cajoling an LD student to complete unfinished assignments. Such nights often end up in shouting matches between parent and child, sometimes with one or both in tears. Other parents spend the year ranting and raving at their child simply trying to get homework brought home or trying to get it back to school. The problems with homework are so numerous.... (Higbee-Mandlebaum, 1992/1993, p. 1)

Despite the negative situations that homework can create for the family, it appears to be gaining in popularity. Researchers have found that homework accounts for about 20% of the time most children spend on academic tasks (Cooper & Nye, 1994). Although many children and their parents would like to see homework "just go away," there are positive relationships between homework and achievement (Bryan, 1995). With the national concern about student achievement, it is unlikely that homework will be discontinued.

General education teachers place importance on homework. They consider homework as a serious part of the instructional program and also as providing opportunities for home–school communication. Many teachers believe that when homework is not completed, parents have not met their expectations (Epstein et al., 1997). So how might communication between teachers and parents improve? Some research gives us guidelines (Jayanthi et al., 1997):

- Parents and teachers need to communicate more about homework, with both parties feeling free to initiate the conversation
- Parents need to tell teachers about homework difficulties
- Teachers need to tell parents about the quality and completion of homework assignments
- Parents need to implement consequences when homework is not completed or is unsatisfactory
- Parents need to know who to contact at school about homework issues
- Teachers need to find ways to communicate with parents who do not speak English
- Teachers need to determine alternate ways for children to get assistance with homework assignments that their parents do not know how to complete

Although many children with learning disabilities believe that homework is too hard, a waste of time, and boring, general education teachers believe that it is valuable and that all students in the class should get the same amount and be graded in the same way (Bryan, 1995; Bryan et al., 1995). Because homework is a reality of school life, some researchers are now attempting to develop methods to make this a more positive experience. Some have explored the effectiveness of cooperative homework teams (O'Melia & Rosenberg, 1994). In this system, peer teams grade and as a group make corrections to homework completed individually the previous evening. Others have created instructional materials, like *Planning for Success*, which is designed to restructure homework activities so they become positive learning experiences (Bryan & Sullivan, 1994a, 1994b). Others use homework planners and suggest graphing and rewarding the number and quality of homework assignments (Bryan & Sullivan-Burstein, 1998; Callahan, Rademacher, & Hildreth, 1998). It is interesting that although middle school students prefer being assigned homework that can be completed at school, they do not prefer being given assignments different from their classmates'. They are afraid that if they had easier work to do it would be perceived as unfair and that might negatively affect their social standing (Nelson et al., 1998).

TECHNOLOGY

Today, microcomputers are common in schools and at home. The 1990s saw expanded capabilities of computers as well as substantial price reductions, making the access to and availability of technology for all students an expectation in most school settings. The benefits to students with disabilities are many, and the possibilities created by technology continue to be discovered. Some educators are suggesting that technology be viewed as a "cognitive prosthesis" for students with learning disabilities (Lewis, 1998). Rapid advances have changed the way educators design instructional opportunities. Let's look at a few of those advances and how they benefit students with learning disabilities. Technology can

- Augment an individual's strengths
- Compensate for effects of disabilities
- Provide alternative modes of performing tasks.

Specifically, technology can also help individuals with disabilities become more efficient and effective learners (Bryant & Bryant, 1998; Lewis, 1998; Raskind & Higgins, 1998). Table 4.5 highlights some of these benefits and how assistive technology can reduce the barriers to success that these individuals face at home, at school, and in daily life.

MICROCOMPUTER TECHNOLOGY

Breakthroughs and improvements in both hardware and software occur almost daily in the computer field. For students with learning disabilities, advances in software are the most important and far-reaching. Thousands upon thousands of instructional software programs are now on the market. While few were specifically developed for students with learning disabilities, many, like those found in Table 4.5, have great benefit to them (Lewis, 1998).

Microcomputer technology also allows for major modifications to instruction. Many of these systems are not new, but are being continually improved in both content and in the way instruction is delivered. For example, **computer-assisted instruction (CAI)** supplements or replaces traditional instruction, and **computer-enhanced instruction** provides for more drill and practice opportunities. An exciting CAI development is **hypertext,** which uses pop-up text windows for further explanation of textbook material. For example, definitions of difficult vocabulary

MAKING CONNECTIONS

For more about technology and students with disabilities see the Technology sections in Chapters 3 through 12.

computer-assisted instruction (CAI). Self-contained instructional software programs that students use to supplement or replace traditional teacher-directed instructional methods. **computer-enhanced instruction.** Software programs that students use to supplement traditional instruction, used primarily for drill and practice. **hypertext.** A computer program that can be used to modify textbook materials through rewording, defining vocabulary, and providing further explanations. **hypermedia.** Computer programs that incorporate text, graphics, sound, photographic images, and video clips.

Table 4.5 Assistive Technology Options for Students with Learning Disabilities

Barriers	Difficulties	Assistive Technology Solution
Print	Reading	Audiotaped books "Talking" computers Captioned film and videos Semantic mapping software (story mapping) Web based texts Hypermedia and hypertext
	Writing	Word processing programs (including grammar assistance) Desktop publishing Computer based thesauruses Editing aids Planning aids Word prediction software
	Spelling	Spellcheckers Voice input devices
Communication	Organization	Manipulating graphics Presentation packages (e.g., Powerpoint, Persuasion) Semantic mapping software
	Speech	E-mail Voice output systems Synthesized speech
Solving Problems	Calculating	Handheld calculators Spreadsheets Graphics programs
Being Organized	Daily Life	Personal organizers Electronic calendars Computer "stickies" Electronic address books
	Study Skills	Organizing software (outlines, graphic organizers) Timing devices
Learning	Researching Topics	CD-ROM based reference books Internet databases Computer based instruction (hypermedia, hypertext)
	Remembering	Outlining systems (main ideas from details)

words, rewording of confusing or complicated text, additional detailed maps, and further explanation of concepts introduced in the text are available to the student with the simple press of a key on the computer keyboard. This feature allows teachers to adapt textbooks so that students with learning disabilities can participate in general education course content. Using hypertext, they can highlight on the screen words that they do not know, concepts they do not understand, or material they would like more information about; a press of a key then gives them additional explanations. **Hypermedia** goes one step further by adding multimedia, such as

Ed Stein. Denver *Rocky Mountain News*.

video clips, and supplements and enriches text with highly interesting visual and auditory presentations (Boone et al., 1997). Multimedia encyclopedias on CD ROM are good examples of hypermedia. Recent research has shown that there are many benefits of this approach for students with learning disabilities (Babbit & Miller, 1996):

- Immediate access to multiple representations of information in a variety of formats
- Access to multiple resources in a nonsequential manner on student demand
- Adaptability to many different learning styles and preferences
- Individually paced

The Internet is having a profound effect on American society, and is also changing classroom instruction and students' interaction with that instruction. The World Wide Web and other related telecommunications applications (like e-mail) can help students with learning disabilities participate more fully in general education curriculum (Peters-Walters, 1998; Smith et al., 1998). Instead of just reading about art and history in textbooks, students can visit virtual museums and libraries all around the world and learn and experience the content of their teacher's lessons. Students can also do their own independent research and retrieve information to use in class reports and term papers. For an active generation that is used to seeing, doing, and participating actively, the Web offers excitement and enrichment that might otherwise be missing from the curriculum. It also might provide the motivation necessary for the extra effort learning requires for students with learning disabilities.

For those students with learning disabilities who find learning to read an insurmountable challenge, new options are now available. For example, the Kurzweil 3000 system can scan any printed material, including pictures and illustrations, and then turn it into an audio output. In other words, the computer "reads" to the student. Students are encouraged to read along with the computer, take notes, and ask the computer to define unknown words by using its 175,000-word online dictionary. This computer system also has the capability of "reading aloud" Web pages and other information found through the Internet. This amazing system holds promise of not only providing an alternative method for teaching reading to those who seem unable to learn through standard methods, but also of allowing students to compensate for poor reading abilities and be able to participate in the general education curriculum alongside their classmates without reading problems.

Educators need to consider many issues when thinking about using technology in their classrooms. What benefits does the technology bring to the student, the teacher, and the instructional program? Are expensive and complicated systems more effective than cheaper methods that do not use computers? In some cases the old tried and true methods of paper-and-pencil tasks are as effective, and the costs of technology cannot be justified (Raskind & Higgins, 1998). However, some effective procedures, like individualized teacher-directed instruction, are so time consuming that using technology which can both optimize learning and free the teacher for more demanding instruction makes the financial costs worthwhile (Wilson et al., 1996).

Advances in technology can serve both as instructional assistants and also compensatory aids. Computers with special devices, like this Kurzweil 3000 computer, includes voice to print, print to voice, word prediction, and Hypermedia options.

WRITING TECHNOLOGY

In particular, the writing process is difficult for students with learning disabilities because this complex task requires the application of many different skills and cognitive abilities. For example, students need to select their topic, generate and organize the content of their paper, revise it, proof and edit it, and produce a final copy (MacArthur, 1996). However, the combination of special writing instruction and the use of a computer with a good word processing program improves both the quality and quantity of these students' writing, and now new software features provide even more assistance to students with writing problems.

The computer supports the writing process naturally. For some students, it is physically less tiring. For others, print on a computer screen is easier to see and read than print on paper. Still others like the use of a computer because the results of the word processing program can be exceptionally attractive. The computer can facilitate collaboration, making it easier for two or more students to work together and merge their components of a writing task.

A feature of many word processing programs helps some students with learning disabilities with their writing. For example, spellcheckers can improve some students' written work (MacArthur et al., 1996). When the spellchecker was unavailable, students corrected only 9% of their spelling mistakes; but when it was available, they corrected 37% of their errors. When a correct suggestion was given for a misspelled word, the students made the right selection 82% of the time. Unfortunately, the spellcheckers did not produce a correct spelling of the intended word between 26% and 37% of the time. For those students whose writing and spelling is so deficient that standard word processing programs are insufficient, other options are now available. For example, some programs provide speech output and word prediction features so that students can determine whether the word they wrote matches the word they hear (MacArthur, 1998). Synthesized speech also supports students' writing by allowing them to listen to the work they have generated. The outcome can be great improvement in students' written work.

CONCEPTS AND CONTROVERSY: IS ADHD A DISABILITY?

- For background about ADHD, see the History section of this chapter.
- Also see the section on ADHD found in the Children with Learning Disabilities section of this chapter.

IDEA was reauthorized twice during the last decade of the twentieth century. During the 1990 reauthorization, attention deficit hyperactivity disorder (ADHD) received considerable attention. Members of Congress heard testimony from parents that their children with ADHD were not being served either appropriately or adequately in public schools. Parents argued that ADHD is a disabling condition that requires intensive special education services. They wanted all children with ADHD to receive special services and the schools to receive extra federal funding so that they could meet these children's educational needs. Since that time, ADHD has received considerable attention in the press, and the public's concern about this condition has increased.

ADHD is not a new condition (Wiederholt, 1991). It was first described by Kurt Goldstein in his observations of young men with brain injuries returning to the States after World War II. It was also described by Strauss and Werner in their studies of children attending the Wayne County Training School in the 1930s and 1940s.

During the 1960s, when the field of learning disabilities actually developed, many of the behaviors that today are considered characteristics of ADHD were included in the description of students with learning disabilities. And in the 1970s, many people were concerned about the use of stimulant drugs, such as Ritalin and Dexedrine, to assist in the control of hyperactivity. So you may wonder why so much attention is directed at this condition in the 1990s. The extra notice is probably due to our lack of knowledge: Neither medical nor education professionals know how to treat or serve these children well. Parents, in their frustration and concern for the well-being of their children, turned to Congress for help. However, the controversy about ADHD was not settled with the 1990 reauthorization of IDEA, nor was it with IDEA '97. Disappointing many parents, Congress did not make ADHD a separate special education category, and did not protect all children with ADHD under IDEA '97.

What is the controversy? Some researchers estimate that 10% to 20% of school-children have ADHD (Shaywitz & Shaywitz, 1992) and that 50% of them do not presently qualify for special education services. But other researchers do not believe that ADHD is even a disorder, let alone a disability (Armstrong, 1995; Reid et al., 1993). Yet others believe that those with attentional problems, rather than hyper-activity, are the ones at risk for academic failure; and those children are already served under the learning disabilities category (Riccio et al., 1994). What would happen if there were a separate category for ADHD? Additional children would un-doubtedly become part of the special education rolls, although no one is sure just how many.

> Can the nation afford to serve more children in special education?
> Do all children with ADHD have disabilities that require unique special education services?
> Is another category necessary if the children with ADHD are already being served by special education, primarily through the learning disabilities and behavior disorders categories?
> Do you think that Congress should create a new special education category for students with ADHD?
> Do you think that ADHD is a separate disability or a symptom of other disabilities?

In Conclusion

The answers to the questions posed in the Advance Organizers section at the beginning of the chapter are found here; use them to review the contents of this chapter.

Summary

Individuals with learning disabilities do not learn in the same way or at the same pace as their nondisabled classmates. Current research is attempting to find better methods of instruction so that these students see further improvement in aca-demic and social performance. When taught by teachers who are well trained and knowledgeable about the newest research findings, many of these individuals should be able to compensate for their disabilities. However, without the best that education can offer, the likelihood is small that individuals with learning disabili-ties will succeed as they should in life.

Self-Test Questions

- *What are the differences and similarities between the two major definitions of learning disabilities?*

  Although many definitions have been proposed, two (or adaptations of them) are generally used to guide the field of learning disabilities: the federal definition found in IDEA '97 and the one put forth by the National Joint Committee on Learning Disabilities (NJCLD). Debate about the best definition of learning disabilities has continued since this field was begun in the 1960s. Since then, almost forty definitions have been proposed, each with a slightly different orientation, philosophy, and thrust. Some definitions, particularly the older ones, are medical in nature. Some definitions address the fact that this is a lifelong disability and might result in deficits in academic and social skills. The basic difference between most of the definitions is due to the originators' beliefs about what causes this disability. The older ones, like the federal definition, have a medical orientation, and the newer ones reflect a more educational perspective. Regardless of what definition is used, professionals recognize some common characteristics. For example, most people with learning disabilities do have normal intelligence but are significantly behind nondisabled peers in academic achievement, a low level often referred to as "unexpected."

- *Why can students be identified as having learning disabilities in one state or school district but not qualify for special education services elsewhere?*

  Nationally, special educators remain concerned about the definition of learning disabilities and the criteria for identification because of inconsistencies in prevalence rates within and across school districts and states and because of the tendency to identify a large number of students as having learning disabilities; estimates range from 3% to 30% of the school population. Prevalence rates vary state by state as definitions and criteria for identification vary as well. Without stringent controls over the number of students served as having learning disabilities, this group of learners seems to grow in number every year. Thus educators fear that children who are not succeeding at school are being misdiagnosed. This may be due to general education teachers, concerned about students who cannot keep up with others in their classes, referring them to special education in hopes that their educational needs will be better met with different arrangements.

- *Why is it correct to consider learning disabilities a lifelong condition?*

  Although recognized by professionals only relatively recently, it is now quite clear: Learning disabilities and their effects present lifelong challenges to these individuals and their families. Those who continue to have difficulties reading often find that their postsecondary education opportunities are limited. They also tend to make career choices based on jobs that do not require them to read or write. For those who dropped out of high school, their adult outcomes appear grim, with their employment opportunities narrow and low-paying. For many adults with learning disabilities, the greatest difficulties center on their lack of friends and social outlets. Changes in curriculum and the expansion of transitional services may alter the adult outcomes for those still in school, but there are many issues to consider (which students receive a college-bound curriculum and which do not) and services to develop.

- *What are some learning characteristics that contribute to these students' poor academic performance?*

  Recent research findings show that many of these learners do not approach learning tasks as others do. They tend to be passive (inactive) learners. Possibly, because of a history of failure, they attribute success with academic tasks to luck or chance rather than effort and ability. These attributions are not innate personality traits but are learned characteristics that can be altered through systematic instruction. However, attributions do affect motivation and influence how hard an individual will work to succeed at a task. These youngsters also have a tendency not to focus on the task or the correct aspect of the task. These students also have difficulties transferring (generalizing) learning from one task, skill, or situation to another. Solving problems, processing information, and applying high-level thinking skills can also present problems for many of these individuals. Children can learn to focus their attention properly, apply their newly learned skills to other situations, learn to learn, and process information more efficiently. They need to learn these skills to be able to compete successfully in basic high school courses such as history, science, and literature. For this to occur, however, requires systematic and intensive instruction. The development of learning strategies and other teaching techniques are proving to help many of these youngsters be more positive and efficient active learners.

- *How might teachers and diagnosticians better identify students with ADHD who qualify for special education services and those who do not?*

  Learning disabilities and ADHD are complex conditions, each with a wide range of variability. These conditions have many common symptoms or characteristics—attention deficits, distractibility, hyperactivity, impulsivity—and in fact almost half of those identified as having ADHD have documented learning disabilities. Many others are identified as having behavior disorders or emotional disturbance, and now ADHD is included in IDEA '97's definition of "other health impairments." All children with ADHD, even those with medical diagnoses, do not qualify for or need special education. The federal government was very clear on the point that IDEA '97 did not make ADHD a special education category or a disability. The defining issue for special education services must be that ADHD significantly affects educational performance. It is here that the teacher is very helpful by creating documentation of how a child's ADHD influences academic work, and whether accommodations help with the problems the condition may cause.

Challenge Question

- *What constitutes an appropriate education for these students and in what setting should it be provided?*

  As the century begins, debate continues about where students with learning disabilities should be educated and what that education should comprise. The use of different options—teams of special education and general education teachers, consulting special educators collaborating with general education teachers, resource rooms, self-contained special education classes, special schools—varies state by state and school district by district. Regardless of the service delivery option used by a school district—categorical or noncategorical—services for students with learning disabilities are available across the nation. These programs vary, but most center on the general education curriculum with strategy instruction or other additional supportive services. They are available from elementary to high school. However, at the end of the century the pattern of service options was changing, with resource rooms being less available. The practices being implemented reflect professionals' and parents' philosophies about the concepts of LRE and full inclusion, the segregation of students, the most appropriate curriculum for these students, and the appropriate roles of general and special education with these students. For this group, in particular, growing consensus is that decisions about education should be made on an individual basis and a full array of services, placements, and curriculum must be available to meet the educational needs of students with disabilities.

 **Supplementary Resources**

Scholarly Readings

Bos, C., & Vaughn, S. (1994). *Strategies for teaching students with learning and behavior problems.* Boston: Allyn and Bacon.

Deshler, D. D., Ellis, E. S., & Lenz, B. K. (1996). *Teaching adolescents with learning disabilities: Strategies and methods* (2nd ed.). Denver: Love Publishing.

Hallahan, D. P., Kauffman, J. M., & Lloyd, J. W. (1996). *Introduction to learning disabilities.* Boston: Allyn and Bacon.

Higgins, K., & Boone, R. (1997). *Technology for students with learning disabilities: Educational applications.* Austin: Pro-Ed.

Lerner, J. (1997). *Learning disabilities: Theories, diagnosis, and teaching strategies* (7th ed.). Boston: Houghton Mifflin.

Reiff, H., Gerber, P., & Ginsberg, R. (1997). *Exceeding expectations: Successful adults with learning disabilities.* Austin, TX: Pro-Ed.

Rivera, D. P., & Smith, D. D. (1997). *Teaching students with learning and behavior problems.* Boston: Allyn and Bacon.

Smith, T. E. C., Dowdy, C. A., Polloway, E. A., & Blalock, G. E. (1997). *Children and adults with learning disabilities.* Boston: Allyn and Bacon.

Popular Books

Brown, C. (1965). *Manchild in the promised land.* New York: Macmillan.

Gantos, J. (1998). *Joey Pigza swallowed the key.* New York: Farrar, Straus, & Giroux.

Moss, P. B. (1989). *An autobiography: P. Buckley Moss: The people's artist.* Waynesboro, VA: Shenandoah Heritage.

Sacks, O. (1985). *The man who mistook his wife for a hat.* New York: Summit Books.

Troyer, P. H. (1986). *Father Bede's misfit.* Monkton, MD: York Press.

Videos and DVDs

The hero who couldn't read. (1984). ABC-TV.
When words don't mean a thing. (1987). ABC.
Read between the lines. (1989). ABC Video Enterprises.

Professional, Parent, and Consumer Organizations and Agencies

Children and Adults with Attention Deficit Disorder (CHADD)
8181 Professional Place, Suite 201
Landover, MD 20785
(800) 233-4050
Web site: http://www.chadd.org

Council for Learning Disabilities (CLD)
P.O. Box 40303
Overland Park, KS 66204
Phone: (913) 429-8755
Web site: http://www.coe.winthrop.edu/CLD

Division for Learning Disabilities (DLD)
Council for Exceptional Children
1920 Association Drive
Reston, VA 22091
Phone: (703) 620-3660
Web site: http://www.cec.sped.org

International Dyslexia Association
8600 LaSalle Road, Chester Building, Suite 382
Baltimore, MD 21286-2044
Phone: (410) 296-0232; (800) 222-3123
E-mail: info@ods.org
Web site: http://www.interdys.org

Learning Disability Association of America (LDA)
(formerly the Association for Children with Learning
Disabilities [ACLD])
4156 Library Road
Pittsburgh, PA 15234-1349
Phone: (412) 341-1515
Web site: http://www.ldanatl.org

National Center for LD (NCLD)
381 Park Avenue S., Suite 1401
New York, NY 10016
Phone: (212) 545-9665
Web site: http://www.ncld.org

Lewis Carroll is probably best known to all of us for his timeless story *Alice in Wonderland.* Born Charles Lutwidge Dodgson in 1832, he was one of ten children and the eldest son of an Anglican minister. He was recognized at school as possessing "a very uncommon share of genius" and particularly excelled in mathematics. He was a nervous boy who had a chronic stuttering problem and was often ridiculed by his classmates. Although he considered following in his father's footsteps as a preacher, his stuttering problem made preaching difficult, and it is suggested that this is why he developed skills as a photographer and pursued a career as a writer (Hinde, 1991). This photograph is of the girl he used as his model for the character Alice.

Princeton University Library. Morris L. Parrish Collection. Department of Rare Books and Special Collections. Princeton University Library. Reprinted by permission.

CHAPTER 5

A Parent's View of a Speech Impairment

Gloria E. Enlow is the mother of two daughters, now ages 25 and 30. Divorced when the children were 5 and 10 years of age, Ms. Enlow raised them on her own for five years, until her remarriage. The younger daughter, Samantha Reid, has cerebral palsy. Ms. Enlow tells her family's story:

Communication is not something that I was thinking about as I held my baby daughter for the first time. As she looked at me with those big, bright brown eyes, though, I knew there was something different about her. She cried a lot, had trouble sucking and chewing, was quite stiff, and startled easily. As time went on and she was not able to sit unassisted or hold objects by herself, my anxiety heightened. Finally, at 18 months of age, she was diagnosed as having cerebral palsy. Samantha's condition is the result of lack of oxygen at birth, causing brain damage, which, for her, means lack of muscle control, including the larynx and tongue. The latter translates into labored and, often, unintelligible speech.

Relieved to know just what the problem was, we launched into a regimen of physical, occupational, and speech therapy, which continued through high school. Even though Samantha had special problems, we always treated her as just another member of the family, and she fully participated in everything from sledding to religious ceremonies. She was beautiful, happy, well adjusted, and developed a positive self-image. Her own personal desire to be involved in as many normal activities as possible prompted me, her teachers, and school administrators to act as advocates to maximize her potential and tap that obvious intelligence, which was masked by her lack of spontaneous, articulate speech.

Speech or Language Impairments

We were fortunate that stable and well-established special education programs were in place by the time Samantha was ready for first grade. Even so, I had to search constantly for the proper care, services, and equipment to help her. A major goal was to enhance her speaking capability. As a result, an administrator and speech therapist identified her first augmentative communication device. By age 10, she had learned to program and use the Autocom, which had a digital display and printout capability. This aid made it easier for her to be integrated into her first regular academic class, a major accomplishment for all of us. Although Samantha liked and appreciated her special education classmates and teachers, she did not want to operate in an isolated environment. As Samantha's integration increased, people realized that she had academic ability. This set the stage for her introduction to newer and more sophisticated communication aids and word processors. This strong support from me, classroom aides, assistive devices, and Samantha's sheer determination all contributed to her ability to accomplish work. Samantha's long-term academic goal was to attend college, and through her ability and will she earned an academic scholarship at the University of New Mexico.

Samantha is very concerned about personal appearance, and she had resisted the idea of accumulating contraptions to carry around on her wheelchair. However, by the time she was completing high school, she knew that an electronic device would be necessary in college. She was introduced to the Touchtalker, a computer with a digital display and synthesized voice. She knew it could be of great assistance to her for communicating her own thoughts in the larger, more unfamiliar environment of the university. It has taken tremendous effort and time for her to learn to use the Touchtalker effectively, but she has mastered it well enough to work it herself and to teach others how to use the equipment.

From reading this story, you may have the impression that Samantha's life and my life were ordered. But that is not the case. I have not discussed my sustained efforts to identify sources of support and necessary resources. I joined committees, councils, and advocacy groups to learn what options and programs were available and to take part in influencing their direction. For many years, I wrote Samantha's dictated answers to homework assignments, spent countless hours at the library, and was intimately involved in her progression of study to assure that she would meet college enrollment requirements. A full-time aide was authorized for high school only after many sessions with numerous levels of school officials. Samantha is considered to be a unique case because of her intelligence and accomplishments despite multiple disabilities. She is determined to earn her degree, live independently, and earn a living. She does not intend to stay dependent on federal or state support. She will require substantial support until she earns a college degree, but the return on investment will be a self-sustaining, accomplished adult.

Today, Samantha is still a college student. Like many others, she interrupted her studies with marriage and the birth of a beautiful little girl, Theresa. I only hope that the future holds a reward for her in the way of acceptance for all that she has to offer.

1. What do you think the future holds for Samantha?

2. How will Samantha's adult life be different from those of individuals with cerebral palsy and severe speech impairments who were born twenty years before her? twenty years after her?

Advance Organizers

 CONNECTIONS MAKING

Use the learning strategy—Advance Organizers—to help focus your study of this chapter's content, and reinforce your learning by reviewing answers to the Focus and Challenge questions found at the end of the chapter.

Overview

When students' primary and secondary disabilities are considered, speech or language impairments is the largest special education category. Most people use oral language for their primary means of communication, and if the communication process is flawed, all facets of interpersonal communication are affected. The relationship between early identification of a language impairment and later identification of a learning disability is strong because language is the foundation for cognition, reading abilities, and social competence. The importance of acquiring language in the normal developmental sequence cannot be underestimated, for it influences the child's overall potential and achievements.

Self-Test Questions

Focus Questions

- What comprises speech impairments and language impairments?
- What is the prevalence of this disability?
- How do language delays, language differences, and language impairments differ?
- How can teachers enhance language development and help to remediate a language impairment?
- What is alternative and augmentative communication, and what are its benefits to this population of learners?

Challenge Question

- What related service provider serves the needs of students with speech or language impairments, their families, and their teachers, and what roles does this professional serve today?

Our society places a high value on oral communication, and for most of us, it is the primary method of interacting with others. We talk with each other to share knowledge, information, and feelings. Most of us, in fact, prefer talking to other forms of communication, such as writing. Notice the intensity of conversations in cafeterias, college dining halls, and restaurants; think about how often we choose to use the telephone instead of writing a letter. Oral communication allows us to interact with others on many dimensions. Clearly, communication is a crucial part of life. Steven Warren (1999) helps us understand the importance of communication and the group of professionals who work to remediate speech or language impairments:

The field of communication and language intervention is truly transdisciplinary due to the fundamental role that these skills play in human functioning. Language is often noted as the most impressive attainment/invention of our species. It is the basis of our culture, of commerce (i.e., the information age), science, religion and so forth. It is what separates us from virtually every other species on this planet. Individuals' fluency and skill with this tool will to a large extent determine their opportunities and options in our society. (Warren, 1999)

This chapter will help you understand people who have difficulty communicating with others because they have either a speech or oral language impairment. Different types of these impairments, what causes them, and how they might be prevented or corrected are discussed. You will learn how this disability affects children during their schoolyears and how speech and language specialists, speech/language pathologists, and classroom teachers can improve children's communicative abilities. You will learn what problems these individuals face as adults and what hope there is in technological advances. You will come away with a clearer understanding of speech or language impairments and the role professionals play in ameliorating them.

Opportunities for the New Millennium

The vast majority of children with disabilities have difficulties with language and its associated skills. The correlation is particularly high for those individuals who also have cognitive impairments. As preschoolers these youngsters are typically late in developing language, and their acquisition patterns are atypical. As they progress through school, oral language problems are compounded by challenges in learning to read, write, and communicate in social situations with others. Although language development is often the root of their difficulties, it remains an area least directly addressed at school.

Legacies from the Twentieth Century Long before the passage of IDEA in 1975, speech/language pathologists (SLPs) worked in schools. However, in those days, the majority of their time was spent with students who had articulation problems, and proportionally little time was devoted to youngsters with cognitive impairments. As the field of special education continued to develop and specialize, teachers assumed the responsibilities of educating students with cognitive and language impairments, but did so with little preparation in the area of language development. Toward the end of the century, SLPs assumed roles as collaborative partners with teachers, assisting them in creating more language development opportunities in the classroom. However, time for these partnerships remains limited because they work with many teachers, many students, and many schools. And SLPs who work intensively with some students with severe language impairments rely on teachers for follow-through efforts to enhance generalization of skills learned in therapy. However, general education and special education teachers remain ill-prepared for these duties.

Thinking About Dilemmas to Solve As you read this chapter, consider your preparation in general and special education. Think about your training in the basic area of language development and also whether the general education curriculum sufficiently addresses language acquisition and fluency. Also, study the interrelationships between language and success in mastering basic academic and social skills. Think about:

- What type of training teachers need in the area of language, whether they work with preschoolers, elementary students, or high school students
- Support services students and teachers need from SLPs
- How delivery systems might be changed so all students receive a language-rich education
- Whether the general education curriculum should be modified
- If more instructional materials should be available that specifically address language development

Sign language, particularly ASL, is discussed in detail in Chapter 10.

communication signals. A variety of messages that announce some immediate event, person, action, or emotion.
communication symbols. Voice, letters of the alphabet, or gestures used to relay communication messages.
vocal symbols. Oral means of relaying messages, such as speech sounds.
written symbols. Graphic means, such as the written alphabet, used to relay messages.
sign language. An organized established system of manual gestures used for communication.

SPEECH OR LANGUAGE IMPAIRMENTS DEFINED

To understand speech or language impairments, we must first understand the communication process people use to interact with others. Think of communication in terms of a game with at least two players (the sender and the receiver) and a message (the purpose of the interaction) (Marvin, 1989). Communication occurs only when the message intended by the sender is understood by the receiver. The sender may have an idea or thought to share with someone else, but the sender's idea needs to be translated from thought to some code the other person can understand.

Coding thoughts into signals or symbols is an important part of the communication game. **Communication signals** announce some immediate event, person, action, or emotion. Signals can be gestures, a social formality, or a vocal pattern, such as a gasp or groan. The U.S. Marine Band playing "Hail to the Chief," for example, signals the appearance of the President of the United States. A teacher rapping on a desk announces an important message. Symbols are used to relay a more complex message. **Communication symbols** refer to something: a past, present, or future event; a person or object; an action; a concept or emotion. Speech sounds are **vocal symbols.** Letters of the alphabet are **written symbols. Sign language** uses gestural symbols. Symbols are used in combination with each other and are governed by rules. Signals, symbols, and the rules that must be followed constitute language and allow language to have meaning.

Once thought is coded, the sender must select a mechanism for delivering the message. The sender chooses from a number of mechanisms: voice, sign language, gestures, writing tools. The delivery system must be useful to the receiver. For example, selecting voice via telephone to transmit a message to a deaf person is useless (unless that person has a voice-decoding telephone device). Sending a written message to someone who cannot read also results in ineffective communication.

Communication messages require the receiver to use eyes, ears, or even tactile (touch) senses (for example, those who use braille) to take the message to the brain where it is understood. Receivers must understand the code the sender uses and be able to interpret the code so that it has meaning. Communication is unsuccessful if the sender or receiver cannot use the signals or symbols adequately. And if either person has a defective mechanism for sending or receiving the information, the

These children are engaged in the communication process. They are taking turns being receivers and senders.

communication process is ineffective. Figure 5.1 illustrates the communication process. As you review this diagram, think about how even a simple message, such as an order at a fast-food restaurant, follows the steps outlined in the diagram.

At this point, it might be helpful for us to distinguish three terms—communication, language, and speech—that are different but related to one another. **Communication** is the process of exchanging knowledge, ideas, opinions, and feelings (Owens, 1998). This transfer is usually accomplished through the use of language. Sometimes, however, communication can occur with the glance of an eye, a gesture, or some other nonverbal behavior. **Language** is a formalized method of communication involving the comprehension and use of the signs and symbols by which ideas are represented. Language also has rules that govern the use of signs and symbols so that the intended message has the correct meaning.

communication. The transfer of knowledge, ideas, opinions, and feelings.

language. The formalized method of communication by which ideas are transmitted to others.

speech. The vocal production of language.

respiratory system. The system of organs whose primary function is to take in oxygen and expel gases.

vocal system. Parts of the respiratory system used to create voice.

vibrating system. The orderly function of the larynx and vocal folds to vibrate and produce sounds and pitch.

resonating system. Oral and nasal cavities where speech sounds are formed.

Speech is the vocal production of language. In most instances, it is the fastest and most efficient means of communicating. Understanding how we produce speech requires knowledge of the neurological, respiratory, vocal, and speech mechanisms that work together in our bodies to produce speech and language. Refer to the diagram of the head and chest cavity shown in Figure 5.2 on page 184 as you read the following description of the process of generating speech.

When we want to speak, the brain sends messages that activate other mechanisms. The **respiratory system's** primary function is to take in oxygen and expel gases from our bodies. However, the diaphragm, chest, and throat muscles of the respiratory system that work to expel air also activate the **vocal system.** Voice is produced in the larynx, which sits on top of the trachea and houses the vocal folds. As air is expelled from the lungs, the flow of air causes the vocal folds to vibrate and produce sounds; the vocal folds lengthen or shorten to cause changes in pitch. The larynx and vocal folds are referred to as the **vibrating system.** As the sounds travel through the throat, mouth, and nasal cavities—the **resonating system**—the voice is shaped into speech sounds by the articulation or **speech mechanisms,** which include the tongue, soft and hard palates, teeth, lips, and jaw.

Now, let's discuss impairments in communication.

TYPES OF SPEECH OR LANGUAGE IMPAIRMENTS

People with speech or language impairments have difficulty using the communication process efficiently. Although considered one special education category, **speech impairments** and **language impairments** are really two separate, though related, disabilities. Each of these major problem areas is further broken down into more specific problems, as shown in Table 5.1 on page 185. Let's look at each type to

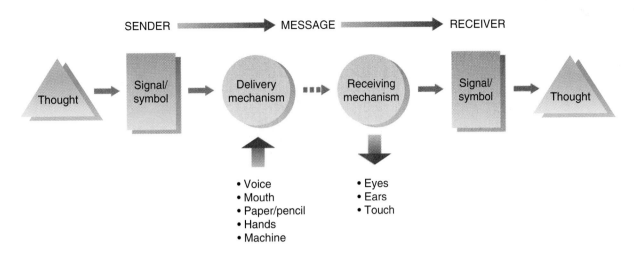

Figure 5.1 **The Communication Process**

Source: "Language and Learning" (p. 148) by C. Marvin, in D. D. Smith, *Teaching Students with Learning and Behavior Problems* (2nd ed.), 1989. Englewood Cliffs, NJ: Prentice-Hall. Reprinted by permission.

SENDER → **MESSAGE** → **RECEIVER**

Thought → Signal/symbol → Delivery mechanism ⋯ Receiving mechanism → Signal/symbol → Thought

- Voice
- Mouth
- Paper/pencil
- Hands
- Machine

- Eyes
- Ears
- Touch

better understand how a problem with any of the areas listed in the table influences the effectiveness of communication.

Speech Impairments. Speech is abnormal when it is unintelligible, is unpleasant, or interferes with communication (Van Riper & Erickson, 1996). The three major types of speech impairments are voice, articulation, and fluency (for example, stuttering). Any one of these three speech impairments is distracting to the listener and can negatively affect the communication process.

VOICE PROBLEMS. One type of speech impairment, **voice problems,** is not very common in schoolchildren, but when this speech impairment does occur it needs immediate attention from a professional. Voice is a measure of self; it is part of one's identity. We can identify many of our friends, for example, simply by hearing their voices. Voice distinguishes each person from others, and we typically do not think about how it functions. But when it does not function as usual, such as when we have laryngitis, we find it frustrating. Many famous personalities are recognized by their unique voices. Think of how impressionists create mental images of famous people through voice and gesture. Our voices also mirror our emotions; we often can tell when people we know well are happy, sad, angry, or scared merely by hearing their voices.

Two aspects of voice are important: pitch and loudness. A voice problem usually involves a problem with one or both of these aspects. **Pitch** is the perceived high or low quality of voice. Men typically have lower voice pitch than women. A man's voice whose pitch is high or a woman's pitch that is low attracts attention. If the receiver of communication pays more attention to the voice than to the message, though, communication is impaired (Van Riper & Erickson, 1996). When young boys' voice pitch changes during puberty, attention is drawn to the boys and their unintentional changes in voice. Of course, this pitch change is a normal part of development and disappears as the boy's body grows and voice pitch becomes stabilized.

speech mechanisms. Includes the various parts of the body—tongue, lips, teeth, mandible, and palate—required for oral speech.

speech impairments. Abnormal speech that is unintelligible, is unpleasant, or interferes with communication.

language impairments. Difficulty or inability to master the various systems of rules in language, which then interferes with communication.

voice problems. An abnormal spoken language production, characterized by unusual pitch, loudness, or quality of sounds.

pitch. An aspect of voice; its perceived high or low sound quality.

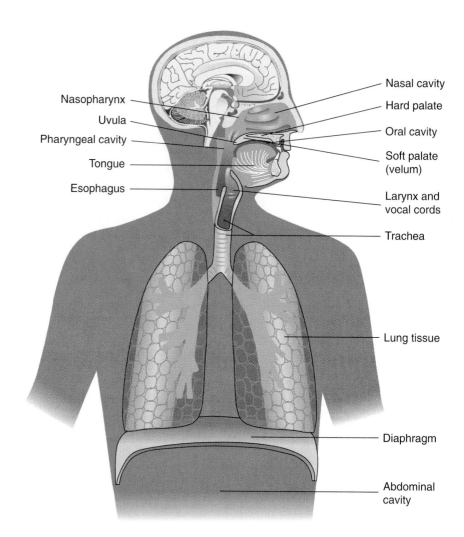

Figure 5.2 The Body's Systems for Generating Voice and Speech

Labels (clockwise from upper left):
Nasopharynx
Uvula
Pharyngeal cavity
Tongue
Esophagus
Nasal cavity
Hard palate
Oral cavity
Soft palate (velum)
Larynx and vocal cords
Trachea
Lung tissue
Diaphragm
Abdominal cavity

Loudness is the other main aspect of voice. In some cases, people are labeled with certain personality traits because of the loudness of their voices: "She is such a soft-spoken individual." "He is loud and brash." Voice can communicate much of the intended message for delivery. In some cases, if the quality of voice is so distracting that the message is misunderstood or lost, speech therapy is probably necessary.

loudness. An aspect of voice, referring to the intensity of the sound produced while speaking.

articulation problems. Abnormal production of speech sounds.

ARTICULATION PROBLEMS. **Articulation problems** are the most common speech impairments (Van Riper & Erickson, 1996). Articulation is the process of producing speech sounds. The receiver of communication must understand the sounds of the words spoken to understand the full message. If speech sounds are incorrectly produced, one sound might be confused with another, changing the meaning of the message. A child who substitutes a *t* for a *k* sound might say "titty tat" instead of "kitty cat." In such cases, if the words are too different or unintelligible, the message has no meaning. Speech/language pathologists, who specialize in correcting speech impairments, spend a considerable portion of their time remediating articulation errors. They also work with language, voice, and fluency problems.

Table 5.1
Types of Speech and Language Impairments

Impairment	Explanation
Speech	Impairment in the production of oral or spoken language
Voice	Absence or abnormal production of vocal quality, pitch, loudness, resonance, and/or duration
Articulation	Abnormal production of speech sounds
Fluency	Interruptions in the flow, rate, and/or rhythm of verbal expression
Language	Delayed or deviant development of comprehension and/or use of the signs and symbols used to express or receive ideas in a spoken, written, or other symbol system
Form	Lack of knowledge or inappropriate application of the rule systems that govern the sounds of language, word structures, and word forms that provide the basic elements of meaning, and the order and combination of words to form sentences
Content	Inability to understand or correctly transmit the intent and meaning of words and sentences
Use	Inability to apply language appropriately in social context and discourse

Articulation is related to the speaker's age, culture, and environment (Plante & Beeson, 1999). Compare the speech of a 3-year-old child, a 10-year-old, and an adult. Some of the most common articulation errors young children make are substitutions and distortions of the *s* and *z* sounds and substituting a *w* for an *l* and a *w* for an *r*. A 3-year-old might say, "Thee Thuzi thwim" for "See Suzi swim," and is perceived by adults as being cute and acceptable. However, the same articulation behavior in a 10-year-old child or an adult is not developmentally correct or acceptable. Articulation behavior that is developmentally normal at one age is not acceptable at another. The chart in Figure 5.3 on page 186 gives the ages when various speech sounds develop. For example, most children learn to articulate *p, m, h, n, w, b* sounds from ages 2 to 3. But the range for learning to articulate *t* and *ng* can be from ages 2 to 6 (Sander, 1972). Some children are able to correctly articulate particular speech sounds earlier than the ages shown in Figure 5.3, and others develop them later.

About 2 to 3% of all children require professional help to overcome or compensate for their articulation errors. Teachers and others working with young children should be aware that children ages 2 to 6 generally make certain articulation mistakes as they go through a normal sequence of speech sound development. Adults should not pay too much attention to such misarticulations. However, if adults become concerned that a child is not acquiring articulation

Children with speech or language impairments may require extra encouragement to practice their newly acquired skills in front of their peers.

Notes: Average-age estimates and upper-age limits of customary consonant production. The solid bar corresponding to each sound starts at the median age of customary articulation; it stops at the age level at which 90% of all children are customarily producing the sound.

The θ symbol stands for the breathed "th" sound, as in the word *bathroom*. The δ symbol stands for the voiced "th" sound, as in the word *feather*. The η symbol stands for the "ing" sound, as in the word *singing*. The zh symbol indicates the sound of the medial consonant in *measure* or *vision*.

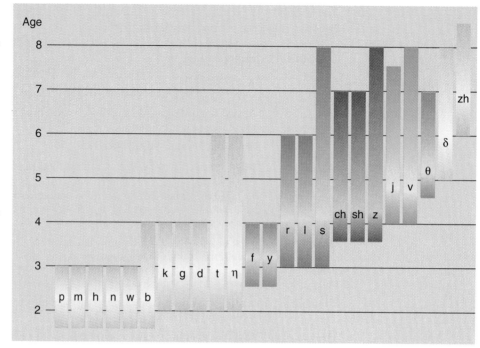

Figure 5.3 Sander's Chart, Indicating When 90% of All Children Typically Produce a Specific Sound Correctly

Source: "When Are Speech Sounds Learned?" by E. K. Sander, 1972, *Journal of Speech and Hearing Disorders, 37*, p. 62. © American Speech-Language-Hearing Association. Reprinted by permission.

skills in a normal manner (see Figure 5.3), the child should be referred to an SLP for a speech evaluation.

Articulation, as mentioned earlier, is also related to the geographical region in which a person lives. For example, some people from certain sections of New York substitute a *d* for the *th* sound, resulting in *dese, dem,* and *dose*. Bostonians often use an *er* sound for an a (*idear* for *idea*), and many Southerners draw out vowels. Although these different articulations are apparent to people who do not reside in a particular locale, they are normal in those regions. Differences in articulation due to regional dialects are not errors. Teachers should be careful not to refer children who have moved from one area of the country to another to an SLP solely because of dialectal differences in their speech.

FLUENCY PROBLEMS. Fluency difficulties are associated with the rate and flow pattern of a person's speech. **Fluency problems** usually involve hesitations or repetitions that interrupt the flow of speech. **Stuttering** is one type of fluency problem.

Some young children (ages 3 to 5) often demonstrate **dysfluencies** (nonfluencies) in the course of normal speech development, but they are not usually indicative of a fluency problem. Adult speech is not always smooth and fluent either. Even the best of speakers find times when they are dysfluent—when they hesitate in the middle of sentences, repeat parts of words, speak very quickly, or insert fillers such as "you know," "like," or "umm" in their speech. Dysfluencies are likely to occur in exciting, stressful, or uncommon situations.

fluency problems. Hesitations or repetitions of sounds or words that interrupt a person's flow of speech.

stuttering. The lack of fluency in an individual's speech pattern, often characterized by hesitations or repetitions of sounds or words.

dysfluencies. Aspects of speech that interrupt the pattern of speech; typical of normal speech development in young children.

As young children search for words or the rules to apply to their messages, they may become disfluent, and their manner of speech may suggest stuttering. The rate of their dysfluencies may even fit a definition of stuttering. However, in young children (below age 6), the rate of spontaneous recovery is great, possibly as high as 75% (Ratner, 1995). As with articulation, excessive attention to a perceived fluency problem early in a child's development can exaggerate rather than eliminate the problem. However, because of the remarkable results now being demonstrated by early intervention programs designed to remediate stuttering, it is inadvisable to delay intervention much beyond the age of 3½ (Onslow et al., 1994). Individuals who have a stuttering problem persisting into childhood frequently experience some difficulty in speaking throughout their lives. Their ability to communicate, their interactions with other people, and their own self-concepts are affected, but their speech generally can be improved with professional help.

Language Impairments. Language is the second major area within the special education category referred to as speech or language impairments. It is the complex system we use to communicate our thoughts to others. Oral language is expressed through the use of speech sounds that are combined to produce words and sentences. Other language systems, such as manual communication or sign language, use gestures or other means of communication, but not speech sounds. There are three aspects of language: form, content, and use.

FORM. The rule systems used in oral language are referred to as **form.** Three rule systems characterize form in language: phonology, morphology, and syntax.

Phonology is the sound system of language; it includes the rules that govern various sound combinations. The phonology of language varies according to language. For example, the speech sounds of Hawaiian are different from those of Spanish and from those of English. The English language, for instance, uses forty-five different speech sound combinations; the Hawaiian language uses only half that number. Swahili and some Native American languages use "clicking" sounds not found in European languages. Rules in each language govern how vowels, consonants, their combinations, and words are used. Researchers now understand the importance of children developing an awareness of sounds in words, and the relationship between phonological awareness during the preschool years and later ease of learning how to read (Ball, 1997; Webster et al., 1997; Torgesen & Wagner, 1998).

The rules that govern the parts of words that form the basic elements of meanings and the structures of words are called **morphology.** For example, prefixes and suffixes change the meanings of the roots of specific words: An *-ed* at the end of a verb changes the tense to past; a *un-* at the beginning of a word means that something is not. Notice the difference in the meanings of the following words: *cover, uncover, covered, uncovered, covers, discovered, discovering, discover, discovery, recover.* We understand the changes in these words' meanings because we understand the rules governing the structure of words.

Syntax determines where a word is placed in a sentence. Like phonology rules, syntax rules vary in different languages. Compare how a sentence is made negative in the English language, in Spanish, or in French, if you are familiar with Spanish or French. The rules within a language determine the meaning of the communication. In English, nouns generally precede verbs in a sentence; but when they do not, the construction might be a question: *It is one o'clock. Is it one o'clock?* The placement of the words in sentences can change their meaning. For example, *The car hit the boy*

form. The rule system of language; it is comprised of phonology, morphology, and syntax.

phonology. The rules within a language used to govern the combination of speech sounds to form words and sentences.

morphology. Rules that govern the structure and form of words and comprise the basic meaning of words.

syntax. Rules that govern word endings and order of words in phrases and sentences.

has a meaning very different from *The boy hit the car.* Rules also structure our placement of adverbs and other parts of speech. *I hardly studied this chapter* and *I studied this chapter hard* show different understandings of how the elements of the English language are put together. Many of these subtleties can be difficult to master.

Form is important in all language (oral, written, and sign); form comprises the rules of language where not all combinations are acceptable. Oral language uses sounds or sound combinations and written language use letters and letter combinations to produce the words and word combinations (sentences) of language. The use of these sounds letters (symbols) and words is governed by the rules of language. What we know about speech sounds, letters, words (or vocabulary), and rules of language influences the way we speak, read, write, and spell. Games like Scrabble, Wheel of Fortune, and Hangman require knowledge about letters and their rules for combinations. Those who play such games well have mastered these rules of language.

CONTENT. The second aspect of language, **content,** relates to the intent and meanings of spoken or written statements. The rules and form of language are important, but for communication to be effective, words must be meaningful. **Semantics** is the system that patterns the intent and meanings of words and sentences to comprise the content of the communication. The key words in a statement, the direct and implied referents to these words, and the order of the words used all affect the meaning of the message. Often we are not clear and precise in our use of words; we use words like *these* and *those, here* and *there,* without being exact. When senders of messages use indirect or implied referents, the receiver might not understand the message that is intended. When a child comes home and tells his mother, for instance, that he "left it at school," she might be unclear about what the child left at school, unless he is answering a direct question like "Where is your jacket?"

USE. The third aspect of language, **use,** concerns the application of language in various communications according to the social context of the situation. Use includes **pragmatics,** which is the study of language in context, and in part focuses on the intention of the communication. For example, an individual may request, order, or give an action or some information through a communication; the communication is different depending on the intent or the social context of the communication. Thus the context of discussion between two children talking to each other during free play is quite different from the context of discussion between a teacher and a child. Blank, Rose, and Berlin (1978) brought the importance of pragmatics to the attention of professionals. They pointed out that a child must know what an object is before it can be labeled meaningfully, described, or referred to in communication. For example, a child must know what a cup is—an object that holds liquid, is picked up, is used to drink from—before that child can develop a concept about cups or use it in conversation. Blank and her colleagues' pragmatics approach integrates the teaching of words and even concepts with instruction that allows children to build and expand on their own experiences. The pragmatic approach serves as the basis for many instructional sequences popular today.

The relationships among language, perception, and cognition are key factors in the development of **communicative competence.** Ruiz (1995) helps us understand this important concept: "[Communicative competence] is what a speaker needs to know to communicate appropriately—what may be said and what should not be said; when, where, and by whom; and for what purposes—in addition to the linguistic knowledge necessary to produce grammatical utterances" (p. 477). Students

content. An aspect of language that governs the intent and meaning of the message delivered in a communication; includes semantics.

semantics. The system within a language that governs content, intent, and meanings of spoken and written language.

use. An aspect of language; applying language appropriately; includes pragmatics.

pragmatics. A key element of communication; the relationship among language, perception, and cognition.

communicative competence. Proficiency in the use of language, allowing people to participate in all aspects of communication in social and learning situations.

For supporting information about communicative competence, see:
- Social Competence (Chapter 4)
- Defined in this chapter

who are not communicatively competent have difficulties understanding teachers' instructions, their lectures, and often interactions with their peers. Ruiz likens this situation to a class being taught in a foreign language the students do not understand. Such students are unable to participate successfully in the communication process that Marvin compared to a game. Many reasons can explain the students' lack of communicative competence. It may be that they have not mastered the necessary language skills because they are still learning English, or it may be due to an actual language impairment.

To achieve competence in communication, a person must be able to use language correctly in a social context. Social competence and communicative competence are related. Being able to communicate effectively is an essential component of being able socially (Walker et al., 1994). Social conventions or rules are used to initiate conversations and to communicate with others. Thus the way we use language at home or with our friends in a casual conversation is different from the way we speak to an employer, a school principal, or people in authority. Not understanding the social rules of language can have serious consequences. For instance, perceived rudeness to a teacher can result in a trip to the principal's office. Remember, mastering the rules and the nuances of language and communication can be difficult for some children. Also, successful conversations require that all aspects of language (form, content, and use) be applied with the rules of conversation (Weiss, 1995).

IDENTIFICATION

Although most people can tell that someone has a speech or language impairment by listening to that person, the formal assessment of speech and language impairments is complicated. Assessment typically involves the use of both standardized tests, such as the *Test of Language Development (TOLD)*, as well as informal testing in contextual situations, like free play. The free play situation is the primary source of the assessment of the child's spontaneous speech, which about 75% of SLPs incorporate into their evaluations (Johnston et al., 1993). Usually, SLPs conduct these assessments because they have the necessary skills, knowledge, and training in normal and abnormal speech and language development. If a hearing loss is suspected as a reason for the speech or language impairment, the SLP is joined by an audiologist.

Speech Impairments. Each of the three aspects of speech—articulation, voice, and fluency—requires a different type of assessment to determine whether the child has an impairment. Given that it is the most common problem in children, let's look at articulation first.

ARTICULATION. These errors are very common in children, but not all occurrences represent a speech impairment. Children learn to articulate the sounds of our language throughout their early childhood. The last sound most U.S. children master at 90% accuracy is the z sound (as in *was*) by age 8½. So the judgment about whether a child has an articulation problem must be made by considering when children typically master various speech sounds. For example, a 6-year-old who cannot produce the z sound correctly probably does not have a speech impairment, but a child of age 12 who is still making many articulation errors probably does have an articulation problem.

Refer again to Figure 5.3 to review the ages when speech sounds are typically mastered.

When considering whether children have a speech impairment, SLPs must consider both age and situation. Professionals understand that children tend to simplify speech and make more articulation errors when they are excited, in an unfamiliar setting, or nervous (Plante & Beeson, 1999). For example, a very young child eager for a freshly baked cupcake might say, "I dan a tutay." Under normal situations, the child would articulate the specific sounds correctly and say, "I want a cupcake." Articulation errors like these, even when made in nonstressful situations, might not represent a speech impairment for a young child but certainly would for an older child or adolescent.

Some children make articulation errors because they do not use the right motor responses to form the sounds correctly. The cause may be a physical problem, such as a **cleft palate,** where the roof of the mouth is not joined together, or an injury to the mouth. The cause may also be errors in the way the individual uses the speech mechanisms—tongue, lips, teeth, mandible (jaw), or palate—to form the speech sounds.

People can make four different kinds of articulation errors: substitutions, distortions, omissions, and additions; Table 5.2 defines and provides an example of each type. Any one of these articulation errors can affect or change the meaning of a communication; more than one error must occur before a child is diagnosed as having an articulation problem. However, no hard-and-fast rules exist regarding the number and types of articulation errors a child must make before a referral for speech therapy is appropriate. SLPs use their professional judgment and weigh a number of factors when identifying children as having an articulation problem. For example, they consider how seriously communication is negatively affected by poor articulation and the frequency, type, and consistency of errors a child makes. Most children with articulation problems, even those whose speech is almost unintelligible, have no apparent physiological reason for their articulation difficulties. In fact, some children can correctly pronounce a sound when it is found at the beginning of words but not when it is in the medial position or in some words and not in others (Rice, 1995). The functional nature of articulation problems can sometimes make it difficult to determine when therapy is actually required.

VOICE. These problems are not common in young children. However, a significant change in voice or a voice quality that deviates substantially from those of one's peers can be a sign of a serious laryngeal disease. For this reason, even very young children with an abnormal voice quality should have a medical examination. Overall, there are two general reasons for voice problems in children: an organic cause (such as a tumor) and a functional cause. Functional causes of voice problems are usually due to individuals using their voices inappropriately. For example, screaming for long periods of time puts undue stress on the vocal folds and larynx, causing damage to the voice mechanisms: The voice will sound hoarse, too low or high in pitch, or breathy. As with articulation, SLPs measure voice by using their clinical judgment—their knowledge and experience—to determine when a child's voice is actually impaired and in need of therapy.

cleft palate. An opening in the roof of the mouth, causing too much air to pass through the nasal cavity when the individual is speaking.

FLUENCY. The third kind of speech impairment is a fluency problem: The flow of speech breaks down because syllables are repeated or a communication includes many hesitations or extraneous words or sounds. Stuttering is a fluency problem, but there are important distinctions between stuttering and dysfluent speech. All of us, particularly young children mastering language, are dysfluent sometimes, and

Table 5.2
Four Kinds of Articulation Errors

Error Type	Definition	Example
Omission	A sound or group of sounds is left out of a word. Small children often leave off the ending of a word (sounds in the final position).	Intended: *I want a banana.* Omission: *I wanna nana.*
Substitution	A common misarticulation among small children, one sound is used for another.	Intended: *I see the rabbit.* Substitution: *I tee the wabbit.*
Distortion	A variation of the intended sound is produced in an unfamiliar manner.	Intended: *Give the pencil to Sally.* Distortion: *Give the pencil to Sally* (the /p/ is nasalized).
Addition	An extra sound is inserted or added to one already correctly produced.	Intended: *I miss her.* Addition: *I missid her.*

this is normal. Adults can distinguish between normal dysfluency and stuttering in children by noticing carefully what aspects of speech are repeated (Plante & Beeson, 1999). One very important aspect is the age of the child. Children around age 3½ are still hesitant in their language use. They spend a lot of energy searching for words and retrieving thoughts. At this age, children often repeat words and phrases. By age 4½, one year later, repetitions of words and phrases have an entirely different purpose. They are used for emphasis.

Another difference between normal dysfluencies and stuttering is in what gets repeated. Children with normal speech often repeat whole words or phrases, like "Give me the, give me the, give me the ball." Children who stutter are more likely to say "Gi-gi-gi-give m-m-m-me the b-b-b-ball"—that is, they repeat specific sounds or syllables. Children who stutter also have a higher frequency of repetitions than do children who are dysfluent. For example, children with normal speech do not repeat more than 3% of what they say, whereas children who stutter repeat syllables in 7% to 14% of what they say (Wingate, 1962). They also tend to show nonverbal signs of struggling with their speech by blinking, grimacing, or becoming tense. SLPs measure a fluency problem by analyzing the frequency and type of an individual's involuntary dysfluencies from samples of oral language taken in various situations, such as free play and answering direct questions.

Language Impairments. Difficulties in language can result in more serious learning problems than speech impairments cause. Lack of language competence influences children's ability to learn to read and write at the pace of their classmates as well as their ability to communicate orally with others. An SLP assesses an individual's language competence through a thorough evaluation, which usually includes assessment of the three aspects of language: form, content, and use. To assess the *form* or structure of an individual's language, the SLP determines how well the child uses the rules of language. Problems with form cause errors in letter or sound formation, grammatical structure usage, or in sentence formation. Many children who have difficulty with the rules of language also have problems recognizing sounds

For more information about the relationship between language impairments and learning problems, see:
- Prevention section (Chapter 4)
- Prevention section (Chapter 6)
- Social Skills section (Chapter 4)
- Preschool section (Chapter 6)

and understanding the meaning of different grammatical constructions, sentence types, and sentence complexities. For example, a child who has not mastered the rules of language might not be able to tell the difference between these two sentences: *Go to the store. Did you go to the store?* The second aspect of language that SLPs assess to determine language competence is *content*. Children with problems in language content often do not understand the meaning of what is said to them and choose inappropriate words for their oral language communications. They might also have difficulty comprehending the written material presented in textbooks. The third aspect of language competence, *use* (pragmatics), is discussed to determine how appropriately a child uses language in social contexts and conversations.

Finally, the SLP prepares an evaluation report that becomes part of the child's permanent record if the evaluation was conducted by or paid for by the school district the child attends. This report presents the status of the child's speech and language and includes a statement about whether the child has a speech or language impairment. It also presents a summary of the child's strengths and weaknesses in speech and language and an overall assessment of the child's language competence. In addition, the report usually includes a suggested remediation plan, a list of the services the child requires, and a statement about the predicted outcome of treatment and remediation. The SLP reviews this report with the parents so that they understand which specific services are being recommended and why. For a child diagnosed as having a speech or language impairment, this process is the beginning of a partnership of parents and professionals working together to remediate the child's disability.

SIGNIFICANCE

Read again the short biographical sketch of Lewis Carroll at the beginning of this chapter to see how his life and career choices were influenced by his stuttering problem

Understanding and being able to use speech and language well influences an individual's success in school, social situations, and employment. A speech impairment affects how a person interacts with others in all kinds of settings. The story of Lewis Carroll is not uncommon among those who stutter. Their impairment often influences career choices, social life, and emotional well-being. It is not uncommon for children to develop emotional problems because of their stuttering. Some researchers (Shames & Ramig, 1998) believe that as listeners, and the individuals themselves, react to this nonfluent speech, feelings of embarrassment, guilt, frustration, or anger are commonly experienced. Stuttering can lead to confusion, feelings of helplessness, and diminished self-concept. The long-term effects can be quite serious. Some individuals respond by acting overly aggressive, denying their disability, and projecting their own negative reactions to their listeners. Others withdraw socially, seeking to avoid all situations in which they have to talk, and ultimately they become isolates.

A language impairment has the potential of being even more serious, for it can impact all aspects of a child's classroom experiences, including the abilities to speak, write, and comprehend what is written and spoken. Language is a complex system to master: Its rules are not consistent, and it has many subtle conventions to learn and follow. Language is an important foundation to the skills children learn at school, however. We know of the relationship between the knowledge of language and the ability to learn to read and write easily. The histories of many children with learning disabilities reveal that they were identified as having a significant language delay or impairment as preschoolers. There are many reasons for a relationship between learning disabilities and language impairment. For example, children who do not understand what is said to them do not develop language at the same rate as children who do understand and benefit from communicative interchanges. Some children with delayed language also do not develop cognitive or thinking skills at the same pace as their nondisabled peers, which can influence all levels of academic achievement, particularly in reading and writing.

Clearly, people who cannot communicate well find that their impairment affects the way they interact with others and how efficiently they communicate and learn. Ultimately, it influences employment options. For example, a receptionist in an office must be able to talk on the phone, take and deliver messages to the public and to other workers in the office, and provide directions to visitors. Thus these individuals should be provided with the services they need to enable them to learn how to communicate successfully with others.

HISTORY OF THE FIELD

Review the ways people with disabilities were treated across history: read again the section called The Essence of Disabilities in Chapter 1.

Speech and language problems have been a part of the human condition since our ancestors began to speak. Even before 1000 B.C., individuals with disabilities were considered fools, buffoons, and sources of entertainment. During Roman times, cages were placed along the Appian Way to display individuals with disabilities. There, Balbus Balaesus the Stutterer would attempt to talk when a coin was thrown into his cage (Van Riper & Erickson, 1996).

There have been many documented cases of speech or language impairments throughout the centuries. Treatment programs also existed; they were not based in schools, and they met with mixed results. In the United States, speech correction was not available in the public schools until the twentieth century. In 1910, the Chicago public schools hired an itinerant teacher to help children who "stammered" (Moore & Kester, 1953). In 1913, the superintendent of the New York City schools began a program for speech training for children with speech impairments. The first speech clinic was opened in 1914 by Smiley Blanton at the University of Wisconsin. In 1925, the American Academy for Speech Correction (later called the American Speech and Hearing Association and now called American Speech-Language-Hearing Association) was formed by a small group of professionals to share their ideas and research. Robert West spearheaded the formation of the academy and is credited by some (Van Riper, 1981) as being the father of his field. Two other pioneers, Lee Travis and Wendell Johnson, developed the program at the University of Iowa and guided this emerging field at the organizational and national level. Through their guidance, the field of speech or language impairments became independent from medicine, psychology, and speech and debate.

In the early part of the twentieth century, public schools hired speech clinicians to work with children who had speech problems, but services were limited. During World War II, the military developed screening procedures to identify persons with speech problems and hearing losses and began their own clinical and research programs. These efforts demonstrated that speech therapy can be effective, and after the war university programs to train SLPs increased in size and number. Correspondingly, public school programs expanded. By 1959, thirty-nine states had laws allowing or requiring school districts to provide services for students with disabilities, including those with speech or language impairments, and to receive state funding.

Throughout the history of the field, professionals who work to remediate children's speech and language problems have had many titles, partly because of their

Robert West, one of the founders of what is now the American Speech-Language-Hearing Association, is considered by many to be the father of this field.

changing roles. At first they were called speech correctionists or speech teachers; these early professionals centered their efforts on remediating stuttering, voice, and articulation difficulties. During the late 1950s and 1960s, professionals began to be called speech therapists and speech clinicians. In this period, they saw more than two hundred children per week, primarily in small groups for as little as thirty minutes per day. However, many children with language problems, with moderate to severe disabilities, with multiple disabilities, or with mental retardation did not receive speech therapy because professionals thought these children were not developmentally able to profit from therapy. During the early 1970s, professionals were called speech pathologists. By the end of that decade, ASHA coined the term *speech/language pathologist* to reflect the broader view of the services they provide.

The 1970s was a period of transition. ASHA and the professionals it represents sought to further improve the quality of services provided to children. Research data indicated that many articulation problems were developmental and were corrected naturally with age. Therefore this period of time also saw a shift in the priorities of speech therapy in the schools. SLPs began to work with fewer children with mild articulation problems and concentrated on youngsters with severe speech or language problems. Today, SLPs often consult and collaborate with general education classroom teachers to remediate minor speech or language problems. SLPs can then work intensively with twenty or thirty children who have serious speech or language impairments.

PREVALENCE

CONNECTIONS MAKING

To see the relationships between language problems and disabilities, scan Chapters 3, 4, 6, and 10.

Many professionals believe that children with speech or language impairments form the largest population of students with disabilities in the schools, and some estimate that the prevalence in schoolchildren may be as high as 10% (Boone & Plante, 1993). However, as noted in Chapters 1 and 4, official reports show that the largest single category of exceptional learners consistently is learning disabilities (U.S. Department of Education, 1998). How can we account for these differing opinions? Remember that children are reported by their primary disabling condition. For a large proportion of children with speech or language impairments, their primary disabling condition is hard of hearing or deafness, learning disabilities, mental retardation, or health impairments. When the children have *only* a speech or language impairment, they are counted in this group, which is the second in prevalence even using this system of counting. In the only study of its kind, the caseloads of SLPs showed that 42% of all the children with communicative difficulties had another primary disabling condition (Dublinski, 1981). As you'll see from the numbers presented next, speech or language impairments would be the largest special education category if primary and secondary disabilities were combined.

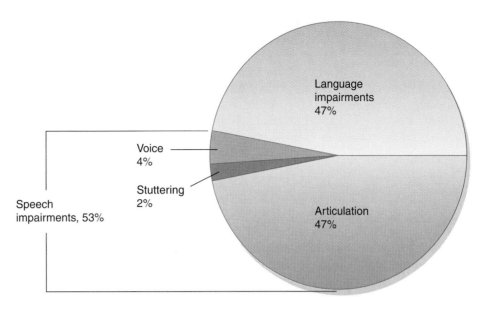

Figure 5.4 The Percentage of Students Having Different Types of Speech and Language Impairments

NEW DIRECTIONS
FOR THE
MILLENNIUM

Legacy: Confusion exists at the early ages between language impairments and learning disabilities; many more young children are identified as having language impairments than learning disabilities, but as children get older the reverse is true.

Opportunities:
- Combine these two disability areas up through the early years of elementary school
- Provide these children with an intensive, integrated language and literacy development curriculum

Data from the *Twentieth Annual Report to Congress on the Implementation of IDEA* (U.S. Department of Education, 1998) indicate that during the 1996–1997 schoolyears 1.7% of the entire school-age population was identified as having a disability because of speech or language impairments or both. Thus more than 2 of every 100 schoolchildren, or a total of 1,050,975 students between the ages of 6 and 17, received services for speech or language impairments as their primary disability. If this comprises 58% of those school-age youngsters SLPs serve, then an additional 441,410 students whose primary disabling condition was not speech or language impairments received supportive services because of speech or language difficulties or both. And of this group, how many have speech impairments and how many have language impairments? Estimates indicate that 53% of the students seen by SLPs have speech impairments and 47% have language impairments (Dublinski, 1981). The percentages of students with language impairments and each type of speech impairment are shown in Figure 5.4.

Of interest to professionals in the field is the relationship between a student's age and these disabilities. Articulation problems, for example, are more common during the preschool and elementary years. Speech or language impairments is definitely a most common label used for children at the age of 6 (the first year they must be identified as belonging to a special education category). For the age group of 6–11, the size of the speech or language impairments category was about 160,000 students smaller than the learning disabilities category (U.S. Department of Education, 1998). However, this comparison is very different for students in the 12–17 age group, where learning disabilities is 1,332,929 larger than the speech or language impairment category. Why might this be so? Do these problems disappear with age? Are early remediation efforts so successful that these impairments are corrected and do not persist through childhood? Or are these youngsters reclassified into another group (such as learning disabilities) as they become older? The answers to these questions rather are most likely based in the expectations and

For overall student dis-abilities rates, see Figure 1.1 (Chapter 1)

Read each of the sec-tions about the causes of specific disabilities to understand that the cause of most cases of disabilities is unknown

demands of different settings. "The earlier diagnosis of language disability often re-flects the expectancies of the preschool curriculum, whereas the later diagnosis of learning disability aligns with the complex demands of a more academic curricu-lum" (Schoenbrodt et al., 1997, p. 264). Clearly, the association between language impairments, often identified in early childhood, and learning disabilities, often identified as the reading demands of academic learning increase, is strong and now widely accepted (Tallal et al., 1996; Wallach & Butler, 1995).

CAUSES AND PREVENTION

Researchers attempt to find what factors cause certain disabilities so that they might be prevented. In this section, you will learn that although there are various theories, professionals still do not know what causes many types of speech or language im-pairments. You will also find that some impairments are preventable and that oth-ers are not.

CAUSES

As with so many disability areas, the most common cause of speech or language im-pairments is unknown. As you read through this section, however, you will find that many causes for some specific impairments are well known.

Speech Impairments. In general, the known causes of speech impairments are varied and include brain damage, malfunction of the respiratory or speech mecha-nisms, or malformation of the articulators. Some types of impairments have an or-ganic cause, meaning that there is a physical reason for the disability. For example, many individuals with severely misaligned teeth cannot articulate well. Once their adult teeth grow in, however, their articulation will probably be fine, so they do not have a speech impairment. This example shows how a problem with an articulator can affect speech; other organic causes of speech impairments are more serious. For example, a cleft lip or palate affects the ability to produce speech. This incidence varies by race/ethnicity: about 1 of every 500 live births for Asian Americans, about 1 of 750 live births for Whites, and 1 of 2,000 for African Americans (McWilliams & Witzel, 1998). The proportions of cleft lips and palates tend to be consistent: about 25% involve the lip, 50% involve the lip and the palate, and the remaining 25% involve the palate. Most cleft lips can be repaired through plastic surgery and do not have a long-term effect on articulation. A cleft palate, however, can present continual problems because the opening of the palate (the roof of the mouth) al-lows excessive air and sound waves to flow through the nasal cavities. The result is a very nasal-sounding voice and difficulties in producing some speech sounds, such as *s* and *z*. A cleft palate is one physical cause of a speech impairment that requires the intensive work of many specialists (plastic surgeons, orthodontists, and SLPs) to help the individual overcome the resulting speech disability.

Too many young children are referred by their teachers to SLPs for articulation problems. These referrals are made because teachers do not remember that speech sounds are mastered at different ages and that individual children acquire specific speech sounds at different times (see Figure 5.3). Many children outgrow their in-ability to properly articulate sounds. Children who make consistent articulation er-rors that are not developmental, however, are less likely to learn to make speech sounds correctly without therapy. In other words, those who make consistent errors tend not to "outgrow" established misarticulation patterns (Van Riper & Erickson, 1996). Therefore all children who are late in acquiring correct production of specific speech sounds and make consistent articulation errors should be referred to an SLP for assessment.

Voice problems are not as common in schoolchildren, although they can be symptomatic of a medical problem. For example, conditions that interfere with muscular activity, such as juvenile arthritis, can result in a vocal disturbance. Voice problems also can be caused by the way the voice is used: Undue abuse of the voice by screaming, shouting, and straining can cause damage to the vocal folds and result in a voice disorder. Rock singers frequently strain their voices so much that they develop nodules (calluses) on the vocal folds, become chronically hoarse, and must stop singing or have the nodules removed surgically. Teachers who notice changes in children's voices that are not associated with puberty should refer the student to an SLP.

Stuttering, a lack of fluency in speaking, may be characterized by severe hesitations or the repetition of sounds and words. Although professionals can describe stuttering, they seem unable to agree on or explain a single cause (Silverman, 1996). It appears that stuttering is not linked to underlying deficiencies in language knowledge or language abilities (Ratner, 1995). In other words, the language capabilities of individuals who stutter are not different from those who do not stutter. Specialists can, however, describe conditions when nonfluency is more likely to occur in stutterers. For example, stuttering is more likely to occur when the conversational situation is very complex or unpredictable (Weiss, 1995). It appears that stress makes its likelihood more probable. It seems that these individuals are less able than those who do not stutter to monitor their speech and recognize when it is not fluent (Finn & Ingham, 1994). Evidently, monitoring their speech is not a natural act and may well prove to be an important instructional target.

Language Impairments. Many problems that fall into the area of language impairments have multiple causes. As with **aphasia,** they can result from brain injury or disease that damages the central nervous system. They can result from the inability to hear well at the time language should be developing. For example, children with chronic **otitis media,** or ear infections, often have associated difficulties with language development, possibly because of interruptions in hearing language during the typical developmental periods or because of related health problems (Vernon-Feagans et al., 1996).

Recent discoveries point to an inherited link to language impairments (Lahey & Edwards, 1995; Rice, 1997). Findings from this line of research clearly show that in some families both immediate and extended family members share similar difficulties in mastering language. Particular aspects of language use, such as correct agreement between subject and verb, presents specific difficulties for these individuals, many of whom do *not* have cognitive impairments. For example, these people are likely to say "She walk home" or "They is happy" instead of using the right noun-verb pattern. The rates of being troubled by such grammar acquisition problems are very high within family units, convincing researchers of a genetic basis for some language impairments. And the further connection between language impairments and reading problems is also thought to have a genetic origin.

Heredity, however, does not explain all language impairments. Poor language development can be caused by environmental factors, including the lack of stimulation

C O N N E C T I O N S
MAKING

For supporting information about factors that can contribute to poor language development, see:
- Causes and Prevention (Chapter 4)
- Causes and Prevention (Chapter 6)

aphasia. Loss or impairment of language ability due to brain injury.

otitis media. Middle ear infection that can result in hearing loss, communication impairments, or learning disabilities if it becomes a chronic condition.

and proper experiences for mental development and learning language. Environmental factors also affect children's abilities to acquire language and become proficient in its use. Some children do not develop language because they have no appropriate role models. Some are left alone too often; others are not spoken to frequently. Some are punished for speaking or are ignored when they try to communicate. Many of these children have no reason to speak; they have nothing to talk about and few experiences to share. Such youngsters are definitely at risk for developing significant language impairments. Fortunately, early intervention programs can reduce or eliminate the probability of acquiring this disability.

As we know, language develops throughout childhood. The ability to use language and follow its rules increases with a child's age. Although individual children acquire language skills at different times, normal language seems to develop in the same sequence, even during the first eighteen months of life (Stark, Bernstein, & Demorest, 1993). Children with typical language development gain skills in an orderly fashion, like the youngster whose profile is shown in Table 5.3. Note that most children after age 3 (40 months) can use some fairly sophisticated language. The child with language impairments at the same age is speaking in only two-word combinations, however.

Differences between children whose language is delayed and those whose language is impaired are apparent to those who analyze children's language development. Children with delayed language generally acquire language in the same sequence as their peers but do so more slowly. Many of these children do not have a disability and catch up with their peers. Some children acquire language in the correct sequence, do so very slowly, and never complete the acquisition of complex language structures. For example, most children with mental retardation have **language delays.** Their language development will remain below that of their peers who have normal intelligence and are developing at expected rates. Some, like Leonard, maintain that these youngsters' language is not impaired, but rather merely delayed. These children profit from intensive language instruction that can be delivered by classroom teachers with the help of SLPs. Leonard (1994) claims that children with language impairments tend to follow a common pattern of language acquisition: They develop slowly and differently. Review Table 5.3 again; notice that the child with disabilities uses the word ending *-ing* after her mean sentence length is two words. The normally developing child is using *-ing* at the same time that she is using two-word combinations. Many children with severe language impairments require intensive remediation efforts, usually delivered by an SLP.

What of the child who is not a native speaker? As discussed in Chapter 3, many teachers have difficulty determining whether a child who is not a native speaker of English is merely **language-different** or has a language impairment (Gonzalez et al., 1997; Langdon & Cheng, 1992). Cultural differences and family values also influence how individual children learn language skills, and it is important to understand that different interaction styles result in communicative competence. Remember, children whose primary language is English can have a language impairment; so, too, can children whose primary language is not English. English being a second language does not result in a disability. And English that reflects dialects of American English is not an impairment either (Payne & Taylor, 1998). Because so many language-different children, including those who come from the African American culture, are misidentified as having a language impairment (and therefore a disability), it is crucial that educators pay close attention to these children and seek

language delay. Development of language skills that is slower than in the majority of peers; may signal language that will require assistance of a specialist to use language proficiently.

language-different. Children who are not native English speakers and those who speak nonstandard English and do not have an impairment even though their language is not typical.

Table 5.3 Pattern of Development Shown by a Child with Language Impairments and by a Normally Developing Child

Child with Language Impairments			Normally Developing Child		
Age	Attainment	Example	Age	Attainment	Example
27 months	First words	*this, mama, bye bye, doggie*	13 months	First words	*here, mama, bye bye, kitty*
38 months	50-word vocabulary		17 months	50-word vocabulary	
40 months	First two-word combinations	*this doggie, more apple, this mama, more play*	18 months	First two-word combinations	*more juice, here ball, more TV, here kitty*
48 months	Later two-word combinations	*Mama purse, Daddy coat, black chair, dolly table*	22 months	Later two-word combinations	*Andy shoe, Mommy ring, cup floor, keys chair*
52 months	Mean sentence length of 2.00 words		24 months	Mean sentence length of 2.00 words	
55 months	First appearance of -ing	*Mommy eating*		First appearance of -ing	*Andy sleeping*
63 months	Mean sentence length of 3.10 words		30 months	Mean sentence length of 3.10 words	
66 months	First appearance of *is*	*The doggie's mad*		First appearance of *is*	*My car's gone!*
73 months	Mean sentence length of 4.10 words		37 months	Mean sentence length of 4.10 words	
79 months	Mean sentence length of 4.50 words			Mean sentence length of 4.50 words	*Can I have some cookies?*
	First appearance of indirect requests	*Can I get the ball?*	40 months	First appearance of indirect requests	

Source: "Language Disorders in Preschool Children" (p. 147) by L. Leonard, in G. H. Shames, E. H. Wiig, and W. A. Secord (Eds.), *Human Communication Disorders: An Introduction* (4th ed.), 1994. New York: Merrill, an imprint of Macmillan. Reprinted by permission.

For supporting information about language differences, see Chapter 3:
- Linguistically Diverse Students (Defined)
- Language and Communication Differences (Diverse Children)

assistance from other professionals when designing the most appropriate educational programs for them (Ruiz, 1995; van Keulen et al., 1998).

What is at issue for bilingual children? Remember that acquiring and mastering a second language is a long process. Many youngsters may appear to be fluent in English because they converse with their classmates on the playground and express their basic needs in the classroom. These abilities, however, are only some of the language skills acquired on the way toward communicative competence. What are the major concerns of students from diverse backgrounds? Dialects affect individuals' accents (the way spoken language sounds) and also can affect the rules for language use (Payne &Taylor, 1998). Dialects result from historical, social, regional, and cultural influences and are sometimes perceived by educators as inferior or nonstandard (Battle, 1996; van Keulen et al., 1998). As with bilingual children, many children

Legacy: Culturally and linguistically diverse students are too often misidentified as having an impairment when they need to be fully taught English as a second language.

Opportunities:

- Assist teachers to learn how to teach English as a second language
- Prepare teachers to understand the differences between language-different students and students with language impairments

MAKING CONNECTIONS

Partnerships with members of culturally and linguistically diverse communities are discussed in Chapter 3 (Collaboration for Inclusive Environments and Families sections).

from diverse backgrounds who use dialects, whether they be from Appalachia or a predominately Black inner-city community, are misidentified as having language impairments. Professionals who can make the distinction between language difference and language impairment must be proficient in the rules of the particular child's dialect and in nondiscriminatory testing procedures. Also, when linguistically diverse children learn in language-sensitive environments, the impression of language impairments is lessened, and they are supported while mastering English. All children benefit from classroom environments that support and enhance language development, and, in turn, unnecessary referrals can be held to a minimum.

PREVENTION

Some types of speech or language impairments can be prevented today. Most of these have a medical basis, and preventive measures for these problems are needed prior to the birth of a baby. For example, polio and rubella can have devastating effects on an unborn baby; proper immunization protects adults and children from these and other diseases. Recent research has shown that a nutritional supplement of folic acid during pregnancy can reduce the risk of cleft palates and lips by 25% to 50% (Maugh, 1995).

Proper prenatal care is important to the health of babies. Good nutrition influences the strength and early development of very young children. Also, the availability of proper medical care at birth is crucial so that conditions like viral encephalitis and otitis media can be avoided or treated early. Although no longer common in the general population, encephalitis is prevalent in poorer communities of our society. If left untreated, encephalitis causes brain damage, which in turn can result in cognitive and language disabilities. The link between poverty and language disabilities is clear. Those who are poor are less likely to have access to information and medical programs, which puts them at risk for disease. Better public education programs available to the entire population inform people of the necessity of good prenatal care, nutrition, and medical care. It may be, however, that innovative approaches to the dissemination of information about the importance of protecting children from disease may need to be implemented. For example, accessing the African American community may require different approaches. Participation in health fairs sponsored by churches, sororities, fraternities, and other community organizations may prove to be more effective ways to communicate important information than are traditional means (CDF, 1997). These services might initially be costly in time and effort, but the positive impact on preventing and overcoming disabilities is significant.

One of the most important ways of reducing the impact of any disability is through early identification, so that treatment can begin as soon as possible. With speech and language impairments, children who receive help and support from highly trained experts can learn to either correct or compensate for their disability. For many of these youngsters, referrals and identification will not occur until their school years, when speech and language are reaching their final stages of development. Alert teachers can be most helpful by conferring with a SLP about specific children's speech or language abilities. Concerns about whether a child's speech or language differences are developmental and will disappear with age, whether they are due to diverse language needs, or whether they are real signs of disabilities require immediate action. Partnerships between experts in speech and language development and classroom teachers result in appropriate and timely referrals.

CHILDREN WITH SPEECH OR LANGUAGE IMPAIRMENTS

Children with speech or language impairments comprise a large and diverse group of youngsters. Some have a speech impairment, others have a language impairment, and still others have both a speech and a language impairment. Naturally, these children have different learning needs. For example, a child with a voice problem will have a different remediation program than a child who has difficulty articulating speech sounds correctly. Certainly, those with speech impairments have entirely different remediation programs than children with language difficulties. Teachers must understand the differences among these types of problems so that they can make better referrals and more effectively assist with treatment programs see Table 5.4).

SPEECH IMPAIRMENTS

Most children whose primary disability is a speech impairment (articulation, voice, or fluency impairment) attend general education classes and function well academically with their peers. Usually their disability does not influence their academic learning. If, however, their speech impairment is severe and sustained, they might have some difficulty with their peers in social interactions. Depending on how the peer group reacts to an individual's disability, the person with a severe disability might have long-term difficulties with self-concept and independence (Van Riper & Erickson, 1996).

Social difficulties are particularly common for those who stutter (Shames & Ramig, 1998). Stuttering can negatively affect a person's sense of adequacy and confidence. To avoid embarrassment, many people who stutter avoid situations in which they have to talk, while some lash out and release their frustration and anger on

Table 5.4 Possible Signs or Characteristics of Speech and Language Impairments

Speech

Makes consistent and age-inappropriate articulation errors

Exhibits dysfluencies (repetitions, prolongations, interruptions) in the flow or rhythm of speech

Has poor voice quality, such as distracting pitch

Is excessively loud or soft

Language

Is unable to follow oral directions

Is unable to match letters with sounds

Has an inadequate vocabulary

Demonstrates poor concept formation

Has difficulty conveying messages or conversing with others

Has difficulty expressing personal needs

others. Consequently, their disability influences the types of jobs they seek, the friends they make, their relationships with others, and their overall quality of life. Think about how you react to people with severe speech impairments. Do you look away from them? Do you try to be helpful to the stutterer by finishing his or her sentence? Do you try to avoid the person? Now think about how young children treat their peers who use different speech sounds, who have a different voice quality, or who stutter. Facing these reactions is an everyday reality for individuals with speech impairments. It is understandable that some would like to withdraw from a society that treats them as different.

Teachers and peers can be most helpful; their actions can make a real difference in the way students with speech or language impairments feel about themselves and others. Environments shape the way people act. Events trigger behavior which in turn is maintained by the events that follow the behavior's occurrence. If stuttering causes peers to laugh and snicker every time it occurs, the individual who stutters will be negatively impacted. The chain of behaviors, however, can be changed through a process called **environmental restructuring.** Using this procedure, peers are taught about behavioral relationships: the causes and effects of actions. They are also taught how to change their behavior to be instructive and supportive. So, now peers learn how to act when their classmate stutters, how to encourage that individual to become involved in activities and groups, and how to monitor their reactions' effects on behavior.

For other useful strategies, see the Achieving Discipline boxes found in each chapter.

LANGUAGE IMPAIRMENTS

Language impairments have many different outcomes. Unlike most speech impairments, however, multiple results—beyond the production of oral language—are observed. Many youngsters' social competence is affected, and a variety of their social skills are inferior to those of peers without this disability. It is also quite common to find correlated cognitive and academic difficulties in children with language impairments.

Social Competence. The relationship between communicative competence and effective social skills is clear. Students with language impairments have a higher than average risk of having difficulties with peer relationships (Asher & Gazelle, 1999). Being able to understand messages and communicate well is important in interactions with peers and adults. For example, part of everyday life at school and in the community is resolving conflicts. It seems that conflict is an inevitable part of life because individuals have incompatible goals or a different understanding about an event or situation. Being able to solve misunderstandings or disagreements is an important skill that requires abilities to solve problems, understand others' points of view, and clearly present one's feelings. Language impairments, particularly in the pragmatic area, negatively influence the skills required for successful conflict resolution (Fujiki et al., 1999).

Language impairments due to problems in the area of pragmatics can result in other difficulties that negatively impact social skills. Many of these youngsters are unable to understand ambiguity in messages (Lloyd, 1994). They seem unable to identify the features that uniquely identify specific objects. For example, they might not be able to successfully play a game in which a target photograph is to be identified by a partner. When the objective is to make as few guesses as possible, the requirement is to describe the distinguishing features of the object using as few clues

environmental restructuring. Peers are instructed and reinforced for encouraging appropriate behavior in their classmate who is exhibiting disruptive behavior.

Achieving Discipline

CHANGING THE CONTEXT: ENVIRONMENTAL RESTRUCTURING

Marcos is a "class clown." Everyone enjoys his jokes and antics. It's hard not to laugh when he imitates the leader of the school's marching band, particularly when he does so during study hall. He blows a kazoo under a Kleenex, and the resulting chaos lands him in the principal's office. Marcos is not a popular child, and he stutters when called on by the teacher. Possibly, his inappropriate behavior serves to draw attention away from his speech impairment, and is also an attempt to gain recognition from his classmates. Marcos's behaviors involve the entire class, for his routines are for their benefit. Whatever it takes to get their attention and to get them to laugh hysterically seems to be within his capability.

Mr. Tyler, Marcos's sixth-grade teacher, understands that the social climate at school is set by everyone's actions. He decided to discuss Marcos's behavior with his fellow teachers and for everyone to come up with a united plan of action. Since Marcos's inappropriate behaviors involved the entire class, the whole class would be involved in the solution. Mr. Tyler discussed the situation with the class. Marcos's peers came to realize that they were partly responsible for encouraging Marcos's inappropriate behavior and it was their responsive actions that resulted in more silly behavior. Mr. Tyler helped the class understand that they could alter this situation. He taught his students not to respond to Marcos's different and outrageous behaviors. Mr. Tyler also helped the class learn not to laugh at Marcos when he stuttered, or when his speech seemed different from typical speech patterns. He also helped them learn how to encourage and reward appropriate behavior in each other and in Marcos. By understanding how they contribute to the creation of supportive environments and by changing the ways they respond to each other, these classmates came to accept individual differences and also help each other behave appropriately and responsibly.

Steps used in environmental restructuring

- Have class discussions that are guided by a teacher or counselor to: pinpoint the behaviors which disturb the learning environment, understand the class's role in encouraging and maintaining them, develop a helping attitude and concern about the target individual
- Help the class recognize their role in the dynamic
- Learn intervention strategies that reduce the likelihood of inappropriate behaviors
- Role-play scenarios where classmates instruct, ignore, and reward behaviors
- Reward class for restructuring their environment
- Reinforce target student for acting appropriately

CONNECTIONS MAKING

Information about the relationship between language skills and social competence is also found in Social Skills section (Chapter 4)

as possible. How would you help a partner know that it was a photo of a zebra and not of a giraffe that was the target? (Try color of its stripes.)

Children who do not have effective communication skills adjust their interaction patterns to avoid uncomfortable or inadequate situations (Asher & Gazelle, 1999; Rice, 1997). They tend to initiate conversations less. They do not engage in communications, and are more likely to rely heavily on adults for their verbal interactions. These students tend to have low social status. They are often ignored and rejected by their peers; children with good verbal abilities are often preferred playmates. The results are often extreme feelings of loneliness and overt harsh treatment by their classmates. Many children who experience general peer rejection, those who are not popular, also do not have friends. Having a close friend—someone with whom to share, seek advice, and gain comfort—is more important for personal adjustment than general popularity (Fujiki et al., 1999). Unfortunately, linguistically diverse students often share this negative status relationship with their classmates with language impairments, probably because of their insecurities about speaking English. To help all of these students, teachers can foster mutually supporting relationships among peers by helping students understand the nature of quality friendships, allow students who like each other to work together on class projects, and help them develop the skills needed for cooperation.

The impact of low social status can be pervasive. It not only influences how children are treated in play situations, it can also affect how they are treated by their classmates during instructional activities (Brinton & Fujiki, 1999). Teachers must be careful and conscious of the relationship between language skills and social status and encourage children to interact with each other on an equal basis. The importance of the concept of communicative competence should be becoming more apparent.

Cognitive and Academic Performance. "Cognition involves the representation and processing of knowledge about physical objects, events, and their relationships" (Stevens & Bliss, 1995, p. 599). Whether it be verbal or nonverbal (e.g., sign language), at the foundation of cognition is language. Research finding after research finding provides substantial evidence that children identified as having a language impairment during the preschool years are very likely to have difficulties mastering reading when they are in elementary school (Ball, 1997). Early abilities to detect sound segments, match beginning sounds, identify sound segments in words and phrases, and to rhyme—the link between these and success in learning to read is definite. Students who do not have these early abilities are at great risk for reading failure. As you have also learned, this situation can be corrected. Specific instruction that teaches phonological awareness and sound segmentation results in improved reading abilities, or provides the prerequisites to learning how to read.

Given the knowledge about the connection between language impairments and reading difficulties, it is not surprising then that other researchers have made a definite connection between language impairments and learning disabilities. Unlike children with speech problems, children with language impairments often have related academic difficulties in school (Wallach & Butler, 1995). Some believe that 80% of all students with learning disabilities have a language impairment (Wiig & Secord, 1998). And a commonly held belief among professionals is that a language impairment diagnosed in a preschooler will result in a learning disability during the schoolyears. Others draw clear connections between early language impairments and later difficulties in developing literacy (Fey et al., 1995). Since literacy is the basis for almost all academic learning in secondary school settings, it is obvious that students with language impairments are vulnerable to school failure.

MAKING CONNECTIONS

Review the sections in Chapter 4 about reading and its necessary precursors (Educational Interventions).

Literacy development begins at a very young age, and books that help children see the connections between sounds and symbols can lay the foundation for later ease in learning how to read.

EDUCATIONAL INTERVENTIONS

A variety of issues in education impact children with speech or language impairments. Today, almost every school in the United States has access to an SLP. In some cases, the SLP is a permanent faculty member. In other cases, the SLP works part-time at several schools or is an itinerant teacher, traveling from one school to another. In all cases, the SLP is available to receive referrals, provide therapy, and consult with teachers concerned about a student's communicative abilities. As noted earlier, the role of the SLP has changed over the last decade. Today these professionals collaborate more with teachers, provide less direct services to children (particularly those with mild disabilities), and guide teachers in the implementation of language development and remediation programs.

General education teachers play a crucial role in children's language development. Teachers must create rich learning environments by providing stimulating instructional settings that encourage oral language and provide the framework necessary for literacy. In the following sections, you'll learn about ways teachers can foster speech and language improvement in their students.

EDUCATION AND THE PRESCHOOL CHILD

NEW DIRECTIONS
FOR THE
MILLENNIUM

Legacy: Although the efficacy of good preschool programs is well documented, many young children with disabilities or at risk for them do not participate.

Opportunities:

- Increase the access and funding for preschool intervention programs
- Insist on high-quality programs that meet adult-to-child recommended ratios and include well-prepared professionals

Preschool programs can make a significant, positive, and long-term difference for young children and their families (Bailey et al., 1999). For most very young children identified as having disabilities, it is their language delays which set them apart from their normally developing peers. Access to preschool programs can make the critical difference in the lives of these individuals. For example, low birth weight infants who received a customized day care program averaged fifteen IQ points higher than the control group (*Education of the Handicapped*, 1992). Only 2% of these youngsters—at risk for speech or language impairments, mental retardation, and learning disabilities—were identified as having a disability later on; the control group was nine times more likely to have a disability. During a child's developmental periods, the acquisition of good communication and language skills is crucial to the child's later development of academic and social skills. However, it is important to remember that preschool programs must be of high quality, with an appropriate adult-to-child ratio. Evidence now exists that when child/staff ratios follow the guidelines set by the American Public Health Association and the American Academy of Pediatrics (3:1 for infants, 4:1 for 2-year-olds, and 7:1 for 3-year-olds), children's readiness for school, particularly in the area of language, is above average (Lombardo, 1999).

Preschool programs for children with or at risk for speech or language impairments should be in accepting and responsive environments that motivate students to communicate. Early intervention programs should foster cooperative play, encourage spontaneous talking, facilitate social interactions with peers, develop responsiveness with conversational partners, and guide parents in the creation of a home environment that fosters language development. Instruction should occur in natural settings where children are free to interact and explore. Because language—its acquisition and generalization—does not occur in isolation, Plante and Beeson (1999) remind us that social interaction must be integrated into the instructional program.

Settings that promote language production are rich in objects and activities that interest and reward young children. Ostrosky & Kaiser (1991) give us some ideas about how to stimulate young children's language, encourage its development, and

Table 5.5 Strategies that Promote Preschoolers' Communication

Interesting materials	The classroom should be rich with materials and activities children are interested in, want to play with, and enjoy.
Out of reach	Some materials should be placed within view of the children but out of their reach, so that they are motivated to make a verbal request for their use.
Inadequate portions	Teachers should arrange the environment to encourage more communication from children—by providing insufficient materials (such as paper, paints, or crayons), for example.
Choice making	Teachers should create situations in which children need to make choices and to ask for the activity they want to engage in or the materials they want to use.
Assistance	Teachers should create situations in which children are likely to need help in order to increase the likelihood that they will communicate their needs to each other or an adult.
Sabotage	Teachers should arrange situations in which children do not have all the materials they need for an activity (painting without brushes, sandbox pails but no shovels) in order to encourage them to request the missing items.
Silly situations	Teachers should create absurd situations (giving them clay instead of crackers at snack time) that surprise the youngsters and encourage their responses.

provide a climate where social interaction is fostered. Their strategies, which are listed and described in Table 5.5, include providing children with reasons to speak, motivating them to interact with others, and making learning interesting and fun. Adults can directly and indirectly create such environments, in which language use is necessary and part of the typical routine. In the Research to Practice box, Ann Kaiser shares the results of her long-term research with young children. The translation of those findings to preschool settings has proven to improve the overall outcomes of these children, particularly in their abilities to use language.

For young children with and at risk for disabilities, good language development does not happen by accident; it occurs through the deliberate actions of preschool teachers and other adults. They must create an environment that fosters language development and thereby promotes early literacy—an environment carefully arranged so that children must imitate, request objects, and obtain the attention of an adult through verbal responses (Warren et al., 1993). Given the importance of play to preschoolers and young children, it is a key to enhanced language and social interaction skills (Clarke, 1996). Through play, children learn skills like cooperation and turn taking; they learn to explore shared concerns and to make friends—in short, they learn to communicate and interact with others. As you have learned, disabilities, particularly language impairments, can be barriers to social interaction and communication. Consequently, teachers must prompt youngsters with disabilities to join groups and play with others. Statements like "Are you going to play with us? Do you want to be a doctor, too?" invite children to play with others, but teachers must create opportunities for them to have social interactions.

The relationship of environment to language, cognition, and reading abilities is clear (Catts et al., 1994). Preschool environments should be rich in experiences and

Research to Practice: Teaching with Confidence

ENHANCED MILIEU TEACHING

ANN P. KAISER
Vanderbilt University

RESEARCH

Enhanced Milieu Teaching (EMT) is a conversation based strategy for teaching young children functional language in the context of everyday interactions. The procedures that comprise EMT are based on an extensive research base demonstrating that children in the early stages of language learning can learn, generalize, and maintain functional use of new language skills taught in the natural environment. Research on EMT shows that children who are beginning to use words and short sentences increase the frequency, diversity, and complexity of their talk. EMT can also benefit children who are using signs or augmented communication systems and children in the later stages of language learning. Research on EMT provides evidence that use of these procedures by parents is especially effective in supporting generalized communication development in young children with disabilities.

PRACTICE

EMT is consistent with the best practice guidelines for communication interventions for young children with disabilities. Immediately functional communication skills are taught in everyday activities and environments. Because early language learning typically occurs in the context of interactions with parents and caregivers, EMT should be implemented by children's significant others and valued communication partners in the context of play and daily living activities as well as by teachers in early intervention or educational contexts.

EMT has three components: (1) environmental arrangement, (2) responsive interactive style, and (3) Milieu Teaching. *Environmental arrangement* provides a context for meaningful and reinforcing communicative interactions. Activities of interest to the child, opportunities for requesting and commenting, and the availability of an interested adult set the occasion for communication and naturalistic teaching. *Responsive interactive style* is the manner in which the teaching adult interacts with the student. The adult follows the child's lead in the interaction and also follows the child's topic and immediate interests as a basis for selecting new language forms to teach. The adult responds to the child's communication, balances her turns with the child, and provides related verbal information contingent on the child's verbal and nonverbal behavior. In the course of responding to the child, the adult models meaningful language both at the child's skill level and at slightly advanced forms. Finally, the adult uses *Milieu Teaching* to prompt the child to produce new forms of language in a functional context. Four Milieu Teaching procedures (elicitive modeling, telling and modeling, time delay, and incidental teaching) are used in response to the child's communicative attempts. Each instance of Milieu Teaching begins with the child's interests, includes one or more prompts for a functional language form, and ends with the child accessing a reinforcing object or event while receiving meaningful feedback from the adult. When EMT is being used, the child is highly engaged in the activity, interaction between the adult and child is positive, and many child-specific language models are used. This teaching system provides opportunities for the child to affect the environment when practicing new language skills.

EMT is most effective when it is based in the collaborative efforts of the classroom teacher, the speech-language clinician, and the child's parents or significant others. Formal assessments by the speech-language clinician identify communication targets for instruction and for generalization to everyday interactions. Teacher and parent observations of the child's functional language skills and interests provide the setting and specific targets for EMT. Classroom teachers embed EMT in instructional activities, daily living activities (e.g., lunch or snack times) and transitions. Parents and significant others use EMT during daily activities (e.g., bath time, mealtimes, riding in the car) or preferred activities (e.g., story reading). Evaluation of children's language development is incorporated into the EMT procedures and conducted in the child's natural settings.

See these sections on
Reading (Chapter 4):
• Education and the
  Schoolchild
• Educational
  Interventions

in literature, including books that are predictable and those that come from children's literature (picture books, storybooks, fairy tales, naming books). Many children begin the reading process by talking about what they think the story says (Katims, 1994). Many come to know every word in the story without being able to actually read a word. Such repetitions enhance both early literacy and language development. Language development is also enhanced by children providing oral narratives of stories (Crais & Lorch, 1994). Story reading provides excellent opportunities for language development, vocabulary building, phonemic awareness, and social exchanges (Owens & Robinson, 1997). The process of reading a story and discussing it at the conclusion of the activity can create many learning opportunities as well as being a social event. Children can be encouraged to answer questions about the story, relate the story to their own experiences, build upon each other's responses, and be guided to develop good language models for each other. Story reading time can also be a time when basic pre-reading skills, like phonics and sound-symbol relationships, can be fostered (Hoffman, 1997). SLPs can be most helpful in showing teachers how to include activities that emphasize these basic skills during story reading time.

EDUCATION AND THE SCHOOLCHILD

Teachers and parents need to be alert to substantial differences in children's speech, language use, and development. Individuals acquire communicative skills at different rates. As you have learned, before becoming overly concerned about an individual's speech or language abilities, teachers should consider several factors: age, setting, and stress. However, if problems persist during the early school years, SLPs are valuable resources who can guide special education and general education teachers and help them adjust their teaching procedures for students with special needs. And, if problems indicate that a child actually has a disability, they stand ready to provide therapy.

Exciting classroom environments stimulate children's language and learning.

Teachers can help all of their students improve their expressive and receptive language skills in many ways. They can modify their standard instructional procedures by adding instructional supports, and they can include units that are meant to directly develop language. Let's look at a few of these.

Instructional Enhancements. The responsibility for creating and fostering a positive learning environment rests with the teacher. Gruenewald and Pollack (1984) illustrate the relationship among the student, the teacher, and the curriculum in all academic settings: Students interact with one another, the teacher, and the curriculum as they participate in classroom activities. By planning both the content and the manner of delivering the instruction, the teacher can match language with the comprehension abilities of the students. The teacher delivering a lecture is the sender; the students are the receivers of the message. Effective teachers (senders) are responsive to their students (receivers) by adjusting, modifying, and supplementing instruction to the needs of their students.

Students who are not native English speakers and are from a cultural background different from their teachers' often need special adjustments from their teachers (van Keulen et al., 1998; Westby, 1995). As discussed in Chapter 3, these youngsters' mastery of English may not yet be sufficient for typical content instruction, and the teacher may need to provide several examples to illustrate a point or explain a concept. They also may need to be cautious in their use of referents and expressions. For example, "We're nearing the two-minute warning" may have no meaning to a child unfamiliar with American sports.

Effective teachers help children with language difficulties in other ways as well. Some use **content enhancement strategies** to help students see relationships among concepts and words (Naremore, 1997; Schoenbrodt et al., 1997). Here are four examples of such visual organizers:

- Attribute web
  Identifies important aspects of a word
    Key word is positioned in the center of the web
    Characteristics of the key word are placed on extensions of the web
    Attributes are grouped by similarities
- Venn diagram
  Compares and contrasts meanings and characteristics of two concepts
    Attributes of the two concepts are identified
    Attributes are written in the appropriate circles
    Similarities of both concepts are moved to the overlapping circle-segments
- Multiple-meaning tree
  Helps students visualize meanings of content words
    The concept is written on the tree's trunk
    Different definitions of the word are written on the branches
    Sentences are generated for each meaning
- Script and story framework
  Organizes knowledge around expected sequences of familiar events
    A framework for remembering event sequences is developed
    A tree-like diagram is used to arrange a story in a hierarchy
    Relationships are grouped and sequences are ordered

content enhancement strategies. Visual organizers of semantic information used in content instruction to teach concepts and vocabulary.

The benefits of content enhancement strategies are many. These instructional techniques not only can improve children's written and oral language skills; they have also been shown to improve their ability to remember information (Hudson & Gillam, 1997). Why do they work so well? Probably because these techniques provide structure for learning concepts based on individuals' experiences. As Naremore (1997) points out, American culture has set expectations for what elements should be included in a story. Stories are suppose to have a point, be goal oriented, be "about something." They have a setting and characters, and are organized by episodes that tend to have an initiating event, a response, a consequence, and an ending. Teachers can take advantage of these routines by helping children understand the predictability of stories and teaching them to use organizing tools like the four content enhancements listed above.

Many teachers find that teaching students learning strategies, whether they are mnemonic based or of the content enhancement variety, is not difficult. What is hard is getting their students to consistently use the right technique. For students who forget to use a strategy or cannot remember which strategy to use when, a clever system can help (Edmunds, 1999). The Cognitive Credit Card (CCC), which is laminated and about the size of a credit card, lists the steps for a specific strategy, such as for taking notes for history or the steps to follow to create an attribute web. A student may have many CCCs, one for each different subject or for different types of tasks, hooked together on a key ring.

Language Instruction. Learning is not merely listening to lectures; it is also mastering the communication game. Students who have a language disability need to be taught how to use language effectively. Language teaching should be part of the curriculum throughout the elementary schoolyears. Just as time is devoted to teaching mathematics, reading, spelling, and social studies, time should be allocated to teaching the language skills that underlie these subjects. During these periods, children should be encouraged to listen, talk, and understand the language of instruction as well as the language of social interactions. All students benefit from this instruction, but for students with language impairments it is essential.

For teachers who are not trained in oral language development, excellent instructional materials are commercially available. For example, the *Peabody Language Development Kits (PLDK–Revised), Levels P and 1; Developing Understanding of Self and Others (DUSO–Revised);* and *Classroom Listening and Speaking (CLAS)* include useful activities to increase language and cognitive skills for students in primary grades. *Let's Talk, Conversations, Communicative Competence, and Directing Discourse* provide ideas for adolescents.

Teachers can use a variety of classroom activities, including games, that encourage children's use of language (Marvin, 1989; Watkins & Rice, 1994). **Barrier games** require children to describe objects while the other players guess what they are describing. In a simple version of this game, the teacher could create a game using picture cards, such as those found in the *Peabody Picture Collection (PPC)* or the CD-ROM picture series called *Fast Sort.* The teacher asks the children to tell about a recent experience or make up stories from a set of sequential pictures.

Another language area often in need of instruction is the use and understanding of metaphors and analogies (Castillo, 1998). Figures of speech are difficult for many students to comprehend, for they are not literal or direct translations of the words used in such phrases. Here are a few examples: "the president is the head of state," "the eyes are windows to the soul," "he's between a rock and a hard place," "my heart goes out to you," "time flies." Students whose abstract thinking skills are not well developed, and those who are learning English as a second language, frequently find it difficult to comprehend the meaning of common metaphors and analogies used in texts and in oral presentations. Teachers should not assume that children understand nonliteral language, and should help their students develop the flexible thinking skills needed to solve the problems such language use presents. Mere exposure to analogies and metaphors is not enough. Teachers need to include direct instruction about **figurative language** use—and when they do, students' facility with language grows in a further dimension. As with most language skills, instruction about these conceptually difficult aspects of language use can be integrated into content lessons.

barrier games. Drill and practice activities that require the application of verbal skills to solve problems, using a game format.
figurative language. Abstract, nonliteral language which uses metaphors and analogies in the creation of various figures of speech.

COLLABORATION FOR INCLUSION

For more suggestions on accommodating students' learning needs in general education settings, see the Accommodating for Inclusive Environments boxes found in Chapters 3 through 12.

Collaborative consultation is the shared responsibility for problem definition, planning, provision of services, and evaluation of outcomes (Schoenbrodt et al., 1997). For students with speech or language impairments this process is critical for good outcomes. The importance of linking speech and language intervention to students' curriculum and classroom experiences is generally accepted by SLPs across the nation. Unfortunately, SLPs have caseloads that do not allow them to work intensively with large numbers of children. They are usually assigned to several different schools, and have to allocate their time carefully so they can provide direct therapy to individual students who are in the greatest need. Almost all students with speech or language impairments (89%) receive their education solely in the general education classroom (an additional 7% attend resource rooms for a small portion of the school day) (U.S. Department of Education, 1998). Therefore, special and general education teachers often work under the guidance of SLPs to implement language intervention programs in the general education classroom and to support SLPs' therapy efforts by fostering generalization. This requires teamwork!

Once a child is identified as having a speech or language impairment and is to receive special services from an SLP, the teacher must work closely and collaborate with the SLP to implement individualized programs for that child. SLPs offer guidance and practical tips to use in the general education class. They work with individual children or small groups. And, increasingly, they work with entire classes of general education students (Owens & Robinson, 1997). For example, an SLP might suggest ways that the teacher can encourage children to expand oral language: be an attentive listener, provide more opportunities for children to talk about what they are interested in, ask open-ended questions that encourage children to talk more.

The integrating of interventions into the fabric of general education instruction requires SLPs, special educators, and general educators to work closely together to form a team. How might these three professionals coordinate instruction? Many SLPs and teachers team-teach special units that integrate language instruction into the standard curriculum. Let's look at some examples. A unit about a local environmental issue might culminate in students preparing short position papers, letters to the editor of the local newspaper, oral presentations by a panel of experts, or a debate. Here's another example, this one in the areas of reading and writing (Norris, 1997): First, the team develops goals and plans for the unit they will share (co-teach). During this time, they choose reading selections and supporting materials. They implement instruction by dividing the tasks and assigning lead responsibilities to each. For this unit, the SLP conducts small reading groups, where she or he helps students translate the basics of sound-symbol relationships from reading to writing. The special educator works with small groups as they explore the topics being studied, and uses content enhancement strategies to help students comprehend the reading materials more effectively and write coherent reports. The general education teacher holds editing conferences with groups of students as they refine and improve their written work. SLPs and teachers find that their collaborative efforts greatly improve the language skills of students with speech and language impairments, and also benefit their other students.

collaborative consultation. Professionals, often from different disciplines, working together to develop and implement students' educational programs.

Let's examine another important way that SLPs can be an invaluable resource to teachers, and another justification for strong collaborative efforts among SLPs and special and general education teachers. As you have learned, children who are not able to rhyme, cannot identify sounds in words, and cannot hear word-sound patterns are

Literacy is also discussed in Chapter 4 under Reading in:
- Education and the Schoolchild
- Educational Interventions

And in Chapter 11 in these sections:
- Methods of Reading and Writing (Children with Low Vision and Blindness)
- Literacy (Educational Intervention

NEW DIRECTIONS
FOR THE
MILLENNIUM

Legacy: Whole language approaches were widely adopted in general education classes during the latter part of the twentieth century; however, research now indicates that these methods are not effective in teaching reading or literacy to students with disabilities

Opportunities:
- Place students with special needs strategically in general education classes where direct instruction is at least one facet of the instructional program
- Provide parallel, separate instruction in phonics for a concentrated part of the school day to those in need

at risk for reading failure. You have also learned that these skills can be taught and reading failure avoided (Ball, 1997). However, you have probably also said to yourself, "But how would I teach these skills to children, when I'm not sure I understand what needs to be mastered?" SLPs can be very helpful in this regard. They can help special education and general education teachers understand the basic units of words and sounds so they are able to develop lessons to teach phonological awareness. And they can help convince educators who do not believe in direct, skill based instruction. They can help them understand that many children will not be successful readers if they are not taught these skills directly, because while many aspects of language development occur naturally, almost spontaneously, phonological awareness does not.

> The argument over whether skills-based instruction with code emphasis is best for children with language/learning disabilities or whether whole language better meets their needs is at best an argument we can no longer afford to indulge. It is an argument that has neither rhyme nor reason, and, at its worst, it is an argument that may deprive too many children access to the world of print. (Ball, 1997, p. 24)

SLPs can help advocate instruction on phonics and basic reading skills, but they can also lend their extensive knowledge about sound-symbol relationships to teachers as they impart these fundamental rules to their students.

Remember, almost all students with speech and language impairments receive the majority of their educational experiences in the general education classroom. These experiences must be positive and successful. How can we make this happen? Teachers must adjust their teaching styles, presentation of content, and expectations for each student in their classes (Geluke & Lovitt, 1992; LaBlance et al., 1994). Effective teachers also understand the role that language plays in learning. They know they must adjust their language and adapt written materials so that students understand the message being delivered. They make these adjustments by moderating their rate of speech, the complexity of their sentences, and their choice of questions (Gruenewald & Pollack, 1984). Almost naturally, teachers adjust their rate of speech depending on the age and level of their students (Cuda & Nelson, 1976). For instance, first-grade teachers speak more slowly than fifth-grade teachers. Effective teachers are also careful in their use of referents. They systematically show students the relationships among items and concepts. They expand discussions about new concepts and ideas. They show children how concepts are related. They also ask questions at graduated levels of difficulty to help students test the accuracy of their new knowledge. Many apply strategies, like those listed in the accompanying box about making accommodations, that facilitate inclusion.

The importance of creating language-sensitive environments was mentioned earlier. Only slight modifications in teaching style and instructional activities can be most helpful and have great benefits for all students (Schoenbrodt et al., 1997). Providing opportunities for language use and incorporating those into standard classroom routines is the support that many students with language impairments, as well as linguistically diverse students, need; and these goals are not difficult to accomplish. Let's look at some easy ways that teachers can take to support students' language development during their typical instructional lessons. The box about making accommodations for students with language impairments gives some helpful suggestions about how to create classrooms where all students' language development is enriched and supported.

Teachers can also enhance the opportunities for discussion and language development by enriching their instruction. For instance, they might include activity centers in their classrooms. One center could have electrical components to create

Accommodating for Inclusive Environments

CREATING LANGUAGE-SENSITIVE CLASSROOMS

- Give children opportunities to talk and hear talk that is appropriate for different purposes (leading discussions, presenting information) and settings (in small groups, to their class, to other classes)
- Provide students with ideas that give them reasons to talk and discuss issues
- Create opportunities for students to interact and use language while they learn academic tasks
- Give students experience in talking about different subjects with different audiences (build self-confidence)
- Have students work together to plan presentations on topics being taught in content subjects
- Insist that students take different roles in group presentations
- Include group debates as part of instructional units
- Allow students to retell the meaning of difficult reading passages

- Create a supportive environment where children trust each other and are encouraged to communicate
- Create a section of the classroom where the physical environment—perhaps a large, round table—encourages sharing and discussion
- Always consider the developmental stages of each student when setting expectations
- Collaborate with the SLP to integrate appropriate language development activities in all academic instruction
- Incorporate activities in class that allow children with language impairments to practice skills mastered in therapy
- Be alert to the possible presence of speech or language impairments and consult with the SLP when one is suspected
- Evaluate student progress and outcomes

circuits so that children can discover cause-and-effect relationships; another center could have magnets and containers of different types of materials. Some part of the day could be set aside for children to talk about their exploration of the materials in the activity centers. Teachers could also use this discussion time to talk about other topics of interest to the children, such as current affairs, environmental issues, or sports.

TRANSITION THROUGH ADULTHOOD

Dropout rates are also discussed in Chapters 3 and 8.

follow-up study. To provide later evaluation, diagnosis, or treatment of a condition.

Adults with speech or language impairments comprise several different subgroups. Some have only a speech impairment, others have only a language impairment, and some have both. Age of onset and causation, however, are what make these subgroups different from one another. Despite having great difficulties as children, the vast majority of adults experience a lifetime of using normal communication (Plante & Beeson, 1999). Problems experienced by adults who were not identified as having speech or language impairments when they were children, typically, are caused by disease, accidents, or aging. Those who had some kind of speech or language impairment during childhood represent but a small percentage of this adult group. To date, very little is known about how children with these impairments fare when they are adults. In the following subsections, we look at their overall adult performance and then describe some of the skills necessary for successful employment.

In a comprehensive **follow-up study** of youth with disabilities, students with learning disabilities and speech impairments appeared to have better outcomes than other youth with disabilities (Wagner et al., 1992). They seem to function fairly well some five years after graduation. Few are socially isolated. By this time they are beginning to move away from home: 40% live independently. They also are employed at about the same rate as their peers without disabilities. Their long-term prospects, however, may not be as good. Although 86% are served in general education classes, only 39% of students with speech impairments graduate with a diploma (U.S. Department of Education, 1998). Serious concerns about their success as adults can be raised. Changing this situation might well demand different types of services while these students are in high school (Aune & Friehe, 1996). These students may require more access to tutoring to remain in academic content courses, services from guidance counselors, experience in advocating for accommodations and special services, and increased instruction on listening and speaking skills.

FAMILIES

For more suggestions about working with families of students with disabilities, see the Families sections in Chapters 3 through 12

Newly developed language skills also need to be facilitated and reinforced at home. The quality of the home's language environment has significant and long-term effects in young children (Hart & Risley, 1995). Some families need guidance as they attempt to develop nurturing environments for their children. For these reasons, most preschool programs include a strong family component. Professionals who work in preschool programs for children with disabilities or those at risk should help parents implement language-learning lessons at home and help these children transfer (or generalize) their learning from school to home. The team effort of teachers and parents enriches children's learning experience and enhances their communication skills.

Involving parents in their children's preschool programs, however, is often difficult. Children (and adults) spend less time at home with family than ever before. For example, about 7 million children of working parents, as early as 11 weeks old, spend thirty hours per week in child care (Children's Defense Fund, 1996). Parent and children share less time together today than they did twenty years ago. Regardless, the child's parents and the home environment provide the foundation for these skills. Even for those children who spend most of their days away from home, those whose home environment is rich in language—where parents talk to their children, where children are given the opportunity to explore the use of language, and where experiences are broad—usually develop fine speech and language skills. When children do not have appropriate language models—when they do not hear language used often, when they do not have experiences to share or a reason to talk—it is not uncommon for their language to be delayed and even become impaired. Children are individuals; so too are parents, and the language environments they provide at home. It is important for educators not to make generalizations about either parents or students. For example, it is unfair and incorrect to assume that parents are responsible for their child's stuttering. Research has shown that parents of stutterers are not different in any characteristics and speech qualities from parents of nonstutterers (Nippold & Rudzinski, 1995). Generalizations about families from diverse backgrounds are inappropriate. Diversity is heterogeneous, where no assumptions are accurate.

Language is normally acquired in a rather orderly fashion (Stark et al., 1993). During the first year of life, infants hear language spoken around them and organize what they hear so that they can gain meaning from it. Toward the end of their first year, infants are able to respond to some of the language they hear. For example, they know their names, respond to greetings, respond to simple verbal commands, and use objects in their immediate environment. At this time, infants also seem to copy the voice patterns they hear by babbling, regardless of the language they hear. Babies begin to talk by first using one- and two-word utterances that are easy to say and have meaning to them (*mama, cookie, doggie*). Throughout their second year of life, children use a growing vocabulary, longer sentences, and more complexity. They are learning the form (the rules) of language and how to apply language rules to give meaning to their oral communications. Regardless of the language heard, children seem to develop language in much the same way across cultures—by interacting with their environment.

To make sense of the language they hear and, ultimately, to learn how to use that language, children employ various strategies. All do not use the same ones, but children who develop language normally apply some structure to make sense of what they hear (Leonard, 1994). For example, some young children, who do not yet understand oral language, might come to understand an adult's intentions by watching nonverbal clues and comprehending the context of the situation. Through such repeated experiences, they come to learn language as well. Other children attend more selectively and learn more vocabulary for objects they can act on or interact with (*ball, key, sock*) or objects that change or move (*clock, car*). Still others focus on specific characteristics of objects (size, shape, sound). All these children are learning to categorize and organize objects and their thoughts, skills that are necessary for learning academic tasks later.

When children do not develop language at the expected rate, intervention is needed. In almost every community, speech and language specialists are available to provide therapy and instruction to children and to assist parents in helping their children acquire language. With training and guidance from SLPs, parents can be excellent language teachers for children with language impairments. In fact, when home-based intervention is provided by parents, children's language scores improve more than when only clinic based instruction is provided by professionals (Cleminshaw et al., 1996).

What kinds of strategies can parents use at home to improve language skills? Specialists suggest that family members specifically label or name objects in the home. They also suggest that simple words be used more often to describe the objects the child is playing with: "This ball is red. It is round. It is soft." They can encourage repetitions of correct productions of sounds and repeat the child's error to help make a comparison. They can play a game of "fill in the blank" sentences. They can ask the child questions that require expanded answers. The family should include the child in activities outside of the home, too, such as visits to the zoo, the market, or a shopping center, so that the child has more to talk about. Practicing good language skills can be incorporated into everyday events. Family members should model language and have the child imitate good language models. For example, a parent might say, "This pencil is blue. What color is this pencil?" and the child should be encouraged to respond that the pencil is blue. Crais and Lorch (1994) also suggest that parents encourage children to engage in the act of "storytelling." Through these stories, children should describe, explain, and interpret their experiences or the stories they have read. Children need a reason to talk, and the home environment can foster children's oral expression by providing many rich and diverse experiences for children to talk about and by providing good language models for children to imitate.

TECHNOLOGY

MAKING CONNECTIONS

For more about technology and students with disabilities, see the Technology sections in Chapters 3 through 12

Technology has had an impact on rehabilitation and the instructional programs for some children with speech or language impairments. For example, an **obturator** can be used to help create a closure between the oral and nasal cavities when the soft palate is missing or has been damaged by a congenital cleft. An artificial larynx can be implanted when the vocal folds become paralyzed or have been removed because of a disease. Because these disabilities are not common in children, however, this technology has affected only a few children with speech or language impairments. More influential to most of these children have been advances in computer technology, which also hold considerable promise for the future. Computer technology also helps the professionals who work with these students by providing a management tool to simplify their work.

ALTERNATIVE AND AUGMENTATIVE COMMUNICATION

The term **alternative and augmentative communication (AAC)** and its definition was provided by ASHA (Beukelman & Mirenda, 1992). AAC includes both low-tech devices (such as communication boards) and high-tech equipment (such as speech talkers). AAC provides alternative ways for individuals with speech or language impairments to interact and communicate with others. AAC devices can be electronic or nonelectronic, they can be constructed for a certain individual, and they can be simple or complex. The common characteristic of AAC systems is that they are used to augment oral or written language production.

A variety of low-tech AAC devices have been in use for many years. For example, communication boards have long been available to persons who are unable to speak; a person wishing to communicate merely points to pictures or words that have been placed on the board. In the near future, these devices will probably be replaced almost entirely by computerized communication devices. Advances in computer technology, particularly area **speech synthesizers,** have changed and will continue to change the mode of communication for many of these individuals. With a computer, a person can type in a message and have it converted to voice or print. Some computers allow the individual to select the voice qualities the machine uses. Some are solely dedicated to speech production, and others have a voice capability as only one of many functions. Some computerized communicative devices are even small enough to be worn on a person's wrist.

The current capabilities of electronic AAC systems are amazing, and the devices continue to improve. AAC systems vary in capability (some can serve multiple purposes) and in price. For example, the Liberator II, which is produced by the Prentke Romich Company and costs under $10,000, can produce both written and oral language. This lightweight equipment can generate ten different age- and gender-appropriate voices, so the individual can select the voice he or she is most comfortable with. Because it uses an icon system, the Liberator (once mastered) is relatively quick and easy to use, and it can be accessed by touch or, for those with limited motor abilities, by switches. The system even includes a calculator and a math scratch pad. What other improvements in the AAC technology can bring more benefits to those who have significant difficulties communicating to others?

Some individuals with severe speech and language impairments and their families resist using electronic communication aids, and certainly individuals' values and those of their families must be considered when professionals recommend an

obturator. A device that creates a closure between the oral and nasal cavities when the soft palate is missing or damaged.
alternative and augmentative communication (AAC). Assistive technology devices that specifically help individuals communicate, including those that actually produce speech.
speech synthesizers. Equipment that creates voice.

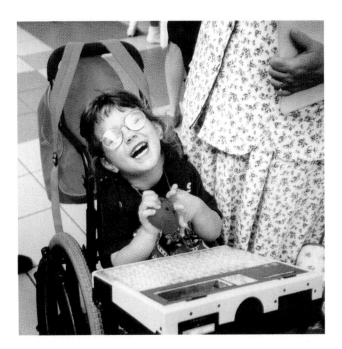

Learning to use electronic communication devices can enable even a student with severe speech or language impairments to engage in a complex interchange of ideas with others. The Liberator II, once mastered, will "speak" for this child.

assistive device (Parette & Angelo, 1996). Professionals have a responsibility to help parents and individuals with disabilities understand the potential benefits of AAC before the devices are rejected. The benefits have now been shown to be great (Romski & Sevcik, 1997). For example, students with little or no speech or language abilities are now able to communicate with others because of AAC devices. And many of these youngsters have developed language abilities that had not been expected from them. The benefits of AAC are still unfolding, but it is clear that they are underestimated. Most users and their families report great satisfaction with AAC, feeling that the child develops communication competence, increases self-esteem, and gains independence.

EMERGING TECHNOLOGIES FOR LANGUAGE INTERVENTION

Advances in CD-ROM technology and its increasing accessibility at schools and at home could revolutionize therapy and treatment of speech or language impairments (Maugh, 1996). The application of research findings, indicating that many youngsters with language impairments do not process speech sounds quickly enough to make them meaningful, to emerging technologies should prove beneficial to a great number of children with disabilities. Speech sounds can now be modified and slowed down so these children can understand them, and the results are new methods and materials for use at school and at home. In the therapy version, the altered speech is applied in a video game format whereby speech sounds are progressively shortened to approximate normal speech sounds. Amazingly, after only a few weeks of therapy, the participating children achieved near-normal language capabilities. This same technology is also available on CD-ROM and audiotapes where expanded speech is available in stories for home use. One can only guess what the future will hold with the increasing use and availability of technology.

New CD-ROM programs, like *Fast Sort*, can save teachers and SLPs time and also produce great instructional benefits because they allow for the creation of individually arranged sets of pictures which contain target sounds or categories of vocabulary words to be learned.

An innovative therapy now holds promise for improved language development (Merzenich et al., 1996; Tallal et al., 1996). The training strategy incorporates computer-generated speech to teach these youngsters to process fast speech sounds, a definite deficit for many children with language impairments and learning disabilities. The experimental program, which uses a computer game format, influenced substantial gains in language comprehension and an increased ability to recognize speech sounds (Peavler, 1996).

CD-ROM technology now makes easier the possibility of using pictures to stimulate children's production of specific sounds and words. Being able to "call up" many different pictures that elicit a particular sound allows SLPs to have many examples of a sound in words readily available for therapy and for teachers to use in follow-up activities. The *Fast Sort* CD-ROM series is just such a program. The sound disk is helpful in programs aimed at remediating articulation problems, and the word disk is extremely useful in developing vocabulary and helping students understand categorizing words and concepts (vehicles: trucks, cars, airplanes; animals: dogs, sheep, cats, lions). The uses of pictures and illustrations for a wide variety of instructional purposes are great. They can be used in barrier games, to stimulate creative writing, to expand the vocabularies of students with disabilities and also linguistically diverse students. Clearly, technology advances are creating new and exciting possibilities for the enhancement and enrichment of instruction.

CONCEPTS AND CONTROVERSY: CAN WE AFFORD NOT TO?

The importance of access to health care and vaccinating young children against dangerous diseases is also discussed in the Prevention sections of Chapters 3 and 6.

When the Great Plague was devastating Russia many years ago, someone asked what was being done about it. The answer was that another thousand coffins had been ordered! To my mind, the tens of billions of tax dollars allocated to various government agencies concerned with our chronic social problems have accomplished little more than buying those coffins. (Anderson, 1972, p. 1)

Two decades ago, Camilla May Anderson called for our government to address the problems of health care. Her special concern was the prevention of diseases causing lifelong disabilities and death. In her book *Society Pays: The High Costs of Minimal Brain Damage in America*, she pointed out that diseases affecting pregnant women and young children can result in brain damage, which, even if minimal, can profoundly influence children's abilities to learn.

The health care issue is a hot topic of debate today, and various proposals for universal health insurance that would cover costs of all Americans' health care needs have been discussed in Congress. Why are there so many proponents for expenses that would place extra burdens on taxpayers? Let's look at the measles virus as an example. Measles is a very dangerous disease that can easily be prevented. The airborne virus can cause death and serious disabling conditions in children (blindness, deafness, brain damage, language impairments), especially if contracted by a pregnant woman or a young child. A vaccine that prevents measles has been available in this country since 1963. During the 1960s, approximately 400,000 cases of measles were reported each year; this number dropped to 1,497 in 1983, and predictions were made that the disease would soon be eradicated. However, a new epidemic of measles raged in the United States recently. Why? Major causes were the unavailability of free vaccinations for the poor, the failure of insurance companies to offer coverage, and the fact that many parents failed to make sure that their children are vaccinated. Nationally, 45 children died of measles in 1989; 40 died during the first four months of 1990. In Los Angeles County, the number of measles cases in 1986 was 42, in 1989 it was 1,202, and in the first four months of 1990 it reached 2,000 (Hilts, 1990). More than 25,000 cases of measles were reported across the nation in 1990; those cases resulted in 60 deaths, over half of them preschoolers (Associated Press, 1991). The epidemic predominantly affected unvaccinated African American and Hispanic preschoolers living in inner cities, but the disease also struck secondary school students, college students, migrant workers, and other adults (Bradley, 1990). Estimates indicated that while 95% of schoolchildren were vaccinated because it is a requirement for school attendance, only 50% of inner-city preschoolers were vaccinated at that time. The disease is most devastating when it strikes young children.

Should the federal government take on the responsibility of a national immunization program? If so, how much would it cost? The cost for an individual child is small; for all children, the cost is quite high. But what are the costs of not preventing diseases like measles and rubella? ASHA's Committee on the Prevention of Speech-Language and Hearing Disorders (1984) cites an excellent example of the cost effectiveness of preventive measures. In 1969, the federal Bureau for the Education of the Handicapped (BEH), now called the Office of Special Education Programs, conducted a study of the impact of the rubella epidemic of the early 1960s; the findings show that if, in 1963, all young females had been vaccinated for rubella, the epidemic would not have occurred. The cost of a national immunization program in the 1960s would have been $10 million; although considered, the program was not implemented. The rubella epidemic left between 20,000 and 30,000 children with impairments. BEH estimated that the projected total expenditure for special education and related services for all the children whose illness resulted in their having a disability because of the rubella epidemic would approach $1 billion; this staggering amount is probably an underestimation of the financial costs. Wisconsin's Department of Health and Social Services developed a series of comparative cost figures for prevention versus treatment of mental retardation, mental illness, and alcoholism. It projected that $1 million could be saved for each individual whose retardation was prevented (ASHA, 1984).

Because of the concerns about the long-term and devastating effects on children, Congress passed the Vaccines for Children Program (VFC) in 1994, and in 1995, federally purchased vaccines became available to low- and moderate-income preschoolers and those whose health insurance providers did not cover them (Children's

Defense Fund [CDF], 1996). The results of this program are impressive. In 1992, only 55% of preschoolers were protected. Now the immunization rate for toddlers exceeds 90% for polio and measles (CDF, 1997). The success of this program rests not only with governmental action, but also with private partnerships like the one with Chase Manhattan Bank, which spent over two million dollars advertising the program. More work still needs to be done to be sure children's immunization records are maintained and to continually make young parents aware of the importance of protecting their children from preventable diseases. With continuing congressional debates about health care, the future is not secure. Is this a federal responsibility? Can the nation afford this program? Can it afford not to have it?

In Conclusion

MAKING CONNECTIONS

Look again at the Advance Organizers found at the beginning of the chapter; to help you study the chapter's content, the answers to the Focus and Challenge questions are found here. Test yourself to see if you have mastered the major points of this chapter.

Summary

Communication does not occur in isolation. It requires at least two parties and a message. Communication is impaired when either the sender or the receiver of the message cannot use the signs, symbols, or rules of language effectively. Communication occurs only when the message intended by the sender is understood by the receiver. The sender may have an idea or thought to share with someone else, but the sender's idea needs to be translated from thought to some code the other person can understand. For most of us, oral language is the primary mode of socializing, learning, and performing on the job. Therefore, communicative competence—what speakers need to know about language to express their thoughts—is the most important goal for students with speech or language impairments. Because oral communication (or sign language for those who are deaf) occurs in a social context, this ability directly affects an individual's social competence as well.

Focus Questions

Self-Test Questions

- *What comprises speech impairments and language impairments?*

  There are two general kinds of impairments: speech and language. A speech impairment is present when the sender's articulation, voice (pitch or loudness), or fluency patterns impair the receiver's attending to or understanding the message. When either the sender or the receiver of the message cannot use the signs, symbols, or rules of language, a language impairment exists. The three aspects of language are form, content, and use (pragmatics). Articulation problems are the most common type of speech impairment in children. Children with articulation problems make consistent errors in producing speech sounds. Articulation errors are part of the normal developmental sequence, with most children able to correctly produce individual speech sounds within the appropriate age ranges. About half of the children seen by SLPs have language impairments. Although the cause of most language impairments is unknown, the relationship between language impairment and delays in cognitive development and the development of social skills is clear.

- *What is the prevalence of this disability?*

  Speech or language impairments is not the largest category of exceptionalities when only a primary disability is considered. Some estimate that when a student's primary and second disability area are considered, as much as 10% of the school-age population may be affected. The U.S. government reports that almost 2% of all students are served with speech or language impairments as their primary disability. However, over 40% of the youngsters seen by SLPs have another primary disabling condition (mental retardation, learning disabilities, deafness and hard of hearing). It is also important to recognize that as children progress through school, the prevalence of this disability decreases but related disabilities (i.e., learning disabilities) increase.

- *How do language delays, language differences, and language impairments differ?*

  Teachers should be careful not to confuse dialect (regional) differences in speech with speech impairments and not to refer young children whose speech is developing normally but is not yet correct. Language differences can also occur when children are acquiring English as their second language (also review Chapter 3 for special considerations for ESL students). Children with language delays acquire language following the normal developmental sequence but do so more slowly than the typical learner. Students with language impairments do not acquire language following the sequence experienced naturally by children without this disability. Professionals do not consider the first two groups of youngsters as having a language impairment.

- *How can teachers enhance language development and help to remediate a language impairment?*

  The teachers' role is important in the educational programs they make available to students with speech or language impairments. Teachers need to integrate language development into the entire curriculum and provide direct instruction about oral language. They should try to match the language they use to the language comprehension skills of their students, and they must create a language-rich environment for all students. Because of their role in the referral process, teachers must be sure that children with these disabilities are identified and receive the specialized services they require. They also assist in remediation programs, collaborate with SLPs, and work to foster maintenance and generalization of skills mastered in therapy.

- *What is alternative and augmentative communication, and what are its benefits to this population of learners?*

  Technology provides many advantages to students with speech or language impairments, and the future holds even more promise. Alternative and augmentative communication (ACC) is particularly beneficial for those with severe speech impairments. The options are many, ranging from low-tech to high-tech devices that actually speak for the user. New breakthroughs signal hope for those with language impairments as well. CD-ROM technology now allows for speech to be systematically altered so it is easier to understand. Such expanded speech, progressively shortened to the rate of normal speech, can even be delivered in game or story formats for use at both school and home.

Challenge Question

- *What related service provider serves the needs of students with speech or language impairments, their families, and their teachers, and what roles does this professional serve today?*

  The field of speech or language impairments has grown and changed over the years. In the past, remediating speech impairments filled the large caseloads of SLPs. More recently, professionals in the field are concerned about children's abilities to communicate with others. Language needs to become a topic of substantial interest for all educators. Speech/language pathologists (SLPs), experts in the field of speech, language, and communication, serve youngsters whose speech or language impairs their ability to communicate effectively with others. Professional SLPs serve in a variety of roles, ranging from consultative services to classroom instruction. They work with families, teachers, small groups of children, and individuals. Depending on the individual's difficulties, SLPs assess and remediate deficits that prevent efficient and effective participation in communication. The most common problems they address are speech impairments; the second most common problem involves language development. SLPs provide both supportive and direct services. They work not only with students whose primary disability is either a speech or language problem, but also with individuals who have a primary disability other than a speech or language impairment.

 # Supplementary Resources

Scholarly Readings

Fey, M. E., Windsor, J., & Warren, S. F. (Eds). (1995). *Language intervention: Preschool through the elementary years.* Baltimore: Paul H. Brookes.

Gonzalez, V., Brusca-Vega, R., & Yawkey, T. (1997). *Assessment and instruction of culturally and linguistically diverse students with or at-risk of learning problems.* Boston: Allyn and Bacon.

Lovitt, T. C. (1995). *Tactics for teaching* (2nd ed.). Columbus, OH: Merrill.

Shames, G. H., Wiig, E. H., & Secord, W. A. (Eds.). (1998). *Human communication disorders: An introduction* (5th ed.). Boston: Allyn and Bacon.

Plante, E., & Beeson, P. M. (1999). *Communication and communication disorders: A clinical introduction.* Boston: Allyn and Bacon.

Van Keulen, J. E., Weddington, G. T., & DeBose, C. E. (1998). *Speech, language, learning and the African American child.* Boston: Allyn and Bacon.

Popular Books

Butler, S. (1936). *The way of all flesh.* New York: Limited Editions Club.

Byars, B. (1970). *The summer of the swans.* New York: Viking.

Caldwell, E. (1948). *Tobacco road.* New York: Grosset and Dunlap.

Johnson, W. (1930). *Because I stutter.* New York: Appleton.

Melville, H. (1962). *Billy Budd.* Chicago: University of Chicago.

Videos and DVDs

The world according to Garp. (1982). Twentieth Century Fox.

This side is good. (1983). Filmmakers Library.

The pain of shyness. (1985). ABC News 20/20–Filmmakers Library.

Life is but a dream. (1985). Filmmakers Library.

Primal fear. (1996). Paramount.

Professional Parent, and Consumer Organizations and Agencies

American Cleft Palate–Craniofacial Association/American Cleft Palate Foundation
104 South Estes Drive, Suite 204
Chapel Hill, NC 27514
(919) 933-9044
Web site: http://www.cleft.com

American Speech-Language-Hearing Association
National Institute of Communication
10801 Rockville Pike
Rockville, MD 20852
Phone: (301) 897-5700
Web site: http://www.asha.org

National Institute on Deafness and Other Communication Disorders (NIDCD)
National Institutes of Health
1 Communication Avenue
Bethesda, MD 20892-3456
Phone: (800) 241-1044; (301) 907-7653
E-mail: nidcd@aerie.com
Web site: http://www.nih.gov/nidcd/

Division for Children with Communication Disorders
The Council for Exceptional Children
1920 Association Drive
Reston, VA 22091
Phone: (888) CEC-SPED; (703) 620-3660
Web site: http://www.cec.sped.org

Stuttering Foundation of America
3100 Walnut Grove Road, Suite 603
P.O. Box 11749
Memphis, TN 38111-0749
Phone: (800) 992-9392; (901) 452-7343
E-mail: stittersfa@aol.com

MAKING CONNECTIONS

Many interesting resources, including scholarly references, popular books, videos and DVDs, are found at the end of every chapter and also in the Students' Resource Manual that accompanies this text.

Gottfried Mind, sometimes called the "Raphael of cats," depicted cats almost exclusively, and was known to have an obsession with the focus of his work and life. It was said that when Mind was not painting or drawing cats, he was carving them out of chestnuts (Foucart-Walter & Rosenberg, 1987). Evidently, his modest apartment was filled with cats and kittens, and when he worked cats were found in his lap and on his shoulders. Mind (1786–1814) was born and lived all of his life in Bern, Switzerland. He was well known all over Europe, and his work was quite popular with cat lovers. Most of his work remains in private collections today, and is rarely seen in public. He is probably one of the few artistic masters of the eighteenth and nineteenth centuries with documented mental retardation. He died of a stroke at the age of 46.

Witt Library, Courtauld Institute of Art, London. Reprinted with permission.

CHAPTER 6

A Mother's Efforts Result in Independent Living Facilities for Her Son

Jean Gibson is one of those very special moms who has never stopped seeing what services are needed, and then making certain that they happen. Probably because of her up-beat personality, Jean seems always able to rally resources, energy, and people. Her continuing dedication to her son has benefited so many. Here's the story of how she is creating supportive independent living arrangements for adults who need assistance but do not have moderate or severe cognitive disabilities.

Brad was five years old before we became aware officially of his disability—although, as I reflect back, I had noticed his lack of interest in toys and his vocabulary was extremely limited. However, he was an attractive blonde, blue-eyed child. His outward appearance did not suggest a disability and he developed physically without incident.

It was our doctor who suggested that we have him tested when we mentioned that Brad didn't seem ready for kindergarten. After many tests and visits to specialists, we were told he had a nonspecific cerebral dysfunction and was neurologically impaired.

The realization that something was "wrong" with our son devastated us. I firmly believed that he would "get better" with the right pill.

He was enrolled in nursery school and his vocabulary improved significantly that year. At age six he was placed in special education at the local school and was

Mental Retardation

eventually mainstreamed for some classes. The school system was recognized statewide for its Special Needs Program, and as years passed I felt that little by little he was gaining. However, as Brad moved closer and closer to age 21, when all school services end, I began to wonder about his future. In fact, it was a time I didn't want to face.

The first year following his graduation, I tried to find some agency, organization, or group that would continue to provide support or assistance for him. The state of New Jersey is mandated to provide homes and services for severely retarded developmentally disabled who have been institutionalized or who are in a crisis situation. But what about those who have always lived at home and were only mildly mentally retarded? They could work at entry-level jobs and contribute to their own well-being—indeed, they would become taxpayers. But they needed minimal assistance and training to do this. Otherwise the skills they had acquired in school would be lost and the state's waiting list for housing and services would continue to grow, since even they would be added eventually.

Two of the special education teachers at the local school discussed the situation with me and stressed the benefits of a transition program of continual education. I knew they were correct, so I kept searching. Finally, after ten months of attending conferences and meetings where parents were asking about these same issues and wondering why it hadn't happened yet, I began to realize that it wasn't going to happen very soon—and I just couldn't wait any longer. It was then I decided to do it myself. I knew there were others like my son who needed the same kind of support and assistance.

I called parents and special education instructors together, and over coffee and brownies we began to set up our plan and organization.

Our group of mildly mentally retarded needed a community based transition program that would give them a chance to live and work as independently as possible on their own, and that meant housing as well. Nearly all of the group grew up and went to school in this locality. They knew their community and the community knew them. They were accepted here. Local government and businesses are often more interested in helping local people. It made more and more sense for them to remain in their own community.

Also, the time to begin independence is while parents or guardians are still active and able to lend support. A gradual process must take place, but it will pay off in the end.

We called our not-for-profit organization the South Brunswick Citizens for Independent Living, Inc., or CIL.

The first requirement was transportation to job sites, since our participant members could not drive. I approached the local municipality and it was agreed to provide a van and driver through a county grant to the municipality.

While our members were still students at the local high school, they participated in a special education program called STEP (Special Training and Employment Program). The STEP coordinator and the department head became members of our CIL core group. The students were employed at competitive jobs and the coordinator provided on-the-job training at the site. The employer received credit for hiring the disabled.

In addition to employment, the disabled population required continual training in living skills to make them self-reliant. When CIL received its first major grant, a director/counselor was hired and a training program was set up. It began in the late afternoon when the participants returned from work. They were taught how to do laundry, cook, clean, manage money, and pay bills. It became clear that managing money and paying bills would be a continual challenge.

An Evening Adult School course was set up by the local Board of Education, in which our group was taught how to use the telephone directory, make medical appointments, choose appropriate clothing, and develop additional cooking skills. The class was called Practical Life Skills.

Recreation became a training ground for acceptable social behavior. Health issues were first addressed by a registered nurse through a grant to CIL. She has remained on as a volunteer.

In just a few short years we began to notice a change in our disabled population. They wanted to do their own shopping lists and purchase their groceries. Even a visit to the local barber shop and washing their own clothes were major steps forward for them. It was then that affordable housing became an essential part of the CIL program.

I began by writing letters, making speeches, networking at conferences, and talking to state and local politicians and put together a funding package. We purchased four condominiums at scattered sites within a local housing development but within walking distance of stores. Seven of our participant members now rent these CIL-owned condos at 30% of their income, a housing provision of the local municipality for people with low incomes and people with disabilities.

However, the need for additional housing was critical, so I approached the local municipal government and requested land so we could build. The desire to help local people became evident again and I put together a larger funding package this time. We called our sister organization CIL Woods, Inc. It took five years from start to the beginning of actual construction. I heard that it couldn't be done, and many obstacles were encountered. They only slowed us down temporarily. This group had to have a chance to live and work and become productive members of society.

Many of the parents, including myself, noticed a difference in themselves as well as their disabled offspring. It was a gradual letting go. Instead of sheltering them, we began to support the independence that they craved. It had to be done!

And what about Brad? He has now lived successfully within the community for eight years. While math and handling money had always been difficult for him, he has discovered a way to pay for his groceries. Part of his recreation now is a trip by himself to the local food market.

Brad's co-workers have nominated him three times for employee of the month. While he has never won, the nomination says it all. Last year, he received a five-year service award.

Brad's three siblings were all honor roll students in high school and college, one a Phi Beta Kappa graduate. While I am very proud of them, it is Brad who I feel has accomplished the most—and I firmly believe it was due to CIL.

1. What lessons can be learned about political action and organizing communities from Jean's and Brad's story?

2. Where should the responsibility for providing supports for adults with more mild cognitive disabilities rest? What role should the state take in these services?

3. What do you think is next for Brad and Jean?

Advance Organizers

MAKING
CONNECTIONS

Use the learning strategy—Advance Organizers—to help focus your study of this chapter's content, and reinforce your learning by reviewing answers to the Focus and Challenge questions at the end of the chapter.

Overview

Mental retardation is a cognitive disability that refers to significant limitations in functioning, measured by a low IQ score and limitations in adaptive skill areas, which are manifested during the developmental period (from conception to the 18th birthday). It is defined by reduced cognitive (intellectual) ability, limited adaptive behavior, and the need for support for full participation in some aspect of life, in school, and in the community. Although people with mental retardation have gained greater access to education, society, and independence over the last twenty years, students with mental retardation still have one of the lowest rates of integration in general education classes.

About 1% of all schoolchildren are identified as having this disability. Most of these students have mild cognitive difficulties and require only limited supports for success in the general education curriculum. Academic and social successes for these students with mental retardation are the results of educators and families working closely together. Although relatively few people have severe mental retardation or multiple disabilities, for them, necessary supports are often intensive, involve many aspects of performance, and come from a variety of sources. For these individuals, planned supports are often required across the life span.

Focus Questions

Self-Test Questions

- What are the key differences between the two AAMR definitions of mental retardation, and why are efforts underway to develop yet another definition?
- How are the causes of mental retardation organized, and what are some of the specific causes within each group?
- Why is it important to identify additional causes of mental retardation?
- What are the learning characteristics of students with mental retardation?
- How can educators be more effective when working with families of students with mental retardation?

Challenge Question

- What are some examples of the four levels of support, and how do they make a difference in the lives of people with mental retardation?

Children and adults with mental retardation are people first. Their mental retardation is only one of many attributes that make up who they are. It is important to remember that they are members of families, they have relationships with friends and neighbors, and they have personalities shaped by their innate characteristics as well as by their life experiences. Youngsters with mental retardation go to school, plan for the future, hope for a good job, wonder whom they will marry, and anticipate adulthood. These people have hopes and dreams like everyone else. They experience joy, sadness, disappointment, pride, love, and all the other emotions that are a part of living.

All disabilities are serious, even when they are considered mild. Those with mental retardation have impaired intellectual or cognitive abilities. These differences in abilities, and the way society reacts to those differences, create obstacles for these individuals and their families. People with this disability must make special efforts to learn, and many need considerable special assistance and supports from teachers and others. Some of the challenges these individuals face, however, are aggravated by prejudice, lack of information, and discrimination. Through persistence and courage, and with support from their families, friends, teachers, and others, people with mental retardation can overcome some of these obstacles.

Opportunities for the New Millennium

People with mental retardation have been persecuted since the beginning of history. They have been denied their access to education and their rightful places in the community. They face discrimination and prejudice in all walks of life. In the last part of the twentieth century—first because of advocacy on the parts of parents and professionals and later from themselves—they are assuming their places in modern society. But the challenges and the supports they need are great, and it is for civil leaders in this new millennium to assure that their participation is both full and with dignity.

Legacies from the Twentieth Century

During the latter part of the twentieth century, the category of mental retardation was limited to include only those students with more moderate and severe disabilities. *Mild* retardation was redefined to include only those with more substantial cognitive deficits, which contributed to the increase in students included in the learning disabilities category. This action played a part in confusion about all mild disabilities and whether they should be considered separate disability areas. A second issue that surrounded these students was where they should receive their education. Some parents and professionals stressed the importance of full integration, in which typical role models are a continuing presence. Full participation in the general education classroom, with a stress on age-appropriate instructional activities, precluded a special curriculum focusing on job and life skills. This raised questions about what constitutes an appropriate education for these students.

Thinking About Dilemmas to Solve

As you read this chapter, ponder these students' needs, the supports they require, and the outcomes they should achieve. Think about:

- How their educational needs can best be met
- How they can be prepared for life's challenges through the general education curriculum
- How the history of their treatment in society cannot be repeated
- How they can achieve a high quality of life
- What the educational system can best provide them

Also see related sections about adaptive behavior in this chapter in:
- History of the Field
- Children with Mental Retardation (adaptive behavior section)
- Educational Interventions (functional curriculum, community based instruction, and transition sections)

mental retardation. A disability characterized by cognitive impairment, limited adapted behavior, need for support, and initial occurrence before age 18.

adaptive behavior. Performance of everyday life skills expected of adults.

paradigm shift. A change in orientation, belief system, or conceptualization of a problem, philosophy, or issue.

adaptive skill areas. Targets of instruction that focus on the ability of an individual to function in a typical environment and on successful adult outcomes (independent living, employment, and community participation).

MENTAL RETARDATION DEFINED

Over the years, many definitions of **mental retardation** have been developed, and most are very similar. They typically refer in some way to intelligence or cognition and an impaired ability to learn. Some definitions also refer to limitations in the everyday behaviors necessary to function independently. Still others stress a certain age by which the condition must have begun, and some require that the disability be incurable. Some definitions require physical proof of the disability or a physical origin for the mental retardation. Throughout the twentieth century, professionals in the field of mental retardation have not been satisfied with the definitions developed to date (Maurer, 1997). Older definitions tend to follow a deficit model, describing the limitations of the individual. A more modern view conceptualizes mental retardation in terms of the levels of supports needed for the individual to function in the community as independently as possible (Polloway, 1997). Let's look at two definitions that represent these two different orientations.

Although the 1983 American Association on Mental Retardation (AAMR) definition of mental retardation represents a deficit view of mental retardation and the individuals affected, it is still used by many groups and is the basis for the definitions developed by many states. (AAMR was formerly called the American Association on Mental Deficiency.) After reading the definition and the ways that it is implemented, you will see some of the reasons why it is still used.

> Mental retardation refers to significantly subaverage general intellectual functioning existing concurrently with deficits in adaptive behavior, and manifested during the developmental period. (Grossman, 1983, p. 1)

The 1983 AAMR definition is implemented by applying criteria to its three major components: intellectual functioning, **adaptive behavior,** and developmental period. Deficits in intellectual functioning are defined by test scores below 70–75 on a standardized test of intelligence. Adaptive behavior is defined by how well an individual meets society's expectations for social responsibility and personal independence in accordance with that person's age and cultural group. The third component, developmental period, requires that the disability occur before age 18. Partly because of the standardized tests available, this definition is fairly easy to use when attempting to qualify students for special education.

In 1992, AAMR supported the development of a new definition of mental retardation (Luckasson et al., 1992). This definition represented a **paradigm shift,** a change from the traditional negative or deficit model to a more positive perspective on this disability area (Polloway, 1997). The definition that resulted addresses the interplay among the capabilities of the individual; the environments in which they live, learn, and work; and how well the individual functions with various levels of support. This definition moved away from a reliance on controversial, and often discriminatory, IQ scores; emphasized **adaptive skills areas;** and created levels of support that would be applied as the individual demonstrated need. Let's look at this definition.

> Mental retardation refers to substantial limitations in present functioning. It is characterized by significantly subaverage intellectual functioning, existing concurrently with related limitations in two or more of the following applicable adaptive skill areas: communication, self-care, home living, social skills, community use, self-direction, health and safety, functional academics, leisure, and work. Mental retardation manifests before age 18.

Legacy: In the last decade of the twentieth century the search for a new definition of mental retardation continued with an effort to rely less on intelligence tests and present a more positive view of the condition, but this definition was difficult to operationalize.

Opportunities:

• Capitalize on the work done that sets a new direction
• Develop easy-to-apply criteria and guidelines for eligibility

The following four assumptions are essential to the application of the definition (Luckasson et al., p. 1):

1. Valid assessment considers cultural and linguistic diversity as well as differences in communication and behavioral factors
2. The existence of limitations in adaptive skills occurs within the context of community environments typical of the individual's age peers and is indexed to the person's individualized needs for supports
3. Specific adaptive limitations often coexist with strengths in other adaptive skills or other personal capabilities
4. With appropriate supports over a sustained period, the life functioning of the person with mental retardation will generally improve

Although clearly presenting a more modern and positive view of mental retardation that emphasizes a person's needs rather than a person's deficits, the 1992 AAMR definition has received considerable criticism (Greenspan, 1997; Smith, 1997). It also has not received widespread adoption by states (Maurer, 1997). So work is underway to develop yet another definition of mental retardation (Greenspan, 1997). Why is there such dissatisfaction with AAMR's current version? Here are a few of the concerns that have been raised:

• Not grounded with a research base
• Difficult to implement
• Few assessment tools available for measurement of the various domains of adaptive skills described in the definition
• Not radical enough, adhering too closely to older conceptualizations of the condition
• Not enough focus on intelligence or cognition
• Too much emphasis on adaptive skills

So where will all this lead? The answer is that a new definition will be developed and adopted. Proposed versions are currently available, but none has yet been ratified or widely accepted in states' regulations (Greenspan, 1997). The next definition of mental retardation will probably: return to a definite association of this disability and intellectual impairments; extend and expand on the concept of supports, accommodations, and protections needed by the individual to live and work in the community; recognize the long-term nature of the condition; and retain the notion that the condition is a result of abnormalities or events occurring during the developmental period or during childhood. It would also not be surprising to see a new name emerge for this special education area; possibly, terms like *cognitive disabilities* or *developmental disabilities* will be viewed as more acceptable, and will be nationally adopted.

Sensitive and well-prepared teachers can help all children learn and have successful experiences.

TYPES

Regardless of the definition used, mental retardation varies along a continuum. Most individuals with mental retardation have mild cognitive impairments and usually require few supports. Typically, those individuals with moderate to severe cognitive impairments require considerable supports.

IQ Based Classification Systems. Since the development of the intelligence (IQ) test, around the turn of the century, people have been grouped, classified, and served on the basis of the score they received on one of these tests. One classification method, popular among educators in the 1960s and 1970s, distinguished educable mental retardation (EMR) from trainable mental retardation (TMR). These subgroups were directly linked to IQ scores. The EMR label was reserved for those individuals who scored between 50 and 80 (the ceiling was higher in those days), and the TMR label was used for those individuals who scored between 25 and 50. The use of EMR and TMR came into disfavor, possibly because educators knew that all people can learn and that education and training should not be separated. Also, perhaps they realized that suggesting that certain human beings were merely trainable sounded like an unfortunate comparison to animals. Since passage of IDEA in 1975, distinctions between education and training have blurred. Today, we understand that all children are capable of learning and have the right to education.

The 1983 AAMR definition attempted to address these problems by dividing mental retardation into four levels: mild, moderate, severe, and profound (Grossman, 1983). These subclassifications were used to compare an individual with others who had mental retardation. Mild mental retardation, as for those in the EMR group, referred to a disability that was less severe. Notice that this classification system has two more groups: severe and profound. Before IDEA, these children were not likely to find their place in public schools, but since its passage in 1975, educators recognize their responsibility to educate *all* children, and these two new groups were added to the 1983 definition.

Support Based Classification Systems. The 1992 AAMR definition, which will probably serve as a model for future definitions, provides a classification system based on an individual's needs for supports. Unlike the older systems, individuals are no longer classified simply by the scores they receive on IQ tests. The 1992 definition describes a profile and intensities of needed supports on levels from least intense to most intense: intermittent (I), limited (L), extensive (E), and pervasive (P). These levels refer to the services and supports the individual, whatever his or her IQ, needs in order to function in the environment. Table 6.1 provides more details about this system. Remember, levels of intensities are not a substitute for the older scheme in which the levels of mild, moderate, severe, and profound were based on IQ scores.

IDENTIFICATION

Disagreements over the definition of intelligence, problems with the delineation of socially expected behaviors, and the inherent bias of IQ tests have prevented universal acceptance of a single measurement tool or procedure. Regardless, the use of standardized tests remains popular, especially for intelligence. Although "mental age" is an outdated and ambiguous concept, it is still used by many professionals.

Table 6.1 The 1992 AAMR Definition and Examples of Intensities of Supports

Intermittent	Supports on an "as needed basis." Characterized by episodic nature; person not always needing the support(s), or short-term supports needed during life span transitions (e.g., job loss or an acute medical crisis). Intermittent supports may be high or low intensity when provided.
Limited	An intensity of supports characterized by consistency over time; time-limited but not of an intermittent nature; may require fewer staff members and less cost than more intense levels of support (e.g., time-limited employment training or transitional supports during the school to adult period provided).
Extensive	Supports characterized by regular involvement (e.g., daily) in at least some environments (such as work or home) and not time-limited (e.g., long-term support and long-term home living support).
Pervasive	Supports characterized by their constancy, high intensity; provided across environments; potential life-sustaining nature. Pervasive supports typically involve more staff members and intrusiveness than do extensive or time-limited supports.

Source: Adapted from *Mental Retardation: Definition, Classification, and Systems of Supports* (p. 26) by R. Luckasson, D. Coulter, E. Polloway, S. Reiss, R. Schalock, M. Snell, D. Spitalnik, and J. Stark, 1992, Washington, DC: American Association on Mental Retardation. Copyright 1992 by American Association on Mental Retardation. Reprinted by permission.

Assessment of individuals' adaptive behavior is also a hallmark of mental retardation identification. So, let's look at these three fundamental constructs of mental retardation.

Intelligence Quotient. The question of what intelligence is has challenged philosophers, scientists, educators, and others for centuries. Because intelligence is a **theoretical construct,** it has been defined in many ways, but the simplest way is to classify according to IQ scores, and probably for that reason this is still the most commonly used way of identifying students with mental retardation (Reschly, 1997). On IQ tests, intelligence is regarded as a trait that is distributed among people in a predictable manner. This statistical distribution can be represented as a bell-shaped curve, called the **normal curve.** As shown in Figure 6.1 on page 234, in this curve the majority of a population falls in the middle of the bell, at or around an intelligence quotient (IQ) score of 100, and fewer and fewer people fall to either end of the distribution, having very low or very high intelligence. IQ level is then determined by the distance a score is from the mean, or average, score. The IQ level of approximately 70–75 or below for mental retardation is also shown in Figure 6.1. Using this system, approximately 2% to 2.5% of the population can be classified as having mental retardation.

Tests of intelligence do not reliably predict an individual's abilities, they discriminate against culturally and linguistically diverse students, and they do not lead to educationally useable results. As you have learned, the use of IQ tests with culturally and linguistically diverse students has led to lawsuits, which motivated the state of California to ban their use when diverse students are being identified for mental retardation. Efforts are underway to develop and implement new ways of determining students' special education eligibility (Reschly, 1997; Reschly et al., in press). For example, Iowa permits the use of CBM and other direct measures of

theoretical construct. A model based on theory, not practice or experience.

normal curve. A theoretical construct of the normal distribution of human traits such as intelligence.

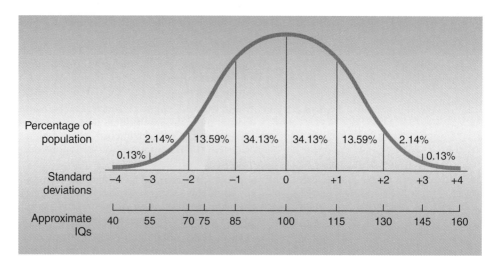

Figure 6.1 The Normal Curve, IQ, and Mental Retardation

See sections about over-representation of culturally and linguistically diverse groups found in the Identification section of Chapter 3.

intellectual function-ing. The actual performance of tasks believed to represent intelligence, such as observing, problem solving, and communicating.

mental age (MA). An age estimate of an individual's mental ability, derived from a comparison of the individual's IQ score and chronological age.

student performance to identify students for special education. Through a waiver system, many school districts are experimenting with more educationally relevant ways to assess children and thereby eliminate the use of IQ tests.

Mental Age. Professionals generally prefer not to use the concept of "mental age" when referring to people with disabilities. It is explained here because it is still used occasionally to describe the **intellectual functioning** of an individual. **Mental age (MA)** is defined as developmental level—or level of acquired ability or knowledge—compared with the age of the individual. Mental age is calculated as the chronological age (CA) of children without mental retardation whose average IQ test performance is equivalent to that of the individual with mental retardation. For example, a man of 35 who has an IQ of 57 might be said to have a mental age of 9 years, 5 months. Such a comparison is imprecise and inaccurate because adults have the physical attributes, interests, and experiences of their nondisabled adult peers. Describing them by mental age underestimates these characteristics. At the same time, the mental age comparison can overestimate certain intellectual skills such as the use of logic and foresight in solving problems.

Adaptive Behavior. Since 1959, professionals have agreed that IQ scores alone are not enough to either qualify individuals for services or assist in the development of appropriate educational programs. Adaptive behavior must also be considered (see Table 6.2 for the ten adaptive skill areas, as outlined in the 1992 AAMR definition). Measures of adaptive skill areas attempt to determine whether the individual actually performs the everyday skills expected of an individual of that age in a typical environment.

Many practitioners have expressed concern about judging individuals' abilities in the adaptive skill area because such judgments are typically made by parents and teachers, who may well be biased in their assessment. The tendency to overestimate an individual's skills or to assess them inaccurately against a nonspecified age-relevant standard is great. A standardized assessment instrument is now available that specifically assesses adaptive behavior. Developed in 1996, the *Assessment of Adaptive*

Table 6.2 The AAMR Adaptive Skills

Adaptive Skill Area	Explanation
Communication	Understanding and expressing messages through either symbolic or nonsymbolic behaviors.
Self-care	Toileting, eating, dressing, and grooming skills.
Home-living	Home environment skills relating to housekeeping, property maintenance, cooking, budgeting, home safety, and scheduling.
Social	Skills related to social exchanges, including interaction with others, as well as the initiation and termination of this interaction.
Community use	Use of appropriate community resources, such as traveling in the community, shopping, purchasing services, and using public transportation.
Self-direction	Skills related to making choices, completing tasks, seeking assistance, and resolving problems.
Health and safety	First aid, physical fitness, illness identification, and safety skills.
Functional academics	Skills related to learning in school, such as basic reading, writing, and practical mathematics.
Leisure	Recreational interests and activities that may involve social interaction, mobility skills, taking turns, and playing appropriately.
Work	Employment (job) skills, such as task completion and money management.

Source: From *Assessment of Adaptive Areas (AAA): Examiner's Manual* (pp. 2–3) by B. R. Bryant, R. L. Taylor, and D. P. Rivera, 1996, Austin, TX: Pro-Ed. Reprinted by permission.

Also see related sections about adaptive behavior in this chapter in:
- Table 6.3
- History of the Field
- Children with Mental Retardation (adaptive behavior section)
- Educational Interventions (functional curriculum, community based instruction, and transition sections)

Areas (AAA) allows the examiner to convert scores to age equivalents in each of the ten adaptive skill areas. This highly useful instrument brings more objectivity to the determination of individuals' abilities in this important area. This is particularly important with the increased weight of adaptive skills in the identification of cases of mental retardation.

SIGNIFICANCE

People with mental retardation often experience the negative effects of unpleasant and unfair stereotypes. For example, many people think of individuals with Down syndrome as "happy, affectionate, music loving, but none too bright," despite the wide variation in ability and personality among those who comprise this group (Thomson et al., 1995). Just as it is wrong to minimize the effects of mental retardation, it is wrong to assume that any individual can achieve only to a certain level or will not be able to master a specific task. It is undeniable: The learning difficulties faced by students with mental retardation are great, particularly because they are usually compounded by communication problems. However, lowering expectations can become self-fulfilling prophecies, dooming people to less independence and autonomy as adults.

Our society places a high value on intelligence. Just think about the comments you hear when someone is being criticized or insulted. Many of these insults—

CONNECTIONS

- Refer to the sections about communicative competence in Chapter 5.
- Also see the section about prevention in Chapter 4.

CONNECTIONS

- See the history section in this chapter for more information about the horrible treatment and discrimination people with mental retardation have experienced across time.
- Chapter 1 also gives background information about the stigma associated with disabilities and with mental retardation in particular.

Participation in group activities improves a wide range of adaptive skills useful throughout people's lives.

stupid, dummy, moron, retarded, or *village idiot*—accuse the person of not being smart. It is not surprising, then, that people whose intelligence is impaired often suffer severe criticism. They may become the victims of prejudice and discrimination solely because of their limited intelligence. Many uninformed people think of individuals with mental retardation as in a perpetual state of childhood. This belief is not accurate and also is unfair, as is demonstrated in Shaun Brewer's case (Loggins, 1999). The courts wanted to force Shaun's mother to uphold visitation rights for his father, even though Shaun is 24 years old. Shaun still lives with his mother. Although Shaun's parents are divorced, and custody and visitation rights are often set by the courts, Shaun is an adult. Is it Shaun's right to decide if and when he wants to see his father?

The stigma that often accompanies mental retardation can be overpowering. Sometimes, the fear of rejection and stigma leads individuals with mental retardation to pretend that they do not have mental retardation. Or it may cause them to be shy or especially reserved. Some people have even lied about their stay in a mental retardation institution, claiming to have been in psychiatric institutions or even prisons (Edgerton, 1967). It should give all of us pause to think that some people are less ashamed of prison than of institutions for mental retardation.

HISTORY OF THE FIELD

Although mental retardation has always been a part of human history, it was only in the late 1700s that it became the focus of sustained study by professionals. Jean-Marc-Gaspard Itard (1806), a French physician, began working in 1798 with the

Review the Essence of
Disabilities and the
Origins of Special
Education sections in
Chapter 1.

NEW DIRECTIONS
FOR THE
MILLENNIUM

Legacy: Public attitudes
about people with men-
tal retardation have
been inconsistent across
time, and efforts to en-
sure a positive climate
where their participation
in the community is
guaranteed must remain
paramount.

Opportunities:

- Ensure that standards
  for community living
  and employment
  arrangements are of
  high quality and offer
  sufficient supports
- Continue to develop
  a wide array of resi-
  dential and employ-
  ment options in
  communities all
  across the country

Later in this chapter, see
the Concepts and
Controversy section.

boy Victor, who had lived all his life in the wild with animals. Itard's work and the progress reports he published provided tangible evidence that it was possible to improve mental disability through skilled teaching.

Residential institutions appeared throughout Europe and Great Britain by the mid-nineteenth century. In the United States, Samuel Gridley Howe, the first director of the Perkins Institute for the Blind in Boston, developed the first U.S. mental retardation institution in 1848. Initially part of the Perkins Institute, it later became a separate institution known as the Walter E. Fernald State School. Ironically, Howe clearly saw the dangers of residential institutions that isolated people with disabilities both geographically and socially. He wrote that there should be only a few residential institutions and they should remain small in size:

> Grave errors were incorporated into the very organic principles of our institutions, which make them already too much like asylums; which threaten to cause real asylums to grow out of them, and to engender other evils ... all such institutions are unnatural, undesirable, and very liable to abuse. We should have as few of them as possible, and those few should be kept as small as possible. (Howe, 1866, p. 39)

Despite warnings to keep the number down and to keep them small, institutions spread over the United States. By 1917, all but four states had institutions for people with mental retardation, and many of them were large. The rise in number and size of institutions for people with mental retardation was based on unjustified fear of these people and their negative effect on society (Winzer, 1993). In 1877, Richard Dugdale, a member of the New York Prison Association, put forth a story about the Jukes family to illustrate that people with mental retardation were a danger to society. Dugdale believed that mental retardation was a hereditary condition and that people with it were the source of crime, poverty, and other social ills found in the country at that time. The logic worked this way: the Jukes, and families like them, were the source of poverty, immorality, crime, and more "feeblemindedness." They also overpopulated. They were a menace to society, and good people should be protected from them. Members of such families therefore should be cast away, put in institutions, and not be allowed to have further offspring. Dugdale was not the only propagator of such theories and reasoning. Henry Goddard, in 1912, released the story of Deborah Kallikak, who came from a family of "feebleminded" people. This condition, Goddard maintained, was passed on by heredity, and nothing could be done to correct the situation. Because of the likelihood that these people would become criminals, and because they were the reason for all of society's ills, they should be removed from society and their population controlled. Reinforcing the notion that feeblemindedness and criminality were related surrounded the attempted assassination of presidential candidate Teddy Roosevelt in 1912. Although they had not personally examined the assailant, three psychiatrists suggested in the press that he was feebleminded (Gelf, 1995). It is quite likely that such inaccurate accounts contributed to factors allowing the terrible state found in institutions for people with mental retardation. It was not until the 1970s and 1980s that abuses came to the public's attention through many exposés. Citing inhumane conditions and standards far below minimum, the courts ordered many closed because they violated residents' constitutional rights.

At about the same time that residential institutions were started, organizations of professionals and parents sprang up to call attention to the needs of these citizens.

The American Association on Mental Retardation (AAMR), the largest and oldest interdisciplinary organization of professionals in the field of mental retardation, was founded in 1876 as the Association of Medical Officers of American Institutions. In 1919, the AAMR formed a committee to develop a definition and classification system for mental retardation (Bryant et al., 1996). Its first manual appeared in 1921. Across time, as more has become known about the condition and as attitudes have changed, the AAMR has refined its definitions and classification systems. For example, the 1959 manual was the first to include limited adaptive behavior skills as part of the condition, and the 1992 version includes the concept of needed support. Founded in 1954, The Arc (formerly the Association for Retarded Citizens) also advocates for people with mental retardation. It was founded by parents to advocate for educational opportunities for these children.

During the 1960s and 1970s, researchers developed and refined new systems of instruction. Behavioral approaches that included token economies, positive reinforcement, direct instruction, and task analysis (breaking tasks down into small teachable units) proved to be highly effective, teaching students with mental retardation skills never mastered with instructional procedures used previously (Ayllon & Azrin, 1964, 1968; Birnbrauer et al., 1965). Jim Lent and his colleagues at the **Mimosa Cottage Project** analyzed many complex tasks and skills used in daily life and on the job (Lent & McLean, 1976). They then taught these complex skills—which some thought students with mental retardation could never learn—to their pupils, residents with mental retardation of a state-funded residential school in Parsons, Kansas. They pioneered work with this population of learners by applying behavioral principles that included systematic instruction, carefully controlled instructional materials, reinforcement for correct responses, and daily evaluation of student progress; these procedures have become commonplace in special education programs.

Also in the 1960s, a new philosophy was stimulated by Benjt Nirje in Sweden (Nirje, 1969). The normalization movement had influence all over the world, including here. Normalization emphasizes that people with mental retardation should have available to them "patterns of life and conditions of everyday living which are as close as possible to the regular circumstances and ways of life of society" (Nirje, 1976). In this country, the principle of normalization as well as the principle of **dignity of risk** (Perske, 1972; Wolfensberger, 1972) helped provide a foundation for civil rights court cases like *Halderman et al. v. Pennhurst State School and Hospital et al.* (1974), which granted people with mental retardation more access to society, schools, and the community. Court actions and the emergence of the **self-advocacy movement** also subsequently led to widespread **deinstitutionalization** of people with mental retardation. The first self-advocacy group began in the 1970s. It was stimulated by the first People First Conference (now an annual meeting) held in Oregon, and helped people with mental retardation learn about and gain access to their rights as U.S. citizens.

Although residential programs in the United States were developed by the middle of the 1800s, the first special class for "defective children" was not opened until 1896 (in Providence, Rhode Island). It was soon followed by others in large cities, and by the early 1900s a few special classes specifically for students with mental retardation dotted the country. Most of these classes had rules about who could attend and usually excluded those who could not walk or were not toilet-trained. It was not until the middle 1970s, by means of court cases, laws passed by some state legislatures, and the passage of IDEA, that all children with mental retardation were allowed to attend public schools.

Mimosa Cottage Project. One of the earliest demonstration and research sites, located at a state-funded institution in Kansas, where institutionalized individuals were shown to be able to learn a variety of tasks.
dignity of risk. The principle that taking ordinary risks and chances is part of growing up and is essentially human.
self-advocacy movement. A social and political movement started by and for people with mental retardation to speak for themselves on important issues such as housing, employment, legal rights, and personal relationships.
deinstitutionalization. Decreasing the number of individuals with mental retardation living in large congregate facilities.

NEW DIRECTIONS
FOR THE
MILLENNIUM

Legacy: In part because of negative associations with the label of mental retardation and in part because instructional approaches used with students with mild disabilities are the same, fewer students (who would otherwise qualify) are being identified as having mild mental retardation.

Opportunities:

- Develop new eligibility requirements for all students with high incidence, mild disabilities
- Create differential, unique curricula for students with different identification profiles

PREVALENCE

Estimates of the prevalence of mental retardation vary from 1% to 3% of the total population. According to the federal government, slightly less than 1% (that is, 1 out of every 100) of our nation's schoolchildren are identified and served as having mental retardation as their primary handicapping condition (U.S. Department of Education, 1998). During the 1996–1997 schoolyear, approximately 592,847 children with mental retardation were served across the country. By far, most of these students have mental retardation at higher IQ levels and need fewer supports.

Some propose that the criteria for inclusion in this group should change and only include those with lower IQs (MacMillan et al., 1996). One reason for this suggestion is the preference of school districts to use other special education categories for students who meet the mental retardation criteria (MacMillan et al., 1998). In other words, educational diagnosticians seem reluctant to identify students as having mental retardation, particularly those individuals who do not have severe disabilities. Although clearly not eligible, children with mild mental retardation, those who need fewer academic supports, are being identified as having learning disabilities.

What are some other reasons for excluding those with mild cases from the mental retardation category? Data indicate that some 75% of the children falling in the mild range are from economically poor backgrounds, while the rate for those with more severe cognitive impairments tends to be quite stable (MacMillan et al., 1996). So, of course, concerns about discrimination and bias are focused on this group of youngsters. Other important differences exist between these two groups. They require very different educational interventions: Those with more severe disabilities require more of a life skills curriculum with many supports. The causes of the more severe disabilities also tend to be of a biological origin, while the causes for those with less severe problems usually cannot be determined. Only time will tell whether a new classification system will be devised, but understand that if the special education category of mental retardation were changed to include only students with moderate, severe, and profound cognitive disabilities, then certainly the prevalence rate for mental retardation would change.

CAUSES AND PREVENTION

Mental retardation is caused by many factors. Understanding a few facts related to causes of mental retardation can be helpful:

1. Specific causes can be associated with treatable health-related problems.
2. The cause itself may be treatable, preventing or minimizing mental retardation.
3. Information about causes is necessary for effective prevention programs.
4. Some research, leading to more effective educational interventions, is more useful if the research subjects can be grouped by the cause of their mental retardation.

The link between identifying specific causes of mental retardation and the development and implementation of preventive measures is clear (Coulter, 1996). When a cause is identified, ways to prevent the debilitating effects of cognitive impairments have often followed soon after. However, the cause in many cases is unknown. In 25% to 40% of individuals with IQs below 50, and in 45% to 62% of the individuals with IQs between 50 and 70, the cause cannot be identified (Coulter, 1996). Therefore, increased funding for research targeted toward identifying the causes of mental retardation has been urged (Stevenson et al., 1996).

CAUSES

Today, it is impossible to single out every cause of mental retardation. Typically, factors interact in complex ways to cause mental retardation. The major causes can be organized in several ways. Sometimes they are divided into four groups: socioeconomic and environmental factors, injury, infections and toxins, and biological causes. However, the dividing lines between these groups are not always clear. For example, lead is a **toxin,** but it is also a socioeconomic and environmental factor because few toxins have been eliminated where poor people live. Similarly, malnutrition of a pregnant woman is a socioeconomic factor, but the damage to the baby is biological. Also, mental retardation is often associated with other conditions (Eriksson et al., 1998). For example, epilepsy frequently accompanies mental retardation, and the rate of seizures increases as the severity of cognitive impairment also increases. Also, individuals who have both cerebral palsy and mental retardation are more likely to have seizures. The interplay of cause and effect, however, is hard to determine.

In the 1992 AAMR manual that includes the current definition of mental retardation, another grouping system is proposed (Luckasson et al., 1992). There, the authors suggest that the causes of mental retardation be grouped according to the **time of onset.** Using this system, the causes of mental retardation are organized into three groups:

1. **Prenatal** causes, including chromosomal disorders, syndromes, inborn errors of metabolism, developmental disorders of brain formation, and environmental influences
2. **Perinatal** causes, including intrauterine disorders and neonatal disorders
3. **Postnatal** causes, including head injuries, infections, toxic-metabolic disorders, malnutrition, environmental deprivation, and any other conditions causing mental retardation after birth

Organizing information about the causes of mental retardation by time of onset helps to group reasons for this disability into meaningful categories, so let's examine the major causes of mental retardation accordingly.

Prenatal Causes. Many cases of mental retardation have their onset before birth, during the prenatal period. Some cases have genetic origins, others do not. For example, maternal infections and toxins ingested by pregnant women can seriously affect their unborn babies, and many of these cases are preventable. Let's first turn our attention to genetic causes.

Genetic Causes. More and more causes of mental retardation, many of them rare biological conditions, are being identified (Bailey et al., 1999). For example, **fragile X syndrome (FXS),** identified in 1991 as an inherited genetic disorder associated with mental retardation, is now thought to be the most common known inherited cause of mental retardation (Abbeduto & Hagerman, 1997). It results from a mutation on the X chromosome. A common associated condition is recurrent otitis media with resulting hearing and language problems. Cognitive deficits can be severe, and it is believed that some 86% of FXS-affected males have mental retardation. Many of these

toxin. A poisonous substance that can cause immediate or long-term harm to the body.

time of onset. When the disability occurred.

prenatal. Before birth.

perinatal. At the time of birth.

postnatal. After birth.

fragile X syndrome (FXS). An inherited genetic disorder associated with disabilities and particularly linked to mental retardation.

individuals are challenged by limited attention spans, hyperactivity, **stereotypic behaviors** (like hand flapping or hand biting), and an inability to relate to others in typical ways. It is now thought that some 6% of boys with autism also have FXS.

Down syndrome is another example of retardation with a biological cause. In England, Down syndrome occurs at a rate of 12.6 per 10,000 live births, and in the United States the rate is 7.63 per 10,000 births (Thomson et al., 1995). In England it accounts for one-third of all children with severe learning difficulties, but here Down syndrome accounts for less than 10% of all individuals with mental retardation. Down syndrome is a chromosomal abnormality. Each human cell normally contains 23 pairs of chromosomes (a total of 46) in its nucleus. In the most common type of Down syndrome, trisomy 21, the twenty-first set of chromosomes contains three rather than the normal pair. Certain identifiable physical characteristics, such as an extra flap of skin over the innermost corner of the eye (an **epicanthic fold**), are usually present in cases of Down syndrome. The child's degree of mental retardation varies, in part depending on the speed with which the disability is identified, the adequacy of the supporting medical care, and the timing of the early intervention. The great majority of people with Down syndrome have multiple problems (Stoel-Gammon, 1997). For example, estimates of hearing loss in this group of individuals are as high as 78%, and because the loss often goes undetected, related problems in language acquisition and development of phonemic awareness are understandable.

Phenylketonuria (PKU), also hereditary, occurs when a person is unable to metabolize phenylalanine, which builds up in the body to toxic levels that damage the brain. If untreated, PKU eventually causes mental retardation. Changes in diet (eliminating certain foods that contain this amino acid, such as milk) can control PKU and prevent mental retardation, although cognitive deficits are typically seen in both treated and untreated individuals with this condition (Dyer, 1999; Koch & de la Cruz, 1999). Because of the devastating effects of PKU, it is critical that the diet of these individuals be strictly controlled. So here is a condition rooted in genetics, but it is a protein in milk that becomes toxic to the individuals affected and causes the mental retardation. Now let's look at other toxins that do not have a hereditary link.

TOXINS. Alcohol, cigarettes, and other drugs taken by mothers during pregnancy can cause mental retardation in their children. Mothers who drink, smoke, or take drugs place their unborn children at serious risk for premature birth, low birth weight, and mental retardation (Ball, 1999). One well-recognized cause of birth defects is **fetal alcohol syndrome (FAS)**. FAS—a condition that manifests with mental impairments, behavior problems, and usually some physical differences, particularly in facial features—is caused by the mother's drinking alcohol during pregnancy. Estimates are that some 5,000 babies with FAS are born each year, and an additional 50,000 show symptoms of Fetal Alcohol Effects (Melner et al., 1998). Research has revealed that some 58% of individuals with FAS have mental retardation and some 94% require supplemental assistance at school. Not all individuals with FAS score low enough on IQ tests to be considered as having mental retardation, but unfortunately most of these people are not free of problems. The majority have deficits in attention, verbal learning, and self-control (Kerns et al., 1997).

DISEASE. Some of the dangers of drugs to unborn babies were just discussed, but there are others. The needle sharing that often accompanies some drug use is one of the culprits in the spread of AIDS, and that spread can be to unborn babies as well. Sexually transmitted diseases such as syphilis, gonorrhea, and **HIV infection** (AIDS)

stereotypic behaviors. Nonproductive behaviors (such as twirling, flapping hands, rocking) that an individual repeats at a high rate.
Down syndrome. A chromosomal disorder that causes identifiable physical characteristics and usually causes delays in physical and intellectual development.
epicanthic fold. A flap of skin over the innermost corners of the eye.
phenylketonuria (PKU). A hereditary condition causing mental retardation that can be avoided by eliminating foods that contain amino acid (like milk) from the diet, which result in a build up of toxins that damage the brain.
fetal alcohol syndrome (FAS). Congenital mental impairments, behavior problems, and perhaps some physical disabilities, caused by the mother's drinking alcohol during pregnancy.
HIV infection. Human immunodeficiency virus; a microorganism that infects the immune system, impairing the body's ability to fight infections.

can cause mental retardation in the unborn child. The HIV virus has been found in blood and other bodily fluids, especially semen and vaginal secretions, and in rare instances in breast milk. HIV infection is transmitted most frequently through needle sharing or unprotected sexual intercourse with an infected person. Many pregnant women who are HIV positive pass the infection to their unborn children, who are then born with a variety of disabilities, including mental retardation. The consequences of HIV infection for infants are devastating. The central nervous system is damaged, opportunistic infections cause progressive disability requiring prolonged hospitalization, and psychosocial factors and nutritional deficiencies lead to a chaotic and painful time before early death.

NEURAL TUBE DEFECTS. Anencephaly—where most of the child's brain is missing at birth—and spina bifida—an incomplete closure of the spinal column—are the two most common examples of neural tube defects, together representing about 80% to 90% of these defects (Sells, 1998). The failure of the neural tube to close during the prenatal period has many different causes, including the health and condition of the expectant mother, heredity, environment, and a combination of these factors (Hall & Solehdin, 1998; Olney & Mulinare, 1998).

Perinatal Causes. Although not as common a cause as prenatal and postnatal factors, problems can develop at the actual time of birth. The birth process can be dangerous to both mother and child and can result in a variety of disabilities, including mental retardation. Let's look at a few of these.

BIRTH INJURIES. Deprivation of sufficient oxygen (**anoxia** or **asphyxia**), umbilical cord accidents, obstetrical trauma, and head trauma can result in serious and permanent damage to the baby. The brain requires a certain amount of oxygen in

Advances in medical technology can save the lives of infants who previously might not have survived, can prevent disabilities, or can lessen the impact of disabilities.

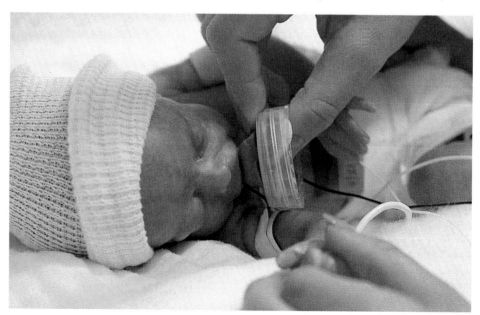

anoxia. Inadequate supply of oxygen to the body, usually at birth.
asphyxia. Deprivation of oxygen, often through near drowning or smoke inhalation.

order to function. Deprivation of oxygen will lead to death in a relatively short period of time. An even shorter period of oxygen deprivation or oxygen saturation can cause damage to the brain, often resulting in cerebral palsy (which may or may not result in mental retardation).

LOW BIRTH WEIGHT. The survival of very tiny premature infants has led to a new cause and increased numbers of individuals with mental retardation. Low birth weight is a major risk factor for disabilities (Ball, 1999). For example, low birth weight babies are 25% more likely to have cerebral palsy. They are 50% more likely to be enrolled in special education when they reach school age. And 31% of them will have repeated a grade by the time they are age 10. Medical advances of the 1980s have greatly increased the likelihood that infants born under two pounds will survive, and thus there are an increasing number of these children. Fortunately, not all of these infants grow up to have a disability. For the others, their disabilities vary greatly—some have visual problems; others have motor problems; some have subtle learning problems; and many have substantial cognitive impairments. Here are some specific results from one study of children who had an average birth weight of $1\frac{1}{2}$ pounds (Haney, 1994): While only 15% of the general population have IQs under 85, half of these children did. While 2% of full-term babies have mental retardation, 21% of these children did. While only 2% of full-term babies have exceptionally poor eyesight, 25% of this group of children had significant visual problems.

Postnatal Causes. Many cases of mental retardation begin after birth. That the environment contributes to individuals' outcomes there is no doubt. Poverty and poor family life can lay the foundation for negative outcomes (Feldman & Walton-Allen, 1997). Early years are crucial to the development of every child, and the events—experiences, illnesses, and accidents—that occur in this period can seriously impact the youngster.

CHILD ABUSE AND NEGLECT. Abused children have lower IQs and reduced response rates to cognitive stimuli (*Youth Record*, 1995). In a study conducted in Canada that compared abused children with nonabused children, the results of abuse become clear. The verbal IQ scores and the pulse rate changes between the two groups of otherwise matched peers were very different: The abused children had an average total IQ score of 88, whereas their nonabused peers' average overall IQ was 101; and the more abuse, the lower was the IQ score. The link between child abuse and impaired intellectual functioning is now definite, but the reasons for the damage are not. Rather than resulting from brain damage, the disruption in language development caused by the abusive situation may be the source of permanent and profound effects on language ability and cognition. Or the abuse may be a result of the frustration and difficulties often associated with children with disabilities. Remember, the connection between neglect and mental retardation has long been recognized, and is part of the early history and documentation of this field. Recall the story of Victor the Wild Child.

MAKING CONNECTIONS

Read again the story of Itard and Victor in Chapter 1, page 12.

Evidence now exits that even family units in which there is no direct abuse can foster negative outcomes. Many parents with mental retardation do not understand basic needs of children. They do not understand basic child care, nourishment, or the importance of positive interactions. Probably due to frustration with the responsibilities of raising children, these parents have higher rates of being abusive. The overall result is that children of parents with mental retardation have problems beyond what one might normally expect (Feldman & Walton-Allen, 1997). These findings help to build a clear case that students with disabilities, and maybe all students, should take courses on child development and parenting during their high school years.

TOXINS. Toxins abound in our environment. All kinds of hazardous wastes are hidden in neighborhoods and communities. In many cases the environment was polluted before the dangers of certain chemicals and poisons were known. In some cases, the environment was polluted because of carelessness. And, unfortunately, in some instances greedy business leaders did not want to spend the money necessary to properly dispose of or clean up waste products.

One toxin now known to cause mental retardation is lead. Two major sources of lead poisoning can be pinpointed. One is exhaust fumes from leaded gasoline, which is no longer sold in the United States. Before it was outlawed, children who lived near freeways and major city streets were at great risk (as were unborn children whose mothers breathed high levels of lead in the air). The other source is lead based paint, which is no longer manufactured. Unfortunately, it remains on the walls of older apartments and houses. Children can get lead poisoning from a paint source by breathing lead directly from the air or eating paint chips. For example, if children touch paint chips or household dust that contains lead particles and then put their fingers in their mouths or touch their food with their hands, they ingest the lead. Clearly, the importance of removing this danger from all children's environments cannot be stressed enough.

ACCIDENTS. Injury, **trauma,** and accidents are major causes of many types of disabilities, including mental retardation. Children under the age of 18 who suffer brain injuries—in automobile or cycle accidents, falls, near drownings—may acquire mental retardation.

PREVENTION

As you can see from the discussion about causes, many cases of mental retardation in this country are preventable. The President's Committee on Mental Retardation (n.d.) reports that more than 50% of all cases of mental retardation could have been prevented through known intervention strategies. Most of these strategies (see Table 6.3) are simple and obvious, but the effects can be significant. For example, in the case of child abuse, teachers have a legal (and many believe moral) responsibility to report suspected cases so that further damage to the child might be avoided (Lowenthal, 1996).

As you can see by studying Table 6.3, many preventive measures are available. Possibly the most important for all pregnant women is to stay healthy. Other prevention strategies involve testing the expectant mother, analyzing the risk factors of the family (genetic history of disabilities or various conditions), and taking action when necessary; screening infants; protecting children from disease through vaccinations; creating positive, nurturing, and rich home and school environments; and implementing safety measures. Notice that not all of these strategies are biological or medical. It is important to use a broad concept that looks at all aspects of the child and the environment for the prevention of mental retardation (Coulter, 1996). Let's look at examples of preventive strategies.

The importance of immunization programs to protect children and their mothers from disease cannot be stressed enough. The incidence of disabilities, including

trauma. An injury.

Table 6.3 Prevention of Mental Retardation

For Women Who Are Pregnant	For Children	For Society
Obtain prenatal medical care.	Ensure proper nutrition.	Eliminate child poverty.
Maintain good health.	Place household chemicals out of reach.	Create appropriate education and habilitation programs for children with retardation.
Avoid alcohol drinking.	Use automobile seatbelts, safety seats, and cycle helmets.	Educate parents, and provide support for good parenting skills.
Avoid drugs.	Provide immunizations.	Protect children from abuse and neglect.
Avoid smoking (fetal tobacco syndrome).	Prevent infections.	Improve sanitation and safety.
Obtain good nutrition.	Provide medical care to treat existing infections.	Provide family planning services; support spacing of children.
Prevent premature births.	Prevent lead intake (from paint and automobile exhaust).	Screen at birth for PKU and other conditions that can lead to retardation if untreated.
Take precautions against injuries and accidents.	Routinely test lead levels.	Provide systematic state prevention programs.
Prevent or immediately treat infections.	Shunt (drain) excess fluid around the brain.	Provide public education on fetal alcohol syndrome.
Avoid sexually transmitted diseases.	Provide neonatal intensive care services.	Provide public education on HIV prevention.
Plan and space pregnancies.	Guarantee proper medical care for all children.	Eliminate environmental toxins such as lead.
Seek genetic counseling and prenatal tests.	Offer early education programs.	Assure proper nutrition for pregnant women.
	Eliminate child abuse.	Assure proper health care for pregnant women.
	Eliminate child neglect.	Assure proper health care for children.

MAKING CONNECTIONS

Immunizations and the prevention of disabilities is discussed in Chapter 5 in these sections:
- Prevention
- Concepts and Controversy

mental retardation, has been greatly reduced because viruses such as rubella, meningitis, and measles are prevented. Access to health care is an important key to keeping in check what has been a major cause of mental retardation. However, immunization programs are still not provided for all children. For example, some families do not have access to immunizations, because a health care facility is unavailable or is too far from home, or because the immunizations are too expensive. Some families ignore or are uninformed about the risks of skipping vaccinations, and other families avoid immunizations for religious reasons or believe that the risk of getting the disease from the vaccination itself is greater than the risk of being unprotected. As a result, easily preventable cases of mental retardation due to infection still occur.

People must not underestimate the importance of prenatal care. Staying healthy means taking proper vitamins and eating well, and there are good examples of why this is essential. For example, folic acid reduces the incidence of neural tube defects. By eating citrus fruits and dark, leafy vegetables (or taking vitamin supplements),

Information about spina bifida is found in Chapter 9.

shunt. A tube used in a medical procedure that draws excess fluid from the brain and head area and disposes of it in a safe area in the body.

one receives the benefits of folic acid—a trace B vitamin that contributes to the prevention of conditions like spina bifida and anencephaly (Sells, 1998).

Infant screening has proven effective in preventing PKU. Using a procedure developed by Robert Guthrie in 1957, a few drops of the newborn's blood are taken from the heel to determine whether the infant has the inherited genetic disorder that prevents metabolizing phenylalanine, a naturally occurring amino acid found in milk. This test, which costs 3 cents, prevents mental retardation because the baby's diet can be changed before the effects of PKU can begin. It also saves over $1 million per PKU victim, the estimated cost for an untreated individual's lifetime of care (NY Times News Service, 1995). Guthrie developed the test because his son and his niece had PKU, and he wanted to prevent the condition from affecting others. New comprehensive procedures that screen all newborns for a variety of conditions will allow for early identification of PKU and other causes of mental retardation—like the blood condition of Rh incompatibility—as well (Chace & Naylor, 1999). These new automated programs are both accurate and cost effective.

Couples can take certain actions before the woman becomes pregnant to reduce the risk of biologically caused mental retardation. For example, gene therapy may soon be available to families who know they are at risk for having offspring with PKU (Eisensmith et al., 1999). Some couples have medical tests before deciding to conceive a child. These tests, combined with genetic counseling, help couples determine whether future children are at risk for certain causes of mental retardation. Tay-Sachs disease, for example, is a cause of mental retardation that can be predicted through genetic testing. Other couples take tests that search for defects after they find out that the woman is pregnant. These tests can determine, in utero, the presence of approximately 270 defects.

Let's look at yet another type of preventive technique that has saved children from mental retardation. Hydrocephaly is the buildup of fluids in the brain ventricles that causes them to expand. This in turn stretches the child's head outward and squeezes and compresses the brain and nerves. After some time, the result is brain damage. Medical procedures can now prevent the damage. Figure 6.2 shows how a **shunt,** or tube, drains excess spinal fluid from the child's brain to another place in the child's body (e.g., the abdomen), where the body can safely absorb, process, and eliminate the fluid. Before this technique was available, children with this condition had irreversible medical problems and mental retardation. And, remarkably, this surgery can now be performed prenatally (Snyder & Sandoval, 1999). Doctors at Vanderbilt University Hospital used this new fetal surgery technique for the first time on March 2, 1999, on baby James Neal Borkowski. In a procedure that took about an hour, a shunt was inserted in this unborn baby's brain and the excess fluid then drained into his mom's uterus. After Neal was born on May 12, he received a more traditional shunt (like the one shown in Figure 6.2). Such corrective surgery will become common in the future, resulting in positive possibilities for families at risk for having children with disabilities.

Remember, not all conditions or factors that cause mental retardation can be prevented. In over half the cases of

Figure 6.2 **How a Shunt Draws Fluid from the Brain**

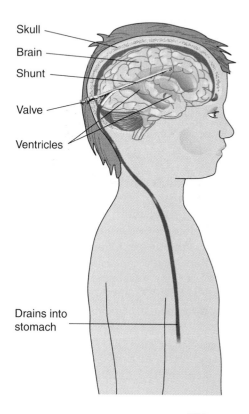

Skull

Brain

Shunt

Valve

Ventricles

Drains into stomach

severe mental retardation, the cause is unknown (Stevenson et al., 1996). Genetic causes account for about 20% of the causes, infections about 11%, trauma another 11%, and prematurity about 4%, with other individual causes making up the total. Until more causes are identified, we will wait for new preventive measures to be developed.

CHILDREN WITH MENTAL RETARDATION

Every person with mental retardation is an individual, and stereotypes can be unfair and inaccurate when applied to individual people. Regardless, it is helpful to understand some of the common characteristics that educators frequently encounter when working with students with mental retardation and their families. Recall that three of the defining characteristics of mental retardation are problems with cognition, adaptive behavior, and the need for supports to sustain independence.

COGNITIVE IMPAIRMENTS

The most common, and perhaps the most defining, characteristic of people with mental retardation is impaired cognitive ability. This trait has pervasive effects, whether the disability is mild or severe. It makes simple tasks difficult to learn. It can interfere with communicative competence because the content of the message is harder to deliver and comprehend. It influences how well one can remember and how flexible a person is with already learned knowledge and skills. Ultimately, the degree of cognitive impairment determines the types of curriculum content these individuals are taught: academic or life skills.

Learning new skills, storing and retrieving information (memory), and transferring knowledge to either new situations or slightly different skills are challenges for individuals with mental retardation. Memory, especially short-term memory, is often impaired. The student may also have trouble with long-term memory—correctly remembering events or the proper sequence of events, particularly when the events are not clearly identified as important. Even when something is remembered, it may be remembered incorrectly, inefficiently, too slowly, or in insufficient detail. Teachers can assist students in developing memory strategies and help them compensate for their lack of abilities in this area in many ways. For example, the student can learn to create picture notebooks that sequence the steps in a task they need to perform, a job that needs to get done, a task to be accomplished, or a checklist of things to do before leaving the house. Another means of enhancing learning is found in the Research to Practice box on page 248. There Herb Rieth and Chuck Kinzer tell us about the benefits of "anchoring" instruction with relevant and meaningful examples through the use of technology. Sometimes enhancing students' attention improves memory. A student, for instance, may have a short attention span for certain tasks; that student needs special help focusing or selecting the appropriate tasks on which to focus attention. By responding to students' leads in attention (Yoder et al., 1993) and preferences in learning materials, activities, and environments, teachers can enhance students' learning.

One limitation of mental retardation is that the individuals with this disability are frequently less able than their peers to acquire knowledge through incidental learning—that is, to accomplish learning that is an unplanned result of their ordinary

MAKING CONNECTIONS

Refer to the section about cognitive and academic performance in the Language Impairment section in Chapter 5.

MAKING CONNECTIONS

See the sections about learning strategies found in Chapter 4:
• Learning Strategies
• Generalization

Research to Practice: Teaching with Confidence

MULTIMEDIA BASED ANCHORED INSTRUCTION

HERBERT J. RIETH
The University of Texas–Austin
CHARLES K. KINZER
Vanderbilt University

RESEARCH

A multimedia based anchored instruction intervention was implemented with junior high school (seventh- and eighth-grade) students with mild disabilities. The students had difficulties learning literacy skills, recalling information outside of learned contexts, and mastering the content of social studies lessons. The students also demonstrated low motivation to attend school. The research's results indicated that academic outcomes increased when students were provided with real-life problem situations shown through a video anchor (movie) to use to "anchor" their discussions and provide context for their learning, Students were better able to link new information with existing knowledge, more interested in learning, and more satisfied with instruction. Teachers reported improved student outcomes and increased student enthusiasm for learning.

PRACTICE

Multimedia anchored instruction is an instructional technique that begins with a focal event or problem situation presented via a video segment or movie. The video provides the opportunity for students to create a mental model or an "anchor" to facilitate learning. It is implemented in four phases.

Phase 1: Watching the Anchor. To begin, all students watch the video anchor as a large group to develop a shared context. The shared context is used as the basis for discussions that enable students to: (1) identify and define real-world problems or issues related to the video, (2) generate strategies for solving problems or addressing issues presented in the video, and (3) identify the concepts and ideas presented in the anchor.

Phase 2: Retelling and Segmenting. Students are divided into two large groups and assigned a portion of the video to retell in their own words. Each group records their retelling of the assigned video segment on sentence strips and displays them for all the groups to preview and discuss. Subsequent discussions enable students to identify contradictions and correct misconceptions about the content. The segmenting activity is designed to develop a shared expertise in the anchor. Small groups of students (three to five students in each group) construct several strategies for breaking sections of video into three or four segments. Prevalent segmenting strategies include: (1) breaking the video into segments based on scene changes, (2) segmenting the anchor based on a character's appearance within a scene, and (3) breaking the video into segments based on shifts in plot sequences.

Phase 3: Characterization. For character analysis, the class is divided into small groups, each group including approximately five students. Each group examines, in detail, one character from the story. They identify their character's basic personality traits, and the societal influences that shaped the character's personality and behavior. Subsequently, they select a single vignette from the anchor to substantiate their analysis of the individual's character traits. Each group presents their character analysis to the class and shows a supporting vignette. Afterward, students ask questions, critically reflect on their classmates' analysis, and discuss related events and actions contained in the video.

Phase 4: Student Research. Each group of students develops a research question from issues arising from their discussions about the anchor. The anchor functions as a focal point as students use textbooks, reference books, photographs, electronic encyclopedias, and the Internet to acquire the information needed to answer their research question. Group members work to divide the workload so each member of the group is required to contribute to the research and to participate in the creation of a multimedia presentation. The presentation is shared with the class to showcase their understandings. During this phase, teachers serve as facilitators. They coach students about research strategies, mediate discussions, help students link new information to previously acquired knowledge, demonstrate presentation techniques, and prompt students to build on each other's work.

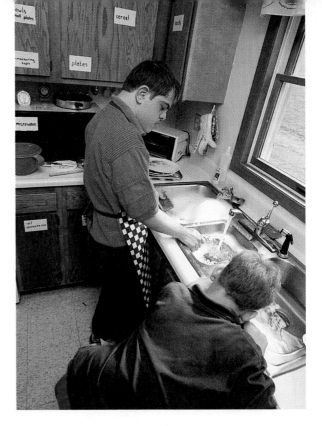

Learning independent living skills at school are best taught in surroundings similar to home settings to ease the generalization process.

daily experiences. For some, it seems that direct instruction is required for almost every task to be learned. Teachers must plan for the generalization (transfer of learning) so that newly learned skills are applied in a variety of settings (school, home, neighborhood), performed with and for different people, and expanded to similar but different skills.

ADAPTIVE BEHAVIOR

Also see related sections about adaptive behavior in this chapter:
- Defined
- Table 6.2
- History of the Field
- Educational Interventions (functional curriculum, community based instruction, and transition sections)

Think about some people you know who are very smart, get great grades in school, but cannot manage daily life. These individuals probably have difficulties with some adaptive skill areas. Now think about people you know who are highly successful on the job but have no social skills. Or those who have great personal hygiene and grooming skills but are unable to balance their personal budgets. All of these people have problems in at least one adaptive skill area. They also are bright (or at least average in intellectual ability), so they do not have mental retardation, just as those people who do not score high on an IQ test but have adequate adaptive skills do not have mental retardation. Review Table 6.2 again, and think about the independence of many of the ten adaptive skill areas. Also think about how important each is to independent functioning in the community. The point here is that mastery of adaptive skills is vital to an individual's successful functioning as an adult in the community. They are not skills that people, regardless of ability or disability, always master without instruction. However, for students with mental retardation, each of these areas should be goals on their IEPs, and effort to attain mastery of each should be vigorous.

Also see related sections about support in this chapter:
- Defined
- Table 6.1
- Transition (Educational Interventions)

For more about inclusive classroom placements, see the Special Education Services section in Chapter 2 and the Collaboration for Inclusive Environments sections in Chapters 3–12.

natural supports. Supports that occur as a natural result of typical family and community living.
nonpaid supports. Ordinary assistance given by friends and neighbors.
generic supports. Non-disability-specific public benefits to which all eligible people have access.
specialized supports. Disability-specific benefits.
Best Buddies. A program that pairs college students with people with mental retardation to build relationships, friendships, and opportunities for support.

SUPPORTS

Everyone needs and uses supports. We ask our friends for advice. We form study teams before a difficult test. We expect help from city services when there is a crime or a fire. We join together for a neighborhood crime watch to help each other be safe. And we share the excitement and joys of accomplishments with family, friends, and colleagues. For all of us, life is a network of supports. Some of us need more support than others, and some need more support at different times of our lives.

Researchers and scholars are studying the types of support needed by people with mental retardation (McDonnell et al., 1996). The 1992 AAMR definition includes support as a defining characteristic of this disability and specifies four types. **Natural supports** are the individual's own resources, family, friends, and neighbors (Bradley et al., 1993). These natural, supportive relationships exist among people in almost every setting and in almost every aspect of life. People help each other in simple and complex day-to-day tasks. **Nonpaid supports** are ordinary neighborhood and community supports. Examples of these kinds of supports include clubs, recreational leagues and groups, and private organizations. **Generic supports** are the type that everyone has access to, such as public transportation or the state human services system. **Specialized supports** are those that are disability-specific, like human services delivered to families of children with disabilities, or even special education. The amount of support needed can vary for each individual and change at different periods of time. Think of support as a fluid concept that is responsive by providing only as much assistance as needed when necessary. Remember, the four levels of support (intermittent, limited, extensive, and pervasive) can be delivered to the same person, at the same time, for different behaviors.

One creative way of helping people with mental retardation receive the support they need was an innovation of Anthony K. Shriver (a nephew of President Kennedy). **Best Buddies** is a program that links college students with individuals with mental retardation. The goal is for these people to become friends, whereby support and companionship are natural outcomes. Many of these relationships exist for years, with the pairs going to movies, sporting events, concerts together. The Best Buddy also helps when the need arises (Best Buddies, n.d.). Many other groups are following the lead of Best Buddy programs. For example, Metropolitan Nashville Public Schools has implemented their own buddy program to facilitate and support inclusion efforts at high schools (Hughes et al., 1999). Interested students without disabilities are able to enroll in an elective course, receive credit, and learn about disabilities and special education teaching techniques (e.g., praising, prompting, reinforcement procedures). These students provide positive role models, support integration efforts in general and vocational education classes, and spend at least one period per day with their special education partner. Participation in extracurricular activities is also encouraged. The results of these peer-support programs have positive effects in both the long term and short term.

FRIENDSHIPS

In the last decade, considerable attention has been directed at the development of friendships between people with mental retardation and people without disabilities. One thought is that if children with and without disabilities make friends early in life, they will continue making comparable friendships as adults as well. One rationale for the "inclusion movement" has been that integrated settings, where students with mental retardation attend general education classes alongside peers with-

NEW DIRECTIONS
FOR THE
MILLENNIUM

Legacy: A major argument for the full inclusion movement for students with moderate to severe mental retardation is that they will form friendships with peers without disabilities; however, little is known about the essence of these relationships or whether full participation in the general education curriculum sacrifices learning other functional life skills.

Opportunities:

- Reshape the argument to reflect the development of positive social relationships
- Embark on full-scale, comprehensive research about the long-term outcomes for people with mental retardation who experienced fully inclusive educational programs

out disabilities, foster friendships. Let's take a look at this belief and what new research findings tell us about friendships.

Social status and friendships are two different types of relationships that all schoolchildren experience. Social status describes how one is perceived by the peer group, but friendship is a reciprocal and mutually beneficial relationship. A third type of relationship experienced by everyone is acquaintanceship. During middle school, children without disabilities form friendships with others of similar backgrounds (e.g., age, gender) and with others who can maintain interactions that can be characterized as equalitarian, enjoyable, balanced, cooperative, and reciprocal (Siperstein et al., 1997). Relationships between students with disabilities and classmates without disabilities tend to follow some patterns, but these patterns are not those of friendships. These relationships cannot be characterized as reciprocal or collaborative. Children do not exchange roles of leader and follower, and they do not work together to make decisions. They do not have fun together, laugh, or mutually share "secrets." These relationships might better be described as acquaintances. If the goal of an inclusive placement for a particular child is improved social acceptance, educators must monitor progress carefully. Possibly, "educators need to exercise caution when utilizing expressed reports about peer relationships as a yardstick for measuring the social outcomes of inclusion" (Siperstein et al., 1997, p.122)

As work continues in this area, more and more interesting and even perplexing findings are being noted. For example, students with more severe disabilities are often viewed as more desirable peers than students with milder disabilities (Cook & Semmel, 1999). Children with mental retardation who are not as friendly and outgoing seem to be accepted more readily by their classmates without disabilities than children with mental retardation who are assertive, friendly, and outgoing (Siperstein & Leffert, 1997). Clearly, teachers need to assist all students, those with and without disabilities, to learn how to interact with each other positively and also effectively.

Although long-term friendships may not be the result of integration of students with disabilities, other benefits have great importance. For example, the attitudes of individuals who attended school alongside students with disabilities may well be different from those who did not attend integrated settings (Ash et al., 1997). Postsecondary students, even those who had experience with inclusionary efforts in public schools, did not interact very much in college with students with disabilities. They did, however, express more positive attitudes and a better understanding of the challenges that peers with disabilities face.

EDUCATIONAL INTERVENTIONS

Students with cognitive impairments require special and intensive instruction, and this instruction needs to begin early. Whether the target of instruction is a life skill, such as making change or cooking a meal, an academic task, or a vocational skill, sound instructional principles must be followed. When the target of instruction is specifically identified and is taught directly, and progress is evaluated systematically and consistently, students with mental retardation achieve well (Jitendra & Nolet, 1995).

These sections examine some special curriculum and instructional areas that these students are more likely to need. Space is devoted to discussing what is involved in functional curricula, community based instruction, learning to make

The importance of early intervention programs is stressed in every Preschool Child (Educational Interventions) section in Chapters 3–12.

choices; and what contributes to achieving a good quality of life, challenging employment, and independence in community living. At the end, you should appreciate what gains can be made, what effort it takes, and what accomplishment is felt when adults with mental retardation take their places in the community.

EDUCATION AND THE PRESCHOOL CHILD

Early identification and intervention are important to children with mental retardation and their families. Early intervention can limit the severity of mental retardation or even prevent it (Guralnick, 1998). Preschool experiences provide the foundation for the development of important skills later in school and in life, and they occur at a time when the family is beginning its long involvement in the education of their child with a disability. The power of early intervention is remarkable, and it is now well recognized that early childhood education programs are essential for young children with disabilities and young children who are at risk for developmental delay.

Children at risk are those whose medical needs or whose environment make it likely that they will have developmental delays if early intervention is not provided. Ramey and his colleagues (1992)—in a pioneering, multisite, randomized study of 985 low birth weight, premature infants—found that young children at risk who received a comprehensive and intensive early intervention program showed significantly increased IQ scores and decreased behavior problems. In fact, the odds of having an IQ score below 70 were 2.7 times greater in the control group that did not receive the early intervention program. Since the late 1960s, research and demonstration efforts have shown the importance of these programs (Bass, 1998). For example, the Susan Gray School of the John F. Kennedy Center at Vanderbilt University, a demonstration site that helped to convince Congress to create Headstart programs across the nation, continues to show that the long-term effects of disabilities can be reduced. However, it is important to recognize that not all programs across the country use proven techniques and get the same results.

Evidence is mounting that the influence of an individual's personality can affect cognitive abilities. Also, evidence now indicates that many children identified with mental retardation during their early years, even those with mild and moderate disabilities, continue to experience problems throughout their school years (Keogh et al., 1997). How could this be so? Well, the ways young children are interacted with can have long-term effects, whether those be casual encounters or planned preschool experiences. And the behaviors displayed by a child contribute to those interactions. Surprisingly, however, it is the children with easy dispositions who experience declines in IQ scores over time, while more difficult children either

Children have a lot to learn when they have opportunities to play together.

Headstart is also discussed in the Preschool sections in Chapters 3 and 5.

remain stable or improve slightly. Why might this be? Maybe these findings reveal that children who are more disruptive and demanding receive more attention than those children who are docile. Policymakers, parents, and educators must recognize the importance of comprehensive and sustained services for these children while they are toddlers and preschoolers.

EDUCATION AND THE SCHOOLCHILD

Most students with mental retardation have mild disabilities. Increasingly, these students are included in general education classes. Frequently, these students' learning goals are similar to or identical with those of their peers without disabilities. Of course, teachers have to adapt their techniques and adjust the curriculum somewhat to accommodate these students' special learning needs. (See the Accommodating for Inclusive Environments box for some ideas about how to make such adjustments.)

Many students with mental retardation, however, have very complex learning needs. They might require intensive, specialized instruction from a variety of professionals in settings away from the traditional school building—for example, learning how to ride a bus by using public transportation. They might even require a different curriculum that includes daily living skills, so that their long-term goal of independent living can be met. And some of these youngsters might need a "balanced curriculum" in which traditional academics are taught along with more functional skills (Hickson et al., 1995).

Accommodating for Inclusive Environments

STEPS FOR SUCCESS IN THE ACADEMIC CURRICULUM

Specify the Instructional Objectives

- List the objectives in observable terms such that they will communicate to others.
- Focus the objectives on what is directly the instructional target.
- Plan how the objectives will be evaluated to ensure continued student progress.

Sequence Skills

- Be sure prerequisite skills are mastered first.
- Sequence easy skills before more difficult ones.
- Plan to teach confusing concepts separately.

Match Instructional Tactic with Topic or Skill to Be Taught

- Select a tactic that has been proven through rigorous research.

- Monitor its effectiveness continuously.
- Change tactics when it is no longer effective.

Provide Many Opportunities for Practice

- Have students apply their learning in different settings.
- Have students apply their learning with slightly different or expanded tasks or skills.

Be Certain That the Skill Is Truly Mastered

- Have the student demonstrate mastery when performing the skill independently.
- Have the student demonstrate mastery in a variety of settings.

For a similar discussion about life skills or functional curricula, see the Education and the Schoolchild and Transition sections in Chapter 4.

For detailed information about IEPs, see Chapter 2.

life skills. Skills used in daily life and independent living.
functional academics. Using life skills as the means to teach academic tasks.
task analysis. Breaking down problems and tasks into smaller, sequenced components.
chaining. A strategy to teach the steps of skills that have been task analyzed, either first step first (forward chaining) or last step first (backward chaining).

Functional Curriculum. A functional curriculum focuses on **life skills.** This type of curriculum answers the needs of those students who have particular difficulties with adaptive behavior. A functional curriculum teaches skills that are used in everyday life or that prepare students for life after graduation. These should include the skills required for personal maintenance and development, homemaking and community life, work and career, recreational activities, and travel within the community (Hickson et al. 1995). Teachers must remember that their lessons should relate to skills that students need for independence.

Functional skills are very important to individual outcomes. Without good life skills, for example, achieving independence in the community is almost impossible. For this reason, some are calling for the curriculum to be judged more important than the placement or setting where students receive instruction (Sandler, 1999). Students with disabilities learn skills that are directly taught to them; they seldom master skills that are not directly taught. Functional skills are typically not the topics of instruction in general education settings. So, either they need to be included there, or educators need to find a place and time for critical instruction in life skills to occur. One way to accomplish mastery of practical skills is by emphasizing **functional academics.** Students' reading, writing, and mathematics instruction focuses on practical skills. The reading program would include reading for protection and information. Here, survival words (street signs: *walk, don't walk, stop*; safety words: *danger, poison, keep out*) might be the topics of instruction. Writing instruction could center on taking phone messages, writing directions for getting to a restaurant, or taking notes on how to do a job. Mathematics instruction would include such topics as time-telling, making change, money skills, cooking measures. All instruction using this system is practical. For example, counting is taught by taking inventory of books in the library rather than by absentmindedly reciting numbers from 1 to 20. A unit on measurement becomes an opportunity to teach cooking, rather than having the students measure lines in a workbook.

When teaching functional or life skills, teachers often find that they need to create their own instructional programs because they are not available from commercial publishing houses. In these circumstances, teachers find that **task analysis** is helpful when breaking skills down into teachable units, and can provide a guide for the sequence of instruction. Simple, linear tasks are easily applied to this system. For example, buttoning a shirt, zipping a jacket, tying shoes, cooking, using public transportation, making change, and telling time are all examples of skills that are often part of these students' IEPs and that are easily submitted to task analyses. Teachers can select two different sequences for **chaining.** In forward chaining, students are taught to perform the first step in the chain first. In the task of zipping a jacket, for example, students would be taught to engage the tab first. Each step up the chain of steps is taught and mastered before the next step in the chain is taught and mastered. In some cases, the teacher might elect to teach the steps in reverse order, which is called backward or reverse chaining. Table 6.4 gives you an example of a skill, zipping a jacket, that was task analyzed and taught to a young child with mental retardation through direct instruction techniques. To complete their instruction, teachers make certain that their students can apply their newly learned skills in real-life situations. For example, the teacher would be sure that the student zips his jacket when going outside to play on a cold day. In some cases, these practical applications should occur away from the school setting, and this is why the concept of community based instruction was developed.

Table 6.4 Task Analysis for Zipping a Jacket

1. Engage zipper
   a. Student stands with unzipped coat on
   b. Left fingers grasp bottom of jacket on left side near zipper
   c. Right hand (thumb and first finger) grasp talon, with talon pointing down
   d. Right hand pulls down firmly
   e. Left hand lifts slider and slides it into the zipper stop
2. Pull up zipper
   a. Left hand maintains downward pull
   b. Right hand pulls up on talon to top of jacket
3. Set zipper
   a. Bend talon down

Community Based Instruction. The strategy for teaching functional skills and adaptive behaviors in the environments in which they should occur naturally is called **community based instruction (CBI).** Remember, generalization abilities are problem areas for many students with a disability, and CBI is designed to help students learn to apply skills in all appropriate settings. Like task analysis, CBI is a crucial teaching tool for many students with mental retardation. Let's look at some examples. Learning how to make change is more natural when using real coins at the neighborhood store than when using paper cutouts of coins in the classroom. Learning how to use public transportation to get from home to work is more effective when actually making such trips on a city bus than when pretending to do so at school. Also, rather than addressing a specific curriculum area such as self-help or language skills in artificial settings, CBI allows for these skills to be taught in at least four important situations: vocational, community, recreation and leisure, and home and family.

CBI also assists students with transferring learning across situations, people, and places by teaching skills in the environment where the behavior is typically expected. Students have the opportunity to learn and practice generalizing their learning from one person to the next. Of what use is it to be able to make change with the teacher if the students forget the skill and cannot make change with the local shopkeeper or a stranger? Generalizing from one place to another can be enhanced by purchasing items in a store rather than from an old refrigerator carton on which the teacher has painted the word *STORE*. Think of more examples about how incidental learning can occur in natural settings through the application of CBI. For example, a trip to the store can include crossing streets, reading road signs, locating the store, finding the items, purchasing them, and interacting politely with the clerk. For those trips beyond walking distance, students learn about bus routes, change for the bus, locating the stop, and similar tasks.

CBI is very effective with students who need to learn adaptive behaviors and have generalization difficulties. However, CBI provides a dilemma for some educators because it is not compatible with inclusive education in age-appropriate general education placements. When a student is learning in the community while age-peers are learning in the school building, the student with mental retardation is

community based instruction (CBI). A strategy of teaching functional skills in the environments in which they occur; for example, shopping skills should be taught in the local market rather than a classroom "store."

Working in the school's snack shop can help children learn important skills they will need later on the job.

MAKING CONNECTIONS

See the sections about generalization in this chapter and in Chapter 4.

deprived of inclusion opportunities with peers. How can the benefits of CBI be weighed against the benefits of inclusive settings? How should this dilemma be resolved?

Making Choices. Learning how to make decisions is a life skill and should be part of a functional curriculum (Wehmeyer et al., 1996). Once acquired, for students with mental retardation to generalize this skill and apply it when appropriate requires application with guided practice in a variety of settings. Learning how to make choices while in community settings increases the probability of being able to use these skills when independent and in the community. Therefore it is also a perfect instructional topic to include in a community based instructional program.

People with mental retardation are allowed fewer choices than other people with disabilities and their nondisabled peers (Wehmeyer & Metzler, 1995). Every day, people make choices for themselves. They decide where to sit, where to eat, what to eat, how long to stay, where to go, and with whom to interact. For people with mental retardation, particularly those who were allowed to make few choices while growing up, the ability to make decisions is unfamiliar. Other people make even the simplest decisions for them. It is not uncommon for people who are paid to be escorts for people with mental retardation to make all of the choices, like what movie to see, at what restaurant to eat, or in what recreational event to participate (Belfiore & Toro-Zambrana, 1994). To avoid such situations, educators may have to teach decision-making skills and be sure these individuals can apply them in a variety of community and home settings.

Teachers can help their students get a head start on decision- and choice-making skills by ensuring that such opportunities exist in the classroom. For example, students could be allowed to choose from an assortment of snacks, from a variety of activities, or whether to work alone or with a partner. This component of education, which will eventually lead to independence and autonomy as adults, can begin during the preschool years. Young children can be encouraged to decide which toys to play with, rather than having someone else pick them out. They can also decide what activities to engage in during different time periods. Although this tactic may seem simple, because the tendency is to make choices for children with mental retardation and because making choices is such an important part of adult life, education and experience with this skill must begin early.

COLLABORATION FOR INCLUSION

Successful integration of people with mental retardation at school and in society requires considerable teamwork and effort. Teachers of students with moderate to severe disabilities, from preschools to high schools, will increasingly work with a greater array of professionals, particularly those from medicine (Bailey et al., 1999). And, of course, collaboration with SLPs to develop and expand these individuals' speech and language abilities will continue to be a major activity in instructional programs. To develop effective partnerships with people from these disciplines will require teachers to learn more about science, genetics, neurology, and biology. Teachers need to understand the vocabulary and concepts of multidisiplinary teams' members to ensure that each student's instructional program is balanced and appropriate.

For people without mental retardation, interacting with others who do not have disabilities, working alongside nondisabled peers, or participating in typical recreational activities does not happen naturally. For example, nondisabled children in play situations offer few positive and many negative comments to their peers with disabilities (Nabors, 1997). Many parents and professionals believe that attending a neighborhood school alongside peers without disabilities will change this pattern of exclusion and segregation (Freeman et al., 1999). However, change requires leadership and a break with tradition; inclusion efforts do not always result in real changes in attitudes or placements (Mamlin, 1999). Clearly, teachers and classmates need to change their interaction patterns, or integration will not have positive results.

Of course, teacher training is one way that educators become more aware of ways to adapt instruction, modify the curriculum, and provide an appropriate education to students with disabilities. Unfortunately, students with disabilities are often ignored by teachers, who typically call on more able students for class discussion. However, students can be taught to facilitate their own participation in the instructional setting. In a novel study, researchers demonstrated that students with disabilities can solicit attention from their teachers by actually prompting teachers to provide them with feedback (Alber & Heward, 1997; Craft et al., 1998). The students were taught to ask their teachers questions like "How am I doing?" or "Look, I'm finished." The result was better academic performance and a substantial increase in teachers' rate of praising students with disabilities.

For many years, inclusionary efforts have been discussed and implemented at schools, but the degree and amount of participation in general education classes is not what you might expect. Keep in mind that the concept of "inclusion" means different things to different people. To some it means participating in public education; to others, it means all-day placements in general education classes (McGregor & Vogelsberg, 1998). And, to some, if "it" is not successful, then "it" must not have

MAKING CONNECTIONS

Information about collaboration and inclusive educational settings is found throughout this text.

NEW DIRECTIONS
FOR THE
MILLENNIUM

Legacy: The focus on supports to ensure successful participation at school and in the community is new, and an understanding of the types and intensity of supports required, and how to ensure their availility, is yet unclear.

Opportunities:

- Develop models for levels and intensities of support applicable in different settings
- Create training modules for teachers, employers, and co-workers about supports and how to deliver them

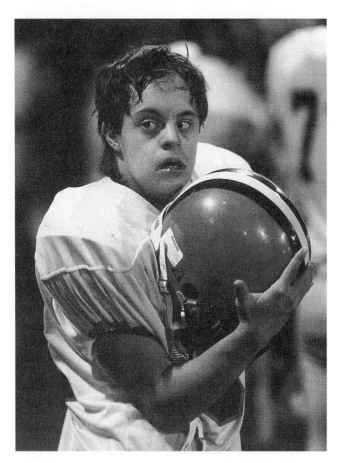

Luke Zimmerman is an important member of his high school football team.

been done right (Mamlin, 1999). For all this discussion and debate, surprisingly, the majority of students with mental retardation—even those with mild cognitive disabilities—still attend segregated settings. Only about 10% of students with mental retardation use the general education classroom as their primary educational placement option. Although some 29% attend resource rooms, almost 54% attend special education classes and almost 7% attend separate schools (U.S. Department of Education, 1998).

Students who attend general education classes must have a positive experience. They not only need to be included in class activities, they also must participate to the fullest extent possible. To remain actively involved in the instructional program offered in the general education class can be challenging for many students with cognitive difficulties. When they lose their places in the group reading activities, when they cannot follow along in the class discussion because the vocabulary is too advanced for them, or when they get tired and stop paying attention, behavior problems can arise. Some smart teachers prompt their students with cognitive disabilities to keep them actively involved in the instructional program; others, as in the example found in the Achieving Discipline box, use positive feedback to avoid behavior problems and retain students' interest in class activities.

TRANSITION THROUGH ADULTHOOD

The topic of discipline is discussed in Chapter 1 (Problems of Special Education and the What IDEA '97 Says about Discipline box) and in the Achieving Discipline boxes in Chapters 3–12.

Individuals with mental retardation can lead satisfying lives as adults. They can work in jobs, establish close relationships with friends and family, live in their home communities, and pursue desired activities. Of course, some may require assistance only from time to time during their lives, while others with more significant cognitive disabilities may always need assistance and support. What should the general goals for people with moderate to severe mental retardation be? Parents and professionals have been grappling with this important question because its answer could provide a framework for curriculum, instruction, and experiences offered to students with mental retardation. This question has stimulated an important discussion about **quality of life** and people with mental retardation. Before talking about employment and community adjustment, more traditional topics related to transition issues, let's spend just a little time thinking about quality of life and how this concept could guide instruction and decisions about adult living arrangements.

Achieving Discipline

KEEPING STUDENTS INFORMED: POSITIVE FEEDBACK

Michael had moderate cognitive disabilities, and attended his neighborhood school. He spent most of his schoolday in Ms. Dismuke's fourth-grade class, and was supported by a special education teacher, an SLP, and an adaptive physical educator. Michael's overall academic performance placed him at about the first-grade level, so keeping up with his classmates was a continuing challenge. Michael was a hard worker and wanted to participate in class activities, but when the level of discussion moved beyond his level of receptive language, he often became distracted, fidgeted, and eventually bothered his peers who were seated near him. The longer he could not keep up with the class, the more disruptive he became. He even began wandering around the room, opening other people's backpacks or rearranging items at various workstations. Ms. Dismuke discussed the problem with Michael's other teachers, and all of them experienced the same pattern of behavior.

All of his teachers had observed that when Michael was actively involved in group activities, he did not bother anyone. They all decided that before more punitive consequences for Michael's inappropriate behavior were implemented, they would try to keep him involved in class activities by providing him with feedback about when he was behaving properly. They decided to implement an intervention that had three components: frequent prompts about what was the expected behavior in the instructional situation, systematic requests for participation, and feedback at the end of the period about his overall performance. The result was a definite reduction in Michael's "off task" behaviors, though occasionally a more serious consequence still needed to be implemented when he was interfering with other students' learning environment.

Keeping students engaged through feedback

- Make the behavioral expectations clear
- Prompt or remind students about how they are suppose to behave
- Remember to continually involve them in the instruction or group activity
- Let the students know how well they are doing
- Be certain that the students understand what will happen if they continually disrupt the learning environment
- Be prepared to resort to more punitive measures

quality of life. A subjective and individual-specific concept dependent on a number of life dimensions, including social relationships, personal satisfaction, employment, choice, leisure, community adjustment, and other factors.

Quality of Life. This elusive concept has been described as being subjective and individually determined (Taylor & Bogdan, 1996). It is certainly complex, and judgments about quality of life must be made by each individual, for what is "good" for one person may not be perceived by another as "good." In other words, no single standard can be applied to all people (Edgerton, 1996). Quality of life relates to a person's satisfaction with life and with life's circumstances. It is associated with a sense of contentment that must result in part from feelings of dignity, worth, and respect (Hughes & Hwang, 1996). Quality of life is multifaceted and is an outcome of many different factors. Table 6.5 on page 260 describes the dimensions and components usually associated with definitions of this concept.

Why might this concept be important to understand? Thinking about quality of life issues can affect decisions and evaluations made about individual people with mental retardation, about their community and vocational placements, and about

Table 6.5 Quality of Life: Its Dimensions and Components

Dimension and Component	Examples
Social relationships and interaction	Friendships, affection, social support networks
Psychological well-being and personal satisfaction	General satisfaction, happiness, personal dignity
Employment	Job satisfaction, work performance, job challenge
Self-determination, autonomy, and personal choice	Independence, personal freedom, empowerment
Recreation and leisure	Visits with friends, movies, sports
Personal competence, community adjustment, and independent living skills	Domestic skills, self-care skills, survival skills
Residential environment	Living arrangement, degree of supervision, number of co-residents
Community integration	Community participation, mobility, community living skills
Normalization	Age-appropriate activities, normalized lifestyle, treated appropriately socially
Support services received	Income support, staff support, quality of care
Individual and social demographic indicators	Access to the community, initiative, persistence, appropriate behavior
Personal development and fulfillment	Academic skills, educational attainment, opportunity for continued learning
Social acceptance, social status, and ecological fit	Community contributions, respect, match with environment
Physical and material well-being	Physical health, safety, financial security
Civic responsibility	Voting, good citizenship, participation

Source: From "Quality of Life in Applied Research: Conceptual Model and Analysis of Measures" by C. Hughes, B. Hwang, J. Kim, L. T. Eisenman, and D. J. Killian, *American Journal of Mental Retardation,* 99, pp. 629–631. Copyright 1995 by American Association on Mental Retardation. Adapted by permission.

their instructional programs (Campo et al., 1997). These factors can also help us judge the merits of an individual's outcomes. In this regard, one set of researchers asked people with disabilities about their desires (Gardner et al., 1997). When asked to identify priority outcomes, which could easily be interpreted as quality-of-life indicators, the people questioned listed these as their top six desires:

- Have economic resources
- Experience security
- Have personal possessions

- Be free from abuse and neglect
- Participate in the community
- Choose free time

Achieving these outcomes is not always guaranteed for people with mental retardation, and the transition from school to life as an independent adult can be a difficult accomplishment. And as they increasingly join the community and experience integration into society, transition goals and instruction assume greater importance. Many factors contribute to a good quality of life. Here, let's consider just two: employment and community living.

Employment. Jobs have become an increasingly important issue for people with mental retardation. Jobs give them the opportunity to earn money, the opportunity for friendships, the opportunity to engage in the social activities of the community, and the opportunity to develop a sense of self-satisfaction and feelings of making a contribution. They also provide opportunities to continue to grow and learn. Unfortunately, jobs are not easy to find or to hold.

One way to gain important vocational skills is through **supported employment,** which not only provides work experience, but also has been suggested as one way to improve the wages of people with mental retardation (Rusch et al., 1997). Through this system students are helped in locating a job, learning the skills needed to be successful in that position, and keeping the job. Many students with mental retardation may need the help of a **job developer** to discover or even design work that they can accomplish. A **job coach** might also be necessary to work alongside the individual, helping the person to learn all parts of the job. Supported employment can have excellent outcomes for many people, even those with very severe disabilities. However, in successful situations, co-workers were trained by job coaches to assist people with severe disabilities as they worked alongside them (Mank et al., 1998).

Community Living. Being able to live independently in the community requires a vast array of skills. Many adults with mental retardation, particularly those who were not trained as young children to make choices, continue to find that they need help in making decisions for themselves and assuming control of their own lives. In fact, although they might need it most, this group of people has been among the last to have **self-determination** become a target of instruction (Wehmeyer & Metzler, 1995). Self-determination refers to the attitudes and abilities required to act on one's own behalf, make decisions for oneself, and make choices. Although the normalization movement is well established, people with mental retardation typically do not have the experience or opportunity to make their own decisions, be independent, or assume the role of self-advocate. They often do not even get the chance to make simple decisions, like what movie to see, what restaurant to eat at, whether to go to church, or whom to visit—even when the person making the decision was hired to assist the person with mental retardation to accomplish his or her needs. Sometimes, decisions are made about the abilities of people—their job skills and the level of independence they can achieve—based on their social competence and not on basic living skills. For this reason, professionals are suggesting that social awareness become an instructional target as early as elementary school, and continue on to instruction in community settings and job placements during high school (Black & Langone, 1997).

A section about self-determination can be found in Chapter 8.

supported employment. Used in job training, whereby students are placed in paying jobs for which they receive significant assistance and support and the employer is helped with the compensation.

job developer. An individual who seeks out, shapes, and designs employment opportunities in the community for people with disabilities.

job coach. An individual who works alongside people with disabilities, helping them to learn all parts of a job.

self-determination. A set of behaviors that includes making decisions, choosing preferences, and practicing self-advocacy.

Not so many years ago, professionals and parents alike shared concerns about people with mental retardation living in community settings. It was suggested that they would not be successful in independent settings, might be victimized, and would not be able to care for themselves. There was also concern about how neighbors would treat them. Cases like Skipper Carrillo's have made people be less worried about individuals with mental retardation living alone in the community (Wielenga, 1997). Skipper lives alone in an apartment in Laguna Beach, California, a community where he has lived for over 34 years. He volunteers his time to the baseball team at the local high school, and is supported by the entire town. Also, long-term research analyses of how well people with mental retardation have fared away from large institutions has proven that community residences, like apartments, are appropriate alternatives (Rubin & Heal, 1996). However, some lessons have been learned since the 1970s. One of these lessons is how important case managers are as supports to successful community living.

FAMILIES

The families of individuals with mental retardation face special challenges. Most of these families require additional services and supports at some time, especially during periods of transition. These supports might include personal care, family support, respite care, financial allowances, subsidies, counseling and guidance, and in-home assistance. Many families also gain strength and information from organizations such as The Arc or other parent support and advocacy groups. However, it is the families themselves who provide the required day-to-day supports. Educators must recognize that families provide lasting and sustaining life connections for their family members with disabilities long after the schooling years are over. When schoolyears are over, educators' work is done, but the family's work is not. As you learned from Jean Gibson (see the Personal Perspective vignette at the beginning of this chapter), although issues change across time, it often seems that families simply move from one challenge to another. For many families, the last major challenge is where their adult family member with mental retardation will live (Freedman et al., 1997). And the fear and worry associated with residential arrangements make many families put off choices until it is almost too late to make good choices and easy transitions. The dilemmas faced by families of individuals with mental retardation can be complex and confusing, and their resolution requires the efforts of the entire family (Thorin et al., 1996). So, in this section your attention is drawn to the support given to family members with disabilities from fathers, grandparents, and siblings.

FAMILY SUPPORT: DADS

Fathers are very important in the lives of their children, and this is no less true for children with disabilities. Fathers of children with disabilities are as involved and spend about the same amount of time with their children as fathers whose children do not have disabilities (Beach Center, 1995a). They just do things differently. These fathers spend more time doing child care. They watch more TV and spend more time at home than other fathers. Those fathers who do help with the rearing of their children with disabilities also tend to have a higher level of satisfaction with their marriage (Willoughby & Glidden, 1995).

Fathers of these children, however, have a serious complaint about service providers: They believe that they are treated like second-class citizens (Beach Center, 1995a). They get the message that mothers are the "experts" about their children. One father even reports that a social worker thanked him for his cooperation and that the worker would check the accuracy of his answers with his wife. Some fathers believe that the predominately female fields that work with children with disabilities are not sensitive to the differences in fathers' emotional perspectives about their children with disabilities. Most fathers seem to understand the importance of their roles. They, more than service providers, know that it takes "two of us to handle all that was happening; service providers would just have to get to know me and learn to accept, if not like, the fact that I was involved with my daughter's life" (p. 4). Children who have positive relationships with their fathers tend to have higher achievement, are more motivated, and have better social skills than those who do not have a dad active in their lives (Beach Center, 1995b). Educators need to remember that fathers are an important part of the family support team. They need to be involved and included in their children's educational programs.

FAMILY SUPPORT: GRANDPARENTS

Grandparents can be important members of the family support team, particularly if they live close to their grandchild with disabilities. The same can be said about the roles of extended family members in some cultures. When planning educational programs and collaborative activities with the home, educators should remember the entire family network. Grandparents, although often overlooked, may provide considerable assistance through babysitting, shopping, and financial support (Sandler et al., 1995). Although there are some reports about grandparents who have difficulties accepting their grandchild's disabilities (even casting blame), there is more evidence that they can be a valuable resource and source of considerable support to their own children, the parents of the child with problems. Professionals should develop better strategies to involve grandparents, as they help build a strong family support system for each child with disabilities.

FAMILY SUPPORT: BROTHERS AND SISTERS

Siblings of people with disabilities have not received much attention from researchers or policymakers. However, recent research shows that siblings play an important role in the lives of their brothers and sisters with disabilities, particularly those with mental retardation (Krauss et al., 1996). Research also shows that siblings of individuals with mental retardation are no more likely to experience stress or emotional problems than people without brothers or sisters with developmental disabilities (Hannah & Midlarksy, 1999). These individuals maintain regular and personal contacts with their less able brothers or sisters and stand ready to assume the role of caregiver. Many, 36% in one study, even intend to co-reside when their parents' health or status prevents their continuing to care for their son or daughter with disabilities. This is particularly true when the adult with mental retardation is in poor health. It is interesting that in most of these cases, the parents are making plans for their adult child with disabilities to live in publicly supported residential services, not co-reside with a sibling (Freedman et al., 1997). Policymakers and community service providers must come to understand and better appreciate the roles that siblings intend to take regarding the care of their brothers and sisters with disabilities.

Medical technology used to prevent mental retardation is found in that section of this chapter.

For more information about assistive technology and augmentative devices, see the Technology section in Chapter 5.

augmentative communication systems. Alternative methods of communicating, such as communication boards, communication books, sign language, and computerized voices. **communication boards.** A flat device on which words, pictures, or other symbols are used to expand the verbal interactions of people with limited vocal abilities.

TECHNOLOGY

Modern technology can make a tremendous difference in the lives of individuals with mental retardation, and the range of technology that has made a difference is wide. Technology can be as simple as letting students with mental retardation use a calculator to perform arithmetic tasks, allowing them to compensate successfully for the difficulties they often face when having to solve mathematical problems used in important life skills like balancing a checkbook. Technology benefiting this group of individuals can also be complex. For example, medical technology has provided interventions and techniques that have lessened the impact of some causes and prevented others. For example, the development of shunt technology has prevented thousands of cases of mental retardation that were inevitable with the onset of hydrocephaly. Some medical techniques can now be performed in utero, before the baby is born. But, when we think of technology, we usually do not think of medical technology. We think of computers, and the applications of computer technology to individuals with disabilities and to classroom settings are far reaching as well.

The ready availability of computer technology has opened up communication possibilities for many students with mental retardation who are unable to communicate with others through speech (Parette & Angelo, 1996). This does not mean that these students cannot communicate. Even children without speech are able to learn other methods of communication. For example, a student may use eye blinks, facial expressions, touches, movement, technology, or sign language to indicate needs and desires. Some children use **augmentative communication systems,** like **communication boards,** to express their needs and feelings (Romski & Sevcik, 1997). In the simple systems, words and/or pictures are placed on a flat surface or in books. The student communicates by pointing to the appropriate symbols. Symbols are customized to the individual; the words or symbols on the board reflect the individual and the needs of the environments in which he or she operates. Some boards are simple homemade projects; others use quite sophisticated technology. The teacher's job is to encourage and shape these techniques into a reliable system of communication for the student. With reliable communication, learning and social interaction can take place.

The ability to communicate is essential to life satisfaction. It can make the difference between a sad, depressed, isolated child and a child who is an enthusiastic participant in the world. Computer technology allows many individuals with severe disabilities to communicate, and communication devices that provide speech output can provide great benefits (Romski et al., 1999). Evidence supports their use, for they allow the individual to convey more information in a more understandable fashion. The result can be better access and participation in the community.

CONCEPTS AND CONTROVERSY: EUGENICS AND ITS LOGICAL EXTENSION

In 1927, under a Supreme Court approved law, the state of Virginia had Virginia Carrie Buck sterilized after her diagnosis as "feebleminded" and the birth of her illegitimate child. She was also committed to an institution for people with mental retardation. It is estimated that following this precedent, some 50,000 people were

Review the question about how people with disabilities have been treated across history (Essence of Disabilities) in Chapter 1 and the History section in this chapter.

sterilized in the United States (Smith, 1994, 1995). In 1933, the German government, using the Virginia law as its model, passed a sterilization law that between 1933 and 1945 sanctioned Nazi sterilization of some 2 million people who were considered defective. The justification for this action (as explained in Hitler's book *Mein Kampf*) was that the "race" needed to be preserved and protected: Defective people should not be allowed to propagate equally defective offspring. The eugenics movement—which was extremely popular in the United States, France, and Germany throughout the beginning of the twentieth century—supported the position that all human characteristics were attributed to heredity and genetic determination. The only way to stop the destruction of society because of an overpopulation of incompetent people was to prohibit their "breeding." The one way to guarantee this event was sterilization.

Of course, support for the eugenics movement diminished after World War II and the atrocities of the Nazi government were revealed. However, some of the attitudes from this movement remain. For example, a survey of obstetricians conducted in 1972 found that 97% of them supported the sterilization of welfare mothers who had illegitimate children (Rodriguez-Trias, 1982). In a 1991 issue of Mensa's Eugenics Special Interest Group's (ESIG) publication, *ESIB Bulletin*, it is recommended that people with Down syndrome not be allowed to reproduce. Herrnstein and Murray (1994), in their book *The Bell Curve*, revive the notion that intelligence is more closely related to heredity than to factors in the environment. Are these isolated and rare examples? Rock (1996) points out at such attitudes are not restricted to birth, but also to death. For example, in discussions about providing life-sustaining medical treatments to individuals with mental retardation, quality-of-life issues qualitatively different from those for people without disabilities are often topics of concern. Who has the right to make decisions about whether specific individuals should become mothers and fathers? How should medical decisions be made? Should benefits to society enter into the decision-making process?

In Conclusion

Look again at the Advance Organizers at the beginning of the chapter; to help you study the content of this chapter, the answers to the Focus and Challenge questions are found here. Test yourself to see if you have mastered the major points of this chapter.

Summary

People with mental retardation have significantly impaired intellectual functioning, have problems with adaptive skills, and require a variety of supports to achieve independence as adults and assume their places in modern society. Their disability must have been manifested during the developmental period, from birth to age 18. But people with mental retardation are people first, with all the emotions, motivations, and complexities of any human being. Thus, attempts to provide education and habilitation to students with mental retardation must be based on the realization of the fundamental similarities of all people.

Self-Test Questions

- *What are the key differences between the two AAMR definitions of mental retardation, and why are efforts underway to develop yet another definition?*

  The American Association on Mental Retardation (AAMR) has offered definitions of this disability since 1921, and since 1959 has included problems with adaptive behavior as a characteristic of the condition. The organization's two most recent definitions were developed in 1983 and in 1992. The 1983 definition has three major components: significant subaverage general intellectual functioning, concurrent deficits in adaptive behavior, and origination before the age of 18. It also divides people with this disability by four levels that are defined by scores individuals receive on standardized tests of intelligence: mild, moderate, severe, and profound. This definition is driven by IQ scores. The 1992 AAMR definition is more flexible, places more emphasis on adaptive skills, and introduces concepts about individuals' needs for support to function independently at home, at work, and in the community. The 1992 definition, however, has proven difficult to implement and few states have adopted it in their regulations for the identification of mental retardation. Therefore, efforts continue to find a better way to describe this disability that will lead to fair and accurate identification as well as the development of appropriate educational programs.

- *How are the causes of mental retardation organized, and what are some of the specific causes within each group?*

  The 1992 AAMR definition classifies causes of mental retardation into three major groups that relate to the time of onset of the disability: prenatal, perinatal, and postnatal. Prenatal causes happen before the child is born and may be caused by factors such as genetic errors, toxins, disease, or neural tube defects. Some examples of genetic causes are fragile X syndrome and Down syndrome. Other genetic causes create predispositions to mental retardation from toxins. PKU is such an example. Toxins are very dangerous to unborn babies. Expectant mothers drinking alcohol can cause fetal alcohol syndrome (FAS). Other drugs taken by expectant mothers, including tobacco, can also cause mental retardation. Diseases—like meningitis, rubella, and measles—can cause retardation, depending on which prenatal period the mother contracted them. Most of these causes of mental retardation can be prevented by vaccines. Other diseases, like AIDS, that are passed on to the unborn child can be devastating as well. Injuries at birth or during the birth process (perinatal causes) often result from oxygen deprivation. Low birth weight is also associated with cognitive impairments that affect these children throughout their lives. Postnatal causes can include child abuse and neglect, accidents, and toxins in the environment.

- *Why is it important to identify additional causes of mental retardation?*

  Many of the causes of mental retardation can be prevented, and more causes need to be discovered so preventive measures can be developed. It is important to recognize that about 50% of the cases of mental retardation could have been prevented by screening pregnant women and their babies for risk factors, protecting children from disease through vaccinations, providing positive and nurturing home and school environments, and implementing safety measures. Most of the effective preventive measures now commonly applied were developed in response to a known cause. For example, mental retardation from PKU is prevented because researchers discovered that the amino acid in milk harms those children who are genetically predisposed to this problem. Shunts and the operations that allow for the safe drainage of excess fluid from the brain were developed when hydrocephaly was understood. History has shown that when a cause is identified, preventive measures soon follow. Increasing the research dollars invested in identifying the causes of mental retardation would greatly decrease the number of cases of this disability.

- *What are the learning characteristics of students with mental retardation?*
The most common characteristic of students with mental retardation is limited cognitive ability. Cognitive impairments manifest themselves in many ways. Clearly, it makes learning more difficult. It also affects memory and the ability to generalize learning to different settings, similar skills, or to different individuals. A common, associated problem is in the area of communication. Both delayed language and speech problems are common among this group of learners. It is also important to recognize that cognitive impairments in these individuals result in difficulties with the ten adaptive skill areas: communication, self-care, home-living, social community use, self-direction, health and safety, functional academics, leisure, and work. Difficulties in adaptive behavior can result in limitations in independence as adults, and for this reason many of these individuals need some support in some adaptive skill areas.

- *How can educators be more effective when working with families of students with mental retardation?*
Educators who develop meaningful partnerships with their students' families find that they are better able to meet their students' educational needs. Unfortunately, many educators do not recognize all significant members of the family unit. For many students with disabilities, the immediate and extended family provide significant support. Family involvement should include not just the mother, but also the father, brothers and sisters, and grandparents. In some cases, it would also include aunts and uncles if they are involved in the student's life on a frequent basis. The supports that family members provide extend far beyond the schoolday and extend to the years after school is completed. Members of the family unit should be included in informational and planning meetings about a student's educational programs, respected as valuable members of the student's support network, and involved in evaluating the effectiveness of school.

Challenge Question

- *What are some examples of the four levels of support, and how do they make a difference in the lives of people with mental retardation?*
The primary goal for most individuals with mental retardation is to achieve a life of autonomy and self-direction. Opportunities to live in normalized living

arrangements in communities, to work, and to have satisfying personal relationships are extremely important. For many of these people, achieving these aims requires supports some of which are naturally available and others needing to be arranged. Types of support include natural (from family, friends, and neighbors), nonpaid (neighborhood and community groups), generic (supports everyone has access to), and specialized (disability-specific). The four levels of support identified in the 1992 AAMR definition are intermittent, limited, extensive, and pervasive. Some individuals need only intermittent (or short-term) support during times of crisis or transition—for example, when they are moving or finding a new job. Others need limited support that is consistent over time (not intermittent) when they are learning new job skills. Extensive and pervasive support includes regular involvement in the person's life and may include supervised living arrangements, money management, and leisure time activities. Support for any individual can be provided on a pervasive basis for some skills and on an intermittent basis for other skills. The intent is to create a flexible and responsive support system that allows the person to live, work, and play in the community with as much independence as possible.

 # Supplementary Resources

Scholarly Readings

Drew, C. J., Logan, D. R., & Hardman, M. L. (1992). *Mental retardation: A life cycle approach.* New York: Merrill.

Hickson, L., Blackman, L. S., & Reis, E. M. (1995). *Mental retardation: Foundations of educational programming.* Boston: Allyn and Bacon.

Polloway, E., & Patton, J. (1996). *Strategies for teaching learners with special needs.* Upper Saddle River, NJ: Merrill.

Popular Books

Arrigoni, R. (1997). *Casa Angelica: Arlene's legacy.* Albuquerque: University of New Mexico Press.

Bérubé, M. (1996). *Life as we know it: A father, a family, and an exceptional child.* New York: Merrill.

Meyers, R. (1978). *Like normal people.* New York: McGraw-Hill.

Perske, R. (1986). *Don't stop the music.* Nashville: Abingdon Press.

Sachs, O. (1987). *The man who mistook his wife for a hat and other clinical tales.* New York: Harper & Row.

Steinbeck, J. (1937). *Of mice and men.* New York: Viking Press.

Videos and DVDs

Charly. (1968). ABC—Selmur Pictures—CBS/FOX.

L'Enfant Sauvage (The wild child). (1969). F. Truffaut (Director).

Being there. (1979). Lorimar/CBS/Fox.

Of mice and men. (1992). MGM/United Artists.

What's eating Gilbert Grape? (1993). Paramount.

Professional, Parent, and Consumer Organizations and Agencies

American Association on Mental Retardation (AAMR)
444 N. Capitol Street NW, Suite 846
Washington, DC 20001-1512
Phone: (800) 424-3688
E-mail: mailbox@aamr.org
Web site: http://www.aamr.org

The Arc (formerly the Association for Retarded Citizens of the United States, ARC-US)
P.O. Box 6109
500 East Border Street, Suite 300
Arlington, TX 76010
Phone: (817) 261-6003
TTY: (817) 277-0553
E-mail: the arc@metronet.com
Web site: http://www.thearc.org

American Association of University Affiliated
Programs for Persons with Developmental Disabilities
8605 Cameron Street, Suite 406
Silver Spring, MD 20910
Phone: (301) 588-8252
E-mail: aaupjones@aol.com
Web site: http://www.waisman.wisc.edu/aauap/
    index.html

Division on Mental Retardation,
Council for Exceptional Children
1920 Association Drive
Reston, VA 22091
Phone: (703) 620-3660; (888) CEC-SPED
Web site: http://www.cec.sped.org

MAKING
CONNECTIONS

Resources to extend your learning of people
with disabilities are found at the end of every
chapter, and a fuller listing is available in
the Students' Resource Manual which
accompanies this text.

Maria **Sibylla Merian** was a natural historian who was born in Germany in 1647. Her genius was noted long before her third birthday. She learned her skills as a painter from her step-father, who was a member of the Dutch painters' colony of that day and was a flower painter. The Dutch were developing trade with their new South American colony, and Maria was able to obtain funding from the government in Amsterdam to study the plants and animals of this "new" land. Quite unusual for women of that time, Maria (at the age of 52) and her daughter spent two years exploring the wilderness areas, as well as the plantations and settlements, of that region. On many occasions they were in great danger, but the result of their expedition was a wonderful collection of botanical and natural history illustrations. The one shown here, from *Dissertation in Insect Generations and Metamorphosis in Surinam* (1719), is owned by the National Museum of Women in the Arts in Washington, DC, and is part of the U.S. Postal Service's stamp collection entitled Botanical Prints, which is available at local post offices throughout the United States.*

*Bound volume of seventy-two hand-colored engravings, 2nd edition. The National Museum of Women in the Arts, Gift of Wallace and Wilhelmina Holladay.

Maria Sibylla Merian (German, 1647–1717). Plate 1 from *Dissertation in Insect Generations and Metamorphosis in Surinam,* 1719. Reprinted by permission.

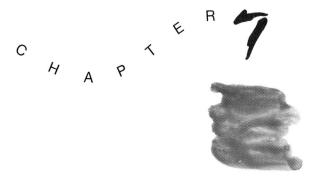

C H A P T E R 7

Personal Perspective:

Students Attending a Class for Gifted Children Share Their Thoughts

Gifted middle school students were interviewed by their teacher. Their responses reveal their feelings about their education and what it is like to be identified as gifted. These children are sixth and seventh graders, attend the same school, and have the same teacher of the gifted for their special education classes.

How does it make you feel to be called gifted?

ROBERT MONTANO: It doesn't really feel any different than how I used to feel, but it makes me feel like good and happy when people say I'm smart and gifted.

KIMBERLY SILVER: It feels strange because I'm the same as everybody else—like everybody's gifted somehow.

JOSHUA BARNARD: Kinda funny because the other kids make fun of you. I guess they are kinda jealous.

ROY BERNALES: I don't know—normal. Just feels like when someone calls me by my name—no different, too.

MICHELLE GOMEZ: It feels neat because you're in higher classes and sometimes you have more fun than in general classes.

DECTRA DIXON: Sometimes it makes you feel like you're ahead of other students. Sometimes they call you nerds, but I like the word *gifted* even if they do call me a nerd.

MARTY FREDERICKSON: I feel singled out. I feel pressured.

JESSICA LUCERO: It feels nice because you have a gift and you should be proud of it.

CHRISTY OLLOWAY: Like everybody thinks you're smart and they ask you to do stuff. Sometimes it bugs me because you don't want to answer the questions, but you're expected to.

Giftedness and Talent Development

What do you like best about your time in gifted class?

GUADALUPE VELASQUEZ: I like it because we dissect things, and it's fun in here, and I think that they teach you more.

KIMBERLY SILVER: I can get more help if I need it, and the teacher explains better.

JOSHUA BARNARD: I like being with only a few people, and I like the teacher. It's nice to be with other people who understand you.

ALIMA MILLS: Things you do in this class are interesting and fun, but still learning.

ROY BERNALES: I like it because there aren't a lot of people—it's not noisy.

DECTRA DIXON: You learn more stuff than in your general classes because in the other one they mess around and in the gifted you have to be serious about what you're doing.

JEREMY CORDOVA: Work is challenging, but more fun. Also, I like working in a small group.

CHRISTY OLLOWAY: You have to try to work extra hard and you feel good about being here.

What does it mean to you to be gifted?

GUADALUPE VELASQUEZ: It means you're more educated. You know more in that subject.

KIMBERLY SILVER: Smart in a different way. Like a different way of learning.

ALIMA MILLS: It's easier for you to learn things, and you are a little smarter than others.

ROY BERNALES: You're special. People think you're all smart and stuff.

MICHELLE GOMEZ: It's like you're smarter in some sections than other people, and you get to show it in higher classes instead of hiding it.

DECTRA DIXON: That you have a faster learning ability than other students.

MARTY FREDERICKSON: Being smarter. Being able to do more. Being singled out.

1. What are the differences between what the children think the term *gifted* means and what it feels like to them to be called gifted?

2. What do these children perceive to be the differences between general and special education?

3. What do you think being called gifted means?

dvance Organizers

MAKING CONNECTIONS

Use the learning strategy—Advance Organizers—to help focus your study of this chapter's content, and reinforce your learning by reviewing answers to the Focus and Challenge questions at the end of the chapter.

Overview Although educational services for gifted students are neither protected nor funded by IDEA, many of the basic principles of special education are applied to this population. In most states, these services are considered part of special education. Currently, professionals in gifted education are questioning the basic tenets of their field: who they serve, what education should comprise, and where services are delivered. Current discussions focus education attention on the development of talent (skills and achievement) with youngsters who possess high potential and abilities.

Self-Test Questions

- Regardless of the definition used, what descriptors can be used for gifted and talented individuals?
- What factors can inhibit giftedness and talent development?
- Why are educators concerned about issues related to underrepresentation and the various subgroups of gifted learners?
- What are three gifted education approaches, and how do they differ from one another?
- What are the four service delivery models often used in gifted education, and how do they differ from one another?

Challenge Question

- Why, across the history of the United States, has there been such an inconsistent commitment to gifted education?

Across time, people living in different periods of history have sometimes exhibited extraordinary levels of particular skills, abilities, or talents. For example, the Indus civilization in northern India between 2400 and 1800 B.C. demonstrated advanced concepts of city planning and architecture. Indus cities were built on a regular grid with major streets running north and south. A drainage system served an entire city, and each home had a bathroom and toilet connected to a sewer system. During the time of the ancient Greeks, athletic prowess and excellence in the fine arts reached peak levels, obvious in the legacies of their civilization: their philosophical writings, dramas, architecture, and sculpture. In ancient China, literary works, architecture, music, and art far surpassed the standards of other cultures. During the second century B.C. the Chinese wrote books, using silk for paper, on topics such as astronomy, medicine, and pharmacology. By the first century B.C., books on mathematics and other topics were produced on paper. Similarly, the temples of the ancient Egyptians stand as testimony to the skills of architects, engineers, and artisans.

A concentration of particular abilities and outstanding achievement can be observed during other segments of history as well. During the height of the Roman civilization, the number of great orators far surpassed the numbers found in many other periods of history. Between A.D. 300 and 750, the Teotihuacan culture in Mexico developed a sophisticated craft industry that produced figurines, pottery, and tools for export throughout the region. During the Renaissance in Europe, a great number of fine artists—Michelangelo, Leonardo da Vinci, Raphael, and others—created beautiful paintings, sculpture, scientific inventions, homes, palaces, churches, and public buildings. Almost two hundred years ago a concentration of musical prodigies (Handel, Haydn, Mozart, Chopin, Liszt) created work that is still valued and enjoyed. Today, computer developers, software designers, and Internet innovators amaze us with their brilliance and technical aptitude.

Why have there been periods in history when particular talents are displayed in abundance? One answer is that periods of brilliance result from a combination of excellent early opportunities, early and continuing guidance, and instruction for the individual (Morelock & Feldman, 1997; Simonton, 1997). These features must be coupled with a major interest of society in a particular ability, opportunities to continually practice and progress, close association and interchange with others of similar abilities, and strong success experiences. Certainly, individuals who demonstrate superiority in a particular area must also have innate talent, but it seems that traits valued by a culture emerge with some frequency when importance is placed on them.

Opportunities for the New Millennium

Gifted and talented people are highly visible in American society. They are credited for advances in medicine, in technology, in business, in theater and cinema, and in the arts. The roads these individuals took to achieve their high levels of contributions to society vary, depending on their families' social class, their socioeconomic status, and the educational opportunities available to them. Unfortunately, opportunities, particularly from the educational system are inconsistent; and many with high potential are lost to society and to themselves.

Legacies from the Twentieth Century 🐾 Attitudes and beliefs about the needs of gifted children are mixed. The public, policymakers, and education professionals do not agree about these children and what constitutes an appropriate education. A commonly held belief is that gifted education is unnecessary. Such rationales are typified by these two statements: "These children will make it on their own" or "The enriched education offered to them will benefit the entire class of general education students." On the other hand, many believe that these children are exceptionally vulnerable, and cannot achieve to their potential without special efforts. Throughout the last two centuries, the popularity and commitment to gifted education waxed and waned. This lack of commitment is one reason why IDEA does not include gifted students in its safeguards and protections. Charges that special education for these students is immoral, racist, morally incorrect, and unfair arose again in the last decade, echoing early Americans' feelings that special treatment for gifted youngsters did not belong in an egalitarian society. And clearly there is no doubt that current identification practices exclude many talented youngsters. So conflict and confusion continues. Even within the gifted education community a great lack of consensus exists about how to best educate gifted students and how to develop their talents.

Thinking About Dilemmas to Solve 🐾 Without a doubt, many dilemmas surround these children and the educational opportunities they should be provided. Think about whether:

- Their educational needs can best be met without special educational programs
- Identification practices can become more flexible, yet not include those who cannot profit from an enriched or accelerated educational program
- Gifted education is unnecessary
- A national law that provides these students with a different education is justified

GIFTEDNESS AND TALENTS DEFINED

Individuals who have high levels of intelligence, are high achievers academically, are extremely creative, or have unique talents are not handicapped in the sense of having a disability. Certainly, they do not face the limitations or the difficulties that most children who receive special education services do. However, many of these individuals, because of their differences, are handicapped by society and our educational systems. They can be stifled by educational approaches that do not challenge or develop their cognitive abilities or that do not allow them to learn academic content at an accelerated pace. Sometimes directly and sometimes indirectly, peers, teachers, and parents discourage them from developing their abilities maximally. Some believe that the result is a significant loss to the individuals and to society in general.

> Failure to help handicapped children reach their potential is a personal tragedy for them and their families; failure to help gifted children reach their potential is a societal tragedy, the extent of which is difficult to measure but which is surely great. How can we measure the loss of the sonata unwritten, the curative drug undiscovered, the absence of political insight? They are the difference between what we are and what we could be as a society. (Gallagher, 1985, p. 4)

TYPES OF GIFTEDNESS AND TALENTS

The field of gifted education is currently experiencing a time of transition (Davis & Rimm, 1998; Tannebaum, 1998). Accepted philosophies, beliefs about what the concept of "giftedness" means, and the value of gifted education are being challenged. The basic foundations of this educational system are being questioned by education professionals. Gallagher (1996, p. 234) distilled the fundamental issues into the following questions that this field must address:

- Is there such a thing as giftedness?
- If there is such an entity, can we find students who possess it or them?
- If we can find such children, can we provide them with quality differentiated services?
- Is it morally right or correct that we put such programs or services into action?

Throughout this chapter, these questions are addressed in hope that you will develop your own answers. Remember, at the present time the professionals working in gifted education are not in agreement, so there is no "right" answer. Let's start by coming to an understanding of how concepts of "gifted" and "talented" have been defined across this century. Such definitions are important because they reflect beliefs about who qualifies and what services they should receive. Across time, the definitions of giftedness have ranged from a narrow view based exclusively on cognition, reasoning, and the score a person receives on a test of intelligence, to a multidimensional view of intelligence, aptitudes, abilities, and talent development.

Traditional Perspectives. As early as 1925, Terman studied individuals with exceptionally high cognitive aptitude. He considered children **gifted** who score in the highest 1% (having scores over 140) on an intelligence (IQ) test. Terman's definition reflects a narrow view of giftedness in which high intelligence is closely associated with high academic achievement. In addition to tying giftedness to a score on an IQ test, Terman also believed that intelligence is a fixed characteristic, one people are born with and one that does not change positively or negatively across time. From

NEW DIRECTIONS
FOR THE
MILLENNIUM

Legacy: Throughout the last century, special programs for gifted students continually gained and then lost support, resulting in inconsistent services.

Opportunities:
- Create a consistent plan for the delivery gifted education across the nation
- Conduct systematic research to study the efficacy and long-term outcomes of gifted education

gifted. A term describing individuals with high levels of intelligence, outstanding abilities, and capacity for high performance.

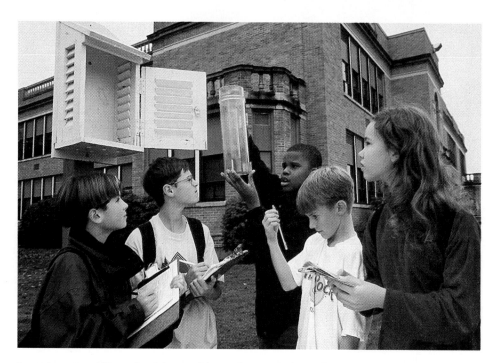

Learning new skills and solving problems does not always have to happen inside the walls of a traditional classroom.

MAKING CONNECTIONS

Review again the sections A Very Special Population: Native Americans (Defined section) and Over- and Underrepresentation of diverse students (Prevalence section) in Chapter 3.

his perspective, intelligence is determined solely by heredity; it is a trait inherited from your parents. Lastly, this view of giftedness reflects many biases about women and people of underrepresented ethnic groups that were prevalent in his time.

Today's professional educators are much less confident than Terman was in the results of standardized tests, believing that such tests can bias against individuals who are not from the dominant American culture. Some tests identify as gifted only persons who have received a strong educational foundation, and this is only one bias that standardized tests present to culturally and linguistically diverse children and youngsters with disabilities. Our understanding of intelligence has changed since Terman's time. In contrast to Terman's view, researchers now believe that intelligence, like any other trait, is influenced by both genetics and environment (Davis & Rimm, 1998; Hunsaker, 1995). It is no longer thought that IQ is a fixed characteristic of the individual. Even though his definition is often criticized, Terman's longitudinal research with gifted individuals continues to be referred to and respected in the professional literature.

In a move toward a less restrictive perspective on giftedness, Sidney Marland, then U.S. Commissioner of Education, offered the nation a definition of the gifted and talented to supplant the Terman definition. The 1972 Marland definition, with minor variations, is still the most widely accepted and is used as the basis for most states' current definitions (Marland, 1972, p. 10):

> Gifted and talented children are those identified by professionally qualified persons who by virtue of outstanding abilities are capable of high performance. These are children who require differentiated educational programs and services beyond those normally provided by the regular school program in order to realize their contribution to self and society. Children capable of high performance include those

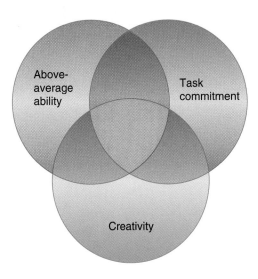

The ingredients of giftedness

Figure 7.1 Renzulli's Three-Ring Concept of Giftedness
Source: "What Makes Giftedness: Reexamining A Definition" by J. S. Renzulli, 1978, *Phi Delta Kappan, 60,* p. 182. Reprinted by permission.

Above-average general ability

with demonstrated achievement and/or potential ability in any of the following areas singly or in combination:

1. General intellectual aptitude.
2. Specific academic aptitude.
3. Creative or productive thinking.
4. Leadership ability.
5. Visual and performing arts.

Notice that there is no reference to a minimal IQ score in this definition of giftedness. In addition, this definition, unlike most presented in the chapters in this book about disabilities, includes a statement that these youngsters should be educated differently from their classmates. The assumption is that under the right conditions (good instructional programs, student motivation, and interest), these students will show overall accelerated performance. This suggestion about a difference between potential and performance implies that if the educational system is not responsive to students' individual needs, achievement will not reflect aptitude and underachievement will occur. Also note that Marland's definition includes discussion of two other issues: (1) who should receive special education services and (2) what that education should comprise.

creativity. A form of intelligence characterized by advanced divergent thought, the production of many original ideas, and the ability to develop flexible and detailed responses and ideas.

Broadened Concepts. Most researchers today believe that giftedness is multidimensional, with high academic aptitude or intelligence being only one factor. For example, Renzulli (1978, 1998; Renzulli & Reis, 1997) suggested that those who have three clusters of characteristics—above-average intelligence, high **creativity,** and substantial task commitment—should be considered gifted. Certainly, Renzulli's view of giftedness is broader than Terman's. As you can see from Renzulli's graphic illustration shown in Figure 7.1, though, some individuals who have obtained high scores on tests of intelligence might not meet his other qualifications for giftedness. However, Renzulli's approach to gifted education is more inclusive than others, for he advocates that 15% to 20% of U.S. schoolchildren should receive enhanced educational services that include many opportunities to develop creativity, critical thinking, and problem solving skills.

Now let's look at an even more multidimensional view of abilities. Gardner, in 1983, proposed a broader view of intelligence and giftedness in a book entitled *Frames of Mind* (Gardner, 1983). According to his multidimensional approach to intelligence, which provides an alternative view to the traditional one of IQ, "human cognitive competence is better described as a set of abilities, talents, or mental skills that we have chosen to call intelligences" (Ramos-Ford & Gardner, 1991, p. 56). Through careful study of human behavior and performance, Gardner concludes that there are seven dimensions of intelligence and that a person can be gifted in any one or more of these areas (Gardner, 1993). A summary of the seven intelligence areas is presented in Table 7.1. By studying this table, you should be able to see how some gifted youngsters are excluded when traditional views of giftedness are applied, resulting in their not receiving the educational services they need to develop their unique abilities and talents.

 Table 7.1 Gardner's Seven Intelligences

Intelligence	Explanation*	Components	Adult Roles
1. Verbal-linguistic	The ability to use language in a number of ways	Syntax, semantics, pragmatics, written and oral language	Novelist, lecturer, lawyer, lyricist
2. Logical-mathematical	The ability to reason and recognize patterns	Deductive reasoning, inductive reasoning, computation	Mathematician, physicist
3. Visual-spatial	The ability to see the world and re-create it	Ability to represent and manipulate spatial configurations, interrelationship of parts	Architect, engineer, mechanic, navigator, sculptor, chess player
4. Body-kinesthetic	The ability to use the body and hands skillfully	Ability to use all or part of one's body	Dancer, athlete, mime, surgeon
5. Musical-rhythmic	The ability to perceive the world through its rhythm	Pitch discrimination; ability to hear themes in music; sensitivity to rhythm, texture, and timbre; production of music through performance or composition	Musician, composer, singer
6. Interpersonal	The ability to notice and respond to other people's needs	Ability to understand and act productively on others' actions and motivations	Teacher, therapist, clergy, politician, salesperson
7. Intrapersonal	The ability to understand one's own feelings	Understanding of self	

Source: "Opportunities to Learn through Multiple Intelligences" (p. 1) by A. D. Morgan, Fall 1994, *School Renewal Update,* Effective Schools Unit, New Mexico State Department of Education.

NEW DIRECTIONS
FOR THE
MILLENNIUM

Legacy: Particularly in the last decade of the twentieth century, demands on general education teachers increased as they included more students with disabilities. The heterogeneity of students—their wide range of skills and abilities—makes meeting all students' educational needs challenging.

Opportunities:

• Reconsider the application of ability grouping

• Carefully study all students' outcomes and achievement results, particularly in classes where children present a wide range of basic skills

paradigm shifts. A change in conceptual framework that is a basic understanding or explanation for a field of study.

Paradigm Shifts. As mentioned at the beginning of this section, gifted education is in a state of transition, self-analysis, and challenge. Some (Margolin, 1996; Sapon-Shevin, 1996) believe that gifted education should be eliminated because it represents a form of legalized tracking that could be a way to disguise racial segregation in school settings. Critics also argue that gifted education is elitist, morally incorrect, unfair, and damaging to general education students who would benefit from more access to these peers. They also maintain that the general education environment and curriculum will be enhanced when more of the gifted instructional methodology is incorporated into these classrooms' educational programs (Rosselli, 1998). The notion is that all students' talents are fostered when general education teachers assume responsibility for talent development.

Although such issues are not yet resolved, important considerations have been raised that support special education and an array of services for gifted students (Borland, 1996; Gallagher, 1996). Consider these provocative questions and reach your own conclusions:

1. Is gifted education and the removal of gifted students from the general education classroom for any time during the school day racist? Or, is not providing differentiated services to those students whose families cannot afford private schooling racist?

2. Is gifted education merely a form of tracking? Or, is it feasible to expect one setting, one broadly prepared teacher, and one curriculum to address the primary educational needs of a heterogeneous group of students who have a great disparity of learning styles and achievement performance?

3. Is it necessary to eliminate gifted education services to bring quality to general education? Or, can the school reform movement be orchestrated along with gifted education services to blend with general education where appropriate and meet the individual needs of students when such specialization is appropriate?

4. Is gifted education (which singles out children of affluence, prepares them for leadership, and provides them with differentiated instruction) morally wrong, a philosophy contributing to inequality, evil social outcomes, and societal oppression? Or, are such points of view misplaced interpretations of equity and equality?

5. Is gifted education unfair to typical learners, making them feel bad because they were not selected as being special or because they were made aware that they could not perform a task (playing a violin, throwing a football, solving calculus problems) as well as someone else? Or, is it unfair to gifted learners not to challenge and accelerate them through an enriched and diversified instructional program that is deep in content and thinking skills?

So, what is the likely future of gifted education? Of course, no one knows for sure, and most likely debates will continue and different options will be implemented in specific locales. Arguments about *equity* will rage on, with questions about egalitarianism and "what's fair" being asked on one side of the debate, and questions about how to achieve and recognize *excellence* on the other. As rhetoric continues, however, the haunting realization about the vulnerability of gifted children must surface:

> Such persons are not just born. True, they are individuals born with strong propensities to learn and to develop intellectually at the high level; they must also be nurtured and provided the educational opportunities required to develop optimally (Benbow & Stanley, p. 278).

Giftedness and Talents Defined **279**

If history is any judge of the future, even in states or school districts where gifted education has been eliminated, it will return. Here the most important question is "when," not "if." Support for educational services for gifted youngsters has waxed and waned since this nation's founding. It is likely that a new conceptual framework for gifted education will be adopted. At least one framework is emerging and gaining considerable support, although specific models and interpretations are still developing and being proposed.

The concept of **talent development** is gaining acceptance and may well be the focus of new and innovative efforts for able youngsters. Feldhusen (1995) believes that the development of talent is the responsibility of the home, school, and community. It is for family members, stimulating teachers, peers who value developing abilities, and experts who are successful in a variety of fields who serve as mentors to help students develop their aptitudes into outstanding abilities and achievements. The Purdue Pyramid (see Figure 7.2) shows one way to think of talent development. Acceptance is the foundation all children need to develop their abilities; the vertical rays represent the wide array of learning experiences required to develop talent; these experiences lead to the necessary self-understanding of the talents and abilities possessed by gifted individuals; and finally the importance of commitment from individuals to develop their abilities into skills and talents is stressed.

According to experts like Treffinger and Feldhusen (1996), an orientation toward talent development will shift and broaden the focus of gifted education. The goal will no longer be solely the development of intellect and academic achievement, but will also include all areas of human activity (e.g., vocational and career domains, art, social-interpersonal skills). Feldhusen (1992) proposed four basic domains that schools can address: academic, artistic, vocational, and personal/social. What might the areas of focus be under a new endeavor toward talent development? Gagné (1996) proposed talent fields relevant to schoolchildren for development: academics, games of strategy (chess, puzzles, video games), technology, arts, social action, business, and athletics. Gardner (Ramos-Ford & Gardner, 1991) would probably propose focusing on talent development for each of his seven multiple intelligences. VanTassel-Baska (1995) advocated an integrated curriculum for talent development that includes the following dimensions: advanced content knowledge, higher-order thinking and processing skills, learning experiences developed along themes and ideas relevant to real-world issues.

Will the term *gifted* be replaced by the term *talent*? Gagné (1996) thinks this unlikely. He believes that gifted education is so much a part of everyday language that it will be retained. However, he believes, as do many other experts in gifted education (Feldhusen, 1995; VanTassel-Baska, 1995), that the terms *giftedness* and *talent* need to be differentiated. Giftedness would be used to describe high natural abilities, but not for a single dimension or trait. Talent would refer to a high level of performance and well-developed skills. Giftedness or aptitude without the work, effort, and unique experiences does not lead to superior mastery or talent development in a particular field of human activity. In other words, for Gagné, giftedness refers to measures of potential and talent is reserved for achievement. For these bright and able students to reach their potential, to turn aptitude into talent and achievement, is not a simple feat. Gallagher (1996) believes that such accomplishments require an array of educational services delivered to gifted students by specialists highly prepared for the responsibility of instructing these students.

MAKING CONNECTIONS

For another discussion of an array of services, see the Service Delivery Options section (Special Educational Services) in Chapter 2.

talent development.
The process of translating ability into achievement.

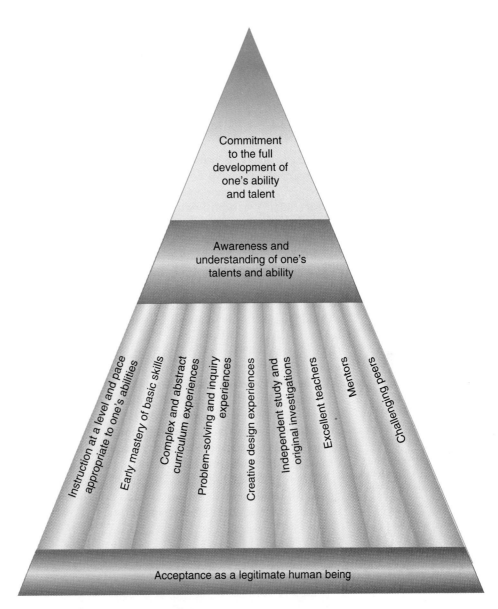

Figure 7.2 **The Purdue Pyramid**

Source: "Talent Development: The New Direction in Gifted Education" by J. F. Feldhusen, 1995, *Roeper Review, 18,* p. 92. Reprinted by permission.

IDENTIFICATION

As you have just learned, the field of gifted education is experiencing a paradigm shift, a time of change. Once giftedness is reconceptualized and agreement about the conceptual framework is achieved, new identification procedures might be developed and implemented. For example, we might one day not use IQ scores to identify students, but might instead use other methods, such as portfolio assessments or teacher nominations, to replace that process (Hunsaker et al., 1997). For the time being, however, most states and school districts will continue to use traditional identification procedures that employ standardized tests.

Although most definitions of giftedness do not include precise criteria to determine eligibility for special programs, the use of IQ scores is still prevalent today to identify students who are gifted. Therefore you should know what these scores mean. Let's look at how intelligence scores are distributed. The assumption is that if measurements of intelligence were given to a large sample of people, the scores obtained would approximate a normal (bell) curve. The scores would cluster around the mean, or average, in a predictable way. Two commonly used tests of intelligence, the *Stanford-Binet* and the *Wechsler Intelligence Scale for Children III (WISC-III)*, use the score of 100 as the mean. Each of these tests breaks scores into groups called a **standard deviation (SD).** On the *Stanford-Binet*, 16 points from the mean equals one standard deviation. On the *WISC-III*, 15 points from the mean equals one SD. So a score of 130 on the *WISC-III* is two SDs from the mean. Figure 7.3 shows a normal curve that has been divided by SDs and the percentage of the population that falls within each SD grouping. Notice that slightly more than 68% of the population falls within one SD below and above the mean (of 100). For a criterion of two SDs higher than the mean, slightly more than 2% of the population should fall above the score of 130 on the *WISC-III*. Thus you often hear that gifted students have IQ scores above 130. Remember, though, that this unidimensional (using a single IQ score) approach to identify gifted students is becoming outdated as theories like Gardner's multiple intelligences are becoming more widely adopted.

The methods used to identify students and ultimately to determine which ones are selected for gifted education programs relate directly to the definition and related selection criteria used for this special education category. Although Marland's definition is used in many states, it is not universally accepted or it is modified because it does not provide specific criteria for identifying gifted students. States concerned about how many children they either desire to serve or can afford to serve in special programs often use specific cutoff scores when they identify and qualify students. Unfortunately, this method often excludes many children, particularly members of certain subgroups who would qualify if more flexible criteria were applied.

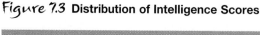

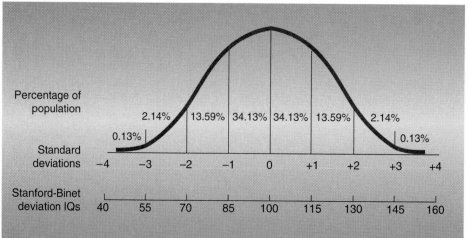

Figure 7.3 Distribution of Intelligence Scores

CONNECTIONS

For another discussion on IQ, see the Defined section in Chapter 6.

standard deviation (SD). A statistical measure that expresses the variability and the distribution from the mean of a set of scores.

To find them, experts suggest that teachers look for characteristics in children, such as: curiosity, experiments with novel things, motivation, inquisitive, observant, creative, and innovative (Fernández et al., 1998).

Let's examine how states actually identify gifted students. The Gifted Education Policy Studies Program at the University of North Carolina at Chapel Hill helps us understand such practices at the state level (Coleman & Gallagher, 1994). A comprehensive study about how students are selected for gifted education services surveyed all 50 states. These researchers found that 49 of the states had regulations in place to guide school districts and that every one of those states uses scores from standardized tests of intelligence and achievement in the identification process. Some states included additional information, such as teacher nominations (46 states), parent nominations (45 states), and student products or work samples (44 states). They also found that in their definitions of *gifted*, 40 states also included creativity, 34 artistic ability, and 28 leadership skills. A more recent study, with a less complete sample, found very similar results (Landrum et al., 1998). So, you can see that even though this field is experiencing a paradigm shift, where scholars are debating crucial issues, practitioners are still using traditional methods for identification.

SIGNIFICANCE

To review the IDEA law, see the Necessity for National Intervention section in Chapter 1.

Gifted individuals are not handicapped by any lack of ability. Rather, the challenge to educators is to provide a stimulating educational environment and a broad curriculum to help these individuals reach their full potential and develop their talents. Unfortunately, gifted education did not receive the full commitment of policymakers during the last century. It is not funded by IDEA, as is education for those with disabilities. Funding for school based programs for gifted children comes from state funds, and it is not consistent across time or locales.

Certain attitudes about giftedness—that education of the gifted is elitist, is socially incorrect, should be merged with general education or even eliminated (Margolin, 1996; Sapon-Shevin, 1996)—place this field in a precarious position. Negative attitudes about gifted education most likely stem from myths about the field and the individuals it serves. For example, many people think that these children will thrive without special programs, that they can make it on their own. Quite sadly, this is simply untrue: gifted individuals often do not reach their potential because their educational programs did not meet their needs (Benbow & Stanley, 1996). Others think that programs for the gifted are elitist. As a result of these attitudes, programs for the gifted have been sporadic since this nation's founding.

While some gifted children achieve their potential without the benefits of special education, many do not. Research findings about these students' achievement clearly support the need for special services and a differentiated educational experience for these youngsters (Cornell et al., 1995). Such findings are also supported by these students' statements of "consumer satisfaction." Elementary, middle, and high school gifted students attending general education classes were asked whether their educational programs in general education were appropriate and meeting their needs (Gallagher et al., 1997). In general, here's what they had to say:

- The curriculum is not challenging
- The instructional pace is too slow
- Too much mastered information is repeated

- Few opportunities are available to study topics of personal interest or in more depth
- Emphasis on mastery of facts, rather than on thinking skills, predominates

All children need to develop the motivation to grow and expand. For many gifted children, the general education classroom alone cannot provide the challenges they require to remain motivated or learn at an accelerated and comfortable pace.

HISTORY OF THE FIELD

Emphasis on educating those with exceptional abilities has been sporadic in human history. Confucius, a Chinese philosopher who lived around 500 B.C., believed that all children should be educated but that education should be tailored to their abilities. His views were implemented during the Tang dynasty in A.D. 618 when gifted and talented children were brought to the imperial court for special education. Because the Chinese valued literacy, leadership, imagination, memory, and reasoning, these topics were part of the curriculum. The Japanese also provided differential educational opportunities to their children. For example, during the Tokugawa period (1604–1868), children born of the samurai nobility were educated in Confucian classics, martial arts, history, moral values, calligraphy, and composition. The children of the poor, however, were educated about the value of loyalty, obedience, humility, and diligence (Davis & Rimm, 1998). In western African cultures, specialized education was provided to children based on the children's status, recognized characteristics, or cleverness. And, as early as 3000 B.C., the Egyptians sent the best students (along with royalty) to court schools or assigned mentors to work in intensive internships to develop their special talents (Hunsaker, 1995).

In Western cultures, attention to people's innate and superior abilities can be attributed to the work of Charles Darwin and Sir Francis Galton in the middle 1800s. Charles Darwin is most famous for his theories about natural selection and the evolution of species. Before his time, no one had studied, on a broad scale, individual differences among people or issues relating to intelligence and heredity (Clark, 1997). In 1869, Galton proposed his theory that genius is solely attributed to heredity and that **eminence** is due to two factors: (1) an internal motivation to excel and (2) intellect, both of which were thought to be genetically inherited. The notion that genetic factors contribute greatly to giftedness is still adhered to today, but the important contributions of the environment are also recognized.

In the United States, our wavering commitment to the education of the gifted reflects our national philosophy about equity and social justice. During the eighteenth century, many leaders of the country leaned toward the view that education was best for the elite. Thomas Jefferson, however, argued against elitism, believing that the purpose of education was to foster democracy. During the nineteenth century, egalitarianism—the notion that no one should get special treatment—became popular. The egalitarian position was extreme, holding that no individual could be considered better than anyone else, regardless of innate abilities, status, or education. Gardner (1984) suggests that it was from this social philosophy that the concept of equal opportunity was developed.

One legacy of egalitarianism is the attitude that special education for gifted children is undemocratic, elitist, unnecessary, and wasteful. Some researchers believe that special programs for gifted youngsters in this country were not advocated "for

eminence. Superiority in ability.

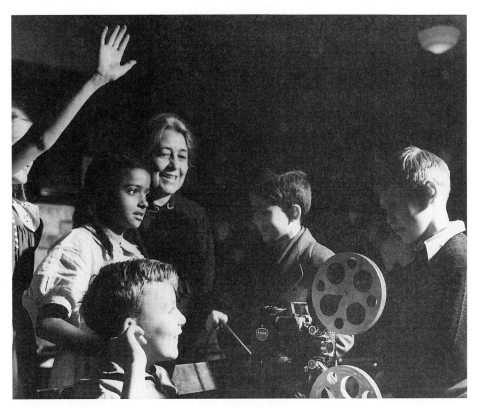

Leta Hollingworth, here working in 1938 with students at the Speyer School (the laboratory school of Teachers College of Columbia University), provided the foundation for many of the methods used today in gifted education.

fear that any attention to their abilities would give rise to a dangerous aristocracy" (Silverman, 1988, p. 136).

Most chroniclers of gifted education in the United States (Clark, 1997; Gallagher, 1988) stress the importance of the development of the Binet Intelligence Test in 1905. Although not originally developed to identify students who are gifted, this test nonetheless marks the beginning of interest in this country about such individuals. Some programs for the gifted were established as early as 1866, but real development and growth in educational services for these individuals did not come until the 1920s. Leta Hollingworth, one of the early pioneers in the field of gifted education, who joined the faculty at Teachers College, Columbia University, in 1916, taught the first course and wrote the first textbook in this area. One of Hollingworth's major contributions to the field was her proposal that giftedness is affected by both heredity and environment, a concept widely held today (Silverman, 1992).

Another pioneer, Lewis Terman, conducted a classic study in 1925 of individuals who were gifted, both as children and as adults. Although dated, it is still highly respected as one of the most comprehensive studies of eminent individuals. This study stimulated interest in gifted education, but efforts were halted by the Great Depression of the 1930s and World War II in the 1940s. Although Terman was most interested in identifying gifted individuals, and not in intervening or enhancing giftedness, his work drew attention to gifted individuals. He also set a priority for gifted education that is still important today.

The 1960s saw a renewed interest in gifted children. The promotion of unique educational services can be linked to a specific historical event: the 1957 Russian launching of the space satellite *Sputnik.* The launch was viewed as a risk to national security and a blow to national pride, and the United States vowed to catch up and surpass the competition. Hence, federal funding was appropriated to establish programs, develop ways to identify students with high academic achievement, particularly in math and science, and conduct research to find effective methods for providing excellent educational experiences. Gifted students were now seen as a great national resource, the persons who would make the United States the leader once again.

During the late 1960s and 1970s, the nation turned its attention to the civil rights movement, to the needs of the culturally and linguistically diverse and poor, and to gifted education. It was thought to be one more advantage for the already advantaged youth of our society, and some of the nation's policymakers adopted the position that these youngsters could make it on their own (Maker, 1986). June Maker, however, continued the research in this field with her pioneering work on behalf of gifted students with learning disabilities. In 1977, she published the results of her research, shedding light on a previously ignored group of learners.

The late 1980s saw the situation change once again, with renewed interest in gifted education. In 1988, for example, more than $200 million was spent by the fifty states for special programs for students who are gifted (Gallagher, 1988). Also, in 1988, Congress passed the Jacob K. Javits Gifted and Talented Students Education Act. This landmark legislation stressed Congress's belief that "unless the special abilities of gifted and talented students are recognized and developed during their elementary and secondary school years, much of their special potential for contributing to the national interest will be lost" (Clark, 1992, p. 163). Enacted in 1990, the act provided $11 million in 1993 in federal funding for research, demonstration, and personnel preparation in this area. The act also reestablished a separate administrative unit in the U.S. Department of Education to serve as a focal point of national leadership and information on the educational needs of gifted and talented students. Despite concern about the quality of our education and the development of our talented youngsters, in 1996 only $10 million was appropriated to this program. Advocates for gifted education continue to seek congressional support for legislation that would support states' efforts to develop and strengthen programs for gifted students (Clarenbach, 1999). However, historic public confusion about the vulnerability of these children, along with concerns about equity, make it difficult to win sustained and substantial support.

PREVALENCE

Gifted students are *not* mandated or funded by IDEA, and their prevalence data are *not* reported in the U.S. Department of Education's annual reports to Congress on the implementation of the Individuals with Disabilities Education Act. The number of children identified as gifted in the United States depends on the definition and concept of giftedness used, and on the number of programs available. We do not, however, have as much information about gifted students and the programs developed for them as we do for students in other special needs categories. So, first let's take a look at the possible percentage of students who could be enrolled in gifted education.

CONNECTIONS

- For a review of learning disabilities see Chapter 4.
- For more about gifted students with disabilities see that section later in this chapter (Gifted Children).

Sputnik. The Russian satellite that was launched in 1957 and caused a renewed interest in the education of the gifted in this country.

NEW DIRECTIONS
FOR THE
MILLENNIUM

Legacy: Most states and school districts which offer gifted education use IQ scores in the identification process, which has excluded many talented youngsters from diverse backgrounds.

Opportunities:

- Develop new and flexible eligibility requirements to ensure identification of all gifted, talented, and creative children

- Involve community partners in decisions about programs offered

The number of students to serve depends on your concept of giftedness. For example, if only those who score in the highest 1% on an intelligence test are considered gifted, then only 1 in every 100 children would qualify for special services. If we consider those who score in the highest 2%, then 2 in every group of 100 children qualify, and so on. Traditional identification methods used in many schools identify about 3% to 5% of the school population as gifted (Davis & Rimm, 1998). But the growing popularity of Renzulli's talent pool/enrichment model increases the percentage receiving special services to somewhere between 10% and 15% (Renzulli & Reis, 1997). When a score from a test of intelligence is the sole means for identifying gifted students, the number who qualify for services is much smaller than when other exceptional characteristics are also considered. For example, under the criterion of IQ score only, children whose primary language is not English who obtain an IQ score of 120 but demonstrate outstanding spatial and interpersonal skills would not qualify for special services.

Only twenty-five states mandate that gifted education be offered to those students who qualify (National Center for Educational Statistics, 1994). Thus estimates of the total number of students with IQ scores above a certain level, based on percentages, exaggerate the number of children actually being served. A long-standing problem in gifted education is that the number of students who receive special services is much lower than it should be. Considerably less than 3% of children receive gifted education. One reason for this is that many school districts and some states do not mandate gifted education. In other words, it is inconsistently offered across the nation. Another reason is that many students from diverse backgrounds, particularly those who live in poor inner-city areas, are overlooked. For example, researchers often find what is called underrepresentation of these children in gifted programs (Brown, 1997; Harry, 1994). Here's one specific example: in one school district where 40% of the students are diverse, fewer than 10% of the participants in gifted classes were diverse students (Tomlinson et al., 1998). Unfortunately, this situation is repeated consistently across the nation. Recall the statistics about Native American students in Alaska, Montana, South Dakota, and Arizona presented in Chapter 3; these students are overwhelmingly identified as having disabilities. In Alaska, for example, Native Americans comprise 25% of the population but only 15% of those students receiving gifted education (Harry, 1994). This is a problem that deserves educators' attention in this new millinneum.

CAUSES: FACTORS THAT ENHANCE OR INHIBIT GIFTEDNESS

Throughout the history of gifted education, people believed that heredity is the primary reason for giftedness. The work of Terman, in the 1920s, also reflected this view. Today, however, researchers recognize the important roles that both the environment and heredity play in the development of the intellect (Reis, 1999; Simonton, 1997).

Research has shown that many factors can influence individuals' outcomes (Brown, 1997; Kitano, 1997,1998; Terman, 1925). Attitudes, expectations, and values expressed in different cultures, societies, and families can shape people's behavior. Also, families' socioeconomic level, a child's birth position (for example, firstborn), and number of children in the family are related to giftedness. Environmental factors correlate both with increased and diminished gifted abilities. For example, children whose early experiences are not rich or diverse often do not develop outstanding cognitive skills, and children who are not challenged in school do not develop their potential.

Educators must not underestimate the power of even subtle events that occur in classrooms and at school. For example, daily, girls (and boys) are taught how to dress and how they are suppose to act, both directly and indirectly. Attitudes and opinions expressed by family, friends, TV, and print media (including textbooks) influence behavior and teach them role expectations (Reis, 1999). Particularly for girls, what is deemed appropriate behavior ("Don't be too aggressive") may impede their ultimate achievement. The power of the peer group and school culture is a critical element that influences all youngsters' behavior (Schroeder-Davis, 1998). For example, 66% of high school students say that athletes receive more attention, including schoolwide celebrations for their accomplishments, than student scholars. "Jocks" and "partyers" are three to five times more popular than "brains." Possibly, educators should seriously reconsider the priorities which are part of the implied message about expectations that is delivered at school. There is no doubt, that schooling and educational experiences can and do make a difference (Parker, 1998). For these reasons many experts are advocating for special programs designed to help gifted individuals achieve their potential.

Intellectual and academic achievement are not the only characteristics that can be influenced by attitudes, expectations, and opportunities. Some time ago, Renzulli (1978) observed that many young children are inherently creative, yet relatively few adults are. What happens to these children during their preschool and early elementary years? Were they really not creative in the first place? Or is creativity discouraged by our society? Teachers favor highly intelligent students who do well academically but are not able in other areas. And schools tend to identify those who are gifted in cognitive and academic areas; they do not consider students who are artistic or creative, particularly those from different cultures and those who live in rural areas (De Leon et al., 1997). Even children's peer groups criticize divergent, independent, and imaginative behavior among their creative friends. Many educators tend to encourage realism instead of imagination: Dolls talk and act like real children; computerized toys teach children the correct answers to arithmetic problems and the correct way to spell words. College students are advised to select majors that will lead to high-paying jobs. Krippner (1967) made the point that the United States is an achievement-oriented society that rewards individuals merely for being competent. Qualities valued are ability to get along with others, ability to work toward a goal, and ability to adapt, not creativity and individual differences. In fact, the need for acceptance causes many people to repress giftedness. If creativity is not fostered, it can be lost (Kirschenbaum, 1998). So, many experts believe that it is important to not only identify academically talented children, but also those who shows signs of creativity (Fishkin & Johnson, 1998).

Educators must come to understand their potential role in inhibiting creativity. Divergent thinking can be a challenge to teachers who are trying to meet the needs of children with a wide range of abilities and interests. Particularly in times of high-stakes, statewide achievement testing, the pressure to have entire classes attain a standard level of achievement can be overwhelming. Many teachers feel that to create order and be able to progress through the curriculum at the required pace demand considerable control, and they place greater emphasis on classroom rules. Rules, however, can be too rigid, resulting in stifled creativity. The Achieving Discipline box gives you an example of how rules can be applied, but how they can also leave room for divergent behavior and creative thinking.

For more about gifted females, see that section later in this chapter (Gifted Children).

For other ideas about behavior management, see the Achieving Discipline boxes in Chapters 3–12.

Achieving Discipline

FOSTERING DIVERGENT AND CREATIVE THINKING: FLEXIBLE RULES

Freesia and Joseph, both highly able and creative mid-schoolers, seemed always to have a different perspective about the content of Ms. Whelan's history lessons. They were easily bored, chatted among themselves, and distracted the class and Ms. Whelan during her lectures and class discussion. Ms. Whelan had implemented strict rules for class conduct. Noise level was to be held to a minimum. Children could speak only when they raised their hands and were called upon, and small-group discussion time was an uncommon occurrence. When the class was asked questions about the historical event being presented, both Freesia and Joseph would often give answers that were interesting but not expected. Their novel contributions often were considered "funny" to their peers, which caused the class to become "out of control." Ms. Whelan had become reluctant to call on either child, for the result seemed to be a loss of instructional time, and it was also hard for her to regain the class's attention. The less these children were called upon, the more disengaged they became.

Ms. Whelan was worried about loosening the structure she had established. She was afraid that less stringent rules about class conduct would lead to more disruptive behavior. She sought help from the school district's talent development specialist, who came to class to observe the quality of Freesia and Joseph's participation and Ms. Whelan's loss of control. Together, the teachers, despite Ms. Whelan's

serious concerns, decided to loosen the class rules. Expectations for "controlled" participation continued, but all of the children were encouraged to think about different views of historical events. Lessons were restructured to provide not only factual presentations, but also to include a multidisciplinary approach (artistic, sociological, and economic perspectives) about the events during the time period being studied. More small group discussions and time for group projects were allocated across every week. All students were encouraged to accept and consider divergent analyses of content. Results of these changes in instructional format and delivery were many. The entire class seemed more engaged in learning, class disruption did not increase, and both Freesia and Joseph were able to develop their creative thinking skills.

Fostering divergent and creative thinking by being more flexible

- Make the behavioral expectations clear
- Let students know the "bottom line" for what is considered acceptable behavior
- Include a range of instructional activities that engage individual students
- Allow all students to "color outside the lines"
- Encourage divergent thinking
- Remember that there usually is no single answer to a problem or question

GIFTED CHILDREN

As with any group of people, it is unfair to generalize group characteristics to individual members. On the other hand, it is easier to understand a group if some commonly observed features are described. Research findings provide us with some common characteristics of gifted people (Clark, 1997; Jenkins-Friedman & Nielsen, 1990; Roberts & Lovett, 1994; VanTassel-Baska, 1996; Yong & McIntyre, 1992). These are found listed in Table 7.2 on page 290. Examine the table before proceeding to the remainder of this section, which is devoted to two other important issues: social behavior and underachieving subgroups.

Table 7.2 Common Characteristics of the Gifted Child

Intellectual/Academic	Social/Emotional
Reasons abstractly	Criticizes self
Conceptualizes and synthesizes	Empathizes
Manages and processes information quickly and meaningfully	Plays with older friends
Solves problems	Persists
Learns quickly	Is intense
Shows intellectual curiosity	Exhibits individualism
Has wide interests	Has strength of character
Dislikes drill and routine	Demonstrates leadership abilities
May show unevenness	Is concerned about ethical issues
Generalizes learning	Takes risks
Remembers great amount of material	Is independent and autonomous
Displays high level of verbal ability	Is highly sensitive to others and self
Prefers learning in a quiet environment	Has mature sense of humor
Adapts to new learning situations	Is nonconforming
Applies varied reasoning and thinking skills	Uses different modes of expression
Uses nonstandard pools of information	Strives for perfection
Is highly motivated by academic tasks	Experiences great stress from failure
Focuses and concentrates on topic or idea for long periods of time	

SOCIAL BEHAVIOR

Misconceptions about gifted individuals' social skills and behavior abound. Historically, gifted learners have been victims of stereotypes and negative descriptors: "thin, nervous, brash, snobbish, difficult to tolerate, and concerned only with books, ideas, and self" (Laycock, 1979, p. 57). Hollingworth (1942) popularized the belief that gifted individuals are likely to develop personality problems. However, research has consistently shown that these negative characteristics do not exist for the group, that these people are not necessarily anxious, nor do they exhibit discipline problems. In general, gifted individuals are better adjusted than the general population (Davis, 1996; Terman, 1925). Remember, however, that many people at different periods of their lives are in need of counseling, and this holds true for everyone, gifted or not.

Current comprehensive research studies consistently show that gifted youngsters are no more likely to exhibit disruptive or problem behaviors in classroom settings than typical learners (Freeman, 1994). They are also no more likely to have behavior disorders than students in the general population (Galluci et al., 1999). Gifted students do, however, complain about being bored at school, which might explain some of the behavior problems noted by some teachers. Certainly, keeping these students engaged can be a challenging experience for educators, particularly those who have a class of students who exhibit a wide range of abilities and achievement levels.

Reprinted with special permission of North American Syndicate.

NEW DIRECTIONS
FOR THE
MILLENNIUM

Legacy: As roles and expectations for women changed in the last part of the twentieth century, gifted women benefited from affirmative action programs that increased their access to high-level positions in business and government. However, many with potential had not developed sufficient skills and knowledge during school to take advantage of these opportunities.

Opportunities:

- Consider implementing and testing the efficacy of special programs specifically for gifted girls, particularly in math and science
- Study factors which would alter girls' underachievement and underrepresentation in gifted programs

Educators should be aware of three common characteristics often seen in these youngsters: sensitivity, perfectionism, and intensity (Piechowski, 1997). For example, they tend to be highly sensitive (Freeman, 1994). This characteristic may lead some of them to overreact to even modest criticism. This, coupled with a need for perfection, causes many gifted students to experience more negative reactions to what they perceive as failure (Roberts & Lovett, 1994). These tendencies may well contribute to underachievement in some gifted students. Another characteristic, intensity, can manifest itself both socially and academically (VanTassel-Baska, 1995). For example, these students often react strongly to the death of a pet or the perceived injustice of a teacher. On the positive side, this characteristic causes these students to become highly focused on an activity they find fascinating, enabling them to concentrate on an intriguing idea for long periods of time and also explore curriculum content in depth. Knowledge of these characteristics and learning styles can help the keen educator understand these students' educational needs and keep them motivated.

SUBGROUPS REQUIRING SPECIAL ATTENTION

Not all gifted children demonstrate high academic achievement; many children with high intelligence are underachievers. Also, because of bias and different perceptions about what constitutes giftedness, other children who could benefit from gifted educational experiences are not included. If not identified and served, the likelihood that they will not achieve to their potential is great. Typically, these children come from one of three subgroups: those with disabilities, females, and culturally and linguistically diverse children. These youngsters need specialized educational services to teach them how to achieve in school, how to approach learning tasks more meaningfully, and how to use their talents in a directed fashion.

Gifted Females. As more and more women have broken from traditional roles and expectations, assumed work responsibilities, and pursued careers outside of the home, people have become more aware of issues related to gender bias both at school and in the workplace (Noble et al., 1999). Clearly, women and girls are underrepresented in both leadership positions in business and in educational programs for the gifted, and this fact appears to be particularly true for Asian American women (Kitano, 1997). A term, "the glass ceiling," has even been coined to refer to the collective barriers women experience in the workplace. And at school, educators often voice concerns about the poor academic achievement of girls, particularly in subjects like science and math (Lupart & Pyryt, 1996).

Allowing students to reinforce their study of content subjects through creative projects, like these students are doing to support their learning about ancient Egypt, helps them remember important content and also have fun learning!

Concern about educational achievement of girls is not new. As early as the 1920s, Hollingworth raised issues regarding bias toward gifted females. She argued that the prevailing notion that women were intellectually inferior to men was incorrect; rather, women did not have equal opportunities to excel and achieve to their potential. Concurrently with Hollingworth's work, Terman studied many individuals identified as gifted; the number of men in his study outnumbered the women. It is interesting that although many of Terman's research associates were women who went on to highly productive academic careers, few women were included as subjects in Terman's research (Rogers, 1999).

Although the numbers of preschool boys and girls identified as gifted are about equal, the proportion of girls to boys in gifted or accelerated programs diminishes across time (Silverman, 1995). Why might this be so? Are there innate differences between the genders that cause giftedness to occur more frequently in men than in women? Innate differences have never been proven in research. Rather, are society's expectations for people and the roles they assume the crucial factors in the achievement levels of either gender? Efforts have begun to conduct retrospective studies of gifted woman to learn more about their characteristics, educational needs, and the interplay of society's and their personal expectations (Arnold et al., 1996; Filippelli & Walberg, 1997; Rogers, 1999). Some of the research has focused on special groups of gifted women, and verify the need to reconsider how gifted girls are educated. For example, gifted Asian girls often do well in school because they focus on educational achievement and apply hard work to their studies, but in later life tend to be ill-prepared for the social challenges of the workplace and the necessity to be assertive and resolve interpersonal conflicts (Kitano, 1997).

The school experience for girls may well be very different from that of their male peers. Traditional role expectations might well be barriers to achievement (Reis,

1999). For example, proper manners ("Don't ask so many questions") and being polite ("Don't interrupt") may conflict with characteristics necessary for girls with high potential to achieve. Not only may others' expectations differ, but so too might personal goals. Some feel that gifted girls, in particular, have to resolve the conflicting demands of being popular and performing well academically (Rakow, 1998). For these reasons, some researchers believe that gifted females need different educational experiences to achieve their potential (Noble et al., 1999). For example, additional instruction might include specific attention to self-actualization, community actualization, risk taking, motivation, and confidence. Support groups, comprised of gifted female peers, could be added to the school experience to help students maintain the motivation to sustain high levels of academic achievement (Frey, 1998). Also, Silverman (1995) suggests that gifted girls must be identified early in their schooling, provided with a challenging curriculum, counseled to achieve in areas not traditionally pursued by women, and given many examples and role models to follow.

For a review of culturally and linguistically diverse children, see Chapter 3.

Culturally and Linguistically Diverse Gifted Students. Culturally and linguistically diverse students, particularly the gifted subgroup, face many challenges. They tend to be overrepresented in disability categories and underrepresented in gifted education programs (Brown, 1997). While they comprise over 50% of students in many school districts, their representation in gifted education does not mirror that proportion (Ford et al., 1996). Why do these youngsters frequently not qualify for gifted special services? A number of reasons have been offered (Callahan & McIntire, 1994; Davis & Rimm, 1998; Fernández et al., 1998; Hébert, 1998; Ford & Harris, 1994; Hunsaker et al., 1997; Tomlinson et al., 1998). First, let's categorize the different explanations given for these students not being identified as gifted at the rate that should be expected:

1. Cultural values at variance with mainstream society and teaching methods used at school
2. Barriers presented because of poverty
3. Bias in traditional methods used for testing and identification
4. Educator's attitudes about and lack of familiarity with culturally and linguistically diverse students
5. Rigid definitions of giftedness

Now let's examine these issues more carefully.

Students from some ethnic groups (African Americans, Hispanics, Pacific Islanders, Native Americans, and others) often do not perform as well as their peers from other groups on standardized tests or on classroom academic tasks. One reason for their poor performance may be their families' different cultural values, different emphasis on cognitive development, or conflict between cultural expectations and teaching methods (Maker & Schiever, 1989; Tomlinson et al., 1998). Sometimes, the culture of the school clashes with the culture of the home. This clash can cause great difficulties for the youngster who cannot discriminate between the expectations of home and those of school. In many cases, students who are not from the dominant culture mask their giftedness in the school environment because they do not believe it is appropriate to demonstrate unique abilities or talents. Some cultures do not value individual achievement or attention; rather, achievement of a group is more important. Some children find it difficult to function well in classes where individual competition is stressed (Kitano, 1997). Others do not perform well in tightly structured classrooms, but do well in less structured situations (Tomlinson et al., 1998). Each culture has different values and norms, of course, and it is impossible to generalize from one culture to another. But it is possible to note differences between the cultures of school and of home. These differences should be considered not only when identifying youngsters for services, but also when planning their educational programs. For example, supportive services, like counseling, can help some students bridge the gap between the cultures of home and school (Ford, 1995).

Unfortunately, one fact of American life is that culturally and linguistically diverse children are more at risk to grow up in poverty than other groups of American children. Poverty is associated with many factors that can result in barriers to school success. How is this so? Borland (1996) helps us understand that socioeconomic status is a variable that should never be underestimated. He notes that students from affluent families are five times more likely to be identified as gifted than are students from poor families. This could be because poor culturally and linguistically diverse children are less likely to have access to health care, and the relationship between good health and intellectual development is clear. Children who do not get proper nutrition, are not inoculated for disease, or do not get appropriate medical treatment for illness are at risk for impaired mental development. Another factor associated with poverty is the instability of the home environment. Many of these children come from families that move frequently and so are not at one school long enough for either identification or services. Finally, underrepresentation related to poverty may be the result of the poor educational levels of parents, the deficiencies of inner-city schools, and lack of exposure to mainstream society.

Clearly, a primary reason for culturally and linguistically diverse children not being identified as gifted is their not meeting stringently applied cutoff scores on standardized tests. Providing the kinds of educational services these underserved gifted students need may require the use of flexible identification procedures. Clearly, we need to broaden our search for talent to include artistic and creative individuals who come from rural and remote areas too (De Leon et al., 1997). Earlier in this text, portfolio assessments were presented as an alternative approach to the evaluation of children, and this procedure is often advocated for students biased against by traditional testing procedures (Ford & Harris, 1994). Portfolio assessment procedures can be implemented in many ways. For gifted youngsters this system is beneficial because it matches well with Gardner's theory of multiple intelligences. Maker, Nielson, and Rogers (1994) also believe that culturally and linguistically diverse students can benefit from a multidimensional identification system based on Gardner's theory. Maker, who is working with Native American students living on a rural reservation, has verified a new method to identify gifted students who have limited proficiency in English. Rejecting the use of standardized tests of intelligence, she is using Gardner's framework and a process in which children solve increasingly complex problems. Most certainly, the process used to identify gifted youngsters from diverse backgrounds itself calls for greater imagination and creativity.

Many educators advocate that alternative assessment procedures be implemented for these students. Peer nominations, teacher nominations, authentic assessments (frequent evaluations of students' classroom work), and curriculum based assessments have all been suggested. Unfortunately, some data indicate that alternative assessments may not offer the solution to this problem as many have hoped (Hunsaker, 1994). Reports from many educators working in local school districts indicate disappointment with alternative assessment procedures because they believe that they do not result in increased placements for culturally and linguistically diverse students: The underrepresented population remains underrepresented. Hunsaker's findings indicate that many educators believe that at the heart of the problem are rigid policies and narrow testing practices.

Unfortunately, identification procedures are not the only source of the problem. Bias, unfair assumptions about groups of children, and low expectations also are reasons for underrepresentation. These factors not only influence identification, but they can also affect students' school performance (Kitano, 1998). For example, if teachers do not expect Hispanic girls to excel at school, they might not reveal their potential through the grades they receive on their report cards or in their academic achievement. Apparently, many educators do not believe that giftedness exists across all groups of students regardless of their ethnic background or economic level. In this case what needs to change is educators' attitudes.

Now let's shift the discussion from identification to services. Educational opportunities make a great difference for these students, but only a few special programs can be found across the country. What special considerations should be included in programs designed specifically for culturally and linguistically diverse students who are gifted? Besides gifted education methods, teachers must be sensitive to their students' cultural differences. Patton and Baytops (1995) provided some specific suggestions for African American students (see Table 7.3 on page 296). They maintained that the heritage, culture, and worldviews of this group demand instruction that both nurtures these students' unique backgrounds and empowers them. To these experts, exemplary programs allow students to explore topics of significance and interest to the individual learner, to respond to real-world issues and problems, to learn advanced content in core curriculum areas (math, language arts, science), and to be challenged by interdisciplinary study that cuts across curriculum areas.

Gifted Individuals with Disabilities. When you think of people with disabilities who are also gifted and have developed outstanding talents, you might think of people like Steven Hawking, the renowned scientist, Ludwig van Beethoven, Thomas Edison, Helen Keller, Franklin D. Roosevelt, Stevie Wonder, Itzhak Perlman, and others. Despite their severe disabilities, their genius and major contributions to their respective fields have brought them considerable recognition. Remember, regardless of disability, anyone can have exceptional abilities, talents, or creativity. Never make an assumption about an individual from a casual meeting. Clearly, society's biases about people with disabilities can overshadow individuals' strengths. In the 1970s, Maker (1977) began to raise the awareness of educators about the needs of gifted learners with disabilities. In her research, Maker (1986) found one key variable leading to these individuals' success: motivation to succeed. Others have followed her lead, coining the term **"twice exceptional students"** to refer to this unique group of learners, particularly those with learning disabilities (Nielsen, Higgins, & Hammond, 1993; Nielsen, Higgins, Hammond, & Williams, 1993).

Unfortunately, students with disabilities often are not included in educational programs for the gifted. A number of factors contribute to this unfortunate situation. Here are a few of those reasons:

1. Despite the severity of the discrepancy between IQ and achievement, if the level of achievement is sufficiently high, the likelihood of being identified as having a learning disability is low (MacMillian et al., 1998).

NEW DIRECTIONS
FOR THE
MILLENNIUM

Legacy: In the latter part of the century an awareness about children who were gifted, but also had a learning disability, emerged. It also became recognized that most of these children received no special programs because their achievement was too high to be identified for learning disability programs and too low for services through gifted education.

Opportunities:

- Determine the prevalence of twice-exceptional students
- Study what constitutes an appropriate and effective education for these special needs children

twice-exceptional students. Students who have a disability and who are gifted.

Table 7.3 Methods of Accentuating Selective Strengths and Learning Modes of African American Gifted Learners

Selective Strengths and Learning Modes	Responsive Teaching-Learning Methodologies
Verbal fluency; stylistic, charismatic use of language	Emphasize creative writing, poetry, public speaking, oral discussion, debating, drama, literature
Expressive movement, advanced kinesthetic ability	Emphasize hands-on learning strategies and allow flexible classroom organization
Advanced aesthetic sensibilities	Integration of arts with core instruction
Resourcefulness, inventiveness, advanced creative abilities	Utilize problem-based learning: opportunities for experimentation with ideas, and seeking solutions to real problems
Preference for person-to-person (over person-to-object) interactions	Emphasize development of social interaction and leadership skills, attention to world affairs, and current issues
Sensitivity for the interconnectedness of humankind with nature	Focus on science, ecology, outdoor field experience, anthropology, and social sciences
Expressed spirituality related to sense of power of external forces of nature, existence of a supreme being, and a heightened sense of responsibility for others within primary reference group	Use of moral, affective overarching themes as base for instructional experiences: study use of parables and proverbs of varying cultures; examine life experiences of selected leaders (those characterized by intense spirituality, individualization, and moral responsibility)

Source: Effective Education of African American Exceptional Learners: New Perspectives (p. 43) by B. A. Ford, F. E. Obiakor, and J. M. Patton (Eds.), 1995, Austin, TX: Pro-Ed. Reprinted by permission.

2. Students are not allowed sufficient (e.g., enough extra) time or appropriate (e.g., assistive) equipment during the testing situation to accommodate for their disabilities.
3. States' regulations for gifted education are not flexible enough (Grimm, 1998).
4. Bias about some disabilities, like cerebral palsy, overshadow actual abilities and talents (Willard-Holt, 1998).
5. Beliefs that high abilities and learning problems cannot possibly coexist (Brody & Mills, 1997).

Gifted students with disabilities tend to share some common characteristics (Willard-Holt, 1998). They often possess skills that allow them to compensate for their disabilities. After years of developing alternative ways to learn and keep up with their classmates, they typically have also developed exceptional problem solving abilities as well. It is often their persistence and determination that have allowed them to succeed, often with no expert assistance. When focusing on gifted students with learning disabilities, experts list a "confusing collection of characteristics," which are shown in Table 7.4 (Robinson, 1999, p. 195). Experts have also noted that these students characterize themselves as being deficient in academic subjects, con-

Table 7.4 Characteristics of a Gifted Student with Learning Disabilities

Perfectionistic

Hypersensitive

Lacks social skills

Socially isolated

Has unrealistic self-expectations

Has low self-esteem

Hyperactive

Distractible

Has psychomotor inefficiency

Chronically inattentive

Frustrated classroom demands

Fails to complete assignments

Excessively critical of self/others

Rebellious against drill and repetition

Disparaging of work required to do

Becomes "expert" in one area and dominates discussions

Source: From "Meeting the Needs of Students Who Are Gifted and Have Learning Disabilities" by Suzanne M. Robinson, 1999, *Intervention in School and Clinic, 34,* p. 196. Reprinted by permission.

tributing to their motivation to avoid academic tasks (Beckley, 1998). Being aware of traits these students typically possess can help educators both identify these children and also provide them an instructional program that is tailored to their needs.

Experts agree: Gifted students with disabilities are in desperate need of intervention (Robinson, 1999). But how should that intervention be focused? Again, there seems to be agreement. These students respond best to an instructional environment that is challenging, highly interesting, and structured yet allows for independence, and builds on each student's strengths. While capitalizing on strengths, however, teachers must work together to remediate individuals' weaker areas, like an inability to focus on tasks for long periods or to read at grade level. Some suggest that students actually be taught (and encouraged) to compensate for their weaknesses (Beckley, 1998). And, finally, it is important that these students come to understand the nature of their disabilities, accept their personal strengths and weakness, and develop a good self-concept. For these goals to be met, support systems and intervention programs are often required. Some professionals argue that at least some of these students may require intensive instruction in separate classes for a part of their educational careers, speaking to the importance of an array of educational alternatives being available to gifted students with disabilities (Brody & Mills, 1997).

A good educational program for these students should include direct instruction in areas in need of remediation, as in any educational program for students with learning disabilities. The educational program must also incorporate gifted education methods. Thus the program would allow students to compensate for their weaker areas and yet foster their development of critical thinking, reasoning, problem solving, and compensatory skills. For example, students might be encouraged to use a broad array of technologies (word processing, spellcheckers,

MAKING CONNECTIONS

Other information about direct instruction techniques is found in Chapter 1 (Development of Informed Solutions), Chapter 4 (Instructional Interventions), and in the Research to Practice boxes in Chapters 3–12.

calculators, database software, and other assistive devices) to compensate for their deficits. Some students might use audio-recorded literature for their reading assignments or tape recorders to take class notes. They would also use technology when they study complex problems, such as the water quality of the local river. To conduct their environmental study, they might tape record interviews with people who live along the river. They might also conduct a variety of tests to assess the water's quality at various points along the river. The students could also visit state and local government offices to determine the policies and regulations regarding pollution, and visit businesses that have been cited for polluting the river to better understand their perspectives as well. The blending of instructional procedures for students with learning disabilities and procedures for gifted students is obviously important for these students' development. Because of these students' unique learning needs, some school districts have developed special programs just for these youngsters.

EDUCATIONAL INTERVENTIONS

Enhanced educational opportunities for gifted individuals have been available, but inconsistently, across time and across the nation. For instance, gifted education is part of special education in some but not all states, since no federal law requires that these students be guaranteed special instructional programs. Remember, gifted education is not part of IDEA and therefore does not receive federal funding for school based programs. Also, remember that this inconsistent commitment to gifted education stems from differing philosophical beliefs about society, elitism, and educational opportunities rooted in our national history. One argument centers on the notion that these children are already advantaged and do not need more benefits. But as you have learned in this chapter, gifted youngsters are atypical learners who need specialized services to make full use of their extraordinary talents. Their potential, if wasted, represents a significant loss. For many years, educators have discussed the educational options that could be made available to students who are gifted. For example, over sixty years ago, Scheidemann in her 1931 text about exceptional children wrote:

> Enrichment of curriculum, rapid progress, or segregation in special classes for only gifted children are advocated by modern educators. The arguments extended by early objectors for these special methods, namely, that attainments of the bright children are needed to stimulate the progress of normal children, or that an IQ aristocracy would be encouraged among school children, are groundless. Even the objections on the basis of the discrepancy between physical and intellectual maturity that would result in permitting the superior child to progress at his individual rate are no longer tenable.... Some specialists urge time-saving by rapid promotions in precollege education, and regular or longer attendance in professional schools, because the gifted mind can spend unlimited time in specialization.
>
> Rapid promotion is urged by many educators because it is easy and inexpensive. The more thoughtful are more inclined to encourage an enrichment program for gifted children, thus keeping their intellectual powers active in association with children who are mentally and physically their equal. Social ostracism, which is the usual fate of the very young high-school child, is thus avoided. Many suggestions in regard to the specific ways in which the curriculum may be enriched are offered. (Scheidemann, 1931, pp. 261–262)

EDUCATION AND THE PRESCHOOL CHILD

What can we do for the preschool child who is gifted? As we know, early stimulation is crucial to the development of all young children, and it is especially important to gifted children. Without early identification *and* services, gifted preschoolers may feel forced to underachieve to remain on par with their typical classmates (Mooij, 1999).

Preschool teachers should be aware of differences between gifted and nongifted preschoolers which can lead to a differentiated education program, offered as soon as the child is identified. What characteristics are commonly observed in these children? At a young age, gifted children show higher levels of curiosity, concentration, problem solving, theoretical thinking, imagination, and enthusiasm (Tucker & Hafenstein, 1997). These children are likely to be healthier, quicker to learn, larger, emotionally better adjusted, and socially more mature; they persist longer at tasks, resist rules, and enjoy competition (Karnes et al., 1982). They are also able to handle complex and abstract language relationships earlier than most (Castillo, 1998). They can come to understand metaphors (e.g., "presidents are heads of state"; "time flies") long before their classmates. And recent research has identified another important difference between these youngsters and their more typically learning peers: They gain phonological awareness and the ability to discriminate speech sounds very early. This ability is a predictor of early reading mastery, a skill highly related to school success (McBride-Chang et al., 1996). Although different in many ways from their classmates, these youngsters tend to associate with the most popular youngsters in the preschool class, rather than playing alone or with others of their intellectual abilities (Schneider & Daniels, 1992).

These young preschoolers are already demonstrating advanced reading and conceptual abilities. Teachers must be alert to continually challenge and support children with giftedness and creativity.

Gifted preschoolers seem to function well in typical preschool settings. They build things, engage in pretend and dramatic play, and converse with others at the same rate as their nongifted classmates. However, those who show signs of accelerated development must be challenged so that their motivation to learn is not dulled. Educators must also understand that sometimes these young children's cognitive abilities far surpass their motor skills (Gallagher & Gallagher, 1994). For example, even those able to read may not be able to write well enough to capture their creative ideas. Researchers also caution that no child should be forced to relearn what is already mastered. Time after time, stories are told about children who come to kindergarten already reading, but instead of being allowed to continue developing their reading skills they are forced to engage in readiness activities with classmates. Instructional time might be better spent on different activities, such as teaching students to classify and organize information or to think critically. The development of critical-thinking skills can begin early in children's education. Units specifically aimed at developing critical thinking can be incorporated as enrichment activities.

EDUCATION AND THE SCHOOLCHILD

A variety of educational services, varying by locale and in philosophy and orientation, are available to gifted students. In this section, several instructional models or approaches to gifted education are discussed. Some approaches are comprehensive and influence the entire schoolday; others modify a portion of the schoolday; still others can be easily integrated into any ongoing instructional program. All seek to develop the unique talents of gifted individuals and serve as illustrative examples of educational systems that are responsive to individual needs by altering traditional educational programs and providing a **differentiated curriculum**.

Approaches. Professionals do not agree on a best educational approach for gifted students, and many different models and instructional practices are used across the nation. A few of the most commonly applied examples of enrichment and acceleration are found in Table 7.5 and are highlighted in the text. Remember that regardless of the approach used, activities always emphasize: cognitive processing, abstract thinking, reasoning, creative problem solving, self-monitoring, content mastery, breadth and depth of topic study, and independent learning.

ENRICHMENT. Broadly speaking, when additional topics or skills are included in the traditional curriculum, the approach is considered **enrichment.** For example, a group of students might spend a small portion of time each week working with instructional materials that enhance creativity or critical-thinking skills. Or enrichment may be the study of a particular academic subject in more depth and detail. Some teachers, when using enrichment in this way, guide students to select a character or an event for research and study. The student's product might be an oral or written report that could become part of a class play or short story, or a nonverbal product such as a painting, construction, or model. The enrichment approach is often used in general classroom settings to meet the needs of advanced learners. To use this approach successfully, however, teachers must be prepared to guide children as they learn and apply skills like critical thinking, problem solving, advanced reasoning, and research.

To better understand the enrichment process, let us look at an example from a history lesson. This lesson involves **interdisciplinary instruction**, which encourages

---

differentiated curriculum. The flexible application of curriculum targets that ensures content mastery, in-depth and independent learning, and exploration of issues and themes and allows for acceleration when needed.

enrichment. Adding topics or skills to the traditional curriculum or presenting a particular topic in more depth.

interdisciplinary instruction. An approach to the education of the gifted that involves studying a topic and its issues in the context of several different disciplines.

Table 7.5 Approaches to Gifted Education

Approach	Explanation
1. Enrichment	
Interdisciplinary instruction	Teaching a topic by presenting different disciplines' perspectives about the issues involved
Independent study	Examining a topic in more depth than is usual in a general education class
Mentorship programs	Pairing students with adults who guide them in applying knowledge to real-life situations
Internship	Programs that allow gifted students, usually during their senior year in high school, to be placed in a job setting that matches their career goals
Enrichment triad/revolving door model	An inclusive and flexible model for gifted education that changes the entire educational system; exposes students to planned activities that seek to develop thinking skills, problem solving, and creativity
Curriculum compacting	Making additional time available for enrichment activities by reducing time spent on traditional instructional topics
2. Acceleration	
Advanced placement	Courses that students take during their high school years resulting in college credit
Honors sections	A form of ability grouping where gifted and nongifted students who demonstrate high achievement in a particular subject are placed together in advanced classes
Ability grouping	Clustering students in courses where all classmates have comparable achievement and skill levels
Individualized instruction	Instruction delivered on a one-to-one basis, with students moving through the curriculum independently at their own pace
3. Eclectic	
Purdue secondary model for gifted and talented youth	A comprehensive high school curriculum for students that incorporates counseling into the standard program for all students

students to study a subject by using different perspectives. As one application of this instructional technique that incorporates multicultural education, Banks (1994) provides this example. The students play a game that Banks calls "Star Power," in which the class is divided into three groups: the stars (who have the most points), the triangles, and the circles (those with the least points). The teacher designs the game so the stars are always in a dominant position, to illustrate the point that highly stratified societies provide little opportunity for mobility. Students study historical examples of groups in positions like the stars, triangles, and circles. Some choices might include the Pilgrims of seventeenth-century England, American colonists in the late 1700s upset with English taxation policies, the Cherokee Indians in the Southeast in the 1830s, the Jews in Germany during the 1940s, and

For her senior-year mentorship, this student has been matched with a local journalist whose specialty is feminist literature.

independent study. A common approach to the education of the gifted that allows a student to pursue and study a topic in depth on an individual basis.

mentorship. A program in which a gifted student is paired with an adult in order to learn to apply knowledge in real-life situations.

internship. A program that places gifted students, usually high school seniors, in job settings related to their career goals in order to challenge them and apply knowledge in real-life skills.

enrichment triad/ revolving door model. A model for gifted education where 15% to 20% rather than 3% of a school's students periodically participate in advanced activities planned to develop thinking skills, problem solving, and creativity.

infused. The incorporation of enrichment activities into the general education curriculum.

African Americans in the South during the 1950s and 1960s. One question students are to answer is how history might have been different if the target group had acted differently. Throughout this process, students learn about history from a sociological perspective. They advance their knowledge of a particular historical period while sharpening their critical-thinking skills.

Three of the many other examples of enrichment are independent study, mentorships, and internships. As an enrichment option, **independent study** is usually used within a traditional course (Sisk, 1987). It allows a student to study a topic in more depth, or to explore a topic that is not part of the general education. Independent study does not mean working alone, but rather learning to be self-directed and to work on problems in which the individual has an interest. **Mentorships** pair students with special interests with adults who have expertise in those areas. **Internships** are used with many gifted high school students who have expressed interest in a particular career, to allow them to gain experience with that profession.

The **enrichment triad/revolving door model** seeks to modify the entire educational system (Renzulli, 1998; Renzulli & Reis, 1997). This is probably the most popular gifted education approach today (Davis & Rimm, 1998). It offers a different view of education for all children by allowing students to move into advanced activities on the basis of their performance in general enrichment offerings. Recall that Renzulli believes that three traits—above-average ability, creativity, and task commitment—constitute giftedness. In support of this flexible definition, Renzulli has developed a model for gifted education in which enrichment activities are **infused** into the general education classroom. In addition to providing enrichment for *all* students, the enrichment triad model directly serves from 15% to 20% of the school population, rather than limiting it to the top 2% to 3%. This highly successful pro-

Renzulli's model was described in the Defined and Identification sections of this chapter.

gram has been adopted in many school districts across the country, and its supporters maintain that it includes students with high potential for creative production. They also believe that this larger pool includes more students from culturally and linguistically diverse backgrounds. How does the program work? Students "revolve" into and out of different levels of their program into three types of skills categories. Here are a few examples of each type:

- *Type 1:* Enrichment activities expose the entire class of general education students to new and exciting topics of study carried out through a variety of instructional approaches (speakers, field trips, demonstrations, videotapes and films, and interest centers).
- *Type 2:* Activities encourage all students to develop their cognitive and affective abilities through their own expressive skills (writing a play, doing a pen-and-ink sketch, using equipment).
- *Type 3:* Opportunities to apply advanced investigative and creative skills are given to students who are motivated, those who show great interest are provided with specialized instruction and activities to explore particular topics, issues, or ideas.

How can general education teachers find time in the busy schoolday to enrich students' curriculum? Instructional time can be recaptured by applying a concept called **curriculum compacting.** Using this instructional strategy, teachers modify or eliminate topics that gifted students have mastered or master in a fraction of the time that their peers need. Research has shown that mathematics and language arts are areas where teachers can learn how to apply curriculum compacting easily and without any reduction in students' achievements (Reis & Purcell, 1993). This study also found that between 24% and 70% of the content across curriculum areas can be eliminated by using this technique. Thus a significant amount of time is left for challenging replacement activities like the enrichment practices discussed in this section.

ACCELERATION. Another approach, **acceleration,** receives considerable support because it does not require separate or special gifted classes or programs, and also because it is effective (Lubinski & Benbow, 1995; Witham, 1997). Look again at Table 7.4. You should notice that acceleration can take a variety of forms, like grade skipping, advanced placement courses, or ability groups such as honors sections. High achievers make great gains when they are accelerated, so let's take a look at a couple of these options.

Advanced placement courses allow students take classes in high school that earn college credit. One older study of advanced placement showed that in only ten states, more than $19 million in college costs was saved in one year alone (Gallagher et al., 1983). Consider inflation and what those savings would be in today's dollars! Advanced placement allows gifted students and those who are high achievers to experience enrichment and acceleration by studying course content in more depth. A side benefit is that they do not have to retake these courses in college.

Another approach, **ability grouping,** has gained considerable support from educators of the gifted because when students are grouped with others of comparable abilities for specific activities or courses in which they excel, they make greater achievement gains (Kulik & Kulik, 1997). Such groups are easily arranged in middle and high schools, where most students travel from class to class. In this approach, gifted students can attend more advanced classes. For example, a ninth grader might attend sophomore- or junior-level mathematics classes; a high school senior might

curriculum compacting. Reducing instructional time spent on typical academic subjects so that enrichment activities can be included in the curriculum.
acceleration. Moving students through a curriculum or years of schooling in a shorter period of time than usual.
advanced placement courses. High school courses that carry college credit.
ability grouping. Placing students with comparable achievement and skill levels in the same classes or courses.

take several classes at a local college. Many high schools provide **honors sections** of academic courses as a form of ability grouping. The criterion for entrance into these classes is outstanding academic achievement in specific subject matters. Ability grouping and honors sections allow gifted students to attend classes with students who are not identified as gifted in subjects where they demonstrate exceptional capabilities. Although used today in many schools as one option for gifted students, ability grouping was struck down in a decision by the Washington, DC District Court in 1967. Ability grouping was deemed discriminatory and a form of racial segregation because so few students from minority groups were included in higher track programs (Hobson v. Hansen, 1967).

What are some benefits of acceleration?

1. Students can complete the traditional general education curriculum in a shorter period of time, being able to finish high school several years early.
2. Academic material can be completed more quickly, allowing students to study related topics in more depth.
3. Educators see more academic gains from students involved with this approach.
4. Some students develop better self-concepts and more positive attitudes about course content and school.
5. The acceleration approach solves the criticism that gifted education segregates these students from more typical learners, because although they are not placed with students of the same age, they are participating in general education programs.

For a review of special education service delivery options, see that section (Special Education Services) in Chapter 2.

Despite these benefits, you need to put this approach into some perspective: Only 17% of gifted students use acceleration (Pendarvais & Howley, 1996).

Service Delivery Options. Enrichment and acceleration can occur in a variety of placements and administrative arrangements. Renzulli (1994/1995) helps us visualize the wide range of programs and the options available; his scheme is displayed in Figure 7.4. Let's look at a few examples of these arrangements.

Cluster grouping is an administrative arrangement where gifted students use the general classroom. The general education teacher, who is supported by a gifted educator, delivers special instructional opportunities (Schuler, 1997). Under this plan, gifted students spend some portion of their schoolday engaged in enriched or accelerated activities, but in the general education classroom setting. For example, these students might be assigned special independent study activities that support and extend topics that are part of the general education curriculum. Sixth graders, studying state history in social studies, might thus prepare a "Who's Who" book of key figures in their state's history. Or they might prepare a position paper on a current issue, like water rights, including the historical reasons for the controversy and concluding with solutions to the problem.

The general education setting has seen the rising popularity of a strategy, **cooperative learning**, designed for mixed ability groups of children to work together in small groups (Slavin, 1990). Cooperative learning is often suggested as a means of providing appropriate educational opportunities for all students, particularly for gifted students attending general education classes. However, this strategy might not be the successful answer to the question, "What teaching technique is effective for a wide range of student abilities, and particularly engages the gifted learner?" Research has found that gifted youngsters find disadvantages with cooperative learning: the

honors sections. Advanced classes for any student who shows high achievement in specific subject areas.
cluster grouping. A plan whereby gifted students spend a part of their day in the general classroom on enriched or accelerated activities.
cooperative learning. Groups of more than two students collaborating as they learn the same material.

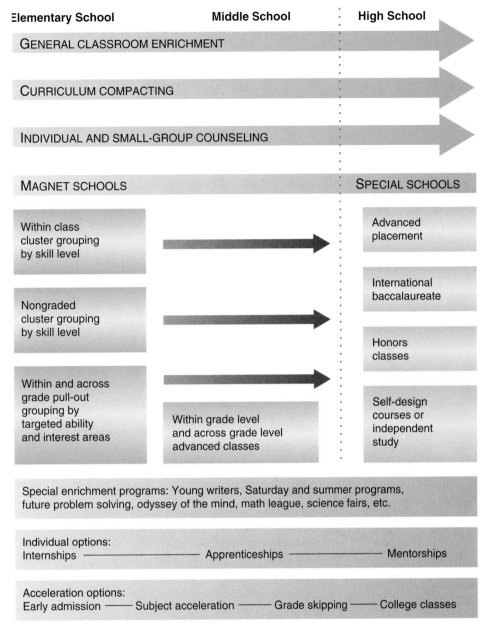

Elementary School	Middle School	High School

GENERAL CLASSROOM ENRICHMENT →

CURRICULUM COMPACTING →

INDIVIDUAL AND SMALL-GROUP COUNSELING →

| MAGNET SCHOOLS | | SPECIAL SCHOOLS |

Within class cluster grouping by skill level → Advanced placement

Nongraded cluster grouping by skill level → International baccalaureate

Honors classes

Within and across grade pull-out grouping by targeted ability and interest areas → Within grade level and across grade level advanced classes — Self-design courses or independent study

Special enrichment programs: Young writers, Saturday and summer programs, future problem solving, odyssey of the mind, math league, science fairs, etc.

Individual options:
Internships ——— Apprenticeships ——— Mentorships

Acceleration options:
Early admission ——— Subject acceleration ——— Grade skipping ——— College classes

Figure 7.4 **The Continuum of Services for Total Talent Development**
Source: "Teachers as Talent Scouts" by J. S. Renzulli, 1994/1995, *Educational Leadership, 52,* p. 78. Reprinted by permission.

pull-out programs. The most common educational placement for gifted students, who spend part of the school day in a special class.

pacing is too slow and group instruction is not challenging enough (Gallagher et al., 1997; Ramsay & Richards, 1997). Maybe the problem is overuse. As with peer tutoring, teachers must apply cooperative learning sparingly, because most bright children resent repeating information over and over again.

Although probably still the most common placement and administrative arrangement for gifted students, **pull-out programs** are decreasing in number

(VanTassel-Baska, 1995). In this service delivery option, students leave the general education class for a portion of their schoolday to attend a special class. Such programs provide services for either several days per week or an hour or so each day. Some schools combine cluster and pull-out programs. Both cluster and pull-out programs rely heavily on the general education classroom for the majority of a child's education.

Other educational options are available to gifted students. For example, students might receive the majority of their instruction in a special class, possibly at their neighborhood school, where they are educated in a homogeneous environment in which all the other students have comparable abilities. Some advantaged youngsters receive their education at exclusive private schools. Today, many of these schools, like Andover, offer scholarships so that students whose families cannot pay the tuition can be included in their educational communities. Some students attend special public schools exclusively for students who are gifted. Hunter Elementary, for instance, administered by Hunter College of the City University of New York, is a public elementary school exclusively for these students; but these schools are usually at the high school level and stress special areas of education. In New York and other cities, for example, **magnet schools** that emphasize a theme, specializing in the performing arts, math, or science, and are available to students who pass qualifying exams or auditions. Finally, a national trend for the development of state-supported, special, residential high schools for students who are gifted and/or creative is emerging (Kolloff, 1997). Six states have already established residential schools for students who require a curriculum different from that offered by most schools, and other states are in the planning stages.

Remember, not all of these educational options exist in every state or local district, and the debate continues about where these students should receive their education, what their education should comprise, and who their classmates should be. On one side of the debate are those who contend that gifted students should receive their education exclusively in the general education classroom from the general education teacher (McDaniel, 1993; Sapon-Shevin, 1996). On the other, people argue that students who are gifted require a unique and challenging educational program in which their classmates comprise a homogeneous ability group (Gallagher, 1996). As in earlier periods of time, equity, elitism, democracy, and fear of an intellectual aristocracy are focal points of one side of the debate. In addition, proponents of this view say that the U.S. classroom should reflect U.S. society: one that is diverse, heterogeneous, and multicultural.

COLLABORATION FOR INCLUSION

Very few gifted students attend segregated special classes or schools. Most attend general education classes and receive enrichment activities, attend "pull-out programs" for a limited portion of the schoolweek, or participate in standard classes with older peers through the acceleration model. These arrangements mean that educators of the gifted and general education teachers need to work closely together to be sure that these students' educational and social needs are being met adequately. Regardless of the approach adopted, effective programming for gifted students requires professionals to work together, and these professionals need to develop partnerships with students' families. All education experts agree about an important key to these individuals' success: Having high yet obtainable expectations contributes to improved school performance. But high expectations alone are not a sufficient

magnet schools. Center schools that serve children who do not live in the immediate neighborhood; some magnet schools are designed to serve children whose parents work in a nearby area; other magnet schools emphasize a particular theme (such as theater arts, math, and science).

Accommodating for Inclusive Environments

ADDRESSING LEARNING DIFFERENCES

Instructional Phase	Accommodations
Initial instruction	Overheads Presentation of software and technology Signals Repetition by partner Study guides Highlighted textbook Thoughtful teacher position
Guided practice	Partially filled-out materials Modeling Partner tutors or partner checks Teacher-controlled practice ("I do it, we do it, you do it") Altered pace Frequent teacher checks
Independent practice	Slower or quick fade from guided practice Home activities More structure Shorter assignment Highlighted textbook Provision of different tasks Peer check
Evaluation	Choice on what is evaluated Portfolios More frequent measures of performance Charts Rubrics to describe quality of work Performance based tasks
Grading	Narrative supplement Different curriculum outcomes

Source: From "Meeting the Needs of Students Who Are Gifted and Have Learning Disabilities" by Suzanne M. Robinson, 1999, *Intervention in School and Clinic, 34,* p. 201. Reprinted by permission.

accommodation; for gifted students to achieve to their potential, they require some unique offerings and opportunities (Dalzell, 1998). General classroom teachers must and do provide educational experiences that are at grade level for the average achievement level of the majority of their students, but as you'll see in the Accommodating for Inclusive Environments box, simple modifications to standard instruction are easy to apply.

In particular, two groups of gifted students deserve extra attention and the development of active partnerships: those with disabilities and those who come from diverse backgrounds. Let's take a closer look at these two groups of students and the

For another discussion of developing partnerships on behalf of diverse students, see the Collaboration (Educational Interventions) and Families sections in Chapter 3.

types of collaborative arrangements that can make a difference in their educational outcomes.

For students with disabilities to succeed and remain able to profit from gifted education requires collaboration among teachers (Robinson, 1999). In effective programs, teachers work together to:

- Define educational problems individual or groups of students are facing
- Research the problem and identify "best practices" that might be effective in this case
- Identify backup or alternative solutions
- Determine how to evaluate the solution's effectiveness (agree on criteria or level of student performance needed to retain the intervention)
- Develop a plan of action
- Decide on a meeting schedule

Students from diverse backgrounds find that they face different issues and have different educational needs (Ford et al., 1996; Patton & Townsend, 1997). Experts maintain that these students avoid underachievement and remain engaged when their educational programs:

- Reflect a multicultural perspective
- Affirm their culture, history, and heritage
- Include culturally sensitive techniques and strategies
- Provide self-affirming experiences and opportunities for better self-understanding
- Stress social responsibility
- Use relevant examples

Of course these points seem self-evident, but they are not easily accomplished, particularly when the teacher is working in isolation. Teachers often find that when they have partnerships with community members and families, instructional units and activities can be quite rewarding. For example, community leaders could link instruction about national American history to information about local heroes and influential figures. Some experts suggest that talent-development specialists, who work as "cultural brokers," help develop, facilitate, implement, and maintain appropriate educational programs for high-ability diverse students (Hébert, 1998). Such specialists also foster meaningful community partnerships. In addition, they assist with the identification of diverse students, in particular Black males, who should be included in gifted education but otherwise might be overlooked. Without very special efforts to support the unique needs of students living in urban settings, it is unlikely that these children will reach their academic potential or fulfill their own goals, dreams, and aspirations.

Community partners and family members can also help students learn about setting-specific behaviors. They can help children sort out when and where some behaviors are appropriate and when they are not. Patton and Townsend (1997) describe this as learning when to **code switch.** Students, through role-playing and demonstrations, can show how they differentially talk to peers in a variety of settings, such as a community center playground, a summer job, church, school, home. Fellow students, family members, and individuals from the community can assist with such activities.

code switch. To use different language and behavior appropriate in different settings.

Whether for particular groups of students or for all students, educators must forge partnerships that are real and authentic. Collaborative efforts should include diverse professionals, students, families, community leaders, and relevant stakeholders (Patton & Townsend, 1997). We are reminded that "(w)hile it is critical for general, special, and gifted educators to collaborate, it is equally important for students, families, and communities to become respected and valued partners" (p. 17). It is only when relationships become true partnerships that negative feelings and perceptions about schools held by diverse parents can turn into efforts that reflect positive attitudes and trust.

TRANSITION THROUGH ADULTHOOD

Terman's perspectives about giftedness are presented in the Defined and Identification sections of this chapter.

One way to understand the transitional needs of any group of people is to study what happens to members of that group as adults. The first comprehensive follow-up study of gifted individuals was conducted by Terman and his colleagues (Terman, 1925; Terman & Oden, 1959; Oden, 1968). Although criticized because of its dated concepts about giftedness, it is still considered a classic study. Terman's work is now supported by other longitudinal studies, and, together, this body of work tends to confirm our beliefs about gifted children and what happens to them as adults. Generally, gifted children assume places of eminence as adults (Filippelli & Walberg, 1997; Kitano, 1997, 1998; Walberg, 1992; Walberg & Zeiser, 1997).

Good outcomes for all gifted individuals, however, are not guaranteed (Benbow & Stanley, 1996). Many do not achieve to their potential; too many do not complete high school or college (Davis & Rimm, 1998). Acceleration programs are often cited as one means of retaining these students by keeping them interested and challenged. Another suggestion is that they be carefully matched with their interest preferences (Achter et al., 1996). Although many people believe that gifted students have broad preferences and talents, this is probably not the case. Rather, their outstanding abilities allow them to "ceiling out" or score well on all subtests of vocational and preference tests, masking their true interests. The amount of individual differences within the gifted group has probably been considerably underestimated, and the myth that these individuals are competent at everything needs to be dispelled. It is quite possible that mismatches between early career exploration and actual preferences explain some of this group's dropout rate.

A subgroup of gifted students also needs special attention. Tragically, the long-term outcomes for "twice exceptional" students appear not to be as good as they should be (Holliday et al., 1999). As adults, these individuals perform more consistently with their learning disabilities than with their intellectual potential. They are more likely to complete high school than their peers with learning disabilities, but unlike their gifted peers, they are more likely to complete only a few semesters of college. Their earnings outcomes reflects their school completion rates; many earn close to minimum wage. To avoid this negative pattern will require intervention. Schools should consider including gifted students with learning disabilities in organized transition programs or including them in career exploration opportunities along with their gifted peers. Realistic career and college counseling should help these individuals understand their potential and select reasonable alternatives for post-secondary experiences.

FAMILIES

The importance of the family cannot be underestimated for any child. Studies of eminent adults clearly show how powerful the influence of family is on gifted children (Filippelli & Walberg, 1997; Hébert, 1998; Kitano, 1997, 1998; Subotnik et al., 1993; Yewchuk, 1995). Definitive common threads run through the early lives of eminent adults. For example, regardless of the father's occupation, learning was valued for its own sake. The family was prepared to commit whatever time and resources were necessary to foster achievement and talent development. These families arranged for instruction, encouraged and supervised practice and study, and were involved in their children's education. Perhaps most important, these parents served as role models by living an achieving lifestyle.

Remember, discussion of underidentification of diverse students in gifted education programs is found in Chapter 3.

As you learned earlier in this chapter, diverse gifted students are at risk for underachievement and underrepresentation (Hébert, 1998). Black boys are at greatest risk. For these children, it is important that parents and family instill a high achievement orientation and a strong belief in self by holding high expectations and recognizing accomplishments. Many educators have found that discussion-group meetings held at private homes allow parents to talk among themselves and share ways to hold high academic expectations for their children.

Parents of gifted children sometimes are confused about what constitutes support. Many of these parents, not unlike most parents, do not have a realistic perspective on their children's abilities. Some deny their child's special abilities in an attempt to keep them normal or well adjusted. Others take the opposite tack and magnify their children's abilities, putting excessive pressure on them to achieve and excel in all areas. All parents, and especially parents of gifted children, need to learn what is realistic for their child and to develop appropriate standards and expectations.

Lastly, many gifted children are extremely verbal and have unusual abstract-thinking skills; they also seem to be more mature than other children of their age (Davis & Rimm, 1998). Such characteristics can be deceptive. These children, like others of their age, are not capable of making complex decisions or setting their own goals and directions. Of course, their interests and feelings should be considered, but parents and teachers must not abdicate responsibility for guidance. According to Davis and Rimm, successful gifted achievers felt confident throughout their schoolyears that adults were concerned about them and made appropriate decisions about their education. They also felt that it was a wise decision to follow the lead of these adults.

Reprinted with special permission of North American Syndicate.

TECHNOLOGY

MAKING CONNECTIONS

To compare different types of technology supports across students with special needs, read the Technology sections in Chapters 3–12.

For gifted people and for people with disabilities, technology can change the quality of their lives, improve the chances for more successful integration in the community, and enhance employment opportunities. The infusion of microcomputer technology into educational settings has been especially beneficial, since it allows for more applications of individualized instruction. Thus, several gifted students can work on different instructional tasks at the same time. For example, one student can work on a tutorial in chemistry or physics while a classmate can be learning how to program the computer to develop an environmental monitoring and control system. Or these students can work on accelerated or enriched topics while their general education classmates work on their own assignments. For gifted students bored by instruction paced too slowly for them or on topics they have already mastered, technology can allow them to study advanced topics more in depth. For gifted students, technology needs to become an essential tool for wide applications in daily life. Technology also has great advantages for these students who live in rural and remote areas. Let's look at these two issues.

TECHNOLOGY AS A FUNCTIONAL SKILL

Computer technology has almost unlimited applications. Computers have become tools of modern life for many Americans, and it is apparent that the technology that computers bring to daily life will continue to expand and develop. For today's students, mastering this tool is just as important as mastering other basic academic skills such as reading, writing, and mathematics. For example, even very young children can learn and apply word processing to their writing assignments. As they become more sophisticated in its use, they can use **desktop publishing** to produce a variety of written products about topics they have researched on the **World Wide Web**.

Teachers at many schools, like Central Virginia Governor's School for Science and Technology, have infused technology into the curriculum and no longer teach these skills and applications as discrete course content (Morgan, 1993). Here, technology is viewed as falling into three categories: increased productivity, awareness of emerging technologies, and enhanced instructional environment. In the first category, students must demonstrate proficiency using software applications in their assignments. For example, they use word processing—along with database, statistical, graphics, and literature search applications—to generate research papers. They also use computers for multimedia presentations of their final reports. In the second category, students come to an awareness of the emerging applications of technology to better understand what is on the horizon. For example, students are given the opportunities to explore robotics, holography, telecommunications, biotechnology, and other developing scientific applications of computer technology. In the last category, the instructional environment is enhanced through the capabilities of technology. In laboratory settings students explore "what if" scenarios to expand on classroom learning. For example, in the study of motion, students can hypothesize what will happen to a velocity or an acceleration curve when a variable (mass, friction, or air resistance) is altered.

Students who have the opportunity to enhance their learning by using technology as a tool rather than an isolated curriculum topic should be enabled to evolve as the practical applications of technology develop. By integrating technology into the instruction of other disciplines, the computer becomes an intellectual tool used to

desktop publishing. Using a microcomputer and special software to prepare written and graphic material in publication format and quality.

World Wide Web. Using the Internet, the Web allows the accessing of information through a personal computer.

Students need to learn how to access information off the internet, and parents can become learning partners by helping children do more in-depth homework projects.

facilitate learning and its generalization to other settings and skills. Such integration also helps extend the standard curriculum. For example, students could construct a database to keep records for a science project on air quality. The database could be used to compare different variables—such as the time of day, temperature, wind conditions, cloud cover, and season of the year—with the amount of air pollution. By using telecommunications (the next topic in this section), students could share the database and the results of various comparisons with other students across the nation.

ELECTRONIC OUTREACH

telecommunications. Various electronic devices that allow students and teachers to access and send materials and information using a computer network system.

e-mail. Uses telecommunications and technology to allow individuals to communicate using computers.

Almost all of us can attest to the benefits of **telecommunications** in our daily lives. We are now able to communicate with friends efficiently and economically through **e-mail.** We are able to find important or interesting information through the Web. Many of you registered for this class online, and use Web editions of your college textbooks as you explore topics discussed in class. It is amazing how quickly this technological application has become popular and in high demand. Its practical benefits to all students, particularly gifted students, cannot be underestimated.

Telecommunications allow students who live miles apart, and maybe have not even met, to work together on joint projects. Students who live in remote areas can access major library facilities and computers that have capabilities to analyze complicated sets of data. They can link up to scientists who work at research laboratories to ask for help in solving a scientific or mathematical question. Telecommunications can also provide opportunities for dialogue between students and practitioners from all across the nation on real issues and problems.

At the Louisiana School for Math, Science and the Arts, a unique outreach program has been developed that allows students who live long distances from the

For Web links to support your study of disabilities, look at the Resources sections at the end of every chapter in this text and the fuller listing found in the Students' Resource Manual that accompanies this text.

See also the sections A Very Special Population: Native Americans (Defined section) and Over- and Underrepresentation of diverse students (Prevalence section) in Chapter 3.

school to participate in many courses not available at their home schools (McBride & Lewis, 1993). This distance learning application provides opportunities for gifted students living in rural areas to take advanced courses in math, foreign languages, science, and the arts without leaving their home schools. Data indicate that this method of delivering instruction is highly effective. First, participating students' scores on national examinations show significant gains. Second, students living across the state in isolated areas become connected not only for the common courses they are taking, but also for other activities of mutual interest. Lastly, these students became so computer literate, through familiarity with the hardware and software used for the distance education component, that they were able to solve their own technical problems when they arose.

CONCEPTS AND CONTROVERSY: DO WE NEED A DIFFERENT WAY TO IDENTIFY AND PROVIDE GIFTED EDUCATION TO NATIVE AMERICAN STUDENTS?

Although somewhere between 3% and 5% of U.S. schoolchildren should qualify for gifted education, culturally and linguistically diverse children are not proportionally represented in those classes. As mentioned in the Giftedness and Talents Defined section of this chapter, most states determine eligibility for programs for gifted students by using scores on tests of intelligence and achievement as a minimum criterion for selection (Coleman & Gallagher, 1994). Typically, to be eligible for gifted education, a child must score at least 130 on a test of intelligence and demonstrate excellence in academics. Unfortunately, these criteria mean that proportionally fewer children from culturally and linguistically diverse groups qualify for gifted education.

Intelligence tests have been criticized for years by political and social leaders as being culturally biased and fostering discriminatory practices. Children from African American, Native American, and Hispanic communities tend not to score over 130 on these tests. Thus it appears that these tests favor the experiential backgrounds of the dominant culture and hinder the performance of children from minority backgrounds (Banks, 1994). While these children are typically overrepresented in disability categories, they are seriously underrepresented in gifted education (Brown, 1997; Harry, 1994; U.S. Department of Education, 1993).

Relatively little attention has been paid to Native American children who might be eligible for educational programs for gifted students. Underrepresentation of these students is significant. Recall that in Alaska, Native Americans comprise 25% of the population but only 15% of those receiving gifted educational services (Harry, 1994). And, in 1992, Hispanics comprised 12% of the nation's student enrollment, but accounted for only 7% of students in gifted education (Brown, 1997). How should eligibility criteria be modified to accommodate these students? Can one identification system be used for all Native American children? Standard systems are used to determine whether youngsters have disabilities and therefore qualify for special education. Should nationally normed standardized tests of intelligence and achievement not be included in the assessment batteries for Native American children? One problem with developing uniform criteria for these youngsters is that they do not come from a homogeneous group. The U.S. government recognizes 177 different tribes in this country, and 187 native languages are spoken. The poverty rate among this population is exceptionally high, moreover.

Are there really fewer Native American children who should receive specialized educational services for the gifted? Or should the process used and the criteria for entrance in such programs be different for Native Americans? If the criteria for selection are determined by the local community, should the number of students included be limited? Definitions and criteria developed at each reservation might exclude some children who would be considered gifted by the dominant culture, and they might include children who would not be typically identified as gifted but who possess certain traits valued by the local culture (Callahan & McIntire, 1994). Maker and her colleagues (1994) believe that traditional methods should be adapted by applying a flexible interpretation of Gardner's theory of multiple intelligences.

A different plan for Native American students leaves us with many questions, however. For example, should the size of these programs be limited to some percentage of the school population? Should a consistent way of identifying students be used across all tribes, or should each local community devise its own system for qualifying youngsters? What would be the content taught in these classes? If a local community decided to emphasize its culture in these classes rather than academic achievement, creativity, and problem solving, would that content be acceptable to the professional community of educators of the gifted? Who should pay for these programs? Would reimbursement (possibly from the Bureau of Indian Affairs or the state educational agency in the state where the tribe is located) be contingent on a curriculum deemed acceptable by an outside community or agency?

Certainly these issues leave considerable room for debate and discussion. How would you assist a Native American community in identifying students who should participate in specialized programs for the gifted?

In Conclusion

Look again at the Advance Organizers at the beginning of the chapter; to help you study the chapter's content, the answers to the Focus and Challenge questions are found here. Test yourself to see if you have mastered the major points of this chapter.

Summary

Gifted individuals do not have a disability that presents obstacles to their learning and participating in society. However, they can be handicapped by our social and educational systems, which present barriers to achieving to their potential. Gifted individuals possess unique intellectual abilities that can be developed into talents. One challenge facing educators is to develop and put into place a consistent array of educational options that will facilitate these individuals' development.

Focus Questions

Self-Test Questions

• *Regardless of the definition used, what descriptors can be used for gifted and talented individuals?*

Although each person is an individual, possessing unique abilities, some common descriptors apply to the group of learners who are called gifted. Under the most common definitions, these individuals are very bright and demonstrate their high intellectual abilities by scoring well on tests of intelligence, learning more quickly than their peers, and applying complex thinking skills. Their academic achievement is significantly higher than their classmates'. These individuals also tend to become leaders. Three common characteristics tend to mark this group: sensitivity, perfectionism, and intensity. Possibly because of these characteristics, many of them become successful adults.

- *What factors can inhibit giftedness and talent development?*

  Educators are interested in identifying the factors that enhance or inhibit giftedness and talent development. Clearly, a strong interplay between heredity and the environment contributes to the intellectual and talent outcomes for all individuals. For example, environmental variables, such as deprivation and lack of stimulation, can impede normal child development. Other factors—like cultural values and expectations, the family's socioeconomic level, the individual's birth position—also are related to giftedness. Also, educational opportunities can be very important to many youngsters with great potential. For them, more educational and social service programs need to be developed and made consistently available to enable these youngsters achieve their potential.

- *Why are educators concerned about issues related to underrepresentation and the various subgroups of gifted learners?*

  The nation serves fewer children as gifted than it should. Estimates indicate that between 3% and 5% of U.S. children should qualify for gifted education. However, substantially less than 3% of children from culturally and linguistically diverse groups in this country receive services. Programs for those who are gifted are not equally available to all students who demonstrate unique and outstanding abilities. Because standardized tests of intelligence and achievement tend to favor children who come from the dominant culture, fewer African American, Hispanic, and Native American children receive educational services for gifted students. These students are underrepresented in gifted education services. Also, individuals from other subgroups—those with disabilities, underachievers, and females—have less access to these programs. Programs need to be put into place that support these subgroups and meet their individual needs.

- *What are three gifted education approaches, and how do they differ from one another?*

  Different types of educational programs are used with gifted students. Some school districts provide a variety of different services, whereas others provide no special services. Few early education programs are specifically designed or available for these children. At the school level, the most common educational arrangement is the pull-out program, which functions like a special education resource room. In general, three approaches are used in gifted education: enrichment (interdisciplinary instruction, independent study, mentorships, internships, enrichment triad/revolving-door model, curriculum compacting), acceleration (advanced placement, honors sections, ability grouping, individualized instruction), and eclectic (e.g., Purdue Secondary Model for Gifted and Talented Youth). The approach most commonly used in high school is acceleration, through honors programs or advanced placement options.

- *What are the four service delivery models often used in gifted education, and how do they differ from one another?*

  Considerable debate about where gifted students should be educated is occurring at the present time. Some educators maintain that they should remain in general education classes and be offered enriched instruction by general education teachers. By enriching the entire general education curriculum, some believe that gifted education will become unnecessary. Many professionals and teachers of gifted students do not agree, believing strongly that these students must spend significant portions of their educational programs with others of comparable abilities engaging in an accelerated and enriched program. Still, the most common arrangement is the pull-out program, in which students spend several hours a day working with a specially trained teacher. Some school districts offer special classes for gifted education in which students receive almost all of their education with peers who are also highly gifted. And, although not common, some special residential schools are available.

Challenge Question

- *Why, across the history of the United States, has there been such an inconsistent commitment to gifted education?*

  Gifted education has experienced periods of great interest and periods of neglect across our nation's history. When leaders sense threats to the country's national security, education of the gifted becomes a priority. For example, education of the gifted flourished after the Russians launched the space satellite *Sputnik* in 1957, and so during the 1960s programs for gifted students were developed and expanded. The 1970s were marked by a diminishing of educational services for students who were gifted. In the 1980s, U.S. leaders again saw external threats to our economy, as standardized test scores revealed that our students were not achieving at levels of students from other nations. As a result, a national interest in gifted education was renewed. The 1990s has seen a paradigm shift in which fundamental questions about gifted education, its merits, its equity, and its value are being asked. Partly because programs for those who are gifted are not mandated by the federal laws that ensure educational programs for those with disabilities, gifted education is subject to such changes in priorities.

 ## Supplementary Resources

Scholarly Readings

Arnold, K. D., Noble, K. D., & Subotnik, R. F. (Eds.) (1996). *Remarkable women: Perspectives on female talent development.* Cresskill, NJ: Hampton Press.

Gallagher, J. J., & Gallagher, S. A. (1994). *Teaching the gifted child* (4th ed.). Boston: Allyn and Bacon.

Davis, G. A., & Rimm, S. B. (1998). *Education of the gifted and talented* (4th ed.). Englewood Cliffs, NJ: Prentice-Hall.

Clark, B. (1997). *Growing up gifted* (5th ed). Upper Saddle River, NJ: Merrill.

Colangelo, N., & Davis, G. A. (Eds.). (1997). *Handbook of gifted education* (2nd ed.). Boston: Allyn and Bacon.

Popular Books

Eberstadt, F. (1991). *Isaac and his devils.* New York: Knopf.

Fitzgerald, J. D. (1985). *The great brain.* New York: Dell.

Kanigel, R. (1991). *The man who knew infinity: A life of the genius Ramanujan.* New York: Scribner.

Kerr, B. A. (1985). *Smart girls, gifted women.* Columbus: Ohio Psychology Publishing.

L'Engle, M. (1962). *A wrinkle in time.* New York: Farrar, Straus, & Giroux.

Videos and DVDs

Amadeus (1984). Republic Pictures.
The Goonies (1985). Warner Brothers/Amblin
　　Entertainment.
Weird science (1985). Universal Pictures.
Little man Tate (1991). Orion.
Class act (1992). Warner Brothers.
Searching for Bobby Fischer (1993). Paramount Pictures.
Good Will Hunting (1998). Miramax.

Professional, Parent, and Consumer Organizations and Agencies

Gifted Child Society
190 Rock Road
Glen Rock, NJ 07452
Phone: (210) 444-6530
Web site: http://www.gifted.org/society

National Association for Gifted Children
1707 L. Street NW
Suite 550
Washington, DC 20036
Phone: (202) 785-4268
Web site: http://www.nagc.org

Mensa, Gifted Children Program
201 Main Street
Suite 1101
Fort Worth, TX 76102
Phone: (817) 649-5232
Web site: http://www.us.mensa.org

The Association for the Gifted (TAG), Council for Exceptional Children
1920 Association Drive
Reston, VA 22091
Phone: (703) 620-3660; (888) CEC-SPED
Web site: http://www.cec.sped.org

The International Center for Gifted Education and Talent Development
210 Lindquist Center
The University of Iowa
Iowa City, IA 53342
Web site: http://www.uiowa.edu/~belinctr
Phone: (319) 356-6248

National Research Center on the Gifted and Talented
362 Fairfield Road, U-7
Storrs, CT 06269-2007
Phone: (860) 486-4678
E-mail: epsadm06@uconnvm.uconn.edu
Web site: http://www.uconn.edu/nrcgt.html

MAKING CONNECTIONS

Resources to extend your learning of people
with disabilities are found at the end of every
chapter, and a fuller listing is available in
the Students' Resource Manual which
accompanies this text.

Edvard Munch, the Norwegian painter who is probably best known for the highly emotional and tormented images in his paintings, himself had a tragic childhood and troubled life. Leaving behind what he thought were the emotionless subjects of the impressionists, he sought to record the anguish of modern humanity's psyche. The result was stark and terrifying images of alienation and despair, emotions that Munch himself experienced. For many years, Munch was plagued by nervous disorders and depression. His first documented hospitalization was at a Swiss clinic in 1900 (Bischoff, 1988). During that decade, Munch had long periods of depression and a series of nervous breakdowns. In 1908, after a nervous breakdown in Copenhagen, he spent half a year in a clinic, and recovered after electroshock treatment (Grolier, 1993). Many of his paintings during this period were of the nurses and doctors who took care of him (Messer, 1985). Possibly, his most well-known painting to Americans is *The Scream.*

Melancholy was painted between 1894 and 1895, and is representative of the despair and psychological torment presented in his paintings of this period. Some believe that the man pictured here is a combination of himself and his best friend. Most certainly, the expression of pain and suffering is clear and haunting.

Edvard Munch, *Melancholy,* 1894–1895, oil on wood, 45.7 × 73.7 cm. Rasmus Meyers Samlinger, Bergen Kommunes Kunstsamlinger. Photograoh by Geir S. Johannessen. Reprinted with permission.

C H A P T E R 8

A Mother Discusses the Stigma of Emotional or Behavioral Disorders

Rebecca Viers is the mother of a teenager classified by special educators as having "emotional or behavioral disorders." Rebecca is the founder of Parents for Behaviorally Different Children. Her experiences of the past seventeen years can teach us a great deal about how to improve services for these children and their families. Here is how she describes her experiences.

Stigma. I know it well. I know stigma intimately as the mother of a 17-year-old daughter with a severe brain disorder. This is our story.

I celebrated the birth of my first and only child as any other young mother would. Jessica was so beautiful and looked so healthy. The first days of her life seemed "average" enough. It would be thirteen difficult years before I was to learn that Jessica was born with a severely abnormal brain structure.

Uncontrolled seizures began when she was 10 months old. By the age of 2, Jessica's behaviors had become quite aggressive, noncompliant, and more difficult than any day care staff cared to handle. She began to talk of "Satchuwa," an imaginary playmate whom she held responsible for the deep scratches on her arms and the handfuls of hair pulled from her head.

I made an appointment with a child specialist, the first in what would become a long line of specialists we consulted across the country. A team of professionals evaluated Jessica and declared that she, in fact, was fine—it was her mother who needed help. Well, I won't pretend that I didn't need help by then. My daughter's behaviors were becoming a greater struggle each day. No one made a connection between the seizures and abnormal behavior.

Emotional or Behavioral Disorders

I was still young and insecure, and I gave in to the professionals' theory that I must be doing something wrong. Within a year, I had tried every behavior management plan, token economy system, and time-out procedure known. All with little success. Her behavior did not improve but, instead, grew steadily worse. As a single working parent, I found myself financially drained and socially isolated. It was difficult to find baby-sitters for Jessica. Most went out the back door as quickly as they came in the front. I had no extended family to rely on. The behavior became more bizarre, and our situation seemed hopeless.

She was expelled from six or seven day care centers. Finally, she was old enough to begin public school, and I was so relieved. But Jessica lasted less than a week that first year in kindergarten. So I found a private religious preschool that would take her. But Jessica came home and told me that her teacher stood her in a circle of tape on the floor. Jessica asked me, "Mommy, how did the devil get inside of me? My teacher said that's why I'm bad. I don't want to be bad."

We endured, and when fall rolled around, I enrolled her in public kindergarten again but had her tested before classes began. She was placed in special education and then in a hospital program where I was told that her problems were a result of my own relationship with my mother and life stressors, and had nothing to do with her neurological makeup.

Challenged, I learned to use the medical library at a local university. I became determined to research "acute, infantile hemiplegia" and related behavior problems, the diagnosis she received when she suffered her first seizure. I dropped dime after dime in the copy machine so that I might enlighten the professionals with copies of the articles. My efforts were in vain. They discounted the articles by saying that research could be found to support anything. I became obsessed with learning everything I could. I found more and more research that suggested a relationship between brain dysfunction and abnormal behavior. I enrolled in graduate school in special education and specialized in behavioral disorders.

I began searching for other parents who had similar experiences with their children, and I attended a "families as allies" conference that changed my life. As I sat in that room and listened to the parents and professionals speak about how families were not responsible for these illnesses and how families have a valuable role in planning the treatment for their children, tears streamed down my face. Unlike previous tears, this time they were tears of liberation. I had been freed of my guilt and pain. Other parents had similar experiences. I clearly remember an older farmer from Idaho who, for the first time in his life, told about his daughter who became ill with schizophrenia at the age of 16. He described the pain and guilt that he and his wife had endured silently all those years. My maternal instinct, that unconditional love for Jessica, had been right all along. I felt empowered when I left the conference.

My story has a somewhat happy ending. I have found great healing in my advocacy work and in freeing other parents from the prison of blame. No parent should be blamed for biologically based disorders. In Jessica's case, her behavioral and emotional problems had more to do with her in utero environment than they ever had to do with her home environment. Programs should be family centered, with parents considered the experts on their children. I wonder how different these past seventeen years might have been for Jessica and me if such a philosophy and program had been available to us.

I would like to say that we all lived happily ever after. The reality is that Jessica, even after her successful brain surgery, still experiences many problems. She did not attend her high school football game last Saturday evening, nor was she invited to the teenage slumber party down the street. But she is getting better. She feels more positively about herself and is beginning to have greater internal control over her emotions. The future is brighter for Jessica and for us as a family.

1. In what ways might professionals have been helpful to Rebecca Viers when her daughter was young?

2. For Rebecca Viers and Jessica, how did stigma influence their situation?

Advance Organizers

Use the learning strategy—Advance Organizers—to help focus your study of this chapter's content, and reinforce your learning by reviewing answers to the Focus and Challenge questions at the end of the chapter.

Overview Children with emotional or behavioral disorders typically fall into one of two categories: externalizing behavior problems or internalizing behavior problems. Aggressive and hostile children have externalizing problems, have the poorest outcome probabilities, are identified at a greater rate, and experience more social rejection than those with withdrawn or internalizing problems. Less than 1% of all schoolchildren are identified as having this disability, but this may well reflect an underidentification of youngsters with internalizing problems and the stigma associated with these conditions.

Self-Test Questions

Focus Questions

- By identifying the components of two definitions—the one in IDEA '97 and the one offered by the National Mental Health and Special Education Coalition—how would you compare them?
- What are the two major subgroups of this disability, and how would you compare the conditions that fall into each subgroup?
- What are the major causes of this disability, and how can it be prevented?
- What are the long-term prospects for these children?
- How can teachers help children with this disability?

Challenge Question

- Why does an array of educational placement options need to be available for students with emotional or behavioral disorders?

Every day we are asked, both subtly and explicitly, to comply with mainstream society's norms and expectations. Most of us find ways to express our individuality and creativity while keeping our behavior within the boundaries of what is considered appropriate. Most children learn very early that life is easier and more pleasant when they conform to certain standards of behavior. Although these standards are rooted in a long history and tend to be rather inflexible, they do vary by situations. Judgments about the appropriateness of someone's actions are made in terms of the parameters of behavioral expectations with respect to an individual's age or the setting in which the behavior occurs.

Just as society and culture provide norms of behavior for different stages of development, it also provides norms of behavior for specific environments. Children in school, for example, are expected to be generally quiet, orderly, cooperative with other children, and attentive to learning. Children at home are expected to be cheerful, loving, helpful, and obedient to their parents. In their communities, children are expected to respect their neighbors' property, abide by curfews and traffic rules, and generally to grow into their roles as the new generation of adult leaders of society. Children whose behavior is inconsistent with expectations of normal behavior in these environments are regarded as having problems.

Sometimes problems are not so obvious. They may be hidden, as in the cases of teenage girls who constantly diet, starving to the point of endangering their health in an exaggerated effort to be fashion-model slim, or the boy who hides his suicidal depression behind a facade of perfect behavior. These hidden disorders are also serious problems, but their signs are often ignored and the conditions untreated. Don't make the mistake of thinking that all disorders are simple violations of age or societal norms. Some emotional or behavioral disorders appear to be unrelated to either; they are obvious at any age or in any culture. For example, psychosis—a major departure from normal acting, thinking, and feeling, sometimes expressed in unprovoked physical aggression toward self or others—would be considered disordered behavior at any age or in any society. Teachers and other professionals can play an important part in helping children with this disability learn in school, have more satisfying relationships with friends and family, and assume adult responsibilities in their communities. Let's see how this might be accomplished.

Opportunities for the New Millennium

Children with emotional or behavioral disorders and people with mental illness do not fare well in American society. In fact, across most of history they have been persecuted and shunned. When compared with other students, even those with disabilities, this group of students seemed to create the greatest challenges to school systems across the nation. And as guns became easier for children to possess and weapons-violence increased at schools, Congress and the public made children with emotional or behavioral disorders accountable for these threats against public safety.

Legacies from the Twentieth Century As the century came to a close, professionals and government officials were becoming alarmed about the composition of this special education category. African American males from poor families were much more likely to be identified as having emotional or behavioral disorders, and fewer of them received their education in the general education classroom. Emotional or behavioral disorders commonly occur along with other disabilities and conditions (learning disabilities, ADHD), making the delivery of an appropriate education more complicated. These students are more likely to be retained at least one grade, fail more courses, and experience an exceptionally high dropout rate; 55% of them leave school before graduating. Clearly, much work is needed to learn more about prevention techniques and educational procedures that are effective and yield better outcomes for this group of learners.

Thinking About Dilemmas to Solve  As you read this chapter, ponder these students' needs, the supports they require, and the outcomes they should achieve. Think about how:

- To reduce the overrepresentation of African American boys in this special education category
- Some schools achieve high outcomes for these students
- Successful programs can be replicated at other schools
- To increase school attendance, grade point averages, and these students' positive feelings about school
- To decrease the dropout rates of these students

EMOTIONAL OR BEHAVIORAL DISORDERS DEFINED

As the introduction makes clear, **emotional or behavioral disorders (EBD)** are difficult to define. In fact, some think that people are identified as having this disability "whenever an adult authority said so" (Hallahan & Kauffman, 2000, p. 249). In other words, in many cases the application of the definition is subjective. Throughout most of the latter part of the twentieth century, definitions of this disability, including the one used in IDEA '97, are based on the one developed by Bower (1960, 1982). Let's first look at the federal definition and then at one that may become the national definition for the new millennium.

Children in school are expected to pay attention to their schoolwork, but this expectation can be difficult for students with behavior disorders and emotional disturbance.

emotional or behavioral disorders (EBD). A condition of disruptive or inappropriate behaviors that interferes with a student's learning, relationships with others, or personal satisfaction to such a degree that intervention is required.

IDEA '97 uses the term **emotional disturbance** to describe children with behavioral or emotional disorders, defining it as follows:

> The term means a condition exhibiting one or more of the following characteristics over a long period of time and to a marked degree that adversely affects a child's educational performance:
>
> - An inability to learn that cannot be explained by intellectual, sensory, or health factors.
> - An inability to build or maintain satisfactory interpersonal relationships with peers and teachers.
> - Inappropriate types of behavior or feelings under normal circumstances.
> - A general pervasive mood of unhappiness or depression.
> - A tendency to develop physical symptoms of fears associated with personal or school problems.
>
> The term includes children who are schizophrenic. The term does not include children who are socially maladjusted, unless it is determined that they have an emotional disturbance. (U.S. Department of Education, 1999, p. 12422)

For a review of IDEA '97, see Chapters 1 and 2 and also the What IDEA '97 Says boxes found in many chapters of this text.

IDEA '97 changed the label for this special education category. Older versions of IDEA used the term *serious emotional disturbance* to describe this disability area, but "serious" was dropped from the IDEA '97 definition. The government did not, however, change the substance of the disability when it changed the term. Here's what it said about the deletion: "[It] is intended to have no substantive or legal significance. It is intended strictly to eliminate the pejorative connotation of the term 'serious'" (U.S. Department of Education, 1999, p. 12542). In addition, some implied parts of the federal definition are important to understand. For example, although only one of the characteristics listed in the IDEA definition needs to be present for the student to qualify for special education, those behaviors must adversely affect the child's educational performance. Because almost everyone has some mild maladjustment for short periods of their lives, the definition also requires that the child exhibit the characteristic for a long time, and to a marked degree or significant level of intensity.

The IDEA term and definition have been criticized by many professionals (Kauffman, 1997). The use only of the word *emotional* in the term seems to exclude students whose disability is interpreted as behavioral. In the definition, the exclusion of students who are "socially maladjusted," which is not defined, contributes to this misunderstanding. And the reference to "school performance" has been narrowly interpreted to mean only academic performance, not behavioral or social performances, not functional or life skills, and not vocational skills.

Responding to these criticisms, a coalition of seventeen organizations, which calls itself the National Mental Health and Special Education Coalition, drafted another definition and continues to lobby federal and state governments to adopt it for the new millenium (Forness & Knitzer, 1992). Here is the coalition's proposed definition:

> The term emotional or behavioral disorder means a disability characterized by behavioral or emotional responses in school so different from appropriate age, cultural, or ethnic norms that they adversely affect educational performance. Educational performance includes academic, social, vocational, and personal skills. Such a disability:
>
> - is more than a temporary, expected response to stressful events in the environment;
> - is consistently exhibited in two different settings, at least one of which is school-related; and

emotional disturbance. A term that is often used interchangeably with emotional or behavioral disorders.

- is unresponsive to direct intervention in general education, or the child's condition is such that general education interventions would be insufficient.

Emotional and behavioral disorders can coexist with other disabilities.

This category may include children or youths with schizophrenic disorders, affective disorders, anxiety disorder, or other sustained disorders of conduct or adjustment when they adversely affect educational performance in accordance with [the opening part of the definition]. (p. 13)

Although not everyone agrees about how to best describe children with emotional or behavioral disorders, consensus about three defining characteristics exists (Hallahan & Kauffman, 2000). The individual's behaviors are: extreme, chronic, and unacceptable. In other words, the behaviors are not just unusual, nor are they short-term or temporary, and they are inappropriate across cultures. Peers and adults frequently respond negatively to students who have these characteristics. Therefore, their needs almost always extend into other areas of their lives outside of school, and multidisciplinary teams—psychologists, psychiatrists, physicians, social workers, family counselors, and others—are required to meet the individual needs of each specific child.

TYPES

Emotional or behavioral disorders are often categorized by whether they are primarily externalizing (typically aggressive) behavior problems, internalizing (typically withdrawn) behavior problems, and low incidence disorders (e.g., schizophrenia). Of course there are other ways of classifying these disorders. For example, the *DSM-IV* (American Psychiatric Association, 1994) provides a section for disorders usually first diagnosed in children. Some of these disorders are considered as disabilities (mental retardation, learning disabilities) by the federal government and the special education community, while others are not (motor skills disorders, tic disorders, mood disorder, oppositional defiant disorder). Since this system is confusing and not easily applied to school situations, the classification scheme of externalizing behaviors and internalizing behaviors is used in this text. Table 8.1 on page 326 defines and explains some of the common behaviors and disorders observed using this system of classification. Remember, conditions that are more disturbing to other people are identified more often and earlier. Internalizing disorders, maybe because they do not bother others, are not always identified, leaving children without appropriate special educational services. Teachers must be alert not only to externalizing disorders but also to the equally serious, although less disruptive, internalizing disorders. Also, emotional or behavioral disorders can coexist with other disabilities. Therefore, a section is devoted to these special challenges.

Externalizing Behavior Problems. **Externalizing behaviors** are aggressive behaviors expressed outwardly, usually toward other persons. Some typical examples are hyperactivity, a high level of irritating behavior that is impulsive and distractible, and persistent **aggression**. Table 8.1 lists some examples of externalizing behavior problems. Here, three common problems are discussed: hyperactivity, aggression, and delinquency.

Hyperactivity is probably one of the most common complaints about children referred for evaluations as having emotional or behavioral disorders. Hyperactivity is also a defining symptom of ADHD. Hyperactivity is difficult to define; the judgment

externalizing behaviors. Behaviors, especially aggressive behaviors, that seem to be directed toward others. **aggression.** Hostile and attacking behavior, which can include verbal communication, directed toward self, others, or the physical environment.

Table 8.1 Examples of Externalizing and Internalizing Behavior Problems

Externalizing Behaviors	Internalizing Behaviors
Violates basic rights of others	Exhibits painful shyness
Violates societal norms or rules	Is teased by peers
Has tantrums	Is neglected by peers
Causes property loss or damage	Is depressed
Is hostile	Is anorexic
Argues	Is bulimic
Is defiant	Is socially withdrawn
Is physically aggressive	Tends to be suicidal
Ignores teachers' reprimands	Has unfounded fears and phobias
Steals	Tends to have low self-esteem
Damages others' property	Has excessive worries
Demonstrates obsessive/compulsive behaviors	Panics
Causes or threatens physical harm to people or animals	
Uses lewd or obscene gestures	
Is hyperactive	

MAKING CONNECTIONS

ADHD is also discussed in these sections of the text: Solutions (Chapter 1), Children with Learning Disabilities (Chapter 4), Co-existing ADHD (Types) in this chapter, Concepts and Controversy in this chapter, and Types of Physical Impairments (Chapter 9).

about whether a certain level of a specific activity is too much or "hyper" is often subjective. If, for example, the activity is admired, the child might be described as energetic or enthusiastic rather than hyperactive. Nevertheless, the *DSM-IV* gives some good examples about which there is considerable consensus. Use their illustratives and see if you can arrive at a definition of hyperactivity:

> Hyperactivity may be manifested by fidgetiness or squirming in one's seat, by not remaining seated when expected to do so, by excessive running or climbing in situations where it is inappropriate, by having difficulty playing or engaging quietly in leisure activities, by appearing to be often "on the go" or as if "driven by a motor," or by talking excessively. (American Psychiatric Association, 1994, p. 79)

Aggression may be turned toward objects, toward the self, or toward others. The *DSM-IV* does not directly define aggression, but it does include elements of aggression in two of the disorders it describes: conduct disorders and oppositional defiant disorder. Of the latter, the manual identifies:

> a recurrent pattern of negativistic, defiant, disobedient, and hostile behavior toward authority figures ... and is characterized by the frequent occurrence of at least four of the following behaviors: losing temper, arguing with adults, actively defying or refusing to comply with the requests or rules of adults, deliberately doing things that will annoy other people, blaming others for his or her mistakes or misbehavior, being touched or easily annoyed by others, being angry and resentful, or being spiteful or vindictive. (American Psychiatric Association, 1994, p. 91)

Aggressive behavior, particularly when it is observed in very young children, is particularly worrisome. This is not just because of the behavior itself—which should not be minimized—it is because of its strong correlation to long-term problems

For more about delinquency and the juvenile justice system, see the "Children with" section in this chapter.

socially maladjusted. A term applied to a group of children who do not act within society's norms but who are excluded from the definition of children with emotional or behavioral disorders.

conduct disorders. Behavior patterns that are externalizing, including "acting out" and hyperactivity; this condition alone does not qualify as a disability according to IDEA.

internalizing behaviors. Behavior that is withdrawn, directed inward, or focused on oneself.

anorexia. Intense fear of gaining weight, disturbed body image, chronic absence or refusal of appetite for food, causing severe weight loss (25% of body weight).

bulimia. Chronically causing oneself to vomit, limiting weight gain.

depression. A state of despair and dejected mood.

(dropping out of school, delinquency, violence). A pattern of early aggressive acts beginning with annoying and bullying, followed by physical fighting, are clear pathways, particularly for boys, leading to violence in late adolescence (Talbott & Thiede, 1999).

Delinquency, or juvenile delinquency, is defined by the criminal justice system rather than the medical or educational systems. Delinquency refers to illegal acts committed by juveniles, which could include crimes such as theft or assault. Remember, some children who are delinquent have emotional or behavioral disorders, but many do not—just as some children with emotional or behavioral disorders are delinquent and many are not. However, it is very important to understand that many of these children are at great risk for being involved with the criminal justice system (Edens & Otto, 1997). Their rates of contact are disproportionately high. While still in high school, 20% have been arrested, as compared to 9% of all students with disabilities. By the time they are two years out of school, 35% have been arrested (2½ times higher than the general population) (Koyanagi & Gaines, 1993).

Two groups of children who exhibit disturbing behavior are not eligible for special education services (unless they have another qualifying condition as well): Children who are **socially maladjusted** and those with **conduct disorders.** *Neither* is included in the IDEA '97 definition. Although social maladjustment is widely discussed, particularly as politicians and educators talk about discipline and violence in the schools, it is not called out as a special education category or a subcategory of emotional or behavioral disorders in IDEA '97. However, Section 504 and ADA do not have exclusions for social maladjustment, so the education system is required to make accommodations for these students despite the fact that they do not qualify for special education services (Zirkel, 1999). Although the law and courts are clear about social maladjustment and conduct disorders not being subsets of emotional or behavioral disorders, practice is not (Costenbader & Buntaine, 1999). There are many reasons for this situation. Some reasons are related to definitional issues. For example, no generally agreed-upon definition of social maladjustment exists, though many people simply refer to these students as "naughty." Conduct disorders are not defined in IDEA, though they are in the *DSM-IV*. According to that manual, the essential feature of this disorder is "a repetitive and persistent pattern of behavior in which the basic rights of others or major age-appropriate societal norms or rules are violated (American Psychiatric Association, 1994, p. 85). Second, many experts are afraid that being more inclusive will cause an explosion in the special education enrollment, increasing their numbers beyond tolerance and acceptability. Third, others strongly feel that they should be included in this special education category, so their needs can better be met by specialists prepared to deal with their problems, and ways should be found to serve and identify them as having emotional or behavioral disorders even if technically they do not qualify (Kauffman, 1997).

Internalizing Behavioral Problems. **Internalizing behaviors** are typically expressed by being socially withdrawn. **Anorexia** and **bulimia** are two examples of internalizing behaviors. Discussions of depression and anxiety, which also fall into the internalizing category, are included here. Surprisingly, students who identify themselves as ADHD describe themselves as having more internalizing behaviors and are more introspective about their problems (Volpe et al., 1999).

Depression is often difficult to recognize in children. Its components—such as guilt, self-blame, feelings of rejection, lethargy, low self-esteem, and negative self-image—are often overlooked or may be expressed by behaviors that look like a

For more about Section 504 of the Rehabilitation Act and the ADA law, see the Necessity for National Intervention section of Chapter 1.

Autism is discussed in Chapter 12.

anxiety disorders.
Conditions causing painful uneasiness, emotional tension, or emotional confusion.
schizophrenia. A rare disorder in children that includes bizarre delusions and dissociation with reality.
Tourette's syndrome.
A low incidence disability that is characterized by multiple and uncontrollable motor and/or verbal tics.
ecological assessment. A procedure that includes observational data collected in the student's natural environments for the purpose of identifying the antecedent events that cause a problem behavior or consequent events that maintain or increase the target behavior.

different problem entirely. Children's behavior when they are depressed may appear so different from the depressed behavior of adults that teachers and parents may have difficulty recognizing the depression. For example, a severely depressed child might attempt to harm himself by running into a busy street or hurling himself off a ledge. An adult might assume the behavior was normal because many children accidentally do those things, or they might minimize its seriousness. In addition, children usually do not have the vocabulary, personal insight, or experience to be able to recognize and label feelings of depression.

Anxiety disorders may be demonstrated as intense anxiety or separation from family, friends, or a familiar environment, excessive shrinking from contact with strangers, or unfocused, excessive worry and fear. Anxiety disorders are difficult to recognize in children. Because withdrawn children engage in very low levels of positive interactions with their peers, peer-rating scales may help educators with identification. Children with internalizing behavior problems, regardless of the type, tend to be underidentified, leaving many of them at risk for being untreated or receiving needed services later than they should.

Low Incidence Emotional or Behavioral Disorders. Some disorders occur very infrequently, but are quite serious when they do occur. For example, schizophrenia, Tourette's syndrome, and autism* can have tragic consequences for the individuals involved and their families, and thankfully do not have high prevalence rates.

Schizophrenia, sometimes considered a form of psychosis or a type of pervasive developmental disability (American Psychological Association, 1994), is an extremely rare disorder in children, although approximately 1% of the general population over the age of 18 has been diagnosed as having schizophrenia. When it occurs, it places great demands on service systems. It usually involves bizarre delusions (such as believing thoughts are controlled by the police), hallucinations (such as voices telling the person what to think), "loosening" of associations (disconnected thoughts), and incoherence. Schizophrenia is most prevalent between the ages of 15 and 45, and experts agree that the earlier the onset, the more severe the disturbance in adulthood (Newcomer, 1993). Children with schizophrenia have serious difficulties with schoolwork and often must live in special hospital and educational settings during part of their childhood. Their IEPs are complex and require the collaboration of members from a multidisciplinary team.

Another low incidence disorder, occurring in about 4 to 5 individuals per 1,000, is **Tourette's syndrome.** This disorder is characterized by multiple tics (sudden, rapid, recurrent, and stereotyped motor movements or vocalizations). These individuals might engage in uncontrollable movements at different locations in the body, or they may make strange noises or say inappropriate words or phrases. Or they may have both motor and verbal tics. The verbal tics may be sounds like grunts, yelps, snorts, barks, or obscenities. This disorder causes considerable distress to the individual involved, and impairs all aspects of the person's life (American Psychiatric Association, 1994).

Coexisting ADHD. Researchers now understand that emotional or behavioral disorders often coexist with other disabilities or conditions, and when this happens

---

*The federal government has decided that autism is in a separate disability category, and therefore it is discussed in Chapter 12. Regardless, it is important to understand that this issue is not resolved and many professionals believe that autism should be considered as one of the conditions included in emotional or behavioral disorders.

ADHD is also discussed in these sections of the text: Solutions (Chapter 1), Children with Learning Disabilities (Chapter 4), Concepts and Controversy in this chapter, and Types of Physical Impairments (Chapter 9).

NEW DIRECTIONS
FOR THE
MILLENNIUM

Legacy: Throughout the last century, concern grew about the overrepresentation of diverse students in special education programs, and professionals and parents were most alarmed by the number of African American boys identified as having emotional or behavioral disorders.

Opportunities:

- Develop early intervention programs aimed at preventing emotional or behavioral disorders
- Create proactive methods and alternative treatment programs for handling inappropriate behavior, particularly in inner-city, high-poverty schools

students need very special help because their problems are very serious (Bussing, Zima et al., 1998). So how common is this situation? In one study of children with ADHD, it was found that 42% received special education services under the emotional or behavioral disorders category (Bussing, Schoenberg, et al., 1998). It is interesting that 25% of the students with ADHD in that study received no mental health services. In another study, researchers learned that, proportionally, ADHD coexists more often with emotional or behavioral disorders than it does with learning disabilities (Bussing, Zima, et al., 1998). And more of these students received medications, like Ritalin, to control their behaviors.

IDENTIFICATION

Standards for normal behavior change as children grow up and move through the stages of their lives. Infants, for example, are expected to be messy and dependent and to communicate through gurgles, facial expressions, and crying. Toddlers, in turn, go through routine stages when temper tantrums and resistance are tolerantly interpreted as the predictable "terrible twos." As children progress through childhood and adolescence, accepted stages of development, including even rebelliousness, are usually viewed as predictable and appropriate for the age of the child. However, some children behave contrary to the predicted stages of child development in our society. An 8-year-old who suddenly begins to wet the bed, clings to his mother, and stops talking creates great concern about his behavior. Even though almost identical behavior would be totally accepted in an infant, an 8-year-old who acts in this way is perceived as having a problem. Think of examples of behavior that draw concerns about children of one age but, if demonstrated by a child of a different age, do not raise questions at all. The subjective judgments about behavior and what constitutes a disability continue to plague educators in this new millennium.

Concerns about this category of special education began in the latter part of the 1990s and are not resolved today. Some concerns center on one particular group of students identified as having this disability. It is now clear that a disproportionate number of African American males, particularly children who are disruptive, are identified as having emotional or behavior disorders (Cluett et al., 1998). While these boys are overrepresented, other groups, like Asian Americans and girls, are underrepresented. In part because there has been little consensus about the definition of emotional or behavioral disorders or the criteria associated with it, a single, reliable method for identifying these children does not exist. Therefore, efforts will continue as the century unfolds to develop new and better diagnostic procedures. Current knowledge can guide educators' actions until more accurate assessment procedures are available:

- Evaluation measures should come from at least two different settings
- Performance in both academics and social skills should be considered
- Information about the child should come from different people who fill different roles
- A variety of methods to assess students' behavior should be used (behavior rating scales, **ecological assessments,** classroom observations, ABC analyses, interviews, projective tests, standardized tests, social work evaluations, psychiatric analyses, functional assessments)

Research continues in an effort to develop more precise assessment instruments. One test is proving to be reliable, efficient, and inexpensive: The *Systematic Screening*

Appropriate services help students with emotional or behavioral disorders enjoy improved self-concepts and satisfying school experiences.

for Behavior Disorders (SSBD) is designed for systematic screening of all students in an elementary school (Walker et al., 1994). This instrument uses the conceptual model of externalizing and internalizing behaviors as the organizing system for this disability area. Professionals believe that by screening all students in a school, early identification and early treatment can prevent some problems from becoming more serious and get services to those who need them as quickly as possible. Another benefit is that groups of students with this disability who have a high probability of being underidentified have a better chance of getting the services they need.

SIGNIFICANCE

This group of special education students can be set apart from their peers with disabilities (U.S. Department of Education, 1994, 1998). They have lower grades than any other group. They are more likely (77% of them) to fail at least one class during high school. They often experience grade retention. Probably because of their lack of success academically, half of them drop out of school, often by tenth grade—the highest dropout rate of all groups of students with disabilities. And they have a high probability of encountering the juvenile justice system (Oswald & Coutinho, 1996; U.S. Department of Education, 1998). Their educational programs are also different from those of their peers with and without disabilities. Possibly because of the excessive number of externalizing behaviors they present, their educational programs focus almost exclusively on behavior management and social adjustment. Unfortunately, the balance of these features with either academic or vocational components is typically not achieved.

Dismal outcomes for students with emotional or behavioral disorders, unfortunately, are typical, and for those with coexisting disabilities they are most often quite certain. For example, when emotional or behavioral disorders coexist with learning disabilities—which could be in about 20% of the cases of learning disabilities—problems compound and tend to be quite severe (Handwerk & Marshall, 1998). Difficulties in both the social and academic areas probably stem from poor language development (Gallagher, 1999). When a student has trouble mastering academic and social skills, intensive instructional and behavioral interventions are necessary. And these interventions should be supported by services from an SLP.

Obviously, emotional or behavioral disorders have grave impacts on the life of the individual, whether child or adult, who has the disability. Without intervention, the person is likely to live with emotional pain and isolation, perhaps even engage in ever-increasing antisocial activity. Once students with behavioral and emotional problems are identified and receive appropriate services, they generally improve their academic skills, enhance their personal relations, and enjoy more satisfying

MAKING CONNECTIONS

Review the section about social competence and language impairments in the Children with Speech or Language Impairments section of Chapter 5 to understand the relationship between language and social skills.

relations with other people. This disability also affects relationships with their family members, adults, their peers, and their teachers—who have the highest turnover rates in the education field (U.S. Department of Education, 1998).

HISTORY OF THE FIELD

MAKING CONNECTIONS

Review the history of care and treatment of people with disabilities by reading again the Origins of Special Education section of Chapter 1 and the History sections in Chapters 3–12.

Throughout history, people have recognized emotional or behavioral disorders particularly in adults, but this disability was often confused with other disorders (Safford & Safford, 1996). It was probably Leo Kanner's 1935 book *Child Psychiatry* that stimulated the development of services for children in America. In ancient times, people believed that individuals who had emotional or behavioral disorders were possessed by the devil or evil spirits. During some periods—as in ancient Egypt— treatment was enlightened and humane (Deutsch, 1949). However, the mystery surrounding mental illness often fostered negative assumptions about its causes and resulted in horrible treatment. Some societies believed that these disorders were contagious, and these people were removed from the community so others would be protected. Treatments of those days reflected such beliefs and commonly included excessive punishment, imprisonment, placement in poorhouses, beatings, chainings, straitjacketing, and other cruel actions.

The first institution for people with mental disorders was established in London in 1547. Officially named St. Mary of Bethlehem, it became known as Bedlam, a term that now means a place of noise and uproar. Individuals in this institution were chained, starved, and beaten. A popular form of entertainment in London was to take the family, including children, for an outing to view the "lunatics" at Bedlam.

By the eighteenth century, changes began to occur through the efforts of reform-minded individuals. For instance, Philippe Pinel, a French psychiatrist, in 1792 ordered humanitarian reform, including unchaining, for mental patients at the Salpêtrière, a Paris asylum for the "insane" (Brigham, 1847). In the United States, major reform in the identification and treatment of children and adults with emotional or behavioral disorders began with the efforts of reformers in the 1800s. Benjamin Rush (1745–1813), considered the father of American psychiatry, proposed more humane methods of caring for children with these problems. (Rush, a signer of the Declaration of Independence, was not only a leader in the American independence movement, but also a founder of the first American antislavery society.)

Samuel Gridley Howe, in addition to his work in blindness and mental retardation, worked to improve the treatment of people with mental disorders. Dorothea Dix influenced the founding of state institutions for people with mental disorders. By 1844, many states had institutions for people with mental disorders, and the Association of Medical Superintendents of American Institutions for the Insane (now the American Psychiatric Association) was founded. But the hope with which early institutions were founded soon gave way to pessimism as the institutions became primarily custodial.

Before the late 1800s and the initiation of public school classes for children with emotional or behavioral disorders, most of these children received no services at all. The passage of compulsory education laws toward the end of that century caused educational services for these students to be developed, even though many attended ungraded classes along with other students who did not adapt well to general education settings. In 1871, a class for students who were regarded as troublemakers was opened in New Haven, Connecticut. It is interesting that many of the early public

Philippe Pinel, chief physician at Salpêtrière, freeing patients with mental disorders from their chains.

wraparound services. A service delivery model whereby all of the child's needs are met through the coordination of the education system, mental health agencies, social services, and community agencies.

school classes provided many noneducational services to these students. These multidisciplinary services often included mental health, health care, and other social services; much like the **wraparound services** being proposed today. In 1909, William Healy founded the Juvenile Psychopathic Institute in Chicago, where he and Augusta Bronner conducted studies of juvenile offenders (Healy & Bronner, 1926). At about this same time, the theoretical work of Sigmund Freud (1856–1939), the founder of psychoanalysis, and his daughter Anna Freud began to influence the education and treatment of children with emotional or behavioral disorders both in Europe and in the United States.

By the twentieth century, professionals realized that children needed special programs, teachers, and teaching techniques. Around 1935, Lauretta Bender at Bellevue Hospital pioneered the development of educational services for children with emotional or behavioral disorders. She even convinced the local public schools to provide the teachers for students living on the wards of the hospital, an exceptionally innovative concept at the time. Meanwhile, Karl Menninger, his father, and his brother revolutionized American psychiatry by stressing a "total environment" of kindness and treatment for patients with mental disorders. Bruno Bettelheim began his work with children with severe emotional disturbance at the University of Chicago in 1944. His ideas about the value of a "therapeutic milieu" continue to be used in many classrooms.

The 1960s and 1970s saw many advances for children with emotional or behavioral disorders, as many researchers, scholars, and educational developers created new ways to teach these students. In 1962, Norris Haring and Lakin Phillips published *Educating Emotionally Disturbed Children*, a book that described their experimental work in the public schools of Arlington, Virginia. Their approach stressed

Dorothea Dix, the social policy activist, changed the course of treatment for people with mental disorders across the United States.

behavioral principles, a structured environment, and interactions between the child's home and school environments. Meanwhile, Eli Bower, working in California, developed a definition of behavioral disorders that is the basis for the federal definition and the definitions used in many states today (Bower & Lambert, 1962).

Two highly successful programs were developed in the 1960s. Project Re-Ed was begun in the 1960s by Nicholas Hobbs. This landmark effort, conducted in Tennessee and North Carolina, clearly showed that an ecological approach, in which children attended residential schools for short periods of time and returned to restructured community and family environments, could effect major changes in the lives of very troubled children. Another major demonstration effort was conducted in California at about the same time. In what was known as the Santa Monica Project, Frank Hewett developed the engineered classroom, a highly structured classroom environment based on behavior management principles.

The publication in 1964 of the classic applied behavioral analysis study of the effects of teacher attention on a preschooler's social interactions with his peers during playtime began the generation of new knowledge about the importance of the environment on people's actions (Allen et al., 1964). The development of applied behavioral analysis techniques with children in applied settings—initiated by Montrose Wolf, Don Baer, and Todd Risley—was instrumental to the application of token economies in classroom settings nationwide. Montrose Wolf became the first editor of the *Journal of Applied Behavior Analysis (JABA)*, which became the primary means for disseminating behavioral research conducted with human subjects during this early period when the knowledge base about behavioral analysis was developing. Wolf is also credited with developing the Teaching-Family Model, which was begun at the University of Kansas with boys with emotional or behavioral disorders who were living in group homes and later extended to a well-known program at Boy's Town in Nebraska. These pioneering efforts have been successfully replicated across the nation, both at schools and in residential settings.

PREVALENCE

It is difficult to accurately estimate the prevalence of emotional or behavioral disorders for two major reasons. First, the definition remains unclear and subjective. Second, because the label is so stigmatizing, many educators and school districts are reluctant to identify many children as having this disability. Only 0.74% of all schoolchildren are identified as having this disability (U.S. Department of Education, 1998). Many believe that this is not due to an actual lower prevalence rate for these youngsters, but rather to a reluctance of educators to so label and identify children (Oswald & Coutinho, 1996). Some believe they are being conservative when estimating that approximately 3% to 6% of all students have this disability (Kauffman, 1997). Clearly, the number of students with emotional or behavioral disorders who receive special education services in the schools is much smaller than the total number of children with emotional or behavioral disorders in this country.

For more about the over- and underrepresentation of diverse students in special education, see the Prevalence section in Chapter 3.

Important factors in prevalence are gender and race. Clear differences show up in the identification of this exceptionality: Most children (some 74%) identified as having emotional or behavioral disorders are male, which is the highest ratio of boys to girls in special education categories. Reasons for this gender difference are not clear, but it is probably linked to boys' higher propensity to be troublesome and violate school rules, and girls' tendency toward less disruptive, internalizing behaviors that are less likely to result in referral. While Asian Americans tend to be underrepresented in this special education category, African Americans are overrepresented: 21% of these students are Black, although they only represent 14% of the student population (McCabe et al., 1999; U.S. Department of Education, 1998). The disproportional representation by racial variables in this special education category is related both to bias and to culture (Peterson & Ishii-Jordon, 1994). For example, more Asian American students are now being identified, but on close examination it has been found that these students are recent immigrants, war refugees who probably do not understand the behavioral expectations of their new homeland (McCabe et al., 1999). As you have learned, new identification practices are being developed, but in the meantime, cultural and gender bias can be reduced by including evaluation of all aspects of the individual's performance through multiple measures—academic achievement, social skills, and classroom behavior (Cluett et al., 1999). Educators must be certain that bias has not influenced their decisions about specific children and their abilities.

CAUSES AND PREVENTION

The causes of emotional or behavioral disorders in an individual are usually unknown, and thus how to prevent this disability also remains elusive. Children are so unique, our scientific study of biological causes so young, the interactions of children and youth with their families and environments so complex, and the interactions with society so individual that we can almost never point to any one variable with certainty as the cause of the emotional or behavioral disorders. We do know, however, that children who experience abuse and turmoil in their daily lives are at great risk for developing this disability. So how substantial is the problem? In 1996, slightly more than 3 million children were reported to social service agencies as suspected cases of neglect or abuse, and these cases are definitely on the increase (Children's Defense Fund, 1999). Almost 40% of these cases were children under the age of 6, and a disproportionate number of them were Black or Native American. Figure 8.1 shows the principle categories of abuse and neglect.

CAUSES

At least three general areas can contribute to emotional or behavioral disorders: biology, home and community, and school. Again, the reasons for problems in a particular child are difficult to identify, and the disability is likely to be the result of multiple and overlapping factors.

Biology. As researchers have discovered and continue to look for biological causes for some types of disorders (e.g., fetal alcohol syndrome [FAS], Down syndrome, autism, Tourette's syndrome), they are seeking biological causes for emotional or behavioral disorders as well. Their efforts are beginning to yield some results. For

- For more about FAS and Down syndrome, see Chapter 6.
- For more about autism, see Chapter 12.

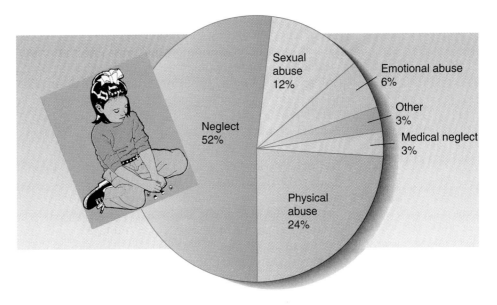

Figure 8.1 **Abuse and Neglect**

Source: Data cited in *The state of America's children: Yearbook 1999* by Children's Defense Fund, 1999, Washington, DC: Author, and U.S. Department of Health and Human Services, Children's Bureau, Administration for Children and Families (1998).

example, there may be a biological dimension to psychological disorders such as anorexia or bulimia. Research now tells us that a definite relationship exists between prenatal drug exposure and childhood emotional or behavioral disorders, with 53% of drug-exposed participants in Headstart preschool programs being identified as having these disabilities as early as kindergarten (Sinclair, 1998). Mood disorders, depression, schizophrenia, and attention deficit hyperactivity disorder may have a genetic foundation (American Psychiatric Association, 1994). Knowing whether biological reasons are part of the cause of a disorder can play a role in treatment. For example, knowing that depression has a biological cause allows for the development and use of medications. Antidepressants are now an important component in many treatment programs for depression. As researchers continue to find biological causes, more medical treatments will become available.

Home and Community. Children, like older people, do not live in a social vacuum. They are members of an immediate family, an extended family, and a variety of communities (neighborhood, church, clubs). All of these comprise the environments that shape and influence each individual's growth and development—whether positive or negative. Rarely does a single negative experience lead to or aggravate emotional problems, but combinations of abuse, neglect, parental stress, inconsistent expectations and rules, confusion and turmoil over long periods of time can. Also, being poor is a contributing factor (Bussing, Zima et al., 1998). So, too, are lack of supervision, erratic and punitive discipline, low rate of positive interactions, high rate of negative interactions, lack of interest and concern, and poor adult role models. For example, children whose parents are violent and have arrest records also tend to become violent and find themselves in trouble with the law (Hallahan & Kauffman, 2000; Rudo et al., 1998). The link with poverty is also clear:

Students whose family incomes are under $12,000 are 2.5 times more likely to drop out of school than those whose families make over $25,000 (Osher & Osher, 1996). On the other hand, healthy interactions, such as warmth and responsiveness, consistent discipline, demand for responsible behavior, along with modeling, teaching, and rewarding desired behaviors can promote positive behaviors in children. Thus, teachers must keep in mind that each child is an individual; there are no general cause-and-effect explanations for why a particular person develops a particular disorder at a particular time.

School. Teachers have tremendous influence in their interactions with students. Teachers' expectations affect the questions they ask students, the feedback they give, and the number and character of their interactions with students. Problems can get better because of teachers' actions, and they can get worse. In other words, what educators do makes a difference. For example, a teacher who is unskilled in managing the classroom or insensitive to students' individual differences may create an environment wherein aggression, frustration, or withdrawal are common responses to the environment or the teacher. And teachers who are skilled at managing classroom behavior, systematically select interventions that match the students' behavior, and are consistent in their application of those interventions can improve students' outcomes (Myles & Simpson, 1998; Rivera & Smith, 1997; Smith & Rivera, 1993). Good teachers are able to analyze their relationships with their students and the learning environment, and they keep close watch on problems and potential problems. Here are some key components of safe and effective schools (McLane, 1997; Walker & Gresham, 1997):

- Consistency of rules, expectations, and consequences across the entire school
- Positive school climate
- Schoolwide strategies for conflict resolution and dealing with student alienation
- High levels of supervision in all school settings
- Cultural sensitivity
- Strong feelings by students of identification, involvement, and bonding with their school
- High level of parent and community involvement
- Well-utilized space and lack of overcrowding

PREVENTION

Prevention of emotional or behavioral disorders can be accomplished. In some cases, techniques can be directed toward eliminating the major causes of these disorders. For example, the behavioral effects of fetal alcohol syndrome can be prevented if pregnant women do not drink. In other cases, prevention consists of eliminating or ameliorating the symptoms of the disability at its initial onset. Standard practices used by teachers in their classrooms can make a real difference and serve to prevent disruption and the need for disciplinary actions (Montague et al., 1997). Teachers can help students learn self-management and other techniques that will actually help them avoid situations that lead to conflict or disruption.

Although knowledge exists about how to reduce or prevent some problems associated with emotional and behavioral disorders, necessary actions are usually not taken. In a provocative commentary, Jim Kauffman (1999) points out that despite discussions about the importance of prevention efforts, actions in the last decade of

MAKING CONNECTIONS

For other ideas about behavior management, see the Achieving Discipline boxes in Chapters 3–12 and the Effective Discipline section (Educational Interventions) of this chapter.

functional assessments. Similar to ecological assessment except that behaviors are manipulated (where they are not in the other system) to determine those events that cause and maintain target behaviors.

ABC model. A behavioral way to analyze and select interventions by looking at whether they occur antecedent to (before), concurrent with (during), or consequent to (after) the target behavior.

NEW DIRECTIONS
FOR THE
MILLENNIUM

Legacy: Despite increased discussions about creating ways to prevent low achievement and unruly school settings while also including students with disabilities who have challenging behaviors, few comprehensive strategies were verified through research and implemented across a variety of school settings.

Opportunities:

- Conduct research and development activities which lead to proven measures to prevent and deal with aggressive and violent behaviors in school settings
- Create a flexible and responsive array of treatment programs for students with, at risk for, emotional or behavioral disorders

More about functional assessments is found in Critical Features of Special Education Programs and the IEP Process sections (Chapter 2) and the Research to Practice box in Chapter 12.

the twentieth century did not match the rhetoric. Possibly for fear of misidentifying children, public systems tend to provide intervention services too late, when chance of success is reduced. Intervention must begin early and deliberately. Clearly, for most children, even those with low risk, classroom interventions can be most successful. However, Kauffman estimates that some 5% to 10% of students in general education may require intensive, intrusive, individualized interventions. But the way the education system is set up "prevents prevention." This is how Kauffman thinks it should work:

- Reward desirable behavior
- Punish, through nonviolent means, undesirable behavior
- Provide direct instruction for both social and academic skills
- Correct the environmental conditions that foster deviant behavior
- Give students clear expectations
- Standardize responses to children across the entire school setting
- Monitor students' behavior closely

In addition to Kauffman's suggestions, other methods can prevent inappropriate behavior. **Functional assessments** help to determine what events cause the behavior to occur and what other events contribute to the behavior's increase or maintenance (Tobin et al., 1996). Many teachers use a less complicated system that helps accomplish this goal. The **ABC model** uses the *antecedent, behavior,* and *consequence* events to target behavior with specific interventions. This model is further explained in the Achieving Discipline box on page 338.

What teachers do in school and classroom settings can make a real difference in reducing *and* preventing behavior problems for both those at risk for emotional or behavioral disorders and those already so identified (Kamps et al., 1999). Here's what works:

- Behavior management, including a point system for appropriate behavior and task completion, charting good behavior, and earning rewards
- Systematic intervention plans, where a hierarchy of tactics is used dependent on students' behavior
- Home–school communication that includes notes home and home-based reward systems
- Peer involvement
- Classroom structure with guided practice and well-organized transitions from activity to activity
- Supervised free periods (recess, hall changes, lunch)
- Consistent standards (held by all school staff members) applied to behavior, with high expectations for academic performance

CHILDREN WITH EMOTIONAL OR BEHAVIORAL DISORDERS

Emotional or behavioral disorders can affect a student's functioning beyond behavior problems or inappropriate emotional expression. The student will likely exhibit learning impairments that affect both academic performance and social interactions with peers and the teacher. Table 8.2 on page 339 lists typical signs or characteristics that these children often exhibit.

Achieving Discipline

GETTING TO KNOW THE BEHAVIOR: ABC ANALYSIS

Damion lived in a housing project with his mother and four sisters. He attended an inner-city, high-poverty school and was in fourth grade. Damion had been identified as being at risk for emotional or behavioral disorders when he was in kindergarten, and was actually identified as having this disability when he was in second grade. Damion's life away from school was in constant turmoil, and his behavior at school seemed to reflect a lack of structure, consistency, and support at home. Some teachers described him as moody. Toward the beginning of the school year, his teachers noticed that his attitude and behaviors were changing; he was becoming more aggressive, hostile, and out of control. He increasingly displayed anger with his peers both in the classroom and during recess and lunch breaks. It seemed to his teachers that his anger began with hostile language and sometimes escalated to a physical action, usually toward an object. He might toss a book, throw a ball away from the sports activity, and even overturn a desk. However, after an incident in which he shoved a classmate, his teachers decided to learn more about this behavior pattern, for they worried that his aggression was accelerating to a point where he might actually hit a peer. Because the seriousness of his aggression was recent and not yet to a level where the school's management team was concerned, Damion did not have a BIP as part of his IEP.

Damion's special education and general education teachers decided to conduct an ABC Analysis. They wanted to see if there was a definite pattern to Damion's behavior, and also to collect more information for the IEP team and others who would conduct a functional behavioral assessment if it was decided that Damion needed a BIP. The first thing they did was carefully observe Damion's behavior and take notes in an organized fashion. The purposes of this process were to discover the events that "caused" or preceded what his teachers were calling aggressive behavior, to describe precisely what constituted aggression for Damion, and to note the events that followed the inappropriate behaviors. To collect this information, his teachers systematically took notes in a three-column format. The first column was labeled "A" (for Antecedent); the second column, "B" (for the Behavior); and the third column, "C" (for Consequences). Here's what they found: 97% of Damion's aggressive behavior was verbal, and resulted from frustration with schoolwork or with a game he was unable to play correctly. And, to everyone's surprise, the response to Damion's aggression was very consistent. He received a lot of attention, more than he received at any other time during the day. Armed with this information his teachers developed a plan and strategy that adjusted schoolwork, provided peer tutoring to help him learn the rules of games played during recess, and set up rewards for academic performance and loss of privileges for even the slightest violation of the classroom rules.

Conducting an ABC Analysis

- Set aside a block of time each day when someone can observe the target student
- Use a three-column format for collecting information
- Write down descriptions of the events that preceded the inappropriate behavior, the behavior of concern in behavioral terms, and the events that followed the behavior
- Fine-tune the descriptions with multiple observations

SOCIAL SKILLS

Students with emotional or behavioral disorders, possibly more than any other group of children with disabilities, present problems with social skills to themselves, their families, their peers, and their teachers. Whether their problems are externalizing or internalizing, developing social competence or behaving appropriately are usually major goals on these children's IEPs. Deficits in social skills, rather than aca-

Table 8.2 Possible Signs or Characteristics of Emotional or Behavioral Disorders

Has problems with
    Adults, particularly those in authority
    Family relationships
    Peers
    Social skills

Demonstrates
    Hyperactivity
    Aggression toward self or others
    Impulsivity
    Distractibility
    Depression and unhappiness
    Suicidal tendencies
    Withdrawal into self
    Anxiety or fearfulness

For other discussions of ADHD, see:
- The question about ADHD in the Solutions section of Chapter 1
- The Prevalence and ADHD (Children with Learning Disabilities) sections, the IDEA '97 box, and the Concepts and Controversy section in Chapter 4
- The Defined section in Chapter 10

demic difficulties, may be the actual reason these students are removed from the academic mainstream (Walker et al., 1994). Being able to use appropriate social skills makes it possible to achieve three important goals:

1. Initiate and develop positive social relationships with others
2. Cope effectively with the behavioral demands and expectations of specific settings
3. Appropriately communicate and assert one's needs, desires, and preferences

Social skills are the foundation for practically all human activities in all contexts (academic, personal, vocational, and community). We use social skills to interact with others and perform most daily tasks. We believe that they should be considered functional life skills that are monitored by educators, just as academic skills are.

Those who are deficient in social skills, and will not be able to develop social competence independently, should receive instruction in this target area. Overwhelming evidence now exists to show that students can profit greatly from instruction in social skills (Locke & Fuchs, 1995; Walker et al., 1994). However, not all social skills training programs are effective (Quinn et al., 1999). Effective programs teach specific skills (e.g., how to interact with others) to individuals rather than teaching global skills (e.g., self-concept, self-esteem) to groups.

Including social skills training as part of the curriculum for students with emotional or behavioral disorders seeks to replace excessive behaviors, specific to the individual, with positive alternatives (Deveres, 1999a). Teaching social skills takes time, and it is wise to allot a minimum of three twenty- to thirty-minute blocks of time each week to a well-researched instructional program.

PEER PERCEPTIONS

What do classmates of students with emotional or behavioral disorders think about these peers? The answers to this question are important because they influence educators' integration efforts. Unfortunately, the answers are not favorable for youngsters with this disability (Safran, 1995). First, educators should recognize that young children without disabilities can clearly discriminate externalizing behavior disorders from nondisordered behavior. They do so by the age of 7. Second, they have exceptionally negative feelings about peers who act out, exhibit aggressive behavior, or are antisocial. Interestingly, girls have stricter standards than boys, and are more sensitive to aggressive behavior. Third, children with externalizing behaviors are considered less desirable for friendship. Fourth, children without disabilities do not recognize internalizing behavior problems—like being socially withdrawn—until about seventh grade. But when they do, the depressed child is less liked, considered less attractive as a friend, and thought to need therapy. During these later school years, externalizing and antisocial behaviors are considered most problematic by peers, and clearly lead to social rejection by these peers. Children without disabilities have much more compassion and understanding for peers with medical problems than for those with psychological disorders.

JUVENILE JUSTICE, DELINQUENCY, AND VIOLENCE

Lack of discipline and increasing violence in American schools have been topics of great concern for some time. That schools are experiencing more violence is of no doubt, and that violence is serious (as evidenced by the 1999 murders at Columbine High School in Colorado and 1997 and 1998 killings at high schools in Pearl, Mississippi; West Paducah, Kentucky; Springfield, Oregon; and Jonesboro, Arkansas). Clearly, aggression—both verbal and physical—is on the increase, but the reasons are open to speculation. Some scholars and social observers, however, do have some ideas (Begley, 1999; Bender & McLaughlin, 1997):

1. Aggression and violence observed in schools is simply a mirror of society in general
2. Children who see a high rate of violence become desensitized and come to believe the behavior is acceptable
3. Fewer hospital and center school placements are available, resulting in more of these students attending general education classes where few supports exist
4. General education teachers are untrained to deal with violence and aggression

Because of the violence in America's high schools during the last part of the twentieth century, the public as well as education professionals understand the importance of being prepared for "worst case scenarios." Weapons violence has become a national concern. As Americans puzzle about the "whys," school personnel must ponder the predictors and prevention. Although the overall incidence of juvenile crime decreased during the last decade of the century, some believe that the intensity of school violence increased (Bender & McLaughlin, 1997). Despite raised public attention, statistics indicate that school violence is not on the increase, and is comparatively rare (Children's Defense Fund, 1999). Regardless, even one case in five years demands that schools be prepared, and researchers are turning their attention to the problem and are providing teachers and administrators with guidance about how to prevent school violence and what actions to take if it does occur (Bender & McLaughlin, 1997; Myles & Simpson, 1998). The Accommodating for Inclusive Environments box provides some sage guidance.

Possibly, the link between delinquency and disabilities is the strongest with children identified as having emotional or behavioral disorders. For example, despite some earlier research to suggest otherwise, a direct relationship between learning and disabilities is *not* strong (Malmgren et al., 1999). This new finding reflects better sta-

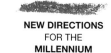

NEW DIRECTIONS
FOR THE
MILLENNIUM

Legacy: During the twentieth century, children with disabilities caught in the juvenile justice system were the most excluded group of students, often not receiving special education services or having modifications made to the little general education instruction they received.

Opportunities:

- Develop seamless transition systems from local schools to juvenile justice and back to the local schools
- Within all juvenile justice systems, create appropriate education programs that support high school graduation and/or the development of vocational skills

Accommodating for Inclusive Environments

BEING PREPARED FOR SCHOOL VIOLENCE

Be alert to

- Whispers and talk of potential confrontation
- Unattended book bags and backpacks
- Students with a history of violence
- Closed classroom doors

Make plans for

- Teacher buddy systems
- The sounds of gunshots
- Hostage crises
- All clear signals

Practice for a crisis by knowing

- Where students should go during an incident
- Who to notify
- Roles for every staff member

Train and inform all school staff members about

- General methods used to resolve conflict
- Standard procedures to follow
- The contents of every Behavior Intervention Plan

Be prepared to

- Develop trust and positive relationships with all students
- Consistently apply behavioral techniques and consequences
- Dress appropriately (comfortable shoes, loose clothing)
- Put valuables and fragile items out of reach

Apply these principles if a crisis occurs

- Remain calm and in control
- Keep tone of voice steady and firm
- Seek assistance
- Ignore accusations

---

tistical analysis methods that can now factor out confounding variables like poverty, age, and ethnicity. However, the relationship between emotional or behavioral disorders and serious juvenile problems is clear. Signals of later problems are clear in young boys and girls (Day & Hunt, 1996; Miller-Johnson et al., 1999; Strain & Timm, 1998; Walker & Sylvester, 1994):

- Problem behaviors are clearly established at ages 4 to 5
- Overt (e.g., bullying) and covert (e.g., stealing) antisocial activities are becoming behavior patterns
- Problems happen across settings (at home, school, and in the community)
- The child is both overactive and inattentive
- Extreme aggression is frequent

Of these five characteristics of young children prone to later problems, the single best predictor is aggression. And without intervention, problems tend to persist. For example, sixth graders referred for special services because of both violent and nonviolent inappropriate social behaviors are likely to present chronic discipline problems during their remaining school years, and also to drop out of school (Tobin & Sugai, 1999). Children with the five characteristics listed above are likely candidates for other negative outcomes: substance abuse, teen pregnancy, suicide, AIDS, poor marital relations, chronic unemployment, and psychiatric disorders (depression and personality disorders). Long-term follow-up studies now prove the effectiveness of early intervention for these individuals, so it is critical that action be taken when these youngsters are preschoolers (Strain & Timm, 1998).

ACADEMIC PERFORMANCE

Students with emotional or behavioral disorders typically do not perform well academically, regardless of intellectual potential (Kauffman, 1997). They could be referred to as underachievers. Many of them lack basic reading and math skills. Of course, the more severe the disability, the greater overall performance is affected. Clearly, being in personal turmoil affects one's ability to attend to school tasks and learning in general. Failure at academic tasks compounds the difficulties these children face not only at school, but also in life. Their frustration with the educational system (and its with them) results in these students having the highest dropout rates of all students (U.S. Department of Education, 1998). The outcomes of students who do not complete high school are not good. Thus, a teacher must, in addition to helping the child with behavior, teach academic skills.

EDUCATIONAL INTERVENTIONS

Education is extremely important for children with emotional or behavioral disorders. As you will learn, unfortunately, most students with this disability have poor educational outcomes. The blame for such dismal results of the last century must rest, in part, with the educational system and its inability to meet the complex needs of these children. As you think about the sections you have read and integrate that information with what you will read next, consider how these goals could be met in classroom settings.

EDUCATION AND THE PRESCHOOL CHILD

Look at Table 8.1 again to refresh your memory about externalizing behavior disorders.

It is difficult to identify some types of emotional or behavioral disorders in young children. For example, internalizing behavior problems are not usually identified until children of school age. However, extreme externalizing behaviors are often obvious by age 4 or 5. Sometimes severe disabilities, such as a psychosis, manifest themselves during the early developmental period as well. Regardless, it is unusual for preschoolers to be identified as having this disability, even though it is advantageous to identify a child's emotional or behavioral disorder as early as possible.

The early identification and management of young children with this disability has many benefits (Feil et al., 1995; Walker et al., 1998). First, problem behaviors seen in preschoolers tend to be very stable over time. In other words, they do not go away without intervention, and they even worsen. The behavior problems seem to follow a progression like the following: disobedient at home, having temper tantrums, teacher reports of fighting or stealing. Second, they are predictive of future learning problems and delinquency. Third, children with early onset of antisocial behavior (e.g., aggression) account for only 3% to 5% of this population, but they account for 50% of all crimes committed by children and youth. Fourth, if children's disorders can be identified early, professionals might be able to intervene with the child and family at an early stage, and avoid predictable negative outcomes.

Early intervention can rectify problems before they become more serious or develop into well-established patterns, help avoid a later need for psychotropic medication to control behavior, reduce stress in the family, and allow for changes in the young child's behavior when the possibility for change is strongest. In a developing strand of longitudinal research, Phil Strain and his colleagues are demonstrating the power of early intervention (Strain et al., 1982; Strain & Timm, 1998, 1999). They are following up the forty individuals, now in their late twenties and early thirties, who participated in the Regional Intervention Project (RIP), a behavioral intervention preschool program for children at risk for behavior disorders. Although data are still being collected, outcomes are amazing and contrary to what is expected for young children displaying the serious aggressive and asocial behaviors of this group. So far, researchers have interviewed eighteen parents, and found that two of the former participants in the RIP program are enrolled in doctoral programs, three have earned master's degrees, three have received bachelor's degrees, five others are enrolled in college programs, three are high school graduates, and the remaining three are high school dropouts. Compare these results with those typically seen for comparable groups, who have a 55% dropout rate. Other early intervention programs have also shown the power of such programs. For example, the one developed by Hill Walker and his colleagues, First Step to Success, again shows that early intervention programs can make a real difference (Walker et al., 1998). This is particularly true when the programs have the following components:

- Parent involvement
- Teaching, through examples, the relationship between behavior and its consequences
- Instruction on appropriate behaviors for different settings (**setting demands**)
- Showing how to make and keep friendships

EDUCATION AND THE SCHOOLCHILD

Many different approaches are used in the education and treatment of schoolchildren with emotional or behavioral disorders. Which approach is selected depends on the conceptual model the professional uses for teaching these children. Table 8.3 on page 344 lists seven major conceptual models of treatment and education. This overview is meant to illustrate the range of options and orientations available—from clinical to behavioral to holistic to eclectic. Generally, educators incorporate various elements of many of these approaches into their educational programs for these children. Since a major focus of school programs is to increase the child's academic success in school, many teachers find the behavioral approach, in combination with elements from one or two others, most useful for educating these children.

In this section, only a few key elements of successful programs are highlighted. Because it is essential that teachers evaluate the effectiveness of their instruction, measuring student progress by using curriculum based assessment techniques is discussed first. Then, your attention is focused on effective discipline techniques, because externalizing behavior problems are of great concern to many of these students' teachers, peers, and families. It is critical that teachers systematically match the best tactic with the specific target behavior; the principles of effective discipline help educators accomplish this goal. Third, because students with this disability are prime candidates for corporal punishment, some cautions and concerns, and some data, about its application in school settings is presented in this section. And,

setting demands. The behavioral requirements, both obvious and subtle, of an environment.

Table 8.3 Conceptual Models in the Treatment of Children with Emotional or Behavioral Disorders

Behavioral approach	Based on the work of B. F. Skinner and other behaviorists, this model focuses on providing children with highly structured learning environments and teaching materials. The student's behaviors are precisely measured, interventions are designed to increase or decrease behaviors, and progress toward goals is measured carefully and frequently.
Psychoanalytic (psychodynamic) view	Based on the work of Sigmund Freud and other psychoanalysts, this model views the problems of the child as having a basis in unconscious conflicts and motivations: based not on the behavior itself, but on the pathology of one's personality. Treatment is generally individual psychotherapy, long term, and designed to uncover and resolve these deep-seated problems.
Psychoeducational approach	The psychoanalytic view is combined with principles of teaching, with treatment measured primarily in terms of learning. Meeting the individual needs of the youngster is emphasized, often through projects and creative arts, through everyday functioning at school and home.
Ecological approach	The problems of the child are seen as a result of interactions with the family, the school, and the community. The child or youth is not the sole focus of treatment, but the family, school, neighborhood, and community also are changed in order to improve the interactions.
Social–cognitive approach	The interactions between the effects of the environment and the youngster's behavior are taught to the child. This approach seeks to integrate and reconceptualize behavioral and cognitive psychology. The result is a view that behavior is the result of interactions in a person's physical and social environments, personal factors (thoughts, feelings, and perceptions), and the behavior itself.
Humanistic education	Love and trust, in teaching and learning, are emphasized; and children are encouraged to be open and free individuals. The approach emphasizes self-direction, self-fulfillment, and self-evaluation. A nonauthoritarian atmosphere in a nontraditional educational setting is developed.
Biogenic approach	Physiological interventions such as diet, medications, and biofeedback are used, based on biological theories of causation and treatment.

Source: Schema is borrowed from *Characteristics of Behavioral Disorders of Children and Youth* (6th ed., pp. 111–124) by J. M. Kauffman, 1997, Columbus, OH: Merrill.

finally, a developing curricular area that holds great promise for students with emotional or behavioral disorders is discussed: self-determination.

Curriculum Based Measurement (CBM). Teachers often use CBM to measure a child's academic gains and thereby evaluate the effectiveness of their instruction. For example, teachers use CBM to measure the percentage of words spelled correctly, the number of new arithmetic facts memorized, reading fluency (how quickly the child reads), and the ability to write topic sentences in writing assignments. They also use this method to measure social behaviors of individual children, to see if they improve with the application of various interventions.

To measure progress in complex areas, the teacher first breaks down those areas into precise behaviors. It is important that the behavior specifically of concern is the one targeted for intervention and measurement. Then, the appropriate data collection system is selected. There are many simple choices for such record keeping, including: tallies (or sheer counts of the frequency of the target behavior's occurrence during a consistent observation period), duration (how long the target behavior lasts during a constant time period), percentage (what proportion of the day the target behavior occurs), or rate (how many times the behavior occurs per minute). The

MAKING CONNECTIONS

Curriculum based measurement is discussed in the Appropriate Evaluations section of Individualized Special Education Programs (Chapter 2).

Learning to take turns is a crucial skill for children to learn. For some it is a difficult learning experience.

measurement of the specific target behavior occurs daily, and across enough time to allow comparisons under different treatments. In other words, how well did the student behave before the teacher implemented a reward system, how well did the student behave while the intervention was in effect, and does that behavior change maintain?

Let us look at an example. Terrell is a kindergartner who has exhibited extreme externalizing behaviors since coming to school. In particular, the multidisciplinary team—which includes the district's school psychologist; a family therapist; a social worker; the school nurse; Ms. Kea, Terrell's special education teacher; Ms. Steppe-Jones, his general education teacher; and members of his family—is concerned about his aggressive behavior. The team discusses what constitutes aggression for Terrell, and these are the behaviors they identify: physically attacking others, bullying, and hitting. They also decide that the setting to begin intervention is the lunch recess, where the problems seem to be the worst. They also decide that after a short assessment phase (to be sure they have targeted the right behaviors and to have a set of data to compare future progress to) the first intervention they will try is contingent instructions ("Don't hit!" after each act) paired with criterion-specific rewards (five minutes of free time at the end of the day for "beating" yesterday's score). Every lunch period, Ms. Kea counted the number of aggressive acts committed by Terrell and noted them on the evaluation chart shown in Figure 8.2 on page 346. As you, and the members of the multidisciplinary team, can see, systematic and careful intervention planning caused remarkable improvement in Terrell's behavior.

MAKING CONNECTIONS

Behavioral Intervention Plans and functional assessments are discussed in the IEP Process (Chapter 2).

Behavioral Intervention Plans. Of this there is no question: The American public's concern about violence at schools and discipline in the classroom is growing. IDEA '97 reflects concerns of Congress and the public about violence, discipline,

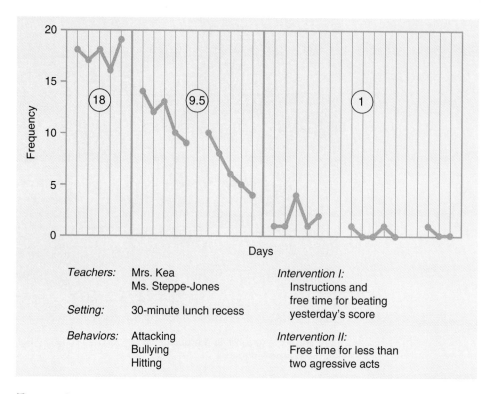

Figure 8.2 Terrell's Evaluation Chart

and special education students. Before this latest version of IDEA was passed, students with disabilities could not be expelled if their disruptive behavior was caused by the disability. Students with emotional or behavioral disorders were typically protected by what used to be called the "stay put provision." Under that provision educational services could not be stopped, and these students could not be expelled from school. IDEA '97 changed that protection. Students with disabilities who violate school rules, particularly in the areas of weapons violence and drugs, are not subject to disciplinary actions like their peers without disabilities. But there are limits, and the end result is that students with disabilities who are violent or "out of control" will have a Behavioral Intervention Plan (BIP), which seeks to eliminate the undesirable behavior and replace it with appropriate ones. The BIP becomes part of the student's IEP and is developed by conducting a functional behavioral assessment. (See the What IDEA '97 Says About box for what the law says about BIPs and functional assessments.)

Most students with emotional or behavioral disorders, particularly those with externalizing behavior problems, have a BIP as part of their IEP. While these plans focus on functional behavioral assessments, they should also stress development of positive social skills (Deveres, 1999a, 1999b). Keep in mind the importance of teaching functional skills and balancing time allotments in favor of instruction over assessment or paperwork. BIPs are a new requirement of IDEA '97, so the basic contents of these plans will probably evolve during the beginning of this century. Some guidelines are now available about these plans and what they should contain (Hartwig & Ruesch, 1998):

Functional Behavioral Assessments and Behavioral Intervention Plans

Either before or not later than ten days after taking a disciplinary action against a student with disabilities because of weapons or drug violations:

- An IEP meeting is called to develop an assessment plan to address the target behavior (for those students without a Behavior Intervention Plan [BIP])
- The IEP team will review and modify the student's BIP (for those who already have a BIP)
- The BIP will include a functional behavioral assessment which operationally defines the behavior in multiple settings, the antecedent and consequent events, and the function or purpose of the behavior
- The BIP will include a hypothesis about the behavior and the intervention likely to positively influence it
- The BIP will describe intervention and acceptable alternative, substitute behaviors to be taught to the student

1. Definition of the behavior(s) and behavioral indicators that had led to the problem behavior previously
2. Description of the classroom rules and the consequences to be implemented when a rule is broken
3. Actions by school personnel resulting from students' behaviors that could be described as aggressive or assaultive are clearly described and followed
4. Consequences and rewards for positive behaviors that are incompatible with unacceptable ones are listed in the plan and delivered

BIPs are now part of an overall strategy to work effectively with students who have behavior problems, but they must coordinate with more general plans and procedures to keep disruption to a minimum.

Effective Discipline. A systematic discipline strategy, in which a hierarchy of interventions is systematically applied, helps to create safe school settings where violence and abuse are eliminated (Myles & Simpson, 1998). Educators are charged with the responsibility of helping students learn maximally, whether the topic of concern is basic academic skills, general or specific knowledge, or social skills. Effective and efficient instruction cannot occur in chaos nor in a repressive environment. What is required is a positive learning climate where children can learn, create, discover, explore, expand their knowledge, and apply new skills. When the amount of disruption is high, causing educators to spend time and energy addressing conduct problems, students do not learn either effectively or efficiently. Disruption—whether from several individuals or most of the class—can be held to a minimum without destroying the climate needed for learning. To accomplish this goal, teachers need to be armed with an array of proven interventions and know when they are most appropriately applied. And interventions applied systematically through a progression, a hierarchy, are most effective (Kamps et al., 1999).

To help teachers better understand how to match interventions with the level and severity of disruptive behavior, Smith and Rivera (1993) use the **Intervention Ladder** (see Figure 8.3). The foundation upon which the ladder stands includes basic preventive measures that good teachers incorporate into all of their instruction. For example, educators are encouraged to make school challenging and exciting, so all students are actively engaged in learning and less likely to be disruptive (Nelson et al., 1996). Also, all members of the school community must be aware of the basic rules or standards of behavior, and everyone must consistently apply the same consequences when the standards are violated (Nelson et al., 1998). The Intervention Ladder illustrates one hierarchy of interventions, starting from the simplest and least intrusive to the most complex and punitive. Only after evaluation procedures indicate that a mild intervention is not successful are more drastic procedures implemented.

Many students with emotional or behavioral disorders need extra special help to maintain self-discipline. For example, the teacher may have to spend much more

Figure 8.3 The Intervention Ladder
Source: From *Effective discipline* (2nd ed.) (p. 17) by D. D. Smith & D. P. Rivera, 1993. Austin, TX: Pro-Ed. Reprinted by permission.

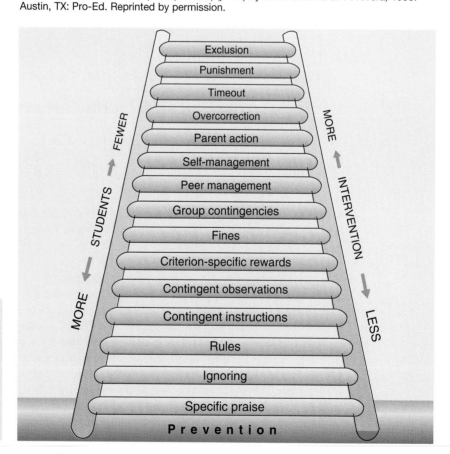

Intervention Ladder. A hierarchy of disciplinary tactics organized from the least intrusive and least complex to the most intrusive and most complicated.

time discussing the school and classroom rules so that these students have a clear idea of the behaviors required. Some of the requirements students must meet in academic environments are obvious, such as keeping quiet when the teacher is talking or joining the other students in the line to go to the lunchroom. But some setting demands are more subtle, and for students with this disability direct and concise instructions are often required so they understand how they are supposed to behave. For example, the student is expected to make eye contact with the teacher when speaking in the hallway, take turns in group games, or sit with good posture when school administrators visit the classroom. Violations of setting demands such as these can lead to students being perceived as lacking in discipline. Problems can be prevented, however, by specifically teaching children to meet the demands of the environment by encouraging them to learn self-management techniques (McDougall, 1998). In this approach, students develop skills required to assess their own performance objectively, measure and monitor their behavior often by keeping data, and determine and schedule rewards for improved behavior. When the rules are broken, however, the teacher must ensure that the consequences are consistently and fairly applied.

Corporal Punishment. Corporal punishment is high on the Intervention Ladder, but I decided to spend a little time discussing this intervention because of its overall negative impact on students and the school environment. All educators should be aware of the potentially devastating effects corporal punishment can have on children. And, despite the negative attention it provides and the lack of research to support its use, corporal punishment persists (Lohrmann-O'Rourke & Zirkel, 1998). Those most vulnerable to its application are students with disabilities, students from poverty, and culturally and linguistically diverse boys.

As you learned in the previous section, there are many alternatives to corporal punishment. Here, let's review what punishment is. Many people mistakenly believe that punishment must necessarily involve physical hitting, screaming, or embarrassment for the child. Punishment, however, is technically defined as any consequence that reduces the rate or strength of the behavior being punished, which means that many different tactics—including corporal punishment—fall within this category. Some teachers find that certain forms of punishment can be an important part of an effective teaching plan to change unwanted behaviors. For example, mild reprimands, temporary withdrawal of attention, or the loss of certain privileges are all punishing tactics (they are intended to reduce the frequency of the target behavior), but do not have the negative long-term effects of corporal punishment (Smith & Rivera, 1993). Some general guidelines for the use of punishment are listed in Table 8.4 on page 350.

Corporal punishment should be *avoided* in school settings. It may temporarily stop undesired behaviors, but it certainly does not teach new skills that students can use to achieve their goals. It may also cause the teacher to become engaged in a power struggle with the student, an unhealthy negative interaction that the youngster has, in effect, dictated. Excessive use of harsh punishment by a teacher can change the classroom to a battleground where the focus is on power and coercion. When a teacher uses corporal punishment, the teacher is modeling a negative style of interaction that other students, as well as the one being punished, may copy in their interactions with others. Remember, any form of punishment should always be accompanied by teaching a new behavior. All classrooms must be safe and orderly environments where students can feel secure to attempt the difficult tasks of learning and trust the educators charged with this important responsibility.

Table 8.4 Guidelines for Using Punishment

1. Punishment should be used only when the behavior is very serious or dangerous.
2. Other tactics should be tried first.
3. Although parental permission is not required for most forms of punishment, Repp and Dietz (1978) suggested that it be granted in writing before the technique occurs so the student will understand why and when punishment will be used.
4. If the behavior does occur, no threats or warnings should be given.
5. The behavior should be stopped as soon as it is noticed.
6. The behavior should be punished each and every time it occurs.
7. The punishment should be of substantial and uniform intensity (it is best not to use mild forms and then gradually increase the intensity).
8. Other positive behaviors of the student should be reinforced. When punishment is used, it should not be the only intervention in effect; there also should be positive elements of the program.

Source: From *Effective Discipline* (pp. 144–145) by D. D. Smith and D. P. Rivera, 1993, Austin, TX: Pro-Ed. Reprinted with permission.

Self-Determination. What is **self-determination**? Because this area is so new, the definition is evolving. However, here are some of the outcomes researchers believe should occur when students have mastered a self-determination curriculum (Martin & Marshall, 1995). After studying these outcomes, even without a proper definition, you should have an understanding of what self-determination is and why gaining these skills is important to individuals with disabilities, particularly those with emotional or behavioral disorders. Successful individuals

- Know how to choose
- Know what they want and how to get it
- Choose goals and persistently pursue them
- Make their needs known
- Evaluate progress toward meeting their goals
- Adjust their performance and create unique approaches to solve problems
- Become their own best advocates

How did researchers arrive at these outcomes? They studied successful people and identified some common characteristics that probably contributed to their achievements. The conclusions they reached also should help you further understand this curriculum area better.

> Successful people know what they want and persistently go after it. They decide upon major goals, set a timeline, develop specific plans to attain their goals, determine the benefits that reaching the goals will bring, close off discouraging influences and thought, and build coalitions with others who share similar goals and who encourage each other in reaching those goals.... When peak performers make decisions, they (a) chose a mission leading to an action; (b) envision and communicate a clear mission; and (c) develop an action plan consisting of specific goals and benchmarks to evaluate the timing, quality, and quantity of the results. (Martin & Marshall, 1995, p. 147)

self-determination. A set of behaviors that include making decisions, choosing preferences, and practicing self-advocacy.

Many individuals with disabilities do not develop the characteristics you just read about. Instead of becoming increasingly independent as they gain years and experience, many become more dependent. Some do not feel comfortable making choices for themselves; while others make inappropriate choices because they do not possess the skills or strategies necessary to make wise decisions. Some researchers suggest that this situation may be due in part to the special education experience (Wall & Dattilo, 1995). Students are not given sufficient opportunities to make choices or decisions. When the opportunities do arise, they are not systematically guided in making decisions. Some believe that instructional environments should be restructured to become more "option-rich, responsive, and informational environments" (Wall & Dattilo, 1995, p. 289) where self-determination opportunities are infused into the schoolday. Others believe that a more direct approach is necessary, where self-determination becomes a topic for instruction.

Several researchers have been working to develop a set of materials or procedures teachers can use to help their students become proficient in the behaviors that comprise self-determination (Serna & Lau-Smith, 1995). By using the list in Table 8.5 on page 352, teachers could develop activities that would help students learn skills that comprise self-determination.

MAKING CONNECTIONS

To review the educational placement options available through special education, see the Special Educational Services section in Chapter 2.

COLLABORATION FOR INCLUSION

Children with emotional or behavioral disorders receive their education in a variety of settings. While many are included in the general classroom, many others can be found in special education classrooms, special schools, community based residential group homes, halfway houses, institutions, and hospitals. Coutinho and Oswald (1996) conducted a four-year study of the educational placement patterns of children with emotional or behavioral disorders. Their findings reveal some interesting information about these students and how their needs are met in America's educational system. First, they found that despite the movement toward inclusion

Although being included in sporting events and learning how to be a member of a team are instructional topics for some students, these important social skills are usually mastered with the aid of systematic instruction.

Table 8.5 Self-Determination Skills List

Prerequisite Social Skills
> Giving positive feedback
> Giving criticism
> Accepting criticism
> Resisting peer pressure
> Negotiation
> Following instruction
> Conversation
> Problem solving

Self-Evaluation Skills
> Evaluating present skills
> Evaluating skills needed for future goals

Self-Direction Skills
> Goal setting
> Goal planning
> Self-management

Networking Skills
> *Informal Networking*
>> Seeking information (trusted adult)
>> Seeking advice (trusted adult)
>> Initiating activities and joining activities
>> Dealing with rejection
>
> *Formal Networking*
>> Enlisting help of others to achieve goals
>> Formal meeting behaviors with network mentors
>> Developing strategies to achieve goals
>> Evaluating outcomes

Collaborative Skills
> Determining team needs
> Teaming to develop goals
> Planning strategies for goal attainment
> Implementing strategies
> Evaluating outcomes

Persistence and Risk-Taking Skills
> Persistence through problem solving
> Risk taking through decision making

Dealing with Stress
> Recognizing feelings
> Expressing feelings appropriately
> Stress reduction skills
> Time-management skills

Source: From "Learning with purpose: Self-determination skills for students who are at risk for school and community failure" by L. A. Serna and J. Lau-Smith, 1995, *Intervention in School and Clinic, 30,* p. 144. Reprinted by permission.

and more integration of special education students into general education classes, the placement rates of students with emotional or behavioral disorders changed little across the time period they studied. Second, the placement pattern for this group of students is different than that of other students with disabilities: They are included less in general education classrooms. Let's take a closer look at placement rates reported by the federal government and others (Edens & Otto, 1997; U.S. Department of Education, 1998):

- Almost 20% of students with emotional or behavioral disorders (as compared to less than 5% of their peers with disabilities) attend school at segregated settings, either separate schools or facilities.
- Less than 24% of them receive services in general education classes (as compared to 46% of all students with disabilities).
- About 50% of all students with disabilities in residential programs are identified as having this disability.
- Some 60% of students in the juvenile justice system may have been identified by schools as having emotional or behavioral disorders.
- For these students, separate special education classes is the most common educational placement option used.

Issues about inclusion spark controversy in special education. For the group of students with emotional or behavioral disorders, it is no different. One report will raise concerns that so few of these students are integrated with nondisabled peers (U.S. Department of Education, 1998), while another stresses the need to maintain a full continuum of services that includes separate, highly specialized programs (Bussing, Zima, et al., 1998). Particularly for those who have externalizing behaviors which are aggressive, general educators seem to agree: They are neither trained nor equipped to handle these children, and general education settings are not equipped to control these children's behaviors nor provide necessary therapeutic instruction (Cheney & Barringer, 1995). In addition, some experts question the benefits experienced by these students when placed in general education classrooms (Hallenbeck & Kauffman, 1995). Although many educators and parents of students with disabilities presume that students benefit from being exposed to socially appropriate peer role models, this may not hold true for students with emotional or behavioral disorders. It is only through intensive direct instruction that these children learn correct social behaviors (Walker et al., 1995).

So it may be that inclusion may not be desirable in some cases and may not be a possibility in others. Students who are being detained by the criminal justice system, for example, are unable to participate in inclusion classes. During the time of their incarceration, it is especially important that their educational needs not be neglected. Students have a right to receive appropriate and individualized special education even if they are in correctional settings such as halfway houses, jails, or prisons. Unfortunately, children in these settings often do not receive the education they need, which many believe should include a functional curriculum, social skills, and skills used in the community (Sinclair et al., 1998; Walker & Gresham, 1997).

TRANSITION THROUGH ADULTHOOD

The outcomes for students with this disability are not good, particularly for those who received no vocational training and left high school without a degree (Rylance, 1998). In fact, they are some of the worst for all students with disabilities (Chesapeake

NEW DIRECTIONS
FOR THE
MILLENNIUM

Legacy: As the new millennium began, it was apparent to special educators that the education system was least successful for students with emotional or behavioral disorders, with almost all markers (academic achievement, graduate rates, dropout, integration, contact with juvenile justice system) being negative.

Opportunities:

- Rethink what comprises an appropriate education for students with emotional or behavioral disorders and research the efficacy of different long-term approaches
- Develop partnerships with an array of agencies (community, medical, legal, social services) to provide supports for individuals with emotional or behavioral disorders and their families

Institute, 1994). Although some of these data were presented in earlier sections of this chapter, the impact of putting them together in the following information points is dramatic. Students with emotional or behavioral disorders:

- Have lower grades than any other groups of students with disabilities
- Fail more courses than other students with disabilities
- Fail minimal competence tests more than other students with disabilities
- Are retained more often
- Do not graduate from high school with a diploma at a rate that should be expected (42% as compared to 50% for all students with disabilities and 76% for all students in the general population)
- Miss more days (eighteen per year) of school due to absenteeism than their peers with disabilities
- Have a high dropout rate (48%), particularly when compared to other students with disabilities (30%) or peers without disabilities (24%)
- Experience a high rate (20%) of being arrested while still in high school (compared to 9% of students with disabilities and 6% of those without)
- Are very likely (58% of them) of being arrested within five years of leaving school (as opposed to 30% for all students with disabilities)

As you have learned, these trends can be changed, but only through systematic intervention that educators and schools do not have to attempt alone. Research has shown that partnerships with community agencies can help keep children and youth out of trouble and succeeding at school (Sinclair et al., 1998; Tobin & Sugai, 1999). Programs like the ones provided by the Chicago Youth Centers (CYC), which provide extracurricular activities, after-school tutoring, mentoring activities, academic support, and programs that teach youngsters conflict resolution and problem solving skills, can keep inner-city children out of trouble. CYC serves over 8,000 children in after-school programs in some of the poorest inner-city areas, most in partnership with the local schools. Unfortunately, not enough of these wonderful programs exist. Because of the terrible results shown for most students with emotional or behavioral disorders, many educators are now advocating a life skills curriculum for them, wherein functional life skills are the focus of much of the instruction (Owens-Johnson & Johnson, 1999). What do you think ought to comprise the educational programs of these youngsters?

FAMILIES

To compare the challenges these families face with those of families of children with different disabilities, see the Family sections in Chapters 3–12.

Parenting a child with emotional or behavioral disorders is usually quite difficult. These families are most likely to be blamed for their children's problems and are also more likely to make significant financial sacrifices to secure services for their children (Ahearn, 1995). Increasingly, though, teachers are paying more attention to both the contributions and the needs of family members, and listening more carefully to parents' concerns. In this section, I decided to call your attention to two common elements in the lives of these children and their families: negotiating the mental health care system and foster home placement.

NEGOTIATING THE MENTAL HEALTH CARE SYSTEM

In 1994, Congress provided funds that support community based services for children with emotional or behavioral disorders and their families. The intent is that these children's multiple health and mental health care needs will be met through a coordi-

"Sam, neither your father nor I consider your response appropriate."

Drawing by Koren, (c) 1983 The New Yorker Magazine, Inc.

nated network of service providers (Children's Defense Fund, 1995). And children and families who use mental health services benefit greatly (Farmer et al., 1997). Although these services are now available, they are not being used at the rate they should. Let's look at some reasons why and how the problem can be solved.

Accessing America's mental health care system can be a daunting experience even for the most capable and most affluent. For those who have limited resources, the barriers can be so great that needed services are not sought or received. Some of those barriers include lack of transportation, lack of child care for other children, lack of information about what services are available and where they can be received, and emotional support. One innovative project is lowering those barriers, and the result is more families and children with emotional or behavioral disorders are accessing the mental health care services they so desperately need (Koroloff et al., 1996). This project uses parents who had negotiated the mental health care system for themselves and their children. These experienced parents are hired as paraprofessionals, and the results are spectacular. Although they cannot help with respite or child care, their assistance in providing transportation, information, and emotional support resulted in a very low dropout rate and a very high contact rate with health care providers. This project is just one example of how challenging problems, even working within the most complex of America's social service systems, can be met when positive thinking, creativity, and people-resources are applied.

FOSTER HOME PLACEMENTS

The number of America's children who are placed in foster care settings is increasing each year. The Children's Defense Fund (1996) estimates that each day in America during 1994, 462,000 children were living in a foster home placement, an increase of almost 20,000 children per day over the previous year. More surprising is the number of infants and toddlers who experience foster care. In a five-state survey, one out of every four children in foster care had entered the system before the age of 1, many of them newborns. The proportion of these children who have disabilities is great, in part due to the large number prenatally exposed to cocaine and other drugs. In fact, it is estimated that the prevalence of disabilities among children in foster care is about double that in the school-age population (Smucker et al., 1996).

Let's look more closely at children with disabilities who live in foster care placements. In one state, Illinois, 30% of children in foster care also receive special education, and almost half of them have been identified as having emotional or behavioral disorders (Smucker et al., 1996). This is the situation when about 10% of

NEW DIRECTIONS
FOR THE
MILLENNIUM

Legacy: At the end of the twentieth century, the foster care programs in many states were in disarray, receiving conflicting information from the public, administrators, legislators, and the courts about the preference of keeping children with their families, the dangers of leaving children in high-risk environments, and difficulties of finding adoptive homes for older children.

Opportunities:

• Develop and consistently apply criteria for removing children from high-risk home environments

• Implement a range of supports to assist families willing to create permanent and stable homes for children with emotional or behavioral disorders who are in the foster care system

To compare different types of technology supports across students with special needs, read the Technology sections in Chapter 3–12.

the school population is identified as having disabilities and only 1% of this group has emotional or behavioral disorders. This is most apparent when they are compared in two groups: (1) those who attend special education and live in foster care settings, and (2) those who attend special education but are not living in foster care placements. The former experience more difficulties in both the academic and behavioral areas. They are more likely to move from school to school, have higher grade-retention rates, and be perceived more negatively by school staffs. It appears that it is the combination of foster care and this disability that makes problems much worse. In fact, for these students, longer stays in foster care seem to cause increases in school-related problems. And some maintain that the likelihood is great that many of these individuals will spend a great portion of their adult lives in jail (Sherman, 1994).

Educators need to be aware of the poor outcomes of these students. What can be done to improve this situation? One thing educators can do is create a positive and consistent classroom environment, where students understand the consequences of their actions, both positive and negative.

TECHNOLOGY

Throughout this text, I have shown how advancements in computerized technology augment and expand students' physical and academic skills. The computer can be especially helpful to a student with emotional or behavioral disorders (Rivera & Smith, 1997). It can serve as an emotionally neutral system with which to interact, have fun, achieve success, and engage actively in learning (Lucent Technologies, 1999).

Computers assist learning without the pressure of subjective judgments; a computer does not criticize or impose feelings about the child who is using it. Answers are simply right or wrong. Thus, a computer serves as a safe environment in which to practice and improve skills. When a teacher incorporates computer-assisted instruction for an individualized learning activity for a child, the computer mirrors many of the attributes of a good teacher:

• It provides immediate attention and feedback
• It individualizes to the particular skill level
• It allows students to work at their own pace
• It makes corrections quickly
• It produces a professional-looking product
• It keeps accurate records of correct and error rates
• It ignores inappropriate behavior
• It focuses on the particular response
• It is nonjudgmental

Using a computer is not a substitute for learning to interact appropriately with other people, however, and a teacher should not rely solely on computer interactions with children with emotional or behavioral disorders. In arithmetic, for example, a teacher might introduce the instruction, allow drill and practice on the computer, and return periodically to check the student's progress. Many computer learning programs are available at different levels. By consulting with computer specialists, teachers can ensure that their judgments about the learning needs of the students are translated into the appropriate computer materials.

CONCEPTS AND CONTROVERSY: BEHAVIORAL CONTROL THROUGH MEDICATION, IS IT NECESSARY?

For other discussions of ADHD, see:

- The question about ADHD in the Solutions section of Chapter 1
- The Prevalence and ADHD (Children with Learning Disabilities) sections, the IDEA '97 box, and the Concepts and Controversy section in Chapter 4
- The Defined section in Chapter 10

More than one million American children take Ritalin to help them control externalizing behaviors. In the last decade of the twentieth century, the use of medication for the treatment of ADHD increased; it has reached a rate of over eight times that of 1990 and five times higher than the rest of the world (Hancock, 1996; Zametkin & Ernst, 1999). And, it appears that students with emotional or behavioral disorders are more likely to have this drug prescribed than their peers (Hallfors et al., 1998). In one research sample, 56% of the students with emotional or behavioral disorders were using this drug (Landrum et al., 1995). It is also interesting to note that across the entire sample, Anglo students (48%) were more likely to be using Ritalin than African American students (33%).

Why are so many American children being placed on behavior control medication? Are doctors better today in diagnosing conditions and prescribing proper medical treatment? Is it that parents and educators are less tolerant of disruptive behavior? Are adults less effective at controlling inappropriate behavior through their actions? Does the medication actually improve learning and behavior? These are some of the questions that professionals in the fields of education and medicine are asking. These are some of the same questions asked during the 1970s when medical management of behavior problems was also popular (Axelrod & Bailey, 1979). In studies conducted then, findings indicated that for the vast majority of students receiving stimulant drugs (e.g., Ritalin, Dexedrine) to control hyperactivity, behavior management techniques were as effective as the drugs (Sulzbacher, 1972; Carpenter & Sells, 1974). New research findings show that classroom interventions can be very successful in remediating inappropriate behaviors in children with ADHD (Ervin et al., 1998; Pancheri & Prater, 1999). The drugs were the same; were the children maybe different thirty years ago?

The controversy over the use of behavior-controlling medication is growing. Some experts believe that the drugs do not improve learning and only improve behavior when paired with behavior modification techniques (Zametkin & Ernst, 1999). Some say they are not effective with all children, while others believe they are a modern miracle (Hancock, 1996). Some are very concerned about side effects such as weight loss and sleeplessness, and feel that the medication is not effective enough to justify its use (Armstrong, 1995). How should these issues be resolved?

Look again at the Advance Organizers at the beginning of the chapter; to help you study the chapter's content, the answers to the Focus and Challenge questions are found here. Test yourself to see if you have mastered the major points of this chapter.

Summary

Precise definitions and criteria for identification of emotional or behavioral disorders have not yet been written. This disability, in part, reflects societal standards for behavior and expectations about the development of children. Many of the behaviors that our society labels as disordered in a particular individual might be acceptable if that person were a different age, lived in a different society, came from a different culture, or exhibited the behaviors under different circumstances. Of course, some conditions are considered disturbed despite age or society's standards.

It is difficult to identify most emotional or behavioral disorders in young children, and there is great reluctance from some professionals to identify preschoolers because of the damage that misidentification can do. However, it is now recognized that this disability has considerable stability over time, particularly for individuals who exhibit severe aggressive behaviors by the time they are four years old. For these people, the benefits of early identification can be great. Some problems can be treated before they become serious, interventions can be developed for the home and community environments, school settings and educational programs can be tailor-made to meet the needs of the youngster from the time of school entrance, and the dismal adult outcomes experienced by many individuals belonging to this group can be avoided.

Focus Questions

Self-Test Questions

- *By identifying the components of two definitions—the one in IDEA '97 and the one offered by the National Mental Health and Special Education Coalition—how would you compare them?*

   The IDEA'97 definition of emotional disturbance—the term used in law—describes these children as unable to develop or sustain positive relationships with peers or teachers, having difficulties with academic tasks, exhibiting inappropriate behaviors, experiencing considerable unhappiness or depression, developing physical symptoms relating to fears about personal or school problems, and having no other (intellectual, sensory, health) reason for the condition. This definition also requires that the condition be severe and long lasting. The National Mental Health and Special Education Coalition's definition also requires that the condition be extreme and long lasting, and also adds that it consists of inappropriate behaviors and negatively affects educational performance. This definition also specifies that the behaviors of concern are observed across settings (both school and home), are unresponsive to direct intervention in general education, and can coexist with other conditions. The IDEA '97 definition continues to be criticized because of its narrow focus. The label used, emotional disturbance, places too much emphasis on emotional problems without mentioning behavioral problems. This definition also tends to provide an older view of schooling that focuses exclusively on academics, rather than incorporating social behavior into a more complete concept of education. The National Coalition's definition attempts to correct these problems.

- *What are the two major subgroups of this disability, and how would you compare the conditions that fall into each subgroup?*

   Emotional or behavioral disorders can be divided into two groups: externalizing behavior problems and internalizing behavior problems. Some have argued that schools dwell too much on externalizing disruptive behaviors, ignoring the equally serious problems of children and youth with internalizing problems, such as depression. This may be the case because aggression, hostility, and defiance disturb others more than internalizing behaviors like being extremely shy, withdrawn, or depressed.

- *What are the major causes of this disability, and how can it be prevented?*

  The specific causes of a behavioral disorder or emotional disturbance in a particular individual are almost always unknown. However, in general three basic areas are often the root of the problem: biology, home and community, and school. As with other disability areas, more and more biological causes are being identified. For example, Tourette's syndrome appears to have a biological basis, and the genetic links for schizophrenia and even for depression are becoming clear. The powerful impact of environment on individuals cannot be denied, particularly on the developing child. The concept of environment must include the home, extended family, and community. Certainly, the family's situation cannot be minimized. The devastation caused by abuse and neglect of young children is an American tragedy, and certainly is a major cause of emotional or behavioral disorders in children today. Although probably more of a reason for the continuation (maintenance) of problems, poorly managed classrooms that provide little consistency and structure and do not produce a positive learning environment can result in students exhibiting externalizing behavior problems. When educators provide safe, positive, and exciting learning environments in which children are actively engaged in learning, many problems are prevented.

- *What are the long-term prospects for these children?*

  Without direct intervention, the long-term prospects for students with externalizing or internalizing behaviors are not promising. Both groups of children are recognized by their peers as different, and they are often rejected. The outcomes for the entire group include high rates of dropping out of school, low academic achievement, failing grades, low high school graduation rates, and contact with the criminal justice system. Those with externalizing behavior problems, particularly those with severe problems with aggression when they were preschoolers, are at risk for even more significant problems as adults. The likelihood is that they will be arrested at rates much higher than other students with disabilities.

- *How can teachers help children with this disability?*

  Research findings are clear: Direct and systematic instruction that includes on-going evaluation to ensure the continued effectiveness of selected interventions produces achievement in these children. Whether the instructional target be in the academic, vocational, or social areas, these procedures and array of teaching tactics are powerful. For example, when behavior is of concern, the tactics found on the Intervention Ladder (specific praise, ignoring, rules, contingent instructions, contingent observation, criterion-specific rewards, fines, group contingencies, peer management, self-management, parent action, overcorrecting, time-out, punishment, exclusion) are paired with functional assessment and curriculum based measurement (CBM) and systematic measurement techniques to assist in determining whether a tactic is sufficiently effective or another one needs to be tried; disruption can be held to a minimum and a positive learning environment fostered. Likewise, when direct instruction (e.g., phonics instruction for acquisition of reading skills, rewards for increased reading rate or fluency) is paired with CBM, academic performance improves dramatically. New curriculum areas are being developed as well. A good example is the work currently being conducted in the area of self-determination, where students are learning to make choices and decisions.

Challenge Question

- *Why does an array of educational placement options need to be available for students with emotional or behavioral disorders?*

Education for children and youth with emotional or behavioral disorders is provided in a variety of environments, including general education classrooms, special education classrooms, community based residential group homes or halfway houses, and even institutions or hospitals. This group of students has the highest rate of placements in segregated settings and the lowest rates of inclusive placements of any group of students with disabilities. Of children and youth with disabilities who are placed in residential programs, about 50% of them have this disability. For those able to participate in programs offered by their local public schools, many do not participate in general education classes because of their aggressive and threatening behavior patterns. General education teachers do not feel prepared to deal with dangerous behaviors in their students, and the settings in which they work are usually not prepared to handle such situations either. Clearly, a fluid and full array of service delivery options must be available for these students and the educators who work with them.

MAKING CONNECTIONS

Resources to extend your learning about people with disabilities are found at the end of every chapter, and a fuller listing is available in the Students' Resource Manual that accompanies this text.

Supplementary Resources

Scholarly Readings

Coleman, M. C. (1996). *Emotional and behavioral disorders: Theory and practice* (3rd ed.). Boston: Allyn and Bacon.

Deveres, L. (1999). *A primer on functional behavioral assessments.* Horsham, PA: LRP Publications.

Kauffman, J. M. (1997). *Characteristics of behavioral disorders of children and youth* (6th ed.). Columbus, OH: Merrill.

Kauffman, J. M. (1999). How we prevent the prevention of emotional and behavioral disorders. *Exceptional Children, 65,* 448–468.

Peterson, R. L., & Ishii-Jordon, S. (1994). *Multicultural issues in the education of students with behavioral disorders.* Cambridge, MA: Brookline.

Rosenberg, M. S., Wilson, R., Maheady, L., & Sindelar, P. T. (1997). *Educating students with behavior disorders* (2nd ed.). Boston: Allyn and Bacon.

Walker, H. M., Colvin, G., & Ramsey, E. (1995). *Antisocial behavior in school: Strategies and best practices.* Pacific Grove, CA: Brooks/Cole.

Popular Books

Atwood, M. (1996). *Alias Grace.* New York: Doubleday.

Duke, P. (1987). *Call me Anna: The autobiography of Patty Duke.* New York: Bantam.

Kesey, K. (1977). *One flew over the cuckoo's nest.* New York: Penguin.

Plath, S. (1971). *The bell jar.* New York: Harper & Row.

Sedaris, D. (1997). *Naked.* Boston: Little, Brown & Co.

Styron, W. (1990). *Darkness visible: A memoir of madness.* New York: Random House.

Videos and DVDs

One flew over the cuckoo's nest. (1975). United Artists.
Camille Claudel. (1989). Orion.
The fisher king. (1991). Columbia Pictures.
The piano. (1993). Miramax.
Twelve monkeys (1995). Universal Studios.
Primal fear. (1996). Paramount.
Seven. (1996). New Line.
Shine. (1996). Pandora Films.
Sling blade. (1996). Miramax.
As good as it gets. (1998). Twentieth Century Fox.

Professional, Parent, and Consumer Organizations and Agencies

American Psychiatric Association
1400 K Street NW
Washington, DC 20005
Phone: (202) 682-6000
Web site: http://www.psych.org

American Psychological Association (APA)
750 First Street NE
Washington, DC 20002-4242
Phone: (202) 336-5500; (800) 374-2721
Web site: http://www.apa.org

Council for Children with Behavioral Disorders (CCBD)
Council for Exceptional Children
1920 Association Drive
Reston, VA 22091
Phone: (703) 620-3660; (888) CEC-SPED
Web site: http://www.cec.sped.org

National Alliance for the Mentally Ill Children and Adolescents Network (NAMICAN)
200 N. Glebe Road, Suite 1015
Arlington, VA 22003-3754
Phone: (800) 950-6264
Web site: http://www.nami.org

National Mental Health Association
1800 N. Kent Street
Arlington, VA 22209
Phone: (703) 684-7722
Web site: http://www.nmha.org

National Mental Health Services Knowledge Exchange Network
P.O. Box 42490
Washington, DC 20015
Phone: (800) 789-2647
Web site: http://www.mentalhealth.org

MAKING CONNECTIONS

For Web links to support your study of disabilities, look at the Resources sections at the end of every chapter in this text. A fuller listing is found in the Students' Resource Manual that accompanies this text.

Henriette Wyeth, an extremely prominent artist in her own right, came from a family of very successful and well-known artists. Her father was the famous artist and illustrator N.C. Wyeth; her brother, Andrew, and her sister, Carolyn, also were well-known artists; and her husband was Peter Hurd, the renowned Western painter. Henriette Wyeth faced many challenges during her youth. She grew up in a high-achieving family that had exceptional expectations for her. She often spoke of the path she took to find the right outlet for her own creativity and talents and how her own special physical challenge helped to shape her future: "I wanted to be a singer. Due to polio at three, I couldn't play the piano. I wanted to be an actress, too. By the age of sixteen I was hooked on painting. I thought everyone drew—like having salt and pepper on the table" (Horgan, 1994, p. 30).

The very special piece shown here was painted in 1940. Doña Nestorita, a blind Mexican woman of 90 years, had lived most of her simple life in the rural Southwest. Wyeth described her as "charming, of great dignity, in a pitiful, tiny, blind person" (Horgan, 1994, p. 58).

Collection of the Roswell Museum and Art Center, Henriette Wyeth, *Dona Nestorita*, oil on canvas, 1940, Gift of Mr. and Mrs. Donald Winston.

C H A P T E R **9**

A Personal Perspective:

The People Who Make Special Education Special

Karen Canellas-U'Ren was a highly successful teacher of students with disabilities. She is now an administrator who is assisting an entire middle school community to accommodate for every student's special learning needs. This dedicated professional continues to be excited about her work.

As I examine how I started my career and compare it to now when I am an advocate for children with special needs, I recognize that several key people and experiences influenced me. In the beginning of my career, I was an elective teacher in a small rural community. That experience taught me that every student has unique qualities and can make a significant contribution to a class or school. Like most first-year teachers, I was open to almost all situations and requests. I am so glad now that my administrator asked me to take some students in my classes who were not successful with some other teachers. Some of my senior colleagues told me that I was being "dumped on," but I did not see it that way. No special education classroom or teacher was available at the school. Intuitively, I knew that another option was needed for many children at my school.

Looking back, I guess I became that option, that special education teacher who helps meet individual students' needs. I provided a classroom that was open to every student at that school. "My" students from that year will always be in my heart. I never worried about what they could or could not do. Rather, I encouraged them to be who they were and to be proud of the talents they possessed.

Physical Impairments and Special Health Care Needs

Mary was about at the end of her high school experience and much older than her peers. She spent almost all day with me. I couldn't have been prouder when Mary graduated from high school and went on to become a mechanic.

My experience with Mary and students like her sparked my interest in special education and students with disabilities. I decided to pursue a master's degree and prepare myself to work with these students and their families. I was hired by the school district near the university on a waiver while I attended school. I learned a lot on the job and at the university. My special education career had begun.

Later, I became a teacher-trainer, and taught other teachers about students with disabilities and their families. I found that most teachers want to know more about special learners but are afraid of the unknown. As an administrator, I once again am educating a school community about students with special needs, particularly those who are being integrated into general education classes for a great part of their school day.

I often wonder what makes me so committed to these students. Maybe it is what I see in their eyes, in their faces, as they struggle to take a breath, utter a response, lift their heads, and participate in their education programs. Maybe it is because they struggle so hard and use every bit of their strength to make their body work. I think the reason for my commitment is basic: It is a result of *their* courage.

The students with severe medical and physical disabilities are, in my opinion, brave beyond words. Their families display unbelievable courage when they entrust their children to us, the teachers and administrators at their neighborhood school, knowing how involved or medically fragile their children are. Whenever I feel frustrated with the discipline problems we have to deal with on a daily basis at school or when I have to deal with difficult people, I "escape" to "my" children and become an active participant in a classroom. There, I can reestablish myself with the children who are the real purpose of my work. Just watching and working with children like Matt and Jason, who really have to struggle to do ordinary tasks, who smile and reach out to me with limbs that are stiff or spastic or weak, reminds me again of their true strength and courage. I can actually feel their psychological strength, despite their physical weaknesses. I get the same feelings as I watch Carissa, another student with severe physical disabilities, sing in a chorus with her peers without disabilities. It is these experiences that restore my faith in children and youth because I can visibly see their compassion and vigor. There is nothing more special than hearing the laughter of children who are so medically fragile that no one knows whether they will survive to adulthood. It is that laughter that makes my job of being their advocate, their facilitator, so important and worthwhile.

I have been fortunate to experience the strength of character of these students and their parents and the tolerance, acceptance, and tenderness of adolescents without disabilities who are these students' peers. Most of these classmates have developed a caring attitude toward others who are different from them, an attitude that I hope they will carry with them throughout their lives. Every day, children and adults in our learning community interact with special learners and, most significantly, embrace them as important individuals in their lives.

1. Why do you think that special educators like Karen Canellas-U'Ren are so dedicated to their profession?
2. How has the field of special education changed since she selected it as a career?

Advance Organizers

CONNECTIONS MAKING

Use the learning strategy—Advance Organizers—to help focus your study of this chapter's content, and reinforce your learning by reviewing answers to the Focus and Challenge questions at the end of the chapter.

Overview

Physical impairments and special health care needs are disability categories that comprise hundreds of conditions and diseases, yet even combined, in children they are low incidence disabilities (comprising only approximately 4% of all schoolchildren with disabilities). Today, most children with physical impairments attend their neighborhood school, but they require modifications in the physical environment. Those with special health care needs tend to have high rates of absenteeism, and they require flexibility and modifications in their instructional programs. Some of these children may present crises to their teachers and require emergency techniques. IDEA '97 now includes children with ADHD in this category as well.

Focus Questions

Self-Test Questions

- Why are there so many different ways to organize and classify these disabilities?
- What are some steps teachers should follow to assist a child who is having a seizure?
- What are the five general causes of physical impairments and special health care needs, and how can they be prevented?
- How can the learning environment be modified to accommodate students with physical impairments and special health care needs?
- Why is the multidisciplinary team approach so necessary for these children, and how can educators improve collaboration among diverse professionals?

Challenge Question

- What are the barriers to the full participation of these individuals in society, and how can they be minimized?

Our society seems obsessed with youth, beauty, and physical fitness. The advertising industry urges us to purchase certain styles of clothes, special cosmetics and hair products, new exercise equipment, and even cars to make ourselves more attractive. Have you noticed messages about physical perfection in television shows, commercials, music videos, and movies? Have you or your friends assigned popularity ratings to others on the basis of physical appearance? Sometimes, we even equate physical perfection with virtue or goodness, imperfection and deformities with evil. Think, for example, of the villain, the deformed Darth Vader, always dressed in black in the *Star Wars* films. This symbolism has been repeated in many books and movies, including *The Hunchback of Notre Dame, Dark Crystal, The Lion King,* and *The Wizard of Oz.*

Children whose health is precarious often do not conform to the standards of strength and energy emphasized by the fashion, advertising, sports, and entertainment industries so admired by our society. Unfortunately, the prejudices of society frequently are reflected in schools as well. These children—whose appearance is unusual because of deformities or muscle problems, or whose walking ability, not to mention athletic prowess, is challenged by wheelchairs or braces—may suffer prejudice and discrimination in school. How can educators eliminate these prejudices in order to provide appropriate learning environments for all children? How can educators address the individual learning needs of children who face physical challenges and require special accommodations because of their health care needs? These are some of the questions and related issues discussed in this chapter.

Organizing the information found here, however, was challenging because so many different diseases, impairments, and conditions can significantly affect children, their lives at school, and those who educate them. It is impossible to describe in any detail every condition leading to a physical impairment or special health care need that educators might encounter at schools. Also, these two disability areas are not mutually exclusive. For example, some impairments are typically grouped under a physical disability or an orthopedic impairment and also result in a long-term health problem. And one more point: Possibly more than any other disability category, many children with physical impairments or health problems do not require special education services.

At this point in your educational career, it is not necessary for you to master all the information about each specific condition, illness, or disease. However, when confronted with a condition rarely seen in children, be certain to learn all about it by seeking out specific information from the many resources available to you: local physicians, the child's multidisciplinary IEP team, and the agencies and organizations representing each condition. In this chapter, only the most common physical disabilities and health impairments that occur in children are discussed. More important, this chapter will stress the ways in which these children's educational needs can be best met through accommodations in physical and learning environments.

Opportunities for the New Millennium

Children with physical disabilities and special health care needs, historically, had been excluded from attending neighborhood schools. Since the original passage of IDEA, access to these schools and participation in the general education curriculum has progressively improved. Particularly for students with physical disabilities, most states no longer provide separate schools. However, inclusion is not consistent, and the pattern of placements varies widely across states.

orthopedic impairments. Conditions related to a physical deformity or disability of the skeletal system and associated motor function.

Legacies from the Twentieth Century
As the century came to a close, more medically fragile children were receiving their education in general education classrooms. Many teachers were concerned about these placements because they felt unprepared to deal with medical crises in their classes and also felt that the time to care for these children would reduce the amount of instructional time they could devote to typical learners. The Supreme Court ruled that school districts would

have to bear the costs of medical assistants for those whose needs were greater than a teacher could provide. School administrators are fearful that these costs will substantially impact overall school budgets. A second issue surrounding this category of learners came to light at the end of the century when ADHD was included as a condition in the health impairments category.

Thinking About Dilemmas to Solve 🌿 As you read this chapter, ponder these students' needs, the supports they require, and the outcomes they should achieve. Think about:

- How the educational system can best respond to their needs
- Why some states use separate special education schools for students with physical disabilities while others do not
- The impact of fully including all medically fragile students in general education classrooms on all of those directly and indirectly involved
- The implications of including ADHD as a condition under the health impairments category
- How teachers should be prepared to work with children with these special needs

PHYSICAL IMPAIRMENTS AND SPECIAL HEALTH CARE NEEDS DEFINED

One confusing aspect about these disability areas is the multiple ways they are organized and defined. For example, IDEA '97 gives two overarching definitions for students with physical impairments and special health care needs. Children with physical impairments—those youngsters who have a problem with the structure or the functioning of their bodies—are referred to as having **orthopedic impairments,** defined in IDEA '97 as a condition

When schools make accommodations to the environment, students with or without disabilities can play and have fun together in natural ways.

> that adversely affects a child's educational performance. The term includes impairments caused by congenital anomaly (e.g., clubfoot, absence of some member, etc.), impairments caused by disease (e.g., poliomyelitis, bone tuberculosis, etc.), and impairments from other causes (e.g., cerebral palsy, amputations, and fractures or burns that cause contractures). (U.S. Department of Education, 1999, p. 12422)

Many children with health impairments—who have limitations to their physical well-being and require ongoing medical attention—have special needs at school. Often, adjustments to school routines are short-term, lessening when the child's health improves. For some, however, accommodations need to increase as a child's illness progresses. Also, note that ADHD is included in the IDEA '97 definition of this special education category. Other conditions, like autism, also at one time were included in the health impairments category. Only time will tell whether ADHD finds its way to another special education category or even becomes a category of its own sometime

NEW DIRECTIONS
FOR THE
MILLENNIUM

Legacy: During the 1990s, parents of children with ADHD asked Congress to recognize this condition as a disability, but calling out ADHD as a health impairment did not resolve parents' concerns because relatively few additional children are included in special education because of this modification in IDEA '97.

Opportunities:

- Develop precise methods for determining whether the presence of ADHD affects the students' educational performance
- Come to understand whether the inclusion of ADHD in this category encompasses more students who need special services than those already served in other special education categories (e.g., learning disabilities; emotional or behavioral disorders)

other health impairments. Chronic or acute health problems resulting in limited strength, vitality, or alertness.

in the future. For now, the federal government in IDEA '97 defines **other health impairments** as

> having limited strength, vitality or alertness, including a heightened alertness to environmental stimuli that results in limited alertness with respect to the educational environment, that is due to chronic or acute health problems such as asthma, attention deficit hyperactivity disorder, diabetes, epilepsy, a heart condition, hemophilia, lead poisoning, leukemia, nephritis, rheumatic fever, and sickle cell anemia; and adversely affects a child's educational performance. (U.S. Department of Education, 1999 p. 12422)

Other experts in the field group these disabilities differently, and even use other terms to describe them. Some use a variety of terms—"orthopedic and neurological impairments" (Sirvis & Caldwell, 1995), "orthopedic and muscular impairments" (Best et al., 1994), "physical disabilities" (Hallahan and Kauffman, 2000), and "physical impairments" (Heller et al., 1996)—to describe what IDEA calls orthopedic impairments. Some experts further cluster specific conditions into major groups, such as neuromotor impairments, degenerative diseases, muscular-skeletal disorders, and major health impairments (Heller et al., 1996), while others talk about all of these children having special health care needs and do not assign them to any group (Urbano, 1992). Probably the primary reason for the differences in the ways professionals discuss these conditions is that there is no simple organizational scheme that uniformly applies. For example, one child with cerebral palsy may face some physical challenges and need considerable assistance from a physical therapist to learn how to control movement and yet have no special health care needs, while another child with the same condition may have both physical limitations and serious health care needs. Students with either disability might require flexible schedules because they are not physically able to participate in six straight hours of school or might need special arrangements (e.g., peer tutors) so they do not fall behind in their studies due to frequent absences. And, remember, some of these children may not require any special education services, or may need relatively few accommodations.

TYPES OF PHYSICAL IMPAIRMENTS AND SPECIAL HEALTH CARE NEEDS

Educators need to know about (1) the conditions that lead to physical impairments and special health care needs, and (2) the common childhood conditions that fall into each group. It is not as important for teachers to know about conditions and diseases that are now prevented in the United States (e.g., polio) or are found in adults but seldom seen in children (e.g, multiple sclerosis). Figure 9.1 uses an organizational scheme that groups the conditions, impairments, disorders, illnesses, and diseases educators might see at school. It lists many different conditions that can result in physical and health impairments, but does not include the much less common conditions. Remember, these conditions, even when combined, are "low incidence" disabilities. The number of children who pertain to this discussion is small, particularly when compared to those with other disabilities, such as learning disabilities.

Neuromuscular/Skeletal Conditions. Study Figure 9.1 to find the names of many of the conditions and impairments that lead to a physical disability. This organizational scheme creates two major groupings: **neuromotor impairments** and **muscular/skeletal conditions**. In Table 9.1, each of these conditions is defined. This chapter's text addresses only those with the highest prevalence: Muscular dystrophy,

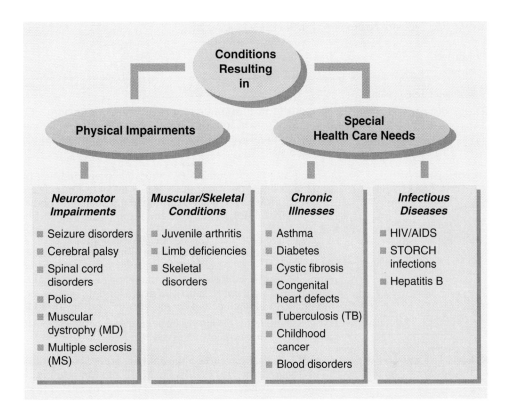

Figure 9.1 An Organizational Scheme for the Conditions, Disorders, Impairments, Illnesses, and Diseases That Can Result in Physical Challenges and Special Health Care Needs in Children.

- Read remaining chapters of this text to learn more about "low incidence disabilities."
- For a division of special education categories into high and low incidence disabilities, see this text's table of contents.

neuromotor impairment. Condition involving both the nerves, muscles, and motor functioning. **muscular/skeletal conditions.** Conditions affecting muscles or bones and resulting in limited functioning. **epilepsy.** A tendency to recurrent seizures.

because of its low prevalence; multiple sclerosis, because it is an adult disease; and polio, because it is almost eradicated, are not discussed. These diseases are, however, described in Table 9.1 on page 370.

NEUROMOTOR IMPAIRMENTS. When the central nervous system (the brain and the spinal cord) is damaged, a serious **neurological impairment** that limits muscular control and movement often results. It is likely that all educators sometime during their careers will work with children who have some type of neuromuscular impairment, probably either epilepsy or cerebral palsy. Although less likely, they might also work with students who have spinal cord (neural tube) disorders. So, these three conditions are discussed in this section. Although ranging in severity from mild to severe, these disabilities are usually very serious and affect these individuals in significant ways throughout their lives. And, in many cases, they are only one of multiple conditions an individual must face (Eriksson et al., 1998). For example, epilepsy is the most frequent additional handicap in children with mental retardation, but remember not to make the terrible error of associating a health or physical impairment with a cognitive one. They do not always go hand in hand.

The most common neuromotor impairment encountered at school is epilepsy, also called a seizure disorder or a convulsive disorder. A person with **epilepsy** often has recurrent seizures resulting from sudden, excessive, spontaneous, and abnormal

Table 9.1 Types of Neuromuscular/Skeletal Conditions

Condition	Description
Neuromotor Impairments	
Seizure disorders	*Epilepsy,* the most common type of neuromotor impairment in children, is a condition of recurrent convulsions or seizures caused by abnormal brain electrical activity. It is treated with medications and frequently is well controlled without any effect on learning or motor skills.
Cerebral palsy (CP)	*Cerebral palsy* is an incurable and nonprogressive condition caused by brain injury that sometimes limits the individual's ability to control muscle groups or motor functioning in specific areas of the body or, infrequently, the entire body. It may be associated with multiple disabilities. Orthopedic and physical therapy offer benefits.
Spinal cord disorders	A neural tube birth defect, *spina bifida* is the improper closure of the protective tissue surrounding the spinal cord. It results in limited neurological control for organs and muscles controlled by nerves that originate below the level of the lesion. Increasing numbers of children have suffered traumatic head or spinal cord injuries resulting in permanent disabilities. Health care needs for both groups include good skin care, management of bladder and bowel care, and orthopedic and physical therapy.
	Typically, the result of injuries from accidents or abuse, *spinal cord injuries* can cause severe motor impairments and even paralysis.
Polio	Caused by a viral infection, almost totally prevented in children immunized in the United States, *polio* attacks the spinal cord and can result in paralysis and motor disabilities. Health care needs parallel those for spinal cord disorders.
Muscular dystrophy (MD)	An exceptionally rare, incurable, and progressive disease, *muscular dystrophy* weakens and then destroys the affected individual's muscles. Health care needs center on lung function support, prevention of pneumonia, and physical therapy.
Multiple sclerosis (MS)	A chronic disease typically occurring in adults, *multiple sclerosis* causes the myelin covering the nerve fibers of the brain and spinal cord to deteriorate, impeding the transmission of electrical signals from the brain to other parts of the body. Health care needs parallel those for MD.
Muscular/Skeletal Conditions	
Juvenile arthritis	*Juvenile arthritis* is a disease caused by an autoimmune process resulting in swelling, immobility, and pain in joints. Health care needs include medication to suppress the process and orthopedic and physical therapy to maintain function in small and large joints.
Limb deficiencies	Skeletal problems in which the individual's limb(s) is shortened, absent, or malformed. They may occur from congenital conditions or from injuries. Health care needs focus on adaptive interventions to support or improve functioning of the missing limb(s).
Skeletal disorders	*Dwarfism,* a condition caused by abnormal development of long bones, may result in varying degrees of motor disabilities. Health care needs may include human growth hormone to improve height.
	Osteogenesis imperfecta, sometimes known as brittle bone disease, is a condition in which normal calcification of the bone does not occur, leading to breakage and abnormal healing of bones with accompanying loss of height. Health care interventions include physical therapy and medical care.
	Scoliosis, a curvature of the spine that occurs in children during puberty, may in severe form limit mobility of the trunk. Health care needs include monitoring of the amount of curvature of the spine and appropriate interventions to arrest the process.

See Table 9.5 for tips on what to do in case of a seizure.

seizure. A spontaneous abnormal discharge of the electrical impulses of the brain, sometimes referred to as a *convulsive disorder.*

aura. A signal of an impending seizure, sometimes called the *preictal stage.*

tonic-clonic seizures. Seizures characterized by a stiff (tonic) phase in which the muscles become rigid, followed by a jerking (clonic) phase in which the arms and legs will snap (formerly referred to as *grand mal seizures*).

absence seizures. Seizures with a short lapse in consciousness (also called *petit mal seizures*).

simple partial seizures. Not always apparent; often affect behavior and feelings.

complex partial seizures. Periods of automatic behavior resulting from discharge in a localized area of the brain (sometimes called psychomotor or focal seizures).

cerebral palsy. A disorder of movement and posture caused by damage to the developing brain.

discharge of neurons in the brain. This can be accompanied by changes in the person's motor or sensory functioning and can also result in loss of consciousness. **Seizures** may involve the entire brain (generalized seizures) or only a portion of the brain (partial seizures). The frequency of seizures may vary from a single isolated incident to hundreds in a day. Some children actually anticipate their seizures because they experience a preictal stage, or an **aura,** and have heightened sensory signals of an impending seizure such as a peculiar smell, taste, vision, sound, or action. Others might experience a change in their behavior. Knowing about an aura pattern is helpful, as an individual can assume a safe position or warn companions before a seizure begins.

The Epilepsy Foundation of America (1994) identifies four main types of seizures: (1) generalized tonic-clonic, (2) absence, (3) simple partial, and (4) complex partial (psychomotor). Generalized **tonic-clonic seizures** (formerly referred to as grand mal seizures) are the most serious type of seizure and are characterized by convulsions and loss of consciousness. The dramatic behaviors exhibited during a tonic-clonic seizure may, at first, be frightening to the teacher and to other students in the class. The child may fall to the floor and usually experiences a stiff (tonic) phase, in which the muscles become rigid, followed by a clonic phase, in which the arms and legs jerk. Other behaviors may accompany the seizure, including teeth grinding, frothing due to inefficient saliva swallowing, and loss of bladder control. These seizures usually last less than five minutes, after which the individual enters the resting (postictal) stage and becomes relaxed, very sleepy, and disoriented. Teachers can help students during and after such a seizure episode; for some guidelines, see Table 9.2.

Absence seizures (also called petit mal seizures) are characterized by short lapses in consciousness. It may even be difficult to determine that the person is experiencing anything out of the ordinary, and in fact the person may not even realize a seizure has occurred after it is over. Typically, someone experiencing an absence seizure simply stares or shows small eye movements like fluttering of the eyelids. Because absence seizures are not dramatic, a teacher might wrongly assume that the child is merely daydreaming or not paying attention.

Not all seizures are obvious to those around the individual experiencing them. Such is often the case with **simple partial seizures,** during which children may think their environments are distorted and strange, that inexplicable events and feelings have occurred. With these seizures, teachers might incorrectly believe that the child is acting out or exhibiting bizarre behavior patterns. **Complex partial seizures** (psychomotor seizures) are the result of a unique electrical dysfunction, localized in a specific part of the brain. For this reason, they are sometimes called focal seizures. After a short period, the child returns to normal activities. Sometimes, teachers interpret the child's behavior during a complex partial seizure as misbehavior or clowning. This mistake can lead to confusion on the part of the child, who is not aware of his or her behavior during a psychomotor seizure, and on the part of the teacher who does not recognize the misbehavior as a seizure.

Another neuromotor impairment frequently encountered in schoolchildren is **cerebral palsy.** Cerebral palsy comprises a family of syndromes associated with disordered movement and posture. This condition is a result of damage, usually because of insufficient oxygen getting to the brain during its developmental period (Cheney & Palmer, 1997). Cerebral palsy is most often congenital, with damage occurring either before (prenatally), during (perinatally), or immediately after (postnatally) the child's birth. Some individuals, however, acquire cerebral palsy later, during the first three years of life. Acquired cerebral palsy is usually caused by brain damage resulting from

Table 9.2 Seizure Recognition

Seizure Type	What It Looks Like	What It Is Not
Generalized tonic-clonic (also called grand mal)	Sudden cry, fall, rigidity, followed by muscle jerks, shallow breathing or temporarily suspended breathing, bluish skin, possible loss of bladder or bowel control, usually lasts a couple of minutes. Normal breathing then starts again. There may be some confusion and/or fatigue, followed by return to full consciousness.	Heart attack Stroke
Absence (also called petit mal)	A blank stare, beginning and ending abruptly, lasting only a few seconds, most common in children. May be accompanied by rapid blinking, some chewing movements of the mouth. Child or adult is unaware of what's going on during the seizure, but quickly returns to full awareness once it has stopped. May result in learning difficulties if not recognized and treated.	Daydreaming Lack of attention Deliberate ignoring of adult instructions
Simple partial	Jerking may begin in one area of the body, arm, leg, or face. Can't be stopped, but patient stays awake and aware. Jerking may proceed from one area of the body to another and sometimes spreads to become a convulsive seizure.	Acting out, bizarre behavior
	Partial sensory seizures may not be obvious to an onlooker. Patient experiences a distorted environment. May see or hear things that aren't there, may feel unexplained fear, sadness, anger, or joy. May have nausea, experience odd smells, and have a generally "funny" feeling in the stomach.	Hysteria Mental illness Psychosomatic illness Parapsychological or mystical experience
Complex partial (also called psychomotor or temporal lobe)	Usually starts with blank stare, followed by chewing, followed by random activity. Person appears unaware of surroundings, may seem dazed and mumble. Unresponsive. Actions clumsy, not directed. May pick at clothing, pick up objects, try to take clothes off. May run, appear afraid. May struggle or flail at restraint. Once pattern established, same set of actions usually occurs with each seizure. Lasts a few minutes, but post-seizure confusion can last substantially longer. No memory of what happened during seizure period.	Drunkenness Intoxication on drugs Mental illness Disorderly conduct

Source: From _Seizure recognition and first aid._ Epilepsy Foundation of America, 1996. Landover, MD: Author. Reprinted with permission.

accidents, brain infections, or child abuse. Cerebral palsy is not a disease, but rather a nonprogressive and noninfectious condition. Regrettably, once acquired, it cannot be cured (at least today).

The severity of the condition depends on the precise location of brain damage, the degree of brain damage, and the extent of involvement of the central nervous system. Individuals with cerebral palsy whose motor functioning is affected show these characteristics alone or in combination: jerky movements, spasms, involuntary movements, and lack of muscle tone. Often, individuals with cerebral palsy have multiple disabilities, probably caused by the same damage to the brain that caused the cerebral palsy. For example, many individuals who have severe difficulties in motor functioning also have difficulties mastering oral speech. These individuals have a speech impairment and a physical disability. Other disabilities that sometimes accompany cerebral palsy include seizures, sensory deficits such as abnormal sensation and perception, visual disabilities, hearing loss, speech or language impairments, and learning problems. Although some degree of mental retardation is present in about half of the children with cerebral palsy, others are intellectually gifted. It is a tragic mistake to assume that cerebral palsy and mental retardation always occur in combination.

Cerebral palsy is usually described in two ways: by mobility or by the affected area. The three main types of cerebral palsy defined by movement are: (1) **spastic,** in which the movements are very stiff; (2) **athetoid,** in which involuntary movements are purposeless and uncontrolled and purposeful movements are contorted; and (3) **ataxia,** in which movements such as walking are disrupted by impairments of balance and depth perception. Many individuals with cerebral palsy have impaired mobility and poor muscle development. Even if they can walk, their efforts may require such exertion and be so inefficient that they need canes, crutches, or a wheelchair to get around. Students with cerebral palsy may also need braces to help support the affected limbs and make them more functional or to prevent **contractures** that would eventually lead to bone deformities and further mobility limitations. Proper positioning of the body also must be considered. Many children need wedges, pillows, and individually designed chairs and worktables so they can be comfortable; breathe easier; avoid injuries, contractures, and deformities; as well as participate in group activities. The classifications of cerebral palsy according to the areas of the body affected are shown in Figure 9.2.

spastic. A type of cerebral palsy characterized by uncontrolled tightening or pulling of muscles.

athetoid. A type of cerebral palsy characterized by purposeless and uncontrolled involuntary movements.

ataxia. A type of cerebral palsy characterized by movement disrupted by impaired balance and depth perception.

contractures. Joint stiffening, often because of muscle shortening, to the point that the joint can no longer move through its normal range.

Figure 9.2 **Areas of the Body Affected by Cerebral Palsy**

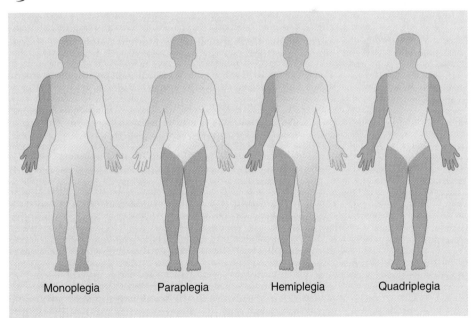

Monoplegia   Paraplegia   Hemiplegia   Quadriplegia

For a review of hydro-cephaly and shunt tech-nology, see Chapter 6:
• Causes and Prevention
• Figure 6.2

The last neuromotor impairment presented in this chapter is **spinal cord disorders,** also called **neural tube disorders.** These conditions involve both the nerves and the muscles of the spinal column. Spinal cord injuries and **spina bifida** are the two most common conditions in this group. In younger children, spinal cord injuries often result from child abuse or car accidents. In older youngsters, many such injuries are caused by sports accidents. In both spinal cord injuries and spina bifida, the defect's seriousness depends on how high the defect is along the spinal column (the closer to the neck, the more serious the impairment) and how much of the spinal cord material is damaged.

Spina bifida, a neural tube birth defect, is caused when the spinal column fails to close properly. The spinal column is the protected area through which nerves transmit messages from the brain to other parts of the body. This bony tube of vertebrae in the back encases and protects the nervous tissue of the **spinal cord** and its covering, the **meninges.** The spinal cord is connected to the brain. Neural tube birth defects occur along the spinal column anywhere from the tailbone (coccyx) to the neck. The defect may range from absence of protective vertebrae to actual protrusion of the spinal cord and its covering. Because of the importance of the spinal cord and the brain, the risks to the infant who has a defect in the spinal column can be grave. Risks include the possibility of infection and further damage to the delicate nervous system, brain damage such as hydrocephaly (expansion of the brain ventricles as spinal fluid collects and does not drain properly), and paralysis. Figure 9.3 shows how the body is affected by the types of spina bifida.

The portion of the central nervous system damaged by spina bifida generally would have controlled the sensations and muscles of the body areas below the location of the lesion. The parts of the body that would have been supplied by sensory and motor nerves branching from the spinal cord at this point or lower are likely to be paralyzed and deprived of sensations. The higher the lesion, the more areas of the body are affected by the damaged nerves. When the lesion is very low on the spine, the child may not be paralyzed but might have some nerve loss or weakness in the legs and feet.

MUSCULAR/SKELETAL CONDITIONS. Like those individuals with spina bifida that affects their mobility, individuals with muscular/skeletal conditions usually have difficulties controlling their movements, but the cause is not neurological. Some need to use special devices and technology to do many of the simple tasks—like walking, eating, or writing—most of us take for granted. Two of these conditions are discussed here: limb deficiencies and juvenile arthritis.

Limb deficiencies can be the result of a missing or nonfunctioning arm or leg and are either acquired or congenital. Regardless of when the impairment occurred, the result is a major impediment to normal physical activity and functioning. Although the root of the disability is physical, many individuals with a limb deficiency have difficulties adjusting to their situation. The attitudes of those who work with these youngsters, and of course the support given by family members, can be major contributors to their psychological health. Emerging technology (particularly robotics) now provides great assistance to those with missing limbs. Artificial limbs now enable movements that only a few years ago were thought to be impossible. And, although hard to believe, limb transplants are possibilities for the future. Matthew Scott, the nation's first hand transplant recipient, believes this to be true: "I hope in 20 or 30 years the science of transplantation and working with limbs has become so commonplace that I am a footnote and not the story" (Holloway, 1999).

spinal cord disorders. Always involve the spinal column, usually both the nerves and muscles.

neural tube disorders. Another name for spinal cord disorders, which always involve the spinal column and usually the spinal cord.

spina bifida. A developmental defect whereby the spinal column fails to close properly.

spinal cord. The cord of nervous tissue that extends through the bony spinal column to the brain.

meninges. Membranes that cover the spinal cord and brain.

limb deficiencies. Resulting from missing or nonfunctioning arms or legs.

374 Chapter 9 Physical Impairments and Special Health Care Needs

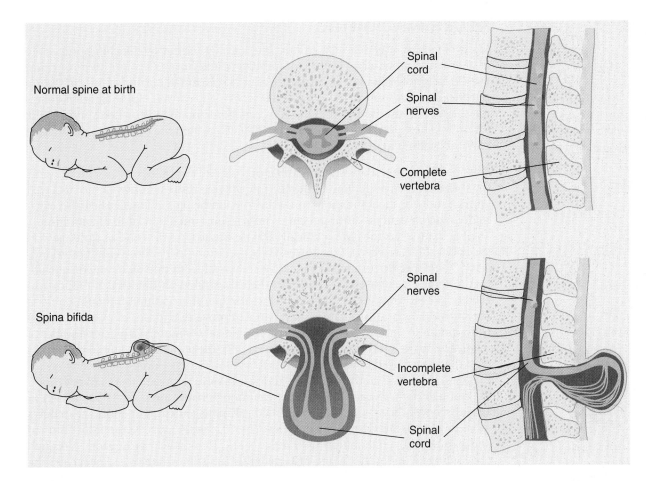

Normal spine at birth

Spinal cord

Spinal nerves

Complete vertebra

Spina bifida

Spinal nerves

Incomplete vertebra

Spinal cord

Figure 9.3 **How the Body Is Affected by the Types of Spina Bifida**

Matthew, whose hand was blown off in a fireworks accident, may well be right, for his doctors report that his progress is excellent.

A relatively common condition affecting joints and the function of muscles is **juvenile arthritis.** Although there are many different forms of this disease, it is typically chronic and painful. Juvenile arthritis usually develops in early childhood and can cause many absences from school. These children often need help keeping up with their classmates because they miss so much class instruction. Teachers must understand that their ability to move may be inconsistent—being better at different times of the day—and that sitting for extended periods of time can cause them to become stiff and experience considerable pain. These children need to be allowed to move around a lot. Those who have a high rate of absences probably need tutoring and extra help to master their academic subjects and keep up with their peers. Fortunately, for many of these youngsters the disease often shows considerable improvement and may even go into remission by the age of 18 (Best et al., 1994). Unfortunately, this is after their elementary and high school years are over. Promising medical treatments can reduce the amount of disability from the disease. However, some medications can have side effects that alter some aspect of personality and physical appearance.

juvenile arthritis. Chronic and painful muscular condition seen in children.

Physical Impairments and Special Health Care Needs Defined **375**

CONNECTIONS

Review Figure 9.1 for names of common health impairments and their groupings.

HEALTH IMPAIRMENTS

Many of us have experienced a serious illness sometime during our childhood; some illnesses, like appendicitis, even require surgery and hospitalization. In most cases, the illness is not long-term and does not affect a substantial portion of our childhood or education. For some of us, the illness is serious and chronic. Some children do not require special education, and if they do (e.g., home-bound instruction), it is usually for only a short period of time. Refer to Table 9.3 to find the definitions of different types of health impairments.

Chronic Illnesses. For a small number of children, their illnesses are chronic, lasting for years, even a lifetime. Children with **chronic illnesses** often do not feel well enough to focus their attention on the instruction being presented. They also experience many absences, causing them to miss a substantial part of their education.

For many years the term **medically fragile** was used to describe all children with special health care needs. It is now usually used to describe those children, regardless of their specific condition, who have complex health care requirements including technological assistance to support their lives (Sirvis & Caldwell, 1995). Medically fragile is a status; it is not assigned to any specific condition but rather reflects the individual's health situation. Students can move in and out of fragile status. It is important to understand that because of medical technology a greater number of medically fragile children survive health crises. In the past, many of these youngsters would not have lived long enough to go to school. Others would have been too sick to attend their neighborhood school and would have received most of their schooling through home-based instruction. Even though many are now stable enough to attend school, they require ongoing medical management. For most, procedures must be planned in case of emergencies. The "if, thens" must be carefully outlined and planned in collaboration with doctors and the medical profession. Although the contingencies for the "worst-case scenarios" must be arranged, in most cases the accommodations required for these children are not terribly dramatic. (However, not having backup power for a child's ventilator could have disastrous results.) Let's look at two conditions that can result in chronic illnesses for some children: asthma and the blood disorder sickle-cell anemia.

Asthma is a pulmonary disease and is the most common chronic illness of children. It is the leading cause of school absences among all the chronic diseases (Getch & Neuharth-Pritchett, 1999). A person with asthma usually has labored breathing that is sometimes accompanied by shortness of breath, wheezing, and a cough. A combination of three events causes the wheezing: (1) tightening of the muscles around the bronchial tubes, (2) swelling of the tissues in these tubes, and (3) an increase of secretions in these tubes. Years ago, many people held a common belief that asthma is a psychological disorder. It is not; its origin is physical. Many factors (e.g., chalk dust, dirt in the environment) can trigger an asthma attack, including physical activity or exertion. Many of these students are unable to participate in sports or even in physical education activities. Teachers can fill a very special role by helping these individuals find other fulfilling activities in which to participate.

Sickle-cell anemia is a hereditary, life-threatening blood disorder. Although prevalent among African Americans and others whose ancestors are from the Mediterranean basin, it is not restricted to these groups of people. This condition causes the red blood cells to become rigid and take on a crescent, or sickle, shape. During what is called a "sickling crisis," this rigidity and shape of the cells do not allow blood to flow through the vessels, depriving some tissues of oxygen and resulting in

chronic illness. Being sick for long periods of time.
medically fragile. Used to describe children with special health care needs.
asthma. A common, chronic condition resulting in difficulty in breathing.
sickle-cell anemia. A hereditary blood disorder that inhibits blood flow.

Table 9.3 Types of Health Impairments

Condition	Description
Chronic Illnesses	
Asthma	*Asthma*, a condition caused by narrowing of airways accompanied by inflammatory changes in the lining of the airways, may result in severe difficulty in breathing with chronic coughing. Health care needs include appropriate medications, environmental modifications, and monitoring and frequently result in no limitation of activities.
Cystic fibrosis	*Cystic fibrosis* is a genetic birth defect that results in chronic lung infections and digestive difficulties. Health care interventions include replacement of required enzymes for aiding digestion and aggressive care of lung infections and function.
Diabetes	*Diabetes* is the loss of the ability of the pancreas to produce enough insulin, resulting in problems with sugar metabolism. Health care needs include the monitoring of blood sugar levels, appropriate diet and exercise regimens, and knowledgeable response for insulin reactions.
Congenital heart defects	*Congenital heart conditions* can result in high rates of school absences for specialized health care. Most have had surgical intervention and medical monitoring by specialists. Health care needs include taking medications during the schoolday.
Tuberculosis (TB)	A disease caused by bacterial infection, *tuberculosis* rarely causes severe disease in children older than infancy. Most often the bacteria remain sequestered and harmless until late adulthood or when the body's immune system fails. The rates of infection are on the rise in many parts of the United States.
Childhood cancer	*Cancer* is the abnormal growth of cells that can affect any organ. The most common types of cancer in children are leukemia and lymphomas. While going through treatment, children may feel too ill to profit from classroom instruction.
	Leukemia causes an abnormal increase in the white blood cells, which are important in the body's defenses against infection. It often results in anemia and enlargement of the lymph glands, spleen, and liver.
	Lymphomas are malignant and cause enlargement of the lymph nodes.
Blood disorders	*Hemophilia*, a genetic condition typically linked with males, is characterized by poor blood clotting, which can result in massive bleeding from cuts and internal hemorrhaging from bruises.
	Sickle cell anemia, a hereditary disorder, causes a distortion in the red blood cells that restricts their passage through the blood vessels.
Infectious Diseases	
HIV and AIDS	*Human immunodeficiency virus (HIV)*, a potentially fatal viral infection that in school-aged children results from transmission from a mother infected with the virus to her newborn child or from transfusion with blood or blood products carrying the virus, causes *acquired immunodeficiency syndrome (AIDS)*. Health care needs include careful monitoring of general health, specialists to care for potentially overwhelming lung infections, and medications that slow or cure infections. The infection is primarily acquired through the exchange of body fluids in older children, through sexual abuse in younger children, through sexual activity in adolescents, and through intravenous drug use. Health care needs include sources of confidential care, counseling, and health education.
STORCH	*STORCH* is the acronym for a group of congenital infections that have the potential of causing severe, multiple impairments. It stands for syphilis, toxoplasmosis, other, rubella, cytomegalovirus, and herpes.
Hepatitis B	A viral disease, *hepatitis B* is infectious and causes inflammation of the liver and is characterized by jaundice and fever. Cases of this dangerous virus are on the increase.

extreme pain, swollen joints, high fever, and even strokes. Some information about this condition is particularly important to educators who have students with sickle-cell anemia. First, there seems to be a correlation between the sickling crisis and emotional stress and strenuous exercise (Best et al., 1994; Heller et al., 1996). Second, many of these children may be absent from school often. To reduce the stress these students experience when they return to school knowing that they have missed assignments and instruction, teachers must work together and develop strategies with the students and their families to compensate for missed schooldays. For example, a neighborhood child could serve as a peer tutor who brings assignments home to the student and explains important instruction for the schoolday.

INFECTIOUS DISEASES. The second type of health impairment is **infectious diseases.** Many different diseases are contracted by schoolchildren. Most, like the common cold or the flu, are relatively short in duration and result in only a few days of missed school. The majority of infectious diseases that children contract at school are not life-threatening or especially serious. Regardless, teachers can help to reduce the spread of these diseases by practicing easy preventive measures. Most of these diseases, however, cannot be avoided for a variety of reasons. For example, some diseases are not contracted at school but are passed on outside of class, before symptoms are apparent. Here are two examples of serious and preventable infectious diseases that teachers have little chance of preventing, but may confront during their classroom experiences.

Human immunodeficiency virus (HIV) is a potentially fatal viral infection transmitted primarily through exchange of bodily fluids in unprotected sex or by contaminated needles. It is the virus responsible for the deadly **acquired immuno-deficiency syndrome (AIDS)** and can be communicated to a child by an infected mother. Before blood-screening procedures were instituted, the virus was also transmitted in blood transfusions. The effects of the infection in children include central nervous system damage, additional infections, developmental delay, motor problems, psychosocial stresses, and death.

STORCH infections are congenital and include many different viruses. Cytomegalovirus (CMV), a virus of the herpes group, is extremely common in children. Approximately 40% of children and most adults have been infected with this virus (Taylor & Taylor, 1989). Although usually harmless, infection by this virus in a fetus can lead to brain damage, blindness, and hearing loss. Therefore, pregnant women who do not have antibodies to the disease must protect themselves and their unborn children from CMV and other STORCH infections (syphilis, rubella, herpes, hepatitis).

IDENTIFICATION

Multidisciplinary teams are required by IDEA '97 as part of the assessment process for all children suspected of having a disability. However, for children with physical impairments and special health care needs, these teams represent the broadest array of professionals from a wide variety of disciplines. The assessment process for these individual students may be extremely complex, involving various professionals and the child's parents throughout the IEP development and implementation process. Each professional uses a variety of assessment tools and techniques. A complete evaluation for a child with cerebral palsy, for example, includes many professionals, all seeking input and consultation from the parents. The report from the

MAKING
CONNECTIONS

For other discussions about preventing infectious diseases, see:
• Causes and Prevention section in Chapter 6
• Concepts and Controversy, Chapter 5

infectious diseases. Contagious diseases.
acquired immuno-deficiency syndrome (AIDS). A usually fatal medical syndrome caused by infection from the human immunodeficiency virus.
STORCH infections. Includes many different congenital viruses.

MAKING CONNECTIONS

To review the IEP process, see Chapter 2.

NEW DIRECTIONS FOR THE MILLENNIUM

Legacy: Although the ADA law requires that all new buildings (and old buildings as they are remodeled) be accessible to people with disabilities, barriers remain an impediment to full participation in American society.

Opportunities:

- Provide federal and state funding to bring all public buildings up to accessibility standards
- Provide tax incentive to private business to renovate physical space to become fully accessible

MAKING CONNECTIONS

For discussions about the biases in U.S. society toward those who do not meet the standards of physical strength or beauty, see in this chapter:

- the opening section
- History

multidisciplinary team for this child will include a physician's evaluation; an evaluation by adapted physical educators, PTs, and OTs; assessments by other professionals such as SLPs and technology experts (depending on the nature and severity of the disability); as well as a thorough academic, vocational, and intellectual evaluation by teachers and diagnosticians. Parent involvement throughout the process is crucial, and the family's culture must also be appreciated and considered.

Physicians are often the first involved with the diagnosis of a physical or health impairment. For these youngsters in particular, doctors (or professionals from the health care community) frequently remain integrally involved in an ongoing way during treatment. They can be of great assistance to educators as instructional programs are planned and appropriate learning environments are designed. Physicians can also be invaluable resources as educators improve their understanding of the individual child's particular condition, resulting limitations, and the accommodations required to provide an appropriate education for the student.

Each discipline and its professionals have unique roles in the assessment of these students' needs and the implementation of their IEPs. For example, PTs evaluate the quality of the person's movement and later teach the student how to compensate and change inefficient motor patterns. OTs work closely with PTs as they assess and later work with upper-body movement, fine motor skills, and daily living activities. Together, PTs and OTs determine the student's physical characteristics and the assistive devices that will benefit the individual (Best et al., 1994). Rehabilitation engineers and assistive technologists recommend and devise mobility and special seating systems and are able to create equipment that will attach other devices (e.g., communication devices) to wheelchairs.

SIGNIFICANCE

Think about how you have reacted in the past to people you have met who look different. The reactions of others have been and continue to be a major problem for students with physical and health impairments and only compound the challenges they face because of their disabilities. Physical differences and health impairments are often obvious, even at first meeting. As a consequence, individuals with these disabilities are forced to deal with the often negative or stereotypical reactions of others in addition to their own feelings about their appearance. They must also address the actual physical and medical requirements of their disabilities and accomplish the tasks of school and daily life. Educators can play an important role in helping these youngsters meet these important challenges and shape satisfying lives for themselves. And the time might now be right as these students enter a changing society with a much more positive outlook for people with disabilities.

Before the Americans with Disabilities Act (ADA) was passed by Congress, and still today, many individuals who face physical impairments were not allowed the opportunity to participate in many aspects of daily life because of physical barriers (e.g., curbs and stairs) and discrimination. Unfortunately, physical barriers still exist in many schools and public buildings because they are old and have not been renovated. Many school doors are too heavy for many students with disabilities to open, school entrances are too steep to maneuver, and many bathrooms are still unsuitable. Although all problems are not yet resolved, important changes signal a better future of access and inclusion in mainstream society.

The junior U.S. Senator from Georgia is certain testimony to changing times in American politics. Senator Max Cleland lost his legs and right arm in a grenade

Joe has waited 20 years for this bus.

Now, thanks to your support of the Americans with Disabilities Act, all public buses ordered after August 1990 must be wheelchair accessible. So for Joe, and others with disabilities, the wait will soon be over.

Because public transportation is for everyone.

accident in Vietnam in 1968. He is a big man with an even bigger zest for life who drives hard political bargains during the day and dances and celebrates his victories at night. It is unlikely that this political centrist and advocate for people with disabilities would have found himself in the U.S. Senate in earlier eras. However, Cleland reports that even the Capitol is not yet fully accessible (Stone, 1997). "It's a real good challenge getting around here," (p. 9D). Cleland is referring to difficulties when maneuvering through the narrow Senate chambers and over the blue, red, and gold carpet, which he says is like riding a bicycle through sand. For another example of people with disabilities finding their places in modern American society you need only to look at how they are now being featured in commercial advertisements. Paula Jean Nicholson-Klimin is the first woman who uses a wheelchair to work for a major modeling agency and was the first woman with a disability to appear on a New York fashion runway (Barry, 1994). Although her debut was only a few years ago, it appears that she is part of a growing trend. Many major stores and manufacturers are now including people with disabilities in their advertisements. This is part of a larger climate of overall acceptance and participation of people with disabilities in everyday life.

Resorts and vacation planners are now seeking out and planning to meet the needs of travelers with

Not too many years ago, individuals with disabilities found it difficult to find jobs as models. But, today, attitudes have changed to allow many like Nicole Parsons, who uses a wheelchair, to have successful modeling careers.

Senator Max Cleland dances with his supporters from Georgia at a victory celebration party.

disabilities. For example, Miami now offers visitors with disabilities a variety of activities and is actively promoting the area's accessibility and vacation opportunities (Samuels, 1995). The city offers a range of usually inaccessible activities—for example, sailing in small boats. Shake-a-Leg, a nonprofit organization, supports a free three-hour ride and even helps in transferring people from wheelchairs to a special boat seat. Some parks have special "surfchairs," specialized chairs with "puffy" wheels that allow movement on soft sand. Even the Everglades National Park has an accessible monorail so that visitors with disabilities can visit the park and see all of the wildlife. This is only a sampling of the special accommodations Miami has created to lure more tourists. Many other sites are seeking out the potentially lucrative tourist business of a previously untapped group of potential travelers. Many business are now also finding that people with disabilities provide a large and profitable market for the travel industry.

As mentioned earlier, athletics is playing a more important role in the lives of many people with disabilities. Wheelchair events are now an integral part of many marathons, with athletes as dedicated as those who win typical events. In addition to wheelchair basketball, tennis, and soccer, special divisions for sports for youngsters with disabilities are being organized in many cities across the nation (Woods, 1994). Special Challenger Division is often where children with disabilities get their start. These special athletic programs allow participation in sports where children with physical limitations are not typically welcome because they might negatively affect the outcomes of the competitions. Early access to sports and team activities can set the stage for an adult life that includes physical activity and social involvement in community events.

MAKING CONNECTIONS

For a reminder about how people with disabilities have been treated across time, reread the Essence of Disabilities section (Chapter 1).

HISTORY OF THE FIELD

The history of physical and health impairments is as long as human history. Anthropologists have discovered skeletons with physical disabilities in grave sites over eleven thousand years old (Frayer et al., 1987). The history of treatment is as long. Evidence of treatment for spinal cord injuries goes back to prehistoric times as well (Maddox, 1987). The earliest documented treatment was the application of meat and honey to the neck. Beginning with Hippocrates (400 B.C.), treatment usually included traction or even a stretching rack to attempt to straighten the back or push in the deformity. Spinal surgery was performed around 600 A.D., even though it was not until the mid-1800s that anesthesia became available and sterile techniques were used. Even with these medical advances, people with spinal cord injuries generally died soon after their injuries occurred. New techniques of treatment and rehabilitation developed after World War II helped many more people survive their spinal cord injuries and their medical treatment.

Descriptions of conditions such as hemophilia, cerebral palsy, and epilepsy can be found in written records from the past. For example, hemophilia, the most common bleeding disorder, was described as early as 200 B.C. Rabbis noted that its transmission was from mothers to sons (Heller et al., 1996). This hereditary condition was traced through royal and noble families in Spain, Germany, Russia, and England. William J. Little, an English surgeon, described the condition now known as cerebral palsy in well-researched case studies in 1861. Hippocrates recognized that epilepsy originated in the brain but believed that it was caused by several factors: blockage of the normal passage of "phlegm" from the brain, the discharge of cold phlegm into warm blood, and unequal heat distribution in the brain from sitting too long in the sun (Scheerenberger, 1983). Epilepsy continued to receive attention through the Middle Ages. It was frequently linked to mental retardation, and individuals who exhibited epileptic seizures were treated in the same manner as those who exhibited mental retardation. Like mental retardation and behavioral disorders, epilepsy was often wrongly believed to have been caused by immoral conduct by the mother or by evil possession of the individual.

The first U.S. educational institution for children with physical disabilities was established in Boston in 1893: the Industrial School for Crippled and Deformed Children (Eberle, 1922). The first public school classes for "crippled children" were established in Chicago at the turn of the century (La Vor, 1976). Later, schools were established in New York City, Philadelphia, and Cleveland. Special schools for students with disabilities resulted from well-intended motives and reasons. They provided a centralized place where expensive equipment (e.g., therapy swimming pools) and highly skilled professionals could work with all the children with very special physical needs from the area. Such treatment, education, and facilities were not feasible when these youngsters were not in a central location. However, they were segregated, and students with disabilities were educated together with no classroom interaction with their neighborhood friends. Advocates with disabilities have called for the closure of all of these special schools, many speaking from their own school experiences in segregated settings (Winzer, 1993).

While children with physical disabilities and special health care needs have always been part of the human experience, the causes of these disabilities and the teachers' responsibilities have changed over the years. Concerns about these children have differed because factors relating to them have differed, factors such as the overall health status of children in society, the ability of medicine and science to address certain health problems, and general views toward children and health. For example, a text published in 1948, *Helping Handicapped Children in School* (Dolch, 1948), included chapters titled "Crippled Children" and "Health Handicaps." The chapter on "crippled children" focused primarily on heart trouble caused by rheumatic fever, measles, scarlet fever, and diphtheria. These diseases, once common, are now rare. Even when children contract them today, the damage can usually be limited by the use of antibiotics and other medical advances. But other causes of these disabilities now demand our attention. Dolch's 1948 chapter on "crippled children" closes by urging prevention by decreasing the accident rate and by providing prenatal and obstetrical care for all mothers and medical care for all children—pleas that continue to be heard today. The chapter on health disabilities also addressed issues

Ed Roberts was a leader in the civil rights movement for people with disabilities. He aggressively advocated for changes in public policy that would promote participation of people with disabilities in an accessible society.

that were a sign of their time: infected and decayed teeth, chronic cold and bronchitis, glandular problems, tuberculosis, and malnutrition.

The U.S. Congress passed significant legislation concerning these disabilities after World War I and World War II. The Soldiers' Rehabilitation Act was passed in 1918 to offer vocational rehabilitation services to wounded soldiers. Two years later, a similar law for civilians with physical disabilities was passed: the Citizens Vocational Rehabilitation Act (La Vor, 1976). (People with mental illness and mental retardation were not added to this law until 1943.) Additional laws were passed following the Vietnam War and other wars. Soldiers returned with war injuries so serious that employers, family members, friends, and the individuals themselves forced major changes in order to reintegrate them into society. Thus in 1965, the National Commission on Architectural Barriers was established to study the problems facing people with physical disabilities.

MAKING

CONNECTIONS

For more about Section 504 of the Rehabilitation Act, the ADA law, and the disability advocacy movement, see the Necessity for National Intervention section of Chapter 1.

Over the past three decades, disability has come to be understood in political terms. People with physical disabilities have played an important part in changing the political, legal, and social climate for all individuals with disabilities. As with many underrepresented groups, the disability community needed a catalyst to begin an organized civil rights movement. In the view of many, Ed Roberts was just that catalyst (Shaw, 1995; Stone, 1995). Although Section 504 of the Rehabilitation Act (prohibiting discrimination) was passed in 1973, it took a wheelchair sit-in, orchestrated by Ed Roberts, in the office of Secretary Califano at the Department of Health, Education and Welfare (now Health and Human Services) four years later to bring about the implementing regulations. The passage of ADA in 1990 is another example of the important role people with physical disabilities have played in improving society's response to all people with disabilities.

At the age of 14, Ed Roberts almost died from polio. After considerable struggle and persistence, in the early 1960s he was ready to attend college, but the University of California (UC) at Berkeley declared that he was "too disabled" for the campus to accommodate. Also, the California Department of Vocational Rehabilitation would not pay for his education because he was "too handicapped." Despite this rejection, he paid for the personal care attendants he needed to attend UC, and he became known as one of the "Rolling Quads" on campus. After receiving his bachelor's and master's degrees, he became the director of the agency that had previously refused to support his education. In 1984, with the monetary award he received from being honored as a MacArthur fellow, Roberts co-founded the World Institute on Disability, which many mark as the formal beginning of the civil rights movement for people with disabilities. In 1995, at the age of 56, he died; but his movement has not, and the voices of people with disabilities are heard across the nation, still demanding acceptance, access, and inclusion.

PREVALENCE

ADHD is also discussed in these sections of the text: Solutions (Chapter 1), Children with Learning Disabilities (Chapter 4), Concepts and Controversy (Chapter 8).

Although the low prevalence rates of physical and health impairments are meaningless to children and their families who are affected, educators should remember that relatively few children have these problems, and many who do have them do not require special education. According to the Twentieth Annual Report to Congress on the Implementation of the Individuals with Disabilities Education Act (U.S. Department of Education, 1998), only .38% (227,224) of all children between the ages of 6 and 21 have physical impairments and special health care needs. Using this terminology and data, approximately 1.3% (66,400) of all children receiving special education services are categorized as having orthopedic impairments; another 3.1% of students enrolled in special education (160,824) are classified as having other health impairments. Thus only some 3% of all children receiving special education services and only 0.4% of all schoolchildren fall within the categories discussed in this chapter. Remember, some of these children have co-existing disabilities that may cause them to be categorized and reported as having multiple disabilities rather than orthopedic or health problems. Also, with ADHD now included in the health impairments category, it is likely that numbers in this category will increase.

The largest group of children with chronic illnesses in America's schools has asthma (Getch & Neuharth-Pritchett, 1999). Asthma is very serious, accounting for 78% of the death rate in children under the age of 19. Approximately 6% of all schoolchildren have asthma, and it is the leading cause of school absenteeism. Regardless, only a small percentage have special education needs. It is wrong to assume that even serious conditions always result in a disability. About 1% of all fetuses contract CMV, but only 10% to 15% of this 1% develop a disability. About 1% of the general population has epilepsy, but substantially less than 1% of the school population has the condition, with 85% of the cases controlled by medication (Epilepsy Education Department of Neurology, University of Minnesota, 1993). About .03% of all children have cerebral palsy, and some of them do not require special education services (United Cerebral Palsy, 1993).

The prevalences of some physical and health problems differ by locale, while others differ by race or ethnicity. For example, the rate of spina bifida in Northern Ireland is 4 to 5 per every 1,000 children, while in Columbia it is 0.1 per 1,000 (Rowley-Kelly & Reigel, 1993). No one knows why rates of spina bifida vary so widely. Sickle-cell anemia, although seen across ethnic groups, is more prevalent in African Americans. A startling 8% of this ethnic group has inherited the condition (Heller et al., 1996). And sadly, the degree and nature of their disability is significant, requiring the fullest efforts of multidisciplinary teams to develop and implement their therapy and educational programs.

Most diseases and conditions that seriously affect children continue to change across time. In some cases, this is good news; in others, it is not. For example, polio, a viral infection that attacks the nerve cells in the spinal cord that control muscle function, is a serious disease that ravaged this country in the 1950s and 1960s, leaving many people with a significant, permanent disability. Hundreds of thousands of Americans contracted the disease, with the worst epidemic, some 56,000 new cases, being in 1952. Many of the senior advocates with disabilities today were disabled by polio. Jonas Salk developed a vaccine, and by the end of the 1960s polio was almost eradicated in the United States. In 1994, only eight cases (caused by the vaccine) were reported in the entire nation, though the disease is still prevalent in developing countries. While the prevalence of polio decreased dramatically, some conditions remained stable. For example, the birth prevalence of cerebral palsy has remained relatively the same for over forty years (Cheney & Palmer, 1997).

Unfortunately, as the prevalence lessens for some conditions, others increase, and new conditions seem to appear unexpectedly. For example, the incidence of asthma is increasing sharply, making it one of only three chronic diseases on the rise throughout the world (the others are AIDS and tuberculosis). Some twenty years ago, HIV infection was never found in children. In 1988 the Centers for Disease Control reported 1,065 cases of pediatric AIDS across the entire nation; 839 were infants and 226 were adolescents. By December 1994, 6,245 cases of pediatric AIDS (below the age of 13) had been reported (Lesar et al., 1995). Its prevalence in infants and children now increases every year, but fortunately current levels have not reached predictions. Although children with AIDS represent less than 2% of the total number of persons with AIDS, the majority of them during their preschool years are not very ill and they live well into their schoolyears (Beverly & Thomas, 1997).

CAUSES AND PREVENTION

To get an overview of how disabilities are caused and how they can be prevented, review the Causes and Prevention sections in this text.

Just as there are many different illnesses, diseases, and conditions that result in disabilities, there are as many different causes, preventions, and treatments. Instead of discussing these specifically for each condition, some common themes and conditions are used as examples. Individual students' programs must reflect the impact of the disability on them, their own and their family's priorities, and the skills that must be mastered to achieve independent living as an adult. The summary in Table 9.4 was designed to help in your understanding of these children's disabilities, what caused them, and how they might have been prevented.

CAUSES

There are almost as many causes for the conditions that result in physical impairments and special health care needs as there are conditions. They can be grouped into some general areas: infections, heredity, accidents and injuries, multiple factors, and "unknown."

Infections. The causes of some disabling conditions are clearly known and understood, although at this time they still cannot be cured. One such case is HIV infections. In children under age 13, the cause of HIV infection can be traced primarily to the risk behaviors of their parents. A few years ago, approximately 75% acquired the infection from their mothers before or at the time of birth and 20% acquired the infection from blood transfusions. In the 1970s and 1980s, the nation's blood supply was contaminated with the HIV virus, and many hemophiliacs, unfortunately, became infected through blood transfusion. In 1982 three cases of AIDS in people with hemophilia could be documented as being caused by blood transfusion. By June 1990, 1,546 people with hemophilia were diagnosed with AIDS. Fortunately, today the blood supply is free from AIDS and hepatitis B viruses (Heller et al., 1996). (Today it is highly unlikely that new cases are caused from blood transfusion.) In contrast, the HIV infections of adolescents are caused primarily by their own risk behaviors.

TABLE 9.4 Causes and Prevention of Physical Disabilities and Health Impairments

Causes	Prevention
Motor vehicle accidents	Child restraints Safety belts Auto air bags Motorcycle helmets
Water and diving accidents	Diving safety Swimming safety
Gunshot wounds	Gun control Weapons training Locked storage of ammunition
Sports injuries (boxing, skiing, football)	Headgear and protective equipment Safe fields and slopes Conditioning/training
Child abuse	Family support services Parenting training
Poisoning/toxins	Knowledge of resources in emergencies Safe storage of poisons
Diseases such as polio, measles	Vaccinations
Premature birth	Prenatal care
Infectious diseases	Vaccinations Good hygiene
HIV infection	Abstinence or safe sex Avoidance of drugs Drug equipment not shared Screening of blood and plasma supplies
Genetic disabilities	Genetic screening
Seizures	Medication
Hydrocephaly	Surgery and medical technology
Asthma	Elimination of allergens from the environment

Heredity. Genetic profiles are the cause of many disabling conditions. As we learn more about many of the conditions thought to have unknown causes, many cases appear to have a genetic link. Hemophilia, which occurs in only 1 in every 10,000 births, seems to be linked to the X chromosome because it is carried by the mother and passed on to the son. Muscular dystrophy, a relatively rare disease (with an incidence of about 2 in every 10,000 people) is another hereditary condition. It is a neuromotor disease in which muscle tissue is replaced by fat tissue, thus decreasing the strength and muscle use of the individual. In most cases of Duchene muscular dystrophy, the condition is carried by the mother and exhibited by some of her children.

Accidents or Injuries. Americans must improve their vigilance against child abuse because the resulting injuries can lead to cerebral palsy, seizure disorders, spinal cord injuries, brain damage, and even death. For example, spinal cord injury in young children, often caused by automobile accidents, can also be the result of child abuse. (A common site of spinal cord dislocation is in the lower back, due to the effects of spanking.) In older children, the most common causes of spinal cord injury are car accidents, falls and jumps, gunshot wounds, and diving accidents. In these cases, the importance of safety equipment (e.g., seat belts, helmets, protective gear) and caution are vitally important.

Multiple Factors. Seizure disorders can be the result of many conditions and circumstances. Dividing them into two groups—primary epilepsies (usually congenital) and secondary epilepsies (acquired)—can help in sorting out some of the common causes of this condition. **Primary epilepsy** appears at a young age, usually in families with some history of epilepsy. Often there is a predictable pattern to the seizure and its response to specific medications. **Secondary (lesional) epilepsy** may appear at any age and can result from accidents or child abuse; degenerative diseases (e.g., Sturge-Weber syndrome); brain tumors and abscesses; lesions, head injury; lead poisoning, infections, like meningitis or encephalitis; or alcohol or drug withdrawal (Epilepsy Foundation of America, 1994).

Another example of a condition that results from different causes is cerebral palsy, which can be caused by impaired development, injury, or disease. It may be congenital (present at birth) or acquired within the first three years of life. Let's look at these categories a little more closely. In congenital cerebral palsy, a developing infant may have been deprived of necessary amounts of oxygen when something went wrong during birth. Cerebral palsy may also result from the effects of premature birth; very low birth weight; blood type (Rh) incompatibility; the mother's infection with rubella, CMV, or other viral diseases; and attacks by other dangerous microorganisms (Nelson & Grether, 1997). Most clearly, the later onset of cerebral palsy typically results from vehicle accidents, brain infections such as meningitis, poisoning through toxins such as lead (ingested in paint chips from walls), serious falls, or injuries from child abuse.

Unknown Causes. With some unknown causes, the medical profession has some good ideas about why the condition exists. Such is the case with asthma: The basic causes of asthma are unknown, but it is believed to be the result of an allergic reaction to certain substances (allergens) in individuals who have a physical predisposition to the condition. The substances that can trigger allergic reactions vary by individual; for some people it may be foods, for others plants, environmental pollutants, chemicals, cigarette smoke, dust mites, cockroaches, or viruses. Daily activity involving heightened periods of exercise may also be a cause. The medical profession is working hard to pinpoint some of these unknown causes. Past experience indicates that when medical researchers can pinpoint the cause of a condition, they are then much closer to finding a way to treat or prevent the condition. A good case in point is polio: The cause was pinpointed as a virus and a vaccine was soon developed to protect individuals from contracting the disease. But those already affected faced a lifetime disability requiring extensive supports.

PREVENTION

Some physical disabilities and health impairments are relatively easy to prevent, but others are not. Remember, many disabilities are caused through no one's fault and cannot be avoided. For most conditions that cannot be prevented, however, the disabling effects can be lessened through treatment. This section is organized with five themes about prevention: prenatal care, vaccinations, avoidance of injuries, prevention of infectious diseases and other illnesses, and treatment.

primary epilepsy. Predictable seizure disorders that appear at a young age and appear to be hereditary.
secondary (lesional) epilepsy. Seizure disorders that appear at any age and seem to occur in response to particular damage.

For more about national immunization programs, see the Concepts and Controversy section of Chapter 5.

**NEW DIRECTIONS
FOR THE
MILLENNIUM**

Legacy: In 1994 Congress passed the Vaccines for Children Program, which guaranteed that vaccines for low- and moderate-income children would be free and available, and this landmark legislation has made a dramatic impact on the reduction of unnecessary illnesses with lifelong effects.

Opportunities:
- Make funding for this program permanent
- Expand the program to include immunizations for all preventable diseases

Prenatal Care. Throughout this text, the importance of pregnant women taking good care of themselves and their unborn babies is stressed. Women who follow some simple measures have a better chance of having healthy babies. Women should be sure they are in good health before they become pregnant and obtain early prenatal care from a physician while pregnant. Prenatal care can ensure access to intensive medical care for the mother and infant if problems occur; provide diagnosis and treatment for diseases in the mother, such as diabetes, that can damage developing infants; and help prevent exposure of the fetus to infections, viruses, drugs, alcohol, and other toxins. Prenatal care also can protect the health of pregnant women so that their babies are born well nourished, healthy, and at full term.

Vaccinations. Vaccines can safeguard children from infectious diseases and avoid millions of dollars in health care costs and millions of lives confronted with unnecessary risks and disabilities. Vaccines have eradicated some diseases. No doubt the medical profession is well on the way toward the discovery of many other vaccines to protect us from potentially devastating diseases.

Smallpox once devastated people all over the world, but today only limited and geographically isolated incidents occur. Vaccines have all but eliminated polio in the United States, with the last naturally occurring case in 1979 (Neergaard, 1995). This news has led some parents, incorrectly, to believe that it is safer not to immunize their children, a situation that can lead to unnecessary cases of dangerous diseases. The Children's Defense Fund (CDF) reports that in 1993 only 67% of all U.S. 2-year-olds were appropriately immunized, a dangerous and unnecessary situation (Finlay, 1995). However, with the passage of the Vaccines for Children Program in 1993, high-cost vaccines are now free to the uninsured and poor children. In 1997 the immunization rate for these toddlers exceeded 90% (CDF, 1997). The remaining barrier is educating parents to understand the importance of protecting their children.

Avoidance of Injuries. Prevention programs designed to promote the protection of children from injury can decrease the number of children subjected to brain damage and serious physical injury. It is important that as many accidents be prevented as possible and that when accidents do occur the individual is protected. The use of seat belts, air bags, helmets, and other protective devices can reduce injuries from motor vehicle and sports-related accidents. Proper child care, child supervision, and family support can help families avoid household accidents and family stresses that can lead to child injury. Family support services and training in effective parenting techniques can help parents understand the harmful physical and emotional effects of physical punishment.

Prevention of Infectious Diseases and Other Illnesses. As already mentioned, teachers cannot prevent many cases of infectious diseases. Children can become infected outside of the school setting and infect other children before they become sick themselves. However, teachers must become more aware and use preventive techniques in their classrooms so that children do not contract infectious diseases. Teachers can play an important role in this regard. For example, when they suspect that a child is sick, they should inform the school nurse and the parents. The longer infected children are playing and learning with their peers, the more the likelihood increases that the classmates will become infected. Diseases can be transmitted from unclean objects in the classroom as well, so all students must learn to wash their hands frequently, keep toys and play areas clean and disinfected, and use some commonsense hygienic precautions at school.

The Centers for Disease Control and physicians stress the importance of universal precautions of sanitation and hygiene, especially with all blood and bodily fluids. The need for these precautions stems from the increased rates of hepatitis-B and HIV among schoolchildren. Disposable gloves should be worn when helping a child who is bleeding from a fall on the playground or perhaps a cut from a pair of scissors used in an art activity. One common mistake of teachers is forgetting to dispose of the gloves and use a new pair whenever the next situation arises. Teachers must be sure not to work with another child while still wearing the used gloves and, after removing the soiled gloves, must be sure to wash their hands. All young children tend to have accidents at school; teachers should have a sufficient supply of gloves on hand to handle those small emergencies common in most classrooms.

The frequency of episodes of some illnesses can be reduced through the efforts of teachers. For example, asthma is often triggered by exposure to specific allergens (Getch & Neuharth-Pritchett, 1999). For some students the chance of an asthma attack is reduced when the classroom is free of chalk dust, plants that generate pollen or mold, cold and dry air, smoke, paint fumes, and chemical smells. Class pets (their fur) can cause an asthma attack. By keeping classrooms free from these sources of pollutants, teachers can help reduce the probability of an attack and resulting illness and absences from school.

Treatment. A variety of treatments, medical and educational, are available for children with physical impairments and special health care needs. The range of treatment options is great. Some treatments must be conducted by medical professionals; others are provided by health related service providers (e.g., SLPs, OTs, PTs); and still others can be conducted by educators and paraprofessionals at schools. At the heart of the multidisciplinary treatment efforts are educators coordinating, delivering, and ensuring an appropriate education and health maintenance program to all of these youngsters.

Medical treatments by physicians are not covered by IDEA; those costs are borne by insurance, government programs, or the family. Regardless, remember that many physical impairments and health problems are solved by medical treatments. Infants born with spinal column (neural tube) defects have surgery to repair the back and to avoid infection or meningitis, which otherwise could result in mental retardation. Some children with spina bifida have hydrocephaly (a buildup of excess fluid in the brain), and to avoid mental retardation a shunt must be surgically implanted to drain excess spinal fluid from the child's brain.

Treatment does not guarantee a "cure" or an improved situation for all individuals with disabilities. For example, many students with cerebral palsy will face significant challenges their entire lives. Only about 85% of those with epilepsy have their seizures controlled through medication (Epilepsy Foundation of America, 1994). And as you know, asthma cannot be cured, but the factors that stimulate episodes can be eliminated or substantially reduced. Even when all precautions have been taken, some asthmatics will still have attacks, and epileptics will still have seizures. Teachers must know what to do for the child during an asthma attack and during a seizure episode. Consultation with the student, the family, and the physician is necessary to monitor medications, to administer breathing treatment, and to plan procedures for assisting the child during an attack. Likewise, teachers must know what to do when a student has a seizure. Table 9.5 on page 390 lists the steps to take in the event of such an emergency at school.

Table 9.5 Treatment Guidelines for Epileptic Seizure

Seizure Type	What to Do	What Not to Do
Generalized tonic-clonic (also called grand mal)	Look for medical identification. Protect from nearby hazards. Loosen ties or shirt collars. Protect head from injury. Turn on side to keep airway clear; reassure when consciousness returns. If single seizure lasted less than 5 minutes, ask if hospital evaluation is wanted. If multiple seizures, or if one seizure lasts longer than 5 minutes, call an ambulance. If person is pregnant, injured, or diabetic, call for aid at once.	Don't put any hard implement in the mouth. Don't try to hold tongue; it can't be swallowed. Don't try to give liquids during or just after seizure. Don't use artificial respiration unless breathing is absent after muscle jerks subside, or unless water has been inhaled. Don't restrain.
Absence (also called petit mal)	No first aid necessary, but if this is the first observation of the seizure(s), medical evaluation should be recommended.	
Simple partial	No first aid necessary unless seizure becomes convulsive, then first aid as above. No immediate action needed other than reassurance and emotional support. Medical evaluation should be recommended.	
Complex partial (also called psychomotor or temporal lobe)	Speak calmly and reassuringly to patient and others. Guide gently away from obvious hazards. Stay with person until completely aware of environment. Offer to help getting home.	Don't grab hold unless sudden danger (such as a cliff edge or an approaching car) threatens. Don't try to restrain. Don't shout. Don't expect verbal instructions to be obeyed.

Source: From *Seizure recognition and first aid,* Epilepsy Foundation of America, 1996. Landover, MD: Author. Reprinted with permission.

CHILDREN WITH PHYSICAL IMPAIRMENTS AND SPECIAL HEALTH CARE NEEDS

The health care needs of some children are so consuming that everything else becomes a secondary priority. Other students—like some with physical impairments—require substantial accommodations to the physical environment so that learning is accessible to them, but their learning characteristics are quite similar to those of their typical classmates. In this section, discussion about the characteristics of these children is divided into two major parts: Characteristics Affecting Learning, and Characteristics Affecting the Classroom and School. My hope is that these global discussions about the characteristics presented by these students will help you understand how better learning environments can be designed for all children in classroom settings.

CHARACTERISTICS AFFECTING LEARNING

To learn more about the accommodations that help these children, see the Instructional Accommodations section (Educational Interventions) in this chapter.

The treatment goal for many of these youngsters is for them to stay strong, healthy, and active and to lead as normal lives as possible. Accomplishing this goal requires considerable attention to many components, including medical management. As with all children, education is also a major component of their childhood, but unlike most of their peers, they face many barriers to efficient learning. Here are a few examples of such obstacles that some students experience:

- Fatigue
- Absences
- Inconsistent abilities to pay attention
- Muscle weakness
- Loss of physical coordination

Review the information about cerebral palsy found in the Types of Physical Disabilities and Special Health Care Needs section in this chapter.

Some of these symptoms are directly related to medications and treatment, and others are a function of the disease, illness, or condition. For example, children who are receiving cancer treatment go through periods of feeling too sick to profit from much of the instructional day, and during this time may have frequent absences. Some may require periods of home-bound instruction. In the case of cerebral palsy, symptoms associated with the condition itself should guide instruction (Horn, 1997). Goals for these students must integrate functional skill development into all activities. Because it is best not to teach skills in isolation, students could be taught good posturing positions while reading motivating and interesting books, or they could be taught improved movement skills while playing games or sports. Current thought emphasizes the importance of children with cerebral palsy learning motor skills that have use and function (Horn, 1997; Palmer, 1997).

Teachers can help these youngsters by using some measures. First, they need to be sensitive to the student's changing condition of wellness. Attentive teachers will be able to notice when the child needs a break. Instructional units might be broken into small, concise elements with key terms and facts emphasized. Long and difficult reading assignments can be shortened. For example, when studying a history unit, classmates often find that summarizing content from a chapter in the textbook, developing time lines, and preparing study notes are good learning exercises for them and a great help to their classmate with a special health care need. Teachers can also prepare summary notes and outlines of the information being presented in the history unit as handouts for all students but with particular thought to the learning characteristics of the child with special needs.

Many accommodations required by children who are medically fragile or chronically ill are rather simple. Remember, for many of these children education may not be their personal priority; they are more preoccupied by their health situation. This is both understandable and natural. Being sensitive to their physical condition is probably the most important consideration you can have. Sometimes, the challenges of being sick affect a child's classroom behavior. An otherwise well-behaved child can become a behavior problem. The Achieving Discipline box on page 392 describes one such case, where the effects of a chronic illness extend far beyond the child's physical well being. Teachers must be alert to such situations as they develop. Other accommodations, like the ones listed here, can make a real difference

Achieving Discipline

ACKNOWLEDGE THE EFFORT: REWARDS

Shaquita has sickle-cell anemia, and experiences frequent and severe sickling crises. She is capable of doing her schoolwork, but because of her illness she is often absent from school and seldom feels well. Even on the best of days, Shaquita's muscles and joints ache. She is frequently frustrated by schoolwork, and it is not uncommon for her to be defiant, rude, and angry. She breaks classroom rules more than her classmates by talking out of turn, crumpling her papers, and even throwing them across the room. Shaquita's peers were beginning to resent her, and fewer and fewer people were willing to bring Shaquita's homework to her house, explain missed assignments, or tutor her on the classwork she had missed. Her anger was compounded because classmates were forgetting to bring classwork to her home, and were not spending time to help her catch up.

Ms. Torres, Shaquita's teacher, had a private conference with Shaquita in which they discussed her behavior, her school progress, and strategies they might use to improve the situation. Shaquita talked with her teacher about her physical condition, and how she did not feel that anyone appreciated the pain and exhaustion she experienced. She also talked about how she felt that it was unfair that she was sick, missed school, and could not participate in sports and other school

activities like her friends. Ms. Torres and Shaquita discussed how she needed to exert extra effort to keep up with the class assignments and that her friends, who were trying to help her, also were making extra efforts. They decided that people were not appreciating each other. So, together they designed a reward system where Shaquita's classmates could earn bonus points toward their grades for helping her, and Shaquita would earn bonus points for each homework and in-class assignment from days when she was absent. They also devised a structured schedule in which Shaquita would earn privileges (being the first in line for recess, being able to stay in the classroom alone during lunch break, getting the assignment of hall monitor) when she behaved appropriately.

Setting up a reward system

- Define the desired behavior specifically
- Have the student create a list of privileges or rewards
- Set criteria for behavior
- Determine a plan for how rewards will be earned
- Be sure to give the student the privilege or reward when criteria are met
- Tell the student why the reward was earned and that you appreciate the effort

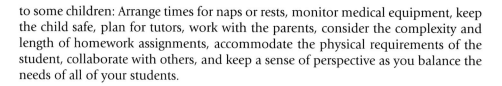

to some children: Arrange times for naps or rests, monitor medical equipment, keep the child safe, plan for tutors, work with the parents, consider the complexity and length of homework assignments, accommodate the physical requirements of the student, collaborate with others, and keep a sense of perspective as you balance the needs of all of your students.

CHARACTERISTICS AFFECTING THE CLASSROOM AND SCHOOL

The challenges facing students with physical limitations and special health care needs and their teachers are great. All schools must meet the special architectural codes required by the ADA law and must be "barrier free." Regardless, these students' world is often filled with physical and social barriers that must be accommodated and overcome before they can achieve independence and a "normal" life.

Eliminating barriers, even obvious physical ones, might be more difficult than you might think. They certainly were for Mattel Toys. The toymaker was quite embarrassed when it was found that the wheelchair of their new doll, Share a Smile Becky, would not fit through the doorway to the Barbie Dream House (*Newsweek*, 1997). This example shows that even those with the best intentions don't always achieve their goals.

Physical Barriers. When considering ways to make an educational environment accessible to a child with a physical problem, educators need to consider all of the places the child needs to go: the bathroom, the lunchroom, the playground, the gymnasium, the music room, the library, the bus, and so on. Remember, the child's educational activities should be chosen on the basis of individual learning needs, not where a wheelchair can and cannot fit.

Every school should have bathroom stalls that accommodate wheelchairs and braces and should have accessible sinks, mirrors, towel dispensers, and door handles. The concept of **accessibility** has many interpretations. It means elevators large enough to hold wheelchairs, handrails along the corridors, chalkboards placed low enough so that children in wheelchairs can write on them, seating arrangements that can accommodate children with a variety of equipment, standing tables so that children can spend time out of wheelchairs, and playground equipment adapted to hold a child with leg braces or in a wheelchair. It also means being able to participate in school activities to the fullest extent.

Integration may require accommodations beyond those required by law (e.g., curb cuts, ramps, elevators, and bathroom alterations). In some cases, it means extra help. For example, teachers of children with spinal cord defects or severe cerebral palsy may need special training to learn how to physically move these children from place to place or to position them for class participation. The PT can provide significant help in this regard and also instruct the teacher on the safest and most appropriate manner to transfer a particular child.

Designing Learning Environments. "Our surroundings affect our moods and temperaments; certain buildings, parks, plazas, and streets lift our spirits; others diminish them" (Sandler, 1989, p. 13). Teachers and children spend a substantial portion of their day in classrooms. Unfortunately, in many classrooms the space and its design restrict learning. For students with physical challenges, poorly designed classroom space can inhibit both academic and social learning. This situation can be remedied and in the process can become an excellent learning opportunity for the entire class.

Buildings and classrooms need to be safe and accessible. Compliance with various construction codes provides basic safety and accessibility, but those codes do not ensure an environment that is functional, scaled to the size and needs of children, and aesthetically pleasing. The physical environment is often overlooked, ignored, and misused (Taylor, 1990). Although teachers and students cannot alter the structure of the school building, they can redesign the space within a classroom. Students can collect data by using simple frequency counts to study the traffic patterns they use in the classroom. They can redesign the organization of desks, tables, work areas, storage space, and learning centers. They can generate visual design alternatives to their environment as it is currently structured through drawings and models. They can work together as a class to evaluate the functionality of these potential re-creations of their learning environment, and as a unit decide how to best

MAKING CONNECTIONS

Review issues related to accessibility and participation of people with physical disabilities by rereading the Significance and History sections in this chapter and the Necessity for National Intervention section in Chapter 1.

accessibility. Barrier-free environments allowing maximal participation by individuals with disabilities.

use the space allocated to them in what is referred to as a classroom. This experience can help to create a more exciting and useful learning environment for every class member and can be particularly helpful to students who face physical challenges.

As the entire class works to create a better learning environment, everyone's learning styles and needs must be considered. Students with physical problems provide a special opportunity for creativity. The class must become sensitive to the physical environment and how it can create unnecessary barriers to learning and social interaction. Students with physical problems may require specially fitted chairs, desks, and worktables and perhaps extra space for maneuvering bulky equipment like crutches or wheelchairs. These factors need to be considered when redesigning physical space. Many students with severe physical impairments require bulky language boards or computers for communication, which present challenges not only during instruction and small-group work activities but also for storage and security. Space must be allocated so that everybody can interact with the child using assistive technology.

As the class seeks to improve other learning environments, keeping everyone's needs in mind, there are many "consultants" who can provide assistance. Architects and design engineers can serve as valuable resources to the class. How do you find such experts to help? Check with the student's parents and school administrators. Call your local college or university to see whether some architecture, engineering, or interior design students would work with the class for several hours. Explore some options with a local construction company. You might be surprised how willing people from the community are to volunteer their time and expertise to this activity. Also consider professionals who are already working with your students. For example, the OT and PT providing direct instruction or itinerant services to the student with physical challenges can also serve as excellent resources to the entire class as they rethink their classroom space. For this activity to meet its potential as an excellent, integrated learning experience, be sure that all of the students remain actively involved.

The benefits of having children participate in creating their classroom learning environment can be great. In addition to designing space conducive to each class member's learning style and physical requirements, the activity itself is a wonderful learning experience that uses many different types of thinking skills as well as integrates many academic areas (e.g., math, reading, and even history). One group of youngsters applied their academic skills and knowledge about barriers to accessible spaces in a service learning project (Long, 1999). A class of middle school students built a nature trail at a local park so classmates could use their wheelchairs on field trips when the class was studying native plants. Taylor and Warden (1994) believe that this practical application of knowledge helps students develop critical thinking skills, solve problems, work cooperatively, apply knowledge to real-life situations, and develop social responsibility. What other benefits can you think of?

EDUCATIONAL INTERVENTIONS

Educators must be aware of the wide variety of potential obstacles to students' education and learning. For students with physical problems and special health care needs, many of these obstacles are different from other "difficult to teach" students. To facilitate an appropriate education for some of these youngsters, teachers need to learn how to assist a child with health care needs, how to deal with frequent absences, how to assist a child who is having a seizure, how to make scheduling accommodations, how to address special issues relating to movement in the classroom, how to adapt the class activities, how to adapt teaching techniques, and how to promote social integration. Even more important is the creation of an exciting learning environment where children are free, both physically and psychologically, to experiment, take risks, interact with one another, and learn.

EDUCATION AND THE PRESCHOOL CHILD

Whether the impairment is physical or health related, early intervention programs provide a strong foundation for the child and family. Parents play an especially crucial educational role during these early years. If the child's intervention program is to be successful, the parents' efforts and enthusiasm must be supported by the other members of the team. In this section, two areas that often are concerns for parents, and the multidisciplinary teams of professionals working with them, are motor development and positioning and developing communication skills. Those are discussed here.

To refresh your memory about IFSPs, see the Individualized Education Plans section in Chapter 2.

Motor Development and Positioning. For some children, early intervention programs focus primarily on motor development. For example, children born with cerebral palsy may have reflex patterns that interfere with typical motor development that sets the stage for maximum independence, including body schema, body awareness, purposeful motor use, and mobility. In many cases, direct instruction is necessary, but before teachers and parents become involved in the educational program they must be trained and supervised to be sure that they do not put the child at risk for injury (Horn, 1997). Enlisting multidisciplinary team members like the OT, PT, and nurse can ensure the development of an effective program and also help properly prepare those who will carry out the program. The student's program usually includes a regimen of special exercises to develop motor skills. The purpose may be to strengthen weak muscle groups through the use of weights or to adapt to and use artificial limbs or orthopedic devices. Once teachers and family members know how to assist the child with the exercises, they should not be afraid and should encourage the youngster to move, play, and interact with the environment.

Because this is a time of tremendous physical and sensorimotor growth, normal motor patterns must be established as early as possible. For those children who already have abnormal motor patterns, repeating those patterns should not be encouraged. The child should always, both at school and at home, be positioned properly so that alignment, muscle tone, and stability are correct during all activities. Specific equipment, such as foam-rubber wedges, Velcro straps, and comfortable mats are used to properly position children with physical disabilities. Although some of this equipment is expensive, other items can be made rather inexpensively. Parents and teachers need to keep in touch with therapists to be certain that they are working properly with their children. Also, teachers must remember

Using a supine stander, this boy shares his science project with his class.

that children should not remain in the same position for too long. They should be repositioned every twenty minutes or so.

Developing Communication Skills. For some students, establishing communication is difficult. Parents and professionals should acknowledge and reinforce every attempt at communication. Although determining how a child with severe disabilities is attempting to communicate can be difficult, an observant person can learn a great deal about the child's communication abilities, even when others believe that the child cannot communicate at all. A good observer will be able to answer questions like these: In what specific ways does the child react to sounds? How does the child respond to certain smells? Does the child have different facial movements when different people enter the room? Does the child gaze at certain objects more than others? How is anger expressed to the family? Through careful observation and experience, parents, teachers, and family members can recognize meaningful communication even when others believe there is none. Parents and professionals should also remember that communication is a two-way street. Children learn to communicate with others by being communicated with: Talk to the child, express feelings with face and body, play games together, and encourage the child to listen to tapes and the radio.

EDUCATION AND THE SCHOOLCHILD

Recall that each child with a physical or a health impairment has individualized needs, even those whose diagnoses seem to be the same. Many of these needs are similar to those of children with other types of disabilities; some, however, require different adjustments to the learning environment. For example, many students with disabilities need flexible schedules, more time to learn academic tasks, and extra assistance. This is also the case for many students with special physical and health care needs. Unlike many of their classmates, some of these students demand a unique learning environment, free from physical barriers that inhibit their movement and their interactions with their peers. The way classroom space is designed affects instruction; it is a very important element of the learning environment and should receive particular attention. Therefore, most of the discussions included in this section focus on adapting both instruction and the learning environment.

For other ideas about accommodating for the needs of special learners, see the Accommodating for Inclusive Environments boxes through out this text (Chapters 3–12).

Instructional Accommodations. When the child is ready to enter school, both the child and the child's family become crucial members of the IEP team, providing recommendations for a program. Sometimes simple schedule flexibility is all that is needed. Here's a tip: Ask students to describe their difficulties and what accommodations they need. They are often the best resource when teachers are planning instruction and the individualized accommodations the student needs.

Some students may often be absent from school because they need medical care or because they are too sick or fragile to come to school on certain days. As mentioned earlier, asthma is the leading cause of school absences, but other conditions are also associated with excessive absences: hemophilia, cystic fibrosis, nephrosis, leukemia, and sickle-cell anemia. To help these children keep up with their classmates, schools can:

- Provide a home or hospital teacher
- Use television, computer, or telephone hookups between the child and the classroom

- Make videotapes of special classroom activities
- Allow classmates to take turns acting as a neighborhood peer to tutor after school
- Incorporate the Web and Internet into classroom instruction

These methods not only help the child's academic progress but also maintain a social connection to the teacher and other students. They help the child feel more comfortable about returning to the classroom later when the physical condition or illness has improved.

We often look for complex answers to difficulties when only simple solutions are required. Such is often the case when adapting instruction. The keys are to anticipate accommodations and to apply your own problem solving skills. Let's look at some ways to create accommodations for children who cannot write as fast and efficiently as others. Teachers could

- Allow students extra time to complete written assignments
- Let students use computers for their written work so they can increase their speed and produce pleasing documents
- Ask a classmate of a student who cannot write to make an extra copy by using carbon paper or photocopying a set of class notes
- Tape children's work papers to their desks
- Provide extra-thick pencils
- Have students tape-record instead of writing their assignments

These simple adjustments give a threefold message: (1) You are willing to give the student a chance, (2) the student is important to you, and (3) even with adjustments, you have high expectations for the student to produce acceptable schoolwork.

Test taking is another area in which teachers can make adjustments. Imagine trying to take a timed test while your body goes through uncontrollable jerky movements. This is just one of the difficulties testing presents to children with physical problems. The risk is that, without accommodations, the test will merely measure the degree of physical difficulty experienced by the individual rather than actual intellectual or academic abilities. How can a teacher give a fair test? Oral testing is one way to measure students' skill level. Remember, ask the student with special needs to help in solving problems presented during instruction. Besides your own thinking skills, they are often the best resource to involve because they know what accommodations have been successful in the past.

COLLABORATION FOR INCLUSION

Perhaps more than any other special education area, an array of professionals from many disciplines participate in these students' educational programs, because their needs demand ongoing collaboration by multidisciplinary teams not only for proper assessment, but also for the delivery of a truly appropriate education. The number of experts who participate in the assessment and planning phases of these students' educational programs seems to expand continually, as new technology and knowledge is developed. And attitudes are changing: More and more students with physical challenges (41%) and those with special health care needs (43%) are receiving their education primarily in general education classes (U.S. Department of Education, 1998). Particularly in some parts of the United States, this number can increase even more because some states are still serving many of these students in center schools. Successful integration and inclusion for increasing numbers of children, however,

Accommodating for Inclusive Environments

ADAPTING ALL ASPECTS OF THE CLASSROOM

Adapt the Physical Environment

- Remove hazards
- Create more workspace
- Provide storage space for equipment
- Make furniture accessible
- Widen aisles
- Use positioning devices
- Change seating arrangements
- Rearrange furniture

Change Student Response Mode

- Allow speaking instead of writing
- Use a speech synthesizer
- Allow writing instead of speaking
- Allow computer-print output

Alter Materials and Equipment

- Give handouts
- Adapt writing tools
- Use special eating utensils
- Explore assistive and adaptive technology

Modify the Activity

- Allow more time to complete the assignments
- Abbreviate assignment
- Create a flexible schedule

Provide Extra Assistance

- Arrange peer tutors
- Have parents or family members help
- Find volunteers to assist
- Video or audiotape lessons
- Use e-mail for help-sessions

To refresh your memory about IEPs, see the Individualized Education Plans section in Chapter 2.

requires considerable supports from multidisciplinary teams. In some cases, it requires considerable effort from teachers, who must make adaptations and accommodations for these students (see the Accommodating for Inclusive Environments box for some ideas).

To meet the specific needs of each individual child, educators must seek the assistance of the entire multidisciplinary team who assisted in the assessment process and the development of that child's IEP. Depending on the individual needs of students, different professionals assume the primary responsibility for students' IEP fulfillment. For example, the teacher of a student with a severe physical impairment needs to collaborate closely with the PT; and for the child who also presents a speech impairment, the SLP must be significantly involved in the child's educational program. However, for many children with special health care needs, these professionals might not be as crucial to the implementation of an appropriate education as the child's physician and the school nurse. What is very important is that educators seek the help of the family and those professionals who can help design the best instructional environment for each child who presents one of these special needs.

Teachers are being called on to assume more responsibilities for the medical management of their students. This is due to several factors. First, more and more of these children are receiving their education alongside their neighborhood peers in the general education classroom. Second, local education budgetary cuts are making a school nurse at every school a rare resource. Teachers are now called on to perform some simple tasks that help children with special health care needs. For example, some children may need assistance with their medication while at school.

NEW DIRECTIONS
FOR THE
MILLENNIUM

Legacy: Congress through IDEA '97, and the courts in a 1999 ruling, make it clear that general education classroom placement for children with special health care needs is a serious options under LRE, and costs for supports is not to be a consideration.

Opportunities:

- Increase federal funding for IDEA and special education so the financial burden of excess costs for extensive supports does not fall on the local school district or the state

- Better prepare teachers to handle children's special health care needs and have school nurses available to every school

Coordination among the child, the child's physician, the family, and the school nurse will be necessary so that the child takes the proper dose at the proper times and so the effects of the type of medication and the dosage can be monitored and changed when necessary.

Teachers can also be called on to perform duties that historically have not been considered part of their role at school. Although it is generally understood that all children should attend school, children with fragile health may spend some of their education time at home or in a hospital. When children are in school, teachers may need to provide personal assistance. For example, while older children with paralysis generally are able to accomplish their bathroom needs independently—through the use of self-administered clean intermittent catheterization (CIC)—many younger children need the teacher's assistance. In these cases, it is important to encourage personal privacy when helping a child with hygiene needs, and it is important to maintain the highest of sanitary conditions possible in a school setting. A good start is to have all children wash their hands often. Other children may need extra rest, or support devices such as ventilators, feeding tubes, and ostomy supplies, all of which need careful monitoring by the teacher.

All school personnel working with students with special health care needs must work together, continually informing each other about students' programs and their health care requirements. Here is an example of an accommodation that is important, requires only minor changes to classroom rules, and can prevent major health complications (Rosenthal-Malek & Greenspan, 1999): The general education teacher has a rule that no one will be excused for a bathroom break in the middle of an exam, so when John, who has diabetes, asked to go to the bathroom and also get a drink, the teacher said no. John, however, told the teacher that he was going anyway, and left the classroom. His action could have easily been interpreted as defiant and a major violation of class rules. In John's case, he was probably acting responsibly. He needed to avoid a serious health crisis by keeping his blood sugar at acceptable levels. Better communication among teachers and the multidisciplinary team might have prevented this unfortunate situation.

Inclusion in recreation has many benefits, including activities where social integration is likely to occur naturally. In addition to all the health benefits of recreation and exercise, recreational skills can allow children with physical impairments to have fun with their classmates and can provide opportunities for enjoyment with their families. Many adapted recreational toys and games are available for people with physical impairments. A Frisbee, for example, has been specially adapted with two adjustable clips on the top so that people with limited hand movements can play. Special sports and fitness programs are also available for individuals with physical disabilities. Little League Baseball's Special Challenger Division for children with physical and mental disabilities has a division in most cities (Woods, 1994). This program allows a wonderful opportunity for children who otherwise would not be able to participate in team sports. Workout tapes for individuals with a variety of disabilities, including people who use a wheelchair, have also been developed. Today, the opportunity to participate in team sports is not restricted to special leagues. Although still criticized and not accepted fully, Casey Martin sued to gain the right to use a golf cart in professional tournaments. Some think that despite his disability—he has a rare circulatory disorder that makes it painful to walk—he has an unfair advantage when using a cart (Associated Press, 1998). While some are complaining about athletes with disabilities in competitions, other athletes are seeking help from coaches with disabilities. Doug Blevins is a kicking coach with the

Compare the adult outcomes of individuals with other disabilities to those with physical disabilities and special health care needs by reading the Transition sections throughout this text (Chapters 3–12).

Miami Dolphins. Belvins has cerebral palsy and uses a wheelchair, but those factors do not lessen his demand with professional football teams (Pacenti, 1997). These are only two examples of a changing society wherein individuals with disabilities can participate fully.

TRANSITION THROUGH ADULTHOOD

About 28% of students with physical impairments and special health care needs complete high school (U.S. Department of Education, 1998). This rate should be higher! Without a high school diploma the chance of attending college is small; and, particularly for students with physical impairments who do not have cognitive impairments, a college degree may be the ticket to a high-paying job. Many individuals with physical impairments and special health care needs do attend college. In fact, many college freshman, some 25,000, have identified themselves as having a health-related disability (Edelman et al., 1998). The conditions reported include many different diseases and conditions, including: severe allergies, arthritis, asthma, cancer, cystic fibrosis, diabetes, epilepsy, sickle-cell anemia. So, in addition to providing physical accommodations and barrier-free environments, colleges also need to provide other accommodations for students with health problems, like extra time to take tests, assisted methods for taking class notes, and help in transcribing class tape recordings. The key is for colleges to provide individualized means for these students to accomplish college work.

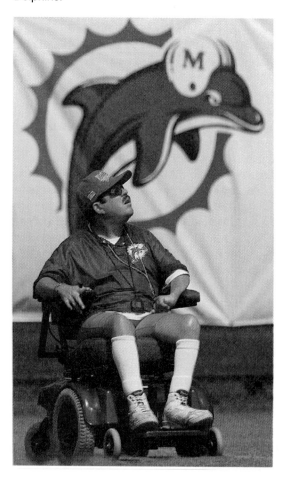

Doug Blevins, unable to kick a football himself, is the highly acclaimed kicking coach for the Miami Dolphins.

Independent living is the goal for many adults with physical disabilities and health impairments. The "independent living movement," people helping themselves to live on their own, has had a great influence on the lives of people with disabilities. Increasingly, adults with physical disabilities and health impairments take control of their lives and their jobs, establish friendships, have families, and exercise political power. Legislation such as the Americans with Disabilities Act (ADA) has had a tremendous impact on the ability of adults with disabilities to pursue their rights and end discrimination, but people with these disabilities must be prepared to take their places in mainstream society. High school transition programs can be very helpful in this regard, by teaching students how to be responsible for their own needs, advocate for themselves, locate the resources they need, and take active roles in their medical management (Edelman et al., 1998). Remember, IDEA does not apply to students after they have left high school, so this important learning time must not be wasted.

Independence is important to all people but is of vital importance to most adolescents and adults with physical impairments or special health care needs. As time goes on, it appears that more and more types of assistance are becoming available. For example, specially trained animals sometimes assist individuals with phys-

Jumar helps Christina Kimm, a special education professor at California State University–Los Angeles, negotiate a large urban college campus and remain as independent as possible; despite her continuing problems with post-polio syndrome.

ical disabilities. Service animals, like Pam Townsend's service dog Astro and Christina Kimm's Jumar, have been trained to pull a wheelchair, pick up things, open doors, push elevator buttons, turn lights off and on, and bring a telephone receiver. When Pam's muscular dystrophy worsened, Canine Assistants provided her with Astro, a golden retriever who helps with many simple and complex things ranging from getting the portable phone when it rings to opening and closing doors (Slaughter, 1999). Dr. Kimm, who is a special educaton professor at California State University, Los Angeles, has achieved more independence and a more balanced life since Canine Companions of San Diego matched her with Jumar, who even hands out papers to Kimm's students (Haynes, 1998). Capuchin monkeys are also used as service animals. Chosen for their small size and ability to perform tasks, they are bred and trained to assist people with physical challenges. These monkeys can feed the individual; dial a speakerphone; get food out of the refrigerator; turn pages of the newspaper; and turn on the television, stereo, and even a VCR (Ferrer, 1996).

To compare the challenges these families face with those of families of children with different disabilities, see the Family sections in Chapters 3–12.

FAMILIES

The families of children with severe physical and health impairments face special issues as they raise their children (Davis, 1993). Martin, Brady, and Kotarba (1992) document the demands that a child's chronic illness can place on a family, including fatigue and low vitality, restricted social life, and preoccupation with decisions related to the child's illness. Often, the costs of the child's health care are staggering. Thus parents' own career decisions may be driven by questions about maintaining family health insurance. Even when health insurance is available, financial record keeping and filing for reimbursements can be complicated and cause a strain. If the child is eligible for government medical benefits, eligibility regulations may be complex. Finally, some families find it necessary to move to a larger city in order to obtain necessary health care and therapies, leaving behind a community in which they have long-term social ties and extended family.

If the child's treatment or health problems require absences from school, the family's routine may be disrupted when one adult has to stay home with the child. Similarly, special planning and complicated arrangements may be necessary to accommodate a weekend away, a family vacation, time spent with other children, or time for the parents alone.

Many homes and apartments are not yet designed for the range of physical needs of the entire population. If a child needs large equipment, a special bathtub, ramps, or other accommodations typical for an individual with physical disabilities, the family may have to move to an accessible apartment or home. Another option for those who are financially able is to remodel their home.

Now let's think about families of children with AIDS and HIV. The outcomes for children with HIV are bleak (Beverly & Thomas, 1997), and families of these children often have to educate educators about their youngsters' prognosis, health conditions, and educational programs. HIV is devastating to the children infected. Pediatric HIV is the greatest infectious cause of mental retardation. It often results in growth, speech, and motor delays; as the disease progresses, skills are lost and functioning levels decline. Of course, at the present it results in early death. Families and teachers must work together to develop relevant curriculum for these individual children. Teachers and families should evaluate the importance of instructional targets on daily functioning as they make curriculum choices for these students. The instructional program should be balanced so it includes opportunities for recreation, social interchange, and fun.

Many families of students with special health care needs, especially those of children with AIDS, share common feelings of isolation, rejection, fear, depression, grief, anger, and guilt (Beverly & Thomas, 1997). Also, many myths are associated with disease and illness—like how they are spread—that educators can help eradicate.

The burdens on families of children with physical problems and health impairments can be great. As we have just discussed, life with a child who has severe physical challenges or who has a chronic illness is very complex, and the stress can be overwhelming. However, many of these parents have difficulties accepting their child's disability. So, in addition to dealing with hospitals, insurance companies, an inaccessible world, financial costs, and a sick child, many have to come to grips with their own situation and personal feelings. Patty McGill Smith (1993), the Executive Director of the National Parent Network on Disabilities and the parent of a child with multiple disabilities, suggests that parents take the following constructive actions as they come to accept and deal with their personal dilemmas, their child, and their family situation:

- Seek the assistance of another parent
- Learn special education terminology
- Seek information from many different sources
- Do not be intimidated
- Maintain a positive outlook
- Keep in touch with reality
- Search for a variety of program alternatives
- Take care of yourself

MAKING CONNECTIONS

AIDS and HIV are discussed in the Infectious Diseases section (Defined) of this chapter.

CONNECTIONS

To compare different types of technology supports across students with special needs, read the Technology sections in Chapters 3–12.

- Avoid pity
- Keep daily routines as normal as possible
- Recognize that you are not alone
- Take one day at a time

Keeping Smith's advice in mind, some parents have found that seeking out others who also have a child with a severe physical or health problem is helpful in many ways. Around the country, these families have joined together in support groups to address common problems and help one another. Often, families share creative ideas for helping the child with the disability to join in the activities of the family, such as inexpensive adaptations of toys, shared baby-sitting, and information exchanges about helpful medical personnel.

TECHNOLOGY

Modern technology can dramatically improve the ability of people with physical impairments and special health needs to gain access to and control the world around them, communicate with others, and benefit from health care. The 1990 reauthorization of IDEA and the courts have clarified the role of assistive technology and the schools: It is a related service that is provided so a student with disabilities can profit from special education. It does not, however, include medical services provided by physicians (Weiss & Dykes, 1995). The adaptations that technology provides these individuals include not only **high-tech devices,** such as computers that control the environment or assist in flying airplanes, but also **low-tech devices,** such as simple built-up spoons and communication booklets. Not all technology is expensive or even sophisticated. In many cases, creativity and individualization are the keys to solving problems.

Deciding what should be considered technology was difficult. Is a wheelchair a piece of technology? What about specially designed chairs for racing or for use in the wilderness? Does a wheelchair become technology if it is motorized or computerized? What if the chair has an electronic switch to permit persons with only partial head or neck control or finger or foot control to move about independently? I also could not decide whether medical advances should be considered technology. Certainly, technology is changing the way we think and act. It might even be the cause of a new special education category: **technology-dependent children** (students who use **ventilators** or other medical equipment to survive). And what about **rehabilitation engineering,** which has brought the benefits of science and engineering to movement, seating, and walking problems, such as those created by cerebral palsy? **Gait training** laboratories (special laboratories for walking) help many children by analyzing their weight-bearing patterns and their normal and abnormal movements. With the aid of PTs and other specialists, these laboratories help to improve children's posture and balance. In the end, I decided to focus on two types of technology used by people with these disabilities: computers, and bionics and robotics.

COMPUTERS

One of the most commonly used technological advances is the personal computer. "When used by a person with a disability, the computer has been likened to the six gun of western mythology—the great equalizer between people of different ability

high-tech devices. Complex technical devices such as computers.

low-tech devices. Simple technical devices such as home-made cushions or a classroom railing.

technology-dependent children. Children who probably could not survive without high-tech devices such as ventilators.

ventilators. Machines to assist with breathing.

rehabilitation engineering. Application of mechanical and engineering principles to improve human physical functioning.

gait training. Analysis and instruction of walking.

or strength" (Maddox, 1987, p. 223). Computers are used for many skills, including augmentative communication, writing and printing, practicing mathematics, and creating "smart rooms" where the thermostat, lights, music, and doors are controlled by a central computer panel. Many adaptations are available for computers so that people with severe physical disabilities can use them. For example, computers can be operated by voice, the gaze of an eye, a mouthstick, a sip-and-puff breath stick, a single finger, a toe, a headstick, or other creative method suitable to an individual's abilities.

What is possible today seemed impossible only a few years ago. What we might have thought were wild visions for science-fiction movies are today's reality. Mike Ward has Lou Gehrig's disease and can only move his eyes (Ramstad, 1995). But Mike goes to work four days a week; with the help of the new computer software called Eyegaze, he is a productive member of a research group at Intel. How is this so? His computer has a camera that follows his eyes and "types" the letters he looks at on the screen. When he is finished with a sentence, he looks at "enter." He uses regular word processing and e-mail software. Right now the cost of this high-tech computer application is high, at $25,000, but think about it: It is this technology that lets him work, be productive, and interact with co-workers and friends.

Aurora Systems now produces software for under $500 that can make any word processing program "speak": It provides auditory feedback as sentences are typed, has advanced word prediction (guesses the word being typed), can convert phonetic spelling into correctly spelled words, and even includes a talking spellchecker.

Computers allow access to other environments and people. This technology can be turned into a great advantage for students who must stay at home for any length of time. Whether an illness requires one day at home or a month, students can use the Internet and **e-mail** to talk to classmates, get tomorrow's homework assignments, or work with their science group on their project. They can also conduct library research by connecting to an information system and even communicate with students around the country about information they are gathering from a central database.

BIONICS AND ROBOTICS

Mobility is an area where the benefits of technology are obvious—freedom of movement, increased privacy, and personal independence. Today, individuals can select artificial limbs that are bionic and resemble human limbs. **Myoelectric limbs** (bionic) are battery powered and aesthetically pleasing. They are hollow but contain a sensor that picks up electrical signals transmitted from the individual's brain through the limb. Although not yet like the **bionic artificial limbs** popularized in the television shows *The Bionic Man* and *The Bionic Woman*, they do allow the individual to control movement and function.

Robotics is another area that holds promise for the future of people with physical disabilities. Robotics is the use of sophisticated devices to accomplish motor skills such as grasping. For example, robotic arms can manipulate objects in at least three directional movements: extension/retraction, swinging/rotating, and elevation/depression. Voice-activated robots are in the developmental stages but offer a promise of great assistance in independent daily living. Manipulator robots have been successfully used in assisting children in such self-help activities as dialing a telephone, turning book pages, and drinking from a cup. Costs, transportability, repairs, and training are currently roadblocks to the wide use of this type of technology, but popular demand for robots that can do household chores is likely in the future and would make robotic technology more economical and widely used.

e-mail. A computerized mail system allowing people using personal computers, the phone system, and a host mainframe computer to communicate.
myoelectric limbs. Artificial limbs, powered by batteries and controlled by electric signals transmitted by the individual's brain (sometimes called *bionic*).
bionic artificial limbs. Artificial arms and legs that replace full functioning of nonfunctional limbs.
robotics. Use of high-tech devices to perform motor skills.

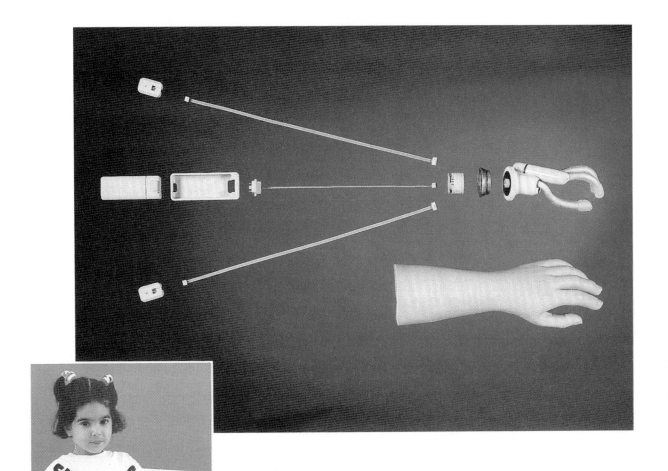

This girl's myloelectric hand allows her to play and learn almost like everyone else.

CONCEPTS AND CONTROVERSY: INCLUSION VERSUS SEGREGATION

Are separate special education classrooms or schools for children with physical disabilities and health impairments necessary? As we have discussed throughout this text, students with disabilities should be educated in the least restrictive environment possible. Sometimes, however, the need for separate classrooms and even separate schools for students with physical disabilities and health impairments is defended. Are they justified? Think about these questions in the context of what you have learned about physical impairments and special health care needs.

According to the U.S. Department of Education (1998), a considerable number of students with physical and health problems do attend general education classes for a substantial portion of their schoolday. However, these rates are very inconsistent across the nation. Let's examine differences in placements more carefully. For example, in the District of Columbia only 2.2% of students with special health care needs attend general education classes, 13% attend resource rooms, none attend separate special classrooms, while 76% go to separate schools for their education. Compare this to the state of Vermont, where 89% of students with special health care needs attend general education classes, 4% attend resource rooms, 3% are in special classes, and only 1% go to separate schools. The case for students with physical impairments is comparable. In Colorado, for example, 79% attend general education classes, 12% are placed in resource rooms, 7% are in separate special classes, and 1% go to center schools. Now, compare these placement rates to the District of Columbia where none attend general education classes, or to the state of Texas where 17% of students with physical impairments go to general education for their education, 39% to resource rooms, 36% to special classes; and about 2% to separate schools. Why do such differences exist?

Clearly, it must be differences in attitudes and philosophy. Perhaps in some states general education teachers are uncomfortable teaching children with physical disabilities because they lack the training. Some believe that it is more efficient and cost effective to locate in one place all of the special equipment and furniture needed by children with physical disabilities. Others argue that because it would be too expensive to make every school totally accessible (beyond ADA codes), only one school in the district should be equipped with state-of-the-art physical accommodations. And others feel that students with very special health care and nursing needs require full-time medical personnel on site, which cannot be accomplished at every school in the district. Do they have so much in common that they need to be in one place? Are there other reasons to explain why different states use different placement standards? Do you think these students should be separated from their nondisabled peers? Why? Why not?

 **In Conclusion**    MAKING CONNECTIONS

Look again at the Advance Organizers at the beginning of the chapter; to help you study the chapter's content, the answers to the Focus and Challenge questions are found here. Test yourself to see if you have mastered the major points of this chapter.

Summary   Children with physical impairments and special health care needs can present special difficulties to their parents and teachers. Even when these two special education categories are combined, the number of students involved is small, about 2% of all schoolchildren with disabilities. Therefore they are considered low-incidence disabilities. Many of these youngsters require substantial adjustments and modifications to their learning environments, but their relatively good high school graduation rates indicate that they are capable of competing in the standard curriculum. For many, independent living remains their greatest challenge.

Focus Questions   **Self-Test Questions**

• *Why are there so many different ways to organize and classify these disabilities?*
Many different systems have been proposed to organize these two special education categories. On one hand, there is great diversity among the disabilities caused by the hundreds of conditions, illnesses, and diseases that lead to phys-

ical impairments and special health care needs. On the other hand, students with physical and health problems share many special educational needs, regardless of the specific condition that caused the disability. To benefit the most from their educational opportunities, every special education student requires an individualized educational program tailored specifically to his or her individual needs. For many of these students, such programs include an array of related services and many accommodations to the physical and learning environments provided at school. This necessitates a multidisciplinary team working collaboratively on behalf of the child and with the family.

- *What are some steps teachers should follow to assist a child who is having a seizure?*

  Teachers can serve a vital role when assisting a child who is having a seizure. Following these simple steps can avoid injury and harm to the student involved. Look for medical identification; create a safe place free from hazards; loosen clothing, particularly around the neck; protect the head from injury; turn the person sideways to ensure free air passage; if the seizure lasts longer than five minutes, call for an ambulance; upon return of consciousness, keep the individual calm; stay with the person until full consciousness is achieved; offer further assistance.

- *What are the five general causes of physical impairments and special health care needs, and how can they be prevented?*

  The five general causes of physical impairments and special health care needs are infection, heredity, accidents or injuries, multiple factors (e.g., brain injury that was hereditary, a combination of injury and illness), and unknown causes (many of which are probably yet undiscovered hereditary conditions). Clearly, the following preventive measures might have lessened or avoided some of the physical and health impairments seen in schools today: prenatal care, vaccines, safety measures to prevent injuries and infectious diseases, and medical treatment. Many of the preventive techniques require access to health care, which, unfortunately, many families with young children do not have.

- *How can the learning environment be modified to accommodate students with physical impairments and special health care needs?*

  The learning environment—classroom space and instructional activities—can be easily modified to better accommodate students with disabilities related to their physical and health conditions. First, the physical environment can be adapted by creating more space, widening aisles, removing hazards, changing seating arrangements, making classroom furniture accessible, and creating room for positioning devices. Second, the demands for the student's response can be changed. The student can speak instead of writing, use a speech synthesizer, write instead of speaking, or have a computer print a response. Third, materials and equipment can be altered. Handouts can be used instead of or to accompany transparencies, or audio versions of books can be assigned. Adaptive equipment such as special writing tools and adapted eating utensils can be provided. Fourth, instructional activities can be modified by allowing more time to complete assignments, abbreviating assignments, or allowing for a flexible schedule. And finally, extra assistance can be given. The student can be assigned tutors (peers, parents, volunteers). Lectures can be audio or videotaped. The teacher or a classmate can answer questions using e-mail at specific times each day.

- *Why is the multidisciplinary team approach so necessary for these children, and how can educators improve collaboration among diverse professionals?*

  The multidisciplinary team approach is important for all students with disabilities, but for those with physical impairments and special health care needs it is a necessity. By bringing together professionals from many different disciplines, the complex needs of these youngsters can be met. Most of these youngsters have difficulties across several areas (e.g., motor, communication, health, mental health), areas in which educators have not received comprehensive training. It is important that parents and educators seek the advice, support, consultation, and training from experts in every field where the student needs special education and related services assistance.

Challenge Question

- *What are the barriers to the full participation of these individuals in society, and how can they be minimized?*

  People with physical disabilities, in particular, face considerable barriers throughout their lives. They face the physical challenge of coping with inaccessible environments, where their impaired mobility hinders their participation in mainstream society. They also face bias, discrimination, and other barriers. Because some of them cannot live independently, it is assumed that they cannot be productive employees either. Although attitudes are changing, people with physical disabilities and those with special health care needs still find rejection in the workplace, difficulties finding jobs, and social rejection by people without disabilities.

  These students may require special teaching, scheduling, counseling, therapies, equipment, and technology. They may frequently be absent from school because of fragile health or medical treatments. They may need special leg braces or wheelchairs; they may need adaptive equipment such as swivel spoons or pencils with extra grips; they may have physical needs such as assistance with medications, assistance with bladder catheterization, or seizure assistance. Some may present potential emergencies and thus require a teacher familiar with emergency techniques. Some may also face powerful emotional issues, such as their impending death or continuous physical dependence, many years before their young friends must face such issues. With accommodations in their instructional programs, the development of new and different learning environments, and the opportunity for full participation in all aspects of school, the lives of the next generation of students with physical impairments and special health care needs will be different.

CONNECTIONS

Resources to extend your learning about people with disabilities are found at the end of every chapter; a fuller listing is available in the Students' Resource Manual that accompanies this text.

Supplementary Resources

Scholarly Reading

Accardo, P. J., & Whitman, B. Y. (1996). *Dictionary of developmental disabilities terminology.* Baltimore: Paul H. Brookes.

Haslam, R. H. A., & Valletutti, P. J. (1996). *Medical problems in the classroom: The teacher's role in diagnosis and management* (3rd ed.). Austin, TX: Pro-Ed.

Heller, K. W., Alberto, P. A., Forney, P. E., & Schwartzman, M. N. (1996). *Understanding physical, sensory, and health impairments.* Pacific Grove: Brooks/Cole.

Urbano, M. T. (1992). *Preschool children with special health care needs.* San Diego: Singular Press.

Popular Books

Brown, C. (1955). *My left foot.* NY: Simon & Schuster.

Gallagher, H. G. (1994). *FDR's splendid deception.* NY: Dodd, Mead.

Mathews, J. (1992). *A mother's touch: The Tiffany Callo story.* NY: Holt.

Pechinpah, S. E. (1993). *Chester: The imperfect all-star.* Agoura Hills, CA: Dasan Publishing.

Reeve, C. (1998). *Still me.* NY: Random House.

Videos and DVDs

Mask. (1985). MCA Home Video.

Gaby: A true story. (1987). Tri-Star Pictures.

Born on the Fourth of July. (1989). Universal.

My left foot. (1989). Miramax Pictures.

Forrest Gump. (1994). Paramount Pictures.

Notting Hill. (1999). Universal

Professional, Parent, and Consumer Organizations and Agencies

Asthma and Allergy Foundation of America
1717 Massachusetts Avenue, Suite 305
Washington, DC 20036
Phone: (800) 7-ASTHMA; (800) 822-2762;
  (202) 466-7643
E-mail: info@aafa.org
Web site: http://www.aafa.org

Council for Exceptional Children
Division of the Physically Handicapped
1920 Association Drive
Reston, VA 22091-11589
Phone: (888) CEC-SPED; (705) 620-3660
Web site: http://www.cec.sped.org

National Easter Seal Society for Crippled Children and Adults
230 W. Monroe Street, Suite 1800
Chicago, IL 60606
Phone: (312) 726-4258; (800) 221-6827
TTY: (312) 726-4258
Web site: http://www.seals.com

Epilepsy Foundation of America
4351 Garden City Drive, Suite 406
Landover, MD 20785
Phone: (800) 332-1000; (301) 459-3700
Voice/TYY: (800) EFA-1000
E-mail: info@efa.org
Web site: http://www.efa.org

March of Dimes Birth Defects Foundation
1275 Mamaroneck Avenue
White Plains, NY 10605
Phone: (888) MODIMES
Web site: http://www.modimes.org

United Cerebral Palsy Association
1660 L Street NW, Suite 700
Washington, DC 20036
Phone: (202) 776-0406; (800) 872-5827
E-mail: ucpnatl@ucpa.org
Web site: http://www.uspa.org

MAKING CONNECTIONS

For Web links to support your study of disabilities, look at the Resources sections at the end of every chapter in this text. A fuller listing is found in the Students' Resource Manual that accompanies this text.

Dorothy Brett was born of a noble British family (Hignett, 1983). Although her childhood was quite sheltered, as a young adult and a student at the Slade Art College in London, she became exposed to young artists like Dora Carrington and the liberal thinking of the day. Her associations with the Bloomsbury Group—two of its more famous members were writer and publisher Virginia Woolf and economist John Maynard Keynes—broadened her horizons. In 1924, Brett followed D. H. Lawrence to New Mexico to be part of a utopian colony. Lawrence returned to England, but Brett remained in America and became part of an artists' colony, often referred to as the Taos Artists. Brett was "partially deaf" almost her entire life; a self-portrait she completed in 1924 shows her with an ear trumpet, which she named Toby, the hearing aid of the day (Hignett, 1983).

Dorothy Brett, *Deer Dancers,* oil on board, 1951, 36 × 24 in. The Albuquerque Museum, gift of Mr. & Mrs. Max L. Ilfeld. Photograph by Damian Andrus.

C H A P T E R 10

A Hearing Mom of a Deaf Middle Schooler Talks About Her Son's Deafness

Ann Park, Ian's mother, shares her story about how she discovered her son was deaf and how her family's life has changed since this discovery:

In February 1984, I learned that my 17-month-old son was deaf. He had been playing with the stereo controls and inadvertently turned them on. It was so loud that the windows rattled in their casements. Even though Ian was only inches away from the stereo speakers, he did not flinch, blink, startle, or cry. We knew at that moment he did not hear like he should, confirming what we had suspected for almost a year. A couple of weeks later our fears were confirmed. Ian was profoundly deaf!

Sitting in the audiology booth with him, I saw the audiologist shaking her head "no" with each presentation of a pure tone that Ian did not respond to. I knew it was bad then. All of my dreams and hopes for him—being a doctor, a pilot, anything—disintegrated. I remember a sudden feeling of relief, almost overwhelming in its magnitude, when the audiologist told us Ian was profoundly deaf. At last, we knew what was wrong! Our suspicions were confirmed. At that moment, I knew what I could do. I would do everything I possibly could to give my son language and a means to communicate. As we left the audiology booth, I started signing, "Let us go down the hall. Then go home," my son watching my hands as we went.

Deafness and Hard of Hearing

It has become a family joke of sorts, the irony of life. I had wanted to be a teacher of the deaf since childhood. So every opportunity I could find, I learned or used the sign language I knew. I remember commenting to the SLP and audiologist working with Ian of this desire, but adding, "I also wanted to send the kids home at three in the afternoon, and get paid every other week. Now, he is all mine, twenty-four hours a day and no pay!" But I still would not change what has happened. I do get paid! Every time he succeeds at a sports event, academically, or in his daily life.

Ian went to a special preschool for deaf children. When he was 6 years old, he attended a class for deaf and hard of hearing students in our local public school. Since second grade, he has been fully mainstreamed. He has had a certified interpreter and been given preferential seating, and his classrooms have been specially adapted with acoustical treatments and special carpeting. He has had support services from an audiologist and an SLP who is fluent in sign language. Ian has also had special equipment such as hearing aids and auditory trainers with an FM microphone worn by his teachers.

Ian has been raised to be independent, to know what his rights are—like having an interpreter. But there are areas not covered by the Americans with Disabilities Act. So when he goes to soccer or baseball practices or games, either his father or myself are always there to interpret for him. We try to teach his team members and coaches the appropriate signs for the sport and those basic for general communication. Regardless, the responsibility of communication rests on our shoulders. Ian's oral speech is often intelligible, especially when the content of the topic is known by those who are listening to him. He tries very hard to speak clearly and slowly for people. But the best of situations would be if others knew how to sign. It is getting better. Ian is not bashful about calling up his deaf and hearing friends on his TTY. Having one of those telephones has given him a new sense of freedom.

In our home, we sign so that Ian is included in all of our family time together. We also get the benefit of reading the TV as well as hearing it by using closed captions. We have a flashing-light system attached to various lights throughout the house that flash in different sequences to tell us when the doorbell or phone is ringing.

It is my deepest hope that Ian will be a self-sufficient, contributing member of society. Ian is a positive example of what children who are deaf can attain, and I know he will always be a positive example for others. I want Ian to bridge the gap between the hearing and the deaf worlds.

The future for deaf and hard of hearing children is so much better than in the past. Children can remain in their homes, and they and their families can receive support services to help them. Early intervention services are now available as soon as the disability is diagnosed, and language development work can begin much sooner. This is important. The disability, and its effects, cannot be erased; but with knowledge, understanding, effort, and support for the child and the family, people with this disability can experience a much better future and life together. Ian is an example of what can be accomplished.

1. What do you think are some of the frustrations and challenges Ian faces because he attends a general education class?

2. What different frustrations and challenges do you think he would face if he attended a special school for deaf students?

3. How does technology help Ian and his family?

Advance Organizers

MAKING CONNECTIONS

Use the learning strategy—Advance Organizers—to help focus your study of this chapter's content, and reinforce your learning by reviewing answers to the Focus and Challenge questions at the end of the chapter.

Overview

Hearing, like vision, is a distance sense and provides us with information from outside our bodies. When hearing is limited, it affects the individual in significant ways: limiting communication, access to orally presented information, and independent living. More so than for any other group of people with disabilities, the Deaf comprise a community united by a rich culture and a unique communication system. Deafness and hard of hearing is a low incidence disability for children, affecting about 0.11% of all schoolchildren.

Focus Questions

Self-Test Questions

- What variables are used to create different subgroups of students who are deaf or hard of hearing?
- What is meant by the concept of Deaf culture?
- What are the major causes of hearing loss?
- What educational support services do many of these students require?
- How do the major instructional methods for deaf children differ, and how should an individual child's communication style affect the choice of instructional method?

Challenge Question

- What types of technology are available to assist the deaf and what advances might the future hold?

The process of hearing is remarkable. Sound waves pass through the air, water, or some other medium. They cause the eardrum to vibrate. These vibrations are carried to the inner ear, where they pass through receptor cells that send impulses to the brain. The brain translates these impulses into sound. The content or associations of sound affect us in different ways. We are warmed by the sound of an old friend's voice, startled by a loud clap of thunder, fascinated by the sound of the wind rushing through trees, lulled by the ocean, excited by the roar of a crowd, consumed by the music of a rock group, and relaxed by the soothing sounds of a symphony. One important way that most of us learn about the thoughts, ideas, and feelings of others is by listening to people tell us their experiences. Through this exchange, we expand our knowledge, share ideas, express emotions, and function in typical workplaces and social settings. Many people who are deaf and hard of hearing participate fully in mainstream society in part because of advances in education and technology such as hearing aids. However, some people cannot be helped by hearing aids and thus have a much more restricted ability to communicate with their nondisabled counterparts.

Opportunities for the New Millennium

The Deaf community has become a visible part of American society, claiming its status as a minority group that should be valued and treasured as an important part of the mix that makes America unique. Awareness of their rich culture that includes dance, literature, arts, and theater was brought to public attention through Deaf individuals' advocacy efforts. Despite the abilities and talents shared by many members of this community, their employment options and overall outcomes are below expectations because they and their culture remain misunderstood, which results in bias and discrimination—a feature shared by other minority groups in this country.

deaf. An inability to usefully perceive sounds in the environment with or without the use of a hearing aid; inability to use hearing as the primary way to gain information.

hard of hearing. Having sufficient residual hearing to be able, with a hearing aid, to comprehend others' speech and oral communication.

prelingually deaf. Having lost the ability to hear before developing language.

postlingually deaf. Having lost the ability to hear after developing language.

eardrum (tympanic membrane). Part of the ear upon which sound waves and their vibrations fall and cause the ossicles to move; separates the outer and middle ear.

Legacies from the Twentieth Century

Controversy has surrounded deaf and hard of hearing people probably since the beginning of time, and it continues today. Throughout the last two centuries, the deaf education community and policymakers have been embroiled in debates about how and where hard of hearing and deaf children should be educated. At the heart of today's continuing debates is communication, the clear distinguishing feature of humans, and values about oral means of interacting with others and the culture that develops from language and social interaction. The use of American Sign Language, a language of manual communication, has become the central feature of the controversy: whether it should become the native language for all deaf children (and English become the second language). New technologies, like cochlear implants, which might someday eradicate deafness are seen by some in the Deaf community as a threat and a devaluation of themselves and their culture. These unresolved controversies influence how children are taught, where they eventually live, who they interact with easily, and employment outcomes.

Thinking About Dilemmas to Solve

As you read this chapter there are many things to consider about deaf and hard of hearing children, their education, and their lives. Think about:

- How language influences human behavior
- Whether deafness and hard of hearing should be clearly separated as we think about the educational needs of children who belong to this group
- The role of Deaf culture in American society
- The special issues hearing families face with the birth of a deaf child
- How the underachievement and poor employment outcomes of many deaf and hard of hearing people can be overcome

CONNECTIONS

For more information, see the section on Deaf culture (Deaf and Hard of Hearing Children) later in this chapter.

hammer (malleus). One of the three tiny bones (ossicles) in the middle ear.

anvil (incus). One of the three tiny bones (ossicles) in the middle ear.

stirrup (stapes). One of the three tiny bones (ossicles) in the middle ear.

ossicles. Three tiny bones in the middle ear that transmit sound waves from the eardrum through the middle ear to the cochlea.

cochlea. Part of the inner ear that contains fluid and hairlike nerve cells that transmit information to the brain.

hair cells. The structures in the inner ear that produce the electrochemical signals that pass through the auditory nerve to the brain, here these signals, which originated as sound waves, are perceived as tones.

DEAFNESS AND HARD OF HEARING DEFINED

People who are **deaf,*** or profoundly hard of hearing, have hearing abilities that provide them with little useful hearing even if they use hearing aids. Although almost all persons who are deaf perceive some sound, they cannot use hearing as their primary way to gain information. People who are **hard of hearing** can process information from sound, usually with the help of a hearing aid.

Although the degree of hearing loss is important, the age when the hearing loss occurs is also important. Individuals who become deaf before they learn to speak and understand language are referred to as **prelingually deaf**. They either are born deaf or lose their hearing as infants. Approximately 95% of all deaf children and youth are prelingually deaf. Their inability to hear language seriously affects their abilities to communicate with others and to learn academic subjects taught later in school. One in ten of those who are prelingually deaf have at least one deaf parent. Children in this group typically learn to communicate during the normal developmental period. However, instead of learning oral communication skills, many learn through a combination of manual communication (sign language) and oral language. Those whose severe hearing loss occurs after they have learned to speak and understand language are called **postlingually deaf.** Many are able to retain their abilities to use speech and communicate with others orally.

What is hearing loss? Hearing loss results when the ear and hearing mechanism are damaged or obstructed. To better understand the definition of hearing loss, we need to understand the process of hearing. Refer to Figure 10.1 on page 416, a picture of the ear, to trace how sound moves through the ear to produce normal hearing. A person speaks and the sound waves from the words pass through the air or some other medium. The sound waves are caught by the pinna or auricle (what we commonly call the ear) and funneled down the auditory canal of the listener; the pinna and the auditory canal are the two parts of the outer ear. Sound waves then travel to the middle ear, which is an air-filled chamber. This chamber contains the eardrum and is connected to the eustachian tube, which equalizes the pressure on the two sides of the eardrum. Sound waves cause the **eardrum (tympanic membrane)** to vibrate. Those vibrations cause the **hammer (malleus)** and **anvil (incus)** to move and the **stirrup (stapes)** to oscillate. These three tiny bones together are called the **ossicles** and are also part of the middle ear. The eardrum converts pressure variations to mechanical vibrations, which are then transmitted to the fluid contained in the compartments of the **cochlea.**

The *inner ear* includes the semicircular canals and the cochlea, which is a hollow, spiral-shaped bone that actually contains the organs of hearing. The mechanical variations produced by the stirrup on the fluid are transmitted to the basement membrane of the cochlea. This membrane supports the **hair cells,** which respond to different frequencies of sounds. Those hair cells closest to the stapes resonate to higher tones; those farther away resonate to lower tones. Each hair cell has about a hundred tiny, rigid spines at its top. When the spines or cilia displace the fluid that surrounds them, this produces electrochemical signals, which are sent through

---

*In this chapter, children with severe hearing losses are referred to in different ways. Sometimes, they are called "children who are deaf," and at other times they are called "deaf children." The latter is preferred by many people in the Deaf community because they believe it better reflects their Deaf culture and identity. The use of the capital letter *D* signifies affiliation with Deaf culture; a small *d* refers to deafness.

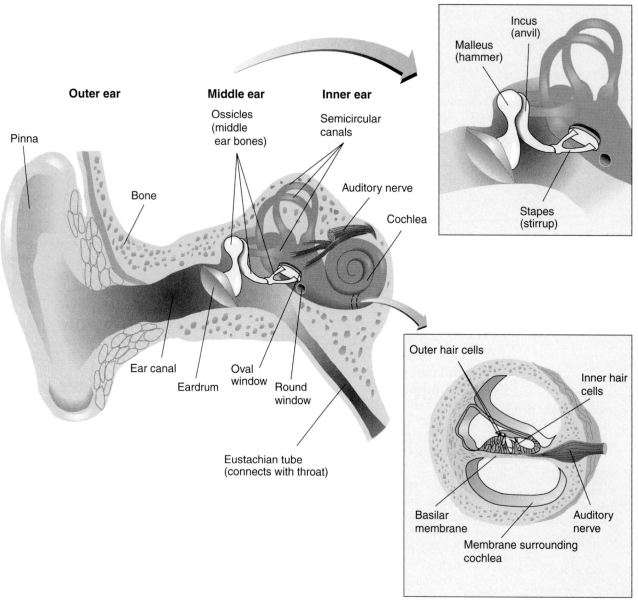

Outer ear

Pinna

Bone

Ear canal

Eardrum

Middle ear

Ossicles
(middle
ear bones)

Oval
window

Round
window

Eustachian tube
(connects with throat)

Inner ear

Semicircular
canals

Auditory nerve

Cochlea

Malleus
(hammer)

Incus
(anvil)

Stapes
(stirrup)

Outer hair cells

Inner hair
cells

Basilar
membrane

Membrane surrounding
cochlea

Auditory
nerve

Cross section of the cochlea

Figure 10.1 **The Structure of the Human Ear**

Source: Physiology of Behavior, 6th ed., by N. R. Carlson, 1998, Boston: Allyn and Bacon. Adapted by permission.

nerve cells along the **auditory nerve** (eighth cranial nerve) to the brain where the signals are perceived as tones.

Hearing losses range in severity, vary in type, and influence each person differently. Let's look first at the various aspects of hearing losses and then at the way they affect the individual.

TYPES OF HEARING LOSS

There are two general types of hearing loss: conductive and sensorineural. **Conductive hearing losses** are due to blockage or damage to the outer or middle ear that prevents sound waves from traveling (being conducted) to the inner ear. Generally, someone with a conductive hearing loss has a mild to moderate disability. Some conductive hearing losses are temporary; in fact, we have all probably experienced a conductive hearing loss at some point in our lives. For example, you may have experienced a temporary loss of hearing due to change of air pressure when flying in an airplane or riding in a car in the mountains. Preschoolers often experience a conductive hearing loss when they have head colds. Because of the high frequency of head colds among children, between 50% and 80% of youngsters attending kindergarten through fifth grade may, at any one time, have a mild hearing loss. The infection causes excessive fluid to accumulate in the middle ear, interfering with the conduction of sound waves there. With a mild loss, the individual can still hear almost all speech sounds and can hear most conversations (Moores, 1996). If the hearing loss was caused by a head cold, once the ear infection clears up, the hearing difficulties also disappear. Most conductive hearing losses can be corrected through surgery or other medical techniques.

The second type of hearing loss, **sensorineural hearing loss,** occurs when there is damage to the inner ear or the auditory nerve and usually cannot be improved medically or surgically. Some people refer to this type of hearing loss as "nerve deafness." Individuals affected by a sensorineural loss are able to hear different frequencies at different intensity levels; their hearing losses are not flat or even. It is also often associated with **recruitment,** which can make correcting the hearing loss and adjusting for loudness when using hearing aids difficult (Boothroyd, 1998). Sensorineural losses are less common in young children than the conductive types, but teachers need to understand that hearing aids can have mixed results with this type of impairment.

IDENTIFICATION

To understand how hearing is measured, let's review some terms and concepts about sound. Sound is produced by the vibration of molecules through air, water, wires, or some other medium. The number of vibrations per second determines the **frequency of sound.** High frequencies are perceived through our ears as high pitch or tone; low frequencies are perceived as low pitch. Frequency is measured in a unit called **hertz (Hz).** The normal ear hears sounds that range from approximately 20 Hz to 20,000 Hz; speech sounds fall approximately in the middle of the human hearing range (between 250 Hz and 4,000 Hz). There are sounds, however, that humans cannot perceive, regardless of hearing abilities. For example, some dog whistles use high frequencies that are beyond humans' hearing range.

Intensity, or loudness, of sound is measured in **decibels (dB).** Softer, quieter sounds have lower decibel measurements; louder sounds have higher decibel numbers. A decibel level of 125 or louder is painful to the average person. Decibel levels ranging from 0 to 120 dB are used to test how well an individual can hear different frequencies; a child with normal hearing should be able to perceive sounds at 0 dB. The scale used to assess hearing has been adjusted so that 0 indicates no loss and numbers greater than 0 indicate the degree or amount of loss. Small numbers indicate mild losses; large numbers indicate moderate to severe or profound losses.

auditory nerve. Nerve that carries messages received through the ear to the brain; known in neurology as the eighth cranial nerve.
conductive hearing losses. Hearing losses caused by damage or obstruction to the outer or middle ear that prevents transfer of sound to the inner ear.
sensorineural hearing loss. Hearing loss caused by damage to the inner ear or the auditory nerve.
recruitment. In many people with sensorineural hearing losses, sounds' loudness does not gradually increase from the level at which it is initially perceived, making the use of analog hearing aids problematic.
frequency of sound. The number of vibrations per second of molecules through some medium like air, water, or wires.
hertz (Hz). Unit of measure for sound frequency.
decibel (dB). Unit of measure for intensity of sound.

NEW DIRECTIONS
FOR THE
MILLENNIUM

Legacy: Despite recent advances in methods for screening newborns for hearing problems, the reduction in costs for these procedures, and documented importance of early intervention, all infants' hearing is not tested across the nation.

Opportunities:

- Mandate universal screening
- Continue research and development to create even less expensive assessment measures

otoacoustic emissions (OAE) test. An inexpensive five-minute procedure that tests newborns' hearing by measuring the vibration of hair cells in the cochlea in the presence of sound.

pure sounds. Sound waves of specific frequencies used to test an individual's hearing ability.

Several different methods are used today to test people's hearing abilities. Some of these methods, like the **otoacoustic emissions (OAE) test,** are even accurate with newborn infants (Martin & Noble, 1998). OAE, a noninvasive procedure, is an inexpensive way to determine if a baby at risk for hearing problems needs early intervention services.

Children's hearing is usually tested differently. Audiologists use **pure sounds—** sound waves of specific frequencies—at various combinations of hertz and decibels and also at various bands of pitch and loudness. They conduct their assessments in soundproof rooms so that distractions like those found in classrooms are eliminated. Besides the traditional approaches to hearing assessment described next, new procedures are being developed that allow audiologists to determine children's abilities to identify common sounds heard in usual speech environments, to understand speech heard in noisy environments, and to localize sound sources (Besing et al., 1998). The results from these assessments can be most useful to therapists and teachers who are implementing instructional programs.

In traditional assessment situations, audiologists use an **audiometer,** an instrument that produces sounds at precise frequencies and intensities. The results of these audiological assessments are plotted on an **audiogram,** which is a grid or graph. Along the top of the graph are hertz levels; the vertical lines represent different levels of sound frequency or hertz. Each ear is tested separately. A **hearing threshold** is determined by noting when the person first perceives the softest sound at each frequency level. Sometimes, hearing threshold is reported only for the better ear, and sometimes an average of an individual's scores at three different frequencies (500, 1,000, 2,000 Hz) is used. Any score falling below the 0 dB line on an audiogram represents some degree of hearing loss because the audiometer is set to indicate that a person has no hearing loss at 0 dB for various hertz levels. Those of you who have some knowledge of music might find Lowenbraun's (1995) explanation of hertz helpful. The frequency of middle C on the piano is approximately 250 Hz. The next vertical line on the audiogram, 500 Hz, is approximately one octave above middle C; 1,000 is two octaves above middle C; and so on. (See the scale in Figure 10.2.)

Now let's review the audiograms of two children—Travis and Heather. Most children's hearing is assessed by the **air conduction audiometry method,** which uses pure-tone sounds generated by an audiometer. Earphones are placed over the child's ears, and the child raises his or her hand when hearing a sound. Such testing is usually done by a pediatrician at a well-child checkup, or by a school nurse.

Because Travis and Heather were suspected of having hearing losses, the audiologist testing them used two procedures: first, the air conduction method and, second, the bone conduction method. It was apparent from the first test that the children had hearing losses, so the audiologist needed to know whether the loss was due to damage in the outer, middle, or inner ear. To determine the location of the damage, the audiologist used the **bone conduction audiometry method,** in which a vibrator is placed on the forehead so that sound can bypass the outer and middle ear and go directly to the inner ear. When the bone conduction thresholds are normal (near 0 dB) and the air conduction thresholds are abnormal, the hearing loss is conductive.

Travis's audiogram, shown in Figure 10.2, indicates that he has a conductive hearing loss. The loss, of about 40 dB, is in the mild range with the amplification of hearing aids. Notice how flat the profile is for Travis's air conduction test. However, the bone conduction test reveals that when the middle ear is bypassed, his hearing is much closer to 0 dB. Travis's hearing loss either is temporary or can be corrected through surgery or other medical treatment. Notice also that a different code is used

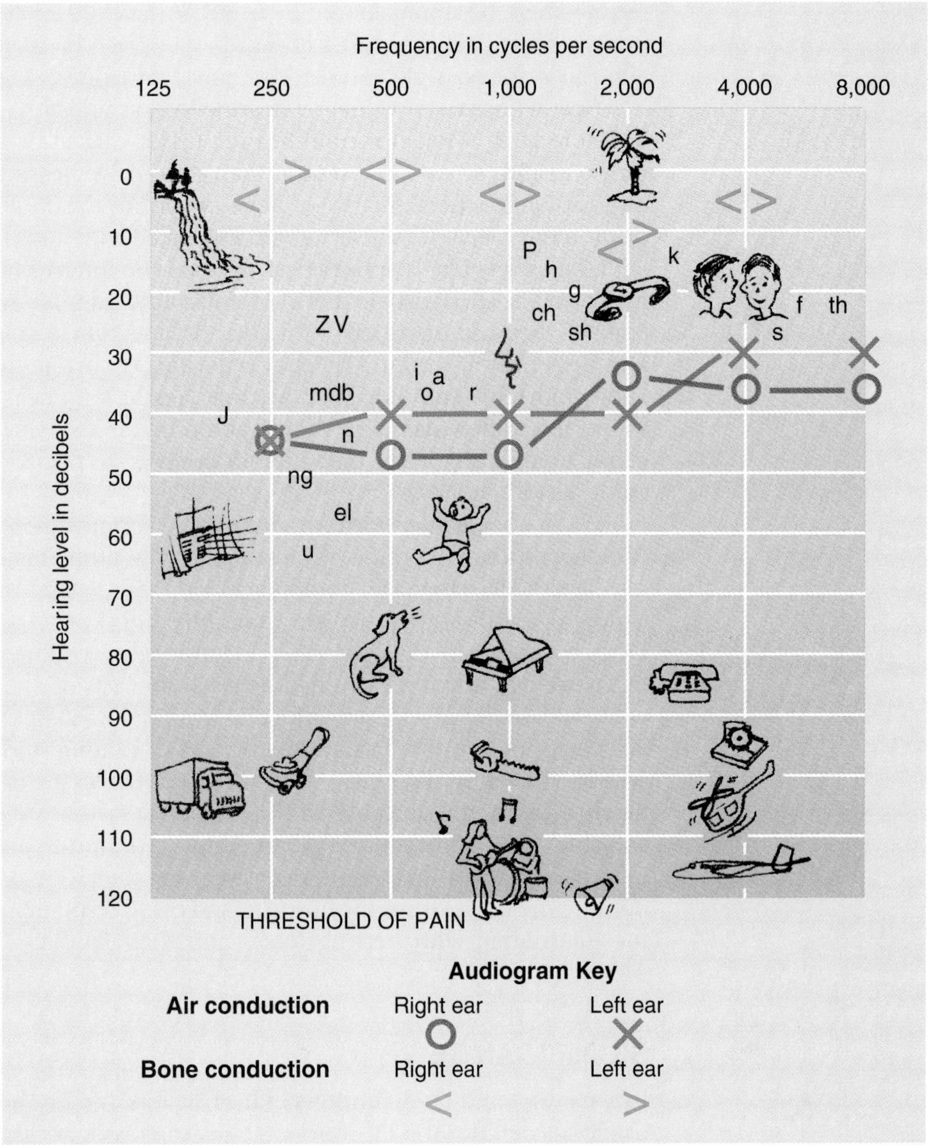

Figure 10.2 Travis's Audiogram

Source: Hearing in Children (p. 7) by J. L. Northern and M. P. Downs, 1984, Baltimore: Williams & Wilkins. Used by permission.

audiometer. An electrical instrument for measuring the threshold of hearing tests using an audiometer; it charts individuals' thresholds of hearing at various frequencies against sound intensities in decibels.

audiogram. The grid or graph used to display a person's hearing abilities.

hearing threshold. The point at which a person can perceive the softest sound at each frequency level.

air conduction audiometry method. A method to test hearing that uses a pure-tone sound generated by an audiometer.

bone conduction audiometry method. A test for conductive hearing loss in which a vibrator is placed on a person's forehead so that sound bypasses the outer and middle ear and goes directly to the inner ear; tests for conductive hearing losses.

for Travis's right and left ears—O for the right ear and X for the left ear. Remember that each ear is tested independently. Travis's hearing threshold for each ear is marked on his audiogram. Most children with normal hearing have auditory thresholds (the points when they first perceive sound) at approximately 0 dB, while Travis's thresholds are considerably below 0.

Travis's hearing abilities are plotted on an audiogram form designed by Northern and Downs (1984) to show where various speech and other sounds occur. This form uses pictures to show where different sounds fall. If the child's pattern is above the picture, then the sound should be heard. If the child's threshold falls below the picture, then the sound pictured cannot be perceived by that child. Without a hearing aid, Travis, for example, can perceive only a few sounds (*ng, el,* and *u*).

Heather has a sensorineural hearing loss, as indicated in her audiogram, shown in Figure 10.3. A sensorineural hearing loss is caused by a defect or damage to the inner ear and can be more serious than conductive hearing losses. Heather has a 30 dB loss. Notice the similarity of her scores from the air conduction and bone conduction tests. Heather's hearing was also tested with her hearing aids on. Notice that with the use of aids, Heather's hearing loss is no longer as serious; it is now at a mild functional level. The shaded area on this audiogram (sometimes called the "speech banana" because of its shape) marks the area where speech sounds fall. Because Heather's hearing abilities lie above this area on her audiogram (see the top of the audiogram), the audiologist knows that Heather can hear the speech sounds at the sound intensities measured during audiological assessment. Along the side of the graph are intensity levels measured in decibels, so horizontal lines represent different levels of loudness.

When should identification occur? The simple answer is: As soon as possible. Children who are identified as having hearing problems before they are 6 months old have better language, comprehension, and general developmental levels than children identified after they are 18 months old (Yoshinaga-Itano & Apuzzo, 1998). Despite continued calls for early identification, children with profound hearing losses are typically not identified between the ages of 1½ and 2½ years old. Those with mild and moderate sensorineural hearing losses are reported to be identified at an average of 5 to 6 years, and many hard of hearing students are not identified by schools (Easterbrooks, 1999). Why is this so? Babies are not universally screened for hearing loss, and even those with definite risk factors are not always tested (Martin & Noble, 1998). Procedures that are simple, nonintrusive, and relatively inexpensive (about $25, a cost that would decrease if the tests were universally applied) can be done before babies leave the hospital, and could result in improved overall outcomes for all children with hearing losses and their families (Gordon-Langbein, 1998, 1999).

SIGNIFICANCE

For a review of communicative competence and speech and language development, see Chapter 5.

Experts vary on their definitions of hearing loss and on the point at which it has educational significance. Of course, all hearing losses are serious, but at some point a hearing loss substantially influences the way in which a child needs to be taught and how well the individual can use the communication modes of nondisabled peers. The amount and type of an individual's hearing loss are related to the ability to understand information presented orally. These two factors also affect how a student might be taught and the types of services needed. For example, a student with a moderate loss might not profit from typical instructional methods (lectures, oral directions) alone.

But what constitutes a mild, a moderate, or a severe hearing loss? Tharpe (1999) considers losses from 26 to 55 dB mild to moderate, losses from 71 to 90 dB severe, and those greater than 91 dB profound. Conductive losses of 30 to 50 dB are relatively common and fall in Tharpe's mild-to-moderate range. Persons with this level of conductive hearing loss cannot hear typical conversations without amplification. Clearly, levels of hearing loss have considerable significance for how people communicate and learn from others. Table 10.1 on page 422 provides definitions for the

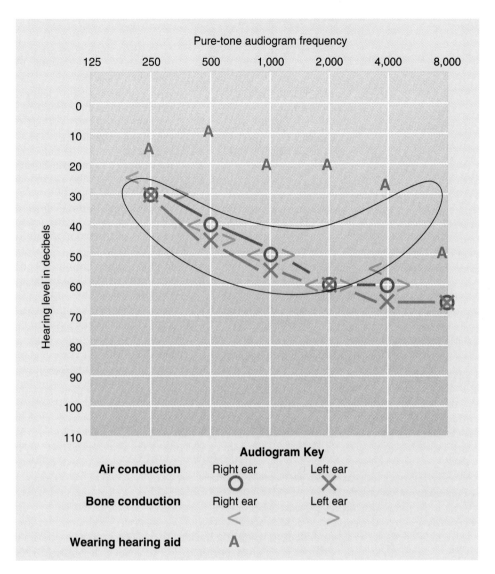

Figure 10.3 Heather's Audiogram

levels of hearing loss. This table also gives explanations of how well individuals can hear for each level of loss, as well as the educational implications for each level.

Compare the story about the Deaf communities on Martha's Vineyard in Chapter 1 with the history of deaf people recounted in this section.

HISTORY OF THE FIELD

As long ago as the days of the ancient Greeks and the early Roman Empire, social leaders like Aristotle, Plato, and the Emperor Justinian wrote about issues facing deaf people of their time. Over the history of Western civilization, attitudes toward people who were deaf have varied. Some societies protected them; others ridiculed, persecuted, and even put them to death. Even in America, attitudes and acceptance of the deaf have changed greatly across time.

Table 10.1 Impact of Hearing Loss

Minimal Hearing Loss (16 to 25 dB HL)	At 15 dB a student can miss up to 10% of the speech signal when a teacher is at a distance greater than 3 feet and when the classroom is noisy.
Mild Hearing Loss (26 to 40 dB HL)	With a 30 dB loss, a student can miss 25–40% of a speech signal. Without amplification, the child with 35–40 dB loss may miss at least 50% of class discussion.
Moderate Hearing Loss (41 to 55 dB HL)	Child understands conversational speech at a distance of 3–5 feet (face-to-face) only if structure and vocabulary are controlled. Without amplification, the amount of speech signal missed can be 50–75% with a 40 dB loss, and 80–100% with a 50 dB loss.
Moderate to Severe Hearing Loss (56 to 70 dB HL)	Without amplification, conversation must be very loud to be understood. A 55 dB loss can cause a child to miss up to 100% of speech information.
Severe Hearing Loss (71 to 90 dB HL)	Without amplification, may hear loud voices about 1 foot from ear. When amplified optimally, children with hearing ability of 90 dB or better should be able to identify environmental sounds and detect all the sounds of speech.
Profound Hearing Loss (≥ 91 dB HL)	Aware of vibrations more than tonal patterns. May rely on vision rather than hearing as primary avenue for communication and learning.
Unilateral Hearing Loss (Normal hearing in one ear with the other ear exhibiting at least a mild permanent loss.)	May have difficulty hearing faint or distant speech. Usually has difficulty localizing sounds and has greater difficulty understanding speech amid background noise.

Source: From "Disorders of Hearing in Children" by A. M. Tharpe, 1999, in *Communication and Communication Disorders: A Clinical Introduction* by E. Plante and P. M. Beeson (p. 100), Boston: Allyn and Bacon. Reprinted and adapted by permission.

The *D* in Deaf has been capitalized here to reflect that deafness here is associated with Deaf culture; for more information, see that section in the Deaf and Hard of Hearing Children section of this chapter.

Documents dating back to the 1500s report of physicians in Europe who worked with people who were deaf. Pedro Ponce de Leon (1520–1584), a Spanish monk credited with being the first teacher of students who were deaf, had remarkable success teaching his students to read, write, and speak. William Holder and John Wallis, who lived during the 1600s, are credited with beginning educational programs in England for individuals who were deaf. Like the Spanish before, they advocated using writing and manual communication to teach speech. By the 1700s, schools for the deaf were established by Henry Baker in England, Thomas Braidwood in Edinburgh, Abbé Charles Michel de l'Epée in France, and Samuel Heinicke in Germany.

By 1817 the first school in the United States for students who were deaf was started in Hartford, Connecticut. Thomas Hopkins Gallaudet, a young divinity student, went to study in England and France in order to start the first special school for deaf in this country. At that time, the French at the school begun by l'Epée were experimenting with methods of manual communication, mainly sign language. Gallaudet was greatly influenced by the effectiveness of these methods, and he brought Laurent Clerc, a deaf Frenchman and a well-known educator of the deaf, to the United States. Clerc is often credited with being the father of education for the deaf in the United States. Other Americans interested in deaf education also went to

Europe and were impressed by the oral approaches in deaf education used in Germany. In most oral approaches of that day, the use of any form of manual communication or sign language was greatly discouraged.

The roots of the debate about the oral versus the manual method of instruction and communication are deep in the history of this field. Although some argument about the best means for communication continue today, the period between the 1860s and 1960s was a time of most heated conflict between those who advocated an oralist approach and those who were proponents of manual signed language. Some even refer to this period of time at the "Hundred Years War" (Drasgow, 1998). The battles were initiated and fueled through the debates of Edward Gallaudet, Thomas Gallaudet's son, and Alexander Graham Bell (Alby, 1962; Adams, 1929). Each of these men had a deaf mother and a highly successful father. Bell invented the telephone and the audiometer and worked on the phonograph. Gallaudet was the president of the nation's college for the deaf and was a renowned legal scholar. These two men clashed. In 1883 and 1884, Bell wrote two papers critical of policies and practices that contributed to segregation of deaf individuals from the rest of society. He believed that residential schools and the use of sign language fostered segregation. Bell proposed legislation that would prevent two adults who were deaf from marrying, eliminate residential schools, ban the use of manual communication, and prohibit the deaf from becoming teachers of deaf students. Gallaudet strongly opposed these positions in both his writings and in public debates. The battle between these two strong individuals and their opposing positions carried over into Congress and even influenced federal funding of teacher preparation programs. Gallaudet's position was supported by Congress, and he received an appropriation to establish a teacher preparation program that emphasized both the oral and manual approach to education of these students. Although Gallaudet won support from Congress, the conflicts were not settled. In fact, for many years the oralist position was more popular, and the use of manual communication in any form was discouraged in classes for deaf and hard of hearing students.

Horace Mann, a leader in education and social reform during the late 1800s, sided with the oral-only camp because the signing system of the manual method did not match English in grammar and structure. Throughout the late nineteenth century and for most of the twentieth century, the oral-only position was commonly followed. It was not until the 1970s that a combined approach—called total communication—was adopted. Total communication uses oral and manual communication systems for the instruction of deaf students. The debate about oralism and a combined oral and sign language method for communicating and instruction continues today, however.

Formal education for the deaf in the United States in the nineteenth century took place primarily in residential schools. Deaf students were sent to boarding schools, as were many students without disabilities in that day. From 1817, when the first school was started, to the eve of the Civil War in 1864, twenty-four schools for the deaf were in operation. **Gallaudet University** (first called the National Deaf-Mute College) was founded in 1864 on the principle of the right of all deaf students to an education. Educators at Gallaudet believed that these students can achieve and learn when expectations are high and a high-quality education is available to them.

The development of the hearing aid had a significant impact on the lives of people who are deaf or hard of hearing, particularly those with conductive hearing losses. The hearing trumpet, as it was called when first developed, made sounds a little louder. At the end of World War II, battery-operated hearing aids were developed,

For a picture of a hearing trumpet, see the photo of Dorothy Brett in the Technology section.

Gallaudet University. The United States' federally funded university serving Deaf undergraduate and graduate students.

CONNECTIONS

For more about
Gallaudet University,
the world's only univer-
sity for the Deaf, and its
importance to the Deaf
community, see in this
chapter:

• the sections about
  Thomas and Edward
  Gallaudet and the
  university earlier in
  the History section
• Deaf Culture in the
  Deaf and Hard of
  Hearing Children
  section
• Overcoming Barriers
  in the Educational
  Interventions section

I. King Jordan, the first Deaf President of Gallaudet University, has become a symbol of Deaf advocacy and Deaf culture.

CONNECTIONS

The advocacy movement
and reasons for it are
also discussed in these
sections:

• Necessity for National
  Intervention
  (Chapter 1)
• Legacies from the
  Twentieth Century
  (Chapter 1)
• History of people with
  physical disabilities
  and special health care
  needs (Chapter 9)
• History section of this
  chapter

but these devices were difficult to use because they were bulky. Behind-the-ear (BTE) hearing aids were created after the development of the transistor in the 1950s and, with refinements, continue in use today. A new generation of hearing aids is being developed today. These digital hearing aids block out background noise, adjust to each individual's hearing profile, and amplify sounds across the entire range of frequencies used in speech.

Since the late 1980s, **Deaf pride** and Deaf culture have gained in numbers and in visibility: The Deaf community is now seen as a significant advocacy group. The Deaf President Now Movement, which galvanized the Deaf community (Gannon, 1989), began in 1988 when a hearing president was appointed to lead Gallaudet University. After protests from Deaf Gallaudet students and the Deaf community, which closed the campus and included a march on the nation's Capitol, the newly appointed president (who could not sign) resigned and I. King Jordan became the first Deaf college president for Gallaudet and the nation. In 1994, a similar protest occurred at the Lexington Center, New York City's only public day school for the deaf. In this case, a hearing chief executive was appointed without input or approval from the Deaf community (Soloman, 1994). Deaf leaders are now taking their proper places in society and in the workplace. One example is Dr. Robert Davila, one of eight children from a migrant farmworker's family. He was the first deaf person to become a vice president at Gallaudet University, and was Assistant Secretary of Education for the U.S. Department of Education from 1989 to 1993.

PREVALENCE

Also see the discussion about prevalence rates when students have multiple disabilities in the Prevalence section of Chapter 11.

Approximately 21 million people in the United States (45% of whom are over age 65) have trouble hearing (Norrix, 1999). Obtaining reliable statistics about the number of children who are deaf or hard of hearing is difficult because states use different criteria for counting who is deaf, hard of hearing, and/or has multiple disabilities. But not all states use the same criteria. In addition, the U.S. Department of Education reports children by their primary disability. So students with mental retardation who also have a hearing loss may be reported only in the mental retardation category or possibly in the multiple disabilities category, but usually not in the deafness and hard of hearing category. Also, those hard of hearing students who do not need special education because hearing aids allow them to hear well enough to participate in typical classroom activities without additional assistance are not included in these counts.

Considering these factors, the number of deaf and hard of hearing students is probably underestimated. Regardless, according to the *Annual Report to Congress on Implementation of the Individuals with Disabilities Education Act* (U.S. Department of Education, 1998), during the 1996–1997 schoolyear, 0.11% of the resident population between the ages of 6 and 21, or 68,641 students, were classified as deaf or hard of hearing.

Almost 44% of deaf schoolchildren are from diverse backgrounds (Gallaudet Research Institute, 1998). Programs for deaf and hard of hearing children serve fewer White and Black students but substantially more Hispanic and Asian/Pacific Islanders. In fact, the rate of Hispanic students identified as having hearing losses has more than doubled since 1974 (Andrews & Martin, 1998). This increasing number of Hispanics, for example, is due in part to their increased representation in demographics relating to deaf and hard of hearing students. What is of great concern is that some of these students are not diagnosed and do not receive intervention services early; few young Mexican American children are identified before the age of 4 and they often are not provided with hearing aids (Walker-Vann, 1998). Being without services during the early years has long-term negative effects that often cannot be overcome.

CAUSES AND PREVENTION

It is not a surprise to learn that hearing loss can result from illness or injury. For example, sustained loud noise can cause a hearing loss. In addition, some types of deafness are the result of heredity. This was the reason that Alexander Graham Bell, in the late 1800s, proposed legislation to ban two deaf people from marrying; fortunately, he was unsuccessful. For educators, understanding the causes of hearing loss can be useful, for the type of loss can have bearing on the accommodations necessary for effective instruction. For everyone, knowing how to prevent hearing loss or minimize its effects is important.

Deaf pride. A term used to signify the accomplishments and achievements of members of the Deaf community.

CAUSES

It appears that heredity accounts for about 35% of childhood deafness in the United States today (Gallaudet Research Institute, 1998). However, as Table 10.2 on page 426 indicates, the cause is unknown for a great many deaf and hard of hearing people.

Table 10.2 Percentage Distribution of Causes of Hearing Loss

Cause[†]	School Year			
	1972–73	1982–83	1987–88	1997–98
Total, all causes	100.0	100.0	100.0	100.0
Cause unknown or not reported	48.6	39.5	48.8	55.2
Cause reported				
Causes at birth				
Maternal rubella	17.6	16.3	5.2	1.0
Heredity	8.5	11.6	12.9	16.5
Prematurity	5.2	4.0	4.8	4.6
Pregnancy complications	3.2	3.4	2.9	3.6
Trauma	2.3	2.4	2.4	2.0
Rh incompatibility	3.1	1.4	0.6	0.3
Cytomegalovirus (CMV)	*	*	0.7	1.7
Causes after birth				
Meningitis	5.3	7.3	8.8	6.2
Otitis media	1.6	3.0	3.4	4.8
High fever	2.3	3.1	2.9	*
Infection	1.5	2.7	2.5	2.4
Trauma	0.9	0.8	0.7	0.8
Measles	2.1	0.8	0.4	*
Mumps	0.6	0.2	0.1	*
Other causes	2.5	8.0	7.2	7.3

*These causes did not appear as a specific category to be checked on questionnaire.

[†]Because some students had more than one reported etiology, the sum of the cause-specific percentages exceeds the total percentage of cases with known causes.

Sources: Demographic Aspects of Hearing Impairment: Questions and Answers (2nd ed., p. 7) by D. Hotchkiss, 1989, Washington, DC: Center for Assessment and Demographic Studies, Gallaudet University. Gallaudet Research Institute. (1998, November). *Regional and National Summary Report Data from the 1997–98 Annual Survey of Deaf and Hard-of-Hearing Children and Youth,* Washington, DC: GRI, Gallaudet University.

Even in these unknown cases, it is likely that heredity and genetics account for many of the hearing losses. The table compares the percentages of students with hearing loss across a twenty-five-year period. Otitis media, meningitis, and heredity are causes that have increased over time. Maternal rubella has decreased dramatically, but unfortunately is still a contributing factor in the number of cases of children with hearing loss today.

Of course, other causes of hearing problems fall outside of these groups. For example, we now know that congenital cytomegalovirus (CMV) infection, a herpes virus, affects about 1% of all newborns and can cause mild to profound sensorineural hearing losses and other disabilities as well. At present, no vaccine or cure is available to prevent or treat CMV; however, avoiding persons affected with the virus, ensuring the safety of blood used in transfusions, and good hygiene are important

CMV is also discussed in the Prevalence and the Causes and Prevention sections in Chapter 9.

preventive measures (Heller et al., 1996). As we eliminate or reduce the incidence of some causes of hearing loss, other causes are discovered. As advances in medical technology continue, many of the unknown causes will be identified. Of course, the hope is that once a cause is identified, a cure or preventive technique will be discovered. Let's look at each of the four major causes of hearing problems.

Maternal Rubella. Rubella (German measles) contracted by a pregnant woman is a devastating disease for an unborn child. Depending on when the expectant mother contracts the virus, the child may be born with a profound hearing loss, a visual disability, or other disabilities alone or in combinations. As with other congenital hearing losses (those present at birth), those caused by maternal rubella are typically sensorineural, with damage to the inner ear or the auditory nerve. The children affected are prelingually deaf. Vaccines are available to prevent women of childbearing age from contracting this disease; therefore the incidence of deafness caused by maternal rubella has declined and should be eliminated.

Meningitis. Meningitis is a disease that affects the central nervous system (specifically the meninges, the coverings of the brain and spinal cord, and its circulating fluid). Most cases that involve a hearing loss are bacterial infections rather than the more lethal viral meningitis. This disease often results in a profound hearing loss and is often associated with other disabilities. Meningitis is the most common cause of postnatal deafness in schoolchildren and is one major cause of sensorineural hearing losses that are not present at birth. These individuals' hearing losses are acquired, and they may have developed some speech and language before they developed the hearing loss. Vaccines do exist that will prevent the disease, but at present there is no national immunization program for meningitis.

Otitis Media. Infection of the middle ear and accumulation of fluid behind the eardrum is called otitis media. The condition can be corrected and treated with antibiotics and other medical procedures. If sustained for long periods of time or not detected in very young children, the condition may result in a language impairment that could affect future academic learning. Chronic otitis media can result in a conductive hearing loss by damaging the eardrum and in about 84% of the cases results in a mild to moderate hearing loss. Typically these youngsters are hard of hearing, and they profit from hearing aids because their hearing loss is conductive.

For other disabilities that have known hereditary origins, see the Causes and Prevention sections of these chapters:
• Chapter 4
• Chapter 6
• Chapter 9

Heredity. More than 150 different types of genetic deafness have been identified, and most likely the unknown causes of deafness are genetic. Genetic causes are congenital and sensorineural. Most children whose deafness is inherited are less likely to have multiple disabilities. Look at Table 10.2 again. Notice that the percentage of cases that can now be documented as being caused by heredity is on the rise.

Noise. Although noise has not traditionally been included as a major cause of hearing loss, employers, federal agencies, and researchers are becoming more aware of its dangers. It is now known that noise is the major cause of hearing loss in this country (Dawson, 1997). While European countries take legal steps to ensure noise abatement, the United States seems to be getting noisier. The U.S. Occupational Safety and Health Administration (OSHA) has set standards indicating that noise louder than 105 dB for longer than an hour is unhealthy, and some believe that this level is way too high (Koran & Oliva, 1997). Imagine the damage caused by the sound levels of

meningitis. A disease that affects the central nervous system and often causes hearing loss.

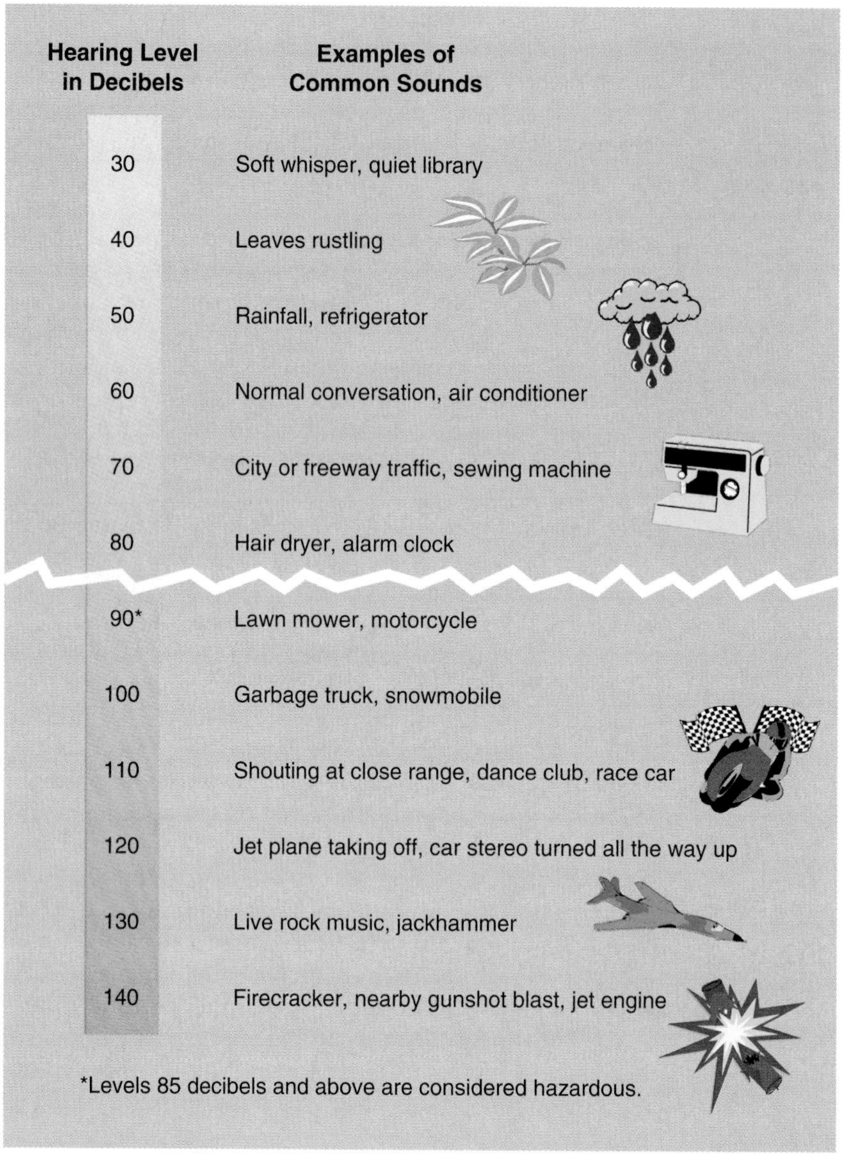

Hearing Level in Decibels	Examples of Common Sounds
30	Soft whisper, quiet library
40	Leaves rustling
50	Rainfall, refrigerator
60	Normal conversation, air conditioner
70	City or freeway traffic, sewing machine
80	Hair dryer, alarm clock
90*	Lawn mower, motorcycle
100	Garbage truck, snowmobile
110	Shouting at close range, dance club, race car
120	Jet plane taking off, car stereo turned all the way up
130	Live rock music, jackhammer
140	Firecracker, nearby gunshot blast, jet engine

*Levels 85 decibels and above are considered hazardous.

Figure 10.4 Decibel Levels of Noise in American Environments
Source: U.S. Congress Select Committee on Children, Youth, and Families.

a rock concert (which often reach 125 dB), a car stereo, or a personal tape player. Indications are that young males are more likely to acquire noise-induced hearing losses because they frequently engage in activities such as mowing the lawn, firing a gun, riding a motorcycle, or fixing a car engine. Even infants and toddlers can sustain irreversible noise-induced hearing losses. And now mounting evidence indicates that loud music typically used in aerobics classes has caused damage to the hearing of millions of people, particularly women. Hearing loss from noise occurs without any pain or notice; and accumulates slowly across years of exposure. Figure 10.4 shows what sounds are considered in the danger zone.

NEW DIRECTIONS
FOR THE
MILLENNIUM

Legacy: The use of cochlear implants with children began late in the last century. It was both applauded and reviled, and remains at the center of great controversy.

Opportunities:

- Carefully determine who are good candidates for this surgery, and apply the procedure accordingly
- Increase the number of SLPs who are skilled in working with children with cochlear implants

MAKING CONNECTIONS

For more information about the debate over cochlear implants, see Concepts and Controversy at the end of this chapter.

cochlear implant. Electronic microprocessor that replaces the cochlea and allows some people who are deaf to process sounds.

PREVENTION

Can some hearing losses be corrected or prevented? The answer, of course, is yes. In some cases, the steps needed for prevention are simple; in other cases, complicated medical technology is required. In many cases, no preventive measures exist today. One cause that can be prevented—noise—requires only some simple measures. People can wear ear protectors when they are around loud sounds. Another preventive measure is to have makers of personal stereos, power lawn mowers, and other noisy equipment install noise-limiting devices or graphic warning lights on their products. Although many preventive measures are simple and seem to be "common sense," other measures are complicated and costly. In the following sections, you will learn how medical technology, early detection, and public awareness can contribute to reducing the number of individuals with hearing loss. And for those whose hearing loss cannot be prevented, many preventive measures can lessen the impact.

Medical Technology. Medical technology can play an important role in the prevention and treatment of hearing problems. As we have discussed, infection can cause hearing loss. But some infections, if diagnosed and treated early, do not have to result in deafness or significant loss. Today, most conductive hearing losses that involve the middle ear can be treated either medically or surgically. And a new laser treatment, OtoLAM, may soon become the common method used to drain fluid from babies' ears, reducing the number of cases where tubes need to be surgically inserted (Marsa, 1999). Also, delicate surgical procedures can repair or replace poorly functioning small bones in the middle ear. Basic research being conducted today further hints at a remarkable future, when hair cells in the cochlea can be regenerated and implants placed in the brain stem transmit signals to the brain, bypassing damaged auditory nerves.

Other medical advances applied today include **cochlear implants.** This technology is currently at the center of great controversy between the Deaf and hearing communities. Because cochlear implants bring only a crude awareness of sound to some deaf people, many in the Deaf community question whether this technology should be applied, particularly to prelingually (congenitally) deaf children. Although it is not beneficial for some, it does improve the hearing of others. And some evidence indicates that children with implants have better reading achievement than those who do not (Spencer et al., 1997). For instance, Linda Benton, who began losing her hearing when she was in her twenties and had severe-to-profound hearing loss by the age of 35, has profited greatly from cochlear implants. She says that the implant allows her to use a regular telephone. It is important to understand that implants do not "cure" deafness, as Benton explains. "Do I want to hear more with my implant? You bet! I would like to listen to music more, understand movies better, and watch TV without captions" (Benton, 1997, p. 21). Regardless, for her implants make an important and real difference. A typical cochlear implant, shown in Figure 10.5 on page 430, converts acoustic information to electrical signals that stimulate the remaining auditory nerve fibers.

Very few American children have received a cochlear implant, which costs between $25,000 and $30,000. In a 1998 survey of deaf and hard of hearing children, only 1,739 were identified who had a cochlear implant (Gallaudet Research Institute, 1998). Although no one really has precise estimates, it is known that some 16% of young children with implants are no longer using them. The cochlear implant

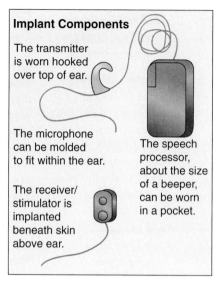

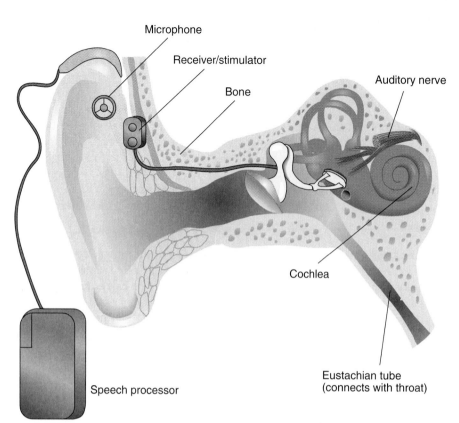

Figure 10.5 Cochlear Implant

procedure involves an incision made behind the ear; when that heals, a wire is wound through the cochlea. The wire is connected to a very small receiver that is placed under the skin behind the ear; then wire and receiver are connected to a small computer, which can be worn on a belt. In the hearing process, the computer detects sound and sends electrical signals to the implanted receiver, which stimulates the auditory nerve, creating sound. Whether that sound is interpreted as noise or as words seems to depend on many factors (how long the person has been deaf, how long the implant has been worn, whether the person knew speech before becoming deaf). In other words, implants do not guarantee the proficient use of oral language in deaf children, particularly in children who have congenital deafness (Lundy, 1997). Some postlingually deaf children, whose hearing loss came early in life, tend to develop moderate ability to perceive sounds, understand language, and develop some intelligible speech. For those born deaf, cochlear implants seem to have the least positive effect (Niparko, 1998). In one research study with children who had used a cochlear implant for at least two years (an average of three years), only some ability to understand information presented orally and little development of intelligible speech occurred (Tye-Murray et al., 1995). In that study, the children could repeat only 22% of the words correctly when retelling a story, their speech intelligibility was very low, they learned speech at a much slower rate than hearing peers, and they continued to use sign language. The successful use of a cochlear implant in everyday communication seems to require a prior knowledge and mastery of spoken language (Lane, 1995).

Early Detection. For all hearing losses, early detection is critical. For those that can be prevented, as in the case of otitis media, further damage can be avoided. For those that cannot be prevented, early intervention can make a significant difference in the individual's overall outcomes, not only in terms of expressive and receptive language abilities, but also in terms of overall development and lower levels of family stress (Drasgow, 1998; Yoshinaga-Itano & Apuzzo, 1998).

Efforts at early detection, however, are not currently sufficient. As you have learned, even children with profound deafness are not typically identified until they are 2½ years old, and early intervention does not begin until a year later (Yoshinaga-Itano & Apuzzo, 1998). This is despite research findings clearly showing that children identified before they are 6 months old experience half the delays of those identified after they are 18 months old. When children with cognitive impairments are removed from the group's analysis, the deaf and hard of hearing children identified early perform close to children without hearing losses.

Despite calls for universal hearing screenings of newborns by ASHA, the National Institutes of Health, and other advocacy groups, only seventeen states currently have passed legislation, and legislation is pending in seven more, requiring infant and newborn hearing testing (ASHA, 1999a; Gordon-Langbein, 1999). In 1992, Rhode Island was the first state to pass a bill requiring hospitals to test all newborns for hearing loss, not just those at risk; the cost of the tests are to be covered by health insurance or the hospital if the family cannot pay. These recent changes are due in part to advances in testing methods; today, the procedures are less expensive, more accurate, and easier to administer. They are also due to better understanding of the numbers of individuals involved (possibly as high as 6 out of every 1,000 live births) and the personal and financial costs involved in not identifying children early. For example, ASHA estimates that the lifetime cost of each case of congenital deafness is over $1,000,000, and with the cost of new universal screening procedures being around $25 for each infant, testing is a good investiment (ASHA, 1999b; Lombardo, 1998). For these reasons, calls for national legislation continue (McGee, 1999). Clearly, all newborns should be tested for hearing loss!

Increased Public Awareness. A more knowledgeable public, availability of good health care for all children, and better-prepared preschool teachers can prevent some hearing losses and provide treatment for others. Another way to prevent hearing loss is to make the public aware of the importance of proper immunization. For example, although the number of children who are deaf because of maternal rubella has been reduced drastically, this disease has not been eliminated. The public needs to be continually reminded of the importance of immunizations. For this reason, you might have noticed an increased number of public service advertisements on television reminding parents of the importance of protecting young children from disease. In addition to raising public awareness, we need to make vaccinations available to all children, even those without the ability to pay for them.

C O N N E C T I O N S
M A K I N G

See the Concepts and Controversy section in Chapter 5 for a discussion regarding whether the federal government has a responsibility to implement a national immunization program.

DEAF AND HARD OF HEARING CHILDREN

CONNECTIONS

- For a review of specific disabilities that may coexist with deafness, see those chapters in this text.
- To review the causes of various disabilities, read the Causes sections in Chapters 3–12.

Deaf and hard of hearing children cannot be stereotyped. They are individuals with different learning styles and abilities, but they do share one common characteristic: Their ability to hear is limited. As we have mentioned earlier, the severity of the hearing loss and the age at which the loss occurred determine how well a person will be able to interact with others orally. Another factor is whether the individual has cognitive impairments along with the hearing loss. Estimates are that about 25% of deaf and hard of hearing children have additional disabilities (Karchmer & Allen, 1999). Additional disabilities may include visual disabilities, mental retardation, learning disabilities, behavior disorders, or cerebral palsy. These accompanying disabilities are often caused by the same disease or accident that caused the hearing loss. For example, rubella (German measles), blood type (Rh) incompatibility between mother and child, and trauma at birth often result in more than one disability. Students whose deafness is inherited tend not to have multiple disabilities. Clearly, for whatever reason, students who cannot hear the communications of others well have a more difficult time learning through traditional instructional methods.

DEAF CULTURE

CONNECTIONS

For a review of the differences between being handicapped and having a disability, see Disabilities Defined section of Chapter 1.

As detailed in a footnote in the Defined section of this chapter, the word *deaf* is begun with a capital letter when it refers to something or someone associated with **Deaf culture.** When the word is begun with a lower-case letter, it refers primarily to an audiological condition or disability. Hard of hearing and deaf persons may be Deaf or deaf, depending on whether they use ASL and associate with the Deaf community. Many consider the Deaf a minority group, much like ethnic and racial minorities in this country (Drasgow, 1998; Lane, 1995). There are many concepts and nuances to understand when learning about the culture of the Deaf; it is important that teachers understand and respect their students' home cultures.

Deafness is viewed in different ways by different individuals and groups. Many hearing people consider deafness a disability, a pathological condition. To many Deaf people, deafness is one aspect binding a minority group together, a minority group rich in culture, history, language, and the arts. The language of the Deaf community is **American Sign Language (ASL),** a language that uses signs, has all of the elements (grammar, syntax, idioms) of other languages, and is not parallel to English in either structure or word order. ASL is not a mere translation of oral speech or the English language (as is **Signed English**); it is a fully developed language. In fact, many states allow ASL as an option to meet the high school foreign language requirement, and the same is true at many colleges and universities. As the language of the Deaf community, ASL is used in all aspects of their culture. For example, plays are written in ASL and performed by deaf theater groups around the world, and a base of folk literature has also developed over the years. This community unites in many ways by coming together socially and for the purpose of advocacy, like when they began the Deaf President Now Movement in 1988.

For many deaf people, being Deaf of Deaf (being born Deaf of Deaf parents), or even a CODA (Child of a Deaf Adult) is a source of considerable pride (Soloman, 1994). Although clearly a minority within a minority, life can be substantially easier for these individuals. They learn sign language as their native language, which they develop naturally just as hearing babies develop oral language. For these individuals, their deafness is a language difference, not a disability (Drasgow, 1998; Lane, 1995). Reports about the Deaf communities that thrived on Martha's Vineyard during the

Deaf culture. The structures of social relationships, language (ASL), dance, theater, and other cultural activities that bind the Deaf community.

American Sign Language (ASL). The sign language or manual communication system preferred by many adults who are deaf in this country.

Signed English. A manual communication system that translates the English language into signs.

Deaf theater groups perform throughout America. Many of these productions express Deaf culture and are performed using American Sign Language.

For a review of the Deaf President Now Movement, see in this chapter:

• History section
• Overcoming Barriers in the Educational Interventions section

To refresh your memory about the Deaf communities on Martha's Vineyard, read again the Disabilities Does Not Equal Handicap box (Chapter 1).

1800s are good examples of how a language difference does not have to be a disability (Groce, 1981; Huntington, 1981). Most of these individuals consider themselves part of the Deaf community and are active in its activities and clubs, attend Deaf Theater, travel in groups, use ASL as their language, and believe that it is important to learn about their culture. Of course, for those who became deaf later in life, do not know ASL, and live in the hearing world, deafness is a disability—one that disconnects them from friends and family. For these people, there is no debate: Deafness is a disability.

What is different in the situation of the Deaf is that only about 5% of these individuals were born of Deaf parents and learn ASL as their native language. The vast majority of others are assimilated into the culture later in life, often at residential schools for the Deaf (Fletcher, 1994). What about the majority of the prelingually deaf? Recall that 95% of deaf children are born of hearing parents. Many of these youngsters do not develop language (either aural or manual) when they should developmentally, which can be devastating to the individual's cognitive and social skills development. The challenges for these youngsters and their families are great. Many parents are afraid that if their children learn ASL as their first language, they will be excluded from mainstream society, seek out the Deaf community, and be lost to their natural family (Goldberg, 1995).

ACADEMIC ACHIEVEMENT

The Gallaudet Research Institute has tracked the academic achievement levels of deaf students consistently across time, and has found that deaf individuals are substantially below the reading and mathematics achievement levels of their peers without disabilities (Allen, 1988; Gallaudet Research Institute, 1994; Moores, 1996). For

Legacy: Due to lack of information, educators and the public continue, into this century, to make erroneous and negative assumptions about deaf students and their needs.

Opportunities:

- Change the attitudes and expectations of teachers, administrators, and the public by publicizing the abilities and skills that deaf and hard of hearing individuals can and do achieve
- Conduct systematic and differential research to determine effective educational practices for deaf and hard of hearing students

example, by age 20 half of the students tested read below the mid-fourth-grade level, leaving them with skills insufficient to read most newspapers, which are written at least at the fifth-grade level. Of course, half of those tested scored over that level, and many deaf people are very efficient readers (Easterbrooks, 1999). But reading and literacy have become major concerns, so in recent years literacy and academic achievement have received increased attention from teachers and researchers. And deaf children's reading performance has been improving. This is in part due to new instructional methods and also to early intervention efforts. Also, more motivation might exist for deaf people to learn to read. Many technological advances developed to benefit people with hearing loss, such as captioned television and films, require an ability to read well, for instance.

SPEECH ABILITY

Being able to hear relates to an ability to speak intelligibly. Research findings indicate that somewhere between 25% and 45% of deaf students have intelligible speech, and most others have speech that sounds "different" from the speech of hearing individuals (Allen, 1986; Wolk & Schildroth, 1986). Intelligibility of speech is related to a number of factors: degree of hearing loss, the communication method the individual uses (speech only, sign only, speech and sign together), age of onset, cultural and linguistic background, and the presence of another disability. The degree of hearing loss appears to be the most crucial factor in determining whether a person's speech is intelligible. Being able to understand someone's speech is also partly determined by the listener's experience (Most et al., 1996). The resulting inconsistency in the ability to understand the speaker is one reason why data about the intelligibility of deaf children's speech is confusing. Unfortunately, a relationship also exists between a person's speech ability and the way the person is perceived by others: As ratings of intelligibility go down, ratings of cognitive competence and personality decline. Learning to speak is a difficult and arduous task for children who are deaf, requiring years of effort and systematic instruction. Because it is so easy to misjudge the intentions and actions of students who have difficulties communicating, teachers must be careful not to harshly interpret deaf students' behaviors. The Achieving Discipline box provides an example of how a situation that a deaf child had thought to be unfair was turned into a learning situation. We all need to be careful not to judge people unfairly. Clearly, judging a person's abilities and character based on how well he or she can speak is an example of how decisions about a person can be made on irrelevant factors.

EDUCATIONAL INTERVENTIONS

As you have learned, deaf and hard of hearing children need to receive an intensive educational experience as early as possible. Professionals in this field may debate about the best educational practices and placements, but they all agree on two points: Education should begin at birth or at the time the hearing loss is discovered, and the entire family needs to be involved. In this section, some suggestions are included for teachers and other professionals on instructing these students more effectively. Throughout these children's schoolyears, an array of professionals and services must be available to guide the development of a responsive program needed by these students.

Achieving Discipline

BE FAIR: MAKE THE PUNISHMENT FIT THE CRIME

Teresa was 8 years old, and attended a neighborhood school. She did very well learning English, but had much left to learn. She had only been in school for three years and had not yet mastered her new language. She was able to converse with her peers and teachers, express her feelings, and—with periodic assistance from a bilingual paraprofessional—learn academic subjects. Members of her multidisciplinary team disagreed about Teresa's level of English proficiency. Some of the confusion stemmed from her difficulties with oral speech, and how intelligible her speech was to others. Teresa was a quick learner, but her moderate hearing loss limited her receptive language abilities. Like many immigrant children, she was not diagnosed early and also did not get hearing aids soon after she was diagnosed. When Teresa was 4 years old, the family's social worker suspected a problem and referred her to a local clinic, where her hearing loss was discovered. After months of delays, Teresa was fitted with hearing aids.

Teresa had great difficulties getting along with her classmates. She accused them of being unfair to her, and they felt that she did not take turns either on the playground or in group activities. Her peers accused her of being demanding and short-tempered. Her teacher, Ms. Tomas, set up a system where Teresa lost privileges for misbehavior, arguments, and bursts of temper. The result was that Teresa remained inside for most recesses and lunch breaks and was always the last to leave the classroom. Her behavior worsened as she became more frustrated. The "behavior

specialist" for Teresa's school, Ms. Garcia, was a special education teacher who served on the IEP teams for children with behavior problems. Ms. Garcia had not been part of Teresa's multidisciplinary team, but asked if she could help resolve the growing crisis. Ms. Garcia discussed the situation with Teresa, and also talked with her classmates separately. Teresa felt that the punishment was unfair, and that everything at school was unfair. Her classmates agreed; most believed the punishment system arranged was too harsh. Instead, they suggested that Teresa earn privileges (not lose them) for getting along and for talking about events that frustrated her. They further suggested that Teresa earn privileges for asking questions when she did not understand the rules of the game. They also thought that they should earn rewards for including Teresa in games that she "ruined." Once the behavior management program was perceived as fair by all, Teresa's interactions with her classmates became positive.

Being fair when implementing behavior management systems

- Consider the current functioning levels of the student
- Include the target student when setting consequences for inappropriate behavior
- Seek suggestions from classmates about behaviors of concern and how they should be handled
- Monitor behavior patterns to be certain that positive outcomes result from interventions

EDUCATION AND THE PRESCHOOL CHILD

Preschool programs are especially important for children with severe to profound hearing losses. As they do for other children with disabilities, good preschool programs can positively affect the lifelong outcomes of these children. Early identification and early implementation of preschool programs allow deaf and hard of hearing students to develop language at the right periods of their lives. These programs also assist families of these children so they can better understand and meet the very special needs of their deaf family members.

NEW DIRECTIONS
FOR THE
MILLENNIUM

Legacy: As the last century came to an end, the power of early intervention became very clear, but preschool programs remain inconsistently available and not always of high quality.

Opportunities:

- Insist on high standards for personnel who work in preschool and early intervention programs
- Increase state and federal funding, and provide incentives for business, so early intervention programs are accessible and widely available

MAKING CONNECTIONS

To review how language typically develops, see the sections on Language Impairments in the Defined section of Chapter 5.

MAKING CONNECTIONS

For more about technology that assists deaf and hard of hearing people, see the Technology section of this chapter.

Evidence connecting language development and academic achievement for deaf children is mounting. You just learned that deaf and hard of hearing students have significantly low academic achievement. New research indicates that this outcome can be avoided (Drasgow, 1998; Yoshinaga-Itano & Apuzzo, 1998). Deaf children of deaf parents learn sign language during their infancy. For those of them without cognitive impairment, by the time they reach school age they are reading at two grade levels above deaf children of hearing parents (Marschark, 1993). This difference occurs because these children of deaf parents learned language during the proper developmental period, while most deaf children of hearing parents are not identified until age 3—an age when language development should be well underway. Building upon the findings from earlier studies, new research provides great optimism. When deaf children learn sign language during infancy, they develop communication skills "on time," and when they then receive instruction that is in their "native" language, they are able to read and write at about the same level as their hearing classmates (Andrews et al., 1997).

Many hearing families, once their child's deafness is identified, choose to learn and use some combination of oral language and a manual communication system so that they can communicate more fully with their child. Some professionals (Drasgow, 1998) propose that infants and their families be taught ASL so these children can acquire it as their "native" language. However, it is important to recognize that like mastering any second language, becoming fluent in ASL is no easy task (Kemp, 1998). Once universal screening is available across the nation, all infants—even those without risk factors—will be screened for hearing losses and those found to have hearing loss will be able to benefit from early intervention and hopefully be able to follow a course of language development similar to that of their hearing peers. Like deaf children of deaf parents, they would use their hands to babble at about the same time that hearing infants make babbling sounds. They would produce two-word utterances at about the same time as their hearing brothers and sisters, but would probably learn English as a second language.

EDUCATION AND THE SCHOOLCHILD

The educational needs of students who are hard of hearing differ from those of deaf students. There are differences in the way they are taught, in what they are taught, and, for some of these students, in where they are taught. For example, 43% are taught using the oral-only approach. Remember, many hard of hearing students do not use sign language. The majority of deaf and hard of hearing students, 51%, use a combination of sign and speech, while only 5% use sign language (Gallaudet Research Institute, 1998). In this section, those differences, along with specific educational options for both deaf and hard of hearing students, are discussed.

Instructional Considerations for Hard of Hearing Students. Since the advent of PL 94–142 in 1975, more and more deaf and hard of hearing students have been educated in general education classes with generally positive results, particularly for hard of hearing students (Easterbrooks, 1999). Remember that most students with hearing loss can hear satisfactorily with amplification (that is, a hearing aid) and therefore can attend school and function well with their nondisabled classmates. In most schools, information is presented orally, and students learn through a combination of textbooks, lectures, and class discussions. Hard of hearing children can cope quite well with these methods as long as an array of supplemental services and assistance is available.

Accommodating for Inclusive Environments

MODIFYING THE DELIVERY OF INSTRUCTION

1. Place the child as close to the speaker as possible.
2. Make certain the child's hearing aid is turned on and functioning properly by listening through it.
3. Reduce the background noise as much as possible.
4. Articulate clearly, but do not talk louder unless you have an unusually soft voice.
5. Make certain to have the student's attention before talking or starting a lesson.
6. Do not exaggerate your lip movements.
7. Do not chew gum or cover your mouth when talking.
8. Do not turn your back to the class.
9. Use an overhead projector instead of a blackboard, so that the student can see your mouth.
10. Avoid moving around the classroom while talking.
11. Speak slowly.
12. Repeat and restate information by paraphrasing.
13. Spend time talking to the child alone so that you become accustomed to each other's speech.
14. Avoid glare when talking or signing by not standing near a light source such as a window.
15. Do not bounce or move around while talking.
16. Bend down so that you are at students' eye level when you talk to individuals or small groups.
17. Use class handouts to support important information from lectures, guest speakers, field trips, and instructional films.
18. Ask classmates to volunteer to be peer assistants, possibly one classmate per class, unit, or topic.
19. Ask classmates to rotate as note takers who make an extra set of lecture notes by using carbon paper as they write, thus freeing the deaf student to watch the teacher more closely.
20. Consult with a certified teacher of the deaf.

Along with acquiring educational benefits, many students learn important social skills in general classroom settings. However, teachers should not assume that social acceptance goes hand in hand with general education placements. Unfortunately, research findings indicate otherwise: Normally hearing peers tend not to have a high social acceptance of deaf or hard of hearing classmates (Antia & Kreimeyer, 1996). Teachers must be proactive, helping to foster good peer relationships among all their students.

With certain modifications to the environment, deaf and hard of hearing students benefit from general education class placements. A number of simple techniques and procedures can help students profit in oral communication situations; some of these methods are listed in the Accommodating for Inclusive Environments box. Another modification to the classroom routine uses handouts listing important points from lectures, films, or movies. Also, a classmate can be asked to help by using carbon paper to make an extra set of lecture notes.

Teachers should seek the help of specialists and others who can provide guidance so that the learning environment is most efficient for all students in the class. For example, classroom teachers have found that the SLP assigned to their school can offer many good ideas about activities that foster better speech and language. The specialist can also provide suggestions about classroom organizers that will assist these students to gain more from traditional classroom settings. Parents are another important source of information. The child's parents can help teachers come to a quicker understanding of their child's preferred learning styles and special needs. For instance, one child might profit from having a classmate serve as a

The wonderful and engaging story of Dina, the Deaf dinosaur, teaches the importance of ASL to those who use it as their primary language.

oral-only approach. One method of instruction advocated for students who are deaf, whereby they learn to communicate (both receiving and sending information) orally, not using sign language.

total communication approach. A system of instruction for deaf students that employs any and all methods of communication (oral speech, manual communication, ASL, gestures) that are easy, efficient, and preferred by the student for communication.

resource to ensure that homework and other assignments are correctly understood. Another child might prefer to tape lectures and listen to them carefully in a quiet setting at home in the evening. Yet another student might benefit by being able to do extra outside reading on specific topics. Teachers need to remember that each child is unique and to capitalize on each child's strengths, not just attend to that student's disabilities.

Instructional Methods for Deaf Students. Best educational practices for deaf students are still developing. Overall, deaf students' academic achievement is improving, but more progress must be made. One factor that makes a difference is the communication system used to convey instruction. Generally, four different approaches are used to deliver instruction to deaf children:

- In the speech or **oral-only approach,** children are taught to use as much of their residual hearing as possible. This method was the most popular for deaf students until the 1970s, and a few programs still use it. Using amplification, children learn how to speech-read (lip-read) and how to speak. The oral approach does not allow children to use any form of manual communication such as finger spelling or signing. In fact, even natural signing, such as using gestures, is discouraged. Those who follow the oral approach believe that indi-

manual communication. Using the hands, not the voice, as the means of communication, as in sign language or finger spelling.
cued speech. Hand signals for "difficult to see" speech sounds that accompany oral speech to assist lipreading.
bilingual-bicultural approach. The application of ESL and bilingual techniques to deaf education where ASL is the native language and reading and writing in English are taught as a second language.

viduals who are deaf must live and work in a world where most people hear normally and communicate through oral expression. This is the method typically used with children who have cochlear implants, and of course is the method used in general education classes with most hard of hearing students.

- The **total communication approach** incorporates aspects of oral speech and **manual communication** (signing). Total communication allows the child to communicate through whatever mode is easiest and most effective. The philosophy behind this approach is that every child should be able to use whatever channels are available to learn and comprehend messages. About 72% of deaf students are now taught using this method (Moores, 1996), and about 51% of all deaf and hard of hearing students (Gallaudet Research Institute, 1998).

- **Cued speech** uses hand signals to accompany oral speech. These hand signals help deaf people read lips to determine, for example, whether the word said was *pan* or *bat*, which look alike to the person reading lips. It is popular with hearing parents because it is easy to learn and follows the English language format and structure (which ASL does not).

- The **bilingual-bicultural approach**, the newest method, is gaining popularity (Stewart, 1997). In the Research to Practice box on page 441, Cindy Bailes (1999) shows us how English is taught as a second language by using ASL.

For another look at bilingual special education methods, reread the Education and the Schoolchild sextion in Chapter 3.

Research findings indicate that achievement levels for many deaf youngsters exposed to this approach are close to those of their hearing peers (Andrews et al., 1997; Easterbrooks, 1999).

Although you might hear a lot about ASL, it is important to recognize that most elementary and secondary teachers of the deaf do *not* use ASL. Only about 5% of teachers for the deaf use ASL in their school classes (Gallaudet Research Institute, 1998). About 55% of deaf and hard of hearing students are taught through a combination of sign and speech, but the sign language used is not typically ASL. Often, a type of manual communication that more closely matches the grammatical form and structure of standard English is used. **Finger spelling,** a form of manual communication different from ASL, assigns each letter of the alphabet a sign. This system is efficient and has been used for centuries; an accomplished person can finger spell at a rate equivalent to typical speech. Finger spelling utilizes English: Words are spelled out, but the rules of grammar and language are the same as for English speech.

COLLABORATION FOR INCLUSIVE ENVIRONMENTS

To review the educational placement options available through special education, see the Special Educational Services section in Chapter 2.

At the national level, a full array of educational services and placements is available for deaf and hard of hearing elementary and secondary students. These educational programs typically include the services of audiologists, SLPs, interpreters, teachers of the deaf, and, for those with multiple disabilities, OTs and PTs. Nationally, placement options include general education classrooms, resource rooms, special classes, special day schools, and residential center schools. When thinking about school placements, the types of accommodations needed by these students, and the professionals who are brought together to form multidisciplinary teams, remember that the educational needs of each student with hearing loss are unique. School placements and methods of instruction are also determined for individual students and their families (Luetke-Stahlman, 1998). And, most important, these decisions must be reconsidered at various points across the students' school careers. Let's first look at how LRE is determined for these students, and then let's consider one particular group of professionals, educational interpreters, who specifically serve many deaf and hard of hearing students, and also work collaboratively with general educators.

For a review of the array of professionals who work with special education students, see the Special Educational Services section of Chapter 2.

Determining LRE. IDEA requires all students with disabilities to receive a free appropriate education (FAPE) in the least restrictive environment (LRE). What is the least restrictive environment for deaf children? The law states that what comprises an appropriate education and what environment is the least restrictive must be individually determined. Many parents and members of the Deaf community believe that the general education classroom is not the least restrictive setting for deaf children (Lane, 1995). "Deaf children deserve to be in an environment where they can communicate with peers, teachers, and staff; to be in an environment that meets their academic, social, emotional and cultural needs; and to be in an environment where they are truly included in every aspect of school" (Hawkins, 1993, p. 7). For students who rely on sign language as their primary means of communication, the general school environment where administrators, teachers, and classmates are not fluent in sign language can result in considerable isolation. It is important to recognize that 45% of general education classes where deaf students attend use an auditory/oral-only approach (Gallaudet Research Institute, 1998).

finger spelling. A form of manual communication that assigns each letter of the alphabet a sign.

Research to Practice: Teaching with Confidence

STRATEGIC USE OF AMERICAN SIGN LANGUAGE (ASL) TO PROMOTE KNOWLEDGE AND MASTERY OF ENGLISH

CYNTHIA NEESE BAILES
Gallaudet University

RESEARCH

Deaf children who use ASL as their primary language must also master English. They must become bilingual. To do so, they need to be able to think about their language, understand the nature of words as abstract concepts, and also be able to define words. This ability allows them to explicitly compare and contrast properties within a given language. The teachers at Metro Deaf School, a bilingual charter school for Deaf children in St. Paul, Minnesota, carry language development a step further. Teachers help children to distinguish between American Sign Language (ASL) and English as distinct languages. The children's growing knowledge about ASL as a first language, mindfully cultivated by their teachers, is applied directly to instruction that teaches the distinction between English and ASL as separate languages.

PRACTICE

Estella Bustamante, a Deaf first-grade teacher at MDS, fosters bridges between ASL and English by comparing and contrasting them explicitly. She draws the students into the discussion in a way that cultivates thinking about ASL and English as two distinct languages.

Estella provides parallel representations of both ASL and English. She signs and points to print, signs and finger spells, signs and writes, finger spells and writes, or uses all combinations to represent language. Finger spelling incorporates the English alphabet and thus provides a visual representation of English through manual communication. Estella uses finger spelling to emphasize English words that have no equivalent ASL translations and English grammatical constructions that are represented differently in ASL (e,g., determiners and verb tense). She involves the children in translating from ASL to English and vice versa, cultivating awareness and knowledge in the process of understanding language. Here's an example from Estella's class.

Estella used *Kites Sail High,* by Ruth Heller, to further compare ASL and English verb usage. The following dialogue, shown here partially in translated English and partially in gloss, a representation of ASL utterances through the use of corresponding English words in capital letters, gives an example of the instructional sequence. (The words she expresses in finger spelling are represented by breaks between letters.)

Estella: What's the title of the story?

Tina: KITES S-A-I-L HIGH.

Estella: What does that mean? Translate the title to ASL. What do you mean by "high"?

Tina: You hold the kite on a string and fly it in the sky.

Estella: Fine. The kite is high. What does the kite do?

Margaret: It moves.

Estella: It moves. The English word to tell how the kite moves is "sail." (Points to "sail" in the title.) S-A-I-L ... KITE-SAIL-HIGH. Now, which would you say: MY DAD HELP ME KITE SELF MOVE-HIGH or MY DAD HELP ME KITE-SAIL HIGH?

Margaret: The second example.

Estella: It is the same with English. K-I-T-E-S S-A-I-L H-I-G-H not K-I-T-E-S M-O-V-E H-I-G-H. (Estella writes "Kites move high" on the board and points to it.) Look at that sentence. It is not the way we say this in English.

Then, Estella crosses out "move" and says that ASL has ways of signing this sentence as well, and using the example of signing KITE MOVE-HIGH and KITE-SAIL-HIGH as examples. As Estella and her students continue through the book, they frequently pause to discuss verb usage in ASL and English. She points out unusual English verbs such as "*horses thunder*" and elicits translations to ASL from her students.

Estella's students were observed to directly apply their growing awareness of the distinctness of ASL and English. When they read stories to each other, they move away from word-to-sign reading, which does little to exhibit ther construction of meaning, to direct translations from English to ASL. When they are unsure of how to translate or when they want to emphasize English words or structures, they use finger spelling. These children also rehearse their writing ideas first in ASL and then in English. And they possessed a budding ability to explain the nature of these differences, a key feature in developing bilingual proficiency.

Research supports some parent concerns about general education placements for deaf students. For instance, deaf students who attend general education classes are often not included in nonacademic activities by their hearing classmates; the major reason for exclusion and rejection is difficulty with communication (Most et al., 1996). Of course, isolation does not have to be the outcome of general education placements, but specific attention to this possible outcome is warranted.

Some deaf students and their families, particularly during the high school years, select the educational option of a residential center school. Although declining in enrollment over the last fifteen years, the fifty-seven all-deaf schools are considered, particularly by members of the Deaf community, an important part of the array of services that should be available to this group of students. The use of schools for the deaf increases as students get older, with 56% of students with profound hearing loss attending residential schools during their high school years (Holden-Pitt, 1997). There also appears to be a relationship between the hearing status of a child's parents and placement in a residential school; 60% of parents of profoundly deaf students attending deaf center high school programs are themselves profoundly deaf. The Deaf community continues to advocate strongly for this educational placement option. What is at issue? At the same time that advocacy groups for people with mental retardation fought to close institutions, the Deaf community fought to keep residential center schools for deaf students open and fully funded. Issues about the best placement for each deaf child are complex, and parents are faced with difficult decisions. Remember that deafness in children is a low incidence disability; in the general school-age population, only a few children have this disability. The result can be that there is only one deaf child at a neighborhood school, or even in an entire school district. Without a critical mass of these youngsters, they are often left with feelings of isolation and rejection where few others use or understand their method of communication. This situation leads the Deaf community, some educators, and many parents to conclude that a separate program best meets the needs of deaf students and also the least restrictive option (Ramsey, 1997).

Determining LRE for students with disabilities can be difficult, particularly for deaf students. A team of professionals and the student's parents come together to create a team that solves this problem. How does the team decide which is the most appropriate service for a deaf student? The team makes the decision on the basis of answers to the following questions:

- How severe is the student's hearing loss?
- Is the student able to use speech?
- Can appropriate educational services be made available locally?
- Are the necessary support services available?

Clearly, many factors must be considered when professionals make decisions about a child's educational placement program and develop an IEP (Cohen, 1994; Schildroth & Hotto, 1994). Some of the factors concerning placement are given in Table 10.3. Meeting these goals requires that a full array of educational services and placements be available.

Teaming with Educational Interpreters. One essential service needed by many deaf students enrolled in general education programs is delivered by **educational interpreters**. These professionals convert spoken messages to the student's preferred communication system, which may be a signed system like ASL or signed English. For many teachers, working with the assistance of an interpreter is a novel experi-

MAKING CONNECTIONS

For a review of FAPE and LRE, see Special Educational Services in Chapter 2.

educational interpreters. Related service providers who translate or convert spoken messages to the deaf person's preferred mode of manual communication.

Table 10.3 Placement and IEP Considerations

<table>
<tr><td></td><td colspan="2" align="center">Type of Hearing Loss</td></tr>
<tr><td></td><td>Hard of Hearing</td><td>Deaf</td></tr>
<tr>
<td>Severity of loss</td>
<td>Youngsters with mild to moderate hearing loss can remain in the general education curriculum with consultative or supportive services from various experts such as SLPs and audiologists.</td>
<td>Students with severe to profound hearing loss require intensive instruction in communication skills and need assistance from an array of related services.</td>
</tr>
<tr>
<td>Potential for using residual hearing</td>
<td>Most of these students profit from hearing aids, thereby allowing them to benefit, with some adaptations, from typical oral methods of instruction.</td>
<td>Most deaf students have little useful residual hearing and require considerable accommodations to benefit from oral instructions.</td>
</tr>
<tr>
<td>Academic achievement</td>
<td>The academic achievement levels of deaf and hard of hearing students tend to be lower than levels of their hearing peers. Students with less hearing loss and no multiple disabilities are usually close to grade level but might need some additional academic instruction.</td>
<td>The academic achievement levels of deaf students are considerably below their hearing peers'. These students need considerable instruction in basic language and communication skills, as well as intensive academic remediation.</td>
</tr>
<tr>
<td>Communicative needs</td>
<td>Many of these students go undetected for a long time. If the loss occurred before or while the youngsters were developing language, it is likely that they will require SLP services as well as academic assistance.</td>
<td>Total communication is the most commonly used approach with deaf youngsters, but the help of educational assistants is necessary, and in many rural regions this expertise is not available.</td>
</tr>
<tr>
<td>Preferred mode of communication</td>
<td>Most of these students should be expected to become proficient using oral language.</td>
<td>Most postlingually deaf students learn (or retain) their use of oral language. Intelligible speech and lipreading are typically unattainable goals for most prelingually deaf children, so for them manual communication is preferred.</td>
</tr>
<tr>
<td>Placement preference</td>
<td>The vast majority of these students attend their neighborhood schools with their hearing peers.</td>
<td>Many deaf students also attend their neighborhood schools. However, a significant number of them prefer center schools where their classmates share their deafness and their mode of communication.</td>
</tr>
</table>

ence, one that might occur only once in their teaching career. For the teacher inexperienced in working with students who use sign language, there is much to learn, plan for, and coordinate. The smooth inclusion of this related service provider as part of the educational team can require considerable communication and teamwork. And for many interpreters, working with students in school settings is also a unique experience (Powers, 1997). This situation necessitates a close working relationship between this related service provider and teachers, where the interpreter needs to learn academic content and the teacher needs to learn how to work with a translator.

The teacher and the interpreter need to coordinate efforts to ensure they understand each other's roles. As responsibilities and duties are defined, it should be clear

Interpreters and classroom teachers work side-by-side in integrated educational settings.

that the teacher has the primary responsibility and the interpreter serves in supporting roles (Salend & Longo, 1994). In other words, the teacher should deliver instruction and remediation (when necessary), and the interpreter should be present to facilitate communication. Because the interpreter may not be an expert in the content of the curriculum, the teacher should give the interpreter copies of lesson plans, lists of key terms, and textbooks to ensure clear and accurate translation of the teacher's lectures and instructions. The teacher and interpreter must also work together on a number of issues, many of which are minor but quite important. For example, the interpreter should sit in a glare-free, well-lit, solid-colored background location that does not block the blackboard or view of the teacher. Some other guidelines for inclusion of interpreters in classroom settings are found in Table 10.4. Possibly the most difficult part of building a team involving the teacher, the school community, the deaf student, and the interpreter is using some good common sense and finding the time for sufficient and ongoing communication.

TRANSITION THROUGH ADULTHOOD

For other information about the outcomes of individuals with disabilities, review the Transition sections in Chapters 3–12.

The purpose of school-to-work transition programs for students who are deaf or hard of hearing is to improve the adult outcomes for these individuals. Of crucial importance are obtaining equitable employment, being able to obtain and hold a job commensurate with the person's abilities, earning a fair wage, and being satisfied with the job. Deaf and hard of hearing people must also be able to participate in their community and in society. Let's consider some issues of transition next.

Educational Options. Like many college students and their families, many deaf people wonder whether college is worth the effort and expense. The answer is a resounding yes. Given that alumni who graduate from Gallaudet tend to be working in the educational field, graduates of Gallaudet University, could in general, be considered relatively affluent by American standards. The 1998 median annual income of the full-time employed alumni who enrolled at Gallaudet as an undergraduate but did not graduate with an undergraduate degree was estimated to be $32,820 per

Table 10.4 Roles and Responsibilities of Educational Interpreters, Teachers, and Deaf Students

The Interpreter	The Teacher	The Deaf Student
Holds long conversations with the student after class	Introduces the interpreter to the class	Makes certain the interpreter uses preferred mode of communication
Asks for clarification when the teacher speaks too fast or was not heard	Talks to the student, not to the interpreter	Notifies the interpreter when there is going to be a change in schedules or when that person will not be needed
Considers teaching hearing students some basic signs	Adjusts pace of speech to allow for the translation	Is clear about whether the interpreter should speak for the student
Only interprets; does not tutor or provide assistance with assignments	Arranges for peers to take notes for their deaf peer	Determines desired role with peers
Maintains confidentiality of personal and private information	Seeks assistance of interpreter when working with others (e.g., SLPs)	Meets with the interpreter on a regular basis to provide feedback, resolve problems, and evaluate progress

year, $39,229 for those whose highest degree from Gallaudet was at the bachelor's level, and $41,000 for those whose highest degree from Gallaudet was at the master's degree level.

Higher education makes a great difference in the lives of people, particularly those who are deaf or hard of hearing. For these students to benefit from higher education, special programs must be available, the students themselves must be ready to participate in these programs, and they must take advantage of these programs. Otherwise, they have a tendency to drop out, and their outcomes become less promising. The federal government supports various types of postsecondary schools with programs for deaf and hard of hearing students. Gallaudet University serves both undergraduate and graduate students and receives federal funding. The National Technical Institute for the Deaf (NTID) at the Rochester Institute of Technology in New York began offering technical and vocational degrees in 1968. Gallaudet and NTID serve a total of about 2,900 students. Four regional, federally funded postsecondary schools—Seattle Community College, California State University–Northridge, St. Paul Technical College, and the University of Tennessee Consortium—serve a total of 534 students.

State and privately funded universities and colleges also offer special programs for deaf and hard of hearing students. *College and Career Programs for Deaf Students* (Rawlings et al., 1999) lists about 150 postsecondary accredited programs designed specifically for deaf students. These programs serve almost 7,000 students with hearing loss, and all have support services, including a coordinator. In 1964 there were only six college programs (excluding those that were federally funded) for these students (Rawlings & King, 1986). Over a three-year period from 1982 to 1985, thirty-seven colleges added programs for students who are deaf (Rawlings et al., 1987). By 1995, 200 college programs were serving over 8,000 students (Cardenas, 1996).

Overcoming Barriers. Although many signs indicate that the situation is improving, some experience significant barriers in their adult lives. As with most other groups of people with disabilities, deaf adults often face discrimination. That's how Stacy

Adam feels about losing her job as a summer lifeguard (Belgum, 1998). Although she is an accredited lifeguard, the YMCA dismissed her as they applied their national rule that lifeguards could not be deaf. She believes that this is unfair, as does retired award-winning lifeguard LeRoy Colombo, who saved more than 907 people from drowning from 1982 to 1991. Stacy thinks that LeRoy's record proves that deaf individuals must cope with unfair bias, and it should be eliminated.

Discrimination and bias can affect individuals' livelihood. Federal laws such as the Americans with Disabilities Act of 1990 attempt to eliminate bias and encourage better access to mainstream society. And there are signs that attitudes are changing. Entertainment that is directed toward Deaf audiences is now gaining wide acceptance. Deaf television programs created by Deaf persons for an audience of Deaf persons, like the show *Deaf Mosaic,* which has been acknowledged with eighteen Emmy awards. This Gallaudet University series was carried by cable networks and presented in ASL with both full voice-over and captions. The Theater of the Deaf also increases in popularity each year with both deaf and hearing audiences.

FAMILIES

For reminders about ASL and the Deaf community, see these sections of this chapter:
• History
• Deaf Culture in the Deaf and Hard of Hearing Children section
• Overcoming Barriers in the Educational Interventions section

Although language, social and emotional development, and technology are important to the overall development of deaf and hard of hearing children, possibly the most important factor in these children's lives is acceptance and inclusion by their families. Some parents and other family members (grandparents, siblings, extended family members) adjust quickly to the demands presented by a child with hearing loss. This is particularly true for children whose parents are deaf. To Deaf parents, the birth of a Deaf child is typically cause for great celebration and also a great relief (Blade, 1994). These parents know ASL, use it as their native language, and will teach it to their infant through the normal developmental process. However, the birth of a deaf child to hearing parents can be frightening, and even devastating to some (Calderon & Greenberg, 1999). Regardless, the event certainly creates many changes for the family. One thing is very clear about families of deaf and hard of hearing children: They are very different from each other, making it almost impossible to develop uniform guidelines about these families or the services they require (Calderon et al., 1998). One distressing fact, however, is that too many of these children and their families receive early intervention services late. The average age of entry into early intervention programs is twenty-one months. This situation leaves deaf and hard of hearing children with little or no means of auditory input for almost two years, two critical years for children's language development. It also means that families have lost almost two years in their learning of manual communication skills.

Although one would imagine that hearing families of deaf and hard of hearing children experience substantial stress because of their child's hearing loss, this stress is not overwhelming (Mapp & Hudson, 1997). Stress typically surrounds the ability to communicate with their children, but these families develop coping strategies fairly quickly. The strategies that they use, however, differ by cultural and ethnic group. In other words, White, African American, and Hispanic families use different coping and problem solving strategies. Regardless, what is of most importance to all families is the development of effective communication modes with their youngsters.

TECHNOLOGY

To compare different types of technology supports across students with special needs, read the technology sections in Chapters 3–12.

A variety of electronic devices have been available to deaf people for some time. **Assistive devices** can improve communication and enhance awareness of environmental sounds. The world of deaf people can be different in so many ways from the world of hearing people. The day might start with a vibrating alarm clock that shakes the bed and the morning news on TV with captions running along the bottom of the screen. Lights flashing wildly in the kitchen signal burnt toast again. Different flashing light patterns indicate the doorbell is ringing. Technology has also changed the way many hard of hearing people participate in daily life. The wide range of assistive listening devices presently available, and those being developed, has reduced the impact of hearing loss for many people.

Unfortunately, finances limit access to these helpful devices for most. Although the cost of many individual technological devices has decreased over the years, the overall cost to a person with hearing loss increases as more equipment is developed. To get a general idea of the typical costs of some assistive devices, see Table 10.5.

Table 10.5 Sample Costs of Assistive Devices Designed for Deaf and Hard of Hearing Individuals

Assistive Device	Cost ($)
Telephone Devices	
TTY	350
TTY cellular phone package	650
Amplified cordless phone with caller ID	169
Portable phone amplifier	30
Loud phone ringer	50
Visual (lamp) phone ringer	50
Alerting Devices	
Alarm clock with bed shaker	70
Vibrating alarm wristwatch	35
Visual fire alarm	90
Doorbell transmitter	70
Visual doorbell	125
Alertmaster signal system	80
Baby cry signaler	40
Smoke detector	189
Listening Systems	
Wireless FM systems	650
Analog hearing aids	500
Digital hearing aids	5,000–7,000
Cochlear implants	25,000
Entertainment and Information	
TV/VCR with superior captioning	429

assistive devices. Any equipment or technology that facilitates people's work, communication, mobility, or any aspect of daily life.

The overall cost of being completely technologically assisted is difficult for most deaf adults. These individuals tend to be underemployed because of their disability. For those who can afford them, assistive devices are most helpful. Let's look at four categories of equipment that can help hard of hearing and deaf people: assistive listening devices, telecommunication devices, computerized speech-to-text translations, and alerting devices.

ASSISTIVE LISTENING DEVICES

Hearing aids and other equipment that help people make better use of their residual hearing are called **assistive listening devices (ALDs).** For those with hearing loss, the **hearing aid** is the most commonly used electronic device; it amplifies sound so that the person can hear more easily. For some individuals, hearing aids allow them to hear well within the normal range. They have eliminated the need for special education for many children who are hard of hearing; with their hearing aids they can profit from general education classes and participate fully in mainstream society. However, it is important to recognize that hearing aids do not solve the problems associated with hearing loss for many hard of hearing people. Current hearing aid technology does not sufficiently correct their disability, but more work being conducted gives great hope for the future.

Hearing aids were designed to solve the problem of reduced hearing acuity by amplifying sounds. They are typically used by people with sensorineural hearing loss, because conductive losses can usually be corrected with medicine or surgery. Hearing aids are most effective in quiet places where speech is the dominant sound in the environment. Even in classroom settings, however, background noise competes with sounds a student might want to focus on. In other settings (lecture halls, auditoriums, recreational centers), background noise can mask all other sounds. Typical hearing aids amplify all sounds, so everything becomes louder, including background noise. For individuals with sensorineural hearing losses, sounds perceived well without a hearing aid are amplified at the same level as those that are heard only faintly. Thus most current versions of hearing aids are often of little help to many people with hearing loss and can even be distracting. Most conventional hearing aids use analog components, and three types of these aids are most common: **behind the ear (BTE), in the ear (ITE),** and **in the canal (ITC).** The new generation of hearing aids uses digital components, and though very expensive at the present time (up to $7,000), they hold great promise.

Dorothy Brett is shown here with her trumpet, "Toby," which is an early version of a hearing aid.

---

assistive listening devices (ALDs). Equipment such as hearing aids that helps deaf and hard of hearing individuals use their residual hearing.

hearing aid. A device that intensifies sound to help hard of hearing people process information presented orally.

behind the ear (BTE). A hearing aid that cups behind the ear with a cord that runs into the person's ear canal.

in the ear (ITE). A hearing aid that fits inside the person's outer ear.

in the canal (ITC). A hearing aid that is worn inside the person's ear canal.

digital hearing aids. A new generation of hearing aids using digitized technology that allows for individualized amplification to match a person's hearing loss profile, and also the ability to mask out background noise.

Digital hearing aids are programmed to each individual's hearing profile and amplify sounds only to the level necessary to compensate for the loss. These assistive devices also are able to mask out background noise, and reports from users indicate extreme satisfaction. Most likely, all hearing aids manufactured in the next five years will be of the digital variety, and with high demand should come price reductions and even more improvements (Harris, 1998).

Because a hearing aid is a sensitive electronic device, it needs special care. Teachers can help students who use hearing aids by helping them master the care and handling of these devices:

- Avoid dust, dirt, and humidity
- Do not drop the hearing aid
- Keep the ear mold clean
- Avoid hair spray
- Do not leave the hearing aid in a hot place
- Be sure the child and the aid are checked frequently by an audiologist

The cost of digital hearing aids places them out of the reach for many students with hearing loss. For the present, one solution to the problems of environmental noise and acoustic feedback faced by hearing aid wearers is the **telecoil** (also called an induction coil). Telephone use is difficult for many people who use hearing aids because of background noise, feedback noise from the hearing aid, and sound distortions, but telecoils are designed to solve these problems (Kaplan, 1999). Telecoils allow sounds to be brought directly into hearing aids from telephones and **FM** (frequency-modulated) **transmission devices.** One version of an FM transmission device, auditory trainers, has been used by teachers and students in classrooms for many years. In this system, the teacher speaks into a microphone, and the sound is received directly by each student's receiver or hearing aid. Background noise is reduced, and teachers may move freely around the classroom without worrying about having their faces in full view of all their students.

Another FM transmission device, the **audio loop,** is an ALD that directs sound from its source directly to the listener's ear through a specially equipped hearing aid or earphone. Sound may travel through a wire connection or through radio waves. Audio loops are inexpensive and easy to install in rooms that seat up to 100 persons. You have probably seen signs in public buildings directing people to areas where this system is installed. Since passage of the Americans with Disabilities Act, audio loops are now found in most concert halls, theaters, airports, and churches across the nation, giving people with hearing losses greater access to events.

TELECOMMUNICATION DEVICES

Telecommunication equipment includes assistive devices that take advantage of sight and hearing to improve communication and also cinema and television listening. A few of the options available are discussed here.

---

telecoil. Also called induction coils, an added option on many hearing aids that allows access to telephones, audio loops, and other assistive listening devices.

FM transmission device. Equipment used in many classes for students with severe hearing loss that allows direct oral transmissions from the teacher to each individual student.

audio loop. A device that directs sound from the source directly to the listener's ear through a specially designed hearing aid.

SO, BUZZ, YOU GOT A NEW HEARING AID?..

WHAT KIND IS IT?

TEN AFTER THREE.

©1993 Tribune Media Services, Inc. / Pluggers, Inc. All rights reserved.

Reprinted with permission from Tribune Media Services.

To have access to information, deaf children who use ASL need interpreters for every instructional activity, whether in a classroom or on a field trip.

Captions, which have been available for many years, are printed words that appear at the bottom of a TV screen, like subtitles that translate foreign films. There are two kinds of captions: open and closed. **Open captions** can be seen by all viewers and were used with certain television programs in the 1970s. *The French Chef* with Julia Child was the first captioned television show, appearing on public television in 1972. Because open captions were unpopular with the general public, **closed captions** (which need an assistive device to be seen) became available in the 1980s. This unpopularity is also why captions have been a long time coming to local theaters and first-run movies.

Captioning is an important tool for deaf people because it allows them to have equal access to public information and entertainment. The Television Decoder Circuitry Act, introduced in 1990 and signed into law in July 1993, requires all television sets sold in the United States to be equipped with an internal, microsized **decoder** that allows captions to be placed anywhere on the screen (to avoid interfering with on-screen titles or other important information in the program) and to appear in different colors. Because these devices are mass produced, they add only a few dollars to the cost of each TV set. Before 1993, use of closed-caption technology required the purchase of a separate decoder; because of the cost ($200), only 10% of people with hearing loss had access to closed captions (Sulzberger, 1990).

Captioning has been much slower coming to the movie theaters, making deaf people wait to see films until they are available in captioned video. Of course, FM sound systems have become increasing available since the passage of the ADA law, but remember that they benefit only those individuals who profit from amplification. Experiments with different captioning systems for movie theaters have been conducted for years to develop more ways for deaf people who desire captions to see them while the rest of the audience is not distracted by them. Rear Window Captioning (RWC) is one example. RWC projects captions from a message board on the theater's rear wall onto a clear plastic screen that attaches to the moviegoer's seat; the individual looks at a transparent Plexiglas panel to see the captions and forward to see the movie (Stanton, 1999). Once a captioning system is developed that

captions. Subtitles that print the words spoken in film or video; can be either *closed* or *open*.
open captions. Captions that appear on the television screen for all viewers to see.
closed captions. Captions that can be seen on the television screen only with the use of a decoder.
decoder. A device that allows closed captions to appear on a television screen.

MAKING CONNECTIONS

To remind yourself about the ADA law, see the Need for National Intervention section in Chapter 1.

satisfies the movie industry, the hearing public, and the deaf and hard of hearing people who use captions, deaf people will be allowed one more way to participate in American life alongside hearing people.

Another important piece of equipment, the **text telephone (TTY)**, formerly referred to as the telecommunication device for the deaf (TDD), enables those who are deaf to make and receive telephone calls. The first device was created by Robert Weitbrecht, a deaf physicist, and used a teletypewriter along with a radio or telephone. TTY prints out the voice message for the person with a hearing loss and can be used to send messages. TTYs are now lightweight (about one pound). They come in portable, battery-operated, and cellular versions, and are commonly available in public buildings (see Table 10.5 again to find some sample prices for TTYs). The next generation of TTYs is already available, though further developments are on the horizon. The Video TTY Videophone allows the "listener" to see sign language or even read lips. The TTY itself is priced under $400, and can use a standard television set and a camcorder as input and output devices (Medugno, 1998).

Most TTYs have one major drawback: A unit is required at both the sending and the receiving end. There are two solutions to this problem. First, the Federal Communications Commission now requires all states to have a **telecommunications relay service (TRS)**, which allows a person using a TTY to communicate with someone using a standard telephone. By using an 800 phone number, the relay service allows deaf individuals to use the phone for everything from calling a

text telephone (TTY). A piece of equipment, formerly called the telecommunication device for the deaf (TDD), that allows people to make and receive telephone calls by typing information over the telephone lines.

telecommunications relay service (TRS). A telephone system required by federal law that allows an operator at a relay center to convert a print-telephone message to a voice telephone message.

Until recently, if you had a hearing disability, you couldn't call anyone who wasn't equipped with a special phone. But now, thanks to the Americans with Disabilities Act, phone companies furnish relay services to anyone who needs them. It's the kind of thing you might take for granted, but to someone who's never been able to, ordering a pizza can be a pretty historic act. *Support Easter Seals.*

Easter Seals

It took an act of Congress to order this pizza.

1 LARGE PEPPERONI

doctor to ordering a pizza. When the person who is deaf uses a TTY in a relay system, an operator at a relay center places the call on a voice line and reads the typed message to the non-TTY user. Although a full conversation can be carried on by using a relay system, it is not very private and thus makes phone calls strained and impersonal. However, for making a doctor's appointment, arranging for a car to be fixed, or checking on a homework assignment, the relay system is invaluable.

Most deaf and hard of hearing people prefer to use their voice on a phone call, and a new device is now available. The **voice carry over (VCO)** is a TTY that includes the option to use both voice and text. For those who want to use their voices but need to receive telephone communication through print, these phones allow for both voice and text transmissions. VCOs have many advantages, particularly for hearing people with deaf family members or friends, for businesses that want both options but do not want to invest in two different phones, and for public places so everyone has access to the telephone system. And now even a TTY/Voice answering machine that takes messages in either format is available.

COMPUTERIZED SPEECH-TO-TEXT TRANSLATIONS

Understanding college lectures is difficult for many deaf students. Those who use sign language can use interpreters during class lectures, but simultaneously taking notes and watching an interpreter is almost impossible. Deaf people in the workplace face similar problems. Several systems have been developed to help deaf people participate in meetings and be free from notetaking, and efforts to create efficient and inexpensive solutions are continuing. One system, called C-print, uses an inexpensive laptop computer, two commercially available software packages, a standard word processing program, and a computer shorthand system to provide **real-time captioning (RTC)** for persons who are deaf. C-print uses a trained operator who listens to the lecture and types special codes that represent words into the computer; the transcription is instantly shown on a special screen that sits on top of an overhead projector. RTC has proven to be beneficial to all students, whether they are deaf or hearing (Steinfeld, 1998). Once the lecture is completed, the student can get a printout. Another system, Computer Assisted Remote Transcription (CART), uses a stenographer who transcribes meetings from a remote location (Preminger & Levitt, 1997), while American Real-Time Captioning Services, which uses court reporters, promises no more than a three- to five-second delay between oral communications and printed text. Many students who attend traditional colleges and universities and who would otherwise have to rely on an interpreter report that RTC does not make them feel different, and even improves social possibilities (Kramlinger, 1996).

ALERTING DEVICES

Alerting devices make people who are deaf aware of an event or important sound in their environment by using the senses of sight or touch. A flashing light, loud gong, or vibration can signal a fire alarm, doorbell, alarm clock, or telephone. Some attach to a lamp that flashes on and off for a signal. Others attach to vibrators (in the bed for an alarm clock, or on a person's belt as a personal signaler). Some alerting devices include sound-sensitive monitors that let the deaf person know about a baby who is crying or an out-of-the-ordinary sound. Signal dogs (or service dogs) also can help alert deaf people to important sounds in their environments (Delta

voice carry over (VCO). A TTY that allows both voice and text use.

real-time captioning (RTC). Practically instantaneous translations of speech into print.

alerting devices. Devices that use sight, sound, or vibration to make individuals aware of an occurrence or an important sound.

For another example of service dogs, see the Educational Interventions section of Chapter 9.

For a fuller discussion of cochlear implants, see the Prevention section in this chapter.

Society, 1999; Ogden, 1992). These dogs are trained to act as "ears." They can distinguish between noises and alerts, and can even recognize specific sounds.

CONCEPTS AND CONTROVERSY: COCHLEAR IMPLANTS: TO DO OR NOT TO DO?

Tension between hearing people and the deaf existed long before Thomas Gallaudet and Alexander Graham Bell debated before Congress on topics such as whether two deaf people should be allowed to marry or whether sign language was an acceptable form of communication. Across time, hearing people viewed deaf people as less than human because they either did not use oral language or did not use it well. With the emergence of Deaf culture and Deaf pride, the acceptance of these individuals has improved. However, the Deaf are engaged in a new and bitter debate, one they believe assaults their worth and integrity.

The debate that continues to rage concerns whether young deaf children should receive a cochlear implant, technology that allows deaf individuals to perceive sound. The position of many hearing parents of deaf children is that the implant may let their child hear sounds in the environment, develop speech, and participate in mainstream society (Venable, 1999). Many parents also fear that if their deaf children do not develop speech, they will lose them to the Deaf community. Many in the Deaf community are opposed to implants. They say it is brutal to open up a child's head, wind wires through the inner ear, and force a child through years of speech therapy without knowing what the outcome will be and possibly seeing little improvement in speech intelligibility. They feel that the child is robbed of his or her right to be a member of the Deaf community, which has a rich language and culture of its own. They also point out that the outcomes for children born deaf are not good, with most not being able to hear well enough to develop intelligible speech or understand oral language (Niparko, 1998; Tye-Murray et al., 1995).

Although the medical profession is seeking to cure deafness, some experts on deafness view implants as a misguided effort (Lane, 1995). The debate extends beyond emotional tension between hearing parents and the Deaf community. Some professionals believe that typical deaf children will not master oral English language with the aid of implants; perhaps they will acquire a few words, but not develop intelligible speech. Others— even some who are deaf themselves—hold different beliefs. They believe that spoken English skills can be acquired by children who are deaf and that oral communication is the key to good jobs and integration into mainstream society. Although current research does not indicate overwhelming results for children born deaf, implants do help some individuals, particularly those deafened as adults, hear better (Benton, 1997; Niparko, 1998). Interestingly, the majority of children with implants use sign and speech as their method of communication (Gallaudet Research Institute, 1998).

Issues beyond surgery and language acquisition are involved in this debate. Many in the Deaf community view the cochlear implant movement as an attack against their culture and worth. Members of the Deaf community believe that implants are a continuation of their history of repression, through which they and their culture are denied and minimized (Laborit, 1998). Many Deaf people believe they do not have a sickness or disability to be pitied and cured, perceptions they feel those who hear have of them. To members of the Deaf community, then, implants reinforce the view that deafness is a pathology, something to be corrected. Others do not understand why parents would put children through a painful operation that they view as useless and cruel. On the other hand, many hearing people believe that those who are Deaf reject the use of implants because they feel threatened by them and fear that their community would not exist if deafness were eliminated.

Is this debate really about choice? Should cochlear implant surgery be withheld from children until the results of experimental studies are better understood? Is this movement really an attack on the Deaf community? Finally, how important is oral language? Should it be a goal for every deaf child? Until these questions are answered, the cochlear implant debate will continue.

 **n Conclusion**

Look again at the Advance Organizers at the beginning of the chapter; to help you study the chapter's content, the answers to the Focus and Challenge questions are found here. Test yourself to see if you have mastered the major points of this chapter.

Summary

Most of us communicate with others through a process of telling and listening. This process is one important way that we learn about the world we live in, subjects at school, and others' perspectives on issues and concerns. The deaf have a more restricted ability to communicate, a difference that should determine the way these students are taught, the content of the curricula, and the related services they require for an appropriate education.

Focus Questions

Self-Test Questions

- *What variables are used to create different subgroups of students who are deaf or hard of hearing?*

  The primary way divides this special education category into three subgroups: amount of loss, age of onset, and type of loss. When classified by the amount of hearing loss, these two groups are used: the deaf and the hard of hearing. The deaf are further divided into two groups relating to age of onset. Those who are prelingually deaf typically lost their hearing at, during, before, or shortly after birth; and those who lost their hearing after they had acquired some language (after the age of 2) are called postlingually deaf. A third way to organize hearing losses is by two general types: conductive and sensorineural. Conductive losses result in a flat profile on an audiogram, respond best to the use of hearing aids, and are caused by damage to the middle or outer ear. Conductive losses are also easier to correct using current medical technology. Sensorineural hearing losses are caused by damage to the inner ear or the auditory nerve and result in an uneven profile on an audiogram.

- *What is meant by the concept of Deaf culture?*

  To many, particularly the Deaf who use American Language (ASL) and who live in the Deaf community, deafness is not a disability. Rather, the Deaf are a historically misunderstood minority group. Deafness has created a language difference, not a disability. The Deaf community and many others support the belief that ASL is a bona fide language with unique elements of all languages. These individuals are proud of their heritage, history, traditions, and art. They have become successful advocates for themselves and their community's way of life. What they desire is respect, independence, and determination, just like most Americans.

- *What are the major causes of hearing loss?*

The five major causes of hearing loss are maternal rubella, meningitis, otitis media, heredity, and noise. Specific causes continue to be identified, particularly those that are due to genetics. Today, many cases of deafness and hard of hearing in children can be prevented or the outcomes of the hearing loss improved. One major cause of deaf and hard of hearing children's poor language and academic skills is late identification and delayed intervention services. The importance of identifying all children with hearing loss during infancy is now acknowledged, and legislation requiring universal hearing screenings conducted right after birth is being passed across the nation.

- *What educational support services do many of these students require?*

With appropriate support systems, many deaf and hard of hearing students can benefit from traditional educational programs at their local neighborhood schools in general education classes where the standard curriculum is presented. This often requires additional services from a variety of specialists: speech/language pathologists, audiologists, educational interpreters, and special education teachers. An important member of the collaborative team created for many of these children is an educational interpreter. Many of these children require some accommodations (seating assignments, handouts, peer assistance) to succeed in general education classes. Also, their general education teachers might need some extra guidance or training from a consulting teacher or an SLP. An expert knowledgeable about hearing can be an important resource to both the teacher and the student.

- *How do the major instructional methods for deaf children differ, and how should an individual child's communication style affect the choice of instructional method?*

Most deaf children do not develop oral language without effort. Debates about the best mode of communication to use when educating deaf students continue. Although some can master oral communication, most cannot. Interest is renewed in the oral-only approach, particularly for those children who are receiving cochlear implants, because it stresses developing the students' facility with oral language. Probably as a response to the Deaf community's advocacy of ASL, the bilingual-bicultural approach is gaining in popularity. This method teaches ASL as the child's native language and written English as a second language. However, the majority of deaf children's parents are able to hear and do not know ASL. For these children, the natural mastery of a communication system is not the norm. For many, a total communication environment—where manual communication (sign language) supports speech—results in increased learning because all channels available for sending and receiving information are used. For family members who are not deaf themselves, implementing this approach requires learning a new communication system, and a very small number have found cued speech to be easier to master. The family and preschool program staff work as a team to provide an educational program that lasts all day, every day, and ensures that some form of language is fully developed.

Challenge Question

● *What types of technology are available to assist the deaf, and what advances might the future hold?*

Technology has had a substantial impact on the lives of the deaf and hard of hearing. First, assistive listening devices such as hearing aids allow many hard of hearing persons to function independently in environments where oral communication is dominant. Hearing aids are continually being refined to accommodate individuals' specific hearing abilities. Second, telecommunication devices help individuals use both their sight and their hearing to improve communication and television listening. The availability of captioned television has greatly broadened the world of those who are deaf. New breakthroughs in the area of computerized speech-to-text translations will dramatically increase the access of deaf people to mainstream society. These new systems allow for real-time translations of daily situations (college lectures, courtroom proceedings, business meetings). Alerting devices help these people become aware of sounds and events in their environments by means other than hearing. Certainly, the digital hearing aids that mask out background noise and adjust to an individual's unique hearing pattern will become less expensive and even more effective in the coming years. It is for the most clever among us to brainstorm future applications of technology that will improve and facilitate the lives of deaf and hard of hearing individuals.

MAKING CONNECTIONS

Resources to extend your learning about people with disabilities are found at the end of every chapter, and a fuller listing is available in the Students' Resource Manual that accompanies this text.

Supplementary Resources

Scholarly Reading

Easterbrooks, S. (1999). Improving practices for students with hearing impairments. *Exceptional Children, 65,* 537–554.

Lane, H. (1995). Construction of deafness. *Disability & Society, 10,* 171–187.

Moores, D. F. (1996). *Educating the deaf: Psychology, principles, and practices* (4th ed.). Boston: Houghton Mifflin.

Tharpe, A. M. (1999). Disorders of hearing in children. In E. Plante & P. M. Beeson (Eds.), *Communication and communication disorders: A clinical introduction.* (pp. 85–116). Boston: Allyn and Bacon.

Popular Books

Davis, L. J. (Ed.). (1999). *Shall I say a kiss: The courtship letters of a Deaf couple, 1936–1938.* Washington, DC: Gallaudet University Press.

Gannon, J. R. (1989). *The week the world heard Gallaudet.* Washington, DC: Gallaudet University Press.

Hairston, E., & Smith, L. (1983). *Black and deaf in America: Are we that different?* Silver Spring, MD: T. J. Publishers.

Laborit, E. (1998). *The cry of the gull.* Washington, DC: Gallaudet University Press.

Ogden, P. (1992). *Chelsea: The story of a signal dog.* Boston: Little, Brown and Company.

Walker, L. A. (1986). *A loss for words: The story of deafness in a family.* NY: Harper & Row.

Videos and DVDs

Johnny Belinda. (1948). Warner Brothers.
The heart is a lonely hunter. (1968). Warner Brothers/7 Arts.
The silent world of Jim. (1974). Film Communicators.
Tin man. (1983). Montage Films.
Children of a lesser god. (1986). Paramount Pictures.
See no evil, hear no evil. (1989). Tri-Star.
Mr. Holland's opus. (1996). Hollywood Home Video.

Professional, Parent, and Consumer Organizations and Agencies

Alexander Graham Bell Association for the Deaf, Inc.
3417 Volta Place NW
Washington, DC 20007
Phone: (202) 337-5220
E-mail: agbell2@aol.com
Web site: http://www.agbell.org

American Speech-Language-Hearing Association (ASHA)
10801 Rockville Pike
Rockville, MD 20852
Voice/TTY: (301) 897-5700
Phone: (800) 638-8255
E-mail: irc@asha.org
Web site: http://www.asha.org

Deafpride, Inc.
1350 Potomac Avenue SE
Washington, DC 20003
TTY: (202) 675-6700

Gallaudet University
800 Florida Avenue NE
Washington, DC 20002-3695
Voice: (202) 651-5000
TDD: (202) 651-5052
Web site: http://www.gallaudet.edu

John Tracy Clinic
806 W. Adams Boulevard
Los Angeles, CA 90007
Voice: (213) 748-5481
TTY: (213) 747-2924
Voice/TTY: (800) 522-4582

Self-help for Hard of Hearing People (SHHH), Inc.
7800 Wisconsin Avenue
Bethesda, MD 20814
Voice: (301) 657-2248
TTY: (301) 657-2249
E-mail: shhh.nancy@genie.com

National Institute on Deafness and Other Communication Disorders (NIDCD) Information Clearinghouse
National Institutes of Health
1 Communication Avenue
Bethesda, MD 20892-3456
Voice: (800) 241-1044
TTY: (800) 241-1055
E-mail: nidc@aerie.com
Web site: http://www.nih.gov/nidcd

The National Theater of the Deaf
5 W. Main Street
P.O. Box 659
Chester, CT 06412
Voice: (860) 526-4971
TTY: (860) 526-4974
E-mail: bookntd@aol.com
Web site: http://www.ntd.org

MAKING CONNECTIONS

For Web links to support your study of disabilities, look at the Resources sections at the end of every chapter in this text; a fuller listing is found in the Students' Resource Manual that accompanies this text.

François **Auguste René Rodin** was born and raised on the Left Bank of Paris. His father was a clerk in the police department. Although the family was not rich, the environment in which Rodin grew up in was. His neighborhood was a community for artists, poets, writers, and creative people. He is said to have once remarked that his native Paris gave him "*millions de pensées*" (millions of thoughts) (Hale, 1969, p. 37). Rodin was probably drawn to art because of his poor success at school. His first school experiences were not positive. It is said that after three years he still could not spell, a problem that followed him the rest of his life. At age 10 he was sent off to a country school, but again was unsuccessful and dropped out of school by the age of 13. It is thought that his frustration and failure at school was because of a severe vision problem, for it is reported that he was so nearsighted that he could not see the blackboard (Hale, 1969). It is probably for these reasons that he chose sculpture as his medium of expression, one that is more tactile than visual. He is considered one of the best sculptors of all time.

The Burghers of Calais, begun in 1884 and completed in 1886, shows the emotions these six city leaders must have felt when they surrendered their lives and city to the conquering English. Rodin broke with tradition, by not depicting these Frenchmen as marching nobly to their deaths, but rather with the weight of defeat showing in their bodies and the fear of death on their faces. These sculptured figures demonstrate Rodin's understanding of the human condition.

Auguste Rodin, *A Burgher of Calais.* Gift of Mrs. John W. Simpson. Photograph © 1999 Board of Trustees, National Gallery of Art, Washington.

C H A P T E R **11**

Two Families of Preschoolers with Visual Impairments Talk About Their Children

Amanda and Vincent attend the New Mexico School for the Visually Handicapped Preschool, which is located in Albuquerque. Amanda is a Native American, and she and her family live at Zia Pueblo. They commute eighty miles round trip so that Amanda can attend this special preschool. Vincent is Hispanic. He and his mom live in town. Both children have a severe visual disability and are classified as legally blind. These parents talk about some experiences and hopes for their children.

Tell me a little bit about yourself.

AMANDA'S DAD: My wife is half Blackfoot from Montana, and she is a quarter Spanish from her mother's side and a quarter Zia. I am seven-eighths Zia blood.

VINCENT'S MOM: I am a single mom. Vincent and I live with my parents here in Albuquerque.

How did you first discover that your child had a visual disability? How did you feel about it?

AMANDA'S DAD: There have been no records of albinos* among our people. It was kind of a different feeling, since she was the first albino in the Zia Pueblo as a whole.

VINCENT'S MOM: I first learned about Vincent's visual impairment from his ophthalmologist. I didn't think he would be able to do the things normal kids do. I couldn't see how he could have a normal life.

*Albinism is a genetic condition that causes abnormal coloration of a person's skin, hair, and eyes because of lack of pigment. These individuals' vision is severely affected because of the eyes' inability to adjust to differences in light and acuity problems associated with the condition.

Low Vision and Blindness

Please share an incident with us about your child at the preschool.

AMANDA'S MOM: When Amanda first went to school, her teachers were calling her Amanda and she wasn't answering to her name. At first, they thought she had a hearing problem. So we had tests taken and that wasn't the problem. I finally stopped and asked, "What are you calling her?" They said that they were calling her Amanda. "I should have told you, her Indian name is Hèshètè and that's the only thing that she understands."

AMANDA'S DAD: So we sat down and we taught them a little bit about our basic language. They took the time when they did not understand what Amanda was saying or doing to ask us. It was just that she was talking in Indian.

VINCENT'S MOM: When Vincent first started going to school, he wasn't even rolling [over] yet. He was about four months old. He wasn't learning how because he couldn't see how to do it. The preschool teachers taught me how to roll him over. We all work with Vincent on a lot of different things. We worked a lot with textures and touching things, and sounds. He is learning a lot.

What are some of the most important things your child has learned at the preschool?

VINCENT'S MOM: When he first started out he didn't like to be around kids his own age. They were too fast for him. Now, he's gotten to where he is one of the kids, and he hangs around with them. The preschool experience has really helped his self-confidence, because he knows he can keep up.

AMANDA'S DAD: We feel Amanda learned to feel good about herself. She is now very competent and portrays this to her younger sister, who is also albino.

What is next for your child after preschool?

VINCENT'S MOM: Vincent will go to a special class for kids with visual impairments in the public school next year. He will spend time in a regular classroom, as well.

AMANDA'S MOM: We want Amanda to go to school at the Pueblo with all of her friends who live nearby.

What are your thoughts about your child's future?

VINCENT'S MOM: Now I think Vincent will be able to do everything but drive.

AMANDA'S MOM: Amanda will be able to attend our Pueblo schools with help from the New Mexico School for the Visually Handicapped Outreach Services.

1. How have these parents' feelings changed about their child? Why do you think this is the case?

2. What do you think are the benefits to a preschooler with severe visual disabilities of a segregated educational setting? What are its disadvantages?

Advance Organizers

CONNECTIONS
MAKING

Use the learning strategy—Advance Organizers—to help focus your study of this chapter's content, and reinforce your learning by reviewing answers to the Focus and Challenge questions at the end of the chapter.

Overview Vision is a distance sense that provides us with information from outside our bodies. When vision is limited, it affects the individual in significant ways: limiting mobility, access to printed information, and independent living. People with visual disabilities also face many stereotypes, social stigma, and barriers to full participation in mainstream society. Some believe that blindness is met with more negative attitudes than is any other physical disability. Visual disabilities (low vision and blindness) in children is a low incidence disability, affecting about 0.5% of all schoolchildren.

Focus Questions

Self-Test Questions

- How is the category of visual disabilities divided into two subgroups?
- What are the major causes of visual disabilities, and what preventive measures protect children from this disability?
- What are some ways the learning environment can be modified to accommodate students with visual disabilities?
- Why must orientation and mobility be long-term curriculum targets for many low vision and most blind students, and what specific skills must be included?
- What technological advances can assist people with visual disabilities at school, in the workplace, and in independent living?

Challenge Question

- Why has braille literacy become such an emotionally charged debate, and how do you think it should be resolved?

For more information about bias and stereotypes people with disabilities face, see these sections:
- Essence of Disabilities (Chapter 1)
- Significance (Defined) sections in Chapters 3–12
- Transitions (Educational Interventions) sections in Chapters 3–12

distance senses.
Senses—hearing and vision—that provide us with information external to our bodies, developed to help alert us to danger.

Although we act on information gained through our sight, we seldom give much thought to the process of seeing. Sometimes, we stop to reflect on the beauty of a particular sunset, the stars at night, a flower in bloom, or the landscape after a snowstorm. We use our sense of sight all of our waking hours, yet we do not think about vision and how it functions. Most of us use vision in our work. For example, people use sight when they use the Internet, write memos, look up telephone numbers, or direct people to various offices. At the zoo, animal caretakers use their vision to be certain that the animals are not acting differently by changing their typical patterns of behavior and are not injured. We use our vision for recreation when we watch a movie, view television, or read a book. Some of us actually prefer learning by reading or looking at information, rather than listening to a lecture or instructions. These people are known as visual learners. We also use our vision for self-defense; for example, we look in all directions before crossing a street by foot or an intersection when driving a car. Unlike touch and taste, vision and hearing are **distance senses**, senses that provide us with information outside our bodies. These senses developed to alert us to the presence of helpful as well as dangerous elements in the environment.

Clearly, those of us with unimpaired vision profit from this sense. We learn by observing events, we use our vision to move freely in our environment, and we are alert to danger by using our sight. People with visual disabilities have limited use of their sight, but with systematic instruction and advances in technology, most can lead fully integrated and independent lives.

This chapter will help you understand visual disabilities and the people they affect. For example, you will learn that the great majority of people who have a visual impairment are able to use their sight to function in society. However, their disability affects the ease with which they can cope with daily life. You will also learn about one of the biggest challenges for those who are blind—learning to be independently mobile. You will become aware of the obstacles these people often confront and come to understand that people with visual disabilities can assume places alongside others who do not share their disability. Finally, you will learn about the stereotypes and barriers that are uniquely centered on this group of people.

Opportunities for the New Millennium

When the Deaf community became united through its culture and acknowledged as an American minority group because of its political action, an example was set for people with visual disabilities. Although not until the late 1990s, they sought the assistance of the federal government to ensure that braille literacy was renewed as an educational option for students with visual disabilities. They were also not silent about the bias and discrimination they experience in society and in the workplace, for despite their skills and abilities they face chronic unemployment, even below levels experienced by other groups of people with disabilities.

Legacies from the Twentieth Century As more and more blind and low vision children were educated at neighborhood schools and in general education settings, fewer of them learned to use braille as their method of reading. As a group, their literacy rates dropped to alarming levels. At the very end of the twentieth century, policymakers learned that many school districts were not providing the option of learning braille as a reading method, supposedly because very few students need this skill and because they attend many different neighborhood schools. So Congress included learning braille as a necessary option in IDEA '97. However, policymakers remain concerned because they know that federal mandates can be difficult to implement, a fact made clear by the problems blind workers have had in finding appropriate jobs despite the Americans with Disabilities Act (ADA).

Thinking About Dilemmas to Solve People with visual disabilities face very unique challenges at school, at home, and across their lives. As you read this chapter, consider:

- How school districts will meet IDEA '97 mandate to offer braille instruction to those who need it when there are insufficient numbers of teachers available who know how to teach this skill to students
- How the general literacy levels of blind and low vision students who read print can be increased
- Ways to eliminate bias and discrimination experienced by people with visual disabilities
- How instruction in life skills can be included when students are fully participating in the general education curriculum
- Methods of improving the employment rates for this group of people

cornea. The transparent, curved part of the front of the eye.
iris. The colored part of the eye.
pupil. Hole in the center of the iris that expands and contracts, admitting light to the eye.
lens. Located behind the iris, brings objects seen into focus.
accommodation. The focusing process of the lens of the eye.
retina. Inside lining of the eye.

VISUAL DISABILITIES DEFINED

optic nerve. The nerve that carries messages from the eye to the visual center of the brain.

visual efficiency. How well a person can use sight.

visual acuity. How well a person can see at various distances.

peripheral vision. The outer area of a person's visual field.

tunnel vision. Severe limitation in peripheral vision.

central vision. The main field of vision in the eye, usually greater than 20 degrees.

To better understand visual disabilities, we must understand how vision normally occurs. For people to see, four elements must be present and operating. The first is light. The second is something that reflects light. The third is the eye processing the reflected image into electrical impulses. The fourth is the brain receiving and giving meaning to these impulses. Use the picture of the eye in Figure 11.1 to trace how the normal visual process works.

Light rays enter the front of the eye through the **cornea.** The cornea is transparent and curved. The **iris,** the colored part of the eye, expands and contracts in response to the intensity of light it receives. In the center of the iris is an opening, the **pupil.** Light rays pass through the pupil to the **lens,** which is behind the iris. The lens brings an object seen into focus by changing its thickness. The process of adjustment by the lens to focus things that are close and those that are far away is called **accommodation.** The lens focuses light rays onto the **retina,** the inside lining at the back of the eye. It is made up of photosensitive cells that react to light rays and send messages along the **optic nerve** to the visual center of the brain.

How well people can use their sight, their **visual efficiency,** is influenced by many factors, including the person's acuity and peripheral vision abilities, environmental conditions, and psychological variables. **Visual acuity** describes how well a person can see at various distances. The width of a person's field of vision, or the ability to perceive objects outside the direct line of vision, is called **peripheral vision.** This aspect of vision helps people move freely through their environment. It helps them see large objects and movement. Severe limitation in peripheral vision is sometimes called **tunnel vision** or restricted **central vision** because of an inability to see

Figure 11.1 How Vision Works

Source: Physiology of Behavior, 5th ed. by N. R. Carlson, 1994, Boston: Allyn and Bacon, Figures 6.4 and 6.12. Adapted by permission.

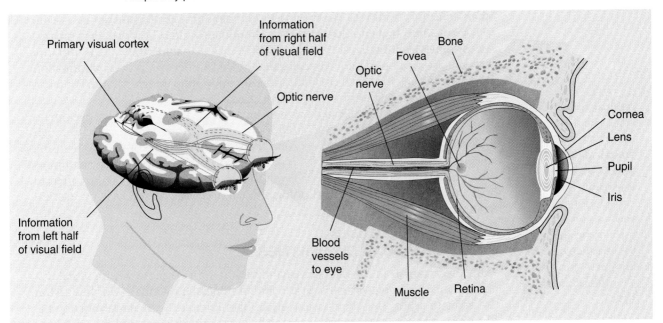

The photo on the left shows what a person with a limited visual field, or tunnel vision, sees; the one on the right shows what a person with restricted visual acuity might see.

a wide area. Some persons with visual disabilities have little functional use of sight, but the great majority have substantial use of their vision, particularly with correction (glasses or contact lenses). Although many people do not realize it, the vast majority of people with visual disabilities use vision as their primary method of learning, and for many the amount of vision they have left, **residual vision,** can be further developed. The vision of some is static, remaining the same from day to day, while others find their ability to see varying by the day, time of day, or setting (Levin, 1996). For some, higher or lower levels of illumination affect how well they can see, but for others, lighting level makes little difference. For some individuals, distance and contrast are important factors affecting how well they can process information presented through the visual channel. Some are color blind; others are not. For most, optical aids such as glasses have a positive effect.

The eye is a very complicated mechanism. Damage to any part of the eye can result in serious limitations in one's abilities to see and process information through the visual channel. Table 11.1 lists conditions of various parts of the eye by using an organizational system suggested by Tuttle and Ferrell (1995). These conditions can result in blindness or severe visual disabilities. Many disorders can be corrected or reduced through medical technology, but not all can be resolved by medical treatment.

TYPES OF VISUAL DISABILITIES

Many professionals in the field of visual disabilities divide persons with visual disabilities into two subgroups: low vision and blindness. Individuals with **low vision** use sight to learn, but their visual disabilities interfere with daily functioning. **Blindness** means that the person uses touch and hearing to learn and does not have

residual vision. The amount and degree of vision that one has functional use of despite a visual disability.
low vision. A level of visual impairment where vision is still useful for learning or the execution of a task.
blindness. Not having a functional use of sight.

Table 11.1 Types of Visual Disabilities

Type	Definition
Conditions of the Eye	
Myopia	Nearsightedness; condition allows focus on objects close but not at a distance.
Hyperopia	Farsightedness; condition allows focus on objects at a distance but not close.
Astigmatism	An eye disorder that produces images on the retina that are not equally in focus.
Conditions of the Eye Muscles	
Strabismus	Improper alignment of the two eyes causes two images to be received by the brain, with the possible result of one eye becoming nonfunctional.
Nystagmus	Rapid, involuntary movements of the eye that interfere with bringing objects into focus.
Conditions of the Cornea, Iris, and Lens	
Glaucoma	Fluid in the eye is restricted, causing pressure to build up and damage the retina.
Aniridia	Undeveloped iris, due to lack of pigment (albinism), results in extreme sensitivity to light.
Cataract (opacity of the crystalline lens)	A cloudy film over the lens of the eye.
Conditions of the Retina	
Diabetic retinopathy	Changes in the eye's blood vessels are caused by diabetes.
Macular degeneration	Damage to a small area near the center of the retina results in restricted fine central vision and difficulties in reading and writing.
Retinopathy of prematurity (ROP)	Excess oxygen to infants causes retinal damage; was called retrolental fibroplasia.
Retinal detachment	Detachment of the retina interrupts transmission of visual information to the brain.
Retinitis pigmentosa	Genetic eye disease leads progressively to blindness; night blindness is the first symptom.
Retinoblastoma	Tumor.
Condition of the Optic Nerve	
Atrophy	Reduced function of the optic nerve.

functional use of sight. Parents and professionals now tend to use functional definitions for these two subgroups. Remember, this classification system is based on how well people can use their sight, even if its use is severely limited.

Low Vision. Corn (1989) defines low vision as "a level of vision which, with standard correction, hinders an individual in the planning and/or execution of a task, but which permits enhancement of the functional vision through the use of optical or nonoptical devices, environmental modifications and/or techniques" (p. 28). In other words, children with low vision use their sight for many school activities, including reading. Barraga and Erin (1992), however, caution us not to assume that all children with low vision use print materials, because some use braille.

Legacy: Because of technological advances, new medical procedures (e.g., laser surgery), and improvements in visual correction devices, many educators erroneously believe that all students with low vision do not require special instruction or accommodations.

Opportunities:
- Ensure that the individual needs of every student with a visual disability are met
- Better educate teachers about the varied needs of low vision students

Blindness. Children without functional use of their vision may only perceive shadows or some movement; these youngsters must be educated through tactile and other sensory channels and are considered functionally blind. Blindness can occur at any age, but its impact varies with age. For those with visual disabilities, as with the deaf and hard of hearing, the age of onset (when the disability occured) is important. Persons born with a severe impairment are **congenitally blind.** Those who acquire a severe visual disability sometime after birth (usually after age 2) are called **adventitiously blind.** People who lose their sight after age 2 retain some memory of what they had seen. They remember what some objects look like. The later the disability occurs, the more they remember. Visual memory is an important factor in learning, for it can influence one's development of concepts and other aspects important to learning.

Despite the movement toward functional definitions of visual disabilities, the nonfunctional definition **legally blind** is still in use. The term legally blind does not relate perfectly to functional use of vision. For example, many people who are considered legally blind use print to gain information. However, being classified as legally blind allows the individual to receive special tax benefits and materials from the federal government and private agencies. To be considered legally blind, a person must meet the following criteria: central visual acuity of 20/200 or less in the better eye, with best correction, or a diameter of visual field that does not subtend an angle greater than 20 degrees at its widest point.

IDENTIFICATION

Important decisions with lifelong implications are often made from those assessments that qualify children with visual disabilities for special education services. Professionals and parents use the information to decide whether a child should learn to read print or to read braille, to specify the level and type of education placements the child will receive, and to determine which assistive services will be included in the child's IEP.

Although parents and professionals are advocating for the use of functional definitions of visual disabilities, many states still use measures of acuity to qualify youngsters for special education services. Normal visual acuity is measured by how accurately a person can see an object or image 20 feet away. Normal vision is thus said to be 20/20. A person whose vision is measured at 20/40 can see at 20 feet what people who do not need visual correction (glasses or contact lenses) can see at 40 feet away. Field of vision is measured in degrees. Those whose visual field is restricted to no more than 20 degrees are classified as legally blind. Although states and school districts vary in the criteria they use to determine eligibility for special services, typically people with visual acuity measuring 20/70 to 20/200 in the better eye with correction are considered to have low vision (Heller et al., 1996). Acuity below 20/200 classifies an individual as legally blind.

When educators use a functional approach, measurement takes on some additional assessment procedures (Blanksby & Langford, 1993). Three factors are considered: visual capacity, visual attention, and visual processing. Visual capacity determines what actually can be seen; it includes acuity, amount of visual field, and how the individual responds to visual information. Visual attention includes four capacities: alertness (ability to maintain sensitivity to environmental stimuli), selection (ability to select information from different sources), degree of attention (ability to maintain attention to a visual stimulus and then change to another), and processing

congenitally blind. Those with severe visual disabilities present at birth.
adventitiously blind. Those who acquired a severe visual disability after the age of two.
legally blind. Visual acuity measured as 20/200 or worse in the better eye with correction, or peripheral vision no greater than 20 degrees.

Reprinted by permission: Tribune Media Services

For a review of IEPs and the services that can be included in special education, read again Chapter 2.

capacity (ability to process visual information). Visual processing is assessed to determine which elements expected in normal visual functioning are impaired.

Assessing visual status can be complicated, imprecise, and frequently inaccurate. Information must be gathered from multiple sources. For example, diagnosticians, the children affected, their parents, educators, school nurses, and eye specialists can all provide important information used in the comprehensive assessment of useful vision. Diagnosticians can help determine visual status for spontaneous visual behaviors in environments in which the child is comfortable. Teachers of blind and low vision students are excellent resources during the assessment process, for they are likely to be the best trained and widely experienced member of the team. Another source of information is the children themselves, but it may be surprising to learn that they are often very unreliable. Possibly motivated by the desire to please a doctor or a diagnostician, many parents report that their blind children both report and simulate a different level of blindness than they actually possess when in the assessment situation (Erin & Corn, 1994). For example, some children indicate that they can see things they cannot: a car coming, the moon at night, the color of an object. Decisions about visual status must be made from accurate information, but surprisingly this task can prove to be quite challenging.

Most states require that all schoolchildren have a visual screening test. Children's visual acuity can be tested in the school nurse's office or by a pediatrician using the **Snellen chart.** The Snellen chart, originally developed by a Dutch ophthalmologist in 1862, comes in two versions. One test uses the letter E placed in various positions in different sizes; the other uses alphabet letters in different sizes. For the screening of substantial numbers of people, a more efficient adaptation of the Snellen chart uses the E version projected on a television monitor placed 10 to 20 feet away from the viewer. The viewer matches a key on a computer with the direction or placement of the E on the screen, allowing the computer to analyze the data.

Although not a requirement, each visual screening of a schoolchild should include teachers' observations about the child's classroom behaviors and performance. For example, teachers should indicate whether a particular child complains about scratchy or itchy eyes or headaches, rubs the eyes excessively, or has difficulty discriminating letters or symbols when completing classroom assignments. Such information is helpful especially when the special services committee makes recommendations about placement and the types of special assistance a child should receive.

Two types of eye specialists provide diagnosis and treatment. **Ophthalmologists** are medical doctors who specialize in eye disorders. They can conduct physical

Snellen chart. A chart used to test visual acuity, developed in 1862. **ophthalmologist.** Medical doctor who specializes in eye disorders.

examinations of the eye, prescribe corrective lenses and medicines, and perform surgery. **Optometrists** are professionals who measure vision and can prescribe corrective lenses and make functional recommendations. They cannot prescribe drugs or perform surgery. An **optician** fills either the ophthalmologist's or optometrist's prescription for glasses or corrective lenses.

SIGNIFICANCE

People experience visual loss due to damage to the eye and the visual processing mechanisms. You have learned through your studies that it is difficult to arrive at a concise definition for most exceptionalities. This is true for visual disabilities as well. Those with visual disabilities range greatly in their abilities, and some of these individuals have multiple disabilities. You have learned so far that visual efficiency is an important concept; think about it as you continue to learn more about this disability and how it impacts the people affected by it. Interestingly, individuals with the same visual acuity or amount of peripheral vision may differ in their abilities to use their sight. A person's visual efficiency influences how that individual learns (through visual, tactile, or auditory channels) and the modifications to instructional methods that teachers must make. For example, a child's visual efficiency could affect how the classroom needs to be organized, where the child should sit, whether additional equipment (microcomputers, braillers) is required, or if adapted materials (texts with enlarged print) are necessary.

Unfortunately, blindness often significantly affects individuals in other ways as well. Hudson (1994) believes it is the attitudes that people with visual disabilities have to contend with in the community and workplace that cause psychological problems in some of these people. She is joined in her belief that the blind face terrible stereotypes and bias by a team of Dutch researchers (Verplanken et al., 1994). In their work, the Dutch team found that sighted people tended to have unfavorable feelings about blind people they had interacted with; unfortunately, more experience and contact did not improve the situation. Verplanken and his colleagues maintain that blindness is met with more negative attitudes than other physical disabilities (Verplanken et al., 1994). Evidently, sighted persons often feel uneasy, afraid, or uncomfortable when interacting with blind people, even if they assess the individual as extremely competent (Hudson, 1994). We must guard against such negative attitudes, which can result in bias in the community, the workplace, and at school. Clearly, bias and negative attitudes can lead to discrimination and missed opportunities for participation in the mainstream of society and should be eliminated. Possibly, sighted people tend to feel uncomfortable with those who are blind because they do not know how to act or whether to offer assistance. Educators can play an important role in helping sighted children learn what is appropriate in social interactions with blind peers and, over time, this may improve the situation for all adults.

HISTORY OF THE FIELD

Our knowledge of people with visual disabilities in Western civilization dates back to the ancient world. Records from ancient Egypt confirm that people with visual disabilities were accepted in society. Homer, the eighth-century B.C. Greek poet who composed the *Odyssey* and the *Iliad*, was blind. The ancient Greeks held Homer and his work in the highest regard, considering him a source of wisdom and a model of

MAKING CONNECTIONS

For suggestions about adapting the classroom setting for blind and low vision students, see the Accommodating for Inclusive Environments box in this chapter.

optometrists. Professionals who measure vision and can prescribe corrective lenses (eyeglasses or contact lenses).

optician. A person who fills either the ophthalmologist's or optometrist's prescriptions for glasses or corrective lenses.

NEW DIRECTIONS
FOR THE
MILLENNIUM

Legacy: More and more students with visual disabilities received their education in general education classes during the last century, which resulted in many benefits (e.g., ability to live at home with their families, integration with nondisabled peers, better access to the general education curriculum) and some disadvantages (e.g., lower rates of literacy, not having close friends who share this disability, more difficulty learning life skills).

Opportunities:

• Focus on the acquisition of reading skills, whether they be print-based or braille

• Ensure that transition programs are available for students with visual disabilities so they master skills needed for: independent living, orientation and mobility, and careers

Tradition holds that Homer, a blind Greek poet, lived around the time of the Trojan War (8th century B.C.) in either Chios or Smyrna. He made his living as a court singer and storyteller and is credited with writing the earliest epic poems, *The Iliad* and *The Odyssey.*

heroic conduct. Despite indications of the acceptance of some blind individuals, there is no record of a systematic attempt to educate and integrate blind people into society until the eighteenth century.

The first school for the blind, the Institution for Blind Youth, was founded in Paris in 1784 by Valentin Haüy. He also conceived a system of raised letters on the printed page. Unfortunately, his developmental efforts ended with the French Revolution in 1789. In the early 1800s, Louis Braille, a Frenchman who was blind, developed a tactile system for reading and writing that used an embossed six-dot cell, the forerunner of the system used today.

The first center school for the blind in the United States, the New England Asylum for the Blind (now the Perkins School for the Blind), directed by Samuel Gridley Howe, opened in 1821. Around 1832, the New York Institute for the Blind and the Pennsylvania Institution for the Instruction of the Blind were founded. These nineteenth-century schools were private boarding schools, usually attended by children from wealthy families.

The first day classes began in Scotland in 1872. The Scottish Education Act required children who were blind to be integrated with their sighted classmates and to attend schools in their local communities. Note that our mainstreaming and "inclusion" movements are not new concepts: Their roots are deep in the history of education of children with disabilities. In the United States, the first concentrated attempts to integrate blind students into local public schools were made in Chicago. In 1900, Frank Hall, the superintendent for the Illinois School for the Blind, convinced people to allow blind students to live at home. Hall developed a plan that divided Chicago into several regions, with one local school in each region to serve blind students. The students attended general classes but also had a special education teacher who taught braille and encouraged students to participate fully in general education programs. Hall developed a mechanical writer, a small, portable machine for taking notes and completing other written tasks.

Edward Allen taught the first class for the partially sighted in 1913 in Boston; later that year, Robert Irwin started a class in Cleveland. These programs were modeled after classes in England in which schoolwork was almost exclusively oral. Reading and writing tasks were kept to a minimum, and students attending these classes participated in general education as much as possible. These classes were generally called "sight saving classes." This method was popular for almost fifty years (from about 1915 to 1965), until Natalie Barraga's research on visual efficiency appeared in 1964 (Barraga, 1964; Barraga & Collins, 1979). She proved that people do not have a limited amount of sight that can be used up; rather, vision can become more limited when it is not used.

Although reading and writing present difficult tasks to many individuals who have visual disabilities, another major area of difficulty is movement. Between 1918 and 1925, dog guides were trained to help French and German veterans of World War I. Guide dogs (Seeing Eye dogs) were introduced in the United States in 1928, but they have not been a popular method of assisting mobility. Less than 4% of people with visual disabilities use Seeing Eye dogs (Tuttle & Ferrell, 1995). Long canes were developed around 1860. Richard Hoover, after whom the **Hoover cane** is named, is credited with developing a mobility and orientation system in 1944. Before this time, there was no systematic method for teaching individuals how to move freely in their environments.

During the 1950s, medical advances that helped save the lives of infants born prematurely ironically caused the disease retinopathy of prematurity (ROP), formally known as retrolental fibroplasia, in surviving infants. ROP results in visual disabilities that range from mild visual loss to blindness. During the 1960s, the rubella (German measles) epidemic left many children with multiple disabilities, often including visual disabilities. The dramatic increase in blind and low vision children strained the capacity of residential schools, which before World War II had served 85% of all schoolchildren with visual disabilities (Sacks & Rosen, 1994). At the same time, parents began to call for their children to attend their local public schools. The result was increased comprehensive programs for these children in local communities. Today, the majority of children with visual disabilities live at home and attend local public schools.

Advances in technology have significantly influenced the lives of blind and low vision individuals. Over the past twenty years, improvements in computer capabilities have allowed for efficient and inexpensive print enlargements and immediate translation of print to braille. The first print-to-voice translator, the **Kurzweil Reader,** was developed in the 1970s and, though crude and expensive when com-

MAKING CONNECTIONS

For other discussions of service animals, see:
• Transition Through Adulthood section in Chapter 9
• Technology section in Chapter 10

Natalie Barraga's work on visual efficiency changed the field's research agenda and influenced how low vision and blind children are taught.

Read the Technology section of this chapter.

For information about other low incidence disabilities, see Chapters 8–12.

MAKING CONNECTIONS

For comparable problems with prevalence figures, see the Prevalence section in Chapter 10.

Hoover cane. Long, white cane used in the mobility and orientation system developed in 1944 by Richard Hoover to help people with visual impairments move through the environment independently.
Kurzweil Reader. One of the first computerized systems designed for people with visual disabilities that translates print into synthesized speech.
multiple disabilities. Possessing more than one handicapping condition.

pared to today's versions of optical scanners, provided immediate access to printed text not available in other formats (braille, enlarged text, audio). This machine provided the breakthrough technology that allows blind individuals immediate access to all printed information, and only hinted at the remarkable innovations now developed and yet to come.

PREVALENCE

According to the American Foundation for the Blind, approximately 4.8 million Americans have severe visual disabilities, with over 220,000 having no useful vision (American Foundation for the Blind, 1999). However, the vast majority of these people are over the age of 65. The proportion of children with visual disabilities is much smaller than the proportion of people with this disability in the general population. This fact is clear when you see the data from the *Twentieth Annual Report to Congress on the Implementation of the Individuals with Disabilities Education Act.* About 4 of every 10,000 schoolchildren (less than .04%) have visual disabilities and receive special services (U.S. Department of Education, 1998). Only 25,800 children between the ages of 6 and 21 are receiving special education because of low vision or blindness. Of this entire group of students, about one-third (5 in every 1,000 students) are legally blind (Tuttle & Ferrell, 1995). Visual disabilities are clearly associated with increasing age.

It is difficult to get an accurate or consistent count of students with visual disabilities. What factors might explain such differences in the numbers of these students from year to year? A primary reason for differences in such counts is that different states use different definitions and criteria to determine eligibility for special services. Also, more than half of those identified as having severe visual disabilities have an additional disability (Tuttle & Ferrell, 1995). Many of these students are counted in the **multiple disabilities** category rather than in the visual disability category, even if the visual disability is their primary, or most serious, disabling condition. Others have their vision corrected with glasses or through surgery. No longer requiring special services, these students do not remain on the special education rolls. Finally, it is possible that many students with mild and even moderate visual loss are not identified and do not receive services for which they are eligible.

CAUSES AND PREVENTION

The prevalence of visual disabilities, particularly in children, varies country by country. For example, the incidence of blindness in developing countries is much greater than in more advanced nations, where access to medical treatment is readily available. In developing nations such as India and countries in Africa, the major causes of childhood blindness are infectious diseases, malnutrition, and vitamin A deficiency, and most of these situations can be prevented or treated.

CAUSES

Visual disabilities may be congenital (present at birth) or acquired. Almost half of the children who are blind have the disability because of prenatal factors, mostly hereditary. Researchers are beginning to identify genes that cause some forms of

To review information about the importance of immunizations, see:
- Concepts and Controversy section in Chapter 5
- Causes and Prevention section in Chapter 3

To review information about low birth weight babies, see:
- Causes and Prevention section in Chapter 6
- Prevalence section in Chapter 9

For more about ROP, see:
- History section of this chapter
- Table 11.1

blindness, which is the first step leading to a cure. For example, the gene that causes retinitis pigmentosa has now been located and isolated, with the hope of a cure in the near future. Fortunately, two causes of visual disabilities were reduced dramatically during the last part of the twentieth century. Today, precautions are being taken to prevent many cases of retinopathy of prematurity (ROP) in low birth weight babies. Rubella, also a significant cause of congenital visual disabilities and multiple disabilities in the past, can today be prevented by a vaccine. That is why it is so important that everyone is immunized.

Advances in medical technology—such as laser treatment, surgery, and corneal implants—help to reduce the incidence or lessen the severity of visual disabilities among children. Although the medical advances that have reduced the prevalence of visual disabilities in children outnumber those that contribute to its increase, medical technology can cause increases in this disability as well. Today more infants survive birth. Premature babies with very low birth weights, even some who weigh less than two pounds, now survive. About half of infants with multiple disabilities have visual disabilities. The cause of the vision problem is often ROP, which can be corrected with eye surgery. Unfortunately, the retina can be reattached successfully only about half the time (Heller et al., 1996).

PREVENTION

Visual screenings can identify children with visual disabilities. However, teachers and parents, alert to possible signs of a visual problem, might be able to identify such students even sooner and ultimately reduce the impact of the disability (Brody, 1993). Table 11.2 lists some common characteristics of children with visual disabilities. Alert teachers, aware of these characteristics, might contribute to the early identification of a child facing a visual problem. Any child who exhibits one or more of these characteristics should be checked by a school nurse, pediatrician, or ophthalmologist.

In many cases visual disabilities can now be prevented, but more can be done. For example, by protecting against eye injuries, the incidence of visual disabilities can be greatly reduced (Prevent Blindness America, 1999). For those visual disabilities that cannot be avoided, their impact can be lessened through early and consistent treatment. Unfortunately, not all U.S. children have early access to health care. In fact, poor children are between 1.2 and 1.8 times more likely to have visual disabilities (Sherman, 1994). Considering the long-term costs to society and these individuals, the problem of access to health care must be addressed.

LOW VISION AND BLIND CHILDREN

You may be surprised to learn that only 10% of students who are legally blind use braille as their primary mode of learning (American Printing House for the Blind, 1992). The great majority of students with visual disabilities are able to learn to read and write, watch television and use their vision to function in society.

CHARACTERISTICS AFFECTING SOCIAL SKILLS

Visual information plays an important role in the acquisition of social skills and the ability to interact appropriately with peers. The process of learning social skills begins in infancy and continues to develop throughout childhood (Baird et al., 1997).

Table 11.2 Possible Signs of Visual Disabilities

- Eyes water excessively.
- Eyes are red or continually inflamed.
- Eyes are crusty in appearance.
- Eyes look dull, wrinkled, or cloudy.
- Eyes look swollen
- One or both pupils (black center of the eye) look gray or white.
- One or both eyes cross, turn in or out, or move differently from the other.
- Baby of three months or more does not look directly at objects.
- Child bumps into or trips over things.
- Child has difficulty seeing after the sun sets (night blindness).
- Child has difficulty reading small print.
- Child has difficulty identifying details in pictures.
- Child has difficulty going up or down stairs, throwing or catching a ball, buttoning clothes, or tying shoes.
- Child is excessively clumsy.
- Child is unable to discriminate letters.
- Child rubs eyes often.
- Child squints.
- Child complains of dizziness or headaches after a reading assignment.
- Child often tilts head.
- Child uses one eye, possibly shutting or covering the other eye when reading.
- Child dislikes or avoids close work.
- Child holds objects abnormally close to the eyes.

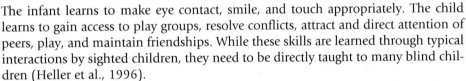

NEW DIRECTIONS
FOR THE
MILLENNIUM

Legacy: During the latter part of the twentieth century, educators came to understand the role social skills play in integration of students with disabilities at school and in the community later in life, but universally effective programs remain illusive.

Opportunities:

- Systematically include guided instruction and opportunities for children to develop good social interaction abilities
- Develop ways to help students with visual disabilities learn to play on par with their sighted peers

The infant learns to make eye contact, smile, and touch appropriately. The child learns to gain access to play groups, resolve conflicts, attract and direct attention of peers, play, and maintain friendships. While these skills are learned through typical interactions by sighted children, they need to be directly taught to many blind children (Heller et al., 1996).

Many blind and low vision children do not understand the social behavior of others because they are deprived of normal social interactions in which most of us gain this awareness (Pring et al., 1998). They seem to be less assertive than their sighted peers, which may disturb the necessary balance and equilibrium in social exchanges (Buhrow et al., 1998). Social skills are important for acceptance by peers, and many blind and low vision students have difficulties in this area as well. Many blind youngsters tend to lack play skills, ask too many irrelevant questions, and engage in inappropriate acts of affection (Rettig, 1994). Many of these individuals also exhibit other inappropriate behaviors, such as rocking, moving their hands strangely in space, and eye poking. Possibly because of their inappropriate or immature social behaviors, they tend to interact with and make friends with the least popular peers in their general education classes (MacCuspie, 1992). And, unfortunately, they tend not to interact with other children naturally or spontaneously (Crocker & Orr, 1996). Being unable to see peers' nonverbal cues, which serve to guide their sighted classmates' social interactions, is a major problem for these youngsters. For them to learn the nuances of socially appropriate interactions often

Achieving Discipline

ESTABLISH BOUNDARIES: EXPLICIT RULES

Ms. Pacheon's third graders' first week of school was difficult. She held high expectations for her students and planned to use many cooperative learning groups during the year. This freer style of instruction was unfamiliar to her students, and would require them to develop independent learning skills and deal with challenging academic materials. Through a community partnership, the summer saw an installation of an Ethernet system in all of the upper elementary classrooms. Six computers, networked to the district's main computer, were now in her class available for the children to use for research through the Web and for writing and other computer applications. The possibilities for enhanced learning were great, but so too were the opportunities for chaos. By the end of the first week of school, everyone realized that achieving a positive learning environment would require cooperation and some structure.

On Monday afternoon, after another frustrating morning, Ms. Pacheon held a class conference. She waited until this time so the students had a clear understanding of the necessity of developing guidelines for their behavior in class. Together, they discussed the opportunities and responsibilities of being able to work in small groups, pairs, or independently. They discussed how they would share the computers and fairly manage time spent using them across the entire day. They talked about the noise level in the class during group time, and shared with each other their own learning styles and needs. They developed a broad, general list of rules. They developed a set of consequences that would be applied when rules were broken and also a reward system for the entire class when standards for their positive learning environment were met. In addition, they all promised to remind each other of the rules during the first-week trial period. Ms. Pacheon told the class that she would hold another class conference on Friday to assess the outcomes, at which time they could review and modify the rules they developed that Monday afternoon.

Steps used to create a positive learning environment

- The teacher actively involved her class in the development of rules
- Together, they generated a list of rules which were broadly and positively stated
- The teacher promoted everyone's understanding of the rules
- The rules were consistently applied
- They were reviewed and modified periodically
- The teacher reminded the students of the rules before situations became high-probability times for infractions

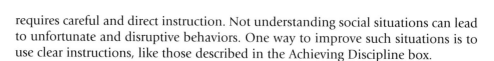

requires careful and direct instruction. Not understanding social situations can lead to unfortunate and disruptive behaviors. One way to improve such situations is to use clear instructions, like those described in the Achieving Discipline box.

Perhaps the way blind children are treated and negative experiences with peers during the schoolyears contribute to the following characteristics often attributed to blind people in the research literature: having low self-esteem and being socially immature, egocentric, self-conscious, isolated, passive, withdrawn, and dependent (Huurre et al., 1999; Tuttle & Ferrell, 1995). Why else are these behavioral characteristics exhibited by some individuals with visual disabilities? Some of these behaviors may be a function of the disability, but some may be caused by a lack of friends and few social relationships. The resulting social isolation and reduced opportunities to develop interpersonal skills often contribute to a poor sense of self-worth. Clearly, the consequences of inadequate personal skills can be great.

Certainly, those with visual disabilities have less information to act on when compared with individuals who have all of their senses intact. This fact has serious ramifications for interpersonal interactions as well as academic learning. Next time you are interacting with friends, consider how nonverbal cues (facial expressions, a shrug of the shoulders) affect the meaning of a message. Now think about how the literal message (without the nonverbal cues) of the interaction would be understood by someone who could not use sight during the interaction.

The lack of effective interpersonal social skills can have a lifelong impact. It can influence leisure-time activities, success on the job, and overall adjustment. The challenge here is to sighted peers, teachers, parents, and to the individuals themselves. Interpersonal skills can be learned, and the opportunities for using those skills can be increased. Sighted peers should be informed about the visual status of their classmates with visual disabilities and can be assigned the role of helper for both academic and social situations. They can also be taught to role-model proper behavior. Teachers can encourage students with visual disabilities to participate fully in all school activities and to communicate their visual needs to others in a straightforward fashion. Teachers can also help these students understand the explicit and implicit rules of games and social interactions. Meanwhile, parents can organize small play groups at home and provide direct feedback about their youngster's interpersonal interactions.

ACADEMIC PERFORMANCE

Today, a large percentage (about 48%) of students with visual disabilities spend over 79% of their schooldays in general education classrooms. Two-thirds of low vision and blind students receive their education at their neighborhood school in the general education classroom, possibly with support from a resource specialist or itinerant teacher (U.S. Department of Education, 1998). These students participate in the general education curriculum with their sighted classmates and, if they do not also have multiple disabilities, perform well academically. Many use aids such as glasses or technology that enlarges type to help them enhance their vision for accessing information from printed material. Others learn to use their tactile senses and employ braille as their reading method, and some rely on audio means for gaining information. One of the singular characteristics of this group of learners is the variety of methods they use for reading and writing. Some of these are highlighted in the next sections.

More information about technology for low vision and blind people is found in the Technology section of this chapter.

Reading Printed Materials. What are some of the methods blind and low vision people use for reading? The majority use their vision and read print. Many low vision students who use their vision to read need specially adapted versions of the texts used in their classes. Many such texts have been produced on microcomputer disks and are available from materials centers. Today, with the availability of scanners and computers, print size and format can be modified quickly and easily. And, of course, materials not originally produced in large type can be enlarged by using common copy machines, making almost all printed materials readily accessible. Technology is adding other methods for reading and writing. For example, speech synthesizers are becoming less expensive, exceptionally portable, and more commonly available, allowing for instant voice-to-print and print-to-voice translations of documents.

As mentioned previously, the size of print in typical books is too small for many students with visual disabilities. If special equipment is not accessible locally or from the state's or school district's materials center, what other options do these students have? Fortunately, many books and materials are broadly available through bookstores and mail-order sources. Large-type dictionaries, thesauruses, and atlases are now available. The Book-of-the-Month Club maintains a Large Print Library; *Reader's Digest* produces a large-type version of its magazine every month, as well as a biography and condensed book series; and the *New York Times* publishes a specially edited weekly version of its newspaper in 16-point type and small page size (12-inch by 14-inch). Such accommodations—essential for most individuals with glaucoma, congenital cataracts, or nystagmus—allow greater participation in American society by blind and low vision people.

For individuals with good central vision but a limited visual field, enlargements may be a hindrance, however. For these students, audiocassette versions of textbooks, **personal readers,** or computer-generated print-to-voice systems may be good alternatives.

Braille. Students with very severe visual disabilities may need to learn to read and write using a very different method: a tactile one. **Braille** uses a coded system of dots embossed on paper so that individuals can feel a page of text. Surrounded in controversy today, braille has been used by shrinking proportions of low vision and blind people in recent years (Schoellkopf, 1995; Wittenstein, 1994). In 1963, over 50% of persons with severe visual disabilities used braille, while in 1978 less than 20% did. By 1992, only 10% of blind students used braille (American Printing House for the Blind, 1992). Also, the literacy levels of these individuals are alarmingly low.

Concern about low vision and blind students' reading abilities is widespread. In a study conducted by the American Printing House for the Blind (1992), which included

For more about braille, see in this chapter:
• The Literacy section (Educational Interventions)
• Concepts and Controversy

Computer technology now makes braille versions of tests, texts, and instructional materials readily available, thus increasing the opportunity for the participation of blind and low vision children in the general education curriculum and also in state-wide assessments.

personal reader. A person who reads text orally to those who cannot read print.

braille. A system of reading and writing that uses dot codes that are embossed on paper, developed by Louis Braille in 1824.

Braille Instruction and Use of Braille

The IEP Team for each student with a visual disability must consider special factors about each child's method of reading:

- All IEPs for children with visual disabilities must address the issue of braille instruction and the use of braille in classroom settings
- Evaluate the child's reading and writing skills, educational needs, and future need for instruction in braille or use of braille
- Provide instruction in braille and allow the child to use braille, if that method is deemed appropriate for that student
- The braille decision cannot be based on factors such as the availability of alternative reading methods or on the availability of braille instruction
- Once the decision is made, services and materials must be delivered without undue delay

elementary and secondary students attending local public schools and those attending state center schools, it was found that 27% were visual readers, 10% were auditory readers, another 10% were braille readers, while 22% of the students were considered prereaders because they were reading at a readiness level and had not yet determined a preferred reading mode, and 31% were nonreaders. Findings like these have caused concern in the field about the low literacy rate among individuals with visual disabilities and have sparked debate about the teaching of braille (Rex et al., 1994). "Braille bills" have been and are being introduced and passed in many state legislatures. IDEA '97 now requires that braille must be considered in the development of these students' IEPs (see the What IDEA '97 Says box for more information). These factors have caused a renewed interest in braille as a reading method for these students.

Many reasons are given to explain why fewer people are using braille as a reading method today. First, braille for many can be very cumbersome and slow. Trent and Truan (1997) report that typical braille readers in high school achieve a rate of only 42 words per minute, and the best reader in their study read 103 words per minute. Try yourself to read that slowly; you will find it quite difficult and laborious. Becoming even minimally proficient at the braille method of reading takes extensive training and practice. Braille also uses different codes for different types of reading, such as math and music, making it even more difficult for students with cognitive impairments to master completely.

Can you think of some other reasons why braille is less popular today? Here is a list: teachers who do not know how to use or teach the braille method, the unavailability of teachers who know how to teach braille to others, increasing availability of audiotapes, immediate computerized print-to-voice translations, difficulty of getting braille versions of books. Braille literacy has become the focus of a great debate. Ironically, advanced technology is both a reason for its resurgence and its unpopularity. The unavailability of braille versions of texts used in the general education classroom was a great hindrance to this method's widespread use. Now, because of scanning capabilities and special microcomputer software and printers that can translate standard print to braille instantaneously, braille editions can be obtained quite quickly through regional materials centers, the American Printing House for the Blind, Library of Congress, and from equipment the student has. Remember that braille is not necessary for all blind students, however. Improved optical corrections and technology are now available that allow more of these individuals to use their own vision as they read and write. Regardless of the method used, reading is an important curriculum area for these students, and often a difficult one to master.

MAKING CONNECTIONS

Background about work in the area of visual efficiency is found in the History section of this chapter.

EDUCATIONAL INTERVENTIONS

The vast majority of low vision and blind students live at home and attend their neighborhood elementary and secondary schools. Many receive the same education as classmates who do not share their disability. They may receive extra assistance from resource specialists and other specialists, particularly in the area of basic skills. Most receive the general education curriculum, with additional instructional support. Students whose functional use of vision is extremely limited require specialized instruction on additional topics such as orientation and mobility and independent living skills.

Like all students with disabilities, for those with visual disabilities, preschool education is vital. During this time, the foundations for social skills, academic success, and independence are formed. These issues are addressed in the next section. In the Education and the Schoolchild section, you will learn about adapting the instructional setting to better meet the educational needs of low vision and blind students, special curriculum topics (e.g., orientation and mobility) unique to this population of learners, and issues surrounding literacy.

EDUCATION AND THE PRESCHOOL CHILD

Preschool programs for individuals with severe visual disabilities help infants and their families from the onset of their visual loss (Barraga & Erin, 1992). Recall that those who are congenitally blind (born blind) and those who became blind at a very early age (adventitiously blind) have little or no memory of how the world looks. These infants are not stimulated like sighted infants and have limited opportunities for learning. They do not see their mother's smile or the toys in their cribs. The right preschool program can give preschoolers with visual disabilities the "right start" so that the disadvantages which this disability can cause are minimized.

A wide variety of programs are available for preschoolers with visual disabilities. In some cities, teachers work with these children and their families at their homes. Sometimes preschool and day care teachers are assisted by special education teachers who travel from school to school (itinerant specialists). In many cities, special preschool programs are available for these children. Sometimes these programs are segregated (attended only by preschoolers with visual disabilities); other times, they are integrated (they include sighted children). Many special preschool programs are supervised and managed by staff from a state center or residential school. No matter what program is chosen, preschoolers should receive the most intensive early educational experiences possible. To provide the fullest attention to the child, the teacher of a preschooler with visual disabilities should coordinate a multidisciplinary team of specialists to work with the child and the family. This team might include an ophthalmologist, occupational therapist, physical therapist, orientation and mobility instructor, and social worker. The makeup of the team depends on the needs of each child and family.

When not stimulated directly, blind infants often withdraw and do not explore their environments as sighted infants do. Many infants who are blind experience a prolonged period of inactivity during their first year, which inhibits their exploration and discovery of their environment. Many develop inappropriate behaviors, such as rocking or inappropriate hand movements. Babies with visual disabilities may acquire some social problems as a result of insufficient interpersonal interactions early in life, so they need assistance as they develop relationships, particularly during the first two years of life (Baird et al., 1997). For example, they may need to be taught when to smile and to make eye contact appropriately. These are skills that parents can teach their children with the help of early childhood specialists. Infants and toddlers with severe visual disabilities do, however, act like sighted babies in other ways. Although there is no difference in the way that these and sighted babies babble, many blind children do have some language delays. However, with some extra guidance from family members, their vocabulary development can be the same as that of sighted babies (Dote-Kwan & Hughes, 1994).

The preschool years provide the foundation for lifelong learning and independence. In that regard, in this section we discuss the development of play skills and initial independence. For many young low vision and blind children and their families, preschool programs are a cornerstone to a good start on the path for strong educational results or outcomes.

The importance of play is also discussed in the Preschool section of Chapter 5.

Play. Researchers are learning that play is a very important part of human development (Recchia, 1997; Skellenger & Hill, 1994). Through play, young children learn to socialize, interact with others, and cooperate. Through discovery and exploration, which are encouraged through play activities, young children also learn about their environment, develop motor skills, and often enhance their language skills. Because of their disability, blind and low vision children play very differently than their sighted peers (Hughes et al., 1998). Both groups of preschoolers with visual disabilities were delayed in their development of play skills, being two years behind sighted peers. Play that could be described as exploration and sensorimotor activities (like banging and mouthing toys) was very immature, accounting for 44% of low vision and 75% of functionally blind preschoolers' play, and these play differences may well have lifelong effects. In this chapter's Research to Practice box on page 480, Jamie Dote-Kwan discusses the results of the work she and her colleagues have conducted.

Blind preschoolers explore their surroundings and interact with their siblings and peers considerably less than do their sighted peers (Tröster & Brambring, 1994). Many blind adults also restrict their environments and tend not to explore unfamiliar areas on their own (Clarke et al., 1994). Tröster and Brambring (1992, 1994) have identified other play characteristics that follow many blind individuals into adulthood: engaging in high rates of solitary play, not playing spontaneously, seeking play with adults rather than other children, and selecting toys that are concrete, familiar items. Delayed play development might well contribute to later difficulties in social interactions and concept formation (Recchia, 1997). Sighted children often find it difficult to adjust their play to the ability levels of blind children who prefer noisy play activities that are not abstract or symbolic (Tröster & Brambring, 1994). They may also find that their play styles are in conflict with blind peers'. The quick and sometimes unpredictable movements of sighted children may disorient children with severe visual disabilities (Rettig, 1994). Such play differences may well inhibit integrated play activities of sighted and nonsighted peers. Some researchers are convinced that adults have to teach blind preschoolers how to play and be sure those skills are well learned before encouraging play with sighted peers (Hughes et al., 1998).

Hughes and her colleagues (1998) suggest that preschool activities be restructured for blind and low vision students, particularly those in inclusive settings. They believe that adults should teach play skills through modeling, direct instruction, and active participation. Teachers must be aware of the possible barriers to parallel play between sighted and blind children; they will need to teach these children to learn how to play together, interact appropriately, and work cooperatively. Teachers

Research to Practice: Teaching with Confidence

FACILITATING CAREGIVER–CHILD INTERACTIONS

JAMIE DOTE-KWAN
California State University–Los Angeles

RESEARCH

Over the past two decades, a substantial amount of experimental research has revealed the importance of the relation of caregiver–child interactions to the developmental outcomes of children, particularly those with severe visual disabilities. These transactional interaction patterns and children's development result not only from the unique characteristics of the caregiver and the child but also from the reciprocity that develops as each partner responds and adapts to the other. My work has shown that interaction styles and patterns begin early in children's lives, and patterns of the ways mothers initiate interactions with their children and respond to their children's initiations are influential in the way children develop. We also know that these interaction patterns can be improved. It is essential that service providers (e.g., early interventionists) assist caregivers and family members in identifying those characteristics of the child's interactions with the social environment that may facilitate development and positive outcomes. These interactions should include natural interactions in the home environment, and also at school if the preschooler is in a center-based program. To develop an intervention plan for children between 20 and 36 months of age, interactions should be assessed in the areas of mother-initiated, mother-responsive, or child-initiated behaviors with a developmental outcome measure designed for young children with visual disabilities.

PRACTICE

Interventions should focus on assisting caregivers and family members in establishing and maintaining interactions that are mutually enjoyable for both the adult and the child. Interventions that increase the caregiver's feelings of competence and promote the child's development can be designed in the following ways:

- Facilitate the caregiver's understanding of the child's visual functioning. For example, identify the physical environmental needs of the child that enhance visual functioning in different settings (e.g., glare, lighting, contrast). Identify for the caregiver the visual features of materials that enhance the child's visual functioning (e. g., contract, color, complexity of the object, and space between objects).

- Support caregiver responsiveness to the child's interests; in objects, events, or people by identifying when the child is ready for interaction and by interpreting nonverbal signals that indicate the child's interest or disinterest in a particular situation. For example, some children become quiet when interested, whereas others increase their body movements; these particular behaviors may indicate disinterest in another child. Some children may open and close their hands while held at their side. These nonverbal cues must be interpreted within the context of an activity by a caregiver who is familiar with the child.

- Assist caregivers in the development of interaction strategies or ways to communicate with the child that are predictable and comprehensible to the child. Some children with visual disabilities may require augmentative communication input that includes using exaggerated vocalization, touch cues (e.g., touching the spoon on the child's lips before inserting food into his or her mouth), object cues (e.g., having the child touch car keys before getting into the car), or auditory cues (e.g., tapping the cup so the child can locate it).

- Help caregivers respond to their children's communicative intents by encouraging them to acknowledge, repeat or rephrase, and expand their child's communicative intent whether verbal or nonverbal. For example, the caregiver is bouncing the child on her lap and stops; the child starts to wiggle and the caregiver interprets this behavior as the child wanting "more" and responds by bouncing the child again. An example of expansion is when the child says "ba" and the caregiver says "ba, you want the ball."

can also create opportunities for play development by selecting activities that are interesting and motivating to blind youngsters, allowing them to select toys and games to play with, and encouraging their active involvement in peer interactions (Recchia, 1997). Fostering these opportunities can require considerable skill and experience. For example, teachers may have to allow blind children extra time to become comfortable in new settings before intruding in play activities. They may need to encourage silly and pretend play, even when it might disrupt the structure of the classroom routine. Finding the balance between routine and flexibility can tax even the most creative teacher.

Learning Independence. Orientation and mobility are major curriculum targets for students with severe visual disabilities. Because instruction in this area needs to begin as early as possible, parents and professionals are encouraging the introduction of the long cane to children between the ages of 2 and 6 (Pogrund et al., 1993). Although some orientation and mobility teachers believe that young children should begin learning how to use a long cane with the adult size that they will use later in life (which would be extra long for their present size), research findings indicate that children are better off learning how to use a mobility cane that is cut to their size (Clarke et al., 1994). Sometimes called the Kiddy Cane or the Connecticut precane, this homemade version of the long cane is tailored to the size of the user, even a preschooler. It is made of rigid, white PVC pipe and is cut at midchest height. It has a red stripe at the bottom and tape across the top for a grip.

Because the home is the most natural setting for infants' and toddlers' educational programs, most include home-based instruction with considerable parent involvement. For later independence, one of the most important lessons parents can learn is to allow their babies to explore the environment. Research shows that parents can

MAKING CONNECTIONS

Orientation and mobility is discussed in the Education and the Schoolchild section of this chapter.

Independent mobility and orientation are two of the greatest challenges that face people with severe visual problems. For them, it is important to begin mobility training as early as possible.

Legacy: As the new millennium began, it was apparent to experts in visual disabilities that specialized instruction in orientation and mobility was not sufficiently available to many students with visual disabilities at all general education settings.

Opportunities:
- Provide more ongoing support from orientation and mobility teachers to students included in general education classes
- Increase outreach services from center schools and state- or district-operated resource centers for blind and low vision students

Also see in this chapter these sections:
- Methods of Reading and Writing (Low Vision and Blind Students)
- Concepts and Controversy

life skills. Those skills used to manage a home, cook, shop, and organize personal living environments.

help their infants become more mobile and independent by teaching them to crawl and walk in a structured program (Joffee, 1988). Some parents of infants with visual disabilities, fearful that their baby will fall or be hurt, are overly protective and controlling—attitudes that can foster dependency (Behl et al., 1996).

EDUCATION AND THE SCHOOLCHILD

The educational needs of low vision students differ from those of blind students. Students with low vision might require some extra tutorial assistance to learn the same number of phonetic rules as their classmates or additional time to read their history assignment. Students who are blind might require the introduction of entirely different curriculum topics. For example, they might need to learn independent **life skills** so that they can manage an apartment, pay their bills, shop for food, and cook their meals without assistance from others. The crucial factor is that the educational and developmental goals, and the instruction designed to meet those goals, reflect the specific needs of each individual (Corn et al., 1995). In the following subsections, guidelines for teaching and suggestions for specific curriculum modifications for low vision and blind students are given. Keep in mind that these two groups are not truly distinct; suggestions for low vision students might well apply to many blind students, and those for blind students to some low vision students.

Literacy. As you have learned, many individuals with severe visual disabilities are not proficient readers, regardless of the reading method they use. Reasons for difficulties in learning to read are numerous and obviously related to visual disabilities. However, accumulating evidence suggests other reasons for this group's reading problems. It appears that somewhere between 14% and 65% of these students also have learning disabilities (Erin & Koenig, 1997). These students may require additional instructional strategies, borrowed from the field of learning disabilities, to master reading. Students learning braille may find great success using the phonics approach, while low vision students with learning disabilities learning to read print may benefit from learning strategies that emphasize comprehension by skimming passages to look for main ideas in texts' content. Literacy is a goal for all Americans and an expectation for all high school graduates. Because literacy presents particular and unique challenges for individuals with visual disabilities, we need to look at literacy in different ways. Being able to gain access to information presented through print and to communicate with others through written and oral modes are components of the literacy goal for students with visual disabilities. In addition, experts include skills such as technology, computing, checkbook balancing, and independent completion of daily living tasks as literacy goals for this population of learners (Newman & Beverstock, 1990).

Clearly, literacy is a diverse and complex concept. For example, reading skills, whether they be through print or braille, are needed to succeed in school and to meet academic demands of high school and college. Other sets of skills are required for achievement in the workplace. To help us better understand what comprises literacy in the adult world, Koenig (1992) provides us with some examples of what he calls functional literacy—the ability to accomplish practical real-life tasks required in the home, school, community, and work environments. Table 11.3 shows examples of these skills and gives us some ideas about what should be included in the curriculum presented to blind and low vision students.

Table 11.3

Literacy Tasks Requiring Communication with Self and Communication with Others in Four Environments

Audience	Home	School	Community	Work
*Communicating with self**	Labeling personal items Maintaining an address and telephone book	Jotting assignments Taking notes in class	Making shopping lists Writing directions to a specific location	Jotting notes to self Making list of "things to do"
Communicating with others†	Writing personal letters to friends Paying bills Reading mail Reading for pleasure Reading newspapers Reading books to others	Reading textbooks and workbooks Reading periodicals Writing term papers Completing assignments Taking tests Completing registration forms	Completing deposit slips at a bank Reading signs Reading menus Signing documents Writing checks at a store Reading labels on items at a store	Reading memos from supervisor Writing reports Reading gauges and dials Filling out forms Reading job manuals Writing work-related correspondence

Source: "A Framework for Understanding the Literacy of Individuals with Visual Impairments" by A. J. Koenig. Reprinted by permission from the *Journal of Visual Impairment and Blindness.* Copyright 1992 by American Foundation for the Blind, 11 Penn Plaza, Suite 300, New York, NY 10001. All rights reserved.

*The individual is both the writer and the intended reader.

†The individual is either the writer or the intended reader, but not both.

orientation. The mental map people use to move through environments.

mobility. The ability to travel safely and efficiently from one place to another.

long cane. White canes used to assist blind people to be independently mobile, developed by Hoover during World War II.

tactile maps. Maps that utilize touch to orient people to specific locales.

Orientation and Mobility. Children with very low visual efficiencies need special training to increase their independence (Clarke et al., 1994). Orientation and mobility training helps those with severe visual disabilities to move around independently. **Orientation** can be described as the mental map people have about their surroundings (Hill, 1986). Most of us use landmarks and other cues to get from one place to another. Think about how you get from your house to a friend's home or from one class to another on campus. What cues or landmarks do you use? These cues or landmarks make up our mental maps and orientation to our environments. **Mobility** is the ability to travel safely and efficiently from one place to another. Many adults use the **long cane** to help them move around independently. Learning how to be independently mobile by using a long cane is a difficult goal to accomplish. This curriculum target should begin when these children are toddlers and continue as a major instructional area across the schoolyears.

The orientation and mobility curriculum includes more than the use of long canes. For example, using maps is important to everyone who must figure out how to travel from place to place. For blind individuals, **tactile maps** can be very helpful. When students are trained in their use, these maps can assist with independent movement in the community, as street maps do for sighted people (Ungar et al., 1997). Recent advances in computers and printers, like American Thermoform's Swell Form Graphics Machine II, now simplify the creation of tactile maps and graphics (Horsfall, 1997).

Service animals are also discussed in these sections:

- Educational Interventions in Chapter 9
- Transition Through Adulthood in the Educational Interventions section of Chapter 10

Review again the discussions of mobility canes in these sections of this chapter:

- Preschool
- History

How do people with visual disabilities orient themselves to their surroundings and increase their mobility? In doing the background research for their book about **guide dog** schools, Eames and Eames estimated that 7,250 people in the United States use guide dogs (*JVIB News Service*, 1995). Relatively few adults who are legally blind (less than 4%) use guide dogs to help them move about independently (Tuttle & Ferrell, 1995). Substantially more blind and low vision people choose to use long canes. The National Center for Health Statistics reported that in 1990, 109,000 used canes to aid their mobility (*JVIB News Service*, 1994). The cane makes a sound as it is tapped on the ground while a person is walking. It helps the user know when a hallway ends, when stairs begin and end, and when doors are reached. However, for many obstacles in our world, a cane is not helpful. Silent traffic signals can be very dangerous to persons with visual disabilities, and many cities have not yet installed beeper traffic signals. Escalators, elevators, and public transportation can present problems as well. In the future, the ADA law should reduce hazards for people with severe visual disabilities. This law provides guidelines that will eliminate protruding and overhanging objects that are undetectable with mobility canes.

Sometimes, like when crossing a busy street or entering an unfamiliar building, blind and low vision people require assistance. But the sighted person must be sensitive to the person's desire to receive help. First, be certain that the individual wants assistance. Ask. If the answer is yes, guide the individual by offering your arm, holding it in a relaxed position. People with a visual disability usually will gently grasp

Eric Weihenmayer is an ambitious and blind outdoorsman who pushes the limits of most people. Eric, who climbed Aconcagua (the highest peak in Argentina at 22,834 feet), El Capitan in Yosemite National Park, and Mt. McKinley, recently taught rock climbing to his father on a recent expedition in the Colorado Rockies.

guide dog. An animal, also called a service animal, trained to assist blind persons to move about independently.

your arm at or above your elbow and will walk slightly behind or to your side. Never push or pull them as you walk. You will find that this system leaves you free to converse and walk with ease.

Sports and recreation programs and activities can have many benefits to children with severe visual disabilities. They not only contribute to better orientation and mobility skills, but also help students become more involved socially. Special events such as the beeping eggs at the White House Easter Egg Hunt make a difference (Associated Press, 1996), but routine activities where consistent participation is possible are best. Many special sports programs are available (for example, skiing, sailing, hiking, baseball, bowling, bicycling, horseback riding), but for everyone it is important to begin the pattern of consistent physical exercise early in life. Many individuals with severe visual disabilities excel in sports and can serve as role models and examples for children. For example, Bill Irwin and his guide dog, Orient, spent eight months hiking the entire 2,167-mile Appalachian Trail, which begins in Georgia and ends in Maine (*New York Times*, 1990). After many different excursions, Orient retired in October 1995 (CNN News, 1995). Erik Weihenmayer, the first blind person to hike the sixty-mile-long Inca Trail in Peru, also was part of the first team of blind people to climb Alaska's Mount McKinley, the highest peak in North America (*Sports Illustrated*, 1995). That 1995 expedition, called AFB HighSights '95, was made up of climbers whose occupations included English and math teacher, computer systems analyst, assistant district attorney, and psychoanalyst. While they climbed the heights, Marla Runyan competed in the finals of the 1,500-meter run in the IAAF World Championships of track and field, which were held in Seville, Spain (Associated Press, 1999a). These are only a few examples that demonstrate that people with visual disabilities can set high goals for themselves and achieve them, if given the opportunity.

COLLABORATION FOR INCLUSION

Estimates indicate that before the 1940s, 85% of students with severe visual disabilities attended special residential schools (Sacks & Rosen, 1994). This situation has changed dramatically. Today, about 8% attend public residential schools, and about 68% attend either general education or resource room programs in their local public schools (U.S. Department of Education, 1998). Except for children with speech or language impairments, this group of youngsters is the most integrated of all students with disabilities.

Many blind and low vision students receive tremendous benefits from attending general education classrooms and living at home. They are taught the same subjects as other children, and generally in the same manner. They grow up where home management (cooking, shopping, cleaning) is part of the daily routine. And they interact socially with many different people, making them better prepared to take their places in society when schooling is completed. Unfortunately, merely attending a local public school or living at home does not guarantee socialization, true integration, nor learning the skills necessary for adult life. Achieving these goals requires many partnerships. Multidisciplinary team members must continually consider placement options for each individual, while special educators, general education teachers, and family members must be vigilant that the student is making progress in attaining his or her IEP goals.

Good inclusive practices for students with visual disabilities require some adjustments to the learning environment and to teaching practices. The suggestions

MAKING CONNECTIONS

For more suggestions about accommodations general education teachers can make to truly include students with disabilities in the instructional program, see the Making Accommodations for Inclusive Environments boxes throughout this text (Chapters 3–12).

Accommodating for Inclusive Environments

IMPLEMENTING THE COURTESY RULES OF BLINDNESS

1. Place the child's desk close to the teacher's desk, the blackboard, and the classroom door.
2. Reduce distracting glare; arrange the child's desk away from a light source but in a well-lit area.
3. Allow the child to relocate in the classroom for different activities to enhance opportunities to see and hear.
4. Open or close doors fully (a half-open door can be a dangerous obstacle).
5. Eliminate unnecessary noise; do not speak too loudly for it tends to increase classroom volume level.
6. Eliminate clutter from the room, particularly in aisles and movement paths.
7. Place materials in consistent places, so students know where particular items are always located.
8. Keep to routine schedules so students know what to expect on specific days and times.
9. Address students by using their names first to get their attention.
10. Do not leave the classroom without telling the student.
11. Explain the implicit and explicit rules for classroom conduct, games, and social situations.
12. Encourage students with visual impairments to express their visual needs.
13. Repeat orally information written on a board or an overhead projector, and give the student a printed version. (Remember that enlargements on an overhead projector are not helpful to all blind and low vision students.)
14. Prepare enlarged print or braille handouts, summarizing key points from lectures (an easy task using computers with braillers and adjustable font and type sizes).
15. Audiotape lectures so students can use tapes as study aids at home.
16. Select bright and contrasting colors for bulletin boards and other instructional materials for those who benefit from such visual contrasts.
17. Increase visual contrast: place yellow plastic overlays over purple ditto worksheets (which will help some students see the worksheets more easily), photocopy dittos, use felt-tip pens.
18. Seek assistance of a specialist in the area of visual impairments, and have high expectations.

Source: Adapted from *Courtesy Rules of Blindness*, courtesy of the National Federation of the Blind.

found in the Accommodating for Inclusive Environments box can easily be incorporated into classroom situations and certainly make the general classroom environment more "friendly" to students with substantial visual limitations (Barraga & Morris, 1992; Harley et al., 1987; Sacks & Kekelis, 1992; Sacks & Reardon, 1992).

Some students with visual disabilities need only minor modifications to succeed in general education classes. Some of these adaptations can help all students gain more from the learning environment and only require some adjustments in teaching style. One such modification is the careful use of language. For example, many of us, when speaking, use words that subsitute for other words, rather than terms that concretely name their referents; we say words like *it, this, that,* and *there* without naming the things we are discussing. For example, an adult might say, "Go get it. It's over there," instead of saying, "Please get the red book on my desk." Adults need to realize how unclear the first set of directions is to many children, particularly those with disabilities. Also, adults need to think about how their written language is indirect and can be made more specific by restating terms they write on the

NEW DIRECTIONS
FOR THE
MILLENNIUM

Legacy: At the end of the twentieth century, very few blind students attended special schools or special programs, resulting in fewer of them mastering braille or developing friendships with people who share common challenges.

Opportunities:

- Make braille instruction more available to students who attend general education programs
- Create opportunities for low vision and blind students who live in the same region to play together, work together, share common interests, become involved in extracurricular activities, and develop friendships

blackboard and also explaining their meanings. Adults are also not always clear about the rules and expectations for school conduct. Without the use of visual cues, it is almost impossible to learn and understand the sometimes subtle distinctions about when a particular behavior is appropriate and when it is not. The process of observing and imitating is incomplete. Therefore, teachers often find it necessary to set the boundaries for acceptable behavior by using explicit instructions, as was described in the Achieving Discipline box. More careful use of language will benefit all members of the class.

All students need to participate actively in the class, should complete assignments independently, and must turn them in at an assigned time. Many blind and low vision students, however, often require more time to complete typical assignments given in general education classes. The teacher can set a different due date, but must enforce this deadline and follow through with contingencies if the assignment is not completed on time. Many teachers find that allowing students to use a computer for in-class assignments and homework is beneficial. Because reading and writing may be physically fatiguing to some students, some teachers suggest making certain exceptions by abbreviating these students' assignments or giving them more time to complete them. Regardless of these accommodations, teachers should not lower their expectations for students with visual disabilities. These students should be encouraged to be full class members who share their work and thoughts with others.

Providing additional structure to both the physical and academic environment can also be helpful. Let us look at the example of Elizabeth, a third grader who is blind. On the first day of school, Mr. Munroe took the time to show Elizabeth the classroom. He made certain that the furniture and materials were in a consistent pattern and placement, but he warned Elizabeth that the classroom would be reorganized periodically. Reorganizing the room every month or so would help Elizabeth learn to adjust to changes in her environment. Other modifications to the classroom's physical space can be important. For example, some of these students use bulky equipment and aids (optical aids, magnifiers, tape recorders) to facilitate their learning. Some use brailling equipment, and others use portable microcomputers. These students need larger desks or a small table near an electrical outlet. They might even need cabinet space to store their belongings.

Many professionals who work with blind and low vision students recommend that teachers use a consistent daily and weekly schedule so that students will know what is expected at various times of the day (math after morning recess) and across the week (spelling tests on Friday). Students need to learn how to manage their study schedule to be sure their work is completed well and on time. The weekly planner shown in Figure 11.2 on page 488 has advantages for many middle and high school students with and without visual disabilities.

Fifty years of experience with inclusion of low vision and blind students has led many parents and professionals to believe that general education placement is not the single answer to questions about how to best meet these students' educational needs. Anne Corn and her colleagues (1995) are advocating for a full array of services for these students, including separate special classes and center or residential schools. Why, after all of these years of inclusion, would there be a call for a change in practice? Many educators are concerned that graduates of general education programs do not possess the skills needed for independence as adults. And, as you will learn in the Transition Through Adulthood section of this chapter, their employment

Date ___1/17___

	MONDAY	√	TUESDAY	√	WEDNESDAY	√	THURSDAY	√	FRIDAY	√	WEEKEND
Tests							English		Science Algebra		To do: Outline English Paper Re-copy History Notes Read Scarlet Letter
Homework/ Papers Due					Algebra Assignment pp 127–130						
Read	Scarlet Letter History Chapter	√ √	Scarlet Letter	√							
Study					for English Test		for Science Test and Algebra				

Figure 11.2 **Weekly Planning Sheet**

rates are dismal. The thought is that for these individuals to achieve adult independence, they need direct instruction in areas that are not part of the typical curriculum, such as social skills, functional life skills, assistive technology, career education, leisure skills, orientation and mobility, and for some, braille. Even model programs of collaboration cannot always address every instructional topic needed for the provision of an appropriate education for an individual student.

The costs, however, of alternative programs are high. When state legislators closed Stevie Wonder's alma mater, the Michigan School for the Blind, they cited costs of about $200,000 per year for each student as the primary reason for its closure (*Albuquerque Journal*, 1995). However, others say even the high costs of residential schools are well worth it for those individuals with intensive needs for instruction in braille, orientation and mobility, and independent living (Spungin, 1997). They argue that without such specialized educational opportunities, some individuals will not be prepared for the challenges they will meet in adult life.

Attending a boarding school during the schoolyear is not the choice of most families of children with severe visual disabilities (Barton, 1997). For these students, their families, and their teachers another type of collaboration is necessary—working with specialists from residential or center schools who deliver **outreach programs** across their state or region, offer short courses and summer programs for both students and their general education teachers. Specialized staff, materials, and equipment enable these schools to provide short courses on mobility and orientation, career education, independent living, and technology instruction not available locally.

outreach programs. Specialized programs offered in local communities by residential schools or centralized agencies serving students with special needs.

TRANSITION THROUGH ADULTHOOD

As was discussed earlier, some young adults with visual disabilities often have a difficult time adjusting to independence and the world of work. They are less experienced in the job world than are many of their sighted peers. Unfortunately, they also seem to be less prepared for adulthood than we might expect. Many of these individuals do not possess the level of literacy necessary to be successful in the community or on the job. Many do not possess other skills (e.g., social interaction, job, self-advocacy) needed to be competitive in the workplace. When such deficiencies are coupled with bias and discrimination, the result is underemployment and a group of individuals not achieving to their capabilities. With education specifically directed toward literacy, career education, and job training, this situation can be corrected.

For discussions of other precollege programs, see these Transitions sections: Chapters 4, 7, 8, and 10.

Transition to Work. Traditionally, employment opportunities have not been very good for blind workers. Their employment rates are even lower than those for many other disability groups (Rumrill & Scheff, 1997). Underemployment or unemployment is commonplace, even in times of record levels of employment and active implementation of the ADA law. Reports that only 40% of clients of the Department of Vocational Rehabilitation are placed in competitive employment persist, and that 79% of blind Americans who want jobs cannot find them, with 30% of those who do, working below their abilities (Associated Press, 1999b). Remember, such statistics reflect employment status, not whether the job held is appropriate for the individual. These unfortunate situations do not have to be the case for people with visual disabilities.

Why are so many blind individuals at a disadvantage in getting good jobs? Possibly, it is partially because their high school years are filled with educational tasks: During high school, many sighted classmates hold jobs after school or during the summer. These sighted peers learn about finding and keeping jobs and also about salaries, wages, and benefits. Students with severe visual disabilities, on the other hand, often spend their summers learning other important skills (such as orientation and mobility) that they need for independence. Unfortunately, not having practical work experience can later put them at a disadvantage in the job market. So, what's the solution to this problem? Internships in real work settings where students get a range of planned experiences may well be one answer (Hanye, 1998). Another may be college graduation. Yet other solutions may be to educate potential employers about the skills and abilities of blind workers and to inform them that the costs of special equipment needed by some is often paid for by state, federal, and private programs (Assoociated Press, 1999b).

Postsecondary education has many benefits for all students but is very important to the increased employability of blind adults. Graduating from college has a significant bearing on a person's career and earning power, but less than half of those with visual disabilities who enter college graduate. Their reasons for leaving college are not usually based on the academic demands, but rather on the difficulties of living independently. Fortunately, the skills needed for successful college life can be taught either before or during college years. The University of Evansville's summer school precollege program teaches students who are blind the mobility, orientation, academic, and life skills needed for college life (Martin, 1999). Here, students learn how to master a college campus, do their own laundry, live in a dormitory, and take notes during lectures. For students who have participated in this twenty-two-year-old program, college is a less frightening and more successful experience. Other options are programs like the College-Success Curriculum, which teach students enrolled in college the skills they need for success (Vancil, 1997). Some of the topics included in this program are: organizational skills, how to hire a reader, gaining access to print material, study skills, being assertive and advocating for oneself, and social skills. Regardless of the method, it is clear that blind and low vision students can improve their chances for success in college and in later life by participating in programs specifically designed to develop skills needed for independence.

Adults with visual disabilities hold jobs at every level. For example, they are scientists, engineers, teachers, office workers, managers of business, and laborers. Unfortunately, despite individual successes and achievements, as a group, people with visual disabilities are generally underemployed. What kind of job can a person with visual disabilities expect? Even for those people with normal intelligence and high school diplomas, individuals with visual disabilities have limited job opportunities that are far below the national average in pay and opportunities for advancement (Kendrick, 1993). Advances in technology, particularly print-to-voice conversions by new equipment, help qualified persons who are blind to have successful careers in a variety of jobs. Unfortunately, many do not work in private industry, but instead hold jobs in sheltered workshops that often do work similar to that done in private industry. Besides offering inferior wages and benefits, these workshops have many disadvantages, among them outdated equipment and techniques. Many of the individuals who work in these settings have the skills needed for work in industry but not the opportunity.

See the Necessity for National Intervention section of Chapter 1 for more information about including people with disabilities in mainstream society.

Fortunately, changes are occurring in law and business. Federal antidiscrimination legislation such as the ADA law forbids discrimination against job applicants with disabilities. Hiring workers with disabilities provides a humanitarian benefit to the individual and an economic benefit to the company. Unfortunately, American society has a long way to go before low vision and blind adults gain access to employment opportunities commensurate with their potential. Although some individuals with severe visual disabilities now have jobs in private industry, employers' attitudes can still be improved so that more qualified people with visual disabilities have an equal opportunity.

Transition to the Community. To better assist their students to make the transition from school to adult life, teachers of students with visual disabilities need to be familiar with a number of different agencies and facts. Particularly at the high school level, teachers of students with visual disabilities should know about the services available to their students after graduation. For example, they need to know how students can become eligible for services from their state's office of vocational rehabilitation.

As we have mentioned, a major problem for people with visual disabilities is their lack of acceptance and the negative attitudes about their disability. These individuals frequently face discrimination in the workplace and in society, and sometimes in the most surprising places. Moira Shea, a blind economist, was a congressional fellow and has worked for the government for over twenty years. In what appeared to be a violation, at least in spirit, of the ADA law, Ms. Shea was denied access to the U.S. Senate chambers during a debate on nuclear waste because some

Karen Chasen Spitzberg creates art for blind people to touch and feel. Some of her work includes reproductions of great masterpieces. This woman is from a Henri de Toulouse-Lautrec painting. Spitzberg's contribution of making art truly accessible to those who can only appreciate art tactilely is unique and important to so many.

senators did not want her to bring her guide dog, Beau, onto the floor (Hebert, 1997). Only a day later, an embarrassed Senate reversed its decision and invited Ms. Shea and Beau onto the Senate floor (Dewar, 1997).

Many adults with visual disabilities feel that their access to recreational, leisure, and cultural activities is also limited. Some positive changes are occurring, however. Cultural events are now more accessible. At concert programs of the New York Philharmonic, the Chamber Music Society, and the Great Performances at Lincoln Center, music programs are available in different versions: braille, large-type, and audiotape. Changed attitudes and the ADA law have brought about other opportunities as well. Not only have museums and entertainment centers become more accessible, but so too have zoos. The San Diego Zoo, and most others, had long-standing bans against guide dogs. These bans existed because many of the wild animals were disturbed by the presence of canines. Now, at least in part, these bans have been discontinued, although some areas of zoos might remain off-limits to guide dogs (McCutcheon, 1994).

MAKING CONNECTIONS

To compare the challenges these families face with those of families of children with different disabilities, see the Family sections in Chapters 3–12.

FAMILIES

No resource is more important to all children than their parents. While teachers are transitory, parents are the major, consistent factor in children's lives. Parents must provide the consistent, sustained, and systematic support their children require.

Family members fill very special roles as they help their children grow up, particularly mothers of children with visual disabilities. Their responsiveness in complying with their children's requests, repeating or rephrasing their communications and facilitating turn-taking, contributes considerably to positive development in expressive and receptive language (Dote-Kwan et al., 1997). Possibly due to their inability to engage in eye contact, important interactions between parent and child that lay the foundations for social interactions, reciprocal language, and affective behaviors are missing in these children's early experiences (Baird et al., 1997). Resolving difficulties in parent–child interactions is critical, and can have lifelong consequences. The importance of early intervention cannot be underestimated.

An important role for family members is to help their blind and low vision children understand that their vision is different from that of others. Erin and Corn (1994) believe that children with visual disabilities must learn that they act on information that is gained differently from seeing people. It is not that their perceptions are faulty but rather are developed through different methods and worked from different sources of information.

As part of understanding their visual differences, these children need to gain knowledge about their visual status, the cause of their vision problem, and the probability of its worsening or improving. Many of the children have great confusion about their disabilities, which is apparent by the kind and content of the questions they ask about their blindness. In one very interesting study, parents were asked to list questions their children had asked about their vision. Among the frequently asked questions were: When would they be able to see? Would they be able to see when they got older? Why did God make them blind? Why could they not see some things (like rainbows)? How do their eyes look? Would anything help them see better? Are they special? Why are they different? What is it like to see? Why did they fail the vision test (Erin & Corn, 1994)?

Sometimes a blind child can overtax a family's resources, both emotional and financial. When this occurs, the family will likely experience stress because family relations are tense or disrupted (Nixon, 1994); the demands on the family are in excess of their available resources. In such situations, many members of the family unit, including the person with the disability, may feel deprived of necessary social support and the family may begin to break apart. Parents and siblings of any child with a disability are at risk for emotional difficulties if their support systems or coping skills are inadequate. An insufficient support system or poor coping skills can affect the child with special needs, too. For example, parents often report a feeling of helplessness. Families must learn to cope with stress, and sometimes this requires outside help, which may be difficult for some family members to accept. In some cases, support from school personnel is helpful. In other cases, support groups of families who also have a blind child meet to share experiences and information and to provide each other with assistance. For some, professional help from counselors or therapists is necessary. Educators can furnish an important service by guiding parents to the best support system to meet their needs.

Throughout this text you have learned that disabilities affect not only the individuals but also their entire families. As Nixon (1994) so aptly put it, "coping with impairment is a shared experience" (p. 329). Educators must understand that many of their students have strong extended families, families where their network of social roles, relationships, and shared commitments bind them together. It is important to recognize that working with the student's parents in these situations means honoring and involving the entire extended family unit. There is great strength to draw from in such situations. Let's think of Ramon and his family. All of Ramon's relatives share their human and financial resources to meet his needs. Ramon's teacher wants him to transfer some of the skills he has learned at school by playing new, more complex games at home. To be successful, she must teach brothers, sisters, cousins, aunts, uncles, grandfathers, and grandmothers, in addition to his parents, how to play the game, for Ramon is the shared responsibility of everybody in the Garcia family. In the culture of the Garcia family, individuals gain strength from the family unit, and it is the family, not just his mother and father, that must be involved in Ramon's educational program. Educators must come to understand that various cultures have different expectations of family units and that some extended family units expect to be involved in the child's education program.

The targets for parents to address with their children are many, particularly for children with severe visual disabilities. These parents must help their children develop many skills across a range of areas: communication, independent living, mobility, sensory development, fine and gross motor skills, cognition, and social skills. Parents also find themselves in a variety of roles. For example, they should provide the support system and continuity needed in their child's life. They are advocates, teachers, and nurturers. Usually, it is for them to provide the most normalized experiences for their children, for they are the ultimate managers of the child's growth and development.

TECHNOLOGY

To compare different types of technology supports across students with special needs, read the technology sections in Chapters 3–12.

Many advances that the general population uses and enjoys have provided great benefits for people with visual disabilities, such as the telephone, developed by Alexander Graham Bell in 1876, and the phonograph, invented by Thomas Edison in 1877. The first radio broadcast occurred in 1906 in the United States and marked access to both entertainment and information for people with visual disabilities. There are many other examples of how items popular with the general population increase access to mainstream society for people with visual disabilities (e.g., large-print books, computerized versions of popular novels, audiotapes of texts). However, it is only their general popularity that makes the price reasonable, allows for mass production, and promotes widespread availability.

For many years, people with visual disabilities have used various kinds of technologies to help them learn and function in society. For example, they have used various types of canes, some electronic, to assist in orientation and mobility. Advances in microcomputer technology provide access to printed information. Because of the popularity of the personal computer, books are now available on computer disks. These electronic books, which may soon be as abundant as conventional books, allow the reader, using a laptop computer, to increase the size of print or to switch from print to voice easily. Many even incorporate animation and a wide variety of graphics, such as maps and diagrams.

Increasingly, people with visual disabilities are gaining access to technology and the assistive devices designed to minimize the effects of their disabilities. Although each of these advances adds to the household budget, the diversity of items is remarkable. For example, talking watches, clocks, calculators, food scales, and machines that tell you the denomination of paper money are now plentiful. Also, braille and enlarged-type versions of games can be purchased for about the same price as games without special adaptations. For example, two large-print decks of colorful playing cards can be purchased for $8.95 (Lighthouse, 1999). Special sets of checkers, chess, Scrabble, poker chips, and many other game items are easy to locate.

These exciting technological advances open up a new world for people with severe visual disabilities. Clearly, these advances give them greater participation and independence in all aspects of modern society. However, two major barriers inhibit access to the broad array of assistive technology available: cost and information. With the average costs of devices ranging from $1,000 to $10,000 and the vast number of options available, careful selection of the right equipment is important. Cost is probably a crucial factor in this situation, and professionals need to seek new avenues for financial assistance to help people acquire the devices. As we have noted, technology affects many aspects of life (reading, mobility) for persons with visual disabilities. These systems use different means of input: visual, auditory, and tactile.

VISUAL AIDS

Closed-circuit television (CCTV) is used to enlarge the print found in printed texts and books. By using a small television camera with a zoom lens and a sliding reading stand on which the printed materials are placed, greatly enlarged printed material can be viewed on a television monitor (up to 60 times the original size). Such equipment provides immediate access to all types of printed materials such as magazines, textbooks, and mimeographed or photocopied handouts. A wide range of CCTVs now exist at more reasonable cost, starting at under $500 but averaging at about $2500, still out of reach of many blind and low vision individuals. One version, the Magni-Cam, uses a handheld camera the size and shape of a large computer mouse that has rollers on the bottom to help track horizontally over a flat surface, and can hook up to a TV set. It costs about $700 (Lighthouse, 1999).

Equipment other than CCTVs can also increase print size. For example, overhead projectors, although not useful to most individuals with low vision, can be used to enlarge printed materials. Microcomputers using special word processing programs can produce large-print displays that allow persons with low vision to adjust the size of print to match their own visual efficiencies. Some programs display print on the microcomputer screen at various sizes, allowing the user to select the type size and style that gives the best readability. In addition, most microcomputers allow the user to select different sizes of print for hard-copy printout or visual display on the monitor, and standard copy machines can now also adjust print size as well. Also, teachers who prepare handouts on a microcomputer can prepare the same material in different-size prints for their students with visual disabilities and their sighted students while still covering the same material.

AUDIO AIDS

Audio aids allow persons with visual disabilities to hear what others can read. **Talking books** have been available through the Library of Congress since 1934, and specially designed record players, tape and compact disc (CD) machines that allow for com-

closed-circuit television (CCTV). A television used for transmissions not accessible to the general public; sometimes, only one camera and television monitor is used.

talking books. Books available in auditory format.

The Kurzweil reader provides immediate access to print for people who cannot read because the machine actually does print-to-voice translations that avoids the need for personal readers or long waiting periods for a resource center to produce a braille version of text.

MAKING CONNECTIONS

The Kurzweil Reader is also discussed in the History section of this chapter.

pressed speech (eliminating natural pauses and accelerating speech) have been developed by the American Printing House for the Blind. A substantial amount of material is available in these forms, but usually it must be ordered from either a regional resource and materials center or a national center. Audiotape versions of many classics and current best-sellers are now available in most bookstores. Although these audiotapes were developed for sale to the general public, they allow greater access to current books for people with visual disabilities.

The Kurzweil 1000, a Stevie Wonder Vision Awards "1998 Product of the Year," changes printed material into synthesized speech. This new reading machine is vastly improved over its 1970s predecessor, which was large, cumbersome, very expensive, unable to recognize all words, and difficult to understand. The Kurzweil 1000 is a personal computer as well as a convenient and quick desktop reading system that turns print into speech or print into braille. The listener can select the rate of speech (how fast it is delivered), the pitch, and the gender of the voice-sound the computer generates. This system has many advantages for individuals who cannot read print. Students can use the same books and materials as their sighted classmates; they are not dependent on the availability of braille or audiotaped materials at a regional materials center. Users of this system also do not have to order special materials or wait for their delivery. Even those who are able to read print benefit from this system. Those who need to use enlarged type do not have to wait for special versions to be prepared. Cost is becoming less of a barrier to accessing this type of equipment.

Although still out of reach for many individuals, the cost of a desktop reading system has dropped dramatically. Only a few years ago the price was between $7,000 and $9,000, and now one can be purchased for a little more than $1,000.

An exciting recent development, **audiodescription,** allows people with severe visual disabilities to better participate in American life and entertainment. Their ability to enjoy plays, movies, television, and home videos is also limited. However, with audiodescription, they hear a narration of the visual cues and nonverbal information presented on the screen or stage. This system, initially developed for television by Margaret Pfanstiehl, uses the added sound track available in stereo televisions to describe aspects (costumes, scenes, sets, body language) important to a fuller understanding of the story. A similar system has been devised for theaters; it uses an earphone and a tiny FM receiver. The explanations occur in the pauses or otherwise silent parts of the film or play. Audiodescriptions are available for movie videos and some public television shows (DVS, 1999).

TACTILE AIDS

As you know, some persons who are blind use braille as their preferred reading method. The Perkins Brailler is a compact and portable machine that uses keys that, when pressed down, emboss special paper with the braille code. It is inexpensive but not as efficient as newer electronic versions that use microprocessors to store and retrieve information. For example, Braille 'n Speak functions as an organizer, note taker, calendar, and talking clock; it costs about $1,500 (Blazie Engineering, 1999). Also, microcomputer systems, even those designed for sighted users, can support various types of braille and can even be networked so that many people can use the braille adaptation simultaneously. As with audiocassettes and talking books, a wealth of materials are available in braille.

Access to braille versions of text is becoming less of a challenge. For example, the Xerox/Kurzweil desktop reading system, discussed earlier, can also scan printed materials and produce a braille version of the text. A braille version of a telephone credit card is available; it stores the user's access number so that he or she can charge the toll and call on any phone. Most major appliance companies now provide braille options for their equipment. For example, GE and Hotpoint provide free braille panels for their ovens, refrigerators, and laundry equipment. Whirlpool also offers braille instructional manuals or audiocassettes to accompany its equipment. Finally, personal computers with special printers transform print to braille. When a specially designed braille printer is attached to a microcomputer, standard text can be translated into braille, allowing a teacher who does not know how to use braille to produce braille copies of handouts, tests, maps, charts, and other class materials. And some new printers, such as the ones made by American Thermoform, can produce braille and print on the same page. Some of these printers cost less than $3,000.

Another limitation of braille versions of text is also now eliminated. Only a few years ago, diagrams and illustrations were omitted from braille versions because of the inability of technology to produce them easily. Today, a new system, Tactile Assess to Education for Visually Impaired Students (TAEVIS), uses a special type of paper, backed with plastic and coated with a heat-sensitive chemical, to produce raised versions of diagrams (*Tennessean*, 1999). Clearly, technology continues to improve access to the world of print for individuals with visual disabilities.

audiodescription. A technique in which trained narrators describe visual and non-verbal information during the pauses in the audio or scripted dialogue of plays, films, and television shows by using FM transmissions or the extra sound track available on stereo televisions.

For other discussions of braille literacy, see these sections in this chapter:

- Methods of Reading and Writing (Low Vision and Blind Children)
- Literacy (Educational Interventions)

CONCEPTS AND CONTROVERSY: IS LITERACY NECESSARY IN THE TWENTY-FIRST CENTURY?

Increasing America's rate of literacy has become a national goal. The federal government has articulated the importance of literacy for the nation in its Goals 2000 document (U.S. Department of Education, 1994) and in the President's 1997 State of the Union address. The declining literacy rate of individuals with severe visual disabilities has become the focus of a national, emotionally charged debate. According to the American Printing House for the Blind (1992), 27% of students who are blind are visual readers and 10% use braille. It is estimated that 10% are auditory readers (primarily using personal readers or recorded materials) and that the remainder is nonliterate. Some estimate that in the last forty years the percentage of blind people who can read and write braille has dropped from 50% to 9% (Schoellkopf, 1995). Judith Heumann, the U.S. Department of Education's assistant secretary for Special Education and Rehabilitative Services, said that data "show that over 90% of working blind people use braille in the performance of their jobs," which led her to conclude that braille literacy is important for blind students (Briand, 1994, p. 6).

Many factors have contributed to the decline in the use of braille by people who are blind or who have low vision. First, less that half (46%) of teachers of students with visual disabilities feel competent in their ability to teach in braille, despite their own proficiency using this reading skill (76%), positive attitudes about braille as a means of reading, and belief that braille should be the primary literacy medium of blind people (Wittenstein, 1994). Second, the availability of teachers of low vision and blind students is limited. In some parts of this country itinerant teachers have caseloads consisting of over fifty students (Corn et al., 1994). Third, there seems to be a growing reliance on audio versions for gaining information from printed materials (audiocassettes, talking books, print-to-voice technology). Fourth, there is an educational philosophy that students with visual disabilities should use their residual vision as much as possible, including reading print. Fifth, there exists a growing number of blind students with multiple impairments who are less able to master either braille or print-based reading skills.

Consider the changes in technology and in American society. Is it necessary to be able to read and write using print? And will it be in the new millennium? Directions for appliances come on videotape. Most people use the telephone instead of writing letters. The technology that converts print to voice and voice to print is now available and will soon be affordable, portable, and commonplace. All Americans will have access to this technology. So will print become outmoded? Can years of instructional time be justified for those who cannot master the skill easily and quickly? Will reading become as obsolete as teaching Greek and Latin? As you think about literacy for those with visual disabilities, broaden your thinking to the entire population.

Why is this national conversation about literacy and the use of braille by blind people so emotional? Of course, one factor is the great concern about the declining literacy rate among people with visual disabilities. Will widespread inability to read print among this group bring them more discrimination and bias? Many of the strongest supporters of braille literacy are blind adults (Augusto, 1993; Schroeder, 1993) who consider braille as a symbol that could unite blind people, as sign language has bonded the Deaf community. Is that reason enough to support the braille literacy movement?

In Conclusion

C O N N E C T I O N S
MAKING

Look again at the Advance Organizers at the beginning of the chapter; to help you study the chapter's content, the answers to the Focus and Challenge questions are found here. Test yourself to see if you have mastered the major points of this chapter.

Summary

For most of us, the primary way we learn is through vision. Often, in the process of learning a new skill, we are shown how to do the task. We observe the actions of others and imitate their behaviors. We gain information by watching television or reading a newspaper, book, or magazine. People with visual disabilities have a restricted ability to use their sight, and that can affect how they function as independent adults. For schoolchildren, visual disabilities is one of the smallest special education categories. The incidence of visual disabilities increases with age: the older a person, the higher the likelihood of that person having some visual impairment. Although these students have been successfully included in general education for many years, they do not find integration the norm when they are adults. Many have not found competitive employment but, rather, work in sheltered workshops. They are not included in the mainstream of American society. In fact, stereotypes and old traditions impede their participation in normal activities as adults. Most clearly, this area will require the concerted efforts of adults with this disability, their families, and their advocates. With changed attitudes, this group will participate more fully in society and take their places alongside sighted people.

Focus Questions

Self-Test Questions

- *How is the category of visual disabilities divided into two subgroups?*

  Individuals with visual disabilities comprise two general groups: those who are blind and those who have low vision. These distinctions relate to the severity of the disability or the amount of functional use of sight an individual has. Another way to divide the category of visual disabilities is by age of onset, when the disability occurred. Those who are congenitally blind have been blind since birth or infancy, while those who are adventitiously blind became profoundly visually impaired sometime after the age of 2. This latter group comprises persons who usually remember what things in their environment look like; these mental images can influence how well they learn about concepts during their school years.

- *What are the major causes of visual disabilities, and what preventive measures protect children from this disability?*

  Many different conditions or situations can cause blindness. Worldwide, the vast majority of cases are caused by poor nutrition or infections and could have been prevented. In the United States, the most common causes are factors related to increasing age. For American children, heredity and accidents are the most frequently cited causes for those who are blind and have a single disability. However, more than half of children with visual disabilities have another disability as well, often placing them in the multiple disabilities category.

- *What are some ways the learning environment can be modified to accommodate students with visual disabilities?*

  The learning environment can be modified and adjusted in many ways to optimize the integration and learning opportunities for low vision and blind students. Some commonsense teaching strategies (using advance organizers, orally summarizing printed information, providing handouts of lectures) often prove to be the most useful. Students should be allowed to position themselves in the best place for them to gain as much as possible from each instructional activity. Sometimes this will be close to the chalkboard, other times away from the glare of an unshaded window. The students must assess their visual efficiencies for each situation. All dangerous obstacles and hazards need to be eliminated, and a consistent organization of both the physical and instructional environments are of great benefit. Teachers must encourage students to participate, let them know what is expected and the consequences when they break the rules (even the subtle ones), have high expectations, and consult with an expert when they need assistance.

- *Why must orientation and mobility be long-term curriculum targets for many low vision and most blind students, and what specific skills must be included?*

  One of the greatest difficulties for blind adults is living independently. Those who are successful are able to move independently to maintain a household, take care of themselves, use transportation necessary to get to and from work, and be independently mobile in the workplace. The development of these orientation and mobility skills takes years of instruction and practice. This is true whether the individual uses a long cane or a guide dog. Although the ADA law will eventually help blind and low vision people by removing the physical hazards in the environment, many challenges will remain: escalators, elevators, public transportation, orientation to new places, use of maps. Participation in sports and leisure activities is important to everyone, and those with severe visual disabilities should participate as well. Although the opportunities through special sports programs are increasing, actual instruction in sports and recreation activities needs to become a consistent instructional topic for these individuals.

- *What technological advances can assist people with visual disabilities at school, in the workplace, and in independent living?*

  Advances and developments in technology have and will continue to change the lives of all Americans, particularly those with disabilities. With the availability and relatively low price of personal computers, persons with severe visual disabilities will use technology based machines to assist them when they need to read and write. Whether their preferred mode is enlarged print, braille, or listening, computers can provide immediate access to all printed documents. Other technologies are beneficial to blind and low vision people. They can be organized into three groups: visual aids, audio aids, and tactile aids. These devices improve independent living opportunities (enlarged print displays, talking watches and clocks, labels for household appliances) and enhance participation in recreational and leisure-time activities (large-print newspapers, audiodescriptions, tactile maps to enjoy museums and national parks).

Challenge Question

- *Why has braille literacy become such an emotionally charged debate, and how do you think it should be resolved?*

Resources to extend your learning about people with disabilities are found at the end of every chapter; a fuller listing is available in the Students' Resource Manual that accompanies this text.

The great majority of persons with visual disabilities use sight to learn and gain information. Although most read print, some require that the print be enlarged. A small number read and write using braille, a system of raised dot codes that requires considerable training and practice to become proficient in its use. For students with substantial cognitive disabilities and visual disabilities, it may not be a skill that can be mastered. At the center of an emotionally charged debate is whether literacy should be a goal for these students. Until the passage of many "braille bills" across the country, instruction in braille was not available to all students who attended their local public school because of the unavailability of teachers proficient in braille instruction. Those states that have passed braille bills now have an option for inclusion on the child's IEP. As with most services in special education, this debate will probably be resolved by encouraging that decisions about braille instruction be made on an individual basis.

Supplementary Resources

Scholarly Reading

Barraga, N. C., & Erin, J. N. (1992). *Visual handicaps and learning* (3rd ed.). Austin, TX: Pro-Ed.

Heller, K. W., Alberto, P. A., Forney, P. E., & Schwartzman, M. N. (1996). *Understanding physical, sensory, and health impairments.* Pacific Grove, CA: Brooks/Cole.

Wilson, J. (1995). *Biography of the blind: Including the lives of all who have distinguished themselves as poets, philosophers, artists, &c., &c.* Washington, DC: Library of Congress.

Popular Books

Hine, R. V. (1993). *Second sight.* Berkeley: University of California Press.

Hull, J. M. (1990). *Touching the rock.* NY: Pantheon Books.

Keller, H. (1988). *The story of my life.* NY: Sig Classics.

Kuusisto, S. (1998). *Planet of the blind.* NY: Dial Press.

Mehta, V. (1989). *The stolen light.* NY: Norton.

Videos and DVDs

The miracle worker (1962). United Artists.
Places in the heart (1984). Tri-Star Pictures.
Sneakers (1991). Universal Pictures.
Scent of a woman (1992). Universal/MCA.
Jennifer 8 (1992). Paramount.

Professional, Parent, and Consumer Organizations and Agencies

American Foundation for the Blind
11 Penn Plaza, Suite 300
New York, NY 10001
Phone: (800) 232-5463; (212) 502-7657
E-mail: afbinfo@afb.org
Web sitre: www.afb.org

Division of the Blind and Visually Impaired, Rehabilitation Services Administration
U.S. Department of Education
Office of Special Education and Rehabilitation Services
330 C Street SW
Washington, DC 20202
Phone: (202) 401-3000
E-mail: chet_avery@ed.gov
Web site: www.ed.gov/offices/osers

American Printing House for the Blind
P.O. Box 6085
1839 Frankfort Avenue
Louisville, KY 40206
Phone: (800) 223-1839; (502) 899-2274
Web site: http://www.aph.org

National Federation of the Blind
1800 Johnson Street
Baltimore, MD 21230
Phone: (410) 659-9314
E-mail: nfb@access.digex.net
Web site: www.nfb.org

Division for the Visual Impairments Council for Exceptional Children
1920 Association Drive
Reston, VA 22091
Phone: (888) CEC-SPED
Web site: www.cec.sped.org

Prevent Blindness America
500 E. Remington Road
Shaumberg, IL 60173-5611
Phone: (800) 331-2020
Web site: http://www.prevent-blindness.org

MAKING CONNECTIONS

For Web links to support your study of disabilities, look at the Resources sections at the end of every chapter in this text; a fuller listing is found in the Students' Resource Manual that accompanies this text.

Stephen Wiltshire is an artist with autism. He was mute as a child, and at age 5 he began to communicate by drawing on scraps of paper. He now talks with reporters and others who want to interview him about his work. Wiltshire lives in England, but has made a number of trips to America. These trips gained him much publicity in America and stimulated his "American Dream" series of art. He uses his visual memory to remember scenes he wants to sketch later. Very seldom does he sketch or paint while he is actually seeing the image for the first time. Most of his early work was done with pen and ink, but he has recently completed art school, where he learned the techniques of using color and paint.

The drawing here is of St. John's Church at the top of Ladbroke Grove in the Notting Hill section of London. The Gothic revival style church was designed and built in 1844 by the well-known architects, J. H. Stevens and G. Alexander.

Stephen Wiltshire, *St. John's, Notting Hill.* © Stephen Wiltshire. Reprinted by permission of the artist.

C H A P T E R **12**

A Family's Continuing Search for the Right Program, or An American Mom in Paris Arranging the Best from Both Worlds

Leslie Palanker, an American who went to Paris on a sojourn from college, met the man who is now her husband and made a life for herself in France. She has two sons, Joey, a precocious 11-year-old who was bilingual by the age of 3, and Luke, who is 8 and autistic. Leslie shares their story, one that is still unfolding. Their experiences can help us understand how confusing it can be for parents who are trying to sort through education and social service systems to arrange for the right services for their children.

Luke's story is like the story heard from many families with autistic children. It starts with a child who seems too fussy, too agitated. Then there is the woman who runs the play group, who suggests having his hearing tested. Then there are the visits to the ear, nose, and throat doctor, with a subsequent (now questionable) operation. And then there are the visits to various child psychiatrists with their requisite archaic attitudes shrouded in Freud or various other psychological theories. The search for answers to questions about Luke's development wasn't leading us anywhere that seemed useful, but our luck changed on a summer visit to America. My father arranged for Luke to be tested though the local public schools. We were now equipped with a label and vocabulary to associate with Luke's problems. We went back to France, and began our search for an educational program in earnest.

With the help of a speech therapist/psychologist from one of the major children's hospitals in Paris, we arranged for Luke to see a psychologist twice a week. Also,

Autism, Deaf-Blindness, and Traumatic Brain Injury: Low Incidence Disabilities

once a week he went to a pre-speech rhythmic class at the hospital, and we also found a bilingual private school that agreed to accept Luke if he were accompanied by a helper. And probably the most important thing was that we all learned how to spend time together in a happier fashion. We continued this system for two years and Luke progressed considerably. Although he still did not express himself verbally, he enjoyed his family, we enjoyed him, and he was generally more manageable.

But as time goes on, needs change; and we looked again for a placement where Luke would continue to grow and develop. We chose, partly because we couldn't find something else, a private school for children with learning difficulties. But within a month of the beginning of the school year, we realized that this school was not adapted for Luke. Having Luke at home by himself at 5½ years old was unthinkable. Every school was full (France's mandatory school law doesn't include children under age 6), and we found that the need for educational places for children like Luke far surpasses the availability. I spent most of that fall calling around and visiting different people and schools, always hoping that I might convince an establishment to take Luke. It was at this time that it became clear that there are very different schools of thought about autism and what makes for an effective program. The psychiatrists analyze and observe. Many people are fervent believers in the TEAACH program. And it goes on. Again, no one answer to our complicated problems. I also discovered the tremendous diversity in special education schools (or day hospitals, as they are called in France).

Our searching provided us with good fortune. We found a speech therapist/teacher who has helped Luke learn to read, write, and do first-grade mathematics. She taught him to sit and do schoolwork for an hour at a time. Then a day hospital (special education school), provided by the national health care system, had an opening. That was two years ago! Our own system of combining public and private services worked well for Luke and for us. His teachers at school and his speech therapist communicate, coordinate, and collaborate about their activities with Luke, something that is rare in France. The special school also provides swimming once a week and a pony club (now that's not usual in America!).

My son grows constantly. We've recently scheduled weekly sessions with a male psychiatrist, to clearly change from the female psychologist who had worked with Luke for years. And, we've seen differences at home. Luke is now more willingly to stay in his bed at night. Recently, he played mini-golf with his brother, Joey, and his friends. His language is clearer, as is his sense of camaraderie and humor. Our most recent shift at home is to speak only French—a major change from our usual bilingualism. Maybe Luke's resistance to speak in any language is linked to the privileged place English has in our household. With Luke's communication problems, it appears that using two languages is confusing to him, and it certainly does cause him a lot of distress. And so our efforts continue, both for Luke and for us. We continue to modify and evolve to help our son become as independent and as happy as possible as he grows up.

1. Could Leslie's experience be repeated here in the United States?

2. What do think is in store for Leslie, Luke, and their family?

Advance Organizers

MAKING CONNECTIONS

Use the learning strategy—Advance Organizers—to help focus your study of this chapter's content, and reinforce your learning by reviewing answers to the Focus and Challenge questions at the end of the chapter.

Overview

Three special education categories can be referred to as very low incidence areas: autism, deaf–blindness, and traumatic brain injury. Children with autism present a complex array of excessive behaviors, an inability to develop relationships, complex speech and language problems, and insistence on sameness. Children with deaf–blindness have very special learning needs because of their dual disabilities. The vast majority of members from both groups also have mental retardation. Children with traumatic brain injury (TBI) possess a range of cognitive and behavior problems, which for some are lifelong and for others only temporary. Many children with these disabilities have very severe problems and require comprehensive, well-coordinated, specialized services.

Focus Questions

Self-Test Questions

- What are the major characteristics of children with autism?
- How would you describe the impact of deaf–blindness on those affected?
- What additional disabilities do children with autism and children with deaf–blindness often possess?
- How can many cases of TBI be prevented?
- How are functional assessments and the development of functionally equivalent behaviors used together?

Challenge Question

- What comprises an appropriate education and the least restrictive environment for students with low incidence disabilities?

This chapter includes information about three very different disabilities: autism, deaf–blindness, and traumatic brain injury. Each is a separate special education category recognized in IDEA '97. One characteristic shared by these three disabilities is their low incidence: They are not very common. It is likely that most educators will not teach many youngsters with these conditions during their careers, in part because of the nature of these disabilities and their relatively low prevalence. Just like other disabilities, these conditions can range in degree from mild to severe. However, most typically, children with these disabilities require substantial and intensive special education services and support. The problems their disabilities present are typically complex and extremely serious.

You will notice that the organization of this chapter is somewhat different from the chapters that focus on only one special education area. There are separate sections for each of the three disabilities, followed by combined discussions of educational interventions, families, and technology.

Opportunities for the New Millennium

Confusion has surrounded people with low incidence disabilities since the beginning of time. Their proper place in society has often been denied them, and questions of how to best educate them so they can achieve their potential continue into this millennium. The challenges they present to themselves, their families, and society are great; these challenges must be met through sustained research and humane consideration.

Legacies from the Twentieth Century
During the latter part of the twentieth century, special attention was given to very low incidence disabilities. Two in particular were designated as separate special education categories. Perhaps the federal government's rationale for this action was to be certain that special attention would be given these individuals who meet the criterion for such identification. The complex problems they present, however, have no simple solutions. Perhaps it is for the medical community to better identify the causes and provide solutions to some of the problems faced by people with these disabilities. For those whose problems can no longer be prevented, it is for the education community to determine through rigorous research how good outcomes can best be achieved.

Thinking About Dilemmas to Solve
As you read this chapter, ponder these students' needs, the supports they require, and the outcomes they should achieve. Think about:

- How their educational needs can best be met
- How they can achieve goals of independent living and full participation in the community
- What supports they require during their schoolyears
- How the curriculum can best provide them with the skills they need
- What technological supports will facilitate their ultimate independence

Autism

autism. A severe disorder of thinking, communication, interpersonal relationships, and behavior.

Although **autism** has probably always been part of the human condition, its discrete identification is recent. Leo Kanner is credited with first coining the term and describing the condition in 1943 (Kanner, 1943). His goal was to separate what he thought was an exceptionally rare condition from the more global classification of childhood psychosis. Autism, as a separate condition, has gained considerable attention across the years. In 1965, Bernard Rimland, a psychologist who has devoted his career to the study of autism and is also a parent of a child with this disability, joined with other parents to form the National Society for Autistic Children (now called the

Children with autism are often excluded from social interactions with peers.

Autism Society of America). This major advocacy group, assisted by the data collected by the Autism Research Institute which was started in 1967, was able in the 1990 reauthorization of IDEA to gain independent classification status for autism. Before that time, autism was included in other special education categories, like mental retardation, physical disabilities, and emotional disturbance. Some professionals still believe that autism should be considered a subgroup of emotional disturbance and behavior disorders (Kauffman, 1997), while others argue that it should be reconceptualized (Attwood, 1998; Myles & Simpson, 1998). Despite these positions, IDEA '97 continues to recognize autism as a separate special education category.

Since autism was first identified, it has been surrounded by considerable confusion and misunderstanding. Let's see whether we can come to an understanding of autism, the nature of this disability, and how it affects these individuals and their families.

AUTISM DEFINED

MAKING CONNECTIONS

For more about autism, see the Autism section of this chapter.

When Kanner originally identified autism, he believed that the condition had two primary symptoms: extreme isolation present from the first years of life, and excessive insistence on preserving "sameness" (Rimland, 1964). Today, many parents and professionals seek to broaden the definition of autism to include children who experience onset of the symptoms often associated with autism later in life, who do not possess all of the symptoms described by Kanner, or who do not experience severe forms of the symptoms. Let's look at two different definitions of autism. Think about who would be included when using each definition and what different curriculum targets teachers must address when different definitions are applied.

According to IDEA '97, autism means:

> A developmental disability significantly affecting verbal and nonverbal communication and social interaction, generally evident before age 3, that adversely affects a child's performance. Other characteristics often associated with autism are engagement in repetitive activities and stereotyped movements, resistance to environmental change or change in daily routines, and unusual responses to sensory experiences. The term does not apply if a child's educational performance is adversely affected primarily because the child has a serious emotional disturbance. (U.S. Department of Education, 1999, p. 12421)

The Autism Society of America defines autism in this way:

> Autism is a developmental disability that typically appears during the first three years of life. The result of a neurological disorder that affects functioning of the brain ... autism impacts the normal development of the brain in the areas of social interaction and communication skills. Children and adults with autism typically have difficulties in verbal and non-verbal communication, social interactions and leisure or play activities. The disorder makes it hard for them to communicate with others and relate to the outside world. They may exhibit repeated body movements (hand flapping, rocking), unusual responses to people or attachments to objects and resist any changes in routines. In some cases, aggressive and/or self-injurious behavior may be present. (Autism Society of America, 1999, p. 1)

Autism is a very serious disability. Great strides are being made in the development of effective teaching strategies that positively change these individuals' patterns of isolation, inability to initiate or sustain meaningful social interchanges, and lack of functional language development. However, more research is needed to better understand this disability and to develop best practices and effective treatment procedures. The outcome for most of these individuals is not good and their ability to function as independent adults is extremely limited. However, as more is learned about the causes of this disability, ways to prevent its occurrence and to reduce its impact are being identified.

TYPES OF AUTISM

autism spectrum. A group of disorders or conditions which share some characteristics and behaviors originally described under the classification of autism.

Asperger syndrome. A little understood disability that shares many symptoms with autism, though in most cases cognitive abilities are average.

Because not all individuals with autism manifest exactly the same or similar characteristics with the same intensity, researchers have been searching for ways to subgroup autism (Sturmey & Sevin, 1994). A number of different dimensions have been explored for subgrouping or even redefining this condition (Attwood, 1998; Myles & Simpson, 1998). For example, some have proposed that different subgroups be created according to level of intellectual functioning, the time of the condition's onset, or the number and severity of the symptoms. As the definition of autism becomes broader, different conditions have been included in the **autism spectrum.** Let's look at one of the most common of the disorders included in this spectrum.

As diagnostic procedures become more and more sophisticated, more unique conditions are being recognized. **Asperger syndrome,** though first identified in the 1940s by Hans Asperger, is an example of a condition that is being identified more often today (Myles & Simpson, 1998). Debate continues about whether Asperger syndrome should be included as part of the autism category or whether it should be considered as a separate disabling condition. (Asperger syndrome is not included in the 1994 *DSM-IV* definition of autism.) Autism and Asperger syndrome share many characteristics like repetitive and stereotypic motor movements, but differ in lan-

Legacy: Experts in the field of autism continue to debate about how restrictive the definition of autism should be and which individuals should be included in this category.

Opportunities:
- Study the impact on schools and the individuals involved as the definition broadens
- Parents, professionals, and state and government officials should decide who should be included in this category

guage and cognitive abilities (Attwood, 1998). Whether Asperger syndrome is the high dimension of the autism spectrum of disabilities or a separate category is probably not as important as it is to recognize that individuals with Asperger syndrome tend to have greater abilities than those who fit the more traditional descriptions of those with autism.

Individuals with Asperger syndrome demonstrate significant impairments in their social interactions with others. Even though they might approach others, they are unable to automatically understand nonverbal cues or the rules of social behavior, maintain eye contact, display socially unacceptable responses, or reciprocate. Their ability to develop language, however, sets them apart from most individuals with autism. Their language development tends to be late; they speak fluently by the age of 5. Their pragmatic language skills tend to remain impaired, particularly when you think about the language needed for effective social interactions. Also, these individuals' cognitive skills can be puzzling. Though their intellectual abilities are often considered average, they have difficulties with some types of thinking skills needed to solve problems, organize information, generalize learning, or discriminate relevant from irrelevant cues.

Probably because of their almost bizarre inconsistencies in ability (being unable to initiate or maintain a conversation yet remembering trivia), people tend to focus considerable attention on **autistic savants.** Remember that this subgroup of individuals with autism is very small, possibly comprising only 5% of those with autism (Begley & Springen, 1996). Needless to say, their abilities and talents are unusual. Some, like the character Raymond in the film *Rain Man,* can instantly count the number of wooden matches that have fallen on the floor, remember the dates and day of the week of important events, or recall the numbers of all of the winning lottery tickets for the past year. Nine-year-old Alex Mont can solve

Alex Mont has unusual mathematical abilities, excelling far beyond even many of his gifted peers. However, like many autistic savants, his abilities are not uniform.

autistic savant. An individual who displays many behaviors associated with autism, yet also possesses discrete abilities and unusual talents.

complicated mathematics problems, even calculus, but has difficulties comprehending social cues. He could not distinguish a horse from a cow until after finishing kindergarten (Levine, 1997). Some have outstanding musical or artistic abilities. Such splinter skills can be fascinating to the observer, but they are rarely functional for the individual.

IDENTIFICATION

One of the first assessment devices used to identify children with autism was a checklist. Developed by Rimland, it is based on Kanner's original definition of the condition (Rimland, 1964). Since that time, many different identification procedures have been developed. Some use checklists, like the *Autism Behavior Checklist (ABC)*, that are easy to use even by untrained people (Krug et al., 1980), while others prefer rating scales, like the *Childhood Autism Rating Scale (CARS)*, that use data gathered from behavioral observations completed by trained observers.

Remember, in most cases of autism the symptoms are so definitive and unique that the diagnosis is obvious to most professionals who specialize in this area. Today, many advocate the use of behavioral or functional assessments. Under this system, which Robert Horner and George Sugai describe in the Research to Practice box, each individual is considered unique, a person whose biological capacities, learning history, and present environment combine to create a set of strengths, behavioral deficits, and special needs. Educators and specialists must grapple with questions such as "When does this maladaptive behavior occur?" "What environmental events may bear upon the expression of that symptom?" and "How can contextual events be manipulated to enable this client to function more effectively?" (Harris et al., 1994, p. 127). Such functional assessments are beneficial in that they identify individuals with autism and provide guidance during design of the treatment program. When functional assessments are conducted in the child's natural (home and school) environments, variables that predict and maintain the problem behavior become apparent (Horner & Carr, 1997). This knowledge can be used to prevent future occurrences of the problem behavior and also to develop effective ways to respond to it when it does occur. This helps teachers understand how to reshape the environment, develop **behavioral support** to reduce the frequency of the inappropriate behaviors, and assist the child in developing more **functionally equivalent behaviors** instead (Koegel et al., 1995).

Unfortunately, most children with autism are not identified until the age of 2, a time when it is apparent that language is not developing normally (Mesibov et al., 1997). However, some interesting retrospective studies now show that signs of autism occur early in life. By analyzing the videotapes of first-year birthday parties of children later identified as having autism, unusual and consistent patterns occurred. These children were less likely to point, show their presents to others, respond to their names, or make direct eye contact with others (Osterling & Dawson, 1994). Awareness of early characteristics of this disorder by physicians could lead to earlier diagnoses and quicker delivery of crucial intervention programs.

SIGNIFICANCE

Individuals with autism process information and understand the world differently from those who do not have this disability (Mesibov, 1994). Most require comprehensive services and extensive supports for their entire lives. Effective services and

MAKING CONNECTIONS

For more information about functional assessments and related topics, see:

- The IEP process in Chapter 2
- Behavioral Intervention Plans in Chapter 8
- ABC Analysis (Achieving Discipline) in Chapter 8
- Teaching Functionally Equivalent Behaviors (Achieving Discipline) in this chapter

behavioral support. Organizing and arranging environments (schools, homes, workplaces) so problem behaviors are less likely to occur.

functionally equivalent behaviors. Appropriate behaviors that can replace inappropriate behaviors because they serve similar purposes.

Research to Practice: Teaching with Confidence

FUNCTIONAL BEHAVIORAL ASSESSMENT

ROBERT H. HORNER AND GEORGE SUGAI
University of Oregon

RESEARCH

Functional behavioral assessment is a process and set of procedures for identifying the events that trigger and maintain problem behaviors. Functional behavioral assessment is based on an extensive body of research documenting the importance of identifying the events that "set the occasion" for problem behaviors, and the events that maintain the problem behaviors over time. The research using functional analysis procedures has demonstrated that behavior support is more likely to be effective if based on information from a functional assessment. In 1997, functional behavioral assessment became part of the Individuals with Disabilities Education Act.

PRACTICE

IDEA '97 indicates that a functional behavioral assessment should be conducted anytime a student with a disability presents significant problem behavior that might affect eligibility, placement, or disciplinary actions and/or represent a significant barrier to a student's education. However, functional behavioral assessment should be viewed and used foremost as a preferred practice for increasing our understanding of the problem behavior presented by any student and for enhancing the effectiveness and efficiency of behavioral interventions and supports. The process can involve many different procedures: (a) *formal interviews* with the student and the people who know the student best, (b) *direct observation* of the student's behavior under different situations, and/or (c) a *functional analysis* that includes systematic manipulations of conditions in the environment while collecting direct observation data. Regardless of the procedures employed, a functional behavioral assessment involves developing hypotheses about the events that trigger and maintain the problem behavior, and then testing those hypotheses to ensure they are correct. The testing always involves either observing the student under typical conditions, or setting up conditions and observing the student under those "special" conditions. The results of a functional behavioral assessment should produce four outcomes: (a) operational definition of the problem behavior(s), (b) clear statement of the conditions (routines/events) that set the occasion for the problem behavior(s), (c) the consequences that maintain the problem behavior (e.g., attention, escape from aversive events, access to food or desired objects, social status), and (d) direct observation data supporting these hypotheses.

The basic goal of a functional assessment is to improve the efficiency and effectiveness of behavior support. The information from a functional assessment should help teachers, special educators, and families modify curricula, social contexts, communication training, social skills instruction, and consequences to improve the behavior of the student. A central focus of functional behavioral assessment is on the features of the environment that affect problem behavior. Functional assessment information is designed to identify how to modify environments so that students are successful, and then build from that success to produce durable reduction of problem behavior. Functional behavioral assessment was developed with students who have more severe disabilities, yet during the past five years has proven useful in the design of behavioral support for students with a full range of disability labels and of problem behavior types.

The range of acceptable methods of conducting functional behavior assessment and developing and implementing behavior support planning is becoming defined more clearly in current research efforts. People who conduct functional behavior assessments should be fluent with why, when, and how they are conducted and what are the necessary outcomes. Specific training and practice increase fluency.

Temple Grandin has recieved considerable attention for her biographical insights into autism and how it affects individuals.

For related information, see Negotiating the Mental Health Care System (Family Section) in Chapter 8.

supports require high levels of coordination and consistency. Unfortunately, these are difficult goals to achieve through the often fragmented services provided by social service agencies, health care providers, and the educational system.

Even high-functioning individuals with autism face considerable challenges. In a fascinating account of her own life, entitled *Thinking in Pictures and Other Reports from My Life with Autism*, Temple Grandin shares with the world what it is like to experience the pains of isolation and being very different from her peers (Grandin, 1995). Excerpts from her biography are found in the accompanying box. Ms. Grandin holds a doctorate in animal science from the University of Illinois and is currently a professor at Colorado State University. She is well known for her designs of livestock holding equipment, and one-third of all of such equipment in this country was designed by her. You might be thinking: How could someone with such a signficant disability as autism be such a successful scientist? Truly, she is unique. However, her insights might help others.

Ms. Grandin writes about her frustration with not being able to talk, though she understood language. She also talks about her sensory problems, like her oversensitivity to sound and touch, that caused her to withdraw from people and the world outside of herself. She also experiences motor problems, having difficulties with balance and coordinating multiple motor responses simultaneously. Even today, she says that she cannot move two or three levers at the same time. She is a strong advocate of early intervention programs. She maintains that young children with autism must not be allowed to "tune out." She believes that these children must remain engaged with others and in activities at least twenty hours per week; they must not be allowed to withdraw into their own worlds and shut everyone and everything out. We can learn a lot from Ms. Grandin, who despite her successful career continues to experience many of the symptoms of autism. Although Ms. Grandin is proof that people with autism can function in the community with supports, most adults with autism do not fare as well.

Insights into Autism

Oliver Sacks, in the foreword to Temple Grandin's (1996) biography, *Thinking in Pictures and Other Reports of My Life with Autism,* underscores the importance of her insights about her disability,

> Unprecedented because there had never before been an "inside narrative" of autism; unthinkable because it had been medical dogma for forty years or more that there was no "inside," no inner life, in the autistic, or that if there was it would be forever denied access or expression; extraordinary because of its extreme (and strange) directness and clarity. Temple Grandin's voice came from a place which had never had a voice, never been granted real existence, before—and she spoke not only for herself, but for thousands of other, often highly gifted, autistic adults in our midst. She provided a glimpse, and indeed a revelation, that there might be people, no less human than ourselves, who constructed their worlds, lived their lives, in almost unimaginably different ways.

> Temple does not romanticize autism, nor does she downplay how much her autism has cut her off from the social whirl, the pleasures, the rewards, the companionships, that for the rest of us may define much of life. But she has a stong, positive sense of her own being and worth, and how autism, paradoxically, may have contributed to this. (pp. 11, 16)

Temple Grandin, an adult with autism, describes her thought processes as being very different from most other people:

> I think in pictures. Words are like a second language to me. I translate both spoken and written words into full-color movies, complete with sound, which run like a VCR tape in my head. When somebody speaks to me, his words are instantly translated into pictures. Language-based thinkers often find this phenomenon difficult to understand, but in my job as an equipment designer for the livestock industry, visual thinking is a tremendous advantage.... [O]ne third of the cattle and hogs in the United States are handled in equipment I have designed. (p. 19)

She helps us understand autism better by explaining how her senses are too active:

> Overly sensitive skin can be a big problem. Washing my hair and dressing to go to church were two things I hated as a child.... Scratchy petticoats were like sandpaper scraping away at raw nerve endings.... When I was little, loud noises were also a problem, often feeling like a dentist's drill hitting a nerve. They actually caused pain. I was scared to death of balloons popping, because the sound was like an explosion in my ear. Minor noises that most people can tune out drove me to distraction.... My ears are like microphones picking up all sounds with equal intensity. (pp. 66–68)

Grandin talks about her emotional differences, which may help us understand different behavior patterns in children with autism:

> Some people believe that people with autism do not have emotions. I definitely do have them, but they are more like the emotions of a child than of an adult. My childhood temper tantrums were not really expressions of emotion so much as circuit overloads.... When I get angry, it is like an afternoon thunderstorm; the anger is intense, but once I get over it, the emotion quickly dissipates.... I don't know what it is like to feel rapturous joy. I know I am missing something when other people swoon over a beautiful sunset. Intellectually I know it is beautiful, but I don't feel it.... [E]motional nuances are still incomprehensible to me, and I value concrete evidence of accomplishment and appreciation.... I still have difficulty understanding and having a relationship with people whose primary motivation in life is governed by complex emotions, as my actions are guided by intellect. (pp. 87–90)

Grandin describes typical autistic behaviors not as an observer, but as the participant. In doing so, she gives us guidance about how educational programs should be developed:

> I would tune out, shut off my ears, and daydream. My daydreams were like Technicolor movies in my head. I would also become completely absorbed in spinning a penny or studying the wood-grain pattern on my desktop. During these times, the rest of the world disappeared, but then my speech teacher would gently grab my chin to pull me back into the real world.... Autistic children will remain in their own little worlds if left to their own devices. (p. 96)

> [Teachers must] be able to determine whether a tantrum or other bad behavior is caused by fear or pain or a learned avoidance response. Sometimes it's because of pain from sounds that hurt their ears or fear of an unexpected change in routine.... Autistics are afraid of the unexpected. (pp. 149–150)

Source: From *Thinking in Pictures and Other Reports from My Life with Autism* by Temple Grandin, 1995, New York: Viking Books. Reprinted with permission.

Deficiencies in adaptive behavior are apparent at very early ages in people with autism (Vig & Jedrysek, 1995). Even at the time of preschool, children with autism show signs of difficulties across many adaptive areas, not just communication and socialization. Significant problems exist in such skill areas as daily living, abstract thinking, problem solving, and motor skills. And it appears that such problems become more serious as these individuals grow older. The reason may be that many of these individuals are less receptive to training (Partington et al., 1994) and do not naturally or spontaneously develop the ability to imitate others (Krantz et al., 1994). The job of learning is a major feat for many of these individuals.

PREVALENCE

How many children are included in any special education category is directly related to the definition used, and for autism this is a significant issue to consider (Peeters, 1997). Some definitions of autism, like Kanner's, are very restrictive. Using this definition results in as few as 0.7 or as many as 2.3 individuals per 10,000 being identified (Locke et al., 1994). Less restrictive definitions would qualify more children, perhaps as many as 7 to 14 per 10,000. According to the Autism Society of America, autism occurs in as many as 1 in 500 individuals, making this condition the third most common developmental disability, surpassing Down syndrome in prevalence (Autism Society of America, 1999). Qualifying more children, however, affects other factors besides the number served under this special education label. It increases the variability in behaviors and symptoms observed in the population, and it results in the inclusion of more children with higher intelligence in this category.

So, how many students are served under this special education category? According to the *Twentieth Annual Report to Congress on the Implementation of IDEA* (U.S. Department of Education, 1998), a total of 34,101 children (ages 6 to 21) across the nation were classified as having autism. This represents about .06% of schoolchildren. It is clear that even though the IDEA '97 definition is much less stringent than Kanner's original conceptualization of the condition, autism is a very low incidence disability.

CAUSES AND PREVENTION

Causes for autism have been sought since the condition was originally identified. Autism was first thought to be an emotional disorder caused by something the child's mother did wrong (Rimland, 1994). This incorrect theory added to mothers' burden. Feelings of guilt and shame were the result of theories of early psychologists like Bruno Bettelheim, who laid clear blame for children's disabilities on mothers' attitudes and poor parenting skills. Eventually, researchers were able to show that autism is a neurological rather than an emotional disorder. Such research findings have changed the beliefs of professionals and the public. Mothers are no longer wrongly blamed for causing autism in their children.

Although definite answers are still unavailable, most experts now agree: Autism is probably organic in nature (Sturmey & Sevin, 1994) and most likely caused by brain damage (Begley & Springen, 1996), possibly in the brain stem (Koegel et al., 1995). Some contend that autism is due to a single gene disorder, similar to what causes PKU (Locke et al., 1994), while others believe that anywhere from two to five

CONNECTIONS

Adaptive behavior is fully explained in Chapter 6 in these sections:

- Mental Retardation Defined
- Children with Mental Retardation

NEW DIRECTIONS FOR THE MILLENNIUM

Legacy: Reports persist that the prevalence of autism is increasing at alarming rates.

Opportunities:

- Develop a consistent definition and criterion for this disability
- Conduct studies to determine how many additional cases are due to definitional changes or due to actual increases in the prevalence rates

CONNECTIONS

For more information about PKU and fragile X syndrome, see the Causes and Prevention section of Chapter 6.

genes may be involved in some complex interaction (Cook, 1998). This theory explains why some cases of autism (or autistic-like behaviors) seem to be associated with fragile X syndrome. Other theories suggest that prenatal or postnatal viral infection may be the culprit (Begley & Springen, 1996; Burger & Warren, 1998). And, recently, because of increased occurrences of autism in specific towns and regions, possible links to environmental toxins are being suspected (Johnson, 1999).

As with all disabilities, it is crucial that researchers focus on identifying the cause(s) of autism. The hope is that once the etiology is understood, a preventive technique will soon follow. For now, some factors have been observed to improve the condition, but the reasons for improvement are not known. For example, vitamin B_6 and magnesium are claimed to have reduced the symptoms of autism in many children, and for those it has not helped it has caused no harm (Rimland, 1994). Temple Grandin maintains that antidepressant medications help control her nervousness. Also, some researchers are beginning to identify a dopamine deficiency in many individuals who are prone to self-injury, and they hypothesize that drugs may prove to be beneficial in controlling SIB and other repetitive behavior problems (Lewis & Bodfish, 1998). Recent findings support a new medication, Secretin (Rimland, 1999). Personal accounts about rapid and dramatic improvements in children with autism seen by parents and professionals is contributing to the great hope and excitement surrounding this drug. Some of the benefits seen are increased eye contact, sociability, and speech. However, the effects seem to be inconsistent. And little is known yet about proper dosage, which group of individuals with autism is more positively affected, or negative side effects.

At the present time, no consistently effective treatment—other than well-designed educational programs based on applied behavior analysis interventions—is available (Maurice et al., 1996; Peeters, 1997). Certainly, much effort needs to be directed toward proving or disproving the many theories that surround autism. Once that happens, reliable techniques can be developed and implemented to prevent the condition and reduce its effects for those who have it.

CHILDREN WITH AUTISM

A unique profile of stereotypic behaviors comprise the symptoms, or characteristics, of autism. Each characteristic alone does not signal autism, but in combination they define a very serious disability. It is a disability that at the present time means challenging outcomes for the individuals with the condition and their families. Table 12.1 on page 516 is an overview of those characteristics—organized into four major groups—that many practitioners, researchers, and family members have identified (Koegel et al., 1995; Mesibov, 1994; Richard, 1997; Rimland, 1994; Sturmey & Sevin, 1994; Travis & Sigman, 1998; Trevarthen et al., 1998; Wilkerson, 1998). Study the table as you read about how some of the outcomes relate to these characteristics.

Data about characteristics of autism that have a lifelong impact are quite significant. Let's look at some data gathered by a number of different researchers (Sturmey & Sevin, 1994). Of children with autism:

self-injurious behaviors (SIB). Self-inflicted injuries (head banging, eye poking).

- 80% have a concurrent diagnosis of mental retardation
- 50% never develop functional speech or language
- 40% engage in high levels of **self-injurious behaviors (SIB)**
- four out of five are males
- 33% develop seizures

Table 12.1 Signs or Characteristics of Autism

Impairment in Reciprocal Social Interactions

Normal attachments to parents, family members, or caregivers do not develop.

Friendships with peers fail to develop.

Cooperative or peer play is rarely observed.

Emotions, like affection and empathy, are rarely displayed.

Nonverbal signals of social intent (smiling, gestures, physical contact) tend not to be used.

Eye contact is not initiated or maintained.

Imaginative play is an activity seldom observed.

The lack of social-communicative gestures and utterances are apparent during the first few months of life.

Preferred interaction style could be characterized as "extreme isolation."

Understanding of others' beliefs, emotions, or motivations is greatly impaired.

Joint attention deficits, not being able to cooperate or share interest with others in the same event or activity, impair normal social reciprocation.

Poor Communication Abilities

Functional language is not acquired fully or mastered.

Content of language is usually unrelated to immediate environmental events.

Utterances are stereotypic and repetitive.

Gestures, facial expressions, and nonverbal cues are poorly understood.

Conversations are not maintained.

Spontaneous conversations are rarely initiated.

Speech can be meaningless, repetitive, and echolalic.

Many fail to use the words *I* and *yes* and have problems with pronouns in general.

Both expressive and receptive language is extremely literal.

Verbal turn-taking, choosing a topic, and contributing properly to a conversation are rare.

Insistence on Sameness

Marked distress is typically experienced over trivial or minor changes in the environment.

Aspects of daily routine can become ritualized.

Obsessive and compulsive behavior is frequently displayed.

The requirement to complete self-imposed, required actions is intense.

Stereotypic behaviors (rocking, hand flapping) are repeated in cycles difficult to stop.

Unusual Behavior Patterns

Hypersensitive and/or inconsistent behaviors are the response to visual, tactile, or auditory stimulation.

Aggression to others is common, particularly when compliance is requested.

Self-injurious or outwardly aggressive behavior (hitting, biting, kicking, head banging) is common and frequent.

Extreme social fears are manifested toward strangers, crowds, unusual situations, and new environments.

Loud noises (barking dogs, street noises) can result in startle or fearful reactions.

Severe sleep problems occur with frequency.

Noncompliant behavior to requests from others results in disruption to the individual and others (tantrums).

Self-stimulation (twirling objects, rocking) consumes a considerable amount of time and energy.

The ability to pretend is lacking.

The disability can be characterized by both behavioral excesses and deficits. Excesses can include ritualistic, bizarre, and stereotypic behaviors. For example, some of these individuals express unfounded fears of changes in the environment, strangers, strange sounds, and pets and other animals. The frequency of self-stimulatory behavior is often high and repetitive, in which the individual engages in such behaviors as loud repetitious verbalizations, rocking, hand flapping, gazing at lights. Their rate of

SIB (hair pulling, hitting, scratching) is exceptionally high, even when compared to others with severe disabilities. For example, SIB among students with mental retardation is estimated to be between 7% and 22%, whereas it is 40% for students with autism. And even more alarming is that SIB continues in adulthood, with 30% of autistic adults exhibiting self-injurious behaviors (Lewis & Bodfish, 1998).

Behavior deficits commonly found in individuals with autism include: inability to pretend, difficulties establishing relationships with others, inappropriate toy play, muteness or **echolalia,** and inappropriate or lack of affect. Many researchers concur: **joint attention deficits** seem to be a characteristic seen in many individuals with autism across their lives (Travis & Sigman, 1998). Joint attention deficits mean that the individual affected is not able to coordinate his or her attention to an event or object with someone else's (Rogers, 1998).

Another area frequently noted as problematic is language, which for most people with autism does not develop completely. These deficits tend to be both verbal and nonverbal. They often take language literally and have trouble understanding gestures and facial expressions (Peeters, 1997). The signs of autism appear during the first few months of life. Family members often note that eye gaze, smiles, desire to be held, recognition of parents, and the ability to be consoled are missing in many of these children.

DEAF-BLINDNESS

The world of children with **deaf-blindness** can be exceptionally restricted. For those whose hearing and vision fall into the ranges of severe or profound losses, their immediate world may well end at their fingertips (Miles, 1995). Some of these students have enough residual vision to allow them to read enlarged print, see sign language, move about in their environment, and recognize friends and family. Some have sufficient hearing to understand some speech sounds or hear loud noises. Some can develop speech themselves, and others have such limited vision and hearing that they profit little from either sense. The majority of these individuals have other disabilities in addition to visual and hearing losses. Most individuals with deaf-blindness need support from others to make their worlds safe and accessible.

DEAF-BLINDNESS DEFINED

A separate funding base for students with deaf-blindness was initiated in 1969. This was the time of a major national crisis, a period when the rubella epidemic caused dramatic increases in the number of babies with disabilities, particularly blindness, deafness, and deaf-blindness. Definitions of deaf-blindness vary by state. The result is inconsistent identification results and service outcomes, which are compounded by the fact that most of these youngsters have disabilities in addition to their visual and hearing problems. For these reasons, many of these youngsters are served in a category referred to as multihandicapped (or multiple disabilities). The category of deaf-blindness is defined in IDEA '97 in this way:

> Deaf-blindness means concomitant hearing and visual impairments, the combination of which causes such severe communication and other developmental and

echolalia. Repeating exactly what was heard, immediately or even days later.
joint attention deficits. Inability to mutually interact or to share interest in events or objects.
deaf-blindness. A dual disability whereby the individual has both vision and hearing problems.

Review the Defined sections in
• Chapter 10
• Chapter 11

learning needs that the persons cannot be appropriately educated in special education programs solely for children and youth with hearing impairments or severe disabilities, without supplementary assistance to address their education needs due to these dual, concurrent disabilities. (U.S. Department of Education, 1999, p. 12422)

The IDEA '97 definition, some professionals believe, does not assist in accurate or correct identification of, and ultimately appropriate services for, all children with this disability (Baldwin, 1996). Many state coordinators therefore advocate for a more functional definition. They are seeking a definition that focuses on the conditions needed for optimal learning and considers the unique conditions caused by the interplay of two sensory impairments. This functional definition is proposed by Victor Baldwin:

> If the deficit in hearing and vision is sufficient to require special adaptations in instruction in both the auditory and visual modes to produce maximum learning, then the person qualifies to be identified as deaf–blind and should be included in the annual census. (Baldwin, 1995, p. 2)

IDENTIFICATION

Most professionals suggest that inclusion in the deaf–blind category requires that "a person needs, at a minimum, to have a visual acuity of 20/70 in the better eye with correction and an auditory deficit of 30 dB in the better ear" (Baldwin, 1995, p. 5).

Helen Keller and her teacher, Anne Sullivan, became a pair who proved that deaf and blind people can achieve beyond many people's expectations.

CONNECTIONS

- For more on methods of reading and writing for students with visual disabilities, see the Low Vision and Blind Children section in Chapter 11
- For more about the development of oral language in deaf children, review the section on speech ability in Deaf or Hard of Hearing Children in Chapter 10

SIGNIFICANCE

The most famous person with deaf–blindness is probably Helen Keller. Keller was a woman of many accomplishments, but her achievements, including graduating from Radcliffe with honors in 1904, would not have been possible without the efforts of her teacher, Anne Sullivan (Holcomb & Wood, 1989). Sullivan's "family tree" is interesting and noteworthy. Samuel Gridley Howe was the founder of the Perkins School for the Blind. Located in Boston, it was the first school for blind students in the United States. One of Howe's pupils was Laura Dewey Bridgman. Bridgman, herself a person with deaf–blindness, talked to other people by tapping letters and using a manual alphabet. She used braille for reading. Bridgman became a teacher, and one of her students was a partially blind girl named Anne Sullivan. When Sullivan grew up, she learned of a 6-year-old girl with deaf–blindness living in Alabama. Sullivan visited young Helen Keller and brought her a gift, a doll given to her by Laura Bridgman. Sullivan became Helen Keller's teacher and lifelong companion. Of her disabilities, Keller said, "Blindness separates a person from things, but deafness separates him from people" (Miles, 1995, p. 4). Clearly, the case of Helen Keller is most unique and remarkable. Although it is unrealistic to expect the outcomes for all individuals with deaf–blindness to be like hers, her story does remind us all of the importance of high expectations, hard work, intensive instruction, and meaningful support.

Just as it would be a mistake to assume that all people with deaf–blindness can become Helen Kellers, it is a mistake to make an alternative assumption about people in this group. Kim Powers is a good example (Rosenberg, 1995). Powers hosts a Saturday television show for kids, *Kim's World*. She is a unique and daring host who has played with tarantulas and tigers, bungee jumped, and ridden horses and elephants. Being a person with deaf–blindness has not stopped her from skiing and scuba diving on TV. The cable network Kaleidoscope, which airs her show, focuses mostly on programs for people with disabilities and hopes to go nationwide soon.

Let's turn our attention to three more common results of this disability, problems that the individuals affected, their family members, and their teachers must address: isolation, communication, and mobility. Feelings of isolation are a particular problem for many individuals with deaf–blindness and an area that educators must address. The world of these individuals is restricted. It is educators' role to expand their "world-view" and connect them with other people and their environments (Haring & Romer, 1995; Heubner et al., 1995). Casey Cook, a deaf–blind triathlete, illustrates the connection that these individuals can make (Boeck, 1998). Cook, winner of an Arete Award for Courage in Sports, has Voigte-Carnegie syndrome, which resulted in his blindness

Kim Powers, who is deaf and blind, stars in Kaleidoscope's Kim's World. Kaleidoscope is a 24-hour cable network that also produces a web site of interesting and useful information (www.ktv-i.com).

MAKING CONNECTIONS

In Chapter 6, review these sections about supports:

- Emerging Classification Systems (Types of Mental Retardation)
- Supports (Children with Mental Retardation)
- Family

MAKING CONNECTIONS

The concept of "age of onset" is discussed in both Chapters 10 and 11 in the Defined sections.

MAKING CONNECTIONS

In Chapter 10:

- Review information about sign language; see the Deaf Culture section (Children Who Are Deaf or Hard of Hearing)
- To find more about different communication systems, including Total Communication, see the Instructional Methods for Deaf Students section (Educational Interventions)

and severe hearing impairments. Despite his disabilities, he races with training partners and says of himself, "I'm a regular guy.... I have a few physical quirks. I'm mystified why others see what I do as a big deal" (p. C3).

Remember, many individuals with deaf–blindness have enough vision to move around, recognize familiar faces, read enlarged print, and even read sign language at close distances. Some have sufficient hearing to understand some sounds, recognize familiar voices, and maybe even develop speech. Many of these students also have mental retardation. So the compounding effects of all of these disabilities result in the vast majority of these individuals requiring extensive supports throughout their lives.

For those of us without disabilities, much of our learning is almost effortless. Through what is called **incidental learning,** we gain knowledge about our environment, we learn the subtle rules and social conventions about interacting with others, and we come to understand how to access our communities. Efficient incidental learning uses intact vision and hearing, for it is through these channels that others communicate and convey important information. Depending on the degree of visual or hearing loss and the age of onset of the disability, the transfer of this knowledge is impaired (Prickett & Welch, 1995). For many of these youngsters, developing communication skills is critical (Engleman et al., 1998). They need to understand what others are saying, and to do so requires them to use their residual senses as best as they can. Accomplishing good communication skills can require a lot of effort, and teachers often need to provide incentives to motivate these children to communicate with others. Because of the severity of their disabilities, they often do not naturally recognize the importance or the need to interact and exchange information with others.

Many deaf–blind individuals use total communication as their means of interchange because it allows for the integrated use of oral and manual communication. And many of these individuals profit from manual communication actually becoming tactile, where the signs are conveyed through touch. What can teachers do to help lessen the impact of both visual and hearing problems on the communication abilities of their students? Prickett (1995, p. 62) provides some suggestions in this regard:

- Interact frequently and consistently
- Use multisensory information
- Use tactile and close-range signing as appropriate
- Focus on individual interaction
- Encourage direct communication among classmates

Movement is important to all of us. We move to exercise, to recreate, to get from one location to another for so many purposes, and to communicate our emotions. The ability to move freely in our environments is a natural human behavior, but for those who have significant visual losses, movement is often restricted and can even be dangerous. The components of purposeful movement need to become instructional targets for students with deaf–blindness. To help us understand the complexity of what is so natural for so many, Groce and Isaacson (1995) identified and defined these components (see Table 12.2).

What should be clear from this discussion is that the significance of deaf–blindness and its associated problems is great. The impact on the individuals affected is substantial. The work and effort to overcome these challenges is considerable and involves teams of dedicated people that include the individuals themselves, their families, educators, and experts from many disciplines.

Table 12.2 Components of Purposeful Movement

Be Aware of Surroundings

The world is comprised of people, places, and things that must be understood independently and in relationship to self.

Initiate and Sustain Movement

Reaching a desired location requires that movement begin and be sustained until the destination is reached.

Recognize Destinations

Movement has an object—the destination—that must be recognized and dealt with appropriately.

Protect Self from Danger

Obstacles and other immediate dangers must be handled safely.

Make Decisions

Choosing when and how to move requires the individual to decide whether there is sufficient reason to move, whether it is the right time to move, whether there is preference for this act of moving, and which mode of transportation to use.

Source: From "Purposeful Movement" by M. M. Groce and A. B. Isaacson, 1995, in K. M. Heubner, J. G. Prickett, R. R. Welch, and E. Joffee (Eds.), *Hand in hand: Essentials of communication and orientation and mobility for your students who are deaf–blind* (pp. 94–95). New York. AFB Press. Adapted by permission.

See the section in Chapter 11 on Orientation and Mobility (Educational Interventions).

incidental learning. Gaining knowledge and skills without being directly taught.

Usher syndrome. A genetic syndrome that includes a nonprogressive sensorineural hearing loss, retinitis pigmentosa and progressively restricted field of vision, loss of the sense of smell, and impaired balance and motor skills.

PREVALENCE

According to the State and Multi-State Service Centers for Children with Deaf–Blindness, in 1995 some 10,415 deaf–blind students—ages birth to 21—were served under IDEA (Baldwin, 1996), while the federal government only reported, 1,286 students in this category. At least 85% of children with deaf–blindness have additional disabilities as well (*JVIB News Service*, 1995). Because students can be reported by the states to the federal government by only one disability area, many deaf–blind students are reported in other categories, so prevalence reports often vary significantly from one source to another.

CAUSES AND PREVENTION

The most frequent specified cause of deaf–blindness is prematurity (Baldwin, 1996). However, it is important to note that in the majority of cases the cause of these multiple disabilities is unknown. Besides prematurity, many causes and factors associated with deaf–blindness are understood. Traces, a federally funded project, has identified over eighteen different hereditary syndromes and nine congential infections that can cause deaf–blindness (Heller & Kennedy, 1994).

Usher syndrome is a hereditary cause of congenital deafness and progressive blindness, along with mental retardation. In addition to these three disabilities, many individuals with Usher syndrome also have walking and motor problems associated with ataxia. Neuropsychological problems are also observed in about 25% of these cases (Accardo et al., 1996). This recessive X-linked genetic syndrome accounts for

MAKING
CONNECTIONS

• For more information about prematurity and its relationship to disabilities, see the section on Low Birth Weight (Causes) in Chapter 6
• For more information about the causes and types of visual disabilities and deafness, see those sections in Chapters 10 and 11

MAKING
CONNECTIONS

For more information about Deaf culture, review Deaf or Hard of Hearing Children in Chapter 10.

about 5% of all children with severe hearing losses, about 2% of children with deaf–blindness, and about 50% of adults with deaf–blindness. This rare syndrome occurs in about 3 out of every 100,000 people. There are several types of deaf–blindness, and with one of these the onset of visual disabilities does not begin until adolescence (Prickett & Welch, 1995). These individuals often face additional emotional challenges because they spent most of their schoolyears alongside deaf peers, included in Deaf culture. As their vision becomes more and more restricted, they find that they can no longer fully participate in the Deaf community, which leads to frustration and disappointment.

Deaf–blindness is associated with other conditions beside Usher syndrome. For example, about 2% of those with deaf–blindness have Down syndrome, about 4% have hydrocephaly, and another 4% were affected by rubella. Prematurity, the most frequently reported cause, accounts for only 9% of the cases of deaf–blindness, and this listed cause itself has many different causes. Thus proportionally few causes are understood, so we do not have reliable preventive measures.

CHILDREN WITH DEAF–BLINDNESS

As mentioned earlier, the vast majority (some 85%) of students who are deaf–blind have additional disabilities beyond their visual and hearing problems (*JVIB News Service*, 1995). The most common additional disability is mental retardation, followed by a speech or language impairment, a physical disability, and a health problem (Baldwin, 1995). Some of these children have more than one additional disability. Their multiple disabilities clearly make meeting their instructional needs challenging and require specially prepared teachers and related service providers. However, it is important to look beyond those disabilities and naturally make accommodations for these individuals' differences (Smith, 1992). As we all seek to be

Figure 12.1 The Frequency of Various Combinations of Hearing and Visual Losses in Children with Deaf-Blindness

Source: From "Summary of Hearing vs. Vision Loss" by V. Baldwin, 1997. Monmouth, OR: Teaching Research, Western Oregon State College.

		Hearing Loss			
		Mild	Moderate	Severe	Profound
Vision Loss	Partially sighted	575	545	470	323
	Legally blind	432	709	685	490
	Light perception only	172	280	305	129
	Totally blind	178	213	212	219

Note: Not included are those children:
(a) not tested (or)
(b) Tested but not conclusive

Table 12.3 Being Disability Sensitive: Fostering a Sense of Belonging for Deaf–Blind Students

Be Courteous

Be human.

Let the person know you are nearby with a gentle touch on the hand that is nearest to you.

If you want to communicate, touch the person's hands gently and then slide your hands underneath the other person's.

Every time you meet the person, identify yourself (maybe with a special sign).

Respect the person. Give him or her time to respond. Let people think for themselves.

Let the person know when you are going to leave the room.

Leave the environment as you found it (furniture should be in its standard places, doors either fully open or closed).

Offer assistance only when necessary.

Include the Individual in Activities

Communicate directly with the deaf–blind student. (Don't ask someone else what that student wants.)

Have the student join in on class discussions by calling on the student as much as you do his or her classmates.

Create cooperative teams for academic tasks.

Be sure to encourage classmates, during recess and free time, to play games in which the deaf–blind student can participate.

Communication

Know the individual's primary mode of communication, and how subtle messages are conveyed (confusion, understanding, request for a restatement).

Communicate clearly. Use direct and descriptive language with clear referents.

Explain the "why" of a situation (why everyone has to move, why you came back without the popcorn).

When serving as an interpreter, the rules of privacy and respect are the same as for interpreters for the deaf.

Review all of the different ways to accommodate and adapt classroom settings by rereading all of the Accommodating for Inclusive Environments boxes throughout this text.

culturally sensitive, we all need to become "disability sensitive." (See Table 12.3 for suggestions about including students with severe disabilities.)

One question that you should be asking relates to the seriousness of these youngsters' visual and hearing disabilities. You should also be wondering about how these degrees of loss combine. For example, do most of these children have a mild vision loss but a profound hearing loss? Do they have little or no functional use of either sense? First consider the levels of loss for hearing and vision separately, then look at their combinations. According to Baldwin (1996), most often these youngsters have a severe hearing loss. So, as a whole, the entire population is more deaf than blind. What is the most common combination of hearing loss and visual loss (e.g., mild loss for vision and severe loss for hearing)? The most frequent combination is being legally blind along with a severe hearing loss (Baldwin, 1997). Figure 12.1 on page 522 displays these overall data.

Strauss and Lehtinen's early work is also discussed in the History section of Chapter 4.

NEW DIRECTIONS
FOR THE
MILLENNIUM

Legacy: Because the symptoms of TBI are quite similar to those of learning disabilities and the instructional procedures used with both groups of students are similar, some wonder whether a separate disability category is necessary for these students.

Opportunities:

- Develop distinct instructional procedures for students with TBI
- Prepare sufficient numbers of teachers who are specialists in this area

TRAUMATIC BRAIN INJURY

Modern medicine has propelled many families into becoming lifelong sources of care and concern for children who experience acquired brain injury resulting in severe disabilities—an unprecedented circumstance in American family life. Prior to the 1960s, most children whose brains were seriously hurt died soon after the trauma. Changes in emergency treatment, imaging technology, and surgical and pharmaceutical treatments have begun to routinely save the lives of approximately 30,000 of these children each year. (Singer et al., 1996, p. xix)

About one million children annually experience a head injury, and about 165,000 of them require hospitalization (Heller et al., 1996). Some youngsters, after their injuries, require special education. Children with **traumatic brain injury (TBI)** have been served in special education since IDEA was originally passed in 1975. In fact, many children with TBI were served long before then. It is quite possible that some were recognized during the 1940s. Strauss and Lehtinen published a groundbreaking book in 1947, *Psychopathology and Education of the Brain-Injured Child,* in which they recommended highly structured educational approaches for children whom they described having many of the characteristics observed in today's students with TBI.

TBI was not, however, considered a separate disability area until the 1990 reauthorization of IDEA (PL 101–476), the special education law. Until that time, these students were counted in the categories that most closely matched their primary learning needs and were educated with peers without disabilities and those with similar learning characteristics. For example, many students with TBI were (as most continue to be) educated alongside those with learning disabilities because of the similarity in their learning and behavioral characteristics. Like their classmates with learning disabilities, these students often exhibit memory deficits, attention problems, language impairments, and reduced academic performance. Many benefit from instructional procedures proven effective with children with learning disabilities: direct instruction, structured schooldays, and organized classes where expectations are clearly specified. Others, because of their head injuries, experience seizures and receive many of the same accommodations as children with epilepsy. Although specific programs for students with TBI are emerging across the nation (Weld County TBI Task Force outside of Greeley, Colorado; Rehabilitation Center in Austin, Texas; Wisconsin Department of Public Instruction), most are served within existing programs for students with other disabilities.

TBI DEFINED

In 1990, Congress added TBI to the list of special education categories. Here's how IDEA '97 defines this disability

> *Traumatic brain injury* means an acquired injury to the brain caused by an external physical force, resulting in total or partial functional disability or psychosocial impairment, or both, that adversely affects a child's educational performance. The term applies to open or closed head injuries resulting in impairments in one or more areas, such as cognition; language; memory; attention; reasoning; abstract thinking; judgment; problem solving; sensory, perceptual, and motor abilities; psychosocial behavior; physical functions; information processing; and speech. The term does

traumatic brain injury (TBI). The result of a head injury; the individual experiences reduced cognitive functioning, limited attention, and impulsivity.

not apply to brain injuries that are congenital or degenerative, or to brain injuries induced by birth trauma. (U.S. Department of Education, 1999, p. 12422)

TBI occurs when a traumatic event "causes a loss of consciousness, memory loss for immediately preceding or subsequent events, confusion, disorientation, or a dazed feeling" (Hux & Hacksley, 1996, p. 158). TBI has several synonyms: acquired brain injury, head injury, closed head injury. It does not include injuries resulting from skull fractures. Table 12.4 provides some explanations of what TBI is and what it is not.

TYPES OF TBI

As with other disabilities, TBI ranges in severity from mild to severe, with most cases falling into the mild range. The vast majority are mild and do not raise alarm with most doctors (Hux & Hacksley, 1996). Mild episodes of brain injury often result in these symptoms: dizziness, headache, selective attention problems, irritability, anxiety, blurred vision, insomnia, fatigue, motor difficulties, language problems, behavior and emotional problems, cognitive problems, and memory problems (Clark, 1996; Heller et al., 1996). These problems can last for a very short time or for years. In many cases the effects eventually disappear, but some cases of TBI result in lifelong problems. Youngsters with moderate to severe injuries often experience dramatic changes in their cognitive, language, motor, sensory, and behavioral performances. Some of these children are typical learners one day, but after their injury have significant disabilities. In these cases, it is also common for the individual to experience depression or withdrawal.

IDENTIFICATION

Many children with TBI are not identified immediately after their injuries. This happens because many of these youngsters show no visible signs (cuts, bruises) of brain

Table 12.4 What Is and What Is Not TBI

TBI	Not TBI
Concussion is another term for TBI.	An internal cause of brain damage—such as a stroke, brain tumor, or infection of the brain—is not TBI.
A TBI can occur without a direct blow to the head—as in shaken baby syndrome and other forms of child abuse.	
A person does *not* have to lose consciousness to sustain a TBI.	A medically documented event potentially causing brain damage but not accompanied by a documentable change in educational performance does not justify TBI verification.
Brain damage resulting from TBI is often *not* visible through medical tests such as EEGs or brain imaging techniques such as computerized tomography scans or magnetic resonance imaging.	
Repeated mild TBIs can have a cumulative effect.	

Source: From "Mild traumatic brain injury: Facilitating school success" by K. Hux and C. Hacksley, 1996, *Intervention in School and Clinic, 31,* p. 160. Reprinted by permission.

Wearing the proper protective gear can prevent head injuries.

injury (NICHCY, 1999). The impact of what has been sometimes called the "silent epidemic" may go misunderstood for months. How can this be? Think about Ryan, who was not wearing a helmet, despite his mother's warnings, and fell while skateboarding. Because he did not want to tell his mother that he was not wearing his helmet, he also did not tell her about the accident. Instead he told his mom that he was tired and went off to his room to take a nap.

Even when accidents are serious, injury to the brain may go unnoticed at first. Too often, families bring their children home from the hospital not knowing that long after the broken bones are mended it is the head injury that could result in long-term disabilities (Singer, 1996). Most families are unaware of the signs associated with TBI, and were not informed by medical staff at the hospital that their children might have long-term cognitive effects from their injuries. Sometimes it is educators who must confirm families' worst (and often unspoken) fears: The accident several weeks ago caused more than a broken leg; it also caused brain injury.

In many cases, families do not inform school personnel of the possibility of mild TBI. This might happen if the accident occurred during the summer. It might be that family members did not make the connection between an accident, physical injuries, and changes in behavior (Hux & Hacksley, 1996). The result can be serious. Educators may spend unnecessary time trying to determine why a child, who never had academic or behavior problems before, is having great difficulty at school. Educators may not know that they should be making specific accommodations for the child's academic or social performance. Since the federal government created its definition of TBI, states have worked toward implementing it. Most states have developed eligibility criteria that require a neurological or medical examination and documentation of the adverse effects of the injury on the student's educational performance. The result is that health specialists and physicians are serving on these children's IEP committees and multidisciplinary teams. Using non-school-district personnel, particularly from the health field, can cause difficulties with scheduling meetings, having the designated team members readily available, understanding or being familiar with educational terms, and budgeting for increased costs. The result could well be that under these circumstances only students with severe disabilities are identified as having TBI. Regardless, multidisciplinary teams are vital to the successful design and implementation of appropriate educational plans for students with disabilities.

MAKING CONNECTIONS

For more about IEPs and how they are developed, see the IEP Process section in Chapter 2.

SIGNIFICANCE

The impact of TBI is related to the severity of the injury. In many minor cases, recovery occurs within a few months (Heller et al., 1996). In devastating situations, recovery and relearning can be a slow and frustrating process. Motor skills usually return first. For those with already well-developed speech and language skills, basic communication abilities tend to recover quickly. More complex language use and comprehension of subtle verbal and nonverbal cues remain difficult for some students. High-level cognitive functions (problem solving, memory, and high-level complex-thinking skills) often return later. The pattern seems to be rapid progress during the first few months after the injury, followed by substantial improvement throughout the first year. Then, gradual improvement is often noted across even a five-year period (Heller et al., 1996).

Educators can play important roles in the recovery of students with TBI. They can provide considerable assistance during the often difficult period when the student is just returning to school and still in the process of adjusting to unusual fatigue, reduced energy, and loss of ability. Educators can also help students learn, once again, how to remember information—an ability frequently impaired with TBI (Hutchinson & Marquardt, 1997). Providing environmental cues, teaching mnemonics, and providing many opportunities to remember previously known information all contribute to improved performance in students with TBI.

PREVALENCE

More than 100,000 children and youth between the ages of birth and 21 are hospitalized each year for injuries to the head. Estimates vary about the long-term effects of these injuries. Some believe that 1 in 500 of these children develop persistent learning and behavior problems (Katsiyannis & Conderman, 1994), and others think that over one-third of those injuries result in lifelong disabilities (Singer, 1996). According to the federal government, 10,378 students were served by special education in the 1996–1997 schoolyear as having TBI (U.S. Department of Education, 1998).

CAUSES AND PREVENTION

The most common causes of TBI are falls, domestic accidents, motor vehicle accidents, pedestrian and bicycle accidents, assaults, and sports accidents (Hux & Hacksley, 1996). These injuries typically occur among older children. Unfortunately, the sad fact is that for children under the age of 2, the most common cause of TBI is child abuse (Heller, et al., 1996).

Those schoolchildren most at risk for TBI are teenage males (Singer, 1996). The majority of cases occur in youngsters 15 and older (West et al., 1996). Why is this so? They are the group who engage in high-risk behaviors such as driving too fast, mixing alcohol or drugs and driving, skateboarding without protective equipment, and participating in contact sports. Preventing many of these accidents merely involves some commonsense measures. For example, wearing helmets when bicycling or skateboarding, not driving a car or motorcycle when using intoxicating substances, or avoiding high-risk behaviors can prevent tragic accidents.

The effects of TBI can be reduced and long-term negative outcomes prevented in many cases by the actions of family members and professionals. The influence of the family on the long-term outcomes of their children with TBI should never be minimized, for the results can be great. In one study, significant improvements in academic and behavioral performance a year after the injury could be attributed directly to the family's involvement (Singer, 1996).

It is obvious that appropriate medical treatment and rehabilitation are critical to preventing the devastating outcomes seen in untreated individuals. Education is also a powerful tool, and students are helped by their special education and general education teachers. Teachers can do many things to enhance these students' ability to succeed. Tyler and Mira (1993) recommend the following steps:

- Retrain and teach cognitive skills
- Consider whether the student is thinking and processing appropriately
- Check on any prerequisite cognitive skills
- Provide frequent feedback
- Refocus student's attention if necessary
- Repeat and review
- Provide examples and models
- Give simple and frequent instructions, both verbal and written
- Provide enough time to respond
- Use computers, especially for drill and practice (p. 25)

CHILDREN WITH TBI

Children with TBI and their families face great emotional turmoil during the time shortly after the injury. They must adjust to changes in ability, performance, and behavior (Hux & Hacksley, 1996). Even those with mild cases of TBI must cope with sudden changes in performance and many of the common symptoms shown in Table 12.5. What came easily one day is filled with frustration and confusion the next. Tasks that were previously easy to perform now present repeated failure. Many youngsters with TBI tend to have uneven abilities, a fact that is confusing to the individuals and to their teachers. These students also often experience reduced stamina, seizures, headaches, hearing losses, and vision problems (Tyler & Myles, 1991).

Table 12.5 Characteristics of TBI

Medical/Neurological	Physical	Cognitive	Behavioral/Emotional
Blurred vision	Decreased motor coordination	Decreased attention	Denial of deficits
Concussion		Decreased organizational skills	Depression
Dizziness	Sensory deficits affecting vision, hearing, taste, or smell	Decreased problem solving	Disinhibition
Headache		Slowed information processing	Distractibility
Seizure activity		Difficulty with abstract reasoning	Flat affect
Skull fracture		Memory deficits	Impulsivity
Sleep disorder		Perceptual deficits	Inappropriate laughing or crying
		Poor judgment	Irritability
		Rigidity of thought	Limited initiation
		Word-finding difficulty	Social isolation

Source: From "Mild traumatic brain injury: Facilitating school success" by K. Hux and C. Hacksley, 1996, *Intervention in School and Clinic, 31,* p. 161. Reprinted by permission.

They get tired easily, so some receive home instruction, often for a year, before returning to school part-time. Many of these youngsters have difficulty adjusting to and accepting their newly acquired disability. Because of the frustrations of having difficulty doing tasks that used to be easy, many display behavior problems and reduced self-esteem.

With some simple adjustments to and accommodations in the classroom routine, though, students with brain injuries can be reintegrated into school settings with relative ease (Mira et al., 1992; Tyler & Myles, 1991). If students spend only half a day at school, the teacher can schedule instruction on important academic tasks during the morning, when they are alert. Homework assignments can be abbreviated to accommodate their reduced stamina. If some students find that their balance, coordination, and ability to carry materials are more limited than before the accident, the teacher can provide another set of textbooks for home use to make life much easier for them and their families. Because many of these students get confused easily, teachers should clearly specify and adhere to classroom rules and expectations. It is also helpful to use instructional tactics that incorporate a considerable amount of drill and practice to help students remember what is being taught.

VERY LOW INCIDENCE DISABILITIES

I have just provided some specific information about three very low incidence disabilities. For each, we talked about definitions, prevalence, causes and preventive techniques, and characteristics. Now let's turn our attention to more general information about three issues: educational interventions, families, and technology. Recognize that the following information will not apply to every individual and that it may pertain to one of these three groups of learners more than the others. Still, we think it is applicable to many children with these disabilities. For example, the supports needed by most individuals with autism, deaf–blindness, and moderate to severe cases of TBI are often both intensive and pervasive. The special needs of these individuals are quite challenging for all who work with them.

EDUCATIONAL INTERVENTIONS

Students with very low incidence disabilities present complex profiles to their families and to their teachers. Despite being assigned to a category, each student should be considered a unique member of a diverse group of learners, all possessing different learning styles and characteristics. As such, instructional programs need to be designed on an individual basis to meet each student's needs. Despite their diversity, these children often share many common goals and desired outcomes. For example, a common goal among children with multiple and severe disabilities is improving communication skills. Another is the development of proficient social skills. These students also experience persistent academic problems, probably because of their poor abilities to generalize their learning of one skill to another. Skills often need to be taught in small increments through consistent, systematic, and direct instructional techniques (Strain et al., 1995). Particularly for students with autism, schedules need to be predictable, teachers need to use concrete examples and avoid ambiguous language, and instruction should be routinely systematic (Peeters, 1997). Many discussions about teaching these skills to preschoolers and schoolchildren with disabilities are found in earlier chapters of this text, so discussion here is limited to two intervention strategies.

But first, educators should never lose sight of the prevailing principles of special education (Maurice et al., 1996; Koegel & Koegel, 1995; Peeters, 1997; Szekeres & Meserve, 1994). These principles should be the foundation for all instruction provided to every child with a disability:

- Instructional procedures, verified through research, are scheduled
- Student assessments are functionally related to instruction
- Educational decisions are made on an individual basis
- Instruction is applied directly to the target behavior
- Collaboration among members of multidisciplinary teams promotes appropriate education
- Accommodations are made for the unique learning styles of each student
- Frequent student evaluation (curriculum based instruction) guides the development and modifications of instructional programs

Functional assessment procedures (described by Rob Horner and George Sugai in the Research to Practice box earlier in this chapter) help parents and educators better understand the relationship between environmental events and target behaviors (Harris et al., 1994; Kennedy & Meyer, 1998); Mullen & Frea, 1995). These techniques often reveal the events that cause inappropriate or undesirable behavior to occur and the reasons why behaviors continue. In many cases, educators find that some unproductive behaviors occur for purposes of escape, attention, or communication. For example, a tantrum—for children who do not know how to ask for help—may be a means of escaping schoolwork that is too difficult or frustrating. When such is the case, educators have found that teaching a student to engage in functionally equivalent behaviors (e.g., "Is this right?" "I need help") often replaces the disruptive behavior (Koegel et al., 1995). These behaviors serve to teach the student very useful skills. (Refer to the Achieving Discipline box for the steps to be followed when teaching functionally equivalent behaviors.) Another intervention that is proving successful, particularly for students with autism, is called **incidental teaching.** Incidental teaching, which was first developed at the University of Kansas and further studied at Emory University, uses many of the principles of the Lovass method (LaRue, 1998). Because the instruction and practice activities are provided in naturally occurring settings, generalization is more likely.

COLLABORATION FOR INCLUSION

It appears that the hopes and promises some parents and professionals have for the full inclusion educational model are not being uniformly achieved. One reason for the disappointment may be different goals that parents have for their sons and daughters. Many parents satisfied with their children's progress in fully inclusive classes believe that they experience more acceptance, increased feelings of belonging, and a larger network of friends (Hunt & Goetz, 1997). These outcomes do not happen by accident, and are achieved only when parents, educators, and multidisciplinary team members work closely together (Kennedy et al., 1997). However, these goals are not uniformly held for students with disabilities (Downing, 1997; Vaughn, 1997). Many parents and professionals, for example, expect curriculum targets to include independent living, academic, and job skills. For them, educational programs in which these skills are not directly taught are not appropriate.

Review the Research to Practice boxes found in Chapters 3–11.

For more information about functional assessments and related topics, see:
- The IEP process in Chapter 2
- Behavioral Intervention Plans in Chapter 8
- ABC Analysis (Achieving Discipline) in Chapter 8
- Teaching Functionally Equivalent Behaviors (Achieving Discipline) in this chapter

incidental teaching.
Expanding skills by reinforcing and teaching behaviors and skills performed by individuals naturally.

Achieving Discipline

TEACHING THE ALTERNATIVES: FUNCTIONALLY EQUIVALENT BEHAVIORS

Jack, a five-year-old child with autism, engaged in high rates of self-stimulation and temper tantrums. He flapped his hands, he rocked back and forth, he repeated words and phrases that had no communicative meaning, and he pounded his hands on his desk. If interrupted he would cry, scream, and be out of control. It seemed that all of Jack's behavior was excessive, and definitely disruptive to his classmates. Ms. Curren, Jack's special education Kindergarten teacher, her assistant, Mrs. Alanya, and Ms. Meers, Jack's general education teacher, conducted a functional assessment of these behaviors. In the classroom and on a home visit, they collected data and information about these inappropriate behaviors. Their intent was to determine the functional relationships between environmental events and the disruptive behaviors. They interviewed family members and other caregivers (babysitters). They discussed the situation among themselves. They directly observed Jack using the ABC model of data collection. In this stage, they described the behaviors in detail, the events (Antecedents) that preceded the self-stimulatory behaviors (the target Behavior), and those events that followed the behaviors (Consequences). When they summarized all of the information while searching for functional relationships, they determined that a significant amount of Jack's disruptive behavior was an attempt to seek attention.

This information, along with knowledge of research findings indicating that developing functionally equivalent behaviors would cause a reduction in the frequency of the related inappropriate behaviors, led them to design an intervention program. They taught Jack to say "Is this right?" when he wanted Ms. Curren's, Ms. Meers's, or Mrs. Alanya's attention. When Jack needed assistance with his work, they taught him to say "I need help." Jack's family members also rewarded Jack when he did not engage in self-stimulation but instead used these two phrases appropriately. Without directly targeting the stereotypic behaviors and instead teaching and reinforcing functionally equivalent behaviors, Jack's parents and teachers saw dramatic improvement in his performance.

Developing functionally equivalent behaviors

- Carefully identify the inappropriate behavior(s) in behavioral terms
- Analyze the behavior and the events that stimulate and maintain it
- Determine substitute behaviors to develop
- Teach and reward alternative behaviors
- Work with everyone to be sure that there is consistency across all settings (home, school, playground)

MAKING
CONNECTIONS

To review LRE and FAPE, see the What Is Special Education sections of Chapter 1 and the Service Delivery Options section (Special Education Services) in Chapter 2.

So despite all of the rhetoric about full inclusion, where do students with severe and multiple disabilities attend school? Let's look at placement patterns. About 12% of children with autism receive the majority of their educational programs in general education class settings (U.S. Department of Education, 1998). About 11% spend somewhere between 21% and 60% of their schoolday attending a resource room, 54% attend separate special education classes, 21% attend special schools, and 3% are placed in residential facilities. The majority of students with deaf–blindness receive their education in special education classes (Baldwin, 1995). Some 40% attend special classes, while 39% attend either public or private special schools. Probably reflecting the complexity of their disabilities, only 11% attend general education classes and 10% attend resource rooms as their primary educational placements. The pattern for students with TBI is somewhat similar to the other two groups (U.S. Department of Education, 1998). The majority of students attend either a general education class (29%) or a resource room (25%). About a third of these students (some 31%) participate for the majority of the schoolday in a special education classroom. A little more than 2% of these students receive hospital or homebound services, and 2% attend school at residential facilities. It is important to understand that the full inclusion movement has made some difference in where these students are educated, but still very few attend general education programs most of the day.

Although integration is clearly important and necessary to achieve adult independence, growing concerns about fully inclusive programs, particularly for children with autism during their early years, is being questioned (Maurice et al., 1996; Peeters, 1997). These experts maintain that effective education often requires specially trained teachers who implement carefully designed instructional programs. Many of the techniques that have proven effective through research are not compatible with the instruction provided to typical learners. For example, structured class schedules, use of concrete examples, controlled teacher language, reduction or elimination of distractions, and rigorously applied behavioral tactics often prove very effective and even necessary for some students with disabilities. For these youngsters, at that point in their educational careers, general education classes are probably not the appropriate placement. However, multidisciplinary teams determining students' placements and evaluating student progress must continually balance the drawbacks and benefits of every educational option available. They must also work together to be sure that the necessary accommodations are in place that will ensure successful outcomes in general education settings. The Accommodatiing for Inclusive Environments box lists some accommodations that many students with autism need to profit from general education placements. Remember, what may be the "correct" educational placement at one point in a child's overall program may later be the "wrong" placement. Frank del Olmo stresses this point. He is certain that his son Frankie would not now be successful in his general education kindergarten class if he had not first participated in a forty-hour-a-week preschool program offered by teachers specially prepared in the Lovass method (del Olmo, 1997). The performance of the student should be at the heart of these decisions.

For more information about functional or life skills, see the Functional Curriculum section (Education and the Schoolchild) in Chapter 6.

TRANSITION TO ADULTHOOD

One important goal of transition programs is for individuals with severe disabilities to achieve social integration in workplace, residential, and recreational settings. This, along with two other goals—holding a job and living independently—provide the core of many education programs during the transition years. Clearly, being employed, possessing functional life skills, and meeting the requirements of daily life (managing a budget, maintaining a household, cooking, shopping) are important to what is considered successful adulthood. However, social integration is thought of by some as associated with quality of life (Chadsey-Rusch & Heal, 1995). Table 12.6 on page 534 lists some important instructional targets that should improve social outcomes of young people.

FAMILIES

Particularly since the 1992 AAMR definition of mental retardation, professionals in the field of special education have been reconceptualizing programs and services for

Accommodating for Inclusive Environments

CREATING SITUATIONS WHERE INDIVIDUALS WITH AUTISM
PARTICIPATE SUCCESSFULLY

Make events predictable

Develop a schedule

Make novel experiences predictable

Avoid surprises

Do not make unannounced changes

Provide structure and a routine

Know how well the individual handles free time

Communicate instructions and consequences carefully

Seek consistency in everyone's responses to inappropriate behavior

Use direct statements

Do not use slang or metaphors

Avoid only using nonverbal cues

Use personal pronouns carefully

Foster positive participation

Provide feedback about the appropriateness of responses

Remember to tell the individual when behavior is proper

Arrange tasks that the person can perform

Translate time into something tangible or visible

Enhance verbal communications with illustrations or pictures

Use concrete examples

For more information about the 1992 AAMR definition of mental retardation, see the Defined section of Chapter 6.

people with disabilities (Luckasson et al., 1992). The worth of these programs is measured in terms of outcomes (or results) for these individuals when they are adults, with their merit being judged by adult independence. The focus is on the type and amount of support the individual needs to remain in the community, living, working, and playing alongside and with people without disabilities (Bradley et al., 1993). The family is one of the most obvious sources of natural support for all individuals with disabilities, particularly those with low incidence disabilities. Support requires commitment. As you read in Leslie Palanker's story (in the Personal Perspective at the beginning of the chapter), you saw how her child impacted on her whole life and how commitment to a child with a disability results in support.

Singer (1996) provides us with some key concepts about creating family supports:

- Service agency personnel should consider the family as the primary unit of concern.
- The family should be assisted in remaining involved in the community and avoiding isolation and withdrawal from friends and activities.
- Support services should be arranged specifically for each family's needs, rather than expecting a family to avail itself of services that happen to be available.
- Many families need a case manager, one person to coordinate all services and supports for the family and the individual.
- Supports must be available across the individual's life span and change as needs change.

Table 12.6 Transition Outcomes

Individuals know how to
- ask for help, offer assistance, ask questions.
- answer questions, respond to criticism.
- interact with others socially at work.
- initiate conversations appropriately.
- advocate for themselves.
- interpret and discriminate social cues.

Personal acceptance is demonstrated by co-workers
- voluntarily eating lunch with the individual.
- seeing the individual after work.
- taking breaks with the individual.
- indicating that the individual is a friend.
- encouraging the individual to attend company social events.

Co-workers or the employer
- initiates social interactions with the individual.
- responds to social interactions initiated by the individual.
- advocates for the individual.
- teaches the individual new social skills.

Individuals participate socially by interacting with co-workers
- about work upon arrival, at breaks, during lunch, several times throughout the day, and after work.
- on nonwork topics upon arrival, at breaks, during lunch, and after work.
- at company-sponsored events.
- social occasions that occur outside of work.

Individuals experience social support as demonstrated by increased
- happiness at work.
- self-esteem.
- friendship network.
- support network.

Individuals are accepted in the workplace as indicated by co-workers
- indicating they like the person.
- advocating or supporting the person.
- considering the person to be an acquaintance.
- considering the person to be a team player.
- displaying positive, general interactions.
- training the person to perform work tasks better.

Source: From "Building consensus from transition experts on social integration outcomes and interventions" by J. Chadsey-Rusch and L. W. Heal, 1995, *Exceptional Children, 62,* pp. 170–174. Adapted with permission.

- Families should be empowered, so they can provide supports and meet challenges without always depending on social service agencies or others.
- People with low incidence disabilities should be an integral part of the community.
- Services that encourage family support must adapt to cultural diversity.

Let's take a look at what these concepts really mean. Simply put, the family's concerns, needs, capacity, and potential for providing support must be moved to the forefront. No longer can the individual with low incidence or severe disabilities be isolated or viewed as an individual who exists without the availability of natural supports. In practice, it means that parents, brothers and sisters, and extended family members should be included in the individual's school, rehabilitation, and social service programs. They should be invited for involvement. When arranging planning sessions, their schedules and desires should be considered. However, it is crucial that their needs be understood. Some may not wish to be involved in the life of the individual with the disability. Professionals from mainstream culture must be sensitive and adapt to others' cultural beliefs and expectations.

Services and programs for individuals with low incidence disabilities should be an integral part of the community. The premise is that sustained family involvement in the lives of those with disabilities increases the probability of success and independence in the community. For example, instead of living in an institution miles from their home communities, these individuals live in settings (homes, apartments, neighborhoods) like everyone else. In many cases, this cannot occur without considerable support from a variety of sources. To prevent the terrible treatment experienced by many individuals with disabilities living in institutions far removed from public scrutiny, those who give family support and community support need to be aware of the signs of abuse. To some, not only is the **family system** the best source of support, but its members have some clear roles to fill (Dell Orto & Power, 1997). If they choose to accept these roles, they should be considered full members of the child's multidisciplinary team. They also can be information providers, active participants in assessment and treatment, and advocates. Individuals from the family system can extend treatment programs to all aspects of the individual's life and assist with generalization. This network of people expresses the hopes and dreams for the achievement of goals for the targeted family member.

MAKING CONNECTIONS

For more about family support, see the Family section of Chapter 6.

family system. Potential sources of support for people with disabilities, including sons and daughters, spouses, parents, siblings, in-laws, aunts and uncles, grandparents, extended family members, and step-family members.

TECHNOLOGY

A major positive change in the lives of people with disabilities and their families has been the development of technology that can address and compensate for their disabilities. Many of these technological advances (alternative and augmentative communication devices, assistive technology, computer-assisted and -enhanced instruction) are very beneficial to individuals with low incidence disabilities. The advent of these devices has allowed students with severe and multiple disabilities to participate in classroom activities in new and important ways. Most students raise their hands to get their teachers' attention, for a turn to participate or to ask for help. Joey, however, cannot raise his hand, but has learned to operate a switch that turns on a light instead. He uses another switch to hear a tape-recorded story when classmates are reading silently, and other switches to use a communication device (Sax et al., 1997).

For the wide array of technological advances that can assist people with disabilities to learn, communicate, see, hear, interact with others, and function better in daily life, see the Technology sections throughout this text.

NEW DIRECTIONS
FOR THE
MILLENNIUM

Legacy: Advances in instructional technology and assistive technology continue to change the lives of people with severe disabilities.

Opportunities:

- Ensure that funding for research and development of technology enhancements continues
- Find ways for people with disabilities to have open access to new and emerging technology

distance education. Uses telecommunications technologies to deliver instruction by experts to areas where particular expertise is needed.

You've learned about the importance of assistive technology in the previous chapters of this text. So in this chapter I have decided to focus on yet another contribution that technology can make to the lives of individuals with disabilities and those who work with them.

A major challenge faced by school administrators who work in rural and remote areas is a lack of sufficient numbers of children who share low incidence disabilities to support the costs of experts from a variety of different disciplines to work with these children and their families. For example, there may be only one deaf–blind child in an entire school district that is hundreds of miles from a large metropolitan area and comprehensive medical services. There may be only two children with autism in adjacent school districts that together cover a thousand square miles. Simply put, it is quite likely that there is insufficient expertise at these school sites to provide an appropriate education for these children, regardless of age and unique learning needs. Compounding the problem are the difficulties of communicating with many people: parents who live many miles from school, members of the multidisciplinary team who come from different parts of the state, itinerant teachers and related service providers, and the student's school based teachers. Table 12.7 lists some ideas about how distance technology can be used to increase communication opportunities with families of students with disabilities.

Today, some of these problems can be solved through technology by using the practices, hardware, and software developed for another purpose: **distance education.** This technology was created to deliver instruction to remote areas, typically a substantial distance from a university campus. Although a great benefit to students with disabilities and their families, the applications of this technology extend far beyond the enhancement of teachers' skills and knowledge. For example, distance education could create "statewide classrooms" where special educators who live even hundreds of miles away can collaborate, team teach, and work together to meet the needs of students with very special learning needs. Consulting teachers and related service providers can work with classroom teachers hundreds of miles away. Through live and interactive television, behavior can be evaluated by a multidisciplinary team as it is occurring in the classroom. Team members can also help the teacher develop and implement an educational program as it is being tested with the child.

Distance education technology can be applied to work with families. Many families have televisions and videotape players in their homes or can arrange to borrow the equipment from the school or a neighbor. This "video connection" can enhance the interaction between the family and the school, even when work and distance make it difficult for family members to make frequent school visits. Teachers can use videotapes to introduce members of the multidisciplinary team to the family, even though their visits to school could not be coordinated to occur at the same time or even on the same day when the parents could be present. Distance education technology can help bridge the gap with families who do not speak sufficient English to understand technical terms and descriptions of how to best work with their child with limited vision and hearing. Lessons might be taped in the family's home language and sent home with the child. Using this strategy, parents can help with generalization by implementing school programs at home that they now understand because they were explained in their primary language (even when none of the teachers at their child's school is proficient in that language). By using a camcorder, the family can also record behaviors they find problematic at home and seek help from the professionals at school.

Table 12.7 Using Distance Technology to Communicate with Families

Exchange Videotapes Between School and Home

The teacher or itinerant specialist might videotape:

A tour of the school and classrooms the child uses

An introduction of all of the teachers and related service messages to the family

Examples of the child's educational programs at school

Demonstrations of activities for follow-up at home

Initial performance and "progress" performances

Activities as a video "report card"

The child engaged in "excellent levels" of performance as examples or models of results that can be achieved

Home language and English comparisons for families who might not be English proficient

The parents or family might videotape:

Introductions of family members, including the extended family and other caregivers (important neighbors, babysitters, close friends)

Introductions of important members of the child's community

The child performing chores and family functions

Behaviors the family would like help in improving

The child participating in significant community events

Messages to the teachers

Use the Internet for More Frequent Communication

Have students create Web sites:

Include descriptions of the classroom, classmates, and teacher(s)

Have students talk about themselves (interests, hobbies, favorite subjects)

Scan photos and pictures into the site

Add in video clips

Use e-mail frequently to:

Share daily progress

Talk about concerns

Create a distribution list to include all multidisciplinary team members

For other discussions about LRE and inclusion, see the What Is Special Education section of Chapter 1, the Service Delivery Options section (Special Education Services) in Chapter 2, and the Collaboration for Inclusion sections in Chapters 3–11.

CONCEPTS AND CONTROVERSY: THE DELICATE BALANCE BETWEEN SEGREGATION AND INTEGRATION

By now you are probably nearing the end of the semester and have almost completed this text. It should be clear: At the heart of great debate and consternation lie issues about where students with disabilities should receive their education. Related issues focus on what that education should comprise and what the first and second priority outcomes for these students should be. In other words, what comprises an appropriate education and what is meant by least restrictive environment? Some parents and professionals believe adamantly that "students with disabilities should be full-time members of age-appropriate, typical classrooms in their home schools (whatever school they would attend if they did not have disabilities) and receive all supports necessary to participate in both the academic and social communities of their peers" (Goetz, 1995, p. 3). The courts, however, do not always agree (*Early Childhood Report*, 1996). In one recent ruling, a 13-year-old student with severe and multiple disabilities, despite his parents' wishes, was denied full-time general education placement. Special education classes with integration in activities across the schoolday was determined to be the LRE. So the debate about LRE continues. But what are its origins, and why is the issue so inflammatory?

Historically, students with severe disabilities were excluded from U.S. public education. For most of these individuals, it took a federal law (PL 94–142, passed in 1975) and many court decisions to guarantee them a place in the educational system. As programs were initiated and services evolved, special classes were developed (some at segregated schools). With all good intentions, these programs were thought to be highly specialized. Students were brought together where they could form a group sufficiently large to allow highly trained specialists (PTs, OTs, SLPs, nurses, assistive technology specialists) to work with expensive special equipment (therapeutic swimming pools, technology). In part because students with severe disabilities were not making hoped-for progress in the development of social skills, were not integrated into mainstream society, and were not generalizing skills learned at school to other settings, The Association for Persons with Severe Disabilities (TASH) has vigorously advocated for all students with disabilities to be educated exclusively in the general education classroom. This model has been referred to as full inclusion.

Consensus still exists among this group: Full inclusion is the best service delivery model for these students (Haring & Romer, 1995). However, some—even those instrumental in creating the full inclusion model—are suggesting modifications (Romer & Haring, 1995). What are the concerns? Inclusion does not guarantee performance outcomes. In fact, no educational placement can make such guarantees. For students with disabilities, if a skill is not directly taught, it is usually not learned. Experts in deaf–blindness make this point well:

> Merely being present with peers without disabilities in general education settings is not sufficient to bring about those outcomes.... We have seen too many students with deaf–blindness included with their peers for many hours a day, only to find that no meaningful relationships were developed with those peers, that no psychological sense of community was felt. We believe this is because, like behavioral technology, we have confused a process, or a behavior, with an outcome. (Romer & Haring, 1995, p. 426)

These experts are not abandoning the concept of integration but are questioning whether placement alone can achieve outcome goals (Kennedy et al., 1997). They also raise an interesting point for those with very low incidence disabilities: Full inclusion could be interpreted as sending a message that the only relationships valued are those with people without disabilities. Being included at the neighborhood school may well mean that no other student with that disability attends school there. Support needs should be met from a variety of communities: families, peers without disabilities, and peers with similar disabilities (Romer & Haring, 1995). People need to be allowed to gain a sense of community with those who have similar interests, concerns, and needs. They need, for example, to band together to advocate for each other when the necessity arises, or share problems and solutions with each other. These connections can be made outside of school, as well as at school. Certainly, issues about placement need continual consideration. This discussion raises an important question: What comprises segregation? Is it being excluded for some part of the schoolday from students without disabilities? Or is segregation not being able to participate with others with similar concerns, interests, and abilities?

In Conclusion

MAKING CONNECTIONS

Look again at the Advance Organizers at the beginning of the chapter; to help you study the chapter's content, the answers to the Focus and Challenge questions are found here. Test yourself to see if you have mastered the major points of this chapter.

Summary

Although the size of the disability group is probably not very important to the individuals or the families affected, these three special education categories are each comprised of very few students. Together, autism, deaf–blindness, and traumatic brain injury account for about .06% of schoolchildren. Although relatively small in numbers, these disabilities are often severe, affecting overall performance significantly. Many of these individuals also have additional problems in one or more of these areas: cognition, language, speech, and motor skills. Many have mental retardation. Individuals with low incidence disabilities have complex learning needs that require the collaborative input of many experts from comprehensive multidisciplinary teams.

Focus Questions

Self-Test Questions

- *What are the major characteristics of children with autism?*

  In 1943, when Leo Kanner first coined the term *autism* and described the condition, he specified two primary characteristics: extreme isolation and excessive insistence on sameness. He also required that these two symptoms be present during infancy. Kanner's is probably the strictest definition of autism, and therefore permits the least number of individuals to be included. Less restrictive definitions also include excessive behaviors, the need for sameness, and social withdrawal. They also describe these behaviors as typifying the condition: stereotyped movements, repetitive activities, unusual responses to auditory and visual stimuli, poor educational performance, inability to initiate or maintain social interactions, and poor language development. Other behaviors are often observed among members of this population. For example, many (about 40%) engage in self-injurious behaviors, such as head banging, eye poking, and biting. The vast majority (some 80%) of these individuals also have mental retardation, and over half do not develop functional speech or language. About a third of the group develop seizures, and four out of five are males. Some individuals exhibit bizarre inconsistencies in their abilities, but only 5% are considered savants and possess unique musical, artistic, or memory abilities.

- *How would you describe the impact of deaf–blindness on those affected?*

  People with deaf–blindness live in very restricted environments. Their dual disability impacts their communication and mobility abilities. As a group, their hearing problems tend to be more severe than their visual disabilities, but their losses in both areas require special adaptations and instruction in both modes for maximal learning to occur. The most typical combination is for the individual to be classified as legally blind and also have a severe hearing loss. Some develop speech and can learn to read print, and others cannot. In almost all cases, these individuals need support from others to make their environments safe and accessible. Because of their limited vision and hearing, many experience significant feelings of isolation. In addition, a great number of these individuals have additional disabilities, such as mental retardation, speech or language impairments, physical disabilities, and health problems.

- *What additional disabilities do children with autism and children with deaf–blindness often possess?*

  The majority of children with autism and children with deaf–blindness could also qualify as belonging to the special education category of multiple disabilities. It is very common for individuals from both groups to also have mental retardation. About 80% of those in the autism category have mental retardation, and this is the most common additional disability for those with deaf–blindness. Speech and language development is a problem area for many of these individuals as well. Those with cognitive impairments often do not fully develop language skills, and those who are deaf usually do not develop speech (and may use sign language instead). Their severe disabilities impact their lives in significant and complex ways.

- *How can many cases of TBI be prevented?*

  The most common causes of traumatic brain injury (TBI) are domestic accidents, motorcycle accidents, car accidents, pedestrian and bicycle accidents, assaults, sports injuries, and child abuse. Except for child abuse, most TBI cases occur among teenage males who engage in high-risk behaviors. Wearing protective gear such as seat belts and helmets can prevent many of these injuries. Avoiding substances such as drugs and alcohol when operating a vehicle can also prevent the accidents that cause many cases of TBI among teenagers. Preventing the dangerous cycle of domestic violence is a complex and major problem in our nation today, but children must be protected and the home environments in which they are raised must be made safe.

- *How are functional assessments and the development of functionally equivalent behaviors used together?*

  Many special educators across many different disability areas use functional assessments (sometimes referred to as an ABC analysis). This behavioral technique helps to more clearly understand an individual's inappropriate behavior patterns. It helps to define the behavior better. For example, for a specific individual self-injurious behavior might include head banging and biting but no other harmful behavior. By analyzing under what conditions the behavior occurs, educators can come to understand what causes and what events maintain the behavior of concern. For instance, head banging occurs most often when the individual is asked to perform a difficult and frustrating task and seems to be maintained because considerable attention is given to the person when that behavior is happening. In this situation, educators will teach the individual how to engage in a functionally equivalent behavior with the aim of replacing the inappropriate behavior with a more useful one. In this case the teacher might encourage the student to raise his hand and say "I need help" when presented with difficult learning situations. The pairing of functional assessments with teaching functionally equivalent behaviors can lead to the reduction of undesirable behaviors and the increase of helpful and productive skills.

Challenge Question

- *What comprises an appropriate education and the least restrictive environment for students with low incidence disabilities?*

MAKING CONNECTIONS

Resources to extend your learning about people with disabilities are found at the end of every chapter, and a fuller listing is available in the Students' Resource Manual that accompanies this text.

There is no single answer to this question. Students with disabilities are very diverse. Their educational goals differ, their abilities are not the same, and the significance of their disabilities is not uniform. Each student's educational goals, effectiveness of instructional methods applied, and desired outcomes for the educational program must drive decisions about what comprises an appropriate education and where it should be delivered.

 ## Supplementary Resources

Scholarly Reading

Haring, N. G., & Romer, L. T. (Eds.). (1995). *Welcoming students who are deaf–blind into typical classrooms: Facilitating school participation, learning, and friendships.* Baltimore: Paul H. Brookes.

Heubner, K. M., Prickett, J. G., Welch, R. R., & Joffee, E. (Eds.). (1995). *Hand in hand: Essentials of communication and orientation and mobility for your students who are deaf–blind.* New York: AFB Press.

Koegel, R. L., & Koegel, L. K. (Eds.). (1995). *Teaching children with autism: Strategies for initiating positive interactions and improving learning opportunities.* Baltimore: Paul H. Brookes.

Mira, M. P., Tucker, B. F., & Tyler, J. S. (1992). *Traumatic brain injury in children and adolescents: A sourcebook for teachers and other school personnel.* Austin, TX: Pro-Ed.

Peeters, T. (1997). *Autism: From theoretical understanding to educational intervention.* San Diego: Singular Publishing Group.

Singer, G. H. S., Glang, A., & Williams, J. M. (Eds.). (1996). *Children with acquired brain injury: Educating and supporting families.* Baltimore: Paul H. Brookes.

Popular Books

Grandin, T. (1995). *Thinking in pictures and other reports from my life with autism.* NY: Viking Books.

Keller, H. (1988). *The story of my life.* NY: Sig Classics.

Sacks, O. (1995). *An anthropologist on Mars: Seven paradoxical tales.* NY: Random House.

Popular Videos

The miracle worker (1962). United Artists.

Rain man (1988). United Artists.

Backstreet dreams (1990). Vidmark Entertainment.

Regarding Henry (1991). Paramount.

The James Brady story (1991). HBO.

House of cards (1993). Penta Pictures Production (A&M Films).

Professional, Parent, and Consumer Organizations and Agencies

American Association of the Deaf–blind
814 Thayer Avenue, Room 300
Silver Spring, MD 20910
Phone: (301) 588-6545 (TTY only)
Web site: http://www.tr.wou.edu/dblink/aadb.htm

Autism Hotline
Autism Services Center
P.O. Box 507
605 Ninth Street
Huntington, WV 25710-0507
Phone: (304) 525-8014

Autism Society of America
7910 Woodmont Avenue, Suite 650
Bethesda, MD 20814-3015
Phone: (800) 3AUTISM; (301) 657-0881
Web site: www.autism-society.org

Brain Injury Association, Inc.
1775 Massachusetts Avenue NW, Suite 100
Washington, DC 20036-1904
Phone: (800) 444-6443; (703) 236-6000
Web site: www.biausa.org

Helen Keller National Center for Deaf–Blind Youths and Adults
111 Middle Neck Road
Sands Point, NY 11050
Phone: (516) 944-8900 (voice/TTY)
Web site: http://www.helenkeller.org

National Information Clearinghouse on Children who are Deaf–Blind (DB-LINK)
345 N. Monmouth Avenue
Monmouth, OR 97361
Phone: (800) 438-9376 (voice); (800) 854-7013 (TTY)
Web site: www.tr.wosc.osshe.edu/dblink

Glossary

ABC model. A behavioral way to analyze and select interventions by looking at whether they occur antecedent to (before), concurrent with (during), or consequent to (after) the target behavior.

ability grouping. Placing students with comparable achievement and skill levels in the same classes or courses.

absence seizures. Seizures with a short lapse in consciousness (also called petit mal seizures).

acceleration. Moving students through a curriculum or years of schooling in a shorter period of time than usual.

accessibility. Barrier-free environments allowing maximal participation by individuals with disabilities.

accommodation. The focusing process of the lens of the eye.

acquired immunodeficiency syndrome (AIDS). A usually fatal medical syndrome caused by infection from the human immunodeficiency virus.

acuity. Sharpness of response to visual, auditory, or tactile stimuli.

adaptive behavior. Performance of everyday life skills expected of adults.

adaptive skill areas. Targets of instruction that focus on the ability of an individual to function in a typical environment and on successful adult outcomes (independent living, employment, and community participation).

advance organizers. Previews to lectures that acquaint students with the content, its organization, and importance.

advanced placement courses. High school courses that carry college credit.

adventitiously blind. Those who acquired severe visual disabilities after the age of two.

aggression. Hostile and attacking behavior, which can include verbal communication, directed toward self, others, or the physical environment.

air conduction audiometry method. A method to test hearing that uses a pure-tone sound generated by an audiometer.

alerting devices. Devices that use sight, sound, or vibration to make individuals aware of an occurrence or an important sound.

alternative and augmentative communication. Assistive technology devices that specifically help individuals communicate, including those that actually produce speech.

American Sign Language (ASL). The sign language or manual communication system preferred by many adults who are deaf in this country.

Americans with Disabilities Act (ADA). Federal disability antidiscrimination legislation passed in 1990.

anchored instruction. The use of videotaped real-life situations to make learning more relevant and meaningful.

anorexia. Intense fear of gaining weight, disturbed body image, chronic absence or refusal of appetite for food, causing severe weight loss (25% of body weight).

anoxia. Inadequate supply of oxygen to the body, usually at birth.

anvil (incus). One of the three tiny bones (ossicles) in the middle ear.

anxiety disorders. Conditions causing painful uneasiness, emotional tension, or emotional confusion.

aphasia. Loss or impairment of language ability due to brain injury.

array of services. A constellation of services, personnel, and educational placements.

articulation problems. Abnormal production of speech sounds.

Asperger syndrome. A little understood disability that shares many symptoms with autism, though in most cases cognitive abilities are average.

asphyxia. Deprivation of oxygen, often through near drowning or smoke inhalation.

assistive devices. Any equipment or technology that facilitates people's work, communication, mobility, or any aspect of daily life.

assistive listening devices (ALDs). Equipment such as hearing aids that helps deaf and hard of hearing individuals use their residual hearing.

assistive technology. Devices that help students with disabilities in their daily lives; they include hearing aids, wheelchairs, computers that offer augmentative communication, and a wide array of equipment that helps compensate for an individual's disabilities.

association. In thinking, the ability to see relationships among different concepts or knowledge bases.

asthma. A common, chronic condition resulting in difficulty in breathing.

at risk. Children whose condition or situation makes it probable for them to develop disabilities.

ataxia. A type of cerebral palsy characterized by movement disrupted by impaired balance and depth perception.

athetoid. A type of cerebral palsy characterized by purposeless and uncontrolled involuntary movements.

attention deficit hyperactivity disorder (ADHD). A condition that describes students who display hyperactive behaviors, have difficulty attending to the task at hand, and tend to be impulsive.

attention deficits. A characteristic often associated with learning disabilities in which students do not pay attention to the task or the correct features of a task to learn how to perform it well.

Attribute Treatment Interaction Approach. Selecting instructional methods that match a student's modality strength; visual learners receive visually-based procedures, and so on.

attributions. The explanations individuals give themselves for their successes or failures.

audio loop. A device that directs sound from the source directly to the listener's ear through a specially designed hearing aid.

audiodescription. A technique in which trained narrators describe visual and nonverbal information during the pauses in the audio or scripted dialogue of plays, films, and television shows by using FM transmissions or the extra sound track available on stereo televisions.

audiogram. The grid or graph used to display a person's hearing abilities.

audiologist. A professional trained to diagnose hearing losses and auditory problems.

audiometer. An electrical instrument for measuring the threshold of hearing tests using an audiometer; charts individuals' thresholds of hearing at various frequencies against sound intensities in decibels.

auditory nerve. Nerve that carries messages received through the ear to the brain; known in neurology as the eighth cranial nerve.

augmentative communication systems. Alternative methods of communicating, such as communication boards, communication books, sign language, and computerized voices.

aura. A signal of an impending seizure, sometimes called the preictal stage.

authentic assessments. Performance measures that use work generated by the student or observational data on social behaviors for assessment and evaluation purposes.

autism. A severe disorder of thinking, communication, interpersonal relationships, and behavior.

autistic savant. An individual who displays many behaviors associated with autism, yet also possesses discrete abilities and unusual talents.

autism spectrum. A group of disorders or conditions which share some characteristics and behaviors originally described under the classification of autism.

barrier games. Drill and practice activities that require the application of verbal skills to solve problems, using a game format.

basic interpersonal communicative skills (BICS). Face-to-face conversational language.

Behavioral Intervention Plan. The plan developed for any student with disabilities that includes a functional behavioral assessment and describes procedures to use to prevent and intervene if the student is violent, brings weapons to school, or is involved in drugs; the result of disciplinary action.

behavioral support. Organizing and arranging environments (schools, homes, workplaces) so problem behaviors are less likely to occur.

behind the ear (BTE). A hearing aid that cups behind the ear with a cord that runs into the person's ear canal.

benchmarks. Indicators of accomplishments for IEP goals and objectives.

Best Buddies. A program that pairs college students with people with mental retardation to build relationships, friendships, and opportunities for support.

best practices. Instructional techniques or methods proven through research to be effective.

bilingual maintenance approach. Teaching students partly in English using ESL strategies and partly in their home language so that they maintain proficiency.

bilingual transitional approach. Teaching students primarily in English and partly in their home language until they learn enough English to learn academic subjects.

bilingual-bicultural approach. The application of ESL and bilingual techniques to deaf education where ASL is the native language and reading and writing in English are taught as a second language.

bionic artificial limbs. Artificial arms and legs that replace full functioning of nonfunctional limbs.

blindness. Not having a functional use of sight.

bone conduction audiometry method. A test for conductive hearing loss in which a vibrator is placed on a person's forehead so that sound bypasses the outer and middle ear and goes directly to the inner ear; tests for conductive hearing losses.

braille. A system of reading and writing that uses dot codes that are embossed on paper, developed by Louis Braille in 1824.

bulimia. Chronically causing oneself to vomit, limiting weight gain.

captions. Subtitles that print the words spoken in film or video; can be either *closed* or *open.*

cascade of services. A linear and sequential model used to describe educational environments from the most to the least restrictive.

categorical. A system of classification using specific categories such as learning disabilities or mental retardation.

center schools. Separate schools (some residential), typically dedicated to serving students with a particular disability.

central nervous system dysfunction. Some brain or neurological damage that impedes individuals' motor and/or learning abilities.

central vision. The main field of vision in the eye, usually greater than 20 degrees.

cerebral palsy. A disorder of movement and posture caused by damage to the developing brain.

chaining. A strategy to teach the steps of skills that have been task analyzed, either first step first (forward chaining) or last step first (backward chaining).

child find. A function or office in each state's department of education that helps refer and identify children with disabilities.

chronic illness. Being sick for long periods of time.

chunking. Grouping information into smaller pieces so that it can be more easily remembered.

classifying. The ability to categorize items or concepts by their common characteristics.

cleft palate. An opening in the roof of the mouth, causing too much air to pass through the nasal cavity when the individual is speaking.

closed captions. Captions that can be seen on the television screen only with the use of a decoder.

closed-circuit television (CCTV). A television used for transmissions not accessible to the general public; sometimes, only one camera and television monitor is used.

cluster grouping. A plan whereby gifted students spend a part of their day in the general classroom on enriched or accelerated activities.

cochlea. Part of the inner ear that contains fluid and hairlike nerve cells that transmit information to the brain.

cochlear implant. Electronic microprocessor that replaces the cochlea and allows some people who are deaf to process sounds.

cognitive behavior modification. Instructional strategies that teach internal control methods (such as self-talk) in structured ways to help students learn how to learn.

cognitive/academic linguistic proficiency (CALP). The abstract language abilities required for academic work.

collaboration. Professionals working cooperatively to provide educational services.

collaborative consultation. Professionals, often from different disciplines, working together to develop and implement students' educational programs.

communication. The transfer of knowledge, ideas, opinions, and feelings.

communication board. A flat device on which words, pictures, or other symbols are used to expand the verbal interactions of people with limited vocal abilities.

communication competence. Proficiency in the use of language allowing people to participate in all aspects of communication in social and learning situations.

communication signals. A variety of messages that announce some immediate event, person, action, or emotion.

communication symbols. Voice, letters of the alphabet, or gestures used to relay communication messages.

community based instruction (CBI). A strategy of teaching functional skills in the environments in which they occur; for example, shopping skills should be taught in the local market rather than a classroom "store."

complex partial seizures. Periods of automatic behavior resulting from discharge in a localized area of the brain (sometimes called psychomotor or focal seizures).

computer-assisted instruction (CAI). Self-contained instructional software programs that students use to supplement or replace traditional teacher-directed instructional methods.

computer-enhanced instruction. Software programs that students use to supplement traditional instruction, used primarily for drill and practice.

computerized language translators. Microcomputers that provide translations of written text from one language to another.

code switching. Using different language and behavior appropriate in different settings.

conduct disorders. Behavior patterns that are externalizing and include "acting out" and hyperactivity, but this condition alone does not qualify as a disability according to IDEA.

conductive hearing loss. Hearing loss caused by damage or obstruction to the outer or middle ear that prevents transfer of sound to the inner ear.

confidential school records. Private files of a student.

congenitally blind. Those with severe visual disabilities present at birth.

consultation/collaborative teaching. General education and special education teachers working together to meet the needs of special needs students.

content. An aspect of language that governs the intent and meaning of the message delivered in a communication; includes semantics.

content enhancement strategies. Visual organizers of semantic information used in content instruction to teach concepts and vocabulary.

continuum of services. A graduated range of educational services, each level of service leading directly to the next one.

contractures. Joint stiffening, often because of muscle shortening, to the point that the joint can no longer move through its normal range.

cooperative learning. Groups of more than two students collaborating as they learn the same material.

cornea. The transparent, curved part of the front of the eye.

co-teaching. General education and special education teachers teaching together in the same classroom for the entire school day.

creativity. A form of intelligence characterized by advanced divergent thought, the production of many original ideas, and the ability to develop flexible and detailed responses and ideas.

cross-cultural dissonance. When the home and school cultures are in conflict.

cued speech. Hand signals for "difficult to see" speech sounds that accompany oral speech to assist lipreading.

cultural pluralism. All cultural groups are valued components of the society, and the language and traditions of each group are maintained.

curriculum based assessment (CBA). A method of evaluating children's performance by collecting data on their daily progress.

curriculum based measurement (CBM). A method of evaluating students' performance by collecting data on their daily progress.

curriculum compacting. Reducing instructional time spent on typical academic subjects so that enrichment activities can be included in the curriculum.

Deaf culture. The structures of social relationships, language (ASL), dance, theater, and other cultural activities that bind the Deaf community.

Deaf pride. A term used to signify the accomplishments and achievements of members of the Deaf community.

deaf–blindness. A dual disability whereby the individual has both vision and hearing problems.

deafness. Inability to usefully perceive sounds in the environment with or without the use of a hearing aid; inability to use hearing as the primary way to gain information.

decibel (dB). Unit of measure for intensity of sound.

decoder. A device that allows closed captions to appear on a television screen.

deinstitutionalization. Decreasing the number of individuals with mental retardation living in large congregate facilities.

demographics. The racial and ethnic composition of a country or regional area.

depression. A state of despair and dejected mood.

desktop publishing. Using a microcomputer and special software to prepare written and graphic material in publication format and quality.

dialect. Words and pronunciation from a particular area, different from the form of the language used by the normative group.

differentiated curriculum. The flexible application of curriculum targets that ensures content mastery, in-depth and independent learning, and exploration of issues and themes and allows for acceleration when needed.

dignity of risk. The principle that taking ordinary risks and chances is part of growing up and is essentially human.

direct instruction. Specifically focusing instruction on the desired, targeted behavior.

discalculia. Severely impaired ability to calculate or perform mathematical functions; presumed to be caused by central nervous system dysfunction.

discrepancy formulas. Formulas developed by state educational agencies or local districts to determine the difference between a child's actual achievement and expected achievement based on the student's IQ scores.

discrepancy scores. The scores used in some states to determine eligibility for services designed for students with learning disabilities.

disgraphia. Severely impaired ability to write; presumed to be caused by central nervous system dysfunction.

distance education. The use of telecommunications technologies to deliver instruction by experts to areas where particular expertise is needed.

distance senses. Senses—hearing and vision—that provide us with information external to our bodies, developed to help alert us to danger.

Down syndrome. A chromosomal disorder that causes identifiable physical characteristics and usually causes delays in physical and intellectual development.

due process hearing. A noncourt proceeding before an impartial hearing officer that can be used if parents and school personnel disagree on a special education issue.

dysfluencies. Aspects of speech that interrupt the pattern of speech; typical of normal speech development in young children.

dyslexia. Severely impaired ability to read; presumed to be caused by a central nervous system dysfunction.

eardrum (tympanic membrane). Part of the ear on which sound waves and their vibrations fall and cause the ossicles to move; separates the outer and middle ear.

Ebonics. A learned and rule-governed social dialect of nonstandard English, spoken by many African American children.

echolalia. Repeating exactly what was heard, immediately or even days later.

ecological assessment. A procedure that includes observational data collected in the student's natural environments for the purpose of identifying the antecedent events that cause a problem behavior or consequent events that maintain or increase the target behavior.

Education for All Handicapped Children Act (EHA) or Public law, PL 94-142. Passed in 1975 with many provisions for assuring free appropriate public education for all students with disabilities; later renamed the Individuals with Disabilities Education Act (IDEA).

educational interpreters. Related service providers who translate or convert spoken messages to the deaf person's preferred mode of manual communication.

e-mail. A computerized mail system allowing people using personal computers, the phone system, and a host mainframe computer to communicate.

eminence. Superiority in ability.

English Language Learners (ELL). *See* limited English proficient (LEP).

emotional disturbance. A term that is often used interchangeably with emotional or behavior disorder.

emotional or behavioral disorders. A condition of disruptive or inappropriate behaviors that interferes with a student's learning, relationships with others, or personal satisfaction to such a degree that intervention is required.

English as a second language (ESL). Instructing children in English in their classrooms or in special classes until English proficiency is achieved.

enrichment. Adding topics or skills to the traditional curriculum or presenting a particular topic in more depth.

enrichment triad/revolving door model. A model for gifted education where 15% to 20% rather than 3% of a school's students periodically participate in advanced activities planned to develop thinking skills, problem solving, and creativity.

environmental restructuring. Peers are instructed and reinforced for encouraging appropriate behavior in their classmate who is exhibiting disruptive behavior.

epicanthic fold. A flap of skin over the innermost corners of the eye.

epilepsy. A tendency to recurrent seizures.

evaluation. Assessment or judgment of special characteristics such as intelligence, physical abilities, sensory abilities, learning preferences, and achievement.

excess cost. Expenses for the education of a child with disabilities that exceed the average expenses of education for a child without disabilities.

extended family. Includes immediate family members—mother, father, and siblings and other relatives—aunts, uncles, grandparents.

externalizing behaviors. Behaviors, especially aggressive behaviors, that seem to be directed toward others.

family system. Potential sources of support for people with disabilities, including sons and daughters, spouses, parents, siblings, in-laws, aunts and uncles, grandparents, extended family members, and step-family members.

fetal alcohol syndrome (FAS). Congenital mental impairments, behavior problems, and perhaps some physical disabilities, caused by the mother's drinking alcohol during pregnancy.

figurative language. Abstract, nonliteral language which uses metaphors and analogies in the creation of various figures of speech.

finger spelling. A form of manual communication that assigns each letter of the alphabet a sign.

fluency problems. Hesitations or repetitions of sounds or words that interrupt a person's flow of speech.

FM transmission device. Equipment used in many classes for students with severe hearing loss that allows direct oral transmissions from the teacher to each individual student.

follow-up study. To provide later evaluation, diagnosis, or treatment of a condition.

form. The rule system of language; it is comprised of phonology, morphology, and syntax.

Fragile X syndrome. An inherited genetic disorder associated with disabilities and particularly linked to mental retardation.

free appropriate public education (FAPE). One of the provisions of IDEA that ensures that children with disabilities receive necessary education and services without cost to the child and family.

frequency of sound. The number of vibrations per second of molecules through some medium like air, water, or wires.

full inclusion. An interpretation that states that the least restrictive environment for all children with disabilities is the general education classroom.

functional academics. Using life skills as the means to teach academic tasks.

functional assessments. Similar to ecological assessment except that behaviors are manipulated (where they are not in the other system) to determine those events that cause and maintain target behaviors.

functional behavioral assessment. A behavioral evaluation technique that determines the exact nature of problem behaviors, the reasons why they occur, and under what conditions the likelihood of their occurrence is reduced.

functionally equivalent behaviors. Appropriate behaviors that can replace inappropriate behaviors because they serve similar purposes.

gait training. Analysis and instruction of walking.

Gallaudet University. The United States' federally funded liberal arts university serving deaf undergraduate and graduate students.

general education. A typical classroom and curriculum designed to serve students without disabilities.

generalization. The transfer of learning from particular instances to other environments, people, times, and events.

generic supports. Non-disability-specific public benefits to which all eligible people have access.

gifted. A term describing individuals with high levels of intelligence, outstanding abilities, and capacity for high performance.

guide dog. An animal trained to assist blind persons to move about independently, also called a service animal.

hair cells. The structures in the inner ear that produce the electrochemical signals that pass through the auditory nerve to the brain, where these signals, which originated as sound waves, are perceived as tones.

hammer (malleus). One of the three tiny bones (ossicles) in the middle ear.

hard of hearing. Having sufficient residual hearing to be able, with a hearing aid, to comprehend others' speech and oral communication.

hearing aid. A device that intensifies sound to help hard of hearing people process information presented orally.

hearing threshold. The point at which a person can perceive the softest sound at each frequency level.

hertz (Hz). Unit of measure for sound frequency.

heterogeneity. Variation among members in a group.

high achievers. Students who expect success and view it as an incentive to work harder.

high stakes testing. Placing incentives and disincentives on schools and school districts for their students' academic achievement.

high-tech devices. Complex technical devices such as computers.

HIV infection. Human immunodeficiency virus; a microorganism that infects the immune system, impairing the body's ability to fight infections.

home or hospital teacher. A special teacher who teaches in the child's home or hospital when the child must be absent from school due to health problems.

honors sections. Advanced classes for any student who shows high achievement in specific subject areas.

Hoover cane. Long, white cane used in the mobility and orientation system developed in 1944 by Richard Hoover to help people with visual disabilities move through the environment independently.

hyperactivity. Impaired ability to sit or concentrate for long periods of time.

Hypermedia. Computer programs that incorporate text, graphics, sound, photographic images, and video clips.

Hypertext. A computer program that can be used to modify textbook materials through rewording, defining vocabulary, and providing further explanations.

identification. The process of seeking out and designating children with disabilities who require special education and related services.

IEP Team. The multidisciplinary team of education professions that develops and evaluates, along with students with disabilities and their parents, the individualized education program plan for each student with a disability.

impulsive. Impaired ability to control one's own behavior.

in the canal (ITC). A hearing aid that is worn inside the person's ear canal.

in the ear (ITE). A hearing aid that fits inside the person's outer ear.

inactive learners. Students who do not become involved in learning situations, do not approach the learning task purposefully, do not ask questions, do not seek help, or do not initiate learning.

incidental teaching. Expanding skills by reinforcing and teaching behaviors and skills performed by individuals naturally.

incidental learning. Gaining knowledge and skills without being directly taught.

independent study. A common approach to the education of the gifted that allows a student to pursue and study a topic in depth on an individual basis.

Individualized Education Program (IEP). A management tool used to identify and organize individualized educational and related services for preschoolers and schoolchildren.

Individualized Family Service Plan (IFSP). A written plan that identifies and organizes services and resources for infants and toddlers with special needs who are under age 3 and their families.

Individualized Transition Plan (ITP). A statement of the transition services required for coordination and delivery of services as the student moves to adulthood.

Individuals with Disabilities Education Act (IDEA). New name given in 1990 to the Education for All Handicapped Children Act (EHA).

infectious diseases. Contagious diseases.

inferences. Incomplete decisions or opinions, based on assumptions or reasoning.

information-processing theory. Suggests that learning disabilities are caused by an inability to organize thinking and approach learning tasks systematically.

infused. The incorporation of enrichment activities into the general education curriculum.

integration. Being included and having full access to mainstream society.

intellectual functioning. The actual performance of tasks believed to represent intelligence, such as observing, problem solving, and communicating.

interdisciplinary instruction. An approach to the education of the gifted that involves studying a topic and its issues in the context of several different disciplines.

interim alternative setting. A temporary (no more than 45 days) educational placement for a student with disabilities who is violent, brings a gun to school, or is involved with drugs; not considered a change in educational placement, and a new IEP is not required for this action.

internalizing behaviors. Behavior that is withdrawn, directed inward, or focused on oneself.

internship. A program that places gifted students, usually high school seniors, in job settings related to their career goals in order to challenge them and apply knowledge in real-life skills.

Intervention Ladder. A hierarchy of disciplinary tactics organized from the least intrusive and least complex to the most intrusive and most complicated.

iris. The colored part of the eye.

itinerant teachers. Teachers who teach students or consult with others in more than one setting.

job coach. An individual who works alongside people with disabilities, helping them to learn all parts of a job.

job developer. An individual who seeks out, shapes, and designs employment opportunities in the community for people with disabilities.

joint attention deficits. Inability to mutually interact or to share interest in events or objects.

judicial hearing. A hearing before a judge in court.

juvenile arthritis. Chronic and painful muscular condition seen in children.

Kurzweil Reader. One of the first computerized systems designed for people with visual disabilities that translates print into synthesized speech.

language. The formalized method of communication by which ideas are transmitted to others.

language delay. Development of language skills that is slower than in the majority of peers; may signal language that will require assistance of a specialist to use language proficiently.

language impairment. Difficulty or inability to master the various systems of rules in language, which then interferes with communication.

language-different. Children who are not native English speakers and those who speak nonstandard English and do not have an impairment even though their language is not typical.

lateral dominance. A preference for using either the right or the left side of the body for one's motoric responses; some believe that mixed dominance or lateral confusion is associated with poor reading performance.

learned helplessness. A phenomenon in which individuals gradually, usually as a result of repeated failure or control by others, become less willing to attempt tasks.

learning disabilities (LD). A disability in which the individual possesses average intelligence but is substantially delayed in academic achievement.

learning strategies. Instructional methods to help students read, comprehend, and study better by helping them organize and collect information strategically.

least restrictive environment (LRE). One of the principles outlined in IDEA that must be balanced when considering the best educational placement for an individual student with disabilities.

legally blind. Visual acuity measured as 20/200 or worse in the better eye with correction, or peripheral vision no greater than 20 degrees.

legislation. Laws passed by a legislature or the Congress and signed by a governor or the President.

lens. Located behind the iris, brings objects seen into focus.

life skills. Those skills used to manage a home, cook, shop, and organize personal living environments.

limb deficiencies. Resulting from missing or nonfunctioning arms or legs.

limited English proficient (LEP). Limited ability to read, write, or speak English.

litigation. A lawsuit or legal proceeding.

long cane. White canes used to assist blind people be independently mobile, developed by Hoover during World War II.

loudness. An aspect of voice, referring to the intensity of the sound produced while speaking.

low achievers. Students who expect failure and see little use in expending effort to learn.

low vision. A level of visual impairment where vision is still useful for learning or the execution of a task.

low-incidence disability. A disability that occurs infrequently; the prevalence and incidence are very low.

low-tech devices. Simple technical devices such as homemade cushions or a classroom railing.

magnet schools. Center schools that serve children who do not live in the immediate neighborhood; some magnet schools are designed to serve children whose parents work in a nearby area; other magnet schools emphasize a particular theme (such as theater arts, math, and science).

mainstreaming. An older term for including students with special needs in general education classrooms for some or all of their school day.

manifestation determination. The result of a process that determines whether or not a student's disciplinary problems are a result of the student's disability.

manual communication. Using the hands, not the voice, as the means of communication, as in sign language or finger spelling.

medically fragile. Used to describe children with special health care needs.

mediation. A meeting of parents and school officials to resolve disagreements about the IEP and the student's placement and services.

melting pot. The concept of an homogenized United States where cultural traditions and home languages are abandoned for the new American culture.

meninges. Membranes that cover the spinal cord and brain.

meningitis. A disease that affects the central nervous system and often causes hearing loss.

mental age (MA). An age estimate of an individual's mental ability, derived from an artificial comparison of the individual's IQ score and chronological age.

mental retardation. A disability characterized by cognitive impairment, limited adapted behavior, need for support, and initial occurrence before age 18.

mentorship. A program in which a gifted student is paired with an adult in order to learn to apply knowledge in real-life situations.

meta-analysis. A research method that allows for the synthesis of many individual research studies to determine the power or effectiveness of an educational practice.

metacognition. Understanding one's own learning process.

Mimosa Cottage Project. One of the earliest demonstration and research sites, located at a state-funded institution in Kansas, where institutionalized individuals were shown to be able to learn a variety of tasks.

mnemonics. A learning strategy that promotes the remembering of names by associating the first letters of items in a list with a word, sentence, or picture.

mobility. The ability to travel safely and efficiently from one place to another.

morphology. Rules that govern the structure and form of words and comprise the basic meaning of words.

motivation. Internal incentives that are influenced by previous success or failure.

multiple disabilities. Possessing more than one handicapping condition.

multiple intelligences. A multidimensional approach to intelligence, providing an alternative view for the concept of IQ, allowing those exceptional in any one of seven areas to be identified as being gifted.

muscular/skeletal conditions. Conditions affecting muscles or bones and resulting in limited functioning.

myoelectric limbs. Artificial limbs, powered by batteries and controlled by electric signals transmitted by the individual's brain (sometimes called *bionic*).

natural supports. Supports that occur as a natural result of typical family and community living.

neural tube disorders. Another name for spinal cord disorders, which always involve the spinal column and usually the spinal cord.

neuromotor impairment. Condition involving the nerves, muscles, and motor functioning.

nondiscriminatory testing. Assessment that properly takes into account a child's cultural and linguistic diversity.

nonpaid supports. Ordinary assistance given by friends and neighbors.

normal curve. A theoretical construct of the normal distribution of human traits such as intelligence.

normalization. Making available ordinary patterns of life and conditions of everyday living.

obturator. A device that creates a closure between the oral and nasal cavities when the soft palate is missing or damaged.

occupational therapist (OT). A professional who directs activities that help improve muscular control and develop self-help skills.

open captions. Captions that appear on the television screen for all viewers to see.

ophthalmologist. Medical doctor who specializes in eye disorders.

optic nerve. The nerve that carries messages from the eye to the visual center of the brain.

optician. A person who fills either the ophthalmologist's or optometrist's prescriptions for glasses or corrective lenses.

optometrist. Professional who measures vision and can prescribe corrective lenses (eyeglasses or contact lenses).

oral-only approach. One method of instruction advocated for students who are deaf, where they learn to communicate (both receiving and sending information) orally, not using sign language.

orientation. The mental map people use to move through environments.

orthopedic impairments. Conditions related to a physical deformity or disability of the skeletal system and associated motor function.

ossicles. Three tiny bones in the middle ear that transmit sound waves from the eardrum through the middle ear to the cochlea.

other health impairments. Chronic or acute health problems resulting in limited strength, vitality, or alertness.

otitis media. Middle ear infection that can result in hearing loss, communication impairments, or learning disabilities if it becomes a chronic condition.

outcomes. The results of decisions and actions.

outreach programs. Specialized programs offered in local communities by residential schools or centralized agencies serving students with special needs.

overrepresentation. Too many students from a cultural or ethnic group participating in a special education category, beyond the level one might expect from their proportion of the overall school population.

paradigm shift. A change in conceptual framework that is a basic understanding or explanation for a field of study. A change in orientation, belief system, or conceptualization of a problem, philosophy, or issue.

perinatal. At the time of birth.

peripheral vision. The outer area of a person's visual field.

personal reader. A person who reads text orally to those who cannot read print.

phenylketonuria (PKU). A hereditary condition causing mental retardation that can be avoided by eliminating foods that contain amino acid (like milk) from the diet, which result in a build up of toxins that damage the brain.

phonemic awareness. An oral language skill that enables children to understand words can be represented in print.

phonology. The rules within a language used to govern the combination of speech sounds to form words and sentences.

physical therapist (PT). A professional who treats physical disabilities through many nonmedical means.

pitch. An aspect of voice; its perceived high or low sound quality.

portfolio assessment. An alternative form of individualized assessment that includes many samples of the student's work across all curriculum targets and reports of teachers and parents about that individual's social skills.

postlingually deaf. Having lost the ability to hear after developing language.

postnatal. After birth.

postsecondary. Education that comes after high school (e.g., community college, technical/vocational school, college, university, continuing education).

pragmatics. A key element of communication; the relationship among language, perception, and cognition.

prelingually deaf. Having lost the ability to hear before developing language.

prenatal. Before birth.

prevalence. The total number of cases at a given time.

primary epilepsy. Predictable seizure disorders that appear at a young age and seem to be hereditary.

problem solving. Finding answers or solutions to situations.

procedural safeguards. IDEA '97 guarantees students with disabilities and their parents the right to a free appropriate public education in the least restrictive environment possible through a process to resolve disagreements and disputes beginning with mediation and ending with civil action.

process/product debate. Argument that either perceptual training or direct instruction was more effective for instruction.

Public Law (PL) 94-142. *See* Education for All Handicapped Children Act (now IDEA).

pull-in programming. Rather than having students with disabilities leave general education classes for special education or for related services, delivering those services to them in the general education classroom.

pull-out programs. The most common educational placement for gifted students, who spend part of the school day in a special class.

pupil. Hole in the center of the iris that expands and contracts, admitting light to the eye.

pure sounds. Sound waves of specific frequencies used to test an individual's hearing ability.

quality of life. A subjective and individual-specific concept dependent on a number of life-dimensions, including social relationships, personal satisfaction, employment, choice, leisure, community adjustment, and other factors.

real-time captioning (RTC). Practically instantaneous translations of speech into print.

reauthorization. The act of amending and renewing a law.

rehabilitation engineering. Application of mechanical and engineering principles to improve human physical functioning.

related services. A part of special education that includes services from professionals from a wide range of disciplines typically outside of education, all designed to meet the learning needs of individual children with disabilities.

residual vision. The amount and degree of vision that one has functional use of despite a visual disability.

resonating system. Oral and nasal cavities where speech sounds are formed.

respiratory system. The system of organs whose primary function is to take in oxygen and expel gases.

retina. Inside lining of the eye.

reversals. Letters, words, or numbers written or read backward.

robotics. Use of high-tech devices to perform motor skills.

schizophrenia. A rare disorder in children that includes bizarre delusions and dissociation with reality.

school nurses. Professionals who participate in delivering FAPE to students with disabilities; they are not listed by IDEA as an actual related service.

school psychologist. A psychologist trained to test and evaluate individual students' abilities.

secondary (lesional) epilepsy. Seizure disorders that appear at any age and seem to occur in response to particular damage.

Section 504 of the Rehabilitation Act of 1973. This law set the stage for both the Individuals with Disabilities Education Act, passed in 1975, and the Americans with Disabilities Act, passed in 1990, by outlining basic civil rights of people with disabilities.

seizure. A spontaneous abnormal discharge of the electrical impulses of the brain, sometimes referred to as a convulsive disorder.

selective attention. Ability to attend to the crucial features of a task.

selective listening. Focusing attention on only one sound in the environment, such as the speaker's voice in a lecture.

self-advocacy movement. A social and political movement started by and for people with mental retardation to speak for themselves on important issues such as housing, employment, legal rights, and personal relationships.

self-determination. A set of behaviors that includes making decisions, choosing preferences, and practicing self-advocacy.

self-injurious behavior (SIB). Self-inflicted injuries (head banging, eye poking).

self-management technique. A set of instructional procedures whereby the individual uses self-instruction, self-monitoring, or self-reinforcement to change behavior.

semantics. The system within a language that governs content, intent, and meanings of spoken and written language.

sensorineural hearing loss. Hearing loss caused by damage to the inner ear or the auditory nerve.

sequencing. Mentally categorizing and putting items, facts, or ideas in order according to various dimensions.

serious emotional disturbance. The term formerly used in IDEA to classify students with behavior disorders and emotional disturbance.

service delivery options. Different special education services and placements sometimes described as a continuum and other times as an array.

service manager. The case manager who oversees the implementation and evaluation of an Individualized Family Service Plan.

setting demands. The behavioral requirements, both obvious and subtle, of an environment.

shunt. A tube used in a medical procedure that draws excess fluid from the brain and head area and disposes of it in a safe area in the body, such as the stomach.

sickle-cell anemia. A hereditary blood disorder that inhibits blood flow.

sign language. An organized, established system of manual gestures used for communication.

simple partial seizures. Not always apparent; often affect behavior and feelings.

Snellen chart. A chart used to test visual acuity, developed in 1862.

social competence. The ability to understand social situations, respond to others appropriately, and interact with other people.

social maladjustment. A term applied to a group of children who do not act within society's norms but who are excluded from the definition of children with emotional or behavioral disorders.

socioeconomic status. The status an individual or family unit holds in society, usually determined by job, level of education, and the amount of money available to spend.

spastic. A type of cerebral palsy characterized by uncontrolled tightening or pulling of muscles.

special education. Individualized education for children and youth with special needs.

specialized supports. Disability-specific benefits.

speech. The vocal production of language.

speech impairment. Abnormal speech that is unintelligible, is unpleasant, or interferes with communication.

speech mechanisms. Includes the various parts of the body—tongue, lips, teeth, mandible, and palate—required for oral speech.

speech synthesizers. Equipment that creates voice.

speech/language pathologist (SLP). A professional who diagnoses and treats problems in the area of speech and language development.

spina bifida. A developmental defect whereby the spinal column fails to close properly.

spinal cord. The cord of nervous tissue that extends through the bony spinal column to the brain.

spinal cord disorders. Always involve the spinal column, usually both the nerves and muscles.

Sputnik. The Russian satellite that was launched in 1957 and caused a renewed interest in the education of the gifted in this country.

standard deviation (SD). A statistical measure that expresses the variability and the distribution from the mean of a set of scores.

standard scores. Converted test scores that equalize scores from different tests to allow comparison.

statewide and districtwide assessments. Part of the national education reform movement that includes annual achievement testing of all schoolchildren for the purpose of increasing the accountability of schools for children's progress in the curriculum.

Stay-Put Provision. The legal mandate prohibiting students with disabilities from being expelled because of behavior associated with their disabilities.

stereotypic behaviors. Nonproductive behaviors (such as twirling, flapping hands, rocking) that an individual repeats at a high rate.

stirrup (stapes). One of the three tiny bones (ossicles) in the middle ear.

STORCH infections. Includes many different congenital viruses.

stuttering. The lack of fluency in an individual's speech pattern, often characterized by hesitations or repetitions of sounds or words.

supported employment. Used in job training, whereby students are placed in paying jobs for which they receive significant assistance and support, and the employer is helped with the compensation.

syntax. Rules that govern word endings and order of words in phrases and sentences.

tactile maps. Maps that utilize touch to orient people to specific locales.

talent development. The process of translating ability into achievement.

talking books. Books available in auditory format.

task analysis. Breaking down problems and tasks into smaller, sequenced components.

technology-dependent children. Children who probably could not survive without high-tech devices such as ventilators.

telecoil. Also called induction coils, an added option on many hearing aids that allows access to telephones, audio loops, and other assistive listening devices.

telecommunications. Various electronic devices that allow students and teachers to access and send materials and information using a computer network system.

telecommunications relay service (TRS). A telephone system required by federal law that allows an operator at a relay center to convert a print-telephone message to a voice telephone message.

text telephone (TTY). A piece of equipment, formerly called the telecommunication device for the deaf (TDD), that allows people to make and receive telephone calls by typing information over the telephone lines.

theoretical construct. A model based on theory, not practice or experience.

time of onset. When the disability occurred.

tonic-clonic seizures. Seizures characterized by a stiff (tonic) phase in which the muscles become rigid, followed by a jerking (clonic) phase in which the arms and legs snap (formerly referred to as grand mal seizures).

total communication approach. A system of instruction for deaf students that employs any and all methods of communication (oral speech, manual communication, ASL, gestures) that are easy, efficient, and preferred by the student for communication.

total immersion. The student is taught entirely in English; all the other students are also non-native English speakers, and the teacher can speak the students' home language.

Tourette's syndrome. A low incidence disability that is characterized by multiple and uncontrollable motor and/or verbal tics.

toxin. A poisonous substance that can cause immediate or long-term harm to the body.

trauma. An injury.

traumatic brain injury (TBI). The result of a head injury; the individual experiences reduced cognitive functioning, limited attention, and impulsivity.

tunnel vision. Severe limitation in peripheral vision.

twice-exceptional students. Students who have a disability and who are gifted.

underrepresentation. The lack of presence of a group or groups of individuals in a special education category; smaller numbers than would be predicted by their proportion in the overall school population.

use. An aspect of language; applying language appropriately; includes pragmatics.

Usher syndrome. A genetic syndrome that includes a nonprogressive sensorineural hearing loss, retinitis pigmentosa and progressively restricted field of vision, loss of the sense of smell, and impaired balance and motor skills.

ventilators. Machines to assist with breathing.

vibrating system. The orderly function of the larynx and vocal folds to vibrate and produce sounds and pitch.

videodisc instruction. An alternative to CAI; instructional discs contain narrated segments of visual images.

visual acuity. How well a person can see at various distances.

visual efficiency. How well a person can use sight.

vocal symbols. Oral means of relaying messages, such as speech sounds.

vocal system. Parts of the respiratory system used to create voice.

voice carryover (VCO). A TTY that allows both voice and text use.

voice problem. An abnormal spoken language production, characterized by unusual pitch, loudness, or quality of sounds.

word banks. Computer-generated lists of words.

World Wide Web. Using the Internet, the Web allows the accessing of information through a personal computer.

wraparound services. A service delivery model whereby all of the child's needs are met through the coordination of the education system, mental health agencies, social services, and community agencies.

written symbols. Graphic means, such as the written alphabet, used to relay messages.

References

CHAPTER 1: The Context of Special Education

Abbott, M., Walton, C., Tapia, Y., & Greenwood, C. R. (1999). Research to practice: A "blueprint" for closing the gap in local schools. *Exceptional Children, 65,* 339–352.

Aiello, B. (1976). Especially for special educators: A sense of our own history. *Exceptional Children, 42,* 244–252.

Albertsons, Inc. v. Kirkingburg, 119 S. Ct. 2162 (1999).

Americans with Disabilities Act of 1990, Pub. L. No. 101–336, 104 Stat. 327.

Artiles, A. J. (1998). The dilemma of difference: Enriching the disproportionality discourse with theory and context. *The Journal of Special Education, 32,* 32–36.

Artiles, A. J., Aguirre-Muñoz, Z., & Abedi, J. (1998). Predicting placement in learning disabilities programs: Do predictors vary by ethnic group? *Exceptional Children, 64,* 543–559.

Artiles, A. J., & Trent, S. C. (1994). Overrepresentation of minority students in special education: A continuing debate. *The Journal of Special Education, 27,* 410–437.

Artiles, A. J., & Zamora-Duran, G. (Eds.). (1997). *Reducing disproportionate representation of culturally diverse students in special and gifted education.* Reston, VA: Council for Exceptional Children.

Audette, B., & Algozzine, B. (1997). Re-inventing government? Let's re-invent special education. *Journal of Learning Disabilities, 30,* 378–383.

Ballard, J., Ramirez, B. A., & Weintraub, F. J. (1982). *Special education in America: Its legal and governmental foundations.* Reston, VA: Council for Exceptional Children.

Bennett, V. (1997, December 18). Ill children in Kyrgyzstan used as pawns. *Los Angeles Times,* pp. A24–A25.

Biklen, D. (1985). *Achieving the complete school: Strategies for effective mainstreaming.* New York: Teachers College Press.

Bragg, L. (1997). From the mute god to the lesser god: Disability in medieval Celtic and Old Norse literature. *Disability & Society, 12,* 165–177.

Briand, X. (Ed.). (1995, May 17). Suspension, special education data reveal mixed picture. *Special Education Report, 21,* 1, 3–4.

Brown v. Board of Education, 347 U.S. 483 (1954).

Burlington School Committee v. Department of Education of the Commonwealth of Massachusetts, 471 U.S. 359 (1985).

Cassuto, L. (1999, March 19). Whose field is it anyway? Disability studies in the academy. *The Chronicle of Higher Education,* p. A60.

Cedar Rapids School District v. Garret F., 106 F.3rd 822 (8th Cir. 1997), cert. gr. 118 S. Ct. 1793 (1998), aff'd, 119 S. Ct. 992 (1999).

Chaifetz, J. (1999, May 30). Saving special ed: System dooms too many children but there is a chance to fix it. *The New York Times* (Soapbox), p. 14.

Cook, B. G., Gerber, M. M., & Semmel, M. I. (1997). Reflections on "Are effective school reforms effective for all students?" The implications of joint outcome production for school reform. *Exceptionality, 7,* 131–137.

Danforth, S., & Rhodes, W. C. (1997). Deconstructing disability: A philosophy for inclusion. *Remedial and Special Education, 18,* 357–366.

Descriptive Video Services (DVS). (1999). *DVS home video catalogue: Described movies for people who have trouble seeing the screen.* Indianapolis, IN: DVS Home Video.

Deveres, L. (1999, April 23). OSEP codifies policy in final regs: ADD/ADHD students may be eligible under OHI. *The Special Educator, 14,* 1, 8–9.

Doe v. Withers, 20 IDELR 422 (1993).

Education Commission of the States (ECS). (1999). *50-state comparison of expenditures and revenues (by source), teacher salaries, teacher/pupil ratios.* Denver: ECS Information Clearinghouse.

Education of Individuals with Disabilities Act. U.S.C. 1988 Title 20, Sections 1400 et seq.

Edgar, E. (1997). School reform, special education, and democracy. *Remedial and Special Education, 18,* 323–325.

Erevelles, N. (1996). Disability and the dialects of difference. *Disability & Society, 11*, 519–537.

Fey, M. E., & Johnson, B. W. (1998). Research to practice (and back again) in speech-language intervention. *Topics in Language Disorders, 18*, 23–34.

Florence County School District Four v. Carter, 950 F.2d 156, 71 Ed. Law Rep. 633 (1991).

Forness, S. R., Kavale, K. A., Blum, I. M., & Lloyd, J. W. (1997). Mega-analysis of meta-analyses: What works in special education and related services. *Teaching Exceptional Children, 29*, 4–9.

Fuchs, L. S., & Fuchs, D. (1998). Treatment validity: A unifying concept for reconceptualizing the identification of learning disabilities. *Learning Disabilities Research and Practice, 13*, 204–219.

Gallagher, H.G. (1994). *FDR's splendid deception* (Rev. ed.) Arlington, VA: Vandamere Press.

Garnett, K. (1996, Spring/Summer). What is wrong with the Senate bill? *The DLD Times, 13*, 7–8.

Gartner, A., & Lipsky, D. K. (1987). Beyond special education: Toward a quality system for all students. *Harvard Educational Review, 57*, 367–395.

Grissmer, D., Flanagan, A., & Williamson, S. (1998). Does money matter for minority and disadvantaged students? Assessing the new empirical evidence. In W. J. Fowler, Jr. (Ed.), *Developments in school finance 1997*. Washington, DC: U.S. Department of Education, Office of Educational Research and Improvement, National Center for Educational Statistics.

Groce, N. E. (1985). *Everyone here spoke sign language: Hereditary deafness on Martha's Vineyard*. Cambridge, MA: Harvard University Press.

Grossman, H. (1998). *Ending discrimination in special education*. Springfield, IL: Charles C. Thomas.

Grupé, B. (Ed.). (1999, May 6). School board members say costs under IDEA are increasing. *Disability Programs, 22*, p. 68.

Gubernick, L., & Conlin, M. (1997, February 10). The special education scandal. *Forbes Magazine*, pp. 66, 69–70.

Harry, B. (1994). *The disproportionate representation of minority students in special education: Theories and recommendations*. Alexandria, VA: National Association of State Directors of Special Education.

Hehir, T. (1996, September). *The achievements of people with disabilities because of IDEA*. Paper presented at the meeting of Project SUCCESS for annual project directors, Washington, DC.

Honig v. Doe, 484 U.S. 305, 108 S. Ct. 592 (1988).

Hungerford, R. H. (1950). On locusts. *American Journal of Mental Deficiency, 54*, 415–418.

Individuals with Disabilities Education Act. Pub. L. No. 104–17, 111 STAT.37.

Irving Independent School District v. Tatro, 468 U.S. 883 (1984).

Itard, J. M. G. (1962). *The wild boy of Aveyron* (G. Humphrey & M. Humphrey, Trans.). Englewood Cliffs, NJ: Prentice-Hall. (Original work published 1806)

Jennings, R. (Ed.). (1999, March 17). Senate republicans amend IDEA in 'Ed Flex.' *Special Education Report, 25*, p. 3.

Johnson, K. (1998). Deinstitutionalization: The management of rights. *Disability & Society, 13*, 375–387.

Kanner, L. (1964). *A history of the care and study of the mentally retarded*. Springfield, IL: Charles C. Thomas.

Kauffman, J. M. (1997). Caricature, science, and exceptionality. *Remedial and Special Education, 18*, 130–132. Newark, NJ: Harwood.

Kitchin, R. (1998). 'Out of place', 'knowing one's place': Space, power and the exclusion of disabled people. *Disability & Society, 13*, 343–356.

Klingner, J. K., Vaughn, S., Schumm, J. S., Cohen, P., & Forgan, J. W. (1998). Inclusion or pull-out: Which do students prefer? *Journal of Learning Disabilities, 31*, 148–158.

Kortering, L. J., & Braziel, P. M. (1999). Staying in school: The perspective of ninth-grade students. *Remedial and Special Education, 20*, 106–113.

Lloyd, J. W., Forness, S. R., & Kavale, K. A. (1998). Some methods are more effective than others. *Intervention in School and Clinic, 33*, 195–200.

Longmore, P. K. (1995, September/October). The second phase: From disability rights to disability culture. *Disability Rag & Resource, 16*, 4–22.

Lovitt, T. C., & Cushing, S. (1999). Parents of youth with disabilities. *Remedial and Special Education, 20*, 134–142.

Lovitt, T. C., Plavins, M., & Cushing, S. (1999). What do pupils with disabilities have to say about their high school experience? *Remedial and Special Education, 20*, 67–76, 83.

MacMillan, D. L., Gresham, F. M., & Bocian, K. M. (1998). Discrepancy between definitions of learning disabilities and school practices: An empirical investigation. *Journal of Learning Disabilities, 31*, 314–326.

Mills v. Board of Education of the District of Columbia, 348 F. Supp. 866 (1972).

Mills, K. (1995, August 27). Disabilities act yet to achieve tricky legal balance. *Albuquerque Journal* (Dimensions), pp. B1, B4.

Murphy v. UPS, 119 S. Ct. 2133 (1999).

Nazzaro, J. N. (1977). *Exceptional timetables: Historic events affecting the handicapped and gifted*. Reston, VA: The Council for Exceptional Children.

Nirje, B. (1969). The normalization principle and its human management implications. In R. B. Kugel & W. Wolfensberger (Eds.), *Changing patterns in residential services for the mentally retarded* (pp. 179–195). Washington, DC: President's Committee on Mental Retardation.

Nirje, B. (1976). The normalization principle. In R. B. Kugel & A. Shearer (Eds.), *Changing patterns in residential services for the mentally retarded* (Rev. ed., pp. 231–240). Washington, DC: President's Committee on Mental Retardation.

Nirje, B. (1985). The basis and logic of the normalization principle. *Australia and New Zealand Journal of Developmental Disabilities, 11,* 65–68.

Oswald, D. P., Coutinho, M. J., Best, A. M., & Singh, N. N. (1999). Ethnic representation in special education: The influence of school-related economic and demographic variables. *The Journal of Special Education, 32,* 194–206.

Parrish, T. B. (1999, Summer). Perspective: What are the costs of special education? *The CSEF Resource,* p. 8.

Patton, J. M. (1998). The disproportionate representation of African Americans in special education: Looking behind the curtain for understanding and solutions. *The Journal of Special Education, 32,* 25–31.

Pennsylvania Association for Retarded Children v. Commonwealth of Pennsylvania, 343 F. Supp. 279 (E. D. Pa., 1972).

Pfeiffer, D. (1996). "We won't go back": The ADA on the grass roots. *Disability & Society, 11,* 271–284.

Powell, B., & Dlugy, Y. (1998, December 21). Human Rights: Russia's gulags for children. *Newsweek,* pp. 40–41.

Rehabilitation Act of 1973. Section 504, 19 U.S.C. section 794.

Reschly, D. J. (1997). Utility of individual ability measures and public policy choices for the 21st century. *School Psychology Review, 26,* 234–241.

Roberts, R., & Mather, N. (1995). Legal protections for individuals with learning disabilities: The IDEA, Section 504, and the ADA, *Learning Disabilities Research and Practice, 10,* 160–168.

Roos, P. (1970). Trends and issues in special education for the mentally retarded. *Education and Training of the Mentally Retarded, 5,* 51–61.

Rose, L. C., & Gallup, A. M. (1998, September). The 30th Annual Phi Delta Kappa/Gallup Poll of the public's attitudes toward the public schools. *Phi Delta Kappan,* 41–56.

Rowley v. Hendrick Hudson School District, 458 U.S. 176 (1982).

Safran, S. P. (1998). The first century of disability portrayal in film: An analysis of the literature. *The Journal of Special Education, 31,* 467–479.

Safran, S. P. (2000). Using movies to teach students about disabilities. *Teaching Exceptional Children, 32* (3), 44–47.

Seguin, E. (1846). *The moral treatment, hygiene, and education of idiots and other backward children.* Paris: Balliere.

Smith v. Robinson, 468 U.S. 992 (1984).

Stainback, S., Stainback, W., East, K., & Sapon-Shevin, M. (1994). A commentary on inclusion and the development of a positive self-identity by people with disabilities. *Exceptional Children, 60,* 486–490.

State ex. rel. Beattie v. Board of Education, 169 Wis. 231, 172 N. W. 153, 154 (1919).

Stein, S. A. (1986). *Van Gogh: A retrospective.* New York: Park Lane.

The summer school for teachers. (1907, February). *Training School Bulletin, 36,* 17.

Sutton v. United Airlines, Inc., 119 S. Ct. 2139 (1999).

Timothy W. v. Rochester, New Hampshire, School District, 1987–88 EHLR DEC. 559:480 (D. N. H. 1988).

Timothy W. v. Rochester, New Hampshire, School District, 875 F.2d 954 (1st Cir. 1989), cert. denied 110 S. Ct. 519 (1989).

Treanor, R. B. (1993). *We overcame: The story of civil rights for disabled people.* Falls Church, VA: Regal Direct Publishing.

Trump, K. S. (1999). *Stopping school violence: An essential guide.* Gaithersburg, MD: Aspen.

U.S. Department of Education. (1998). *The twentieth annual report to Congress on the implementation of the Individuals with Disabilities Education Act.* Washington, DC: U.S. Government Printing Office.

U.S. Department of Education. (1999). Assistance to states for the education of children with disabilities program and the early intervention program for infants and toddlers with disabilities; final regulations. *Federal Register, 34,* CRF Parts 300 and 303.

Vukelich, D. (1995, November). Serving disabled clients pays. *The Albuquerque Tribune,* p. C6.

Walther, I. F., & Metzger, R. (1993). *Vincent van Gogh: The complete paintings (Vol. 1).* Germany: Benedikt Taschen.

Warby, D. B., Greene, M. T., Higgins, K., & Lovitt, T. C. (1999). Suggestions for translating research into classroom practices. *Intervention in School and Clinic, 34,* 205–211, 223.

Werne, S. (1995, November 12). Accessible by design. *Albuquerque Journal,* (Trends), pp. I-1, I-7.

West, J. (1994). *Federal Implementation of the Americans with Disabilities Act, 1991–1994.* New York: Milbank Memorial Fund.

Wilcox, M. J., Hadley, P. A., & Bacon, C. K. (1998). Linking science and practice in management of childhood language disorders: Models and problem-solving strategies. *Topics in Language Disorders, 18,* 10–22.

Winzer, M. A. (1993). *The history of special education: From isolation to integration.* Washington, DC: Gallaudet University Press.

Wolfensberger, W. (Ed.). (1972). *The principle of normalization in human services.* Toronto: National Institute on Mental Retardation.

Wolfensberger, W. (1995). Of "normalization," lifestyles, the Special Olympics, deinstitutionalization, mainstreaming, integration, cabbages and kings. *Mental Retardation, 33,* 128–131.

Zobrest v. Catalina Foothills School District, 963 F.2d 190.

Chapter 2: Individualized Educational Programs: Planning and Delivering Services

Henri de Toulouse-Lautrec

Art Institute of Chicago (1999). *Henri de Toulouse-Lautrec.* [On-line]. Available: www.artic.edu

Denvir, B. (1991). *Toulouse-Lautrec.* London: Thames and Hudson.

Perruchot, H. (1962). *Toulouse-Lautrec.* NY: Collier Books.

Special Education Services

Cook, B. G., Gerber, M. M., & Semmel, M. I. (1997). Reflections on "Are effective schools reforms effective for all students?" The implications of joint outcome production for school reform. *Exceptionality, 7,* 131–137.

Deno, E. (1970). Special education as developmental capital. *Exceptional Children, 37,* 229–237.

Elliott, S. N., Kratochwill, T. R., & Schulte, A. G. (1998). The assessment accommodation checklist. *Teaching Exceptional Children, 31,* 10–14.

Fox, N. E., & Ysseldyke, J. E. (1997). Implementing inclusion at the middle school level: Lessons from a negative example. *Exceptional Children, 64,* 81–98.

Hunt, P., & Goetz, L. (1997). Research on inclusive educational programs, practices, and outcomes for students with severe disabilities. *The Journal of Special Education, 31,* 3–29.

Kennedy, C. H., Shukla, S., & Fryxell, D., (1997). Comparing the effects of educational placement on the social relationships of intermediate school students with severe disabilities. *Exceptional Children, 64,* 31–47.

Klingner, J. K., Vaughn, S., Schumm, J. S., Cohen, P., & Forgan, J. W. (1998). Inclusion or pull-out: Which do students prefer? *Journal of Learning Disabilities, 31,* 148–158.

Landau, J. K., Vohs, J. R., & Romano, C. (1998). *Statewide assessment: Policy issues, questions, and strategies.* Boston: The Federation for Children with Special Needs, Inc.

Manset, G., & Semmel, M. I. (1997). Are inclusive programs for students with mild disabilities effective? A comparative review of model programs. *The Journal of Special Education, 31,* 155–180.

McLaughlin, M. J., & Warren, S. H. (1995). *Individualized education programs: Issues and options for change.* College Park, MD: University of Maryland, Center for Policy Options in Special Education.

Menlove, M. (1996). A checklist for identifying funding sources for assistive technology. *Teaching Exceptional Children, 28,* 20–24.

Project Forum. (1999, February). Issue: Linkage of the IEP to the general education curriculum. *Quick Turn Around.* Washington, DC: NASDSE.

Roberts, R., & Mather, N. (1995). The return of students with learning disabilities to regular classrooms: A sellout? *Learning Disabilities Practice, 10,* 46–58.

Rose, L.C., & Gallup, A. M. (1998, September). The 30th annual Phi Delta Kappa/Gallup poll of the public's attitudes toward the public schools. *Phi Delta Kappan,* pp. 41–56.

Salend, S. J., & Duhaney, J. M. G. (1999). The impact of inclusion on students with and without disabilities and their educators. *Remedial and Special Education, 20,* 114–126.

Thurlow, M. L. (1998). *Assessment: A key component of education reform.* Boston: The Federation for Children with Special Needs, Inc.

U.S. Department of Education. (1998). *Twentieth annual report to Congress on the implementation of the Individuals with Disabilities Education Act.* Washington, DC: U.S. Government Printing Office.

Vanderwood, M., McGrew, K. S., & Ysseldyke, J. E. (1998). Why we can't say much about students with disabilities during education reform. *Exceptional Children, 64,* 359–370.

VanEtten, S. (1998). *The participation of students with disabilities in large-scale assessments.* Unpublished doctoral dissertation, University of New Mexico, Albuquerque.

Vaughn, S., Elbaum, B. E., & Schumm, J. S. (1996). The effects of inclusion on the social functioning of students with learning disabilities. *Journal of Learning Disabilities, 29,* 598–608.

Vaughn, S., Elbaum, B. E., Schumm, J. S., & Hughes, M. T. (1998). Social outcomes for students with and without learning disabilities. *Journal of Learning Disabilities, 31,* 428–436.

Waldron, N. L., & McLeskey, J. (1998). The effects of an inclusive school program on students with mild and severe learning disabilities. *Exceptional Children, 64,* 395–405.

Welch, M., Richards, G., Okada, R., Richards, J., & Prescott, S. (1995). A consultation and paraprofessional pull-in system of service delivery. *Remedial and Special Education, 16,* 16–28.

Williams, B. T., & Katsiyannis, A. (1998, January). The 1997 IDEA amendments: Implications for school principals. *NASSP Bulletin, 82,* 12–18.

Winzer, M. A., & Mazurek, K. (1998). *Special education in multicultural contexts.* Columbus, OH: Merrill.

Yell, M. L., & Shriner, J. G. (1997, September). The IDEA amendments of 1997: Implications for special and general education teachers, administrators, and teacher trainers. *Focus on Exceptional Children, 30,* 1–19.

Individualized Special Education Programs

Algozzine, B., Ysseldyke, J. E., & Christenson, S. (1983). An analysis of the incidence of special class placement: The masses are burgeoning. *The Journal of Special Education, 17,* 141–147.

Bateman, B., & Linden, M. A. (1998). *Better IEPs: How to develop legally correct and educationally useful programs* (3rd ed.). Longmont, CO: Sopris West.

Bear, G. G. (1999). *Interim alternative educational settings: Related research and program considerations.* Alexandria, VA: National Association of State Directors of Special Education (NASDSE).

Blalock, G. (1996). Community transition teams as the foundation for transition services for youth with learning disabilities. *Journal of Learning Disabilities, 29,* 148–159.

Bloom, L., & Bacon, E. (1995). Using portfolios for individual learning and assessment. *Teacher Education and Special Education, 18,* 1–9.

Clark, G. M. (1996). Transition planning assessment for secondary-level students with learning disabilities. *Journal of Learning Disabilities, 29,* 79–92.

Commission on the Education of the Deaf. (1988). *Toward equality: Education of the deaf.* Washington, DC: U.S. Government Printing Office.

Council for Exceptional Children (CEC). (1999). *IEP Team Guide.* Reston, VA: Author.

Curran, C. M., & Harris, M. B. (1996). *Uses and purposes of portfolio assessment for general and special educators.* Albuquerque: University of New Mexico.

Edgar, E., & Polloway, E. A. (1994). Education for adolescents with disabilities: Curriculum and placement issues. *The Journal of Special Education, 27,* 438–452.

Fitzsimmons, M. K. (1998, November). Functional behavior assessment and behavior intervention plans. *ERIC/OSEP Digest,* EDO-EC-98-9. Reston, VA: ERIC Clearinghouse on Disabilities and Gifted Education, Council for Exceptional Children.

Fuchs, L. S., & Deno, S. L. (1994). Must instructionally useful performance assessment be based in the curriculum? *Exceptional Children, 61,* 15–24.

Fuchs, L. S., & Fuchs, D. (1998). Treatment validity: A unifying concept for reconceptualizing the identification of learning disabilities. *Learning Disabilities Research & Practice, 13,* 204–219.

Hallahan, D. P., & Kauffman, J. M. (1995). *The illusion of inclusion.* Austin, TX: Pro-Ed.

Hasazi, S. B., Furney, K. S., & Destefano, L. (1999). Implementing the IDEA transition mandates. *Exceptional Children, 65,* 555–566.

Horner, R. H. (1994). Functional assessment: Contributions and future directions. *Journal of Applied Behavior Analysis, 27,* 401–404.

Katsiyannis, A., & Maag, J. W. (1998). Disciplining students with disabilities: Issues and considerations for implementing IDEA '97. *Behavioral Disorders, 23,* 276–289.

Keogh, B. K. (1988). Perspectives on the regular education initiative. *Learning Disabilities Focus, 4,* 3–5.

Klingner, J. K., Vaughn, S., Schumm, J. S., Cohen, P., & Forgan, J. W. (1998). Inclusion or pull-out: Which do students prefer? *Journal of Learning Disabilities, 31,* 148–158.

Kroth, R. (1990). *A report of the referral and identification rate of students in the Albuquerque public schools.* Unpublished manuscript, University of New Mexico, Albuquerque.

Larson, P. J., & Maag, J. W. (1998). Applying functional assessment in general education classrooms: Issues and recommendations. *Remedial and Special Education, 19,* 338–349.

Lehmann, J. P., Bassett,. D. S., & Sands, D. J. (1999). Students' participation in transition-related actions: A qualitative study. *Remedial and Special Education, 20,* 160–169.

Levine, P., & Edgar, E. (1994). An analysis by gender of long-term postschool outcomes for youth with and without disabilities. *Exceptional Children, 61,* 282–300.

Lovitt, T. C., Cushing, S. S., & Stump, C. (1994). High school students rate their IEPs: Low opinions and lack of ownership. *Intervention in School and Clinic, 30,* 34–37.

Lovitt, T. C., Plavins, M., & Cushing, S. (1999). What do pupils with disabilities have to say about their experience in high school? *Remedial and Special Education, 20,* 67–76, 83.

MacMillan, D., & Forness, S. R. (1998). The role of IQ in special education placement decisions: Primary and determinative or peripheral and inconsequential? *Remedial and Special Education, 19,* 239–253.

NICHCY (1998, June). The IDEA Amendments of 1997 (Special Issue). *News Digest, 26,* 1–39.

Office of Special Education Programs (1999). *IDEA '97 Training Module.* www.ed.gov/offices/osers/osep

Padeliadu, S., & Zigmond, N. (1996). Perspectives of students with learning disabilities about special education placement. *Learning Disabilities Research and Practice, 11,* 15–23.

Parette, Jr., H. P., Murdick, N. L., & Gartin, B. C. (1996). Minigrant to the rescue. *Teaching Exceptional Children, 28,* 20–23.

Patton, J. R., & Blalock, G. (1996). *Transition and students with learning disabilities: Facilitating the movement from school to adult life.* Austin, TX: Pro-Ed.

Patton, J. R., Cronin, M. E., & Jairrels, V. (1997). Curricular implications of transition: Life skills instruction as an integral part of transition education. *Remedial and Special Education, 18,* 294–306.

Pautier, N. F. (1995, April 6). Area high schools flunk in attempt to teach learning disabled. *University Week,* p. 5.

Reschly, D. J. (1996). *Disproportionate minority representation in general and special education programs: Patterns, issues, and alternatives.* Des Moines, IA: Iowa Department of Education.

Reschly, D. (1999, March). *Curriculum based measurement: A self-correcting method.* Presentation made at the Alliance Project Seminar on Placement of Students of Color in Special Education, Marina del Rey, California.

Robinson, T. R., & Rapport, M. J. K. (1999). Providing special education in the juvenile justice system. *Remedial and Special Education, 20,* 19–26, 35.

Sailor, W. (1991). Special education in the restructured school. *Remedial and Special Education, 12,* 8–22.

Salend, S. J. (1998). Using portfolios to assess student performance. *Teaching Exceptional Children, 31,* 36–43.

Sands, D. J. (1999). *Best practices in transition: What school professionals can do to promote high student participation in transition services.* Denver: Technology and Special Services Division, College of Education, University of Colorado at Denver.

Smith, D. D. (1988). No more noses to the glass: A response. *Exceptional Children, 54,* 476.

Snell, M. E. (1988). Gartner and Lipsky's "Beyond special education: Toward a quality system for all students": Messages to TASH. *Journal of the Association for Persons with Severe Handicaps, 13,* 137–140.

Stainback, S., Stainback, W., East, K., & Sapon-Shevin, M. (1994). A commentary on inclusion and the development of a positive self-identity by people with disabilities. *Exceptional Children, 60,* 486–490.

Turnbull, H. R., III, Turnbull, A., Shank, M., & Leal, D. (1995). *Exceptional Lives: Special education in today's schools.* Columbus, OH: Merrill.

U.S. Department of Education. (1999). Assistance to states for the education of children with disabilities program and the early intervention program for infants and toddlers with disabilities; final regulations. *Federal Register, 34,* CRF Parts 300 and 303.

Vaughn, S., & Schumm, J. S. (1995). Responsible inclusion for students with learning disabilities. *Journal of Learning Disabilities, 28,* 264–290.

Vaughn, S., Elbaum, B. E., Schumm, J. S., & Hughes, M. T. (1998). Social outcomes for students with and without learning disabilities. *Journal of Learning Disabilities, 31,* 428–436.

Voyles, L. (1999). Special focus issue: A primer on IDEA 1997 and its regulations. *CEC Today, 5,* 1, 5, 9, 12.

Winzer, M. A., & Mazurek, K. (1998). *Special education in multicultural contexts.* Columbus, OH: Merrill.

Concepts and Controversy

Consortium on Renewing Education (1998). *20/20 Vision: A strategy for doubling America's academic achievement by the year 2020.* Nashville: Peabody Center for Educational Policy, Vanderbilt University.

Tindal, G., Heath, B., Hollenbeck, K., Almond, P., & Harniss, M. (1998). Accommodating students with disabilities on large-scale tests: An experimental study. *Exceptional Children, 64,* 439–450.

Voyles, L. (1998). Assessments fail to give teachers relevant information. *CEC Today, 5,* 1, 9.

Ysseldyke, J., & Olsen, K. (1999). Putting alternative assessments into practice: What to measure and possible sources of data. *Exceptional Children, 65,* 175–185.

Chapter 3: Multicultural and Bilingual Special Education

Introduction

Artiles, A. J. (1998). The dilemma of difference: Enriching the disproportionality discourse with theory and context. *The Journal of Special Education, 32,* 32–36.

Multicultural and Bilingual Special Education Defined

Amos, R. L. (1997). A review of psychological and educational assessment of Northern American Indian/Alaska Native children. *Rural Special Education Quarterly, 16,* 33–43.

Baca, L. M. (1998). The diversity of America's schoolchildren. In R. Tharp, *Teaching Alive,* CD Rom. Santa Cruz, CA: The Center for Research on Education, Diversity and Excellence, University of California, Santa Cruz.

Baca, L. M., & Cervantes, H. T. (Eds.). (1998). *The bilingual special education interface* (3rd ed.). Columbus, OH: Merrill.

Banks, J. A. (1994). *An introduction to multicultural education.* Boston: Allyn and Bacon.

Cheng, L. L. (Ed.). (1995). *Integrating language and learning for inclusion: An Asian-Pacific focus.* San Diego, CA: Singular Publishing Group.

Cuccaro, K. (1996, April 3). Teacher observations key in bilingual assessment. *Special Education Report, 22,* pp. 1, 3.

Diana v. State Board of Education, No. C–70–37 Rfp (N.D. Calif. 1970).

Gardner, H. (1983). *Frames of mind: The theory of multiple intelligences.* New York: Basic Books.

Gollnick, D. M., & Chinn, P. C. (1998). *Multicultural education in a pluralistic society* (5th ed.). Upper Saddle River, NJ: Prentice-Hall.

Holman, L. J. (1997). Working effectively with Hispanic immigrant families. *Phi Delta Kappan, 78,* 647–649

Krause, M. (1992). Testimony to the Select Senate Committee on Indian Affairs on S. 2044, *Native American Languages Act of 1991,* to assist Native Americans in assuring the survival and continuing vitality of their languages, pp. 16–18.

Larry P. v. Riles, Civil Action No. C–70–37 (N.D. Calif. 1971).

Maker, C. J., Nielson, A. B., & Rogers, J. A. (1994). Giftedness, diversity and problem solving. *Teaching Exceptional Children, 27,* 4–18.

National Center for Educational Statistics (NCES). (1997). *Enrollment in public elementary and secondary schools, by race or ethnicity and state: Fall 1986 and fall 1995.* Washington, DC: NCES, Common Core of Data survey.

Ochoa, S. H., Robles-Pina, R., Garcia, S. B., & Breunig, N. (1999). School psychologists' perspectives on referrals of language minority students. *Multiple Voices, 3,* 1–14.

Ogbu, J. U. (1992). Understanding cultural diversity and learning. *Educational Researcher, 21,* 5–14.

Ortiz, A. A. (1997). Learning disabilities occurring concomitantly with linguistic differences. *Journal of Learning Disabilities, 30*, 321–332.

Patton, J. M. (1998). The disproportionate representation of African Americans in special education: Looking behind the curtain for understanding and solutions. *The Journal of Special Education, 32*, 25–31.

Patton, J. M., & Baytops, J. L. (1995). Identifying and transforming the potential of young gifted African Americans: A clarion call for action. In B. A. Ford, F. E. Obiakor, and J. M. Patton (Eds.), *Effective education of African American exceptional learners: New perspectives* (pp. 27–68). Austin, TX: Pro-Ed.

Reschly, D. J. (1997). Utility of individual ability measures and public policy choices for the 21st century. *School Psychology Review, 26*, 234–241.

Reschly, D. J., Tilly, W. D., III, & Grimes, J. P. (Eds.) (1999). *Functional and noncategorical identification and intervention in special education.* Longmont, CO: Sopris West.

Rogers-Dulan, J. (1998). Religious connectedness among urban African American families who have a child with disabilities. *Mental Retardation, 36*, 91–103.

Rueda, R., & Garcia, E. (1997). Do portfolios make a difference for diverse students? The influence of type of data on making instructional decisions. *Learning Disabilities Research & Practice, 12*, 114–122.

Tiedt, P. L., & Tiedt, I. M. (1999). *Multicultural teaching: A handbook of activities, information, and resources* (5th ed.). Boston: Allyn and Bacon.

Tomlinson, C. A., Callahan, C. M., & Lelli, K. M. (1998). Challenging expectations: Case studies of high-potential, culturally diverse young children. *Gifted Child Quarterly, 41*, 5–17.

U.S. Department of Education, National Center for Education Statistics. (1999). *Dropout Rates in the United States,* NCES 1999-082, by Phillip Kaufman, Steve Klein, and Mary Frase.

U.S. Office of Education, Office of Bilingual Education. (1980). Manual for application for grants under bilingual education, 1974. In A. H. Leivbowitz, *The bilingual education act: A legislative analysis.* Rosslyn, VA: National Clearinghouse for Bilingual Education.

Winzer, M. A., & Mazurek, K. (1998). *Special education in multicultural contexts.* Columbus, OH: Merrill.

Yates, J. R., & Ortiz, A. A. (1995). Linguistically and culturally diverse students. In R. S. Podemski, G. E. Marsh, II, T. E. C. Smith, & B. J. Price (Eds.), *Comprehensive administration of special education* (2nd ed., pp. 129–155). Englewood Cliffs, NJ: Prentice-Hall.

History of the Field

Baca, L. M., & Cervantes, H. T. (Eds.). (1984). *The bilingual special education interface.* St. Louis, MO: Times Mirror/Mosby.

Banks, J. A. (1994). *An introduction to multicultural education.* Boston: Allyn and Bacon.

Bransford, L., Baca, L., & Lane, K. (Eds.). (1974). Special issue: Cultural diversity. *Exceptional Children, 40.*

Diana v. State Board of Education, No. C–70–37 Rfp (N.D. Calif. 1970).

Dunn, L. M. (1968). Special education for the mildly retarded: Is much of it justifiable? *Exceptional Children, 35*, 5–22.

Gollnick, D. M., & Chinn, P. C. (1983). *Multicultural education in a pluralistic society.* New York: Macmillan.

Gonzales, E. (1989). Issues in the assessment of minorities. In H. L. Swanson and B. Watson (Eds.), *Educational and psychological assessment of exceptional children: Theories, strategies, and applications* (pp. 383–402). Columbus, OH: Merrill.

Larry P. v. Riles, Civil Action No. C–70–37 (N.D. Calif. 1971).

Lau v. Nichols, 414 U.S. 563 (1974).

Mercer, J. (1973). *Labeling the mentally retarded.* Berkeley: University of California Press.

Mercer, J. R., & Lewis, J. F. (1978). *System of multicultural pluralistic assessment: Student assessment manual.* New York: Psychological Corporation.

Phyler v. Doe, 102 S. Ct. 2382 (1982).

President's Committee on Mental Retardation. (1970). *The six hour retarded child.* Washington, DC: U.S. Government Printing Office.

Prevalence

Artiles, A. J., Aguirre-Muñoz, Z., & Abedi, J. (1998). Predicting placement in learning disabilities programs: Do predictors vary by ethnic group? *Exceptional Children, 64*, 543–559.

Baca, L. M. (1998). The diversity of America's schoolchildren. In R. Tharp, *Teaching Alive,* CD Rom. Santa Cruz, CA: The Center for Research on Education, Diversity and Excellence, University of California, Santa Cruz.

Children's Defense Fund (CDF). (1999). *The state of America's children: Yearbook.* Washington, DC: Author.

Chinn, P. (1999, March). *Changing demographics in America.* Presentation at Alliance Seminar "Placement of Students of Color in Special Education," Marina del Rey, California.

Daniels, V. I. (1998). Minority students in gifted and special education programs: The case for educational equity. *The Journal of Special Education, 32*, 41–43.

Deno, E. (1970). Special education as developmental capital. *Exceptional Children, 37*, 229–237.

Diana v. State Board of Education, No. C–70–37 Rfp (N.D. Calif. 1970).

Dunn, L. M. (1968). Special education for the mildly retarded: Is much of it justifiable? *Exceptional Children, 23*, 5–21.

Ford, D. Y. (1998). The underrepresentation of minority students in gifted education: Problems and promises in recruitment and retention. *The Journal of Special Education, 32*, 4–14.

Gottlieb, J., Alter, M., Gottlieb, B. W., & Wishner, J. (1994). Special education in urban America: It's not justified for many. *The Journal of Special Education, 27*, 453–465.

Harry, B. (1994). *The disproportionate representation of minority students in special education: Theories and recommendations.* Alexandria, VA: National Association of State Directors of Special Education.

Individuals with Disabilities Education Act (IDEA), Pub. L. No. 101–476, 104 Stat.

Kauffman, J. M., Hallahan, D. P., & Ford, D. Y. (Eds.). (1998). Special issue. *The Journal of Special Education, 32*, 3–62.

Larry P. v. Riles, Civil Action No. C–70–37 (N.D. Calif. 1971).

Lau v. Nichols, 414 U.S. 563 (1974).

MacMillan, D. L., Gresham, F. M., & Bocian, K. M. (1998). Discrepancy between definitions of learning disabilities and school practices: An empirical investigation. *Journal of Learning Disabilities, 31*, 314–326.

National Center for Educational Statistics (NCES). (1997). *Enrollment in public elementary and secondary schools, by race or ethnicity and state: Fall 1986 and fall 1995.* Washington, DC: NCES, Common Core of Data survey.

Oswald, D. P., Coutinho, M. J., Best, A. M., & Singh, N. N. (1999). Ethnic representation in special education: The influence of school-related economic and demographic variables. *The Journal of Special Education, 32*, 194–206.

Patton, J. M. (1998). The disproportionate representation of African Americans in special education: Looking behind the curtain for understanding and solutions. *The Journal of Special Education, 32*, 25–31.

Reschly, D. J. (1997). Utility of individual ability measures and public policy choices for the 21st century. *School Psychology Review, 26*, 234–241.

Reschly, D. J., Tilly, W. D., III, & Grimes, J. P. (Eds.) (1999). *Functional and noncategorical identification and intervention in special education.* Longmont, CO: Sopris West.

U.S. Department of Education. (1993). *Fifteenth annual report to Congress on the implementation of the Individuals with Disabilities Education Act.* Washington, DC: U.S. Government Printing Office.

U.S. Department of Education. (1998). *Twentieth annual report to Congress on the implementation of the Individuals with Disabilities Education Act.* Washington, DC: U.S. Government Printing Office.

Causes and Prevention

Amos, R. L. (1997). A review of psychological and educational assessment of Northern American Indian / Alaska Native children. *Rural Special Education Quarterly, 16*, 33–43.

Artiles, A. J., Aguirre-Muñoz, Z., Abedi, J. (1998). Predicting placement in learning disabilities programs: Do predictors vary by ethnic group? *Exceptional Children, 64*, 543–559.

Cheng, L. L. (Ed.). (1995). *Integrating language and learning for inclusion: An Asian–Pacific focus.* San Diego: Singular Publishing Group.

Children's Defense Fund (CDF). (1997). *Poverty matters: The cost of child poverty in America.* Washington, DC: Author.

Children's Defense Fund (CDF). (1998). *The state of America's children: Yearbook.* Washington, DC: Author.

Fujiura, G. T., & Yamaki, K. (1997). Analysis of ethnic variations in the developmental disability prevalence and household income. *Mental Retardation, 35*, 286–294.

Holman, L. J. (1997). Working effectively with Hispanic immigrant families. *Phi Delta Kappan, 78*, 647–649.

Kozol, J. (1991). *Savage inequalities: Children in America's schools.* New York: Crown.

Kozol, J. (1995). *Amazing grace: The lives of children and the conscience of a nation.* New York: Crown.

Lynch, E. W., & Hanson, M. J. (1998). *Developing cross-cultural competence: A guide for working with young children and their families* (2nd ed.). Baltimore: Brookes.

Obiakor, F. E., & Utley, C. A. (1997). Rethinking preservice preparation for teachers in the learning disabilities field: Workable multicultural strategies. *Learning Disabilities Research & Practice, 12*, 100–106.

Oswald, D. P., Coutinho, M. J., Best, A. M., & Singh, N. N. (1999). Ethnic representation in special education: The influence of school-related economic and demographic variables. *The Journal of Special Education, 32*, 194–206.

Reed, S., & Sautter, R. C. (1990, June). Children of poverty: Kappan special report. *Phi Delta Kappan, 71*, K1–K12.

Rivera, D. P., & Smith, D. D. (1997). *Teaching students with learning and behavior problems.* Boston: Allyn and Bacon.

Rueda, R., & Garcia, E. (1997). Do portfolios make a difference for diverse students? The influence of type of data on making instructional decisions. *Learning Disabilities Research & Practice, 12*, 114–122.

Sileo, R. W., & Prater, M. A. (1998). Preparing professionals for partnerships with parents of students with disabilities: Textbook considerations regarding cultural diversity. *Exceptional Children, 64*, 513–528.

U.S. Department of Education. (1998). *Twentieth annual report to Congress on the implementation of the Individuals with Disabilities Education Act.* Washington, DC: U.S. Government Printing Office.

Voltz, D. (1998). Cultural diversity and special education teacher preparation: Critical issues confronting the field. *Teacher Education and Special Education, 21*, 63–70.

Exceptional Culturally and Linguistically Diverse Children

Baca, L. M. (1998). The diversity of America's schoolchildren. In R. Tharp, *Teaching Alive*, CD Rom. Santa Cruz, CA: The Center for Research on Education, Diversity and Excellence, University of California, Santa Cruz.

Cheng, L. L. (Ed.). (1995). *Integrating language and learning for inclusion: An Asian-Pacific focus.* San Diego, CA: Singular Publishing Group.

Cheng, L. L. (1999). Moving beyond accent: Social and cultural realities of living with many tongues. *Topics in Language Disorders, 19,* 1–10.

Cheng, L. L., & Chang, J. (1995). Asian/Pacific islander students in need of effective services. In L. L. Cheng (Ed.), *Integrating language and learning for inclusion: An Asian-Pacific focus* (pp. 3–59). San Diego, CA: Singular Publishing Group.

Cummins, J. (1984). *Bilingualism and special education: Issues in assessment and pedagogy.* San Diego, CA: College-Hill.

Henning-Stout, M. (1996). ¿Que Podemos Hacer?: Roles for school psychologists with Mexican and Latino migrant children and families. *School Psychology Review, 25,* 152–164.

Kozol, J. (1988). *Rachel and her children: Homeless families in America.* New York: Crown.

Krause, M. (1992). Testimony to the Select Senate Committee on Indian Affairs on S. 2044, *Native American Languages Act of 1991,* to assist Native Americans in assuring the survival and continuing vitality of their languages, pp. 16–18.

McLean, Z. Y. (1999). Distinctions between language differences and language disorders. Unpublished diagram, Vanderbilt University, Special Education Department, Nashville, TN.

Obiakor, F. E. (1994). *The eight-step multicultural approach: Learning and teaching with a smile.* Dubuque, IA: Kendall/Hunt.

Ruiz, N. (1995). The social construction of ability and disability: I. Profile types of Latino children identified as language learning disabled. *Journal of Learning Disabilities, 29,* 491–502.

Seymour, H. N., Abdulkarim, L., & Johnson, V. (1999). The Ebonics controversy: An educational and clinical dilemma. *Topics in Language Disorders, 19,* 66–77.

Sileo, T. W., Sileo, A. P., & Prater, M. A. (1996). Parent and professional partnerships in special education: Multicultural considerations. *Intervention in School and Clinic, 31,* 145–153.

Taylor, O. L. (1997). *Testimony of Orlando L. Taylor on the subject of "Ebonics" to the United States Senate Committee on Appropriations Subcommittee on Labor, Health and Human Services and Education.* Washington, DC: United States Senate.

Walther-Thomas, C., Korinek, L., McLaughlin, V. L., & Williams, B. T. (1996) Improving educational opportunities for students with disabilities who are homeless. *Journal of Children and Poverty, 2,* 57–75.

Zima, B. T., Forness, S. R., Bussing, R., & Benjamin, B. (1998). Homeless children in emergency shelters: Need for prereferral intervention and potential eligibility for special education. *Behavioral Disorders, 23,* 98–110.

Educational Interventions

Amos, R. L. (1997). A review of psychological and educational assessment of Northern American Indian/Alaska Native children. *Rural Special Education Quarterly, 16,* 33–43.

Artiles, A. J. (1998). The dilemma of difference: Enriching the disproportionality discourse with theory and context. *The Journal of Special Education, 32,* 32–36.

Artiles, A. J., & Zamora-Duran, G. (Eds.). (1997). *Reducing disproportionate representation of culturally diverse students in special and gifted education.* Reston, VA: Council for Exceptional Children.

Artiles, A. J., Trent, S. C., & Kuan, L. A. (1997). Learning disabilities empirical research on ethnic minority students: An analysis of 22 years of studies published in selected referee journals. *Learning Disabilities Research & Practice, 12,* 82–91.

Cheng, L. R. (1996). Beyond bilingualism: A quest for communication competence. *Topics in Language Disorders, 16,* 9–21.

Chicago Youth Centers (CYC). (1999). *CYC informational materials.* [On-line]. Available: www.chicagoyouthcenters.org

Children's Defense Fund. (1995). *The state of America's children: Yearbook.* Washington, DC: Author.

Chinn, P. (1999, March). *Changing demographics in America.* Presentation at Alliance Seminar "Placement of Students of Color in Special Education," Marina del Rey, California.

Collier, V. P. (1995). *Acquiring a second language for school. Directions in Language & Education.* Washington, DC: National Clearinghouse for Bilingual Education.

Cummins, J. (1984). *Bilingualism and special education: Issues in assessment and pedagogy.* San Diego, CA: College-Hill.

Currie, J., & Thomas, D. (1995). *Does Head Start make a difference?* Santa Monica: Rand.

Fletcher, T. V., Bos, C. S., & Johnson, L. M. (1999). Accommodating English language learners with language and learning disabilities in bilingual education classrooms. *Learning Disabilities Research & Practice, 14,* 80–91.

Gersten, R., Brengilman, S., & Jiménez, R. (1994). Effective instruction for culturally and linguistically diverse students: A reconceptualization. *Focus on Exceptional Children, 27,* 12–16.

Gollnick, D. M., & Chinn, P. C. (1998). *Multicultural education in a pluralistic society* (5th ed.). Columbus, OH: Merrill.

Hoff, D. (Ed.). (1995, June 15). New York City special ed suit targets preschoolers. *Special Education Reports, 21,* 2–3.

Housman, N., & Simmons, A. (1998, Summer). The bilingual ed debate heats up—As the need for qualified teachers continues to rise. *RNT Future Teacher, 5,* 1–2.

Jairrels, V., Brazil, N., & Patton, J. R. (1999). Incorporating popular literature into the curriculum for diverse learners. *Intervention in School and Clinic, 34,* 303–306.

Jordan, E., French, L., & Tempest, P. (1997). Assessing Navajo psychological and educational needs in New Mexico. *Rural Special Education Quarterly, 16,* 24–32.

Kea, C. D., & Utley, C. A. (1998). To teach me is to know me. *The Journal of Special Education, 32,* 44–47.

King, E. W, Chipman, M., & Cruz-Janzen, M. (1994). *Educating young children in a diverse society.* Boston: Allyn and Bacon.

Lemberger, N. (1996). Factors affecting language development from the perspectives of four bilingual teachers. *The Journal of Educational Issues of Language Minority Students, 18*, 17–34.

Lopez-Reyna, N. A. (1997). The relation of interactions and story quality among Mexican American and Anglo American students with learning disabilities. *Exceptionality, 7*, 245–261.

Lynch, E. W., & Hanson, M. J. (1998). *Developing cross-cultural competence: A guide for working with young children and their families* (2nd ed.). Baltimore: Brookes.

Lyons, J. (1998, August). *Bilingual education.* Presentation at the BUENO Center and Alliance Project Conference on Language Diversity, Vail, CO.

Pyle, A. (1996, January 14). Long-term study touts bilingual education. *Albuquerque Journal*, p. A7.

Ramasamy, R. (1996). Post–high school employment: A follow-up of Apache Native American youth. *Journal of Learning Disabilities, 29*, 174–179.

Rogers-Dulan, J. (1998). Religious connectedness among urban African American families who have a child with disabilities. *Mental Retardation, 36*, 91–103.

Salend, S. J., Dorney, J. A., & Mazo, M. (1997). The roles of bilingual special educators in creating inclusive classrooms. *Remedial and Special Education, 18*, 54–64.

Sexton, D., Lobman, M., Constans, T., Snyder, P., & Ernest, J. (1997). Early interventionists' perspectives of multicultural practices with African-American families. *Exceptional Children, 63*, 313–328.

Siccone, F. (1995). *Celebrating diversity: Building self-esteem in today's multicultural classrooms.* Boston: Allyn and Bacon.

Sileo, T. W., & Prater, M. A. (1998). Creating classroom environments that address the linguistic and cultural backgrounds of students with disabilities: An Asian Pacific American perspective. *Remedial and Special Education, 19*, 323–337.

Thorp, E. K. (1997). Increasing opportunities for partnership with culturally and linguistically diverse families. *Intervention in School and Clinic, 32*, 261–269.

U.S. Department of Education, National Center for Education Statistics. (1999). *Dropout Rates in the United States*, NCES 1999-2082, by Phillip Kaufman, Steve Klein, and Mary Frase.

Vraniak, D. (1998, Summer). Developing systems of support with American Indian families of youth with disabilities. *Health Issues for Children & Youth & Their Families, 6*, 9-10.

Walther-Thomas, C., Korinek, L., McLaughlin, V. L., & Williams, B. T. (1996). Improving educational opportunities for students with disabilities who are homeless. *Journal of Children and Poverty, 2*, 57–75.

Families

Bailey, D. B., Jr., Skinner, D., Rodriguez, P., Gut, D., & Correa, V. (1999). Awareness, use, and satisfaction with services for Latino parents of young children with disabilities. *Exceptional Children, 65*, 367–381.

Holman, L. J. (1997). Working effectively with Hispanic immigrant families. *Phi Delta Kappan, 78*, 647–649.

Harry, B. (1992). Restructuring the participation of African-American parents in special education. *Exceptional Children, 59*, 123–131.

Linan-Thompson, S., & Jean, R. E. (1997). Completing the parent participation puzzle: Accepting diversity. *Teaching Exceptional Children, 30*, 46–50.

Little, L. (1998, Summer). Toward a more diverse cultural community. *Early Developments, 2*, 8–9.

Milian, M. (1999). Schools and family involvement: Attitudes among Latinos who have children with visual impairments. *Journal of Visual Impairment & Blindness, 93*, 277–290.

Prater, L. P., & Tanner, M. P. (1995). Collaboration with families: An imperative for managing problem behaviors. In F. E. Obiakor & R. Algozzine (Eds.), *Managing problem behaviors: Perspectives for general and special educators* (pp. 178–206). Dubuque, IA: Kendall/Hunt.

Rogers-Dulan, J. (1998). Religious connectedness among urban African American families who have a child with disabilities. *Mental Retardation, 36*, 91–103.

Thorp, E. K. (1997). Increasing opportunities for partnership with culturally and linguistically diverse families. *Intervention in School and Clinic, 32*, 261–269.

Voltz, D. (1994). Developing collaborative parent–teacher relationships with culturally diverse parents. *Intervention in School and Clinic, 29*, 288–291.

Vraniak, D. (1998, Summer). Developing systems of support with American Indian families of youth with disabilities. *Health Issues for Children & Youth & Their Families, 6*, 9–10.

Concepts and Controversy

Lyons, J. (1998, August). *Bilingual education.* Presentation at the BUENO Center and Alliance Project Conference on Language Diversity, Vail, CO.

Pachon, H. P. (1998, October, 15). ... but the measure's flaws make it hard to implement. *Los Angeles Times*, p. A-2.

Piatt, B. (1990). *¿Only English? Law and language policy in the United States.* Albuquerque: University of New Mexico.

Portes, A., & Rumbaut, R. (1996). *Immigrant America: A portrait.* Berkeley: University of California Press.

Smith, D. D. (1998, November). *Language diversity and students with learning disabilities.* Presentation at the National Council for Learning Disabilities Conference, Albuquerque, NM.

Tatalovich, R. (1995). *Nativism reborn? The official English language movement and the American states.* Lexington: University of Kentucky Press.

Chapter 4: Learning Disabilities

P. Buckley Moss

Moss, P. B. (1989). *P. Buckley Moss: The people's artist: An autobiography.* Waynesboro, VA: Shenandoah Heritage.

Learning Disabilities Defined

Abrahamsen, E. P., & Sprouse, P. T. (1995). Fable comprehension by children with learning disabilities. *Journal of Learning Disabilities, 28,* 302–308.

Cannon, L. (1998, March/April). To promote or to retain: NJCLD Responds. *LDA Newsbriefs, 33,* 1.

Fletcher, J. M., Francis, D. J., Shaywitz, S. E., Lyon, G. R., Foorman, B. R., Stuebing, K. K., & Shaywitz, B. A. (1998). Intelligent testing and the discrepancy model for children with learning disabilities. *Learning Disabilities Research & Practice, 13,* 186–203.

Fuchs, L. S., & Fuchs, D. (1998). Treatment validity: A unifying concept for reconceptualizing the identification of learning disabilities. *Learning Disabilities Research & Practice, 13,* 204–219.

Haager, D., & Vaughn, S. (1995). Parent, teacher, peer, and self-reports of the social competence of students with learning disabilities. *Journal of Learning Disabilities, 28,* 205–231.

Harrison, D. (Ed.). (1997, August 11). Learning disability tests coming under scrutiny. *Education USA, 39,* pp. 1, 3.

Kauffman, J. M., Hallahan, D. P., & Lloyd, J. W. (1998). Politics, science, and the future of learning disabilities. *Learning Disabilities Quarterly, 21,* 276–280.

Kavale, K. A., & Forness, S. R. (1996). Social skill deficits and learning disabilities: A meta-analysis. *Journal of Learning Disabilities, 29,* 226–237.

Kavale, K. A., & Forness, S. R. (1998). The politics of learning disabilities. *Learning Disabilities Quarterly, 21,* 245–274.

Kavale, K. A., & Reese, J. H. (1992). The character of learning disabilities: An Iowa profile. *Learning Disabilities Quarterly, 15,* 74–94.

King, P. (1998, June 15). Politics of promotion: An old idea—keeping kids back—is hot again. *Newsweek,* p. 27.

Lester, G., & Kelman, M. (1997). State disparities in the diagnosis and placement of pupils with learning disabilities. *Journal of Learning Disabilities, 30,* 599–607.

MacMillan, D. L., Gresham, F. M., & Bocian, K. M. (1998). Discrepancy between definitions of learning disabilities and school practices: An empirical investigation. *Journal of Learning Disabilities, 31,* 314–326.

Maker, J. M. (1986). Education of the gifted: Significant trends. In R. J. Morris & B. Blatt (Eds.), *Special education: Research and trends* (pp. 190–221). NY: Pergamon.

McLeskey, J. (1992). Students with learning disabilities at primary, intermediate, and secondary grade levels. *Learning Disabilities Quarterly, 15,* 13–19.

Mercer, C. D., Jordan, L., Allsopp, D. H., & Mercer, A. R. (1996). Learning disabilities definitions and criteria used by state education departments. *Learning Disabilities Quarterly, 19,* 217–232.

National Joint Committee on Learning Disabilities (NJCLD). (1994). *Collective perspectives on issues affecting learning disabilities.* Austin, TX: Pro-Ed.

National Joint Committee on Learning Disabilities (NJCLD). (1998). Operationalizing the NJCLD definition of learning disabilities for ongoing assessment in schools. *Learning Disabilities Quarterly, 21,* 186–193.

New Mexico Learning Disabilities Association. (Spring 1994). Grade retention may not help students catch up. *LDA Newsletter,* pp. 1–3.

Padget, S. Y. (1998). Lessons from research on dyslexia: Implications for a classification system for learning disabilities. *Learning Disabilities Quarterly, 21,* 167–178.

Reschly, D. J. (1996). *Disproportionate minority representation in general and special education programs: Patterns, issues, and alternatives.* Des Moines: Iowa Department of Education.

Robinson, S. M. (1999), Meeting the needs of students who are gifted and have learning disabilities. *Intervention, 34,* 195–211.

Rock, E. E., Fessler, M. A., & Church, R. P. (1997). The concomitance of learning disablties and emotional/behavioral disorders: A conceptual model. *Journal of Learning Disabilities, 30,* 245–263.

Rosenberg, M. (1997). Learning disabilities occurring concomitantly with other disability and exceptional conditions: Introduction to the special series. *Journal of Learning Disabilities, 30,* 242–244.

Rourke, B. P. (1994). Neurological assessment of children with learning disabilities: Measurement issues. In G. R. Lyon (Ed.), *Frames of reference for the assessment of learning disabilities: New views on measurement issues.* Baltimore: Paul H. Brookes.

Schoenbrodt, L., Kumin, L., & Sloan, J. M. (1997). Learning disabilities existing concomitantly with communication disorder. *Journal of Learning Disabilities, 30,* 264–281.

Shafrir, U., & Siegel, L. S. (1994). Subtypes of learning disabilities in adolescents and adults. *Journal of Learning Disabilities, 27,* 123–134.

Swanson, H. L. (1998). Politics and learning disabilities—Editor's comments on special issue. *Learning Disabilities Quarterly, 21,* 243–244.

Tomasi, S. F., & Weinberg, S. L. (1999). Classifying children as LD: An analysis of current practice in an urban setting. *Learning Disabilities Quarterly, 22,* 31–42.

U.S. Department of Education. (1999). Assistance to states for the education of children with disabilities program and the early intervention program for infants and toddlers with disabilities; final regulations. *Federal Register, 34,* CRF Parts 300 and 303.

History of the Field

Hammill, D., & Larsen, S. (1974). The effectiveness of psycholinguistic abilities. *Exceptional Children, 41,* 5–14.

Kavale, K. A., Hirshoren, A., & Forness, S. R. (1998). Meta-analytic validation of the Dunn and Dunn model of learning-style preferences: A critique of what was Dunn. *Learning Disabilities Research and Practice, 13,* 75–80.

Wiederholt, J. L. (1974). Historical perspectives on the education of the learning disabled. In L. Mann and D. Sabatino (Eds.), *The second review of special education* (pp. 103–152). Philadelphia: Journal of Special Education Press.

Prevalence

MacMillan, D. L., Gresham, F. M., & Bocian, K. M. (1998). Discrepancy between definitions of learning disabilities and school practices: An empirical investigation. *Journal of Learning Disabilities, 31,* 314–326.

Parrish, T. B. (1995). *What is far? Special education and finance equity.* Palo Alto, CA: American Institutes for Research.

Reschly, D. J. (1996). *Disproportionate minority representation in general and special education programs: Patterns, issues, and alternatives.* Des Moines: Iowa Department of Education.

Causes and Prevention

Bender, W. N. (1998). *Learning disabilities: Characteristics, identification, and teaching strategies* (3rd ed.). Boston: Allyn and Bacon.

Bos, C. S., & Vaughn, S. (1994). *Strategies for teaching students with learning and behavior problems.* Boston: Allyn and Bacon.

Currie, J., & Thomas, D. (1995). *Does Head Start make a difference?* Santa Monica, CA: Rand.

Decker, S. N., & Defries, J. C. (1980). Cognitive abilities in families of reading disabled children. *Journal of Learning Disabilities, 13,* 517–522.

Decker, S. N., & Defries, J. C. (1981). Cognitive ability profiles in families of reading disabled children. *Developmental Medicine and Child Neurology, 23,* 217–227.

Deshler, D. D., & Schumaker, J. B. (1986). Learning strategies: An instructional alternative for low-achieving adolescents. *Exceptional Children, 52,* 583–590.

Hallahan, D. P., Kauffman, J. M., & Lloyd, J. W. (1996). *Introduction to learning disabilities.* Boston: Allyn and Bacon.

Lerner, J. (1997). *Learning disabilities: Theories, diagnosis, and teaching strategies* (7th ed.). Boston: Houghton Mifflin.

New Mexico Learning Disabilities Association. (Fall 1994). Dyslexia gene region identified. *New Mexico LDA Newsletter,* p. 1.

Oliver, J. M., Cole, N. H., & Hollingsworth, H. (1991). Learning disabilities as functions of familial learning problems and developmental problems. *Exceptional Children, 57,* 427–440.

Schoenbrodt, L., Kumin, L., & Sloan, J. M. (1997). Learning disabilities existing concomitantly with communication disorders. *Journal of Learning Disabilities, 30,* 264–281.

Wallach, G. P., & Butler, K. G. (1995). Language learning disabilities: Moving in from the edge. *Topics in Language Disorders, 16,* 1–26.

Children with Learning Disabilities

Abrahamsen, E. P., & Sprouse, P. T. (1995). Fable comprehension by children with learning disabilities. *Journal of Learning Disabilities, 28,* 302–308.

American Psychiatric Association. (1994). *Diagnostic and statistical manual of mental disorders* (4th ed.) (*DSM-IV*). Washington, DC: American Psychiatric Association.

Armstrong, T. (1995). *The myth of the ADD child.* New York: Dutton.

Bryan, T. (1994). The social competence of students with learning disabilities over time: A response to Vaughn and Hogan. *Journal of Learning Disabilities, 27,* 304–308.

Bryan, T. (1997). Assessing the personal and social status of students with learning disabilities. *Learning Disabilities Research & Practice, 12,* 63–76.

Dev, P. C. (1997) Intrinsic motivation and academic achievement: What does their relationship imply for the classroom teacher? *Remedial and Special Education, 18,* 12–19.

Dohrn, E., & Bryan, T. (1994). Attribution instruction. *Teaching Exceptional Children, 26,* 61–63.

Donahue, M. L. (1997). Beliefs about listening in students with learning disabilities: "Is the speaker always right?" *Topics in Language Disorders, 17,* 41–61.

DuPaul, G. J., Ervin, R. A., Hook, C. L., & McGoey, K. E. (1998). Peer tutoring for children with attention deficit hyperactivity disorder: Effects on classroom behavior and academic performance. *Journal of Applied Behavior Analysis, 31,* 579–592.

Ellis, E. S. (1986). The role of motivation and pedagogy on the generalization of cognitive strategy training. *Journal of Learning Disabilities, 19,* 66–70.

Fuchs, D., & Fuchs, L. S. (1998). Researchers and teachers working together to adapt instruction for diverse learnings. *Learning Disabilities Research & Practice, 13,* 126–137.

Fulk, B. M. (1996). The effects of combined strategy and attribution training on LD adolescents' spelling performance. *Exceptionality, 6,* 13–17.

Fulk, B. M., Brigham, F. J., & Lohman, D. A. (1998). Motivation and self-regulation: A comparison of students with learning and behavior problems. *Remedial and Special Education, 19,* 300–309.

Geisthardt, C., & Munsch, J. (1996). Coping with school stress: A comparison of adolescents with and without learning disabilities. *Journal of Learning Disabilities, 29,* 287–296.

Gresham, F. M., MacMillan, D. L., & Bocian, K. M. (1996). Learning disabilities, low achievement, and mild mental retardation: More alike than different? *Journal of Learning Disabilities, 29,* 570–581.

Gulley, V., & Northup, J. (1997). Comprehensive school-based behavioral assessment of the effects of methylphenidate. *Journal of Applied Behavior Analysis, 30*, 627–638.

Haager, D., & Vaughn, S. (1995). Parent, teacher, peer, and self-reports of the social competence of students with learning disabilities. *Journal of Learning Disabilities, 28*, 205–231.

Hartas, F., & Donahue, M. L. (1997). Conversational and social problem-solving skills in adolescents with learning disabilities. *Learning Disabilities Research & Practice, 12*, 213–220.

Hock, M. (1997, June). Student motivation and commitment: A cornerstone of strategy instruction. *Strategram, 9*, 1–2.

Kavale, K. A., & Forness, S. R. (1996). Social skill deficits and learning disabilities: A meta-analysis. *Journal of Learning Disabilities, 29*, 226–237.

Lenz, B. K., Alley, G. R., & Schumaker, J. B. (1987). Activating the inactive learner: Advance organizers in the secondary content classroom. *Learning Disabilities Quarterly, 10*, 53–67.

Lerner, J. (1993). *Learning disabilities: Theories, diagnosis, and teaching strategies* (6th ed.). Boston: Houghton Mifflin.

Lerner, J. W., Lowenthal, B., & Lerner, S. R. (1995). *Attention deficit disorder*. Pacific Grove, CA: Brooks/Cole.

Margalit, M. (1998). Loneliness and coherence among preschool children with learning disabilities. *Journal of Learning Disabilities, 31*, 173–180.

Mercer, C. D. (1997). *Students with learning disabilities* (5th ed.). Columbus, OH: Merrill.

Pearl, R. (1982). LD children's attributions for success and failure: A replication with a labeled LD sample. *Learning Disabilities Quarterly, 5*, 173–176.

Powell, S., & Nelson, B. (1997). Effects of choosing academic assignments on a student with attention deficit hyperactivity disorder. *Journal of Applied Behavior Analysis, 30*, 181–183.

Reason, R. (1999). ADHD: A psychological response to an evolving concept (Report of a working part of the British Psychological Society). *Journal of Learning Disabilities, 32*, 85–91.

Riccio, C. A., Gonzalez, J. J., & Hynd, G. W. (1994). Attention-deficit hyperactivity disorder (ADHD) and learning disabilities. *Learning Disabilities Quarterly, 17*, 311–322.

Rivera, D. P., & Smith, D. D. (1997). *Teaching students with learning and behavior problems*. Boston: Allyn and Bacon.

Roberts, C., & Zubrick, S. (1993). Factors influencing the social status of children with mild academic disabilities in regular classrooms. *Exceptional Children, 59*, 192–202.

Sabornie, E. J. (1994). Social-affective characteristics in early adolescents identified as learning disabled and nondisabled. *Learning Disabilities Quarterly, 17*, 268–279.

Sexton, M., Harris, K. R., & Graham, S. (1998). Self-regulated strategy development and the writing process: Effects on essay writing and attributions. *Exceptional Children, 64*, 295–311.

Shapiro, E. S., DuPaul, G. J., & Bradley-Klug, K. L. (1998). Self-management as a strategy to improve the classroom behavior of adolescents with ADHD. *Journal of Learning Disabilities, 31*, 545–555.

Shaywitz, S. E., & Shaywitz, B. A. (Eds.). (1992). *Attention deficit disorder comes of age: Toward the twenty-first century*. Austin, TX: Pro-Ed.

Shelton, T. L., & Barkley, R. A. (1994). Critical issues in the assessment of attention deficit disorders in children. *Topics in Language Disorders, 14*, 26–41.

Stormont-Spurgin, M. (1997). I lost my homework: Strategies for improving organization in students with ADHD. *Intervention in School and Clinic, 32*, 270–274.

Swanson, H. L. (1987). Information processing theory and learning disabilities: An overview. *Journal of Learning Disabilities, 20*, 3–7.

Swanson, H. L. (1990). Intelligence and learning disabilities: An introduction. In H. L. Swanson and B. Keogh (Eds.), *Learning disabilities: Theoretical and research issues* (pp. 23–39). Hillsdale, NJ: Erlbaum.

Switzky, H. N., & Schultz, G. F. (1988). Intrinsic motivation and learning performance: Implications for individual educational programming for learners with mild handicaps. *Remedial and Special Education, 9*, 7–14.

Torgesen, J. K., & Licht, B. G. (1983). The learning disabled child as an inactive learner: Retrospect and prospects. In J. D. McKinney and F. Feagan (Eds.), *Current topics in learning disabilities* (Vol. 1, pp. 3–31). Norwood, NJ: Ablex.

Tur-Kaspa, H., & Bryan, T. (1995). Teachers' ratings of the social competence and school adjustment of students with LD in elementary and junior high school. *Journal of Learning Disabilities, 28*, 44–52, 64.

Tur-Kaspa, H., Weisel, A., & Segev, L. (1998). Attributions for feelings of loneliness of students with learning disabilities. *Learning Disabilities Research & Practice, 13*, 89–94.

Wiener, J., & Sunohara, G. (1998). Parents' perceptions of the quality of friendship of their children with learning disabilities. *Learning Disabilities Research & Practice, 13*, 242–257.

Yasutake, D., & Bryan, T. (1995). The influence of affect on the achievement and behavior of students with learning disabilities. *Journal of Learning Disabilities, 28*, 329–334.

Educational Interventions

American Academy of Pediatrics. (1992). *Infant health and development program for low birth weight, premature infants: Program elements, family participation, and child intelligence*. Elk Grove Village, IL: Author.

Aune, B., & Friehe, M. (1996). Transition to postsecondary education: Institutional and individual issues. *Topics in Language Disorders, 16*, 1–22.

Badian, N. A. (1998). A validation of the role of preschool phonological and orthographic skills in the prediction of reading. *Journal of Learning Disabilities, 31*, 472–481.

Bakken, J. P., Mastropieri, M. A., & Scruggs, T. E. (1997). Reading comprehension of expository science material and students with learning disabilities: A comparison of strategies. *The Journal of Special Education, 31,* 300–324.

Bassett, D. S., & Smith, T. E. C. (1996). Transition in an era of reform. *Journal of Learning Disabilities, 29,* 161–166.

Biemiller, A., & Siegel, L. S. (1997). A longitudinal study of the effects of the Bridge reading program for children at risk for reading failure. *Learning Disabilities Quarterly, 20,* 83–92.

Blalock, G. (1997). Transition. In D. P. Rivera and D. D. Smith, *Teaching students with learning and behavior problems* (3rd ed., pp. 414–449). Boston: Allyn and Bacon.

CEC Today. (1995, October). Research shows phonological awareness key to reading success. Reston, VA: Council for Exceptional Children.

Chard, D. J., & Dickson, S. V., (1999). Phonological awareness: Instructional assessment and guidelines. *Intervention in School and Clinic, 34,* 261–270.

Colvin, R. L. (1996, April 30). Word of honor. *Los Angeles Times,* pp. E1, E5.

Council for Learning Disabilities Board of Trustees. (1993). Council for Learning Disabilities position statement, April 1993. *Learning Disabilities Quarterly, 16,* 126.

Cronin, M. E. (1996). Life skills curricula for students with learning disabilities: A review of the literature. *Journal of Learning Disabilities, 29,* 53–68.

Deshler, D. D., Ellis, E. S., & Lenz, B. K. (1996). *Teaching adolescents with learning disabilities: Strategies and methods* (2nd ed.). Denver: Love Publishing.

Deshler, D. D., & Schumaker, J. B. (1986). Learning strategies: An instructional alternative for low-achieving adolescents. *Exceptional Children, 52,* 583–590.

Dunn, C. (1996). A status report on transition planning for individuals with learning disabilities. *Journal of Learning Disabilities, 29,* 17–30.

Ellis, E. S., (1997). Watering up the curriculum for adolescents with learning disabilities: Goals of the knowledge dimension. *Remedial and Special Education, 18,* 326–346.

Friend, M., & Bursuck, W. D. (1999). *Including students with special needs: A practical guide for classroom teachers* (2nd ed.). Boston: Allyn and Bacon.

Fuchs, D., & Fuchs, L. S. (1998). Researchers and teachers working together to adapt instruction for diverse learnings. *Learning Disabilities Research & Practice, 13,* 126–137.

Fuchs, D., Fuchs, L. S., Mathes, P. G., & Simmons, D. C. (1997). Peer-assisted learning strategies: Making classrooms more responsive to diversity. *American Educational Research Journal, 34,* 174–206.

Ganschow, L., Coyne, J., Parks, A. W., & Antonoff, S. J. (1999). A 10-year follow-up survey of programs and services for students with learning disabilities in graduate and professional schools. *Journal of Learning Disabilities, 32,* 72–84.

Greenbaum, B., Graham, S., & Scales, W. (1995). Adults with learning disabilities: Educational and social experiences during college. *Exceptional Children, 61,* 460–471.

Greenbaum, B., Graham, S., & Scales, W. (1996). Adults with learning disabilities: Occupational and social status after college. *Journal of Learning Disabilities, 29,* 167–173.

Greene, G. (1994). The magic of mnemonics. *LD Forum, 19,* 34–37.

Guterman, B. R. (1995). The validity of categorical learning disabilities services: The consumer's view. *Exceptional Children, 62,* 111–124.

Haring, K. A., Lovett, D. L., & Smith, D. D. (1990). Recent special education graduates of learning disabilities programs. *Journal of Learning Disabilities, 23,* 108–113.

Hishinuma, E. S., & Fremstad, J. S. (1997). NCAA college freshmen academic requirements: Academic standards or unfair roadblocks for students with learning disabilities? *Journal of Learning Disabilities, 30,* 589–598.

Hoehn, T. P., & Baumeister, A. A. (1994). A critique of the application of sensory integration therapy to children with learning disabilities. *Journal of Learning Disabilities, 27,* 338–350.

Johnson, D. J., & Blalock, J. W. (1987). *Adults with learning disabilities: Clinical studies.* Orlando, FL: Grune & Stratton.

Kahn, K. R. (Ed.). (1996, August 2). LRE/Inclusion: Inclusion which made student feel "different" was inappropriate. *The Special Educator,* pp. 14–15.

Katims, D. S. (1994). Emergence of literacy in preschool children with disabilities. *Learning Disabilities Quarterly, 17,* 58–69.

Klingner, J. K., Vaughn, S., Hughes, M. T., Schumm, F. S., & Elbaum, B. (1998). Outcomes for students with and without learning disabilities in inclusive classrooms. *Learning Disabilities Research & Practice, 13,* 153–161.

Kortering, L. J., & Braziel, P. M. (1999). Staying in school: The perspective of ninth-grade students. *Remedial and Special Education, 20,* 106–113.

Kravets, M. (1999). *The K & W guide to colleges for the learning disabled: A resource book for students, parents, and professionals* (5th ed.). New York: Random House.

Learning Disabilities Association of America. (September/October 1994). Adults with learning disabilities: Preliminary analysis of survey data. *LDA Newsletter, 29,* 3–4.

Lebzelter, S. M., & Nowacek, E. J. (1999). Reading strategies for secondary students with mild disabilities. *Intervention in School and Clinic, 34,* 212–219.

Lovett, M. W., & Steinback, K. A. (1997). *Learning Disabilities Quarterly, 20,* 189–210.

Lovitt, T. C. (1995). *Tactics for teaching* (2nd ed.). Columbus, OH: Merrill.

Lyon, G. R., & Moats, L. C. (1997). Critical conceptual and methodological considerations in reading intervention research. *Journal of Learning Disabilities, 30,* 578–588.

MacMillan, D. L., Gresham, F. M., & Bocian, K. M. (1998). Discrepancy between definitions of learning disabilities and school practices: An empirical investigation. *Journal of Learning Disabilities, 31*, 314–326.

Majsterek, D. J., & Ellenwood, A. E. (1995). Phonological awareness and beginning reading: Evaluation of a school-based screening procedure. *Journal of Learning Disabilities, 28*, 449–456.

Mangrum, C. T., II, & Strichart, S. S. (Eds.). (1997). *Peterson's colleges with programs for students with learning disabilities* (5th ed.). Princeton, NJ: Peterson's Guides.

Markell, M., A., & Deno, S. L. (1997). Effects of increasing oral reading: Generalization across reading tasks. *The Journal of Special Education, 31*, 233–250.

Mastropieri, M. A., & Scruggs, T. E. (1997). Best practices in promoting reading comprehension in students with learning disabilities: 1976–1996. *Remedial and Special Education, 18*, 197–213.

Mastropieri, M. A., & Scruggs, T. E. (1998). Constructing more meaningful relationships in the classroom: Mnemonic research into practice. *Learning Disabilities Research & Practice, 13*, 138–145.

Mastropieri, M. A., Scruggs, T. E., & Whedon, C. (1997). Using mnemonic strategies to teach information about U.S. presidents: A classroom-based investigation. *Learning Disabilities Quarterly, 20*, 13–21.

Mather, N. (1992). Whole language reading instruction for students with learning disabilities: Caught in the cross fire. *Learning Disabilities Research & Practice, 7*, 87–95.

Mathes, P. G., Fuchs, D., & Fuchs, L. S. (1997). Cooperative story mapping. *Remedial and Special Education, 18*, 20–27.

McCarthy, J. M., Harris, M. J., & Reeves, K. K. (1997). Specific learning disabilities in preschool children: Shifting paradigms in the middle of the stream. *Learning Disabilities Research & Practice, 12*, 146–150.

McIntosh, R., Vaughn, S., Schumm, J. S., Haager, D., & Lee, O. (1993). Observations of students with learning disabilities in general education classrooms. *Exceptional Children, 60*, 249–261.

Murray, C., Goldstein, D. E., & Edgar, E. (1997). The employment and engagement status of high school graduates with learning disabilities through the first decade after graduation. *Learning Disabilities Research & Practice, 12*, 151–160.

National Joint Committee on Learning Disabilities (NJCLD). (1993). Providing appropriate education for students with learning disabilities in regular education classrooms. *Journal of Learning Disabilities, 26*, 330–332.

New York Times. (1997, January 25). Teaching Johnny to read. Author, p. C–1.

O'Connor, R. E., & Jenkins, J. R. (1996a). Cooperative learning as an inclusion strategy: A closer look. *Exceptionality, 6*, 29–51.

O'Connor, R. E., & Jenkins, J. R. (1996b). Choosing individuals as the focus to study cooperative learning. *Exceptionality, 6*, 65–68.

O'Connor, S. C., & Spreen, O. (1988). The relationship between parents' socioeconomic status and education level, and adult occupational and educational achievement of children with learning disabilities. *Journal of Learning Disabilities, 21*, 148–153.

Padeliadu, S., & Zigmond, N. (1996). Perspectives of students with learning disabilities about special education placement. *Learning Disabilities Research & Practice, 11*, 15–23.

Patton, J. R., & Blalock, G. (Eds.). (1996a). *Transition and students with learning disabilities: Facilitating the movement from school to adult life.* Austin, TX: Pro-Ed.

Patton, J. R., & Blalock, G. (1996b). Transition and students with learning disabilities: Creating sound futures. *Journal of Learning Disabilities, 29*, 7–16.

Patton, J. R., Cronin, M. E., Bassett, D. S., Koppel, A. E. (1997). A life skills approach to mathematics instructions: Preparing students with learning disabilities for the real-life math demands of adulthood. *Journal of Learning Disabilities, 30*, 178–187.

Prater, M. A., Bruhl, S., & Serna, L. A. (1998). Acquiring social skills through cooperative learning and teacher-directed instruction. *Remedial and Special Education, 19*, 160–172.

Pressley, M., & Rankin, J. (1994). More about whole language methods of reading instruction for students at risk for early reading failure. *Learning Disabilities Research & Practice, 9*, 157–168.

Roberts, R., & Mather, N. (1995). The return of students with learning disabilities to regular classrooms: A sellout. *Learning Disabilities Research & Practice, 10*, 46–58.

Scanlon, D., Deshler, D. D., & Schumaker, J. B. (1996). Can a strategy be taught and learned in secondary inclusive classrooms? *Learning Disabilities Research & Practice, 11*, 41–57.

Schalock, R. L., Holl, C., Elliott, B., & Ross, I. (1992). A longitudinal follow-up of graduates from a rural special education program. *Learning Disabilities Quarterly, 15*, 29–38.

Schoenbrodt, L., Kumin, L., & Sloan, J. M. (1997). Learning disabilities existing concomitantly with communication disorder. *Journal of Learning Disabilities, 30*, 264–281.

Sitlington, P. L., & Frank, A. R. (1993). Dropouts with learning disabilities: What happens to them as young adults. *Learning Disabilities Research & Practice, 8*, 244–252.

Slavin, R. E. (1997). *Sand, bricks, and seeds: School change strategies and readiness for reform.* Baltimore: Johns Hopkins University, Center for Research on the Education of Students Placed at Risk.

Smith, C. R. (1998). From gibberish phonemic awareness: Effective decoding instruction. *Teaching Exceptional Children, 31*, 20–25.

Swanson, P. N., & De La Paz, S. (1998). Teaching effective comprehension strategies to students with learning and reading disabilities. *Intervention in School and Clinic, 33*, 209–218.

Talbott, E., Lloyd, J. W., & Tankersley, M. (1994). Effects of reading comprehension interventions for students with learning disabilities. *Learning Disabilities Quarterly, 17*, 223–232.

Thomas, A. (1997, February 17). *Changes and proposed changes concerning students with disabilities.* Letter to the University of New Mexico faculty.

Thurlow, M. L., Ysseldyke, J. E., & Reid, C. L. (1997). High school graduation requirements for students with disabilities. *Journal of Learning Disabilities, 30,* 608–616.

Torgesen, J. K., & Wagner, R. K. (1998). Alternative diagnostic approaches for specific developmental reading disabilities. *Learning Disabilities Research & Practice, 13,* 220–232.

Torgesen, J. K., Wagner, R. K., & Rashotte, C. A. (1994). Longitudinal studies of phonological processing and reading. *Journal of Learning Disabilities, 27,* 276–286.

Torgesen, J. K., Wagner, R. K., Rashotte, C. A., Alexander, A. W., & Conway, T. (1997). Preventive and remedial interventions for children with severe reading disabilities. *Learning Disabilities: A Multidisciplinary Journal, 8,* 51–61.

U.S. Department of Education. (1998). *Twentieth annual report to Congress on the implementation of IDEA.* Washington, DC: U.S. Government Printing Office.

Vandervelden, M. C., & Siegel, L. S. (1997). Teaching phonological processing skills in early literacy: A developmental approach. *Learning Disabilities Quarterly, 20,* 63–81.

Vaughn, S., Elbaum, B. E., Schumm, J. S., & Hughes, M. R. (1998). Social outcomes for students with and without learning disabilities in inclusive classrooms. *Journal of Learning Disabilities, 31,* 428–436.

Webster, P. E., Plante, A. S., & Couvillion, L. M. (1997). Phonological impairment and prereading: Update on a longitudinal study. *Journal of Learning Disabilities, 30,* 365–375.

White, W. J. (1992). The postschool adjustment of persons with learning disabilities: Current status and future projections. *Journal of Learning Disabilities, 25,* 448–456.

Winnery, K. W., & Fuchs, L. S. (1993). Effects of goal and test-taking strategies on the computation performance of students with learning disabilities. *Learning Disabilities Research & Practice, 8,* 204–214.

Zigmond, N., & Baker, J. M. (1994). Is the mainstream a more appropriate educational setting for Randy? A case study of one student with learning disabilities. *Learning Disabilities Research & Practice, 9,* 108–117.

Zumwalt School District v. Missouri State Board of Education, 24 IDELR 222 (E.D. Mo. 1996).

Families

Bryan, T. (1995). *Strategies for improving homework completion and the home–school connection.* Paper presented at the Council for Learning Disabilities Conference, Chicago, October 1995.

Bryan, T., Nelson, C., & Mathur, S. (1995). Doing homework: Perspectives of primary students in mainstream, resource, and self-contained special education classrooms. *Learning Disabilities Research & Practice, 10,* 85–90.

Bryan, T., & Sullivan, K. (1994a). *Planning for success: A teacher's self-study guide to homework.* Phoenix, AZ: Planning for Success.

Bryan, T., & Sullivan, K. (1994b). *Planning for success: A parent's self-study guide to homework.* Phoenix, AZ: Planning for Success

Bryan, T., & Sullivan-Burstein, K. (1998). Teacher-selected strategies for improving homework completion. *Remedial and Special Education, 19,* 263–275.

Callahan, K., Rademacher, J. A., & Hildreth, B. L. (1998). *Remedial and Special Education, 19,* 131–141.

Cooper, H., & Nye, B. (1994). Homework for students with learning disabilities: The implications of research for policy and practice. *Journal of Learning Disabilities, 27,* 465–536.

Dyson, L. L. (1996). The experiences of families of children with learning disabilities: Parental stress, family functioning, and sibling self-concept. *Journal of Learning Disabilities, 29,* 280–286.

Epstein, M. H., Polloway, E. A., Buck, G. H., Bursuck, W. D., Wissinger, L. M., Whitehouse, F., & Jayanthi, M. (1997). Homework-related communication problems: Perspectives of general education teachers. *Learning Disabilities Research & Practice, 12,* 221–227.

Higbee-Mandelbaum, L. (1992/1993). Homework: Getting it done. *New Mexico LDA Newsletter,* pp. 1–2.

Jayanthi, M., Bursuck. W., Epstein, M. H., & Polloway, E. A. (1997). Strategies for successful homework. *Teaching Exceptional Children, 30,* 4–7.

Jayanthi, M., Swayer, V., Nelson, J. S., Bursuck, W. D., & Epstein, M. H. (1995). Recommendations for homework-communication problems. *Remedial and Special Education, 16,* 212–225.

Kroth, R. (1978). Parents: Powerful and necessary allies. *Teaching Exceptional Children, 10,* 88–91.

Kroth, R. L., & Edge, D. (1997). *Strategies for communicating with parents and families of exceptional children* (3rd ed.). Denver, CO: Love.

Nelson, J. S., Epstein, M. H., Bursuck, W. D., Jayanthi, M., & Sawyer, V. (1998). The preferences of middle school students for homework adaptions made by general education teachers. *Learning Disabilities Research & Practice, 13,* 109–117.

O'Melia, M. C., & Rosenberg, M. S. (1994). Effects of cooperative homework teams on the acquisition of mathematics skills by secondary students with mild disabilities. *Exceptional Children, 60,* 538–548.

O'Shea, D. J., O'Shea, L. J., & Hammitte, D. J. (1994). Expanding roles for teachers of students with learning disabilities: Working with family members. *LD Forum, 19,* 28–30.

Simpson, R. L. (1996). *Working with parents and families of exceptional children and youth: Techniques for successful conferencing and collaboration* (3rd ed.). Austin, TX: Pro-Ed.

Technology

Babbitt, B. C., & Miller, S. P. (1996). Using hypermedia to improve the mathematics problem solving skills of students with learning disabilities. *Journal of Learning Disabilities, 29,* 391–401.

Boone, R., Higgins, K., & Williams, D. (1997). Computer-based multimedia and videodiscs: Uses in supporting content-area instruction for students with LD. *Intervention in School and Home, 32*, 302–311.

Bryant, D. P., & Bryant, B. R. (1998). Using assistive technology adaptations to include students with learning disabilities in cooperative learning activities. *Journal of Learning Disabilities, 31*, 41–54.

Lewis, R. B. (1998). Assistive technology and learning disabilities: Today's realities and tomorrow's promises. *Journal of Learning Disabilities, 31*, 16–54.

MacArthur, C. A. (1996). Using technology to enhance the writing process of students with learning disabilities. *Journal of Learning Disabilities, 29*, 344–355.

MacArthur, C. A. (1998). Word processing with speech synthesis and word prediction: Effects on the dialogue journal writing of students with learning disabilities. *Learning Disabilities Quarterly, 21*, 151–166.

MacArthur, C. A., Graham, S., Haynes, J. B., & De La Paz, S. (1996). Spelling checkers and students with learning disabilities: Performance comparisons and impact on spelling. *The Journal of Special Education, 30*, 35–57.

Peters-Walters, S. (1998). Accessible Web site design. *Teaching Exceptional Children, 30*, 42–47.

Raskind, M. H., & Higgins, E. L. (1998). Assistive technology for post-secondary students with learning disabilities: An overview. *Journal of Learning Disabilities, 31*, 27–40.

Smith, S., Boone, R., & Higgins, K. (1998). Expanding the writing process to the Web. *Teaching Exceptional Children, 30*, 22–26.

Wilson, R., Majsterek, D., & Simmons, D. (1996). The effects of computer-assisted versus teacher-directed instruction on the multiplication performance of elementary students with learning disabilities. *Journal of Learning Disabilities, 29*, 382–290.

Concepts and Controversy: Is ADHD a Disability?

Armstrong, T. (1995). *The myth of the ADD child*. New York: Dutton.

Reid, R., Maag, J. W., & Vasa, S. F. (1993). Attention deficit hyperactivity disorder as a disability category: A critique. *Exceptional Children, 60*, 198–214.

Riccio, C. A., Gonzalez, J. J., & Hynd, G. W. (1994). Attention deficit hyperactivity disorder (ADHD) and learning disabilities. *Learning Disabilities Quarterly, 17*, 311–322.

Shaywitz, S. E., & Shaywitz, B. A. (Eds.). (1992). *Attention deficit disorder comes of age: Toward the twenty-first century.* Austin, TX: Pro-Ed.

Wiederholt, J. L. (1991). Editor's comments. *Journal of Learning Disabilities, 24*, 68.

Chapter 5: Speech or Language Impairments

Lewis Carroll

Hinde, T. (1991). *Lewis Carroll: Looking-glass letters.* New York: Rizzoli.

Introduction

Warren, S. F. (1999). The transdisciplinary view of communication. Personal communication.

Speech and Language Impairments Defined

Ball, E. W. (1997). Phonological awareness: Implications for whole language and emergent literacy programs. *Topics in Language Disorders, 17*, 14–26.

Blank, M., Rose, S. A., & Berlin, L. J. (1978). *The language of learning: The preschool years.* New York: Grune & Stratton.

Johnston, J. R., Miller, J. F., Curtiss, S., & Tallal, P. (1993). Conversations with children who are language impaired: Asking questions. *Journal of Speech and Hearing Research, 36*, 973–978.

Marvin, C. (1989). Language and learning. In D. D. Smith, *Teaching students with learning and behavior problems* (pp. 147–181). Englewood Cliffs, NJ: Prentice-Hall.

Newcomer, P. L., & Hammill, D. D. (1988). *Test of Language Development (TOLD)*. Austin, TX: Pro-Ed.

Onslow, M., Andrews, C., & Lincoln, M. (1994). A control/experimental trial of an operant treatment for early stuttering. *Journal of Speech and Hearing Research, 37*, 1244–1259.

Owens, R. E., Jr. (1998). Development of communication, language, and speech. In G. H. Shames, E. H. Wiig, and W. A. Secord (Eds.), *Human communication disorders: An introduction* (5th ed., pp. 27–68). Boston: Allyn and Bacon.

Plante, E., & Beeson, P. M. (1999). *Communication and communication disorders: A clinical introduction.* Boston: Allyn and Bacon.

Ratner, N. B. (1995). Language complexity and stuttering in children. *Topics in Language Disorders, 15*, 32–47.

Rice, M. L. (1995). Speech and language impairments. In E. L. Meyen and T. M. Skrtic (Eds.), *Special education and student disability: An introduction* (4th ed., pp. 339–376). Denver, CO: Love.

Ruiz, N. T. (1995). The social construction of ability and disability: I. Profile types of Latino children identified as language learning disabled. *Journal of Learning Disabilities, 28*, 476–490.

Sander, E. K. (1972). When are speech sounds learned? *Journal of Speech and Hearing Disorders, 37*, 62.

Shames, G. H., & Ramig, P. R. (1998). Stuttering and other disorders of fluency. In G. H. Shames, E. H. Wiig, and W. A. Secord (Eds.), *Human communication disorders: An introduction* (5th ed., pp. 308–349). Boston: Allyn and Bacon.

Torgesen, J. K., & Wagner, R. K. (1998). Alternative diagnostic approaches for specific developmental reading disabilities. *Learning Disabilities Research & Practice, 13,* 220–232.

Van Riper, C., & Erickson, R. L. (1996). *Speech correction: An introduction to speech pathology and audiology* (9th ed.). Boston: Allyn and Bacon.

Walker, H. M., Schwarz, I. E., Nippold, M. A., Irving, L. K., & Noell, J. W. (1994). Social skills in school-age children and youth: Issues and best practices in assessment and intervention. *Topics in Language Disorders, 14,* 70–82.

Webster, P. E., Plante, A. S., & Couvillion, L. M. (1997). Phonologic impairment and prereading: Update on a longitudinal study. *Journal of Learning Disabilities, 30,* 365–375.

Weiss, A. L. (1995). Conversational demands and their effects on fluency and stuttering. *Topics in Language Disorders, 15,* 18–31.

Wingate, M. E. (1962). Personality needs of stutterers. *Logos, 5,* 35–37.

History of the Field

Moore, G. P., & Kester, D. (1953). Historical notes on speech correction in the preassociation era. *Journal of Speech and Hearing Disorders, 18,* 48–53.

Van Riper, C. (1981). An early history of ASHA. *ASHA, 23,* 855–858.

Van Riper, C., & Erickson, R. L. (1996). *Speech correction: An introduction to speech pathology and audiology* (9th ed.). Boston: Allyn and Bacon.

Prevalence

Boone, D. R., & Plante, E. (1993). *Human communication and its disorders* (2nd ed.). Englewood Cliffs, NJ: Prentice-Hall.

Dublinski, S. (1981). Block grant proposal introduced: What does it mean? *Language, Speech, and Hearing Services in the Schools, 12,* 192–199.

Schoenbrodt, L., Kumin, L., & Sloan, J. M. (1997). Learning disabilities existing concomitantly with communication disorder. *Journal of Learning Disabilities, 30,* 264–281.

Tallal, P. Miller, S. L., Bedi, G., Byma, G., Wang, X., Nagarajan, S. S., Schreenei, C., Jenkins, W. M., & Merzenich, M. M. (1996). Language comprehension in language learning impaired children improved with acoustically modified speech. *Science, 27,* 81–84.

U.S. Department of Education. (1998). *Twentieth annual report to Congress on the implementation of the Individuals with Disabilities Education Act.* Washington, DC: U.S. Government Printing Office.

Wallach, G. P., & Butler, K. G. (1995). Language learning disabilities: Moving in from the edge. *Topics in Language Disorders, 16,* 1–26.

Causes and Prevention

Battle, D. (1996). Language learning and use by African American children. *Topics in Language Disorders, 16,* 22–37.

Children's Defense Fund (CDF). (1997). Child immunizations hit all-time high. *CDF Reports.*

Finn, P., & Ingham, R. J. (1994). Stutterers' self-rating of how natural speech sounds and feels. *Journal of Speech and Hearing Research, 37,* 326–340.

Gonzalez, V., Brusca-Vega, R., & Yawkey, T. (1997). *Assessment and instruction of culturally and linguistically diverse students with or at-risk of learning problems.* Boston: Allyn and Bacon.

Lahey, M., & Edwards, J. (1995). Specific language impairment: Preliminary investigation of factors associated with family history and with patterns of language performance. *Journal of Speech and Hearing Research, 38,* 634–657.

Langdon, H. W., & Cheng, L.-R. L. (1992). *Hispanic children and adults with communication disorders.* Gaithersburg, MD: Aspen.

Leonard, L. (1994). Language disorders in preschool children. In G. H. Shames, E. H. Wiig, and W. A. Secord (Eds.), *Human communication disorders: An introduction* (4th ed., pp. 174–211). New York: Merrill.

Maugh, T. H., II. (August 11, 1995). Study finds folic acid cuts risk of cleft palate. *Los Angeles Times,* p. A20.

McWilliams, B. J., & Witzel, M. A. (1998). Cleft palate. In G. H. Shames, E. H. Wiig, and W. A. Secord (Eds.), *Human communication disorders: An introduction* (5th ed., pp. 438–479). Boston: Allyn and Bacon.

Payne, K. T., & Taylor, O. L. (1998). Differences and disorders of language. In G. H. Shames, E. H. Wiig, and W. A. Secord (Eds.), *Human communication disorders: An introduction* (5th ed., pp. 118–154). Boston: Allyn and Bacon.

Ratner, N. B. (1995). Language complexity and stuttering in children. *Topics in Language Disorders, 15,* 32–47.

Rice, M. L. (1997). Specific language impairments: In search of diagnostic markers and genetic contributions. *Mental Retardation and Developmental Disabilities, 3,* 350–357.

Ruiz, N. T. (1995). The social construction of ability and disability: I. Profile types of Latino children identified as language learning disabled. *Journal of Learning Disabilities, 28,* 476–490.

Silverman, F. H. (1996). *Stuttering and other fluency disorders* (2nd ed.). Boston: Allyn and Bacon.

Stark, R. E., Bernstein, L. E., & Demorest, M. E. (1993). Vocal communication in the first 18 months of life. *Journal of Speech and Hearing Research, 36,* 548–558.

van Keulen, J. E., Weddinton, G. T., & DeBose, C. E. (1998). *Speech, language, learning, and the African American child.* Boston: Allyn and Bacon.

Van Riper, C., & Erickson, R. L. (1996). *Speech correction: An introduction to speech pathology and audiology* (9th ed.). Boston: Allyn and Bacon.

Vernon-Feagans, L., Manlove, E. E., & Volling, B. L. (1996). Otitis media and the social behavior of daycare-attending children. *Child Development, 67,* 1528–1539.

Weiss, A. L. (1995). Conversational demands and their effects on fluency and stuttering. *Topics in Language Disorders, 15*, 18–31.

Children with Speech or Language Impairments

Asher, S. R., & Gazelle, H. (1999). Loneliness, peer relationships, and language disorder in childhood. *Topics in Language Disorders, 19*, 16–33.

Ball, E. W. (1997). Phonological awareness: Implications for whole language and emergent literacy programs. *Topics in Language Disorders, 17*, 14–26.

Brinton, B., & Fujiki, M. (1999). Social interactional behaviors of children with specific language impairment. *Topics in Language Disorders, 19*, 49–69.

Fey, M. E., Windsor, J., & Warren, S. F. (Eds). (1995). *Language intervention: Preschool through the elementary years.* Baltimore: Paul H. Brookes.

Fujiki, M., Brinton, B., Hart, C. H., & Fitzgerald, A. H. (1999). Peer acceptance and friendship in children with specific language impairment. *Topics in Language Disorders, 19*, 34–48.

Lloyd, P. (1994). Referential communication: Assessment and intervention. *Topics in Language Disorders, 14*, 55–59.

Rice, M. L. (1997). Specific language impairments: In search of diagnostic markers and genetic contributions. *Mental Retardation and Developmental Disabilities, 3*, 350–357.

Shames, G. H., & Ramig, P. R. (1998). Stuttering and other disorders of fluency. In G. H. Shames, E. H. Wiig, and W. A. Secord (Eds.), *Human communication disorders: An introduction* (5th ed., pp. 308–349). Boston: Allyn and Bacon.

Stevens, L. J., & Bliss, L. S. (1995). Conflict resolution abilities of children with specific language impairment and children with normal language. *Journal of Speech and Hearing Research, 38*, 599–611.

Van Riper, C., & Erickson, R. L. (1996). *Speech correction: An introduction to speech pathology and audiology* (9th ed.). Boston: Allyn and Bacon.

Wallach, G. P., & Butler, K. G. (1995). Language learning disabilities: Moving in from the edge. *Topics in Language Disorders, 16*, 1–26.

Wiig, E. H., & Secord, W. A. (1998). Language disabilities in school-age children and youth. In G. H. Shames, E. H. Wiig, and W. A. Secord (Eds.), *Human communication disorders: An introduction* (5th ed., pp. 185–226). Boston: Allyn and Bacon.

Educational Interventions

Aune, B., & Friehe, M. (1996). Transition to postsecondary education: Institutional and individual issues. *Topics in Language Disorders, 16*, 1–22.

Bailey, D. B., Jr., Aytch, L. S., Odom, S. L., Symons, F., & Wolery, M. (1999). Early intervention as we know it. *Mental Retardation and Developmental Disabilities Research Reviews, 5*, 11–20.

Ball, E. W. (1997). Phonological awareness: Implications for whole language and emergent literacy programs. *Topics in Language Disorders, 17*, 14–26.

Blank, M., & Marquis, A. M. (1987). *Directing discourse.* Tucson, AZ: Communication Skill Builders.

Castillo, L. C. (1998). The effect of analogy instruction on young children's metaphor comprehension. *Roeper Review, 21*, 27–31.

Catts, H. W., Hu, C.-F., Larrivee, L., & Swank, L. (1994). Early identification of reading disabilities in children with speech-language impairments. In R. V. Watkins and M. L. Rice (Eds.), *Specific language impairments in children* (pp. 145–160). Baltimore: Paul H. Brookes.

Clarke, J. (1996). Language development in children prenatally drug exposed: Consideration for assessment and intervention. *The Source, 6*, 12–14.

Crais, E. R., & Lorch, N. (1994). Oral narratives in school-age children. *Topics in Language Disorders, 14*, 13–28.

Cuda, R. A., & Nelson, N. (1976). *Analysis of teacher speaking rate, syntactic complexity and hesitation phenomena as a function of grade level.* Paper presented at the annual meeting of the American Speech-Language-Hearing Association, Houston. As reported in G. Wallach and K. Butler (Eds.). (1984). *Language learning disabilities in school-age children.* Baltimore: Williams & Wilkins.

Dinkmeyer, D., & Dinkmeyer, D. (1982). *DUSO-revised: Developing understanding of self and others.* Circle Pines, MN: American Guidance Service.

Dunn, L. M., Dunn, L. M., Smith, J. O., Smith, D. D., & Horton, K. (1983). *Peabody picture collection.* Circle Pines, MN: American Guidance Service.

Dunn, L. M., Smith, J. O., Dunn, L. M., Horton, K., & Smith, D. D. (1981). *Peabody language development kits (rev. ed.), levels P & 1.* Circle Pines, MN: American Guidance Service.

Edmunds, A. L. (1999). Cognitive credit cards: Acquiring learning strategies. *Teaching Exceptional Children, 31*, 68–73.

Education of the Handicapped (February 26, 1992). Early intervention greatly reduces learning problems, study says. Author, p. 7.

Geluke, N., & Lovitt, T. C. (1992). *Conversations with general education teachers about their work with mainstreamed students.* Unpublished paper, High School Curriculum Project, University of Washington, Seattle.

Gruenewald, L., & Pollack, S. (1984). *Language interaction in teaching and learning.* Austin, TX: Pro-Ed.

Hoffman, P. R. (1997). Phonological intervention within storybook reading. *Topics in Language Disorders, 17*, 69–88.

Hoskins, B. (1987). *Conversations: Language intervention for adolescents.* Allen, TX: DLM–Teaching Resources.

Hudson, J. A., & Gillam, R. B. (1997). "Oh, I remember now!" Facilitating children's long term memory for events. *Topics in Language Disorders, 18*, 1–15.

Katims, D. S. (1994). Emergence of literacy in preschool children with disabilities. *Learning Disabilities Quarterly, 17,* 58–69.

LaBlance, G. R., Steckol, K. F., & Smith, V. L. (1994). Stuttering: The role of the classroom teacher. *Teaching Exceptional Children, 27,* 10–12.

Lombardo, L. A. (1999, July). Children score higher on tests when child care meets standards. *Early Childhood Reports, 10,* 4.

Marvin, C. (1989). Language and learning. In D. D. Smith, *Teaching students with learning and behavior problems* (pp. 147–181). Englewood Cliffs, NJ: Prentice-Hall.

Naremore, R. C. (1997). Making it hang together: Children's use of mental frameworks to structure narratives. *Topics in Language Disorders, 18,* 16–31.

Norris, J. A. (1997). Functional language intervention in the classroom: Avoiding the tutoring trap. *Topics in Language Disorders, 17,* 49–68.

Ostrosky, M. M., & Kaiser, A. P. (1991). Preschool classroom environments that promote communication. *Teaching Exceptional Children, 23,* 6–10.

Owens, R. E., Jr., & Robinson, L. A. (1997). Once upon a time: Use of children's literature in the preschool classroom. *Topics in Language Disorders, 17,* 19–48.

Plante, E., & Beeson, P. M. (1999). *Communication and communication disorders: A clinical introduction.* Boston: Allyn and Bacon.

Plourde, L. (1985). *Classroom listening and speaking (CLAS).* Tucson, AZ: Communication Skill Builders.

Schoenbrodt, L., Kumin, L., & Sloan, J. M. (1997). Learning disabilities existing concomitantly with communication disorder. *Journal of Learning Disabilities, 30,* 264–281.

Simon, C. (1981). *Communicative competence: A functional-pragmatic approach to language therapy.* Tucson, AZ: Communication Skill Builders.

Smith, D. D., & VanEtten-Luaces, S. (in press). *Fast Sort.* Boston: Allyn and Bacon.

U.S. Department of Education. (1998). *Twentieth annual report to Congress on the implementation of the Individuals with Disabilities Education Act.* Washington, DC: U.S. Government Printing Office.

van Keulen, J. E., Weddington, G. T., & DeBose, C. E. (1998). *Speech, language, learning and the African American child.* Boston: Allyn and Bacon.

Wagner, M. M., D'Amico, R., Marder, C., Newman, L., & Blackorby, J. (1992). *What happens next? Trends in postschool outcomes of youth with disabilities. The second comprehensive report from the National Longitudinal Transition Study of Special Education Students.* Menlo Park, CA: SRI International.

Warren, S. F., Yoder, P. J., Gazden, G. E., Kim, K., & Jones, H. A. (1993). Facilitating prelinguistic communication skills in young children with developmental delay. *Journal of Speech and Hearing Research, 36,* 83–97.

Watkins, R. V., & Rice, M. L. (Eds.). (1994). *Specific language impairments in children.* Baltimore: Paul H. Brookes.

Westby, C. E. (1995). Culture and literacy: Frameworks for understanding. *Topics in Language Disorders, 16,* 50–66.

Wiig, E. (1982). *Let's talk: Developing prosocial communication skills.* Columbus, OH: Merrill.

Families

Children's Defense Fund. (1996). *The state of America's children: Yearbook 1996.* Washington, DC: Author.

Cleminshaw, H., DePompei, R., Crais, E. R., Blosser, J., Gillette, Y., & Hooper, C. R. (1996). Working with families. *ASHA, 38,* 34–45.

Crais, E. R., & Lorch, N. (1994). Oral narratives in school-age children. *Topics in Language Disorders, 14,* 13–28.

Hart, B., & Risley, T. (1995). *Meaningful differences in the everyday lives of American Children.* Baltimore: Paul H. Brookes.

Leonard, L. (1994). Language disorders in preschool children. In G. H. Shames, E. H. Wiig, and W. A. Secord (Eds.), *Human communication disorders: An introduction* (4th ed., pp. 174–211). New York: Merrill.

Nippold, M. A., & Rudzinski, M. (1995). Parents' speech and children's stuttering: A critique of the literature. *Journal of Speech and Hearing Research, 38,* 978–989.

Stark, R. E., Bernstein, L. E., & Demorest, M. E. (1993). Vocal communication in the first 18 months of life. *Journal of Speech and Hearing Research, 36,* 548–558.

Technology

Beukelman, D. R., & Mirenda, P. (1992). *Augmentative and alternative communication: Management of severe communication disorders in children and adults.* Baltimore: Brookes.

Maugh, T. H., II. (January 5, 1996). New therapy aids pupils with speech problems. *The Los Angeles Times,* pp. A1, A25.

Merzenich, M. M., Jenkins, W. M., Johnston, P., Schreiner, C., Miller, S. L., Tallal, P. (January 5, 1996). Temporal processing deficits of language-learning impaired children ameliorated by training. *Science, 271,* 77–80.

Parette, H. P., & Angelo, D. H. (1996). Augmentative and alternative communication impact on families: Trends and future directions. *The Journal of Special Education, 30,* 77–99.

Peavler, B. (Spring 1996). New studies may yield treatment for language-based learning disabilities. *New Mexico Learning Disabilities Association Newsletter,* pp. 1–2, 8.

Romski, M. A., & Sevcik, R. A. (1997). Augmentative and alternative communication for children with developmental disabilities. *Mental Retardation and Developmental Disabilities Research Reviews, 3,* 363–368.

Smith, D. D., & VanEtten-Luaces, S. (in press). *Fast Sort.* Boston: Allyn and Bacon.

Tallal, P., Miller, S. L., Bedi, G., Byma, G., Wang, X., Nagarajan, S. S., Schreenei, C., Jenkins, W. M., & Merzenich, M. M. (1996). Language comprehension in language learning impaired children improved with acoustically modified speech. *Science, 27,* 81–84.

Concepts and Controversy

Anderson, C. (1972). *Society pays: The high costs of minimal brain damage in America.* New York: Walker.

ASHA Committee on Prevention of Speech-Language and Hearing Problems. (1984). Prevention: A challenge for the profession. *ASHA, 26,* 35–37.

Associated Press. (January 9, 1991). Panel urges measles-vaccination fund boost. *Albuquerque Journal,* p. D10.

Bradley, A. (May 16, 1990). Lack of funds halts measles-vaccination program. *Education Week,* p. 5.

Children's Defense Fund (CDF) (1996). *The state of America's children: Yearbook 1996.* Washington, DC: Author.

Children's Defense Fund (CDF) (1997). Child immunizations hit all-time high. *CDF Reports.*

Hilts, P. J. (May 9, 1990). Fight measles stalls on money: U.S. runs out of funds for emergency vaccinations to fight the epidemic. *New York Times,* p. A13.

Chapter 6: Mental Retardation

Gottfried Mind

Foucart-Walter, E., & Rosenberg, P. (1987). *The painted cat: The cat in Western painting from the fifteenth to the twentieth century.* New York: Rizzoli.

Mental Retardation Defined

Bryant, B. R., Taylor, R. L., & Rivera, D. P. (1996). *Assessment of adaptive areas (AAA): Examiner's manual.* Austin, TX: Pro-Ed.

Edgerton, R. (1967). *The cloak of competence.* Berkeley: University of California.

Greenspan, S. (1997). Dead manual walking? Why the 1992 AAMR definition needs redoing. *Education and Training in Mental Retardation and Developmental Disabilities, 32,* 179–190.

Grossman, H. J. (Ed.). (1983). *Classification in mental retardation.* Washington, DC: American Association on Mental Retardation.

Loggins, K. (1999, April 4). Adult son wants out of visitation: Ruling may affect many with disabilities. *The Tennessean,* p. B1.

Luckasson, R., Coulter, D. L., Polloway, E. A., Reis, S., Schalock, R. L., Snell, M. E., Spitalnik, D. M., & Stark, J. A. (1992). *Mental retardation: Definition, classification, and systems of supports.* Washington, DC: American Association on Mental Retardation.

Maurer, S. (1997). Struggling with the definitional issue: A state level perspective. *Education and Training in Mental Retardation and Developmental Disabilities, 32,* 191–193.

Polloway, E. A. (1997). Developmental principles of the Luckasson et al. (1992) AAMR Definition of mental retardation: A retrospective. *Education and Training in Mental Retardation and Developmental Disabilities, 32,* 174–178.

Reschly, D. J. (1997). Utility of individual ability measures and public policy choices for the 21st century. *School Psychology Review, 26,* 234–241.

Reschly, D. J., Tilly, W. D., III, & Grimes, J. P. (Eds.) (in press). *Functional and noncategorical identification and intervention in special education.* Longmont, CO: Sopris West.

Smith, J. D. (1997). Mental retardation as an educational construct: Time for a new shared view? *Education and Training in Mental Retardation and Developmental Disabilities, 32,* 167–173.

Thomson, G. O. B., Ward, K. M., & Wishart, J. G. (1995). The transition to adulthood for children with Down's syndrome. *Disability and Society, 10,* 325–339.

History of the Field

Ayllon, T., & Azrin, N. H. (1964). Reinforcement and instructions with mental patients. *Journal of Experimental Analysis of Behavior, 7,* 327–331.

Ayllon, R., & Azrin, N. H. (1968). Reinforcer sampling: A technique for increasing the behavior of mental patients. *Journal of Applied Behavior Analysis, 1,* 13–20.

Birnbrauer, J. S., Wolf, M. M., Kidder, J. D., & Tague, C. E. (1965). Classroom behavior of retarded pupils with token reinforcement. *Journal of Experimental Child Psychology, 2,* 219–235.

Bryant, B. R., Taylor, R. L., & Rivera, D. P. (1996). *Assessment of adaptive areas (AAA): Examiner's manual.* Austin, TX: Pro-Ed.

Gelf, S. (1995). The beast in man: Degenerationism and mental retardation, 1900–1920. *Mental Retardation, 33,* 1–9.

Halderman et al. v. Pennhurst State School and Hospital et al. (1974) E.D. Pa., No. 74-1345.

Howe, S. G. (1866). *On the proper role of state institutions for the disabled.* Speech given at ceremonies on laying the cornerstone of the New York State Institution for the Blind at Batavia, Genesee County, New York. Batavia, NY: Henry Todd.

Itard, J. M. G. (1806). *Wild boy of Aveyron.* (G. Humphrey and M. Humphrey, Trans.). (1962). Englewood Cliffs, NJ: Prentice-Hall. Originally published Paris: Gouyon (1801).

Lent, J. R., & McLean, B. M. (1976). The trainable retarded: The technology of teaching. In N. G. Haring and R. L. Schiefelbush (Eds.), *Teaching special children* (pp. 197–223). New York: McGraw-Hill.

Nirje, B. (1969). The normalization principle and its human management implications. In R. Kugel and W. Wolfensberger (Eds.), *Changing patterns in residential services for the mentally retarded* (pp. 179–195). Washington, DC: President's Committee on Mental Retardation.

Nirje, B. (1976). The normalization principle. In R. Kugel and A. Schearer (Eds.), *Changing patterns in residential services for the mentally retarded* (pp. 231–240). Washington, DC: President's Committee on Mental Retardation.

Perske, R. (1972). The dignity of risk. In W. Wolfensberger (Ed.), *The principle of normalization in human services* (pp. 194–200). Toronto: National Institute on Mental Retardation.

Winzer, M. A. (1993). *The history of special education: From isolation to integration.* Washington, DC: Gallaudet University Press.

Wolfensberger, W. (1972). *The principle of normalization in human services.* Toronto: National Institute on Mental Retardation.

Prevalence

MacMillan, D. L., Gresham, F. M., & Bocian, K. M. (1998). Discrepancy between definitions of learning disabilities and school practices: An empirical investigation. *Journal of Learning Disabilities, 31,* 314–326.

MacMillan, D. L., Siperstein, G. N., & Gresham, F. M. (1996). A challenge to the viability of mild mental retardation as a diagnostic category. *Exceptional Children, 62,* 356–371.

U.S. Department of Education. (1998). *Twentieth annual report to Congress on the implementation of the Individuals with Disabilities Education Act.* Washington, DC: U.S. Government Printing Office.

Causes and Prevention

Abbeduto, L., & Hagerman, R. J. (1997). Language and communication in fragile X syndrome. *Mental Retardation and Developmental Disabilities Research Reviews, 3,* 313–322.

Bailey, D. B., Jr., Aytch, L. S., Odom, S. L., Symons, F., & Wolery, M. (1999). Early intervention as we know it. *Mental Retardation and Developmental Disabilities Research Reviews, 5,* 11–20.

Ball, W. (1999, April). Examining the link between tobacco use and low birth weight. *Early Childhood Reports, 10,* p. 3.

Chace, D. H., & Naylor, E. W. (1999). Expansion of newborn screening programs using automated tandem mass spectrometry. *Mental Retardation and Developmental Disabilities Research Reviews, 5,* 150–154.

Coulter, D. L. (1996). Prevention as a form of support: Implications for the new definition. *Mental Retardation, 34,* 108–116.

Dyer, C. A. (1999). Pathophysiology of phenylketonuria. *Mental Retardation and Developmental Disabilities Research Reviews, 5,* 104–112.

Eisensmith, R. C., Kuzmin, A. I., & Krougliak, V. A. (1999). Prospects for treatment of phenylketonuria by gene therapy. *Mental Retardation and Developmental Disabilities Research Reviews, 5,* 150–154.

Eriksson, K., Erilä, R., Kivimäki, R. & Koivikko, M. (1998). Evolution of epilepsy in children with mental retardation: Five-year experience in 78 cases. *American Journal on Mental Retardation, 102,* 464–472.

Feldman, M. A., & Walton-Allen, N. (1997). Effects of maternal mental retardation and poverty on intellectual, academic, and behavioral status of school-age children. *American Journal on Mental Retardation, 101,* 352–364.

Hall, J. G., & Solehdin, F. (1998). *Mental Retardation and Developmental Disabilities Research Reviews, 4,* 269–281.

Haney, D. Q. (1994, September 22). Disabilities plague the tiniest preemies: Medical miracle has a dark side. *Albuquerque Journal,* p. A4.

Kerns, K. A., Don, A., Mateer, C. A., & Streissguth, A. P. (1997). Cognitive deficits in nonretarded adults with fetal alcohol syndrome. *Journal of Learning Disabilities, 30,* 685–693.

Koch, R., & de la Cruz, F. (1999). Historical aspects and overview of research on phenylketonuria. *Mental Retardation and Developmental Disabilities Research Reviews, 5,* 101–103.

Lowenthal, B. (1996). Educational Implications of child abuse. *Intervention in School and Clinic, 32,* 21–25.

Luckasson, R., Coulter, D. L., Polloway, E. A., Reis, S., Schalock, R. L., Snell, M. E., Spitalnik, D. M., & Stark, J. A. (1992). *Mental retardation: Definition, classification, and systems of supports.* Washington, DC: American Association on Mental Retardation.

Melner, J., Shackelford, J., Hargrove, E., & Daulton, D. (1998). *Resources related to children and their families affected by alcohol and other drugs* (3rd ed.). Chapel Hill: NEC*TAS.

New York Times News Service. (1995, June 28). Dr. Robert Guthrie saved thousands from mental retardation. *Albuquerque Tribune,* p. C12.

Olney, R., & Mulinare, J. (1998). Epidemology of neural tube defects. *Mental Retardation and Developmental Disabilities Research Reviews, 4,* 241–246.

President's Committee on Mental Retardation. (n.d.). *A guide for state planning: For the prevention of mental retardation and related disabilities.* Washington, DC: Author.

Sells, C. J. (1998). Overview: Neural tube defects. *Mental Retardation and Developmental Disabilities Research Reviews, 4,* 239–240.

Snyder, B., & Sandoval, E. (1999, June 19). Fetal patient an emerging joy: Experimental surgery shows hope. *The Tennessean,* pp. 1A, 8A.

Stevenson, R. E., Massey, P. S., Schroer, R. J., McDermott, S., & Richter, B. (1996). Preventable fraction of mental retardation: Analysis based on individuals with severe mental retardation. *Mental Retardation, 34,* 182–188.

Stoel-Gammon, C. (1997). Phonological development in Down syndrome. *Mental Retardation and Developmental Disabilities Research Reviews, 3,* 300–306.

Thomson, G. O. B., Ward, K. M., & Wishart, J. G. (1995). The transition to adulthood for children with Down's syndrome. *Disability and Society, 10,* 325–339.

Youth Record. (1995, August 15). Child abuse leads to lower IQ and body responsiveness, p. 1.

Children with Mental Retardation

Ash, A., Bellew, J., Davies, M., Newman, T., & Richardson, L. (1997). Everybody in? The experience of disabled students in further education. *Disability and Society, 12,* 605–621.

Best Buddies. (n.d.). *Best buddies colleges.* Miami, FL: Best Buddies Headquarters.

Bradley, V. J., Ashbough, J. W., & Blaney, B. (Eds.). (1993). *Creating individual supports for people with developmental disabilities: A mandate for change at many levels.* Baltimore: Brookes.

Cook, B. G., & Semmel, M. I. (1999). Peer acceptance of included students with disabilities as a function of severity of disability and classroom composition. *The Journal of Special Education, 33,* 50–61.

Hughes, C., Guth, C., Hall, S., Presley, J., Dye, M., & Byers, C. (1999). "They are my best friends": Peer buddies promote inclusion in high school. *Teaching Exceptional Children, 31,* 32–37.

McDonnell, J., Mathot-Buckner, C., & Ferguson, B. (1996). *Transition programs for students with moderate/severe disabilities.* Pacific Grove, CA: Brooks/Cole.

Siperstein, G. N., & Leffert, J. S. (1997). Comparison of socially accepted and rejected children with mental retardation. *American Journal on Mental Retardation, 101,* 339–351.

Siperstein, G. N., Leffert, J. S., & Wenz-Gross, M. (1997). The quality of friendships between children with and without learning problems. *American Journal on Mental Retardation, 102,* 111–125.

Yoder, P. J., Kaiser, A. P., & Alpert, C. (1993). Following the child's lead when teaching nouns to preschoolers with mental retardation. *Journal of Speech and Hearing Research, 36,* 158–167.

Educational Interventions

Alber, S. R., & Heward, W. L. (1997). Recruit it or lose it! Training students to recruit positive teacher attention. *Intervention in School and Clinic, 32,* 275–282.

Bailey, D. B., Jr., Aytch, L. S., Odom, S. L., Symons, F., & Wolery, M. (1999). Early intervention as we know it. *Mental Retardation and Developmental Disabilities Research Reviews, 5,* 11–20.

Bass, M. R. (1998). A place for every child: Susan Gray School improves children's lives through early intervention. *Vanderbilt Magazine, 80,* 17–21.

Belfiore, P. J., & Toro-Zambrana, W. (1994). *Recognizing choices in community settings by people with significant disabilities.* Washington, DC: American Association on Mental Retardation.

Black, R. S., & Langone, J. (1997). Social awareness and transition to employment for adolescents with mental retardation. *Remedial and Special Education, 18,* 214–222.

Campo, S. F., Sharpton, W. R., Thompson, B., & Sexton, D. (1997). Correlates of the quality of life of adults with severe or profound mental retardation. *Mental Retardation, 35,* 329–337.

Craft, M. A., Alber, S. R., & Heward, W. L. (1998). Teaching elementary students with developmental disabilities to recruit teacher attention in a general education classroom: Effects on teacher praise and academic productivity. *Journal of Applied Behavior Analysis, 31,* 399–415.

Edgerton, R. B. (1996). A longitudinal-ethnographic research perspective on quality of life. In R. L. Schalock (Ed.), *Quality of life: Conceptualization and measurement* (pp. 83–90). Washington, DC: American Association on Mental Retardation.

Freeman, S. F. N., Alkin, M. D., & Kasari, C. L. (1999). Satisfaction and desire for change in educational placement for children with Down syndrome. *Remedial and Special Education, 20,* 143–151.

Gardner, J. F., Nudler, S., & Chapman, M. S. (1997). Personal outcomes as measures of quality. *Mental Retardation, 35,* 295–305.

Guralnick, M. J. (1998). Effectiveness of early intervention for vulnerable children: A developmental perspective. *American Journal on Mental Retardation, 102,* 319–345.

Hickson, L., Blackman, L. S., & Reis, E. M. (1995). *Mental retardation: Foundations of educational programming.* Boston: Allyn and Bacon.

Hughes, C., & Hwang, B. (1996). Attempts to conceptualize and measure quality of life. In R. L. Schalock (Ed.), *Quality of life: Conceptualization and measurement* (pp. 51–62). Washington, DC: American Association on Mental Retardation.

Hughes, C., Hwang, B., Kim, J., Eisenman, L. T., & Killian, D. J. (1995). Quality of life in applied research: Conceptual model and analysis of measures. *American Journal of Mental Retardation, 99,* 623–641.

Jitendra, A., & Nolet, V. (1995). Teaching how to use a check register: Procedures for instruction and selection. *Intervention in School and Clinic, 31,* 28–33.

Keogh, B. K., Bernheimer, L. P., & Guthrie, D. (1997). Stability and change over time in cognitive level of children with delays. *American Journal on Mental Retardation, 101,* 365–373.

Mamlin, N. (1999). Despite best intentions: When inclusion fails. *The Journal of Special Education, 33,* 36–49.

Mank, D., Cioffi, A., & Yovanoff, P. (1998). Employment outcomes for people with severe disabilities: Opportunities for improvement. *Mental Retardation, 36,* 205–216.

McGregor, G., & Vogelsberg, R. T. (1998). *Inclusive schooling practices: Pedagogical and Research Foundation.* Billings, MT: Consortium on Inclusive Schooling Practices, University of Montana.

Nabors, L. (1997). Playmate preferences of children who are typically developing for their classmates with special needs. *Mental Retardation, 35,* 107–113,

Ramey, C. T., Bryant, D. M., Wasik, B. H., Sparling, J. J., Fendt, K. H., & LaVange, L. M. (1992, March). Infant health and development program for low birth weight, premature infants: Program elements, family participation, and child intelligence. *Pediatrics, 3,* 454–465.

Rubin, S. S., & Heal, L. W. (1996) Revisiting 10 adults with developmental disabilities after 13 years in their own apartments. *Exceptionality, 6,* 231–245.

Rusch, F. R., Heal, L. W., & Cimera, R. E. (1997). Predicting the earnings of supported employees with mental retardation: A longitudinal study. *American Journal on Mental Retardation, 101,* 630–644.

Sandler, A. G. (1999). Short-changed in the name of socialization? Acquisition of functional skills by students with severe disabilities. *Mental Retardation, 37,* 148–150.

Taylor, S. J., & Bogdan, R. (1996). Quality of life and the individual's perspective. In R. L. Schalock (Ed.), *Quality of life: Conceptualization and measurement* (pp. 11–22). Washington, DC: American Association on Mental Retardation.

U.S. Department of Education. (1998). *Twentieth annual report to Congress on the implementation of the Individuals with Disabilities Education Act.* Washington, DC: U.S. Government Printing Office.

Wehmeyer, M. L., Kelchner, K., & Richards, S. (1996). Essential characteristics of self-determined behavior of individuals with mental retardation. *American Journal on Mental Retardation, 100,* 632–642.

Wehmeyer, M. L., & Metzler, C. A. (1995). How self-determined are people with mental retardation? The national consumer survey. *Mental Retardation, 33,* 111–119.

Wielenga, D. (1997, April 4). Safe at home. *Los Angeles Times,* pp. E1, E6.

Families

Beach Center on Families and Disability. (1995a). Dads feel left out. *Families and Disability Newsletter, 6,* p. 4.

Beach Center on Families and Disability. (1995b). How to involve fathers more with their children with special needs. *Families and Disability Newsletter, 6,* pp. 5–6.

Freedman, R. I., Krauss, M. W., & Seltzer, M. M. (1997). Aging parents' residential plans for adult children with mental retardation. *Mental Retardation, 35,* 114–123.

Hannah, M. E., & Midlarsky, E. (1999). Competence and adjustment of siblings of children with mental retardation. *American Journal on Mental Retardation, 104,* 22–37.

Krauss, M. W., Seltzer, M. M., Gordon, R. M., & Friedman, D. H. (1996). Binding ties: The roles of adult siblings of persons with mental retardation. *Mental Retardation, 34,* 83–93.

Sandler, A. G., Warren, S. H., & Raver, S. A. (1995). Grandparents as a source of support for parents of children with disabilities: A brief report. *Mental Retardation, 33,* 248–250.

Thorin, E., Yovanoff, P., & Irvin, L. (1966). Dilemmas faced by families during their young adults' transitions to adulthood: A brief report. *Mental Retardation, 34,* 117–120.

Willoughby, J. C., & Glidden, L. M. (1995). Fathers helping out: Shared child care and marital satisfaction of parents of children with disabilities. *American Journal on Mental Retardation, 99,* 399–406.

Technology

Parette, H. P., & Angelo, D. H. (1996). Augmentative and alternative communication impact on families: Trends and future directions. *The Journal of Special Education, 30,* 77–98.

Romski, M. A., & Sevcik, R. A. (1997). Augmentative and alternative communication for children with developmental disabilities. *Mental Retardation and Developmental Disabilities Research Reviews, 3,* 363–368.

Romski, M. A., Sevcik, R. A., & Adamson, L. B. (1999). *American Journal on Mental Retardation, 104,* 249–259.

Concepts and Controversy

Herrnstein, R., & Murray, C. (1994). *The bell curve: Intelligence and class structure in American life.* New York: The Free Press.

Rock, R. J. (1996). Eugenics and euthanasia: A cause for concern for disabled people, particularly disabled women. *Disability and Society, 11,* 121–127.

Rodriguez-Trias, H. (1982). Sterilization abuse. In R. Hubbard, M. S. Henitin, and B. Fried (Eds.), *Biological woman: The convenient myth.* Cambridge, MA: Schenkman.

Smith, J. D. (October 1994). Mental retardation and eugenics: The persistent argument. *The Front Line, 1,* pp. 6–11. Pacific Grove, CA: Brooks/Cole.

Smith, J. D. (1995). For whom the bell curves: Old texts, mental retardation, and the persistent argument. *Mental Retardation, 33,* 199–202.

Chapter 7: Giftedness and Talent Development

Introduction

Morelock, M. J., & Feldman, D. H. (1997). High IQ children, extreme precocity, and savant syndrome. In N. Colangelo and G. A. Davis (Eds.), *Handbook of gifted education* (2nd ed., pp. 439–459). Boston: Allyn and Bacon.

Simonton, D. K. (1997). When giftedness becomes genius: How does talent achieve eminence? In N. Colangelo and G. A. Davis (Eds.), *Handbook of gifted education* (2nd ed., pp. 335–349). Boston: Allyn and Bacon.

Giftedness and Talent Defined

Benbow, C. P., & Stanley, J. C. (1996). Inequity in equity: How "equity" can lead to inequity for high-potential students. *Psychology, Public Policy, and Law, 2,* 249–292.

Borland, J. H. (1996). Gifted education and the threat of irrelevance. *Journal for the Education of the Gifted, 19,* 129–147.

Coleman, M. R., & Gallagher, J. J. (1994). *Report on states' policies related to the identification of gifted students.* Chapel Hill: Gifted Education Policy Studies Program.

Cornell, D. G., Delcourt, M. A. B., Goldberg, M. D., & Bland, L. C. (1995). Achievement and self-concept of minority students in elementary school gifted programs. *Journal for the Education of the Gifted, 18,* 189–209.

Davis, G. A., & Rimm, S. B. (1998). *Education of the gifted and talented* (4th ed.). Boston: Allyn and Bacon.

Feldhusen, J. F. (1992). *TIDE: Talent identification and development in education.* Sarasota, FL: Center for Creative Learning.

Feldhusen, J. F. (Ed.). (1995). Talent development: The new direction in gifted education. *Roeper Review, 18*, 92.

Fernández, A. T., Gay, L. R., Lucky, L. F., & Gavilan, M. R. (1998). Teacher perceptions of gifted Hispanic limited English proficient students. *Journal for the Education of the Gifted, 21*, 335–351.

Gagné, F. (1996). From giftedness to talent: A developmental model and its impact on the language of the field. *Roeper Review, 18*, 92, 103–111.

Gallagher, J. J. (1985). *Teaching the gifted child* (3rd ed.). Boston: Allyn and Bacon.

Gallagher, J. J. (1996). A critique of critiques of gifted education. *Journal for the Education of the Gifted, 19*, 234–249.

Gallagher, J., Harradine, C. C., & Coleman, M. R. (1997). Gifted students in the classroom: Challenge or boredom? Gifted students' views on their schooling. *Roeper Review, 19*, 132–136.

Gardner, H. (1983). *Frames of mind: The theory of multiple intelligences.* New York: Basic Books.

Gardner, H. (1993). *Multiple intelligences: The theory in practice.* New York: Basic Books.

Hunsaker, S. L. (1995). The gifted metaphor from the perspective of traditional civilizations. *Journal for the Education of the Gifted, 18*, 255–268.

Hunsaker, S. L., Finley, V. S., Frank, E. L. (1997). An analysis of teacher nominations and student performance in gifted programs. *Gifted Child Quarterly, 41*, 19–24.

Landrum, M. S., Katsiyannis, A., & DeWaard, J. (1998). A national survey of current legislative and policy trends in gifted education: Life after the National Excellence report. *Journal for the Education of the Gifted, 21*, 352–371.

Margolin, L. (1996). A pedagogy of privilege. *Journal for the Education of the Gifted, 19*, 164–180.

Marland, S. (1972). *Education of the gifted and talented* (Report to the Congress of the United States by the U.S. Commissioner of Education). Washington, DC: U.S. Government Printing Office.

Morgan, A. D. (1994, Fall). Opportunities to learn through multiple intelligences. *School Renewal Update.* Santa Fe: Effective Schools Unit, New Mexico State Department of Education.

Ramos-Ford, V., & Gardner, H. (1991). Giftedness from a multiple intelligence perspective. In N. Colangelo and G. A. Davis (Eds.), *Handbook of gifted education* (pp. 55–64). Boston: Allyn and Bacon.

Renzulli, J. (1978). What makes giftedness? Reexamining a definition. *Phi Delta Kappan, 60*, 180–184, 261.

Renzulli, J. S. (1998, October). A rising tide lifts all ships: Developing the gifts and talents of all students. *Phi Delta Kappan, 80*, 104–111.

Renzulli, J. S., & Reis, S. M. (1997). The schoolwide enrichment model: New directions for developing high-end learning. In N. Colangelo and G. A. Davis (Eds.), *Handbook of gifted education* (2nd ed., pp. 136–154). Boston: Allyn and Bacon.

Rosselli, H. C. (1998). From Passow to Gardner: Curriculum for talent development. *Gifted Child Quarterly, 42*, 245–252.

Sapon-Shevin, M. (1996). Beyond gifted education: Building a shared agenda for school reform. *Journal for the Education of the Gifted, 19*, 192–214.

Tannenbaum, A. J. (1998). Programs for the gifted: To be or not to be. *Journal for the Education of the Gifted, 22*, 3–36.

Terman, L. (1925). *Genetic studies of genius* (Vol. 1). Stanford, CA: Stanford University Press.

Thornkike, R. L., Hagen, E. P., & Sattler, J. M. (1996). *Stanford-Binet Intelligence Scale* (4th ed.). Itasca, Illinois: Riverside.

Treffinger, D. J., & Feldhusen, J. F. (1996). Talent recognition and development: Successor to gifted education. *Journal for the Education of the Gifted, 19*, 181–193.

VanTassel-Baska, J. (1995). The development of talent through curriculum. *Roeper Review, 18*, 98–102.

Wechsler, D. (1991). *Wechsler Intelligence Scale for Children III (WISC-III).* San Antonio, Texas: Psychological Corporation.

History of the Field

Clarenbach, J. (1999, April). !!Legislative alert!! *National Association for Gifted Children Communique*, pp. 1, 4.

Clark, B. (1992). *Growing up gifted* (4th ed.). New York: Merrill-Macmillan.

Clark, B. (1997). *Growing up gifted* (5th ed.). Upper Saddle River, NJ: Merrill.

Davis, G. A., & Rimm, S. B. (1998). *Education of the gifted and talented* (4th ed.). Boston: Allyn and Bacon.

Gallagher, J. J. (1988). National agenda for educating gifted students: Statement of priorities. *Exceptional Children, 55*, 107–114.

Gardner, J. W. (1984). *Excellence: Can we be equal and excellent too?* (Rev. ed.). New York: Norton.

Hunsaker, S. L. (1995). The gifted metaphor from the perspective of traditional civilizations. *Journal for the Education of the Gifted, 18*, 255–268.

Maker, C. J. (1986). Education of the gifted: Significant trends. In R. J. Morris and B. Blatt (Eds.), *Special education: Research and trends* (pp. 190–221). New York: Pergamon.

Silverman, L. K. (1988). Gifted and talented. In E. G. Meyen and T. M. Skrtic (Eds.), *Exceptional children and youth: An introduction* (3rd ed., pp. 263–292). Denver, CO: Love.

Silverman, L. K. (1992). Leta Stetter Hollingworth: Champion of the psychology of women and gifted children. *Journal of Educational Psychology, 84*, 20–27.

Prevalence

Brown, C. N. (1997). Legal issues and gifted education: Gifted identification as a constitutional issue. *Roeper Review, 19*, 157–160.

Davis, G. A., & Rimm, S. B. (1998). *Education of the gifted and talented* (4th ed.). Boston: Allyn and Bacon.

Harry, B. (1994). *The disproportionate representation of minority students in special education: Theories and recommendations.* Alexandria, VA: National Association of State Directors of Special Education.

National Center for Education Statistics. (1994). *Digest of Education Statistics.* Washington, DC: U.S. Government Printing Office.

Renzulli, J. S., & Reis, S. M. (1997). The schoolwide enrichment model: New directions for developing high-end learning. In N. Colangelo and G. A. Davis (Eds.), *Handbook of gifted education* (2nd ed., pp. 136–154). Boston: Allyn and Bacon.

Tomlinson, C. A., Callahan, C. M., & Lelli, K. M. (1998). Challenging expectations: Case studies of high-potential, culturally diverse young children. *Gifted Child Quarterly, 41,* 5–17.

Causes: Factors That Enhance or Inhibit Giftedness

Brown, C. N. (1997). Legal issues and gifted education: Gifted identification as a constitutional issue. *Roeper Review, 19,* 157–160.

De Leon, J., Argus-Calvo, B., & Medina, C. (1997). A model project for identifying rural gifted and talented students in the visual arts. *Rural Special Education Quarterly, 16,* 16–23.

Fishkin, A. S., & Johnson, A. S. (1998). Who is creative? Identifying children's creative abilities. *Roeper Review, 21,* 40–46.

Kirschenbaum, R. J. (1998). The creativity classification systems: An assessment theory. *Roeper Review, 21,* 20–26.

Kitano, M. K. (1997). Gifted Asian American women. *Journal for the Education of the Gifted, 21,* 3–37.

Kitano, M. K. (1998). Gifted Latina women. *Journal for the Education of the Gifted, 21,* 131–159.

Krippner, S. (1967). The ten commandments that block creativity. *Gifted Child Quarterly, 11,* 144–151.

Parker, J. (1998). The Torrance Creative Scholars Program. *Roeper Review, 21,* 32–35.

Reis, S. (1999, March). Overcoming barriers to girls' talent development. *Parenting for High Potential,* pp. 18–21.

Renzulli, J. (1978). What makes giftedness? Reexamining a definition. *Phi Delta Kappan, 60,* 180–184, 261.

Schroeder-Davis, S. (1998, December). Parenting high achievers: Swimming upstream against the cultural current. *Parenting for High Potential,* pp. 8–10.

Simonton, D. K. (1997). When giftedness becomes genius: How does talent achieve eminence? In N. Colangelo and G. A. Davis (Eds.), *Handbook of gifted education* (2nd ed., pp. 335–349). Boston: Allyn and Bacon.

Terman, L. (1925). *Genetic studies of genius* (Vol. 1). Stanford, CA: Stanford University Press.

Gifted Children

Arnold, K. D., Noble, K. D., & Subotnick, R. F. (Eds.) (1996). *Remarkable women: Perspectives on female talent development.* Cresskill, NJ: Hampton Press.

Beckley, D. (1998, Spring). Gifted and learning disabled: Twice exceptional students. *The National Research Center on the Gifted and Talented Newsletter,* pp. 6–10.

Borland, J. H. (1996). Gifted education and the threat of irrelevance. *Journal for the Education of the Gifted, 19,* 129–147.

Brody, L. E., & Mills, C. J. (1997). Gifted children with learning disabilities: A review of the issues. *Journal of Learning Disabilities, 30,* 282–296.

Brown, C. N. (1997). Legal issues and gifted education: Gifted identification as a constitutional issue. *Roeper Review, 19,* 157–160.

Callahan, C. M., & McIntire, J. A. (1994). *Identifying outstanding talent in American Indian and Alaska Native students.* Washington, DC: U.S. Department of Education, Office of Educational Research and Improvement.

Clark, B. (1997). *Growing up gifted* (5th ed.) Upper Saddle River, NJ: Merrill.

Davis, G. A. (1996). Review of giftedness and talent development for Smith and Luckasson. Personal communication.

Davis, G. A., & Rimm, S. B. (1998). *Education of the gifted and talented* (4th ed.). Boston: Allyn and Bacon.

De Leon, J., Argus-Calvo, B., & Medina, C. (1997). A model project for identifying rural gifted and talented students in the visual arts. *Rural Special Education Quarterly, 16,* 16–23.

Fernández, A. T., Gay, L. R., Lucky, L. F., & Gavilan, M. R. (1998). Teacher perceptions of gifted hispanic limited English proficient students. *Journal for the Education of the Gifted, 21,* 335–351.

Filippelli, K. A., & Walberg, H. J. (1997). Childhood traits and conditions of eminent women scientists. *Gifted Child Quarterly, 41,* 95–103.

Frey, C. P. (1998). Struggling with identity: Working with seventh- and eighth-grade gifted girls to air issues of concern. *Journal for the Education of the Gifted, 21,* 437–451.

Ford, B. A., Obiakor, F. E., & Patton J. M. (Eds.). (1995). *Effective education of African American exceptional learners: New perspectives.* Austin, TX: Pro-Ed.

Ford, D. Y. (1995). *Counseling gifted African American students: Promoting achievement, identity, and social and emotional well-being.* Storrs, CT: National Research Center on the Gifted and Talented, University of Connecticut.

Ford, D. Y., Grantham, T. C., & Harris, J. J., III. (1996). Multicultural gifted education: A wakeup call to the profession. *Roeper Review, 19,* 72–78.

Ford, D. Y., & Harris, J. J. (1994). Reform and gifted black students: Promising practices in Kentucky. *Journal of Gifted Education, 17,* 216–240.

Freeman, J. (1994). Some emotional aspects of being gifted. *Journal for the Education of the Gifted, 17,* 180–197.

Gallucci, N. T., Middleton, G., & Kline, A. (1999). The independence of creative potential and behavior disorders in gifted children. *Gifted Child Quarterly, 43,* 194–203.

Grimm, J. (1998). The participation of gifted students with disabilities in gifted programs. *Roeper Review, 20*, 285–286.

Hébert, T. P. (1998). Gifted black males in an urban high school: Factors that influence achievement and underachievement. *Journal for the Education of the Gifted, 21*, 385–414.

Hollingworth, L. S. (1942). *Children above 180 IQ, Stanford-Binet: Origin and development.* Yonkers, NY: World Book.

Hunsaker, S. L. (1994). Adjustments to traditional procedures for identifying underserved students: Successes and failures. *Exceptional Children, 61*, 72–76.

Hunsaker, S. L., Finley, V. S., Frank, E. L. (1997). An analysis of teacher nominations and student performance in gifted programs. *Gifted Child Quarterly, 41*, 19–24.

Jenkins-Friedman, R., & Nielsen, M. E. (1990). Gifted and talented students. In E. L. Meyen (Ed.), *Exceptional children in today's schools* (2nd ed., pp. 451–493). Denver, CO: Love.

Kitano, M. K. (1997). Gifted Asian American women. *Journal for the Education of the Gifted, 21*, 3–37.

Kitano, M. K. (1998). Gifted Latina women. *Journal for the Education of the Gifted, 21*, 131–159.

Laycock, F. (1979) *Gifted children.* Glenview, IL: Scott, Foresman.

Lupart, J. L., & Pyryt, M. C. (1996). "Hidden gifted" students: Underachiever prevalence and profile. *Journal for the Education of the Gifted, 20*, 36–53.

MacMillan, D. L., Gresham, F. M., & Bocian, K. M. (1998). Discrepancy between definitions of learning disabilities and school practices: An empirical investigation. *Journal of Learning Disabilities, 31*, 314–326.

Maker, C. J. (1977). *Providing programs for the gifted handicapped.* Reston, VA: Council for Exceptional Children.

Maker, C. J. (1986). Education of the gifted: Significant trends. In R. J. Morris and B. Blatt (Eds.), *Special education: Research and trends* (pp. 190–221). New York: Pergamon.

Maker, C. J., Nielson, A. B., & Rogers, J. A. (1994). Giftedness, diversity and problem solving. *Teaching Exceptional Children, 27*, 4–19.

Maker, C. J., & Schiever, S. W. (1989). Defining the Hispanic population. In C. J. Maker and S. W. Schiever (Eds.), *Critical issues in gifted education: Defensible programs for cultural and ethnic minorities* (Vol. 2, pp. 1–4). Austin, TX: Pro-Ed.

Nielsen, M. E., Higgins, L. D., & Hammond, A. E. (1993). The twice-exceptional child project: Identifying and serving gifted/handicapped learners. In C. M. Callahan, D. A. Tomlinson, and P. M. Pizzat (Eds.), *Contexts for promise: Noteworthy practices and innovations in the identification of gifted students* (pp. 145–168). Charlottesville, VA: National Research Center on the Gifted and Talented.

Nielsen, M. E., Higgins, L. D., Hammond. A. E., & Williams, R. A. (1993). Gifted children with disabilities: The twice-exceptional child project. *Gifted Child Today, 16*, 9–12.

Noble, K. D., Subotnik, R. F., & Arnold, K. D. (1999). To thine own self be true: A new model of female talent development. *Gifted Child Quarterly, 43*, 140–149.

Patton, J. M., & Baytops, J. L. (1995). Identifying and transforming the potential of young, gifted African Americans: A clarion call for action. In B. A. Ford, F. E. Obiakor, and J. M. Patton (Eds.), *Effective education of African American exceptional learners: New perspectives* (pp. 27–58). Austin, TX: Pro-Ed.

Piechowski, M. (1997). Emotional giftedness: The measure of intrapersonal intelligence. In N. Colangelo and G. A. Davis (Eds.), *Handbook of gifted education* (2nd ed., pp. 366–381). Boston: Allyn and Bacon.

Rakow, S. R. (1998, March). Middle matters: Guiding gifted girls through the middle school maze. *Parenting for High Potential,* pp. 20–30.

Reis, S. (1999, March). Overcoming barriers to girls' talent development. *Parenting for High Potential,* pp. 18–21.

Roberts, S. M., & Lovett, S. B. (1994). Examining the "F" in gifted: Academically gifted adolescents' physiological and affective responses to scholastic failure. *Journal for the Education of the Gifted, 17*, 241–259.

Robinson, S. M. (1999). Meeting the needs of students who are gifted and have learning disabilities. *Intervention in School and Clinic, 34*, 195–204.

Rogers, K. B. (1999). The lifelong productivity of the female researchers in Terman's genetic studies of genius longitudinal study. *Gifted Child Quarterly, 43*, 150–169.

Silverman, L. K. (1995). Gifted and talented. In E. L. Meyen and T. M. Skrtic (Eds.), *Exceptional children and youth: An introduction* (4th ed., pp. 377–414). Denver, CO: Love.

Terman, L. (1925). *Genetic studies of genius* (Vol. 1). Stanford, CA: Stanford University Press.

Tomlinson, C. A., Callahan, C. M., & Lelli, K. M. (1998). Challenging expectations: Case studies of high-potential, culturally diverse young children. *Gifted Child Quarterly, 41*, 5–17.

VanTassel-Baska, J. (1995). The development of talent through curriculum. *Roeper Review, 18*, 98–102.

Willard-Holt, C. (1998). Academic and personality characteristics of gifted students with cerebral palsy: A multiple case study. *Exceptional Children, 65*, 37–50.

Yong, F. L., & McIntyre, J. D. (1992). A comparative study of the learning style preferences of students with learning disabilities and students who are gifted. *Journal of Learning Disabilities, 25*, 124–132.

Educational Interventions

Achter, J. A., Lubinski, D., & Benbow, C. P. (1996). Multipotentiality among the intellectually gifted: "It was never there and already it's vanishing." *Journal of Counseling Psychology, 43*, 65–76.

Banks, J. A. (1994). *An introduction to multicultural education.* Boston: Allyn and Bacon.

Benbow, D. P., & Stanley, J. C. (1996). Inequity in equity: How "equity" can lead to inequity for high-potential students. *Psychology, Public Policy, and Law, 2*, 249–292.

Castillo, L. C. (1998). The effect of analogy instruction on young children's metaphor comprehension. *Roeper Review, 21*, 27–31.

Dalzell, H. J. (1998). Giftedness: Infancy to adolescence: A developmental perspective. *Roeper Review, 20*, 259–264.

Davis, G. A., & Rimm, S. B. (1998). *Education of the gifted and talented* (4th ed.). Boston: Allyn and Bacon.

Filippelli, K. A., & Walberg, H. J. (1997). Childhood traits and conditions of eminent women scientists. *Gifted Child Quarterly, 41*, 95–103.

Ford, D. Y., Grantham, T. C., & Harris, J. J., III. (1996). Multicultural gifted education: A wakeup call to the profession. *Roeper Review, 19*, 72–78.

Gallagher, J. J. (1996). A critique of critiques of gifted education. *Journal for the Education of the Gifted, 19*, 234–249.

Gallagher, J. J., & Gallagher, S. A. (1994). *Teaching the gifted child* (4th ed.). Boston: Allyn and Bacon.

Gallagher, J., Harradine, C. C., & Coleman, M. R. (1997). Gifted students in the classroom: Challenge or boredom? Gifted students' views on their schooling. *Roeper Review, 19*, 132–136.

Gallagher, J. J., Weiss, P., Oglesby, K., & Thomas, T. (1983). *The status of gifted/talented education: United States survey of needs, practices, and policies.* Ventura, CA: Ventura County Superintendent of Schools Office.

Hébert, T. P. (1998). Gifted black males in an urban high school: Factors that influence achievement and underachievement. *Journal for the Education of the Gifted, 21*, 385–414.

Hobson v. Hansen, 269 F. Supp. 401 (D. D. C. 1967), affirmed subnom. Smuck v. Hobson, 408 F. 2d 175 (DC Cir 1969).

Holliday, G. A., Koller, J. R., & Thomas, C. D. (1999). *Journal for the Education of the Gifted, 22*, 266–281.

Karnes, M. B., Shwedel, A. M., & Linnemeyer, S. A. (1982). The young gifted/talented child: Programs at the University of Illinois. *Elementary School Journal, 82*, 196–213.

Kitano, M. K. (1997). Gifted Asian American women. *Journal for the Education of the Gifted, 21*, 3–37.

Kitano, M. K. (1998). Gifted Latina women. *Journal for the Education of the Gifted, 21*, 131–159.

Kolloff, P. B. (1997). Special residential high schools. In N. Colangelo and G. A. Davis (Eds.), *Handbook of gifted education* (2nd ed., pp. 198–206). Boston: Allyn and Bacon.

Kulik, J. A., & Kulik, C. L. C. (1997). Ability grouping. In N. Colangelo and G. A. Davis (Eds.), *Handbook of gifted education* (2nd ed., pp. 230–242). Boston: Allyn and Bacon.

Lubinski, D., & Benbow, C. P. (1995). Optimal development of talent: Respond educationally to individual differences in personality. *The Educational Forum, 59*, 381–392.

McBride-Chang, C., Manis, F. R., & Wagner, R. K. (1996). Correlates of phonological awareness: Implications for gifted education. *Roeper Review, 19*, 27–30.

McDaniel, T. R. (1993). Education of the gifted and the excellence-equity debate: Lessons from history. In C. J. Maker (Ed.), *Critical issues in gifted education: Programs for the gifted in regular classrooms* (pp. 6–18). Austin, TX: Pro-Ed.

Mooij, T. (1999). Integrating gifted children into kindergarten by improving educational processes. *Gifted Child Quarterly, 43*, 63–74.

Oden, M. H. (1968). The fulfillment of promise: 40-year follow-up of the Terman gifted group. *Genetic Psychology Monographs, 77*, 3–93.

Patton, J. M., & Townsend, B. L. (1997). Creating inclusive environments for African American children and youth with gifts and talents. *Roeper Review, 20*, 13–17.

Pendarvis, E., & Howley, A. (1996). Playing fair: The possibilities of gifted education. *Journal for the Education of the Gifted, 19*, 215–233.

Ramsay, S. G., & Richards, H. C. (1997). Cooperative learning environments: Effects on academic attitudes of gifted students. *Gifted Child Quarterly, 41*, 160–168.

Reis, S. M., & Purcell, J. H. (1993). An analysis of content elimination and strategies used by elementary classroom teachers in the curriculum compacting process. *Journal for the Education of the Gifted, 16*, 147–170.

Renzulli, J. S. (1994/1995). Teachers as talent scouts. *Educational Leadership, 52*, 75–81.

Renzulli, J. S. (1998, October). A rising tide lifts all ships: Developing the gifts and talents of all students. *Phi Delta Kappan, 80*, 104–111.

Renzulli, J. S., & Reis, S. M. (1997). The schoolwide enrichment model: New directions for developing high-end learning. In N. Colangelo and G. A. Davis (Eds.), *Handbook of gifted education* (2nd ed., pp. 136–154). Boston: Allyn and Bacon.

Robinson, S. M. (1999). Meeting the needs of students who are gifted and have learning disabilities. *Intervention in School and Clinic, 34*, 195–204.

Sapon-Shevin, M. (1996). Beyond gifted education: Building a shared agenda for school reform. *Journal for the Education of the Gifted, 19*, 192–214.

Scheidemann, N. V. (1931). *The psychology of exceptional children.* New York: Houghton Mifflin.

Schneider, B. H., & Daniels, T. (1992). Peer acceptance and social play of gifted kindergarten children. *Exceptionality, 3*, 17–29.

Schuler, P. A. (1997). Cluster grouping coast to coast. *National Research Center on the Gifted and Talented Winter Newsletter*, pp. 11–14.

Sisk, D. (1987). *Creative teaching of the gifted.* New York: McGraw-Hill.

Slavin, R. E. (1990). Ability grouping, cooperative learning and the gifted. *Journal for the Education of the Gifted, 14*, 3–8.

Terman, L. (1925). *Genetic studies of genius* (Vol. 1). Stanford, CA: Stanford University Press.

Terman, L. M., & Oden, M. H. (1959). *The gifted group at midlife*. Stanford, CA: Stanford University Press.

Tucker, B., & Hafenstein, N. L. (1997). Psychological intensities in young gifted children. *Gifted Child Quarterly, 41*, 66–75.

VanTassel-Baska, J. (1995). The development of talent through curriculum. *Roeper Review, 18*, 98–102.

Walberg, H. J. (1982). Child traits and environmental conditions of highly eminent adults. *Gifted Child Quarterly, 25*, 103–107.

Walberg, H. J., & Zeiser, S. (1997). Productivity, accomplishment, and eminence. In N. Colangelo & G. A. Davis (Eds.), *Handbook of gifted education* (2nd ed., 238–334). Boston: Allyn and Bacon.

Witham, J. H. (1997). Public or private schools: A dilemma for gifted students? *Roeper Review, 19*, 137–141.

Families

Davis, G. A., & Rimm, S. B. (1998). *Education of the gifted and talented* (4th ed.). Boston: Allyn and Bacon.

Filippelli, K. A., & Walberg, H. J. (1997). Childhood traits and conditions of eminent women scientists. *Gifted Child Quarterly, 41*, 95–103.

Hébert, T. P. (1998). Gifted black males in an urban high school: Factors that influence achievement and underachievement. *Journal for the Education of the Gifted, 21*, 385–414.

Kitano, M. K. (1997). Gifted Asian American women. *Journal for the Education of the Gifted, 21*, 3–37.

Kitano, M. K. (1998). Gifted Latina women. *Journal for the Education of the Gifted, 21*, 131–159.

Subotnik, R., Kassan, L., Summers, E., & Wasser, A. (1993). *Genius revisited: High IQ children grow up*. Norwood, NJ: Ablex Publishing.

Yewchuk, C. R. (1995). The "mad genius" controversy: Implications for gifted education. *Journal for the Education of the Gifted, 19*, 3–29.

Technology

McBride, R. O., & Lewis, G. (1993). Sharing the resources: Electronic outreach programs. *Journal for the Education of the Gifted, 16*, 372–386.

Morgan, T. D. (1993). Technology: An essential tool for gifted and talented education. *Journal for the Education of the Gifted, 16*, 358–371.

Concepts and Controversy

Banks, J. A. (1994). *An introduction to multicultural education*. Boston: Allyn and Bacon.

Brown, C. N. (1997). Legal issues and gifted education: Gifted identification as a constitutional issue. *Roeper Review, 19*, 157–160.

Callahan, C. M., & McIntire, J. A. (1994). *Identifying outstanding talent in American Indian and Alaska Native students*. Washington, DC: U.S. Department of Education, Office of Educational Research and Improvement.

Coleman, M. R., & Gallagher, J. J. (1994). *Report on states' policies related to the identification of gifted students*. Chapel Hill: Gifted Education Policy Studies Program.

Harry, B. (1994). *The disproportionate representation of minority students in special education: Theories and recommendations*. Alexandria, VA: National Association of State Directors of Special Education.

Maker, C. J., Nielson, A. B., & Rogers, J. A. (1994). Giftedness, diversity and problem solving. *Teaching Exceptional Children, 27*, 4–19.

U.S. Department of Education. (1993). *Fifteenth annual report to Congress on the implementation of the Individuals with Disabilities Education Act*. Washington, DC: U.S. Government Printing Office.

Chapter 8: Emotional or Behavioral Disorders

Edvard Munch

Bischoff, U. (1988). *Edvard Munch: 1863–1944*. Köln, Germany: Benedikt Taschen Verlag GmbH & Co.

Grolier. (1993). *The new Grolier multimedia encyclopedia*. Danbury, CT: Grolier Electronic Publishing.

Messer, T. M. (1985). *Munch*. New York: Harry N. Abrams.

Emotional or Behavioral Disorders Defined

American Psychiatric Association. (1994). *Diagnostic and statistical manual of mental disorders (DSM-IV)* (4th ed.). Washington, DC: Author.

Bower, E. M. (1960). *Early identification of emotionally disturbed children in school* (Rev. ed.). Springfield, IL: Thomas.

Bower, E. M. (1982). Defining emotional disturbance: Public policy and research. *Psychology in the Schools, 19*, 55–60.

Bussing, R., Schoenberg, N. E., Rogers, K. M., Zima, B. T., & Angus, S. (1998). Explanatory models of ADHD: Do they differ by ethnicity, child gender, or treatment status? *Journal of Emotional and Behavior Disorders, 6*, 233–242.

Bussing, R., Zima, B. T., Belin, T. R., & Forness, S. R. (1998). Children who qualify for LD & SED programs: Do they differ in level of ADHD symptoms and co-morbid psychiatric conditions? *Behavioral Disorders, 23*, 85–97.

Cluett, S. E., Forness, S. R., Ramey, S. R., Ramey, C. T., Hsu, C., Kavale, K. A., & Gresham, F. M. (1998). Consequences of differential diagnostic criteria in identification rates of children with emotional or behavioral disorders. *Journal of Emotional and Behavioral Disorders, 6*, 130–140.

Costenbader, V., & Buntaine, R. (1999). Diagnostic discrimination between social maladjustment and emotional disturbance. *Journal of Emotional and Behavioral Disorders, 7*, 2–10.

Edens, J. F., & Otto, R. K. (1997). Prevalence of mental disorders among youth in the juvenile justice system. *Focal Point, 11*, 1, 6–7.

Forness, S. R., & Knitzer, J. (1992). A new proposed definition and terminology to replace "serious emotional disturbance" in IDEA. *School Psychology Review, 21*, 12–20.

Gallagher, T. M. (1999). Interrelationships among children's language, behavior, and emotional problems. *Topics in Language Disorders, 19*, 1–15.

Hallahan, D. P., & Kauffman, J. M. (2000). *Exceptional children: Introduction to special education* (8th ed.). Boston: Allyn and Bacon.

Handwerk, M. L., & Marshall, R. M. (1998). Behavioral and Emotional problems of students with learning disabilities, serious emotional disturbance or both conditions. *Journal of Learning Disabilities, 31*, 327–338.

Kauffman, J. M. (1997). *Characteristics of behavioral disorders of children and youth* (6th ed.). Columbus, OH: Merrill.

Koyanagi, C., & Gaines, S. (1993). *All systems failure.* Alexandria, VA: National Mental Health Association

Newcomer, P. L. (1993). *Understanding and teaching emotionally disturbed children and adolescents* (2nd ed.). Austin, TX: Pro-Ed.

Oswald, D. P., & Coutinho, M. J. (1996). Identification and placement of students with serious emotional disturbance. Part I: Correlates of state child-count data. *Journal of Emotional and Behavioral Disorders, 3*, 224–229.

Talbott, E., & Thiede, K. (1999). Pathways to antisocial behavior among adolescent girls. *Journal of Emotional and Behavioral Disorders, 7*, 31–39.

U.S. Department of Education. (1994). *Sixteenth annual report to Congress on the implementation of the Individuals with Disabilities Education Act.* Washington, DC: U.S. Government Printing Office.

U.S. Department of Education. (1998). *Twentieth annual report to Congress on the implementation of the Individuals with Disabilities Education Act.* Washington, DC: U.S. Government Printing Office.

U.S. Department of Education. (1999). Assistance to state for the education of children with disabilities and the early intervention program for infants and toddlers with disabilities: Final regulations. *Federal Register, 64 (48)*, CFR Parts 300 and 303.

Volpe, R. J., DuPaul, G. J., Loney, J., & Salisbury, H. (1999). Alternative selection criteria for identifying children with ADHD: Observed behavior and self-reported internalizing symptoms. *Journal of Emotional and Behavioral Disorders, 7*, 103–109.

Walker, H. M., Severson, H. H., Nicholson, F., Kehle, T., Jenson, W. R., & Clark, E. (1994). Replication of the systematic screening of behavior disorders (SSBD) procedure for the identification of at-risk children. *Journal of Emotional and Behavioral Disorders, 2*, 66–77.

Zirkel, P. (1999, February 12). How to determine eligibility of students with problem behaviors. *The Special Educator, 17*, 1, 7–8.

History of the Field

Allen, K. M., Hart, B. M., Buell, J. S., Harris, F. R., & Wolf, M. M. (1964). Effects of social reinforcement on isolated behavior of a nursery school child. *Child Development, 35*, 511–518.

Bower, E. M., & Lambert, N. M. (1962). *A process for in-school screening of children with emotional handicaps.* Princeton, NJ: Educational Testing Service.

Brigham, A. (1847). The moral treatment of insanity. *American Journal of Insanity, 4*, 1–15.

Deutsch, A. (1949). *The mentally ill in America: A history of their care and treatment from colonial times* (2nd ed.). New York: Columbia University Press.

Haring, N. J., & Phillips, E. L. (1962). *Educating emotionally disturbed children.* New York: McGraw-Hill.

Healy, W., & Bronner, A. F. (1926). *Delinquents and criminals: Their making and unmaking.* New York: Macmillan.

Safford, P. L., & Safford, E. J. (1996). *A history of childhood and disability.* New York: Teachers College Press.

Prevalence

Cluett, S. E., Forness, S. R., Ramey, S. R., Ramey, C. T., Hsu, C., Kavale, K. A., & Gresham, F. M. (1998). Consequences of differential diagnostic criteria in identification rates of children with emotional or behavioral disorders. *Journal of Emotional and Behavioral Disorders, 6*, 130–140.

Kauffman, J. M. (1997). *Characteristics of behavioral disorders of children and youth* (5th ed.). Columbus, OH: Merrill.

McCabe, K., Yeh, M., Hough, R. L., Landsverk, J., Hurlburt, M. S., Culver, S. W., & Reynolds, B. (1999). Racial/ethnic representation across five public sectors of care for youth. *Journal of Emotional and Behavioral Disorders, 7*, 72–82.

Oswald, D. P., & Coutinho, M. J. (1996). Identification and placement of students with serious emotional disturbance. Part I: Correlates of state child-count data. *Journal of Emotional and Behavioral Disorders, 3*, 224–229.

Peterson, R. L., & Ishii-Jordon, S. (Eds.). (1994). *Multicultural issues in the education of students with behavioral disorders.* Cambridge, MA: Brookline.

U.S. Department of Education. (1998). *Twentieth annual report to Congress on the implementation of the Individuals with Disabilities Education Act.* Washington, DC: U.S. Government Printing Office.

Causes and Prevention

American Psychiatric Association. (1994). *Diagnostic and statistical manual of mental disorders (DSM-IV)* (4th ed.). Washington, DC: Author.

Bussing, R., Zima, B. T., Belin, T. R., & Forness, S. R. (1998). Children who qualify for LD & SED programs: Do they differ in level of ADHD symptoms and comorbid psychiatric conditions? *Behavioral Disorders, 23*, 85–97.

Children's Defense Fund. (1999). *The state of America's children: Yearbook 1999.* Washington, DC: Author.

Hallahan, D. P., & Kauffman, J. M. (2000). *Exceptional children: Introduction to special education* (8th ed.). Boston: Allyn and Bacon.

Kamps, D., Kravits, T., Stolze, J., & Swaggart, B. (1999). Prevention strategies for at-risk students and students with EBD in urban elementary schools. *Journal of Emotional and Behavioral Disorders, 7*, 178–188.

Kauffman, J. M. (1999). How we prevent the prevention of emotional and behavioral disorders. *Exceptional Children, 65*, 448–468.

McLane, K. (1997). School-wide behavioral management systems. *Research Connections in Special Education, 1*, 1–5.

Montague, M., Bergeron, J., & Lago-Delello, E. (1997). Using prevention strategies in general education. *Focus on Exceptional Children, 29*, 1–12.

Myles, B. S., & Simpson, R. L. (1998). Aggression and violence by school-age children and youth: Understanding the aggression cycle and prevention/intervention strategies. *Intervention in School and Clinic, 33*, 259–264.

Osher, D. M., & Osher, T. W. (1996). The national agenda for children and youth with serious emotional disturbance (SED). In C. M. Nelson, R. B. Rutherford, Jr., & B. I. Wolford (Eds.), *Comprehensive and Collaborative Systems That Work for Troubled Youth: A National Agenda* (pp. 149–164). Richmond, KY: Eastern Kentucky University, National Juvenile Detention Association.

Rivera, D. P., & Smith, D. D. (1997). *Teaching students with learning and behavior problems.* Boston: Allyn and Bacon.

Rudo, Z. H., Powell, D. S., & Dunlap, G. (1998). The effects of violence in the home on children's emotional, behavioral, and social functioning: A review of the literature. *Journal of Emotional and Behavioral Disorders, 6*, 94–113.

Sinclair, E. (1998). Head Start children at risk: Relationship of prenatal drug exposure to identification of special needs and subsequent special education kindergarten placement. *Behavioral Disorders, 23*, 125–133.

Smith, D. D., & Rivera, D. P. (1993). *Effective discipline.* Austin, TX: Pro-Ed.

Tobin, T., Sugai, G., & Colvin, G. (1996). Patterns in middle school discipline records. *Journal of Emotional and Behavioral Disorders, 4*, 82–94.

Walker, H. M., & Gresham, F. M. (1997). Making schools safer and violence free. *Intervention in School and Clinic, 32*, 199–204.

Children with Emotional and Behavioral Disorders

Begley, S. (1999, May 3). Why the young kill. *Newsweek,* pp. 32–35.

Bender, W. N., & McLaughlin, P. J. (1997). Weapons violence in schools: Strategies for teachers confronting violence and hostage situations. *Intervention in School and Clinic, 32*, 211–216.

Children's Defense Fund. (1999). *The state of America's children: Yearbook 1999.* Washington, DC: Author.

Day, D. M., & Hunt, A. C. (1996). A multivariate assessment of a risk model for juvenile delinquency with an "under 12 offender" sample. *Journal of Emotional and Behavioral Disorders, 4*, 66–72.

Deveres, L. (1999a, August 27). Social skills training aids students in life's lessons. *The Special Educator, 15*, 1, 8–9.

Kauffman, J. M. (1997). *Characteristics of behavioral disorders of children and youth* (6th ed.). Columbus, OH: Merrill.

Locke, W. R., & Fuchs, L. S. (1995). Effects of peer-mediated reading instruction on the on-task behavior and social interaction of children with behavior disorders. *Journal of Emotional and Behavioral Disorders, 3*, 92–99.

Malmgren, K., Abbott, R. D., & Hawkins, J. D. (1999). LD and delinquency: Rethinking the link. *Journal of Learning Disabilities, 32*, 194–200.

Miller-Johnson, S., Coie, J. E., Maumary-Gremaud, A., Lockman, J., & Terry, R. (1999). Relationship between childhood peer rejection and aggression and adolescent delinquency severity and type among African-American youth. *Journal of Emotional and Behavioral Disorders, 7*, 137–146.

Myles, B. S., & Simpson, R. L. (1998). Aggression and violence by school-age children and youth: Understanding the aggression cycle and prevention/intervention strategies. *Intervention in School and Clinic, 33*, 259–264.

Quinn, M. M., Kavale, K. A., Mathur, S. R., Rutherford, R. B., Jr., & Forness, S. R. (1999). A meta-analysis of social skill interventions for students with emotional or behavioral disorders. *Journal of Emotional and Behavioral Disorders, 7*, 54–64.

Safran, S. P. (1995). Peers' perceptions of emotional and behavioral disorders: What are students thinking? *Journal of Emotional and Behavioral Disorders, 3*, 66–75.

Strain, P. S., & Timm, M. A. (1999). Preliminary results from the early childhood intervention study. Nashville: Regional Intervention Project (RIP). Unpublished paper.

Tobin, T. J., & Sugai, G. M. (1999). Using sixth-grade school records to predict school violence, chronic discipline problems, and high school outcomes. *Journal of Emotional and Behavioral Disorders, 7*, 40–53.

U.S. Department of Education. (1998). *Twentieth annual report to Congress on the implementation of the Individuals with Disabilities Education Act.* Washington, DC: U.S. Government Printing Office.

Walker, H. M., Schwarz, I. E., Nippold, M. A., Irvin, L. K., & Noell, J. W. (1994). Social skills in school-age children and youth: Issues and best practices in assessment and intervention. *Topics in Language Disorders, 14*, 70–82.

Walker, H. M., & Sylvester, R. (1994). Where is school along the path to prison? *The Frontline, 1*, 3–6.

Educational Interventions

Bussing, R., Zima, B. T., Belin, T. R., & Forness, S. R. (1998). Children who qualify for LD & SED programs: Do they differ in level of ADHD symptoms and co-morbid psychiatric conditions? *Behavioral Disorders, 23*, 85–97.

Cheney, D., & Barringer, C. (1995). Teacher competence, student diversity, and staff training for the inclusion of middle school students with emotional and behavioral disorders. *Journal of Emotional and Behavioral Disorders, 3*, 174–182.

Chesapeake Institute. (1994). *National agenda for achieving better results for children and youth with serious emotional disturbance.* Washington, DC: U.S. Department of Education Office of Special Education Programs.

Coutinho, M. J., & Oswald, D. (1996). Identification and placement of students with serious emotional disturbance. Part II: Nation and state trends in the implementation of LRE. *Journal of Emotional and Behavioral Disorders, 4*, 40–52.

Deveres, L. (1999a, August 27). Social skills training aids students in life's lessons. *The Special Educator, 15*, 1, 8–9.

Deveres, L. (1999b). *A primer on functional behavioral assessments.* Horsham, PA: LRP Publications.

Edens, J. F., & Otto, R. K. (1997). Prevalence of mental disorders among youth in the juvenile justice system. *Focal Point, 11*, 1, 6–7.

Feil, E. G., Walker, H. M., & Severson, H. H. (1995). The early screening project for young children with behavior problems. *Journal of Emotional and Behavioral Disorders, 3*, 194–202.

Hallenbeck, B. A., & Kauffman, J. M. (1995). How does observational learning affect the behavior of students with emotional or behavioral disorders? A review of research. *The Journal of Special Education, 29*, 45–71.

Hartwig, E., & Ruesch, G. (1998). *Discipline in the Schools.* Horsham, PA: LRP Publications.

Kamps, D., Kravits, T., Stolze, J., & Swaggart, B. (1999). Prevention strategies for at-risk students and students with EBD in urban elementary schools. *Journal of Emotional and Behavioral Disorders, 7*, 178–188.

Lohrmann-O'Rourke, S., & Zirkel, P. A. (1998). The case law on aversive interventions for students with disabilities. *Exceptional Children, 65*, 101–123.

Martin, J. E., & Marshall, L. H. (1995). Choicemaker: A comprehensive self-determination transition program. *Intervention in School and Clinic, 30*, 147–156.

Myles, B. S., & Simpson, R. L. (1998). Aggression and violence by school-age children and youth: Understanding the aggression cycle and prevention/intervention strategies. *Intervention in School and Clinic, 33*, 259–264.

Nelson, J. R., Crabtree, M., Marchand-Martella, N., & Martella, R. (1998). Teaching good behavior in the whole school. *Teaching Exceptional Children, 30*, 4–9

Nelson, J. R., Johnson, A., & Marchand-Martella, N. (1996). Effects of direct instruction, cooperative learning, and independent learning practices on the classroom behavior of students with behavioral disorders: A comparative analysis. *Journal of Emotional and Behavioral Disorders, 4*, 53–62.

McDougall, D. (1998). Research on self-management techniques used by students with disabilities in general education settings. *Remedial and Special Education, 19*, 310–320.

Owens-Johnson, L., & Johnson, J. (1999). The local employer survey project: An effective school-to-work curriculum. *Teaching Exceptional Children, 31*, 18–23.

Rylance, R. J. (1998). Predictors of post–high school employment for youth identified as severely emotionally disturbed. *The Journal of Special Education, 32*, 184–192.

Serna, L. A., & Lau-Smith, J. (1995). Learning with purpose: Self-determination skills for students who are at risk for school and community failure. *Intervention in School and Clinic, 30*, 142–146.

Sinclair, M. F., Christenson, S. L., Evelo, D. L., & Hurley, C. M. (1998). Dropout prevention for youth with disabilities: Efficacy of a sustained school engagement procedure. *Exceptional Children, 65*, 7–21.

Smith, D. D., & Rivera, D. P. (1993). *Effective discipline* (2nd ed.). Austin, TX: Pro-Ed.

Strain, P. S., & Timm, M. A. (1998). The early childhood intervention study. Nashville: Regional Intervention Project (RIP). Unpublished paper.

Strain, P. S., & Timm, M. A. (1999). Preliminary results from the early childhood intervention study. Nashville: Regional Intervention Project (RIP). Unpublished paper.

Strain, P. S., Steele, P., Ellis, R., & Timm, M. (1982). Long-term effects of oppositional child treatment with mothers as therapists and therapist trainers. *Journal of Applied Behavior Analysis, 15*, 163–169.

Tobin, T. J., & Sugai, G. M. (1999). Using sixth-grade school records to predict school violence, chronic discipline problems, and high school outcomes. *Journal of Emotional and Behavioral Disorders, 7*, 40–53.

U.S. Department of Education. (1998). *Twentieth annual report to Congress on the implementation of the Individuals with Disabilities Education Act.* Washington, DC: U.S. Government Printing Office.

Walker, H. M., Colvin, G., & Ramsey, E. (1995). *Antisocial behavior in school: Strategies and best practices.* Pacific Grove, CA: Brooks/Cole.

Walker, H. M., & Gresham, F. M. (1997). Making schools safer and violence free. *Intervention in School and Clinic, 32*, 199–204.

Walker, H. M., Kavanagh, K., Stiller, B., Golly, A., Severson, H. H., & Feil, E. G. (1998). First Step to Success: An early intervention approach for preventing school antisocial behavior. *Journal of Emotional and Behavioral Disorders, 6*, 66–80.

Wall, M. E., & Dattilo, J. (1995). Creating option-rich learning environments: Facilitating self-determination. *The Journal of Special Education, 29*, 276–294.

Families

Ahearn, E. (Ed.). (1995, February). Summary of the 16th annual report to Congress on special education. *Liaison Bulletin*, pp. 1–3. Alexandria: NASDSE.

Children's Defense Fund. (1995). *The state of America's children: Yearbook 1995*. Washington, DC: Author.

Children's Defense Fund. (1996). *The state of America's children: Yearbook 1996*. Washington, DC: Author

Farmer, E. M. Z., Burns, B. J., Angold, A., & Costello, E. J. (1997). Impact of children's mental health problems on families: Relationships with service use. *Journal of Emotional and Behavioral Disorders, 5*, 230–238.

Koroloff, N. M., Elliott, D. J., Koren, P. E., & Friesen, B. J. (1996). Linking low-income families to children's mental health services: An outcome study. *Journal of Emotional and Behavioral Disorders, 4*, 2–11.

Sherman, A. (1994). *Wasting America's future: The Children's Defense Fund report on the costs of child poverty*. Boston: Beacon Press.

Smucker, K. S., Kauffman, J. M., & Ball, D. W. (1996). School-related problems of special education foster-care students with emotional or behavioral disorders: A comparison to other groups. *Journal of Emotional and Behavioral Disorders, 4*, 30–39.

Technology

Lucent Technologies (1999). Reinventing today's classrooms with wireless technology. Bell Labs Innovations: www.wavelan.com/educational

Rivera, D. P., & Smith, D. D. (1997). *Teaching students with learning and behavior problems* (3rd ed.). Boston: Allyn and Bacon.

Concepts and Controversy

Armstrong, T. (1995). *The myth of the ADD child*. New York: Dutton.

Axelrod, S., & Bailey, S. L. (1979). Drug treatment for hyperactivity: Controversies, alternatives, and guidelines. *Exceptional Children, 45*, 544–550.

Carpenter, R. L., & Sells, C. J. (1974). Measuring effects of psychoactive medication in a child with a learning disability. *Journal of Learning Disabilities, 7*, 545–550.

Ervin, R. A., DuPaul, G. J. Kern, L., & Friman, P. C. (1998). Classroom-based functional and adjunctive assessments: Proactive approaches to intervention selection for adolescents with attention deficit hyperactivity disorder. *Journal of Applied Behavior Analysis, 31*, 65–88.

Hallfors, D., Fallon, T., Jr., & Watson, K. (1998). An examination of psychotropic drug treatment for children with serious emotional disturbance. *Journal of Emotional and Behavioral Disorders, 6*, 56–64.

Hancock, L. N. (1996, March 18). Mother's little helper. *Newsweek*, pp. 51–56.

Landrum, T. J., Singh, N. N., Nemil, M. S., Ellis, C. R., & Best, A. M. (1995). Characteristics of children and adolescents with serious emotional disturbance in systems of care. Part II: Community-based services. *Journal of Emotional and Behavioral Disorders, 3*, 141–149.

Pancheri, C., & Prater, M. A. (1999). What teachers and parents should know about Ritalin. *Teaching Exceptional Children, 31*, 20–26.

Sulzbacher, S. I. (1972). Behavior analysis of drug effects in the classroom. In G. Semb (Ed.), *Behavior analysis and education— 1972* (pp. 37–52). Lawrence: University of Kansas Support and Development Center for Follow Through.

Zametkin, A. J., & Ernst, M. (1999). Problems in the management of attention-deficit-hyperactivity disorder. *New England Journal of Medicine, 340*, 40–46.

Chapter 9: Physical Impairments and Special Health Care Needs

Henriette Wyeth

Horgan, P. (1994). *The artifice of blue light: Henriette Wyeth*. Santa Fe: Museum of New Mexico.

Physical Impairments and Special Health Care Needs Defined

Barry, J. (1994, December 13). Disabled model makes comeback—a step at a time. *Albuquerque Journal*, p. B4.

Best, S. J., Bigge, J. L., & Sirvis, B. P. (1994). Physical and health impairments. In N. G. Haring, L. McCormick, and T. G. Haring, *Exceptional children and youth* (6th ed., pp. 300–341). New York: Macmillan College Publishing.

Cheney, P. D., & Palmer, F. B. (Eds.) (1997). Special issue: Cerebral palsy. *Mental Retardation and Developmental Disabilities Research Reviews, 3*, 109–219.

Epilepsy Foundation of America. (1994). *Epilepsy: Questions and Answers*. Landover, MD: Author.

Eriksson, K., Erilä, T., Kivimäki, T., & Koivikko, M. (1998). Evolution of epilepsy in children with mental retardation: Five-year experience in 78 cases. *American Journal on Mental Retardation, 102*, 464–472.

Getch, Y. Q., & Neuharth-Pritchett, S. (1999). Children with asthma: Strategies for educators. *Teaching Exceptional Children, 31*, 30–36.

Hallahan, D. P., & Kauffman, J. M. (2000). *Exceptional children: Introduction to special education* (7th ed.). Boston: Allyn and Bacon.

Heller, K. W., Alberto, P. A., Forney, P. E., & Schwartzman, M. N. (1996). *Understanding physical, sensory, and health impairments*. Pacific Grove: Brooks/Cole.

Holloway, T. (Ed.) (1999, February 16). Fresh start now within reach. *The Tennessean*, p. 4A

Samuels, R. (1995, April 2). South beach access: Miami offers disabled visitors a variety of activities. *Albuquerque Journal*, p. C1.

Sirvis, B. P., & Caldwell, T. H. (1995). Physical disabilities and chronic health impairments. In E. L. Meyen & T. M. Skrtic (Eds.), *Special education and student disability: An introduction* (4th ed., pp. 533–564). Denver, CO: Love.

Stone, A. (1997, April 2). A man of determination: 'Scars become my stars' for Ga. senator. *USA Today*, p. 9D.

Taylor, J. M., & Taylor, W. S. (1989). *Communicable disease and young children in group settings*. Boston: College-Hill.

Urbano, M. T. (1992). *Preschool children with special health care needs*. San Diego: Singular Press.

U.S. Department of Education. (1999). Assistance to state for the education of children with disabilities and the early intervention program for infants and toddlers with disabilities: Final regulations. *Federal Register, 64 (48)*, CFR Parts 300 and 303.

Woods, E. (1994, May 14). Spirit of the game. *Albuquerque Tribune*, p. C1.

History of the Field

Dolch, E. W. (1948). *Helping handicapped children in school.* Champaign, IL: Garrard Press.

Eberle, L. (1922, August). The maimed, the halt and the race. *Hospital Social Service, 6*, 59–63. Reprinted in R. H. Bremner (Ed.), *Children and youth in America, A documentary history: Vol. II, 1866–1932* (pp. 1026–1928). Cambridge, MA: Harvard University Press.

Frayer, D. W., Horton, W. A., Macchiarelli, R., & Mussi, M. (1987, November 5). Dwarfism in an adolescent from the Italian late Upper Palaeolithic. *Nature, 330*, 60–61.

Heller, K. W., Alberto, P. A., Forney, P. E., & Schwartzman, M. N. (1996). *Understanding physical, sensory, and health impairments.* Pacific Grove: Brooks/Cole.

La Vor, M. L. (1976). Federal legislation for exceptional persons: A history. In F. J. Weintraub, A. Abeson, J. Ballard, and M. L. La Vor (Eds.), *Public policy and the education of exceptional children* (pp. 96–111). Reston, VA: Council for Exceptional Children.

Maddox, S. (Ed.). (1987). *Spinal network: The total resource for the wheelchair community.* Boulder, CO: Author.

Scheerenberger, R. C. (1983). *A history of mental retardation.* Baltimore: Brookes.

Shaw, B. (1995, May/June). Ed Roberts: 1939–1995. *Disability Rag,* p. 25.

Stone, K. G. (1995, March 19). Disability rights pioneer inspired his community. *Albuquerque Journal,* p. C6.

Winzer, M. A. (1993). *The history of special education: From isolation to integration.* Washington, DC: Gallaudet University.

Prevalence

Beverly, C. L., & Thomas, S. B. (1997). Developmental and psycho-social effects of HIV in school-aged population: Educational implications. *Education and Training in Mental Retardation and Developmental Disabilities, 32*, 32–41.

Cheney, P. D., & Palmer, F. B. (1997). Overview: Cerebral palsy. *Mental Retardation and Developmental Disabilities Research Reviews, 3*, 109–111.

Epilepsy Education Department of Neurology University of Minnesota. (1993). *Epilepsy: Medical aspects.* Landover, MD: Author.

Getch, Y. Q., & Neuharth-Pritchett, S. (1999). Children with asthma: Strategies for educators. *Teaching Exceptional Children, 31*, 30–36.

Heller, K. W., Alberto, P. A., Forney, P. E., & Schwartzman, M. N. (1996). *Understanding physical, sensory, and health impairments.* Pacific Grove: Brooks/Cole.

Lesar, S., Gerber, M. M., & Semmel, M. I. (1995). The HIV infection in children: Family stress, social support, and adaptation. *Exceptional Children, 62*, 224–236.

Rowley-Kelly, F. L., & Reigel, D. H. (1993). *Teaching the student with spina bifida.* Baltimore: Paul H. Brookes.

United Cerebral Palsy Associations. (1993). *Cerebral palsy—Facts and figures.* Washington, DC: Author.

U.S. Department of Education. (1998). *Twentieth annual report to Congress on the implementation of the Individuals with Disabilities Education Act.* Washington, DC: U.S. Government Printing Office.

Causes and Prevention

Children's Defense Fund (CDF). (1997). Child immunizations hit all time high. *CDF Reports.*

Epilepsy Foundation of America. (1994). *Epilepsy: Questions and answers.* Landover, MD: Author.

Finlay, B. (1995, May). Service clubs promote immunizations. *Children's Defense Fund, CDF Reports, 16*, 13.

Getch, Y. Q., & Neuharth-Pritchett, S. (1999). Children with asthma: Strategies for educators. *Teaching Exceptional Children, 31*, 30–36.

Heller, K. W., Alberto, P. A., Forney, P. E., & Schwartzman, M. N. (1996). *Understanding physical, sensory, and health impairments.* Pacific Grove: Brooks/Cole.

Neergaard, L. (1995, July 11). Safer polio vaccines raise fears of new epidemics. *Albuquerque Journal,* pp. A1, A5.

Nelson, K.B., & Grether, J. K. (1997). Cerebral palsy in low-birthweight infants: Etiology and strategies for prevention. *Mental Retardation and Developmental Disabilities Research Reviews, 3*, 112–117.

Children with Physical Impairments and Special Health Care Needs

Horn, E. M. (1997). Achieving meaningful motor skills: Conceptual and empirical bases of a neurobehavorial intervention approach. *Mental Retardation and Developmental Disabilities Research Reviews, 3*, 138–144.

Long, D. (1999, May 27). Students plan nature trail for handicapped. *The Tennessean,* p. 5B.

Newsweek (1997, June 23). Perspectives. Author, p. 27.

Palmer, F. B. (1997). Evaluation of developmental therapies in cerebral palsy. *Mental Retardation and Developmental Disabilities Research Reviews, 3*, 145–152.

Sandler, A. (1989). Learning by design: The AIA elementary and secondary education program. *Art Education, 42*, 13–16.

Taylor, A. (1990). The place of design education in art education. *Design for Arts in Education, 43*, 22–28.

Taylor, A., & Warden, M. G. (1994). Learning environments for the twenty-first century. *Curriculum in Context, 22*, 12–14.

Educational Interventions

Associated Press. (1998, March 4). Martin is surprised by celebrity status. *The Tennessean*, p. C2.

Edelman, A., Schuyler, V. E., & White, P. H. (1998). *Maximizing success for young adults with chronic health-related illnesses: Transition planning for education after high school.* Washington, DC: American Council on Education, HEATH Resource Center.

Ferrer, S. H. (1996, August 29). Monkeys give helping hand to paralyzed. *Albuquerque Journal*, p. A8.

Haynes, K. A. (1998, June 16). Teacher's pet. *Los Angeles Times*, p. B12.

Horn, E. M. (1997). Achieving meaningful motor skills: Conceptual and empirical bases of a neurobehavorial intervention approach. *Mental Retardation and Developmental Disabilities Research Reviews, 3*, 138–144.

Pacenti, J. (1997, August 3). Coach is getting his kicks: Wheelchair doesn't stop Dolphins' aide. *Albuquerque Journal*, pp. C1, C8.

Rosenthal-Malek, A., & Greenspan, J. (1999). A student with diabetes is in my class. *Teaching Exceptional Children, 31*, 38–43.

Slaughter, S. (1999, January 31). Lending a helping paw: Agency's specially trained dogs quickly become partners for disabled clients. *The Tennessean*, pp. F1, F9.

U.S. Department of Education. (1998). *Twentieth annual report to Congress on the implementation of the Individuals with Disabilities Education Act.* Washington, DC: U.S. Government Printing Office.

Woods, E. (1994, May 14). Spirit of the game. *Albuquerque Tribune*, p. C1.

Families

Beverly, C. L., & Thomas, S. B. (1997). Developmental and psycho-social effects of HIV in school-aged population: Educational implications. *Education and Training in Mental Retardation and Developmental Disabilities, 32*, 32–41.

Davis, H. (1983). *Counseling parents of children with chronic illness or disability.* Baltimore: Brookes.

Martin, S. S., Brady, M. P., & Kotarba, J. A. (1992). Families with chronically ill young children: The unsinkable family. *Remedial and Special Education, 13*, 6–15.

Smith, P. M. (1993). You are not alone: For parents when they learn that their child has a disability. *NICHCY News Digest, 3*, 1–15.

Technology

Maddox, S. (Ed.). (1987). *Spinal network: The total resource for the wheelchair community.* Boulder, CO: Author.

Ramstad, E. (1995, April 2). High tech helps engineer work despite his disease. *Albuquerque Journal*, p. E15.

Weiss, K. E., & Dykes, M. K. (1995). Legal issues in special education: Assistive technology and support services. *Physical Disabilities: Education and Related Services 11*, 1, 29–36.

Concepts and Controversy

U.S. Department of Education. (1998). *Twentieth annual report to Congress on the implementation of the Individuals with Disabilities Education Act.* Washington, DC: U.S. Government Printing Office.

Chapter 10: Deafness and Hard of Hearing

Dorothy Brett

Hignett, S. (1983). *Brett from Bloomsbury to New Mexico: A biography.* New York: Franklin Watts.

Deafness and Hard of Hearing Defined

Besing, J., Koehnke, J., Abouchacra, K., & Letowski, T. (1998). Contemporary approaches to audiological assessment in young children. *Topics in Language Disorders, 18*, 52–70.

Boothroyd, A. (1988). Recruitment and dynamic range in sensorineural hearing loss. *Hearing Loss, 19*, 11–13.

Easterbrooks, S. (1999). Improving practices for students with hearing impairments. *Exceptional Children, 65*, 537–554.

Gordon-Langbein, A. L. (1998). What is universal newborn hearing screening and why is it important? *Hearing Loss, 19*, 7–10.

Gordon-Langbein, A. L. (1999). Screening newborns for hearing loss—The time is hear! *Volta Voices, 6*, 7–10.

Lowenbraun, S. (1995). Hearing impairment. In E. L. Meyen and T. M. Skrtic (Eds.), *Exceptional children and youth: An introduction* (4th ed., pp. 453–486). Denver, CO: Love.

Martin, F. N., & Noble, B. E. (1998). Hearing and hearing disorders. In G. H. Shames, E. H. Wiig, and W. A. Secord (Eds.), *Human communication disorders: An introduction* (5th ed., pp. 350–394). Boston: Allyn and Bacon.

Moores, D. F. (1996). *Educating the deaf: Psychology, principles, and practices* (4th ed.). Boston: Houghton Mifflin.

Northern, J. L., & Downs, M. P. (1984). *Hearing in children* (3rd ed.). Los Angeles: Williams & Wilkins.

Tharpe, A. M. (1999). Disorders of hearing in children. In E. Plante and P. M. Beeson (Eds.), *Communication and communication disorders: A clinical introduction* (pp. 85–116). Boston: Allyn and Bacon.

Yoshinaga-Itano, C. Y., & Apuzzo, M. L. (1998). Identification of hearing loss after age 18 months is not early enough. *American Annals of the Deaf, 143,* 380–387.

History of the Field

Adams, M. E. (1929). 1865–1935: A few memories of Alexander Graham Bell. *American Annals of the Deaf, 74,* 467–479.

Alby, J. F. (1962, Spring). The educational philosophy of Thomas Hopkins Gallaudet. *Buff and Blue,* pp. 17–23.

Drasgow, E. (1998). American Sign Language as a pathway to linguistic competence. *Exceptional Children, 64,* 329–342.

Gannon, J. R. (1989). *The week the world heard Gallaudet.* Washington, DC: Gallaudet University Press.

Soloman, A. (1994, August 28). Defiantly deaf. *New York Times Magazine,* pp. 38–45, 64–68.

Prevalence

Andrews, J. F., & Martin, G. (1998). Hopwood, affirmative action, and deaf education. *American Annals of the Deaf, 143,* 305–313.

Gallaudet Research Institute. (1998, November). *Regional and national summary report of data from the 1997–1998 annual survey of deaf and hard-of-hearing children and youth.* Washington, DC: GRI, Gallaudet University.

Norrix, L. (1999). Disorders of hearing in adults. In E. Plante and P. M. Beeson (Eds.), *Communication and communication disorders: A clinical introduction* (pp. 117–146). Boston: Allyn and Bacon.

U.S. Department of Education. (1998). *Twentieth annual report to Congress on the implementation of the Individuals with Disabilities Education Act.* Washington, DC: U.S. Government Printing Office.

Walker-Vann, C. (1998). Profiling hispanic deaf students: A first step toward solving the greater problems. *American Annals of the Deaf, 143,* 46–54.

Causes and Prevention

ASHA (1999a). *Newborn and infant hearing screening: Status of state universal newborn and infant hearing screening legislation and laws.* [On-line]. Available: www.asha.org

ASHA (1999b). *Issue brief: State highlights: Universal newborn hearing screening.* [On-line]. Available: www.asha.org

Benton, L. F. (1997). Paradise regained: Personal reflections of a cochlear implant user. *Hearing Loss, 18,* 18–21.

Dawson, N. (1997). Noise-induced hearing loss. *Wired for Sound, 7,* 1–2.

Drasgow, E. (1998). American Sign Language as a pathway to linguistic competence. *Exceptional Children, 64,* 329–342.

Gallaudet Research Institute. (1998, November). *Regional and national summary report of data from the 1997–1998 annual survey of deaf and hard-of-hearing children and youth.* Washington, DC: GRI, Gallaudet University.

Gordon-Langbein, A. L. (1999). Screening newborns for hearing loss—The time is hear! *Volta Voices, 6,* 7–10.

Heller, K. W., Alberto, P. A., Forney, P. E., & Schwartzman, M. N. (1996). *Understanding physical, sensory, and health impairments.* Pacific Grove, CA: Brooks/Cole.

Koran, N., & Oliva, G. (1997). Bring your earplugs: Loud aerobics music may be hazardous to your hearing. *Hearing Loss, 18,* 10–13.

Lane, H. (1995). Construction of deafness. *Disability & Society, 10,* 171–187.

Lombardo, L. A. (1998, August). Electronic screening, reporting help Wyo. detect hearing problems early. *Early Childhood Report, 9,* 1, 6–7.

Lundy, J. (1997, April 28). Letter to the author. Denver, CO: Metropolitan State College of Denver.

Marsa, L. (1999, March). Does your child really need ear tubes? *Parents,* pp. 41–44.

McGee, D. (1999). The Newborn and Infant Hearing Screening and Intervention Act of 1999 (HR 1193). *Volta Voices, 6,* 3.

Niparko, J. K. (1998). An update on cochlear implants: Part III. Results and rehabilitation. *Hearing Loss, 19,* 19–23.

Spencer, L., Tomblin, J. B., & Gantz, B. J. (1997). Reading skills in children with multichannel cochlear-implant experience. *The Volta Review, 99,* 193–202.

Tye-Murray, N., Spencer, L., & Woodworth G. G. (1995). Acquisition of speech by children who have prolonged cochlear implant experience. *Journal of Speech and Hearing Research, 38,* 327–337.

Yoshinaga-Itano, C. Y., & Apuzzo, M. L. (1998). Identification of hearing loss after age 18 months is not early enough. *American Annals of the Deaf, 143,* 380–387.

Deaf and Hard of Hearing Children

Allen, T. E. (1988, Winter/Spring). A demographic view of deaf students and mainstreaming in the United States. *Research at Gallaudet,* p. 6.

Drasgow, E. (1998). American Sign Language as a pathway to linguistic competence. *Exceptional Children, 64,* 329–342.

Easterbrooks, S. (1999). Improving practices for students with hearing impairments. *Exceptional Children, 65,* 537–554.

Fletcher, R. (1994). On Deaf culture and cultures. *Border Walking, 2,* 2.

Gallaudet Research Institute. (1994). *Working Papers 89-3.* Washington, DC: Gallaudet University.

Goldberg, B. (1995). Families facing choices: Options for parents of children who are deaf or hard of hearing. *ASHA, 37,* 38–45.

Groce, N. (1981). A lesson in human understanding. *The Dukes County Intelligencer, 22,* 83–97.

Huntington, G. (1981). Chilmark's deaf: Valued citizens. *The Dukes County Intelligencer, 22,* 98–102.

Karchmer, M. A., & Allen, T. E. (1999). The functional assessment of deaf and hard of hearing students. *American Annals of the Deaf, 144,* 68–77.

Lane, H. (1995). Construction of deafness. *Disability & Society, 10,* 171–187.

Moores, D. F. (1996). *Educating the deaf: Psychology, principles, and practices* (4th ed.). Boston: Houghton Mifflin.

Most, T., Weisel, A., & Lev-Matezky, A. (1996). Speech intelligibility and the evaluation of personal qualities by experienced and inexperienced listeners. *The Volta Review, 98,* 181–190.

Soloman, A. (1994, August 28). Defiantly deaf. *New York Times Magazine,* pp. 38–45, 64–68.

Wolk, S., & Schildroth, A. N. (1986). Deaf children and speech intelligibility: A national study. In A. N. Schildroth and M. A. Karchmer (Eds.), *Deaf children in America* (pp. 139–159). Austin, TX: Pro-Ed.

Educational Interventions

Andrews, J. F., Ferguson, C., Roberts, S., & Hodges, P. (1997). What's up, Billy Jo? Deaf children and bilingual-bicultural instruction in East-Central Texas. *American Annals of the Deaf, 142,* 16–25.

Antia, S. D., & Kreimeyer, K. H. (1996). Social interaction and acceptance of deaf or hard-of-hearing children and their peers: A comparison of social-skills and familiarity-based interventions. *The Volta Review, 98,* 157–180.

Bailes, C. N. (1998). Primary-grade teacher's strategic use of American Sign Language in teaching English literacy in a bilingual school setting. Gallaudet Research Institute Report, UMI No. 9926724.

Belgum, D. (1998, March 2). Deaf lifeguard, fired by YMCA, sues. *Los Angeles Times,* pp. B10–B11.

Cardenas, J. (1996, April 5). Magnet: Deaf and hearing students together. *Los Angeles Times* (Valley ed.), pp. B1, B6–B7.

Cohen, O. P. (1994). Introduction. In R. C. Johnson and O. P. Cole (Eds.), *Implications and complications for Deaf students of the full inclusion movement* (pp. 1–6). Washington, DC: Gallaudet Research Institute, Gallaudet University.

Drasgow, E. (1998). American Sign Language as a pathway to linguistic competence. *Exceptional Children, 64,* 329–342.

Easterbrooks, S. (1999). Improving practices for students with hearing impairments. *Exceptional Children, 65,* 537–554.

Gallaudet Research Institute. (1998, November). *Regional and national summary report of data from the 1997–1998 annual survey of deaf and hard-of-hearing children and youth.* Washington, DC: GRI, Gallaudet University.

Hawkins, L. (1993). Opinion: full inclusion or isolation? *The Endeavor, 2,* 7.

Holden-Pitt, L. (1997). A look at residential school placement patterns for students from deaf- and hearing-parented families: A ten-year perspective. *American Annals of the Deaf, 142,* 108–114.

Kemp, M. (1998). Why is learning American Sign Language a challenge? *American Annals of the Deaf, 143,* 255, 259.

Lane, H. (1995). Construction of deafness. *Disability & Society, 10,* 171–187.

Luetke-Stahlman, B. (1998). Providing the support services needed by students who are deaf or hard of hearing. *American Annals of the Deaf, 143,* 388–391.

Marschark, M. (1993). *Psychological development of deaf children.* New York: Oxford University Press.

Moores, D. F. (1996). *Educating the deaf: Psychology, principles, and practices* (4th ed.). Boston: Houghton Mifflin.

Most, T., Weisel, A., & Lev-Matezky, A. (1996). Speech intelligibility and the evaluation of personal qualities by experienced and inexperienced listeners. *The Volta Review, 98,* 181–190.

Powers, A. R. (1997). The preparation of educational interpreters for rural education settings. *Rural Special Education Quarterly, 16,* 24–32.

Ramsey, C. L. (1997). *Deaf children in public schools.* Washington, DC: Gallaudet University Press.

Rawlings, B. W., Karchmer, M. A., & DeCaro, J. J. (1987). Postsecondary programs for deaf students at the peak of the rubella bulge. *American Annals for the Deaf, 132,* 36–42.

Rawlings, B. W., Karchmer, M. A., Allen, T. E., & DeCaro, J. J. (1999). *College and career programs for deaf students* (10th ed.). Washington, DC and Rochester, NY: Gallaudet University and National Technical Institute for the Deaf.

Rawlings, B. W., & King, S. J. (1986). Postsecondary educational opportunities for deaf students. In A. N. Schildroth and M. A. Karchmer (Eds.), *Deaf children in America* (pp. 231–257). Austin, TX: Pro-Ed.

Salend, S. J., & Longo, M. (1994). The roles of the educational interpreter in mainstreaming. *Teaching Exceptional Children, 26,* 22–28.

Schildroth, A. N., & Hotto, S. A. (1994). Deaf students and full inclusion: Who wants to be excluded? In R. C. Johnson and O. P. Cole (Eds.), *Implications and complications for Deaf students of the full inclusion movement* (pp. 31–40). Washington, DC: Gallaudet Research Institute, Gallaudet University.

Stewart, D. A. (1997). Bi-Bi- to MCE. *American Annals of the Deaf, 142,* 106–111.

Yoshinaga-Itano, C. Y., & Apuzzo, M. L. (1998). Identification of hearing loss after age 18 months is not early enough. *American Annals of the Deaf, 143,* 380–387.

Families

Blade, R. (1994, October 31). Sign language is beautiful, close-knit Deaf community says. *Albuquerque Tribune,* p. A5.

Calderon, R., Bargones, J., & Sidman, S. (1998). Characteristics of hearing families and their young deaf and hard of hearing children: Early intervention follow-up. *American Annals of the Deaf, 143,* 347–362.

Calderon, R., & Greenberg, M. T. (1999). Stress and coping in hearing mothers of children with hearing loss: Factors affecting mother and child adjustment. *American Annals of the Deaf, 144,* 7–23.

Mapp, I., & Hudson, R. (1997). Stess and coping among African American and Hispanic parents of deaf children. *American Annals of the Deaf, 142,* 48–56.

Technology

Delta Society. (1999). Information from Delta Society Web site: www.deltasociety.org

Harris, B. (1998). Digital hearing aids: You asked the questions and we found the answers. *Hearing Loss, 19,* 8–15.

Kaplan, H. (1999). Hearing aid technology: What consumers need to know. *Hearing Loss, 20,* 15–19.

Kramlinger, J. (1996). Making noise in a silent world: A profile of the deaf college experience. *Volta Voices, 3,* 20–21.

Medugno, R. (1998). *Via TV Phone* (advertising brochure). Santa Clara, CA: 8x8, Inc.

Ogden, P. (1992). *Chelsea: The story of a signal dog.* Boston: Little, Brown and Company.

Preminger, J. E., & Levitt, H. (1997). Computer-assisted remote transcription (CART): A tool to aid people who are deaf or hard of hearing in the workplace. *The Volta Review, 99,* 219–230.

Stanton, J. F. (1999). Captions and the movies: Where we're going. *Volta Voices, 6,* 20–21.

Steinfeld, A. (1998). The benefit of real-time captioning as measured by working memory. *The Volta Review, 100,* 29–44.

Sulzberger, A. O. (1990, October 16). Closed-caption law: Victory for the deaf. *New York Times,* p. A11.

Concepts and Controversy

Benton, L. F. (1997). Paradise regained: Personal reflections of a cochlear implant user. *Hearing Loss, 18,* 18–21.

Gallaudet Research Institute. (1998). *Who and where are our children with coclear implants?* Washington, DC: Gallaudet Research Institute Web site.

Laborit, E. (1998). *The cry of the gull.* Washington, DC: Gallaudet University Press.

Lane, H. (1995). Construction of deafness. *Disability & Society, 10,* 171–187.

Niparko, J. K. (1998). An update on cochlear implants: Part III. Results and rehabilitiation. *Hearing Loss, 19,* 19–23.

Tye-Murray, N., Spencer, L., & Woodworth, G. G. (1995). Acquisition of speech by children who have prolonged cochlear implant experience. *Journal of Speech and Hearing Research, 38,* 327–337.

Venable, D. (1999). The gift of a cochlear implant. *Volta Voices, 6,* 30–31.

Chapter 11: Blindness and Low Vision
Auguste Rodin

Hale, W. H., and the editors of Time-Life. (1969). *The world of Rodin: 1840–1917.* New York: Time-Life Books.

Visual Disabilities Defined

Barraga, N. C., & Erin, J. N. (1992). *Visual handicaps and learning* (3rd ed.). Austin, TX: Pro-Ed.

Blanksby, D. C., & Langford, P. E. (1993). VAP-CAP: A procedure to assess the visual functioning of young visually impaired children. *Journal of Visual Impairment and Blindness, 86,* 46–49.

Corn, A. L. (1989). Instruction in the use of vision for children and adults with low vision: A proposed program model. *RE:view, 21,* 26–38.

Erin, J. N., & Corn, A. L. (1994). A survey of children's first understanding of being visually impaired. *Journal of Visual Impairment and Blindness, 88,* 132–139.

Heller, K. W., Alberto, P. A., Forney, P. E., & Schwartzman, M. N. (1996). *Understanding physical, sensory, and health impairments.* Pacific Grove: Brooks/Cole.

Hudson, D. (1994). Causes of emotional and psychological reactions to adventitious blindness. *Journal of Visual Impairment and Blindness, 88,* 498–503.

Levin, A. V. (1996). Common visual problems in classrooms. In R. H. A. Haslam & P. J. Valletutti (Eds.), *Medical problems in the classroom: The teacher's role in diagnosis and management* (pp. 161–180). Austin, TX: Pro-Ed.

Tuttle, D. W., & Ferrell, K. A. (1995). Visually impaired. In E. L. Meyen & T. M. Skrtic (Eds.), *Exceptional children and youth: An introduction* (4th ed., pp. 487–532). Denver, CO: Love.

Verplanken, B., Meijnders, A., & van de Wege, A. (1994). Emotion and cognition: Attitudes toward persons who are visually impaired. *Journal of Visual Impairment and Blindness, 88,* 504–511.

History of the Field

Barraga, N. C. (1964). *Increased visual behavior in low vision children.* New York: American Foundation for the Blind.

Barraga, N. C., & Collins, M. E. (1979). Development of efficiency in visual functioning: Rationale for a comprehensive program. *Journal of Visual Impairment and Blindness, 73,* 121–126.

Sacks, S. Z., & Rosen, S. (1994). Visual impairment. In N. G. Haring, L. McCormick, & T. G. Haring (Eds.), *Exceptional children and youth* (6th ed., pp. 403–446). Columbus, OH: Merrill.

Tuttle, D. W., & Ferrell., K. A. (1995). Visually impaired. In E. L. Meyen & T. M. Skrtic (Eds.), *Exceptional children and youth: An introduction* (4th ed., pp. 487–531). Denver, CO: Love.

Prevalence

American Foundation for the Blind. (1999). *Prevalence estimates of blindness and visual impairment in the United States.* New York: Programs and Policy Research.

Tuttle, D. W., & Ferrell, K. A. (1995). Visually impaired. In E. L. Meyen & T. M. Skrtic (Eds.), *Exceptional children and youth: An introduction* (4th ed., pp. 487–532). Denver, CO: Love.

U.S. Department of Education. (1998). *Twentieth annual report to Congress on the implementation of the Individuals with Disabilities Education Act.* Washington, DC: U.S. Government Printing Office.

Causes and Prevention

Brody, J. W. (1993, November 3). Vision problems in children often go undetected. *The New York Times* (Health), p. B8.

Heller, K. W., Alberto, P. A., Forney, P. E., & Schwartzman, M. N. (1996). *Understanding physical, sensory, and health impairments.* Pacific Grove: Brooks/Cole.

Prevent Blindness America (1999). *Publications and video catalog.* Schaumburg, IL: Author.

Sherman, A. (1994). *Wasting America's future: The Children's Defense Fund on the cost of child poverty.* Boston: Beacon Press.

Low Vision and Blind Children

American Printing House for the Blind. (1992). *Annual report.* Louisville, KY: Author.

Baird, S. M., Mayfield, P., & Baker, P. (1997). Mothers' interpretations of the behavior of their infants with visual and other impairments during interactions. *Journal of Visual Impairment and Blindness, 91,* 467–483.

Buhrow, M. M., Hartshorne, T. S., & Bradley-Johnson, S. (1998). Parents' and teachers' ratings of the social skills of elementary-age students who are blind. *Journal of Visual Impairment and Blindness, 92,* 503–511.

Crocker, A. D., & Orr, R. R. (1996). Social behaviors of children with visual impairments enrolled in preschool programs. *Exceptional Children, 62,* 451–462.

Heller, K. W., Alberto, P. A., Forney, P. E., & Schwartzman, M. N. (1996). *Understanding physical, sensory, and health impairments.* Pacific Grove: Brooks/Cole.

Huurre, T. M., Komulainen, E. J., & Aro, H. M. (1999). Social support and self-esteem among adolescents with visual impairments. *Journal of Visual Impairment and Blindness, 93,* 26–38.

MacCuspie, P. A. (1992). The social acceptance and interaction of visually impaired children in integrated settings. In S. Z. Sacks, L. S. Kekelis, and R. J. Gaylord-Ross (Eds.), *The development of social skills by blind and visually impaired students* (pp. 83–102). New York: American Foundation for the Blind.

Pring, L., Dewart, H., & Brockbank, M. (1998). Social cognition in children with visual impairments. *Journal of Visual Impairment and Blindness, 92,* 754–768.

Rettig, M. (1994). The play of young children with visual impairments: Characteristics and interventions. *Journal of Visual Impairment and Blindness, 88,* 410–420.

Rex, E. J., Koenig, A. J., Wormsley, D. P., & Baker, R. L. (1994). *Foundations of braille literacy.* New York: AFB Press.

Schoellkopf, A. (1995, March 25). Declining braille skills alarm advocates. *Albuquerque Journal* (Metropolitan), p. B1.

Trent, S. D., & Truan, M. B. (1997). Speed, accuracy, and comprehension of adolescent braille readers in a specialized school. *Journal of Visual Impairment and Blindness, 91,* 494–500.

Tuttle, D. W., & Ferrell, K. A. (1995). Visually impaired. In E. L. Meyen and T. M. Skrtic (Eds.), *Exceptional children and youth: An introduction* (4th ed., pp. 487–532). Denver, CO: Love.

Wittenstein, S. H. (1994). Braille literacy: Preservice training and teacher's attitudes. *Journal of Visual Impairment and Blindness, 88,* 516–524.

U.S. Department of Education. (1998). *Twentieth annual report to Congress on the implementation of the Individuals with Disabilities Education Act.* Washington, DC: U.S. Government Printing Office.

Educational Interventions

Albuquerque Journal. (1995, September 7). Alma mater closing doors. p. A2.

Associated Press. (1996, April 9). Clintons forgo bunny suit, see Easter egg roll hopping. *The Los Angeles Times,* p. A11.

Associated Press (1999a, August 28). Blind runner gains finals. *The Tennessean,* p. C5.

Associated Press (1999b, July 3). Blind workers idle in desperate labor market. *The Tennessean,* pp. E1, E3.

Baird, S. M., Mayfield, P., & Baker, P. (1997). Mothers' interpretations of the behavior of their infants with visual and other impairments during interactions. *Journal of Visual Impairment and Blindness, 91,* 467–483.

Barraga, N. C., & Erin, J. N. (1992). *Visual handicaps and learning* (3rd. ed.). Austin, TX: Pro-Ed.

Barraga, N. C., & Morris, J. E. (1992). *Program to develop efficiency in visual function: Source book on low vision.* Louisville, KY: American Printing House for the Blind.

Barton, D. D. (1997). Growing up with Jed: Parents' experiences raising an adolescent son who is blind. *Journal of Visual Impairment and Blindness, 91,* 203–212.

Behl, D. D., Akers, J. F., Boyce, G. C., & Taylor, M. J. (1996). Do mothers interact differently with children who are visually impaired? *Journal of Visual Impairment and Blindness, 90,* 501–511.

Clarke, K. L., Sainato, D. M., & Ward, M. E. (1994). Travel performance of preschoolers: The effects of mobility training with a long cane versus a precane. *Journal of Visual Impairment and Blindness, 88,* 19–30.

CNN Headline News. (1995, October & November). *Orient the guide dog retires.*

Corn, A. L., Hatlen, P., Huebner, K. M., Ryan, F., & Siller, M. A. (1995). *The national agenda for the education of children and youths with visual impairments, including those with multiple disabilities.* New York: AFB Press, American Foundation for the Blind.

Dewar, H. (1997, April 16). Senate drops ban against guide dog: Canine allowed under resolution. *Albuquerque Journal*, p. A7.

Dote-Kwan, J., & Hughes, M. (1994). The home environments of young blind children. *Journal of Visual Impairment and Blindness, 88,* 31–42.

Erin, J. N., & Koenig, A. J. (1997). The student with a visual disability and a learning disability. *Journal of Learning Disabilities, 30,* 309–320.

Hanye, R. (1998). The missing link: Real work experiences for people who are visually impaired. *Journal of Visual Impairment and Blindness, 92,* 884–847.

Harley, R. K., Truan, M. B., & Sanford, L. D. (1987). *Communication skills for visually impaired learners.* Springfield, IL: Thomas.

Hebert, H. J. (1997, April 15). Guide dog can't pass senate floor. *Albuquerque Journal*, p. A2.

Hill, E. W. (1986). Orientation and mobility. In G. R. Scholl (Ed.), *Foundations of education for blind and visually handicapped children and youth: Theory and practice* (pp. 315–340). New York: American Foundation for the Blind.

Horsfall, B. (1997). Tactile maps: New materials and improved designs. *Journal of Visual Impairment and Blindness, 91,* 61–65.

Hughes, M., Dote-Kwan, J., & Dolendo, J. (1998). A close look at the cognitive play of preschoolers with visual impairments in the home. *Exceptional Children, 64,* 451–462.

Joffee, E. (1988). A home-based orientation and mobility program for infants and toddlers. *Journal of Visual Impairment and Blindness, 82,* 282–285.

JVIB News Service. (1994, January-February). Demographics update: Use of "white" ("long") canes. *Journal of Visual Impairment and Blindness, 88,* 4.

JVIB News Service. (1995, March-April). Demographics update: Alternate estimate of the number of guide dog users. *Journal of Visual Impairment and Blindness, 89,* 4.

Kendrick, D. (1993). *Jobs to be proud of: Profiles of workers who are visually impaired.* New York: American Foundation for the Blind.

Kim, Y., & Corn, A. L. (1998). The effects of teachers' characteristics on placement recommendations for students with visual impairments. *Journal of Visual Impairment and Blindness, 92,* 491–502.

Koenig, A. J. (1992). A framework for understanding the literacy of individuals with visual impairments. *Journal of Visual Impairment and Blindness, 85,* 277–284.

Martin, K. (1999). *Summer college program for students with disabilities on the campus of the University of Evansville.* Evansville, IN: Evansville Association for the Blind.

McCutcheon, C. (1994, May 5). First guide dog goes to the zoo. *Albuquerque Journal* (Metropolitan), p. C1.

Newman, A. P., & Beverstock, C. (1990). *Adult literacy: Contexts and challenges.* Newark, DE: International Reading Association.

New York Times. (1990, November 22). Blind hiker finishes an 8-month journey, p. A14.

Pogrund, R. L., Fazzi, D. L., & Schreier, E. M. (1993). Development of a preschool "Kiddy Cane." *Journal of Visual Impairment and Blindness, 86,* 52–54.

Recchia, S. L. (1997). Play and concept development in infants and young children with severe visual impairments: A constructivist view. *Journal of Visual Impairment and Blindness, 91,* 401–406.

Rettig, M. (1994). The play of young children with visual impairments: Characteristics and interventions. *Journal of Visual Impairment and Blindness, 88,* 410–420.

Rumrill, P. D., Jr., & Scheff, C. M. (1997). Impact of the ADA on the employment and promotion of persons who are visually impaired. *Journal of Visual Impairment and Blindness, 91,* 460–466.

Sacks, S. Z., & Kekelis, L. S. (1992). Guidelines for mainstreaming blind and visually impaired children. In S. Z. Sacks, L. S. Kekelis, and R. J. Gaylord-Ross (Eds.), *The development of social skills by blind and visually impaired students* (pp. 133–149). New York: American Foundation for the Blind.

Sacks, S. Z., & Reardon, M. P. (1992). Maximizing social integration for visually impaired students: Applications and practice. In S. Z. Sacks, L. S. Kekelis, & R. J. Gaylord-Ross (Eds.), *The development of social skills by blind and visually impaired students* (pp. 151–170). New York: American Foundation for the Blind.

Sacks, S. Z., & Rosen, S. (1994). Visual impairment. In N. G. Haring, L. McCormick, & T. G. Haring (Eds.), *Exceptional children and youth* (6th ed., pp. 403–446). Columbus, OH: Merrill.

Skellenger, A. C., & Hill, E. W. (1994). Effects of a shared teacher-child play intervention on the play skills of three young children who are blind. *Journal of Visual Impairment and Blindness, 88,* 433–445.

Sports Illustrated. (1995, August 7). Faces in the crowd: Erik Weihenmayer, p. 10.

Spungin, S. J. (1997). Specialized schools still in jeopardy. *JVIB News Service, 91,* 1, 3–5.

Tröster, H., & Brambring, M. (1992). Early social-emotional development in blind infants. *Child: Care, Health and Development, 18,* 421–432.

Tröster, H., & Brambring, M. (1994). The play behavior and play materials of blind and sighted infants and preschoolers. *Journal of Visual Impairment and Blindness, 88,* 421–432.

Tuttle, D. W., & Ferrell., K. A. (1995). Visually impaired. In E. L. Meyen and T. M. Skrtic (Eds.), *Exceptional children and youth: An introduction* (4th ed., pp. 487–531). Denver, CO: Love.

Ungar, S., Blades, M., & Spencer, C. (1997). Teaching visually impaired children to make distance judgments from a tactile map. *Journal of Visual Impairment and Blindness, 91,* 163–169.

U.S. Department of Education. (1998). *Twentieth annual report to Congress on the implementation of the Individuals with Disabilities Education Act.* Washington, DC: U.S. Government Printing Office.

Vancil, D. (1997). Steps to success in college for students with visual impairments. *Journal of Visual Impairment and Blindness, 91,* 219–223.

Families

Baird, S. M., Mayfield, P., & Baker, P. (1997). Mothers' interpretations of the behavior of their infants with visual and other impairments during interactions. *Journal of Visual Impairment and Blindness, 91,* 467–483.

Dote-Kwan, J., Hughes, M., & Taylor, S. L. (1997). Impact of early experiences on the development of young children with visual impairments: Revisited. *Journal of Visual Impairment and Blindness, 91,* 131–144.

Erin, J. N., & Corn, A. L. (1994). A survey of children's first understanding of being visually impaired. *Journal of Visual Impairment and Blindness, 88,* 132–139.

Nixon, H. L., II. (1994). Looking sociologically at family coping with visual impairments. *Journal of Visual Impairment and Blindness, 88,* 329–337.

Technology

Blazie Engineering. (1999). Catalog of products for blind and visually impaired people. MD: Forest Hill.

Descriptive Video Services (DVS). (1999). *DVS home video catalogue: Described movies for people who have trouble seeing the screen.* Indianapolis, IN: DVS Home Video.

Lighthouse International. (1999). *Lighthouse catalog.* New York: The Lighthouse Store.

The Tennessean (1999, February 16). 'Net lets blind "see" diagrams, p. A4.

Concepts and Controversy

American Printing House for the Blind. (1992). *Annual report.* Louisville, KY: Author.

Augusto, C. R. (1993). Reading, writing, and literacy. *AFB News, 28,* pp. 1, 8.

Briand, X. (1994, July 13). ED top set new guidelines promoting braille instruction. *Special Education Report,* p. 6.

Corn, A. L., Hatlen, P., Huebner, K. M., Ryan, F., & Siller, M. A. (1995). *The national agenda for the education of children and youths with visual impairments, including those with multiple disabilities.* New York: AFB Press, American Foundation for the Blind.

Schoellkopf, A. (1995, March 25). Declining braille skills alarm advocates. *Albuquerque Journal* (Metropolitan), p. B1.

Schroeder, F. K. (1993). *Braille usage: Perspectives of legally blind adults and policy implications for school administrators.* Unpublished doctoral dissertation, University of New Mexico.

U.S. Department of Education. (1994). *The Goals 2000: Educate America Act—Launching a new era in education.* Washington, DC: U.S. Government Printing Office.

Wittenstein, S. H. (1994). Braille literacy: Preservice training and teacher's attitudes. *Journal of Visual Impairment and Blindness, 88,* 516–524.

Chapter 12: Very Low-Incidence Disabilities

Autism

Attwood, R. (1998). *Asperger's syndrome: A guide for parents and professionals.* Philadelphia: Jessica Kingsley Publishers.

Kanner, L. (1943). Autistic disturbances of affective contact. *Nervous Child, 2,* 217–250.

Kauffman, J. M. (1997). *Characteristics of behavioral disorders of children and youth* (5th ed.). Columbus, OH: Merrill.

Myles, B. S., & Simpson, R. L. (1998). *Asperger syndrome: A guide for educators and parents.* Austin, TX: Pro-Ed.

Autism Defined

Attwood, R. (1998). *Asperger's syndrome: A guide for parents and professionals.* Philadelphia: Jessica Kingsley Publishers.

Autism Society of America. (1999). Autism Society of America Brochure. Bethesda, MD: Author.

Begley, S., & Springen, K. (1996, May 13). Life in a parallel world: A bold new approach to the mystery of autism. *Newsweek,* p. 70.

Grandin, T. (1995). *Thinking in pictures and other reports from my life with autism.* NY: Viking Books.

Harris, S. L., Belchic, J., Blum, L., & Celiberti, D. (1994). Behavioral assessment of autistic disorder. In J. L. Matson (Ed.), *Autism in children and adults: Etiology, assessment, and intervention* (pp. 127–146). Pacific Grove, CA: Brooks/Cole.

Horner, R. H., & Carr, E. G. (1997). Behavioral support for students with severe disabilities: Functional assessment and comprehensive intervention. *The Journal of Special Education, 31,* 84–104.

Koegel, R. L., Koegel, L. K., Frea, W. D., & Smith, A. E. (1995). Emerging interventions for children with autism: Longitudinal and lifestyle implications. In R. L. Koegel and L. K. Koegel (Eds.), *Teaching children with autism: Strategies for initiating positive interactions and improving learning opportunities* (pp. 1–16). Baltimore: Paul H. Brookes.

Krantz, P. J., McClannahan, L. E., & Poulson, C. L. (1994). Generalized imitation and response—class formation in children with autism. *Journal of Applied Behavior Analysis, 27,* 685–697.

Krug, D. A., Arick, J., & Almond, P. (1980). Behavior checklist for identifying severely handicapped individuals with high levels of autistic behavior. *Journal of Child Psychology and Psychiatry, 21,* 221–229.

Levine, S. (1997, August 4). Capabilities & cruelties of the mind. *Albuquerque Journal* (Health), pp. C1–C2.

Mesibov, G. B. (1994). A comprehensive program for serving people with autism and their families: The TEACCH model. In J. L. Matson (Ed.), *Autism in children and adults: Etiology, assessment, and intervention* (pp. 85–98). Pacific Grove, CA: Brooks/Cole.

Mesibov, G. B., Adams, L. W., & Klinger, L. G. (1997). *Autism: Understanding the disorder.* New York: Plenum Press.

Myles, B. S., & Simpson, R. L. (1998). *Asperger syndrome: A guide for educators and parents.* Austin, TX: Pro-Ed.

Osterling, J., & Dawson, G. (1994). Early recognition of children with autism: A study of first birthday home videotapes. *Journal of Autism and Developmental Disorders, 24,* 247–257.

Partington, J. W., Sundberg, M. L., Newhouse, L., & Spengler, S. M. (1994). Overcoming an autistic child's failure to acquire a tact repertoire. *Journal of Applied Behavior Analysis, 27,* 733–734.

Rimland, B. (1964). *Infantile autism: The syndrome and its implications for neural theory of behavior.* Englewood Cliffs, NJ: Prentice-Hall.

Schopler, E., Reichler, R. J., & Renner, B. R. (1988). *The Childhood Autism Rating Scale (CARS).* Los Angeles: Western Psychological Services.

Sturmey, P., & Sevin, J. A. (1994). Defining and assessing autism. In J. L. Matson (Ed.), *Autism in children and adults: Etiology, assessment, and intervention* (pp. 13–36). Pacific Grove, CA: Brooks/Cole.

Vig, S., & Jedrysek, E. (1995). Adaptive behavior of young urban children with developmental disabilities. *Mental Retardation, 33,* 90–98.

U.S. Department of Education. (1999). Assistance to state for the education of children with disabilities and the early intervention program for infants and toddlers with disabilities: Final regulations. *Federal Register, 64 (48),* CFR Parts 300 and 303.

Prevalence

Autism Society of America. (1999). What is autism? [On-line]. Available: www.autism-society.org

Locke, B. J., Banken, J. A., & Mahone, C. H. (1994). The graying of autism: Etiology and prevalence at fifty. In J. L. Matson (Ed.), *Autism in children and adults: Etiology, assessment, and intervention* (pp. 37–58). Pacific Grove, CA: Brooks/Cole.

Peeters, T. (1997). *Autism: From theoretical understanding to educational intervention.* San Diego: Singular Publishing Group.

U.S. Department of Education. (1998). *Twentieth annual report to Congress on the implementation of the Individuals with Disabilities Education Act.* Washington, DC: U.S. Government Printing Office.

Causes and Prevention

Begley, S., & Springen, K. (1996, May 13). Life in a parallel world: A bold new approach to the mystery of autism. *Newsweek,* p. 70.

Burger, R. A., & Warren, R. P. (1998) Possible immunogenetic basis for autism. *Mental Retardation and Developmental Disabilities Research Reviews, 4,* 137–141.

Cook, E. H. (1998). Genetics of autism. *Mental Retardation and Developmental Disabilities Research Reviews, 4,* 113–120.

Grandin, T. (1995). *Thinking in pictures and other reports from my life with autism.* New York: Viking Books.

Johnson, L. A. (1999, January 20). NJ town might have rare cluster of autism. *USA Today,* p. 10A.

Koegel, R. L., Koegel, L. K., Frea, W. D., & Smith, A. E. (1995). Emerging interventions for children with autism: Longitudinal and lifestyle implications. In R. L. Koegel & L. K. Koegel (Eds.), *Teaching children with autism: Strategies for initiating positive interactions and improving learning opportunities* (pp. 1–16). Baltimore: Paul H. Brookes.

Lewis, M. H., & Bodfish, J. W. (1998). Repetitive behavior disorders in autism. *Mental Retardation and Developmental Disabilities Research Reviews, 4,* 80–89.

Locke, B. J., Banken, J. A., & Mahone, C. H. (1994). The graying of autism: Etiology and prevalence at fifty. In J. L. Matson (Ed.), *Autism in children and adults: Etiology, assessment, and intervention* (pp. 37–58). Pacific Grove, CA: Brooks/Cole. 89.

Maurice, C., Green, G., & Luce, S. C. (1996). *Behavioral intervention for young children with autism: A manual for parents and professionals.* Austin, TX: Pro-Ed.

Peeters, T. (1997). *Autism: From theoretical understanding to educational intervention.* San Diego: Singular Publishing Group.

Rimland, B. (1994). The modern history of autism: A personal perspective. In J. L. Matson (Ed.), *Autism in children and adults: Etiology, assessment, and intervention* (pp. 1–12). Pacific Grove, CA: Brooks/Cole.

Rimland, B. (1999). The use of secretin in autism: Some preliminary answers. [On-line]. Available: www.autism-society.org

Sturmey, P., & Sevin, J. A. (1994). Defining and assessing autism. In J. L. Matson (Ed.), *Autism in children and adults: Etiology, assessment, and intervention* (pp. 13–36). Pacific Grove, CA: Brooks/Cole.

Children with Autism

Koegel, R. L., Koegel, L. K., Frea, W. D., & Smith, A. E. (1995). Emerging interventions for children with autism: Longitudinal and lifestyle implications. In R. L. Koegel & L. K. Koegel (Eds.), *Teaching children with autism: Strategies for initiating positive interactions and improving learning opportunities* (pp. 1–16). Baltimore: Paul H. Brookes.

Lewis, M. H., & Bodfish, J. W. (1998). Repetitive behavior disorders in autism. *Mental Retardation and Developmental Disabilities Research Reviews, 4,* 80–89.

Mesibov, G. B. (1994). A comprehensive program for serving people with autism and their families: The TEACCH model. In J. L. Matson (Ed.), *Autism in children and adults: Etiology, assessment, and intervention* (pp. 85–98). Pacific Grove, CA: Brooks/Cole.

Peeters, T. (1997). *Autism: From theoretical understanding to educational intervention.* San Diego: Singular Publishing Group.

Richard, G. J. (1997). *The source for autism.* East Moline, IL: LinguiSystems.

Rimland, B. (1994). The modern history of autism: A personal perspective. In J. L. Matson (Ed.), *Autism in children and adults: Etiology, assessment, and intervention* (pp. 1–12). Pacific Grove, CA: Brooks/Cole.

Rogers, S. J. (1998). Neuropsychology of autism in young children and its implications for early interventions. *Mental Retardation and Developmental Disabilities Research Reviews, 4,* 104–112.

Sturmey, P., & Sevin, J. A. (1994). Defining and assessing autism. In J. L. Matson (Ed.), *Autism in children and adults: Etiology, assessment, and intervention* (pp. 13–36). Pacific Grove, CA: Brooks/Cole.

Travis, L. L., & Sigman, M. (1998). Social deficits and interpersonal relationships in autism. *Mental Retardation and Developmental Disabilities Research Reviews, 4,* 65–72.

Trevarthen, D., Aitken, K., Papoudi, D., & Robarts, J. (1998). *Children with autism: Diagnosis and interventions to meet their needs* (2nd ed.). Philadelphia: Jessica Kingsley Publishers.

Wilkinson, K. M. (1998). Profiles of language and communication skills in autism. *Mental Retardation and Developmental Disabilities Research Reviews, 4,* 73–79.

Deaf–Blindness

Miles, B. (1995, December). *Overview on deaf–blindness.* Monmouth, OR: DB-LINK, The National Information Clearinghouse on Children Who Are Deaf–Blind.

Deaf–Blindness Defined

Baldwin, V. (1995). *Annual Deaf–Blind Census.* Monmouth, OR: Teaching Research, Western Oregon State College.

Baldwin, V. (1996). *Population/Demographics.* Monmouth, OR: Teaching Research, Western Oregon State College.

Boeck, S. (1998, November 4). Blind, deaf triathelete honored. *USA Today Sports,* p. C3.

Engleman, M. D., Griffin, H. C., & Wheeler, L. (1998). Deaf-blindness and communication: Practical knowledge and strategies. *Journal of Visual Impairment & Blindness, 92,* 783–798.

Groce, M. M., & Isaacson, A. B. (1995). Purposeful movement. In K. M. Heubner, J. G. Prickett, R. R. Welch, and E. Joffee (Eds.), *Hand in hand: Essentials of communication and orientation and mobility for your students who are deaf–blind* (pp. 91–110). New York: AFB Press.

Haring, N. G., & Romer, L. T. (Eds.). (1995). *Welcoming students who are deaf–blind into typical classrooms: Facilitating school participation, learning, and friendships.* Baltimore: Paul H. Brookes.

Heubner, K. M., Prickett, J. G., Welch, R. R., & Joffee, E. (Eds.). (1995). *Hand in hand: Essentials of communication and orientation and mobility for your students who are deaf–blind.* New York: AFB Press.

Holcomb, M., & Wood, S. (1989). *Deaf woman: A parade through the decades.* Berkeley, CA: DawnSignPress.

Miles, B. (1995, December). *Overview on deaf–blindness.* Monmouth, OR: DB-LINK, The National Information Clearinghouse on Children Who Are Deaf–Blind.

Prickett, J. G. (1995). Deaf-blindness and communication. In K. M. Heubner, J. G. Prickett, R. R. Welch, and E. Joffee (Eds.), *Hand in hand: Essentials of communication and orientation and mobility for your students who are deaf–blind* (pp. 61–90). New York: AFB Press.

Prickett, J. G., & Welch, T. R. (1995). Deaf-blindness: Implications for learning. In K. M. Heubner, J. G. Prickett, R. R. Welch, and E. Joffee (Eds.), *Hand in hand: Essentials of communication and orientation and mobility for your students who are deaf–blind* (pp. 25–60). New York: AFB Press.

Rosenberg, H. (1995, February 27). "Kim's World" open to disabled and beyond. *Los Angeles Times* (Calendar), pp. F1, F10.

U.S. Department of Education. (1999). Assistance to state for the education of children with disabilities and the early intervention program for infants and toddlers with disabilities: Final regulations. *Federal Register, 64 (48),* CFR Parts 300 and 303.

Prevalence

Baldwin, V. (1996). *Population/Demographics.* Monmouth, OR: Teaching Research, Western Oregon State College.

JVIB News Service. (1995, May–June). Demographics update: The number of deaf–blind children in the U.S., 89, 13–14.

Causes and Prevention

Accardo, P. J., Whitman, B. U., Laszewski, C., Haake, C. A., & Morrow, J. D. (1996). *Dictionary of developmental disabilities terminology.* Baltimore: Paul H. Brookes.

Baldwin, V. (1996). *Population/Demographics.* Monmouth, OR: Teaching Research, Western Oregon State College.

Prickett, J. G., & Welch, T. R. (1995). Deaf-blindness: Implications for learning. In K. M. Heubner, J. G. Prickett, R. R. Welch, and E. Joffee (Eds.), *Hand in hand: Essentials of communication and orientation and mobility for your students who are deaf–blind* (pp. 25–60). New York: AFB Press.

Heller, K. W., & Kennedy, C. (1994). *Etiologies and characteristics of deaf–blindness.* Monmouth, OR: Teaching Research Publications.

Children with Deaf–Blindness

Baldwin, V. (1995). *Annual deaf–blind census.* Monmouth, OR: Teaching Research, Western Oregon State College.

Baldwin, V. (1997). *Annual deaf–blind census.* Monmouth, OR: Teaching Research, Western Oregon State College.

Baldwin, V. (1996). *Population/Demographics*. Monmouth, OR: Teaching Research, Western Oregon State College.

JVIB News Service. (1995, May–June). Demographics update: The number of deaf–blind children in the U.S., *89*, 13–14.

Smith, T. B. (1992). *Guidelines for working and playing with deaf–blind people*. Monmouth, OR: DB-LINK (the National Information Clearinghouse on Children Who Are Deaf–Blind).

Traumatic Brain Injury

Heller, K. W., Alberto. P. A., Forney, P. E., & Schwartzman, M. N. (1996). *Understanding physical, sensory, and health impairments*. Pacific Grove, CA: Brooks/Cole.

Singer, G. H. S., Glang, A., & Williams, J. M. (Eds.). (1996). *Children with acquired brain injury: Educating and supporting families*. Baltimore: Paul H. Brookes.

Strauss, A., & Lehtinen, L. (1947). *Psychopathology and education of the brain-injured child*. New York: Grune & Stratton.

TBI Defined

Clark, E. (1996). Children and adolescents with traumatic brain injury: Reintegration challenges in educational settings. *Journal of Learning Disabilities, 29*, 549–560.

Heller, K. W., Alberto, P. A., Forney, P. E., & Schwartzman, M. N. (1996). *Understanding physical, sensory, and health impairments*. Pacific Grove, CA: Brooks/Cole.

Hux, K., & Hacksley, C. (1996). Mild traumatic brain injury: Facilitating school success. *Intervention in School and Clinic, 31*, 158–165.

Hutchinson, J., & Marquardt, T. P. (1997). Functional treatment approaches to memory impairment following brain injury. *Topics in Language Disorders, 18*, 45–57.

Katsiyannis, A., & Conderman, G. (1994). Serving individuals with traumatic brain injury: A national survey. *Remedial and Special Education, 13*, 319–325.

NICHCY. (1994). *General information about traumatic brain injury: Fact Sheet #18*. Washington, DC: National Information Center for Children and Youth with Disabilities.

Singer, G. H. S. (1996). Constructing supports: Helping families of children with acquired brain injury. In G. H. S. Singer, A. Glang, and J. M. Williams (Eds.), *Children with acquired brain injury: Educating and supporting families* (pp. 1–22). Baltimore: Paul H. Brookes.

U.S. Department of Education. (1999). Assistance to state for the education of children with disabilities and the early intervention program for infants and toddlers with disabilities: Final regulations. *Federal Register, 64 (48)*, CFR Parts 300 and 303.

Prevalence

Katsiyannis, A., & Conderman, G. (1994). Serving individuals with traumatic brain injury: A national survey. *Remedial and Special Education, 13*, 319–325.

Singer, G. H. S. (1996). Constructing supports: Helping families of children with acquired brain injury. In G. H. S. Singer, A. Glang, and J. M. Williams (Eds.), *Children with acquired brain injury: Educating and supporting families* (pp. 1–22). Baltimore: Paul H. Brookes.

U.S. Department of Education. (1998). *Twentieth annual report to Congress on the implementation of the Individuals with Disabilities Education Act*. Washington, DC: U.S. Government Printing Office.

Causes and Prevention

Heller, K. W., Alberto, P. A., Forney, P. E., & Schwartzman, M. N. (1996). *Understanding physical, sensory, and health impairments*. Pacific Grove, CA: Brooks/Cole.

Hux, K., & Hacksley, C. (1996). Mild traumatic brain injury: Facilitating school success. *Intervention in School and Clinic, 31*, 158–165.

Singer, G. H. S. (1996). Constructing supports: Helping families of children with acquired brain injury. In G. H. S. Singer, A. Glang, and J. M. Williams (Eds.), *Children with acquired brain injury: Educating and supporting families* (pp. 1–22). Baltimore: Paul H. Brookes.

Tyler, J. S. , & Mira, M. P. (1993). Educational modifications for students with head injuries. *Teaching Exceptional Children, 25*, 24–27.

West, M. D., Gibson, K., & Unger, D. (1996). The role of the family in school-to-work transition. In G. H. S. Singer, A. Glang, and J. M. Williams (Eds.), *Children with acquired brain injury: Educating and supporting families* (pp. 197–220). Baltimore: Paul H. Brookes.

Children with TBI

Hux, K., & Hacksley, C. (1996). Mild traumatic brain injury: Facilitating school success. *Intervention in School and Clinic, 31*, 158–165.

Mira, M. P., Tucker, B. F., & Tyler, J. S. (1992). *Traumatic brain injury in children and adolescents: A sourcebook for teachers and other school personnel*. Austin, TX: Pro-Ed.

Tyler, J. S., & Myles, B. S. (1991). Serving students with traumatic brain injury: A new challenge for teachers of students with learning disabilities. *LD Forum, 16*, 69–74.

Very Low-Incidence Disabilities
Educational Interventions

Baldwin, V. (1997). *Annual deaf–blind census*. Monmouth, OR: Teaching Research, Western Oregon State College.

LaRue, S. (1998, January). Program aims to introduce autistic children to incidental learning. *Early Childhood Report, 9*, 1, 4–5.

Chadsey-Rusch, J., & Heal, L. W. (1995). Building consensus from transition experts on social integration outcomes and interventions. *Exceptional Children, 62*, 165–187.

del Olmo, F. (1997, December 21). Perspective on autism: To gift of hope, add a bonus: Love. *Los Angeles Times* (Commentary), p. M-5.

Downing, J. (1997). Responses to Hunt and Goetz. *The Journal of Special Education, 31*, 32–33.

Harris, S. L., Belchic, J., Blum, L., & Celiberti, D. (1994). Behavioral assessment of autistic disorder. In J. L. Matson (Ed.), *Autism in children and adults: Etiology, assessment, and intervention* (pp. 127–146). Pacific Grove, CA: Brooks/Cole.

Hunt, P., & Goetz, L. (1997). Research on inclusive educational programs, practices, and outcomes for students with severe disabilities. *The Journal of Special Education, 31*, 3–29.

Kennedy, C. H., & Meyer, K. A.. (1998). Establishing operations and the motivation of problem behavior. In J. Luselli and M. Cameron (Eds.), *Antecedent-based approaches to reducing problem behavior* (pp. 329–346). Baltimore: Paul H. Brookes.

Kennedy, C. H., Shukla, S., & Fryxell, D. (1997). Comparing the effects of educational placement on the social relationships of intermediate school students with severe disabilities. *Exceptional Children, 64*, 31–47.

Koegel, R. L., & Koegel, L. K. (Eds.). (1995). *Teaching children with autism: Strategies for initiating positive interactions and improving learning opportunities.* Baltimore: Paul H. Brookes.

Koegel, R. L., Koegel, L. K., Frea, W. D., & Smith, A. E. (1995). Emerging interventions for children with autism: Longitudinal and lifestyle implications. In R. L. Koegel & L. K. Koegel (Eds.), *Teaching children with autism: Strategies for initiating positive interactions and improving learning opportunities* (pp. 1–16). Baltimore: Paul H. Brookes.

Maurice, C., Green, G., & Luce, S. C. (1996). *Behavioral intervention for young children with autism: A manual for parents and professionals.* Austin, TX: Pro-Ed.

Mullen, K. B., & Frea, W. D. (1995). A parent-professional collaboration model for functional analysis. In R. L. Koegel & L. K. Koegel (Eds.), *Teaching children with autism: Strategies for initiating positive interactions and improving learning opportunities* (pp. 175–188). Baltimore: Paul H. Brookes.

Peeters, T. (1997). *Autism: From theoretical understanding to educational intervention.* San Diego: Singular Publishing Group.

Strain, P. S., Danko, C. D., & Kohler, F. (1995). Activity engagement and social interaction development in young children with autism: An examination of "free" intervention effects. *Journal of Emotional and Behavioral Disorders, 3*, 108–123.

Szekeres, S. F., & Meserve, N. F. (1994). Collaborative intervention in schools after traumatic brain injury. *Topics in Language Disorders, 15*, 21–36.

U.S. Department of Education. (1998). *Twentieth annual report to Congress on the implementation of the Individuals with Disabilities Education Act.* Washington, DC: U.S. Government Printing Office.

Vaughn, S. (1997). Responses to Hunt and Goetz. *The Journal of Special Education, 31*, 32–33.

Families

Bradley, V. J., Ashbough, J. W., & Blaney, B. (Eds.). (1993). *Creating individual supports for people with developmental disabilities: A mandate for change at many levels.* Baltimore: Paul H. Brookes.

Dell Orto, A. E., & Power, P. W. (1997). *Head injury and the family: A life and living perspective.* Boca Raton, FL: GR/St. Lucie Press.

Luckasson, R., Coulter, D. L., Polloway, E. A., Reis, S., Schalock, R. L., Snell, M. E., Spitalnik, D. M., & Stark, J. A. (1992). *Mental retardation: Definition, classification, and systems of supports.* Washington, DC: American Association on Mental Retardation.

Singer, G. H. S. (1996). Constructing supports: Helping families of children with acquired brain injury. In G. H. S. Singer, A. Glang, and J. M. Williams (Eds.), *Children with acquired brain injury: Educating and supporting families* (pp. 1–22). Baltimore: Paul H. Brookes.

Technology

Sax, C., Pumpian, I., & Fisher, D. (1997, March). Assistive technology and inclusion. *CISP Issue Brief.* Pittsburgh, PA: Allegheny University of Health Sciences.

Concepts and Controversy

Early Childhood Report. (1996, July). Special education LRE for 12-year-old student with multiple disabilities, p. 8. Horsham, PA: LRP Publications.

Goetz, L. (1995). Inclusion of students who are deaf–blind: What does the future hold? In N. G. Haring and L. T. Romer (Eds.), *Welcoming students who are deaf–blind into typical classrooms: Facilitating school participation, learning, and friendships* (pp. 3–16). Baltimore: Paul H. Brookes.

Haring, N. G., & Romer, L. T. (Eds.). (1995). *Welcoming students who are deaf–blind into typical classrooms: Facilitating school participation, learning, and friendships.* Baltimore: Paul H. Brookes.

Kennedy, C. H., Shukla, S., & Fryxell, D. (1997). Comparing the effects of educational placement on the social relationships of intermediate school students with severe disabilities. Exceptional Children, 64, 31–47.

Romer, L. R., & Haring, N. G. (1995). Including educational outcomes for students with deaf-blindness: Rethinking current practices. In N. G. Haring and L. T. Romer (Eds.), *Welcoming students who are deaf–blind into typical classrooms: Facilitating school participation, learning, and friendships* (pp. 421–430). Baltimore: Paul H. Brookes.

Name Index

Note: Page numbers followed by letters *f* and *t* indicate figures and tables, respectively.

Benton, L. F., 453
Bergeron, J., 336
Berlin, L. J., 188
Bernheimer, L. P., 252
Bernstein, L. E., 198, 214
Besing, J., 418
Best, A. M., 28, 90–91, 95, 357
Best, S. J., 368, 375, 378–379
Bettelheim, B., 332, 514
Beukelman, D. R., 216
Beverly, C. L., 385, 402
Beverstock, C., 482
Biemiller, A., 153
Bigge, J. L., 368, 375, 378–379
Biklen, D., 22, 40
Birnbrauer, J. S., 238
Bischoff, U., 318
Black, R. S., 261
Blackman, L. S., 253–254
Blackorby, J., 214
Blade, R., 446
Blades, M., 483
Blalock, G., 66, 70, 159–160
Blalock, J. W., 160
Bland, L. C., 283
Blaney, B., 250, 533
Blank, M., 188
Blanksby, D. C., 466
Blatt, B., 40
Blevins, D., 399–400
Bliss, L. S., 204
Bloom, L., 57
Blosser, J., 215
Blum, I. M., 33
Blum, L., 510, 530
Bocian, K. M., 28, 92–93, 127, 129,
    131–132, 136–137, 139, 162,
    239, 295
Bodfish, J. W., 515, 517
Boeck, S., 519
Bogdan, R., 40, 259
Boone, D. R., 194
Boone, R., 167–168
Boothroyd, A., 417
Borland, J. H., 279, 294
Bos, C. S., 106, 108, 138
Bower, E. M., 323, 333
Boyce, G. C., 482
Bradley, A., 219
Bradley, V. J., 250, 533
Bradley-Johnson, S., 473
Bradley-Klug, K. L., 148
Brady, M. P., 401
Bragg, L., 10
Braidwood, T., 422
Braille, L., 469
Brambring, M., 479
Bransford, L., 88–89
Braziel, P. M., 32, 161
Brazil, N., 104

Brengilman, S., 106
Brett, D., 410, 448
Breunig, N., 85
Briand, X., 31, 497
Bridgman, L. D., 519
Brigham, A., 331
Brigham, F. J., 144
Brinton, B., 202–204
Brock, W., 23
Brockbank, M., 473
Brody, L. E., 296–297
Bronner, A., 332
Brown, C. N., 287, 293, 313
Bruhl, S., 153
Brusca-Vega, R., 198
Bryan, T., 140, 144, 147, 165–166
Bryant, B. R., 166, 238
Bryant, D. M., 252
Bryant, D. P., 166
Buck, G. H., 165
Buell, J. S., 333
Buhrow, M. M., 473
Buntaine, R., 327
Burger, R. A., 515
Burns, B. J., 355
Bursuck, W. D., 156, 165–166, 346
Bush, G., 17
Bussing, R., 101, 329, 335, 353
Butler, K. G., 138, 196, 204
Byers, C., 250
Byma, G., 196, 218

Calderon, R., 446
Caldwell, T. H., 368, 376
Callahan, C. M., 85, 287, 293–294,
    314
Callahan, K., 166
Campbell, A., Jr., 23
Campo, S. F., 260
Canellas-U'Ren, K., 363–364
Cannon, L., 132
Cardenas, J., 445
Carpenter, R. L., 357
Carr, E. G., 510
Carroll, L., 176, 192
Cassuto, L., 23
Castillo, L. C., 210, 299
Catts, H. W., 206
CEC Today, 150
Celiberti, D., 510, 530
Cervantes, H. T., 82t, 83, 87, 89
Chace, D. H., 246
Chadsey-Rusch, J., 532, 534t
Chaifetz, J., 6
Chang, J., 98
Chapman, M. S., 260
Chard, D. J., 150
Cheney, D., 353
Cheney, P. D., 371, 385

Cheng, L. L., 82, 95, 97–98
Cheng, L. R., 106
Cheng, L. R. L., 198
Chesapeake Institute, 353–354
Children's Defense Fund, 90, 93–95,
    113, 200, 214, 219–220, 334,
    340, 355, 388
Chinn, P., 89, 102
Chinn, P. C., 82t, 83, 87, 89, 105
Chipman, M., 103–104
Christenson, S., 62
Christenson, S. L., 353–354
Church, R. P., 128
Cimera, R. E., 261
Cioffi, A., 261
Clarenbach, J., 286
Clark, B., 284–286, 289
Clark, E., 329–330, 525
Clark, G. M., 70
Clarke, J., 206
Clarke, K. L., 481, 483
Cleland, M., 379–381
Cleminshaw, H., 215
Clerc, L., 422
Cluett, S. E., 329, 334
Cohen, O. P., 442
Cohen, P., 29, 44, 56
Coie, J. E., 341
Cole, N. H., 138
Coleman, M. R., 283, 305, 313
Collier, V. P., 106
Collins, M. E., 470
Colombo, L., 446
Colvin, G., 337, 353
Colvin, R. L., 159
Conderman, G., 527
Confucius, 284
Conlin, M., 6, 27
Constans, T., 104
Conway, T., 157
Cook, B. G., 33, 44, 251
Cook, C., 519–520
Cook, E. H., 515
Cooper, H., 165
Corn, A. L., 465, 467, 482, 487, 492,
    497
Cornell, D. G., 283
Correa, V., 114–115
Costello, E. J., 355
Costenbader, V., 327
Coulter, D. L., 230–231, 239–240,
    244, 533
Coutinho, M. J., 28, 90–91, 95, 330,
    333, 351–353
Couvillion, L. M., 149, 187
Coyne, J., 162–163
Crabtree, M., 348
Craft, M. A., 257
Crais, E. R., 208, 215
Crocker, A. D., 473

Hobbs, N., 333
Hock, M., 140
Hodges, P., 436, 440
Hoehn, T. P., 151
Hoff, D., 108
Hoffman, P. R., 208
Holcomb, M., 519
Holden-Pitt, L., 442
Holder, W., 422
Holl, C., 160
Hollenbeck, K., 72
Holliday, G. A., 309
Hollingsworth, H., 138
Hollingworth, L., 285, 292
Hollingworth, L. S., 290
Holloway, T., 374
Holman, L. J., 83, 95, 113, 115
Hook, C. L., 147
Hooper, C. R., 215
Hoover, R., 470–471
Horgan, P., 362
Horn, E. M., 391, 395
Horner, R., 510–511, 530
Horner, R. H., 58, 510
Horsfall, B., 483
Horton, W. A., 381
Hotto, S. A., 442
Hough, R. L., 334
Housman, N., 107
Howe, S. G., 13, 237, 331, 469, 519
Howley, A., 304
Hsu, C., 329, 334
Hu, C. F., 206
Hudson, D., 468
Hudson, J. A., 209
Hudson, R., 446
Huebner, K. M., 482, 487, 497, 521t
Hughes, C., 250, 259, 260t
Hughes, M., 479, 492
Hughes, M. R., 157
Hughes, M. T., 44, 157
Hungerford, R. H., 6
Hunsaker, S. L., 276, 281, 284, 293–295
Hunt, A. C., 341
Hunt, P., 44, 530
Huntington, G., 433
Hurlburt, M. S., 334
Hurley, C. M., 353–354
Hutchinson, J., 527
Huurre, T. M., 474
Hux, K., 525–528
Hwang, B., 259
Hynd, G. W., 147, 171

Ingham, R. J., 197
Irvin, L., 262
Irving, L. K., 189, 330, 339, 341
Irwin, B., 485

Irwin, R., 470
Isaacson, A. B., 520, 521t
Ishii-Jordon, S., 334
Itard, J. M. G., 11–12, 236–237

Jairrels, V., 70, 104
Jayanthi, M., 165–166, 346
Jean, R. E., 113, 115
Jedrysek, E., 514
Jefferson, T., 284
Jenkins, J. R., 156
Jenkins, W. M., 196, 218
Jenkins-Friedman, R., 289
Jennings, R., 32
Jenson, W. R., 329–330
Jiménez, R., 106
Jitendra, A., 251
Joffee, E., 482, 521t
Johnson, A., 348
Johnson, A. S., 288
Johnson, B. W., 33
Johnson, D. J., 160
Johnson, J., 354
Johnson, K., 23
Johnson, L. A., 515
Johnson, L. M., 106, 108
Johnson, V., 99
Johnson, W., 193
Johnston, J. R., 189
Johnston, P., 218
Jones, H. A., 206
Jordan, E., 113
Jordan, I. K., 424
Jordan, L., 127
Justinian, 421

Kahn, K. R., 155
Kaiser, A. P., 205–207, 206t, 247
Kamps, D., 337, 348
Kanner, L., 13, 331, 506–507
Kaplan, H., 449
Karchmer, M. A., 432, 445
Karnes, M. B., 299
Kasari, C. L., 257
Kassan, L., 310
Katims, D. S., 151, 208
Katsiyannis, A., 49, 63, 283, 527
Kauffman, J. M., 7, 34, 55, 92–93, 129, 137, 323–325, 327, 333, 335–337, 342, 353, 355, 368, 507
Kavale, K. A., 33–34, 126, 129–130, 132–133, 135, 139–140, 144–145, 329, 334, 339
Kavanaugh, K., 342–343
Kea, C. D., 104
Kehle, T., 329–330
Kekelis, L. S., 486

Kelchner, K., 256
Keller, H., 518–519
Kelman, M., 127, 131
Kemp, M., 436
Kendrick, D., 490
Kennedy, C., 521
Kennedy, C. H., 44, 530, 538
Keogh, B. K., 55, 252
Kephart, N., 133–135
Kern, G. J., 357
Kerns, K. A., 241
Kester, D., 193
Kidder, J. D., 238
Killian, D. J., 260t
Kim, J., 260t
Kim, K., 206
King, E. W., 103–104
King, P., 132
King, S. J., 445
Kinzer, C. K., 247–248
Kirk, S., 133–135
Kirschenbaum, R. J., 288
Kitano, M. K., 287, 291–293, 295, 309–310
Kitchin, R., 25
Kivimäki, R., 240, 369
Kline, A., 290
Klinger, L. G., 510
Klingner, J. K., 29, 44, 56, 157
Knitzer, J., 324
Koch, R., 241
Koegel, L. K., 510, 514–515, 530
Koegel, R. L., 510, 514–515, 530
Koehnke, J., 418
Koenig, A. J., 477, 482, 483t
Kohler, F., 529
Koivikko, M., 240, 369
Koller, J. R., 309
Kolloff, P. B., 306
Komulainen, E. J., 474
Koppel, A. E., 162
Koran, N., 427
Koren, P. E., 355
Korinek, L., 101, 108
Koroloff, N. M., 355
Kortering, L. J., 32, 161
Kotarba, J. A., 401
Koyangi, C., 327
Kozol, J., 94, 102
Kramlinger, J., 452
Krantz, P. J., 514
Kratochwill, T. R., 52
Krause, M., 84, 98
Krauss, M. W., 262–263
Kravets, M., 162
Kravits, T., 337, 348
Kreimeyer, K. H., 437
Krippner, S., 288
Kroth, R., 62, 163
Kroth, R. L., 163

McLean, B. M., 238
McLean, Z. Y., 98, 99t
McLeskey, J., 44, 132
McWilliams, B. J., 196
Medina, C., 288, 294
Medugno, R., 451
Meijnders, A., 468
Melner, J., 241
Menlove, M., 49
Menninger, K., 332
Mercer, A. R., 127
Mercer, C. D., 127, 141
Mercer, J., 88
Merian, M. S., 270
Merzenich, M. M., 196, 218
Meserve, N. F., 530
Mesibov, G. B., 510, 515
Messer, T. M., 318
Metzger, R., 2
Metzler, C. A., 256, 261
Meyer, K. A., 530
Middleton, G., 290
Midlarsky, E., 263
Miles, B., 517, 519
Milian, M., 114–115
Miller, J. F., 189
Miller, S. L., 196, 218
Miller, S. P., 168
Miller-Johnson, S., 341
Mills, C. J., 296–297
Mills, K., 19
Mind, G., 224
Mira, M. P., 528–529
Mirenda, P., 216
Moats, L. C., 150, 152
Montague, M., 336
Montessori, M., 13
Mooij, T., 299
Moore, G. P., 193
Moores, D. F., 417, 433, 439
Morelock, M. J., 274
Morgan, A. D., 278t
Morgan, T. D., 311
Morris, J. E., 486
Morrow, J. D., 521
Moss, P. B., 122
Most, T., 434, 442
Mulinare, J., 242
Mullen, K. B., 530
Munch, E., 318
Munsch, J., 145
Murdick, N. L., 54
Murray, C., 159, 265
Mussi, M., 381
Myles, B. S., 336, 340, 347, 507–508,
    528–529

Nabors, L., 257
Nagarajan, S. S., 196, 218

Naremore, R. C., 209
Naylor, E. W., 246
Nazzaro, J. N., 26
Neergaard, L., 388
Nelson, B., 147
Nelson, C., 165
Nelson, J. R., 348
Nelson, J. S., 165–166, 346
Nelson, K. B., 387
Nelson, N., 212
Nemil, M. S., 357
Neuharth-Pritchett, S., 376, 384,
    389
Newcomer, P. L., 189, 328
Newhouse, L., 514
Newman, A. P., 482
Newman, L., 214
Newman, T., 251
Nicholson, F., 329–330
Nicholson-Klimin, P. J., 380
Nielsen, M. E., 289, 295
Nielson, A. B., 86, 294, 314
Niparko, J. K., 430, 453
Nippold, M. A., 189, 214, 330, 339,
    341
Nirje, B., 22–23, 238
Nixon, H. L., II, 492
Noble, B. E., 418, 420
Noble, K. D., 291–293
Noell, J. W., 189, 330, 339, 341
Nolet, V., 251
Norris, J. A., 211
Norrix, L., 425
Northern, J. L., 419
Northup, J., 149
Nowacek, E. J., 153
Nudler, S., 260
Nye, B., 165

Obiakor, F. E., 95, 100, 296t
Ochoa, S. H., 85
O'Connor, R. E., 156
O'Connor, S. C., 160
Oden, M. H., 309
Odom, S. L., 205, 240, 257
Ogbu, J. U., 83
Ogden, P., 92, 452–453
Oglesby K., 303
Okada, R., 44
Oliva, G., 427
Oliver, J. M., 138
Olney, R., 242
Olsen, K., 72
O'Meila, M. C., 165
Onslow, M., 187
Orr, R. R., 473
Ortiz, A. A., 86
Orton, S., 133
O'Shea, D. J., 163

O'Shea, L. J., 163
Osher, D. M., 336
Osher, T. W., 336
Osterling, J., 510
Ostrosky, M. M., 205–206, 206t
Oswald, D. P., 28, 90–91, 95, 330,
    333, 351–353
Otto, R. K., 327, 353
Owens, R. E., Jr., 182, 208, 211
Owens-Johnson, L., 354

Pacenti, J., 400
Pachon, H. P., 117
Padeliadu, S., 56, 157–159
Padget, S. Y., 129–130
Palanker, L., 503–504
Palmer, F. B., 371, 385, 391
Pancheri, C., 357
Papoudi, D., 515
Parette, H. P., 216–217, 264
Parette, H. P., Jr., 54
Park, A., 411–412
Parker, J., 288
Parks, A. W., 162–163
Parrish, T. B., 30, 135
Parsons, N., 380
Partington, J. W., 514
Patton, J. M., 28–29, 86, 92–93, 295,
    296t, 308–309
Patton, J. R., 66, 70, 104, 159–160,
    162
Pautier, N. F., 66
Payne, K. T., 198–199
Pearl, R., 140
Peavler, B., 218
Peeters, T., 514–515, 517, 530, 532
Pendarvais, E., 304
Perruchot, H., 38
Perske, R., 238
Peterson, R. L., 334
Peters-Walters, S., 168
Pfanstiehl, M., 496
Pfeiffer, D., 20
Phillips, L., 332–333
Piatt, B., 117
Piechowski, M., 291
Pinel, P., 331–332
Plante, A. S., 149, 187
Plante, E., 190–191, 194, 205, 213
Plato, 421
Plavins, M., 29, 56, 70
Pogrund, R. L., 481
Pollack, S., 208–209, 212
Polloway, E. A., 54, 165, 230–231,
    240, 533
Ponce de Leon, P., 422
Portes, A., 117
Poulson, C. L., 514
Powell, B., 11

Subject Index

Note: Page numbers followed by letters *f* and *t* indicate figures and tables, respectively.

American Occupational Therapy
      Association, 20–21
American Physical Therapy
      Association, 20–21
American Printing House for the
      Blind, 494–495
American Sign Language, 414,
      432–433, 439–441
American Speech-Language-Hearing
      Association, 20, 193–194
Americanization, 87
Americans with Disabilities Act, 8,
      17–20, 379, 383, 392
   and social maladjustment, 327
   and visual disabilities, 484, 490–491
Analogies, 210
Anchored instruction, 247–248
Anencephaly, 242, 245–246
Animals, service, 400–401, 452–453,
      470, 484, 490–491
Aniridia, 465t
Anorexia, 327
Anoxia, 242
Antidepressants, 335, 515
Antisocial behavior, 342–343
Anvil (incus), 415, 416f
Anxiety disorders, 327–328
Aphasia, 197
The Arc, 21, 238, 262
Array of services, 47
Arthritis, juvenile, 370t, 375
Articulation, normal development of,
      185, 186f
Articulation problems, 180, 184–186,
      185t
   causes of, 196–197
   definition of, 184
   versus dialect, 186
   identification of, 189–190
   types of, 190, 191t
Asian/Pacific Islanders, 82, 425
Asperger syndrome, 508–509
Asphyxia, 242
Assessment, 57–58
   authentic, 56–57, 86
   of autism, 510
   of culturally and linguistically
      diverse students, 85–88, 96,
      293–295
   of deaf–blindness, 518
   ecological, 329
   of emotional or behavioral
      disorders, 329–330, 336–338
   functional, 58, 336–337, 347,
      510–511
   of giftedness, 281–283
   of hearing loss, 417–420, 419f, 421f
   in IEP process, 61–62
   of learning disabilities, 131–132
   of mental retardation, 232–235

nondiscriminatory, 85–86
of physical impairments and special
      health care needs, 378–379
portfolio, 57–58, 86, 96, 294
of speech or language impairments,
      189–192
statewide or districtwide,
      participation in, 51–52, 71–72
of traumatic brain injury, 525–526
of visual impairments, 466–468
Assessment of Adaptive Areas (AAA),
      234–235
Assistive devices. *See also* Technology
   for deaf or hard-of-hearing people,
      447t, 447–452
   definition of, 447
   for people with visual disabilities,
      493–496
Assistive listening devices, 447t,
      448–449
Assistive technology specialist, 49
The Association for Persons with
      Severe Disabilities (TASH), 538
Association, of concepts, 144
Asthma, 376, 377t, 384–385, 386t,
      389, 396
Astigmatism, 465t
At risk children, 103, 252
Ataxia, in cerebral palsy, 373
Athetoid cerebral palsy, 373
Athletics, inclusion in, 381, 399–400
Attention deficit(s)
   definition of, 141
   learning disabilities and, 141
Attention-deficit disorder (ADD), 146.
      See also Attention-deficit/
      hyperactivity disorder
Attention-deficit/hyperactivity
      disorder, 146–149, 325
   controversy over, 170–171
   definitions of
      DSM-IV, 147
      WHO, 147
   DSM-IV diagnostic criteria for, 147,
      148t
   emotional or behavioral disorders
      with, 327–329
   IDEA classification of, 29–30,
      136–137, 171, 365, 367, 384
   learning disabilities with, 125–126,
      130–131, 136–137, 141–142
   medication for, 149, 171, 357
   prevalence of, 146
   and social skills, 147–148
Attribute Treatment Interaction
      Approach, for learning
      disabilities, 135
Attribute webs, 209
Attribution
   definition of, 140
   learning disabilities and, 140–141

Audio aids, for people with visual
      disabilities, 494–495
Audio loop, 449
Audiodescription, 496
Audiogram, 418–420, 419f, 421f
Audiologists, 44, 49, 189, 418–420
Audiometer, 418–419
Auditory nerve, 415–417, 416f
Auditory trainers, 449
Augmentative and alternative
      communication (AAC), 178,
      214–216, 264
Aura, in epilepsy, 371
Authentic assessment, 56–57, 86
Autism, 328, 502–504, 506–517
   causes of, 514–515
   characteristics of children with,
      515–517, 516t
   definitions of, 506–508
   educational interventions in,
      529–532
   families and, 532–535
   IDEA classification of, 507–508
   identification of, 510
   and inclusion, 530–533
   prevalence of, 514
   prevention of, 514–515
   significance of, 510–514
   technology for, 535–536, 537t
   and transition through adulthood,
      532, 534t
   types of, 508–510
Autism Behavior Checklist (ABC), 510
Autism Research Institute, 507
Autism Society of America, 506–508
Autism spectrum, 508
Autistic savants, 509–510

Barrier games, 210
Barrier-free, 392–393
Barriers, physical, 379, 383, 392–393
Basic interpersonal communicative
      skills (BICS), 108
Bedlam, 331
Behavior control medication, 329, 357
Behavior problems. *See also* Emotional
      or behavioral disorders
   externalizing, 321, 325–327, 326t,
      340, 345, 353
   internalizing, 321, 325, 326t,
      327–328, 340
   learning disabilities and, 130–131,
      139t
Behavioral analysis. *See* Functional
      assessment
Behavioral approach, in emotional or
      behavioral disorders, 344t
Behavioral intervention plan (BIP),
      62–63, 345–347

Behavioral support, 510
Behind-the-ear hearing aids, 424, 448
The Bell Curve (Herrnstein and
    Murray), 265
Benchmarks
    definition of, 62
    in IEP, 62–63
Best Buddies, 250
Best practices
    definition of, 151
    for learning disabilities, 151–152
Bilingual education, 76–121
    approaches in, 106–108, 107t
    assessment in, 85–88, 96
    banning of, 89, 116–118
    changing policies affecting,
        116–118
    cooperative learning in, 108, 110
    definition of, 81, 82t
    families and, 108–109, 113–116
    family-school partnerships in,
        115–116
    history of, 87–89
    inclusion in
        collaboration for, 108–112, 111f
        cultural sensitivity and, 105
        interventions in, 102–113
        preschool, 103–104
        schoolchild, 104–108
        speech or language assessment in,
            198–200
        surface and deeper language
            proficiency in, 107–108, 109f
        technology and, 116
Bilingual maintenance approach, 107,
    107t
Bilingual special education, definition
    of, 81, 82t
The Bilingual Special Education Interface
    (Baca and Cervantes), 89
Bilingual transitional approach, 107,
    107t
Bilingual-bicultural approach, for deaf
    students, 439–441
Binet Intelligence Test, 285
Biogenic approach, in emotional or
    behavioral disorders, 344t
Bionic artificial limbs, 404
Bionics, 404–405
BIP. *See* Behavioral intervention plan
    (BIP)
Birth injuries, and mental retardation,
    242–243
Blacks. *See* African American(s)
Blind children
    academic performance of, 475–477
    characteristics of, 472–477
    educational interventions for,
        478–491
    families of, 491–493

inclusion of, 485–488
independence of, 481–482
interactions with caregivers, 480
literacy of, 462, 477, 482, 483t, 497
mobility of, 481–485
orientation of, 481–485
play of, 479–481
preschool, 478–482
schoolchildren, 482–485
social skills of, 472–475
Blindness, 458–501. *See also*
    Deaf–blindness
    adventitious, 466
    causes of, 471–472
    congenital, 466
    courtesy rules of, 486
    definition of, 464–465
    history of field, 468–471
    identification of, 466–468
    legal, 466
    prevalence of, 471
    prevention of, 471–472
    significance of, 468
    technology for, 470–471, 493–496
    and transition through adulthood,
        489–491
    types of, 466
Blood disorders, 377t
Body-kinesthetic intelligence, 86, 278t
Bone conduction audiometry method,
    418–419
Boys' Town, 333
Braille, 469, 476–477, 496
Braille literacy, 462, 477, 497
Brain injury. *See also* Traumatic brain
    injury
    and learning disabilities, 128,
        133–135, 137–138
Brothers, support from, 263
Brown v. Board of Education, 16t
Bulimia, 327
*Burlington School Committee v.
    Department of Education*, 21t

CAI. *See* Computer-assisted instruction
California Proposition 187, 89
California Proposition 209, 118
California Proposition 227, 89,
    116–117
California State University-Northridge,
    445
CALP, 108
Cancer, childhood, 377t, 391
Canes, for people with visual
    disabilities, 470–471, 481, 483
Canine Assistants, 401
Canine Companions, 401
Captions, for deaf or hard-of-hearing
    people, 450–451

Capuchin monkeys, as service
    animals, 401
Cascade of services, 47–48
Cataract, 465t
Categorical approach, to disabilities,
    7–8
Catheterization, 399
CBI. *See* Community based instruction
CBM. *See* Curriculum based
    measurement
CD-ROMs, in speech or language
    therapy, 216–217
Cedar Rapids School District v. Garret F.,
    21t, 31
Census classifications, 81
Center school, 44, 46t, 55–56
Central nervous system dysfunction.
    See also Neuromotor
    impairments
    definition of, 128
    and learning disabilities, 128,
        137–138
Central vision, 463–464, 464f
Cerebral palsy, 177–178, 243, 369,
    370t, 371–373, 382
    areas of body affected by, 373f
    assessment of, 378–379
    causes of, 387
    functional skill development in, 391
    with mental retardation, 240, 373
    motor development and positioning
        in, 395–396
    other disabilities with, 373
    prevalence of, 385
    types of, 373
Chaining, 254
Chicago Youth Centers, 111–112, 354
Child abuse. *See* Abuse
Child find, 54–55
Child Psychiatry (Kanner), 331
Childhood Autism Rating Scale (CARS),
    510
Choice-making skills, in mental
    retardation, 256–257
Christmas in Purgatory (Blatt), 40
Chronic illnesses, 369f, 376–378
Chronological age, 234
Chunking, 144
Citizens Vocational Rehabilitation Act,
    383
Classifying, 144
*Classroom Listening and Speaking
    (CLAS)*, 210
Clean intermittent catheterization, 399
Cleft lips, 196, 200
Cleft palate
    assistive technology for, 214
    definition of, 190
    prevention of, 200
    speech impairments with, 190, 196

Closed captions, 450
Closed-circuit television, 494
Cluster grouping, in gifted education, 304
CMV infection. *See* Cytomegalovirus infection
Cochlea, 415, 416f
Cochlear implants, 414, 429–431, 430f, 447t, 453–454
Code switching, 308
Cognitive Credit Card, 210
Cognitive disabilities, 228, 231. *See also* Mental retardation
  language impairments with, 180
  personality and, 252–253
Cognitive/academic linguistic proficiency (CALP), 108
Collaboration, definition of, 49
Collaborative consultation
  definition of, 211
  in speech or language impairments, 180, 211–213
College. *See* Postsecondary education
College and Career Programs for Deaf Students (Rawlings), 445
College Success Curriculum, 490
Communication
  assistive technology for, 178, 214–216, 264
  in children with physical or health impairments, development of, 396
  definition of, 182
  manual, 423, 520. *See also* Sign language
  preschool, strategies for promoting, 205–208, 206t
  process of, 181–182, 183f
  total, 438–439, 520
Communication boards, 264
Communication differences, 84, 97–100
Communication signals, 181
Communication symbols, 181
Communicative Competence, 210
Communicative competence, 188–189
  definition of, 188
  learning disabilities and, 144–145
  and social competence, 189, 202–204
Community living, for people with mental retardation, 261–262
Community support, in multicultural education, 108–112, 111f
Community based instruction (CBI)
  definition of, 255
  for students with mental retardation, 255–256
Complete Guide to America's National Parks (Fodor), 19

Complex partial seizures, 371, 372t, 390t
Computer(s). *See also* Technology
  for students with physical or health impairments, 403–404
Computer Assisted Remote Transcription, 452
Computer-assisted instruction (CAI)
  definition of, 166
  for students with emotional or behavioral disorders, 356
  for students with learning disabilities, 166–167
Computer-enhanced instruction
  definition of, 166
  for students with learning disabilities, 166
Computerized language translators, 116
Computerized speech-to-text translations, 452
Concussion. *See* Traumatic brain injury
Conduct disorders, 326–327
Conductive hearing loss, 417–419, 419f
Congenital heart defects, 377t
Congenitally blind, 466
Connecticut precane, 481
Consultation/collaborative teaching, 44–45, 46t
Content enhancement strategies
  definition of, 209
  for students with language impairments, 209–210
Continuum of services, 47–48
Contractures, with cerebral palsy, 373
Conversations, 210
Convulsive disorders. *See* Epilepsy
Cooperative homework teams, 165–166
Cooperative learning
  definition of, 304
  explicit rules for, 474
  in gifted education, 304–305
  for multicultural/bilingual students, 108, 110
  peer management in, 142
Cooperative story mapping, 153
Cornea, 462–463, 463f
  conditions of, 465t
Corporal punishment, 349
Co-teaching, 44–45, 46t
Council for Citizens with Disabilities, 22
Council for the Education of Exceptional Children, 20
C-print, 452
Creativity
  definition of, 277
  and discipline, 289

as giftedness criterion, 277f, 277–278
  inhibition of, 288
Crisis teaching, 153
Cross-cultural dissonance, 114–115
Cued speech, 439
Cultural differences, 100
Cultural diversity, 104–105
Cultural pluralism, 80, 88
Cultural sensitivity, 105–106
Culturally diverse students, 83
  changing policies affecting, 116–118
  disabilities in
    causes of, 93–95
    prevention of, 93, 95–96
  educational interventions for, 102–113
  exceptional, 96–102
  families of, 108–109, 113–116
  gifted, 293–295, 296t, 307–309
  identification of, for services, 85–87
  inclusion of
    collaboration for, 108–112, 111f
    cultural sensitivity and, 105
  overrepresentation of
    in emotional or behavioral disorder category, 322, 329, 334
    in special education, 28–29, 80, 85–88, 90–93, 92t
  prevalence of, 89–90, 91f
  transition through adulthood, 113
  types of, 81–85
  underrepresentation of, in gifted education, 80, 85–87, 93, 287, 293–295, 310, 313–314
Curriculum compacting, in gifted education, 301, 301t, 303
Curriculum based measurement (CBM), 57
  for culturally and linguistically diverse students, 86
  definition of, 57
  for students with emotional or behavioral disorders, 344–345, 346f
  for students with learning disabilities, 132, 152–153
  for students with mental retardation, 233–234
Cystic fibrosis, 377t
Cytomegalovirus (CMV) infection, 378, 384, 426–427

Deaf children
  academic achievement of, 433–434, 443t
  characteristics of, 432–434

Diversity. *See also* Multicultural education
  dimensions of, 79–80
  prevalence of, 89–90, 91*f*
  significance of, 87
Diving accidents, 386*t*
Doe v. Withers, 21*t*
Dogs, as service animals, 400–401, 452–453, 470, 484, 490–491
Dopamine deficiency, in autism, 515
Down syndrome, 235, 241
Dropout rates
  of multicultural/bilingual students, 87, 113
  poverty and, 113
  of students with emotional or behavioral disorders, 330–331, 353–354
  of students with learning disabilities, 132, 161–162
Drug exposure, and emotional or behavioral disorders, 335
DSM-IV. *See Diagnostic and Statistical Manual of Mental Disorders,* fourth edition
Duchenne muscular dystrophy, 386
Due process hearing, 59–60
Dwarfism, 370*t*
Dysfluencies, 185*t*, 186–187, 190–191
Dyslexia, 128, 130, 133

Ear, 415–416, 416*f*
Eardrum, 414–415, 416*f*
Early childhood education. *See* Preschool children
Eating disorders, 327
EBD. *See* Emotional or behavioral disorders
Ebonics, 98–99
Echolalia, 517
Eclectic approach, for gifted children, 301*t*
Ecological approach, in emotional or behavioral disorders, 344*t*
Ecological assessment, 329
Educable mental retardation, 232
Educating Emotionally Disturbed Children (Haring and Phillips), 332–333
Education for All Handicapped Children Act, 7, 16–17. *See also* Individuals with Disabilities Education Act
Education for Homeless Children's Act, 102
Educational interpreters, for deaf students, 442–444, 445*t*
Egalitarianism, and gifted education, 284–285

Electronic outreach, 312–313
E-mail, 312, 404, 537*t*
Eminence, 284
Emotional disturbance. *See also* Emotional or behavioral disorders
  IDEA definition of, 324
Emotional or behavioral disorders, 318–361
  ABC model for, 336–338
  and academic performance, 342
  with attention deficit hyperactivity disorder, 327–329
  behavioral intervention plan in, 345–347
  causes of, 334–336
    biological, 334–335
    in home and community, 335–336
    school-related, 336
  characteristics of children with, 337–342, 339*t*
  curriculum based measurement in, 344–345, 346*f*
  definitions of, 323–325
  and delinquency, 325–327, 340–342
  discipline in, 338, 347–349
  educational interventions for, 342–351
  families and, 354–356
  functional assessment of, 336–337, 347
  gender difference in, 334
  history of field, 331–333
  identification of, 329–330
  and inclusion, 341, 351–353
  and juvenile justice, 340–342
  with learning disabilities, 330
  low incidence, 328
  medication for, 357
  negotiating mental health care systems in, 354–355
  overrepresentation of culturally diverse students in category of, 322, 329, 334
  peer perceptions of, 339–340
  in preschool children, 342–343
  prevalence of, 333–334
  prevention of, 336–337
  in schoolchildren, 343–351
  self-determination in, 350–351, 352*t*
  significance of, 330–331
  social skills in, 338–339
  technology for, 356
  and transition through adulthood, 353–354
  treatment of, conceptual models in, 344*t*

  types of, 325–329, 326*t*
  and violence, 340–342
Employment
  IEP transitional services and, 70
  mental retardation and, 261
  supported, 261
  visual disabilities and, 489–490
Encephalitis, 200
English as a second language (ESL), 107, 107*t*
English Language Learners (ELL). *See* Limited English proficient
English only, 89, 116–118
English Plus, 118
Enhanced milieu teaching, 207
Enrichment
  definition of, 300
  in gifted education, 300–303, 301*t*
Enrichment triad/revolving door model, in gifted education, 301*t*, 301–303
Environmental arrangement, 207
Environmental restructuring, 202–203
Epicanthic fold, 241
Epilepsy, 369–371, 370*t*
  causes of, 387
  definition of, 369
  historical perspective on, 382
  with mental retardation, 240
  prevalence of, 384
  primary, 387
  procedure guidelines for, 390*t*
  secondary (lesional), 387
  seizures in
    recognition of, 372*t*
    types of, 371
  treatment of, 389, 390*t*
Epilepsy Foundation of America, 22, 371
ESL. *See* English as a second language
Eugenics, 264–265
Evaluation. *See also* Assessment
  appropriate, 57–58
  definition of, 56
  in IEP process, 61–62
Exceptional Children, 88–89
Excess cost, 30–31
Extended family, 115, 263
Externalizing behaviors, 321, 325–327, 326*t*, 340, 345, 353
Eye, 463*f*, 463–464
Eye conditions, 465*t*
Eye muscles, conditions of, 465*t*

Fads, 33
Families
  of culturally and linguistically diverse students, 108–109, 113–116

Health care needs, special, 362–409
    characteristics of children with, 390–394
        affecting classroom and school, 392–394
        affecting learning, 391–392
    definition of, 367–368
    educational interventions in, 394–401
    families and, 401–403
    history of field, 381–383
    identification of, 378–379
    and inclusion, 397–400, 405–406
    instructional accommodations for, 396–397
    organizational scheme for, 368, 369f
    in preschool children, 395–396
    in schoolchildren, 396–397
    significance of, 379–381
    technology and, 403–404
    and transition through adulthood, 400–401
Health impairments, 376–378, 377t
    accidents or injuries and, 386t, 386–387
    causes of, 385–387, 386t
        unknown, 387
    and communication skills, 396
    heredity and, 386
    IDEA classification of, 29, 367–368
    motor development and positioning in, 395–396
    multiple factors in, 387
    prevalence of, 384–385
    prevention of, 386t, 387–389
    treatment of, 389
    types of, 368–378
Health insurance, 401
Hearing aids, 423–424, 447t, 448–449
Hearing loss, 189, 410–457
    and academic achievement, 433–434, 443t
    assistive technology for, 447t, 447–452
    causes of, 425–428, 426t
    characteristics of children with, 432–434
    conductive, 417–419, 419f
    early detection of, 431
    educational interventions for, 434–446
    families and, 446
    heredity and, 427
    history of field, 421–424
    identification of, 417–420, 419f, 421f
    and inclusion, 436–438, 440–444
    instructional considerations/methods in, 436–440

levels of, 420–421, 422t
with mental retardation, 240–241, 432
noise and, 427–428, 428f
and peer relationships, 437
placement and IEP considerations in, 443t
in preschool children, 435–436
prevalence of, 425
prevention of, 429–431
public awareness of, 431
in schoolchildren, 436–440
sensorineural, 417, 420, 421f
significance of, 420–421
and transition through adulthood, 444–446
treatment of, medical technology for, 429–431, 430f
types of, 417
Hearing process, 413, 415–416, 416f
Hearing threshold, 419
Heart defects, 377t
Helping Handicapped Children in School (Dolch), 382
Hemophilia, 382, 385
Hepatitis B infection, 377t, 389
Heritage Foundation, 41
Hertz (Hz), 417
Heterogeneity
    definition of, 126
    of learning disabilities, 126, 139
High achievers, 140–141
High school options
    for deaf students, 442
    for students with learning disabilities, 161–162
High stakes testing, 52, 71–72
High-tech devices, 403
Hispanic(s)
    hearing losses in, 425
    as linguistically diverse students, 82
    overrepresentation of, in special education, 91–93, 92t
    underrepresentation of, in gifted education, 93, 313
HIV. *See* Human immunodeficiency virus infection (HIV)
Hobson v. Hansen, 304
Home teacher, 49
Homeless children, 100–102
Homework, learning disabilities and, 165–166
Honig v. Doe, 21t
Honors sections, 301t, 304
Hoover cane, 470–471
Hospital teacher, 49
Human immunodeficiency virus infection (HIV)
    in children, 377t, 378, 385, 386t, 389, 402

definition of, 241
maternal, and mental retardation, 241–242
precautions with, 389
Humanistic education, in emotional or behavioral disorders, 344t
Hydrocephaly, 246, 246f, 386t, 389
Hyperactivity, 325–326
    in attention deficit hyperactivity disorder, 131, 147–149, 148t, 325
    definition of, 131
Hypermedia
    definition of, 166
    for students with learning disabilities, 167–168
Hyperopia, 465t
Hypertext
    definition of, 166
    for students with learning disabilities, 166–167

IDEA. *See* Individuals with Disabilities Education Act (1997)
Identification, 57–58
    of autism, 510
    of culturally and linguistically diverse students, 85–88, 96, 293–295
    of deaf-blindness, 518
    definition of, 60
    of emotional or behavioral disorders, 329–330, 336–338
    of giftedness, 281–283
    of hearing loss, 417–420, 419f, 421f
    of learning disabilities, 131–132
    of mental retardation, 232–235
    of physical impairments and special health care needs, 378–379
    of speech or language impairments, 189–192
    of traumatic brain injury, 525–526
    of visual impairments, 466–468
IEP. *See* Individualized education program
IFSP. *See* Individualized family service plan
Illinois School for the Blind, 469–470
Illinois Test of Psycholinguistic Abilities (ITPA), 135
Illnesses
    chronic, 369f, 376–378
    prevention of, 388–389
Immunizations, 219–220, 244–245, 388, 427, 431
Improving America's Schools Act, 41
Impulsivity
    in attention deficit hyperactivity disorder, 131, 141, 148t
    definition of, 131

Continuation of Photo Credits

p. 332: North Wind Picture Archives; p. 345: Will Faller; p. 351: Brian Smith; p. 367: Dana White/PhotoEdit; p. 380: (top) Courtesy of the National Easter Seal Society; (bottom) Shahn Kermani/Gamma Liaison; p. 381: © Steve Barrett; p. 383: Lydia Gans/World Institute on Disability; 395: Will Faller; p. 400: AP/Wide World Photos; p. 401: Jayne Kamin-Oncea/*Los Angeles Times*; p. 405: Courtesy of Otto Bock, Orthopedic Industry of Canada, © Otto Bock 1995; p. 424: Copyright 1997 *USA Today,* reprinted with permission; p. 433: Bob Daemmrich/Image Works; pp. 438–439: From *Dina the Deaf Dinosaur* by Carole Addabbo; illustrated by Valentine. Stamford, CT: Hannacroix Creek Books. Text copyright © 1998 by Carole Addabbo; Illustrations copyright © 1998 by Patti Zimmer (Valentine). Reprinted by permission; p. 444: Will Hart; p. 448: Reprinted from Sean Hignett, *Brett: From Bloomsbury to New Mexico: A Biography.* (London and New York: Hodder Stoughton and Franklin Watts. Copyright © 1984 by Sean Hignett.); p. 450: Jim Pickerell; p. 451: Courtesy of the National Easter Seal Society; p. 464 (both) Joe McNally/Sygma; p. 469: North Wind Picture Archives; p. 470: Courtesy of Natalie Barraga, the University of Texas; p. 476: Will Hart; p. 481: Robin L. Sachs/PhotoEdit; p. 484: Beth Wald/Aurora; p. 491: (*left*) From the CBS Sunday Morning Show with Charles Osgood, "Art for the Blind," featuring Karen Chasen Spitzberg. Used with permission. (*right*) Photo courtesy of Karen Chasen Spitzberg; p. 495: © Lernout & Hauspie Speech Products, Burlington, MA; p. 507: Will Hart; p. 509: Photo by Carol Guzy © 1977, *The Washington Post.* Reprinted with permission; p. 512: Michael Schwarz/ Liaison Agency; p. 518: Library of Congress; p. 519: Courtesy of Kaleidoscope; p. 526: Will Faller.

Chapter	Achieving Discipline	What IDEA '97 Says About	Accommodating for Inclusive Environments	Research to Practice
1		Least restrictive environment and free appropriate public education, discipline		
2		Access to general education curriculum, procedural safeguards, IEP team members, transition services		
3	Schoolwide disciplinary actions: Consistency	Nondiscriminatory testing	Helping everyone become culturally sensitive	Using cooperative learning structures to optimize learning for all students
4	Create a community of helpers: Peer management	Attention deficit hyperactivity disorder (ADHD)	Steps for success in the academic curriculum	Peer-assisted learning strategies (PALS): Helping teachers face the challenge of student diversity
5	Changing the context: Environmental restructuring		Creating language-sensitive environments	Enhanced milieu instruction
6	Keeping students informed: Positive feedback		Steps for success in the academic curriculum	Multimedia based anchored instruction
7	Fostering divergent and creative thinking: Flexible rules		Addressing learning differences	
8	Getting to know the behavior: ABC analysis	Functional behavioral assessments and behavioral intervention plans	Being prepared for school violence	
9	Acknowledge the effort: Rewards		Adapting all aspects of the classroom	
10	Being fair: make the punishment fit the crime		Modifying the delivery of instruction	Strategic use of ASL to promote knowledge and mastery of English
11	Establish boundaries: Explicit rules	Braille instruction and use of braille	Implementing the courtesy rules of blindness	Facilitating caregiver-child interactions
12	Teach the alternatives: Functionally equivalent behaviors		Creating situations where individuals with autism participate successfully	Functional behavior assessment